Montgomery's
AUDITING
Eleventh Edition

This book contains quotations and adaptations from publications copyrighted by the American Institute of Certified Public Accountants, Inc., the Financial Accounting Standards Board, and The Institute of Internal Auditors, Inc. Those materials have been reprinted or adapted with the permission of those organizations, from whom copies of the complete documents are available.

Montgomery's
AUDITING
Eleventh Edition

VINCENT M. O'REILLY, CPA
Deputy Chairman, Accounting and Auditing,
Coopers & Lybrand

MURRAY B. HIRSCH, CPA
Vice Chairman, Auditing, Coopers & Lybrand

PHILIP L. DEFLIESE, CPA
Professor Emeritus, Graduate School of Business,
Columbia University

HENRY R. JAENICKE, Ph.D., CPA
C.D. Clarkson Professor of Accounting,
College of Business and Administration,
Drexel University

JOHN WILEY & SONS
New York   Chichester   Brisbane   Toronto   Singapore

Library of Congress Cataloging in Publication Data:

Montgomery, Robert Hiester, 1872–1953.
 Montgomery's Auditing.

 Includes index.
 1. Auditing. I. O'Reilly, Vincent M. II. Title.
III. Title: Auditing.

HF5667.M7 1990   657'.45   84-27103
ISBN 0-471-50522-6

Printed in the United States of America

10 9 8 7 6 5 4 3

About the Authors

Vincent M. O'Reilly, CPA, is Deputy Chairman, Accounting and Auditing, and a member of the Executive Committee at Coopers & Lybrand. Previously he was the Regional Managing Partner responsible for the firm's Northeast operations. He is a member of the SEC Practice Section Executive Committee of the AICPA and also a member of the Accounting Education Change Commission.

Murray B. Hirsch, CPA, is Vice Chairman, Auditing, at Coopers & Lybrand. He is a member of the Auditing Standards Board of the AICPA and of Coopers & Lybrand's International Accounting and Auditing Committee. He is also a member of the Accreditation Management Committee of the American Assembly of Collegiate Schools of Business. He was formerly National Director of Professional Education and Regional Managing Partner in the Actuarial, Benefits and Compensation Consulting Division of Coopers & Lybrand.

Philip L. Defliese, D.C.S. (Hon.) and CPA, is a co-author of the 8th, 9th, and 10th editions of this book. He is the retired Chairman of Coopers & Lybrand, former Chairman of the AICPA, former Chairman of the Accounting Principles Board, former Chairman of the Auditing Standards Board, and former Chairman of the Audit Committee for New York City. He is Professor Emeritus at Columbia University and a member of the Governmental Accounting Standards Board. He was elected to the Accounting Hall of Fame and is a recipient of the AICPA Gold Medal for Distinguished Service to the Accounting Profession.

Henry R. Jaenicke, Ph.D. and CPA, is the C.D. Clarkson Professor of Accounting at Drexel University. He was the principal research consultant to the Commission on Auditors' Responsibilities, and authored the commission's research study on *The Effect of Litigation on Independent Auditors*. He was the Project Director of the AICPA's Special Committee on Governance and Structure of the Institute and the Profession. He won the American Accounting Association's Wildman Medal for his FASB research study, *Survey of Present Practices in Recognizing Revenues, Expenses, Gains, and Losses*. He is also co-author of *Evaluating Internal Control*, published by John Wiley & Sons, and of *A Framework for Evaluating an Internal Audit Function*, published by the Institute of Internal Auditors.

Historical Perspective

Robert H. Montgomery (1872–1953) together with William M. Lybrand (1867–1960), Adam Ross (1869–1929), and T. Edward Ross (1867–1963) founded the firm of Lybrand, Ross Bros. & Montgomery (now Coopers & Lybrand) in 1898, two years after the first CPA law was passed. The four had for some time previously practiced public accounting in Philadelphia.

Montgomery was a prolific writer and leader of his profession. He was instrumental in the organization of what is now the American Institute of Certified Public Accountants and served as its president. Earlier, he also taught at Columbia University, New York University, and the University of Pennsylvania.[1] He saw the need for a practical book on auditing and in 1905 and 1909 published American editions of Dicksee's *Auditing*, a British work. Noting the radical departure of American practice from Dicksee's work, however, he wrote the first American book on the subject, *Auditing: Theory and Practice*, in 1912. Nine subsequent editions followed from 1916 through 1985. For the seventh edition, co-authors Alvin R. Jennings and Norman J. Lenhart joined him and the book was renamed *Montgomery's Auditing*. The eighth edition, published after his death, was co-authored by Norman J. Lenhart and Philip L. Defliese in 1957. The ninth edition, published in 1975, was co-authored by Philip L. Defliese, Kenneth P. Johnson, and Roderick K. Macleod. The tenth edition, co-authored by Jerry D. Sullivan, Richard A. Gnospelius, Philip L. Defliese, and Henry R. Jaenicke, was published in 1985; college versions of the tenth edition (adapted for classroom use) were also begun at this time. Comparisons of the various editions reveal the development of accounting and auditing in the United States.

In 1956, in recognition of the growing needs of international practice, Cooper Bros. & Co. in the United Kingdom and other countries (founded in 1854), MacDonald Currie & Co. in Canada (founded in 1910), and Lybrand, Ross Bros. & Montgomery formed the multinational firm of Coopers & Lybrand. Dropping the Montgomery name from a firm that had so long celebrated his contributions was not easy. The continued association of the Montgomery name, however, with his major contribution to the literature of the profession is a proper tribute to his memory.

---

[1]For a full account of Montgomery's contributions, see his autobiography, *Fifty Years of Accountancy* (New York: The Ronald Press Co., 1939).

Preface

Before the profession formalized the standard-setting process following the landmark *McKesson & Robbins* case in 1938, auditing practice was governed by views expressed in books and articles. Montgomery was a pioneer among the writers of the time, and his *Auditing* was revered as the practitioner's manual. There was no professional standard-setting organization or process at that time, and Montgomery's views were his own, based on many years of practice and observation. Auditing standard-setting today—50 years later—has evolved into a formal and complex process, in which pronouncements reflect a consensus, arrived at after healthy debate, among the appointed members of the profession's standard-setting board. This process brings together the collective wisdom of those individuals, often aiding in articulating and fine-tuning pronouncements.

We have just passed through a period of reexamination and revision of some of the basic standards—most visibly a radical change in the wording of the auditor's standard report on financial statements, the first such change in 40 years. The standard on detecting fraudulent financial reporting is the fourth during that period, each reflecting an attempt to clarify earlier thinking and refocus the emphasis in keeping with the times. The standard on internal control is a reworking of a Statement on Auditing Procedure issued in 1972; the standard on analytical procedures supersedes one originally issued in 1978; the standards on communicating internal control deficiencies and on "going concern uncertainties" replace standards issued in 1977 and 1981.

Other standards—those on auditing accounting estimates and communicating with audit committees—are new pronouncements that recognized the need for guidance in areas previously not specifically covered in official pronouncements. Underscoring the growing importance of another area—testing and reporting on compliance with laws and regulations—the Auditing Standards Board issued a standard on compliance auditing.

Much of the Auditing Standards Board's recent efforts was inspired by the same series of events that led to the creation of the National Commission on Fraudulent Financial Reporting (Treadway Commission), a two-year, private-sector study by knowledgeable lawyers, bankers, financiers, and accountants. Its objective was to make recommendations that would stem the tide of misleading financial reporting. Most of the 49 recommendations in the 1987 Treadway report focused on the role of management, regulators, and educators rather than on the auditing profession. Treadway's major points for the profession suggested a clarification of and greater emphasis on the auditor's role in detecting fraudulent financial reporting and in communicating with the public; the new auditing standards in these areas were developed contemporaneously with those recommendations and harmonized well with them. Both the new auditing standards and the Treadway recommendations in these areas were responsive to the gap between the assurance that an audit actually provides and the public's perception that an audit provides absolute assurance of the quality of an entity's financial statements and the ongoing viability of its business operations—two things an audit could never give.

The Treadway Commission recognized this, as Montgomery had in the early years of this century. The limitations of auditing remain with us today, as the following quotes from the Treadway report show:

> The responsibility for reliable financial reporting resides first and foremost at the corporate level. Top management—starting with the chief executive officer—sets the tone and establishes the financial reporting environment. Therefore, reducing the risk of fraudulent financial reporting must start within the reporting company. . . .

> Prior efforts to reduce the risk of fraudulent financial reporting have tended to focus heavily on the independent public accountant and, as such, were inherently limited. Independent public accountants play a crucial, but secondary role. They are not guarantors. Their role, however, can be enhanced, particularly with respect to detecting fraudulent financial reporting, and financial statement preparers and users should be made to understand the enhanced role. . . .

> Yet, implementing all 49 of the Commission's recommendations would still not guarantee that fraudulent financial reporting will disappear. Similarly, failure to implement some or all of the recommendations should not automatically establish liability if fraudulent financial reporting occurs. Those who allege that fraud has occurred must still offer affirmative proof of any actual wrong doing.

> A further word of caution also is in order. While increased awareness of fraudulent financial reporting within the business and professional community and among the investing public generally is important, it is equally important that public expectations not be raised unduly because even full implementation of the Commission's recommendations will not completely eradicate fraudulent financial reporting. Fraudulent financial reporting must not be assumed merely because a business fails. The public must recognize and understand the clear line that distinguishes the failure of the top management to manage well from the intentional or reckless conduct that amounts to fraud. . . .

Since fraudulent financial reporting will never be completely eradicated, an auditor signing an opinion will always be taking a risk even when the audit has been conducted in accordance with generally accepted auditing standards and an appropriately low level of audit risk has been achieved. The consideration of this exposure and the assessment of audit risk are not new ideas, nor were they new with the 1983 standard on audit risk. Montgomery's second edition (1916) described audit risk in the following way:

> Opportunities for wrong-doing vary, as a rule, with the size of the undertaking. In a small business the details are apt to be supervised by one or all of the

proprietors, while in a large business much of the detail is necessarily left to subordinates. The auditor must be governed by the circumstances surrounding each engagement and then determine the amount of detail to be covered. (p. 13)

In the preface to the tenth edition, the authors stated that "the more things change, the more they remain the same," and quoted excerpts from prefaces of earlier editions of this book as evidence that basic audit concepts and objectives remained largely unchanged, while techniques, terminology, and approaches varied from time to time. Many of the events of the intervening five years seem to substantiate that view. Careful analysis of the new standards will reveal that the underlying conceptual basis of auditing continues to be sound and unchanged. What was needed were new ways for the professional literature to respond to the challenges posed by the current business environment and, in particular, the "expectation gap," a large part of which may be perhaps better described as a "communication gap," between the public's expectations for audits and its perception of auditors' performance.

The current business environment poses another challenge to the profession. We expressed our concern in the preface to the tenth edition over the increased competition within the accounting profession and the resulting lower fees and emphasis on audit efficiency. The recent mergers in the accounting profession can also trace their roots to the competitive environment. With the greater competition comes a concern for maintaining the level of audit quality. Regardless of size and competitive pressures, the auditing profession has a responsibility to the public to perform high-quality audits. The profession has taken many steps to create incentives to achieve and maintain that quality. In the final analysis, however, quality work is the result of a sense of professionalism on the part of individual auditors and an environment of professionalism created by individual firms.

We acknowledge with thanks the permission granted to us by the American Institute of Certified Public Accountants, the Financial Accounting Standards Board, and The Institute of Internal Auditors to quote or paraphrase passages from their publications. Copies of the complete documents can be obtained from those organizations.

This book represents the efforts and ideas of many people. The following individuals, presently or formerly associated with Coopers & Lybrand, contributed to various portions of the book: Murray S. Akresh, Thomas E. Alberto, John T. Baily, Alan M. Bangser, Harvey J. Bazaar, Boris Benic, Clark L. Bernard, Bhaskar H. Bhave, Clark A. Cable, Robert Chakrin, Clark Chandler, David J. Checkosky, Kevin L. Colburn, David S. Colwell, Victor V. Coppola, Chris E. Corrie, F. Richard Couture, Vincent A. D'Angelo, Robert L. DeNormandie, Raymond L. Dever, Richard D. Dole, Lawrence P. Doss, Richard W. Ellis, Stephen J. Emanuel, David J. Farling, Joseph J. Feeley, Joseph B. Feiten, Robert T. Forrester, Jerry L. Frengou, Michael R. Galper, John F. Garry, Joel L. Gauthier, James S. Gerson, Tambra L. Giddens, Edwin J. Gillis, John P. Glynn, Richard P. Graff, Lynford E. Graham, Jr., Robert D. Greenbaum, Alan D. Greene, Edward R. Hansen, James A. Hogan, Margaret R. Horvath, John Christopher Jenkins, Dennis R. Jennings, Lawrence S. Jones.

Also, Charles Kachmarik, Jr., Shelly Kassen, Jack M. Keen, Robert T. Kern, James F. Lafond, Stephen J. Lis, John J. Lynch, Ronald T. Maheu, Kenneth K. Marshall, Alan May, Jr., John H. McCarthy, Martin S. McDermut, David L. McLean, James C. Meehan, Mark E. Mildner, Maribess Miller, David L. Millstein, Frank C. Munn, Ronald J. Murray, Stephen N. Nevers, Ann L. Payne, Dennis E. Peavey, Kevin C. Piccoli, William J. Powers, Jane S. Pressly, James J. Quinn, Gary C. Ratajczak, Ann E. Rhoads, Walter G. Ricciardi, Mitchell M. Roschelle, Jon B. Rosen, Thomas B. Sabol, Gregory C. Scates, Henry J. Schultzel, Glenn A. Shively, Alan G. Siemek, Christopher S. Stafford, Kim B. Staudt, Richard M. Steinberg, John H. Swords, Robert W. Uek, John V. Valorz, J. Donald Warren, Jr., Sandra Ormsby Wheeler, Paul Ray Williams, Jr., David W. Wilson, David T. Wright.

We are deeply indebted to our co-author of the tenth edition and the former Director of Audit Policy at Coopers & Lybrand, Jerry D. Sullivan, for his major contribution to this revision. As Chairman of the Auditing Standards Board from 1985 to 1988, he was a driving force behind the Board's recently issued "expectation gap" standards. The authors of this edition are the beneficiaries of his insights into the thinking behind those standards. We are greatly appreciative of his efforts in drafting and reviewing the manuscript of this edition.

We owe a special acknowledgment to A. J. Lorie, partner at Coopers & Lybrand, for his invaluable assistance in drafting sections of this book and for his careful and thoughtful review of the entire manuscript. His scrutiny of the book from beginning to end provided a needed continuity to an undertaking of this scope. Our thanks are also due to Myra D. Cleary, who was the senior editor of the book and managed the administrative aspects of its creation. In that role, she endeavored, by editing and rewriting the manuscript, to shape it into a coherent work. Finally, we are grateful to Jill Spelman, who copyedited the manuscript, for her efforts to streamline the writing and enhance the readability of the book. To all those individuals, and any who were inadvertently omitted, go not only our thanks, but also the usual absolution from blame for errors and omissions.

V. M. O.
M. B. H.
P. L. D.
H. R. J.

Contents

Chapter 4   Professional Responsibility and Legal Liability   85

PART 2   THEORY AND CONCEPTS

Chapter 5   The Audit Process   127

Chapter 6   Audit Risk, Materiality, and Engagement Strategy   167

Chapter 7   The Internal Control Structure   187

Chapter 8   Assessing Inherent and Control Risk   213

Chapter 9   Controlling Detection Risk: Substantive Tests   257

Chapter 10   The Extent of Testing: Audit Sampling   277

PART 3   AUDITING SPECIFIC CYCLES AND ACCOUNTS

Chapter 12   Auditing the Revenue Cycle   369

Chapter 13   Auditing the Buying Cycle   415

Chapter 19   Auditing Income Taxes   563

Chapter 20   Auditing Debt and Equity   575

PART 4   COMPLETING THE WORK AND REPORTING THE RESULTS

Chapter 21   Completing the Audit   591

Chapter 22   The Auditor's Report   631

Chapter 23   Special Reporting Situations   673

Chapter 24   Attestation Engagements   717

Chapter 25   Compliance Auditing   745

PART 5   AUDITING SPECIALIZED INDUSTRIES

Chapter 26   Auditing Banks   771

Chapter 27   Auditing Colleges, Universities, and Independent Schools   789

Chapter 31   Auditing High Technology Companies   871

Chapter 32   Auditing Insurance Companies   881

Chapter 33   Auditing Investment Companies   903

Chapter 34   Auditing Mining Companies   919

Chapter 35   Auditing Oil and Gas Producing Activities   939

Chapter 36   Auditing Pension Plans   969

Chapter 37   Auditing Public Utilities   1003

Chapter 38   Auditing Real Estate Companies   1027

Chapter 39   Auditing Securities and Commodities Broker-Dealers   1047

Chapter 40   Auditing State and Local Governmental Entities   1089

Index   1107

Abbreviations
and References

Abbreviations

References in this book to names of organizations, committees, and publications are often abbreviated, as follows (abbreviations used in Part 5 of the book are excluded):

AAA	American Accounting Association
AcSEC	Accounting Standards Executive Committee
AAER	Accounting and Auditing Enforcement Release
AICPA	American Institute of Certified Public Accountants
ALI	American Law Institute
APB	Accounting Principles Board
ARB	Accounting Research Bulletin
ASB	Auditing Standards Board
ASR	Accounting Series Release
AudSEC	Auditing Standards Executive Committee
EITF	Emerging Issues Task Force
FASB	Financial Accounting Standards Board
FRR	Financial Reporting Release
GAO	General Accounting Office
GASB	Governmental Accounting Standards Board
IAPC	International Auditing Practices Committee
IFAC	International Federation of Accountants
IIA	Institute of Internal Auditors
IRS	Internal Revenue Service
SAB	Staff Accounting Bulletin
SAP	Statement on Auditing Procedure
SAS	Statement on Auditing Standards
SEC	Securities and Exchange Commission
SFAS	Statement of Financial Accounting Standards
SOP	Statement of Position
SSARS	Statement on Standards for Accounting and Review Services
SSAE	Statement on Standards for Attestation Engagements
SSMAS	Statement on Standards for Management Advisory Services

References

References in this book to AICPA and FASB pronouncements are current as of September 1, 1989. In addition to citations to original AICPA or FASB pronouncements (or later codifications, where applicable), second references are provided wherever possible. For pronouncements contained in *AICPA Professional Standards*, second references are to the appropriate section in that publication. Second references for accounting pronouncements are to the General Standards volume of the *Current Text* of FASB Accounting Standards; however, all quotations from the accounting literature are taken from the original pronouncements.

PART 1

The Audit Environment

1

An Overview of Auditing

This book covers auditing—what auditors do and should do when they perform an audit—and the auditing profession—the institutional framework within which the practice of auditing takes place. An understanding of what an audit is and how it is performed is needed to understand the social function of an audit and the professional responsibilities auditors assume when they fill that function. To understand the background and logic behind the methods and techniques auditors use and the care they exercise in conducting an audit, one must also understand the environment and institutions within which an audit occurs. Knowing what constitutes an audit performed with due professional care and why particular auditing procedures are followed enables the auditor to adapt to changing circumstances in order to meet social, legal, and professional responsibilities. This book is based on the premise that an auditor who understands the theory and concepts of auditing—discussed in detail in Part 2 of this book—is more effective and efficient than an auditor who has merely memorized a series of steps to be performed. That understanding is enhanced by the broad overview of the audit function that this chapter provides.

Definition of Auditing

Different types of audits and the purposes of audits have evolved over many years, and this evolution is still taking place. Accordingly, auditing should be defined broadly enough to cover the various types and purposes of audits. The definition of auditing that appeared in *A Statement of Basic Auditing Concepts*, published in 1973 by the American Accounting Association (AAA) Committee on Basic Auditing Concepts, embraces both the process and purposes of auditing.

> Auditing is a systematic process of objectively obtaining and evaluating evidence regarding assertions about economic actions and events to ascertain the degree of correspondence between those assertions and established criteria and communicating the results to interested users. (p. 2)

The AAA Committee noted that its definition was intentionally quite broad to cover "the many different purposes for which an audit might be conducted and the variety of subject matter that might be focused on in a specific audit engagement" (p. 2). The following discussion of each key phrase in the definition is couched primarily in the context of an audit of the financial statements of a business organization, usually referred to as a financial audit. Chapter 2 discusses compliance audits and performance audits as well as financial audits.

Assertions About Economic Actions and Events. The assertions of management that are embodied in a set of financial statements are the subject matter of an audit of those statements. For example, the item "inventories . . . $5,426,000" in a balance sheet of a manufacturing company embodies the following assertions, among others: The inventories physically exist; they are held for sale or use in operations; they include all products and materials;

$5,426,000 is the lower of their cost or market value (as both terms are defined under generally accepted accounting principles); they are properly classified on the balance sheet; and appropriate disclosures related to inventories have been made, such as their major categories and amounts pledged or assigned. Comparable assertions are embodied in all the other specific items and amounts in financial statements. Those assertions can be conveniently grouped into a few broad categories, which are discussed in Chapter 5. Chapters 12 through 20 explain how those assertions apply to specific accounts in financial statements.

The assertions are made by the preparer of the financial statements—management—and communicated to the readers of the statements; they are not assertions by the auditor. The auditor's responsibility is to express an opinion on management's assertions in the context of the financial statements taken as a whole, and to communicate that opinion to the readers in the form of the auditor's report. Similar assertions are also the subject matter of compliance and performance audits.

Since the subject matter of auditing usually is information about economic actions and events, assertions must be quantifiable to be auditable. Building costs are quantifiable, as is the number of stock options outstanding; the morale of employees is not. Information that is quantifiable is also generally verifiable; information that is not verifiable is by definition not auditable. Information is verifiable if it "provides results that would be substantially duplicated by independent measures using the same measurement methods" (Accounting Principles Board Statement No. 4, para. 90).

Degree of Correspondence Between Assertions and Established Criteria. Everything that takes place during an audit has one primary objective: the formation of an opinion by the auditor on the assertions about economic actions and events that have been audited. The auditor's opinion will specify how well those assertions conform to established criteria or standards. In financial audits, generally accepted accounting principles (GAAP) are the established criteria against which the assertions are measured; GAAP require that inventories exist and be owned by the enterprise before they can be included among its assets. If the inventories exist and are owned by the reporting enterprise, and if the other assertions implicit in the item "inventories . . . $5,426,000" also conform to generally accepted accounting principles, the auditor will conclude that there is complete correspondence between those assertions and established criteria.

GAAP are, for the most part, explicit and precisely defined, as are the criteria for comprehensive bases of accounting other than GAAP. (See the discussions of the meaning of fair presentation in conformity with GAAP in Chapter 22 and of reporting on other bases of accounting in Chapter 23.) The same may be true in the case of many compliance audits. For example, the established criteria against which the assertions on a tax return are measured are the tax laws, regulations, and rulings that pertain to the particular tax return. In other instances, such as a performance audit of an enterprise's capital budgeting system, the criteria are far less precise and are generally ill defined. In those situations, the auditor and the client will have to agree on the criteria to be used, and those criteria should be explicitly stated in the auditor's report. (See the discussion of established and stated criteria in Chapter 24, "Attestation Engagements.")

Objectively Obtaining and Evaluating Evidence.   In essence, auditing consists of obtaining and evaluating evidence that will support the auditor's opinion that the assertions conform to established criteria. "The types of evidence obtained and the criteria employed to evaluate evidence may vary from audit to audit, but all audits center on the process of obtaining and evaluating evidence" (*A Statement of Basic Auditing Concepts*, p. 2). In a financial audit, for example, evidence about the degree of correspondence between assertions in the financial statements and generally accepted accounting principles consists of underlying accounting data (such as journals, ledgers, and files) and corroborating information (such as invoices, checks, and information obtained by inquiry, observation, physical inspection of assets, and correspondence with customers). To continue with the inventory example, the auditor may examine purchase contracts or paid invoices to ascertain that the enterprise owns the inventory, observe an inventory count to determine that it exists, and retotal the perpetual inventory ledger to ascertain the mathematical accuracy of the dollar amount of inventory reported on the balance sheet.

The auditor must also interpret and evaluate the evidence obtained before reaching the conclusion that the assertions conform to objective criteria. The judgments required are often extremely difficult and call for significant analytical and interpretive skills. For example, judging whether inventories are properly valued at the lower of cost or market requires the auditor to understand and evaluate how the enterprise determined cost. This may be particularly difficult if sophisticated last-in, first-out costing methods are used or if a standard cost system is employed, to cite just two examples. That same inventory valuation assertion also requires the auditor to evaluate how management determined replacement cost, estimated selling price, and normal profit margins in the course of ascertaining "market" value. Finally, the auditor must evaluate whether provisions for losses on obsolete and slow-moving items are adequate. Conclusive evidence is rarely available to support these judgments, but they are crucial to an audit of financial statements. The different types of evidence used in a financial statement audit and criteria for evaluating the evidence are discussed in Chapter 5.

The definition of auditing specifies that the process of obtaining and evaluating evidence must be carried out objectively. Objectivity in the process of obtaining and evaluating evidence is not the same as objectivity of the evidence itself. Objectivity of evidence relates to how useful the evidence will be in achieving the auditor's purpose, a matter that is discussed in Chapter 5. Objectivity of the process refers to the auditor's ability to maintain an impartial attitude in selecting and evaluating evidence. That impartial attitude is part of the concept of auditor independence, which is discussed at length in Chapter 3.

Systematic Process.   The word "systematic" implies that planning the audit and formulating an audit strategy are important parts of the audit process.

Moreover, evidence should be selected and evaluated in relation to specific audit objectives, many of which are interrelated. This requires the auditor to make many decisions in the course of planning and performing an audit.

A *Statement of Basic Auditing Concepts* notes that the phrase "systematic process" suggests that "auditing is based, in part at least, on the discipline and philosophy of scientific method" (p. 2). Most auditors, however, do not think of themselves as applying the scientific method, probably because the term implies a more highly structured method of inquiry than is possible or even desirable in most audits. Certainly an audit should be founded on a carefully conceived audit strategy, but that strategy is subject to extensive modification during an audit as the auditor obtains and evaluates evidence relating to specific assertions about the various, often interrelated components of financial statements.

Communicating the Results to Interested Users.   The end and aim of all audits is a report that communicates to the reader the degree to which the client's assertions meet the agreed-upon criteria. In an audit of financial statements, the communication, called an auditor's report, states the conclusions reached on whether or not the financial statements conform to generally accepted accounting principles. (This kind of report is discussed at length in Chapter 22.) In other types of audits, the auditor similarly reports the findings to interested parties. Thus, the definition of auditing includes the reporting phase, when the auditor communicates an opinion or evaluation to interested parties, as well as the investigative phase, when the auditor gathers and evaluates evidence to form that opinion or evaluation.

Relationship Between Accounting and Auditing.   It should be clear from the definition of auditing and the references to various types of possible audits that there *need not* be any relationship between auditing and accounting. Virtually any information that is quantifiable and verifiable can be audited, as long as the auditor and the auditee agree on the criteria to be used as the basis for determining the degree of correspondence. For example, an auditor for the United States General Accounting Office may be requested to audit the effectiveness of a particular airplane. The criteria for measuring effectiveness, which will have to be agreed on before the audit takes place, will most likely be concerned with speed, acceleration, cruising altitude, number and type of armaments, and so on. None of these criteria involve accounting data.

The subject matter of most audits, however, and all financial audits, is usually accounting data that is contained in the books, records, and financial statements of the audited entity. The assertions about economic actions and events that the auditor is concerned with are often assertions about accounting transactions and the resulting account balances. The established criteria that accounting assertions are ordinarily measured by are generally accepted accounting principles. Thus, while an accountant need not be knowledgeable about auditing, an auditor must be knowledgeable about accounting. The accounting process creates financial statements and other useful information; auditing generally does not create accounting data or other information. Rather, auditing enhances the value of the information created by the accounting process by critically evaluating that information and communicating the resulting opinion to interested parties.

Origins and Early History of Auditing[1]

Historians believe that record keeping originated about 4000 B.C., when ancient civilizations in the Near East began to establish organized governments and businesses. From the beginning, governments were concerned with accounting for receipts and disbursements and collecting taxes. An integral part of this concern was establishing controls, including audits, to reduce errors and fraud on the part of incompetent or dishonest officials. Several "modern" forms of internal control are described in the Bible, which is generally viewed as covering the period between 1800 B.C. and A.D. 95, and the explanation of the logic behind instituting controls—that if employees have an opportunity to steal they may take advantage of it—reflects the same professional skepticism expected of auditors today. Specifically, the Bible discusses dual custody of assets, the need for competent and honest employees, restricted access, and segregation of duties.

The government accounting system of the Zhao dynasty (1122–256 B.C.) in China included an elaborate budgetary process and audits of all government departments. In fifth-century B.C. Athens, the popular Assembly controlled the receipt and disbursement of public funds. The public finance system included government auditors who examined the records of all officeholders at the expiration of their terms. In the private sector, managers of estates conducted audits of the accounts. Public finance in the Roman Republic was under control of the Senate, and public accounts were examined by a staff of auditors supervised by the treasurer. The Romans maintained segregation of duties between the officials who authorized taxes and expenditures and those who handled receipts and payments, and, like the Greeks, devised an elaborate system of checks and counterchecks.

The oldest surviving accounting records and references to audits in English-speaking countries are those of the Exchequers of England and Scotland, which date back to 1130. There are references to auditors and auditing in the thirteenth century in both England and Italy, and a French work on estate management written in the same century recommends an annual audit of the accounts. The City of London was audited at least as early as the 1200s, and in the early fourteenth century auditors were among the elected officials. From that time on, there is extensive evidence that the value of audits was widely recognized and that the accounts of municipalities, private landholdings, and craft guilds were audited regularly.

The early audits in Great Britain were of two types. Audits of cities and towns were held publicly before the governing officials and citizens and

---

[1]Much of the material in this section is based on Richard Brown, *A History of Accounting and Accountants* (Edinburgh: T. C. and E. C. Jack, 1905); and Michael Chatfield, *A History of Accounting Thought*, rev. ed. (Huntington, NY: Robert E. Kreiger Publishing Company, 1977).

consisted of the auditors' hearing the accounts[2] read by the treasurer. Similarly, audits of guilds were heard before the membership. By the middle of the sixteenth century, auditors of cities often annotated the accounts with phrases such as "heard by the auditors undersigned." Reporting by auditors can be traced to this preliminary form of "audit certificate." The second type of audit involved a detailed examination of the "charge and discharge" accounts maintained by the financial officers of large manors, followed by a "declaration of audit," that is, an oral report before the lord of the manor and the council. Typically, the auditor was a member of the manorial council, and thus was the precursor of the modern internal auditor.

Both types of audits performed in Great Britain before the seventeenth century were directed primarily at ensuring the accountability of funds entrusted to public or private officials. Those audits were not designed to test the quality of the accounts, except insofar as inaccuracies might point to the existence of fraud. The economic changes between 1600 and 1800—which saw the growth of towns in place of manors, and factories in place of guilds, and the beginning of widespread commerce—introduced new accounting concerns. These focused on the ownership of property and the calculation of profits and losses in a business sense. Auditing also began to evolve from a listening process to a close examination of written records and testing of supporting evidence. At the end of the seventeenth century, the first law was enacted (in Scotland) prohibiting certain officials from serving as auditors of a town, thus introducing the modern notion of auditor independence to the Western world.

Despite these advances in auditing practices, it was not until well into the nineteenth century—which brought the construction of railways and the growth of insurance companies, banks, and other joint-stock companies—that the professional auditor became an important part of the business scene. The railroad industry in the United States was among the first employers of internal auditors. By the latter part of the nineteenth century, so-called traveling auditors visited widely dispersed ticket agencies to evaluate management's accountability for assets and its reporting systems.

Historical Development of External Auditing in the United States[3]

The development of external auditing in this country owes much to the various Companies Acts enacted in Britain during the second half of the nineteenth century. Before 1850, audits were a minor part of an accountant's practice and were not routinely performed. When they were performed, they were viewed as a way to make managers and directors accountable to absentee stockholders for the stewardship of assets. The auditor's primary objective was the detection

---

[2]The practice of "hearing the accounts," which originated in the days when few people could read, continued until the seventeenth century. The word "audit," in fact, derives from the Latin word for a hearing.

[3]A more comprehensive history of American auditing appears in C. A. Moyer, "Early Developments in American Auditing," *The Accounting Review* (January 1951), pp. 3–8.

of fraud. Moreover, there were no standards governing what the examination should consist of or the qualifications of those performing it. The Companies Acts aimed to establish auditing and reporting standards, beginning with the 1845 Act, which required that one or more of a company's stockholders be appointed to audit the balance sheet but did not address the issues of qualifications or responsibilities. The Companies Acts of 1855–1856 removed the requirement that auditors had to be stockholders and thus gave companies the option of engaging an external auditor. In addition, a petition by 20 percent of the stockholders could compel a company to appoint an external auditor. This was the first step toward compulsory independent audits. The Act of 1862 included a detailed description of an audit examination, as well as the first standard form of the auditor's report. It took until 1900, however, for annual audits to become mandatory for all limited companies. Standards for qualification of auditors, however, along with accounting and disclosure requirements, were not incorporated into British regulations until the twentieth century. The first comprehensive text on auditing, *Auditing: A Practical Manual for Auditors*, by Lawrence R. Dicksee, was published in England in 1892.

Independent audits in the United States up to the turn of the century were modeled on British practices. The audit work consisted of detailed scrutinies of clerical data relating to the balance sheet. Robert H. Montgomery, in the first edition of this book, called the early American audits "bookkeeper audits," and he estimated that three quarters of the audit time was spent on footings and postings. Since there were no statutory requirements for audits in America, and since most audits were performed by auditors from Britain who were sent by British investors in U.S. companies, the profession grew slowly at first. Only a small amount of auditing literature was published in the United States prior to the 1900s. H. J. Mettenheim's 16-page work entitled *Auditor's Guide* (1869) contained suggestions for preventing fraud and instructions for auditing cash. *Science of Accounts* by G. P. Greer, published in 1882, described auditing procedures for various accounts; significantly, those procedures included gathering evidence from outside the books. In 1905 and again in 1909, Montgomery published American editions of *Dicksee's Auditing*, and in 1912, recognizing the departures of U.S. practice from the British, he wrote the first American auditing book, *Auditing: Theory and Practice*, subsequently to be retitled *Montgomery's Auditing*.

Gradually, American audits evolved into "test audits" as procedures were adapted to rapidly expanding American business, which considered British-style detailed checking of footings and postings too time-consuming and expensive. In addition to increased use of testing methods, auditors began to obtain evidence from outside clients' records as a means of examining transactions. Because of investors' concerns, they began to pay closer attention to the valuations of assets and liabilities. These developments reflected a broadening of audit objectives beyond checking clerical accuracy and detecting fraud. Independent auditing in the modern sense was emerging in the United States, motivated largely by the demands of creditors, especially banks, for reliable financial information on which to base credit decisions.

Financial statement users in the early years of this century continued to focus on the balance sheet as the primary indicator of a company's health, and, for the most part, auditors emphasized the balance sheet in their work. The first U.S. authoritative auditing pronouncement, prepared by the American Institute of Accountants (now the American Institute of Certified Public Accountants [AICPA]) at the request of the Federal Trade Commission, was published in 1917 and referred to "balance-sheet audits." A revised pamphlet was published in 1929, under the title "Verification of Financial Statements." Although the pamphlet still emphasized the balance sheet audit, it discussed income statement accounts in detail, thus reflecting the growing interest in results of operations. The 1929 pamphlet also covered reporting practices and stressed reliance on internal controls.

The 1936 edition of the pamphlet was entitled "Examination of Financial Statements by Independent Public Accountants." The use of the word "examination" rather than "verification" indicated the fundamental changes in auditing theory and practice that had occurred by that time. In 1936 it was generally acknowledged that the independent auditor's function was more accurately described as an examination (i.e., auditing by testing selected items) than a verification, which implies a detailed audit of all data. The 1936 revision was influenced by a number of significant events of the previous few years, most notably the AICPA's collaboration with the New York Stock Exchange in an effort to improve reporting standards and the enactment of the Securities Act of 1933 and the Securities Exchange Act of 1934, which required listed companies to file audited financial statements.

The modern era of audit standard-setting began in 1939, when the AICPA created the Committee on Auditing Procedure and that committee issued the first Statement on Auditing Procedure (SAP). Fifty-four SAPs were issued through 1972, at which time the name of the committee was changed to the Auditing Standards Executive Committee (later renamed the Auditing Standards Board), which codified all the SAPs in Statement on Auditing Standards (SAS) No. 1; that series of statements continues to the present.

The 1970s and 1980s were marked by heightened public interest in the responsibilities and performance of auditors. The period was marked by a succession of alleged audit failures, followed by congressional hearings, the creation of special commissions to determine the role and responsibilities of auditors, the conclusion that a gap existed between the public's perception of what an audit was supposed to do and the limitations of the actual audit process, and heightened activity by the Auditing Standards Board to help close that gap.

The nature of auditing has evolved in response to business, professional, regulatory, and other events, as well as to changes in the public's perceptions and expectations. The history of auditing is clearly an evolutionary process, which will continue in response to further changes in the social, legal, and business environment. Certain key events in that evolution are highlighted in Figure 1.1.

The Role of Independent Audits

The social purpose that independent audits serve today has been concisely stated by the Financial Accounting Standards Board in Statement of Financial

Figure 1.1 Historical Perspective of Auditing—Key Events

Date	Event
c. 4000 B.C.	First audits of tax collections in Babylonia
1800 B.C.–A.D. 95	Biblical references to internal controls and surprise audits
c. 1130	Audits of revenue and expenditures by Exchequers of England and Scotland
c. 1200	City of London audited
1500s	Manorial accounts audited by member of council—precursor of internal auditor
Mid-1500s	City accounts annotated by auditors—preliminary form of "audit certificate"
Late 1600s	Earliest law prohibiting town officials from serving as auditors—first notion of auditor independence
1845–1900	First auditing and reporting standards established by British Companies Acts
1854	First professional charter to Scottish Institute—creation of the "Chartered Accountant" (CA) designation
Late 1800s	Internal auditors employed by U.S. railroad companies
1887	American Institute of Accountants (now American Institute of Certified Public Accountants) established
1892	Publication of Dicksee's Auditing: A Practical Manual for Auditors
1896	First CPA law (in New York State)—creation of the CPA designation
1899	First woman CPA (Christine Ross)
1900	Annual audits made compulsory for limited companies in Britain
1905–1912	Publication of Montgomery's editions of Dicksee's Auditing, and of the first edition of Montgomery's Auditing
Early 1900s	Evolution of U.S. audits from "detailed" audits to "test" audits
1917	First U.S. authoritative auditing pronouncement published by American Institute of Accountants
1921	General Accounting Office (GAO) created by the Budget and Accounting Act
1933 and 1934	Passage of the federal securities acts
1936	Revised auditing pronouncement entitled "Examination of Financial Statements by Independent Public Accountants"
1939	First Statement on Auditing Procedure issued
1941	Institute of Internal Auditors (IIA) founded
1948	Ten "generally accepted auditing standards" adopted by AICPA membership
1961	Publication of The Philosophy of Auditing by Mautz and Sharaf
1972	First Statement on Auditing Standards, Codification of Auditing Standards and Procedures, issued
Mid-1970s	Congressional hearings on the accounting profession
1977	Division for CPA Firms created by AICPA; member firms required to undergo peer review

Figure 1.1 *Continued*

Date	Event
1978	*Report, Conclusions, and Recommendations* of the Commission on Auditors' Responsibilities (Cohen Commission)
Mid-1980s	Congressional hearings on the accounting profession
1986	First Statement on Standards for Attestation Engagements issued
1987	Report of the National Commission on Fraudulent Financial Reporting (Treadway Commission)
1988	Nine "expectation gap" Statements on Auditing Standards issued by Auditing Standards Board

Accounting Concepts No. 1, *Objectives of Financial Reporting by Business Enterprises*, as follows:

> The effectiveness of individuals, enterprises, markets, and government in allocating scarce resources among competing uses is enhanced if those who make economic decisions have information that reflects the relative standing and performance of business enterprises to assist them in evaluating alternative courses of action and the expected returns, costs, and risks of each. . . . Independent auditors commonly examine or review financial statements and perhaps other information, and both those who provide and those who use that information often view an independent auditor's opinion as enhancing the reliability or credibility of the information. (para. 16)

Users of audited financial information are often actual or potential investors and creditors. Members of the public at large generally are also interested in audited financial information, however, because their present and future income and wealth may also depend on reliable financial information. Accordingly, this book will refer to "the public" as a way of acknowledging the large number of individuals who are served by reliable financial reporting, in addition to those who use financial information to make investing and lending decisions.

By enhancing the credibility of financial information, an audit reduces the "information risk" to financial statement users. "Information risk" is the risk that information, in this case information contained in financial reports, is incorrect. Information risk is distinguishable from business risk, which is the risk that, even with correct information, the return on an investment will be less than expected because of some unforeseen circumstance or event. Investors and lenders demand, and the "market" pays, a return for assuming risk. Reducing the information risk in financial information reduces the risk premium that must be paid by an enterprise. This lowers the audited enterprise's cost of capital, thereby promoting the efficient allocation of scarce economic resources among competing uses. Of course, audits are not the only way to reduce information risk. Accounting standard-setting bodies in both the public sector (the Securities and Exchange Commission) and the private sector (the Financial Accounting Standards Board and the Governmental

Accounting Standards Board) promote uniformity of accounting measurement principles and full disclosure of relevant financial information.

There has been considerable research in recent years on the value of annual financial statements to investment and credit decision makers. That research, with its focus on the "efficient market hypothesis," seems to suggest that annual financial statements have little effect on security prices. Information is available to investors in the financial press and from investment analysts and is acted on before the annual financial statements are published. There is widespread agreement, however, that *audited* financial statements do have "information content," that is, they contain *new* information merely by virtue of their having been audited. The Commission on Auditors' Responsibilities, also known as the Cohen Commission, after its chairman, Manuel C. Cohen, concluded that "audited financial statements provide a means of confirming or correcting the information received earlier by the market. In effect, the audited statements help to assure the efficiency of the market by limiting the life of inaccurate information or by deterring its dissemination."[4]

In addition to the credibility dimension, the AAA Committee on Basic Auditing Concepts considered the control dimension as another aspect of the value an audit adds to financial information.

> The addition of the audit function serves as a *control* over the quality of information because:
>
> 1. It provides an independent check on the accounting information against established criteria presumably reflecting the user's needs and desires.
> 2. It motivates the preparer of the information to carry out the accounting process under his control in a way that conforms to the user's criteria since he (the preparer) knows his efforts will be subjected to independent, expert review.[5]

The motivational aspect of an audit has long been recognized: Knowing that an audit will be performed is a strong deterrent to disseminating erroneous information.

Objectives of Audits of Financial Statements.   In contrast to the social role filled by an audit of financial statements, the AICPA has stated, in SAS No. 1, *Codification of Auditing Standards and Procedures*, the immediate objective of an audit, as follows:

> The objective of the ordinary audit of financial statements by the independent auditor is the expression of an opinion on the fairness with which they present . . . , in all material respects, financial position, results of operations, and its cash flows in conformity with generally accepted accounting principles. (para. 110.01)

---

[4]*Report, Conclusions, and Recommendations*, 1978, p. 6.
[5]*A Statement of Basic Auditing Concepts*, 1973, p. 13.

Thus, meeting the needs of the people who require an entity to present audited financial statements can be thought of as the immediate objective of an audit. Several groups or organizations have the power or authority to require that specific entities be audited. (The authors are not suggesting that without those specific requirements audits would not occur.) Those groups include creditors and potential creditors, the SEC and the various stock exchanges acting on behalf of actual and potential investors, and government agencies that require nonbusiness organizations to file audited financial statements.

Lending institutions, such as banks and insurance companies, frequently want audited financial statements of borrowers and prospective borrowers. Other creditors, such as vendors, may request audited financial statements to help them make credit and lending decisions. All of those organizations may want audited financial statements throughout the life of the credit or loan agreement. To a great extent, audits are performed because lenders and creditors demand them. In addition, the Securities Act of 1933 and the Securities Exchange Act of 1934 require that companies (with several exceptions) that issue securities to the public or seek to have their securities publicly traded on the various securities exchanges and in the securities market must file audited financial statements with the SEC. Since 1933, the New York Stock Exchange has required independently audited financial statements to be filed with listing applications and to be published annually after a security has been listed for trading on the exchange.

An additional objective of financial statement audits is to provide the client with information about its internal control structure. Auditors are required to inform the audit committee (or its equivalent) about significant deficiencies in the design or operation of the internal control structure that come to their attention in the course of an audit. In practice, auditors often extend that communication to include less significant deficiencies as well, along with suggestions for improving the internal control structure. The latter communication is ordinarily in writing, although it is customary to review its contents with management before the document, known as either a ''management letter'' or an ''internal control letter,'' is finalized. The management letter is provided to the client as a service and is an important by-product or secondary objective of an audit. Performing an audit also gives the auditor substantial knowledge of the client's business and financial operations. That knowledge often enables the auditor to provide other, nonaudit services, such as tax planning advice and recommendations on the financial statement effects of alternative acceptable accounting principles.

Expectations of Users of Financial Information.   The National Commission on Fraudulent Financial Reporting, also known as the Treadway Commission, after its chairman, James C. Treadway, Jr., stated that

> The financial statements are first and foremost the responsibility of the management of the reporting entity. But the independent public accountant plays a crucial role in the financial reporting process.

Users of financial statements expect auditors to bring to the reporting process technical competence, integrity, independence, and objectivity. Users also expect auditors to search for and detect material misstatements, whether intentional or unintentional, and to prevent the issuance of misleading financial statements.[6]

Recent survey research in Canada indicates, however, that

The public at large and even some quite sophisticated members of the financial community have only a vague understanding of the responsibilities undertaken and work done by the auditor. To the public it is the end result, the financial disclosure, that is important. The auditor is quite likely to be the first to be blamed for errors or inadequacies in financial disclosure almost without regard to his or her audit responsibility.[7]

The Canadian survey results parallel those of earlier surveys taken in the United States and other countries, and are confirmed by views expressed in Congress, in the media, and in the 1987 report of the Treadway Commission.

Inaccurate or misleading financial reporting happens in one of two ways. First, financial statements or other financial information may be misstated unintentionally because of errors in processing or recording transactions (such as failure to record an authorized sale that actually took place) or because of incorrect judgments in interpreting facts or presenting them in conformity with GAAP. For example, management may truly believe a particular lease is an operating lease when, in fact, under GAAP it should be classified as a capital lease.

Second, the financial reporting may be deficient because of deliberate financial statement misrepresentations by management or because assets have been stolen or otherwise misappropriated and the loss not properly shown in the financial statements. Examples of these types of fraud are, respectively, the deliberate recording of sales that never occurred, and the undiscovered theft of customers' remittances.

The public's concern about being misinformed by financial statements stems from an awareness of the inherent potential conflict of interest between preparers and users of financial statements. This is not to say that there is or must be a conflict of interest; nor does it suggest that managements are dishonest. It merely suggests that preparers may have certain biases in preparing financial information, as do those who use the information. Audits have a restraining influence in that auditors serve as independent third-party intermediaries between preparers and users of financial information.

Addressing User Expectations.   In performing audits aimed at meeting financial statement users' expectations, independent auditors perform two functions. One of them is serving as an expert gatherer and evaluator of evidence to

[6]*Report of the National Commission on Fraudulent Financial Reporting* (Treadway Commission), 1987, p. 49.

[7]*Report of the Commission to Study the Public's Expectations of Audits* (Macdonald Commission) (Toronto: Canadian Institute of Chartered Accountants, 1988), p. 11.

corroborate the completeness, genuineness, and arithmetical accuracy of the information presented in the financial statements. For example, the item "accounts receivable—trade" shown in a balance sheet implies that the accounts receivable exist, that the enterprise owns them, and that all existing and owned trade accounts receivable are included in the total. It also implies that the computations behind the amount shown are mechanically accurate—that is, the arithmetic involved in preparing customer invoices, posting the invoice amounts to individual customer accounts, and summarizing the individual accounts was done correctly—and that the effects of transactions with non-trade debtors (e.g., enterprise officers and other related parties) have not been included. An auditor will obtain and evaluate evidence to corroborate those assertions.

The auditor's other function involves management's assertions concerning financial statement disclosures and valuations in conformity with generally accepted accounting principles. To make the financial statements useful or, at a minimum, ensure that they are not misleading, certain disclosures about the accounts receivable may be necessary. Also, generally accepted accounting principles require that accounts receivable be valued net of appropriate allowances, such as for uncollectible accounts and returns. Deciding what to disclose and estimating the necessary allowances require the financial statement preparer to exercise considerable judgment. An integral part of the auditor's function is to interpret the facts supporting the preparer's judgments and evaluate the judgments made. To do this, the auditor must have a thorough understanding of the client's business as well as of generally accepted accounting principles.

Over the years, and particularly in the last two decades, the evidence-gathering function has become less important and the interpreting/evaluating function more so. This is not to suggest that the former is unimportant or that it is not time-consuming, but merely that the more judgmental function has taken on greater significance. In part, this has resulted from management's increasing success in developing internal control structures that ensure mechanically correct accounting information. Auditors often find it more efficient to test the client's internal control structure to obtain evidence that it is designed and operating effectively than to test the output of the accounting system. Another reason for this change in audit emphasis is the proliferation of complex and innovative transactions and the need to evaluate how management has chosen to account for them. Still another reason is the increase in both the number and level of specificity of accounting standards, especially disclosure requirements, in recent years. These all demand increased time and effort from the auditor to obtain the facts defining the underlying substance—rather than merely the legal form—of the transactions and evaluate the judgments management made in accounting for them.

The Limitations of Auditing.   No audit provides complete assurance that the financial statements are free from material misstatement. Errors can exist, because of either incorrect processing of accounting data or incorrect judgments in selecting and applying accounting principles, and not be found even though the audit was performed according to generally accepted auditing standards. As the Cohen Commission noted,

> Audited financial statements cannot be perfectly accurate, in part because of the ambiguity of the accounting concepts they reflect. . . . [Also,] accounting results—the financial statements—cannot be more accurate and reliable than the underlying accounting measurement methods permit. For example, no one, including accountants, can foresee the results of many uncertain future events. To the extent that the accuracy of an accounting presentation is dependent on an unpredictable future event, the accounting presentation will be inaccurate. The *audited* accounting presentation can be no more accurate, for the auditor cannot add certainty where it does not exist.[8]

Moreover, accounting measurement principles frequently provide more than one way to account for a given transaction or event. For example, there are several acceptable ways of accounting for the flow of inventory costs through an enterprise and for the depreciation of tangible assets. Neither the authoritative accounting literature nor logic supports one alternative over another. This flexibility of generally accepted accounting principles allows enterprises to influence the financial information they present. Also, reasonable financial statement preparers and auditors can disagree about the interpretation and application of accounting principles.

In addition to limitations imposed by the existing accounting framework, there are limitations imposed by management's decisions about the accounting and control procedures to use in processing transactions. Management makes decisions, based largely on weighing costs and benefits, about the design of its internal control structure. No cost-effective control structure can provide absolute assurance that management's financial reporting objectives will be met with 100 percent accuracy. Similarly, the audit process itself and auditing technology limit the assurance that can be attained from an audit. Ideally, an auditor would like to have sufficient firsthand evidence to provide absolute assurance about every assertion implicit in a set of financial statements, but that is usually impracticable if not impossible. For one thing, even if that goal could be achieved, it would probably not be worth the cost, to either the client or the financial statement user. Accordingly, in corroborating an assertion about an account balance or a class of transactions, the auditor will often examine less than 100 percent of the items involved. Moreover, the auditor cannot audit the results of events and transactions that were never recorded. If control procedures to ensure the completeness of processing and recording data are nonexistent or ineffective, it may be impossible to audit some aspects of the financial statements or even the statements as a whole. In addition, the need for judgment and the fact that much of the evidence available to the auditor is persuasive, rather than conclusive, preclude the auditor from attaining absolute assurance.

Generally accepted auditing standards recognize these limitations by requiring only that the auditor obtain sufficient evidence to provide a reasonable basis for forming an opinion on the financial statements. The auditor's stan-

[8]*Report, Conclusions, and Recommendations, op. cit.*, p. 7.

dard report acknowledges this by stating that auditing standards "require that we plan and perform the audit to obtain reasonable assurance about whether the financial statements are free of material misstatements."

The Expectation Gap—An Ongoing Concern

The limitations of auditing are generally well known to auditors, but not to most users of audited financial information. In addition, the public probably perceives the quality of auditor performance as lower than it actually is, because of the mistaken assumption that fraudulent financial reporting (and, by implication, an audit failure) is involved whenever there is a business failure. As a result, the public's expectations for audits greatly exceed its perception of auditors' performance, thereby creating what has come to be called the expectation gap.

The 1988 Report of the Commission to Study the Public's Expectations of Audits (Macdonald Commission) illustrated the expectation gap, its components, and the conceptual means of resolving it, as shown in Figure 1.2. The shaded horizontal line represents the full gap possible between the highest expectations from audits (point A) to public perceptions of what audits actually provide (point E). Point C represents auditor performance and financial information quality called for by present standards. The line segment A to C (labeled the "Standards Gap") represents public expectations that go beyond existing auditing and accounting standards. The line segment C to E (labeled the "Performance Gap") represents public perceptions that auditor performance or audited financial information falls short of what is required by existing standards.

The Macdonald Commission Report notes that

> The emphasis in this diagram [Figure 1.2] is on public expectations and public perceptions. Those expectations may or may not be reasonable, and those perceptions may or may not be realistic. An unrealistic expectation that is disappointed, or an erroneous perception of performance, can be just as damaging to the public's trust in auditors and audited information as real shortcomings in auditing and accounting standards or performance. It is, nevertheless, important to appraise the realism of public expectations and perceptions when the profession seeks remedies to the expectation gap. If the public has reasonable expectations not met by existing professional standards (line segment B to C) or the profession's performance falls short of its standards (line segment C to D), then it can and should act to improve standards or improve performance. On the other hand, if the problem is that the public's expectations are unreasonable (line segment A to B) or its perceptions of performance are mistaken (line segment D to E), then the logical course is to attempt to improve public understanding. Should that not be feasible, the profession must be prepared to cope with the consequences.[9]

The Commission also recognized that the figure "does not illustrate separately expectation gaps related to the quality of work the auditor does, which is

---

[9]*Report of the Commission to Study the Public's Expectations of Audits, op. cit.*, pp. 6–7.

Figure 1.2   Components of the Expectation Gap

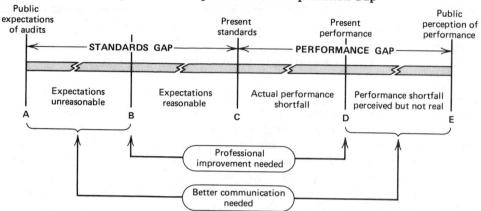

Source: Reprinted, with permission, from *Report of the Commission to Study the Public's Expectations of Audits*, The Canadian Institute of Chartered Accountants, Toronto, 1988, p. 6.

the subject of auditing standards, and gaps related to the quality of financial information with which the auditor is associated, which is the subject of accounting standards.'' (The Canadian Institute of Chartered Accountants is responsible for developing both authoritative accounting and auditing standards. In the United States, the Financial Accounting Standards Board and the Governmental Accounting Standards Board are the private-sector bodies responsible for developing authoritative accounting standards, while the Auditing Standards Board is responsible for developing authoritative auditing standards.)

Efforts have been made to reduce the actual performance shortfall. This book details, particularly in Chapters 3 and 4, what steps the auditing profession in the United States has taken to maintain the level of audit quality, and what sanctions are imposed when audit failures do occur. In 1988, the Auditing Standards Board issued nine new authoritative auditing pronouncements designed to narrow the expectation gap by raising performance and reporting standards. Those ''standards gap'' pronouncements, as well as others in various stages of development, are discussed throughout the book, starting in Chapter 4.

2

The Organization and Structure of the Auditing Profession

Types of Services

Although the focus of this book is on financial audits, the definition of auditing is sufficiently broad to include other types of audits. Auditors are often called on to express opinions on the reliability of information other than historical financial statements. Some of these services continue to be referred to as "audits," while others—particularly some of the newer ones—are called "attest engagements."

Financial Audits. In a financial audit, the auditor seeks evidence about assertions related mainly to financial information, usually contained in a set of financial statements or some component thereof. The established criteria that information is measured against are generally accepted accounting principles or some other specified basis of accounting (such as might be stipulated in a rental agreement). Generally, the information will be used by parties other than the management of the entity that prepared it. Sometimes, however, the information is intended to be used primarily by management for internal decision-making purposes. In that event, it may include nonfinancial as well as financial data. While financial audits are most often associated with independent auditors whose work results in an opinion on financial statements, both internal auditors and government auditors also perform financial audits, often in conjunction with compliance or performance audits.

Compliance Audits. Compliance audits are intended to determine whether an entity has complied with specified policies, procedures, laws, regulations, or contracts that affect operations or reports. Examples of compliance audits include auditing a tax return by an Internal Revenue Service agent, auditing components of financial statements to determine compliance with a bond indenture, auditing a researcher's expenditures under a government grant to determine compliance with the terms of the grant, and auditing an entity's hiring policies to determine whether the Equal Employment Opportunity Act has been complied with. As with all audits, a compliance audit requires established criteria (such as those contained in a law or regulation) to measure the relevant assertions against. Compliance audits are performed by independent auditors and by internal and government auditors (often as part of a performance audit).

If a policy, contract, law, or regulation has a direct and material effect on the entity's financial statements, determining the extent of compliance with it will usually be an integral part of a financial statement audit.[1] For example, an auditor reviews an enterprise's conformity with the restrictive covenants in a long-term debt agreement to ascertain that a violation of the covenant has not made the entire bond issue due and payable at the lender's option, which might

---

[1]SAS No. 54 indicates that a law or regulation has a direct effect on financial statements if it relates to financial and accounting matters. It cites as an example (in paragraph 5) a tax law that affects accruals and the amount recognized as expense in the accounting period.

require that the debt be reclassified as a current liability. Independent auditors do not, however, plan their audits of financial statements to provide assurance about an enterprise's compliance with policies, contracts, laws, and regulations that do not have a direct and material effect on the financial statements. Chapter 4 describes the auditor's responsibilities when a possible illegal act is detected. Compliance audits are discussed further in Chapter 25.

Performance Audits. Performance audits, also referred to as operational audits, include economy and efficiency audits and program audits. *Government Auditing Standards: Standards for Audit of Governmental Organizations, Programs, Activities, and Functions*, issued by the U.S. General Accounting Office in 1988, defines those audits as follows:

> Economy and efficiency audits include determining (1) whether the entity is acquiring, protecting, and using its resources (such as personnel, property, and space) economically and efficiently, (2) the causes of inefficiencies or uneconomical practices, and (3) whether the entity has complied with laws and regulations concerning matters of economy and efficiency.

> Program audits include determining (1) the extent to which the desired results or benefits established by the legislature or other authorizing body are being achieved, (2) the effectiveness of organizations, programs, activities, or functions, and (3) whether the entity has complied with laws and regulations applicable to the program.

Using resources economically means achieving a specified output or performance level at the lowest possible cost. An enterprise that met or exceeded the specified level at the lowest cost would be using its resources economically. Using resources efficiently means attaining the highest possible output or performance level at a specified cost. If output or performance can be increased without incurring additional costs, the implication is that a more efficient use of resources is possible. The achievement of desired results or benefits refers to the extent to which a program meets objectives and goals that are proper, suitable, or relevant. Results that are consistent with established objectives and goals indicate that the program is being carried out effectively.

Objectives and goals may be established by federal or state legislatures or granting agencies or they may be set by management of an enterprise. As noted in Chapter 1, the subject matter of auditing usually is quantifiable information about economic actions and events. Some quantifiable objectives and goals may not relate to economic actions and events, however, which raises the question of whether their evaluation falls within the definition of auditing. For example, in an "audit" of program results in a state's prison system, program objectives and goals will almost surely not be stated in terms of economic actions or events; instead, they may be stated in terms of the number of prisoners rehabilitated and released, the number of repeat offenders, or the percentage of prison capacity utilized. While such program audits may at times stretch the definition of auditing, they are widely performed, particularly by government auditors, and are almost always referred to as audits.

Attest Engagements.   An attest engagement is defined in Statement on Standards for Attestation Engagements, *Attestation Standards* (AT Section 100), as "one in which a practitioner is engaged to issue or does issue a written communication that expresses a conclusion about the reliability of a written assertion that is the responsibility of another party." The scope of services covered by this definition is similar, if not identical, to that in the American Accounting Association's definition of auditing, which was discussed in Chapter 1. Examples of attest services include testing and reporting on representations about the characteristics of computer software, investment performance statistics, internal control structures, prospective financial information, and historical occupancy data for hospitals.

The profession has not yet reached a consensus about which services should be called audits and which attest engagements. For the foreseeable future, however, it is clear that attest services related to historical financial statements will continue to be called audits. Also, the term "attest engagement" will be limited to an engagement in which the CPA issues a *written* opinion about a *written* assertion. Many of the services auditors currently perform do not fall into either of these categories, and these services will continue to be described by terms like performance audit.

Types of Auditors

A popular classification of auditors uses three categories: independent, internal, and government.

Independent auditors are also referred to as external auditors, and frequently as CPAs, public accountants, or "outside" auditors. Independent auditors are never owners or employees of the organization that retains them to perform an audit (their client), although they receive a fee from the client for their services. Independent auditors perform financial statement audits to meet the needs of investors and creditors and the requirements of regulatory bodies like the Securities and Exchange Commission (SEC). The audits result in an opinion on whether the financial statements are fairly stated, in all material respects, in conformity with generally accepted accounting principles. Occasionally, independent auditors perform performance audits. Increasingly, they perform attest engagements.

Internal auditors are employed by the enterprise they audit. The Institute of Internal Auditors has defined internal auditing as "an independent appraisal function established within an organization to examine and evaluate its activities as a service to the organization. The objective of internal auditing is to assist members of the organization in the effective discharge of their responsibilities. . . . The internal auditing department is an integral part of the organization and functions under the policies established by management and the board [of directors]."[2] The primary function of internal auditors is to examine their organization's internal control structure and evaluate how adequate and effective it is. In performing that function, internal auditors often

[2]*Standards for the Professional Practice of Internal Auditing.* The Institute of Internal Auditors, Inc., 1978, p. 1.

conduct performance (or operational) audits that are broadly designed to accomplish financial and compliance audit objectives as well.

The independence of internal auditors is different from that of independent (i.e., external) auditors. Internal auditors' independence comes from their organizational status—essentially, their function and to whom they report—and their objectivity. For external auditors, independence derives instead from the absence of any obligation to or financial interest in their client, its management, or its owners.

Government auditors are employed by agencies of federal, state, and local governments. When the audit is of the government agency or department that employs them, they function as internal auditors; when they audit recipients of government funds (including other government agencies), they act as external auditors. For example, auditors employed by the U.S. Department of Agriculture may audit the internal operations of that department; they may also audit the economy, efficiency, and program results of research funded by the Department of Agriculture but performed by others, such as colleges and universities. Most audits performed by government auditors are performance audits of economy, efficiency, and programs, which include determining whether the entity being audited has complied with laws and regulations concerning economy and efficiency as well as those applicable to the program. Some audits, such as those by the Internal Revenue Service, are performed almost exclusively for compliance purposes.

There are many different groups of government auditors; virtually every level of government and every government agency has its own auditors. One group in particular warrants further discussion—the General Accounting Office (GAO). A nonpolitical agency headed by the Comptroller General of the United States, it was created by and reports directly to Congress. The GAO has the authority to audit virtually every federal agency and expenditure. The GAO formulated the notion of and standards for economy, efficiency, and program audits, which are the major part of its activities.

As suggested by the foregoing discussion, the work performed by independent, internal, and government auditors is not mutually exclusive. The classification scheme used in this book is of necessity limited, and does not fully describe the three branches of the auditing profession. There is considerable overlap in the types of audits they perform, and all possess varying degrees of independence.

The Organization of an Accounting Firm

Accounting firms range in size from an individual CPA in business as a sole practitioner to large firms with an international practice, hundreds of offices worldwide, and thousands of partners and employees. In between these two extremes are countless small and medium-sized firms of professional accountants. In general, the larger firms offer a broader range of services to clients than do the smaller ones. The majority of medium-sized and large accounting firms are multicapability firms, meaning that they serve clients in several major practice areas, including accounting and auditing, taxation, management consulting, and actuarial, benefits, and compensation consulting. Although the structure of individual firms varies, it is possible to make some generalizations about the services typically offered by the majority of accounting firms.

Auditing Services.   The most basic practice area of a CPA firm is accounting and auditing, which consists primarily of performing independent audits of companies' financial statements. In addition, a number of audit-related services are generally offered to clients, either in conjunction with an audit or as separate engagements. One of these services is a communication to management containing recommendations for improvements in the internal control structure and other matters, such as comments on operating efficiencies and profitability. Additional audit-related services include acquisition audits of entities that clients are contemplating acquiring, and issuing letters reporting whether a client is in compliance with the covenants of debt instruments. Some of these services qualify as attest engagements. While attest engagements are typically undertaken by audit personnel, at times they are performed by personnel specializing in some of the "other services" offered by accounting firms, as described below. (Attest engagements are described further in Chapter 24.)

An audit requires personnel with a blend of skills and technical expertise. For example, if the engagement is extremely complex technically, the audit team may require members who have industry expertise, a high level of knowledge of computer auditing, tax expertise, or the ability to understand difficult actuarial computations. A team with such expertise will frequently find and recommend ways to improve the client's financial and operating policies, a client service that is derived from the audit process.

Compilation and Review Services.   CPAs also perform compilation and review services. A compilation consists of presenting information in the form of financial statements without expressing any opinion on them. A review consists of applying certain limited procedures to financial statements so as to express limited assurance that there are no material modifications that should be made to them. Compilation and review services for nonpublic entities were defined by the American Institute of Certified Public Accountants (AICPA) in 1978 in the first of a series of Statements on Standards for Accounting and Review Services (SSARSs). Those statements resulted from the AICPA's recognition of the need for professional services that are less than an audit, but that provide some assurance about the reliability of a nonpublic entity's financial statements. The SSARSs establish guidelines for performing and reporting on compilation and review engagements. Compilations and reviews are discussed further in Chapter 23.

Other Services.   Another major service provided by accounting firms is in the area of taxation—tax and business planning and compliance services offered to corporations, other businesses, and individuals. Tax services offered to businesses by accounting firms cover a broad spectrum, including preparing federal, state, and local tax returns; advising on merger or acquisition approaches to minimize taxes and on structuring operations to take advantage of tax opportunities; and reviewing tax returns for compliance with applicable laws and regulations. Services to individuals include tax, financial, and estate planning.

A firm's tax practice often includes one or more special service groups that address complex issues related to taxation. For instance, some accounting firms maintain support groups composed of senior tax professionals who monitor new tax laws, regulations, rulings, cases, and other related developments and communicate this specialized knowledge to the rest of the firm. Many firms employ lawyers and engineers to advise clients on tax aspects of various transactions. Other groups that combine both tax and financial accounting expertise may be established to provide tax services relating to state and local tax matters; mergers, acquisitions, divestitures, sales of businesses, and related financing transactions; specialized industries that are affected by legislative, regulatory, and judicial proceedings; and international tax developments that concern multinational clients.

Management advisory services (MAS), sometimes called management consulting services, are offered in several diversified areas, such as strategic planning, finance, inventory and supply, transportation, computers, and human resources. For example, professionals working in the MAS practice area of an accounting firm may undertake work and make recommendations to client management in one or more of the following areas:

- Establishing long-range strategic planning programs.
- Analyzing and improving administration—organization, methods, procedures, and productivity.
- Developing data processing strategy, equipment and software evaluation and selection, and telecommunications network and security evaluation.
- Designing and implementing information systems.
- Applying techniques, such as just-in-time inventory planning, to improve profits.
- Improving materials controls, from consumer goods sales forecasting to manufacturing planning and control.

Actuarial, benefits, and compensation consulting professionals employed by accounting firms can advise clients about

- Planning executive compensation arrangements, conducting salary surveys, and devising wage programs.
- Designing pension and profit-sharing plans, performing annual actuarial valuations, and implementing medical, life, and disability insurance programs.
- Communicating benefits and compensation policies to employees.
- Developing benefits and compensation administration systems.
- Determining compliance with government reporting requirements.

Those consultants may also provide technical support to audit engagement teams.

Firm Structure.   It is difficult to generalize about the organization of accounting firms because each one has its own structure and no two are exactly alike. Some multioffice firms are organized by groups or regions, with one partner designated overall responsibility for the practice offices in each group or region. The group or regional partners may report to a number of vice chairmen or other designated partners. Each practice office is headed by a partner, often called the managing partner or partner in charge of the office, who is responsible for day-to-day operations. Within each practice office, there may be separate units for auditing, tax, MAS, and perhaps one or more specialized practice areas. In addition to professional personnel, each practice office may have an administrative staff to handle personnel management, including recruiting, and to support the office's accounting and reporting function.

In addition to their practice offices, many large accounting firms have a number of specialized departments, usually organized as part of a national office, that provide support to the practice. Examples of such resource groups are industry specialization, marketing and planning, professional education, and accounting and auditing policy setting, research, and consulting. Firms that practice in different countries are further organized under an international structure usually governed by a committee of representatives from the various member firms or geographic areas.

The Audit Engagement Team.   Each audit is staffed by a team headed by a partner who signs the audit report and is ultimately responsible for the audit and its results. Especially on large or complex engagements, there may be more than one partner, or the partner may delegate many functions to one or more managers; however, one partner retains responsibility for the quality of the audit and thus should be actively involved in its planning and in evaluating the results, as documented and summarized by the members of the engagement team. The team usually includes a manager (or more than one on a large engagement) and other personnel with varying degrees of experience and professional expertise and competence. Firms establish staff classifications through which employees progress and policies that set forth the responsibilities of audit personnel on each level. While these responsibilities vary from one firm to another, the typical functions and duties of each classification can be described generally.

Partner.   The partner has primary responsibility for accounting and auditing services and is usually the direct contact with the client. The partner is responsible for all decisions made in the course of the engagement, including those about the scope of services, the audit strategy, and the resolution of significant accounting and auditing technical issues. In short, the partner is responsible for ensuring that the audit has been planned, conducted, and reported on in accordance with the firm's policies and professional standards.

As noted in Chapter 3, firms that are members of the AICPA's SEC Practice Section are required to assign a second, or concurring, partner on SEC engagements to provide additional assurance that those objectives are achieved. Because of the perceived benefits of such additional partner review, many firms assign a concurring partner to other engagements as well.

The concurring partner on an engagement generally assesses the audit strategy, including auditing procedures to be performed in sensitive or high-risk areas, and may suggest additional matters to be addressed or recommend ways of enhancing audit efficiency. The concurring partner reviews the draft audit report, related financial information and disclosures, and, where applicable, published reports and filings to be made with the SEC and other regulatory bodies. In some circumstances, the concurring partner's review may be more detailed and include inquiring of members of the engagement team and reviewing working papers to determine that the scope of auditing procedures and related documentation comply with the firm's policies and professional standards.

Manager.   Under the direction of a partner, a manager is responsible for administering all aspects of an engagement, including planning and coordinating activities with client personnel, delegating duties to team members, coaching them, supervising and reviewing their work, controlling engagement time and expenses, and overseeing billings and collections. A manager is expected to have attained a degree of technical competence in accounting and auditing sufficient to ensure that an audit complies with all applicable professional standards and firm policies. The manager is also responsible for keeping the partner informed of all significant developments throughout the audit. Among other things, the manager is often delegated the responsibility for reviewing the report to management covering control structure related matters, the financial statements first in draft form and then in final form, the documentation of the engagement, and proposed changes in the audit program.

Other Personnel.   One or more experienced accountants are responsible, under the manager's direction, for the overall quality, timeliness, and efficiency of the field work in an audit. This involves assisting the manager with administrative matters during the planning phase of the engagement as well as during and after the field work. During the field work, these individuals are responsible for understanding the client's business, industry, and control structure; assessing risk; reviewing working papers prepared by other engagement team personnel; drafting the report on control structure related matters and the proposed audit report; and preparing a summary of audit findings for the partner's attention.

Less experienced personnel are responsible for completing assigned tasks under supervision. Their assignments, which vary with the size and complexity of the engagement, generally include preparing documentation of the understanding of the client and its control structure, performing various types of audit tests and documenting the results, and keeping higher-level personnel informed of all findings.

The Audit Pyramid.   The engagement team members at the various levels are commonly viewed as forming a "staffing pyramid." There are generally large numbers of less experienced personnel on an engagement team, with proportionately fewer people at each higher level and one partner, with ultimate responsibility for the audit, at the top. The exact shape of the pyramid varies both by the size and organization of the accounting firm and by the circumstances of the client's business and industry. For example, on multilocation, technically complex engagements, there may be several individuals with differing amounts of experience; those less experienced will be assigned responsibility for specific aspects of the field work, under the supervision of a more experienced individual who will direct the overall field work. The specific needs of the engagement, as determined by the client's operations and industry, also affect the shape of the pyramid. For instance, if the audit work includes extensive detailed testing, such as counting securities or confirming customers' accounts receivable, a larger number of less experienced personnel may be necessary than on an engagement in which detailed testing is limited.

The Organization of the Auditing Profession

The auditing profession in the United States has formed numerous voluntary groups with various purposes, among them the AICPA, state societies or institutes of CPAs, and the Institute of Internal Auditors, all of which have broadly based memberships. In addition, there are more specialized organizations of government auditors, computer auditors, teachers of auditing, and internal auditors with particular industry interests. The designation "Certified Public Accountant" is granted by state boards of accountancy, discussed in the next section of this chapter.

American Institute of CPAs.   The mission of the AICPA is "to act on behalf of its members and provide necessary support to assure that CPAs serve the public interest in performing quality professional services." Just under half of the AICPA's approximately 280,000 members, who are required to be CPAs, are in public practice either with CPA firms or as sole practitioners. (The rest are in business and industry, government, or education; or are retired.) The AICPA provides a broad range of services to members, including continuing professional education, technical accounting and auditing assistance, auditing standards, self-regulation of the profession, and assistance in managing an accounting practice.

Ultimate authority over the AICPA is vested in its Council. Its 21-member Board of Directors, which includes 3 non-Institute members who represent the public, administers resources and sets policy. Pronouncements in the form of technical and ethical standards are issued by senior technical committees composed of Institute members in public practice and, to some extent, in industry, government, and academe. The Institute's bylaws authorize eight senior technical committees to make public statements, sometimes in the form of authoritative pronouncements, on matters related to their areas of practice, without clearance by Council or the Board of Directors. Those senior technical committees and the public statements they issue are shown in Figure 2.1.

Figure 2.1   Public Statements Issued by AICPA Senior Technical Committees

Senior Technical Committee[a]	Public Statements Issued
Accounting and Review Services Committee	Statements on Standards for Accounting and Review Services[b] Accounting and Review Services Interpretations Statements on Standards for Attestation Engagements[b]
Accounting Standards Executive Committee	Statements of Position Issues Papers Practice Bulletins
Auditing Standards Board	Statements on Auditing Standards[b] Auditing Interpretations Statements on Standards for Attestation Engagements[b] Interpretations of Attestation Standards Statements on Standards for Accountants' Services on Prospective Financial Information[b] Notices to Practitioners Statements of Position
Federal Taxation Executive Committee	Statements on Responsibilities in Tax Practice
Management Advisory Services Executive Committee	Statements on Standards for Management Advisory Services[b] Statements on Standards for Attestation Engagements[b]
Professional Ethics Executive Committee	Interpretations of Rules of Conduct[b] Ethics Rulings[b]
Quality Review Executive Committee	Standards for Performing and Reporting on Quality Reviews

[a]The Personal Financial Planning Executive Committee has also been designated as a senior technical committee and is authorized to make public statements on matters related to its area of practice. At the time of this writing, however, it has not issued any public statements.

[b]The Rules of the AICPA Code of Professional Conduct and implementing resolutions of Council require AICPA members to comply with standards contained in these pronouncements; departures therefrom must be justified by those members who do not follow them.

In addition, the AICPA has four voluntary membership divisions. Three are for individual members with a special interest in tax, management advisory services, or personal financial planning. The fourth is the Division for CPA Firms, which comprises an SEC Practice Section and a Private Companies Practice Section. The Division for CPA Firms is discussed in Chapter 3.

Through its Continuing Professional Education Division, the AICPA provides programs covering a wide range of technical and professional subjects of interest to members in public practice, business, teaching, and government. The Institute also publishes the *Journal of Accountancy* and *The Tax Adviser* monthly, which are available to nonmembers as well as members; several newsletters of interest to practicing members; and numerous pamphlets, reports, and studies. The Institute's Board of Examiners prepares, administers, and grades the semiannual CPA examinations on behalf of the 50 states and other licensing jurisdictions. Through its Professional Ethics Division, the AICPA issues interpretations of the Principles and Rules of the Code of Professional Conduct, investigates complaints against members regarding unethical practices, and assists in investigating and presenting ethics cases referred to the Joint Trial Board.

State Societies of CPAs.   In addition to belonging to the AICPA, most CPAs belong to a state society of CPAs. The purpose of the state societies is also to improve the profession and help their members better serve the public interest. To accomplish this, the state societies offer members continuing professional education courses, provide consultation services, maintain liaison with members of state legislatures and relevant administrative agencies of state governments, publish professional journals, clarify and enforce professional technical and ethical standards, and provide other services to members, such as various types of group insurance. Members of a state society are automatically members of a specific local chapter within the state, which holds regular meetings and coordinates its activities with those of the state society.

The Institute of Internal Auditors.   The Institute of Internal Auditors (IIA) was formed in 1941 to promote the professionalism and education of internal auditors. The organization now has more than 32,000 members in over 180 chapters throughout the world. The Institute actively sponsors training seminars, conferences, research, and books and other publications, including a bimonthly professional journal entitled *The Internal Auditor*. The Institute's International Board of Directors and other international committees set Institute policy. The IIA offers a certification program leading to the professional designation of Certified Internal Auditor (CIA). IIA achievements include codifying ethics, developing professional standards, and identifying a common body of practitioner knowledge.

Other Organizations.   Auditors with specialized interests have formed various organizations, usually with more precisely defined objectives than the broadly based AICPA and IIA. Among those groups are computer, insurance company, government, and bank auditors. Members of the American Accounting Association who are interested in auditing research and teaching have established an Auditing Section of the Association, which publishes *Auditing: A Journal of Practice and Theory*. Membership in some of these organizations is limited to auditors practicing in a specific field or industry.

Professional Certification and Licensing

The main professional designations relating to the practice of auditing are "Certified Public Accountant," "Certified Internal Auditor," and "Certified Information Systems Auditor."

Certified Public Accountant (CPA).   Starting in 1896, the various states have licensed and regulated individuals who have met specified education, experience, and examination requirements and who hold themselves out to the public as CPAs. Accountancy laws governing the licensing of professional accountants and establishing state boards of accountancy to administer and enforce them have been enacted in all 50 states, the District of Columbia, Guam, Puerto Rico, and the U.S. Virgin Islands. Only individuals who pass the CPA examination and meet the education and experience requirements of their state boards are granted a license to practice by the state and are entitled to use the designation "Certified Public Accountant" or "CPA." The CPA certificate is granted to qualified candidates to ensure the professional competence of those who offer their services to the public as professional accountants.

The semiannual, two-and-one-half-day CPA examination is prepared by the Board of Examiners of the AICPA and is given uniformly throughout the United States in May and November. The examination in all states currently consists of the following four parts:

- Accounting Theory—tests the candidate's conceptual knowledge of accounting.
- Accounting Practice—tests the candidate's ability to apply accounting concepts, authoritative accounting pronouncements, cost accounting concepts, and federal tax accounting principles and procedures.
- Auditing—tests the candidate's knowledge of professional responsibilities, auditing standards and procedures, and standards relating to nonauditing services provided by CPAs.
- Business Law—tests the candidate's knowledge of the legal implications of business transactions, particularly as they relate to accounting and auditing, and auditors' legal liability.

Some states may require candidates to be tested in other subjects as well.

All state boards of accountancy use the AICPA Uniform CPA Examination and Advisory Grading Service. Even though the papers are graded by the AICPA, the state boards are responsible for the quality, composition, and grading of the examination and for licensing individuals, and thus may review the Institute's grading. Education and experience requirements differ from state to state. Although in some states individuals receive a CPA certificate on passing the examination, most states require a period of experience before they issue a license to practice.

Additional information concerning a state's regulations and requirements can be obtained from the following sources:

- The appropriate state education department or state board of accountancy.
- National Association of State Boards of Accountancy, 545 Fifth Avenue, New York, New York 10017.
- American Institute of Certified Public Accountants, 1211 Avenue of the Americas, New York, New York 10036.
- The appropriate state society of certified public accountants.

Publications that may have information about the CPA examination and state accountancy laws include

- *Information for CPA Candidates*, published by the American Institute of Certified Public Accountants.
- *Digest of State Accountancy Laws and State Board Regulations*, which includes a listing of the state boards of accountancy, published by the National Association of State Boards of Accountancy and the AICPA.
- *Accountancy Law Reporter*, published by Commerce Clearing House.

Certified Internal Auditor (CIA).   The Certified Internal Auditor examination measures technical competence in the practice of internal auditing and is administered by the Board of Regents of the Institute of Internal Auditors (IIA). The IIA's Director of Professional Practices is responsible for preparing, administering, and grading the examination within the guidelines established by IIA's Board of Regents and Board of Directors. The Certified Internal Auditor examination is open to internal auditors and others who have the required professional qualifications. To maintain the CIA designation, a holder of a CIA certificate must meet specific CPE requirements. The certificate confers professional recognition, but does not include a license to practice. Because CIAs do not offer their services to the public, states do not license them.

Additional information relating to the experience and education requirements for the CIA examination can be obtained by writing to The Institute of Internal Auditors, Inc., 249 Maitland Avenue, Altamonte Springs, Florida 32701.

Certified Information Systems Auditor (CISA).   In 1979, the EDP Auditors Foundation engaged Educational Testing Service to develop a certification examination for Certified Information Systems Auditor (CISA), to test knowledge and skills in the various fields of EDP auditing. The EDP Auditors Foundation appointed a Certification Board to supervise and control the program and the content of the test. To retain certification, a CISA must meet certain CPE requirements or retake the examination. The CISA program is also one of professional recognition rather than state licensure.

Additional information about the experience and education requirements for the CISA examination can be obtained by writing to the EDP Auditors Foundation, Inc., 455 East Kehoe Boulevard, Suite 106, Carol Stream, Illinois 60188.

Professional Standards and Standard-Setting Bodies

Auditing standards, in the broadest sense, are guidelines for performing professionally responsible audits. The AICPA, IIA, and General Accounting Office have all formulated auditing standards to guide their members.

Generally Accepted Auditing Standards.   The membership of the AICPA has approved and adopted ten broad statements collectively entitled "generally accepted auditing standards," often abbreviated as "GAAS." Nine of them were originally adopted in 1948 and have not changed basically since (although our understanding of several of them has changed significantly over the years). The tenth was adopted some years later, but the basic principle had existed before. Two of the standards were amended in 1988. Of the ten standards, three are concerned with personal qualities that the auditor should possess (general standards), three with how an audit should be conducted (field work standards), and four with the form and content of the auditor's report (reporting standards). The ten GAAS are discussed in detail in Chapter 3.

The authority to amplify and interpret the ten original GAAS resides in a senior technical committee of the AICPA. From 1939 to 1972, that committee was called the Committee on Auditing Procedure and issued 54 pronouncements called Statements on Auditing Procedure. The Committee on Auditing Procedure was replaced in 1972 by the Auditing Standards Executive Committee, and in 1978 the Auditing Standards Board (ASB) was formed to succeed the Executive Committee. The ASB is now responsible for promulgating auditing standards and procedures to be observed by AICPA members in accordance with the Institute's Code of Professional Conduct. The pronouncements of the Auditing Standards Executive Committee and the Auditing Standards Board are called Statements on Auditing Standards (SASs). They define the nature and extent of auditors' responsibilities and provide guidance to auditors in carrying out their duties. From 1972 through mid-1989 the two committees issued 63 Statements on Auditing Standards. While statements issued by all three committees are technically amplifications and interpretations of the ten original GAAS, they and the ten GAAS are frequently referred to collectively as generally accepted auditing standards.

In addition to issuing SASs, the Auditing Standards Board approves for publication auditing interpretations of the SASs; the interpretations are prepared by the staff of the Auditing Standards Division of the AICPA. As they are issued, Statements on Auditing Standards, auditing interpretations, and other AICPA professional standards are incorporated in the AICPA's looseleaf service, *Professional Standards*, which results in a continuous codification of those pronouncements. Once a year, a bound version of the latest *Professional Standards* is published for Institute members by the AICPA and for non-Institute members by Commerce Clearing House.

In an effort to promote international uniformity in auditing, the International Auditing Practices Committee (IAPC) of the International Federation of Accountants (IFAC) issues guidelines on generally accepted auditing practices and audit reports. The guidelines are not authoritative in the way AICPA professional standards are in the United States, but IAPC members have agreed to work toward implementing them to the extent practicable. Twenty-seven international guidelines have been issued through mid-1989; for the most part, their provisions conform with comparable U.S. GAAS. If a guideline is issued that deviates significantly from GAAS, the Auditing Standards Board considers ways of resolving the differences.

The Role of the SEC and the Courts in Setting Auditing Standards. The various federal acts that the Securities and Exchange Commission administers give it broad powers. Those powers probably include promulgating auditing standards and may extend even to prescribing specific steps to be followed by auditors of financial statements filed with the Commission. The Commission has, however, adopted the general policy of relying on the public accounting profession to establish auditing standards, largely because of the profession's willingness to address issues the SEC deems significant. The policy stated by the Commission in 1940 in Accounting Series Release No. 19 continues to be effective.

> Until experience should prove the contrary, we feel that this program is preferable to its alternative—the detailed prescription of the scope of and procedures to be followed in the audit for the various types of issuers of securities who file statements with us—and will allow for further consideration of varying audit procedures and for the development of different treatment for specific types of issuers.

This is not to suggest that the SEC has not or will not influence the development of auditing standards. Indeed, it has done so on several occasions and is likely to continue doing so. That influence takes essentially two forms: stimulating the Auditing Standards Board to issue a pronouncement when the Commission believes one is needed (as occurred with SAS No. 36, *Review of Interim Financial Information* [AU Section 722]) and informing the Auditing Standards Board of its views during the standard-setting process. The Auditing Standards Board must continually acknowledge the presence of the SEC throughout its deliberations, but must not sacrifice the independence and objectivity that are essential to its standard-setting function.

Despite numerous opportunities to interpret auditing standards when auditors have been the subject of litigation, only rarely have the courts failed to apply the profession's own auditing standards, and then it was primarily in areas involving reporting standards. Conformity with promulgated professional auditing standards has generally been an effective defense for auditors.

Attestation Standards.   In March 1986, the AICPA's Auditing Standards Board and its Accounting and Review Services Committee (ARSC) jointly issued Statement on Standards for Attestation Engagements (SSAE), *Attestation Standards* (AT Section 100), the first in a new series of statements. (The AICPA's Management Advisory Services Executive Committee is also authorized to issue SSAEs.) The attestation standards provide guidance and establish a broad framework for performing and reporting on attest services generally. The standards do not supersede any existing SASs or other authoritative standards, but are a natural extension of the ten GAAS. Because of their breadth, the attestation standards can serve as a basis for establishing interpretive standards for a wide range of services in the future, while at the same time setting reasonable boundaries around the attest function. The attestation standards are discussed in Chapter 24.

Standards for Tax Practice.   The AICPA's Tax Division issues Statements on Responsibilities in Tax Practice, which provide guidance on tax practice and accountants' responsibilities in this area. They are not as authoritative as SASs because they are not enforceable under the Rules of the AICPA Code of Professional Conduct. Rather, they constitute advice on standards of good tax practice, covering the CPA's responsibility to his or her client, the public, the government, and the accounting profession.

Standards for MAS Practice.   In 1981, the AICPA's Management Advisory Services Executive Committee issued Statement on Standards for Management Advisory Services (SSMAS) No. 1, which defines two types of management advisory services—MAS engagements and MAS consultations—and sets forth a number of general and technical standards for MAS practice. Two subsequent statements provide guidance on the application of the standards in SSMAS No. 1 and establish additional standards. Compliance with the MAS standards is required under the Code of Professional Conduct. The MAS general and technical standards, adapted from *AICPA Professional Standards* MS Sections 11.05, 11.06, and 31.11, are summarized in Figure 2.2.

Standards for Internal Auditing.   The Institute of Internal Auditors in 1978 adopted a series of *Standards for the Professional Practice of Internal Auditing.* Those standards, which are reproduced in Figure 2.3, address the independence of

Figure 2.2   Standards for MAS Practice

General Standards:

Professional competence. A member shall undertake only those engagements which he or his firm can reasonably expect to complete with professional competence.

Due professional care. A member shall exercise due professional care in the performance of an engagement.

Planning and supervision. A member shall adequately plan and supervise an engagement.

Sufficient relevant data. A member shall obtain sufficient relevant data to afford a reasonable basis for conclusions or recommendations in relation to an engagement.

Forecasts. A member shall not permit his name to be used in conjunction with any forecast of future transactions in a manner that may lead to the belief that the member vouches for the achievability of the forecast.

Technical Standards:

Role of MAS practitioner. In performing an MAS engagement (consultation), an MAS practitioner should not assume the role of management or take any positions that might impair the MAS practitioner's objectivity.

Understanding with client. An oral or written understanding should be reached with the client concerning the nature, scope, and limitations of the MAS engagement (consultation) to be performed.

Client benefit. Since the potential benefits to be derived by the client are a major consideration in MAS engagements (consultations), such potential benefits should be viewed objectively and the client should be notified of reservations regarding them. In offering and providing MAS engagements (consultations), results should not be explicitly or implicitly guaranteed. When estimates of quantifiable results are presented, they should be clearly identified as estimates and the support for such estimates should be disclosed.

Communication of results. Significant information pertinent to the results of an MAS engagement (consultation), together with any limitations, qualifications, or reservations needed to assist the client in making its decision, should be communicated to the client orally or in writing.

Figure 2.3   Summary of General and Specific Standards
for the Professional Practice of Internal Auditing

100   **INDEPENDENCE**—Internal auditors should be independent of the activities they audit.

    110   ***Organizational Status***—The organizational status of the internal auditing department should be sufficient to permit the accomplishment of its audit responsibilities.

    120   ***Objectivity***—Internal auditors should be objective in performing audits.

200   **PROFESSIONAL PROFICIENCY**—Internal audits should be performed with proficiency and due professional care.

    The Internal Auditing Department

    210   ***Staffing***—The internal auditing department should provide assurance that the technical proficiency and educational background of internal auditors are appropriate for the audits to be performed.

    220   ***Knowledge, Skills, and Disciplines***—The internal auditing department should possess or should obtain the knowledge, skills, and disciplines needed to carry out its audit responsibilities.

    230   ***Supervision***—The internal auditing department should provide assurance that internal audits are properly supervised.

    The Internal Auditor

    240   ***Compliance with Standards of Conduct***—Internal auditors should comply with professional standards of conduct.

    250   ***Knowledge, Skills, and Disciplines***—Internal auditors should possess the knowledge, skills, and disciplines essential to the performance of internal audits.

    260   ***Human Relations and Communications***—Internal auditors should be skilled in dealing with people and in communicating effectively.

    270   ***Continuing Education***—Internal auditors should maintain their technical competence through continuing education.

    280   ***Due Professional Care***—Internal auditors should exercise due professional care in performing internal audits.

300   **SCOPE OF WORK**—The scope of the internal audit should encompass the examination and evaluation of the adequacy and effectiveness of the organization's system of internal control and the quality of performance in carrying out assigned responsibilities.

    310   ***Reliability and Integrity of Information***—Internal auditors should review the reliability and integrity of financial and operating information and the means used to identify, measure, classify, and report such information.

    320   ***Compliance with Policies, Plans, Procedures, Laws, and Regulations***—Internal auditors should review the systems established to ensure compliance with those policies, plans, procedures, laws, and regulations which could have a significant impact on operations and reports and should determine whether the organization is in compliance.

Figure 2.3   Continued

330   *Safeguarding of Assets*—Internal auditors should review the means of safeguarding assets and, as appropriate, verify the existence of such assets.

340   *Economical and Efficient Use of Resources*—Internal auditors should appraise the economy and efficiency with which resources are employed.

350   *Accomplishment of Established Objectives and Goals for Operations or Programs*—Internal auditors should review operations or programs to ascertain whether results are consistent with established objectives and goals and whether the operations or programs are being carried out as planned.

400   **PERFORMANCE OF AUDIT WORK—Audit work should include planning the audit, examining and evaluating information, communicating results, and following up.**

410   *Planning the Audit*—Internal auditors should plan each audit.

420   *Examining and Evaluating Information*—Internal auditors should collect, analyze, interpret, and document information to support audit results.

430   *Communicating Results*—Internal auditors should report the results of their audit work.

440   *Following Up*—Internal auditors should follow up to ascertain that appropriate action is taken on reported audit findings.

500   **MANAGEMENT OF THE INTERNAL AUDITING DEPARTMENT—The director of internal auditing should properly manage the internal auditing department.**

510   *Purpose, Authority, and Responsibility*—The director of internal auditing should have a statement of purpose, authority, and responsibility for the internal auditing department.

520   *Planning*—The director of internal auditing should establish plans to carry out the responsibilities of the internal auditing department.

530   *Policies and Procedures*—The director of internal auditing should provide written policies and procedures to guide the audit staff.

540   *Personnel Management and Development*—The director of internal auditing should establish a program for selecting and developing the human resources of the internal auditing department.

550   *External Auditors*—The director of internal auditing should coordinate internal and external audit efforts.

560   *Quality Assurance*—The director of internal auditing should establish and maintain a quality assurance program to evaluate the operations of the internal auditing department.

Source: Reproduced from *Standards for the Professional Practice of Internal Auditing* with the permission of The Institute of Internal Auditors, Inc.

internal auditors, their professional proficiency, the scope and performance of their work, and the management of internal auditing departments. The IIA standards differ somewhat in their philosophy from the AICPA standards for external auditors in that the former represent the practice of internal auditing as it *should be*, whereas to a large extent Statements on Auditing Standards represent the Auditing Standards Board's view of the consensus among practitioners—what is "generally accepted." That difference should not be exaggerated, however; the IIA standards are also a consensus, but of the best of practice rather than of what is minimally acceptable. The IIA also periodically issues Statements on Internal Auditing Standards to provide guidance on issues of interest to internal auditors.

Standards for Government Auditing. The General Accounting Office, the largest employer of government auditors in the United States, has issued a set of *Government Auditing Standards: Standards for Audit of Governmental Organizations, Programs, Activities, and Functions,* popularly referred to as the "Yellow Book." The standards were first published in 1972 and have been revised several times since then, most recently in 1988. Adherence to the standards is required not only for audits of federal organizations, programs, activities, and functions but also for federal funds received by nonprofit organizations and other nongovernmental entities. The GAO recommends that the standards be followed for state and local government audits performed by government auditors or CPAs, and several state and local audit agencies have adopted them. The GAO standards incorporate the AICPA's auditing standards and are compatible with the standards issued by the IIA.

The GAO standards define two types of government audits: financial audits (which include financial statements and financial-related audits) and performance audits (which include economy and efficiency audits and program audits). The standards consist of general standards, including independence and due professional care, and field work and reporting standards. The GAO standards are discussed further in Chapters 25 and 40.

3

Auditing Standards and Professional Conduct

All professions have technical and ethical standards to guide members in carrying out their duties and in their relationships with the various groups with which they come in contact. Also, all professions have means for enforcing those standards. Compliance with the public accounting profession's technical and ethical standards is enforced through various mechanisms created by the American Institute of Certified Public Accountants (AICPA) and by state societies of CPAs, state boards of accountancy, the Securities and Exchange Commission (SEC), the courts, and accounting firms themselves.

AUDITING AS A PROFESSION

While various writers and organizations have different criteria for defining an activity as a profession, there seems to be widespread agreement that the following characteristics must be present:

1. Formal recognition of professional status by means of a license issued by a government body after admission standards have been met.
2. A body of specialized knowledge, usually acquired through formal education.
3. A code of ethics to provide standards of conduct, and a means of enforcing compliance with the code.
4. Informal recognition and acceptance of professional status by the public, and public interest in the work performed.
5. Recognition by the professionals of a social obligation beyond the service performed for a particular client.

There can be little doubt that auditing has the attributes necessary to qualify as a profession. In a majority of jurisdictions in the United States, the privilege of practicing as a public accountant is limited by the statutes of the various states and territories to those who have been granted the designation of Certified Public Accountant (CPA) by a particular state or territory. The certification is granted only to those who have passed the CPA examination and, in many jurisdictions, who have also met specified education and experience requirements. At least in part because the CPA examination is uniform throughout all licensing jurisdictions and has a well-deserved reputation of being difficult, the public has come to expect a high level of expertise in accounting and auditing from a person who is a CPA.

The specialized knowledge of accounting and auditing that an auditor must have is usually acquired initially through an academic program at the undergraduate level, the graduate level, or both. The necessary knowledge is also acquired through on-the-job training and continuing education courses, sometimes to meet licensing or membership requirements of various bodies. For example, many states require an average of 40 hours of annual continuing education credits for CPAs to keep their license to practice; the AICPA's membership requirements also stipulate that members in public practice meet a similar level of professional education, with fewer credits required for members not in public practice. CPAs must also supplement their knowledge through an ongoing program of reading and self-study to keep current with new professional standards and stay abreast of economic and business issues.

As discussed later in this chapter, membership in the AICPA requires adherence to the Institute's Code of Professional Conduct. The Institute of Internal Auditors also has such a code, adherence to which is required of those internal auditors who have qualified as Certified Internal Auditors by virtue of having met examination, education, and experience requirements. The AICPA's Code of Professional Conduct and its enforcement are designed to ensure that CPAs who are members of the AICPA accept and achieve a high level of responsibility to the public, clients, and colleagues.

It is apparent that the public considers public accountancy a profession. Universities have established schools and programs of professional accountancy, and a mechanism is in place for separate accreditation of those programs by the American Assembly of Collegiate Schools of Business (AACSB). There is a high level of public interest in the work performed by CPAs, particularly auditing services. It is unusual for someone other than a CPA to be asked to attest to financial or other information that will be disseminated outside the enterprise.

Lastly, it is clear that the profession has long recognized an obligation to the public at large that extends well beyond the services performed for a particular client. While auditors realize that they have an obligation or responsibility to the client that has retained them, they are also aware that their audience is much larger. Audited financial statements are read, used, and relied on by many other groups—present and potential investors and creditors, suppliers, employees, customers, and government agencies. Testimony before legislative bodies at all levels of government and other less formal recommendations regarding tax laws, securities acts, and other relevant legislation have indicated a concern for the public interest that extends far beyond the parochial interests of auditors whose livelihood could be enhanced or diminished by the proposed legislation. Often, the positions an auditor takes publicly on such matters conflict with the specific interests of one or more clients, but professionals should place the interests of the public ahead of their own or those of a particular client. Above all, however, CPAs have an awareness of a professional's responsibilities to the public at large, an awareness that is continually enhanced by Congress, the media, the courts, the SEC, the AICPA, and other organizations, such as the Commission on Auditors' Responsibilities (the Cohen Commission) and the National Commission on Fraudulent Financial Reporting (the Treadway Commission).

GENERALLY ACCEPTED AUDITING STANDARDS

Professions set technical standards to ensure a specified minimum level of performance and quality, primarily because they recognize that the public has an interest in and relies on the work of professionals—and this is undoubtedly true for the auditing profession. Standards set the minimum level of performance and quality that auditors are expected, by their clients and the public, to achieve. In contrast to auditing procedures—which are steps to be performed and vary depending on factors unique to each audit, such as client size, industry, accounting system, and other circumstances—standards are measures of the quality of performance. Auditing standards should be unvarying over a wide spectrum of audit engagements over long periods of time.

The balance between the exercise of professional judgment and the establishment of specific rules to guide professional conduct pervades every aspect of accounting and auditing. The auditing profession has clearly rejected the two extremes: On the one hand, "cookbook" rules are not and never will be sufficient to cover every possible combination of circumstances and thereby allow auditors to shed their responsibility to exercise professional judgment; on the other hand, a framework exists to provide guidance for exercising judgment in all significant aspects of audit practice. It is between the two extremes that tensions and controversies arise: for example, how much uniformity should be required in auditing practice versus how much flexibility should be permitted, or to what extent standard sample sizes and auditing procedures should be spelled out versus the extent to which an auditor's pragmatic judgments should be required. Although the specific subject matter of debate changes from time to time, it is likely that the philosophical debate itself will never be concluded. It should be noted that this same tension between rules and individual judgment pervades most professions.

The membership of the AICPA officially adopted ten generally accepted auditing standards in 1948. AICPA pronouncements—Statements on Auditing Procedure and Statements on Auditing Standards—have amplified and interpreted the ten GAAS. Fifty-four Statements on Auditing Procedure (SAPs) were issued between 1939 and 1972; 63 Statements on Auditing Standards (SASs) have been issued since then, and others are in draft. Statement on Auditing Standards No. 1 codified the 54 SAPs; updated codifications of SAPs and SASs that are still effective are issued annually by the AICPA.

Practitioners and others who need to understand auditors' work and reports should be thoroughly familiar with the SASs, for they constitute the authoritative professional auditing literature. The ten generally accepted auditing standards—the source of all subsequent SAPs and SASs—are found in SAS No. 1 (AU Section 150 of *AICPA Professional Standards*), as follows:

General Standards

1. The audit is to be performed by a person or persons having adequate technical training and proficiency as an auditor.
2. In all matters relating to the assignment, an independence in mental attitude is to be maintained by the auditor or auditors.
3. Due professional care is to be exercised in the performance of the audit and the preparation of the report.

Standards of Field Work

1. The work is to be adequately planned and assistants, if any, are to be properly supervised.

2. A sufficient understanding of the internal control structure is to be obtained to plan the audit and to determine the nature, timing, and extent of tests to be performed.
3. Sufficient competent evidential matter is to be obtained through inspection, observation, inquiries, and confirmations to afford a reasonable basis for an opinion regarding the financial statements under audit.

Standards of Reporting

1. The report shall state whether the financial statements are presented in accordance with generally accepted accounting principles.
2. The report shall identify those circumstances in which such principles have not been consistently observed in the current period in relation to the preceding period.
3. Informative disclosures in the financial statements are to be regarded as reasonably adequate unless otherwise stated in the report.
4. The report shall either contain an expression of opinion regarding the financial statements, taken as a whole, or an assertion to the effect that an opinion cannot be expressed. When an overall opinion cannot be expressed, the reasons therefor should be stated. In all cases where an auditor's name is associated with financial statements, the report should contain a clear-cut indication of the character of the auditor's work, and the degree of responsibility the auditor is taking.

General Standards

The general standards relate to the qualifications of an auditor and the quality of the audit work. They are personal in nature and are distinct from the standards governing the performance of field work and reporting.

Training and Proficiency.   The first general standard suggests that the auditor must have proper education and experience in the field of auditing to meet the profession's requirements for adequate training and proficiency. Training begins with formal education and continues with proper supervision and review on the job, as well as formal continuing professional education and self-study. Formal continuing education and self-study are necessary parts of this standard, especially as new developments in accounting, auditing, finance, data processing, taxes, and other aspects of business management continue to force change on practitioners. The need for formal continuing education and self-study, however, does not diminish the importance of on-the-job training, planned development of well-rounded experience, and adequate supervision and review in maintaining proficiency.

Independence.   The second general standard requires that the auditor not be biased toward the client. Furthermore, to safeguard the confidence of the public and users of financial statements in auditor independence, auditors must also be "recognized" as independent. SAS No. 1 (AU Section 220.03) provides the following amplification of this:

To *be* independent, the auditor must be intellectually honest; to be *recognized* as independent, he must be free from any obligation to or interest in the client, its management, or its owners. For example, an independent auditor auditing a company of which he was also a director might be intellectually honest, but it is unlikely that the public would accept him as independent since he would be in effect auditing decisions which he had a part in making. Likewise, an auditor with a substantial financial interest in a company might be unbiased in expressing his opinion on the financial statements of the company, but the public would be reluctant to believe that he was unbiased. Independent auditors should not only be independent in fact; they should avoid situations that may lead outsiders to doubt their independence.

The distinction drawn in this quotation is often referred to as that of "independence in fact" contrasted with "independence in appearance." The former—intellectual honesty—cannot be ensured by rules or prohibitions. The latter—avoiding potentially compromising situations—can, at least partially, be. To guard against any appearance or "presumption" of loss of independence, the AICPA has established specific rules on independence in its Code of Professional Conduct, as discussed in the next section of this chapter. Likewise, the Securities and Exchange Commission has emphasized the importance of independence and has issued rules relating to it.

Due Care.   SAS No. 1 (AU Section 230.04) notes that due care relates to what independent auditors do and how well they do it. Due care imposes a responsibility on each person in an auditing firm to exercise the skills he or she possesses with reasonable care and diligence; due care also requires critical review of the work done and of the judgments made. For example, due care is not exercised if the auditor fails to corroborate representations of client management that are significant to the financial statements, such as representations regarding the collectibility of long-outstanding accounts receivable.

Standards of Field Work

The standards of field work cover planning and supervising the audit, understanding the internal control structure, and obtaining audit evidence.

Adequate Planning and Supervision.   Planning an audit engagement involves both technical and administrative considerations. The technical aspect of planning entails formulating an overall audit strategy for the engagement. Implementing the audit strategy includes numerous planning decisions of an administrative nature, such as scheduling the work, assigning personnel, and similar matters.

Early appointment of the independent auditor facilitates audit planning. In particular, it makes it possible to consider performing certain auditing procedures during the year rather than at year-end. This increases both audit efficiency and the likelihood of identifying problems at an early date. In the planning stage, analytical procedures are performed to help determine the nature, timing, and extent of other auditing procedures by identifying significant matters the auditor should address.

SAS No. 22, *Planning and Supervision* (AU Section 311.11), states that supervision involves directing the work of assistants and determining whether the objectives of that work were accomplished. On many engagements, as much as one-fifth to one-fourth of the total audit time is spent on supervision. The time is well spent, because the total audit time is likely to be much greater without effective supervision.

Supervision starts with assigning tasks and ensuring that each task and its objectives are understood. It continues with frequent discussions between supervisor and assistants for the purpose of both keeping informed, especially about significant problems encountered, and providing ongoing advice and direction to assistants. That means discussions among the partner, manager, and staff members on an engagement; on large audits personal visits to many different groups and locations may be required. Supervision also entails dealing with differences of opinion among staff members concerning accounting and auditing issues. A final element of supervision is reviewing the completed work of assistants, discussing the review with them, and evaluating their performance.

Understanding the Internal Control Structure.   The importance of the second standard of field work has increased as the role of the control environment in preventing and detecting fraud and error has received increasing recognition, as specialists have learned to construct highly reliable computerized accounting systems, and as auditors have become concerned with conducting efficient as well as effective audits. This standard requires the auditor to obtain a sufficient understanding of the client's control structure to adequately plan the tests of transactions and account balances to be performed; the standard does not require that the entire control structure, or even a part of it, be tested *unless* the auditor plans to use the knowledge obtained from such tests to restrict the testing of transactions and account balances. Subsequent chapters discuss the elements of the control structure, how the auditor assesses it, and how that assessment affects the tests the auditor applies to account balances and underlying transactions.

Obtaining Competent Evidence.   A detailed understanding of the third standard of field work is important to all phases of auditing. The standard covers both the "competence" and the "sufficiency" of evidence. The competence of evidence relates to its relevance and reliability; sufficiency depends on the amount of assurance the auditor believes is needed to support an opinion that the financial statements are not materially misstated.

Standards of Reporting

Four standards of reporting govern this aspect of the audit effort.

Adherence to Generally Accepted Accounting Principles.   The auditor is required first to be thoroughly familiar with generally accepted accounting principles, and second to determine whether the financial statements reported on "present fairly" the client's financial position, results of operations, and cash flows in conformity with those principles. Chapter 22, "The Auditor's Report," deals in depth with the auditor's reporting responsibilities relating to generally accepted accounting principles and fairness, and presents examples of appropriate auditors' reports in cases of departures from generally accepted accounting principles.

Consistent Application.   The consistency standard requires the auditor to identify in the auditor's report circumstances in which generally accepted accounting principles have not been applied consistently from period to period. The objective is to ensure either that changes in accounting principles or methods of applying them do not materially affect the comparability of financial statements between periods or that the effect is disclosed.

Adequate Disclosure.   The intent of the third standard of reporting is that issuers of financial statements and auditors have a responsibility to ensure that disclosures are adequate, regardless of whether a specific authoritative pronouncement covers the matter. It is thus the auditor's responsibility to identify matters of potential interest to users of the financial statements and to form a conclusion about whether and how they should be disclosed. If the client does not make the necessary disclosures, the auditor must qualify the opinion.

Expression of Opinion.   An auditor's report must be painstakingly precise in spelling out the opinion expressed. Leaving the meaning of an auditor's opinion open to readers' inferences is both inappropriate and dangerous. In some instances, an auditor's failure to state the reasons for disclaiming an opinion has permitted inferences that were either more or less favorable to a client than was warranted. In other instances, financial statement users cited ambiguity in an auditor's report as grounds for claims against the auditor. From the time of its adoption, the fourth standard of reporting has been accompanied by detailed recommendations for reporting in all conceivable circumstances. The intention of those detailed prescriptions is to ensure that all auditors use precisely the same words in the same circumstances to prevent misinterpretation of their opinions and the responsibility they assume.

THE AICPA CODE OF PROFESSIONAL CONDUCT

The Code of Professional Conduct of the American Institute of Certified Public Accountants covers both the profession's responsibility to the public and the CPA's responsibility to clients and colleagues. While the AICPA Code is directly enforceable only against individual AICPA members, in reality its applicability is much more pervasive. Most of the significant portions of the Code have been adopted by the various state societies or institutes of CPAs and in many cases have also been incorporated into state statutes or the regulations of state boards of accountancy that license CPAs to practice before the public. In effect, all of these organizations enforce ethical behavior by CPAs.

Codes of ethical conduct are not unique to the practice of accounting. All professionals, including doctors, lawyers, and actuaries, to name a few, have deemed it essential to promulgate codes of professional conduct and to establish means for ensuring their observance. Such codes define the type of behavior that the public has a right to expect from the professionals, and thereby enhance the public's confidence in the quality of professional services rendered.

Most codes of professional conduct, including the AICPA's, contain general ethical principles that are aspirational in character and represent the objectives toward which every member of the profession should strive. The codes also usually contain a set of specific, mandatory rules that state the minimum level of conduct the professional must maintain to avoid being subject to disciplinary action. In the past, some sections of many codes of conduct have also had an ancillary effect of reducing competition, through prohibitions against advertising, solicitation of clients, and encroachment on the practice of a fellow professional. In recent years, however, the courts have deemed such prohibitions to be illegal. Accordingly, most professional associations, including the AICPA, have revised their codes to permit advertising and other forms of solicitation, so long as the professional does not seek to obtain clients by false, misleading, or deceptive advertising or other forms of solicitation.

The AICPA's ethical standards fall into four categories: Principles, Rules, Interpretations of the Rules, and Ethics Rulings. The Principles and Rules comprise the Code of Professional Conduct, the latest version of which was adopted by vote of the AICPA membership in 1988. The Principles express the basic tenets of ethical and professional conduct. The Rules consist of enforceable ethical standards to which AICPA members must adhere: Members must be prepared to justify departures from the Rules. Interpretations of the Rules have been adopted by the AICPA to provide guidelines on the scope and application of the Rules. Ethics Rulings summarize the application of the Rules and Interpretations to a particular set of factual circumstances. The Code as a whole is intended to provide guidance and rules for all AICPA members in the performance of their professional responsibilities, regardless of whether the members are in the public practice of accountancy, in industry, in government, or in academe. Some of the Rules, however, are specifically relevant and stated to be applicable only to CPAs in public practice.

The Preamble to the Principles of Professional Conduct emphasizes the professional's responsibility to the public, clients, and colleagues. The Principles of the Code of Professional Conduct are goal oriented, describing general ideals accountants should aspire to, while the Rules set forth minimum levels of acceptable conduct. The high level of conduct for which CPAs should strive is embodied in the more philosophical Principles, which ''call for an unswerving commitment to honorable behavior, even at the sacrifice of personal advantage.''

The six Principles of the Code are as follows:

Responsibilities. In carrying out their responsibilities as professionals, members should exercise sensitive professional and moral judgments in all their activities.

The Public Interest. Members should accept the obligation to act in a way that will serve the public interest, honor the public trust, and demonstrate commitment to professionalism.

Integrity. To maintain and broaden public confidence, members should perform all professional responsibilities with the highest sense of integrity.

Objectivity and Independence. A member should maintain objectivity and be free of conflicts of interest in discharging professional responsibilities. A member in public practice should be independent in fact and appearance when providing auditing and other attestation services.

Due Care. A member should observe the profession's technical and ethical standards, strive continually to improve competence and the quality of services, and discharge professional responsibility to the best of the member's ability.

Scope and Nature of Services. A member in public practice should observe the Principles of the Code of Professional Conduct in determining the scope and nature of services to be provided.

A discussion of each of the Rules, along with the related Interpretations and Rulings, follows.

Independence, Integrity, and Objectivity

According to the Principles of the Code of Professional Conduct,

> Integrity is an element of character fundamental to professional recognition. It is the quality from which the public trust derives and the benchmark against which a member must ultimately test all decisions. . . . Integrity also requires a member to observe the principles of objectivity and independence and of due care.
>
> Objectivity is a state of mind, a quality that lends value to a member's services. It is a distinguishing feature of the profession. The principle of objectivity imposes the obligation to be impartial, intellectually honest, and free of conflicts of interest. Independence precludes relationships that may appear to impair a member's objectivity in rendering attestation services.

The importance of independence is indicated by the prevalence of the subject in the profession's authoritative literature. It is found not only in the Principles of the Code of Professional Conduct and Rule 101, but also in the corresponding rules of professional conduct of the various state societies and state regulatory agencies; in SAS No. 1 (AU Section 220) (discussed in an earlier section of this chapter); in Statement on Quality Control Standards No. 1, *System of Quality Control for a CPA Firm* (QC Section 10); and in Rule 2–01 of SEC Regulation S-X. Independence enhances the auditor's ability to act with integrity and objectivity.

Rule 101 (Independence) requires AICPA members in public practice to be independent in the performance of auditing and other attestation services. Auditors, like practitioners in other professions, offer clients specialized technical skills and knowledge based on training and experience, but that is not all.

Clients and others rely on auditors because of their belief in the auditors' professional integrity, independence, and objectivity. Clearly, the published opinion of an auditor has little value unless it rests unquestionably on those qualities. They are personal, inward qualities not susceptible to precise determination or definition, and are best maintained by the individual auditor's own conscience and the recognition that a professional's principal asset is a reputation for integrity, independence, and objectivity. It is also important to the public's confidence in an auditor's opinion that the auditor's respect for those qualities be as apparent as possible.

The Code of Professional Conduct, like SAS No. 1, emphasizes *appearing* to be independent as well as *being* independent. Both the accounting profession and the SEC have spelled out detailed prohibitions, not only against those activities or relationships that might actually erode the mental attitude of independence but also against those that might even suggest or imply a possibility of lack of independence.

Interpretation 101-1 (ET Section 101.02) provides examples of situations that impair independence.

Interpretation of Rule 101. Independence shall be considered to be impaired if, for example, a member had any of the following transactions, interests, or relationships:

A. During the period of a professional engagement or at the time of expressing an opinion, a member or a member's firm

   1. Had or was committed to acquire any direct or material indirect financial interest in the enterprise.
   2. Was a trustee of any trust or executor or administrator of any estate if such trust or estate had or was committed to acquire any direct or material indirect financial interest in the enterprise.
   3. Had any joint, closely held business investment with the enterprise or with any officer, director, or principal stockholders thereof that was material in relation to the member's net worth or to the net worth of the member's firm.
   4. Had any loan to or from the enterprise or any officer, director, or principal stockholder of the enterprise. This proscription does not apply to the following loans from a financial institution when made under normal lending procedures, terms, and requirements:
      a. Loans obtained by a member or a member's firm that are not material in relation to the net worth of such borrower.
      b. Home mortgages.
      c. Other secured loans, except loans guaranteed by a member's firm which are otherwise unsecured.

B. During the period covered by the financial statements, during the period of the professional engagement, or at the time of expressing an opinion, a member or a member's firm

   1. Was connected with the enterprise as a promoter, underwriter or voting trustee, as a director or officer, or in any capacity equivalent to that of a member of management or of an employee.

2. Was a trustee for any pension or profit-sharing trust of the enterprise.

The above examples are not intended to be all-inclusive.

Regulation S-X, Rule 2–01, "Qualifications of Accountants," specifies the SEC's independence requirements.

> The Commission will not recognize any certified public accountant or public accountant as independent who is not in fact independent. For example, an accountant will be considered not independent with respect to any person or any of its parents, its subsidiaries, or other affiliates (1) in which, during the period of his professional engagement to examine the financial statements being reported on or at the date of his report, he, his firm, or a member of his firm had, or was committed to acquire, any direct financial interest or any material indirect financial interest; (2) with which, during the period of his professional engagement to examine the financial statements being reported on, at the date of his report or during the period covered by the financial statements, he, his firm, or a member of his firm was connected as a promoter, underwriter, voting trustee, director, officer, or employee. A firm's independence will not be deemed to be affected adversely where a former officer or employee of a particular person is employed by or becomes a partner, shareholder or other principal in the firm and such individual has completely disassociated himself from the person and its affiliates and does not participate in auditing financial statements of the person or its affiliates covering any period of his employment by the person. For the purposes of Rule 2–01 the term "member" means (i) all partners, shareholders, and other principals in the firm, (ii) any professional employee involved in providing any professional service to the person, its parents, subsidiaries, or other affiliates, and (iii) any professional employee having managerial responsibilities and located in the engagement office or other office of the firm which participates in a significant portion of the audit.
>
> In determining whether an accountant may in fact be not independent with respect to a particular person, the Commission will give appropriate consideration to all relevant circumstances, including evidence bearing on all relationships between the accountant and that person or any affiliate thereof, and will not confine itself to the relationships existing in connection with the filing of reports with the Commission.

Many of the foregoing prohibitions reach extremes that might appear ridiculous to a nonprofessional, but they reflect the profession's concern about the appearance of independence. For example, no partner in an auditing firm or member of the partner's immediate family is permitted to own even one share of stock of a client or affiliated company or even to participate in an investment club that holds such shares, no matter what the individual's personal net worth, the size of the company, or the partner's distance from the actual audit work. Some firms also prohibit ownership of a client's stock by any staff member, regardless of what office is performing the audit. As another example, an auditing firm may not have its employees' pension fund managed by an investment counselor that also manages a mutual fund client; even though there is no actual financial relationship, there might be an appearance of lack of independence. In addition, other Interpretations and Ethics Rulings under Rule 101 outline specific prohibitions in this area.

The AICPA's and SEC's prohibitions relating to independence are not entirely free of social costs. Weighing the costs and benefits of prohibitions on individual or firm conduct in order to enhance independence is a matter of public policy and social choice. The current independence rules indicate the importance that both the profession and the public attach to the auditor's independence, integrity, and objectivity.

Accounting Services. Interpretation 101-3 (ET Section 101.05) permits members to provide bookkeeping or data processing services to audit clients only if the following requirements are met:

- There must be no relationship or conflict of interest between the CPA and the client that would impair the CPA's integrity and objectivity.
- The client's management must accept responsibility for the financial statements.
- The CPA must not assume the role of an employee or management of the client.
- In auditing the financial statements, the CPA must comply with generally accepted auditing standards, i.e., must perform sufficient audit tests of statements prepared from records that the CPA has maintained or processed.

The SEC has noted that an accountant's maintaining the records of an SEC registrant either manually or through EDP equipment may be indicative of a lack of independence. (Many of the SEC's independence requirements extend to the entire period covered by the financial statements, which generally cover three years of operations and cash flows.)

Family Relationships. Interpretation 101-9 (ET Section 101.10) addresses two categories of family relationships that may affect the independence of members. The first category comprises a member's spouse, dependent children, and any other dependent person living in the same household as or supported by the member. The financial interests and business relationships of such individuals are ascribed to the member and thus are governed by Rule 101. The second category is nondependent close relatives, defined as nondependent children, brothers and sisters, grandparents, parents, parents-in-law, and the spouses of any of those individuals. Relatives in this category are not permitted to have a material financial interest or investment in or business relationship with a client of a member, nor may they hold a position with a client in which they can exercise significant influence over its operating, financial, or accounting policies.

Independence and Attest Engagements. Statement on Standards for Attestation Engagements, *Attestation Standards* (AT Section 100.22–.24), requires members to be independent in performing engagements covered by that Statement. In January 1989, the Professional Ethics Executive Committee issued for exposure a proposed Interpretation under Rule 101 to provide guidance regarding independence for attest engagements not covered by Statements on Auditing Standards, Statements on Standards for Accounting and Review Services, or Statements on Standards for Accountants' Services on Prospective Financial Information.

Under the proposed Interpretation,

> Independence will be considered to be impaired if an individual on the attest engagement team
>
> 1. Has either directly or beneficially, through his or her firm,[a] a relationship with the asserter or the subject matter of the assertion ("the subject") that is proscribed under Interpretation 101-1 of Rule 101, or
> 2. Has knowledge that a nondependent close relative[b] has either a position of significant influence with or a financial interest material to the close relative in the asserter or the subject.
>
> Independence will also be considered to be impaired if an individual on the attest engagement team has knowledge that (1) a partner or shareholder in his or her office has a relationship with the asserter or the subject that is proscribed under Interpretation 101-1 or (2) a partner or shareholder in another office has a position of significant influence with the asserter or the subject.
>
> [a]For the purpose of this Interpretation, firm shall mean the sole proprietorship, partnership or professional corporation of which an individual on the attest engagement team is an owner, partner, shareholder or employee.
> [b]For the purpose of this Interpretation, these terms shall mean the same as in Interpretation 101-9, "The Meaning of Certain Independence Terminology and the Effect of Family Relationships on Independence."

The proposed Interpretation is noteworthy in that it proscribes relationships with both the subject matter of the assertion and the asserter, and provides guidance or examples for each situation. However, the prohibited relationships apply only to the attest engagement team (which is precisely defined in the Interpretation) and certain individuals whose relationships are known to members of the team. In contrast, prohibited relationships in *audit* engagements apply to all partners or proprietors in the accounting firm and to all managerial employees in an office that participates in a significant portion of the engagement.

Past-Due Fees.   Ethics Ruling 52 (ET Section 191.103–.104) addresses the effect of past-due fees on the independence of a member's firm. The Ruling states that independence may be impaired if more than one year's fees are unpaid when the member issues a report on the client's financial statements for the current year. The reason for this ruling is that past-due fees may make it appear that the auditor is providing working capital for the client and that collecting the past-due fees may depend on the nature of the auditor's report on the financial statements. (The SEC's rules in this regard are more restrictive than those of the AICPA.)

Conflicts of Interest.   Rule 101 on independence is applicable only to members in public practice. That Rule (and the Interpretations under it) are intended, according to the Principles of the Code of Professional Conduct, to preclude "relationships that may appear to impair a member's objectivity in rendering attestation services." Rule 102 is intended to prohibit members, whether or not in public practice, from subordinating their judgment to others when performing *any* professional service.

Rule 102 (Integrity and Objectivity) states

> In the performance of any professional service, a member shall maintain objectivity and integrity, shall be free of conflicts of interest, and shall not knowingly misrepresent facts or subordinate his or her judgment to others.

In 1989, the Professional Ethics Executive Committee adopted an Interpretation (102–2) under Rule 102 that addresses conflicts of interest. This Interpretation states

> A conflict of interest may occur if a member performs a professional service for a client or employer and the member or his or her firm has a significant relationship with another person, entity, product, or service that could be viewed as impairing the member's objectivity. If this significant relationship is disclosed to and consent is obtained from such client, employer, or other appropriate parties, the rule shall not operate to prohibit the performance of the professional service. When making this disclosure, the member should consider Rule 301, "Confidential Client Information."

> Certain professional engagements require independence. Independence impairments under Rule 101 and its interpretations cannot be eliminated by such disclosure and consent.

Until 1988, members engaged in the practice of public accounting were explicitly prohibited from concurrently engaging in any business or occupation that would create a conflict of interest in rendering professional services. That rule was deleted because the Principles provide guidance on conflicts of interest and Rule 102 requires AICPA members to avoid such conflicts.

General and Technical Standards

The Rules require adherence to standards related to the conduct of the CPA's work.

General Standards.   Rule 201 sets forth the following general standards:

> A member shall comply with the following standards and with any interpretations thereof by bodies designated by Council.

> A. *Professional Competence.* Undertake only those professional services that the member or the member's firm can reasonably expect to be completed with professional competence.

B. *Due Professional Care.* Exercise due professional care in the performance of professional services.

C. *Planning and Supervision.* Adequately plan and supervise the performance of professional services.

D. *Sufficient Relevant Data.* Obtain sufficient relevant data to afford a reasonable basis for conclusions or recommendations in relation to any professional services performed.

Technical Standards.   Rules 202 and 203 are as follows:

Compliance With Standards. A member who performs auditing, review, compilation, management advisory, tax, or other professional services shall comply with standards promulgated by bodies designated by Council.

Accounting Principles. A member shall not (1) express an opinion or state affirmatively that the financial statements or other financial data of any entity are presented in conformity with generally accepted accounting principles or (2) state that he or she is not aware of any material modifications that should be made to such statements or data in order for them to be in conformity with generally accepted accounting principles, if such statements or data contain any departure from an accounting principle promulgated by bodies designated by Council to establish such principles that has a material effect on the statements or data taken as a whole. If, however, the statements or data contain such a departure and the member can demonstrate that due to unusual circumstances the financial statements or data would otherwise have been misleading, the member can comply with the rule by describing the departure, its approximate effects, if practicable, and the reasons why compliance with the principle would result in a misleading statement.

Rules 202 and 203 were adopted to require compliance with the profession's practice standards and accounting principles. There is a strong presumption that adherence to accounting principles promulgated by the FASB and the Governmental Accounting Standards Board (GASB) will result in financial statements that are not misleading.

Rule 203 and Interpretation 203–1 also recognize that occasionally there may be unusual circumstances in which the literal application of pronouncements on accounting principles would have the effect of rendering financial statements misleading. In such unusual cases, the proper accounting treatment is one that will render the financial statements not misleading. Chapter 22 discusses the appropriate wording of the auditor's report in these circumstances.

Responsibilities to Clients

The Principles of the Code of Professional Conduct note that a CPA has responsibilities to clients as well as to the public. CPAs should serve their clients with competence and with regard for the clients' interests. They must also, however, maintain their obligation to the public as evidenced by their independence, integrity, and objectivity.

A fundamental responsibility of the CPA concerns the confidentiality of client information. Rule 301 states that "a member in public practice shall not disclose any confidential information without the specific consent of the client."[1]

Need for Confidentiality.   Both common sense and the independence concept dictate that the auditor, not the client, should decide what information the auditor needs to conduct an effective audit. That decision should not be influenced by a client's belief that certain information is confidential. An efficient and effective audit requires that the client have the necessary trust in the auditor to be extremely candid in supplying information. Therefore, the client must be assured of confidentiality and that, except for disclosures required by generally accepted accounting principles, information shared with the auditor will go no further without explicit permission.

Despite the profession's emphasis on confidentiality, executives of some companies are concerned about losing control of sensitive material through an auditor's staff. They may believe that certain material is so sensitive that they cannot be comfortable with an auditor's general assurances about the character and training of the audit staff. If access to the material is necessary to the auditor's opinion, the client's executives have no alternative but to grant access; if they wish to limit that access to specified individuals on the audit team, that condition should be respected. Although awareness of clients' sensibilities is important, the authors have observed that clients' fears generally tend to subside as the working relationship is strengthened, confidence grows, and mutually satisfactory arrangements are made.

Confidentiality Versus Privilege.   Except as noted earlier, communications between the client and the auditor are confidential; that is, the auditor should not reveal the information contained in the communication without the client's permission. Under common law, however, that information is not "privileged." Information is privileged if the client can prevent a court or government agency from gaining access to it through a summons or subpoena. Information given to an auditor by a client is often not privileged; it is subject to summons or subpoena in many jurisdictions, including the federal courts. (In those states where an auditor–client privilege does exist, it can be waived only by the client. While it exists for the client's benefit, it also serves to enhance full and honest disclosure between client and auditor.) Auditors and

---

[1]Rule 301 states that "this rule shall not be construed (1) to relieve a member of his or her professional obligations under rules 202 and 203, (2) to affect in any way the member's obligation to comply with a validly issued and enforceable subpoena or summons, (3) to prohibit review of a member's professional practice under AICPA or state CPA society authorization, or (4) to preclude a member from initiating a complaint with or responding to any inquiry made by a recognized investigative or disciplinary body."

In 1989, the Professional Ethics Executive Committee adopted an Interpretation (301-2) under Rule 301 that provides that "exemption (2) is interpreted to provide that Rule 301 should not be construed to prohibit or interfere with a member's compliance with applicable laws and government regulations"; and also specifies that the recognized investigative or disciplinary bodies noted in exemption (4) are only AICPA bodies or other participants in the Joint Ethics Enforcement Program.

their professional organizations generally support clients' legal resistance to summonses and subpoenas to produce documents or other communications given to or received from their auditors, when it appears that there are legitimate reasons for maintaining confidentiality.

One particularly sensitive area involves the auditor's review of the client's analysis of the provision for income taxes. As a result of Internal Revenue Service subpoenas of auditors' tax provision working papers, and several lawsuits resulting from CPA firms' refusal to comply, many clients are reluctant to provide the auditor with such tax analyses. Regardless of a client's fears, however, the auditor must review sufficient evidential matter to conclude that the tax provision is adequate. Fortunately for the public as well as for the profession, the courts have placed significant limitations on the extent to which these working papers may be subpoenaed.

Insider Information.   Auditors and their staff have the same responsibilities as management for handling insider information: not to turn it to personal profit or to disclose it to others who may do so. Those responsibilities are clearly covered by the general injunctions of the Code of Professional Conduct: Independence forbids personal profit, and confidentiality forbids aiding others in that pursuit. The ways in which insider information may be used, even inadvertently, are many and subtle; society's heightened standards of accountability have focused attention on the responsibility of all insiders to use insider information only for the benefit of the enterprise.

Problems Involving Confidentiality.   Some clients' fears that secrets will be passed on to competitors are so great that they refuse to engage an auditor whose clients include a competitor; others are satisfied with assurances that the staff on their engagement has no contact with a competitor's personnel. The price paid by a client for so high a degree of confidentiality is the loss of industry expertise that can be provided by auditors who are familiar with more than one company in an industry. Experience suggests that the risk of leakage of information that has competitive value is extremely slight.

A more difficult and quite common dilemma results if two of an auditor's clients do business with each other. For example, an auditor of a commercial bank is likely also to have clients among the bank's depositors and borrowers. Suppose the auditor observes the September 30th physical inventory of a company that is also a borrower at the client bank, and finds a substantial shortage. Under the terms of the company's loan agreement with the bank, audited financial statements are not due at the bank until the next March 31. The client understandably wants time to determine the cause of the shortage. What does the auditor do? This is a practical dilemma quite apart from problems of potential formal legal liability or expression of an opinion on either set of financial statements. On the one hand, the auditor must not use insider information from one client to profit by improving his or her relationship with the other client. On the other hand, it is absurd for the auditor to pretend not to know something that he or she does know. One party will be unhappy if the auditor does nothing; the other party will be upset if the auditor does anything.

The solution to the dilemma is clear in principle, though following it in practice may be difficult. Court cases have clarified the client's responsibility: As soon as a significant event—good or bad—happens, it should be disclosed to all concerned. Neither the client bank nor the client borrower has priority, and the incidental fact of their parallel relationship with the auditor should not affect the handling of the matter. The auditor's duty is to persuade the client borrower to make the necessary prompt disclosures—to the other party if it affects only the two, and publicly if it affects the public.

Before information is publicly disclosed, however, the auditor needs to obtain and document all available pertinent facts, discuss them with the client, and evaluate their effect on the financial statements. All of this takes time, but the resulting delay in making the disclosure is justified: Disclosing information prematurely or inappropriately, that is, before it has been adequately investigated, may create more problems than it solves.

If the client's management refuses to disclose information that the auditor has concluded should be disclosed, the auditor must decide whether it is possible to continue to serve the client. The auditor may want to seek legal counsel in this situation. Usually the auditor will consider going to the board of directors, and in some cases to the SEC and the stock exchanges, and to anyone else known to be affected. Those are very serious steps, and whether to take them is as difficult a decision as an auditor can ever be called on to make. The auditor would risk even more serious problems, however, by favoring a client over other concerned parties. The courts have made clear, as indicated by the *Fund of Funds*[2] case, that an auditor who has reason to believe, from whatever source, that a client's financial statements are materially misstated cannot issue an unqualified opinion.

Another problem of confidentiality may result if a client that is considering acquiring another company engages its own auditor to audit that company. What happens to the auditor's findings and to whom is the duty of confidentiality owed? Common practice in those circumstances is to obtain written confirmations from the chief executives of both companies regarding the extent and limitations of the auditor's responsibilities to each. The confirmation letter to the company to be acquired often includes a statement that the auditor has no responsibility to that company other than the obvious requirement to act in a professional manner. Usually the confirmations approve delivering the findings to the acquiring company, but only after discussing them with the company to be acquired.

Responsibilities to Colleagues

While there are currently no specific Rules governing a CPA's responsibility to colleagues, the Principles set forth the fundamental tenet of cooperation among members of the profession by stating that AICPA members should "cooperate with each other to improve the art of accounting, maintain the public's confidence, and carry out the profession's special responsibilities for self-governance."

---

[2]*Fund of Funds, Ltd.* v. *Arthur Andersen & Co.*, 545 F. Supp. 1314 (S.D.N.Y. 1982).

Other Responsibilities and Practices

Acts Discreditable to the Profession. Rule 501 states: "A member shall not commit an act discreditable to the profession." Interpretations under Rule 501 (ET Section 501.01–.05) provide examples of specific acts that would be discreditable to the profession.

1. Retention of client records after a demand is made for them.
2. Discrimination based on race, color, religion, sex, age, or national origin in hiring, promotion, or salary practices.
3. Failure to follow government audit standards, guides, procedures, statutes, rules, and regulations (in addition to generally accepted auditing standards) that may be specified in an audit of government grants, government units, or other recipients of government monies if an engagement has been accepted under those conditions.
4. Negligence in the preparation of financial statements or records (thus explicitly including CPAs who are not in public practice and who serve as preparers rather than auditors of financial statements).

Form of Practice and Name and Ownership of Practice Units. Rule 505 states

> A member may practice public accounting only in the form of a proprietorship, a partnership, or a professional corporation whose characteristics conform to resolutions of Council.
>
> A member shall not practice public accounting under a firm name that is misleading. Names of one or more past partners or shareholders may be included in the firm name of a successor partnership or corporation. Also, a partner or shareholder surviving the death or withdrawal of all other partners or shareholders may continue to practice under such name which includes the name of past partners or shareholders for up to two years after becoming a sole practitioner.
>
> A firm may not designate itself as "Members of the American Institute of Certified Public Accountants" unless all of its partners or shareholders are members of the Institute.

The current rule revises a previous rule that prohibited a firm name that included a fictitious name or indicated specialization. The previous rule was revised because the prohibition against fictitious names was vulnerable to antitrust attack and was inconsistent with the rule on advertising and solicitation, which prohibits only claims that are false, misleading, or deceptive. Since a member may advertise a specialty, there is no reason a firm should not be allowed to do so in its name, provided the false, misleading, or deceptive test is met.

Appendix B to the Code contains a resolution of AICPA Council that specifies the characteristics that a professional corporation must have to comply with Rule 505. That resolution restricts ownership of a professional corporation to persons engaged in the practice of public accounting, and is intended to make the owners of practice units subject to the Institute's technical, ethical, and practice-monitoring requirements and its self-regulatory and disciplinary processes.

The contrary view, which has been expressed by the Federal Trade Commission (FTC), is that this rule may deter the use of more efficient forms of practice and thereby restrain competition. The ownership question raises complex economic and social issues, which are likely to be of significant concern to the SEC, other regulatory bodies, and congressional oversight committees. At the time of this writing, the FTC is consulting with those bodies.

Marketing Professional Services

Traditionally, CPAs marketed their services by performing quality work and relying on word of mouth to inform potential clients about their professional qualifications. Until the late 1970s, the AICPA code of ethics prohibited members from advertising and using all forms of direct solicitation, including competitive bidding. Such activities were viewed as potentially encroaching on the practice of other members, which was considered unprofessional.

The Rules of the AICPA Code of Professional Conduct presently address the marketing of professional services in three ways. Rule 302 generally prohibits performing services for contingent fees; Rule 502 sets restraints on advertising and solicitation; and Rule 503 prohibits paying or receiving commissions or referral fees. Each of those rules is discussed below. Since those rules, or related interpretations, are currently being questioned by the FTC, the discussion concludes with a summary of the AICPA's consent agreement with the FTC.

Contingent Fees.   Rule 302 states

> Professional services shall not be offered or rendered under an arrangement whereby no fee will be charged unless a specified finding or result is attained, or where the fee is otherwise contingent upon the finding or results of such services. However, a member's fees may vary depending, for example, on the complexity of services rendered.

There is a presumption that a CPA will perform professional services in a competent manner and that the fee charged will not depend on the CPA's findings or the outcome of the work. For example, specific Ethics Rulings prohibit fees as a percentage of a bond issue, finder's fees based on a percentage of the acquisition price, and fees as an expert witness based on the amount awarded the plaintiff.

Fees are not regarded as being contingent if, for any type of engagement, they are fixed by courts or other public authorities or, in tax matters, if they are determined based on the results of court decisions or the resolution of controversies with government agencies. An Ethics Ruling explicitly states, however, that basing a fee for preparing a tax return on the amount of tax savings to the client would violate Rule 302.

Advertising and Solicitation. Following U.S. Supreme Court rulings that the Virginia bar association's minimum fee schedule was a violation of the Sherman Act[3] and that the Arizona bar association's restrictions on advertising violated the right of free speech guaranteed by the First Amendment to the U.S. Constitution,[4] the AICPA in 1978 lifted the ban on advertising by accountants. One year later, the AICPA removed its prohibition against direct solicitation of clients when it abolished Rule 401 (Encroachment). That Rule stated that "a member shall not endeavor to provide a person or entity with a professional service which is currently provided by another public accountant."

The present Rule 502 on advertising and solicitation is as follows: "A member in public practice shall not seek to obtain clients by advertising or other forms of solicitation in a manner that is false, misleading, or deceptive. Solicitation by the use of coercion, over-reaching, or harassing conduct is prohibited." There are no restrictions on the type of advertising media or frequency of placement.

Commissions and Referral Fees. Rule 503 states

> The acceptance by a member in public practice of a payment for the referral of products or services of others to a client is prohibited. Such action is considered to create a conflict of interest that results in a loss of objectivity and independence.

> A member shall not make a payment to obtain a client. This rule shall not prohibit payments for the purchase of an accounting practice or retirement payments to individuals formerly engaged in the practice of public accounting or payments to their heirs or estates.

AICPA–FTC Consent Agreement. In 1989, the FTC approved for public comment a consent agreement with the AICPA under which the Institute agreed to cease and desist from enforcing some portions of its Code of Professional Conduct relating to contingent fees, commissions, referral fees, solicitation, advertising, and the use of "trade names" in designating a practice unit. At the time of this writing, the FTC has not issued a final Rule on these matters, even though the comment period has already expired. Under the consent agreement, the AICPA agreed to cease and desist from

> Restricting, regulating, impeding, declaring unethical, advising members against, or interfering with any of the following practices by any CPA:

> 1. The offering or rendering of professional services for, or the receipt of, a contingent fee by a CPA, provided that the offering or rendering by a CPA for a contingent fee of professional services for, or the receipt of such a fee from, any person for whom the CPA also performs attest services may be prohibited by the AICPA during the period of the attest services engagement and the

---

[3]*Goldfarb* v. *Virginia State Bar*, 421 U.S. 773 (1975).
[4]*Bates* v. *State Bar of Arizona,* 433 U.S. 350 (1977).

period covered by any historical financial statements involved in such attest services;

2. The offering or rendering of professional services for, or the receipt of, a disclosed commission by a CPA, provided that the offering or rendering of professional services by a CPA for a commission for any person for whom the CPA also performs attest services may be prohibited by the AICPA during the period of the attest services engagement and the period covered by any historical financial statements involved in such attest services;

3. The payment or acceptance of any disclosed referral fee;

4. The solicitation of any potential client by any means, including direct solicitation;

5. Advertising, including, but not limited to:

   (a) any self-laudatory or comparative claim;

   (b) any testimonial or endorsement; and

   (c) any advertisement not considered by AICPA to be professionally dignified or in good taste; and

6. The use of any trade name;

PROVIDED THAT nothing contained in this order shall prohibit AICPA from formulating, adopting, disseminating, and enforcing reasonable ethical guidelines governing the conduct of its members with respect to solicitation, advertising or trade names, including unsubstantiated representations, that AICPA reasonably believes would be false or deceptive within the meaning of Section 5 of the Federal Trade Commission Act. . . .

Attest service is defined in the agreement as "(1) any audit, (2) any review of a financial statement, (3) any compilation of a financial statement when the certified public accountant ('CPA') expects, or reasonably might expect, that a third party will use the compilation and the CPA does not disclose a lack of independence, and (4) any examination of prospective financial information."

An important aspect of the consent agreement that many auditors believe constitutes a major victory for the profession is that the Institute can continue to prohibit members from receiving commissions or contingent fees for services performed for attest *clients* (even if such commissions or contingent fees are not related to an attest *engagement*); and can require members to disclose to clients any permissible referral fees or commissions they do receive. The AICPA's keeping and exercising those rights could mitigate the perception that CPAs will now be able to act with less objectivity and independence than previously.

At the time of this writing, significant issues relating to the AICPA-FTC consent agreement are still unsettled. Most significantly, because the FTC has not issued a final Rule, the AICPA has not yet promulgated new Rules on commissions, contingent fees, and referral fees consistent with the consent agreement. In addition, the codes of conduct of many state societies of CPAs and the rules of many state boards of accountancy proscribe the same types of activities the FTC consent agreement would bar the AICPA from proscribing.[5]

[5]At least one state (California) has passed legislation that may, depending on its interpretation and enforcement, also proscribe those activities, and similar legislation has been introduced in several other states.

Those state proscriptions are not directly affected by the consent agreement and thus may still serve to restrain CPAs from engaging in activities that may be acceptable under a revised AICPA Code of Professional Conduct.

INCENTIVES FOR MAINTAINING AUDIT QUALITY

Introduction

Audit quality embraces the concepts of professional competence and the meeting or exceeding of professional standards (both technical and ethical) in expressing an opinion on audited financial statements, reporting on prospective financial information, being associated with unaudited financial statements, and providing other types of accounting services.

Audit quality proceeds primarily from a firm's enlightened self-interest and from the concept of integrity. The first step in ensuring the quality of a firm's accounting and audit practice is to incorporate quality control measures into the audit itself—requirements, at the engagement level, for documentation, the use of practice aids, and reviews by various knowledgeable personnel. While each firm's specific policies concerning documentation, use of practice aids, consultation, and review, and its means of enforcing them, depend largely on its size, organizational structure, and style or philosophy of management, each of those elements must be present in one way or another. In addition to building audit quality into individual engagements as a means of achieving and maintaining a reputation for professional excellence, incentives for maintaining audit quality are provided through regulatory mechanisms and other means.

The regulatory mechanisms include both the self-regulatory system of the profession and the disciplinary systems provided by government agencies like the SEC and individual state boards of accountancy. The self-regulatory system of the profession imposes penalties for performance or conduct that departs from professional standards. In addition, the profession has developed recommendations for quality control systems to provide reasonable assurance that CPA firms conform with professional standards in the conduct of their accounting and auditing practices.

Furthermore, since 1988 the AICPA has required members engaged in the practice of public accounting in the United States or its territories to practice as proprietors, partners, shareholders, or employees of firms enrolled in an approved practice-monitoring program in order to retain their membership in the Institute beyond specified periods. There are two approved practice-monitoring programs.

- The peer review programs of the AICPA Division for CPA Firms.
- The quality review program the AICPA has established in cooperation with state CPA societies.

Both of those programs are discussed later in the chapter.

Other incentives for maintaining audit quality also exist. For one thing, firms are increasingly exposed to litigation in the conduct of their audit practices and to sanctions by the SEC. This subject is covered in detail in Chapter 4. In addition, clients, and particularly audit committees, are putting increasing pressure on firms to maintain high audit quality. Audit quality is also a significant factor in a firm's ability to attract and retain clients and high-caliber personnel. Furthermore, through the efforts of financial writers and other news media, there is increasing public awareness of a firm's image and of the events that shape it.

The remainder of this section describes the profession's quality control and practice-monitoring programs, and the disciplinary systems of the profession and the state boards of accountancy.

Quality Controls

The objectives of quality control policies and procedures are to improve individual and firm performance and to ensure compliance with technical and ethical standards. The relationship of generally accepted auditing standards to quality control standards is discussed in SAS No. 25, *The Relationship of Generally Accepted Auditing Standards to Quality Control Standards* (AU Section 161.03).

> Generally accepted auditing standards relate to the conduct of individual audit engagements; quality control standards relate to the conduct of a firm's audit practice as a whole. Thus, generally accepted auditing standards and quality control standards are related, and the quality control policies and procedures that a firm adopts may affect both the conduct of individual audit engagements and the conduct of a firm's audit practice as a whole.

Statement on Quality Control Standards (SQCS) No. 1, *System of Quality Control for a CPA Firm* (QC Section 10), requires CPA firms to have a system of quality control. Issued in November 1979 by the AICPA Quality Control Standards Committee—the Institute's senior technical committee designated at that time to issue pronouncements on quality control standards—SQCS No. 1 superseded SAS No. 4, *Quality Control Considerations for a Firm of Independent Auditors*, which first gave formal recognition to a CPA firm's need for quality control policies and procedures.

SQCS No. 1 describes nine elements of quality control and requires that a firm consider each of them, to the extent applicable to its practice, in establishing its quality control policies and procedures. The nine elements of quality control, as listed below, are interrelated (e.g., a firm's hiring practices affect its policies relating to training).

1. *Acceptance and continuance of clients.* Policies and procedures should be established for deciding whether to accept or continue a client in order to minimize the likelihood of association with a client whose management lacks integrity.
2. *Assigning personnel to engagements.* Policies and procedures for assigning personnel to engagements should be established to provide the firm with reasonable assurance that work will be performed by persons having the required degree of technical training and proficiency.

3. *Supervision*. Policies and procedures for the conduct and supervision of work at all organizational levels should be established to provide the firm with reasonable assurance that the work performed meets the firm's standards of quality.

4. *Hiring*. Policies and procedures for hiring should be established to provide the firm with reasonable assurance that employees possess the appropriate characteristics to enable them to perform competently.

5. *Professional development*. Policies and procedures for professional development should be established to provide the firm with reasonable assurance that personnel will have the knowledge required to enable them to fulfill their responsibilities.

6. *Advancement*. Policies and procedures for advancing personnel should be established to provide the firm with reasonable assurance that those selected for advancement will have the qualifications necessary to fulfill the responsibilities they will be called on to assume.

7. *Consultation*. Policies and procedures for consultation should be established to provide the firm with reasonable assurance that personnel will seek assistance, to the extent required, from persons having appropriate levels of knowledge, competence, judgment, and authority.

8. *Independence*. Policies and procedures should be established to provide the firm with reasonable assurance that persons at all organizational levels maintain independence to the extent required by the AICPA's Code of Professional Conduct.

9. *Inspection*. Policies and procedures for inspection should be established to provide the firm with reasonable assurance that the procedures relating to the other elements of quality control are being effectively applied.

Acceptance of Clients. The element relating to accepting clients formalizes a long-standing practice by auditors of seeking to ascertain the reputation and business integrity of potential clients as a means of protecting their own reputation and avoiding inadvertently accepting an audit of high or unknown risk. The extent of the inquiry varies with the circumstances. It will be informal and brief, for example, if the potential client is well known in the community or can be easily investigated through mutual business associates. In other instances, more extreme and formal inquiries are called for, as often happens with companies having new management or diverse private ownership, or companies in industries or areas with which the auditor is relatively unfamiliar.

Sources of information that are useful in the investigation include

- Recent financial statements, both annual and interim and both audited and unaudited.
- Forms 8-K filed with the SEC, if the company is registered.
- Predecessor auditors.
- Outside legal counsel and bankers.
- Regulatory authorities.

- Investigatory or credit rating services.
- Industry associations and publications.

Continuance of Clients.   The investigation process should be ongoing and not end when the client is accepted. The auditor should be alert to changed circumstances that might call for reconsideration of the relationship with the client. For example, if a client company is purchased or client management is replaced by individuals unknown to the auditor, another investigation would be in order.

Personnel Policies and Procedures.   These policies and procedures include assigning personnel to engagements, supervision, hiring, professional development, and advancement. Firm management should ensure that the firm is adequately staffed and that each staff level possesses the skills necessary to achieve the desired level of professional excellence. Supervision is usually exercised on an engagement-by-engagement basis, and it commonly depends on factors such as the nature of the service performed, including the complexity of the client's business; the size of the engagement team necessary to serve the client and the extent of the team's training; and the intended use of the financial statements (e.g., whether they will be included in an SEC document, or restricted to management's internal use only).

Consultation.   Consultation with individuals in a firm who have specialized expertise occurs when an auditing or accounting issue is complex or unusual. Examples are the application of newly issued technical pronouncements; industries with special accounting, auditing, or reporting requirements; emerging practice problems; choices among alternative GAAP when an accounting change is to be made; and filing requirements of regulatory agencies. The nature of a firm's consultation organization depends on, among other things, the size of the firm and the level of knowledge, the competence, and the judgment of the persons performing the work.

Independence.   Public accounting firms are required to be independent of clients for whom they perform attestation services, such as audits. Thus, all of a CPA firm's professional personnel must adhere to applicable independence rules, regulations, interpretations, and rulings of the AICPA, state societies of CPAs, state boards of accountancy, state statutes, and if applicable the SEC and other regulatory agencies. Firms should communicate the independence policies and procedures to appropriate personnel and monitor compliance with them. Typically, one or more individuals will be designated to maintain and monitor a firm's independence policies and procedures.

Inspection.   The inspection element is performed internally by individuals acting on behalf of the firm's management, as contrasted with peer reviews, discussed below, which are conducted by individuals not associated with the firm being reviewed. SQCS No. 1 (QC Section 10.10) also requires firms to maintain a monitoring function, of which inspection is one aspect. In monitoring the effectiveness of its system of quality control, a firm should modify its policies and procedures in a timely manner to address not only findings from its inspection program and peer review but also changed circumstances in its practice and new authoritative pronouncements.

Practice-Monitoring Programs

AICPA Division for CPA Firms. The AICPA Division for CPA Firms comprises two sections, one for SEC practice and the other for private company practice. The principal objective of each section is to improve the quality of CPA firms' practice by establishing requirements for member firms and an effective system of self-regulation. Following are requirements that have the most direct effect on audit quality.

Requirements common to both sections:

- Adhere to quality control standards established by the AICPA Quality Control Standards Committee.
- Submit to peer reviews of the firm's accounting and audit practice every three years or at such additional times as designated by the section's executive committee. The reviews will be conducted in accordance with review standards established by the section's peer review committee.
- Ensure that all professionals in the firm achieve at least the minimum hours of continuing professional education prescribed by the section.

Additional SEC Practice Section Requirements for All SEC Engagements[6]:

- Periodically rotate partners.
- Have a partner other than the audit partner in charge review and concur with the audit report on the financial statements before it is issued.
- Refrain from performing certain management advisory services. Such services include psychological testing; public opinion polls; merger and acquisition assistance for a finder's fee; recruitment for managerial, executive, or director positions; and, in certain situations, actuarial services to insurance companies.
- Communicate at least annually with the audit committee or, if there is no audit committee, with the board of directors (or its equivalent in a partnership) the total fees received from the client for management advisory services during the year under audit and a description of the types of such services rendered.[7]
- Report to the Quality Control Inquiry Committee (described below) any litigation (including criminal indictments) against the firm or its personnel or any proceeding or investigation publicly announced by a regula-

---

[6]The section's definition of an SEC engagement includes audits of certain banks and other lending institutions and certain sponsors or managers of investment funds, even though they are not registered with the SEC.

[7]In addition, SAS No. 61 requires auditors of SEC clients and other entities that have an audit committee or its equivalent to communicate certain other matters to the committee, as discussed in Chapter 21.

tory agency that alleges deficiencies in the conduct of an audit of the financial statements or reporting thereon of a present or former SEC client. Any allegations made in such formal litigation, proceeding, or investigation that the firm or its personnel have violated the federal securities laws in connection with services other than audit services must also be reported.

- Communicate in writing to all professional firm personnel the broad principles that influence the firm's quality control and operating policies and procedures on, as a minimum, matters related to the recommendation and approval of accounting principles, present and potential client relationships, and the types of services provided; and inform professional firm personnel periodically that compliance with those principles is mandatory.

- Notify the Chief Accountant of the SEC within five business days when the auditor–client relationship with an SEC registrant ceases (because the auditor has resigned, declined to stand for reelection, or been dismissed).

There are no significant additional requirements for membership in the Private Companies Practice Section.

Each section is governed by an executive committee composed of representatives from member firms that establishes the section's general policies and oversees its activities. Each section also has a peer review committee that administers its peer review program. The Executive Committee of the SEC Practice Section has in addition organized a Quality Control Inquiry Committee to identify corrective measures, if any, that should be taken by a member firm involved in a specific alleged audit failure. The activities of the SEC Practice Section are also subject to review by an independent Public Oversight Board that issues public reports.

Peer Review.   Peer reviews must be conducted in conformity with the confidentiality requirements in the AICPA Code of Professional Conduct. (Rule 301 contains an exception that allows a peer review of a member's practice.) Information obtained concerning a reviewed firm or any of its clients is confidential and should not be disclosed by review team members to anyone not "associated with the review." (The executive and peer review committees and the Public Oversight Board are encompassed by the phrase "associated with the review.") While the AICPA Code of Professional Conduct does not deal specifically with independence in relationships between reviewers, reviewed firms, and clients of reviewed firms, the concepts of independence expressed in the Code are considered in regard to these relationships. The firm under review has the option of either having the Peer Review Committee appoint the review team or engaging another member firm to conduct the review; however, reciprocal reviews are not permitted.

The peer review team evaluates whether the reviewed firm's quality control system met the objectives of the quality control standards established by the AICPA, whether it was complied with to provide reasonable assurance of conforming with professional standards, and whether the firm was in compliance with the membership requirements of the section. Some tests made by the review team are performed at the practice office level, others on a firm-wide basis, and still others on an individual engagement basis. The review is of the firm's accounting and auditing practice, but other segments, such as tax, are covered in the review (1) to the extent that personnel from those segments assist on accounting and auditing engagements, and (2) as to compliance with membership requirements.[8] At the completion of the peer review, the review team furnishes the reviewed firm with a formal peer review report and, if applicable, a letter of comments on matters that may require action by the firm, both of which are available to the public. The SEC Practice Section manual presents an example of an unqualified peer review report, which is reproduced in Figure 3.1.

With respect to member firms with SEC clients, a procedure has been established to enable the SEC to make its own evaluation of whether the peer review process and the Public Oversight Board's oversight of it are adequate. The procedure permits the SEC access, during a limited period following the Peer Review Committee's acceptance of the peer review report, to defined areas of the peer review working papers, with appropriate safeguards to prevent the SEC from identifying the clients whose audit working papers were reviewed. After their review of the working papers on a specific peer review, the SEC representatives discuss with representatives of the Public Oversight Board and the Peer Review Committee any matters that they believe the committee should consider.

The following circumstances ordinarily would require a modified report:

- The scope of the review is limited by conditions that preclude the application of one or more review procedures considered necessary.
- The system of quality control as designed fails to meet one or more applicable objectives of quality control standards established by the AICPA, resulting in a condition in which the firm did not have reasonable assurance of conforming with professional standards.
- The degree of noncompliance with the reviewed firm's quality control policies and procedures was such that the reviewed firm did not have reasonable assurance of conforming with professional standards.
- The reviewed firm did not comply with the membership requirements of the Section in all material respects.

The objective of the letter of comments is to report to the reviewed firm matters that resulted in a modified report or that the review team believes created a condition in which there is more than a remote (i.e., slight) possibility that the firm would not conform with professional standards on accounting and auditing engagements. The letter should include appropriate

[8]The Division for CPA Firms has defined a firm's accounting and auditing practice as being "limited to all auditing, and all accounting, review, and compilation services covered by generally accepted auditing standards, standards for accounting and review services, standards for accountants' services on prospective financial information, and standards for financial and compliance audits contained in *Standards for Audit of Governmental Organizations, Programs, Activities, and Functions* issued by the U.S. General Accounting Office."

Figure 3.1   Unqualified Peer Review Report

[AICPA or Other Appropriate Letterhead]

September 15, 19____

To the Partners
Jones, Smith & Co.

We have reviewed the system of quality control for the accounting and auditing practice of Jones, Smith & Co. (the firm) in effect for the year ended June 30, 19____. Our review was conducted in conformity with standards for peer reviews promulgated by the peer review committee of the SEC Practice Section of the AICPA Division for CPA Firms (the section). We tested compliance with the firm's quality control policies and procedures (at the firm's executive office and at selected practice offices in the United States)* and with the membership requirements of the section to the extent we considered appropriate. These tests included the application of the firm's policies and procedures on selected accounting and auditing engagements. (We tested the supervision and control of portions of engagements performed outside the United States.)**

In performing our review, we have given consideration to the general characteristics of a system of quality control as described in quality control standards issued by the AICPA. Such a system should be appropriately comprehensive and suitably designed in relation to the firm's organizational structure, its policies, and the nature of its practice. Variance in individual performance can affect the degree of compliance with a firm's prescribed quality control policies and procedures. Therefore, adherence to all policies and procedures in every case may not be possible. (As is customary in a peer review, we are issuing a letter under this date that sets forth comments related to certain policies and procedures or compliance with them. None of these matters were considered to be of sufficient significance to affect the opinion expressed in this report.)***

comments regarding the design of the reviewed firm's system of quality control, its compliance with that system (including professional standards), and its compliance with the membership requirements of the Section. The review team may also communicate orally to senior management of the reviewed firm comments that were not deemed significant enough to be included in the letter of comments.

Quality Review Program.   The quality review program, which applies to firms that are not members of the Division, is similar to the peer review program of the Private Companies Practice Section of the Division for CPA Firms. There are some differences, however, between the two programs, particularly in the reporting requirements and distribution of review reports.

Standards for the quality review program are applicable to firms enrolled in the program, individuals and firms that perform and report on reviews, state societies that participate in the administration of the program, associations of CPA firms that assist their members in arranging and carrying out quality

Figure 3.1 *Continued*

In our opinion, the system of quality control for the accounting and auditing practice of Jones, Smith & Co. in effect for the year ended June 30, 19____, met the objectives of quality control standards established by the AICPA and was being complied with during the year then ended to provide the firm with reasonable assurance of conforming with professional standards. Also, in our opinion the firm was in conformity with the membership requirements of the section in all material respects.

AICPA Review Team No._____

William Brown
Team Captain

or

Johnson & Co.   [for review by a firm]

or

_____   [for review by an association-
John Doe   or state society-sponsored re-
Team Captain   view team]

*To be included, as appropriate, for reviews of multioffice firms.

**To be included for reviewed firms with offices, correspondents, or affiliates outside the United States. Appropriately modified wording should be used if the reviewed firm uses correspondents or affiliates domestically, if that is significant to the scope of the review.

***To be included if the review team issues a letter of comments along with the unqualified report.

---

reviews, and the AICPA Quality Review Division itself. Specifically, the standards

- Provide distinctly different performance and reporting standards for two types of quality reviews—an on-site review for firms that examine historical or prospective financial statements, and an off-site review for firms that issue compilation or review reports but perform no examinations of historical or prospective financial statements.
- Provide guidance on general considerations applicable to all quality reviews.
- Describe how review teams are formed and what qualifications they must possess.
- Define the responsibilities of the review team, the reviewed firm, and the entity administering the review, and provide standards, procedures, and guidelines to be followed by each participant in the process.

Disciplinary System

The AICPA (in conjunction with state societies of CPAs), state boards of accountancy, the courts, and the SEC may impose sanctions on individuals and firms for performance or conduct that violates professional standards or civil or criminal laws. The paragraphs that follow discuss disciplinary actions of the profession and state boards of accountancy; legal and other sanctions are covered in Chapter 4.

Disciplinary System Within the Profession for Individuals. The AICPA's self-disciplinary mechanism for individual members consists of the Institute's Professional Ethics Division (the Division) and the Joint Trial Board.

The Division is responsible for interpreting the Code of Professional Conduct and proposing amendments to it. The Division is also responsible for investigating alleged violations of the Code for possible disciplinary or rehabilitative action, including hearings before panels of the Joint Trial Board. The Division may initiate an investigation on the basis of complaints from individuals, state societies of CPAs, or government agencies, or on the basis of information from news media, the SEC *Docket*, or the IRS *Bulletin*.

The Executive Committee of the Division can take the following types of disciplinary actions against individual members:

- If the Executive Committee concludes that a prima facie violation of the Code of Professional Conduct or bylaws is not of sufficient gravity to warrant further formal action, it may direct the member or members concerned to complete specified continuing professional education courses or to take other remedial or corrective action. There is no publication of that action in the Institute's principal membership periodical, *The CPA Letter*. The member has the right to reject the direction. If he or she does, the Executive Committee determines whether to bring the matter to a panel of the Joint Trial Board for a hearing.
- Presentation of a prima facie case to a panel of the Joint Trial Board, a proceeding that is used for serious violations that may require suspension or expulsion from membership or public censure. Publication of the names of members found guilty of the charges is required.

The AICPA's bylaws provide for automatic termination of membership (with publication of name) if a member is convicted of (1) a crime punishable by imprisonment for more than one year, (2) the willful failure to file any income tax return that he or she is required to file as an individual taxpayer, (3) filing a false or fraudulent income tax return on the member's own or a client's behalf, or (4) the willful aiding in the preparation and presentation of a false and fraudulent income tax return of a client.

Disciplinary System Within the Profession for Firms. The executive committee of each section of the AICPA Division for CPA Firms has the authority to impose sanctions on member firms for failing to meet membership requirements, either on its own initiative or on the basis of recommendations from that Section's Peer Review Committee. The following types of sanctions may be imposed on member firms:

- Corrective measures by the firm, including consideration by the firm of appropriate actions with respect to individual firm personnel.

- Additional requirements for continuing professional education.
- Accelerated or special peer reviews.
- Admonishments, censures, or reprimands.
- Monetary fines.
- Suspension or expulsion from membership.

State Boards of Accountancy.   A state board of accountancy is charged with enforcing laws that regulate the practice of public accounting in that state. Generally, a board has the power to revoke or suspend the certificates of CPAs; to revoke, suspend, or refuse to renew permits to practice; and to censure the holders of licenses or permits to practice.[9] Those penalties can be imposed for a wide variety of acts or omissions specified in accountancy laws. Several states also require the registration of firms, issue permits for firms to practice in the state, and have the power to revoke or suspend those permits. An increasing number of states have required firms to participate in "Positive Enforcement Programs"—a type of quality review—as a condition for practicing within those states.

ENHANCING THE INDEPENDENCE OF AUDITORS

Generally accepted auditing standards, the AICPA Code of Professional Conduct, the Securities and Exchange Commission, and individual accounting firms require auditors to maintain an attitude of independence and prohibit certain relationships with clients.[10] Nevertheless, some people believe that there are potential threats to auditor independence because the client selects the auditor and pays the fee and because the auditor may undertake nonaudit services for the client. Since auditors are often selected and paid, retained, or replaced at the sole discretion of the management on whose representations they are expected to report, many people believe that total professional independence is impossible. While "total" independence may be impossible, auditors are extremely conscious that their independence is vital and that they must preserve the standards of the profession for the sake of their own reputation.

The profession, the SEC, and responsible leaders of the financial community have recognized this alleged threat and have taken steps to deal with it. Some companies require that the selection and retention of auditors be ratified by the stockholders. In the case of companies whose securities are publicly traded, the SEC requires public notice of the termination of auditors, disclosure of any accounting or auditing disputes within two years between the client and the former auditor, and a letter from the former auditor concurring in such disclosure. Those are worthwhile steps, but they mitigate rather than eliminate the threat to auditor independence.

[9]It should be noted that the AICPA has no such powers, since it does not issue certificates or permits to practice. AICPA disciplinary actions are related only to membership in the Institute.

[10]As discussed earlier in this chapter, an AICPA Interpretation of its Code of Professional Conduct distinguishes the independence requirements appropriate for audit engagements from those appropriate for attest engagements other than audits.

Another alleged threat to auditor independence arises from the various types of nonaudit services provided to audit clients by public accounting firms. Such services include tax services (such as tax return preparation, tax planning advice, and representation before the IRS); management services, some that are related to accounting and auditing (such as advice on systems, control procedures, data processing, and cost accounting) and some that are not (for instance, market studies or studies of factory layout); and accounting services (such as compilations and reviews for nonpublic companies and advice on selection and application of accounting principles and the accounting implications of proposed management decisions). There is no general proscription by either the SEC or the AICPA against performing nonauditing services for audit clients. The SEC has at times in the past monitored such relationships and required their disclosure, and the AICPA Division for CPA Firms prohibits members of its SEC Practice Section from providing certain management advisory services.

Many proposals have been made to strengthen auditor independence. They fall into two broad categories.

- Protecting the auditor from management influence, through the use of audit committees, requiring that a successor auditor communicate with the predecessor auditor, SEC scrutiny of auditor changes, and rotation of audit personnel.

- Other proposals to increase auditor independence, including transfer of the audit function to the public sector, auditor selection of generally accepted accounting principles for clients, and prohibiting auditors from performing management advisory services for audit clients.

The Cohen Commission considered and evaluated those proposals in its 1978 report; several of them were restudied by the Treadway Commission in its 1987 report. The remainder of this chapter discusses and evaluates each of the proposals.

Protecting the Auditor from Management Influence

Neither audit effectiveness nor audit efficiency would be strengthened if the auditor were isolated from client management. An auditor must work with management because management's active and positive cooperation is required in conducting an audit, and that in turn requires the auditor and management to have a high degree of confidence in one another. Yet auditor independence must be maintained despite the need for cooperation. Another difficulty auditors face in maintaining their independence is that they are members of a profit-making firm that depends on fees over which client management may exert considerable control. Several proposals to increase the auditor's ability to resist pressure from management are discussed next.

Audit Committees. Over the years, several professional and regulatory bodies have suggested requiring companies to have audit committees of boards of directors as a means of reinforcing auditors' independence from management. The SEC endorsed the establishment of audit committees composed of outside directors in 1972 (ASR No. 123) and subsequently adopted nonbinding rules underscoring this commitment. The AICPA recommended in 1967 that audit committees be established for all publicly held companies. In 1978, the New York Stock Exchange mandated that domestic companies with listed securities establish audit committees made up entirely of outside directors; in 1979, the American Stock Exchange strongly recommended similar action. A special House subcommittee in 1976 also noted the desirability of audit committees. The Cohen Commission strongly endorsed the use of audit committees to recommend to shareholders the appointment of independent auditors and to evaluate the relationship between auditor and management. The Institute of Internal Auditors also endorsed the establishment of audit committees consisting of outside directors by both public companies and other organizations, such as not-for-profit and governmental bodies. Finally, the Treadway Commission recommended that the SEC require all public companies to establish audit committees composed solely of outside directors. It also provided guidance on how audit committees could serve as "informed, vigilant, and effective overseers of the financial reporting process and the company's internal controls."[11]

Today, although not universally required, audit committees are an important part of our corporate structure. They oversee a company's accounting and financial reporting policies and practices, help the board of directors fulfill its corporate reporting responsibilities, and help maintain a direct line of communication between the board and the company's external and internal auditors. Although occasionally the entire board may turn to the independent auditors for assistance in reviewing the financial statements or other data, contact between the board and the auditors is generally through the audit committee.

Over the years, the AICPA and the New York Stock Exchange have issued general guidelines for audit committees but have not mandated specific duties, responsibilities, or activities. Since specific functions have not been prescribed for audit committees, their activities vary from one company to the next. Effective committees, however, should generally perform at least the following:

- Recommend the appointment of the independent auditor and review the fee arrangements.
- Review the proposed scope of the independent audit.
- Communicate with the internal auditors and review their activities, effectiveness, and recommendations for improving the company's control structure.
- Review the financial statements and the results of the independent audit.
- Review the report by management (discussed in Chapter 23) containing management's opinion on the effectiveness of the company's control structure and the basis for that opinion.
- Consider the selection of accounting policies.

[11]*Report of the National Commission on Fraudulent Financial Reporting* (Treadway Commission), 1987, p. 41.

- Scrutinize the required communications from the independent auditor regarding deficiencies in the company's control structure, irregularities discovered in the course of the audit, and many other matters related to the audit (all of which are discussed in Chapter 21).
- Oversee or conduct special investigations or other functions on behalf of the board of directors.

In the authors' opinion, the trend toward establishing audit committees of outside directors has been beneficial to management, directors, stockholders, and the auditing profession. Auditors and outside directors have common interests that are vastly strengthened by interaction between the two groups. An active and involved audit committee serves to protect corporate interests by overseeing the activities of the auditor and, at least to some extent in matters of financial reporting, company management. The existence of an audit committee of outside directors demonstrates that all parties with responsibility for reliable financial reporting—management, the independent auditors, and the board of directors acting in an oversight capacity—are diligently carrying out their duties to the stockholders. An audit committee reinforces the auditor's independence, while the auditor provides an independent source of information to the directors; management's support of the relationship demonstrates a sense of accountability.

Communicating with Predecessor Auditors.   SAS No. 7, *Communications Between Predecessor and Successor Auditors* (AU Section 315.01–.09), issued in 1975, requires a successor auditor to attempt to communicate with the predecessor as part of the process of determining whether to accept an engagement. The SAS outlines, in paragraph 6 (AU Section 315.06), the procedures to be followed by a successor auditor.

> The successor auditor should make specific and reasonable inquiries of the predecessor regarding matters that the successor believes will assist him in determining whether to accept the engagement. His inquiries should include specific questions regarding, among other things, facts that might bear on the integrity of management; on disagreements with management as to accounting principles, auditing procedures, or other similarly significant matters; and on the predecessor's understanding as to the reasons for the change of auditors.

AU Section 315 indicates that the predecessor auditor is obligated to ''respond promptly and fully'' to any ''reasonable'' question, but it also recognizes that, in unusual situations such as when litigation is or may be involved, the predecessor may need to advise the successor that the response is limited. In that event, the successor auditor should consider whether the information obtained from all sources is adequate to support accepting the client. If the client refuses to allow the successor auditor to talk to the predecessor auditor, the successor auditor should also consider whether to accept the engagement.

After a successor auditor has been appointed, there are two occasions when communications between the predecessor and the successor auditors are appropriate. One reflects the successor's need to review the prior auditor's working papers, and the other arises if the successor believes that there is an error in the financial statements on which the predecessor auditor expressed an opinion.

Working papers are the property of the auditor who prepared them, who is under no compulsion to share them with a successor auditor. In the absence of unusual circumstances, however, such as litigation between the client and the predecessor auditor or amounts owed to the predecessor auditor by the client, predecessor auditors customarily allow successor auditors access to at least certain working papers.

Scrutiny of Auditor Changes.   Management sometimes threatens to dismiss the auditor when there is a disagreement on accounting principles. Management might then ''shop around'' for a more compliant auditor. Requiring auditor changes to be ratified by an audit committee is one way of relieving pressure on the auditor from management. Outside scrutiny of the dismissal of an auditor also inhibits the tendency to apply such pressure. The scrutiny of auditor changes has been enhanced by SEC requirements to disclose potential ''opinion shopping'' situations and disagreements between the client and the auditor when there is a change in auditors.

Opinion Shopping.   An auditor may be asked by another accountant's client for professional advice on an accounting or auditing technical matter. In some situations, the client and its auditor may have disagreed about the matter in question. When the client's purpose in seeking another professional opinion is to find an accountant willing to support a proposed accounting treatment that would favor a particular reporting objective but that is not necessarily in conformity with GAAP and is not supported by the client's auditor, the practice is commonly referred to as ''opinion shopping.'' SAS No. 50, *Reports on the Application of Accounting Principles* (AU Section 625), contains standards to be followed by an accountant who is asked to give an opinion on GAAP to another auditor's client (see discussion in Chapter 23).

The SEC has noted that the search for an auditor who would support a proposed accounting treatment may indicate an effort by management to avoid the requirement for an independent audit, and that an auditor's willingness to support a proposed accounting treatment that may frustrate reliable reporting may suggest a lack of professional skepticism and independence on the part of the auditor. The SEC requires disclosure of possible opinion shopping situations in connection with a change in auditors if the registrant consulted the newly engaged auditor within approximately two years before the engagement.[12] (The SEC rule specifies the matters covered by the consultation and the information required to be disclosed.)

Disagreements with Clients.   Since 1971, the SEC has required disclosure in a timely Form 8-K filing of a change in auditors made by the registrant, including disclosure of certain disagreements between the registrant and the

---

[12]SEC Financial Reporting Release No. 31, April 7, 1988.

predecessor auditor during the two most recent fiscal years and any subsequent interim period. The predecessor auditor provides a letter, which is generally filed by the company with its Form 8-K, either concurring with the company's disclosures or setting forth any disagreements that were omitted or require further explanation. In addition, if the predecessor auditor objected to an accounting method or disclosure that had a material effect on the financial statements and the successor auditor agrees to it, Item 304 of Regulation S-K requires the registrant to disclose the disagreement and the effect on the financial statements that would have resulted if the method advocated by the former auditor had been followed.[13]

SEC Financial Reporting Release No. 31 clarified the meaning of the term "disagreements," identified certain "reportable events" that require the same disclosures as for disagreements, and specified the required disclosures for disagreements and reportable events. (As noted above, it also provided for disclosure of possible opinion shopping situations.)

The SEC rules emphasize that the term "disagreements" should be interpreted broadly to include any differences of opinion regarding accounting principles or practices, financial statement disclosure, or auditing scope or procedure that, if not resolved to the satisfaction of the former auditor, would have caused him or her to refer to the disagreement in the audit report. Further, the rules indicate that a disagreement means a difference of opinion, not necessarily an argument. Both disagreements that were resolved to the former auditor's satisfaction and those that were not are required to be reported. However, initial differences of opinion based on incomplete facts or preliminary information that were later resolved to the former auditor's satisfaction (before his or her dismissal or resignation) are not disagreements.

Certain other events also require the same disclosures as for disagreements, when there is a change in auditors (even if the registrant and the former auditor did not have a difference of opinion regarding the event). These reportable events include situations in which the former auditor advised the registrant that

- Internal controls necessary for the registrant to develop reliable financial statements did not exist.
- He or she was unwilling to rely on management's representations or be associated with the registrant's financial statements.
- He or she would have had to significantly expand the scope of the audit and was not permitted to do so.
- Information came to his or her attention that he or she has concluded materially affects the fairness or reliability of either a prior audit report or the underlying financial statements, or the current financial statements, and, for whatever reason, the issue was not resolved.

---

[13]SEC Financial Reporting Release No. 34, issued in March 1989, revised the SEC's rules with respect to the timing of Form 8-K filings relating to changes in auditors, as well as the required Regulation S-K disclosures.

The registrant must also disclose whether

- The former auditor resigned, declined to stand for reelection, or was dismissed.
- The audit committee of the board of directors or the board discussed the subject matter of each disagreement or reportable event with the former auditor.
- The registrant has authorized the former auditor to respond fully to the inquiries of the successor auditor regarding the subject matter of each disagreement or reportable event.

Members of the SEC Practice Section of the AICPA Division for CPA Firms must report disagreements (as defined) to the audit committee or board of directors of SEC clients, even when there has not been a change in auditors. As previously noted, members of the SEC Practice Section must also notify the Chief Accountant of the SEC within five business days when the auditor–client relationship with an SEC registrant ceases, regardless of whether the client has reported a change in auditors in a Form 8-K filing.

Rotation of Audit Personnel.   To decrease the auditor's incentive for yielding to pressure from management, some people have proposed mandatory rotation of auditors, with a new auditor to be appointed every three to five years. Also, some argue that a new auditor would bring a fresh viewpoint to the engagement. Rotation would considerably increase audit costs, however, because of the start-up and learning time necessary on a new engagement. In addition, the Cohen Commission, noting that most cases of substandard performance by auditors were first- or second-year audits, stated, "Once an auditor becomes well acquainted with the operation of a client, audit risks are reduced" (p. 109).

Because of this, the Cohen Commission concluded that rotation of audit firms should not be required. The Commission also pointed out that the primary advantage of rotation—the fresh viewpoint—can be achieved if the personnel assigned to an engagement are systematically rotated.[14] This recommendation is reflected in the membership requirement of the SEC Practice Section of the AICPA Division for CPA Firms that certain personnel on audits of SEC engagements be periodically rotated.

Other Proposals to Enhance Independence

Over the years, there have been many other proposals to enhance auditor independence, several of which would require a sweeping change in the relationship between auditor and client. They have not been supported, however, by the AICPA, the SEC, the Cohen and Treadway Commissions, or the

[14]*Report, Conclusions, and Recommendations*, 1978, pp. 108–9.

authors of this book. Three of the more frequently presented of those proposals are discussed next.

Transfer to the Public Sector.   In order to sever the ties between auditor and management, proposals have been made to have independent auditors approved, assigned, or compensated by a government agency or by the stock exchanges or to have audits conducted by a group of government auditors. The Cohen Commission concluded that having auditors approved, assigned, or compensated by the government is not warranted either by the magnitude of deficiencies in present practice or by the promise of potential improvements. It also noted that the government may use accounting information to accomplish its own economic or political objectives, which suggests that increased government involvement in audits may well create problems of independence and objectivity.[15]

Auditor Selection of GAAP for Clients.   Traditionally, management has had the primary responsibility for the financial statements, including selecting what accounting principles to use and what disclosures to make. Proposals have been made to require the auditor to assume those responsibilities. The authors believe that the present division of responsibility is sound and should not be changed. Management, with firsthand knowledge of what has occurred, should be responsible for ensuring that events and transactions are properly reported. Furthermore, management is in the best position to make the judgments and estimates necessary to prepare the financial statements, and the auditor is in the best position to challenge and evaluate those judgments and estimates.

Occasionally, an issue involving reporting standards or the application of generally accepted accounting principles becomes a ''disagreement'' between management and the auditor. Such disagreements are frequently resolved by the auditor's convincing management of the propriety of an accounting principle or the necessity and justification for a particular disclosure. If, however, the auditor is not successful, a qualification results. Probably the most effective way of avoiding this is for the client to seek the auditor's early involvement and consultation in the formative stages of nonroutine transactions. In that way, neither party is faced with an unavoidable accounting or auditing outcome that is unsatisfactory to the client.

The linkage between selecting accounting principles and accumulating and classifying accounting data is very close. If auditors were responsible for selecting accounting principles and disclosures, they would lose the independent evaluation function that they perform today. Auditors should use their expertise to advise and counsel management in preparing financial statements, with management retaining the ultimate responsibility for the presentation.

Prohibition of Management Advisory Services.   The potential adverse effect on auditor independence of performing management advisory services for

---

[15]*Ibid.*, p. 105.

audit clients has been debated for more than three decades. The Treadway Commission noted that

> Some argue that the independent public accountant's performance of management advisory services improves the quality of audits. They claim that in the process of advising management the independent public accountant acquires a deeper understanding of the client's business. Many in the public accounting profession also maintain that benefits accrue to the audit process when the independent public accountant is already familiar with the company's operations.
>
> Others believe that some management advisory services place independent public accountants in the role of management, add commercial pressures to the audit examination and, as a result, impair independence. These individuals also argue that, at the very least, the public accountant's performance of management advisory services raises the perception of impaired independence. (p. 43)

Like the Cohen Commission before it, the Treadway Commission reviewed previous studies of the issue and sponsored its own research study. Neither commission found any actual case in which an auditor's independence was compromised by providing management advisory services. The Treadway Commission cited several empirical studies, however, that indicated that "a substantial percentage of members of key public groups involved in the financial reporting process believe that performing certain management advisory services can impair a public auditor's objectivity and independence."[16]

The Treadway Commission concluded that the existence of that perception should not be ignored. It noted that members of the SEC Practice Section of the AICPA's Division for CPA Firms must disclose to the audit committee or board of directors the total fees received from an SEC audit client for management advisory services during the past year and a description of the types of such services rendered. The Treadway Commission recommended that the audit committee should oversee management judgments relating to management advisory services and the auditor's independence.

> The Commission recommends that the audit committee, in its oversight capacity, also review management's plans to engage the independent public accountant to perform management advisory services during the coming year. This entails reviewing the types or categories of services that management may engage the independent public accountant to perform as well as the projected fees. The audit committee should weigh carefully the possible advantages of such use against the possible effects it may have on the independence—or even the perceived independence—of the public accountant, considering, among other factors, the type of service to be performed, helpful knowledge of the company that the independent public accountant may bring to the task because of its audit services, the extent to which audit and management advisory services staffs are positioned to take advantage of each other's knowledge, and the amount of the management advisory services fee relative to the audit fee. (p. 44)

[16]Treadway Commission, p. 44.

4

Professional Responsibility and Legal Liability

The terms "auditors' responsibility" and "auditors' legal liability" are often confused by nonauditors. The distinction is subtle, yet it must be drawn in order for auditors and nonauditors to communicate with each other. This entire book, with the exception of the second section of this chapter, "Auditors' Legal Liability," is concerned with auditors' responsibilities.

An appropriate way of viewing the relationship between responsibility and liability is to think of "responsibilities" as synonymous with "professional duties," and "legal liabilities" as relating to society's means of enforcing adherence to those professional duties—that is, compliance with professional standards—and providing compensation to victims of wrongful conduct. The concept of auditor responsibility usually arises in two related contexts: responsibility for what, and to whom? Answers to both questions are found primarily in the technical and ethical standards of the public accounting profession; they are also occasionally specified in state and federal statutes and court decisions. All of these sources provide guidance to auditors on how to conduct audits with due professional care and thus meet their professional responsibilities, and on the duties that auditors owe to their clients and third parties.

Chapter 3 described the various mechanisms the AICPA and state boards of accountancy have for maintaining the quality of audit practice. The legal process is another mechanism that helps ensure that auditors meet their responsibilities. Litigation and threats of litigation serve as enforcers of duties; they also help define auditors' responsibilities and, on rare occasions, create what some perceive to be new responsibilities. The Commission on Auditors' Responsibilities (Cohen Commission) noted that "court decisions are particularly useful [in defining auditors' responsibilities] because they involve consideration of competing theories of responsibility. However, they must be considered carefully because a decision is usually closely related to the facts of a particular case. Consequently, the language used in a particular decision may not be the best expression of the technical issues involved."[1] The outcome of a specific legal case also may not be a reliable indicator of auditors' responsibilities because it is often impossible to discern the rationale of a jury verdict, and appellate decisions are often clouded by procedural rules, such as the requirement that factual determinations not be disturbed.

AUDITORS' PROFESSIONAL RESPONSIBILITY

To a great degree, auditors' responsibilities reflect the expectations of users of audited financial statements. Users expect an auditor to evaluate the measurements and disclosures made by management and determine whether the financial statements contain material misstatements, either unintentional or not. Auditors have long accepted the responsibility to design their audits to detect material unintentional errors in financial statements; after all, if that is not a purpose of an audit, what is? The auditor's responsibility for designing audits to detect deliberate misstatements in financial statements has been less clear over the years, mainly because of the difficulty, or even impossibility, of

---

[1]*Report, Conclusions, and Recommendations,* 1978, p. 2.

detecting skillfully contrived employee or management fraud, particularly if any form of collusion is present.[2] Although management fraud is only one of several categories of misstatements affecting financial statements, it has probably received more attention from the public and been alleged in more instances of litigation involving auditors than any other category.

Responding to Public Expectations

In 1978, the Cohen Commission concluded that a gap existed between the performance of auditors and the expectations of financial statement users, and that, with certain exceptions, the users' expectations were generally reasonable. The Commission recommended a number of ways to respond to user expectations by clarifying and tightening auditing standards and improving communication of the auditor's role and work to the public. Several of those recommendations were acted on by the auditing profession, but others were either rejected or ignored.

By the mid-1980s, the "expectation gap" not only continued to exist but was exacerbated by difficult economic times in certain industries and several notable bankruptcies traceable to questionable business practices or to management's lack of awareness of the risks it was incurring. Unfortunately, many investors mistakenly believe that a business failure equates with an audit failure. Also, highly publicized instances of fraudulent financial reporting and illegal corporate activities had raised questions about auditors' responsibility for detecting and reporting fraud and illegalities, and also about their role in assessing an entity's policies and procedures that might prevent such irregularities. In addition, senior management and directors of major corporations were expressing a desire for the independent auditor to provide them with more assistance in meeting their responsibilities for overseeing the corporate financial reporting process.

The expectation gap and the expressed needs of corporate officers and directors resulted in efforts by three diverse bodies to consider how independent auditors can better meet and communicate their responsibilities. First, the House Subcommittee on Oversight and Investigations, chaired by Congressman John Dingell of Michigan, conducted a series of hearings regarding auditing and financial reporting problems under the federal securities laws. The Subcommittee focused public attention on several notorious business failures and frauds.

Second, the National Commission on Fraudulent Financial Reporting (Treadway Commission) was established under the sponsorship of the AICPA, American Accounting Association, Financial Executives Institute, Institute of Internal Auditors, and National Association of Accountants. The Commission's objectives were to develop initiatives for the prevention and detection of fraud and, in particular, to determine what the role of the independent auditor should be in detecting management fraud. The Treadway Commission's recommendations were published in October 1987. The five sponsoring organiza-

---

[2]"Management" as used in this chapter includes both top management and all lower levels of management that may have reasons to deceive top management.

tions have set up a committee—the Treadway Oversight Implementation Committee—to monitor the business community's reaction to the Commission's recommendations.

Third, the AICPA's Auditing Standards Board (ASB) issued nine new Statements on Auditing Standards (SASs) that represent a major attempt to respond to the public's expectations of auditors and to the needs of senior management and corporate directors. In addition, the ASB has issued guidance on implementing various aspects of the new SASs. It is also likely that additional SASs will be issued in response to regulatory rule-making, research, and other activities undertaken as a result of the Treadway Commission's recommendations.

The authors of this book believe that the recently issued SASs address in many significant respects the needs of financial statement users, senior management and boards of directors, and the public. It is clear, however, that the issues surrounding the expectations of those groups do not simply concern auditor performance and responsibilities, but are far more complex. There are, for example, fundamental concerns about the accounting measurement and disclosure principles that enter into the preparation of financial statements, about business ethics and conduct, and about the responsibilities of corporate directors and management. The ASB can address only the auditor's performance and responsibilities. The authors believe it has done so in a way that will help to close the expectation gap and that is also responsive to many of the concerns of the Dingell Committee and the Treadway Commission relating to auditors' responsibilities in performing an audit and communicating their findings.

Responsibility for Detecting Misstatements

The authoritative auditing literature for many years reflected the view that auditors were not responsible for detecting deliberate financial statement misstatements unless the application of generally accepted auditing standards (GAAS) would result in such detection. Many financial statement users, however, believe that one of the primary purposes of an audit is to detect management fraud or other intentional misstatements in *all* circumstances. The Securities and Exchange Commission (SEC) has long taken the position that an audit can be expected to detect certain kinds of fraud, stating in Accounting Series Release (ASR) No. 19, "In the Matter of McKesson & Robbins, Inc.," issued in 1940

> Moreover, we believe that, even in balance sheet examinations for corporations whose securities are held by the public, accountants can be expected to detect gross overstatements of assets and profits whether resulting from collusive fraud or otherwise. We believe that alertness on the part of the entire [audit] staff, coupled with intelligent analysis by experienced accountants of the manner of doing business, should detect overstatements in the accounts, regardless of their cause, long before they assume the magnitude reached in this case. Furthermore, an examination of this kind should not, in our opinion, exclude the highest officers of the corporation from its appraisal of the manner in which the business under review is conducted. Without underestimating the important service

rendered by independent public accountants in their review of the accounting principles employed in the preparation of financial statements filed with us and issued to stockholders, we feel that the discovery of gross overstatements in the accounts is a major purpose of such an audit even though it be conceded that it might not disclose every minor defalcation.

AICPA Professional Requirements.   Many commentators both inside and outside the accounting profession believe that until 1988, official pronouncements on auditors' responsibilities were broad, vague, and sometimes overly defensive and self-serving. However, the latest AICPA pronouncement on the auditor's responsibility to detect financial statement misstatements, SAS No. 53, *The Auditor's Responsibility to Detect and Report Errors and Irregularities* (AU Section 316.05 and .08), issued in April 1988, explicitly states

> The auditor should assess the risk that errors and irregularities may cause the financial statements to contain a material misstatement. Based on that assessment, the auditor should design the audit to provide reasonable assurance of detecting errors and irregularities that are material to the financial statements. . . .
>
> The auditor should exercise (a) due care in planning, performing, and evaluating the results of audit procedures, and (b) the proper degree of professional skepticism to achieve reasonable assurance that material errors or irregularities will be detected.

On the other hand, the SAS makes it clear (as was stated in prior pronouncements) that the auditor is not an insurer or guarantor that the financial statements are free of material misstatement.

> Since the auditor's opinion on the financial statements is based on the concept of reasonable assurance, the auditor is not an insurer and his report does not constitute a guarantee. Therefore, the subsequent discovery that a material misstatement exists in the financial statements does not, in and of itself, evidence inadequate planning, performance, or judgment on the part of the auditor. (AU Section 316.08)

The reason for this is that even a properly designed and executed audit may not detect material irregularities, because of their multifaceted characteristics. For example, an irregularity may involve forgery and collusion. Auditors are not trained to authenticate signatures or documents, and skillful collusion between client personnel and third parties or among management or employees may make otherwise appropriate auditing procedures totally ineffective. Also, auditing procedures that are effective for detecting an unintentional misstatement may be ineffective when the same misstatement is intentional, cleverly executed, or concealed through collusion.

Definitions.   As used in SAS No. 53, the terms ''errors'' and ''irregularities'' are precisely defined (AU Section 316.02 – .04).

> The term *errors* refers to *unintentional* misstatements or omissions of amounts or disclosures in financial statements. Errors may involve—

- Mistakes in gathering or processing accounting data from which financial statements are prepared.
- Incorrect accounting estimates arising from oversight or misinterpretation of facts.
- Mistakes in the application of accounting principles relating to amount, classification, manner of presentation, or disclosure.

The term *irregularities* refers to *intentional* misstatements or omissions of amounts or disclosures in financial statements. Irregularities include fraudulent financial reporting undertaken to render financial statements misleading, sometimes called *management fraud*, and misappropriation of assets, sometimes called *defalcations*. Irregularities may involve acts such as the following:

- Manipulation, falsification, or alteration of accounting records or supporting documents from which financial statements are prepared.
- Misrepresentation or intentional omission of events, transactions, or other significant information.
- Intentional misapplication of accounting principles relating to amounts, classification, manner of presentation, or disclosure.

The primary factor that distinguishes errors from irregularities is whether the underlying cause of a misstatement in financial statements is intentional or unintentional. Intent, however, is often difficult to determine, particularly in matters involving accounting estimates or the application of accounting principles. For example, an unreasonable accounting estimate may result from unintentional bias or may be an intentional attempt to misstate the financial statements.

Management fraud often involves the deliberate misapplication of accounting principles, such as the failure to provide for uncollectible accounts receivable or the deliberate overstatement of inventory. Often it is done to further a management goal, such as higher reported earnings, rather than for direct personal enrichment. Such irregularities are likely to have a significant effect on financial statements. Management fraud sometimes includes misappropriation of assets or services. That type of management fraud is difficult to detect, because it involves management override of control structure policies and procedures, and is less likely than other types of management fraud to be material to the financial statements.

Employee defalcations are generally less significant than management fraud. Clever concealment of defalcations can result in overstatements of assets (paid receivables reported as still due) or understatements of liabilities (cash misappropriated and reported as payments made). In many instances of defalcation, however, the financial statements are not actually misstated, because the asset that has been misappropriated is no longer included in the balance sheet and total expenses on the income statement are correct, although amounts related to the misappropriation are misclassified. (For example, inventory that was stolen may have been properly removed from the balance sheet, but charged to cost of sales rather than to a loss account.)

Considering the Risk of Irregularities.   As cited above, SAS No. 53 states that the auditor's responsibility under GAAS is to "design the audit to provide reasonable assurance of detecting errors and irregularities that are material to the financial statements,'' and to ''exercise (a) due care in planning, performing, and evaluating the results of audit procedures, and (b) the proper degree of professional skepticism. . . .'' Neither SAS No. 53 nor any other auditing standards, however, describe specific procedures that should be performed to accomplish these objectives. Instead, the emphasis is placed on the auditor's awareness of factors that influence the risk of material misstatements in the client's particular situation. Those factors may be related to particular account balances or classes of transactions, or they may have effects that are pervasive to the financial statements taken as a whole. As an example of the former, a management that places undue stress on increased earnings may be disinclined to provide adequate allowances for uncollectible accounts receivable or unsalable inventory. To illustrate the latter, pressure on divisional executives to meet unrealistic budgets, or a downturn in the economy, may lead to recording sales in advance of shipments, nonrecognition of expenses, unreasonably low estimates of annual depreciation, or other means of artificially inflating income.

A management orientation toward a favorable earnings trend, however, or the imposition of tight budgets on divisions, does not necessarily mean there is a likelihood of management fraud. Also, while a perceived reluctance by management to segregate responsibilities appropriately among employees, or an accounting function that is distinctly less effective than one would expect in a particular organization, may increase the possibility of errors, management fraud, and defalcations, it does not necessarily imply that they are probable. However, when factors are present that increase the risk of material errors or irregularities, the auditor should respond to that higher risk. For example, more experienced personnel could be assigned to the audit, the extent of procedures applied in particular areas (for example, the size of the sample in a particular test) could be increased, or the type of procedure used could be changed to obtain evidence that is more persuasive than would have otherwise been appropriate. A higher risk should also cause the auditor to exercise a heightened degree of professional skepticism in conducting the audit.

Management Integrity and Professional Skepticism.   An auditor should neither assume that management is dishonest nor assume unquestioned honesty. As SAS No. 53 (AU Section 316.17) points out,

> A presumption of management dishonesty . . . would be contrary to the accumulated experience of auditors. Moreover, if dishonesty were presumed, the auditor would potentially need to question the genuineness of all records and documents obtained from the client and would require conclusive rather than persuasive evidence to corroborate all management representations. An audit conducted on these terms would be unreasonably costly and impractical.

The way the auditor meets the obligation to not assume unquestioningly that management is honest is by maintaining an attitude of professional skepticism throughout the audit, especially when gathering and evaluating evidence, including management's answers to audit inquiries. For example, the auditor may detect conditions or circumstances that serve as "red flags," that is, that indicate a material misstatement could exist. Typically, these are conditions or circumstances that differ from the auditor's expectations; for example, errors are detected in an audit test that apparently were known to management but were not voluntarily disclosed to the auditor. Professional skepticism requires that when such "red flags" appear, the auditor should reconsider the audit testing plan in order to obtain sufficient competent evidence that the financial statements are free of material misstatements. Audit planning and audit evidence are covered at length in later chapters of this book.

Illegal Acts by Clients. In the 1970s, various government bodies, particularly the SEC, focused attention on illegal or questionable corporate acts, such as bribes, political payoffs, and kickbacks—usually made at least ostensibly for the benefit of the enterprise. One consequence of this scrutiny was the Foreign Corrupt Practices Act, discussed in Chapter 7. At the same time, the SEC, members of Congress, the Cohen Commission, and others in the profession proposed that independent auditors assume more responsibility for the detection and disclosure of illegal or questionable acts by clients. As a result, in 1977, the ASB issued SAS No. 17, *Illegal Acts by Clients*. In the 1980s, public attention once again focused on auditors' responsibilities with respect to clients that were alleged to have committed illegal acts; that attention resulted in the issuance in April 1988 of SAS No. 54 (AU Section 317), which superseded SAS No. 17. Illegal acts by clients are violations of laws or government regulations, perpetrated by an entity or by management or employees acting on behalf of the entity; they do not include personal misconduct unrelated to the client's business.

Some laws and regulations have a direct and material effect on the determination of amounts in financial statement line items. For example, tax laws affect the provision for income taxes and the related tax liability; federal laws and regulations may affect the amount of revenue that should be recognized under a government contract. The auditor, however, considers such laws and regulations from the perspective of their known relation to audit objectives and the corresponding financial statement assertions, rather than from the perspective of legality per se. The auditor's responsibility to detect misstatements resulting from illegal acts that have a direct and material effect on financial statement amounts is the same as for errors and irregularities.

SAS No. 54 (AU Section 317.06) explains, however, that there is another class of illegal acts for which the auditor has far less detection responsibility.

> Entities may be affected by many other laws or regulations, including those related to securities trading, occupational safety and health, food and drug administration, environmental protection, equal employment, and price-fixing or other antitrust violations. Generally, these laws and regulations relate more to an entity's operating aspects than to its financial and accounting aspects, and their financial statement effect is indirect. An auditor ordinarily does not have sufficient basis for recognizing possible violations of such laws and regulations. Their indirect effect is normally the result of the need to disclose a contingent

liability because of the allegation or determination of illegality. For example, securities may be purchased or sold based on inside information. While the direct effects of the purchase or sale may be recorded appropriately, their indirect effect, the possible contingent liability for violating securities laws, may not be appropriately disclosed. Even when violations of such laws and regulations can have consequences material to the financial statements, the auditor may not become aware of the existence of the illegal act unless he is informed by the client, or there is evidence of a governmental agency investigation or enforcement proceeding in the records, documents, or other information normally inspected in an audit of financial statements.

The auditor should be aware of the possibility that these kinds of illegal acts may have occurred. Normally, an audit performed in accordance with generally accepted auditing standards does not include procedures specifically designed to detect these illegal acts. Only if specific information comes to the auditor's attention indicating that such acts might exist and might need to be disclosed in the financial statements, should the auditor apply procedures specifically directed to ascertaining whether such an illegal act has occurred. An audit conducted in accordance with generally accepted auditing standards provides no assurance that this type of illegal act will be detected or that any resultant contingent liabilities will be disclosed.

Procedures that would otherwise be applied, however, for the purpose of forming an opinion on the financial statements, may bring possible illegal acts to the auditor's attention. Such procedures include reading minutes of directors' meetings; inquiring of the client's management and legal counsel concerning litigation, claims, and assessments; and performing tests of the various account balances. The auditor may also make inquiries of management concerning the client's

- Compliance with laws and regulations.
- Policies relating to the prevention of illegal acts.
- Communications to, and the receipt of representations from, its own management at appropriate levels of authority concerning compliance with laws and regulations. Those representations often include statements, signed annually by all levels of management, that they have not violated company policy—which is usually defined to cover all of the actions proscribed by the Foreign Corrupt Practices Act, as well as conflicts of interest—and that they are not aware of any such violations.

Finally, through the performance of procedures (including communication with attorneys) to determine the existence of loss contingencies, the auditor may uncover violations of laws.

Responsibilities on Discovering an Error, Irregularity, or Illegal Act. An auditor who becomes aware of an error or a possible irregularity or illegal act should determine the potential effect on the financial statements being audited. The auditor must be aware of the sensitivity of these matters and the need for substantial evidence before making any allegations of irregularities or illegal acts. If the auditor concludes that the financial statements are materially misstated, because of either errors or possible irregularities or illegal acts, or that loss contingencies or the potential effects of an illegal act on the entity's operations are inadequately disclosed, the auditor should insist that the statements be revised. If they are not, he or she should express a qualified or an adverse opinion on the financial statements. In addition, the auditor should bring immaterial irregularities to the attention of management at a level high enough to be able to deal appropriately with the matter, including further investigation if considered necessary. This level should be at least one level above those involved. Also, the auditor should be sure that the audit committee has been informed about all irregularities and illegal acts of which the auditor becomes aware, unless they are clearly inconsequential.

Disclosure of irregularities or illegal acts to parties other than the client's senior management and its audit committee, however, is not ordinarily part of the auditor's responsibility (unless the matter affects the opinion on the financial statements), and would be precluded by the auditor's ethical and legal obligation of confidentiality. There are four circumstances, however, in which a duty to notify parties outside the client may exist: (a) disclosure to the SEC when an auditor change is reported,[3] (b) disclosure to a successor auditor upon appropriate inquiry, (c) disclosure in response to a subpoena, and (d) disclosure to a governmental agency in accordance with requirements for audits of entities that receive financial assistance from a governmental agency. The SASs note that "because potential conflicts with the auditor's ethical and legal obligations for confidentiality may be complex, the auditor may wish to consult with legal counsel before discussing [irregularities or illegal acts] with parties outside the client" (AU Sections 316.29 and 317.23).

SAS No. 53 indicates that in some cases the auditor may not be able to determine the extent of a possible irregularity. If the auditor is precluded by the client from applying necessary procedures or is otherwise unable to conclude whether irregularities may materially affect the financial statements, an opinion qualified because of a scope limitation or a disclaimer of opinion should be issued. SAS No. 54 contains similar guidance with respect to an illegal act. The auditor could be precluded by the client from evaluating whether a possible illegal act is, in fact, illegal and material to the financial statements. In those instances, the auditor should generally disclaim an opinion on the financial statements. If, however, the auditor's inability to determine whether an act is illegal does not result from client-imposed restrictions, a scope qualification, or explanatory language because of an uncertainty, may be appropriate.

If the client refuses to accept the auditor's report as modified for the reasons described above, the auditor should withdraw from the engagement and indicate the reasons for withdrawal to the audit committee or board of directors. Withdrawal might also be appropriate in other circumstances, such as when the client continues to retain a known perpetrator of an irregularity in a position with a significant role in the entity's internal control structure, or

---

[3]As noted in Chapter 3, CPA firms that are members of the AICPA's SEC Practice Section have an obligation to notify the SEC when a firm has resigned, declined to stand for reelection, or been dismissed.

when the client refuses to take remedial action the auditor considers appropriate when an illegal act has occurred. Withdrawal from an engagement would cause a change of auditors, which, for a publicly traded company, would trigger the SEC Form 8-K filing discussed on pages 79 to 81, thereby publicizing the reasons for the withdrawal.

Engagement Letters.   Most auditors recognize the need for a written communication to the client specifying the responsibilities of both the client and auditor. That communication, called an "engagement letter," is not required by generally accepted auditing standards, but is widely employed to avoid misunderstandings about the auditor's responsibility for discovering errors, irregularities, and illegal acts, and to remind clients of the inherent limitations of an audit. (Some auditors also include fee terms and other arrangements in the letter, and may wish to include a statement that consistent application of generally accepted accounting principles is assumed unless otherwise stated in the auditor's report.) A typical engagement letter (for an entity that has an audit committee) is shown in Figure 4.1. Some auditors ask clients to sign and return a copy of the engagement letter to indicate their acceptance of, and agreement with, its contents.

Figure 4.1   Typical Engagement Letter

Audit Committee
X Corporation

This letter sets forth our understanding of the terms and objectives of our engagement, and the nature and scope of the services we will provide.

We will audit your financial statements as of and for the year ended December 31, 19XX, in accordance with generally accepted auditing standards. The objective of an audit is the expression of our opinion on whether the financial statements present fairly, in all material respects, the financial position, results of operations, and cash flows in conformity with generally accepted accounting principles.

As a part of our audit, we will consider the Company's internal control structure, as required by generally accepted auditing standards, for the purpose of establishing a basis for determining the nature, timing, and extent of auditing procedures necessary for expressing our opinion on the financial statements. We will also read information included in the annual report to shareholders and consider whether such information, including the manner of its presentation, is consistent with information appearing in the financial statements.

Our audit will include procedures designed to provide reasonable assurance of detecting errors and irregularities that are material to the financial statements. As you are aware, however, there are inherent limitations in the auditing process. For example, audits are based on the concept of selective testing of the data being examined and are, therefore, subject to the limitation that such matters, if they exist, may not be detected. Also, because of the characteristics of irreg-

Figure 4.1 *Continued*

٠ ularities, including attempts at concealment through collusion and forgery, a properly designed and executed audit may not detect a material irregularity.

Similarly, in performing our audit we will be aware of the possibility that illegal acts may have occurred. However, it should be recognized that our audit provides no assurance that illegal acts, other than those having a direct and material effect on the determination of financial statement amounts, will be detected. We will inform you with respect to illegal acts or material errors and irregularities that come to our attention during the course of our audit.

You recognize that the financial statements and the establishment and maintenance of an internal control structure are the responsibility of management. Appropriate supervisory review procedures are necessary to provide reasonable assurance that adopted policies and prescribed procedures are adhered to and to identify errors and irregularities or illegal acts. As part of our aforementioned consideration of the Company's internal control structure, we will inform you of matters that come to our attention that represent significant deficiencies in the design or functioning of the internal control structure.

Generally accepted auditing standards require that we communicate certain additional matters to you or, alternatively, assure ourselves that management has appropriately made you aware of those matters. Such matters specifically include (1) the initial selection of and changes in significant accounting policies and their application; (2) the process used by management in formulating particularly sensitive accounting estimates and the basis for our conclusions regarding the reasonableness of those estimates; (3) audit adjustments that could, in our judgment, either individually or in the aggregate, have a significant effect on your financial reporting process; (4) any disagreements with management, whether or not satisfactorily resolved, about matters that individually or in the aggregate could be significant to the financial statements or our report; (5) our views about matters that were the subject of management's consultation with other accountants about auditing and accounting matters; (6) major issues that were discussed with management in connection with the retention of our services, including, among other matters, any discussions regarding the application of accounting principles and auditing standards; and (7) serious difficulties that we encountered in dealing with management related to the performance of the audit.

At the conclusion of the engagement, we will be supplied with a representation letter that, among other things, will confirm management's responsibility for the preparation of the financial statements in conformity with generally accepted accounting principles, the availability of financial records and related data, the completeness and availability of all minutes of board of directors (and committee) meetings, and the absence of irregularities involving management or those employees who have significant roles in the control structure.

We shall be pleased to discuss this letter with you.

[Firm name, manually signed]

AUDITORS' LEGAL LIABILITY

Beyond the disciplinary system of the profession discussed in the previous chapter, auditors,[4] in common with other professionals, are subject to legal and other sanctions as a consequence of deficiencies, that is, failure to meet professional standards in the performance of their work. Unlike some other professionals, however, whose liability is limited to their clients and patients, independent auditors are also liable to growing numbers of nonclient third parties, mainly investors and creditors, who rely on audited financial statements in making decisions that expose them to substantial potential losses. As a result, auditors' exposure to possible loss is great, and the amount of potential loss is usually indeterminate at the time the audit is performed. This section of the chapter examines auditors' civil liabilities to clients and third parties, as well as criminal liability and civil regulatory remedies. It starts with an overview of the American legal system.

Overview of the American Legal System

The American legal system consists of state and federal courts and administrative agencies. Auditors' legal liability under that system derives from both common and statutory law as applied by the courts and the rulings of administrative agencies. Common law evolves from judicial rulings on matters of law in specific cases. Statutory law may codify or change common law. Judicial interpretation of statutory law, in turn, leads to the development of case law precedents. This interaction permits the courts to continually redefine the auditor's role and duties. Administrative agencies, which are created by state legislatures and Congress, have the power to enact and enforce regulations affecting auditors.

Federal Courts.   A court must have subject matter jurisdiction over a particular case and personal jurisdiction over a defendant in the case before it has the power to try the case. Generally, the subject matter jurisdiction of the federal courts is based on one of two concepts: diversity jurisdiction or federal question jurisdiction. The *diversity jurisdiction* of the federal courts is derived from the U.S. Constitution and was created to prevent prejudicial treatment of out-of-state litigants in state courts. Diversity jurisdiction exists when the parties to a lawsuit are from different states and the amount in controversy exceeds $50,000.[5] For there to be diversity jurisdiction, none of the plaintiffs (the parties who brought the suit) can be citizens of the state of any of the defendants (the parties against whom the suit was brought). The citizenship of a corporation is based on its place of incorporation and its principal place of

---

[4]In this section of the chapter, the words "auditor" and "auditors" apply to both individuals, whether sole practitioners or employees of CPA firms, and auditing firms, unless otherwise specified or indicated by context.

[5]In November 1988, Congress passed the Judicial Improvements and Access to Justice Act, which limits the availability of a federal court forum for diversity jurisdiction in some respects for cases filed after May 18, 1989. The most prominent change was an increase in the necessary amount in controversy from $10,000 to $50,000.

business; if they differ, it is considered a citizen of both states. The citizenship of a partnership is determined by the citizenship of its partners.

Federal question jurisdiction is present when a plaintiff asserts a right under the Constitution, a federal statute, or a federal regulation. Federal courts also have jurisdiction over claims brought by the United States.

In addition to subject matter jurisdiction, a court must also have *personal jurisdiction* over a defendant. Generally, if a defendant is present in a court's district, the court will have personal jurisdiction over the individual. Courts also have "long-arm" jurisdiction that applies when a person from outside the district provides services that cause injury within the district.

To hear a case, the court must have subject matter jurisdiction and personal jurisdiction over the defendants, and be a proper "venue," that is, an appropriate location for the trial. In general, cases based on diversity jurisdiction may be brought in the judicial district where all plaintiffs or all defendants reside or where the claim arose. Cases based on federal question jurisdiction may be brought where all defendants reside or where the claim arose. In rare circumstances, a court with subject matter jurisdiction, personal jurisdiction, and venue will transfer a case to a more convenient forum, such as where all the witnesses are located, under a doctrine known as *forum non conveniens*.

A defendant may raise any claim it has against the plaintiff in a counterclaim and may bring a related claim against nonparties in a third-party complaint. For example, if a company sued its auditor for failing to prevent an embezzlement loss, the auditor could counterclaim for fees owed by the company and could file a third-party claim against the embezzler.

Administrative Agencies. Administrative agencies, such as the SEC, have the power, delegated by state legislatures and Congress, to enact and enforce regulations and punish violators of them. Thus, the SEC has the power to enact a regulation requiring auditors of companies registered with it to comply with GAAS, investigate whether a violation of that regulation occurred, file a complaint against an alleged violator, decide the merits of the complaint, and determine the penalty for the violation. The judges employed by federal administrative agencies to decide complaints brought by the agency are referred to as administrative law judges.

Federal courts will overturn an administrative agency's decision only if the agency's action violates the Constitution or a statute, is arbitrary or capricious, or is not supported by the record created by the agency to support its decision. However, if there is conflicting evidence, the agency's decision will not be overturned by the courts.

State Courts. State courts hear and decide legal disputes that a federal court may not have jurisdiction over. These disputes may involve state statutes, some of which parallel federal statutes, such as the federal securities laws, or common law.

Common law includes contract law, which concerns the enforcement of promises, and the law of torts, which involves the duty to not cause harm to others. The law of torts covers negligence, which is the failure to conform one's conduct to the standard of a reasonable person, and fraud, which is an intentional misstatement made for the purpose of monetary gain. Professional malpractice, the failure of a licensed professional to conform his or her conduct to professional standards, falls under the law of negligence. For auditors, professional standards are contained in generally accepted auditing standards. In almost all cases, a licensed professional must testify that there has been a deviation from professional standards in order to support a charge of professional malpractice. Thus, unless a violation is so egregious that it would be obvious to a lay person, a plaintiff generally must retain an "expert" witness in order to prevail in a malpractice claim.

Judicial Procedures.   A civil case is brought by filing a complaint with a court; the complaint is served or delivered, with a summons, to the defendant. The summons is a document that tells the defendant he or she has been sued and must respond to the complaint. The complaint must contain a plain and concise statement of the facts and the legal theories that the plaintiff believes entitle him or her to relief.

Generally, the defendant files an answer to the complaint, admitting or denying each of the allegations in the complaint, or files a motion to dismiss the complaint or a motion for summary judgment. A motion to dismiss accepts the truth of the allegations but argues they are insufficient to entitle the plaintiff to relief. A motion to dismiss may also be based on deficiencies in the complaint. For example, allegations of fraud must be specific and particular, and the plaintiff's failure to detail facts in support of a charge of fraud is a basis for dismissal of a complaint. Deficiencies also include a lack of personal or subject matter jurisdiction.

A motion for summary judgment argues there is no genuine issue of material fact and the party filing the motion is entitled to dismissal or relief as a matter of law. Motions for summary judgment are often accompanied by documents or statements under oath, called affidavits. If the sworn statements or documents conflict on material issues, those issues must be resolved at trial, which may be before a jury if any party requests one. Before the trial, both parties to the dispute are entitled to discovery of all facts relevant to the dispute, including facts that may lead to relevant evidence. The parties are required to produce documents and provide pretrial testimony under oath at depositions. The parties may also obtain subpoenas from the court to compel persons who are not parties to the lawsuit to provide documents or testimony at a deposition or at the trial.

The only relevant information not available to a litigant is information protected by a privilege, such as the attorney–client privilege. The attorney-client privilege protects confidential communications between a client and his or her attorney made for the purpose of obtaining legal advice. Courts also recognize an attorney work product privilege, which protects material that would provide insight into the attorney's theories on a legal dispute, such as a memorandum recording the attorney's assessment of the strengths or weaknesses of the case. Disclosure of privileged information to a third party, such as an accountant, may constitute a waiver of the privilege. Thus, there is tension between a client's obligation to disclose material information to its accountants and to the public, and the desire to protect privileged information from disclosure to its opponents in litigation. Many states recognize by statute an accountant–client privilege. However, federal courts do not recognize such a privilege in cases involving federal claims. In every state, with the possible exception of Illinois and Tennessee, the client may waive the privilege and obtain the accountant's files and testimony. (Clients may also waive the attorney–client privilege.)

At trial, the plaintiff has the burden of producing evidence in support of his or her claim and of persuading the fact finder of each element of the claim. Thus, the plaintiff must convince the jury, or the judge if there is no jury and the judge is serving as the fact finder, that it is more likely than not that the facts supporting his or her claim occurred.

The federal appellate courts and most state appellate courts will not decide an issue until there is a final ruling that resolves the entire case, such as dismissal of the case or a jury verdict. Moreover, the appellate courts will not disturb the fact finder's determination unless it is clearly erroneous or there was legal error—such as the exclusion of admissible evidence or an improper instruction to the jury on the applicable legal standards. Most court opinions that establish legal precedents are decisions on motions prior to trial or decisions on appeals of dismissals or jury verdicts.

The Litigation Explosion

Few lawsuits were brought against accountants prior to 1965. In the late 1960s, several court decisions signaled dramatic changes in the attitude of the courts and the expectations of the public concerning auditors' responsibilities and their legal liability to third parties. By the mid-1970s, hundreds of lawsuits were pending against accountants. Lawsuits against accountants received new impetus in the early 1980s, with jury awards of damages in the tens of millions of dollars, including an $80 million award in 1981. Such awards initiated a new wave of litigation against accountants.

The extent of litigation facing accounting firms is reflected also by the size of their internal legal staffs. The first time a lawyer joined an accounting firm to provide legal advice was in 1968. In 1983, 40 lawyers were employed for such purposes by the 11 largest accounting firms. By 1989, 103 lawyers were providing legal advice to the 14 largest accounting firms. In addition, in 1988, the eight largest accounting firms spent over $100 million in out-of-pocket expenses, including attorney's fees paid to outside lawyers, in defending litigation. This amount does not include the cost of verdicts or settlements, or of liability insurance, when it is available.[6] Moreover, it is estimated there are over $1 billion in claims pending against accountants. Undoubtedly, auditors' legal liability is one of the most important issues currently facing the profession.

A number of factors have contributed to the increase in litigation against auditors since the 1960s, including technical legal developments that made

[6]An October 10, 1988, article in *Crain Business Insurance* (M. Bradford, "Accountants E&O Market Stable—for Now," p. 14) included an estimate that small firms pay from $1000 to $2500 per professional for liability insurance, while the largest firms pay at least twice that amount. Some small firms have difficulty obtaining professional liability insurance.

legal remedies available to third parties (discussed in a later section) and social changes that influenced the public's expectations of auditors. Most notable of these social changes are the growth of consumerism and the perception of auditors as "insurers" of the reliability of a company's financial statements.

Consumerism.   It was inevitable with the passage of the federal securities laws in the early 1930s and the growth of the securities markets that investors and creditors would make increased use of audited financial statements. Paralleling this development has been the growth of an attitude that just as consumers of the products and services of American business are entitled to expect more from their purchases than they did in the past, so too are investors and creditors, as consumers of financial information. When people's expectations are not met, they are increasingly likely to contact legal counsel, especially since many attorneys are willing to take cases on a contingency basis.

This attitude has been buttressed by the access that disappointed consumers of financial information have to new and far-reaching remedies, perhaps the most significant of which from the auditor's point of view is the class action lawsuit (discussed later in this chapter). The result of these developments has been a heightening of the public's expectations of auditors and their work, and a far greater willingness on the part of investors and creditors who relied on that work to seek recovery from auditors for losses suffered. Rightly or wrongly, many people believe auditors can act to prevent investor and creditor losses and are thus a logical choice to bear those losses.

Auditors as "Insurers."   A second important influence on the legal environment is the public's perception of auditors as "guarantors" of the reliability of a company's financial statements. The public, perhaps because of the perceived precision of financial statements and the prominence of the auditor's report accompanying them, often does not recognize that a company's management has primary responsibility for its financial statements and that the auditor's role inherently involves numerous difficult judgments. (As noted elsewhere, the auditor's standard report adopted by the Auditing Standards Board in 1988 specifically addresses these user misperceptions.)

Thus, when the "guarantor" is viewed as a large, successful organization with substantial resources (including professional liability insurance), and frequently in troubled situations is also the only financially viable entity available to sue, it should not be surprising that auditors are looked to for their "deep pockets" and are sued by injured persons primarily because of their ability to pay, regardless of culpability. The fact that an auditor's fees for an engagement rarely bear any reasonable relationship to the auditor's potential liability, and that the auditor derived no "equity" benefit from the operations of the entity, rarely elicits sympathy from disappointed investor-plaintiffs.

Substantial numbers of lawsuits against auditors alleging inadequacies in their professional services will probably continue to be a fact of life, at least for the foreseeable future. The nine auditing pronouncements issued in 1988 in an attempt to narrow the "expectation gap," and other efforts by the profession to articulate its objectives, responsibilities, and the limitations of those responsibilities, may have an effect on the public's expectations and perception of auditors. In the meantime, an auditor's best protection against liability (in addition to adequate malpractice insurance, when available) is to do competent work and to keep in mind an understanding of how the courts perceive the professional's role and responsibilities, as expressed in judicial rulings under common law and as codified in the securities laws.

Liability to Clients

An auditor's liability to clients is based on the direct contractual relationship between them, referred to as "privity," and on the law of torts. Under common law, a professional is liable to a client for breach of contract (e.g., an auditor's issuing an unqualified opinion without conducting an audit in accordance with GAAS when that has been contracted for) and also, under tort law, for ordinary negligence. Obviously, if an auditor is liable to a client for ordinary negligence, gross negligence and fraud on the part of the auditor are also grounds for liability to a client.

Most lawsuits by clients are brought on grounds of ordinary negligence, which is defined as the failure to exercise due professional care. For auditors, due care essentially means adhering to generally accepted auditing standards. Gross negligence is the lack of even slight care. The client has a cause for action against the auditor if the financial statements contain a misrepresentation of a material fact—that is, a material error or irregularity—that was not detected because of the auditor's failure to exercise due care, and that injured the client.

Suits by clients arise in a variety of contexts, but certain patterns are evident. Many instances of litigation against auditors involve the situation in which an audit does not detect an ongoing embezzlement by an employee of the client, and additional money is taken after the audit is completed. The client contends the losses occurring after the audit would have been prevented if the auditor had detected the embezzlement. A client may also contend that internal control deficiencies enabled losses to go undetected, and the auditor failed to bring such deficiencies to the attention of management.

Clients often have fidelity bond coverage to protect against such losses. In many circumstances, after a fidelity bond carrier pays on a loss, it becomes "subrogated" to the client's claim against the auditor, that is, it "steps into the shoes" of the client and may assert the client's rights.[7]

Clients also bring suits against their accountants in a variety of other contexts. For example, suits by clients may arise out of business acquisitions, when the accountant has performed a review prior to the acquisition. The purchase price may be based on the assets of the acquired company as reflected by the financial statements. If the client determines later that the assets were overstated, a suit against the accountant may result. Clients have also sued

---

[7]In 1945, the predecessor of the American Institute of Certified Public Accountants reached an agreement with the industry trade group representing the surety bond companies. The agreement provided that accountants would encourage their clients to rely on fidelity bond coverage to protect themselves from losses from embezzlements. In exchange, a number of fidelity bond carriers agreed not to sue an accountant for failing to detect such losses unless they could first prove to an independent panel that the accountant was grossly negligent. A number of courts have enforced the agreement.

when they discovered that certain divisions they thought were profitable based on the financial statements were actually losing money. The client contends it would have closed the unprofitable divisions had it known about the losses and thereby would have prevented additional injury.

A claim by a client for failing to detect an embezzlement scheme or an overstatement of assets or income is generally based on negligence. It is alleged the accountant failed to comply with professional standards; had such standards been followed, the subsequent losses would have been prevented. Since such a claim is brought by the client, privity is satisfied. The person who embezzled the money or who sold the business is also made a party to such litigation in most cases. By the time the loss is discovered, however, the embezzler has often spent the stolen funds and will be "judgment-proof," that is, will lack assets to collect a court judgment against. In addition, the seller may have been released from liability by the buyer as part of the sale contract.

Besides defending the quality of their audits, auditors also defend themselves in such cases by pointing to negligence on the part of officers and employees of the client—in selecting or supervising the embezzler or in evaluating the acquisition. This concept is known as contributory negligence. In addition, auditors point to management's primary responsibility for the financial statements and the internal control structure. In states where contributory negligence is still the rule, proof of such negligence will completely bar the client's claim.

Today, however, most states follow the concept of comparative negligence, and the client's negligence will not bar the claim. Instead, it will be compared with any negligence of the auditor on a percentage basis, and liability will be apportioned based on the parties' relative degrees of fault. Most of those states, however, also follow the rule of "joint and several liability," under which claimants can collect all or part of their damages from any defendant found liable, irrespective of that defendant's proportionate fault. In many cases, the other defendants are "judgment-proof" because they have few assets and no insurance, leaving the auditor, who usually has "deep pockets," responsible for all the damages awarded. Many auditors believe that the prevailing rule of "joint and several liability" should be replaced by a "several liability" rule, under which defendants would not be required to pay more than their proportionate share of the claimant's losses.

Under what is often termed the *National Surety* doctrine, some states require that the negligence of the client must contribute to the accountant's failure to properly perform the audit before such negligence will constitute a defense under either the comparative or contributory negligence concept.[8] Under the *National Surety* doctrine, the accountant could not raise as a defense the fact that management negligently failed to discover an embezzlement scheme, because such negligence would not interfere with the conduct of the audit. However, if management failed to follow the auditor's recommendations about internal control, for example, the auditor would be able to raise the client's negligence as a defense. The client's negligence could also be raised as a defense if the client failed to provide material information to the auditor that would have had

---

[8]*National Surety Corp.* v. *Lybrand*, 256 A.D. 226 (N.Y. App. Div. 1939).

an effect on the scope of the audit —such as any suspicious acts by an employee that came to the attention of management or other employees.[9]

At some point, fraud by a client company may become so pervasive that it will bar any claim against the accountant. In *Cenco Inc.* v. *Seidman & Seidman*,[10] managerial employees of the client engaged in a massive fraud that involved the overstatement of inventories. The inflated value of inventory increased the price of the client's stock, and enabled the company to buy other companies cheaply, obtain overstated insurance recoveries for lost inventory, and borrow money at lower rates. The chairman and president were aware of the fraud, but seven of the nine members of the board were not. The company brought a negligence claim against the accountant for failing to detect the fraud. The court held that the company could not recover against the accountants "if the fraud permeates the top management of the company and if, moreover, the managers are not stealing from the company—that is, from its current stockholders—but instead are turning the company into an engine of theft against outsiders—creditors, prospective stockholders, insurers, etc."

An accounting firm may be liable for a loss resulting from an embezzlement, even if it provides only review or compilation services and does not conduct an audit. In *Robert Wooler Co.* v. *Fidelity Bank*[11] the court held that the accounting firm, which had not performed an audit, nevertheless had an obligation "to warn its client of known deficiencies in the client's internal operating procedures which enhanced opportunities for employee defalcations." In *1136 Tenants' Corp.* v. *Max Rothenberg & Co.*,[12] an accountant engaged to perform nonaudit accounting services was liable for failing to inform the client of missing invoices, which enabled an employee's embezzlement to go unnoticed.

Auditors should try to avoid misunderstandings with clients about their responsibility for detecting errors or irregularities and illegal acts. Because this is a sensitive area, most auditors discuss these matters with their clients and follow up with a written communication spelling out a mutual understanding of functions, objectives, and responsibilities regarding the audit (see Figure 4.1). Such communications do not, however, relieve the auditor of legal liability for failing to exercise due professional care.

Potential liability also arises from the auditor's quasi-fiduciary relationship with a client. As discussed in Chapter 3, the auditor has a professional responsibility not to disclose confidential information obtained during an audit unless disclosure is required to fairly present the client's financial information in conformity with generally accepted accounting principles. In *Fund of Funds, Ltd.* v. *Arthur Andersen & Co.*,[13] the auditors were found liable as a result of, among other things, failing to use information they obtained from another client to determine which of the two clients' financial statements accurately

---

[9]In general, an employer is legally responsible for the negligent acts of an employee, but not for acts of intentional dishonesty for the personal benefit of the employee.

[10]686 F.2d 449 (7th Cir.), *cert. denied*, 459 U.S. 880 (1982).

[11]479 A.2d 1027 (Pa. App. 1984).

[12]36 A.D.2d 804 (App. Div. 1971), *aff'd*, 281 N.E.2d 846 (N.Y. 1972).

[13]545 F. Supp. 1314 (S.D.N.Y. 1982).

portrayed the facts of the same transaction. Thus, there may be a legal precedent for holding an auditor liable for not disclosing and using information obtained from services rendered to one client that is relevant to the audit of another client. The auditor's professional responsibility in this situation is discussed in Chapter 3.

Civil Liability to Third Parties Under Common Law

Most civil suits brought by third parties against auditors under common law allege losses resulting from reliance on financial statements. Such suits arise when lenders or investors lose money on a loan to or an investment in a company and contend, with the benefit of hindsight, that the financial statements materially misstated the company's financial condition. Suits of this type have increased as a result of a number of judicial decisions beginning in the 1960s that expanded the class to whom the auditor owed a duty of care and also raised the level of care owed to third parties. Today an auditor may be liable for ordinary negligence to any reasonably limited and reasonably definable class of persons the auditor might reasonably expect to rely on the opinion. Liability for gross negligence and fraud extends to all third parties.

Privity of Contract Doctrine.   Unlike the auditor–client relationship, there is no privity of contract between the auditor and third parties. Traditionally, claims by third parties under common law were based on the law of torts, and only fraud, not ordinary negligence from failure to exercise due care, was considered a wrongful act by an auditor. The first case to test the privity of contract doctrine involving auditors was *Ultramares Corp.* v. *Touche*[14] in 1931. The plaintiff, without the defendant's knowledge, had relied on financial statements audited by the defendant to make loans to a company that later became insolvent. The plaintiff alleged that the auditors were guilty of negligence and fraudulent misrepresentation in not detecting fictitious amounts included in accounts receivable and accounts payable. The court upheld the doctrine of privity of contract as a limitation on the auditors' liability to the unforeseen third party for ordinary negligence, based, at least in part, on Judge Cardozo's reasoning that auditors' liability for negligence should not be extended to third parties because doing so would have the potential effect of deterring people from entering the profession, which would be detrimental to society. Cardozo described the consequences of extending the auditor's duty to third parties as follows:

> If liability for negligence exists, a thoughtless slip or blunder, the failure to detect a theft or forgery beneath the cover of deceptive entries, may expose accountants to a liability in an indeterminate amount for an indeterminate time to an indeterminate class. The hazards of a business conducted on these terms are so extreme as to enkindle doubt whether a flaw may not exist in an implication of a duty that exposes to these consequences.

[14]255 N.Y. 170 (1931).

Primary Benefit Rule.   Subsequently, however, courts in some states have attempted to increase the auditor's liability to third parties for ordinary negligence by undermining the privity doctrine. The first crack in the privity rule occurred in the *Ultramares* case itself with the formulation of the "primary benefit rule," which held that an auditor would be liable to a third party for ordinary negligence if the auditor knew that the audit was being performed for the primary benefit of a specifically identified third party. Before the mid-1960s, however, most third-party plaintiffs bringing suit against auditors pursuant to the primary benefit rule were not successful, even in cases in which the auditor knew specific persons might rely on the opinion. For example, in *State St. Trust Co.* v. *Ernst*[15] the auditor was found not liable to a lender for negligence, even though the auditor knew the particular lender intended to rely on the audited financial statements.

Further weakening of the privity of contract doctrine in cases of professionals' liability did not occur until 1963, 32 years after *Ultramares*. It began with a series of cases that represented an attack on the primary benefit rule. The *Hedley Byrne* case[16] was decided by the highest court of England, the House of Lords, in 1963. The case did not involve auditors, but a negligently stated accommodation credit report by a bank on which a third person relied, to his damage. In their opinions, the justices stated that "where there is a relationship equivalent to contract . . . , there is a duty of care." The court's finding, however, was intended to have somewhat limited application in that it extended the duty of care to only a restricted class of third parties, as in *Ultramares*.

Foreseen Third Parties.   In 1965, the American Law Institute (ALI) issued its Second Restatement of the Law of Torts, a compendium of tort principles. Partly in reliance on *Hedley Byrne*, the ALI interpreted the law of negligent misrepresentations by professionals to third parties more broadly than before. The Restatement provides that an accountant is liable to a person who justifiably relies on false information when the accountant fails to exercise reasonable care in obtaining or communicating the information, if: (1) the loss is suffered "by the person or one of a limited group of persons for whose benefit and guidance . . . [the accountant] knows that the recipient intends to supply" the information; and (2) the loss is suffered "through reliance upon" the information in a transaction that the accountant knows the recipient intends the information to influence or in a substantially similar transaction. Thus, the Restatement extended liability to a member of a limited group that the accountant is aware will receive information that is provided with regard to a transaction the accountant is aware of or a substantially similar transaction. This can be described as a "foreseen" class of recipients, as opposed to a "foreseeable" class, defined as an unlimited class of persons not identified by the auditor who may foreseeably be expected to rely on information.

---

[15]278 N.Y. 104 (1938).

[16]*Hedley Byrne & Co. Ltd.* v. *Heller & Partners, Ltd.*, 1964 A.C. 465 [1963] 2 *All E.R.* 575 (H.L. 1963).

The distinction in the Restatement's interpretation of a professional's duty to third parties between *foreseen* and *foreseeable* persons is critical to an understanding of post-1965 legal decisions based on common law. In several significant cases, courts accepted the foreseen class concept of the Restatement. In *Rusch Factors, Inc.* v. *Levin*,[17] the court ruled that the auditor could be liable to the third-party plaintiff, a lender of the client, for negligence. In this case, the audit was performed at the specific request of the plaintiff-lender. In another case, *Rhode Island Hospital Trust National Bank* v. *Swartz, Bresenoff, Yavner & Jacobs*,[18] the court found the auditors liable for negligence to a foreseen party; the auditors knew that the plaintiff-bank required audited financial statements of the client, even though they did not know the specific identity of the plaintiff.

Foreseeable Third Parties.   Until 1983, auditors' common law liability for negligence extended no further than foreseen third parties. In that year, the New Jersey Supreme Court ruled in a motion for partial summary judgment that an auditor has a duty to reasonably foreseeable but unidentifiable third-party users who may rely on financial statements for appropriate business purposes.[19] The plaintiffs had alleged that they relied on financial statements audited by the defendants in making an investment that subsequently proved to be worthless, after the financial statements were found to be misstated. The plaintiffs were not members of an identifiable group of users to whom the financial statements were intended to be furnished. In handing down the opinion, the court quoted the court's opinion in *Rusch Factors*, which questioned the wisdom of the *Ultramares* decision, as follows:

> Why should an innocent reliant party be forced to carry the weighty burden of an accountant's professional malpractice? Isn't the risk of loss more easily distributed and fairly spread by imposing it on the accounting profession, which can pass the cost of insuring against the risk onto its customers, who can in turn pass the cost onto the entire consuming public? Finally, wouldn't a rule of foreseeability elevate the cautionary techniques of the accounting profession?[20]

The court added its own belief that

> When the independent auditor furnishes an opinion with no limitation in the certificate as to whom the company may disseminate the financial statements, he has a duty to all those whom that auditor should reasonably foresee as recipients from the company of the statements for its proper business purposes, provided that the recipients rely on the statements pursuant to those business purposes.

The key distinction between the Restatement rule and the liberalized standard recognized in New Jersey is the accountant's knowledge at the time the

[17]284 F. Supp. 85 (D.R.I. 1968).
[18]482 F.2nd 1000 (4th Cir. 1973).
[19]*H. Rosenblum, Inc.* v. *Adler*, 93 N.J. 324 (1983).
[20]*Rusch Factors, Inc.* v. *Levin*, 284 F. Supp. 85 (D.R.I. 1968).

audit is performed with regard to who will be supplied with financial statements and for what purpose. Under the Restatement rule, the accountant must have been aware of a limited group of parties and the particular or a substantially similar transaction in which it was intended that a party would rely on the financial statements. For example, if a certain investor was considering purchasing a company, the accountant would have to have known about the investor's intended reliance on the financial statements in connection with the proposed purchase. Under the liberalized test, the accountant would be liable for negligence to an unforeseen investor with regard to an unexpected transaction if such an event was foreseeable.

Soon after the decision by the New Jersey Supreme Court in *Rosenblum*, the Wisconsin Supreme Court reached the same result in *Citizens State Bank* v. *Timm, Schmidt & Co.*[21] In the *Timm* case, the court stated that "the fundamental principle of Wisconsin negligence law is that a tortfeasor is fully liable for all foreseeable consequences of his act." The court rejected any policy consideration that might have justified a more restrictive rule of liability for accountants.

In 1985, however, the highest court in New York rigorously adhered to the *Ultramares* rule in *Credit Alliance Corp.* v. *Arthur Andersen & Co.*[22] The court in *Credit Alliance* set forth three "prerequisites that must be satisfied before accountants would be held liable in negligence to third parties who rely to their detriment on inaccurate financial reports: (1) the accountants must have been aware that the financial reports were to be used for a particular purpose or purposes; (2) in the furtherance of which a known party or parties was intended to rely; and (3) there must have been some conduct on the part of the accountants linking them to that party or parties, which evinces the accountants' understanding of that party or parties' reliance."

Since the decision in *Credit Alliance*, other state courts have taken various positions. In 1986, in *International Mortgage Co.* v. *John P. Butler Accountancy Corp.*[23] an intermediate appellate court in California rejected the New York rule and followed New Jersey and Wisconsin, holding that an accountant was liable to a lender for failing to detect that a preexisting mortgage was not reflected on a real estate firm's financial statements, even though the lender first contacted the real estate firm after the report was issued.

In 1988 the highest court in New York reaffirmed the test set forth in *Credit Alliance* and applied it in the context of a review of financial statements (see Chapter 23).[24] A year later, in *Law Offices of Lawrence J. Stockler, P.C.* v. *Rose*,[25] the Michigan Court of Appeals followed the Restatement test, holding that the accountant could be liable for negligence to the purchaser of a company that relied on the financial statements. In this case, the accountant was aware, at the time the report was issued, that the purchaser would rely on the financial statements for purposes of purchasing the company. The court rejected the

[21]113 Wis. 2d 376 (1983).

[22]65 N.Y. 2d 536 (1985).

[23]177 Cal. App. 3d 806 (1986).

[24]*William Iselin & Co.* v. *Mann Judd Landau*, 71 N.Y. 2d 420 (1988).

[25]174 Mich. App. 14 (1989).

"foreseeable" test followed by California, New Jersey, and Wisconsin on the following ground:

> The reasons for taking this more restricted approach in third party actions against the accountant have been a recognition that the financial statements themselves are the representations of the client (with the auditor's liability arising from the opinion rendered concerning the accuracy of the client's records) and the accountant's inability to control the distribution of the report or the content of some of the statements he is assessing.

In 1989 the Idaho and Nebraska supreme courts and the intermediate court of appeals in Florida adopted the *Ultramares* rule.[26]

At the time of this writing, the following jurisdictions, in addition to those cited above, appear to be adhering to the *Ultramares* rule: Arkansas,[27] Delaware,[28] Indiana,[29] Kansas,[30] and Pennsylvania.[31] The following jurisdictions are apparently following the Restatement approach: Georgia,[32] Hawaii,[33] Iowa,[34] Minnesota,[35] Missouri,[36] New Hampshire,[37] New Mexico,[38] North Carolina,[39] Ohio,[40] Tennessee,[41] Texas,[42] Utah,[43] and Washington.[44] The only court to join New Jersey, California, and Wisconsin since the California decision in 1986 was the supreme court of Mississippi in August 1987.[45] In that case the accountant provided a copy of the financial statements to a third party.

[26]*Idaho Bank & Trust Co.* v. *First Bancorp*, Idaho LEXIS 68 (1989); *Citizens National Bank* v. *Kennedy & Coe*, 232 Neb. 477 (1989); *First Florida Bank* v. *Max Mitchell & Co.*, 541 So.2d 155 Fla. App. (1989).

[27]*Robertson* v. *White*, 633 F. Supp. 954 (W.D. Ark. 1986).

[28]*McLean* v. *Alexander*, 599 F.2d 1190 (3d Cir. 1979).

[29]*Toro Co.* v. *Krouse, Kern & Co.*, 827 F.2d 155 (7th Cir. 1987).

[30]*Nortek, Inc.* v. *Alexander Grant & Co.*, 532 F.2d 1013 (10th Cir. 1974), *cert. denied*, 429 U.S. 1042 (1977).

[31]*Hartford Accident & Indemnity Co.* v. *Parente, Randolph, Orlando, Carey & Associates*, 642 F. Supp. 38 (M.D. Pa. 1985); *Pennine Resources, Inc.* v. *Dorwart Andrew & Co.*, 639 F. Supp. 1071 (E.D. Pa. 1986).

[32]*Badische Corp.* v. *Caylor*, 257 Ga. 131 (1987).

[33]*Chun* v. *Park*, 51 Haw. 462 (1969).

[34]*Pahre* v. *Auditor*, 422 N.W. 2d 178 (Iowa 1988).

[35]*Bonhiver* v. *Graff*, 311 Minn. 111 (1976).

[36]*Lindner Fund* v. *Abney*, 770 S.W.2d 437 (Mo. App. 1989); *Aluma Craft Mfg. Co.* v. *Elmer Fox & Co.*, 493 S.W. 2d 378 (Mo. App. 1973).

[37]*Spherex, Inc.* v. *Alexander Grant & Co.*, 122 N.H. 898 (1982).

[38]*Stotlar* v. *Hester*, 92 N.M. 26 (Ct. App. 1978).

[39]*Raritan River Steel Co.* v. *Cherry, Bekaert & Holland*, 332 N.C. 200 (1988).

[40]*BancOhio National Bank* v. *Schiesswohl*, 515 N.E. 2d 997 (Ohio 1986).

[41]*Stinson* v. *Brand*, 738 S.W.2d 186 (Tenn. 1987).

[42]*Blue Bell, Inc.* v. *Peat, Marwick, Mitchell & Co.*, 715 S.W.2d 408 (Tex. Ct. App. Dallas 1986); *Shatterproof Glass Corp.* v. *James*, 466 S.W.2d 873 (Tex. Civ. App. 1971).

[43]*Milliner* v. *Elmer Fox & Co.*, 529 P.2d 806 (Utah 1974).

[44]*Haberman* v. *WPPSS*, 109 Wash. 2d 107 (1987).

[45]*Touche Ross & Company* v. *Commercial Union Insurance Co.*, 514 So. 2d 315 (Miss. 1987).

An interesting development on this issue occurred in 1987, when the Illinois legislature enacted a statute that codified the *Ultramares* rule.[46] More recently, Arkansas and Kansas enacted similar statutes.[47] These statutes provide that accountants are not liable for negligence to anyone other than their clients, unless it can be established that the auditor knew of and acceded to third parties' reliance on the auditor's report. In addition, the Illinois and Arkansas statutes provide a mechanism by which accountants may limit their liability by formally identifying in writing to the third parties and the client the third parties they know to be relying on the report. That communication is known as a ''privity letter.'' Accountants are in the process of lobbying other states for similar relief.

Some third parties have attempted to satisfy the privity requirement imposed by common law, such as *Credit Alliance*, or the above statutes by notifying the accountants in writing *after* the report has been issued that they are relying on it. Accountants have been advised to respond to such letters by communicating in writing that they were not aware at the time the report was issued that the parties would be relying on it.

Scienter Requirement. In addition to actions on the grounds of negligence, third parties may bring suit against auditors on the grounds of fraud or constructive fraud that is inferred from evidence of gross negligence. Constructive fraud differs from actual fraud in that the former involves the lack of a reasonable basis for believing that a representation is true, whereas the latter involves actual knowledge that a representation is false. Actions grounded in fraud (actual or constructive) require the plaintiff to prove some form of knowledge on the auditor's part of the falsity (or its equivalent) of a representation. This knowledge is commonly referred to as ''scienter'' and the requirement to prove it as the ''scienter'' requirement. Essentially, it is a requirement to prove an intent to injure. In some jurisdictions, scienter may be established by proof of any one of the following three elements:

1. Actual knowledge of the falsity of the representation.
2. A lack of knowledge of the truth of the representation.
3. A reckless disregard for the truth or falsity of the representation.

Under common law, the distinction between negligence and fraud rests essentially on the requirement for scienter. If a jury were to find that the defendant-auditors expressed an unqualified opinion on the financial statements when they had no knowledge of the facts, and if this would support an allegation of fraud in other respects,[48] then liability for the tort of deceit (fraud) could extend to all injured third parties. Without scienter, the case would not involve fraud. The question of the requirement to prove scienter and the elements that constitute scienter are further explored in the discussion, later in

[46]Ill. Rev. Stat. ch. 111 ¶5535.1 (1987).

[47]Ark. Stat. Ann. § 16-114-302 (Supp. 1987); Kan. Stat. Ann. §1-402 (Supp. 1988).

[48]Those ''other respects'' include proof of false representation that was relied on by and caused damages to the plaintiff.

the chapter, of the auditor's liability under Section 10(b) of the Securities Exchange Act of 1934 and related Rule 10b-5.

Civil Liability to Third Parties Under the Federal Securities Acts

The principal provisions of the federal securities acts that have determined the auditor's civil liability are Section 11 of the Securities Act of 1933 and Section 10(b) of the Securities Exchange Act of 1934 and related Rule 10b-5. Class action suits against auditors under the federal securities laws became common after 1966, when the procedural rules governing them were liberalized. Class actions are litigations in which one or a relatively small number of plaintiffs sue on behalf of a very large number of allegedly injured persons. One of the prerequisites of a class action is that the number of potential claimants is so large that it would be impracticable for each of them to sue individually. The dollar amount of potential liability in class actions can run into the hundreds of millions of dollars, thereby making the class action technique a formidable weapon.

The Securities Act of 1933.   The Securities Act of 1933 regulates public offerings of securities and contains provisions intended to protect purchasers of securities. Section 11(a) reads, in part, as follows:

> In case any part of the registration statement . . . contained an untrue statement of a material fact or omitted to state a material fact required to be stated therein or necessary to make the statements therein not misleading, any person acquiring such security . . . may . . . sue . . . every accountant . . . who has with his consent been named as having . . . certified any part of the registration statement . . . with respect to the statement in such registration statement . . . which purports to have been . . . certified by him.

Thus, Section 11 of the Securities Act of 1933 imposes civil liability on auditors for misrepresentations or omissions of material facts in a registration statement. The measure of damages under the civil provisions of the 1933 Act is based on the difference between the amount the plaintiff paid for the security and either the market price at the time of the suit or, if the security was sold, the selling price.

Section 11 expands the elements of an auditor's liability to third parties beyond that of common law in the following significant ways:

1. Privity with the plaintiff is not a necessary element; unnamed third parties, that is, the purchasers of securities in a public offering, may sue auditors.
2. Liability to third parties does not require proof of fraud or gross negligence; ordinary negligence is a basis for liability.
3. The burden of proof of negligence is shifted from the plaintiff to the defendant. The plaintiff has to prove only a material misstatement of fact.
4. The auditor is held to a standard of care described as the exercise of "due diligence"—a reasonable investigation leading to a belief that the financial statements are neither false nor misleading.

5. The plaintiff need not prove reliance on the financial statements or the auditor's report on them, but the defendant-auditor will prevail if the plaintiff's knowledge of the "untruth or omission" is proved.

The first, and still the most significant, judicial interpretation of Section 11, *Escott* v. *BarChris Construction Corp.*,[49] did not occur until 1968. The *BarChris* case was a class action against a bowling alley construction corporation that had issued debentures and subsequently declared bankruptcy, and against its auditors. The suit was brought by the purchasers of the debentures for damages sustained as a result of false statements and material omissions in the prospectus contained in the registration statement. The court ruled that the auditors were liable on the grounds that they had not met the minimum standard of "due diligence" in their review for subsequent events occurring to the effective date of the registration statement (required under the 1933 Act and known as an S-1 review) because the auditor performing the review failed to appropriately follow up management's answers to his inquiries.

A defense to a Section 11 action against auditors would require demonstrating that a reasonable investigation (defined in Section 11[c]) had been made and that the auditors had reasonable grounds for believing and did believe that the financial statements were true and not misleading. In the *BarChris* case, the court stated that "accountants should not be held to a higher standard than that recognized in their profession," but held that the individual accountant responsible for the S-1 review, who had little practical auditing experience, had not met even that standard. As a direct result of this case, professional standards governing auditing procedures in the subsequent period (described in Chapter 21) were made stricter, and auditing firms began to place more emphasis on staff members' knowledge of a client's business and industry.

A controversial aspect of the 1933 Act concerns the issues of reliance and causation. An auditor is liable to purchasers of securities who may not have relied on the financial statements or the auditor's opinion or who may not even have known of their existence. If the auditor can prove, however, that something other than the misleading financial statements caused the plaintiff's loss, the amount of loss related to those other factors is not recoverable. Section 11 thus provides a causation defense, but it clearly places the burden of proof on the defendant-auditor; it requires the defendant to prove that factors other than the misleading statements caused the loss (in whole or in part). The courts have rarely considered the causation defense in Section 11 cases against auditors because damages in such cases have usually been determined in out-of-court settlements, as happened in *BarChris*.

Before 1988, accountants were often charged with violating Section 12(2) of the 1933 Act. This statute imposes liability on any person who "offers or sells" a security "by means of a prospectus or oral communication, which contains an untrue statement of a material fact or omits to state a material fact necessary in order to make the statements, in the light of the circumstances under which they are made, not misleading." Some courts took the position that any party, including accountants, that provided "substantial assistance"

[49]283 F. Supp. 643 (S.D.N.Y. 1968).

in connection with a sale could be charged with violating the section. In 1988, the U.S. Supreme Court ruled in *Pinter* v. *Dahl*[50] that to be liable under Section 12 one had to be a "substantial factor" or "substantial participant" in a sale. In *Pinter*, the Court held that liability under Section 12 extended only to the person who successfully solicited the purchase.

The Securities Exchange Act of 1934.   Many more suits alleging civil liability against auditors have been brought under the Securities Exchange Act of 1934 than under the 1933 Act. The 1934 Act, which requires all companies whose securities are traded to file annual audited financial statements and quarterly and other financial information, regulates trading of securities and thus has broad applicability. Auditors' liability under the 1934 Act, however, is not as extensive as under the 1933 Act in the following significant respects:

1. As established by the *Hochfelder* case (described below) in 1976, ordinary negligence is not a basis for liability to third parties under Section 10(b) and Rule 10b-5. Thus the auditor's liability to unforeseen third parties under the 1934 Act is essentially the same as it is under common law following *Ultramares* and *Credit Alliance*.
2. The burden of proof of both reliance on the financial statements and causation (i.e., that the loss was caused by reliance on the statements, known as "proximate cause") rests with the plaintiff, as it does under common law.

On the other hand, the 1934 Act is accessible to both buyers and sellers of securities; Section 11 of the 1933 Act applies only to buyers.

Damages recoverable under the civil provisions of the 1934 Act are the plaintiff's "out of pocket" losses, determined by the difference between the contract price of the securities and their actual value on the date of the transaction. Actual value is ordinarily considered to be the market value on the date the misrepresentation or omission is discovered and rectified.

The majority of civil lawsuits against auditors have been based on Section 10(b) and Rule 10b-5. Their provisions apply to any purchase or sale of any security, and thus they can be used by a plaintiff with respect to both registered public offerings (also covered by the 1933 Act) and most other transactions in securities. Moreover, the statute of limitations in some states is quite long, and it is not uncommon to have a lawsuit four to five years after the event for which liability is claimed.[51] Rule 10b-5 states, in part, that

It shall be unlawful for any person . . . (a) To employ any device, scheme, or artifice to defraud, (b) To make any untrue statement of a material fact or to

---

[50] 108 S. Ct. 2063 (1988).

[51] In litigation under Section 10(b), most courts apply the statute of limitations of the jurisdiction where the plaintiff is domiciled, and this varies from state to state. Under the 1933 Act, suit must be brought within one year of the discovery of the untrue statement or omission, or after such discovery should have been made by the exercise of reasonable diligence, and in any event within three years after the security was offered to the public. Suits brought under common law follow the statute of limitations of the state in which the suit is brought.

omit to state a material fact necessary in order to make the statements made, in light of the circumstances under which they were made, not misleading, or (c) To engage in any act, practice, or course of business which operates or would operate as a fraud or deceit upon any person, in connection with the purchase or sale of any security.

Section 10(b) and Rule 10b-5 do not provide a good-faith defense; rather, the defendant must refute the specific charges brought by the plaintiff. On the other hand, in a Rule 10b-5 action, the burden of proof that the auditor acted fraudulently rests with the plaintiff; under Section 11 of the 1933 Act, the burden of proof that the auditor was not culpable rests with the defendant-auditor.

The SEC enacted Rule 10b-5 in 1942 as a disciplinary measure for its own use against fraudulent purchasers of securities. A series of judicial interpretations subsequently made the rule accessible to private claimants who were able to prove damages resulting from their reliance on financial statements containing misrepresentations or omissions. Unfortunately, Rule 10b-5 is not at all precise in defining standards for liability, and it does not include a due-diligence defense. Between the time of its enactment and the *Hochfelder* ruling in 1976 (discussed below), the courts interpreted the rule in disparate ways. Thus, in some jurisdictions auditors were found liable to third parties for ordinary negligence (absence of due diligence) in rendering their opinions; in other jurisdictions the courts held that an element of knowledge of the wrongful act or an intent to commit fraud (scienter) was required. Much of the controversy was resolved by the U.S. Supreme Court in 1976 with its decision in *Ernst & Ernst* v. *Hochfelder*.[52]

The complaint in *Hochfelder* charged that the auditors had violated Rule 10b-5 by their failure to conduct proper audits and thereby aided and abetted a fraud perpetrated by the president of a securities firm. The plaintiff's case rested on a charge of negligence and did not allege fraud or intentional misconduct on the part of the auditors. The Supreme Court ruled that a private suit for damages under Section 10(b) and Rule 10b-5 required an allegation of scienter. The Court's opinion stated, in part,

> When a statute speaks so specifically in terms of manipulation and deception, and of implementing devices and contrivances—the commonly understood terminology of intentional wrongdoing—and when its history reflects no more expansive intent, we are quite unwilling to extend the scope of the statute to negligent conduct.

It is important to note that this decision did not impose any general standard for liability under the federal securities laws. It applied specifically to Section 10(b) and Rule 10b-5. The negligence standard under the federal securities laws continues to apply to those sections where Congress expressly intended it to apply or where the courts have determined that imposing liability without scienter in the implied liability sections of the law is compatible with

[52]425 U.S. 185 (1976).

the overall structure and philosophy of the statutes. For example, a negligence standard is still applicable to liability under Section 11 of the 1933 Act.

The Court noted in *Hochfelder* that "in certain areas of the law, recklessness is considered to be a form of intentional conduct for purposes of imposing liability for some act." Thus, although the Court declined to address the question of reckless behavior in that case, most courts have since held that recklessness is sufficient to meet the scienter test.

In an action under Section 10(b), a buyer or seller of a security must also demonstrate reliance on the misstatement. This defense can be important in cases where the plaintiff did not know of the misstatement, such as when he or she never read the financial statements. One exception to the reliance requirement is the "fraud on the market" theory of liability, which the Supreme Court adopted in 1988 in *Basic, Inc.* v. *Levinson*.[53] This doctrine provides that a misstatement or omission that has a general effect on the market price of the security can result in liability, even without actual reliance by the plaintiff. The rule is based on the theory that the purchaser or seller relies on the integrity of the market price, which should reflect all relevant information available in the market. However, at least for the present, the doctrine is limited to securities traded on the national public markets, such as the New York or American Stock Exchange.

A party can also be held liable for aiding and abetting a violation of Section 10(b). In *Roberts* v. *Peat, Marwick, Mitchell & Co.*,[54] the U.S. Court of Appeals for the Ninth Circuit ruled that an accounting firm could be liable for aiding and abetting a violation of Section 10(b). In that case the offering documents indicated that the accounting firm agreed to perform accounting services for the partnership, and the plaintiffs alleged that the firm knew that the documents were false and that it furthered the fraud by consenting to the inclusion of its name in the offering material. According to the court, "the investors relied on Peat, Marwick's reputation when deciding to invest and . . . they would not have invested had Peat, Marwick disclosed the alleged fraud."

RICO

Since the early 1980s, more and more suits have been brought against accountants for violations of the Racketeer Influenced and Corrupt Organizations (RICO) statute of the Organized Crime Control Act of 1970. In general, RICO provides a remedy of triple damages and attorney's fees to any person injured by reason of the operation of an enterprise through "a pattern of racketeering." The statute defines a pattern of racketeering as two violations of a list of statutes, including mail fraud, wire fraud, and securities fraud. In 1989, the U.S. Supreme Court held that such a "pattern" of racketeering activities may be satisfied by a series of actions that are part of a single fraudulent scheme.[55]

Although the statute, which provides a remedy to any victim of a common-

[53]485 U.S. 224 (1988).

[54]857 F.2d 646 (9th Cir. 1988).

[55]*H. J. Inc.* v. *Northwestern Bell Telephone Co.*, 109 S. Ct. 2893 (1989).

law fraud, was designed to attack organized crime, courts have generally followed the literal language of the statute. Moreover, the Supreme Court has stated that there is no record that Congress intended its use to be limited to organized crime activities. In 1988, it was estimated that over 50 such claims were pending against accountants, and the first RICO case to go to trial against an accountant resulted in a verdict against the accountant.[56] The accounting profession, and others, are currently lobbying Congress for a change in the RICO statute.

Criminal Liability

Violations of the securities acts that give rise to civil liability for association with misleading financial statements also subject auditors to criminal penalties (fines of up to $10,000 or imprisonment for not more than five years, or both) under Section 24 of the Securities Act of 1933 and Section 32 of the Securities Exchange Act of 1934 if the violations can be shown to be willful or intentional. Auditors are also exposed to criminal penalties under the federal mail fraud and conspiracy statutes.

Perhaps because of the availability of other legal remedies (including injunctions, administrative proceedings, and civil suits by third parties) and the absence of the element of personal gain, there have been few criminal actions against auditors. Four of the most widely publicized criminal prosecutions were *Continental Vending*,[57] *Four Seasons*,[58] *National Student Marketing*,[59] and *Equity Funding*,[60] which together produced the conviction of eight individuals. Those cases demonstrate that auditors' errors of judgment in not insisting on appropriate accounting, including adequate disclosure, of certain matters known to them may result in criminal liability in certain circumstances, even though no motive can be proved and no personal gain can be shown to have resulted.

John C. Burton, former Chief Accountant of the SEC, stated the Commission's position on bringing criminal charges against auditors.

> While virtually all Commission cases are civil in character, on rare occasions it is concluded that a case is sufficiently serious that it should be referred to the Department of Justice for consideration of criminal prosecution. Referrals in regard to accountants have only been made when the Commission and the staff believed that the evidence indicated that a professional accountant certified financial statements that he knew to be false when he reported on them. The Commission does not make criminal references in cases that it believes are simply matters of professional judgment even if the judgments appear to be bad ones.[61]

[56] *The Wall Street Journal*, May 9, 1988, p. 43. The case was settled for $15 million after the defendant said it would appeal a jury verdict in the amount of $60 million.

[57] *United States* v. *Simon*, 425 F.2d 796 (2d Cir. 1969), *cert. denied*, 397 U.S. 1006 (1970).

[58] *United States* v. *Clark*, 360 F. Supp. 936 (S.D.N.Y. 1973).

[59] *United States* v. *Natelli*, 527 F.2d 311 (2d Cir. 1975), *cert. denied*, 425 U.S. 934 (1976).

[60] *United States* v. *Weiner*, 578 F.2d 757 (9th Cir.), *cert. denied*, 439 U.S. 981 (1978).

[61] John C. Burton, "SEC Enforcement and Professional Accountants: Philosophy, Objectives and Approach," *Vanderbilt Law Review* 28 (January 1975), p. 28.

The consequences of criminal prosecution to an auditor may go beyond the obvious ones of the costs of defense and the resulting fines and imprisonment. A successful criminal prosecution may help to establish civil liability and will generally preclude the individual from continuing to practice as an auditor.

Other SEC Sanctions

Auditors are also subject under the federal securities acts to legal sanctions that do not involve criminal penalties or the payment of damages. The SEC, as the principal government regulatory agency charged with enforcing financial reporting standards, has two civil remedies available to it: civil injunctive actions and disciplinary (administrative) proceedings under Rule 2(e) of its Rules of Practice. Either remedy may be sought against an individual auditor or an entire firm.

Injunctive Proceedings.   The SEC has the authority under Section 20 of the 1933 Act and Section 21 of the 1934 Act to initiate injunctive actions in the courts to restrain future violations of the provisions of those acts (including Section 10[b] of the 1934 Act). Under currently prevailing standards, discussed below, such injunctions are available only against those the SEC can persuade a court are likely to violate the federal securities laws again if not enjoined. In a case tried in 1980, *Aaron v. SEC*,[62] the Supreme Court held that injunctions under Section 10(b) of the 1934 Act (and one subsection of Section 17[a] of the 1933 Act) require scienter.[63]

The consequences of an injunction may extend far beyond an admonition to obey the law in the future. The injunction can be useful to plaintiffs in subsequent civil suits for damages, and the person enjoined is exposed to civil and criminal contempt proceedings. Moreover, an injunction resulting from a consent decree, in which guilt is neither admitted nor denied, may require the auditor or firm to adopt and comply with certain procedures to prevent future violations.

Requests for permanent injunctions are tried publicly before a judge without a jury. Thus, the injunctions are granted or denied largely at the discretion of the trial judge. The SEC must prove not only that a violation of the securities laws has occurred but also that there is a reasonable likelihood that future violations will occur if an injunction is not imposed. For example, in *SEC v. Geotek*,[64] the court found there was no evidence of a past violation. The issue of what constitutes a ''reasonable likelihood'' of future violations remains unresolved. On the one hand, the courts tend to give great weight to the SEC's expert judgment of the immediate need for an injunction. On the other hand, however, in *SEC v. Bausch & Lomb, Inc.*,[65] the court ruled against

---

[62]446 U.S. 680 (1980).

[63]The Supreme Court decided, however, that injunctions under two other subsections of Section 17(a) do not require scienter.

[64]426 F. Supp. 715 (N.D. Cal. 1976), *aff'd sub nom. SEC v. Arthur Young & Co.*, 590 F. 2d 785 (9th Cir. 1979).

[65]420 F. Supp. 1226 (S.D.N.Y. 1976), *aff'd*, 565 F. 2d 8 (2d Cir. 1977).

enjoining the auditors, on the grounds of insufficient evidence that they were likely to commit further violations.

Administrative (Rule 2[e]) Proceedings. Rule 2(e) of the SEC's Rules of Practice states that the Commission

> May deny, temporarily or permanently, the privilege of appearing or practicing before it in any way to any person who is found . . . (i) not to possess the requisite qualifications to represent others, (ii) to be lacking in character or integrity or have engaged in unethical or improper professional conduct, or (iii) to have willfully violated or willfully aided and abetted the violation of any provision of the federal securities laws . . . or the rules and regulations thereunder.

Before 1989, proceedings under Rule 2(e) were generally conducted in private hearings. Such proceedings are now public, unless the SEC directs otherwise in a particular case. In addition, the resulting Accounting and Auditing Enforcement Releases, which set forth the SEC's allegations and the terms of settlement, attract a great deal of publicity. Rule 2(e) gives the SEC the explicit authority to suspend from appearing or practicing before it auditors who have been permanently enjoined from violation of the securities laws or convicted of a felony or of a misdemeanor involving immoral conduct.

Over the years, the SEC has devised imaginative, often sweeping sanctions against auditing firms under Rule 2(e), many of which involved agreements to institute new or improved control procedures and to subject those procedures to an independent compliance review. In the past, these sanctions were often announced in Accounting Series Releases (ASRs), and are now published in Accounting and Auditing Enforcement Releases (AAERs). Among the sanctions that have been imposed on accounting firms are the following:

1. Required a firm to conduct a study of the use of a specific accounting method and to establish guidelines for the firm's practice in this area. (ASR No. 173 [July 2, 1975])
2. Required a firm to employ consultants to review and evaluate the firm's auditing procedures for publicly held companies. (ASR No. 176 [July 22, 1975])
3. Prohibited a firm from merging or combining practices with another accounting firm. (ASR No. 196 [September 1, 1976])
4. Prohibited a firm for 60 days from undertaking new engagements likely to result in filings with the SEC. (ASR No. 209 [February 16, 1977])
5. Required a firm to conduct or sponsor a research project relating to reliance on internal controls and to incorporate, to the extent deemed appropriate, the results into the firm's audit practice. (ASR No. 241 [February 10, 1978])
6. Censured a firm, other than following a permanent injunction or criminal conviction. (ASR No. 248 [May 31, 1978])
7. Required a firm to name a new managing partner of one of its offices. (ASR No. 288 [February 26, 1981])

8. Required a firm to create a Special Review Committee to review its audit practice, and required it to adopt and implement any and all recommendations of the committee. (AAER No. 9 [June 30, 1983])

9. Required a firm to emphasize audit documentation and revenue recognition in firm training programs. (AAER No. 78 [October 10, 1985])

10. Required that audit work on the firm's publicly held client must be reviewed by an independent auditor who is a member of the AICPA's SEC Practice Section and is approved by the SEC Office of the Chief Accountant; and that working papers must be made available to the SEC. (AAER No. 86 [February 10, 1986])

11. Required a CPA or his firm to join the AICPA's SEC Practice Section and receive an unqualified peer review report, and the CPA to take 50 hours of courses on GAAP and GAAS in each of two years. (AAER No. 150 [September 3, 1987])

SEC sanctions such as these are generally publicly disclosed and can obviously have a significant impact on a CPA firm's practice. Almost all recent Rule 2(e) proceedings, however, have involved consent decrees, in which the auditing firm neither denied nor admitted guilt.

Like all the other sanctions imposed on auditors, these raise the question of what standard of care the auditor must observe to avoid action under Rule 2(e). The grounds for SEC-imposed sanctions, including temporary or permanent suspension as well as the more innovative actions described above, fall into three categories.

1. A finding that the auditor lacked certain personal qualities, for example, character or integrity, or the qualifications to represent others.

2. An adverse finding by a court, the SEC, or a state licensing body of actions involving something more than ordinary negligence.

3. A finding by the Commission of unethical or improper professional conduct.

Rule 2(e) proceedings following a permanent injunction fall into the second category, which generally requires either willful intent or an act so evidently reprehensible that it leads to criminal conviction or loss of license resulting from violation of the securities laws. The SEC believes, however, and the Supreme Court has agreed to some extent at least (see above), that ordinary negligence is sufficient for it to seek and obtain a civil injunction. Ordinary negligence thus appears sufficient to sustain a Rule 2(e) proceeding following an injunction under Section 10(b).

Some of the more innovative procedures required by the SEC in settlement of Rule 2(e) proceedings are evidence of the Commission's ability to create or influence specific professional standards. This has taken basically two forms.

1. Language in a proceeding indicating auditing responsibilities not prescribed by the profession. (An example is the view expressed in ASR No. 153 [1974] that successor auditors must review the work of predecessor

auditors, and that a refusal by the client to permit the necessary communication should be grounds for rejecting the engagement. Professional literature at the time did not make predecessor–successor communications mandatory. Moreover, present standards, while requiring such communication, leave room for the exercise of professional judgment on the effect of a prospective client's forbidding such communication.)

2. Language in a consent decree requiring an auditing firm to develop specific auditing procedures not addressed in the professional literature. (An example is the auditing firm's consent in ASR No. 153 to develop and submit to the SEC procedures for the audit of related party transactions. An SAS on the subject did not exist at the time of ASR No. 153.)

As discussed in Chapter 2, the SEC has traditionally left the specific implementation and interpretation of GAAS to the auditing profession. At the least, Rule 2(e) proceedings and the accompanying consent decrees provide a vehicle for selective departure from that policy.

The Profession's Responses to the Litigious Environment

The litigious environment has encouraged the public accounting profession as a whole and individual firms to reexamine and strengthen auditing standards and ways of encouraging compliance with them. Since the increase in litigation against auditors, the AICPA has issued a great many authoritative auditing pronouncements (48 SASs were promulgated between 1977 and March 1989) and has twice revised its code of ethics. The Institute has also devoted considerable attention to the design and implementation of quality control reviews of firms. Individual firms have devoted increasingly more resources to their own policies and procedures for maintaining and raising the quality of practice.

Authoritative Pronouncements.   Many of the Statements on Auditing Procedure (SAPs) and SASs were issued following audit failures that led to litigation. In addition, other auditing pronouncements originated from accounting pronouncements that, in turn, can be traced to alleged misconduct of one kind or another that led to litigation. For example, SAPs No. 47, *Subsequent Events*, and No. 48, *Letters for Underwriters* (both issued in 1971), can be traced to the *BarChris* case, discussed earlier. SAS No. 7, *Communications Between Predecessor and Successor Auditors* (1975), was related to the *U.S. Financial*[66] case. The origin of SAP No. 44 (1971), *Reports Following a Pooling of Interests*, was Accounting Principles Board Opinion No. 16, *Business Combinations* (1970). This in turn had its source in the deterioration of accounting principles evidenced at least in part by litigation, like the *Westec*[67] case, that raised questions of the propriety of the accounting principles selected and applied to account for particular com-

---

[66]*In re U.S. Financial Securities Litigation*, 609 F.2d 411 (9th Cir. 1979), *cert. denied*, 446 U.S. 929 (1980).
[67]*In re Westec Corp.*, 434 F.2d 195 (5th Cir. 1970).

binations. Moreover, a number of auditing pronouncements further refined or clarified previous pronouncements that were traceable to litigation involving auditors. For example, several subsequent pronouncements further clarified the auditor's responsibilities set forth in SAP No. 1, *Extensions of Auditing Procedure*, which had its source in the *McKesson & Robbins*[68] case.

Other auditing pronouncements, while not individually traceable to specific audit failures that led to litigation, represent part of the accounting profession's program to close the "expectation gap," discussed both in Chapter 1 and earlier in this chapter, which had its roots in several audit failures and attendant litigation and investigations. SAS Nos. 53 through 61, issued in 1988, were all responsive to the issues underlying the expectation gap, namely, a series of business failures that revealed material misstatements in audited financial statements. Those SASs increased the auditor's responsibility to detect errors and irregularities, sharpened the guidance on how to meet that heightened responsibility, and created new responsibilities to communicate both the existence of errors and irregularities and the conditions that enabled them to occur.

Increased Attention to Quality Control.   Both the auditing profession and individual firms have recognized the need for more effective controls over the quality of audit practice. Statement on Quality Control Standards No. 1, *System of Quality Control for a CPA Firm* (QC Section 10), requires CPA firms to establish quality control policies and procedures. Efforts by the AICPA to improve and monitor the quality of audit practice are described in Chapter 3. Both the profession and the state boards of accountancy have disciplinary systems through which sanctions are imposed on auditing firms and individual auditors for violations of the Code of Professional Conduct and state accountancy laws. These self-regulatory measures are also discussed in Chapter 3.

Measures to Protect Against Legal Liability.   Individual firms have also designed and implemented programs for monitoring their audit practices, including, among other things

- Increased resources devoted to continuing education.
- Institution of second-partner and interoffice reviews of working papers and reports.
- Practice bulletins directed at both accounting and auditing issues.
- Policy statements on internal quality control programs.
- Engagement of other auditing firms to conduct independent quality reviews.
- Increased emphasis on research in auditing theory and applications, including the use of sophisticated technology to enhance the quality of audit performance.

[68]ASR No. 19, "In the Matter of McKesson & Robbins, Inc." (1940).

The practice many auditing firms have adopted of having a second-partner review of engagements has been traced directly to the *Continental Vending* case.[69] Second-partner reviews are discussed in Chapter 21. As mentioned earlier, most auditors follow the practice of setting forth the scope and inherent limitations of an audit in an engagement letter to the client. Many of the points covered in a typical engagement letter are also addressed in the representation letter from management, which SAS No. 19, *Client Representations* (AU Section 333), requires the auditor to obtain. As discussed in Chapter 21, management's representation letter provides written evidence of, among other matters, inquiries made by the auditor and management's responses to them. Both the engagement letter and the management representation letter may constitute important evidence in the event of a lawsuit.

In very general terms, the best protection against legal liability for both CPA firms and individual practitioners is meticulous adherence to the technical and ethical standards of the profession, described in Chapter 3, and establishing and implementing policies and procedures designed to ensure that all audits are systematically planned and performed, that the work is done with a high degree of professional skepticism by people who understand the client's business circumstances, that appropriate evidence is obtained and objectively evaluated, and that all work done is carefully documented. These objectives are the underlying structure of the theory and practice of auditing described throughout this book.

[69]A. A. Sommer, Jr., "Legal Liability of Accountants," *Financial Executive* 42 (March 1974), p. 24.

PART 2

Theory and Concepts

5

The Audit Process

Most of the auditor's work in forming an opinion on financial statements consists of obtaining and evaluating evidence about management's assertions that are embodied in those statements. To be able to express an opinion on financial statements, the auditor must establish specific audit objectives related to those assertions and then design and perform audit tests to obtain and evaluate evidence about whether the objectives have been met. Throughout the process, the auditor must make decisions about whether the evidence obtained is competent and sufficient for formulating an opinion.

The approach the auditor takes can be broken down into a series of systematic steps. The steps are usually the same in every audit, but the types of tests performed and the evidence obtained vary with each engagement. This chapter explores the concepts of audit objectives, risk, theory, and evidence, and presents an overall framework for viewing the steps in an audit. The chapter concludes with a discussion of working papers—the principal means of documenting the work performed, the evidence obtained, and the conclusions reached—and of certain auditor–client relationships.

AUDIT ASSERTIONS, OBJECTIVES, AND PROCEDURES

An entity's financial statements can be thought of as embodying a set of assertions by management. SAS No. 31, *Evidential Matter* (AU Section 326), groups financial statement assertions into the following broad categories:

- Existence or occurrence.
- Completeness.
- Rights and obligations.
- Valuation or allocation.
- Presentation and disclosure.

Many auditors find it helpful to consider explicitly two additional categories of assertions that are implicit in the SAS No. 31 list, namely

- Accuracy.
- Cutoff.

Assertions about existence relate to whether assets, liabilities, and ownership interests exist at a specific date. These assertions pertain to both physical items—such as inventory, plant and equipment, and cash—and accounts without physical substance—such as accounts receivable and accounts payable. Assertions about occurrence are concerned with whether recorded transactions, such as purchases and sales, represent economic events that actually occurred during a certain period. Assertions about existence and occurrence state that transactions and balances recorded in the accounts have real-world counterparts, for example, that there are real-world asset equivalents to the financial statement accounts representing the assets.

Assertions about completeness pertain to whether all transactions and other events and circumstances that occurred during a specific period and should have been recognized in that period have in fact been recorded. For example, *all* purchases of goods and services should be recorded and included in the financial statements. The completeness assertion also states that all recognizable financial statement items are in fact included in the financial statements. For example, management asserts that accounts payable reported on the balance sheet include all such obligations of the enterprise.

Assertions about rights and obligations relate to whether assets are the rights, and liabilities are the obligations, of the entity at a given date. For example, the reporting of capitalized leases in the balance sheet is an assertion that the amount capitalized is the unamortized cost of rights to leased property and that the amount of the lease liability is the unamortized obligation of the enterprise.

Assertions about valuation or allocation pertain to whether financial statement items are recorded at appropriate amounts in conformity with generally accepted accounting principles. For example, the financial statements represent that depreciation expense for the year and the carrying value of property, plant, and equipment are based on the systematic amortization of the historical cost of the assets, and that trade accounts receivable are stated at their net realizable value.

Assertions about presentation and disclosure relate to the proper classification, description, and disclosure of items in the financial statements; for example, that the settlement of long-term liabilities will not require the use of assets classified as current, and that the accounting policy note to the financial statements includes the disclosures required by generally accepted accounting principles.

Assertions about accuracy relate to the mathematical correctness of recorded transactions that are reflected in the financial statements and the appropriate summarization and posting of those transactions to the general ledger. For example, the financial statements represent that accounts payable reflect purchases of goods and services that are based on correct prices and quantities and on invoices that have been accurately computed.

Assertions about cutoff relate to the recording of transactions in the proper accounting period. For example, a check to a vendor that is mailed on December 31 should be recorded in December and not, through either oversight or intent, in January.

SAS No. 31 is written in terms of financial statement assertions; auditors generally translate those assertions into audit objectives that they seek to achieve by performing auditing procedures. For each assertion embodied in each item in the financial statements, the auditor develops a corresponding audit objective. Then the auditor designs procedures for obtaining sufficient competent evidential matter to either corroborate or contradict each assertion and thereby achieve the related audit objective or reveal a deficiency in the financial statements.

Chapter 1 discussed two functions that auditors perform: first, gathering and evaluating evidence about verifiable ''facts'' and, second, interpreting those facts once they are known, which includes evaluating accounting estimates and judgments made by the client's management. Although the two functions of auditing are distinguishable by the type of assertion for which evidence is primarily gathered, in practice they are interrelated. Moreover, the auditor must evaluate all evidence obtained, regardless of why it was gathered. Hence, the function of interpreting/evaluating permeates all audit work.

In developing audit objectives and related auditing procedures for certain categories of assertions—existence or occurrence, completeness, accuracy, cutoff, and rights and obligations—the auditor's function is primarily evidence gathering. Interpreting and evaluating relate mainly to formulating audit objectives and designing auditing procedures to test the assertions relating to valuation or allocation and presentation and disclosure. These assertions reflect the client's selection and application of accounting measurement and disclosure principles, including the estimates that are an inherent part of the accounting process.

Figure 5.1 illustrates how auditors consider these seven broad categories of assertions in formulating audit objectives and designing auditing procedures to obtain evidence supporting them. In the figure, a single auditing procedure is linked to each stated audit objective. In an actual audit, a combination of auditing procedures will generally be necessary to achieve a single objective, and some auditing procedures will relate to more than one objective. For example, in addition to observing physical inventory counts by client personnel to obtain evidence that inventories included in the balance sheet physically exist, the auditor may also confirm the existence and amount of inventories stored in public warehouses or with other custodians at locations outside the entity's premises. Moreover, observing inventory counts also provides evidence that the inventory quantities include all products, materials, and supplies on hand (completeness objective).

Relating the evidence obtained from auditing procedures to the audit objectives is an iterative process of accumulating, analyzing, and interpreting information in light of the auditor's expectations, past experience with the client, generally accepted accounting principles, and good management practices. Procedures performed to meet one audit objective for one account frequently generate information that requires further action by the auditor to achieve that particular audit objective or other audit objectives related to that particular account or other accounts. Evidence that raises questions, for example, about revenues recorded may also raise questions about the adequacy of the allowance for inventory obsolescence, which in turn will require the auditor to accumulate and analyze additional evidence.

AUDIT RISK

Audit risk is the risk that the auditor will issue an inappropriate opinion on financial statements. Although an auditor could conceivably report that financial statements are not fairly presented when they are, for practical purposes audit risk refers to the risk of reporting that financial statements are fairly

Figure 5.1   Examples of Audit Objectives and Procedures

Management Assertion	*Example of Audit Objective*	*Example of Auditing Procedure*	*Primary Audit Function*
Existence or occurrence	Inventories in the balance sheet physically exist.	Observe physical inventory counts by client personnel.	Evidence gathering
Completeness	Sales revenues include all items shipped to customers.	Review the client's periodic accounting for the numerical sequence of shipping documents and invoices.	Evidence gathering
Accuracy	Accounts receivable reflect sales transactions that are based on correct prices and quantities and are accurately computed.	Compare prices on invoices with master price list and quantities with customer's sales order and client's shipping records; recalculate amounts on invoices.	Evidence gathering
Cutoff	Sales transactions are reported in the proper period.	Compare shipping dates with dates of journal entries for sales recorded in the last several days of the old year and the first several days of the new year.	Evidence gathering
Rights and obligations	Real estate in the balance sheet is owned by the entity.	Inspect deeds, purchase contracts, settlement papers, insurance policies, minutes, and related correspondence.	Evidence gathering
Valuation or allocation	Receivables are stated at net realizable value.	Review client's aging of receivables to evaluate adequacy of allowance for uncollectible accounts.	Interpreting/ evaluating
Presentation and disclosure	Loss contingencies not required to be recorded are appropriately disclosed.	Inquire of the client's lawyers concerning litigation, claims, and assessments and evaluate the related disclosures.	Interpreting/ evaluating

presented when they are not. The auditor's objective is to design and perform auditing procedures that will restrict audit risk to a low level.

Audit risk has two components: the risk that the financial statements contain misstatements and the risk that the auditor will not detect them. The former risk is not under the auditor's control; the auditor assesses the risks that are associated with the entity, but cannot in any way change them. The latter risk, called detection risk, is controlled by the auditor through the selection and performance of tests directed at specific assertions relating to specific transactions and account balances. The auditor's assessment of the risk of the financial statements containing misstatements determines the level of detection risk he or she can accept, and still restrict audit risk to an appropriately low level.

The risk of misstatement occurring in the financial statements has two aspects—inherent risk and control risk. Inherent risk is the susceptibility of an account balance or a class of transactions to material misstatements, without consideration of the control structure. That susceptibility may result from either conditions affecting the entity as a whole or characteristics of specific transactions or accounts. Control risk is the risk that the control structure will not prevent or detect material misstatements on a timely basis. The auditor assesses inherent risk conditions and characteristics to identify areas where the risk of material misstatement may be high. In assessing control risk, the auditor considers the elements of the entity's control structure and, if appropriate, tests them to determine to what extent they are designed and operating effectively and thus can be expected to prevent or detect misstatements. The resulting evidence reduces the evidence the auditor needs from tests of transactions and account balances to restrict audit risk to an acceptably low level. Audit risk is covered in detail in Chapter 6; the auditor's assessment of inherent and control risk is the subject of Chapter 8.

AUDIT EVIDENCE AND AUDIT TESTS

The third standard of field work states

> Sufficient competent evidential matter is to be obtained through inspection, observation, inquiries, and confirmations to afford a reasonable basis for an opinion regarding the financial statements under audit. (AU Section 326.01)

The evidence necessary to either corroborate or contradict the assertions in the financial statements and thus provide the auditor with a basis for an opinion is obtained by designing and performing auditing procedures. This section of the chapter describes the various kinds of evidence that are available to the auditor and the types of procedures that the auditor performs to obtain evidence.

Types of Evidence

SAS No. 31 (AU Section 326) points out that evidential matter necessary to support the assertions in the financial statements consists of *underlying accounting data* and all *corroborating information* available to the auditor. Underlying evidence for the most part is available to the auditor from within the client company. It consists of the accounting data from which the financial statements are prepared, and includes journals, ledgers, and computer files; accounting manuals; and memoranda and worksheets supporting such items as cost allocations, computations, and reconciliations.

Corroborating evidence is information that supports the underlying evidence, and generally is available to the auditor from both the client and outside sources. Client sources include documentary material closely related to accounting data, such as checks, invoices, contracts, minutes of meetings, correspondence, written representations by knowledgeable employees of the client, and information obtained by the auditor by inquiry of officers and employees and observation of employees at work. Additional types of corroborating evidence include confirmations of amounts due or assets held by third parties (such as customers and custodians), correspondence with experts such as attorneys and engineers, and physical examination or inspection of assets such as marketable securities and inventories.

Examination of underlying accounting data alone is not sufficient to meet the third standard of field work. The auditor must obtain satisfaction about the quality of the underlying evidence through corroborating evidence. For example, an auditor usually finds it necessary to confirm open accounts receivable to support receivable balances in the accounts receivable subsidiary ledger. To cite another example, the auditor should ordinarily corroborate lists of inventory items counted by client personnel by observing the client's physical inventory counting procedures and making some test counts.

Auditors use various methods, or procedures—inquiry, observation, inspecting assets, confirmation, examination of documents, reperformance, and analytical procedures—to obtain sufficient competent evidential matter. How the evidence is classified is not very important; what is important is the auditor's ability to evaluate each kind of evidence in terms of its relevance and reliability, as discussed later in this chapter.

Inquiry.   Inquiry means asking questions. The questions may be oral or written and may be directed to the client or to third parties. At the planning stage of the audit, the auditor needs to develop an understanding of the client's business and its internal control structure; one of the easiest ways to do this initially is through inquiry. (Later in the audit, the understanding is either corroborated or contradicted by the results of other tests.) At various stages in the audit, the auditor may ask the client's employees specific questions about matters arising in the course of the audit work. The auditor makes inquiries of management as part of evaluating accounting principles and estimates. Requesting a representation letter from client management as to the recording of all known liabilities, the existence of contingent liabilities, and the existence and carrying value of inventory is a form of inquiry. The auditor may also inquire of third parties, such as the client's outside legal counsel regarding legal matters, on matters outside the auditor's expertise. In all instances, the auditor's evaluation of responses is an integral part of the inquiry process.

Observation.   Observation involves direct visual viewing of client employees in their work environment, and of other facts and events. It is a useful technique that can be employed in many phases of an audit. The auditor should consider, however, that employees may not perform in the same way when the auditor is not present. At the beginning of the audit, the auditor may tour the client's facilities as part of gaining an understanding of the client's business. That tour may also provide possible indications of slow-moving or obsolete goods. Observation of the client's employees taking a physical inventory can provide firsthand knowledge to help the auditor assess the adequacy of the inventory taking. Watching employees whose functions have accounting significance perform their assigned tasks can help the auditor assess whether specific control procedures are operating effectively.

Inspection and Counting of Assets.   The auditor may obtain evidence by inspecting or counting assets. For example, the auditor may count cash or marketable securities on hand to ascertain that the assets in the accounts actually exist and are accurately recorded.

Confirmation.   Confirmation involves obtaining a representation of a fact or condition from a third party, preferably in writing. Examples are a confirmation from a bank of the amount on deposit or of a loan outstanding, or a confirmation from a customer of the existence of a receivable balance at a certain date. Auditors most often associate confirmations with cash (confirmation from a bank) and accounts receivable (confirmation from customers). Confirmation, however, has widespread applicability; depending on the circumstances, virtually any transaction, event, or account balance can be confirmed with a third party. For example, creditors can confirm accounts and notes payable; both customers and creditors can confirm specific transactions; insurance companies can confirm insurance premiums paid during the year and balances due at year-end, as well as borrowings on life insurance policies; transfer agents and registrars can confirm shares of stock outstanding; trustees can confirm balances due under long-term borrowings and payments required and made under bond sinking fund requirements. The list of items that can be confirmed is virtually endless.

Examination of Documents and Records.   Examining documents includes reading, tracing, looking at supporting documentation, comparing, and reconciling. The auditor may read the minutes of the board of directors' meetings for authorization of new financing. The auditor may trace postings from customers' sales invoices to individual customer accounts, or may examine invoices, purchase orders, and receiving reports to ascertain that the charges to a particular asset or expense account are adequately supported. The auditor may look at evidence in the form of signatures or initials on a purchase invoice, indicating that the invoice has been compared, by appropriate client personnel, with the corresponding purchase order and receiving report, and that the footings and extensions on the invoice have been recalculated. The auditor may compare purchase invoices with related receiving reports for evidence that merchandise has been received for bills rendered by creditors. The auditor may examine the client's reconciliation of accounts receivable subsidiary ledgers with control accounts.

Reperformance.   Reperformance involves repeating, either in whole or in part, the same procedures performed by the client's employees, particularly recalculations to ensure mathematical accuracy. Reperformance may involve some of the other techniques previously mentioned, such as comparing or counting. For example, comparing a vendor's invoice with the corresponding purchase order and receiving report, where there is evidence in the form of initials on a document that the client's employees previously made that comparison, is reperformance. Reperformance may also involve recounting some of the client's physical inventory counts, recalculating the client's extensions and footings on sales invoices and inventory listings, repeating the client's calculations of depreciation expense, and reconstructing a client-prepared bank reconciliation. In addition, in evaluating management's accounting estimates and its choice and application of accounting principles, the auditor may "reperform" the processes followed by management. Auditing procedures for evaluating accounting estimates are described in detail in Chapter 9.

Analytical Procedures. Analytical procedures are reasonableness tests of financial information made by studying and comparing relationships among data and trends in the data. Analytical procedures include scanning or scrutinizing accounting records, such as entries to an inventory control account for a period, looking for evidence of unusual amounts or unusual sources of input, which, if found, would be further investigated. Other examples of analytical procedures typically performed in an audit include fluctuation analyses, ratio analyses, comparisons of accounting data with operating data, and comparisons of recorded amounts with expectations developed by the auditor. Analytical procedures are performed early in the audit to help the auditor in planning other auditing procedures, as substantive tests to obtain evidence about specific assertions and accounts, and at the end of the audit as an overall review of the financial statements. Analytical procedures are discussed in Chapters 8, 9, and 21.

Competence of Evidential Matter

The third standard of field work requires the auditor to obtain evidential matter that is both competent and sufficient. In other words, the auditor must reach a decision, based on experience and judgment, on whether the evidence obtained is good or useful (competent evidential matter) and whether enough useful evidence has been obtained (sufficient evidential matter).

To be competent, evidence must be both relevant and reliable. To be relevant, evidence must affect the auditor's ability to accept or reject a specific financial statement assertion. The auditor reaches a conclusion on the financial statements taken as a whole through a series of judgments made throughout the audit about specific financial statement assertions. Each piece of evidence obtained is evaluated in terms of its usefulness either in corroborating or contradicting an assertion by management or in the auditor's evaluation of evidence obtained at other stages of the audit. Evidence is relevant to the extent that it serves either of those purposes.

An example or two will illustrate the concept of relevance of evidence. Confirming accounts receivable by requesting the client's customers to inform the auditor about any differences between their records of amounts they owe the client and the client's records of open balances is a commonly performed auditing procedure. When considered in conjunction with other evidence, a signed confirmation returned to the auditor indicating agreement with the open balance on the client's books can provide support for the implicit management assertion that the account receivable exists and is not overstated. Confirmations, however, do not provide evidence about collectibility, completeness, or rights and obligations. A confirmed account may not be collectible because the debtor does not intend or is unable to pay; receivables may exist that have not been recorded and therefore cannot possibly be selected for confirmation; or the client may have sold the receivables to another party and may be merely acting as a collection agent for that party. Similarly, physically inspecting and counting inventory gives the auditor evidence about its existence, but not about its valuation or about the client's title to it. Using irrelevant evidence to support an audit conclusion about a management assertion is a major source of "nonsampling error," as discussed in Chapter 10.

Evidence must also be reliable if it is to be useful to the auditor. The FASB's definition of reliability is also appropriate in the context of audit evidence. Reliability is "the quality of information that assures that information is reasonably free from error and bias and faithfully represents what it purports to represent."[1] Synonyms for reliability are "dependability" and "trustworthiness." The reliability of audit evidence is influenced by several factors.

- *Independence of the source.*   Evidential matter obtained by the auditor from independent sources outside the entity being audited is usually more reliable than that from within the entity. Examples of evidence from independent sources include a confirmation from a state agency of the number of shares of common stock authorized to be issued, and a confirmation from a bank of a cash balance, a loan balance, or securities held as collateral. (The high level of reliability that such evidence provides does not mean that errors in confirmations of this nature never occur.) In contrast, evidence arising from inquiries of the client or from inspecting documents provided by the client is usually considered less reliable from the auditor's viewpoint.

- *Qualifications of the source.*   For audit evidence to be reliable, it must be obtained from people who are competent and have the qualifications to make the information free from error. (The independence-of-the-source criterion addresses the possibility of deliberate errors in the evidence; the qualifications-of-the-source criterion addresses the possibility of unintentional errors in the evidence.) For instance, confirmations provided by business customers are usually more reliable than confirmations provided by individuals. Answers to inquiries about pending litigation from client counsel are usually more reliable than answers from persons not working in the legal department. The auditor should not necessarily assume that the higher a person is in the client's organization, the better qualified that person is to provide evidence. The accounts payable clerk probably knows the "true" routine in the accounts payable section of the accounting department better than the corporate controller does. Furthermore, auditors should challenge their own qualifications

---

[1]Statement of Financial Accounting Concepts No. 2, "Glossary of Terms."

when evaluating evidence they have gathered. When inspecting or counting precious gems in a jeweler's inventory, for example, the auditor is probably not qualified to distinguish between diamonds and pieces of glass.

• *Internal control structure.*   Underlying accounting data developed within a satisfactory internal control structure is more reliable than similar data developed within a less adequate internal control structure. The auditor does not accept the client's description of the control structure without corroboration. Instead, if the auditor plans to look to the control structure as a source of audit evidence, he or she observes the activities of company personnel and performs other tests of policies and procedures that are part of the control structure to determine that they are designed and operating effectively.

• *Objectivity of the evidence.*   Evidence is objective if it requires little judgment to evaluate its reliability. Evidence obtained by an auditor's direct, personal knowledge through counting, observing, calculating, or examining documents is generally more objective than evidence based on the opinions of others, such as the opinion of an appraiser about the value of an asset acquired by the client in a nonmonetary transaction, the opinion of a lawyer about the outcome of pending litigation, or the opinion of the client's credit manager about the collectibility of outstanding receivables. Sometimes, however, more objective evidence is not attainable.

The auditor's twofold objective in performing an audit in accordance with generally accepted auditing standards is to achieve the necessary assurance to support the audit opinion and to perform the audit as efficiently as possible. Thus, in addition to considering the relevance and reliability of evidence, the auditor must also consider its availability, timeliness, and cost. Sometimes a desirable form of evidence is simply not available. For example, an auditor who is retained by the client after its accounting year-end cannot be present to observe and test-count the ending inventory. Also, time constraints may not permit an auditor to consider a particular source of evidence. For example, confirming a foreign account receivable might delay the completion of the audit by weeks or even months. Different types of evidence have different costs associated with them, and the auditor must consider cost–benefit trade-offs.

Fortunately, auditors usually have available more than one source or method of obtaining evidence to corroborate a particular financial statement assertion. If one source or method is not practicable to use, another can often be substituted. For example, a customer who may not be able to confirm an account receivable balance may be able to confirm specific sales transactions and cash remittances. Or a more costly source of evidence may be substituted for a less costly source that is not as reliable. For instance, a petroleum engineer who is independent of the client could be retained instead of the auditor's relying on engineers employed by the client for estimates of proven oil reserves. The auditor should choose the type of evidence (corroborating evidence often is sought using more than one method) that meets the audit objectives at the lowest cost.

What the auditor normally expects to achieve through this process of gathering and evaluating audit evidence is the assurance needed to support an unqualified opinion on the financial statements. The auditor cannot be satisfied with anything less and still express such an opinion. The type of evidence, the amount needed, and the timing of the procedures used to obtain the evidence, however, can all be varied to fit the circumstances of the individual engagement and thus enhance efficiency.

Sufficiency of Evidential Matter

Determining the sufficiency of evidential matter is a question of deciding how much evidence is enough to achieve the reasonable assurance necessary to support the auditor's opinion. The sufficiency of evidence depends partly on the thoroughness of the auditor's search for it and partly on the auditor's ability to evaluate it objectively. For some auditing procedures, the amount of evidence needed corresponds precisely with the decision to use a certain procedure at all: The auditor either performs or does not perform the procedure. For example, in the audit of a client with a single cash fund, a decision to count cash on hand is a decision to count *all* cash on hand. If the client had numerous cash funds, however, the auditor could count only some of the cash funds. In that case, the question of sufficiency becomes one of determining the extent of testing. The extent of testing, including the use of sampling, is discussed in Chapter 10.

Types of Audit Tests

The types of evidence and the procedures for obtaining it described previously could also be classified according to the purpose for which the evidence is gathered. Viewed in terms of their purpose, auditing procedures can for the most part be classified as one of two major types: *tests of controls* and *substantive tests*. These two types of audit tests and their respective purposes are discussed at length in Chapters 8 and 9. They are described briefly here to set the stage for the overview of an audit that is presented later in this chapter.

Tests of controls are performed to provide the auditor with evidence about the effectiveness of the design and operation of internal control structure policies and procedures. That evidence supports an assessment of control risk below the maximum for one or more assertions. Based on that assessment, the assurance needed from substantive tests, which are tests of transactions and account balances, is reduced. To illustrate a test of controls, consider a client's internal control structure that requires the accounts payable clerk to recalculate the extensions and footings on vendors' invoices as a means of determining that the vendors' calculations are mathematically accurate. As evidence that the control procedure has been applied, the clerk initials the invoice after performing the calculations. To test the effectiveness of the control procedure, the auditor should inspect the invoice for the presence of the clerk's initials and may reperform the calculations that the clerk was supposed to have made. If the initials are present and the extensions and footings are correct, the auditor would conclude that the control procedure operated effectively in that specific instance.

Substantive tests consist of tests of the details of transactions and account balances, and analytical procedures. The purpose of substantive tests is to provide the auditor with evidence supporting management's assertions that are implicit in the financial statements or, conversely, to discover errors or irregularities in the financial statements. Analytical procedures used as substantive tests are discussed in detail in Chapter 9. An example of a test of the details of transactions is the auditor's examination of underlying documents that support purchases, sales, and retirements of property, plant, and equipment during the year. The auditor examines them as a means of forming a conclusion about the assertions concerning existence, rights and obligations, and accuracy that are implicit in the balance reported for that account in the balance sheet. An example of a test of the details of an account balance is the confirming of accounts receivable in order to form a conclusion about their existence.

Other key auditing procedures, which do not fit the literal definition of substantive tests, include reading minutes of meetings of the board of directors and its important committees, obtaining letters from outside counsel regarding legal matters, and obtaining a letter of representation from management about the completeness of recorded liabilities.

Audit Evidence Decisions

The amount and kinds of evidence that the auditor decides are necessary to provide a reasonable basis for forming an opinion on the financial statements taken as a whole, and the timing of procedures used to obtain the evidence, are matters of professional judgment. The auditor makes these decisions only after carefully deliberating on the circumstances of a particular engagement and considering the various risks related to the audit. The goal in every audit should be to perform the work in an effective and efficient manner.

As discussed in Chapter 1, usually an auditor finds it necessary to rely on evidence that is persuasive rather than convincing. In deciding how much persuasive evidence is enough, by necessity the auditor must work within time constraints, considering the cost of obtaining evidence and evaluating the usefulness of the evidence obtained. In making these decisions, the auditor cannot ignore the risk of issuing an inappropriate opinion or justify omitting a particular test solely because it is difficult or expensive to perform. While an auditor is seldom convinced beyond all doubt with respect to all the assertions embodied in the financial statements, he or she must achieve the level of assurance necessary to support the opinion given.

An unqualified opinion requires that the auditor have reasonable assurance about the fairness of presentation of all material items in the financial statements. (The meaning of fair presentation is discussed in Chapter 22.) The auditor must refrain from forming an opinion until sufficient competent evidential matter has been obtained to remove all substantial doubt. For example, if the auditor tries to communicate with a customer to confirm a material amount owed to the entity and the customer fails to respond after repeated requests, the auditor should use alternative procedures—such as examining evidence of subsequent cash receipts, cash remittance advices, the customer's purchase orders, and sales and shipping documents—to obtain satisfaction that the account receivable exists and the balance is accurate.

In deciding on the nature, timing, and extent of auditing procedures to be performed, the auditor can choose from a number of alternative strategies. For example, for some audit objectives for specific accounts, the auditor might decide to perform tests of controls. The tests would be designed to provide evidence that the accounting system from which the account balances were derived and the other elements of the internal control structure were operating consistently and effectively, and would be combined with limited substantive tests of the account balances themselves. For other audit objectives or accounts, the auditor might decide to obtain evidence mainly from substantive tests. These decisions will be influenced by answers to such questions as: which approach provides the needed assurance most efficiently; are the accounting system and related control procedures satisfactory; what are the principal risks of the client's business; and what are the significant account balances in the financial statements? These questions are not all-inclusive, but are indicative of the kinds of considerations and judgments the auditor must make. They are discussed throughout this book and particularly in Chapter 6.

AUDITING THEORY

Earlier sections of this chapter discussed the specific objectives the auditor seeks to achieve in an audit of financial statements, the different types of evidence that are available for meeting those objectives, and the kinds of decisions the auditor must make concerning the most effective and efficient sources and methods of obtaining evidence. A later section presents a framework for viewing the various phases of the audit process in which the work, as determined by the audit objectives and evidence decisions, is carried out, resulting in an audit that meets the requirements of professional standards. This section of the chapter covers the nature of and need for a theory of auditing, the various elements of auditing theory, the basic postulates that underlie that theory, and auditing concepts that help to explain the audit process.

Nature of and Need for Auditing Theory

Webster's New World Dictionary contains several definitions of "theory," at least two of which are appropriate in the present context.

- A formulation of apparent relationships or underlying principles of certain observed phenomena which has been verified to some degree.
- That branch of an art or science consisting in a knowledge of its principles and methods rather than in its practice.[2]

Mautz and Sharaf, in their landmark work, *The Philosophy of Auditing*, note the importance of a theory of auditing: "Auditing deals with abstract ideas; it has its foundations in the most basic types of learning; it has a rational structure of

[2] *Webster's New World Dictionary*, 3rd college ed. (New York: Simon & Schuster, 1988).

postulates, concepts, techniques, and precepts; adequately understood, it is a rigorous intellectual study worthy to be called a 'discipline' in the current sense of that term."[3] Auditing theory is primarily derived from current practice and as a result is largely descriptive of that practice. To a lesser extent, auditing theory is also normative, that is, it provides guidance about what auditing practice should be. Thus, "the purpose of a theory of auditing is to provide a rational, coherent, conceptual framework for determining the auditing procedures (and extent thereof) necessary to fulfill defined auditing objectives."[4] The authors would add that a theory of auditing also provides a framework for continually evaluating current practice and procedures for the purpose of improving them.

Elements of Auditing Theory

The preceding paragraph suggests the necessary components of a theory of auditing.

- *Audit objectives*—The overall objectives of an audit were discussed in Chapter 1 of this book; specific audit objectives were described in the first section of this chapter; how those specific objectives can be related to classes of transactions and account balances is explained in Chapter 9 and illustrated throughout the book.
- *Standards*—Generally accepted auditing standards were introduced in Chapter 2 and are discussed throughout the book, especially in Chapter 3.
- *Postulates*—Underlying assumptions, not subject to direct verification, that are essential to the development of a discipline. Postulates are discussed in this chapter.
- *Concepts*—Generalized ideas about various aspects of a discipline, derived from observations and experience. Auditing concepts are also discussed in this chapter.
- *Techniques*—In auditing, various methods of obtaining evidence. Types of evidence were discussed earlier in this chapter, as were types of audit tests, which are covered in more detail in Chapters 8 and 9.

The components of a theory of auditing are not unlike those of a theory of accounting or, for that matter, of many other disciplines. The FASB's conceptual framework is intended to provide a theory of accounting—what the Board hopes will serve as a constitution for accounting. No similar project has yet been undertaken by an authoritative auditing standard-setting body, although the Auditing Standards Board, its predecessor committees, the Commission on Auditors' Responsibilities, and several individuals (notably Mautz and Sharaf)

---

[3] R. K. Mautz and H. A. Sharaf, *The Philosophy of Auditing* (Sarasota, FL: American Accounting Association, 1961), p. 16.

[4] R. J. Anderson, *The External Audit 1: Concepts and Techniques* (Toronto: Pitman Publishing, 1977), p. 119.

have made significant contributions toward a theory of auditing.[5] As previously noted, audit objectives, standards, and techniques are discussed throughout this book. The postulates and concepts of auditing help to explain the rest of the theoretical structure and are discussed next.

Postulates of Auditing[6]

All fields of knowledge have basic assumptions or postulates that serve as the starting point for reasoning. They cannot be directly verified, but propositions derived from them can be, thereby indicating the validity of the postulates. While postulates are taken for granted at a particular time, they are not unchanging; new knowledge and changing events or circumstances can challenge a postulate and even demonstrate that it is invalid.

As might be expected, different authors have different lists of postulates. The postulates listed and explained below reflect the current environment in which audits of financial statements are performed.

1. Financial statements and financial data are verifiable. If this fundamental assumption were not valid, auditing would have no purpose and would not exist. Verification does not imply incontrovertible proof, but rather suggests the concept of reasonable assurance. Mautz and Sharaf note that "based on this single postulate, we find (1) the theory of evidence, (2) the procedure of verification, (3) the application of probability theory to auditing, and (4) some establishment of the bounds of the auditor's responsibilities" (p. 44).

2. There is no necessary conflict of interest between the auditor and the management of the enterprise under audit. However, some critics of the profession believe that the more notorious management frauds perpetrated in recent years render this postulate invalid, and suggest that auditors should assume that a potential conflict between the two parties always exists. The authors of this book do not believe that there is necessarily a conflict of interest, although the potential for one exists.

The fundamental need for audits of financial statements rests on the potential conflict of interest between the party that is being held accountable (management) and the parties to whom that accountability is being rendered (all financial statement users), with the auditor serving as an unbiased third-party intermediary. All of management's assertions, whether made in the form of the financial statements or presented as evidence in the course of an audit, must be viewed with professional skepticism and must be tested by the auditor. To do otherwise would result in an audit not conducted in accordance with professional standards.

[5]Some contemporary observers have suggested that SAS No. 31, *Evidential Matter* (AU Section 326), SAS No. 47, *Audit Risk and Materiality in Conducting an Audit* (AU Section 312), and the SSAE, *Attestation Standards* (AT Section 100), effectively serve as the beginning of an authoritative conceptual framework for attest engagements, particularly audits.

[6]Much of the material in this and the following section is adapted from Mautz and Sharaf, *op. cit.*

SAS No. 53, *The Auditor's Responsibility to Detect and Report Errors and Irregularities* (AU Section 316.16–.17) specifies that

> An audit of financial statements in accordance with generally accepted auditing standards should be planned and performed with an attitude of professional skepticism. The auditor neither assumes that management is dishonest nor assumes unquestioned honesty. Rather, the auditor recognizes that conditions observed and evidential matter obtained, including information from prior audits, need to be objectively evaluated to determine whether the financial statements are free of material misstatement.

> Management integrity is important because management can direct subordinates to record transactions or conceal information in a manner that can materially misstate financial statements. When approaching difficult-to-substantiate assertions, the auditor should recognize the increased importance of his consideration of factors that bear on management integrity. A presumption of management dishonesty, however, would be contrary to the accumulated experience of auditors. Moreover, if dishonesty were presumed, the auditor would potentially need to question the genuineness of all records and documents obtained from the client and would require conclusive rather than persuasive evidence to corroborate all management representations. An audit conducted on these terms would be unreasonably costly and impractical.

3. Properly designed and executed audits provide only reasonable, but not absolute, assurance that material misstatements, particularly those caused by irregularities, will be detected. The basis for this postulate is found in the characteristics of irregularities, particularly those involving forgery or collusion. Auditors are not trained to authenticate documents, nor is that required by auditing standards. SAS No. 53 (AU Section 316.07) also recognizes that "audit procedures that are effective for detecting a misstatement that is unintentional may be ineffective for a misstatement that is intentional and is concealed through collusion between client personnel and third parties or among management or employees of the client."

This postulate, however, does not completely relieve the auditor of responsibility for detecting irregularities. As discussed in Chapter 4, the auditor has the responsibility, stated in SAS No. 53 (AU Section 316.05), to "design the audit to provide reasonable assurance of detecting errors and irregularities that are material to the financial statements." The SAS acknowledges, however (AU Section 316.08), that "since the auditor's opinion on the financial statements is based on the concept of reasonable assurance, the auditor is not an insurer and his report does not constitute a guarantee. Therefore, the subsequent discovery that a material misstatement exists in the financial statements does not, in and of itself, evidence inadequate planning, performance, or judgment on the part of the auditor."

4. The existence of a satisfactory internal control structure reduces the probability of errors and irregularities. This assumption is embodied in the second standard of field work; it also underlies the importance of the auditor's understanding and assessment of the client's control structure as a basis for determining the nature, timing, and extent of substantive procedures to be employed. The postulate states that the probability of errors and irregularities

is *reduced*, not eliminated. As a result, the auditor needs additional evidence beyond that supplied by knowledge of an effective control structure as a basis for the necessary reasonable assurance about the financial statement assertions. That thought is expressed in SAS No. 55 (AU Section 319.63), which states that "ordinarily the assessed level of control risk cannot be sufficiently low to eliminate the need to perform any substantive tests to restrict detection risk for all of the assertions relevant to significant account balances or transaction classes. Consequently, regardless of the assessed level of control risk, the auditor should perform substantive tests for significant account balances and transaction classes."

5. Recurring audits are structured on the basis of experience and knowledge accumulated from auditing a client in prior years. Accordingly, unless there is evidence to the contrary, the auditor may assume that what has generally held true in the past for the enterprise under audit will hold true in the future. This postulate supports the view taken by most auditors that planning the current engagement should be based—in the absence of known changes in the client's control structure, operations, and personnel—on evidence accumulated in past audits. This does not mean that the audit plan should not be looked at anew every year. As indicated throughout this book, the audit plan is not an immutable document; it changes throughout the course of the audit as evidence is accumulated and evaluated. As a basis for planning, however, this postulate enhances audit efficiency. Of course, the auditor should not ignore new evidence as it is accumulated.

6. Independence is the essence of auditing; anything that tends to infringe on it should be viewed with concern. When examining financial data for the purpose of expressing an independent opinion on it, however, the auditor often gains knowledge that is useful for and leads to the performance of other services, such as accounting, tax, and management advisory services. As discussed in Chapter 3, providing such services should not be viewed as infringing on the auditor's independence.

7. The professional status of the independent auditor imposes commensurate professional obligations. Those obligations are discussed in Chapters 3 and 4 and are not repeated here. Generally accepted auditing standards recognize this obligation specifically in the standard of due professional care and generally in all of the Statements on Auditing Standards as well as in the AICPA Code of Professional Conduct.

Concepts in Auditing Theory

Concepts are general ideas derived from the observed particulars. They take shape gradually, appearing first as crude descriptions and then as broad generalizations. For example, familiar accounting concepts include "accrual accounting," "asset," "liability," "realization," "economic entity," and many others. As Mautz and Sharaf point out, all of these, and concepts generally, are "abstracted forms derived from observation and experience, generalized ideas which help us to see similarities and differences and to understand better the subject matter in question" (p. 54).

As with postulates, different authors have different lists of auditing concepts. The concepts that Mautz and Sharaf consider primary are few: evidence, due audit care, fair presentation, independence, and ethical conduct (p. 67). Other auditing concepts that are important to the development of auditing as a discipline are objectivity; materiality; competence and sufficiency of evidence; generally accepted accounting principles; reasonable assurance; audit risk (and its components); audit efficiency; and audit effectiveness. These concepts are not discussed here because they are dealt with in depth throughout this book.

Auditing and the Scientific Method

One of the dictionary definitions of "scientific" is "designating the method of research in which a hypothesis, formulated after systematic, objective collection of data, is tested empirically."[7] With certain caveats, auditing can be thought of as an application of the scientific method in which hypotheses are formulated and tested empirically. The hypotheses consist of financial statement assertions and audit decisions about the most efficient way to obtain the necessary reasonable assurance about those assertions. Both the financial statement assertions and the audit plan are tested empirically through the collection and evaluation of audit evidence. Either type of hypothesis can be rejected or accepted based on the evaluation of the evidence.

Auditors, however, do not generally think of themselves as applying the scientific method, and with few exceptions they do not prepare audit programs or working papers following the specific steps that natural and social scientists adhere to in conducting research. Auditors speak in terms of financial statement assertions, audit decisions, and audit objectives, not in terms of hypothesis testing. One reason for this is that the term "scientific method" usually connotes a high level of mathematical precision or at least a precise measure of certainty, which auditing in its present state surely does not have (except in specific instances in which statistical sampling techniques have been applied). Accordingly, this book does not present audit judgments and decisions as hypotheses. It does, however, emphasize the primary role of audit objectives in both planning and carrying out an audit engagement. Those objectives—developed from financial statement assertions that, if corroborated, state that the financial statements taken as a whole are presented fairly, in all material respects, in conformity with generally accepted accounting principles—are the equivalent of hypotheses and must be tested empirically through the accumulation of evidence.

THE STEPS IN AN AUDIT

Every audit includes the following major steps:

1. Carrying out such initial audit activities as staffing and budgeting.
2. Obtaining (or updating) and documenting information about the client

---

[7] *Webster's New World dictionary, op. cit.*

and its control structure as a basis for assessing inherent and control risk, including, in many situations, performing some tests of controls.

3. Developing the audit testing plan.
4. For specific audit objectives and account balances, where appropriate, performing additional tests of controls to further reduce the assurance needed from substantive tests.
5. Performing substantive tests to obtain, evaluate, and document sufficient competent evidence to corroborate that the management assertions embodied in account balances and in the financial statements as a whole, including the disclosures, are reasonable and thus to determine that the corresponding audit objectives have been met.
6. Performing final analytical and other procedures, and reviewing and evaluating the audit findings.
7. Formulating the auditor's report and communicating deficiencies in the control structure.

The nature, timing, and extent of the work in each step vary from one audit client to another and may vary from year to year for a given client. Moreover, the steps seldom appear as separate, isolated, specifically identifiable activities. These steps are elaborated on in this section and graphically displayed in Figure 5.2. With the exception of the reporting phase of the audit process, all the steps involve activities that affect audit strategy decisions. As depicted in the figure, strategy considerations are most intense during the risk assessment activities and when the auditor evaluates the results of those activities and develops the audit testing plan. The key strategy decision made at that time is whether to perform additional tests of controls to further reduce the assurance needed from substantive tests or to proceed directly to the substantive testing step.

Initial Audit Activities

Before a new client or a recurring engagement is accepted, appropriate information is gathered and evaluated as a basis for deciding whether to accept or retain the engagement. Once the engagement has been accepted, the terms and engagement goals have to be established. A number of administrative and strategy decisions also need to be made, namely, whether to use the work of internal auditors and specialists (for example, actuaries, appraisers), determining whether to use the work and reports of other firms that have been engaged to audit one or more components of the client, assigning staff, preparing time budgets, and other similar scheduling and administrative activities. In addition, opportunities to improve client relations and to maximize the quality of client services may be identified at this initial stage of the audit.

Obtaining and Documenting Information About the Client

At an early stage in the audit, the auditor obtains (or updates) information about the client. This information is used to assess inherent and control risk as

Figure 5.2   Summary of the Audit Process

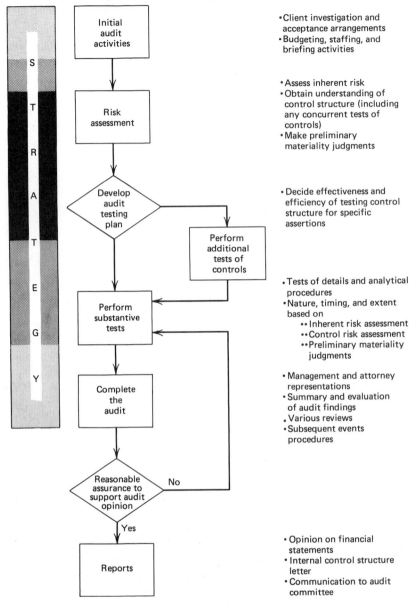

a basis for developing the audit testing plan. Among other things, the auditor gathers information about

- The nature, size, and organization of the enterprise and its operations.
- Matters affecting the business and industry in which the enterprise operates, such as
  - —The business environment
  - —Legal constraints and requirements.

- The control environment and significant management and accounting policies, practices, and methods.
- The accounting system and significant control procedures.
- Significant accounts or groups of accounts and the interrelationships among significant financial and operating data.
- Important dates, such as
    - Dates of the auditor's meetings with the audit committee of the board of directors
    - Dates by which the client will have assembled the data, records, and documents required by the auditor
    - Date or dates on which the client plans to physically count inventories or other assets
    - Deadlines for issuing the report on the financial statements and any other audit-related reports.

The information is obtained in a number of ways. The auditor may begin by consulting such materials as the client's recent annual reports and interim earnings or other news releases; general business or industry publications; industry accounting and auditing guides developed by the AICPA, the auditor's firm, and others; and trade association materials. For a recurring engagement, prior years' working papers and current correspondence files are also valuable sources of information. For an initial engagement, the auditor makes inquiries and reviews preceding years' working papers of the predecessor auditor, if the client has been audited in the past. The auditor supplements this knowledge by interviewing officers and employees of the client and others knowledgeable about and experienced in the industry. Additionally, the auditor typically reviews the company's policy and procedures manuals; tours its major plants and offices; reads the minutes of recent meetings of the board of directors, its important committees, and the stockholders; reads the client's significant contracts and other agreements; and compares the client's significant financial and operating data with that of its competitors, analyzing relationships and trends in the data.

Understanding the Control Structure.   Generally accepted auditing standards require the auditor to obtain an understanding of the client's control structure, which comprises the control environment, accounting system, and control procedures. On a recurring engagement, the auditor should focus on aspects of the control structure that have been added, changed, or assumed increased importance since the previous audit. At a minimum, the understanding must be sufficient for planning the audit, that is, for the auditor to identify and respond to the risk of material misstatements in the financial statements and design appropriate substantive tests to detect them. In obtaining the understanding of the control structure, the auditor identifies the critical points in the accounting system where significant errors or irregularities could occur and determines whether policies and procedures to prevent or detect such errors or irregularities have been designed and placed in operation at those critical points.

The auditor obtains (or updates) an understanding of the client's control structure mainly through observing and inquiring of client personnel, referring to relevant policy and procedures manuals, and inspecting books, records, forms, and reports. As a practical matter, the auditor generally does not "relearn" or redocument the client's control structure in each year's engagement. Most audits are recurring engagements, for which the auditor carries forward the knowledge and documentation developed in prior years and updates them for significant changes since the preceding year's audit. Most (if not all) of those changes generally come to the auditor's attention through continuing contact with the client between one year's audit and the next. If the auditor is concerned that the documented understanding of the client's accounting system may be incorrect or incomplete, perhaps because of changes since the preceding audit, it may be efficient to trace one or a few representative transactions through the system (sometimes called a transaction review or "walkthrough") before formalizing the audit testing plan.

A record of the information obtained by the auditor is needed to plan and control the audit and document the auditor's compliance with generally accepted auditing standards. Some auditors document all the information in narrative form; others prefer to use narratives for general information about the industry and company, and overview flowcharts to describe the accounting system and key control procedures. How much information is necessary to design and carry out subsequent auditing procedures depends on whether there have been significant changes in matters affecting the client, its business, or its control structure since the preceding audit, as well as on the audit testing plan contemplated.

Concurrent Tests of Controls.   The auditor uses the information about the client to make preliminary materiality judgments and assess inherent and control risk. As part of the assessment of control risk, the auditor often performs tests of controls concurrently with obtaining the understanding of the control structure. Those tests of controls provide evidence about whether control structure policies and procedures have been properly designed to prevent or detect errors on a timely basis and have operated effectively and continuously. They may include inquiring of client personnel who apply policies and procedures, as well as others in a position to be aware of control breakdowns; observing how the policies and procedures are applied; examining records and documents for evidence that they have been applied; and reperforming control procedures by duplicating the actions of the client's personnel. If the results of the tests of controls are positive, the auditor then considers whether, based on the work done so far, he or she can reduce the assurance needed from substantive tests for specific accounts and audit objectives. This will ordinarily be possible.

Developing the Audit Testing Plan

The auditor's materiality judgments and risk assessments determine the nature, timing, and extent of auditing procedures for each account or group of accounts. The auditor's aim is to choose an audit strategy that will most efficiently limit audit risk—that is, the risk that he or she will unknowingly fail to modify the opinion appropriately if the financial statements are materially misstated—to a low level.

As explained in Chapter 1, the auditor typically tests less than 100 percent of the items in an account balance or class of transactions. Most auditors start with the presumption that it will not be necessary to perform substantive tests on every item that supports an account balance in the financial statements. From information gathered or updated about the client (particularly about its control environment and accounting system), and from any concurrent tests of controls performed, the auditor usually has some evidence that the client has established policies and procedures that reduce the risk of material misstatement, either in particular accounts or groups of accounts or in the financial statements as a whole.

After the auditor has completed the risk assessment activities, he or she develops the audit testing plan. Concurrent tests of controls may have been performed as part of obtaining the understanding of the control structure, and the auditor may have assessed control risk at below the maximum. He or she then considers whether additional evidence about the effectiveness of control structure policies and procedures is likely to be available and whether it would be efficient to obtain it in order to further reduce substantive tests for specific audit objectives. If so, the auditor will perform additional tests of controls.

Performing Additional Tests of Controls

Performing additional tests of controls will be efficient only if the audit time and effort saved by reducing substantive testing exceeds the time and effort spent in performing the tests of controls. Therefore, additional tests of controls are generally performed only when achieving the relevant audit objectives solely by substantive testing would require substantial audit time and effort. Moreover, tests of controls are usually performed only on those policies and procedures that the auditor has assessed as potentially capable of limiting control risk to a low level. The auditor should not automatically decide to perform additional tests of controls, even if it appears that they will provide the necessary evidence, without considering whether performing them will be efficient.

The auditor should discuss with appropriate client personnel any significant deficiencies in the design of control structure policies and procedures and any significant breakdowns in their operation. The auditor should also consider how such deficiencies and breakdowns affect the risk that account balances could be materially misstated, and should plan the nature, timing, and extent of substantive procedures accordingly.

The basic audit strategy alternatives are either to perform additional tests of controls and thus significantly reduce substantive procedures, or to perform substantive tests without significant restriction based on tests of controls. The auditor usually adopts different strategies for different parts of the audit. Thus, it is possible to achieve one or more audit objectives for an account or a group of accounts by performing additional tests of controls and restricting substantive tests, while achieving other audit objectives entirely by performing substantive procedures. This flexibility also applies to different client locations, subsidiaries, and components of business activities.

Regardless of the audit strategy chosen, auditors have traditionally focused more on audit objectives related to balance sheet accounts than on their income statement counterparts, since that is frequently the most efficient way to conduct an audit. Emphasizing balance sheet accounts is also conceptually sound: Balance sheet accounts represent the enterprise's economic resources and claims to those resources at a point in time, reflecting the cumulative effects of transactions and other events and circumstances on the enterprise. Income statement accounts reflect the enterprise's performance during a period between two points in time, measuring its revenues, expenses, gains, and losses that occurred during the period. Income statement accounts are logically and inextricably related to one or more balance sheet accounts. Often, evidence that helps achieve an audit objective for a balance sheet account also helps achieve a corresponding audit objective for an income statement account. For example, evidence about the existence of trade accounts receivable at the beginning and end of a period is also a source of assurance about the occurrence of sales transactions during the period. In some cases, however, it may be more efficient to achieve audit objectives for balance sheet accounts by achieving the corresponding audit objectives for related income statement accounts. For example, the completeness of trade accounts receivable at the end of a period may be audited most efficiently by auditing the completeness of sales recorded for the period.

The audit strategy selected for each part of the audit and the significant reasons for choosing that strategy should be documented. The accounting system and control procedures and related tests of controls are documented on various forms, such as systems flowcharts, questionnaires, or other practice aids. Audit strategy documentation should also include the decisions made about certain other aspects of the audit plan, such as locations where work will be performed, analyses to be prepared by the client, the need to use the work of other auditing firms or specialists (such as actuaries), and the effects of an internal audit function on the audit strategy. The audit plan as initially determined and documented should be reviewed, and revised if necessary, as the audit progresses and new information becomes available.

The auditor may decide on the audit strategy for each account or group of accounts, develop the audit program, and plan and schedule the work, particularly for recurring engagements, before performing additional tests of controls. If those tests then indicate that control structure elements may not have operated effectively throughout the period, the auditor may have to reassess the risk that account balances could be materially misstated, and revise the audit plan accordingly. In formulating the audit plan before completing tests of controls, the auditor assumes the test results will be satisfactory. On a new engagement, the basis for that assumption is generally derived from knowledge (which may perhaps be limited in scope) obtained through inquiries, observation, and inspection of documents, records, and reports undertaken as part of developing an understanding of the control structure and from any concurrent tests of controls performed at that time. On a recurring engagement, that assumption is also supported by the prior year's audit experience, preliminary inquiries of knowledgeable client personnel, and the auditor's recognition that, except in extraordinary circumstances, a client's control structure generally does not deteriorate markedly from one year to the next.

Performing Substantive Tests

Substantive tests provide evidence about management's assertions and the corresponding audit objectives. In the substantive testing phase, the auditor obtains, evaluates, and documents evidence to corroborate management's assertions embodied in the accounts and other information in the financial statements and related notes. The auditor's purpose in performing substantive tests is to determine whether the audit objectives have been achieved. Substantive procedures include tests of details of account balances and transactions, and analytical comparisons and other procedures. The nature of substantive tests, when they are performed, and the extent to which they are performed depend on the auditor's materiality judgments and risk assessments. Furthermore, the assurance required from substantive tests may be obtained from tests of details, analytical procedures, or some combination of both, with the assurance obtained from one reducing the assurance needed from the other.

Substantive tests may also provide evidence about the control structure, such as when a misstatement discovered through a substantive test is, upon further investigation, found to have resulted from a deficiency in the control structure. In that situation, the auditor may have to reassess his or her prior conclusions about the control structure.

Completing the Audit

After all the previous steps in the audit have been performed, the auditor performs final analytical and certain other procedures, such as reading minutes of recent board and committee meetings and obtaining representation letters. Then he or she makes final materiality judgments, summarizes and evaluates the audit findings, reviews the working papers and reviews the financial statement presentation and disclosures for adequacy, and considers subsequent events. Those procedures require the exercise of considerable professional judgment and thus are generally performed by the senior members of the engagement team.

Formulating the Auditor's Report and Communicating Control Structure Deficiencies

Finally, the auditor prepares the audit report and generally also communicates to management and the audit committee significant control structure deficiencies noted during the course of the audit.

RESEARCHING AUDITING PROBLEMS

The profession has set high standards for the technical and ethical conduct of CPAs. Many of those standards establish precise requirements for auditor performance in a variety of circumstances. In meeting their obligation under those standards, auditors need to become familiar with the requirements of the 10 generally accepted auditing standards (GAAS); in addition, often they need to refer to the Statements on Auditing Standards and other professional literature for guidance on interpreting and adhering to GAAS.

Generally accepted auditing standards serve a dual purpose: They implicitly require an auditor to be aware of all pertinent literature—the first general standard—and they serve as a first level of research to resolve auditing problems. For example, an auditor may be confronted for the first time with the need to issue a letter for underwriters on an engagement that includes filing the auditor's report with the SEC under the Securities Act of 1933. The accepted form and content of the letter, as well as important suggestions for procedures to follow and cautions to observe, can be readily researched in SAS No. 49, *Letters for Underwriters* (AU Section 634).

The auditor should also be familiar with AICPA auditing interpretations (AU Section 9000). Interpretations are not as authoritative as pronouncements of the Auditing Standards Board, but they are issued by the staff of the Auditing Standards Division of the AICPA to provide guidance on the application of Statements on Auditing Standards, and CPAs may have to justify departures from auditing interpretations. Thus, if faced with an auditing problem with respect to, for example, related party transactions (dealt with in AU Section 334), the auditor should consult interpretations in AU Section 9334 for additional guidance.

An auditor who does not have prior experience in an industry may be engaged to audit a company in that industry. He or she should, among other considerations, determine whether a relevant industry audit (or audit and accounting) guide has been issued by the AICPA. An auditor engaged, for example, by an investment company should read the latest edition of the audit and accounting guide for that industry. The guides have authoritative status similar to that of auditing interpretations. Chapters 26 to 40 of this book may also be helpful.

Auditors sometimes need to research issues in the latest authoritative accounting pronouncements in order to determine whether the assertions in financial statements are in conformity with generally accepted accounting principles. Standards issued by the FASB and the GASB (and related interpretations) and Statements of Position issued by the AICPA Accounting Standards Executive Committee and the SEC should be available and consulted as necessary.

Most auditors should be familiar with and have available a copy of the latest edition of *Accounting Trends and Techniques*, published by the AICPA. Issues of disclosure and presentation can be readily researched in this publication. It also contains wording of auditor's reports in unusual situations. While the publication is nonauthoritative, it includes examples from recent practice and can serve to document an auditor's diligence.

An auditor may be faced with a question regarding independence, which is an ethical consideration. In that case, the auditor should refer to the AICPA's Code of Professional Conduct and similar pronouncements of the relevant state society, state board of accountancy, and the SEC.

Other research sources that the auditor may consult include

- Statements of Position (SOPs) of the AICPA's Auditing Standards Division, which revise or clarify recommendations in industry audit guides. SOPs are published as separate documents and are also included in reprints of audit guides and in the AICPA's *Technical Practice Aids.*
- Notices to Practitioners issued by the AICPA's Auditing Standards Division, which are published in *The CPA Letter,* a semimonthly news report published by the AICPA. Notices to Practitioners are used to disseminate important information quickly.
- AICPA Auditing Research Monographs and Auditing Procedures Studies, which address various areas of practice, such as auditing small businesses and applying confirmation procedures.
- *AICPA Audit and Accounting Manual,* a set of nonauthoritative audit tools and illustrations prepared by the AICPA staff.
- Publications of federal agencies that provide guidance for audits of entities under their jurisdiction. Examples are the U.S. General Accounting Office's *Standards for Audit of Governmental Organizations, Programs, Activities, and Functions* (the "Yellow Book") and the SEC's Financial Reporting Releases and Accounting and Auditing Enforcement Releases.
- Periodicals, such as the *Journal of Accountancy* and *The CPA Journal,* that contain practical guidance on interpreting and applying auditing pronouncements. These journals also report on the publication of the other research materials described here.

Thus, a substantial body of authoritative and nonauthoritative literature exists which is (or should be) available from libraries to help auditors solve problems concerning auditing standards and procedures. In practice, most auditors are familiar with these sources and refer to them frequently. Practitioners and firms should receive, review, and maintain all authoritative pronouncements and interpretations as well as other professional literature, such as industry audit guides, for reference purposes. Larger firms maintain research departments for consultation.

Not all problems encountered, however, can be so readily researched. Many state societies of CPAs and the AICPA offer technical services to assist in research; a local university may also be of help. These organizations as well as many firms often use computer-assisted research sources, such as NAARS, LEXIS, and INFORM. Some firms also have their own research data bases. An auditor may also consult relevant trade associations or fellow practitioners with appropriate background and experience.

When a problem is identified, the auditor must document the related issues, develop an approach to obtaining research assistance, evaluate the material uncovered as to relevance and authoritative status, and reach a conclusion. For engagement efficiency and good client relations, problems should be identified early, so that the time spent solving them does not unduly delay completion of the audit work. The means by which auditing problems have been resolved should be clearly documented in the working papers.

WORKING PAPERS

Statement on Auditing Standards No. 41, *Working Papers* (AU Section 339), specifies that the auditor should prepare and maintain working papers as a record of the work done and conclusions reached on significant matters. Working papers also help the auditor in planning, conducting, and supervising the work.

More specifically, the working papers document

- The understanding of the client's business.
- The consideration of inherent risk.
- The understanding of the internal control structure.
- The basis for the conclusion about whether control structure policies and procedures are designed and operating effectively.
- The audit strategy decisions made.
- Tests of controls performed.
- Substantive procedures applied to transactions, account balances, and other information presented in the financial statements.
- That the work of any assistants was supervised and reviewed.
- Resolution of exceptions and unusual matters.
- Recommendations for improving control structure policies and procedures, as noted throughout the engagement.
- Support for the auditor's opinion on the financial statements.[8]

In addition, the working papers provide information needed for SEC reports, tax returns, and reports to other government agencies, and they serve as a source of information for succeeding audits.

Working papers are the property of the auditor and not a substitute for the client's accounting records. (In some cases, as an accommodation to the client, working papers are transmitted to and accepted by the client as a substitute for a record that it would otherwise prepare.) The auditor should adopt reasonable procedures for the safekeeping and retention of working papers long enough to meet his or her own practice needs and to satisfy any pertinent legal requirements for records retention.

---

[8]As noted in footnote 3 to AU Section 339.01, however, "there is no intention to imply that the auditor would be precluded from supporting his report by other means in addition to working papers."

Form and Content of Working Papers

Working papers include audit programs, trial balances, schedules, analyses, memoranda, letters of confirmation, representative abstracts of company documents, narratives, flowcharts, questionnaires, and various other forms and practice aids. They may be handwritten, typewritten, or in the form of computer printouts or data stored on electronic media. Often, portions of working papers are prepared by client personnel according to auditor-determined specifications; the auditor should, of course, test the accuracy of client-prepared working papers.

The *content* of working papers generally cannot be standardized. Certain types of working papers, however, lend themselves to standardization, such as a summary of accounts receivable confirmation coverage and results. Working papers should be legible, complete, readily understandable, and designed to fit the circumstances and needs of the auditor for the particular engagement and subject matter under audit.

Unnecessary or irrelevant working papers that do not serve a useful purpose should not be prepared. If such working papers are inadvertently prepared, they should generally not be kept.

Although the content of working papers varies with the engagement, there are several advantages to adopting a standardized approach to their *format*. It facilitates the systematic organization of working papers for use during an engagement, enhances their ready access for reference or review, and aids in their orderly filing for future reference. Thus, every working paper should be headed, dated, and initialed by the preparer at the time the work is performed.

A *heading* identifies the client and the subject of the working paper.

Dating not only provides evidence of the time of preparation but also makes it easier to trace the sequence in which steps were performed and to plan the timing of similar work in the next audit.

Initialing establishes responsibility for the work and also directs reviewers or subsequent users to personnel who might be able to furnish additional information.

Every working paper should contain an explanation of the procedures followed (unless the information is included elsewhere in the working papers, such as in an audit program) and the results of those procedures. Figure 5.3 shows a working paper that illustrates this. Sometimes the procedures are obvious from the computations or other data recorded; sometimes a narrative explanation is required. When an explanation is required, it is frequently placed at the end of the working paper and assigned a symbol or ''tick mark,'' which is placed next to the appropriate item (generally a dollar amount) in the body of the working paper. For example, a working paper listing the details of notes receivable at a particular date may have the letter ''E'' after the details of each note, with the following explanation at the end of the working paper— ''E = note examined,'' meaning that the auditor physically inspected the notes. Some auditors use a standardized set of symbols to document procedures.

Figure 5.3   Analysis of Notes Receivable and Related Interest Accounts

Date Prepared: 3/10/89
Prepared By:
a) C&L EF
b) Client and
   Examined By
Reviewed By:
   C&L Sr Sup

COOPERS CABINET COMPANY
NOTES RECEIVABLE
12/31/88

⑦ DEBTOR	INTEREST RATE	NOTE DATE / DUE DATE	BALANCE 12/31/87	PRINCIPAL – A/C 116 ADDITIONS	RECEIPTS	BALANCE 12/31/88	CURRENT PORTION	LONG-TERM PORTION	BALANCE 12/31/87	ACCRUED INTEREST – A/C 117 INTEREST INCOME	RECEIPTS	BALANCE 12/31/88
④ WATTS ENGINEERING	c 15	6/30/86 DEMAND	32 7 5 00 ℗			② 3275 00	3275		245 62	ℝ 491 26	491 26	245 62
⑤ MATCHOMATIC	c 16 Ⓘ	4/4/86 ℗/87 Payable 7/1/870 annually plus interest		71 250 00 ℗		③④ 7850 00 ℗ 7/1/87	1,570	6280	1015 58	1015 58	1015 58	1015 58
⑥ POWER BELT CONVEYORS	c 12	3/1/86 7/1/86 Payable 2215 annually plus interest	6 375 00 ℗			③ 6375 00	4250	2,125	491 38	765 00	724 58	138 80
⑥ BORLAND PLUMBING	c 8	3/1/78 DEMAND	535000		⑤ 5350 00	–			856 00	33 16	② 894 16	
			1 500 000 0	71 850 00	5350 00	11 500 00 ℗f ✓T/B	9,095	8405	1200 00	231 000	211 000	140 000 ✓T/B

℗-Footed cf-cross footed
℗-Agreed to prior year's w/p's
T/B-Agreed to the trial balance.
c-Agreed all details to confirmation on w/p 512.2 to 52.5
℗-Recomputed classifications based on terms of the notes
ℝ-Recomputed; appears reasonable.
Ⓘ-Agreed to copy of executed note in permanent file. Reviewed note for unusual terms, collateral arrangements and significant requirements, restrictions or other covenants. None noted other than the note is collateralized by inventory (see confirmation on 52.3)
②-Agreed to customer remittance advice, paid 2/3/86, totaling # 6,244.16 including interest
Traced to cash receipts journal and agreed to deposit slip on 2/3/88

③ – Agreed to remittance advice for collection of note installment and/or interest, date indicated next to tickmark.

④ – Reviewed stated interest rate for reasonableness.

⑥ – Note not collected at 3/10/89. Discussion with treasurer disclosed that demand for payment will be 6/1/89. D&B report of Watts Engineering indicate good credit rating. Balance appears collectible; no allowance deemed necessary.

⑤ – First installment due 3/1/88 was made on 2/3/89. Client indicated customer has experienced a cash flow problem in early 1988, which has now been remedied. Customer has indicated the second installment will be paid on time. D&B report of Power Belt indicates improved rating. Balance appears collectible; no allowance deemed necessary.

⑦ – Per review of the notes and discussion with Treasurer, none of these are related parties as defined by SAS No. 45.

⑨ – Reclassification entry for financial statements:
    116 Notes receivable – short-term 8405
    116   Notes receivable – long term 8405
                    A&E No. 47

⑨ – For footnote disclosures, notes collateralized by inventory. See confirmations 52.1

Each working paper or set of working papers covering an audit objective should contain a clear record of all work performed. This record should include an explanation of exceptions noted by the auditor as a result of the procedures performed and identification of proposed adjustments to account balances. Language such as "are fairly stated" and "appear to be fairly stated" should be avoided, however, because the conclusion could be misinterpreted as having been reached in the context of the financial statements taken as a whole. That inference would be inappropriate and unsupportable since the conclusion is based on only a portion of the work done during the audit of the overall financial statements.

Most working papers contain quantitative information. Some working papers, however, are prepared based on inquiry or observation procedures and contain no quantitative information. For example, the auditor may inquire of management about the existence of transactions with related parties or observe the physical condition of inventory during the client's year-end inventory count. In these instances, the auditor should prepare working papers that clearly document the inquiries made, the client personnel involved, any tests resulting from the inquiry, or a description of the condition observed and the conclusion reached.

Working Paper Organization

There are no rigid guidelines for organizing a set of audit working papers. What follows should be viewed as general guidance that is subject to substantial modification by individual auditors and firms.

Detailed working papers are often summarized through the use of lead schedules for each financial statement caption. This technique provides an overview of an entire audit area for the preparer, as well as reviewers. In addition, a lead schedule enables a reviewer to look at as much or as little detail as is considered necessary in the circumstances.

Detailed support for lead schedules or other summary working papers is often filed behind the summary in order of relative significance or other meaningful sequence. There should always be an easy-to-follow trail between the detailed working papers and the amounts in the financial statements. Each working paper should be able to stand on its own; that is, it should be complete and understandable in itself. Reference may be made to other working papers to document audit findings. Cross-referencing of working papers should be specific rather than general. The "to–from" technique is used to make the "direction" of referencing apparent; that is, it shows which number is the source and which is the summary (see Figure 5.4).

Typical Working Papers

As suggested above, the variety of conditions encountered in practice generates a wide variety of working papers. Nevertheless, some types of working

Figure 5.4   Working Paper Organization

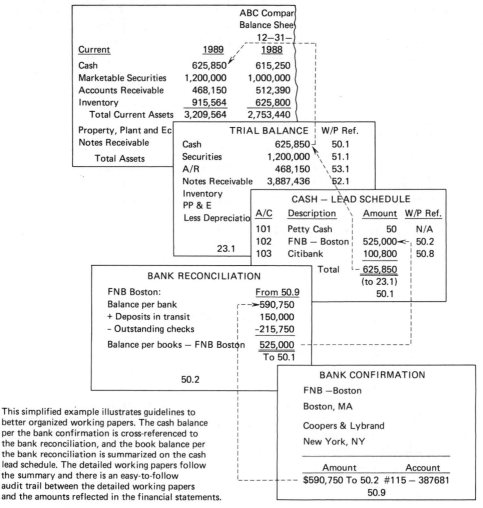

This simplified example illustrates guidelines to better organized working papers. The cash balance per the bank confirmation is cross-referenced to the bank reconciliation, and the book balance per the bank reconciliation is summarized on the cash lead schedule. The detailed working papers follow the summary and there is an easy-to-follow audit trail between the detailed working papers and the amounts reflected in the financial statements.

papers have common characteristics, which are explained in this section of the chapter.

The Trial Balance.   The trial balance is the key working paper in many audits because it is the one where data from all underlying working papers is integrated, referenced, and summarized into the amounts appearing in the financial statements. There are a number of ways to prepare the trial balance, and each of them has its advantages. Often it is prepared in a form that compares the current figures with those of the previous period. It may be prepared in balance sheet and income statement order, and amounts may be grouped into subtotals to make it easier to identify trial balance amounts with those in the financial statements. Client adjustments made as a result of the audit and financial statement reclassification entries (made only on the trial balance) are shown in additional columns. The adjusted trial balance is usually cross-referenced to supporting working papers.

Schedules and Analyses.   Auditing procedures are documented on a variety of schedules and analyses, as well as in narrative form.

- *Tests of controls* may be documented in narrative form by describing what tests were performed and which control structure policies and procedures were tested. Sometimes a test of controls requires preparing a list of items to be extracted from the files or compared with data in another location. If so, the schedule or listing prepared can serve as the working paper. In some instances, tests of controls are documented on the same form—for example, a questionnaire—that lists what policies and procedures were tested.

- *Substantive tests* are most often evidenced by some kind of analysis; the form depends on the nature of the auditing procedures performed. For example, the working papers might include an analysis showing the composition of the ending balance in a particular account, or perhaps a summary of the account. They also might include an analysis of the activity in the particular account for the period, showing the beginning balance, a summary of the transactions during the period (logically classified so that relationships with related accounts are apparent), and the ending balance. The working papers should present both the account information and an indication of what evidence was examined and what other auditing procedures were performed; sometimes the dollar amount or the percentage of the total tested is also shown.

- *Analytical procedures* involve a study and comparison of relationships among data; they are often evidenced by computations the auditor makes as part of the comparison. The working paper evidence usually consists of a narrative description of the procedures, their results, further investigation of matters identified as having a significant effect on the audit, and any resulting changes in the scope of the audit of related accounts.

Memoranda.   Questions, errors discovered by procedures performed, or unusual matters that arise during the audit should be documented. A memorandum should explain what steps were taken to resolve them (such as additional auditing procedures, consultation with the client, the auditor's own research and reasoning), what people were involved in the resolution, and the resulting conclusions. It is undesirable simply to check off a question or record a cryptic answer such as "cleared." Explanations of material matters should be complete and conclusive.

Permanent Working Papers.   Working papers for recurring engagements usually contain files that are carried forward from preceding years' audits; these are often referred to as permanent files. These files should include data having continuing use and not subject to frequent change. Examples of such data include copies or abstracts of the certificate of incorporation, bylaws, bond and note indentures, union agreements, important contracts having historical significance, organization charts, the client's accounting policies and procedures, key personnel, and location of plants. The file may also include activity schedules not maintained by the client, for example, schedules of future amortization or depreciation (sometimes referred to as "lapse schedules"), and analyses and other working papers that have historical significance, such as analyses of various capital accounts. Audit programs, descriptions of the accounting system, flowcharts, and questionnaires or other documentation of the control structure are also often kept in the permanent files.

Common Working Paper Deficiencies

Deficiencies in working papers often result in confusion and wasted time at several stages—carrying out auditing procedures, assisting new staff in the following year's audit, and reconstructing at a later date the work performed and judgments made. Those deficiencies are generally discovered during the working paper review process, which is discussed in Chapter 21. Some of the more common working paper deficiencies are listed in Figure 5.5.

AUDITOR–CLIENT RELATIONSHIPS

To an outsider, the practice of auditing often appears to consist mainly of comparing figures, examining documents, and reviewing financial statements, all of which involve little contact with people. In reality, however, auditing is concerned with the activities of people, for it is people who define the entity's control environment, design accounting systems, keep accounting records, perform control procedures, program computers to process accounting data, enter into contractual agreements, prepare financial statements, and engage auditors. Further, an audit is carried out on the client's premises with the help of the client's personnel, and, ultimately, the auditor is responsible to people—the client's board of directors, trustees, and stockholders. Auditing is to a great extent a process of dealing with people.

The auditor needs to develop and maintain a network of contacts at all levels throughout the client's organization. Depending on the type of information the auditor needs, he or she may obtain it most expeditiously from the client's nonmanagement personnel, operating management, financial management, the chief executive officer, the chief financial officer, the internal auditors, or others.

Working with the Client's Management and Other Personnel

The auditor should discuss the audit plan with client personnel, primarily to establish timetables and assignments. The auditor is then more likely to receive client data and access to client personnel when they are needed. Careful, cooperative planning does not compromise the auditor's independence or

Figure 5.5   Common Working Paper Deficiencies

- Working paper not initialed and dated by preparer or reviewer.
- Working paper not properly "headed."
- Cross-referencing too general; reviewer unable to find referenced working papers.
- Reason for cross-referencing missing or not apparent.
- Tick marks appearing on the working paper without a descriptive legend.
- Purpose of working paper not apparent; no explanation given.
- Working papers sloppy or cluttered.
- Exceptions or unusual items not properly explained or evaluated.
- Working paper content illogical.
- Amounts not in agreement with trial balance.
- Poor quality, illegible photocopy placed in the working papers.
- Detailed explanation given for insignificant items or differences, for which a simple notation, such as "Amounts insignificant; no audit work deemed necessary," would be sufficient.
- Arrangement of working papers not logical.
- Too much reliance placed on the prior year's working papers, which resulted in a lack of focus on unusual items or changes in significant account balances.
- Preparing a working paper because the client-prepared working paper was not in the exact format preferred by the auditor.
- Nature of auditing procedures performed not described fully and clearly.
- Use of similar tick marks to denote different procedures.

responsibility for determining audit scope. The auditor always retains that responsibility, but the client can facilitate the process.

Even in the best-planned, smoothest running engagement, an auditor needs to ask many questions and make many requests of a client's staff. The client's staff may also help the auditor directly by preparing schedules and analyses, searching files, accumulating data, confirming accounts receivable (under the auditor's control), and giving the auditor access to computers and computer files for testing purposes. Clearly, courtesy and consideration are required, and the auditor should minimize the number and duration of interruptions.

Operating management can be a valuable source of information to the auditor. For example, in a manufacturing business, the production manager may be able to provide information relevant to the auditor's assessment of the allowances for inventory valuation and obsolescence; in a retail business, buyers can often provide this information.

Chief Executive Officer.   It is important for the auditor to establish and maintain meaningful contact with the client's chief executive officer (CEO). Such contact leads to the development of a professional relationship in which both parties are comfortable discussing relevant issues with each other. For example, the CEO may consult the auditor about a contemplated acquisition or other transaction, or the auditor may contact the CEO to discuss observations made during the audit concerning operating or financial matters.

Chief Financial Officer.   An auditor who is broadly experienced and has a good understanding of the client is inevitably a valuable adjunct to the chief financial officer (CFO). The auditor can contribute expertise in accounting and financial reporting drawn from experience with other clients and can provide an objective point of view. In addition, the auditor is a source of informed, knowledgeable comments on events and decisions facing the CFO. As with the CEO, the auditor should foster a professional relationship with the CFO that includes open lines of communication between the two.

Head of Internal Audit.   In the interests of audit efficiency, the external auditor tries to coordinate the overall audit work with the internal auditors as far as possible. This involves meeting with the head of internal audit to discuss the scope of work done by the internal auditors and to consider the following: whether the external auditor can use that work, the rotation of certain audit coverage, the sharing of working papers, and the exchange of audit reports and communications with management. Using the work of internal auditors is discussed in Chapter 6.

Corporate Staff.   In all but the smallest audits, an auditor will be involved with a variety of members of the client's corporate staff who are working on problems directly or indirectly related to accounting and auditing. The range of possible problems covers the whole spectrum of business activity and could involve merger negotiations, labor contracts, lease or purchase decisions, fair trade laws, or environmental protection restrictions, to name a few. An auditor should be asked to review and approve the accounting treatment of proposed transactions before the fact rather than afterward. Because of their expertise and experience, auditors frequently can offer suggestions for improvements.

Working with Audit Committees and Boards of Directors

Audit Committees.   Audit committees of outside directors are now an integral part of the American corporate structure, appearing not only in large organizations but also in smaller businesses and in other institutions like hospitals and universities. Chapter 3 describes the role of audit committees in enhancing independence; it also discusses the responsibilities typically undertaken by audit committees.

Since 1988, auditors have been required to determine that certain matters are communicated to an audit committee (or equivalent group), if the client has one, or if the client is an SEC engagement. SAS No. 61, *Communication With Audit Committees* (AU Section 380), further states that the matters may be communicated by either the auditor or management, and that the communication may be oral or written.

The following are matters that must be communicated to the audit committee or equivalent group responsible for overseeing the financial reporting process:

- The auditor's responsibility under generally accepted auditing standards. (This is generally communicated in the engagement letter discussed in Chapter 4.)
- Significant accounting policies.
- Sensitive accounting estimates by management and the basis for the auditor's conclusions about their reasonableness (see Chapter 9).
- Significant audit adjustments (discussed in Chapter 21).
- Other information in documents containing audited financial statements (see Chapters 22 and 23).
- Disagreements with management.
- Consultation with other accountants (discussed in Chapter 23).
- Major issues discussed with management prior to the auditor's retention.
- Difficulties encountered in performing the audit.

In addition, other auditing standards require specific communications with the audit committee. Communication of control structure related matters is discussed in Chapter 8; Chapter 4 covers reporting material irregularities, and illegal acts by clients; and communication of deficiencies in an entity's system of interim financial controls is discussed in Chapter 23.

SAS No. 61 underscores the importance of audit committees in overseeing the financial reporting process and facilitating communication between the full board of directors and the auditor. The matters required to be communicated help the audit committee understand what kind of assurance the audit provides: reasonable, but not absolute, assurance. The communication also aids the committee in its oversight of management's activities.

Boards of Directors.   In the normal course of events, contact between the board of directors and the independent auditor is generally through the audit committee. Because the SEC requires a majority of the members of the board of directors to sign a registered company's annual report on Form 10-K, however, the entire board may turn to the auditor for assistance in reviewing the financial statements and other financial data contained in the 10-K. Some independent auditors routinely provide the board with fairly detailed reports describing the nature and extent of their involvement with the company. In addition, if an SEC client does not have an audit committee or its equivalent, the communication required by SAS No. 61 is generally directed to the board.

Stockholder Meetings.   While there is no professional or regulatory requirement that the independent auditor attend the annual stockholders' meeting, auditors generally attend when invited to do so. The auditor should be prepared to answer questions regarding the CPA firm, the audit just concluded, and the financial statements. The auditor can also help management prepare for the meeting. Typical questions shareholders ask financial management and the independent auditor relate to the following topics:

- Whether the internal control structure is adequate.
- What the responsibilities of the audit committee are.
- How much was paid in fees to independent auditors.
- Whether the internal audit function is adequate.
- Whether compensation of executives is appropriate.
- Whether the company can remain liquid.
- What effects tax legislation will have on the company.

6

Audit Risk, Materiality, and Engagement Strategy

The first standard of field work requires that the audit be adequately planned; good management practices require that it be controlled to ensure that it is performed efficiently and on a timely basis as well as in accordance with professional standards—that is, effectively. Planning and control are closely related aspects of engagement management. Engagement management is a continuous activity that involves determining the strategy to use on an audit, planning how to implement that strategy, and controlling the way the audit is performed in accordance with the audit plan. Throughout the audit, the auditor makes numerous decisions, ranging from determining the overall strategy to choosing specific auditing procedures and deciding how to implement them. The most significant factor in all those decisions is the auditor's assessment of the principal risks associated with the client's financial statements.

AUDIT RISK

Generally accepted auditing standards (GAAS), user expectations, and sound business practices require the auditor to design and perform auditing procedures that will permit expressing an opinion on the financial statements with a low risk that the opinion will be inappropriate. The complement of that risk is an expression of the level of assurance that the opinion will be appropriate. Stated another way, the auditor seeks to have a low risk that the opinion expressed is inappropriate or a high level of assurance that the financial statements are free from material misstatements. Obtaining audit assurance and restricting audit risk are alternative ways of looking at the same process.

There is no practical way to reduce audit risk to zero. The auditor's determination of how much risk is acceptable is a business decision constrained by users' expectations. To users, an audit opinion indicates that professional standards were adhered to and sufficient evidence was accumulated and evaluated to support the opinion. The auditor should design the audit so that the risk of an inappropriate opinion is sufficiently low to meet those expectations.

The auditor varies the nature, timing, and extent of auditing procedures in response to his or her perception of risk. Thus, when risk is perceived to be high, more reliable evidence (see Chapter 5), larger sample sizes, and procedures timed at or near the end of the period under audit are common. Risk analysis is also used to balance the mix of tests of controls, substantive tests of details, and analytical procedures to achieve an efficient audit.

The term "overall audit risk" is used to describe the risk that the auditor will issue an inappropriate opinion. That opinion may be either that the financial statements taken as a whole are fairly stated when they are not, or that they are not fairly stated when they are.[1] For practical reasons, auditors

---

[1]Statement on Auditing Standards No. 47, *Audit Risk and Materiality in Conducting an Audit* (AU Section 312), defines audit risk as "the risk that the auditor may unknowingly fail to appropriately modify his opinion on financial statements that are materially misstated." Even though this definition does not include the risk that the auditor might erroneously conclude that the financial statements are materially misstated when they are not, it logically follows that the auditor should obtain sufficient evidence to give the proper opinion in all circumstances.

are particularly attuned to the risk of issuing a "clean" opinion on materially misstated financial statements. Issuing a qualified or an adverse opinion on fairly stated financial statements is considered unlikely, because client concern over the adverse consequences of such opinions normally leads to a protracted study and investigation that would probably clear up the misperception before the auditor issued such an opinion. Nevertheless, both aspects of overall audit risk have cost implications for auditors.[2]

Overall audit risk is the combination of the various audit risks for each assertion related to each account balance or group of account balances. Considering overall audit risk in relation to the financial statements taken as a whole is usually impracticable. It ordinarily is practicable, however, to consider audit risk for particular assertions associated with particular account balances, groups of account balances, or related classes of transactions, because they are likely to have different patterns of risk, and the auditing procedures applied to them are likely to have different relative costs.

The primary objective in engagement management is limiting the audit risk in individual balances or classes of transactions so that, at the completion of the audit, overall audit risk is limited to a level sufficiently low—or conversely, that the level of assurance is sufficiently high—to permit the auditor to express an opinion on the financial statements taken as a whole. A secondary objective is to achieve the desired assurance as efficiently as possible.

Many attempts have been made to develop mathematically based risk assessment models, but there is no requirement that audit risk or its components (discussed later) be quantified. In fact, it may not be practicable to objectively quantify certain components of audit risk because of the large number of variables affecting them and the subjective nature of many of those variables. Accordingly, many auditors do not attempt to assign specific values to risk factors. The auditor should always consider audit risk for each assertion related to each significant account or class of transactions.

The Components of Audit Risk

Audit risk at the account-balance or class-of-transactions level has the following two major components for each assertion:

- The risk (consisting of inherent risk and control risk) that misstatements (from either errors or irregularities) that are material, either individually or in the aggregate, are contained within the financial statements. *Inherent risk* is the susceptibility of an account balance or a class of transactions to

[2]SAS No. 47 (footnote to AU Section 312.02) notes that

> In addition to audit risk, the auditor is also exposed to loss or injury to his professional practice from litigation, adverse publicity, or other events arising in connection with financial statements that he has audited and reported on. This exposure is present even though the auditor has performed his audit in accordance with generally accepted auditing standards and has reported appropriately on those financial statements. Even if an auditor assesses this exposure as low, he should not perform less extensive procedures than would otherwise be appropriate under generally accepted auditing standards.

Audit exposure is one aspect of the business risk an accountant faces in accepting any engagement to perform professional services.

material misstatements, without consideration of the control structure. *Control risk* is the risk that the client's control structure policies and procedures will not prevent or detect material misstatements on a timely basis.

- The risk (called *detection risk*) that misstatements that are material, either individually or in the aggregate, in the financial statements will not be detected by the auditor's substantive tests (including both tests of details and analytical procedures).

Inherent and control risks differ from detection risk in that the auditor can only assess them but cannot control them. The auditor's assessment of inherent and control risks leads to a better understanding of them, but does not reduce or otherwise change them. The auditor can, however, control detection risk by varying the nature, timing, and extent of specific substantive tests.

Inherent Risk.   Financial statement misstatements may be caused by a condition (referred to in this book as an "inherent risk condition") that exists at the macroeconomic, industry, or company level or by a characteristic of an account balance or a class of transactions (referred to in this book as an "inherent risk characteristic"). The auditor's understanding of inherent risk conditions and characteristics comes from knowing the client's business and industry, performing analytical procedures, studying prior years' audit results, and understanding the entity's transactions, their flow through the accounting system, and the account balances they generate.

Inherent Risk Conditions.   Some aspects of inherent risk are not limited to specific transactions or accounts but stem from factors outside the entity that are related to its business environment. These *inherent risk conditions* usually cannot be controlled by the enterprise; they include changes in general business conditions, new governmental regulations, and other economic factors. Examples of the latter are a declining industry characterized by bankruptcies, other indications of financial distress, and a lack of financial flexibility, which might either affect the realization of assets or incurrence of liabilities, or influence client management or other personnel to deliberately misstate financial statements. Conversely, overrapid expansion (with or without concomitant demand) can create quality failures resulting in potential sales returns or unsalable inventory.

The audit objectives most likely to be affected by inherent risk conditions are valuation, rights and obligations, and presentation and disclosure. Certain inherent risk conditions might have such a pervasive effect on the client's financial statements as a whole as to warrant special audit attention. For example, a severe recession might lead to substantial doubt about a company's ability to continue to operate as a going concern. The auditor's responsibility in this situation is described in Chapter 22.

While inherent risk conditions cannot be controlled by the enterprise, the control environment set by management (the "tone at the top") can help ensure that the financial statements reflect the underlying economic realities that those conditions create. In addition, the client may establish special control procedures or perform special year-end procedures in response to inherent risk conditions. Examples include special reviews of inventory obsolescence or the provision for uncollectible accounts receivable.

Inherent Risk Characteristics.   Other aspects of inherent risk are peculiar to the specific class of transactions or account being audited (i.e., they are *characteristics* of the transaction or account). The risk of errors or irregularities is greater for some classes of transactions or accounts than others. In general, transactions that require considerable accounting judgment by the client are more likely to produce errors. Similarly, some assets are more susceptible to theft than others; cash is more prone to misappropriation than are steel beams. Account balances derived from accounting estimates are more likely to be misstated than account balances composed of more factual data. The characteristics of accounts with generic titles differ from one company to another and even within a company. For example, not all inventories are the same. Consequently, in assessing risk, the auditor considers the characteristics of the specific items underlying the particular account. In some instances the auditor is mainly concerned with whether the inventory exists, while in other situations the auditor might be more concerned with its valuation.

Inherent risk characteristics should be, and usually are, addressed by the entity's control structure. If so, and if, based on efficiency considerations, the auditor plans to test the effectiveness of control structure policies or procedures, then the assessment of the inherent risk characteristics becomes inseparable from the assessment of control risk, and only a joint assessment of the two is useful. For example, the auditor may determine in planning the audit that an asset (such as cash) with characteristics (liquidity and transferability) that make it extremely prone to theft is nevertheless subject to extremely effective control structure policies and procedures. In effect, the enterprise has designed specific policies and procedures in light of the asset's characteristics. In this environment the auditor may find it efficient to test how well the policies and procedures are designed and operating. If they are effective, the auditor may then be able to assess the risk of misappropriation—and thus the risk of a financial statement misstatement—as low.

Control Risk.   There are likely to be errors in the accounting process that the client does not detect because no affordable control structure can be 100 percent effective. Therefore, some risk is normally associated with every control structure; effective structures carry a relatively lower risk, less effective structures, a relatively higher risk.

The auditor may be able to assess control risk as low by determining whether the policies and procedures an enterprise applies to transactions and balances have been appropriately designed and testing whether they are operating effectively. If those tests indicate that appropriately designed policies and procedures are operating effectively, the auditor will be able to conclude that the risk of misstatement occurring is low.

Some assertions and some transactions and balances are not specifically addressed—either intentionally or otherwise—by the client's control structure. For example, discretionary bonuses and unusual transactions may not be subject to control procedures; in addition, management override of control procedures is always possible. If control risk for transactions or accounts is at the maximum—either because the transactions or accounts are not specifically addressed by the control structure or because the auditor does not plan, for reasons of efficiency or otherwise, to seek evidence to support an assessment below the maximum—the risk of misstatement occurring is determined by inherent risk only.

Detection Risk.   Detection risk is the possibility that misstatements, in a cumulatively material amount, will go undetected by both analytical procedures and substantive tests of details. Since analytical procedures and substantive tests of details complement each other, the assurance derived from one reduces proportionately the assurance the auditor needs from the other to reduce detection risk to the desired level. In other words, the risks associated with them are multiplicative, as the following illustrates. As a conceptual exercise—recalling that it is not practicable to try to assign specific values to the various risk factors—suppose an auditor performs no substantive tests of details or analytical procedures. If there is an error in the financial statements, there is a 100 percent chance that it will not be detected (detection risk is 100 percent). On the other hand, if both substantive tests of details and analytical procedures are performed and there is a 40 percent risk that analytical procedures will not detect cumulatively material misstatements and a 20 percent risk that substantive tests of details will not detect them, the chance that neither procedure will detect the error is the product of 40 percent and 20 percent—8 percent. For a misstatement in the financial statements to go undetected by the auditor, both substantive tests of details and analytical procedures must fail to detect it.

Summary of the Risk Model

The components of overall audit risk and of audit risk associated with specific accounts and specific assertions are summarized in Figure 6.1. For a given desired level of audit risk, the acceptable level of detection risk varies inversely with the auditor's assessment of the risk of material misstatement occurring. That is, the higher the perceived risk of material irregularities or errors, the more assurance the auditor needs from substantive tests (i.e., the lower the acceptable level of detection risk) to achieve a specified (presumably low) level of audit risk, and vice versa. Similarly, given the assurance desired from substantive tests, the assurance the auditor needs from substantive tests of details will vary inversely with the assurance obtained from analytical procedures. In high-risk situations where a great deal of assurance is needed, the auditor may choose to perform a combination of tests of details and analytical procedures aimed at the same accounts and assertions.

Various combinations of audit effort devoted to risk assessment activities, analytical procedures, and substantive tests of details can restrict audit risk to the same low level, but some combinations will be more efficient (i.e., less costly) than others. Based on his or her expectations about inherent and control risks, the auditor formulates an audit strategy that will, in a cost-effective manner, provide sufficient competent evidence to (1) confirm those expecta-

Figure 6.1   Basic Audit Risk Components

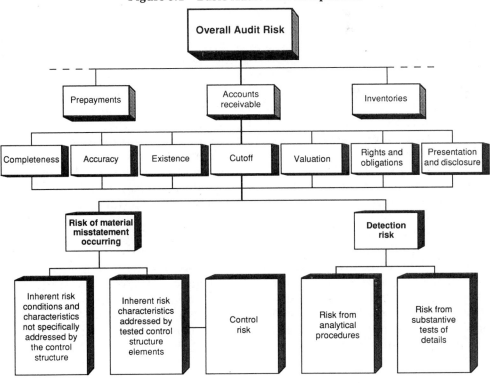

tions about inherent and control risk, and (2) reduce detection risk sufficiently to achieve a low level of audit risk.

Before issuing an unqualified opinion, the auditor should be satisfied that *overall* audit risk is appropriately low. In considering overall audit risk, the individual audit risks for the various account balances and assertions should be combined. To date, however, no single, simple, generally agreed-on mathematical approach to combining these risks has been developed. Nor has the profession been able to agree on what an appropriately low level of overall risk is. While the auditor may at times think in quantitative terms when considering alternative audit strategies and assessing risk, risk management ultimately requires seasoned judgment based on experience, training, and business sense. The way the audit results of each component of the financial statements are combined depends on how the auditor apportions materiality and combines risk. Normative models for apportioning materiality and combining risk for the financial statements taken as a whole have been a subject of academic research for some years, but do not seem likely to yield practical benefits in the foreseeable future.

MATERIALITY

A concept of materiality is a practical necessity in both auditing and accounting. Allowing immaterial items to complicate and clutter up the auditing process or financial statements is uneconomical and diverts users' attention from significant matters in the financial statements. Materiality judgments influence audit planning and, in the evaluation of audit results, are critical to determining whether the financial statements are fairly presented. Inherent in rendering an audit opinion is the recognition that financial statements cannot "precisely" or "exactly" present financial position, results of operations, and cash flows. Such precision is unattainable because of limitations in the accounting measurement process and constraints imposed by the audit process and auditing technology, as discussed in Chapter 1. Since 1988, the wording of the standard auditor's report has explicitly recognized this by stating that the financial statements are presented fairly, in all material respects.

Materiality is "the magnitude of an omission or misstatement of accounting information that, in the light of surrounding circumstances, makes it probable that the judgment of a reasonable person relying on the information would have been changed or influenced by the omission or misstatement" (FASB Statement of Financial Concepts No. 2, *Qualitative Characteristics of Accounting Information*). Ultimately, the user of financial statements determines what is material. There are many users, however, including enterprise management, shareholders, creditors, audit committees, financial analysts, investors, and labor unions, and each may have a different view of what is important. Investors rely on information to assess long-term prospects such as trends of cash flows and income; short-term creditors focus more on asset liquidity in the immediate future.

SEC Regulation S-X (Rule 1–02) defines "materiality" as follows:

> The term "material," when used to qualify a requirement for the furnishing of information as to any subject, limits the information required to those matters about which an average prudent investor ought reasonably to be informed.

This definition has been reinforced by court decisions such as the *BarChris* case[3] in which the judge clearly indicated that the materiality issue involved amounts he believed would motivate the "average prudent investor," not the average banker or security analyst. In developing a standard of materiality for a particular situation, other court cases refer to the "reasonable shareholder"[4]; FASB Concepts Statement No. 2, to the "reasonable person"; and an American Accounting Association publication,[5] to the "informed investor." Thus, the consensus seems to be that materiality is determined by the user, who may be informed, but is not necessarily sophisticated, about financial statements.

Materiality has both qualitative and quantitative aspects. A financial statement misstatement may be quantitatively immaterial, but may nevertheless warrant disclosure in the financial statements. SAS No. 47, *Audit Risk and Materiality in Conducting an Audit* (AU Section 312.07), cites as an example "an

---

[3]*Escott v. BarChris Construction Corp.*, 283 F. Supp. 643 (S.D.N.Y. 1968).

[4]For example, *TSC Industries v. Northway, Inc.*, 44 U.S.L.W. 4852 (1976).

[5]*Accounting and Reporting Standards for Corporate Financial Statements* (Evanston, IL: American Accounting Association, 1957).

illegal payment of an otherwise immaterial amount [that] could be material if there is a reasonable possibility that it could lead to a material contingent liability or a material loss of revenue." Moreover, such matters may have broad implications regarding the integrity of management, and thus may warrant further investigation. The auditor may need to assess the possible pervasiveness of the problem, reassess the effectiveness of the control structure, and report the findings to appropriate company officials. Similarly, qualitatively innocuous mistakes in the form of small unintentional errors can add up to quantitatively material dollar misstatements that would cause the auditor to qualify the opinion if adjustments were not made to the accounts. Materiality judgments also influence items that are or should be disclosed without directly affecting the financial statement amounts. Because of the dual influence of qualitative and quantitative factors in determining materiality, the concept is difficult to operationalize, and trying to establish a single, agreed-on quantitative standard is an exercise in futility.

The assessment of materiality takes place throughout an audit, particularly during planning and when evaluating the results of auditing procedures. SAS No. 47 (AU Section 312.10) requires the auditor, in planning an engagement, to consider a "preliminary judgment about materiality levels for audit purposes." That preliminary judgment may include assessments of what constitutes materiality for significant captions in the balance sheet, income statement, and statement of cash flows individually, and for the financial statements taken as a whole. One purpose of this preliminary materiality judgment is to focus the auditor's attention on the more significant financial statement items while he or she is determining the audit strategy. As a practical matter, however, SAS No. 47 indicates that the preliminary judgment about materiality for the financial statements taken as a whole is generally the smallest aggregate level of errors that could be considered material to any one of the financial statements (AU Section 312.12).

As an example of how an auditor might set materiality levels in planning the audit, he or she may consider misstatements aggregating less than $100,000 not to be material to net income, but may establish a higher materiality threshold for misstatements that affect only the balance sheet (such as misclassifications). This would be because the relatively higher magnitude of the balance sheet components might cause the $100,000 to be immaterial to the balance sheet. Similarly, when planning procedures at the line item level (such as receivables or inventories), the auditor must consider that immaterial misstatements in separate line items might aggregate to a material amount. Thus, auditing procedures in one area—for example, receivables—might have to be designed to detect income statement misstatements of much less than $100,000, because of possible misstatements in other areas of the balance sheet. The auditor should consider materiality levels in planning the nature, timing, and extent of all auditing procedures.

To perform an effective and efficient audit, the auditor must continually assess the results of procedures performed and repeatedly reevaluate whether, based on those results, the scope of procedures planned for the various accounts is adequate, or possibly excessive. For example, individually immaterial misstatements of certain expenses may aggregate to a material amount. As audit work progresses, the auditor may find that the individually immaterial misstatements do not offset each other but cause income to be overstated. In these circumstances, the auditor may need to adjust the scope of procedures for the expenses remaining to be examined, to gain assurance that a material aggregate misstatement will be detected if it exists. It may also be necessary to apply additional procedures to areas that have already been audited.

New facts and circumstances may also change the amount the auditor considers material to individual financial statement line items or to the financial statements taken as a whole. For example, if adjustments are made to the accounts during the course of the audit, the parameters the auditor used to determine materiality in the planning stage (e.g., amounts for net income, revenues, and shareholders' equity) may change. By the end of the audit, materiality may be different than at the planning stage. An auditor who does not continually reassess materiality and audit scope as the engagement progresses assumes a greater risk of performing an inefficient or ineffective audit. Materiality assessments and audit planning should be viewed as dynamic rather than static auditing concepts.

To keep track of misstatements discovered through the various tests and procedures performed during an audit and to help in drawing conclusions about their effect on the financial statements, the auditor often maintains a summary of potential audit adjustments. This practice tool assists the auditor in accumulating known misstatements found through audit tests, misstatements based on projections developed from sampling procedures, and misstatements relating to client accounting estimates that the auditor believes are unreasonable. Ordinarily, management adjusts the records for many of the known misstatements. The auditor then considers the effect of the remaining unadjusted items on the financial statements. Sometimes the auditor believes that further adjustments are necessary for an unqualified opinion to be given. The summary also assists in evaluating whether misstatements, if uncorrected, would affect only the balance sheet, only the income statement, or both. The summary of adjustments is discussed in further detail and illustrated in the section on ''Summarizing and Evaluating the Audit Findings'' in Chapter 21.

AUDIT STRATEGY

From the time an engagement is first considered—even before it is accepted—until the results are summarized and evaluated at the end of the engagement, the auditor makes numerous decisions, which collectively constitute the audit strategy for the engagement. Formulating the audit strategy involves making broad-level planning decisions, such as whether to use the work of the client's internal auditors; whether the assistance of a specialist is needed; whether, in the audit of a multilocation or multicomponent client, to vary the locations or components visited each year; and whether to use the work of other independent auditors who have audited any of the client's components. Formulating the audit strategy also involves making detailed decisions about the nature, timing, and extent of auditing procedures for each significant account balance or class of transactions in the financial statements.

Generally, the most significant and sophisticated strategy decision the auditor makes is whether, and to what extent, to perform tests of controls to reduce the assurance needed from substantive tests. This aspect of audit strategy results in an audit testing plan for each account balance and each assertion, based on the auditor's assessment of inherent and control risk.

As indicated in the overview of the audit process in Chapter 5 and explained in detail in Chapter 8, during the risk assessment phase the auditor often performs some tests of controls concurrently with obtaining the required understanding of the control structure. If the results of those tests are positive, the auditor will be able to reduce the amount of assurance needed from substantive tests. After evaluating the results of concurrent tests of controls, the auditor makes a strategy decision about whether to perform additional tests of controls to support a further, significant reduction in substantive tests. Because additional tests of controls require substantial audit effort, performing them is efficient only if they can be expected to support a significant reduction in substantive tests.

Several factors determine the audit testing plan that will most efficiently enable the auditor to achieve the audit objectives related to each account balance. The most important of these is the auditor's assessment of inherent and control risk in the context of materiality. Other factors include

- *The cost of performing specific tests of controls versus the cost of performing specific substantive procedures.* ''Cost'' includes more than simply the number of hours of auditor time; it also involves optimal staff utilization, on-the-job training, and similar factors, as well as the level of client support needed. All of these influence what combination and timing of auditing procedures the auditor will choose. Cost is also affected by the availability of computer resources. Instead of performing tests manually, the auditor may use computer-assisted audit techniques, which are often more cost effective. Chapter 11 discusses using computers to enhance audit effectiveness and efficiency.

- *Prior decisions about the nature, timing, and extent of specific procedures.* For example, if the client wants the audit report shortly after year-end, the auditor might decide to perform substantive tests of details early and then to perform tests of controls and analytical procedures to obtain satisfaction about account balances at year-end. As another example, the decision to use negative rather than positive confirmations may ultimately lead the auditor to confirm more receivables or perform certain analytical procedures, because negative confirmations that are not returned are less conclusive evidence than positive confirmations.

- *Client expectations about the auditor's consideration of the control structure.* In setting the audit strategy, the auditor should consider whether additional responsibilities arise from requests of the client (e.g., a request for a review of the control structure beyond what the auditor believes is required for planning the audit), or because the company is subject to special regulatory or other requirements.

- *The auditor's ability to obtain corroborating evidence from outside the accounting system.* For example, the auditor may be able to obtain reliable information from operating personnel directly involved in sales or purchasing activities, or from knowledgeable third parties.

Audit strategy decisions are normally made by experienced staff members because such decisions require a high degree of professional judgment; approval of the audit testing plan should rest with the partner.

Audit strategy documentation varies in form and substance among auditing firms. As discussed in detail in Chapter 8, professional standards require the auditor to document his or her understanding of the control structure elements and the assessment of control risk. In addition, the auditor normally documents the understanding of the client's business, the assessment of inherent risk conditions, judgments about materiality, and the audit strategy adopted for major account balances and classes of transactions in the financial statements. Many auditors incorporate other materials in the planning section of the working papers, for example, detailed time budgets, the audit timetable, and certain audit-related correspondence such as communications with internal auditors.

PLANNING AND CONTROLLING THE AUDIT

Audit planning and control are essential to managing an engagement so that it both meets generally accepted auditing standards and is performed efficiently and within the client's time constraints.

Implementation Planning

Planning is the process of implementing the audit strategy decisions. Planning takes place throughout the audit, especially during the risk assessment activities and when the auditor develops the audit testing plan and formalizes it in a detailed audit program. The activities involved in planning the audit and the order in which they are done vary with the engagement; often the various activities overlap.

The auditor should establish a timetable for completing the principal segments of the engagement. The timetable sets forth the planned audit work and provides a way of controlling the engagement. The client's scheduling requirements should be considered in establishing the timetable.

The auditor should then prepare an audit program listing the detailed procedures to be undertaken on the engagement. The audit program is the basis for the detailed time and expense budgets. Preliminary budgets are sometimes prepared based on the initial audit activities and certain risk assessments, and revised, if necessary, when the audit strategy is finalized. Budgets help keep the work within the client's and the auditor's time requirements and are the basis for establishing the audit fee. The budgets should cover all the different tasks and levels of personnel to be employed on the engagement. They should be sufficiently detailed so that staff members can complete tasks in relatively short periods and thereby manage their time efficiently. The complexity of audits of multilocation and multinational companies makes detailed time and expense budgets critical to the timely and efficient conduct of those engagements. Both during the field work and at the end of the audit, time or expense overruns should be evaluated. If they were caused by inefficiencies, the evaluation can help ensure that they will not be repeated in the following year. If overruns were caused by the discovery of client errors or irregularities, the evaluation serves as a reminder to the auditor to determine that the matter has been properly disposed of. Finally, the evaluation helps ensure that next year's budget will be realistic, and also promotes more efficient use of staff.

Personnel for the engagement must be identified and assigned. In assigning people to a particular engagement, the manager and partner generally consider: how technically complex the engagement is and whether it calls for industry expertise; the continuity of the engagement team; personnel career development; and staff commitments to other engagements. Staff availability and cost considerations sometimes lead to adjustments in the timing of certain procedures and other strategy decisions.

If the client uses computers in significant accounting applications, the audit team may need specialized audit skills. AU Section 311.10 specifies that if the work of a professional with such skills (whether a member of the audit team or an outside professional) is used, the auditor must have sufficient computer-related knowledge to communicate audit objectives to that professional, evaluate whether the procedures he or she applies meet the auditor's objectives, and determine how the results of those procedures affect the nature, timing, and extent of other planned auditing procedures. A computer audit professional who is a member of the audit team requires the same supervision and review as any other member.

Personnel to whom work is delegated should be told what their responsibilities are, what objectives their procedures are meant to achieve, and when their work should be completed within the overall audit timetable. They should also be informed about matters that may affect the nature, timing, and extent of auditing procedures, such as the nature of the client's business and potential accounting and auditing problems. The audit plan should be communicated to the audit team, including other offices involved in the engagement. The principal auditor should establish communication links with other independent auditors involved in the engagement. Timetables, procedures to be performed, and the type of report the principal auditor needs should be communicated early in the audit.

The auditor usually should discuss the general audit strategy with the client's management. Some planning details (e.g., when to observe inventory, what schedules and analyses the client's staff should prepare, and what other ways client personnel can assist the auditor; and considering using the work of internal auditors) will almost inevitably need to be discussed and agreed on beforehand.

Using the Work of Internal Auditors

In some companies, the internal audit department operates with few or no restrictions and reports to the board of directors or audit committee on a wide range of matters. In other companies, the department may be limited in its duties and may not enjoy organizational independence. Internal audit departments can operate in a variety of ways. They may

- Perform specific control procedures, focusing heavily on activities like surprise cash counts and inventory counts.
- Function essentially parallel with the external audit function as described in this book, examining and evaluating control structure policies and procedures and substantiating account balances.
- Have broad responsibility for evaluating compliance with company policies and practices.
- Conduct performance audits, which are described in Chapter 2, in addition to financial and compliance audits.
- Work on special projects or be responsible for specific aspects of the control structure.

SAS No. 55 (AU Section 319.09) categorizes the internal audit function as part of the control environment, specifically, one of management's ways of monitoring whether the other aspects of the control structure—the accounting system and internal control procedures—are appropriately designed and operating effectively. For example, an entity may have a control procedure that calls for an employee to perform bank reconciliations. The internal auditor might evaluate how well the reconciliation process is designed and whether it is effectively performed by the employee, and report on it to management. In some organizations, internal auditors perform the reconciliations as part of their review of cash disbursements procedures; although not an internal audit function, this enhances the control environment by formalizing separation of duties.

As part of obtaining an understanding of the control structure as required by SAS No. 55, the external auditor considers the activities performed by the internal auditors to determine whether their work is related to areas of interest to the external auditor and whether he or she can use that work in assessing control risk.[6] In making that determination, the external auditor should first obtain an understanding of the operation of the internal audit function. The principal matters considered in obtaining that understanding are

- The standing and responsibilities of the person(s) to whom the head of internal audit reports and the resulting objectivity of internal audit personnel.

---

[6]SAS No. 9, *The Effect of an Internal Audit Function on the Scope of the Independent Audit* (AU Section 322), provides guidance on the factors that affect the external auditor's consideration of the work of internal auditors. At the time of this writing, the Auditing Standards Board is considering whether SAS No. 9 should be revised. The guidance presented in this section reflects the authors' views on how SAS No. 9 should be applied in light of subsequent SASs, including SAS No. 47 (AU Section 312) and SAS No. 55.

- The responsibilities assigned to the internal auditors. These responsibilities are frequently set forth in an internal audit department charter.
- The size and professional competence of the internal audit department, taking into consideration the complexity of the control structure. For example, if the circumstances require tests of general computer control procedures, the internal auditors should have an adequate knowledge of computer audit techniques. Hiring, training, advancement, assignment, and consultation practices of the internal audit function also should be considered.
- The extent of supervision and review of work. For example, the work carried out by the internal auditors should be supervised by senior internal audit personnel.
- The extent, if any, to which the internal auditors' access to records, documentation, and personnel is restricted.
- The adequacy of the evidence of the work done by the internal auditors.
- The nature, timing, and extent of the internal audit coverage.
- The nature and frequency of, and response to, reports issued by the internal auditors.

If, based on the understanding, the external auditor believes that it may be possible to use the work of the internal auditors, he or she should seek additional evidence of the effectiveness of that work. This usually involves reviewing internal audit working papers and related reports with respect to the internal control structure to determine whether the internal auditors' work appears to be adequately supervised and appears to support the external auditor's assessment of the internal audit function and the role it plays in the control structure.

If the external auditor concludes that he or she can use the internal auditors' work in assessing control risk, the following techniques may enhance the efficiency of the audit effort:

- Preparing integrated audit testing plans.
- Exchanging reports.
- Holding regularly scheduled coordination meetings.
- Granting free and open access to each other's working papers.
- Providing the internal auditors with audit software and training, or requesting that the internal auditors write computer programs for the external auditor's use.
- Making joint presentations to the audit committee or the board of directors.
- Adopting common documentation techniques and establishing common user files.

Using the Work of a Specialist

In considering evidence to corroborate management's assertions, an auditor may occasionally encounter a matter that requires special expertise. The auditor cannot be expected to have or develop the expertise of a person in another profession or occupation, and may thus decide to arrange for a specialist to help obtain competent evidential matter. The need to do so should be established in the planning stage of the audit, so that the necessary arrangements can be made on a timely basis.

Specialists may be used on a recurring basis or only for special matters. An actuary will ordinarily be engaged to perform certain calculations in determining pension plan costs. An appraiser may be used to establish fair market value of real estate collateralizing bank loans. Lawyers may be used as specialists in matters outside of litigation, claims, or assessments. Petroleum engineers may be used to estimate oil reserves, and gemologists to appraise precious gems.

The auditor should be satisfied with the competence, reputation, and standing of the specialist in the particular field. The specialist's competence may be demonstrated by professional certification, license, or other formal recognition. Peers or others familiar with the specialist's work may be able to vouch for the individual's reputation and standing.

As indicated in paragraph 6 of SAS No. 11, *Using the Work of a Specialist* (AU Section 336.06), the "work of a specialist unrelated to the client will usually provide the auditor with greater assurance of reliability because of the absence of a relationship that might impair objectivity." The auditor should take steps to ascertain the nature of any relationship the specialist may have with the client. Specialists are not required to be "independent" in the same sense as auditors are; however, the auditor must evaluate whether any relationship is material. If the specialist has a relationship with the client that might impair the specialist's objectivity, the auditor should consider performing additional procedures with respect to some or all of the specialist's assumptions, methods, or findings to determine that the findings are not unreasonable.

The work of a specialist may be used as an auditing procedure to obtain competent evidential matter, but it is not sufficient in itself. Additional auditing procedures must be performed to meet the requirements of particular circumstances. The procedures should not duplicate any of the specialist's work, but are generally needed to corroborate accounting data the client provides to the specialist. The specialist is responsible for the appropriateness, reasonableness, and application of any methods or assumptions used. The auditor must understand the methods or assumptions used, however, to determine whether the specialist's findings are suitable for corroborating the related information in the financial statements. The auditor is not required to conclude that the specialist's findings are reasonable, but only that they are not unreasonable. For example, an appraisal of real estate owned may indicate a 25 percent increase in fair market value over the previous year. This finding would appear to be unreasonable if current market conditions generally indicated a decline in values of comparable real estate during the same period. An auditor who believes that the specialist's findings are unreasonable should perform additional procedures, including inquiry of the specialist.

If the auditor is not able to resolve a matter after performing additional procedures, he or she should consider obtaining the opinion of another specialist. An unresolved matter will result in a qualified opinion or a disclaimer of opinion because the inability to obtain sufficient competent evidential matter constitutes a scope limitation (paragraphs 40 and 41 of SAS No. 58, *Reports on Audited Financial Statements* [AU Sections 508.40 and .41]). The auditor should not mention the work or findings of a specialist when expressing an unqualified opinion on financial statements.

Rotating Audit Emphasis

If the auditor has assessed the control environment as highly effective, it may be practical to rotate the audit emphasis from year to year and limit the number of locations where auditing procedures are performed in a specific engagement. This strategy may enhance audit efficiency and make a complex engagement (such as a multilocation audit) less costly. The way to accomplish this varies with the circumstances of the engagement. The auditor must ensure, however, that each year's audit work is adequate to support a conclusion on the fairness of the financial statements for that year. Subject to audit risk considerations, auditors may vary both the locations visited and the strategies employed at various locations. In a large multilocation engagement, often only a few, if any, locations are individually material to a specific account balance or class of transactions. For example, a retail chain store operation might consist of 300 separate stores of varying size, none of which is individually material to the enterprise in terms of its sales volume or inventory.

Using the Work of Other Auditors

In reporting on the financial statements of a company or group of companies, an auditor may use the work and report of other auditors who have audited one or more components (subsidiaries or divisions) of the entity. Other auditors may also be used to carry out part of an engagement on grounds of efficiency. Physical distance and language barriers among components of an entity may also be overcome most economically through these arrangements. When more than one auditor is involved in the engagement, one usually serves as principal auditor. Determining who is the principal auditor involves considering what proportion of the entire engagement each auditor performs and the auditor's overall knowledge of the engagement.

Even though each auditor has individual responsibility for the work performed and the opinion rendered, the principal auditor should apply certain procedures in order to be able to use another auditor's report and express an opinion on the overall financial statements. SAS No. 1 (AU Section 543) contains guidelines about what procedures should be performed. They include inquiring about the other auditor's professional reputation and ascertaining that the other auditor is independent; is aware of the intended use of the financial statements and report; is familiar with GAAP, GAAS, and other (e.g., SEC) reporting requirements; and has been informed about matters affecting the elimination of intercompany transactions and the uniformity of accounting principles among the components. In some circumstances, the principal auditor may review the other auditor's audit programs or working papers, read summaries of the work performed and conclusions reached by the other auditor, or attend key meetings between the other auditor and management. The principal auditor may also visit the other auditor's premises or obtain written representations about various matters. The need for such steps should be considered early in the planning process and continually reviewed during the engagement. When another auditor's work is used, the opinion may or may not refer to the other auditor's involvement. That issue is discussed in Chapter 22, "The Auditor's Report."

Using a Report on Internal Control at a Service Organization

A client may use a service organization, such as a data processing center, to record certain transactions, process data, or even execute transactions and maintain the related accounting records and assets such as securities. Transactions may flow through an accounting system that is, wholly or partially, separate from the client's organization, and the auditor may find it necessary or efficient in understanding and assessing the client's control structure to consider procedures performed at the service organization. To do that, the auditor may obtain a report prepared by the service organization's auditor covering aspects of internal control at the service organization.

SAS No. 44, *Special-Purpose Reports on Internal Accounting Control at Service Organizations* (AU Section 324), provides guidance on the auditor's use of a special-purpose report of another independent auditor on internal control at a service organization. In deciding whether to obtain such a report, the auditor considers both the nature of the procedures the service organization provides and their relationship to the client's control structure.

The service organization may both record significant classes of client transactions and process related data. In that situation, the auditor often considers it necessary, in order to obtain a sufficient understanding of the flow of transactions and to plan substantive tests, to obtain a report prepared by the service organization's auditor on the *design* of its internal control structure. If accounting and control procedures located at the service organization are essential to achieve one or more of the client's control objectives, and the auditor seeks to assess control risk at less than the maximum, he or she will find it necessary to obtain a report from the service organization's auditor about the *effectiveness* of its control structure or specific control procedures therein as well. In these circumstances, the auditor should assess control risk based on the combination of control structure policies and procedures of both the client and the service organization.

If the service organization executes transactions and maintains the related accounts, the client will be unable to maintain independent records of the transactions. In these circumstances, the auditor will need either to obtain a report from the service organization's auditor about the effectiveness of the control structure as a basis for evaluating whether relevant control objectives have been achieved, or to apply (or ask the service organization's auditor to apply) substantive tests at the service organization in order to meet the related audit objectives.

The decision to use a report on the service organization's internal control, along with appropriate inquiries and other steps necessary to implement that decision, should be made during the planning phase of the audit. Reporting considerations when a service organization's auditor's report is used are discussed in Chapter 23. SAS No. 44 also provides guidance on the responsibilities of the auditor who issues a report on internal control at a service organization. See Chapter 23 for further discussion.

Controlling the Engagement

Supervision and review are essential parts of managing an engagement. The partner is ultimately responsible for forming and expressing an opinion on the financial statements and cannot delegate this responsibility. The manager or other experienced individual is usually responsible for supervising and monitoring the work done to ensure that it is in accordance with the audit testing plan. Supervision also entails comparing the completed work with established timetables and budgets, training and coaching, and identifying differences in professional judgment among personnel and referring them to the appropriate level for resolution, as well as directly reviewing the work performed. The work done by each member of the audit team is supervised, reviewed, and approved by another, more experienced member. Queries raised during the review process should be followed up and resolved before completing the engagement and issuing the audit opinion.

7

The Internal Control Structure

An enterprise's internal control structure comprises three elements: the control environment, the accounting system, and control procedures. Each of these elements consists of policies, procedures, methods, and records designed by management to safeguard its assets, generate reliable financial information, promote operational efficiency, and encourage adherence to prescribed managerial policies. Collectively, the elements of the internal control structure operate within an enterprise to reduce its unintended exposure to business, financial, and accounting risks.

RELEVANCE OF AN ENTITY'S INTERNAL CONTROL STRUCTURE TO AN AUDIT

The auditor's responsibility regarding a client's internal control structure is formalized in the second standard of field work, stated in paragraph 1 of Statement on Auditing Standards No. 55, *Consideration of the Internal Control Structure in a Financial Statement Audit* (AU Section 319), as follows:

> A sufficient understanding of the internal control structure is to be obtained to plan the audit and to determine the nature, timing, and extent of tests to be performed.

In addition, as discussed in Chapter 6, the auditor assesses control risk to determine the acceptable level of detection risk with respect to financial statement assertions related to account balances. (Those assertions are described in Chapter 5.) For some assertions, the auditor will assess control risk at the maximum level, but is often able to assess it at below the maximum by performing tests that provide evidence that the control structure is designed and operating effectively. The auditor can then limit the substantive tests applied to account balances for those assertions. For example, if the auditor is satisfied, based on the results of tests performed in assessing control risk related to revenue, that control procedures applied to sales transactions are adequate to ensure that all authorized shipments of products, and only authorized shipments, are accurately billed and recorded, the auditor can reduce the substantive tests related to the completeness, accuracy, and existence of sales and the related charges to accounts receivable.

An entity establishes internal control structure policies and procedures for a variety of reasons, only some of which may be relevant to an audit of its financial statements. In general, the policies and procedures that are relevant to an audit concern the entity's ability to record, process, summarize, and report financial information consistent with the assertions embodied in the financial statements. Other policies and procedures, however, may also be relevant to an audit if they are related to information the auditor uses in performing auditing procedures, even though the information itself is not part of the financial statements. An example might be policies and procedures related to production statistics that are used by the auditor in certain analytical procedures.

Still other control structure policies and procedures are not relevant to an audit of financial statements, but relate to the effectiveness and efficiency of certain management decision-making processes. Although auditors have no responsibility to do so, they often report deficiencies in such policies and procedures as a client service, when they become aware of them in the course of an audit. For example, an auditor who noticed that the monthly sales analysis used by management was prepared from an ancillary system that did not include all adjustments made in the general ledger might suggest that the client reexamine how the sales analysis is prepared.

AN OVERVIEW OF THE CONTROL STRUCTURE

Internal control structure policies and procedures can generally be classified into three elements—the control environment, the accounting system, and control procedures.[1] Whether individual control structure policies and procedures are relevant to an audit is determined not by what category they fall in, but by whether they affect, directly or indirectly, financial statement assertions or the auditor's ability to form judgments about those assertions.

The *control environment* comprises the attitudes, abilities, awareness, and actions of an enterprise's personnel, especially its management, as they affect the overall operation and control of the business. In the words of the National Commission on Fraudulent Financial Reporting (Treadway Commission), it is the "tone at the top." The control environment represents the collective effect of various factors (described in detail later) on the effectiveness of specific control structure policies and procedures. Management's actions in enforcing the company's code of conduct, for example, would be one aspect of the control environment.

The *accounting system* consists of the procedures established to identify, assemble, classify, analyze, and record an entity's transactions, as well as the documents produced as a result of those procedures. These procedures and documents help management operate the business effectively and enable it to prepare proper financial statements. For example, the way in which a purchase transaction is recorded and posted to ledger accounts is part of the accounting system.

Control procedures are the policies and procedures, in addition to those that are part of the control environment and accounting system, that have been established to provide reasonable assurance that the entity's objectives regarding the processing of transactions, the preservation of related data on files, and the safeguarding (or protection) of assets will be achieved. While control procedures are conceptually separate from the control environment and accounting system, they may at times be integrated into various components of the latter two elements. For example, recording a sale of merchandise based on a prenumbered invoice is a procedure that is part of the accounting system. Accounting for the numerical sequence of the invoices is a control procedure to ensure that all items billed to customers have been recorded.

---

[1]In this book, the term "internal control *structure policies and procedures*" or "control *structure policies and procedures*" will be used to denote the totality of an entity's control structure. In contrast, policies and procedures that constitute the third element of the control structure will be referred to as "control *procedures*."

The Concept of "Reasonable Assurance"

Auditors have long recognized the inherent limitations on the effectiveness of an internal control structure. SAS No. 55 notes the following factors that may reduce or eliminate the effectiveness of the internal control structure:

Misunderstanding of instructions, mistakes of judgment, personal careless-ness, distraction, or fatigue on the part of the person responsible for performing a control procedure.

Collusion among individuals, circumventing control procedures whose effectiveness depends on segregation of duties.

Management override of certain policies or procedures.

In view of these as well as cost limitations, an internal control structure can provide reasonable, but not absolute, assurance that its objectives will be accomplished. This is recognized by SAS No. 55, the Foreign Corrupt Prac-tices Act of 1977 (the Act), and sound financial management. Management will always have to make economic judgments about relative benefits and costs. SAS No. 55 expresses it in this way.

The concept of reasonable assurance recognizes that the cost of an entity's internal control structure should not exceed the benefits that are expected to be derived. Although the cost–benefit relationship is a primary criterion that should be considered in designing an internal control structure, the precise measurement of costs and benefits usually is not possible. Accordingly, manage-ment makes both quantitative and qualitative estimates and judgments in eval-uating the cost–benefit relationship. (AU Section 319.14)

TRANSACTION CYCLES

The approach to the internal control structure described in this book views business activities in terms of "cycles" into which related transactions can be conveniently grouped and for which specific policies and procedures are established by an entity's management.[2]

Each cycle comprises several transaction classes that vary with the opera-tions of a particular business. For example, sales of goods and services, cash receipts, and customer returns may be three distinct transaction classes mak-ing up the revenue cycle. Further, each class of transactions may have two or more subclasses; for instance, sales of goods and services may be subdivided into cash sales and credit sales, or into foreign sales and domestic sales. Transaction classes and subclasses are distinguished from each other primarily by differences in the control structure policies and procedures applied to them.

---

[2]The FASB defines a "transaction" as "an external event involving transfer of something of value . . . between two (or more) entities" (Statement of Financial Accounting Concepts No. 3, para. 77). The term is used more broadly in this book to include all events and circumstances that require accounting recognition. In the context of computerized systems, the term is used even more broadly to encompass any change to the computerized records.

Three major transaction cycles are identified in this book and discussed in detail in Chapters 12 through 14. They are the revenue, buying, and production cycles, and may be described as follows[3]:

Revenue Cycle—Transactions relating to revenue generating and collecting, and related control structure policies and procedures applied to such activities as recording sales orders, shipping, and cash collection.

Buying Cycle—Transactions relating to purchases and payments, and related control structure policies and procedures applied to such activities as ordering and receiving purchases, payroll functions, and cash disbursements.

Production Cycle—Transactions relating to producing goods or services, and related control structure policies and procedures applied to such activities as maintaining inventory balances, inventory transfers, and charges to production for labor and overhead.

The essence of the cycle concept is its focus on whether appropriate control structure policies and procedures are applied to each class of transactions as they flow through the processing system. The auditor considers each transaction class or subclass to determine whether adequate control structure policies and procedures have been designed and are operating effectively to achieve their intended objectives.

CONTROL OBJECTIVES

Control structure policies and procedures that are relevant to an audit are established to meet specific objectives related to

- Processing transactions,
- Preserving the integrity of files on which those transactions and related data are stored, and
- Protecting assets.

Processing Transactions

Five control objectives relate to transaction processing. They are referred to as

Completeness of input—that all transactions that occurred are initially entered into the accounting records and accepted for processing.

Accuracy of input—that transactions are initially recorded at the correct amount, in the appropriate account, and on a timely basis.

---

[3]Other transaction cycles—for example, determining, recording, and paying income taxes—may be identified, if the client has created specific control structure policies and procedures unique to classes of transactions.

Authorization of transactions—that all recorded transactions represent economic events that actually occurred and relate to the organization, and were approved by designated personnel.

Completeness of updating—that the data files and the records and reports generated at each stage of processing reflect all transactions that have occurred.

Accuracy of updating—that transactions are accurately recorded at each stage of their processing.

Maintaining Files

The five objectives outlined above also apply to storing recorded accounting data on files.[4] For ease of reference, in discussing files the above five control objectives have been grouped together and designated as

File control objective—that the transactions and related data contained on a file continue to be complete, accurate, and authorized until they are affected by subsequent transactions that are similarly complete, accurate, and authorized.

Protecting Assets

An additional control objective relates to the safeguarding of assets and is referred to as

Asset protection—that access to assets and to the documents that control their movement and the records of their existence is suitably restricted to authorized personnel.

Conceptually, the seven control objectives fit every enterprise and apply to all transactions into which it enters (and the related files and assets), regardless of the specific control structure policies and procedures established to achieve them. For purposes of this chapter, however, the control objectives will be considered only as they apply to major classes and subclasses of transactions, such as sales, purchases, cash receipts, and cash disbursements. Those are generally the high-volume transactions within transaction cycles; in addition, certain entities may enter into other high-volume transactions, depending on the nature of their business.

In considering how the control objectives apply to classes or subclasses of transactions, the auditor formulates control objectives specific to each class or subclass of transactions. For example, Figure 7.1 identifies the specific control objectives for credit sales transactions processed by computer in the revenue cycle.

Two pervasive aspects of the control structure facilitate achieving the control objectives, namely,

---

[4]A file is an accumulation of transactions or other data and may be in the form of a computerized file or a manual journal or ledger.

Figure 7.1   Control Objectives for Credit Sales Transactions

Control Objective	Specific Control Objective for Credit Sales Transactions in a Computerized Accounting System
Completeness of input	All credit sales transactions are input and accepted for processing.
Accuracy of input	Sales are correctly recorded as to amounts, quantities, dates, and customers in the proper period; are accurately converted into computer-readable form; and are accurately input to the computer.
Authorization of transactions	All recorded sales transactions represent actual shipments of goods or rendering of services to nonfictitious customers of the entity and were approved by responsible personnel.
Completeness of updating	The sales and accounts receivable data files are updated by all sales transaction data input and accepted for processing.
Accuracy of updating	The sales and accounts receivable data files are accurately updated by the data input.
File control	The integrity of both individual accounts receivable in the subsidiary ledger and the general ledger control account, after sales transactions have been accumulated in them, is preserved.
Asset protection	Only authorized personnel have access to accounts receivable records or data stored on files.

- Arrangements to segregate duties so that the same person is not responsible for both accounting or control procedures for a particular transaction and the safeguarding of related assets.
- Arrangements to ensure that employees are adequately supervised.

ELEMENTS OF THE INTERNAL CONTROL STRUCTURE—A CLOSER LOOK

The three elements of the internal control structure and their relevance to an audit are discussed in the following sections. Although all three elements contribute to the achievement of the control objectives, those objectives are generally met more directly by the accounting system and control procedures than by the control environment.

Control Environment

An enterprise's management can foster an environment that encourages maintaining an effective accounting system and control procedures. Such a control environment can have a "significant impact on the selection and effectiveness of a company's . . . control procedures and techniques"[5] and, in accordance with SAS No. 55, is required to be considered in planning an audit engagement.

Knowledge about the control environment enables the auditor to determine (1) whether it appears to be conducive to maintaining an effective accounting system and control procedures, and (2) whether it minimizes the incentives and opportunities for management to deliberately distort the financial statements.

Various factors that affect an enterprise's control environment can have a pervasive effect on the management assertions underlying the financial statements. These factors typically include

1. Management's philosophy and operating style.
2. The organizational structure of the entity.
3. The composition and activities of the board of directors and its committees, particularly the audit committee.
4. Methods of assigning authority and responsibility.
5. The control methods used by management for monitoring and following up on performance, including an internal audit function.
6. The personnel policies and practices of the entity.
7. Various external influences that affect an entity's operations and practices.

The following paragraphs discuss each of these factors and indicate their relevance to the audit.

Management's Philosophy and Operating Style. Management's philosophy and operating style are expressed through its attitudes toward a broad range of matters, including taking business risks, reporting financial information, adhering to an appropriate code of conduct, and achieving financial or operating goals. In addition, management's integrity, which has a pervasive influence on the control environment, is an integral part of its philosophy and operating style. If management is dominated by one or a few individuals, their philosophy and operating style are likely to have a particularly significant influence on the control environment.

Management's attitude about adhering to standards of ethical behavior is reflected in its establishment and enforcement of a formal or informal code of conduct. By demonstrating its own compliance with the code, management sets an example for employees to follow. Management further communicates its expectations by the way it monitors employees' behavior and reacts to violations of the code.

Direct indications of management's philosophy and operating style can often be found in how candidly management discusses matters with the auditor, whether management has previously tried to materially misstate financial

---

[5]*Report of the Special Advisory Committee on Internal Accounting Control* (New York: American Institute of Certified Public Accountants, 1979), p. 12.

information, and whether there are frequent disputes over the application of accounting principles. Management's philosophy and operating style are indirectly reflected in events such as frequent turnover of operating management personnel, which may result from top management's overemphasis on unreasonable operating or financial goals, possibly through tying a significant portion of operating management's compensation to meeting those goals. This type of pressure to meet unreasonable expectations may also encourage management to intentionally misstate financial information.

The attitudes and attributes of management that characterize its philosophy and operating style have a significant impact on both the entity's ability to maintain an effective accounting system and control procedures, and the likelihood of attempts by management to deliberately distort the financial statements. Accordingly, the auditor needs to identify those attitudes and attributes and develop an understanding of them. Because they are subjective, it may take more judgment and experience on the part of the auditor to understand them than any of the other factors.

Organizational Structure.   All business entities have an organizational structure within which their operations are planned, executed, controlled, and monitored. Defining key areas of responsibility and establishing appropriate lines of reporting are significant aspects of the organizational structure. For example, the director of internal audit should report to a higher level than the individuals responsible for the areas under audit. Without the appropriate line of reporting, the internal audit department's work, including recommendations for corrective action, may lack objectivity.

The appropriateness of an entity's organizational structure, for example, whether it is centralized or decentralized, depends, in part, on the size and nature of the entity. A highly structured arrangement, including formal documentation of reporting lines and responsibilities, may be appropriate for a larger entity, but could impede the necessary flow of information and thus be inappropriate in a small entity, such as an owner-operated business. The auditor should judge the effectiveness of the entity's organizational structure in light of the size and nature of the entity.

Composition and Activities of the Board of Directors and Committees.   The effectiveness of the board of directors and committees, especially the audit committee, is an important factor in the control environment. The more effective the board and audit committee are in overseeing the entity's policies and practices, the less likely management is to have the opportunity to misappropriate resources, involve the entity in illegal acts, subject the entity or its assets to inordinate risk, or materially misstate financial information. The effectiveness of the board of directors and audit committee is evidenced by whether board members are independent from management, how frequently the board and the audit committee hold meetings, and how well they analyze relevant accounting and financial information. In addition, the presence of an audit committee that fosters a direct line of communication between the board and the external and internal auditors is a further indication that the board of directors is monitoring management appropriately.

The auditor should consider how effectively the board of directors appears to be overseeing the entity's accounting and financial reporting policies and practices. If the board does not exercise adequate oversight, management may have greater opportunity to override control structure policies and procedures, and thereby render them ineffective. An active and involved audit committee of independent directors, in particular, is often a good indication that management is effectively monitored.

Assigning Authority and Responsibility.   To ensure that the activities of the business are properly carried out, individuals within the organization must have an adequate understanding of their authority and responsibilities. Adequately communicating expectations to personnel and monitoring their achievement help to ensure that the business will be run properly. Ways of doing this in large entities include written codes of conduct, job descriptions, policy bulletins, and operating manuals. In smaller entities, codes of conduct may be implicit in the operating style of the owner-manager. Whether disseminated formally or informally, policies governing the delegation of authority, responsibilities, and reporting relationships must be effectively communicated to employees. As discussed earlier, management's attitude about adhering to these policies is an important aspect of its philosophy and operating style.

Considering whether the appropriate methods are used to assign and communicate authority and responsibilities, including ethical responsibilities, will help the auditor judge whether personnel understand their responsibilities and therefore can be expected to carry them out properly. If management does not effectively communicate its expectations, control structure policies and procedures may not be complied with.

Control Methods Used by Management.   Management uses various methods to monitor the entity's activities, including the performance of individuals in authority and the systems used to process and report information. These methods include establishing an internal audit function that evaluates and reports on the effectiveness of other control structure policies and procedures. Management also exercises control by comparing actual financial and operating results with benchmarks or predetermined expectations and investigating variances. For this aspect of the control environment to be effective, management must also follow up on findings and implement corrective action where needed. Management's follow-up includes identifying the specific activities and individuals affected by the matter in question.

Understanding the process by which management institutes systems for developing and reporting performance and financial information, and reviews the resulting reports, helps the auditor judge whether management is likely to become aware of material misstatements in financial information. In particular, management's comparison of financial data, such as an aged accounts receivable listing, with benchmarks, goals, or expectations based on knowledge of the business may provide the auditor with evidence of how reliable the financial information is. The auditor's identification of those key management reports may also be useful in designing audit tests.

Personnel Policies and Practices.   To operate effectively, the entity needs appropriate policies and procedures to hire, train, supervise, and evaluate employees to ensure that they have sufficient knowledge and experience to carry out their assigned responsibilities. Further, there must be a sufficient number of employees, and the employees must have adequate equipment. The entity's personnel policies and practices should be directed toward achieving those goals. For example, the proper functioning of computer operations and processing depends on EDP personnel with appropriate skills and on adequate computer equipment to meet the entity's processing needs.

If the auditor concludes that the entity's personnel policies and practices appear to be adequate, the personnel who operate the accounting system and apply control procedures are likely to be competent. That, in turn, reduces the likelihood that financial information will contain misstatements.

External Influences.   Outside parties, while generally not subject to management's control, may have an influence on the entity. Management may react to such external influences with a heightened awareness of the need to monitor and report certain entity operations, or by deciding to establish specific control structure policies or procedures. For example, the Securities and Exchange Commission's requirements for quarterly securities counts by broker-dealers may focus management's attention more closely on control procedures relating to securities.

Knowing management is focusing special attention on certain aspects of operations can help the auditor determine what areas are most likely to have effective control structure policies and procedures. On the other hand, knowing the entity is subject to scrutiny by regulatory agencies may cause the auditor to seek additional evidence that relevant control structure policies and procedures are effective.

After considering the factors that contribute to the control environment, the auditor should be able to reach an overall conclusion about whether the environment is conducive to maintaining an effective accounting system and control procedures, and how much it reduces the incentives and opportunities for intentional distortion of the financial statements by management. If the auditor concludes that the control environment is favorable, there is a lower risk that control structure policies and procedures will be overridden or neglected and that misstatements may occur. That conclusion helps the auditor determine the nature, timing, and extent of other auditing procedures. In addition, knowledge about the control environment provides the auditor with certain information that can be helpful in developing the audit testing plan, for example, significant reports and procedures that management uses to control the business.

Accounting System

All active businesses enter into transactions and use resources, and have some form of accounting system consisting of a series of procedures to gather data and to process and record transactions. Such procedures may be performed manually, for example, the manual recording of goods received or the manual calculation of invoices. Accounting procedures may also be performed by computer, for example, the automatic generation of checks to pay suppliers or the computerized preparation of invoices. These computerized accounting procedures are referred to as *programmed accounting procedures*. A computerized system normally comprises a series of both manual and computerized procedures that record transactions from their inception to their entry in the general ledger.

An effective accounting system includes appropriate methods and records to

1. Identify and record all authorized transactions.
2. Describe the transaction on a timely basis, in sufficient detail to classify it properly for financial reporting.
3. Measure the value of the transaction so that its monetary value can be recorded in the financial statements.
4. Determine when the transaction occurred, to ensure that it is recorded in the proper accounting period.
5. Present the transaction and related disclosures properly in the financial statements.

The documents produced by the accounting system provide third parties, management, and employees with information about the processing and recording of transactions. These documents, for example, checks, bills of lading, and accounts receivable aging schedules, are often subject to scrutiny by those users, who may detect errors in the information resulting from the failure of accounting procedures or related control procedures to operate effectively.

Two principal types of data are used by the accounting system, *standing data* (also called *master file data*) and *transaction data*. Standing data is data of a permanent or semipermanent nature that is used repeatedly during processing. Examples are rates of pay used to calculate salaries, and customer credit limits used to decide whether to accept customer orders. Transaction data relates to individual transactions, for example, the number of hours an individual employee worked in a particular week, which is used to calculate that person's salary. Errors in standing data are likely to be of greater significance than errors in transaction data, because errors in standing data will affect many transactions until they are corrected. This is particularly true of computerized systems in which standing data is usually reviewed only when originally set up on files and not each time it is used.

Conceptually, the accounting system is separate from the control procedures that constitute the third element of the control structure. However, it is generally not practical to separate the contribution of the accounting system toward achieving the control objectives from that of the control procedures that are applied to the transactions that flow through the accounting system. That is because the appropriateness of control procedures depends on the attributes of the accounting system, such as the means of processing, volume of transactions, level of sophistication, and so forth. A simple manual accounting system and a sophisticated computerized one may both contribute toward meeting the control objectives, if the control procedures applied to transactions processed by each system are appropriate to that system.

For example, a manual accounting system for processing sales invoices may contribute toward meeting the completeness control objective for sales and accounts receivable if all invoices and shipping documents are prenumbered and the numerical sequence is accounted for; missing or unmatched items are investigated and followed up by persons independent of the shipping and invoicing functions; and supervisory personnel review and approve the performance of the above procedures. For a sophisticated computerized system, appropriate control procedures would generally include computer matching of shipping orders to an outstanding order file and sales transaction file, the generation of an exception report by the computer, and control procedures applied to ensure program and data file security, in addition to follow-up and supervision by responsible personnel. The appropriateness of the control procedures, in each instance, is determined by the attributes of the accounting system.

Control Procedures

In contrast to the policies and procedures that are part of the control environment and accounting system, which relate to all relevant transactions an entity enters into, control procedures are generally established only for high-volume or high-risk classes of transactions. The design of control procedures is influenced by the size, complexity, and nature of the business as well as the nature of the entity's control environment and accounting system, including the method of data processing. For example, for a large entity with a complex data processing environment, it is usually necessary to establish formal approved vendor or customer lists, credit policies, and program and data file security control procedures. For a small entity with a relatively simple data processing environment, such control procedures may not always be considered necessary to meet the control objectives.

Entities meet the control objectives by designing and applying control procedures at various organizational and data processing levels. Some control procedures are applied directly to transactions, files, data, records, and assets. The effectiveness of those control procedures is enhanced if they are routinely overseen or reviewed and if functions are assigned in ways that help protect assets and prevent or detect misstatements in the accounts. In computerized environments, there are control procedures, commonly called general control procedures, that do not relate to specific transactions or files but have a pervasive effect on an entire transaction cycle or more than one cycle, or on the entity as a whole. General control procedures, which are increasingly being referred to by the more descriptive term "information technology control procedures," are discussed in detail in Chapter 11.

As discussed in SAS No. 55, control procedures fall into several broad categories, including, but not limited to

- Proper authorization of transactions and activities.
- Segregation of duties so that a person's opportunity to both perpetrate and conceal errors or irregularities in the normal course of his or her

duties is reduced—for example, assigning the responsibilities for authorizing transactions, recording transactions, and safeguarding assets to different people.

- Design and use of adequate documents and records to help ensure the proper recording of transactions and events, such as monitoring the use of prenumbered shipping documents.
- Adequate safeguards over access to and use of assets and records, such as secured facilities and authorization for access to computer programs and data files.
- Independent (including supervisory) reviews of performance and of the valuation of recorded amounts, such as clerical checks, reconciliations, comparison of assets with recorded amounts, control procedures performed by a computer, management review of reports that summarize the detail of account balances (e.g., an aged trial balance of accounts receivable), and user review of computer-generated reports.

In noncomputerized environments, all control procedures are, of course, performed manually. In computerized environments, certain control procedures are carried out by computer programs. These control procedures are referred to as *programmed control procedures*; an example is the computer matching of purchase invoices with goods received records held on file. To be effective, control procedures must cover the entire processing system from the initial recording of transactions to their ultimate recording and storage in manual ledgers or computer files. In a computerized environment, this requires a combination of programmed control procedures that generate reports, and manual operations that are applied to those reports. For example, before a vendor's invoice is paid on its due date, a computer program may match all open invoices due on that date with the file of open receiving reports. If there is a match, the computer removes both the invoices and the receiving reports from their respective files, puts them into a paid invoice file, and prints out the vendor's check. If there is no match, either because there is no receiving report or because the data on the receiving report differs from the data on the invoice, the computer does not print out the check but instead prints out an "exception report" of invoices due for which no receiving report exists or for which the data on the two documents does not agree. An accounting supervisor reviews and "clears" the exception report by determining that, in fact, the goods have not been received and no receiving report should have been created, or that the data does not otherwise agree and the vendor should not be paid. The computerized matching and the generation of the exception report are programmed control procedures; the review and clearing of the exception report is a manual control procedure. Both operations are necessary for the control objective to be achieved—in this case, that all payments to vendors are authorized.

In computerized systems, computer programs can create certain transactions without specific manual intervention. Examples of computer-generated transactions include

- Automatic posting of standard journal entries during month-end processing.

- Automatic reversal of monthly accrual or prepaid accounts in a subsequent month.
- Automatic payment of recurring operating expenditures (e.g., rents, royalties, etc.).

From a control perspective, the stored (i.e., standing) data that processes those transactions should be complete, accurate, and authorized, and the parameters, conditions, and programs used to initiate the transactions should be appropriately set up and maintained.

As noted earlier, entities design and implement control procedures to ensure that all transactions that actually occurred are authorized and are recorded completely and accurately, that errors in execution or recording are detected as soon as possible (regardless of whether the error is the processing of an unauthorized transaction, the failure to process an authorized one, or the failure to process it accurately), that the integrity of recorded accounting data is preserved on computer files and in ledgers, and that access to assets and related records is restricted. That is, the control procedures ensure that the control objectives of completeness, accuracy, authorization, file control, and asset protection are achieved and reliable financial information is thereby generated. The following paragraphs discuss different ways of achieving those objectives.

Completeness.   *Completeness-of-input* control procedures in a computerized environment are designed to ensure that all transactions are initially input and accepted for processing. The initial recording of transactions frequently involves manual procedures performed before transactions are entered into the computer, although in many on-line systems, transactions are input at terminals as they occur, with no prior manual recording. In a manual system, control procedures are designed to ensure that all transactions that occur are entered on a control document (e.g., a receiving report or shipping advice) and then recorded. Without adequate completeness control procedures, there is a possibility that documents may be lost or misplaced, and this could result in a failure to record transactions that occurred. Regardless of the means of processing, control procedures should be established for correcting and resubmitting rejected items. Examples of control procedures designed to ensure completeness are described below.

- *Numbering all transactions as soon as they originate (or, preferably, prenumbering them) and then accounting for all the transactions after they have been processed.* Numbering documents is an accounting procedure; the control procedure is the act of reviewing to see that all numbered documents complete the expected processing. In a computer-based system, a technique known as a computer sequence check can be used to have the computer ascertain that the sequence of serially numbered documents is maintained and to report missing or duplicate numbers for manual investigation. The possibility of purposeful or accidental errors in the numbering process is reduced if the numerical sequence is printed in advance on the forms. If the risk of error or misuse is not considered significant, the numbering is often originated simultaneously with the document.

- *Determining that all data is processed by using "control totals."* This can be done in a computerized system by batching source documents and controlling batch totals, or in a manual system by totaling the critical numbers for a batch of transactions before and after processing; the assumption is that the processing is correct if the two totals agree. There is, of course, a possibility of one error exactly offsetting another error or omission, but the possibility is slight. Control totals do not provide control in themselves; they provide information for exercising control. The control procedure is comparing two totals and searching out and correcting errors that caused differences. Control totals appear in many forms. The double-entry system provides control totals in the sense that the totals of the debits must always equal the totals of the credits, both in individual entries and in the accounts as a whole.
- *Matching data from different sources.* Examples are computer matching of transactions input to other data within the system (such as matching the receipt of goods to the open purchase order file), and periodic reviews, either manual or by computer, of unmatched documents (such as receiving reports or vendors' invoices) and the investigation of long-outstanding items to ascertain that a document has not been lost in the processing.
- *Determining that all transactions are entered in a register.* For example, in a manual system, all chargeable service hours may be recorded in a service register that is reconciled to the hours that customers are billed for.
- *One-for-one comparison of input with retained source documents.* This technique is often used for standing data in a computerized system, because of the limited volume of changes and the importance of the data. An example is comparing changes in wage rates used to calculate employees' salaries with an approved listing of wage rate changes.

Completeness control procedures are also needed to ensure that information is properly summarized and financial reports are properly prepared for both internal and external purposes. Such control procedures are particularly important if general ledger entries come from sources other than books of original entry. For example, it is relatively easy to ascertain the completeness of postings to the general ledger for sales transactions if the postings are made directly from the summarized totals in the sales journal. A simple review to ensure that there are 12 monthly postings in the general ledger may suffice. If, however, general ledger entries arise from other sources as well, additional control procedures may be needed to ensure that all transactions are summarized and posted. Using standard journal entry numbers, with reviews to determine that all appropriate standard journal entries were made, may facilitate achieving this control objective.

Control procedures that relate to *completeness of updating* in computerized systems are designed to ensure that all transaction data input and accepted for processing updates the appropriate data file. In some cases the completeness-of-input control procedures might also control completeness of updating. Examples are a one-for-one comparison carried out on a report produced after updating or, where updating takes place at the same time as input, a sequence check carried out on an updated file. More commonly, some form of control total is used to ensure completeness of updating. This may include manual batch totals reconciled to updated file totals, or computer-generated totals and control records that report out-of-balance situations. Completeness of updating of computer-generated data should also be controlled, including calculations and summarizations of transaction data that are carried out by programmed accounting procedures as the data is processed. Examples are programmed accounting procedures that calculate sales invoices from a transaction file of goods shipped and that summarize invoices for posting to the accounts receivable control account.

Accuracy. Control procedures are necessary to ensure that each transaction is recorded at the correct amount, in the right account, and on a timely basis. Accuracy of amount and account is most frequently achieved by establishing control procedures to review calculations, extensions, additions, and account classifications. Such reviews might be performed and evidenced by the performer's initialing sales invoices, credit memoranda, or payroll summaries. In manual systems, where there is a possibility of random error in processing transactions, occasionally an additional "double check" is made by another individual who repeats the calculations, extensions, and additions, and reviews the account classifications.

In a computerized environment, *accuracy-of-input* controls are designed to ensure that data is accurately recorded and accurately input to the computer. Although the control procedures are usually applied mainly to key financial data that directly affects balances in the financial statements, reference data such as customer number or invoice date may also be subject to control procedures.

Control procedures to ensure that transactions are recorded on a timely basis are also essential to achieve the accuracy objective. This requires procedures to establish what date a transaction took place. (Those procedures also help to ensure a proper "cutoff," that is, that transactions are recorded and reported in the proper accounting period.) As an example, goods received are inspected and recorded at the time of their receipt. Usually the receiving records are matched to related vendors' invoices as part of a subsequent control procedure to ensure the timely recording of transactions.

Various procedures for processing transactions through the accounting system may generate "exception reports" that are used by management for operational purposes. These reports may also provide evidence that certain types of errors are absent. For example, before cash receipts from customers are credited to their accounts, they may be matched to specific sales charged to the customers' accounts and an exception report of unmatched receipts may be generated. The purpose of the match and the exception report is to ensure that the full amount of specific invoices is collected. The matching of receipts to sales on the accounts receivable file and the follow-up of the exception report, however, also provide evidence of the accuracy and genuineness of the sales transactions. Furthermore, as noted earlier, management's review and follow-up of exception reports is itself an important aspect of an effective control structure.

Certain techniques used to ensure completeness of input may also ensure accuracy of input of some types of data. Examples are one-for-one comparison, establishing batch totals for certain data, and computer matching of data. Specific techniques to achieve accuracy usually include a wide range of edit checks, many of which may be carried out directly at terminals as transactions are input. These edit checks depend on the operation of programmed control procedures, for example, matching a customer number input at a terminal to the customer master file, followed by the system displaying the customer name on the screen for visual checking.

Control procedures that relate to *accuracy of updating* in a computerized environment are designed to ensure that the appropriate files are accurately updated by the data input. Accuracy of the most significant data, for example, monetary amount and date for open accounts receivable balances, is often ensured by control procedures used for completeness of updating. Except for the most significant data, accuracy of updating is often not specifically controlled, and the client relies on the effective operation of relevant programmed procedures.

Authorization.   Recorded transactions can be controlled in various ways to ensure that they represent economic events that actually occurred. The most elementary control procedure to do this consists of requiring transactions to be approved by persons having the authority to do so, as specified by the entity's established policies and procedures. In more sophisticated systems, control procedures to ensure authorization are built into the system so that transactions are automatically tested against predetermined expectations; exceptions must then be reviewed by someone who is authorized to approve them. Control procedures to ensure that fictitious transactions are not recorded include segregating responsibilities for processing transactions (such as credit sales) from responsibilities for corresponding with other parties to the transaction (such as mailing monthly statements and opening customer correspondence).

Typical authorization techniques include approval by a responsible official, exception reporting (such as reporting employees working more than a given number of hours in a week, with a subsequent review by a responsible official), computer matching to authorized standing or transaction data (for example, matching customers' orders to authorized credit limits or matching goods received to authorized orders), and procedures that restrict access to programs and data files to authorized users. A responsible official can give approval online by inputting an appropriate password and authorization code at a terminal. Except for manual authorization, the effectiveness of the above techniques is likely to depend on the operation of programmed control procedures and on the security procedures applied to files.

Some authorization control procedures are designed to ensure that only transactions that actually occurred are recorded, and that no transactions are recorded more than once. For example,

• Accounting procedures are normally established to record goods received on receiving reports, and goods shipped on shipping reports. Control procedures designed to ensure the authorization of these transactions include inspecting the related goods to determine that their description, condition, and quantities are correct and comparing that information with data on sales and vendors' invoices. (Any significant discrepancies noted must also be investigated and resolved if these control procedures are to be effective.)

- Canceling the voucher and related documents supporting a purchase transaction at the time of payment prevents their being recorded a second time and being reused to support a duplicate payment or a payment for a nonexistent purchase.

Other authorization control procedures are designed to ensure that individual transactions are approved by responsible personnel in accordance with established guidelines. Such authorization can be general or specific. A general authorization may take the form of giving a department or function permission to enter into transactions against some budgeted amount. Budget approval for a capital expenditure, for example, in effect serves as authorization for expenditures up to the budgeted amount. Another example, from the retail industry, is the "open to buy" concept in which a buyer is authorized to buy merchandise up to a specified amount. A specific authorization, on the other hand, would grant permission to a person to enter into a specific transaction, for example, to buy a specific amount of raw material needed to produce a made-to-order item.

Control procedures to ensure the authorization of transactions are increasingly being automated by specifying in advance the conditions under which a transaction will be automatically authorized and executed. For example, a production order can be automatically authorized when the on-hand amount of an inventory item falls to a predetermined point and needs replenishing. Even in nonautomated systems, general authorizations can be used to accomplish the same objective.

File Control.   File control procedures are designed to ensure that transaction data and standing data contained on files continue to be complete, accurate, and authorized until the files are updated by subsequent transactions that are similarly complete, accurate, and authorized. Examples of techniques for ensuring the integrity of files are reconciling the accounts receivable detail ledger to the general ledger, matching cash receipts to the accounts receivable file, and reconciling an inventory count to the recorded inventory. If file control procedures are absent or ineffective, the files may be incomplete or inaccurate, or may contain unauthorized data. For example, if an entity failed to periodically reconcile subsidiary ledgers to the general ledger control account, misstatements that management would not be aware of could exist in either the control account or the detailed accounts.

In a manual accounting system, the file control objective is achieved largely by periodically reconciling subsidiary ledgers to general ledgers. In a computerized accounting system, achieving file control means ensuring the integrity of stored data on computer files, at both the file total level and the detail level. File control in a computerized system also requires procedures to ensure that transactions are processed using only the most recently updated files and that the current files can be recovered in the event of a computer failure.

Some control procedures that achieve one or more transaction processing control objectives also achieve the file control objective. For example, matching cash receipts to the accounts receivable file is performed mainly to ensure that cash receipts are accurately posted, but it also serves to ensure the integrity of the detail of unpaid balances on the accounts receivable file; that is, that all unpaid accounts receivable remain on the file and the details of individual accounts (customer name, invoice number, and dollar amount) remain accurate on the file. That matching procedure, or other similar procedures, would be likely to disclose errors in files if transaction processing was disrupted for any reason, although the errors might not be revealed on a timely basis. In a computerized environment, file control at the file total level might be ensured by the general control procedures within computer operations (as discussed in Chapter 11), especially those pertaining to recovery from processing failures and to the use of correct files.

As an illustration of how account balances could be misstated if file control procedures were not effective, assume that during the year a company disposed of some spoiled raw materials. The quantities disposed of were removed from the detailed perpetual inventory records, but the control account was inadvertently not adjusted. In this situation, an adequate transaction processing control procedure for raw material disposal was not sufficient to prevent misstatement of the inventory balance. File control procedures, such as reconciling the perpetual inventory records to the control account and investigating differences, would also have been necessary. And if the materials disposed of were not removed from either the detailed perpetual inventory records *or* the control account, neither one would properly reflect the existing assets. Physically counting the inventory, reconciling the count to the accounting records, and investigating differences would be the appropriate file control procedures.

Asset Protection. Control procedures designed to safeguard assets are based on restricting access to assets to authorized personnel. Effective asset protection depends on adequate division of duties. To prevent theft or simply well-intended activity not consistent with established policies and procedures, it is necessary to restrict access to anything that could be used to initiate or process a transaction. Asset protection is most commonly thought of in connection with negotiable assets—cash, securities, and sometimes inventory and other items easily convertible to cash or personal use. But the concept of limited access applies equally to the books and records and the means of altering them, such as unused forms, unissued checks, check signature plates, files, and ledgers.

In its simplest form, asset protection is evidenced by such things as a safe, a vault, a locked door, a storeroom with a custodian, a guarded fence, or other means of preventing unauthorized persons from gaining access to assets and records. Control procedures should also protect assets and records from physical harm such as accidental destruction, deterioration, or simply being mislaid.

In computerized systems, control procedures to limit access to data stored on files to authorized persons are especially important because assets can be moved by manipulating data (for example, transactions generating an automatic check payment), and fraud or theft can be obscured by processing unauthorized transactions. Control procedures to ensure the security of computer programs and stored data are of key importance in computerized systems where there may be potentially wide access to programs and data through terminals. Such control is normally achieved by general control procedures relating to program and data file security, as discussed further in Chapter 11.

Segregation of Duties.   If the internal control structure is to be effective, there needs to be an adequate division of duties among those who perform accounting and control procedures and handle assets. Although division of duties relates to all three elements of the control structure, it is most prevalent in the performance of control procedures. It consists of assigning different people to authorize a particular class of transactions, perform control procedures when the transactions are processed, supervise those procedures, maintain the related accounting records, and handle the related assets. Such arrangements reduce the risk of error and limit opportunities to misappropriate assets or conceal other intentional misrepresentations in the financial statements. For example, to reduce the risk of error, management may establish procedures for monthly reconciliations of a control account to be reviewed and approved by someone who did not perform the reconciliations.

If two accounting procedures related to a single transaction are handled by different people, each serves as a control mechanism on the other; a further control procedure should be applied to the transaction by a third person. For example, one bookkeeper can process a day's cash receipts received through the mail, and another can post the receipts to the accounts receivable records. A third person's comparison of the total of the postings with the total receipts provides evidence that each operation was accurately performed. If the comparison of the postings total with the total receipts is not performed by a third person, there is an increased risk of misstatement in the accounting records.

Segregation of duties also serves as a deterrent to fraud or concealment of error because of the need to recruit another individual's cooperation (collusion) to conceal it. For example, separating responsibility for physically protecting assets from the related record keeping is a significant control mechanism over the fraudulent conversion of the assets. Similarly, the treasurer who signs checks should not be able to make entries in the disbursements records and thereby hide unauthorized disbursements. Control is even further enhanced if neither the treasurer nor the bookkeeper is responsible for periodically comparing cash on hand and in the bank with the cash records and taking appropriate action if there are any differences. In a computerized system, for example, personnel responsible for sensitive standing data should not be responsible for processing transaction data.

Supervision.   Supervisory control procedures lower the risk that accounting and control procedures are not functioning as designed at all times, as opposed to solely in those instances observed by the auditor. Supervisory control procedures also help ensure that errors that do occur are detected on a timely basis. Supervising the manual aspects of accounting and control procedures has an obvious effect on the quality of the accounting records. With effective supervision, personnel performing accounting and control procedures can be directed to make necessary modifications when new types of transactions occur, take corrective action when errors are revealed, and follow up when deficiencies in those procedures become evident.

Many supervisory control procedures consist of specific, observable administrative routines for regularly assuring supervisors that the prescribed control procedures are operating. These routines must be documented, for example, by means of checklists; exception reports; initials evidencing review of batch controls, bank reconciliations, and vouchers; log books for review routines; and written reports.

RELEVANCE OF CONTROL OBJECTIVES TO THE ACHIEVEMENT OF AUDIT OBJECTIVES

As indicated at the beginning of this chapter, the auditor is required by generally accepted auditing standards to assess control risk, that is, to reach a conclusion about how effective the entity's control structure policies and procedures are in reducing the risk that the financial statements will contain misstatements. To whatever extent the auditor concludes that control structure policies and procedures achieve the control objectives, he or she can restrict substantive tests for the related account balances and audit objectives. This section of the chapter discusses briefly the relationship between control objectives and audit objectives. It also discusses the relevance of the control objectives to the auditor's assessment of risk.

The control objectives of completeness, accuracy, and authorization are closely related to the audit objectives of completeness, accuracy, and existence/occurrence. For example, control procedures related to the control objective of accuracy are designed to prevent or detect sales transaction processing errors that could arise because incorrect prices were used, invoices were improperly computed, or shipments were billed to the wrong customer. From the auditor's point of view, these procedures reduce the risk that sales in the income statement and accounts receivable in the balance sheet are not accurate. Clearly, if there are control procedures to ensure the accuracy of recorded transactions and related files and the auditor has tested the control procedures and found them to be effective, that reduces the amount of assurance the auditor must obtain from substantive tests to meet the audit objective of accuracy.

While the control objectives of completeness and authorization are related to the audit objectives of completeness and existence/occurrence, the relationship is more complex than it is with the accuracy objective. This is primarily because of the double-entry system, which records two aspects of every transaction. Consider sales transactions: If a sale is made and goods are shipped, but the transaction is not recorded, the control objective of completeness of transaction processing is not achieved, resulting in both sales in the income statement and accounts receivable in the balance sheet being incomplete. If, however, ineffective control procedures permit the incomplete recording of cash receipts from charge customers, but the receipts have been properly deposited, then the cash account is not complete and accounts receivable contain nonexistent receivables. In this instance, an ineffective completeness control procedure has resulted in a misstatement with respect to existence.

The same type of analysis for the authorization objective leads to the conclusion that while ineffective control procedures that permit unauthorized transactions to be recorded may lead to recording nonexistent assets (for example, a fictitious sale that generates a nonexistent account receivable), in some circumstances those procedures may result in assets or liabilities being omitted from the balance sheet (for example, removing a receivable due from an employee by recording a fictitious sales return). Delineating the relationship between control objectives and audit objectives for all classes of transactions and related accounts is not practicable, because of the immense number of possible combinations of transactions and errors that could occur. In practice, auditors determine what could go wrong in the processing of specific transactions or in their preservation on files (ineffective control procedures), determine how that could affect specific audit objectives and accounts in the financial statements, and then design and perform substantive tests to detect possible financial statement misstatements.

Control procedures to ensure completeness may have an especially significant effect on the conduct of an audit. Auditors often find it particularly difficult to obtain sufficient evidence regarding the completeness of transaction recording. Because the control objectives of accuracy and authorization are concerned mainly with *recorded* transactions and balances, the auditor can usually obtain sufficient evidence about their accuracy and existence, even if control procedures are inadequate, by performing substantive tests of those balances or of the underlying transactions, for example, examining supporting documentation and reperforming accounting procedures.

When assessing the completeness of transaction processing and the resultant accounting records, the auditor is concerned with the possibility of *unrecorded* transactions, for which there is usually no evidence. For example, if prenumbered documents are used to record transactions, the auditor can account for the numerical sequence of documents and thus obtain evidence that all transactions for which a prenumbered document was prepared have been recorded. However, this will not detect unrecorded transactions if documents were not prepared for all transactions. The auditor should therefore pay particular attention to control procedures designed to ensure that all transactions are recorded on a document, for example, a requirement that a shipping document be prepared before a storeroom clerk releases merchandise for shipment.

Authoritative auditing literature notes that ''in the great majority of cases, the auditor finds it necessary to rely on evidence that is persuasive rather than convincing'' (SAS No. 31, *Evidential Matter* [AU Section 326.19]). This is particularly true for evidence supporting the completeness of recording of transactions that have occurred. In most instances, persuasive evidence about completeness can be obtained, but in extreme circumstances where completeness control procedures are absent or particularly ineffective, the auditor should question the auditability of the accounting records. Not all classes of transactions of a particular enterprise may be auditable; at the extreme, the significance of unauditable classes of transactions may be so great as to make the enterprise as a whole unauditable.

As discussed earlier, the file control objective is concerned with preserving the integrity of files that contain accumulated transactions and related accounting data. Accordingly, an entity's failure to achieve the file control objective could lead to account balances that are incomplete, inaccurate, or nonexistent. For example, if an entity fails to periodically reconcile the accounts receivable subsidiary ledger to the general ledger control account, the accounts receivable balance may be missing receivables for which goods were shipped, or may include receivables that were already paid or were fictitious. This increases the amount of assurance the auditor must obtain from substantive tests to achieve the completeness, accuracy, and existence audit objectives.

Inadequate control procedures to protect assets and the documents that control their movement might allow unauthorized access to those assets and could result in unrecorded loss of assets. In that situation, assets that did not exist would continue to be recorded, thus affecting the auditor's achievement of the existence audit objective.

The absence of adequate control procedures to safeguard assets and records affects the timing and extent of substantive tests. For example, the absence of adequate control procedures to limit physical access to inventories may mean that a complete inventory count must be performed at the balance sheet date, even if other control procedures applied to the inventory records are adequate. If adequate control procedures to protect assets and records exist, the auditor may either (1) observe and make some test counts of the client's cycle counts of portions of the inventory or (2) observe a physical inventory count at an interim date and then roll forward inventory balances on the balance sheet date based on recorded activity.

The relationships between control objectives and audit objectives discussed in the preceding paragraphs are summarized in Figure 7.2. Note that several of the audit objectives discussed in Chapter 5—namely, cutoff, valuation, rights and obligations, and presentation and disclosure—are not included in that figure. That is because those objectives, with the exception of the cutoff objective, are rarely specifically addressed by an entity's control procedures. The cutoff objective is sometimes addressed, in part, by control procedures related to the completeness and accuracy of transactions occurring near the year-end. The audit objectives not addressed by control procedures (and all audit objectives for accounts that are not related to a major class of transactions) may be achieved, to varying degrees in different entities, through many of the factors that make up the control environment. For example, management's review of operating reports may provide evidence relevant to meeting the valuation objective for certain accounts.

MANAGEMENT'S RESPONSIBILITY FOR INTERNAL ACCOUNTING CONTROL UNDER THE FOREIGN CORRUPT PRACTICES ACT

Changes in the business and legal environment and in particular the Foreign Corrupt Practices Act of 1977 (the Act) have magnified the importance of the

Figure 7.2   Relationship of Control Objectives to Audit Objectives

		Control Objectives			
	Completeness	Accuracy	Authorization	File Control	Asset Protection
Audit Objectives					
Completeness	X		X	X	
Accuracy		X		X	
Existence	X		X	X	X

internal control structure to management. The Act, which amended the Securities Exchange Act of 1934, has two parts: One deals with specific acts and penalties associated with certain corrupt practices; the second, with standards relating to internal accounting controls (i.e., internal control procedures).

Illegal Payments

The Act prohibits any domestic company—or its officers, directors, employees, agents, or stockholders—from paying or offering to pay a foreign official to obtain, retain, or direct business to any person. Specifically, the law prohibits payments to foreign officials, political parties, and candidates for the purpose of obtaining or retaining business by influencing any act or decision of foreign parties in their official capacity, or by inducing such foreign parties to use their influence with a foreign government to sway any act or decision of such government. This section of the Act applies to virtually all U.S. businesses, and noncompliance with its provisions, as amended in August 1988, can result in fines of up to $2 million for corporations and up to $100,000 for individuals who willfully participate in the bribery of a foreign official. Violators may also be subject to imprisonment for up to five years.

Internal Accounting Control

The section of the Act addressing internal accounting control imposes additional legal obligations on publicly held companies. Failure by such companies to maintain appropriate books and records and internal accounting controls violates the Securities Exchange Act of 1934. In addition, the 1988 amendments to the Act created criminal liability for failing to comply with the internal accounting control provisions if an individual knowingly circumvents or knowingly fails to implement a system of internal accounting controls or knowingly falsifies any book, record, or account.

Specifically, the Foreign Corrupt Practices Act establishes a legal requirement that every SEC registrant

(A) Make and keep books, records and accounts, which, in reasonable detail, accurately and fairly reflect the transactions and dispositions of the assets of the issuer; and

(B) Devise and maintain a system of internal accounting controls sufficient to provide reasonable assurances that the following four objectives are met:

      (i)   transactions are executed in accordance with management's general or specific authorization;

      (ii) transactions are recorded as necessary (I) to permit preparation of financial statements in conformity with generally accepted accounting principles or any other criteria applicable to such statements, and (II) to maintain accountability for assets;

      (iii) access to assets is permitted only in accordance with management's general or specific authorization; and

      (iv) the recorded accountability for assets is compared with the existing assets at reasonable intervals and appropriate action is taken with respect to any differences.

The requirements in (B) are compatible with the control objectives discussed earlier in this chapter. (The language dealing with internal accounting control was taken directly from the relevant authoritative auditing literature [AU Section 320] in effect when the Act was drafted. AU Section 320 was superseded by SAS No. 55.) The 1988 amendments to the Act clarified the terms "reasonable detail" and "reasonable assurances" by describing them as the level of detail and degree of assurance that would satisfy prudent officials in the conduct of their own affairs.

It is clear from the legislative history of the Act that Congress' primary intent was to prevent corrupt payments to foreign officials, and that the requirements for accurate books and records and for internal accounting controls were intended mainly to help accomplish that objective. But those requirements are considerably more far reaching, since they cover all transactions, not only those related to illegal foreign payments. The SEC has enforced these provisions of the law in connection with domestic improprieties as well as illegal foreign payments.

While the Act has necessitated more direct management involvement in designing and maintaining the internal control structure, it does not specifically affect the auditor's responsibility. The auditor's responsibility with respect to the control structure remains as prescribed by the second standard of field work in SAS No. 55. This was explicitly articulated in an AICPA interpretation dealing with illegal acts by clients, which noted that the Foreign Corrupt Practices Act created new responsibilities for *companies* subject to the Securities Exchange Act of 1934, but not for their *auditors*.

8

Assessing Inherent and Control Risk

The two major components of audit risk were discussed in Chapter 6 in connection with planning and controlling an engagement. The first component, the risk that the financial statements contain material misstatements, is beyond the auditor's ability to control or change; however, the auditor can and should assess that risk as a basis for determining the nature, timing, and extent of auditing procedures.

Risk assessment is the process of arriving at an informed judgment of the risk that the financial statements contain material misstatements. That risk has two aspects, inherent risk and control risk, and the auditor assesses them within the context of materiality as a basis for determining the assurance he or she will need from substantive tests. Inherent and control risks should be assessed at the account balance and class of transactions level, and the assessment should address individual financial statement assertions and corresponding audit objectives.

Risk assessment aids the auditor in identifying

- Inherent risk conditions and characteristics that create a high risk of material misstatement and thus require emphasis on particular audit objectives and accounts.
- Internal control structure policies and procedures that may reduce the risk of material misstatement and enable the auditor to restrict substantive tests for particular audit objectives and accounts.
- Accounts that can be subjected to limited substantive tests because the risk of material misstatement is low.

The basis for the auditor's assessment of inherent and control risk is information about various aspects of the client and its business. Much of that information is general and relates to the nature of the entity's business; the industry it operates in, including legal and regulatory requirements peculiar to the industry; and the entity's significant accounts and interrelationships among financial and operating data. The auditor is also required to obtain an understanding of the entity's control structure in order to assess control risk as part of planning the audit.

OBTAINING INFORMATION TO ASSESS INHERENT AND CONTROL RISK

As discussed in Chapter 6, inherent risks result from both conditions that are not under the entity's control and the characteristics of its transactions and related account balances. Inherent risk *conditions* exist at the macroeconomic, industry, and company level, and sometimes relate to factors outside the entity. These conditions may relate to changes in the general business environment, government regulations, and other economic factors. Inherent risk *characteristics* relate to the particular attributes of the entity's transactions and related accounts. The auditor considers both aspects of inherent risk in planning the audit. Information about inherent risk conditions comes mostly from outside sources. Inherent risk conditions generally are not addressed by specific accounting and control procedures; however, an effective control environment provides evidence of management's ability to monitor inherent risk conditions and respond to changes in them. In contrast, management designs control structure policies and procedures in response to the particular characteristics of its classes of transactions and account balances, so that inherent risk characteristics often are addressed by all three control structure elements. For that reason, inherent risk characteristics are ordinarily assessed concurrently with control risk, as discussed later in the chapter.

For a recurring audit engagement, much of the general information relevant to assessing inherent and control risk is available from prior years' working papers and needs only to be updated, not gathered all over again. Both client personnel and the auditor must be careful not to treat changed circumstances perfunctorily. A client's personnel can easily forget changes that took place during the year because they have become routine by the time the auditor makes inquiries; the auditor can easily treat significant changes as trivial if their implications are not thoroughly considered. An auditor approaching a recurring engagement must remember that changed conditions can make last year's risk assessments obsolete and a misleading guide to the nature and extent of procedures required. The auditor should not perform auditing procedures based on the previous year's assessments before reviewing changed circumstances.

The information needed to assess inherent and control risk is obtained from many sources and is documented in a number of places in the audit working papers. Most of the information-gathering procedures are performed during the early stages of the audit; however, the auditor is likely to obtain additional information about the client throughout the engagement and should consider that information in determining the nature, timing, and extent of auditing procedures.

Information about the client's business and industry, recent financial information, and a knowledge of applicable accounting, auditing, and regulatory standards are useful for identifying inherent risk conditions, inherent risk characteristics, and the control structure policies and procedures the client may have implemented in response to those characteristics. The paragraphs that follow describe how the auditor gathers or updates that information.

Obtaining Knowledge of the Client's Business and Industry

Relevant information about the client's business includes its product lines, sources and methods of supply, marketing and distribution methods, sources of financing, and production methods. The auditor should also obtain information about the locations and relative size of the client's operating plants, divisions, and subsidiaries, and the extent to which management is decentralized. Concerning the client's industry, the auditor needs to know such matters as industry characteristics and the client's position in the industry. Industry conditions that can affect a client include its market share and relative size, industry practices (for example, with regard to quantity discounts and consignment sales), and its competition. If the client operates in more than one industry, the auditor should obtain information about each industry in which the client has significant activities. The auditor can do this through a variety of information sources, including government statistics; economic, financial, industry, and trade journals; client publications and brochures; internal audit reports, where applicable; and reports prepared on the entity, its competitors, or its industry by underwriters, merchant bankers, and securities dealers and analysts.

The auditor should also learn about economic conditions that affect the client's business and industry. Economic conditions affect an entity's continuing ability to generate and collect revenues, operate profitably, and provide a return to investors. Unfavorable economic conditions may raise questions about whether the entity's assets are recoverable, how its liabilities should be measured, and, ultimately, whether it can remain in business. Unfavorable economic conditions may also increase the likelihood of intentional financial statement misrepresentations.

Analyzing Recent Financial Information

SAS No. 56, *Analytical Procedures* (AU Section 329), requires the auditor to use analytical procedures in planning the audit. In meeting that requirement, the auditor typically reviews recent financial statements and other available financial information and performance indicators to highlight changes in the client's business, to identify which account balances and classes of transactions are material and which are immaterial, and to identify unusual or unexpected relationships among accounts. Such relationships may indicate material misstatements in specific account balances, or inherent risk conditions such as declining liquidity or poor operating performance, that may have a pervasive effect on the financial statements. In addition, comparing recent financial information with prior-year financial data and with budgets for the current period may alert the auditor to favorable or unfavorable operating trends, significant deviations from expected results, recent financing or investment activities, and other changes in the entity's business. Unusual or unexpected balances or relationships among data aggregated at a high level, such as financial statement line items or their major components, could serve as an early warning of specific risks. Also, comparing a client's financial results with those of other companies in its industry group as a whole may be a useful way to determine whether the client's performance is consistent with that of other similar entities. Information compiled by services like Dun & Bradstreet, Robert Morris Associates, or Standard & Poor's can give the auditor standard "benchmarks" against which to measure performance. Auditors are increasingly using computers to access such information from public data bases. The nature and extent of analytical procedures depend on how large and complex the client's business is and what financial information is available.

In addition to financial data, analytical procedures used in planning the audit are sometimes based on relationships between financial and nonfinancial information, particularly for enterprises in industries in which an "average" rate has meaning. For example, in the hotel industry, the overall reasonableness of revenue from room occupancy may be tested by considering the result of multiplying the number of rooms by the occupancy rate by the average room rate.

Updating Knowledge of Applicable Accounting, Auditing, and Regulatory Standards

The auditor's understanding of the business also includes knowledge of the client's accounting policies and practices. The auditor should evaluate whether those policies and practices are appropriate for the way the client conducts its business and in light of generally accepted accounting principles. If the client has changed any accounting policies or practices during the current year, the auditor should determine whether those changes were made in response to changes in its methods of doing business or in accounting or regulatory standards, or to better reflect operating results, and should consider their possible effects on the audit.

The auditor should identify any accounting and auditing standards that warrant special attention in the current year, such as standards that have become applicable or have taken on increased significance because of changes in the client's business or because of significant, unusual, or nonrecurring transactions. The client may not be aware that such standards apply to its financial statements or may not fully understand how to apply the standards. New or changed regulatory standards may have a similar impact on the client's financial statements. The auditor should consider discussing such standards with management at the earliest possible date so that it can take action to address them properly and on a timely basis.

Related Party Transactions

In understanding the client's business, the auditor has a specific responsibility to consider the client's relationships and transactions with related parties. Statement of Financial Accounting Standards (SFAS) No. 57, *Related Party Disclosures* (Accounting Standards Section R36), sets forth disclosure requirements with regard to related parties and contains (in Section R36.406) the following definition of related parties:

> Affiliates of the enterprise; entities for which investments are accounted for by the equity method by the enterprise; trusts for the benefit of employees, such as pension and profit-sharing trusts that are managed by or under the trusteeship of management; principal owners of the enterprise; its management; members of the immediate families of principal owners of the enterprise and its management; and other parties with which the enterprise may deal if one party controls or can significantly influence the management or operating policies of the other to an extent that one of the transacting parties might be prevented from fully pursuing its own separate interests. Another party also is a related party if it can significantly influence the management or operating policies of the transacting parties or if it has an ownership interest in one of the transacting parties and can significantly influence the other to an extent that one or more of the transacting parties might be prevented from fully pursuing its own separate interests.

The terms "affiliates," "control," "immediate family," "management," and "principal owners" are further defined in SFAS No. 57.

Under AU Section 334, *Related Parties*, the auditor has the responsibility to understand the client's business activities well enough to evaluate whether the client's disclosures regarding related parties are appropriate, including the propriety of any client representations that related party transactions took place at terms equivalent to arm's-length transactions. AU Section 334 sets forth specific auditing procedures the auditor should consider in determining the existence of related parties, procedures to help identify material transactions with related parties, and procedures the auditor should consider when examining any related party transactions identified.

The client has the ultimate responsibility for identifying, recording, and disclosing related party transactions, and the auditor should obtain specific representation from client management that it is aware of, and has fulfilled, that responsibility. The auditor's procedures, however, should extend beyond inquiry of, and obtaining such representations from, management. The auditor should also review other potential sources of information, such as proxy material, stockholder listings, and minutes of meetings of the board of directors and executive or operating committees. As far as possible, related parties should be identified at the beginning of the audit and their names distributed to all members of the audit team, including those responsible for auditing other divisions or subsidiaries of the enterprise, to help them identify related party transactions in the course of their work. The auditor should assess the client's procedures for identifying related parties and transactions to determine the nature and extent of auditing procedures he or she will have to perform to identify such transactions.

OBTAINING AN UNDERSTANDING OF THE CONTROL STRUCTURE ELEMENTS

The previous section described how the auditor obtains general information to assess inherent and control risk as part of planning an audit. The second standard of field work specifically requires that the auditor obtain a sufficient understanding of the client's internal control structure for planning purposes. As indicated in Chapter 6, the auditor's assessment of inherent and control risk in the context of materiality is a key factor in planning the audit.

A "sufficient" understanding of the control structure is one that, when considered together with other information about the client, such as that from prior years' experience, enables the auditor to identify what types of misstatements could occur, consider the risks of their occurring, and design appropriate substantive tests to detect them. The auditor develops this understanding by determining the *design* of relevant policies and procedures *in each element of the control structure* and whether they have been *placed in operation*, that is, whether the entity is actually using them. The auditor is *not required*, as part of developing the *understanding* of the control structure, to obtain evidence about whether those policies and procedures are *effectively designed* or are *operating effectively*. (Tests designed to provide evidence about effectiveness are discussed later in the chapter.) Often, however, in the course of developing the understanding of control structure policies and procedures, particularly those that are part of the accounting system or control environment, the auditor also obtains evidence about their effectiveness. The auditor considers that evidence when assessing control risk with respect to relevant assertions and account balances.

The understanding of the control structure required for audit planning (that is, for identifying and responding to the risk of material misstatements) is obtained by considering previous experience with the entity, reviewing prior-year audit results, interviewing client personnel and observing them in the performance of their duties, and examining client-prepared descriptions of policies and procedures and other appropriate documentation. As explained in Chapter 5, observation involves direct viewing of client employees in the work environment. Inquiry (interviewing) entails asking specific questions of the client's management and employees, which may be done informally or in formal interviews. The auditor examines records, documents, reconciliations, and reports for evidence that a policy or procedure has been properly applied. What procedures the auditor performs to obtain the necessary understanding of the control structure, and the extent to which they are performed on a particular audit, vary according to the client's size and complexity, the auditor's previous experience with the client, the particular policy or procedure, and the client's documentation. As a result of prior years' experience with the client, the auditor will likely have some idea of the level at which control risk will be assessed in the current audit. This may in some cases also affect the nature and extent of procedures performed in updating the understanding of the control structure.

Developing an Understanding of the Control Environment and Accounting System

The auditor obtains information about the control environment to determine whether it appears to be conducive to maintaining an effective accounting system and control procedures and whether it minimizes the incentives and opportunities for management to deliberately distort the financial statements. An understanding of the flow of transactions through the accounting system gives the auditor a general knowledge of the various classes of transactions, their volume and typical dollar values, and the procedures for authorizing, executing, initially recording, and subsequently processing them, including the methods of data processing. While obtaining an understanding of the accounting system, the auditor should consider whether client personnel who use the information the system generates would be likely to detect and report potential errors in data underlying the financial statements. In a recurring engagement, much of the relevant information about the control environment and the flow of transactions is already available in the prior years' working papers. The auditor should use this information as much as possible; however, it should be thoroughly reviewed and updated each year.

Reviewing Prior Years' Audit Results.   Reviewing prior years' audit results can help the auditor determine the likelihood of material misstatements in current-year account balances. For example, if the control environment was found to be effective in prior years and there have been no changes in the people and procedures that generate information that management uses to monitor business activities, the auditor should consider this when planning substantive tests of accounts requiring management estimates and judgments.

Prior-year working papers the auditor ordinarily reviews include financial information, the understanding of the client's business and industry, and risk assessments. The auditor should also refer to the prior year's documentation of matters brought to the attention of the partner, particularly significant accounting and auditing matters such as the nature, cause, and amounts of errors the auditor found—both those that were material and resulted in adjustment of the financial statements and those that were not.

If a client changes auditors, professional courtesy calls for the predecessor auditor to make certain information in the working papers available to the successor auditor. The predecessor auditor's working papers can be a convenient source of information about the accounting system, control procedures, and accounting principles used by the client, as well as the composition of beginning balances of individual accounts, although most of this information can also be obtained from the client.

Interviews and Client Manuals.   Interviewing is one of the most effective ways to gain an initial understanding of the client's accounting system and related control procedures. Interviews with client personnel who are knowledgeable about the accounting system and control procedures can give the auditor an understanding of how the company's accounting, internal control, and related activities are carried out. Interviewing personnel who are immediately responsible for performing procedures enables the auditor to learn about the main features of the accounting system and control procedures and about potential problem areas with implications for the internal control structure or the financial statements. In those interviews, questions and answers can be highly detailed, specific, and directed because both the auditor and knowledgeable client personnel know what information the auditor needs.

Deciding how many interviews are required is a matter of judgment, and avoiding omissions or duplications may be difficult in a large and complex operation. Some auditors like to interview both those who perform accounting functions and their supervisors early in the audit; others defer interviews with nonsupervisory personnel until later. In conjunction with interviews, some auditors observe accounting personnel performing their tasks; client personnel may prefer to explain what they do by showing the auditor specific examples of their work.

Many companies, particularly large and complex ones, maintain extensive manuals of policies and procedures. The auditor should normally obtain or have access to a complete set of procedures manuals covering accounting and internal control activities; familiarity with those manuals will help the auditor conduct more insightful interviews with client accounting personnel. Manuals of activities peripheral to accounting, such as purchasing and personnel policies, may also be useful. But although those manuals can often help clarify a particular phase of a client's operations, they are often too detailed and extensive to contribute effectively to the auditor's initial effort to understand the client's accounting system and control procedures. Instead, these manuals often serve as reference sources as the audit progresses.

Computerized Systems. Presuming that the client's accounting system is computerized, the auditor also needs a general understanding of the principles of computers and computer processing and how those principles are applied in the client's system. The auditor should become familiar with the hardware and software used to process financially significant transactions. This information serves as a basis for ascertaining the likelihood that the client will have appropriate general control procedures, and determining whether audit software can be used in the audit. The auditor generally obtains this information by inquiry of data processing management. The auditor should also consider whether specialized skills are needed to assess the effect of the computer environment on the audit.

Transaction Reviews. In some situations, the auditor may be concerned that his or her understanding of the design of the accounting system may not be correct or complete enough to provide an adequate basis for planning the audit. In that event, the auditor may decide to trace one or a few transactions of each relevant class of transactions completely through the system to determine whether relevant accounting procedures have been placed in operation. This process is sometimes referred to as a "transaction review" or "walk-through." By revealing what types of misstatements could occur because of absent or ineffective procedures or documents, a transaction review can help the auditor in designing substantive tests to detect those misstatements. To decide whether to perform transaction reviews to obtain evidence that accounting procedures have been placed in operation, the auditor considers whether it would be more efficient to obtain that evidence by other means, such as examining documents and information produced by the system.

Developing an Understanding of Control Procedures

In developing an understanding of control procedures, the auditor is concerned with whether such procedures have been designed and placed in operation to determine whether the entity's objectives for processing transactions, storing data on files, and safeguarding assets will be met. That information helps the auditor to design and carry out more efficient substantive tests to detect possible misstatements.

Some of the procedures that achieve the control objectives may be integrated into components of the control environment and the accounting system. Accordingly, the auditor is likely to obtain some information about the presence or absence of control procedures as part of obtaining an understanding of the control environment and accounting system. The auditor should consider that information in determining what, if any, additional understanding of control procedures is necessary to plan the audit. In addition, the auditor may want to obtain an understanding of certain control procedures in order to understand the accounting system. SAS No. 55 (AU Section 319) notes that audit planning ordinarily does not require an understanding of all control procedures related to an individual account balance or audit objective.

DOCUMENTING THE UNDERSTANDING OF THE CONTROL STRUCTURE

Professional standards require the auditor to document the understanding of the control structure elements, but do not specify the form and extent of documentation. Thus, the documentation will vary with the size and complexity of the entity and the nature of its control structure. In general, the more complex the control structure, the more detailed the documentation will be.

The documentation of accounting systems that process financially significant transactions usually includes a record of the significant classes of transactions and principal accounting procedures, files, ledgers, and reports. It may be in the form of narratives or flowcharts. Flowcharts are symbolic diagrams that show procedures in graphic form and thus make it easy to understand and communicate information. Commonly used flowcharting symbols are depicted and explained in Figure 8.1. Flowcharts usually flow from top to bottom or from left to right and should be clear and simple. Only procedures, documents, and reports that have audit significance need be shown.

Auditors frequently document accounting systems on a type of flowchart called an *overview flowchart*, which illustrates the flow of significant classes of transactions from initiation, through processing, to the reports generated by the system, including those that are used to update the general ledger. The degree of detail required in an overview flowchart varies, depending on the entity's accounting system and whether the auditor plans to test the effectiveness of control procedures. While the overview flowchart is used primarily to document the accounting system, it may also be a convenient place to document the auditor's understanding of the design of key control procedures, if he or she does not plan to specifically test their effectiveness. On the other hand, if the auditor plans to test control procedures, they will be documented on other forms (discussed below) and generally will not be indicated on the overview flowchart. In any event, an overview flowchart should contain sufficient information to facilitate the design of substantive tests. An example of an overview flowchart for a computerized revenue cycle is shown in Figure 8.2.

Flowcharts are appropriate for all engagements, regardless of size or complexity. On many recurring engagements, flowcharts will already have been prepared; they should be reviewed and updated annually and used as long as they continue to be relevant. A complete redrawing of flowcharts annually is usually unnecessary unless the underlying procedures have changed or previous amendments have impaired a flowchart's clarity. Supporting documentation—such as copies of (or extracts from) accounting records, procedures manuals, and filled-in specimen forms or documents—should be cross-referenced to and filed with the flowcharts to help the auditor understand the accounting system.

The auditor may need to prepare more than one flowchart to cover an entire transaction cycle. For example, within the buying cycle, separate flowcharts may be necessary to show goods or services purchased and wages paid. The decision to prepare separate flowcharts depends on how significant the transactions are and whether the accounting procedures and reports generated are different for different classes of transactions.

It is not necessary to include on the flowchart every transaction that is

Figure 8.1   Flowcharting Symbols

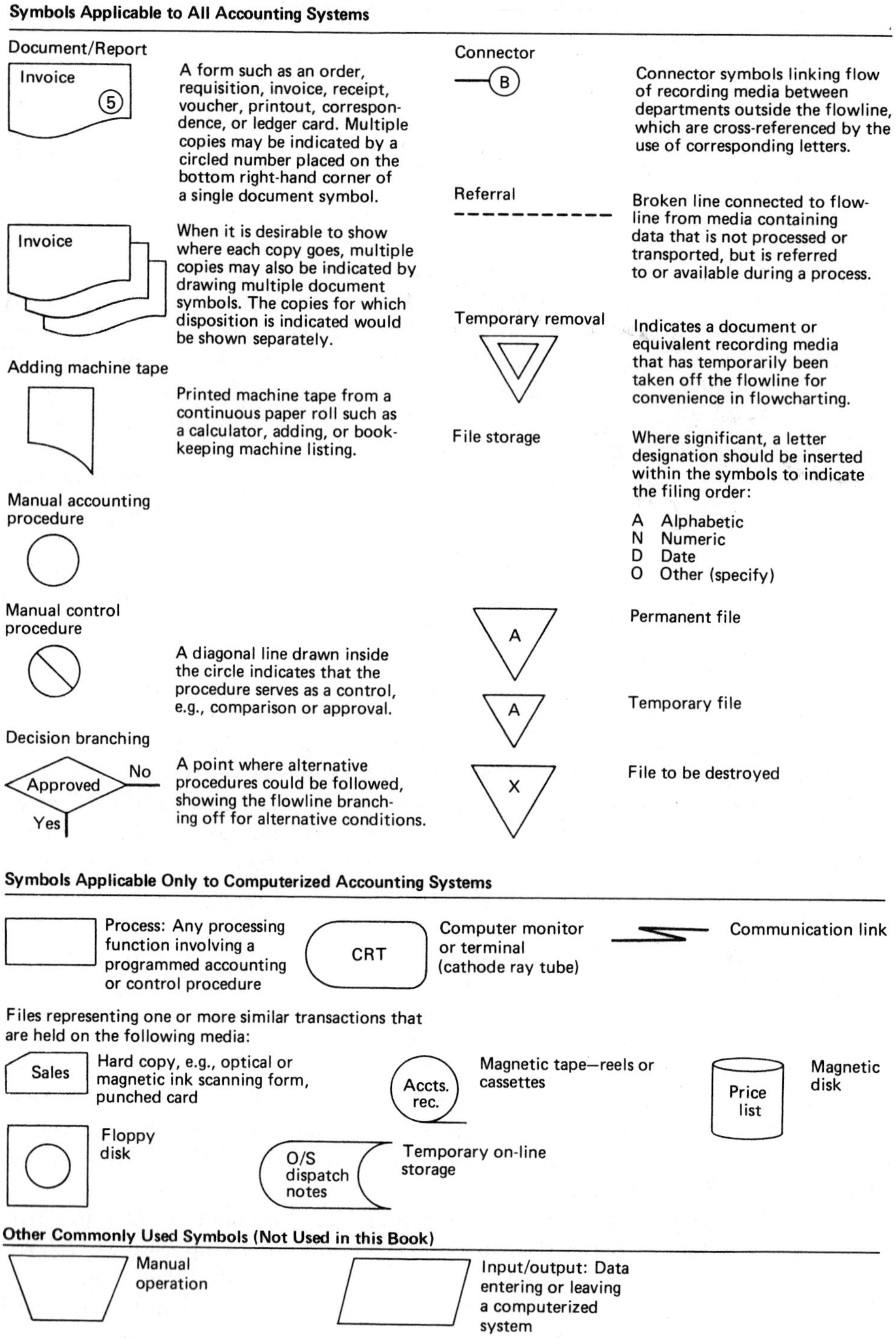

Symbols Applicable to All Accounting Systems

Document/Report

Invoice ⑤

A form such as an order, requisition, invoice, receipt, voucher, printout, correspondence, or ledger card. Multiple copies may be indicated by a circled number placed on the bottom right-hand corner of a single document symbol.

Invoice

When it is desirable to show where each copy goes, multiple copies may also be indicated by drawing multiple document symbols. The copies for which disposition is indicated would be shown separately.

Adding machine tape

Printed machine tape from a continuous paper roll such as a calculator, adding, or bookkeeping machine listing.

Manual accounting procedure

Manual control procedure

A diagonal line drawn inside the circle indicates that the procedure serves as a control, e.g., comparison or approval.

Decision branching

Approved — No — Yes

A point where alternative procedures could be followed, showing the flowline branching off for alternative conditions.

Connector

— B

Connector symbols linking flow of recording media between departments outside the flowline, which are cross-referenced by the use of corresponding letters.

Referral

- - - - - - - - - -

Broken line connected to flowline from media containing data that is not processed or transported, but is referred to or available during a process.

Temporary removal

Indicates a document or equivalent recording media that has temporarily been taken off the flowline for convenience in flowcharting.

File storage

Where significant, a letter designation should be inserted within the symbols to indicate the filing order:

A   Alphabetic
N   Numeric
D   Date
O   Other (specify)

A — Permanent file

A — Temporary file

X — File to be destroyed

Symbols Applicable Only to Computerized Accounting Systems

Process: Any processing function involving a programmed accounting or control procedure

CRT — Computer monitor or terminal (cathode ray tube)

Communication link

Files representing one or more similar transactions that are held on the following media:

Sales — Hard copy, e.g., optical or magnetic ink scanning form, punched card

Accts. rec. — Magnetic tape—reels or cassettes

Price list — Magnetic disk

Floppy disk

O/S dispatch notes — Temporary on-line storage

Other Commonly Used Symbols (Not Used in this Book)

Manual operation

Input/output: Data entering or leaving a computerized system

Figure 8.2 Overview Flowchart

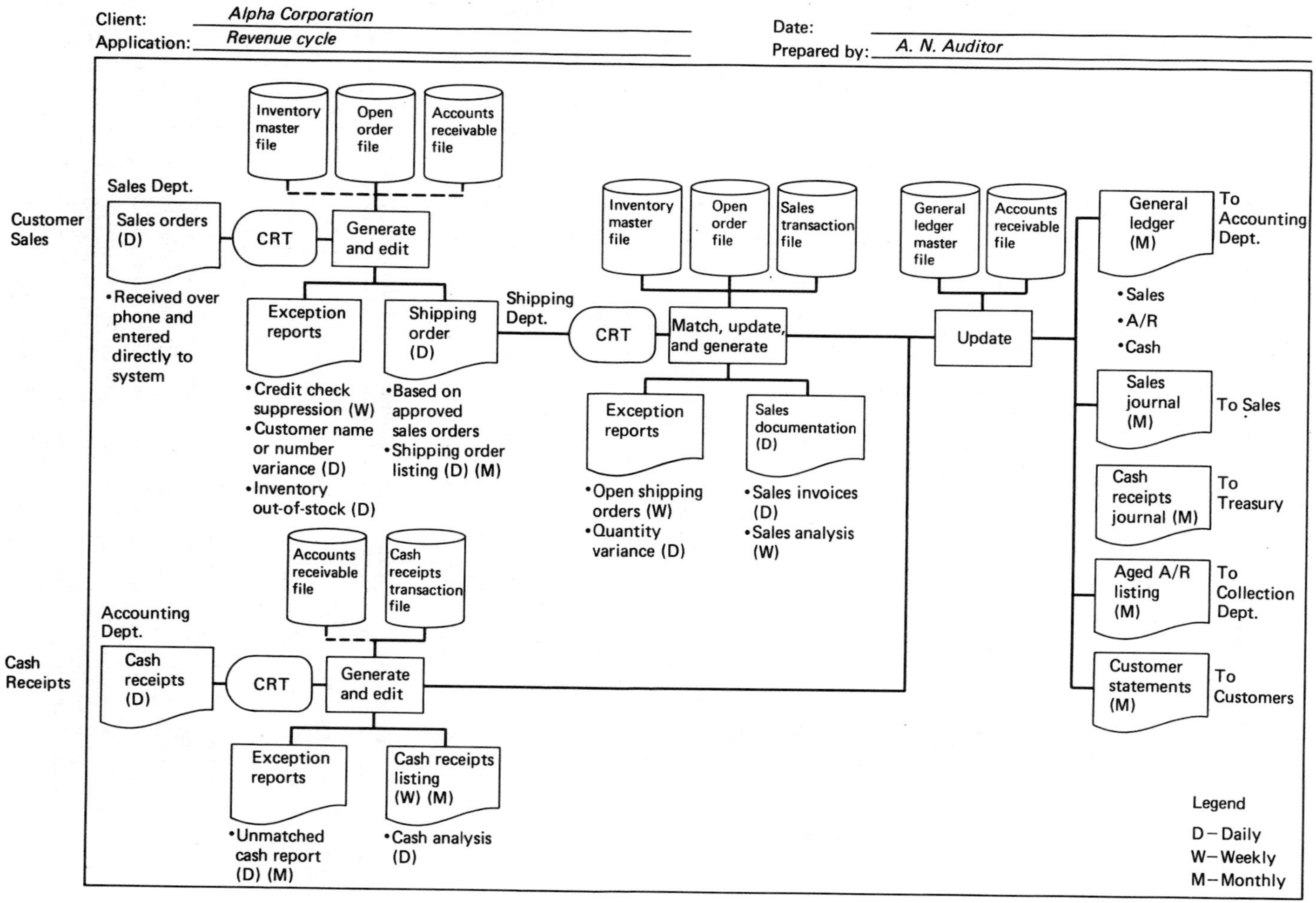

Client: _Alpha Corporation_   Date: _____

Application: _Revenue cycle_   Prepared by: _A. N. Auditor_

Legend

D — Daily
W — Weekly
M — Monthly

225

processed by a particular system. Only significant transactions should be documented. Transactions outside the main flow of information, such as adjustments, standing data amendments, and the like, may be documented in supplementary narratives as necessary. Such a narrative is illustrated in Figure 8.3.

An overview flowchart displays, normally on one or two pages, the accounting system for a transaction cycle in summary form. It provides the auditor with information about the nature of transactions that flow through the system. An overview flowchart should depict the principal features of the accounting system, including the following:

1. The nature and source of significant transactions.
2. The key processes and flow of significant transactions.
3. Principal files or ledgers supporting account balances and the process by which they are updated.
4. Reports of accounting significance produced, their frequency and distribution, and the files from which they are derived.

Each of those features is described below with reference to the computerized revenue cycle accounting system flowcharted in Figure 8.2 and the supplementary narrative shown in Figure 8.3.

Nature and source of significant transactions—The significant transactions flowcharted for the revenue cycle are customer sales and cash receipts. Other revenue cycle transactions outside the main flow of information, such as adjustments to accounts receivable and standing data amendments, are described in the supplementary narrative to the flowchart. The flowchart shows that customer sales transactions originate with the input of sales orders from customers and the automatic generation and further processing of shipping orders. This information helps the auditor identify what source documents to use in designing substantive tests and which information

Figure 8.3   Supplementary Narrative to Overview Flowchart

Client: *Alpha Corporation*
Application: *Revenue cycle*

Adjustments to Accounts Receivable
Adjustments to accounts receivable balances are made by processing credit memos (which are initiated by the sales department, entered directly to the system, and processed similar to sales orders) or by processing accounts receivable adjustment sheets for account write-offs (which are initiated by the accounting department based on discussions with the collection department and processed directly against the accounts receivable and general ledger master files).

Standing Data Amendments
Unit sales price data stored on the inventory master file is updated monthly by the accounting department based on the price change list received from the sales department.

processing points might have completeness control procedures related to customer sales.

Key processes and flow of significant transactions—The flowchart shows how sales transactions flow from initiation (when the sales order is received over the phone and recorded on a sales order document), through processing (when the sales order is input to the system and used in connection with master file data to generate a shipping order and sales invoice), to updating significant accounting files and producing the ultimate reports from the system (the general ledger, sales journal, and aged accounts receivable listing). Also shown are the processes, called editing and matching, that compare sales orders and shipping orders with data on file to determine whether there are exceptions that must be cleared by a responsible person before processing can continue. This information helps the auditor understand how certain key files are updated and reports produced, so that he or she can design substantive tests or identify control procedures relating to transaction processing.

Principal files or ledgers supporting account balances and the process by which they are updated—The flowchart shows the principal file supporting the accounts receivable balance (the accounts receivable file) and how it is updated (e.g., by accessing data on the sales and cash receipts transaction files). This information helps the auditor identify key files that should be subjected to manual or automated substantive tests. It also helps identify key files that should be subject to control procedures and therefore be considered when testing the effectiveness of the control procedures.

Reports of accounting significance produced, their frequency and distribution, and the files from which they are derived—The flowchart shows how significant accounting reports (e.g., the aged accounts receivable listing and the general ledger) are produced, where they are distributed and how frequently, and what files they were derived from (the accounts receivable and general ledger master files). This information helps the auditor identify reports to use in designing substantive tests. The flowchart also shows how and when exception reports are produced. This helps identify documents the client may use in performing certain control procedures.

If the client's operations are computerized, the auditor should obtain an understanding and record information about computer hardware and software used in financially significant applications. Some auditors document the relevant information on a form designed to record, concisely and in one place, the organization of the EDP installation, the hardware and software in use, the configuration of the network, and the details of the application environment, such as packages used, type of processing, access security software, and so on. Part of such a form is illustrated in Figure 8.4.

Generally, the auditor documents the understanding of the control environment and the design of many control procedures as part of documenting the assessment of control risk, as described later in this chapter. However, the auditor's understanding of the design of certain key control procedures may be documented on the overview flowchart by a narrative description, or by notations in the audit program, particularly if the auditor does not plan to test those control procedures as part of the process of assessing control risk. Often

Figure 8.4   Computer Environment Form

```
PART 1: PROCESSING ENVIRONMENT

MIS Organization
MIS Contact name and title: _____ Phone: _____
Installation address: _____
Size and structure of the department: _____
_____
_____


Hardware
Computer manufacturer and model: _____
Magnetic Storage Media:
    Magnetic tape _____
    Magnetic disk _____
    Diskettes _____
    Other (specify) _____
Software
Operating system: _____.
Communications software: _____
Major programming languages: _____
Inquiry/report writer packages available: _____
_____
_____
```

these are key control procedures that must be understood before the auditor
can design efficient substantive tests; for example, the matching of shipping
documents to invoices to ensure the completeness of recorded sales, and client
procedures relating to physical inventory counts.

ASSESSING CONTROL RISK

Both SAS No. 47 and SAS No. 55 require the auditor to assess control risk to
determine what level of detection risk is acceptable in an audit. Assessing
control risk is defined in SAS No. 55 (AU Section 319.29) as the "process of
evaluating the effectiveness of an entity's internal control structure policies and
procedures in preventing or detecting material misstatements in the financial
statements." The conclusion reached from this process is referred to as the
"assessed level of control risk" and is a combined judgment, based on evidence obtained about all three control structure elements. While SAS No. 55
does not require the auditor to evaluate separately the effectiveness of each of
the elements of the control structure, in most cases it is practical to do so in
arriving at an assessed level of control risk. Figure 8.5 depicts the assessment of
control risk in flowchart form, including the various decisions the auditor
makes and their consequences for the audit strategy. The steps in the flowchart
are expanded on in the following sections of the chapter.

Risk Assessment and Audit Strategy

Control risk should be assessed in relation to the audit objectives derived from
the financial statement assertions. The auditor may assess control risk at the

Figure 8.5   Control Risk Assessment*

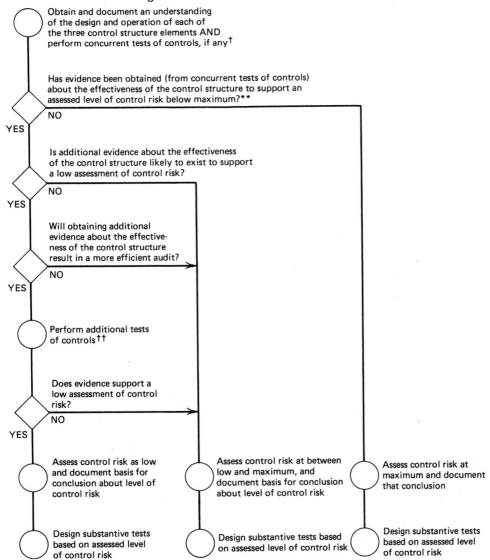

*Relevant management assertions/audit objectives related to specific account balances or classes of transactions should be considered separately in assessing control risk and designing substantive tests.

†Conceptually it would be possible for the author not to perform any tests of controls until after obtaining the understanding of the control structure. In practice, however, the auditor is unlikely to plan to perform tests of controls after obtaining the understanding without having performed some concurrent tests of controls.

**Evidence about the effectiveness of control structure policies and procedures may result from auditing procedures *planned* as concurrent tests of controls; alternatively, such evidence may be obtained from concurrent tests of controls that are *incidental* to auditing procedures directed at obtaining the understanding.

††On a recurring engagement where the auditor intends to again perform additional tests of controls, he or she may begin at this point and update the understanding and perform tests of controls simultaneously.

maximum level (that is, 100 percent) for all or certain audit objectives and decide to proceed directly to substantive tests to obtain assurance for those audit objectives, without doing any further work related to the control structure.

Assessing control risk at the maximum for an audit objective can result from a belief that control structure policies and procedures have not been effectively designed or have not operated effectively. The auditor can arrive at that belief based on the information gathered or updated about the client and the understanding of its control structure.

In order to assess control risk at below the maximum level, the auditor must be able to *identify* specific control structure policies and procedures that are in place and are likely to prevent or detect material misstatements in specific financial statement assertions, and must *test* whether those policies and procedures are designed and operating effectively.[1] In identifying control structure policies and procedures relevant to specific assertions, the auditor should keep in mind that some policies and procedures have a pervasive effect on many account balances or classes of transactions and on numerous assertions, while others have a specific effect on only one account or class of transactions and one assertion.

The effect of policies and procedures varies with the particular control structure element. The control environment and accounting system often have a pervasive effect on many account balances or classes of transactions and thus frequently affect several assertions. For example, the conclusion that an entity's decentralized accounting system is highly effective may affect the auditor's decision about the number of locations where he or she will perform auditing procedures or whether to perform certain auditing procedures in some locations at an interim date. Those decisions, in turn, affect the way in which auditing procedures are applied with respect to the completeness, accuracy, and existence/occurrence assertions, even though the auditor may not specifically consider each of those assertions. Control procedures, on the other hand, often have a specific effect on an individual assertion related to a particular account balance or class of transactions. For instance, control procedures established to ensure that all items reported on a receiving report log are included in accounts payable relate directly to the completeness assertion for accounts payable.

The relationship of control structure policies and procedures to assertions may be either direct or indirect. The degree of directness, or closeness, of the relationship determines, in part, how likely a specific policy or procedure is to have an effect on a particular assertion for a specific account balance or class of transactions. For example, accounting for the numerical sequence of sales invoices is directly related to the completeness assertion for accounts receivable

---

[1]The auditor may believe that such "tests of controls" (defined later) could lead to an assessment of control risk below the maximum level but that it would not be efficient to perform those tests. As noted in the section of the chapter on "Tests of Controls," however, tests of controls performed concurrently with developing the required understanding of the control structure will usually support an assessment of control risk at below the maximum for one or more specific assertions and account balances.

and sales, while management's review of monthly sales analyses indirectly relates to the completeness assertion for those account balances.

The tests the auditor performs to support an assessment of control risk at less than the maximum level are directed at the *effectiveness* of *both* the design *and* the operation of control structure policies and procedures. Those tests are referred to as "tests of controls" in SAS No. 55 and are discussed in a later section of this chapter. Effective design relates to whether the policy or procedure is suitably designed to prevent or detect material misstatements with respect to specific assertions. Effective operation is concerned with how the policy or procedure was applied, whether it was consistently applied throughout the period, and the person(s) who applied it. (As used in this chapter in the context of the operation of policies and procedures, the terms "effectiveness" and "effective" incorporate the concept of consistent, or continuous, operation.)

Assessing the Control Environment

In assessing the control environment, the auditor considers factors that contribute to its quality, tests whether those factors are operating effectively, and forms an overall conclusion about the environment. The factors that affect an enterprise's control environment were described in Chapter 7. Some of them affect the entity's ability to maintain an effective accounting system and control procedures. Others affect management's ability to make the informed judgments and estimates necessary to prepare financial statements. Still other factors affect the entity's ability to restrict the opportunity for management fraud. All of those factors are interrelated. The auditor should consider them both individually and collectively in assessing the extent to which they contribute to the control environment.

Management's review of various operating reports is an aspect of the control environment that the auditor frequently considers important and tests because it may provide evidence about the entity's accounting system and control procedures. (Knowing what reports management reviews may also serve as a basis for designing substantive tests.) In assessing how useful their reviews are, the auditor should consider

- The competence of the individuals reviewing the reports. They should have an adequate level of business knowledge and technical expertise and be familiar with the entity's operations.
- The authority of the individuals performing the reviews to take corrective action. They should be adequately positioned within the organization to act effectively.
- The objectivity of the individuals performing the reviews. The individuals should be independent of those who perform the work, both functionally (that is, there should be adequate segregation of duties) and motivationally (for example, an officer's review might be of less value from the auditor's standpoint if the officer's compensation is based on operating results being reviewed).

The objectivity of the manager who reviews operating reports is particularly important in audits of small businesses that are dominated by owner-managers or others who have the authority to establish policies and make decisions about how to pursue business objectives. On the one hand, owner-manager reviews may enhance the control structure because of the close attention with which they are carried out. They may also provide an additional level of segregation of duties in the accounting function. On the other hand, if there is no level of review above that of management (such as a review by nonmanagement members of the board of directors), the contribution of management reviews to the control environment may be limited because of a possible lack of objectivity. This would be particularly true if management's objectives regarding the financial statements did not coincide with those of the auditor—as would be the case if management's primary concern were maximizing (or minimizing) reported earnings rather than fair presentation in conformity with GAAP.

After testing the various policies and procedures that contribute to the control environment and assessing their effectiveness, the auditor reaches an overall conclusion about to what extent the environment is conducive to maintaining an effective accounting system and control procedures, and reduces the likelihood that management would intentionally distort the financial statements. If the auditor concludes that the control environment is favorable, there is a lower risk that other control structure policies and procedures will be overridden or bypassed and that misstatements may occur. That conclusion helps the auditor determine the nature, timing, and extent of other auditing procedures, including both tests of control procedures and substantive tests.

Auditors sometimes document the assessment of the control environment on a form that lists the various factors that make up the control environment and provides space for the auditor's comments and conclusions about each factor. Figure 8.6 illustrates part of such a form, dealing with the availability and reliability of information for management to use in reviewing and evaluating its operations.

Assessing the Accounting System

As described earlier in the chapter, the auditor obtains an understanding of the flow of transactions through the client's accounting system. That understanding covers the significant classes of transactions and key accounting procedures, files, ledgers, and reports. In the process of obtaining and documenting the understanding, the auditor considers whether the accounting system appears to be effectively designed and operated. The auditor's review of prior-year working papers, interviews of accounting personnel, and transaction reviews (if performed) provide evidence about the accounting system. In addition, tests performed in assessing the control environment and control procedures provide evidence about the effectiveness of accounting procedures as well. In practice, the auditor does not make a separate assessment of the accounting system because it is not feasible to isolate the effect of the accounting system on specific assertions and account balances. Instead, the auditor incorporates the assessment of the accounting system into the overall assess-

Figure 8.6   Assessment of Control Environment

SECTION D: AVAILABILITY AND RELIABILITY OF MANAGEMENT INFORMATION

To monitor effectively the activities of the business, management must have sufficient, reliable information on a timely basis to review and evaluate its operations. In addition, appropriate actions must be taken as a result of management's reviews and evaluations. In evaluating whether appropriate reliable management information exists, consider the following factors:

Factors	*Comments*
The adequacy of financial, statistical, or other information used by management with respect to: • its relevance to the respective managers' responsibilities • its sufficiency • the frequency and timeliness with which it is received • its reliability (e.g., the adequacy of the accounting procedures to ensure the reliability of periodic financial statements—see also factors below) • its informational value (e.g., the appropriateness of its level of detail or aggregation).	Monthly Management Package* is given to each manager responsible for analyzing performance. —Reports are generated within ten working days —Reports are generated by the system or by accounting clerks and reviewed by the controller before going to users —Operating reports are produced in both detail and aggregated versions appropriate for various levels of management. (Note: There is no report that analyzes inventory levels.)
The comparison of current conditions or results with appropriate benchmarks (e.g., the preceding year's conditions or results, or a practicably achievable budget or plan).	Compared with prior year and month.
The explanations obtained for current variations from reasonable benchmarks and implementation of corrective action.	They obtain explanations for the differences in results between the prior year and prior month.
With respect to the explanations and corrective actions: • documentation of explanations • evaluation of explanations by the appropriate levels of management or the board of directors • implementation of corrective actions by the appropriate levels of management and follow-up by senior management.	Due to structure/size of company, explanations are seldom documented. They are discussed among management monthly and with Board quarterly. Corrective actions are agreed upon at those meetings. Corrective action plans are monitored and progress is reported at the next regularly scheduled meeting.

(Continued)

Figure 8.6 *Continued*

Personal involvement of managers in activities relating to their respective areas of responsibility, and their accessibility to subordinates.	Key management personnel make periodic reports to the Board describing actions they have taken to meet the objectives of their department.
Other factors considered (list): —Close scrutiny of A/R status by key management	—Communications throughout the company are informal but effective based on prior audits and conversations with key/middle management. —President, Treasurer, and V.P.–Sales meet to review weekly aged A/R listing, at which time they decide whether to put delinquent accounts on a cash basis for future orders and adjust credit limits for other accounts. V.P.–Sales continuously receives input from salespeople on business climate in their territories and apparent health of customers' operations. On V.P.–Sales' instructions, salespeople visit delinquent accounts and press for payment.

Conclusions

It appears that management generally receives the type and level of information necessary to make informed judgments about the operations of the entity. In addition, the information is timely and corrective action, when necessary, seems appropriate. However, they do not monitor inventory levels on a current basis and obsolescence is considered only at year-end.

*Package Contains:
• Financial Statements
• Monthly Financial Statement Analysis
• Production, Cost, and Sales Information by Product
• Past Due A/R Analysis by Customer

ment of control risk relating to specific assertions for particular account balances and classes of transactions.

Assessing Control Procedures

In assessing control procedures, the auditor identifies the specific procedures designed and placed in operation by the client to achieve the control objectives of completeness, accuracy, authorization, file control, and asset protection for a particular transaction cycle. The auditor then develops and performs appropriate tests of the effectiveness of the design and operation of those control procedures. As a practical matter, tests of control procedures are normally restricted to major transaction classes, because other transactions are relatively low volume and the related accounts can be more efficiently audited by substantive tests.

TESTS OF CONTROLS

The auditor performs tests of controls to determine whether the policies and procedures to prevent or detect misstatements have been effectively designed and have operated effectively throughout the period under audit.

Concurrent Tests of Controls

The auditor may perform some tests of controls concurrently with developing an understanding of the design of control structure policies and procedures and whether they have been placed in operation. Those tests are referred to in this book as "concurrent tests of controls." Evidence about the effectiveness of control structure policies and procedures may result from auditing procedures *planned* as concurrent tests of controls; alternatively, such evidence may be obtained from concurrent tests of controls that are *incidental* to auditing procedures directed at obtaining the understanding. In both situations, the auditor will ordinarily have obtained, concurrent with the understanding of the control structure, evidence to support an assessment of control risk at below the maximum for one or more specific assertions and account balances. Concurrent tests of controls are more likely to focus on the control environment and accounting system than on specific control procedures (the third element of the control structure). Because of the audit effort involved in testing control procedures, concurrent tests of control procedures are generally limited or in some cases not performed at all.

The authors believe that, because of evidence from concurrent tests of controls, auditors are rarely in a position where they must assess control risk at the maximum level for all audit objectives for all account balances. SAS No. 55 (AU Section 319.41) cites, as an example of concurrent tests of controls (although the term itself is not used in the SAS), the following procedures: inquiry about management's use of budgets, observing management's comparison of monthly budgeted with actual expenses, and inspecting reports of the investigation of variances between budgeted and actual amounts. Although those auditing procedures were directed at ascertaining the *design* of the entity's budgeting policies and whether they had been *placed in operation*, the procedures may also provide evidence about *how effectively the policies are designed and operating* to prevent or detect material misstatements in classifying expenses. In some circumstances, that evidence may support an assessment of control risk that is below the maximum level for the presentation and disclosure objective relating to expenses in the income statement.

Another example of how procedures performed in obtaining the required understanding of the control structure can also provide evidence of its effectiveness involves division of duties. In the course of obtaining an understanding of the accounting system, the auditor usually observes whether duties over cash receipts and deposits are adequately segregated. In doing this, the auditor will at the same time have obtained evidence about how effectively the separation procedure is designed and operating. This evidence may support a control risk assessment below the maximum level for, in this instance, the existence objective relating to cash. A third example involves the accounting system. In inquiring about how the accounting system for a particular class of transactions is designed and how the transactions flow through it, the auditor generally obtains evidence as well about whether the system is operating effectively. The authors believe that in most situations such evidence will support an assessment of control risk below the maximum.

Additional Tests of Controls

After evaluating the evidence about the effectiveness of the control structure that was obtained concurrently with obtaining the understanding of the control structure, the auditor decides whether to seek additional evidence through ''additional tests of controls.'' Conceptually, the decision to perform tests of controls might not be made until after the understanding of the control structure has been obtained. In practice, however, the auditor is not likely to consider performing additional tests of controls unless he or she has obtained evidence of the effectiveness of the control structure concurrently with developing the understanding. The purpose of performing additional tests of controls is to support a further reduction in the assessed level of control risk for certain audit objectives and account balances. The decision is based mainly on the auditor's judgment about what evidence is likely to be available (discussed later) and whether testing the control structure in order to further restrict substantive tests of accounts in a particular transaction cycle will be efficient, as compared with proceeding directly to substantive testing. On a recurring engagement where the auditor intends to again perform additional tests of controls, he or she may update the understanding of the control structure and perform tests of controls simultaneously. Because of the substantial audit effort involved in performing additional tests of controls, it is usually not efficient to undertake them unless the auditor believes that they will support a low control risk assessment for specific assertions and account balances.

SAS No. 55 (AU Section 319.44) discusses audit efficiency considerations as follows:

> In considering efficiency, the auditor recognizes that additional evidential matter that supports a further reduction in the assessed level of control risk for an assertion would result in less audit effort for the substantive tests of that assertion. The auditor weighs the increase in audit effort associated with the additional tests of controls that is necessary to obtain such evidential matter against the resulting decrease in audit effort associated with the reduced substantive tests. When the auditor concludes it is inefficient to obtain additional evidential matter for specific assertions, the auditor uses the assessed level of control risk based on the understanding of the internal control structure in planning the substantive tests for those assertions.

The auditor usually decides that it would not be efficient to seek a further reduction in the assessed level of control risk when one or more of the following circumstances are present:

1. Volumes of transactions are low, or inherent risk characteristics make substantive tests relatively easy to apply.
2. The client has a manual system, or its computerized systems are neither complex nor pervasive.
3. The necessary tests of controls entail testing a large number of control procedures, as might be the case, for example, if relevant general control procedures in a computerized system do not ensure the effectiveness of programmed control procedures.

In these circumstances, the auditor designs and performs substantive tests for all relevant audit objectives and account balances, taking into consideration the results of the materiality and risk assessment activities already carried out.

Outside of the situations just described, the auditor may consider it efficient to perform additional tests of controls in one or more transaction cycles in order to further reduce the assessed level of control risk for specific assertions and account balances. In most instances, this strategy will enable the auditor to further reduce the assurance needed from substantive tests with respect to the audit objectives of completeness, accuracy, and existence/occurrence (and, in some cases, cutoff) for accounts that are derived from transaction cycles. This strategy will be particularly effective if it is possible to also obtain indirect evidence about the ongoing effective operation of control structure policies and procedures from such factors as management reviews of accounting reports and the absence of recurring problems in using data produced by those policies and procedures.

For large clients with pervasive, complex, and integrated computerized systems, it may be readily apparent that performing additional tests of control structure policies and procedures in all transaction cycles is an efficient strategy. For such clients, the auditor usually expects to be able to significantly reduce the assurance needed from substantive tests of accounts derived from transaction cycles, although some specific deficiencies in control structure policies and procedures may have to be taken into consideration.

Other enterprises, whether large or small, may have relatively complex computerized accounting systems, but the number and expertise of computer personnel may be limited. In other instances, there may be extensive control structure policies and procedures, but some general control procedures may be informal and not well documented. There are frequently deficiencies in control procedures related to program and data file security, although some of these deficiencies may be mitigated if the client uses purchased accounting packages for which the source code is not readily available (that is, the client's personnel are effectively unable to amend the programs). On these types of engagements it is often more difficult for the auditor to decide whether to perform additional tests of controls to support a further reduction in the assessed level of control risk.

Tests of controls focused on the control environment and accounting system do not require as much audit effort as tests of specific control procedures (the third element of the control structure). The evidence obtained from tests of the control environment and accounting system relates to several assertions and accounts, and thus is not sufficient in itself to support a low control risk assessment for specific assertions and account balances. To assess control risk as low for a particular assertion and account, the auditor will almost always have to perform additional tests of relevant control procedures and may also perform additional tests of controls directed at the control environment and accounting system.

In most engagements the auditor may believe he or she needs evidence of the effective operation of certain key control procedures in order to design efficient substantive tests with respect to a particular audit objective. The auditor then plans, at an early stage, to assess the effectiveness of those control procedures. Even if the results of such tests are not expected to support a low control risk assessment, they may affect the nature, timing, and extent of substantive tests. Examples of such key control procedures are physical inventory cycle count procedures, which the auditor might test to help establish the accuracy of inventory quantities, and cash reconciliations, tests of which might help establish the accuracy of the cash account balance.

The auditor's expectation when he or she performs tests of individual control procedures is that the tests will support a low risk assessment; that is, an assessment that all the control structure elements interacting together reduce to a low level the risk of material misstatement relating to an audit objective. This aggregate assessment will influence the auditor's decision about what specific tests to perform on which individual control procedures, what techniques to use, when to perform them, and how much testing to do. If the auditor assesses control risk as low for one or more assertions related to an account balance or class of transactions, he or she may be able to eliminate or significantly curtail substantive tests. SAS No. 55 cautions that regardless of the assessed level of control risk, some substantive tests should be performed for every significant account balance and class of transactions. However, if the auditor assesses the risk of material misstatement related to an assertion as low, it is not necessary to direct substantive tests to that particular assertion.

Figure 12.1 on pages 390 to 391 provides an example of the control objectives applicable to a client's sales of goods and services and of the control procedures an entity may have established to achieve the objectives.[2] As the figure indicates, one or more control procedures that the auditor expects will support a restriction of substantive tests would be identified for each control objective as a basis for designing tests of controls.

Sources of Evidence and Techniques Used to Test Controls

The evidence needed to support a specific assessed level of control risk is a matter of auditor judgment. In determining the evidence that is sufficient to support a specific assessed level of control risk below the maximum level, the auditor should consider the source of evidence, its timeliness, and whether related evidence exists. Those considerations in turn determine what specific techniques the auditor will use in performing tests of controls to obtain the needed evidence.

The techniques used in testing control structure policies and procedures are observation, inquiry of client personnel, examination of documents and rec-

[2]Figures 12.2, 13.1, 13.2, 13.3, and 14.1 illustrate the same principles for other classes of transactions.

ords, and, in some cases, reperformance of the application of policies and procedures. (With the exception of reperformance, the techniques used in performing tests of controls are the same as those used in obtaining the understanding of the control structure elements, as described earlier in the chapter.)

There may be no client documentation of the design or operation of some policies or procedures, such as certain control environment factors and arrangements for segregating duties. In that event, evidence may be obtained through observation. In general, evidence the auditor obtains directly, for example, by observation, is more reliable than that obtained indirectly, such as by inquiry. However, this must be weighed against the possibility that the observed procedure may not be performed in the same way when the auditor is not present.

During the inquiry process, the auditor should, wherever possible, corroborate the explanations received by inspecting procedures manuals and reports or other similar documents evidencing control structure policies and procedures. The auditor also may make corroborative inquiries of individuals other than those implementing the policies and procedures. SAS No. 55 states that inquiry alone generally does not provide sufficient evidence to support a conclusion about whether a specific policy or procedure is effective. Accordingly, if the auditor believes a policy or procedure may have a significant effect in reducing control risk to a low level for a specific assertion, he or she usually must perform tests in addition to inquiry to obtain sufficient evidence that it is designed and operating effectively.

For aspects of the control structure that are performed manually (such as the follow-up of items contained in computer-generated exception reports), the auditor should examine documents and records of the application when they may reasonably be expected to exist (for example, there may be written explanations, check marks, or other indications of performance on a copy of a report used in applying a control procedure). The auditor generally examines documentation of the performance of supervisory control procedures.

Tests based on observation, inquiry, and examination of documents ordinarily provide sufficient evidence about the effective design of a control structure policy or procedure, and often provide evidence about its operating effectiveness as well. That is, these tests provide evidence of how the policy or procedure was applied, whether it was applied consistently throughout the period, and the person(s) who applied it. However, in some instances, the auditor may also have to reperform the application of the policy or procedure to obtain adequate evidence that it is operating effectively. When the auditor believes a control structure policy or procedure is so significant that further evidence of its effectiveness is necessary, it is appropriate to reperform its application. For example, a bank's control procedure designed to ensure the completeness and accuracy of updating a standing data file of interest rates may be so significant to the accuracy of interest charged to loan customers that the auditor may wish to reperform the updating procedure a few times to gain additional evidence that it is operating as prescribed. If extensive reperformance of control procedures is likely to be necessary, the auditor should reconsider whether it is still efficient to perform tests of controls in order to restrict the scope of substantive testing.

Timeliness of Evidence. If observation is used as a test of controls, the auditor should consider that the evidence obtained from that test is relevant only to the time when the observation took place. Accordingly, the evidence may not be sufficient to assess effectiveness for untested periods. In that situation, the auditor may decide to perform other tests of controls to obtain evidence about whether the policy or procedure was operating during the entire period under audit. For example, the auditor may observe cycle counting of inventory at a point in time and examine documents evidencing the counting procedure during other time periods.

In considering evidence to support the assessment of the control structure in the current year, the auditor may consider prior-year audit evidence. In determining whether such evidence is relevant to the current audit, the auditor should consider the audit objective involved, the specific policies and procedures, the degree to which they were assessed in prior years, the results of the tests of controls performed, and the evidence about design or operation that may be expected from substantive tests in the current audit. The auditor should obtain information currently about whether changes in the control structure have occurred and, if so, their nature and extent. All of these considerations may support either increasing or decreasing the evidence needed in the current period.

Continuous Operation of Control Structure Policies and Procedures. When assessing whether tests of controls can reduce the assessed level of control risk sufficiently to permit the planned restriction of substantive tests, the auditor needs to determine that relevant control structure policies and procedures have operated continuously during the period.

Manually applied control structure policies and procedures are prone to random failures. When assessing those policies and procedures, the auditor should obtain evidence of their application, and if necessary reperform them, for control events occurring at different times during the period of assessment. These tests need not necessarily be extensive. Supervisory control procedures that the auditor can test may provide evidence that underlying manually performed control procedures were operating continuously.

Spreading tests throughout the period is not always necessary to obtain evidence about continuous operation. For example, if a control procedure involves reviewing and following up an exception report that is cumulative, transactions or circumstances meeting specified criteria continue to be reported and reviewed as long as the criteria are met (examples would be reports of "goods shipped but not billed" or "goods received but not invoiced"). For such control procedures, tests that provide evidence that a procedure operated effectively at a point in time will also provide evidence about the proper operation of the underlying accounting procedures throughout the period up to that point in time.

Accounting and control procedures performed by a computer program are not subject to random failures or deterioration over time, provided that the relevant general computer control procedures, including those for program maintenance, are operating effectively. This suggests that if general control procedures appear to be operating appropriately and effectively, the auditor could choose to test them as a basis for determining that accounting and control procedures performed by a computer program operated continuously throughout the period.

In addition, users of information affected by control structure policies and procedures would become aware of control breakdowns and report them to appropriate levels of management. Thus, the auditor can sometimes obtain indirect evidence, from the ongoing operation of business activities, that policies and procedures operated continuously.

Dual-Purpose Tests.   Tests of controls normally precede substantive tests, because the results of tests of controls affect the auditor's decision about the appropriate nature, timing, and extent of substantive tests. Sometimes, however, to achieve greater audit efficiency, the two types of tests may be performed simultaneously using the same document or record. For example, the same accounts receivable balances selected for confirmation (a substantive test) may be used to determine that the customers' files contain documents showing that the sales orders were appropriately approved (a test of controls). Moreover, a test of controls may provide evidence about dollar errors in the accounts. Also, a substantive test may provide evidence about the control structure if no errors were found as a result of the substantive test or if errors that were found were investigated and determined to be the result of a control structure deficiency.

Interrelationship of Evidence.   In assessing control risk for a specific audit objective, the auditor should consider evidence in its entirety: Evidence provided by tests of one element of the control structure should be considered in relation to evidence about the other elements. Evidence produced by different tests of controls should be considered in combination. Evidence from various tests that supports the same conclusion is more reliable than evidence obtained from a single test. When audit evidence from more than one source leads to different conclusions, however, the auditor should reconsider his or her original assessment. For example, if tests of the control environment indicate that it should prevent or detect unauthorized changes in a computer program, but tests of the effective operation of the program reveal that unauthorized changes were made and were not detected, the auditor would reassess the conclusion about the control environment.

Evaluating the Results of Tests of Controls.   The auditor should review the results of the tests of controls and consider whether the expected reduction in the assessed level of control risk has been attained. If the auditor finds that the risk of material misstatement for a particular financial statement assertion is higher than originally expected, he or she will have to reconsider the assurance needed from substantive tests.

If the tests of controls reveal a departure from or breakdown in prescribed policies and procedures, the auditor should consider its cause and document his or her conclusions. What amendments need to be made to planned substantive tests will depend in part on the reasons for the departure. For example, the appropriate audit response to control structure breakdowns should be different if the cause was a poorly trained clerk who substituted for a highly trained clerk during the latter's three-week vacation than if the cause was incompetent work or ineffective supervision throughout the year. The auditor can sometimes ascertain the reason for a control breakdown by inquiring and examining the circumstances; in other cases, the auditor may have to extend the testing. Before extending the testing, however, the auditor should ensure that it will help determine the cause and extent of the breakdown. Depending on the nature of the policy or procedure, if a departure or breakdown is corrected long enough before year-end, and this is confirmed by appropriate tests, no amendment to other audit tests will normally be necessary.

Departures from and breakdowns in control structure policies and procedures should be considered for reporting to the client, as discussed later. Also, the documentation of the control structure should be amended as required.

DOCUMENTING THE ASSESSMENT AND TESTS

Professional standards require the auditor to document the basis for the conclusions reached concerning the assessed level of control risk for specific audit objectives related to the account balances and classes of transactions reflected in the financial statements. (For audit objectives for which control risk is assessed at the maximum level, however, the basis for the conclusion does not have to be documented.) The nature and extent of documentation will vary according to the assessed level of control risk and the nature of the control structure and the entity's related documentation.

Techniques for documenting the understanding of the control environment and the accounting system were discussed earlier in this chapter. This section presents several alternative formats for documenting the assessment of control procedures, provides examples, and explains when each could be used. Individual auditors and firms often express a preference for one type of documentation by means of their internal policy pronouncements and the practice aids (for example, forms, checklists, and questionnaires) they provide, which may be either required or optional. Regardless of the type of documentation the auditor uses, it must provide a means for recording in the working papers a description of the relevant control procedures and the tests the auditor performed to assess how effectively they were designed and operating.

Documenting Control Procedures

Control procedures are typically documented by narratives, flowcharts, control matrices, questionnaires, or other forms designed for this purpose.

Narratives.   While many auditors prefer flowcharting as the means of documenting the design and assessment of the accounting system and related control procedures, narratives are often useful and, particularly for unsophisticated control structures, may be more cost effective. When narratives are used, the auditor should ensure that they contain all relevant information.

Flowcharts.   Control procedures are sometimes documented on a flowchart, often called a *systems flowchart*, that depicts, for each significant class of transactions, the path of a transaction from its inception (that is, the point where the transaction first enters the accounting system) to the update of the general ledger. It provides, in a convenient form, a combined description of the accounting system and related control procedures and contains information necessary for the auditor to design tests of those control procedures. A systems flowchart typically contains, for each significant class of transactions,

1. The details of significant accounting and control procedures, including division of duties and supervision.
2. The job titles of the people performing the procedures.
3. The frequency of the operation of the procedures.

The information is usually organized by area of responsibility within the system. Depending on the responsibilities involved, an organizational unit may vary from a large department (such as a sales department) to one individual (the credit manager). The names of the organizational units the transactions flow through should be shown at the top of the flowchart. The flow of transactions usually is from top left to bottom right. Control procedures should be distinctly marked on the flowchart by a diagonal line inside a procedure symbol and may include a narrative supplement noting the nature of the control procedure (e.g., ''approval'').

Systems flowcharts need not be excessively detailed, as only significant procedures should be depicted. One or more accounting and related control procedures may be depicted by one symbol, with a narrative explanation of each significant procedure provided separately on the flowchart. This normally makes it possible to show each transaction cycle on one or two pages. An illustration of part of a systems flowchart for the sales order and billing portions of a computerized revenue cycle is provided in Figure 8.7.

Control Matrices.   Some auditors capture information about the principal control procedures and any apparent deficiencies in them (such as omitted procedures) through the use of control matrices. Control matrices may be designed to record control procedures related to transaction processing, file control, asset protection, or any other relevant types of control procedures, whether computerized or manual. Figure 8.8 shows a control matrix covering the processing of transactions relating to both shipments and cash receipts in a computerized revenue cycle. It describes the principal control procedures the client designed to meet the control objectives relating to transaction processing and serves as an aid in understanding those procedures and designing tests of controls. It may even serve as a substitute for an internal control questionnaire or other similar form of documentation, as discussed later.

An explanation of the columns in the illustrated control matrix follows.

- The *significant transactions/key files receiving initial input (volumes)* column describes briefly each significant class of transactions (manually initiated or computer generated), including amendments to standing data, with an estimate of the annual volume of transactions processed. Significant transactions are transactions that could have a material effect on the key data file(s) that support account balances.

Figure 8.7 Systems Flowchart—Revenue Cycle, Shipping and Billing

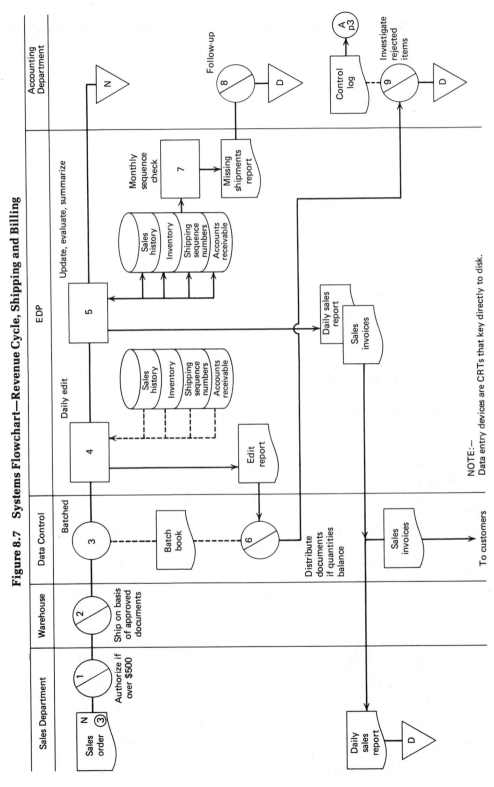

NOTE:–
Data entry devices are CRTs that key directly to disk.

Figure 8.8 Transaction Control Matrix

Client/Location   Alpha Corporation/Middlebury

Application/Class of transactions   Revenue Cycle

Prepared by/Date

Reviewed by/Date

| Significant transactions/Key files receiving initial input (volumes) | Input/Generation | | | | Updates | | | Division of duties |
	Completeness	Accuracy (specify fields)	Standing data used	Authorization	Key file(s)	Completeness and accuracy		
Shipments Open order file Sales transaction file (160,000 shipments per year)	Shipments matched against open order file; numerically sequenced invoices generated; shipments recorded on sales transaction file. Investigation of long-outstanding open orders and review for integrity of numerical sequence of invoices & bills of lading on sales transaction listing.	Matching sales order to inventory master file and A/R file • customer no. • product code • price Matching shipping order to open order file • customer no. • product code • quantity	Product no. Price Customer no.	As orders are input, they are matched against preestablished credit limits and sales terms. Orders outside preestablished limits are investigated before being updated to the open order file.	A/R file, G/L master file		Comparison of A/R balance with G/L master file. Comparison of sales with monthly activity on G/L master file. Sequence check of invoice numbers.	Initiate order; approve order; input shipment; compare account activity & balances with G/L master file; follow-up on exceptions.
Cash remittances Cash receipts transaction file (45,000 cash remittances per year)	Cash receipts listing reconciled to bank's deposit control report.	Matching cash remittances to open invoices on A/R file	N/A	N/A	A/R file, G/L master file		Comparison of A/R balance with G/L master file. Comparison of cash receipts listings with deposits recorded on bank statements.	Receipt of cash; deposit of cash; input of cash remittance; comparison of A/R with G/L & comparison of cash receipts listing with bank deposits; follow-up on exceptions.

- The *completeness of input/generation* column identifies the principal control procedures used to ensure that all such transactions are initiated, recorded, and accepted for further processing.

- The *accuracy of input/generation* column identifies the principal control procedures used to ensure that the key data fields are accurately recorded.

- The *input/generation—standing data used* column indicates the key data file(s) involved.

- The *authorization for input/generation* column identifies and records the principal control procedures used to prevent or detect unauthorized transactions.

- The *updates—key file(s)* column records the key file(s) updated by the key transaction fields.

- The *completeness and accuracy of updates* column records the principal control procedures used to ensure that the key file(s) listed in the previous column are completely and accurately updated by the transaction.

- The *division of duties* column records what duties are performed by separate persons, i.e., showing that those responsible for control procedures related to transaction processing are separate from those who have access to the related assets.

Internal Control Questionnaires.   Since control objectives and the means of achieving them are much the same from one control structure to another, some auditors find it efficient to design an internal control questionnaire (ICQ) that identifies and lists expected control procedures and then use the questionnaire to document control procedures on all or most engagements. The questionnaire is usually divided into transaction cycles that cover the main transaction flows, and is organized in terms of the control objectives that should be achieved by the client's control procedures at each stage of transaction processing. The questions relating to each control objective are sometimes further subdivided between

1. Those that seek information concerning *accounting procedures* that are not in themselves control procedures, but that form the basis for the exercise of control procedures.

2. Those that seek to determine whether or not *control procedures* are present.

A portion of this type of questionnaire for a manual revenue cycle is illustrated in Figure 8.9. Questions in an ICQ also frequently indicate the type of control procedure being addressed: transaction processing, file control, asset protection, segregation of duties, supervisory, or general computer. While it is not necessary to have this degree of subdivision for an ICQ to be effective, it may allow for a better understanding of the internal control structure and is helpful in designing both tests of controls and substantive tests.

   The ICQ is also a convenient way of documenting the specific internal control procedures that the auditor intends to test. If systems flowcharts have

Figure 8.9   Internal Control Questionnaire

Control Procedures Applied to Goods Shipped and Services Performed	Flowchart Reference	Yes	No
Completeness			
Accounting Procedures—Basis for Control Procedures			
1. Are the accounting records maintained in such a way that it can subsequently be established whether all the related transactions have been accounted for (e.g., by sequentially prenumbering delivery slips) in respect of: (a) Goods? (b) Services?			
2. Are records maintained of goods shipped and services performed that have not been matched with the related sales invoices in respect of: (a) Goods? (b) Services?			
Control Procedures			
3. If sequentially prenumbered forms are used, are all numbers accounted for as part of the procedure for ascertaining unmatched items in respect of: (a) Goods? (b) Services?			
4. Are unmatched records of goods shipped and services performed reviewed on a regular basis (e.g., monthly) to determine the reasons for any such items that have not been matched within a reasonable period of time in respect of: (a) Goods? (b) Services?			
5. Are the results of the procedure in question 4 reviewed and approved by a responsible official?			

been prepared, the information contained in them should be used, as much as possible, in answering the ICQ questions. The questions in the ICQ are usually phrased so that they may be answered ''Yes'' or ''No'' to indicate, respectively, the presence or absence of a control procedure. If a question does not apply to a specific client or location, the appropriate response is N/A (Not Applicable).

The ICQ is often completed concurrently with obtaining the understanding of the design of control procedures, which is in part the basis for the auditor's decision to perform tests of controls. The auditor should reconsider the answers to the ICQ questions during subsequent stages of the audit, particularly after performing tests of controls and substantive tests. Departures from or deficiencies in prescribed control procedures may be disclosed by substantive tests. In that event, the ICQ should be amended to reflect the new information.

Documenting Tests of Control Procedures

When tests of controls are performed, they must be documented, and auditors use many different means of doing so. The choice, once again, depends on such factors as the type of test (for example, observing that a control procedure is operating versus reperforming it) and the policies of the particular CPA firm. Some tests of controls can conveniently be recorded directly on control matrices or internal control questionnaires, in which case the matrices and ICQs, with minor adaptations, document both the control procedures identified and the tests performed to ensure that they are operating effectively. (Conceptually, tests of controls can also be documented as part of a narrative description of accounting and control procedures or on a flowchart, but those documentation methods can make it difficult for a reviewer to evaluate the tests performed.) Alternatively, separate working papers could be used to document the tests performed; this method is particularly useful when a test consists of examining evidence of the operation of a control procedure (such as authorization of payroll changes by department heads and personnel managers) or reperformance of a control procedure (such as reperforming, at year-end, the client's monthly follow-up of all unmatched cash receipts included in a suspense account, for evidence that the receipts were credited to the proper account).

Some auditing firms have designed forms specifically for both recording the client's control procedures and documenting the results of tests of those procedures. The form may be organized like an ICQ; that is, it may be divided into sections by control objectives and list under each control objective questions related to the control procedures that achieve that objective. The auditor indicates a "Yes" or "No" answer to each question and describes, either directly on the form or on an attached working paper, the relevant control procedure and the tests of controls performed.

Control procedures should be described in sufficient detail to support the auditor's conclusion as to whether the control objective has been achieved. Typically, the following information is recorded for each procedure:

a. The name and job title of the person performing the procedure.
b. A description of the procedure.
c. How frequently the procedure is performed.
d. What report(s) are used in performing the procedure or generated by it.

Similarly, tests of controls should be recorded in enough detail to support the auditor's conclusion about whether the procedures are operating effectively. This generally includes

a. The name and job title of the person the auditor discussed the procedure with or observed performing it.

b. The date of the discussion or observation.

c. A description of the discussion or observation.

d. Details of any documents, reports, or other evidence examined or tests performed.

A question may be included at the end of each section that prompts the auditor to draw an overall conclusion about whether the control procedures, taken as a whole, are appropriately designed to achieve the control objective and are operating effectively, and to document the reasons for the conclusion.

Figure 8.10 shows part of a form used to document control procedures and tests of controls. The two pages illustrated relate to the completeness-of-input control objective for shipments in a computerized revenue cycle. The control procedures described are based on the same set of facts recorded on the control matrix shown in Figure 8.8.

Documenting Control Deficiencies

It is often helpful for the auditor to prepare a document summarizing the deficiencies found in the design or operation of control procedures. This permits the auditor to consider the effect of the deficiencies on planned substantive tests. It also facilitates preparing the communication on control structure deficiencies (discussed in the next section). The documentation should be amended whenever pertinent information is found in the course of the audit, whether in performing tests of controls or substantive tests. The working paper documentation will usually include a description of the nature of the deficiency and its possible effect on the financial statements, a decision on whether the deficiency could give rise to material misstatement in the financial statements and the justification for this decision, and an explanation of the audit response to the deficiency, including any amendment to the nature, timing, or extent of substantive procedures.

COMMUNICATING CONTROL STRUCTURE DEFICIENCIES

While management has primary responsibility for reliable financial reporting, the board of directors, generally acting through its audit committee (if there is one), is responsible for overseeing the financial reporting process. That responsibility can be most effectively carried out if the board or audit committee is informed of deficiencies in the internal control structure that the auditor becomes aware of. Management also is usually interested in the auditor's observations about internal control deficiencies and ways of remedying them, and in suggestions the auditor may have for improving the enterprise's operations and profitability.

SAS No. 60, *Communication of Internal Control Structure Related Matters Noted in an Audit* (AU Section 325.02), requires the auditor to communicate to the audit committee of the board of directors, or its equivalent, matters coming to his or her attention in the course of the audit that represent ''significant deficiencies'' in the design or operation of any of the elements of the internal control

Figure 8.10   Record of Control Procedures and Tests

Control Objective 3—Revenue Cycle (Shipments)—Completeness of Input

Questions and control procedures	Yes	No	Tests
Transactions controlled by matching 3.1 Are the procedures for setting up and maintaining expected transactions on the control file adequate to ensure that the matching process could ensure completeness of processing? Shipments are matched against the items flagged on the open order file as having generated a bill of lading.	✔		Information provided by Jim Miller (Controller) and the EDP Manager
3.2 Is the matching process adequate to: (a) form a basis for identifying all unmatched transactions. (b) identify duplicates and other mismatching transactions? Twice a day, a list summarizing orders entered since the last transmission and a bill of lading for each order are generated. The items in the open order file are flagged as having generated a bill of lading. After shipment, the shipping input clerk enters the sales order number and quantity shipped via CRT. The customer and item number are compared with the order information appearing on the CRT. (a) Items flagged as having generated a bill of lading that have not been confirmed as shipped are reported on the unmatched bill of lading report. (b) Invoices are generated for items confirmed as shipped and the order is flagged as completed on the open order file.	✔		On 4/4/X3 we discussed the review of the unmatched bill of lading report with Jake O'Leary, accounts receivable supervisor. He indicated that normally the items are the result of orders received late in the day, which they were unable to ship until the following day. We examined the reports for the following days: June 8 and 15, September 17 and 19, November 10 and 25, and April 1 and noted fewer than 10 items appeared on each day (see workpapers 101.9–101.15). All orders were noted as being shipped the following day. The orders did not appear on the next day's report. O'Leary had approved the reports.

Figure 8.10   Continued

Questions and control procedures	Yes	No	Tests
3.3 Are all changes and deletions to the control file of expected transactions approved? Changes to and deletions from the open order file require the approval of the sales manager prior to input. A report listing all the changes is generated, and a one-for-one comparison is performed.	✔		The sales manager indicated that changes to the open order file normally result from changes to orders that were on backorder, had price overrides, or had credit limit overrides. We examined the file of daily change order reports for the month of March, noting that only 10 changes had been made that month. All reports were approved. We examined the March 12 report, noting that it contained only one item, which was a change in the order quantity that was made to keep the customer within its credit limit. Notations on the report indicated that the customer had been contacted and wished to reduce its order.
3.4 Is a report of long outstanding transactions or aged analysis produced at regular intervals? The unmatched bill of lading report is produced daily. The unmatched order report is cumulative; therefore any correction not made would reappear as an exception on the next day's report.	✔		During our performance of step 3.2 we observed that the client's files contained daily cumulative reports.
3.5 Are there adequate procedures to investigate and, if necessary, correct: (a) long outstanding items: (b) all duplicates, mismatches, and rejections? (a) Items appearing on the unmatched bill of lading report are investigated each day. The report and corrections are approved by the accounts receivable supervisor. (b) The integrity of the numerical sequence of the invoices and the bills of lading on the sales transaction listing is reviewed monthly. Mismatched bills of lading are investigated in (a).	✔		(a) See testing of 3.2. (b) We discussed the procedure with the accounts receivable supervisor and examined the June and November reports. One duplicate invoice and two missing bill of lading numbers were identified on the reports. We noted that the items were corrected and the supervisor had approved the reports and corrections.

structure that could adversely affect the organization's ability to "record, process, summarize, and report financial data consistent with the assertions of management in the financial statements." The SAS refers to these matters as "reportable conditions," and expresses a preference that they be communicated in writing rather than orally. The SAS explicitly permits the auditor to comment on other matters that do not meet the criteria of "reportable conditions" but that the auditor deems to be of value to the audit committee, and those comments may be segregated from observations about reportable conditions.

Although the auditor is required to communicate reportable conditions only to the audit committee or its equivalent, the authors believe it is good practice to communicate such matters to management as well. If there is no audit committee or board of directors or the equivalent, the communication would be made only to management (which is likely to be an owner-manager) or to the party that engaged the auditor.

The auditor may come across matters other than reportable conditions in the course of an audit that would be helpful to management in carrying out its duties. These are matters that either may be below the threshold of significance for reporting to the audit committee, or may be financial and business suggestions that would enhance operational efficiency and profitability. The auditor usually discusses such matters with management and may also communicate them in writing.

It is good practice for the auditor to discuss all comments on the internal control structure with the client before drafting a written communication. If the auditor's understanding of the control structure was mistaken in some respect, discussing the comments will clarify the misunderstanding and save the auditor the embarrassment of discovering it later. In many instances, management's responses to the auditor's suggestions are included in the communication. The best time to discuss deficiencies in the control structure and related problems and to draft a written communication is at the conclusion of tests of controls. Ideally, that point occurs when both auditor and management have time to consider the auditor's findings. It should preferably take place far enough before year-end to permit corrective action that could affect the auditor's remaining work.

The auditor has no obligation to extend auditing procedures in order to search for reportable conditions, but merely an obligation to report those coming to his or her attention as a result of procedures that are performed as part of the audit. Many practitioners believe that reports on the internal control structure that are based solely on what the auditor learns in the course of an audit are likely to be often misunderstood or misinterpreted by the public at large, who may read into them a greater degree of assurance than is warranted. Accordingly, the SAS specifies that "the report should state that the communication is intended solely for the information and the use of the audit committee, management, and others within the organization" (AU Section 325.10). The report may also discuss the inherent limitations of internal control in general and the specific nature and extent of the auditor's consideration of the internal control structure.

Figure 8.11   Report on Internal Control Structure Related Matters

April 12, 19XY

Audit Committee of the Board of Directors
ABC Manufacturing Co., Inc.
123 Industrial Road
Anytown, U.S.A. 12345

Gentlemen:

In planning and performing our audit of the financial statements of the ABC Manufacturing Co., Inc., for the year ended December 31, 19XX, we considered its internal control structure in order to determine our auditing procedures for the purpose of expressing our opinion on the financial statements and not to provide assurance on the internal control structure. However, we noted certain matters involving the internal control structure and its operation that we consider to be reportable conditions under standards established by the American Institute of Certified Public Accountants. Reportable conditions involve matters coming to our attention relating to significant deficiencies in the design or operation of the internal control structure that, in our judgment, could adversely affect the organization's ability to record, process, summarize, and report financial data consistent with the assertions of management in the financial statements.

Access Controls to Data by Terminals Can Be Bypassed

At the present time, there is a critical "file protect" system that prohibits the access of production data by remote terminal users. Our review disclosed a method (special coding of a control card) by which this system can be bypassed and remote terminal users can access and/or alter financial data in computer files. Unauthorized access to data files can result in inaccurate financial data being reported by the systems or confidential data being available to unauthorized personnel. Management is currently studying various means of correcting this situation.

The Director of Internal Audit Reports to the Controller

The objectivity of the internal audit function is enhanced when the director of internal audit reports to an individual or group in the company with sufficient authority to promote independence, provide adequate consideration of findings and recommendations in audit reports, ensure that appropriate action is taken on audit recommendations, and resolve conflicts between internal auditors and various levels of management. At ABC Manufacturing Co., Inc., the director

(Continued)

Figure 8.11   *Continued*

of internal audit for each subsidiary reports to the subsidiary controller; the corporate director of internal audit reports to the corporate controller. We believe that the directors' objectivity would be enhanced if they reported to the vice-president and treasurer of each subsidiary and the corporate vice-president and treasurer, respectively, with summaries of all internal audit reports presented to the audit committee of the board of directors.

Inadequate Systems for Preparing Consolidated Satements

The accounting department does not presently have sufficient staff to prepare consolidated reports of worldwide operations in time to meet the company's requirements for preparing quarterly and year-end financial information. Those requirements are presently met, in part, through the assistance of both the internal auditors and ourselves. Preparing consolidated financial statements is not an appropriate service for either the internal or external auditors to provide. Financial management agrees with our views and is currently undertaking to add sufficient competent personnel and appropriate computer software to the accounting department to enable it to prepare consolidated quarterly and year-end financial statements on a timely basis.

This report is intended solely for the information and use of the audit committee, management, and others within the organization.

Very truly yours,

Smith and Jones, CPAs

Determining whether a deficiency in the design or operation of an entity's control environment, accounting system, or control procedures is a reportable condition requires considerable judgment on the part of the auditor. In making that judgment, the auditor considers various factors relating to the specific client, such as its organizational structure, ownership characteristics, size, complexity, and diversity of operations.

Reportable conditions may be of such magnitude as to be considered material weaknesses in the internal control structure. A material weakness is "a reportable condition in which the design or operation of the specific internal control structure elements do not reduce to a relatively low level the risk that errors or irregularities in amounts that would be material in relation to the financial statements being audited may occur and not be detected within a timely period by employees in the normal course of performing their assigned functions." Although not required to do so, an auditor may choose to separately identify those reportable conditions that meet this definition. Or, if it is appropriate to do so, the auditor may state that none of the reportable conditions communicated were believed to be a material weakness. However, the auditor should not issue a written representation that no reportable conditions were noted during the audit, because of the potential for misinterpretation of the limited degree of assurance that such a report would provide. Figure 8.11 presents an example of a report to an audit committee on internal control structure related matters.

The client may already be aware of the existence of reportable conditions related to internal control structure design or operation, and may have decided to accept the accompanying degree of control risk because of cost or other considerations. If the audit committee has acknowledged that it understands and has considered a deficiency and the related risks, the auditor need not continue to report the matter after it has been initially reported to the committee. Changes in management or in the audit committee, or merely the passage of time, may nevertheless make continued reporting of such matters appropriate and timely.

Many auditors believe that all recommendations for improvements in the control structure that are communicated to any level of management should be brought to the attention of the client's audit committee. One way to do this would be to include a statement in the report to the audit committee that the auditor has, in a separate communication to management, made suggestions for control structure improvements that do not involve reportable conditions. A copy of that communication could also be sent to the audit committee.

As discussed previously, the auditor may report conditions noted during the audit that he or she believes will be helpful to management, but that do not reach the threshold level of a reportable condition. Similarly, management may request the auditor to be alert to certain matters that might not be considered reportable conditions and to submit a report on the findings. These agreed-upon arrangements, which may be particularly useful to the client, do not relieve the auditor of the basic responsibility to communicate reportable conditions.

9

Controlling Detection Risk: Substantive Tests

As stated in earlier chapters of this book, the primary purpose of an audit is the expression of an opinion on whether the entity's financial statements are presented fairly, in all material respects, in conformity with generally accepted accounting principles. The auditor needs a high level of assurance that the opinion is appropriate; that is, audit risk must be limited to a low level. Audit risk was defined in Chapter 6 as consisting of the risk of material misstatement occurring (comprising inherent and control risks), and the risk, known as detection risk, of not detecting a material misstatement that is contained in the financial statements. The auditor assesses inherent and control risks as part of developing the audit testing plan, and controls detection risk by performing substantive tests to gain the necessary assurance regarding the various assertions embodied in the financial statements.

REVIEW: AUDIT OBJECTIVES, RISK ASSESSMENT, AND AUDIT STRATEGY DECISIONS

Audit Objectives

Each auditing procedure performed on an engagement should be designed to meet one or more specific audit objectives that, in turn, correspond with specific assertions embodied in the financial statements. Seven categories of management assertions and corresponding audit objectives were identified in Chapter 5: existence or occurrence, completeness, accuracy, cutoff, rights and obligations, valuation or allocation, and presentation and disclosure. The audit objectives are the same for all engagements; the emphasis given to particular objectives for specific account balances and classes of transactions varies according to the auditor's materiality judgments and risk assessments. Accordingly, the nature, timing, and extent of auditing procedures performed to achieve the audit objectives also vary.

Risk Assessment and Audit Strategy Decisions

The process by which inherent and control risks are assessed was described in Chapter 8. The results of those assessments have an inverse relationship to the acceptable level of detection risk. That is, the lower the risk of a material misstatement occurring, the higher the level of detection risk the auditor can accept in planning substantive tests to gain the assurance needed to limit audit risk to a sufficiently low level. Conversely, the greater the risk of a material misstatement occurring, the lower the acceptable level of detection risk.

Generally accepted auditing standards require that, on all engagements, the auditor obtain an understanding of the entity's control environment, the flow of transactions through its accounting system, and its control procedures, and assess how effective they are in preventing or detecting material misstatements in the financial statements. Each of the auditor's risk assessment activities— assessing inherent risk conditions and characteristics and assessing, for purposes of audit planning, the elements of the control structure (including any concurrent tests of controls performed)—can result in a reduction in the perceived level of risk that a material misstatement has occurred, which in turn reduces the assurance needed from substantive tests. As discussed in Chapter 8, in most situations those risk assessment activities would enable the auditor to reduce to some degree the assurance needed from substantive tests.

Beyond that, the auditor makes a key strategy decision about whether to perform additional tests of controls, particularly of control procedures, to support a further reduction in the assessed level of control risk. Those additional tests of controls would generally be directed toward completeness, accuracy, or existence. As explained in Chapter 7, those are the audit objectives that can often be related to control objectives specifically addressed by an entity's control structure. A key factor in the decision to perform additional tests of controls is whether it will be more efficient than performing substantive tests without seeking to further reduce the assessed level of control risk.

Both additional tests of controls and substantive tests help the auditor achieve specific audit objectives for specific accounts. For example, a set of financial statements generally includes management's assertion that accounts receivable exist and are the result of sales of goods and services to customers. The auditor seeks evidence to support this assertion, which corresponds with the audit objective of existence/occurrence. The audit objective may be achieved, in part, by confirming accounts receivable (a substantive test), or by testing the control procedures the client has established to ensure that only authorized sales of goods and services, and all cash collections, are properly processed and recorded (a test of controls).

The audit strategy for each significant class of transactions or account balance will depend both on the auditor's judgment about how effectively the relevant control procedures are designed and are operating and whether it will be more efficient to test the control procedures or to test the account balances themselves. The auditor *may* choose to obtain evidence entirely from substantive tests of account balances, but, as stated in Statement on Auditing Standards (SAS) No. 55 (AU Section 319.63), *may not* choose to omit substantive tests entirely for *all* of the audit objectives relevant to significant account balances or transaction classes. The evidence obtained from performing substantive tests will either confirm or contradict the conclusions the auditor reached when assessing inherent and control risks. If the auditor learns those risks are higher than was previously thought, the decision about how much assurance is needed from substantive tests should be reconsidered. Chapter 8 described tests of controls; this chapter covers substantive tests performed to obtain assurance about financial statement assertions.

DESIGNING AND PERFORMING SUBSTANTIVE TESTS

Substantive tests consist of tests of details of account balances and related transactions, and analytical procedures. The nature, timing, and extent of the substantive tests to be performed to meet specific audit objectives for each account balance and class of transactions are determined primarily by the results of the auditor's risk assessment activities. Assessing how much assurance can be attained from a particular substantive procedure is a matter of professional judgment and cannot be specified without knowledge of the full context in which the procedure is to be performed. This chapter describes many substantive procedures. Auditors rarely perform all of them on an engagement. Instead, after considering the evidence obtained from tests of controls and from other risk assessment activities, they select the specific procedures, for each audit objective relevant to each financial statement account and disclosure, that will provide the evidence needed in the particular circumstances. This section of the chapter describes the major considerations that determine what substantive tests should be performed in varying circumstances.

The key to selecting appropriate substantive tests is the auditor's understanding of management's assertions and the corresponding audit objectives. The auditor identifies specific audit objectives for each significant account balance and designs auditing procedures to provide the necessary assurance that those objectives have been achieved. Figure 9.1 illustrates the audit objectives that may be applicable to an entity's trade accounts receivable and sales, and provides examples (which are not intended to be exhaustive) of substantive tests the auditor may perform to satisfy the objectives.

Types of Accounts

The nature, timing, and extent of substantive tests appropriate for a particular audit objective and account vary with the type of account. Accounts may be classified into three types.

1. Accounts that are derived from a major class of transactions within a transaction cycle that typically involves high volumes of transactions. As explained in Chapter 7, these accounts are commonly subjected to control procedures that address the control objectives of completeness, accuracy, and authorization of transactions and files. Examples are cash, accounts receivable, inventory, accounts payable, purchases, salaries and wages, and sales. Decisions about whether the audit strategy for these accounts should include additional tests of controls are generally related to whether that would be the most efficient way to achieve the completeness, accuracy, and existence/occurrence audit objectives.

2. Accounts that reflect internal allocations of revenues or expenses over time through the accrual, deferral, amortization, or valuation of assets or liabilities. These accounts often require management to exercise judgment in determining the period or method of allocation and also in selecting and applying accounting measurement and recognition principles. While the transactions that form the basis for these accounts are sometimes subjected to control procedures, it is usually more efficient not to perform additional tests of controls related to these accounts. Examples of such accounts include accrued receivables and payables, deferred charges and credits, and asset valuation and estimated liability accounts.

3. Accounts that typically reflect a relatively small number of material transactions in an accounting period. These accounts are carried forward from one year to the next, unless transactions affecting them take place. Examples of

these accounts include bonds payable, property and equipment, and contributed capital accounts. Because transactions affecting these accounts occur infrequently, control procedures may not be established to ensure their completeness, accuracy, and authorization. Even when the transactions affecting these accounts are subject to control procedures, it is usually not efficient to perform tests of controls for these accounts.

For the first type, accounts derived from a major class of transactions, the auditor will often face a strategy decision with respect to achieving the completeness, accuracy, and existence/occurrence audit objectives. For other accounts, however, the risks associated with completeness, accuracy, and existence/occurrence, and for all accounts, the risks associated with the audit objectives of valuation, rights and obligations, and presentation and disclosure, may not be addressed by control procedures, although policies and procedures that are part of the control environment and accounting system may affect the achievement of those audit objectives. Even if they do, the auditor is still likely to require a significant amount of assurance from substantive tests directed at the valuation, rights and obligations, and presentation and disclosure objectives. Although an enterprise may have control procedures to ensure a proper cutoff of purchases, sales, cash receipts, and cash disbursements, the auditor generally finds it more efficient not to perform additional tests of controls with respect to the cutoff objective but instead to obtain evidence primarily from substantive tests.

Tests of Details and Their Relationship to Audit Objectives

Tests of details of account balances and transactions are most commonly thought of in connection with providing assurance about specific audit objectives. This section discusses the different techniques used in performing tests of details and when they can be performed. Chapter 10 discusses the extent of testing—how many items to test.

Substantive tests of details of transactions and account balances or of other information in the financial statements normally involve the techniques of inquiry, observation, examining documents and records, reperformance, inspecting assets, and confirmation. The following paragraphs describe each of these and suggest how they relate to the audit objectives.

Frequently, one of the auditor's first steps in testing an account balance or class of transactions is making *inquiries* of client management and employees; the responses are then corroborated by other tests. At various stages in the audit, discussions with management or employees and subsequent follow-up may bring errors to the auditor's attention. As an example, the auditor inquires about management's plans as part of considering the entity's ability to continue as a going concern, as discussed in Chapter 22. In addition, the auditor obtains letters from the client's lawyers regarding legal matters and letters of representation from management concerning the recording of known liabilities, the existence of contingent liabilities, and the existence and carrying value of inventory. Inquiries may provide evidence about many audit objectives, depending on the specific accounts or transactions involved. Lawyers'

Figure 9.1 Audit Objectives for Trade Accounts Receivable and Sales

Audit Objective	Specific Audit Objectives for Trade Accounts Receivable and Sales	Illustrative Substantive Tests[a]
Completeness	Trade accounts receivable represent all amounts owed to the entity at the balance sheet date arising from sales transactions. All shipments or services rendered during the period covered by the financial statements and all returns or allowances provided are reflected in the financial statements.	On a test basis, compare records of goods shipped and services performed with recorded transactions.
Accuracy	Sales transactions are based on correct prices and quantities and are accurately computed and classified in the appropriate general ledger and accounts receivable subsidiary ledger accounts. The accounts receivable subsidiary ledger is mathematically correct and agrees with the general ledger.	On a test basis, compare shipping documents and invoices with supporting documents and recorded transactions. (Confirmation of customers' accounts to some extent also indicates the accuracy of the balances.) Using audit software, calculate invoice amounts and total the accounts receivable subsidiary ledger.
Existence or Occurrence	Recorded accounts receivable represent amounts owed to the entity at the balance sheet date. Recorded sales transactions represent goods actually shipped or services actually rendered during the period covered by the financial statements.	Select customers' accounts for confirmation and the method of confirmation (positive, negative, or a combination), investigate any discrepancies reported or questions raised, and determine whether any adjustments are necessary. For positive confirmations not responded to, agree amounts to subsequent cash receipts or supporting sales documents.
Cutoff	Sales transactions, cash receipts, and returns and claims are recorded in the proper period.	Perform cutoff tests: (a) Determine that sales invoices are recorded as sales in the proper period by comparing the related records of goods shipped and services performed with recorded sales for several days before and after year-end.

Assertion		
		(b) Determine that credit memos are recorded in the proper period by examining the related records of returns and claims from customers for several days before and after year-end. (*Note:* Improper cutoff of cash receipts is generally a low risk, since only the composition of current assets could be in error.)
Valuation or Allocation	Accounts receivable are stated at net realizable value (i.e., net of appropriate allowances for uncollectible accounts, discounts, returns, and similar items). Revenue is recognized only when appropriate accounting recognition and measurement criteria are met.	Determine whether the allowance for uncollectible accounts is adequate by reviewing the aged trial balances, discussing the allowance and composition of the receivable balance with management, and identifying significant old receivables and receivables in dispute or changes in the collectibility of current receivables. Review cash collections after the balance sheet date and examine related remittance advices or other supporting documentation to ascertain that payments relate to the balance that was due at the balance sheet date. Determine the adequacy of collateral, if any. Review relevant credit file information, such as customer financial data and correspondence. Discuss all significant potentially uncollectible accounts with management.
Rights and Obligations	Accounts receivable are legal rights of the entity at the balance sheet date (i.e., customer accounts that have been sold or factored are excluded from the accounts receivable balance).	Make inquiries and read agreements relating to the possible sale of receivables that the client continues to service.
Presentation and Disclosure	Accounts receivable, sales, and related accounts are properly described and classified in the financial statements. Accounts receivable pledged as collateral are properly disclosed.	Identify liens, security interests, and assets pledged as loan collateral by reviewing debt and lease agreements; confirmation replies, particularly from financial institutions; and minutes of directors' meetings. Inquire of management about those items.

[a]Analytical procedures, such as analysis of monthly sales trends compared with prior years and budget, may be designed to provide assurance relating to audit objectives for trade accounts receivable and sales.

and client representation letters provide assurance relating especially to rights and obligations, and presentation and disclosure.

The auditor may *observe* the client's employees as they perform various tasks, like counting inventory. The auditor's observation of how the client conducts a physical inventory can provide firsthand knowledge of the reliability of the inventory count.

The auditor often *examines documents or records* supporting a transaction or item in the financial statements and *reperforms*, usually on a test basis, the client's related procedures in order to determine that the transaction was both authorized and accurately accounted for. Accordingly, examining documentation often provides assurance that recorded assets or liabilities are accurate and, depending on the specific transaction under consideration, exist or are complete. The cutoff objective is often achieved by examining documentation for transactions recorded shortly before and after the client's year-end. The auditor normally examines documents to obtain evidence that the client has performed all prescribed procedures, reperforms those procedures (on a test basis, if appropriate), and determines that no aspects of the transaction appear unreasonable (such as a supplier's invoice not addressed to the client). That evidence may have been generated wholly or partly by entities outside the client (such as suppliers' invoices, customers' orders, signed contracts) or by the client itself (such as purchase orders, receiving reports, marketing plans). If external evidence is available, it is usually considered more reliable than internal evidence. One specific form of internal documentation the auditor reads at various stages in the audit is minutes of meetings of the board of directors and its important committees.

In many instances an account balance may represent the result of a computation or an accumulation of computations. To substantiate the accuracy of such an account balance, the auditor often reperforms some or all of the detailed computations or otherwise makes an overall evaluation of the balance. If judgment is the basis of a computation, such as in the valuation of accounts receivable, the auditor reperforming the computation must also understand and evaluate the reasoning process underlying the judgment. For example, if the provision for uncollectible accounts is based on a formula (giving appropriate consideration to past experience) related to the age of the receivables, the auditor should consider the reasonableness of the formula as well as reperform the mathematical calculations. (The auditor would also perform other procedures regarding the collectibility of accounts receivable in reviewing the adequacy of the provision for uncollectible accounts.)

If the client compares accounting records with physical assets, such as inventory, or with documents, such as an invoice, the auditor may be able to use these comparisons and their documentation in performing substantive tests. That is, the auditor may choose to test the client's matching procedures, which is what typically happens during the client's physical inventory count, rather than perform similar or duplicative procedures. If the client has supervisory control procedures over those comparisons, as part of the substantive tests the auditor may examine the documentation of those procedures to obtain evidence that they operated effectively. As an example, the auditor's tests of the client's physical inventory count would ordinarily include tests of the client's supervision of its counting personnel. In addition, management's review of reports, which is an aspect of the client's control environment that the auditor often tests in assessing control risk, can also serve as the basis for a substantive procedure, depending on the type of report involved. For example, management's review of reports of write-offs or dispositions of obsolete inventory could be one source of evidence that the financial statements do not reflect inventory carried at more than its net realizable value.

Inspecting assets involves counting or examining physical items represented by accounts in the financial statements. This procedure is generally performed by client personnel, with the auditor participating or observing, although on occasion the auditor actually performs the function. A typical example of inspection, combined with observation, is the tests of the client's counting procedures and recounting of some of the client's counts during a physical inventory. Other items subject to inspection (which may be counted or examined directly by the auditor) include cash, marketable securities, and property, plant, and equipment. Inspecting assets is a principal source of assurance about their existence and about the accuracy of the related accounts, and may provide some assurance about completeness, that is, that all items counted were recorded.

Confirmation consists of obtaining a representation of a fact or condition from a third party, preferably in writing. Although many facts can be confirmed, this procedure is generally applied to items making up an account balance and often serves as the principal test of details related to that balance. Confirmations obtained from parties that are independent of the client frequently provide strong support for the existence of the relevant fact or account balance and often provide some evidence with respect to the accuracy objective as well. For example, a customer's acknowledgment that it owes the client $1500 is strong evidence that the debt exists and that it is not overstated (absent valuation considerations). Confirmations also provide some evidence that the transactions underlying the account balances were recorded in the proper period. Confirmation provides little or no evidence, however, with respect to completeness, valuation, rights and obligations, or presentation and disclosure of receivables.

The level in the organization at which a fact or an account balance is confirmed is also relevant to how much assurance the confirmation provides. For example, an auditor seeking to confirm the existence and terms of a major contract between the client and a supplier would consider to whom the confirmation should appropriately be addressed. On receiving the signed confirmation, the auditor would note whether the signature was that of someone in a position to know and understand the details of the contract.

Many substantive tests of the details of transactions and account balances involve procedures, such as examining documents or reperforming calculations, that are the same as procedures used in performing tests of controls. This is not surprising; whether a particular procedure is a test of controls or a substantive test depends not on the procedure itself, but on the purpose for which it is performed. For example, footing and extending a purchase invoice could be part of a test of controls performed to obtain evidence about whether a control procedure designed to prevent purchase transactions from being recorded inaccurately was operating effectively; it could also be a substantive test of the accuracy of recorded machinery and equipment. Similarly, reperforming the client's bank reconciliation could be a test of the client's performance of periodic reconciliations of the cash account (a test of controls); the auditor's reconciliation at year-end would be a substantive test of the accuracy and existence of the cash balance. As a general rule, tests of details of transactions to which control procedures are applied are tests of controls; tests of details of ending balances of balance sheet accounts are substantive tests. Regardless of the purpose for performing a particular test, however, many tests provide evidence that serves the other purpose as well.

Timing of Tests of Details

It is often desirable to perform tests of details before year-end (early substantive testing), particularly if the client wants the audit to be completed shortly after year-end. This may be done in appropriate circumstances without impairing the effectiveness of the audit, although before doing so the auditor should assess the difficulty of controlling the incremental audit risk (AU Section 313.04–.07).

It is usually efficient to perform substantive tests on related accounts as of a common date. Therefore, when considering early substantive testing of a specific account, the auditor should consider the relationship of that account to others in the financial statements and the extent to which a single substantive test may apply to more than one account. For example, a cutoff test of shipments relates to sales, accounts receivable, cost of sales, and inventory accounts.

If early substantive testing is done, the auditor will have to obtain satisfaction that, for the balances tested early, the risk of material misstatement is low during the intervening period between the early testing date and year-end. Generally, the auditor obtains that satisfaction by performing tests of controls directed at the design and operation of relevant control structure policies and procedures during the intervening period.[1] Such tests of controls might include reviewing reconciliations of individual ledger balances to control accounts and investigating any unusual items in the reconciliations. The auditor should also perform analytical and other substantive procedures, as described later, to obtain assurance that transactions were properly recorded during the intervening period.

In certain circumstances, the auditor might obtain satisfaction about transactions during the intervening period by examining evidence of the operation

---

[1]AU Section 313.05 states that "assessing control risk at below the maximum is not required in order to have a reasonable basis for extending audit conclusions from an interim date to the balance-sheet date; however, if the auditor assesses control risk at the maximum during the remaining period, he should consider whether the effectiveness of certain of the substantive tests to cover that period will be impaired." The authors believe an auditor would rarely have the required "reasonable basis" if control risk was assessed at the maximum. However, as noted in Chapter 8, the authors also believe it would be rare for an auditor to assess control risk at the maximum for the completeness, accuracy, and authorization objectives for accounts derived from transaction cycles.

of special procedures established by the client for that period. As an example, a management review of sales transactions recorded around year-end performed to ensure a proper cutoff would provide some evidence about the authorization and accuracy of sales recorded after an early accounts receivable confirmation.

If early substantive testing is performed, the auditor should link the balances tested early to year-end balances by one or more of the following procedures, as appropriate in light of the assessment of control risk:

- Review key performance indicators and management information for unexpected variations in account balances at the balance sheet date, and investigate any material fluctuations in account balances and any unusual activity since the time of the early substantive tests.
- Scan entries in the relevant general ledger accounts (including control accounts) or review summaries of recorded transactions to determine whether any expected entries have been omitted and whether the entries appear to be reasonable in relation to the normal level of activity.
- Review any special procedures the client has carried out on the year-end figures.
- Review reconciliations of individual ledger balances to control accounts, and investigate any unusual items in the reconciliations.
- Ensure that any relevant matters brought forward from the early substantive testing date have been satisfactorily resolved.
- Reassess any valuation accounts (e.g., allowance for uncollectible accounts) in light of the latest available information.

In most instances, early substantive testing is not appropriate unless the auditor has obtained evidence, through tests of controls, that control structure policies and procedures related to transactions and account balances tested early are effective. In addition, early substantive testing is not usually done for all assertions relating to an account balance. For example, the existence of accounts receivable may be confirmed at an early date, but their valuation tested at year-end. In particular, if control procedures necessary to safeguard assets (such as inventories) are ineffective, early substantive testing (such as observing early physical inventory counts) is normally not appropriate, because the auditor will be unable to obtain evidence that those assets were safeguarded in the intervening period, and will therefore not have evidence about their existence at year-end.

Significant changes in the client's circumstances after the date of early substantive testing may require the auditor to perform additional procedures. To avoid unnecessary work, the auditor should consider the possibility of such changes when determining the audit testing plan. AU Section 313 contains the authoritative guidance on performing substantive tests before the balance sheet date.

Analytical Procedures

Analytical procedures are an integral part of the audit process. They are reasonableness tests of account balances and classes of transactions and, as stated in SAS No. 56, *Analytical Procedures* (AU Section 329.02), ''consist of evaluations of financial information made by a study of plausible relationships among both financial and nonfinancial data.'' Examples of analytical procedures routinely performed in an audit include fluctuation analyses, ratio analyses, comparisons of financial statements, and scanning accounting records for unusual entries or entries that do not meet the auditor's expectations. SAS No. 56 requires analytical procedures to be used in the planning and overall review stages of the audit, as discussed in Chapters 8 and 21, respectively, and encourages their use as substantive tests to provide assurance with respect to specific audit objectives for particular account balances or classes of transactions. Analytical procedures, together with tests of controls and substantive tests of details of transactions and balances, provide the evidential matter required by the third standard of field work.[2]

Developing Expectations. The basic premise underlying analytical procedures is that relationships among data may reasonably be expected to exist and continue in the absence of known conditions to the contrary. Examples of those conditions include specific unusual transactions or events, accounting changes, business changes, random fluctuations, and errors or irregularities. Changes in relationships among data in the absence of conditions known to the auditor could suggest that the financial statements were misstated because of unknown errors or irregularities.

In performing analytical procedures, the auditor first develops expectations of recorded amounts or ratios derived therefrom, by considering plausible relationships among data. The bases for the auditor's expectations are knowledge obtained about the nature of the entity's business, the industry in which it operates, inherent risk conditions, and the characteristics of individual account balances and classes of transactions. The auditor then compares the expectations with the recorded amounts or ratios. The comparisons may be simple or complex, and may involve single or multiple relationships.

Typically, the auditor uses the following sources of information, either individually or in combination, in developing expectations:

a. Financial information of comparable prior periods, adjusted for known current changes. (For example, an expectation of current year's sales might be formed from the prior period's sales adjusted for known price and volume increases. That expectation would then be compared with the current period's recorded sales.)

b. Anticipated results. (For example, expectations could be developed from budgets, forecasts, and extrapolations of interim results, which would then be compared with recorded results.)

c. Relationships among elements of financial information within the period. (For example, an expectation of commission expense in relation to sales could be developed from knowledge of the entity's commission

---

[2]Analytical procedures are also used in complying with professional standards in connection with various reports on unaudited financial information, as discussed in Chapter 23.

policies, and then compared with the relationship between recorded commission expense and recorded sales.)

d. Information regarding the industry in which the client operates. (For example, expectations of gross margin could be developed from industry-wide statistics for particular product lines.)

e. Relationships between financial information and relevant nonfinancial information. (For example, expectations might be developed concerning available square footage related to revenue in a retail operation, labor hours related to labor costs, average rent related to rent revenue, or number of properties related to real estate tax expense.)

Unexpected relationships or other items that appear to be unusual should be investigated if the auditor believes they indicate matters that may have a significant effect on the audit. In investigating unusual items, the auditor generally considers them in the light of the information obtained about the client and its business, and makes inquiries of management. The auditor then seeks additional evidence to corroborate management's replies. Analytical procedures are effective only if the auditor exercises skepticism in evaluating management's explanations of unexpected results and seeks relevant and reliable evidence to support those explanations.

Using Analytical Procedures to Achieve Audit Objectives.   A major decision the auditor makes in designing substantive tests is whether to perform an analytical procedure, a test of details, or a combination of the two. That decision is based on the auditor's judgment about the expected effectiveness and efficiency of available procedures, considering the total assurance sought from substantive tests with respect to a specific audit objective for a particular account balance or class of transactions. In many situations, it is possible to design analytical procedures that, when considered in combination with other auditing procedures, will provide relatively large amounts of assurance, so that the auditor will need less assurance from other substantive procedures. In designing and performing both analytical procedures and tests of details, the auditor should consider the relationship among accounts and the likelihood that evidence obtained about one or more audit objectives with respect to a particular account balance or class of transactions may also provide assurance about other account balances or classes of transactions.

The effectiveness and efficiency of an analytical procedure in identifying potential errors or irregularities depends on, among other things, (a) the plausibility and predictability of the relationship among the data analyzed, (b) the availability and reliability of the data used to develop the expectation, (c) the precision of the expectation, and (d) the nature of the account balances or classes of transactions and the particular audit objectives.

Plausibility and Predictability of the Relationship.   It is important for the auditor to understand what makes relationships among data plausible. Data sets sometimes appear to be related when they are not, which could lead the auditor to erroneous conclusions.

Relationships in a stable environment are usually more predictable than relationships in a dynamic or unstable environment. Relationships among income statement accounts tend to be more predictable since they represent transactions over a period of time, whereas relationships among balance sheet accounts tend to be less predictable because a balance at a point in time may be subject to many random influences. Relationships involving transactions subject to management discretion are usually less predictable; for example, management may influence the timing of maintenance or advertising expenditures.

Availability and Reliability of the Data Used to Develop the Expectation. The availability of the data needed to develop expectations for a particular assertion will vary. SAS No. 56 notes, as an example, that for some entities expected sales might be developed from production statistics or from square feet of selling space as a means of testing the completeness of sales. For other entities, however, data relevant to that assertion may not be readily available, and it may be more effective or efficient to perform substantive tests of details on the entity's shipping records.

The auditor should also consider whether the underlying financial and nonfinancial data used to develop the expectation is reliable. In considering the likelihood of misstatements in such data, the auditor considers, among other things, knowledge obtained during previous audits, the results of the assessment of control risk, and the results of tests of details of account balances and transactions. How reliable data used in analytical procedures must be depends on how much assurance the auditor desires from the procedure. For example, in analytical procedures used in planning the audit, untested industry data may be appropriate for developing an expectation about the level of business activity. Expectations developed using information from a variety of independent sources may be more reliable than expectations developed using data from a single source.

Precision of the Expectation.   The precision of the expectation depends on, among other things, how thoroughly the auditor considers the factors that affect the amount being audited, and the level of detail of the data used to develop the expectation.

Many factors affect financial relationships. For example, sales may be affected by prices, volume, and product mix, each of which, in turn, may be affected by a number of factors. In developing expectations, the auditor should consider the factors that might have a significant impact on the relationship. The more assurance desired from analytical procedures, the more thoroughly factors affecting the relationship should be considered.

Analytical procedures based on expectations developed at a more detailed level have a greater chance of detecting misstatements of a given amount—and thus provide greater assurance—than do broader comparisons. Comparisons of monthly amounts may be more effective than those of annual amounts, and comparisons by location or lines of business may be more effective than companywide comparisons. What level of detail is appropriate may be influenced by the nature of the entity, its size and complexity, and the level of detail available in its records. Generally, the possibility that material misstatements could be obscured by offsetting factors increases as an entity's operations become more complex and more diversified. For example, the auditor's expectations regarding profit margins on sales in a diversified business will be more precise if they are based on an analysis using disaggregated data, such as gross profit margin by facility or product line rather than on an analysis of the consolidated gross profit margin.

Nature of the Account Balance and Audit Objective. For some accounts, analytical procedures may be the most effective means for achieving certain audit objectives and may sometimes be the only procedure performed. For example, in some situations, two common analytical procedures, comparing the allowance for uncollectible accounts as a percentage of accounts receivable and as a percentage of overdue receivables with expectations developed from similar percentages for the prior years, might provide sufficient evidence with respect to the valuation objective for accounts receivable. (However, in other situations some substantive tests of details, such as investigating specific overdue items, might also be done.) Or, in auditing accrued payroll at year-end the auditor may test the reasonableness of the accrual by multiplying the gross pay for the weekly, semi-monthly, and monthly payrolls by the ratio of days accrued at year-end to total number of days for the pay periods. Analytical procedures may also be particularly effective when potential misstatements would not be detectable by examining details of transactions, especially when the relevant audit objective is the completeness of recorded transactions.

On the other hand, examining documentation (a test of details) may be the most appropriate means of obtaining assurance regarding the accuracy of fixed asset additions. In obtaining assurance regarding the accuracy of depreciation expense, a combination of analytical procedures and tests of details (such as recalculation of individually significant amounts) may be appropriate. Like other auditing procedures, analytical procedures that are directed specifically at one or more audit objectives for a particular account balance or class of transactions may simultaneously address other accounts or objectives as well; the auditor should take this into consideration when deciding how to obtain the necessary assurance for a particular account or objective.

Other Considerations in Using Analytical Procedures. Many companies, as part of controlling the operation of their business, perform analytical procedures to identify unusual transactions, balances, or relationships on a timely basis. Depending on how relevant and reliable those procedures and the underlying data are, the information generated may be useful to the auditor. In addition, when assessing the control environment, the auditor may identify key performance indicators and management and budgetary information that management reviews and that may be useful in performing analytical procedures. Examples include operating budgets and results, sales analyses, inventory turnover and obsolescence reports, cash flow analyses, and forecasts.

The auditor may choose to use analytical procedures to help determine sample size, to stratify a population, or to assist in the design of other substantive tests. In determining the sample size necessary for auditing procedures related to inventory obsolescence, for example, the auditor may examine the change in inventory turnover rates for various components of inventory to decide which inventory items should be given more attention. Analytical procedures provide corroborative evidence about the accounting treatment of transactions and balances, and can also be good detectors of changes in accounting principles, but of course they will not alert the auditor to a misstatement if an inappropriate accounting principle remains unchanged. Analytical procedures may be particularly useful in helping the auditor to identify transactions that have not been recorded. Similarly, as discussed earlier, if the auditor performs substantive tests of details before year-end, analytical procedures can often provide evidence about the proper recording of transactions in the period between early testing and year-end.

The results of analytical procedures may possibly lead the auditor to extend testing. For example, the auditor might calculate the number of days' sales outstanding and observe that it had increased significantly, and he or she might not be satisfied with management's explanation of that trend. In those circumstances, the auditor might decide to confirm more customer accounts than planned and to confirm them at the end of the year to ensure that fictitious receivables had not been created. The auditor might also expand tests for collectibility, to ensure that the allowance for uncollectible accounts was adequate.

Scanning can be a particularly effective analytical procedure, provided the auditor has a thorough understanding of the account or schedule being scanned and the types of misstatements that could occur. For example, in scanning an inventory listing, the auditor needs to know how the listing is categorized (that is, what items have been grouped together) and what constitutes a reasonable set of parameters for both quantity and price for each group. A larger than expected quantity of an inventory item might indicate an error in transferring information from the count sheets to the listing, or it might be indicative of slow-moving merchandise that needs to be considered in the valuation allowance. In addition, the auditor would investigate any price that was unexpectedly high or low. Similarly, an auditor scanning accounts receivable would be alert to negative amounts that might indicate the misapplication of cash or incomplete recording of sales, and would also be watchful for account balances with related parties. Scanning a listing of monthly charges to expense accounts can alert the auditor to abnormal items that may reflect errors. Scanning may also be used to test the remaining portion of an account balance after the auditor has examined several large items that constitute a significant portion of the balance.

Analytical procedures may be performed using monetary amounts, physical quantities, ratios, or percentages; they may be applied to overall financial information of the entity, to financial information of components such as subsidiaries or divisions, and to individual elements of financial information. Some auditors have developed specialized software programs to extract appropriate client data from computer files and perform standardized procedures. Other software packages require the auditor to input client data to a computer (often a microcomputer), which processes the data and generates analytical reports.

Testing Accounting Judgments and Estimates

The auditor has a responsibility to perform substantive tests as part of evaluating accounting judgments and estimates made by management, which was described in Chapter 5 as the interpreting/evaluating function. The substantive tests performed to do this consist of a combination of tests of details and analytical procedures.

Evaluating Accounting Judgments.   The auditor's responsibility entails more than merely substantiating facts about specific transactions and other events and circumstances in order to achieve specific audit objectives for relevant accounts. The auditor also has the responsibility to evaluate how the client has translated those facts into appropriate accounting presentations. As part of that process, the auditor should evaluate what accounting principles are selected and how they are applied. He or she should evaluate accounting judgments to address the risk that generally accepted accounting principles (GAAP) could be misused, intentionally or unintentionally, with respect to how transactions are accounted for and measured and how they are presented and disclosed in the financial statements. This is a pervasive aspect of audit risk that the auditor should keep in mind at all times.

The auditor's evaluation of the selection and application of GAAP requires consideration of the industry involved, the client environment, economic conditions, and numerous other intangible factors. Meeting that responsibility requires an extensive knowledge of accounting principles and of the ways in which they should be applied to produce financial statements that reflect, in all material respects, the substance of the client's transactions and present a picture of the enterprise that is not misleading. Many audit failures in the past have resulted from the auditor's failure to evaluate whether GAAP were properly applied, even when all of the relevant facts were available. The valuation and the presentation and disclosure audit objectives are pervasive; accordingly, the auditor should keep them in mind throughout the audit, not only when performing specific substantive tests directly related to those objectives.

Auditing Accounting Estimates.   An important aspect of evaluating the application of accounting principles, particularly as they relate to the valuation objective for many accounts, involves evaluating accounting estimates. Accounting estimates are financial statement approximations that are necessary because the measurement of an account is uncertain until the outcome of future events is known, or because relevant data concerning events that have already occurred cannot be accumulated on a timely, cost-effective basis. Examples of the first type of accounting estimates include uncollectible receivables, obsolete inventory, useful lives of equipment, actuarial assumptions in pension plans, and warranty claims. Examples of the second type of accounting estimates include allocating passenger ticket revenues to airlines other than those issuing the tickets, and telephone company revenues from long distance calls involving more than one company. SAS No. 57, *Auditing Accounting Esti-*

mates (AU Section 342), provides guidance to the auditor in auditing both types of estimates.

Management is responsible for making the necessary accounting estimates; the auditor is responsible for evaluating their reasonableness. Even when management's estimating process involves competent personnel using relevant and reliable data and the most likely assumptions about the factors that affect an accounting estimate, the subjectivity that enters into those estimates introduces the potential for bias. As a result, the auditor should evaluate accounting estimates with an attitude of professional skepticism. The auditor's objective in evaluating accounting estimates is to obtain sufficient competent evidence to provide reasonable assurance that all material accounting estimates have been developed, are reasonable, and are presented and disclosed in conformity with GAAP.

In evaluating the reasonableness of an estimate, the auditor should use one or a combination of three basic approaches.

1. Review and test the process management used to develop the estimate.
2. Independently develop an expectation of the estimate to corroborate the reasonableness of management's estimate.
3. Review events or transactions occurring after the date of the financial statements (but before the audit is completed) that provide an actual amount to compare the estimate with.

When following the first of these approaches, the auditor should

- Obtain an understanding of the process management established to develop each significant accounting estimate.
- Assess the inherent and control risks related to management's process for developing the estimate.
- Identify and evaluate the key factors and assumptions management used to formulate the estimate, concentrating on those key factors and assumptions that are
  - •• Material to the estimate.
  - •• Sensitive to variations.
  - •• Deviations from historical patterns.
  - •• Subjective, and therefore susceptible to misstatement and bias.
- Assess the reliability of the underlying data that enters into the estimate.
- Determine that the calculations used to translate the underlying data and assumptions into the accounting estimate are accurate.

The first two and last two of the above steps do not need further clarification here, since they involve procedures that are discussed throughout the book. However, procedures helpful in identifying and evaluating the key factors and assumptions are unique to auditing accounting estimates. They may involve some or all of the following steps:

- Identifying the sources of information that management used to formulate the assumptions and considering, based on information gathered from other audit tests, whether the information is relevant, reliable, and sufficient for the purpose.

- Considering whether there are additional key factors or alternative assumptions.
- Evaluating whether the assumptions are consistent with one another, with the supporting data, and with relevant historical data.
- Analyzing historical data used in developing the assumptions to assess whether it is comparable and consistent with data of the period under audit, and determining whether it is sufficiently reliable.
- Considering whether changes in the business or industry or in other facts or circumstances may cause factors different from those considered in the past to become significant to the accounting estimate.
- Reviewing available documentation of the assumptions used in developing the accounting estimate, and inquiring about any other relevant plans, goals, and objectives of the entity; and considering their relationship to the assumptions.
- Considering using the work of a specialist (SAS No. 11, *Using the Work of a Specialist* [AU Section 336]).

Evaluating the Results of Substantive Tests

Substantive tests may reveal errors or irregularities in account balances or classes of transactions. As explained in Chapter 21, auditors often maintain a summary of all misstatements found as a result of their auditing procedures. At the completion of the audit, the summary is evaluated to determine whether adjustments to account balances are needed before the auditor can conclude that the financial statements are presented fairly, in all material respects, in conformity with generally accepted accounting principles.

When errors or irregularities are found as a result of substantive tests, the auditor should ascertain the reason for them and consider the implications. If the nature or frequency of errors or irregularities indicates the possibility of a significant misstatement in the account balance in which they were found or in related account balances, the auditor should consider whether to increase the extent of substantive tests or to change their nature or timing. The auditor should also consider the implications of a misstatement in terms of the client's control structure and the auditor's assessment of control risk. For example, if the auditor's tests indicate that, contrary to expectations formed as a result of assessing control risk, not all transactions have been recorded, the auditor should reevaluate the assessed level of control risk. In addition, if substantive tests reveal a deficiency not previously identified in assessing control risk, the relevant documentation should be amended.

AUDIT PROGRAMS

Auditing procedures are compiled into a document referred to as an audit program. An audit program is a list of steps to be performed in the course of an audit. It typically specifies the nature and extent of the audit work, aids in scheduling and assigning the work, guards against possible omissions and duplications, and provides part of the documentation of the work done. An audit program is necessary for adequate planning and supervision of an engagement under the first standard of field work and is required by SAS No. 22, *Planning and Supervision* (AU Section 311). The audit program should be revised as new information is gathered during subsequent stages of the audit.

The audit program should be organized in a way that will provide for the efficient performance of the procedures listed. More specifically, the program should be organized so that when a particular document is examined, as many of the planned auditing procedures as possible are performed on it. For example, assume that one auditing procedure calls for examining vendor invoices for initials indicating the invoice was reviewed for mathematical accuracy and matched to a purchase order and receiving document, and that another auditing procedure calls for examining vendor invoices for evidence that they were authorized for payment. Combining these auditing procedures into one audit program step will enhance audit efficiency. Since the authors believe that audit programs should be tailored to the specific circumstances of individual clients, a "complete" audit program as such is not presented in this book, although specific tests of controls and substantive tests are presented and discussed in Part 3 in the context of auditing the various transaction cycles and account balances.

Auditors differ among themselves over the degree of detail that should be included in an audit program. Some auditors believe that an audit program should be as general as possible and that someone wanting to know what detailed audit steps were performed can find that information by looking at the working papers that report the results of the audit tests. At the extreme, such an audit program might, for example, include the step: "Perform tests of controls applied to shipments." Other auditors believe that the audit program should be as detailed and specific as possible. The advantage of this is that two people reading the audit program would perform exactly the same audit tests on the same number of transactions or balances. An audit program that reflected this attitude to the extreme might contain the step: "Examine 75 shipping documents for signature of individual authorized to release merchandise from warehouse." The disadvantage of this approach is that it could eliminate much judgment from the audit process and make that process somewhat mechanical. Either approach may be consistent with an efficient and effective audit as long as the work is planned and supervised appropriately for the particular type of audit program, and the education and training of the auditor performing the procedures are adequate to enable the individual to make the necessary judgments.

10

The Extent of Testing: Audit Sampling

This book has noted on several occasions that the auditor has several decisions to make in gathering evidence about each assertion implicit in the individual measurements and disclosures in a set of financial statements. Those decisions include how much evidence to acquire, that is, decisions about the extent of audit tests. This chapter addresses those decisions. In the first edition of this book, published in 1912, Montgomery recognized as an "obvious conclusion" the notion that "no audit can or should embrace a complete verification of all the transactions of the period under review."[1] If for every procedure selected by the auditor for gathering evidence, or even if for a few of those procedures, the auditor were to examine every item that could possibly be selected for examination, it would be virtually impossible to complete an audit on a timely basis, not to mention at a reasonable cost. Neither the client nor the public expects the auditor to examine every transaction. Consequently, the auditor is continually faced with the question: How much testing is enough?

In some instances, that question is answered by deciding not to perform a specific procedure at all. For example, if control procedures applied to payroll disbursements are tested and found to be effective, the auditor may decide neither to prepare a reconciliation of the payroll bank account at year-end nor even to review the client's year-end reconciliation. (In that situation, the decisions about what kind of evidence and how much evidence to acquire are identical.) In other instances, the question is answered by deciding to perform some procedure, but not to apply it to all the items in an account or to all transactions of a specific class. For example, the auditor may decide to confirm accounts receivable, but to limit the procedure to only a portion of receivables under $10,000. Testing less than the entire population for the purpose of evaluating it is referred to as audit sampling.

Statement on Auditing Standards (SAS) No. 39, *Audit Sampling* (AU Section 350.01), provides a formal definition of audit sampling: "Audit sampling is the application of an audit procedure to less than 100 percent of the items within an account balance or class of transactions for the purpose of evaluating some characteristic of the balance or class."

Based on the results of applying an auditing procedure to a representative sample of items, the auditor can make an inference (by projecting or extrapolating the sample results) about the entire population from which the sample was selected. In fact, SAS No. 39 requires that the items be selected in such a way that the sample can be expected to be representative of the population. After performing the necessary auditing procedures, the auditor is required to project the sample results to the population. When evaluating whether the financial statements as a whole may be materially misstated, the auditor should aggregate all projected misstatements (discussed later) determined from sampling applications and other likely misstatements[2] determined from nonsampling procedures.

---

[1]R. H. Montgomery, *Auditing Theory and Practice* (New York: Ronald Press, 1912), p. 81.

[2]In addition to projected misstatement, likely misstatement includes known misstatements specifically identified by the auditor in nonsampling procedures and differences between unreasonable estimates in the financial statements and the closest reasonable amount in a range of acceptable amounts.

Audit sampling is used by auditors in both tests of controls and substantive tests. It is especially useful when the auditor's selection of items to be tested is drawn from a large population and the auditor has no specific knowledge about the characteristics of the population being tested, such as the frequency, size, and direction of misstatements. For example, accounts receivable, inventory, and accounts payable balances could be overstated or understated as a result of using incorrect quantities or prices or because of errors in posting or arithmetical extensions and footings.

PROCEDURES NOT INVOLVING SAMPLING

SAS No. 39 promulgated professional standards for all uses of audit sampling. Although in the past the term "sampling" was used to describe virtually all forms of detailed audit testing in which not every item was examined, the definition of sampling in SAS No. 39, cited earlier, excludes several types of tests frequently performed in an audit. To clarify the circumstances in which an auditor's examination of less than 100 percent of the items in a class of transactions or an account balance would not be considered audit sampling, in January 1985 the ASB issued an auditing interpretation of SAS No. 39 (AU Section 9350.01–.02).

The auditor's purpose in applying a procedure is the governing factor in determining whether the procedure constitutes sampling. Sampling is not involved if the auditor does not intend to extend the conclusion reached by performing the procedure to the remainder of the items in the class or account balance. Thus, sampling does not generally apply to procedures performed to obtain an understanding of the control structure. For example, the auditor might trace one or two transactions through the client's accounting system only for the purpose of understanding the flow of transactions through the system, and not for assessing the effectiveness of specific control procedures. Similarly, auditors sometimes reperform calculations or trace journal entries to ledger accounts on a test basis for the purpose of obtaining additional evidence relating to a financial statement assertion. SAS No. 39 does not apply in those situations because the auditor's intent is not to evaluate a characteristic of all transactions passing through the system or all balances in the account. Other auditing procedures, for example, reading the minutes of meetings of the board of directors, also do not involve sampling.

Furthermore, sampling is not involved when the auditor separates a class of transactions or an account balance into two groups based on specific criteria and then examines 100 percent of the items in one group and tests the other by other means or does not test it at all because it is immaterial. For example, in what is known as the "high dollar coverage" approach, the auditor might divide the accounts receivable balance into two groups: (1) several large items that constitute a significant portion of the balance, and (2) the remaining (smaller) items. All the accounts in the first group may be confirmed, while assurance for those in the second group, which may be material in the aggregate, may be obtained from other auditing procedures, for example, analytical procedures using scanning techniques. The auditor would be using sampling only if an auditing procedure were applied to individual items that constituted less than 100 percent of the population in the second group for the purpose of drawing a conclusion about all of the items in that group.

Sampling does not apply to many tests of controls, such as tests of control structure policies and procedures based on segregation of duties or other procedures that provide no documentary evidence of performance. In addition, sampling may not apply to tests of certain documented control structure policies and procedures. Those tests often consist of inquiry and observation. An example is an auditor's observation of a client's physical inventory count procedures, such as inventory movement and counting procedures. (Audit sampling may be involved in certain tests of inventory, such as tracing selected test counts into inventory records.) Generally, sampling applies less often to tests of controls directed at the control environment and accounting system than to tests of control procedures.

A substantive testing method in which less than 100 percent of an account balance is examined and that is similar to, but is not, sampling is referred to as "accept–reject" testing. It is used when projecting a misstatement amount (discussed later) is not practical, for example, test counts made as part of a physical inventory observation and tests of reconciling items. In those circumstances, the auditor either "accepts" that the test supports its objective (that is, no or few misstatements are found) or "rejects" the test (more than negligible misstatements are found) and performs other procedures to achieve the objective. However, the auditor still must consider the extent of testing (that is, assurance needed and materiality) in planning to use "accept–reject" testing and must adequately document the test results.

Other examples of auditing procedures that usually do not involve sampling are cutoff tests in which the auditor examines all significant transactions around the cutoff date and analytical procedures. Also, sampling may not always be necessary in testing control procedures that operate repeatedly throughout the period. Sometimes, if such a control procedure operates cumulatively, the auditor can achieve the test objective by examining a single item. For example, a review of the year-end bank reconciliation may be sufficient to achieve the auditor's objective with respect to control procedures for bank reconciliations generally. Similarly, examination of other year-end cumulative reconciliations (such as a reconciliation of the accounts receivable subsidiary ledger to the control account) may be sufficient to achieve the relevant test objectives.

Generally accepted auditing standards do not require auditors to use sampling (statistical or nonstatistical); they do require that auditors obtain sufficient competent evidence to afford a reasonable basis for an opinion regarding the financial statements, and that auditors document their sources of audit evidence, regardless of whether sampling is employed.

AUDIT RISK AND SAMPLING

Having decided that a particular auditing procedure will be applied to a sample of an audit population, the auditor must then determine the minimum sample size that is needed to control the risk of an undetected material misstatement in the financial statements. That risk—referred to as audit risk—is the risk that an improper conclusion may be reached about the client's financial statements. Audit risk was discussed in Chapter 6 in the context of formulating the audit strategy on an overall basis. How that discussion relates to sampling is explained here.

Nonsampling Risk

Nonsampling risk encompasses all risks that are not specifically the result of sampling. Nonsampling risk is the risk that any factor other than the size of the sample selected will cause the auditor to draw an incorrect conclusion about an account balance or about the effectiveness of a control structure policy or procedure. Examples of nonsampling risk are

- Omitting necessary auditing procedures (e.g., failing to review management or board minutes).
- Applying auditing procedures improperly (e.g., giving confirmation requests to the client for mailing).
- Applying auditing procedures to an inappropriate or incomplete population (e.g., excluding an entire class of purchases from the process of selecting a sample for substantive tests of the accuracy of recorded transactions and then concluding that all purchase transactions have been accurately recorded).
- Failing to recognize a deviation in a control procedure when it is encountered in a test of controls.
- Failing to detect that accounting recognition, measurement, or disclosure principles have been improperly selected or applied.
- Failing to take action either in response to audit findings or because factors requiring attention have been overlooked.

Sample size is not a consideration in assessing nonsampling risk. Analyses of past alleged audit failures indicate that such nonsampling risk factors as failure to understand business situations or risks, errors in interpreting accounting principles, mistakes in interpreting and applying standards, and misstatements caused by client fraud are among the most significant audit risk factors and sources of auditor liability. Since sample size is irrelevant if the auditor fails to apply appropriate auditing procedures or examines an inappropriate population, adequate control over nonsampling risk is a prerequisite to controlling sampling risk.

Most auditors deal with nonsampling risk, in part, by carefully planning the audit and maintaining high standards of audit quality. Quality standards address matters such as independence and professional development of staff, independent review of working papers, and senior and managerial personnel's supervision of the performance of procedures. These are covered in detail in Chapter 3.

Sampling Risk

Sampling risk is the risk that, when an audit test is restricted to a sample, the conclusion reached from the test will differ from the conclusion that would have been reached if the same test had been applied to all items in the population rather than to just a sample. It is the chance that the test will indicate that a control structure policy or procedure is effective or an account is not materially misstated when the opposite is true, or that the policy or procedure is not effective or an account is materially misstated when the opposite is true. Sampling risk can also be viewed as the complement of the desired level of assurance from a particular sample. Thus, if the auditor seeks a high level of assurance from a test, a low sampling risk should be specified. Sampling risk is inversely related to sample size (i.e., with all other factors remaining the same, the larger the sample, the lower the sampling risk).

Sampling risk has the following aspects:

1. In the context of tests of controls
   a) The *risk of assessing control risk too low* is the risk that the auditor will conclude, based on the sample, that the control structure policy or procedure is operating more effectively than it actually is.[3]
   b) The *risk of assessing control risk too high* is the risk that the auditor will conclude, based on the sample, that the control structure policy or procedure is operating less effectively than it actually is.[4]
2. In the context of substantive tests of account balances
   a) The *risk of incorrect acceptance* is the risk that the auditor will conclude, based on a sample, that the recorded account balance is not materially misstated when examination of every item in the population would reveal that it is materially misstated.[5]
   b) The *risk of incorrect rejection* is the risk that the auditor will conclude, based on a sample, that the recorded account balance is materially misstated when examination of every item in the population would reveal that it is not materially misstated.[6]

The risks of assessing control risk too high and of incorrect rejection relate primarily to audit efficiency. For example, if the auditor initially concludes, based on an evaluation of an audit sample, that an account balance is materially misstated when it is not, performing additional auditing procedures and considering other audit evidence would ordinarily lead the auditor to the

[3]SAS No. 39 (AU Section 350.12) describes this risk as the risk that the auditor will conclude, based on a sample, that the assessed level of control risk is less than the true operating effectiveness of the control structure policy or procedure. This type of risk is sometimes referred to in statistical literature as the *beta* risk.

[4]SAS No. 39 (AU Section 350.12) describes this risk as the risk that the auditor will conclude, based on a sample, that the assessed level of control risk is greater than the true operating effectiveness of the control structure policy or procedure. This type of risk is sometimes referred to in statistical literature as the *alpha* risk.

[5]This risk is sometimes referred to in statistical literature as the *beta* risk.

[6]This risk is sometimes referred to in statistical literature as the *alpha* risk.

correct audit conclusion. Similarly, if the auditor's evaluation of a sample leads to a higher assessed level of control risk for an assertion than is necessary, substantive tests are likely to be increased to compensate for the perceived control structure ineffectiveness. Although the audit might be less efficient in those circumstances, it would nevertheless be effective.

The risks of incorrect acceptance and of assessing control risk too low are of greater concern to the auditor, since they relate directly to the effectiveness of an audit in detecting material misstatements. It is thus necessary to ensure that the extent of testing (sample size) is adequate to keep those risks from exceeding acceptable levels. The complement of the risks of assessing control risk too low and of incorrect acceptance is the desired level of assurance, which is sometimes referred to as the "reliability" or "confidence level." For example, an auditor's willingness to accept a 5 percent risk of assessing control risk too low for a test of a particular control procedure could also be expressed as seeking a confidence level of 95 percent.

DETERMINANTS OF SAMPLE SIZE

In planning a sampling application, an auditor must consider three factors: how much risk can be accepted that the sample results will be misleading (sampling risk), how much misstatement can be accepted (tolerable misstatement), and how much misstatement there might be in the population (expected misstatement). The auditor then determines an appropriate sample size, either by applying statistical sampling techniques, described later in this chapter, that incorporate those factors, or on a nonstatistical[7] basis by applying professional judgment in considering each factor's relative impact on sample size. The population size is sometimes important to the statistical computations, but when the population is large (e.g., over 2000 items), the effect on the computations is often minimal. For small samples taken from large populations, the population size has the least influence of all the relevant factors on sample size. This emphasis on the planning aspects of sampling applications means that the auditor must thoroughly develop the sampling strategy before the testing begins.

Sampling Risk

As noted previously, sampling risk is inversely related to sample size. The auditor determines the acceptable level of sampling risk after considering the evidence obtained from other procedures performed on the account or control structure policy or procedure being tested. Thus, a higher level of sampling risk may be accepted for detailed substantive tests when control risk for the financial statement assertion being tested has been assessed as low.

---

[7]The term "nonstatistical sampling" is used in SAS No. 39 to describe what many auditors previously referred to as "judgmental sampling." Statistical sampling procedures involve the exercise of substantial amounts of audit judgment, as, of course, does nonstatistical sampling.

The following example will illustrate these relationships. If an auditor has assessed control risk as low and is performing extensive analytical procedures for a specific assertion, then a high sampling risk (small sample size) is acceptable for related substantive tests of details (or perhaps it may not even be necessary to perform any detailed tests). On the other hand, if the auditor has assessed control risk as high and is not performing extensive analytical procedures for an assertion, then a low sampling risk (large sample size) is required. Very low levels of sampling risk are normally attainable only with very large sample sizes (i.e., several hundred items).

Tolerable Deviation Rate or Misstatement Amount

The *tolerable deviation rate* (usually shortened to "tolerable rate") is the rate of deviation from a prescribed procedure that can be found, as a result of performing tests of controls, without causing the auditor to either revise the assessed level of control risk or modify planned substantive tests.[8] The *tolerable misstatement amount* (usually shortened to "tolerable misstatement") is the amount of dollar misstatement in an account balance that may be discovered as a result of performing a substantive test and not require performing other auditing procedures or affect the auditor's opinion on the financial statements. For substantive test samples, the tolerable misstatement cannot be larger than the smaller of the materiality amount for the individual item or for the financial statements taken as a whole (which is the smaller of balance sheet or income statement materiality). For example, if balance sheet materiality is $200,000 and income statement materiality is $100,000, the tolerable misstatement should be no larger than $100,000 or the materiality amount for the individual item, if smaller. Determining materiality levels is discussed in Chapter 6.

The chance of the true misstatement in every sampling application equaling tolerable misstatement is remote, and thus auditors normally plan auditing procedures so that the sum of the individual tolerable misstatements exceeds the amount considered "tolerable" (material) for the financial statements as a whole. In other words, tolerable misstatement for an account balance is usually set somewhere between overall materiality and a proportional allocation of overall tolerable misstatement to that account.

As the tolerable rate or misstatement amount increases, the sample size required to achieve the auditor's objective at a given level of sampling risk (or of its complement, reliability) decreases. (This conclusion is derived from the sample size table for statistical samples, Table 10.1, on page 293; the same concept applies to nonstatistical samples.) Thus, with all other factors remaining the same, sample size can be almost halved if the tolerable rate or misstatement amount is doubled (e.g., from 5 percent to 10 percent) at a confidence

---

[8]Some auditors use the term "tolerable misstatement rate" instead of "tolerable deviation rate." Although an ineffective control structure policy or procedure *may* cause financial statement misstatements, it does not necessarily do so. Thus, the word "deviation" is used in this book in referring to a departure from a prescribed policy or procedure.

level of 95 percent with an expected deviation rate or misstatement amount (discussed later) of one-half of 1 percent. For tests of controls using statistical sampling, the examples in SAS No. 39 suggest a range of possible tolerable deviation rates between 5 percent and 10 percent. No such guidelines can be given for substantive tests, however, since tolerable misstatement for a specific account must be determined judgmentally based on a number of factors— overall materiality, account balance materiality, and type and amount of individual items within an account balance—that are not precisely definable. For example, if inventory has a larger account balance than accounts receivable, then inventory may be allocated a larger tolerable misstatement than accounts receivable.

Designing a sample with a high tolerable rate or misstatement may produce evidence that is too imprecise to support a conclusion at a low risk level that the account and the financial statements taken as a whole are not materially misstated. Also, a large sample can generally detect both frequent and infrequent deviations or misstatements that aggregate to a material amount, but a small sample can be relied on to detect only frequent deviations or misstatements. At the extreme, some items in an account may individually be so material or may have such a high likelihood of misstatement that the auditor should be unwilling to accept any sampling risk; those items should not be sampled but should be examined 100 percent.

Expected Deviation Rate or Misstatement Amount

Expected deviation rate or misstatement amount also has an impact on sample size. As the expected rate or amount increases, the sample size necessary to meet the auditor's specified sampling risk at a given tolerable deviation rate or misstatement amount increases as well. The auditor's specification of the expected deviation rate or misstatement amount in the population to be sampled is the best estimate of the true deviation rate or misstatement amount in that population. Auditors commonly use the results of prior years' tests of controls to estimate the expected deviation rate; if those results are not available, a small preliminary sample from the current year's population can be used for that purpose, or the auditor's "best guess" can be used. The estimate need not be exact, since it affects only the determination of sample size and not the auditor's evaluation of sample results.

In a statistical sampling context, the relationship between the increase in expected deviation rate or misstatement amount and the increase in sample size is not proportionate. For example, if the auditor estimates the expected deviation rate at 2 percent for a particular test of controls and specifies a tolerable deviation rate of 5 percent at a 95 percent confidence level, the appropriate minimum statistical sample size is 190. If, given the same circumstances, the expected rate were estimated at 3 percent, the sample size would be 370. (This can be seen by referring to Table 10.1 on page 293.) When the expected deviation rate is close to the tolerable deviation rate, very large sample sizes are often necessary. On the other hand, if the auditor sets an expected deviation rate that is below the true deviation rate, the sample is likely not to be large enough to support, at the desired level of reliability, a conclusion that the true deviation rate does not exceed the tolerable rate.

Figure 10.1   Factors Influencing Sample Size in a Test of Controls

	Conditions Leading to	
	Smaller Sample Size	Larger Sample Size
Desired assessed level of control risk	Higher	Lower
Expected deviation rate	Lower	Higher
Tolerable deviation rate	Higher	Lower
Number of items in population	Virtually no effect on sample size unless population is very small (fewer than 2000 items)	

Figures 10.1 and 10.2 summarize the effect of the factors discussed previously on sample size.

Other Planning Considerations

SAS No. 39 (AU Section 350.17) requires the auditor to ''determine that the population from which he draws the sample is appropriate for the specific audit objective. For example, an auditor would not be able to detect understatements of an account due to omitted items by sampling the recorded items. An appropriate sampling plan for detecting such understatements would involve

Figure 10.2   Factors Influencing Sample Size in a Substantive Test of Details

	Conditions Leading to	
	Smaller Sample Size	Larger Sample Size
Assessed level of control risk	Lower	Higher
Stratification[a]	Greater	Lesser
Expected misstatement:		
Size of expected individual misstatement	Smaller	Larger
Frequency and aggregate amount of expected misstatement	Lower	Higher[b]
Tolerable misstatement	Higher	Lower
Assurance from other substantive tests (e.g., analytical procedures)	Significant	Little or none
Number of items in population	Virtually no effect on sample size unless population is very small (fewer than 2000 items)	

[a]Stratification is the separation of population items into groups or strata on the basis of some characteristic related to the specific audit objective.

[b]If the auditor's assessment of the amount of expected misstatement exceeds an acceptable level of materiality, it may be inadvisable to perform the test on a sample basis.

selecting from a source in which the omitted items are included.'' In general, audit sampling (or any testing) directed at a recorded balance will not provide assurance as to the completeness of the balance. To test the completeness of an account balance (e.g., accounts receivable), it is often necessary to test some other source in which the potentially omitted items are included (e.g., the shipping log).

CHOOSING STATISTICAL OR NONSTATISTICAL METHODS

SAS No. 39 explicitly recognizes that both statistical and nonstatistical approaches to audit sampling, when properly applied, can provide sufficient evidential matter. Moreover, the guidance in SAS No. 39 applies equally to both approaches. Both approaches have advantages and disadvantages, and the auditor should choose between them after considering those advantages and disadvantages.

The major advantages of statistical sampling are the opportunity to determine the minimum sample size needed to meet the objectives of audit tests and the opportunity to express the results quantitatively. In statistical sampling, sampling risk can be measured in quantitative terms and objectively evaluated and controlled. This is because the process of determining the appropriate sample size entails specifying a level of reliability[9] and a desired degree of precision.[10]

There are also disadvantages to using statistical sampling, however, and they can result in practical problems that might make the use of statistical techniques less efficient than nonstatistical sampling procedures. For example, the statistical sampler *must* use random sample selection techniques, which can be more time consuming than the unsystematic (haphazard) techniques available to the nonstatistical sampler. In selecting a random sample, the auditor may have practical problems establishing a correlation between a table or computer printout of random numbers and the population under audit. For example, an auditor who plans to use random number selection of unpaid invoices in the audit of accounts receivable may face a population that is made up of invoices from three client locations, with the invoice numbers assigned at

[9]As noted on page 284, reliability may be thought of as the auditor's level of assurance or confidence—expressed as a percentage—that the statistical results provide correct information about the true population value. A 95 percent reliability level is considered a high level of audit assurance for substantive tests of details. If control risk is assessed below the maximum or if additional assurance is obtained from other substantive tests such as analytical procedures, the auditor often designs a substantive test sample at a level below 95 percent.

[10]Precision may be defined as the difference between the rates or amounts specified for tolerable misstatement and expected misstatement (both of which were explained on pages 285–286) in planning a sample. For example, if tolerable misstatement is set at 5 percent and expected misstatement is set at 1 percent, the desired precision of the test is 4 percent. In some types of sampling, such as attributes sampling used in tests of controls, precision is stated in terms of a rate of occurrence (e.g., 5 percent). In other types, such as variables sampling used in substantive tests of details, it is expressed as a dollar amount (e.g., $25,000). SAS No. 39 (AU Section 350) uses the concepts of ''tolerable misstatement'' and an ''allowance for sampling risk'' instead of precision.

each location without regard to the numbers assigned at the other locations. Not only will problems be caused by missing numbers in the population as a result of paid invoices, but duplicate numbers could also exist because of the lack of coordination among locations in assigning invoice numbers. Thus, the auditor might have to renumber the population in order to use random number selection.

The use of specialized audit software to extract a sample from a population stored in machine-readable form may greatly reduce the costs of selecting a statistical sample. When appropriate audit software is used, statistical samples may not be more costly than nonstatistical samples. As a result, the availability of computerized sample selection and evaluation programs is often a deciding factor in determining whether it is efficient to use statistical sampling techniques. Before deciding whether to use a statistical sampling procedure in a particular circumstance, the auditor should make a cost–benefit analysis, weighing the additional costs of determining sample size, extracting the sample, and evaluating the results using appropriate formulas against the benefits of knowing the reliability and precision associated with the sample results.

STATISTICAL TESTS OF CONTROLS

A statistical technique called *attributes sampling* that deals with proportions and rates may be used for tests of controls. Attributes sampling techniques are used to estimate the true proportion (not dollar value) of an attribute in a population. The auditor must carefully define the attribute being measured—such as proper approval of an invoice for payment—because the person who examines each sample item must have criteria for determining whether the sample item possesses that attribute or not. The sample results are then projected to the population and statistical computations made to measure the precision and reliability associated with the sample results.

In tests of controls, departures from prescribed procedures (i.e., deviations) are generally measured in rates of incidence. For example, in a sample of 50 disbursement checks, the absence of evidence of proper authorization of 1 check is generally expressed as a 2 percent sample deviation rate (1/50). Since the control procedure either operates or not, percentages are a convenient way to express test sample results.

The true deviation rate in the population is likely to be higher or lower than the rate found in a sample. The statistical sampler can make a statement about how high the true deviation rate could be, at a given level of reliability. For example, an auditor, having evaluated a statistical sample, could state

> One deviation was found in a random sample of 50 items (a 2 percent deviation rate); thus, there is a 90 percent level of reliability (10 percent sampling risk) that the true deviation rate in the population is less than 8 percent.

In the authors' view, a mathematical statement of risk based on statistical attributes sampling often has limited applicability in assessing the effectiveness of a control procedure in a typical engagement. Since statistical procedures (e.g., formal random selection) introduce additional expense, and statistical and nonstatistical procedures may provide essentially equivalent audit information, the extra expense is rarely justified. Additionally, because of the existence of other, corroborative sources of audit evidence and the interrelatedness of many auditing procedures, a single test is rarely the sole source of audit evidence about whether a control procedure is effective. Furthermore, even after assessing the effectiveness of a control procedure statistically, the auditor must still exercise judgment to determine whether, and to what extent, the control procedure contributes to a low control risk assessment. As noted in Chapter 8, the assessment of control risk for a specific audit objective should be based on evidence provided by tests of controls in their entirety. The statistical measurement of sampling risk associated with a test of controls does not diminish the need to consider the interrelationships among elements of the control structure. However, in environments such as engagements to determine compliance with governmental laws and regulations (see Chapter 25), the precise measurement of risk that statistical attributes sampling provides may be more appropriate, since a specific test may more often be the sole source of evidence about compliance with a regulation.

Basic Concepts of Attributes Sampling

If the true deviation rate in a population were known, the exact (discrete) probability of obtaining a specific sample result (such as 1 deviation in a sample of 50 items) could be computed. The auditor does not, however, know the true deviation rate and thus can only infer what it could be, based on sample results. Because the auditor samples from a finite population and removes each item from the population as it is sampled (i.e., sampled items are not replaced), the auditor must use the appropriate statistical formulas to compute the reliability and precision of the sample results.

To illustrate the attributes sampling technique, consider a simple example in which the true population deviation rate is known. The example is later varied to resemble more closely a realistic audit situation. Assume the following:

Population	= 1000 invoices
Properly approved invoices	= 950 items
Improperly approved invoices	= 50 items

The attribute being measured by the auditor is the approval of invoices for payment. In assessing the approval control procedure to reduce the amount of substantive testing, the auditor might use the following decision rule: If no deviations were found in a sample of five items, the control procedure would be considered effective, but if one or more deviations were found in the sample (a 20 percent or more sample deviation rate), the control procedure would not be considered effective. (Small sample sizes are used to illustrate the concepts and computations and are not indicative of suggested sample sizes.) What is the chance the auditor would find no deviations in a random sample of five items from this population?

If a sample of five invoices is taken from the population, one item at a time, there will be 950 chances out of the total population of 1000 of drawing a properly approved invoice as the first sample item. If the first invoice was properly approved and is not placed back into the population, there will be 949 properly approved invoices out of the total of 999 items in the population available for the second draw. The probability of a sample of five invoices from this population containing no deviations is

$$\frac{950}{1000} \times \frac{949}{999} \times \frac{948}{998} \times \frac{947}{997} \times \frac{946}{996} = .7734$$

That is, there is a 77 percent chance of finding no deviations in a sample of five items when the true deviation rate in the population is 5 percent (50/1000).[11]

Ordinarily, the auditor would not know the true deviation rate in the population. Assume that the auditor would not consider the control procedure to be effective if he or she believed that the true deviation rate exceeded 5 percent. In other words, a 5 percent deviation rate is "tolerable," but a greater deviation rate is not. In this case, having drawn a sample of five invoices, all of which were found to be properly approved, the auditor would be accepting a 77 percent sampling risk (the risk of assessing control risk too low, as defined in SAS No. 39) that the true deviation rate might not be acceptable, even if no deviations were found in the sample of five items. The complement of the sampling risk (100% − 77% = 23%) is the reliability level of the test. Stated another way, the auditor obtained from the sample of five items a 23 percent level of reliability that the true deviation rate does not exceed 5 percent.

Increasing the sample size will reduce the sampling risk and thus increase the reliability of the test. For example, if one more item were added to the sample, the sampling risk would be reduced from 77 percent to 73 percent (.7734 × 945/995 = .7345). To achieve a 90 percent reliability level (10 percent sampling risk) for the conclusion that the true deviation rate does not exceed 5 percent, a sample of approximately 45 items would be required, with no exceptions noted. Thus, by setting a tolerable deviation rate (5 percent) and a reliability level (90 percent) in the planning stage of the sampling application, the auditor could estimate, using statistical formulas, the minimum required sample size (45) to satisfy a stated audit objective.

The relationship among reliability, tolerable deviation rate, and sample size is particularly significant. For a given sample size (e.g., 60) and a tolerable deviation rate (e.g., 5 percent), only a certain level of reliability (in this case, 95 percent) can be obtained. To obtain a higher level of reliability or to be able to set a lower tolerable deviation rate (or both), the sample size must be

[11]The proper general formula for computing probabilities in this situation is the hypergeometric formula, which can be found in most introductory statistics books. In certain circumstances, calculations using the binomial and Poisson probability distributions can yield approximations close to the exact hypergeometric probabilities. Normal distribution theory, however, is often inappropriate for attributes sampling in auditing because it approximates the hypergeometric probabilities only when deviation rates are between 30 and 70 percent. Generally, much lower deviation rates are found in audit populations. The mean-per-unit estimation technique, discussed later in this chapter, is an appropriate application of normal distribution theory.

increased. That is the price that must be paid by the auditor to reduce the risk of assessing control risk too low (the *beta* risk).

The auditor may also buy ''insurance'' that the sample will not contain so many deviations that control risk will be assessed too high (the *alpha* risk). This insurance is bought at the cost of a larger sample size. To control this risk (i.e., the risk that the sample will indicate that the deviation rate in the population may be unacceptable when, in reality, it is acceptable), the auditor must take a larger sample. By specifying a conservative (higher) expected deviation rate, the auditor protects somewhat against concluding that the control structure is operating less effectively than it actually is when one or more deviations appear in the sample. Another way to control this risk is for the auditor to specify an acceptable deviation rate, lower than the tolerable deviation rate, at which the risk of assessing control risk too high is to be controlled, and a reliability level commensurate with that specified risk. For example, the auditor may wish to be able to conclude at a 90 percent reliability level (10 percent risk) that the true deviation rate does not exceed the tolerable deviation rate of 5 percent, and may also wish to be assured at an 80 percent reliability level that, if the population deviation rate is actually 2 percent (the lower acceptable deviation rate), the sample results will not include so many deviations that they will lead to the conclusion that the population may contain an unacceptable deviation rate, that is, more than 5 percent. The closer the lower acceptable rate is set to the tolerable rate, and the higher the associated reliability level is set, the larger will be the sample size necessary to protect against the risk of assessing control risk too high. In practice, controlling that risk at a meaningful level is often inefficient, given the significant flexibility available to the auditor in designing additional substantive procedures when sample results may indicate that control risk is higher than was desired. Controlling this risk is covered in more advanced statistical sampling discussions.

Determining Sample Sizes in Statistical Attributes Tests

When designing an attributes test, the auditor should decide if it is necessary to estimate the range within which the true deviation rate lies (i.e., whether upper and lower deviation limits are relevant) or if it is sufficient to test whether the true deviation rate either exceeds or falls below a certain tolerable level. (For example, the auditor may only need to know whether the true deviation rate exceeds the tolerable rate.) That decision affects the size of the sample that is appropriate for performing the test. A sample in which the auditor is concerned with both the upper and lower limits is evaluated on a two-sided basis; if only one limit is of interest, the sample is evaluated on a one-sided basis. A possible conclusion for a two-sided estimate is

- The auditor can be 95 percent assured that the true deviation rate is between 2 percent and 8 percent.

A possible conclusion for a one-sided test is

- The auditor can be 95 percent assured that the true deviation rate is not greater than 8 percent.

Usually the auditor needs assurance only that the true deviation rate does not exceed the tolerable rate. Knowing the lower limit of the true rate would not add to the audit usefulness of the information from a sample. Sometimes, however, the client asks the auditor to estimate the range within which the true deviation rate may lie. Internal auditors may appropriately design two-sided estimates for internal reporting purposes to aid in making the cost–benefit determinations associated with improving the control structure.

If the auditor needs only a one-sided evaluation, the sample should be designed accordingly. One-sided testing is efficient because it is generally possible to use a smaller sample size to meet the same reliability level and tolerable deviation rate for one-sided tests than for two-sided estimates. Most standard attributes tables and some computer programs designed for audit use assume a one-sided testing plan. If a two-sided plan is desired, the documentation for the one-sided computer program or table usually explains how to make the conversion.

Table 10.1 is an abbreviated table for sample sizes at the 95 percent reliability level. To use the table, the auditor specifies a tolerable deviation rate and an expected population deviation rate, and locates the column for the tolerable rate along the top of the table and the row for the expected rate along the left-hand side of the table. The intersection of the row and column indicates the minimum necessary sample size. For example, if the tolerable rate is 6 percent and the expected rate is 1 percent, the minimum sample size is 80 items.

Reliability levels for tests of controls are generally set high (e.g., as high as 90 percent or 95 percent) if the test is the auditor's primary source of evidence about whether a control structure policy or procedure is effective. However, lower reliability levels are usually warranted, because additional evidence about the effectiveness of the policy or procedure will ordinarily be obtained through extensive observation and inquiries, tests of controls of related policies or procedures, and examination of the control aspects of sample items selected for substantive tests. Tolerable deviation rates of between 5 percent and 10 percent are common; the more critical the policy or procedure and the more

Table 10.1 Determination of Sample Size (Reliability = 95%)

Expected Deviation Rate (Percent)	Tolerable Deviation Rate (Percent)											
	1	2	3	4	5	6	7	8	9	10	12	14
0.00	300	150	100	75	60	50	45	40	35	30	25	20
0.50		320	160	120	95	80	70	60	55	50	40	35
1.0			260	160	95	80	70	60	55	50	40	35
2.0				300	190	130	90	80	70	50	40	35
3.0					370	200	130	95	85	65	55	35
4.0						430	230	150	100	90	65	45
5.0							480	240	160	120	75	55
6.0									270	180	100	65
7.0										300	130	85
8.0											200	100

likely that a deviation will cause a financial statement misstatement, the lower the tolerable deviation rate should be set. Appendix A to this chapter contains tables for determining sample size (one-sided tests) in statistical attributes sampling at reliability levels of 60, 80, 90, and 95 percent. Because of rounding in those and other tables, however, the auditor should consider using computer software to determine the most efficient sample size. Computer programs may be particularly helpful in determining sample sizes in situations not covered by tables or where the population size is small, requiring more precise computations than are possible using tables.

Selecting the Sample

A statistical sample must be selected randomly, regardless of whether it is expensive, inconvenient, or time-consuming to do so. (A nonstatistical sample does not have to be selected randomly; however, knowing how to select a true random sample may help an auditor using nonstatistical sampling to select a representative sample.) Random sample selection is any method of selection in which every item (element) in the population has an equal (or, more technically, calculable) probability of being included in the sample. The two most common methods of achieving a random sample are random number selection and systematic selection.

For random number selection, the auditor needs a source of random numbers, such as random number tables or a computer program for generating random numbers, and a scheme establishing a one-to-one correspondence between each random number selected and a particular population item. The correspondence scheme is simple if the documents are numbered and can be retrieved based on the numbers. If documents are unnumbered or are filed other than numerically, the auditor may have to assign sequential numbers to them. If it is not easy to make the numbers correspond, or the auditor cannot determine the size of the population, it may be difficult to conclude that the population is complete.

In systematic sample selection, the auditor calculates a sampling interval (n) by dividing population size by sample size, randomly identifies a starting point between 1 and n, and then methodically selects every nth item in the entire population to be sampled. Alternatively, the auditor may use multiple random starts to overcome any possible nonrandomness in the population arrangement and to avoid potential criticism about the randomness of a sampling population. Using computer programs to generate random numbers or batch programs to select items randomly is often an efficient way of selecting specific items for examination.

Often the auditor finds it efficient to perform more than one test of controls using the same sample. For example, the auditor may wish to reperform, using a reliability level of 95 percent, an expected deviation rate of 1 percent, and a tolerable deviation rate of 8 percent, a control procedure the client applies to ensure the mathematical accuracy of cash disbursement vouchers. Using Table 10.1, the auditor can determine that the appropriate sample size is 60. If a sample of 80 disbursements had already been selected to test a control procedure relating to authorization, the auditor could randomly (or systematically) select 60 items from the initial 80 items for purposes of testing the control procedure relating to mathematical accuracy. Or, both tests may be performed using 80 items (the larger of the two sample sizes) when it is not too costly to do so.

Evaluating Statistical Attributes Sample Results

After the auditor has performed the auditing procedures, the results must be evaluated, using mathematical formulas, tables, or computer programs, to determine the upper (and, if desired, lower) deviation rate limits for a specified reliability level, based on the sample results. To determine the upper limit on the deviation rate, the auditor must have four pieces of information.

- The reliability level (which is selected judgmentally).
- The sample size.
- The number of observed deviations in the sample.
- The population size.

Table 10.2 is an abbreviated table for evaluating sample results at a desired reliability level of 95 percent in a large population. The sample size used is located along the left-hand column and the number of deviations found in the sample is located along the sample size row. The achieved upper deviation rate limit is read from the top of the column. The auditor compares this with the tolerable deviation rate to determine whether the objective of the test has been met. Alternatively, some auditors may seek to know the achieved reliability of

Table 10.2   Evaluation of Results Based on Number of Observed Deviations (Reliability = 95%)

Sample Size	*Achieved Upper Deviation Rate Limit (Percent)*											
	1	*2*	*3*	*4*	*5*	*6*	*7*	*8*	*9*	*10*	*12*	*14*
30										0		
35									0			1
40								0			1	
45							0				1	2
50						0				1		2
55						0			1		2	3
60					0			1			2	3
65					0			1		2	3	4
70					0		1		2		3	4
75				0			1		2		4	5
80				0		1		2		3	4	5
85				0		1		2	3		5	6
90				0		1	2		3	4	5	6
95				0	1		2	3		4	5	7
100			0		1		2	3	4		6	8

the test for a fixed tolerable deviation rate; this would require using several tables for varying reliability levels. Appendix B to this chapter contains tables for evaluating sample results in attributes sampling at reliability levels of 60, 80, 90, and 95 percent.

Continuing with the earlier example, suppose in the test of 80 disbursement checks for proper authorization, 1 deviation was found. By using Table 10.2, the auditor determines an upper deviation rate limit of 6 percent. If the tolerable rate is 6 percent, the objective of the test has been met. If, however, 2 deviations were found in the test of disbursement vouchers for mathematical accuracy, from a sample of 60 items, the upper deviation rate limit would be 12 percent, which would exceed the specified tolerable deviation rate of 8 percent. In this instance, the auditor does not have the assurance sought from the test, and the assessed level of control risk is higher than planned.

Discovery Sampling

Discovery sampling is a special application of attributes sampling and is used when the attribute being tested is of such critical importance that a single exception in the sample may have audit significance. This single instance is a ''red flag'' that indicates the existence of a problem or a need for further investigation. Some examples of such significant attributes are

- Inaccuracies in an inventory of securities held in trust.
- Fraudulent transactions.
- Illegal payments.
- Circumvented control procedures.
- Fictitious employees.

When setting a discovery sample size, the auditor determines how many items to examine to gain assurance at a high level of reliability (e.g., 95 percent) that, if the true deviation rate in the population is at some low level (e.g., 1 percent), one or more instances will be found in the sample. Since the attribute being examined is critical, auditors often use high reliability levels (95 percent or above) and low ''tolerable'' deviation rates (less than 5 percent). The procedure for determining sample size is the same for discovery sampling as for attributes sampling in general, except that since no deviations are expected, the expected deviation rate is assumed to be zero.

To find an appropriate sample size, the auditor may use tables or computer programs. For example, in a population of over 10,000 items, the auditor would require a sample of about 300 items to be assured at a 95 percent reliability level that if the population incidence was 1 percent or more, 1 instance would appear in the sample (see Table 10.1).

Evaluating discovery sampling results is straightforward: If no instances of the critical attribute appear in the sample, the auditor has the assurance specified when the sample was designed. No evaluation tables or computer programs are necessary.

Although discovery sampling has been described in terms of tests of controls, the auditor may use any random sample of items—whether selected for tests of controls or for substantive testing—to gain assurance that a deviation from, or an instance of, a defined critical attribute would have appeared in the sample under certain conditions. For example, in a random sample of 300 accounts receivable selected for confirmation from a population of 2000 or more, the auditor may use computer programs or standard tables to determine that, at a 95 percent level of reliability, the sample would have contained at least 1 instance of a fictitious receivable if 1 percent of the items in the population were fictitious.

Sequential Sampling

In the previous discussion of attributes sampling, the sample was designed using a fixed-sized sampling plan. Another form of attributes sampling is sequential sampling, in which the auditor selects the sample in several stages, using computer programs or tables specifically designed for sequential sampling to determine the sample size for each stage. After selecting items in the first stage of the sample and performing tests, the auditor evaluates the results and either (1) concludes that the sample meets or does not meet the criteria for reliability and tolerable deviation rate, and discontinues sampling, or (2) determines that a conclusion cannot be reached and selects and evaluates additional items (this is the second stage of the process). The sampling continues until a decision is ultimately reached. Sequential plans may be designed to include any number of stages. The risk of assessing control risk too high may or may not be specifically controlled, and the sample sizes at each stage may be varied; for example, some plans have larger initial sample sizes and smaller second-stage sizes, while others have smaller initial sample sizes and larger second-stage sample sizes. Regardless of the plan adopted, the auditor must follow the rules established for the plan to obtain the desired level of assurance.

An excerpt of a two-stage sequential sampling plan is presented in Table 10.3. The sampling plan was designed for a 95 percent level of reliability. By following the decision rules, the auditor will be able to determine whether the specified criteria have been met or not. In the illustration, the auditor stops testing after the first-stage sample if no deviations or if two or more deviations are found, but goes on to the second stage if one deviation is found. Separate sample evaluation tables are unnecessary, because the decision rules are an integral part of the sampling plan. Appendix C to this chapter contains tables for two-stage sequential sampling plans at reliability levels of 80, 85, 90, and 95 percent.

A sequential plan allows the auditor to examine additional sample items if an unexpected deviation is found in the sample, or to stop the work after examining a small number of items if no deviations are found in the first sample. Thus, it may be efficient for the auditor to use a sequential sampling plan if a zero or very low deviation rate is expected or if it is difficult to estimate an expected deviation rate. In a fixed sample plan, if unfavorable results were obtained from the first sample, the auditor would be precluded

Table 10.3 Two-Stage Sequential Sampling Plan (Reliability = 95%)

Tolerable Deviation Rate (Percent)	Initial Sample Size	Second-Stage Sample Size
10	31	23
9	34	29
8	39	30
7	45	33
6	53	38
5	65	42

	Decision Rules		
	No Deviations	*One Deviation*	*Two or More Deviations*
Initial sample	Stop—achieved goal	Go to next stage	Stop—failed
Second stage	Stop—achieved goal	Stop—failed	Stop—failed

from simply extending the sample and evaluating the combined results using a fixed sample table as though they were a single sample. To evaluate the results of a sequential plan properly, the exact plan and all the decision rules must be specified before the sample sizes are determined.

STATISTICAL SUBSTANTIVE TESTING

A group of statistical techniques called *variables sampling* can be used in substantive testing. Variables sampling techniques are used to estimate the true dollar value of a population or the total misstatement amount in the population and thereby permit the auditor to conclude that a recorded balance is not materially misstated. Since variables techniques deal with dollar values, their use in substantive testing is common. Although a variety of variables techniques may be used, two—monetary unit sampling and stratified mean-per-unit sampling—are particularly effective in auditing and are widely used. Two others—difference and ratio estimation techniques—are also effective in certain circumstances.

From a statistical variables sampling test, the following type of conclusion can usually be drawn:

> The amount of population misstatement projected from the sample is $20,000. It can be stated with a 95 percent level of reliability, however, that the true amount of misstatement in the population is between $10,000 and $30,000.

This means that the direct projection, or point estimate, of the misstatement in this account or class of transactions is $20,000, but the true misstatement amount at a 95 percent level of reliability may be anywhere between $10,000 and $30,000. The auditor must decide whether a $30,000 misstatement would be material to the account or class of transactions being examined. If it is not material, the auditor may conclude, exclusive of the results of other tests, that there is a 95 percent reliability level that no material misstatement exists in the population. If an amount less than $30,000 but greater than $20,000 could be material, the auditor's assurance that a material misstatement does not exist is reduced to less than a 95 percent level of reliability. After considering the results of this and all other tests performed, if the auditor still does not have reasonable assurance that the account or class is not materially misstated, he or she may have to perform additional auditing procedures.

Some variables techniques project sample results in terms of audited amounts; others project sample results in terms of the amount of misstatement—or difference (recorded amount minus audited amount)—as in the foregoing example. If the results are in terms of the misstatement amount, it must be added to or subtracted from the total recorded amount to produce an estimate of the total audited amount.

Applying Variables Sampling

An auditor using variables sampling relies on statistical theory (including the auditor judgments that must be made) to draw conclusions about whether material misstatement is present in the population sampled. SAS No. 39 (AU Section 350) requires that before sampling, the auditor remove from the population for 100 percent examination those items for which, based on auditor judgment, potential misstatements could individually equal or exceed tolerable misstatement. Those items are not considered as sample items. In some circumstances, the auditor may be able to achieve high dollar coverage of the population by examining a relatively small number of items, and by doing so may reduce the risk of an undetected material misstatement to an acceptably low level. Examining items to achieve a specified level of dollar coverage is not sampling according to the definition in SAS No. 39. If risk is reduced to an acceptably low level by nonsampling procedures, sampling the remaining items may not be necessary.

In general, variables sampling may be an efficient sampling approach in any of the following situations:

- The population consists of a large number of items.
- High dollar coverage cannot be achieved by examining an economical number of items.
- The auditor is unable to determine which specific items in the population should be examined to meet the audit objectives.
- The auditor desires a quantitative evaluation of sampling risk from the audit test, as might be appropriate in an unusually high-risk situation.

As in attributes sampling, the auditor can buy "insurance" against concluding that the population may be materially misstated when examining all items in the population would reveal that the population was not materially misstated—the *alpha* risk. Controlling this risk requires the auditor to increase the sample size, which is determined by setting an acceptable, less than material, amount of misstatement and an associated reliability level.

Monetary Unit Sampling (MUS)

In this statistical technique, the individual monetary unit in the population (i.e., the dollar) is the sampling unit. Thus, the sample is composed of random dollars, not random items, in the population. When a particular dollar is identified for examination, the auditor examines the entire item or transaction of which the identified dollar is a part and determines an audited value for the entire transaction. The ratio of the misstatement amount, if any, found in the transaction to the recorded amount is used to ''taint'' the sample dollar. For example, a recorded transaction value of $200 with an audited value of $150 yields a 25 percent tainting of the identified dollar. This tainted dollar information is used to project a point estimate of the misstatement and create an upper (and, if desired, a lower) misstatement limit at a specified reliability level.

Since the sample in monetary unit sampling is randomly selected from a population of dollars, large value transactions have more chances of being selected and are more likely to enter the sample than are small value transactions. Consequently, a transaction containing an understatement would have relatively fewer chances of being selected than would a properly stated transaction or a transaction containing an overstatement. MUS is one of the variables sampling evaluation methods that utilizes a probability-proportional-to-size (PPS) sample selection technique. This selection method is often appropriate in an audit, because large value transactions are often of greater concern to auditors than small value transactions.[12] Common applications where MUS may be an effective audit tool include

- Selecting accounts for confirmation of receivables.
- Testing the pricing of inventory.
- Determining the accuracy of recorded amounts of fixed assets.
- Selecting employees for payroll tests.

There are both advantages and disadvantages to MUS. Some of its advantages are

- The sample sizes used with MUS are generally efficient.
- It is usually easy to apply.
- It is an effective statistical technique for substantiating that an expected low misstatement population is not materially misstated.

[12]Stratification can be used with an item-based sample selection method to accomplish a similar objective. Stratification is discussed later in this chapter in connection with mean-per-unit estimation.

The disadvantages of MUS are

- It requires that the population be cumulatively totaled so that random dollars can be identified.
- It is less likely to detect understated balances than overstated ones.
- It cannot select zero-value items for examination.
- Either credit balance items must be sampled as a separate population or the selection of sample items must be based on the absolute recorded value of the population items.

Determining Sample Size. Determining sample size for an MUS sample is similar to the method used for attributes sampling in tests of controls, as discussed previously. The auditor must specify the dollar value of the population, a level of reliability, a maximum tolerable misstatement rate expressed as a percentage of the dollar value of the population, and an expected misstatement rate expressed as a percentage of the dollar value of the population. The auditor may use the same tables or computer programs as for attributes sampling to determine sample size.

For example, assume that accounts receivable has a balance of $1,000,000 as of the confirmation date and the auditor has specified a reliability level of 95 percent. If the maximum tolerable misstatement amount is $50,000, the maximum tolerable misstatement rate is 5 percent $\left(\frac{\$50,000}{\$1,000,000}\right)$. If the expected misstatement amount is $10,000, the expected misstatement rate is 1 percent $\left(\frac{\$10,000}{\$1,000,000}\right)$. Using Table 10.1 on page 293, the auditor can determine that the sample size is 95. Before determining sample size, the auditor should consider whether any population items exceed the maximum tolerable misstatement amount—in this case, $50,000. Any items in excess of that amount should be segregated from the population for 100 percent examination, and their value should be subtracted from the total population value.

Selecting the Sample. To determine which items in the population contain the selected dollar units, the population is cumulatively totaled by item. If the records are computerized, those totals should be easy to obtain; however, if the records are manual, this process may be time-consuming. MUS sample selection can then be made using random or systematic selection to identify unique dollars in the cumulatively subtotaled population, resulting in a random selection of dollar units from the population since each item has a chance of selection proportional to its dollar value.

The most common method of MUS sample selection is systematic selection with at least one random starting point between $1 and the sampling interval (the population value divided by sample size—in the illustration, $1,000,000 divided by 95, or $10,526). When using systematic selection, the auditor is assured that all items in the population greater in value than the sampling

Figure 10.3   Calculation of Misstatement-Tainting Amounts

	Amount			
Error	Recorded	Audited	Difference	Tainting
1	$100	$ 60	$40	.40
2	200	180	20	.10
3	80	76	4	.05

interval will be selected; those items should be treated as items selected for 100 percent examination, because there is no chance that they will not be selected. Alternatively, the auditor may remove these large value items from the population before selecting the sample items, reducing the population by the dollar value of the items removed.

Evaluating MUS Results.   After selecting the sample, the auditor applies the planned auditing procedures to the sample items, determines an audited value for each item examined, and evaluates the results. The first step in the evaluation is to calculate the "tainting" of the misstatements found in the sample. The tainting is determined by computing the ratio of each misstatement amount found in the sample items to the recorded amount.[13] To continue with the earlier illustration of accounts receivable confirmations, the three misstatements in Figure 10.3 are assumed to have been found in a population of $1,000,000 from which a sample of 95 items had been chosen.

The next step is to calculate the projected misstatement for the population. This is done by dividing the sum of the individual tainting factors by the sample size, in this case (.40 + .10 + .05) ÷ 95, or .0058, and multiplying the result by the population amount ($1,000,000), yielding the point estimate of the misstatement amount, in this case $5800. (Had all three errors been 100 percent tainted—that is, had the audited amounts been zero in each case—the point estimate of the misstatement amount for the population would have been $31,579, derived as follows: [(1.00 + 1.00 + 1.00) ÷ 95] x $1,000,000.)

The last step is to compute an upper misstatement dollar limit. This requires two calculations. First, the auditor uses the table for evaluating the results of an attributes sample to calculate an upper misstatement rate limit for 3 misstatements in a sample of 95 items at a 95 percent reliability level.[14] Since the misstatements were not 100 percent taintings, a more precise upper

[13]Misstatement amounts found in sample items are those differences between recorded values and audited values that the auditor determines, after applying auditing procedures to the sample items, are in fact misstatements. For example, a response to a confirmation request might indicate that the recorded balance of an account receivable is incorrect because the balance had been paid before the confirmation was received. The auditor should determine whether a payment for that amount was in fact received within several days of the mailing of the confirmation. If it was, the audited value of the customer's balance and the recorded value would be in agreement as of the date of the confirmation and no misstatement would exist.

[14]More precise results may be obtained by using other tables or computer programs that are less subject to rounding errors than the attributes evaluation tables. Another method of computing the upper misstatement dollar limit that uses a different set of tables is illustrated in the AICPA Audit and Accounting Guide, *Audit Sampling* (New York: AICPA, March 1983).

Figure 10.4   Calculation of Upper Misstatement Rate Limit

Number of Misstatements	Upper Misstatement Rate Limit[a]	Increment	Tainting	Product
0	.04	.04	1.00	.0400
1	.05	.01	.40	.0040
2	.07	.02	.10	.0020
3	.08	.01	.05	.0005
		Upper misstatement rate limit		.0465

[a]Determined by reference to Table 10.2, "Evaluation of Results Based on Number of Observed Deviations (Reliability = 95%)," on p. 295.

misstatement rate limit can be obtained by using a "building block" approach, that is, by multiplying the increment in the upper misstatement rate limit for each misstatement by the individual tainting factors and adding the products to calculate the upper misstatement rate limit, as illustrated in Figure 10.4.

For conservatism, the misstatements are arranged in descending order according to the size of the tainting. Also, an allowance for possible, but unfound, misstatements is labeled "0" and is conservatively assigned a tainting of 1.00. (This is done to consider the possibility that misstatements existed in the population, even if no misstatements had been found in the sample.)

Next, the auditor converts the upper misstatement rate limit to a dollar amount by multiplying it by the total population amount, in this case $1,000,000 x .0465, or $46,500. (Had all three misstatements been 100 percent tainted misstatements, the auditor would have used the attributes evaluation table [Table 10.2] to determine an upper misstatement rate limit of 8 percent, which would have been converted directly to dollars by multiplying it by the population dollar amount [$1,000,000 x 8%, or $80,000].)

In the foregoing example, the auditor can conclude that, at a 95 percent level of reliability, the true amount of misstatement in the population is less than $46,500.[15] This upper misstatement dollar limit of $46,500 is then compared with the tolerable misstatement amount used in determining the sample size, $50,000. If at the specified reliability level the tolerable misstatement is greater than the upper misstatement dollar limit, the results support accepting the recorded amount as not being materially misstated. If at the specified reliability level the tolerable misstatement is less than the upper misstatement dollar limit, the true population misstatement amount could exceed the tolerable misstatement.[16] When the tolerable misstatement is only slightly below the upper misstatement dollar limit (i.e., there is a higher than desired sampling

[15]Other ways to state this conclusion are as follows:

1. The auditor is 95 percent confident that the true amount of the population is at least $1,000,000 – $46,500, or $953,500.

2. The auditor is 95 percent confident that the true amount of misstatement in the population is not more than $5800 + $40,700.

[16]If at the specified reliability level the tolerable misstatement is also less than the point estimate, there is a high risk (greater than 50 percent) of misstatement.

risk that the true misstatement amount may exceed the tolerable misstatement), the auditor may wish to recalculate the upper misstatement dollar limit at successively lower reliability levels until the tolerable misstatement and upper misstatement dollar limit are approximately equal, to determine the additional risk implied by the test results. This may help the auditor choose among several possible courses of action, among them to (1) reconsider additional assurance obtained or obtainable from other substantive tests, such as analytical procedures; (2) modify planned substantive procedures; (3) select highly suspect elements in the population for more work by the client; and (4) request the client to correct the misstatements found or considered likely in the population.

In any event, misstatements found in the sample should always be considered for adjustment. Any additional amount relating to projected misstatements proposed as an adjustment is a matter of auditor judgment. Knowing the upper misstatement dollar limit and point estimate may help the auditor determine the appropriate amount of any proposed adjustment.

Considering Other Techniques.   Although it would be cost effective to be able to use one variables technique in all audit situations, the auditor should be knowledgeable about several techniques to be able to choose the technique that will yield the most precise and relevant statistical results in a particular sampling application. For example, some audit tests, such as those involving samples from accounts payable, have as their specific objective to detect and evaluate understated amounts within the population of recorded accounts. In other cases, such as some inventory pricing tests, a number of understatements may be expected, even if the primary audit objective is to detect and evaluate overstatements. Because MUS is more likely to detect overstatements, its use in situations in which understatements are suspected may not be desirable. Furthermore, MUS methods of evaluating understatements found in the sample and methods that suggest netting them with overstatements in the sample remain an area of controversy and require further research. MUS may also sometimes be less efficient than other statistical techniques in situations where expected misstatement rates are high.

The following techniques are based on normal distribution theory. Although their use in auditing has diminished as a result of advancements in MUS technology, they remain important and effective techniques.

Mean-Per-Unit Estimation

In the mean-per-unit (MPU) technique, the auditor selects a random sample of accounts or items from the population, and, using the audited values of the sample items or balances, projects the average (or mean) value of the audited sample values to the population to create a population point estimate. For example, if the auditor selected a sample of 50 items from a population of 10,000 items and found their average audited value to be $20.25, the point estimate of the population amount would be $202,500 ($20.25 x 10,000). The auditor would have very little confidence, however, that the point estimate of $202,500 was the true population amount. Confidence can be expressed only in terms of the upper and lower precision limits that are determined in a statistical test. If upper and lower precision[17] limits have been calculated, the auditor can make the following type of statement:

> I am 95 percent confident that the true amount of the population falls within the interval of $202,500 plus or minus 10 percent (or, plus or minus $20,250).

One advantage of MPU is that it can be used on populations that do not have detailed recorded amounts. For example, it may be used to estimate the audited value of an inventory where only quantity information is recorded. Although MPU can be an effective technique in a wide variety of audit situations (e.g., those in which expected misstatement rates might be either low or high and those in which understatement is as likely as overstatement), the large sample sizes necessary to achieve the precision that is commonly sought in many audit tests may not always make it the most efficient statistical technique to use, unless the auditor stratifies (explained later in this chapter) the population.

A key factor in determining how close the point estimate of the population value will be to the true population value is the degree of variability (also referred to as dispersion) in the population. For example, if the average audited value of $20.25 in the foregoing example was developed from 50 invoices that were each valued at exactly $20.25, the auditor would intuitively be more comfortable with the point estimate than if the sample revealed 20 zero-value items, 20 items valued at $1.00, and 10 items valued at $99.25. Statistical computations of the upper and lower precision limits for the population (or misstatement) amount at a given level of reliability take into consideration the observed variability in the sample data. The more variable the sample data, the wider the range between the upper and lower precision limits will be (i.e., precision deteriorates as variability increases).

Because of the key role that sample values and their variability play in determining the point estimate and upper and lower precision limits, the sample should be as representative of the population as possible. Very small samples cannot be relied on to provide representative sample values, since the selection of one or several unusually large or small items in the sample would significantly affect the point estimate.

Basic MPU Concepts. SAS No. 39 requires the auditor to project sample results to the population as a basis for considering whether material misstatement exists in the population. In meeting this requirement, the auditor uses the information obtained from a sample to estimate the extent of misstatement in the population or the true value of the population.

To make statistical inferences about the dollar value or misstatements in a population from a sample, the auditor must compute the sample mean and the sample standard deviation. For example, an auditor, not knowing the audited values of the population of 10,000 accounts receivable, might take a random sample of 100 items totaling $3318.73. The sample mean is computed by

---

[17]SAS No. 39 uses the term ''allowance for sampling risk'' rather than ''precision.''

dividing $3318.73 by 100, to get $33.19, which is multiplied by the number of items in the population ($33.19 x 10,000) to compute an estimate, or projection, of the total value of the population ($331,900).

It is extremely unusual for any one sample mean to be exactly the same as the true mean in the population. Each different random sample of items from the population would most likely yield a different sample mean. For audit purposes, it is desirable for the sample mean to be close to the true mean. This is accomplished by both taking a representative sample from the population and choosing an adequate sample size.

A second measure that must be computed for the mean-per-unit technique is the sample standard deviation, which is a measure of the variability of particular item values around the mean value of the sample and serves as an estimate of the population standard deviation. In a sample whose values are very close to each other, and thus to the mean, the standard deviation will be very small. If there are both very large and very small values in the sample, however, the standard deviation will be larger. The sample standard deviation is computed using the following formula:

$$\text{Sample standard deviation} = \sqrt{\frac{\text{Sum of squared differences between sample audited values and mean value}}{\text{Sample size} - 1}}$$

Applying the Concepts.   The calculation of a sample standard deviation is illustrated in Figure 10.5. The example assumes that a sample of 100 items drawn from a population of 10,000 items produced a sample mean of $33.19.

The individual sample audited values are listed in Column (*1*). In Column (*2*), the average or mean value of the sample items is shown, and in Column (*3*), the differences between the individual audited sample values and the mean value are computed. In Column (*4*), the differences are squared and totaled. [The differences are squared to keep them from netting out to zero, as they do in Column (*3*).] The total of the squared differences is divided by the sample size minus one, and the square root of the result is taken, giving the standard deviation of the sample, in this case $27.729.

The calculations involved in computing the standard deviation can be confusing, but it is important that the auditor grasp the mathematical relationships involved. The standard deviation decreases as the variability of the sample values around the mean value decreases (holding sample size constant), and it also decreases as the sample size increases (holding the variability constant). (As mentioned earlier, very small sample sizes do not generally give reliable information about the total population, because small samples sometimes contain one or more items that are unrepresentative of the population and that can significantly distort the point estimate of the population value and the calculations of variability among items.)

The standard deviation (a sample statistic) is used to compute the standard error (a statistic related to the population value). The standard error, in turn, determines the upper and lower precision limits of the point estimate of the population value, which in this example is $331,900 (mean value of $33.19 x

Figure 10.5   Calculation of a Sample Standard Deviation

Sample Observation	(1) Audited Value	(2) Mean Value	(3) Difference	(4) Difference Squared
1	$ 80.29	$33.19	$47.10	$ 2,218.41
2	6.97	33.19	– 26.22	687.49
.	.	.	.	.
.	.	.	.	.
.	.	.	.	.
100	10.30	33.19	– 22.89	523.95
Totals	$3,318.73			$76,120.85

$$\sqrt{\frac{\$76,120.85}{100-1}} = \$27.729$$

population size of 10,000 items). The standard error of the estimate is the population size multiplied by the sample standard deviation divided by the square root of the sample size,[18] as follows:

$$\text{Standard error} = \frac{10,000 \times \$27.729}{\sqrt{100}} = \$27,729$$

The upper and lower precision limits can then be computed by multiplying the standard error ($27,729) by a reliability factor (discussed later) appropriate for the desired level of reliability (e.g., the factor for 95 percent reliability is 1.96; for 90 percent reliability, 1.64), and calculating an interval on either side (plus or minus) of the projected population value (in this example, $331,900 ± [1.96 × $27,729]). The conclusion, at a 95 percent reliability level, is that the lower precision limit is $277,551 and the upper precision limit is $386,249.

The statistical sampling results can be summarized by the statement that the total population amount is between $277,551 and $386,249 with 95 percent reliability. Thus, there is only a 5 percent risk (the complement of reliability) that the true value falls outside this range. SAS No. 39 refers to this risk for substantive test sampling applications as the risk of incorrect acceptance. If the true value of the population can be in the interval between $277,551 and $386,249 without causing the auditor to conclude that material misstatement exists in the population, then the auditor can say with 95 percent confidence that no material misstatement exists in this population. The limits are of

[18]The sample standard deviation should also be multiplied by a finite population correction factor $\left(\sqrt{1 - \dfrac{\text{size of sample}}{\text{size of population}}} \right)$ when computing the standard error. However, when the sample size is small relative to the population (less than 10 percent), the factor has little influence on the computations. For many audit sampling applications this factor will not be significant and therefore is not illustrated in this chapter.

primary importance when MPU sampling is employed. Point estimates are less important; they are used to compute the interval, or limits, on the population value. A reliability percentage can be associated only with computed upper and lower precision limits. No statistical statement or reliability level can be associated with point estimates.

In the preceding calculations, a 95 percent reliability level has been used. Sampling results, especially in the audit environment, do not always require a 95 percent level of reliability. Auditors often have information in addition to their sample results that they can rely on in reaching audit conclusions, and thus a reliability level of less than 95 percent frequently is appropriate for audit applications. The Appendix to SAS No. 39 contains an illustration leading to a substantive test sampling application with a desired reliability level of less than 50 percent. For practical purposes, if sampling is such a minor element in the auditor's strategy or if the sampling effort is minimal, it is rarely economical to perform a statistical procedure to be able to measure precisely the reliability of the sample.

Reliability Factors.   The concept of reliability factors, as illustrated earlier, is derived from statistical theory based on the known mathematical properties of the normal, or bell-shape, distribution. The theory is that if repeated large samples from the population are taken and the frequency distribution of the point estimates of the population value from each sample is plotted (with the values along the horizontal axis and the frequency along the vertical axis), the distribution of the point estimates would create the distribution commonly referred to as the normal distribution. The normal, or bell-shape, distribution is illustrated in Figure 10.6.

The properties of the normal distribution that are used in the MPU technique have the following effect: If repeated samples were taken from the population and a point estimate of the population value from each sample was computed, 68 percent of the point estimates would lie at less than 1 standard error on either side of the true population value and 95 percent of the point estimates would lie at less than 1.96 standard errors on either side of the true population value. That result is adapted to fit the audit situation (i.e., the auditor takes a single sample and makes inferences about the true population value from that sample). Thus, the auditor can determine, at a particular reliability level, upper and lower precision limits between which the true population value is expected to lie.

Reliability factors associated with different reliability levels are shown in Figure 10.7. Thus, if the auditor wanted to evaluate sample results at a 90

Figure 10.6   Normal Distribution

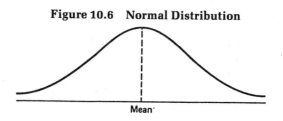

Mean

Figure 10.7   Factors for Different Reliability Levels

Two-Sided Evaluation

Reliability	Factor
60%	.842
70%	1.036
80%	1.282
85%	1.440
90%	1.645
95%	1.960
99%	2.576

One-Sided Evaluation

Reliability	Factor
60%	.253
70%	.524
80%	.842
85%	1.036
90%	1.282
95%	1.645
99%	2.326

percent level of reliability and if a two-sided evaluation was appropriate (see subsequent discussion), the standard error would be multiplied by 1.645 to measure the allowance for sampling risk, or precision. Similarly, for a 99 percent reliability level, the auditor would multiply the standard error by 2.576 to measure the allowance for sampling risk.

When designing a statistical test, the auditor should consider whether a two-sided estimate is needed, or whether a one-sided test is sufficient to determine whether the true value either exceeds or falls below a certain tolerable level. By designing a one-sided evaluation, the auditor may be able to draw the desired conclusion using a smaller sample size than that necessary for a two-sided evaluation. Alternatively, for the same sample size and reliability level, a one-sided evaluation yields greater precision (a smaller allowance for sampling risk). For example, the auditor may use statistical techniques in lieu of determining exact amounts for inventory values. In that event, the auditor may desire a two-sided estimate, using the "plus and minus" as a benchmark for evaluating the precision of the sample result. However, when the auditor assesses the principal risk as either overstatement or understatement, such as in evaluating accounts receivable (in which the principal risk is generally overstatement), a one-sided test may be sufficient for audit purposes. Other procedures may be applied (e.g., analytical procedures) to assess the risk of understatement.

Stratified Mean-Per-Unit Estimation.   One method of improving the precision of the mean-per-unit technique without increasing the sample size is to stratify the population and sample each stratum independently. In stratification, the auditor segments the population into groups of items that are likely to be close to each other in audited value. After the mean and standard error in each stratum have been calculated, the results for the individual strata can be combined to create an overall estimate. The first several strata dramatically reduce the required sample size (or reduce the allowance for sampling risk for the same sample size). Although increasing the number of strata generally improves the precision of the estimate (or reduces the required sample size necessary to achieve a specific precision), diminishing returns and other factors often lead the auditor to use between three and ten strata in most circumstances.

Research has shown the stratified mean-per-unit technique to be a very effective audit tool. It can be used in suspected low-misstatement and high-misstatement situations and, with the use of a sufficient number of strata, can often result in relatively efficient sample sizes. Since, unlike MUS, the technique requires a random selection of items, zero (recorded) value items have a chance for selection. The technique can be equally effective for evaluating overstatements and understatements of recorded values and net misstatement amounts.

Despite the advantages of stratified MPU, however, there are a number of significant constraints on its efficiency. Stratifying the population often requires reorganizing the underlying data, which, unless there is extensive computer assistance in data manipulation and sample selection, can be expensive. To compute the sample size required to meet the auditor's objectives, estimates of the variability among audited values need to be developed. Since estimates are somewhat difficult to develop, auditors often use the recorded values to estimate the necessary sample size and then include a safety factor (add extra sample items to the computed sample size). If the auditor performed a statistical application in the prior year, past experience is often a useful guide in estimating variability.

The steps required to apply stratified mean-per-unit estimation are summarized in the following paragraphs. Some of the steps in the evaluation process require the use of computations discussed earlier in the chapter. The steps are as follows:

1. Determine the number of strata to be used.
2. Determine stratum boundaries (the high and low population values for each stratum).
3. Determine an appropriate overall sample size.
4. Allocate the overall sample size to the individual strata.
5. Randomly select the sample items from each stratum.
6. Perform auditing procedures to determine an audited value for each sample item.
7. Compute an overall point estimate (projection) of the population value.
8. Compute the overall upper and lower precision limits at the desired reliability level.

As previously indicated, between three and ten strata are generally sufficient to meet audit objectives efficiently. A number of formulas (or judgment) can be used to satisfy steps 2, 3, and 4. One formula option for steps 2 and 4 determines stratum boundaries so that each stratum contains an approximately equal proportion of population dollars, and allocates sample size so that each stratum is allocated approximately the same sample size. Another option attempts to minimize the overall sample size by determining stratum boundaries and allocating sample size in such a way that the overall standard error is minimized.[19] As a rule of thumb, the auditor should plan for at least 20 to 25 items in each stratum so that representative results for each stratum are more likely.

The computations in steps 3 and 4 are often based on recorded values or small preliminary samples from the population. (As noted, because these figures may not be exactly representative of the final sample audited values, the auditor may want to add a "cushion" [10 percent is common] to the computed stratum sample sizes to ensure that the desired precision of the sample will be achieved.) Computer software can be designed to accomplish steps 2 through 5, 7, and 8 with a minimum of effort on the auditor's part, except for supplying the key judgments or information (such as reliability, precision, population size, and other options). Computer software can efficiently analyze a population, stratify it, determine sample sizes, allocate them to different strata, select a valid random sample from each stratum, and evaluate sample results. In this as well as other statistical sampling applications, manual computations of the formulas are often unnecessary and inefficient, given the current availability of timesharing and microcomputer software.

To evaluate the results of a stratified sample, the auditor calculates a sample mean, sample standard deviation, point estimate, and standard error for each stratum; finally, the auditor combines the results from the individual strata (steps 7 and 8). The combined (overall) point estimate is simply the sum of the individual point estimates. The combined standard error is computed as the square root of the sum of the squared individual standard errors.

To illustrate, assume the following facts:

	Stratum 1	Stratum 2
Population	4,000	1,200
Sample size	50	50
Sample mean	$343.19	$989.91
Standard deviation	$21.98	$85.42
Point estimate	$1,372,760	$1,187,892
Standard error	$12,434	$14,496

Based on these facts, the results of the two strata can be combined as follows:

1. Combining of sample results
   (a) Point estimate = $1,372,760 + $1,187,892 = $2,560,652
   (b) (Standard error)^2 = $154,604,356 + $210,134,016 = $364,738,372
   Standard error = $\sqrt{\$364,738,372}$ = $19,098

---

[19]For more details, see Donald M. Roberts, *Statistical Auditing* (New York: AICPA, 1978).

2. Calculation of two-sided precision limits and total audited amount, 95% reliability

$$\$2,560,652 \pm 1.96\,(\$19,098)$$
$$\$2,560,652 \pm \$37,432$$

3. Summary of misstatement limits

Recorded value	$2,787,200	$2,787,200
Lower precision limit	2,523,220	
Upper precision limit		2,598,084
Misstatement limits	$ 263,980	$ 189,116

Although the recorded value lies outside the computed precision limits of $2,523,220 and $2,598,084, the auditor may be able to accept it if the difference between the recorded value ($2,787,200) and the farthest limit ($2,523,220) is not material. Another way to arrive at the same conclusion is to compare the computed upper misstatement limit ($263,980) with the tolerable misstatement amount used in planning the sample. Even if the sample supports accepting the recorded amount, the auditor may propose that the accounts be adjusted for misstatements found in the sample as well as misstatements identified as a result of other procedures performed on the account.

Difference and Ratio Estimation

Difference and ratio estimation techniques are other variables sampling techniques also based on random item selection. They have many features in common with mean-per-unit sampling and can be used in stratified or unstratified populations, but are most effective when stratification is employed. These techniques have long been used in audit tests because of their apparent ability to generate precise results with relatively small sample sizes. Research has demonstrated, however, that they may not be dependable (i.e., the auditor may believe the sample yielded a 95 percent level of reliability when it actually yielded a lower reliability) in populations with low misstatement rates or when used in unstratified form with small sample sizes.[20] For this reason, their use is recommended only when high misstatement rates are expected, such as in some inventory pricing situations (even if the misstatement rates are high, the amounts may still be small and offsetting) or for conversions of inventory bases (such as FIFO to LIFO conversions in which each item can be expected to show a "difference"). Either technique can be used in tests for both overstatements and understatements. Whether one technique is superior to the other in producing a more precise estimate depends on the characteristics of the misstatements found in the sample.

The computations used in these techniques are based on the differences between the recorded and audited amounts of the sample items. The techniques require estimating a standard deviation and, if stratification is used, employ similar formulas for obtaining stratum limits and combining them to obtain overall limits.

---

[20]See John Neter and James K. Loebbecke, *Behavior of Major Statistical Estimators in Sampling Accounting Populations*, Auditing Research Monograph No. 2 (New York: AICPA, 1975).

In the difference estimation approach, the auditor calculates the point estimate of the population misstatement amount (or difference) by computing the average sample misstatement and multiplying it by the number of items in the population. In the ratio approach, the point estimate of the population value is based on the ratio of the audited amount to the recorded amount of the sample items. In both approaches, the auditor should ascertain that the sample contains differences that are representative of those in the population. Unlike mean-per-unit sampling, difference and ratio estimation techniques require that each population item have a recorded amount.

These techniques are most effective if many small differences are expected between the recorded and audited amounts of the sample items. As a rule of thumb, 20 or more differences are considered sufficient. If no differences are found in the sample, these techniques cannot be used, and the auditor should consider evaluating the sample as a mean-per-unit sample.

An example of how an auditor might evaluate a sample using difference estimation at a 95 percent reliability level and with two-sided limits is summarized here.

1. Assumed facts
   (a) Population
       Size   100,000
       Amount $1,700,000
   (b) Sample
       Size   100
       Audited amount $1,500
       Recorded amount $1,600
       Difference amount   – $100
       Mean difference   – $1
       Standard deviation of sample differences[21] $2
2. Calculations
   (a) Point estimate of difference
       Population size × mean difference
       $100,000 \times -\$1 = -\$100,000$
   (b) Standard error
       $$\frac{\text{Population size} \times \text{standard deviation of sample differences}}{\text{Square root of sample size}}$$

       $$\frac{100,000 \times \$2}{\sqrt{100}} = \$20,000$$

   (c) Upper and lower error limits
       Point estimate ± standard error × reliability factor
       $\$100,000 \pm \$20,000 \times 1.96$
       $\$100,000 \pm \$39,200$

---

[21]The standard deviation of sample differences is a measure of variability of *differences* between recorded values and audit values around the mean of those *differences*. In the earlier discussion of MPU estimation, the sample standard deviation was a measure of variability of audited *values* around the mean of those *values*.

Thus, the true amount of misstatement is indicated as falling between $60,800 and $139,200 at a 95 percent reliability level. Provided these possible misstatement amounts do not exceed the tolerable misstatement for the account, the auditor may be able to conclude at the desired reliability level that the balance is not materially misstated.

An example of a ratio estimation computation is not presented, but the calculations would be similar to those for difference estimation. The ratio technique point estimate is based on a ratio of the audited sample values to the recorded sample values (using the foregoing example, $1500/$1600 x $1,700,000 = $1,593,750; $1,700,000 − $1,593,750 = $106,250 projected misstatement amount), and the precision is calculated by measuring the variability of the sample ratios, using a computational formula.[22]

The difference estimation technique is often more precise when all the differences found in the sample are of a similar amount and are not related to the recorded values for the items containing the misstatements. The ratio estimation technique may be more precise when the differences in the sample are roughly proportional to the recorded values of the items containing the misstatements (i.e., when large items contain the large differences and small items contain the small differences).

NONSTATISTICAL SAMPLING

The auditor is faced with the same decisions in applying both nonstatistical and statistical sampling, namely, determining an appropriate sample size, selecting the sample, performing the tests, and evaluating the results. This section provides guidance to the auditor in applying nonstatistical sampling techniques. Much of that guidance is, of course, based on statistical sampling principles and techniques.

Determining Sample Size

If the sampling application involves nonstatistical sampling, only the most general guidance can be given regarding the appropriate sample size in different circumstances. No rule of thumb is appropriate for all applications. Many auditors, in an effort to provide some uniformity among nonstatistical sampling applications throughout their practice, have developed more specific guidance for nonstatistical sampling applications, in some cases based on

---

[22]One such computational formula to measure the variability of the sample ratios (i.e., the standard deviation $[SD_R]$ for an unstratified ratio estimator) is

$$SD_R = \sqrt{\frac{\Sigma x_i^2 + \hat{R}^2 \Sigma y_i^2 - 2\hat{R}\Sigma x_i y_i}{n-1}}$$

where:

x_i = individual sample audited values

y_i = individual sample recorded values

$\hat{R}$ = the computed overall sample ratio $\left(\dfrac{\Sigma x_i}{\Sigma y_i}\right)$

n = sample size

Σ = summation.

sample sizes used in similar circumstances on other engagements, and in other cases based on statistical sampling concepts and technology.

The guidance that follows represents the authors' views on appropriate sample sizes in nonstatistical applications, also based in part on experience and in part on conclusions reached in statistical sampling applications. This discussion, however, is clearly only one approach to providing guidance for the auditor's judgment process.

Some auditors establish a minimum sample size for tests of controls because they believe that there is some amount of testing below which the assessment of control risk will be unaffected. No minimum sample size can be established for substantive tests of details since the extent of these tests depends on the assessed level of control risk and on the extent of analytical procedures and other substantive tests of details. Therefore, a small sample size may be appropriate if a low level of assurance from the sample is acceptable.

A sample size of 260 for both tests of controls and substantive tests of details is a practical ceiling above which diminishing returns limit the incremental value of a few additional sample items. An auditor contemplating selecting more than 260 items for a nonstatistical sample should either consider using statistical sampling to increase the efficiency and effectiveness of the sampling application or ascertain that the cost–benefit trade-off of sampling versus other auditing procedures has been fully assessed. Experience has demonstrated that in many audit situations statistical samples of fewer than 260 items will achieve the audit objectives.

Selecting Representative Samples

Whenever sampling is used in an audit, SAS No. 39 requires that sample items be selected in such a way that they can be expected to be representative of the population from which they are drawn. The dictionary defines "representative" as "typical of a group or class." If each item in a population or subpopulation has a chance (not necessarily an equal chance) of being selected, the resulting sample is potentially representative of the characteristics contained in the population or subpopulation. For example, a sample cannot be relied on to be representative if it is made up of one or a few blocks of items in sequence (such as all items in a particular time period, on a particular page, or in a particular alphabetical section of a ledger) or if it is not drawn from the whole population. As another example, sample items that will be used to evaluate the reasonableness of a client's entire accounts receivable balance should be selected from the details of that entire balance, so that each item in the population has a chance of being selected. Conversely, sample items that will be used exclusively to evaluate balances outstanding for more than 90 days should be potentially representative of that group of balances, but may not necessarily be representative of the entire accounts receivable balance. Other procedures or a separate sample may be necessary to draw conclusions about the remainder of the receivables.

The auditor may achieve representative samples through either unsystematic, systematic, or dollar-weighted selection techniques. In the first two methods, the population may be stratified or unstratified. Unsystematic sample selection (sometimes referred to as haphazard sample selection) attempts to avoid personal bias in selecting items for testing. It is called haphazard selection because auditors intend it to approximate random sample selection; the term does not imply any element of carelessness. It can be affected by personal bias toward selecting certain items, however, such as a subconscious tendency to favor items in a particular location on each page or never to pick the first or last items in a listing. In its purest hypothetical form, unsystematic selection would involve blindfolded selection from a thoroughly mixed pile of all the records. More commonly, an auditor will choose a number of items from throughout the ledger or other records, after gaining satisfaction about the completeness of the population from which the sample is selected.

The only difference between the nonstatistical and statistical sampler's use of systematic sample selection is that the nonstatistical sampler often does not specifically identify a random starting point. Systematic selection is currently a commonly used nonstatistical sample selection method and in all likelihood will continue to be, because it is usually a cost-effective approach to extracting a potentially representative sample.

For substantive tests of details, sampling risk can be reduced without increasing sample size by stratifying the population by size or nature in order to permit different intensities of sampling for different strata. This technique may be effectively used to help ensure representative samples in either statistical or nonstatistical sampling applications. Often the auditor can use strata already inherent in the client data (e.g., location or product line). The sample sizes would be varied in accordance with the auditor's assessment of the risk of material misstatement associated with each stratum; that is, a larger number of sample items should be apportioned to those strata in which the auditor has assessed a higher risk of material misstatement. Either systematic or unsystematic selection methods can be used with a stratified population.

Dollar-weighted selection techniques can lead to sample sizes that are nearly as efficient as those used with stratified techniques. Dollar-weighted selection is similar to the unsystematic method except that the auditor judgmentally "weights" the selection of sample items based on their recorded amount, giving more weight to items with large recorded values. (This should not be confused with 100 percent examination of items above a specified dollar level and a sample of other items, or with a formal stratification plan.)[23]

Evaluating Sample Results

Regardless of whether statistical or nonstatistical techniques are applied, the auditor should extrapolate (project) the sample results to the whole population. Because conclusions based on sample results apply only to the population from which the sample items were drawn, it is important that the auditor carefully define the population (i.e., the aggregate of items about which information is desired) and keep it in mind when evaluating the sample results. For example, conclusions about the entire accounts receivable balance cannot be supported

---

[23]For a discussion of dollar-weighted sample selection, see page 301.

on the basis of a sample selected only from accounts outstanding for more than 90 days.

Tests of Controls. Sample results for tests of controls are appropriately stated as deviation rates, which are determined by dividing the number of sample deviations by the sample size. The deviation rate in the sample is the best estimate of the deviation rate in the population from which the sample was selected.

The auditor should follow up on identified deviations from control structure policies and procedures to determine if they are "isolated incidents," such as a clerk's being on vacation, or indications of a possible control structure deficiency. Isolated incidents should always be included as sample deviations and projected to the population; their impact on the assessment of control risk should be carefully evaluated. If the projected deviation rate exceeds the tolerable rate, the auditor should reconsider the control risk assessment. Either a single instance of a control structure deficiency (e.g., circumvention of a control procedure) or the aggregate effect of a number of instances (whether "isolated" or not) may be sufficient to change the assessed level of control risk.

Substantive Tests. There are several acceptable methods of projecting the impact of dollar misstatements in a substantive test sample to the population. In the *ratio approach*, for example, the projected population misstatement is determined by multiplying the total dollar amount of the population by a misstatement rate obtained by dividing the total dollar amount of sample misstatements by the total dolar amount of the sample, as follows:

$$\frac{\$1,000,000}{\text{(population amount)}} \times \frac{\$100 \text{ (sample misstatements)}}{\$1000 \text{ (sample amount)}} = \$100,000 \text{ (projected population misstatement)}$$

In the *average-difference approach*, the total number of items in the population is multiplied by the average misstatement amount obtained by dividing the total dollar amount of sample misstatements by the number of sample items, as follows:

$$\frac{15,000}{\text{(population items)}} \times \frac{\$1000 \text{ (sample misstatements)}}{140 \text{ (sample items)}} = \$107,143 \text{ (projected population misstatement)}$$

The ratio approach is generally the more appropriate technique when the misstatement amounts are roughly proportional to the recorded values of the sample items (i.e., the larger dollar misstatements are from the larger sample items). The average-difference approach is more appropriate when the misstatement amounts are disproportionate to the recorded values of the sample items (e.g., large items have small dollar misstatements and small items have large dollar misstatements, or the dollar misstatements are all about the same size regardless of recorded amount).

Another acceptable (but infrequently used) method is the *projection of average audit values*. This approach is used, for example, in constructing a balance sheet value for inventory if recorded values are not available and only quantity (not price) information can be obtained from the client.[24] This approach may also be most appropriate if there are recorded amounts but the general ledger control account does not agree with the sum of the individual recorded amounts. In the average-audit-value approach, the total number of items in the population is multiplied by the quotient obtained by dividing the total "audited" dollar amount of the sample items by the number of sample items, as follows:

$$\begin{array}{l}150{,}000 \\ \text{(population items)}\end{array} \times \frac{\$900 \text{ (total sample audited value)}}{150 \text{ (sample items)}} = \begin{array}{l}\$900{,}000 \text{ (projected} \\ \text{population amount)}\end{array}$$

In this technique, the misstatement projection is the difference between the recorded and projected population dollar amounts.

Other methods of projection may also be appropriate. It is important to remember that different projection techniques often result in different projected misstatement amounts. Auditors may find the ratio approach useful for a wide variety of situations, but no one method of projecting the misstatement is necessarily "better" than the others in all circumstances.

To ascertain the total projected misstatement for the account balance being examined, the projected misstatement from the sample results should be added to any known misstatements discovered as a result of nonsampling procedures performed, such as misstatements identified in 100 percent examinations of selected items or from high dollar coverage tests. Since, by definition, the dollar amount of the projection of sample results already includes the sample misstatements found, those misstatements should not be separately added to the projected misstatement. Similarly, misstatements affecting the account balance that were found in related tests of controls should also not be separately added to the projected misstatement.

An auditor using stratification in the sampling plan should project the results for each stratum separately and then add the stratum projections to determine the projected misstatement for the account or class of transactions being examined.

The auditor should compare the projected misstatement obtained from sampling procedures and other likely misstatements with the tolerable misstatement. (If the tolerable misstatement was not quantified for purposes of determining sample size, the auditor may find it useful to use overall financial statement materiality or some smaller amount for this comparison.) Even if the projected misstatement from sampling procedures plus other likely misstatements are less than tolerable misstatement—the misstatement the auditor can accept before modifying the opinion—the auditor should post the projected misstatement to a working paper that summarizes misstatements and potential adjustments, discussed in Chapter 21, to determine whether all likely misstate-

---

[24]In developing estimated amounts for financial reporting or tax reporting purposes, statistical samples are generally employed.

ments discovered during the audit equal or exceed the auditor's determination of materiality. The auditor should also evaluate the nature of the misstatements and discuss them with the client. In some circumstances it may be practicable for client personnel to review the remaining population for items having characteristics similar to those in the sample that were found to contain misstatements. When adjustments are made to the recorded balance, the related projected misstatement should be reduced by the amount of the adjustments. For example, if the auditor calculated a projected overstatement of $20,000 in an inventory balance based on misstatements found in the sample, but by investigating a few instances of a particular problem was able to identify $11,000 of overstatement that the client agreed to record as an adjustment to the recorded inventory balance, the projected misstatement would be reduced to $9000.

If the projected misstatement from sampling combined with other likely misstatements is greater than the tolerable misstatement (or financial statement materiality), the auditor must consider the implications for the audit opinion and audit testing plan and take appropriate action. Possible auditor actions include

- Asking the client to adjust for all of the known and some or all of the projected misstatements.
- Asking the client to perform additional work either to identify the sources of misstatements in the account balance and correct the account balance or to justify the balance.
- Extending the planned auditing procedures to identify and correct the misstatements or to demonstrate that the account balance is not materially misstated. Since extended sampling of the same population is usually not cost effective, this would likely involve designing other auditing procedures. For example, additional samples may "target" high-misstatement segments of the original test population.
- Concluding that the financial statements are materially misstated and modifying the audit report accordingly.

Allowance for Sampling Risk. Even if the projected misstatement or deviation rate is less than the tolerable misstatement or deviation rate, the auditor still must consider the risk that the true misstatement in the population exceeds the tolerable misstatement or rate. Thus, an allowance for sampling risk, defined as a margin for inaccuracy or imprecision in the sample result, must be determined. (The concept is similar to "precision," a term defined earlier in connection with statistical sampling applications.) When statistical sampling is applied, the allowance for sampling risk is computed. However, the non-statistical sampler must rely on rules of thumb and judgment to consider the allowance for sampling risk. For example, assume that the tolerable misstatement in an account balance of $2,000,000 is $80,000 and that the total projected misstatement based on an appropriately sized sample is $20,000. A statistical test might result in a computed precision of plus or minus $40,000 for a specified level of reliability, such as 95 percent. Since the projected misstatement (i.e., $20,000) plus the allowance for sampling risk (i.e., $40,000) does not exceed the tolerable misstatement, the auditor may conclude that there is an acceptably low sampling risk (i.e., 5 percent, the complement of the 95 percent reliability level) that the true population misstatement does not exceed the tolerable misstatement. In part because of the difference between the $20,000 projected misstatement and the $80,000 tolerable misstatement, the nonstatistical sampler, not knowing the exact precision, would make a judgment that he or she may be reasonably assured that there is an acceptably low sampling risk that the true monetary misstatement in the population exceeds the tolerable misstatement. On the other hand, if the total projected misstatement approaches or exceeds the tolerable misstatement, the auditor may conclude that there is a higher-than-planned sampling risk that the true monetary misstatement in the population exceeds the tolerable misstatement.

A possible rule of thumb for the nonstatistical sampler when considering an allowance for sampling risk is: If the deviation rate or number or amount of misstatements actually identified in the sample does not exceed the expected rate or misstatement used in determining the sample size, the auditor can generally conclude that the risk that the true deviation rate or misstatement amount exceeds the tolerable rate or amount is consistent with the risk considered acceptable when the sample was initially planned. For example, if an auditor performing a test of controls had established expected and tolerable deviation rates of 1 percent and 5 percent, respectively, a deviation rate approximating 1 percent would be a satisfactory result consistent with the risk considered acceptable when the sample was planned. Conversely, if the deviation rate identified in the sample exceeds the expected deviation rate used in determining the sample size, the auditor should generally conclude that there is a higher-than-planned sampling risk that the true rate exceeds the tolerable rate.

If, based on this rule of thumb, the auditor concludes that there is an unacceptably high risk that the true deviation rate or misstatement amount in the population exceeds the tolerable deviation rate or misstatement amount (or financial statement materiality), appropriate action is necessary. For tests of controls, the auditor should consider revising the control risk assessment. For substantive tests, the auditor's possible actions are the same as those discussed in the preceding section as being appropriate when projected misstatement exceeds tolerable misstatement. In using this rule of thumb for substantive tests, the auditor may encounter situations in which the acceptability of the achieved sampling risk for a particular account balance or class of transactions is not clear—for example, if the sampling risk indicated by the sample only slightly exceeds the level the auditor originally desired from the test, and other auditing procedures have not yet been applied to the account or related accounts. In these cases, the auditor should consider deferring further action until the aggregation and evaluation of misstatements for the remaining areas in the financial statements have been completed.

Aggregating Misstatements.   The auditor should consider the aggregate of all projected misstatement results from all sampling applications and all other likely misstatements from nonsampling applications and other relevant auditing procedures in evaluating whether the financial statements taken as a whole may be materially misstated. The aggregation and the disposition of the misstatements should be documented in the working papers. The summary discussed in Chapters 6 and 21 is an effective way of doing the aggregation.

After the projected misstatements have been aggregated, the auditor must determine an appropriate overall allowance for sampling risk to compensate for the fact that sample results may indicate the absence of material misstatements even though the true misstatements in the populations exceed the tolerable amount (financial statement materiality). This overall allowance is not the sum of the allowances for individual samples, because it is very unlikely that the true amount of misstatement in each sample is the extreme high or low of the range of possible values and because misstatements may be offsetting. Practically, the auditor must decide if the dollar difference between the aggregation of projected misstatements plus other likely misstatements and the amount deemed material to the financial statements is large enough to provide an adequate overall allowance for sampling risk.

For nonstatistical applications, the allowance should be based on the number of individual sampling applications and the size of the samples. For example, if the amount of misstatement material to the financial statements as a whole is $1,000,000 and there are net projected misstatements of $800,000 from sampling procedures and other likely misstatements of $20,000 from nonsampling procedures, the auditor must judge whether $180,000 ($1,000,000 – $820,000) is an adequate allowance for sampling risk. If a total of 1000 to 1200 items were examined in numerous (e.g., 8 to 10) sampling applications, $180,000 may be adequate, because those sample sizes would be likely to yield quite precise results. Alternatively, if the auditor examined 100 to 200 items in the same number of sampling applications, $180,000 might not be adequate, because the smaller sample sizes would produce less precise results. The deciding factor in determining the allowance for sampling risk in nonstatistical sampling is the probable preciseness of the results of individual samples, which is generally related to sample size.

If the auditor judges the allowance for sampling risk to be adequate, he or she should document that decision in the working papers and conclude that the financial statements as a whole are not materially misstated. Conversely, if the allowance for sampling risk is considered inadequate, the auditor's actions may include

- Requesting the client to perform additional work in those areas that were subject to large misstatement projections and to adjust for all or some of the misstatements.
- Extending the tests in those areas that were subject to large misstatement projections.

DOCUMENTING AUDIT SAMPLING

Documentation of the sampling applications used on an audit must satisfy the professional standards for working papers promulgated in Statement on Audit-

Figure 10.8   Summary of Audit Sampling Documentation

Type of Information	Documentation Needed	
	Related to Planning the Sample	Related to Performing and Evaluating the Results of the Sample
Objective and description of test	X	
Definition of misstatements (deviations)	X	
Population:		
1. Definition	X	
2. Description of how completeness was ensured	X	
3. Identification of items for 100 percent examination, if any	X	
Sample size determination factors:		
1. Degree of assurance/sampling risk	X	
2. Tolerable misstatement	X	
3. Expected misstatement	X	
4. Other factors, if any	X	
Sample size, including how determined	X	
Description of sample selection methods, including stratification	X	
Evaluation of sample results:		
1. Projection of misstatements		X
2. Aggregation with items examined 100 percent		X
3. Investigation of misstatement sources (causes)		X
4. Consideration of allowance for sampling risk		X
5. Conclusion on test		X
Aggregation with other test results and consideration of overall allowance for sampling risk		X

ing Standards No. 41, *Working Papers* (AU Section 339). Working paper documentation of auditing procedures is discussed in Chapter 5 of this book. The documentation should relate to planning the sampling application, and performing it and evaluating the results. Figure 10.8 identifies and categorizes information that should be documented.

Appendix A:
TABLES FOR DETERMINING SAMPLE SIZE: ATTRIBUTES SAMPLING

Reliability Levels of 60, 80, 90, and 95 Percent

Appendix A: Table 1 Determination of Sample Size (Reliability = 60%)

Expected Deviation Rate (Percent)	Tolerable Deviation Rate (Percent)														
	1	2	3	4	5	6	7	8	9	10	12	14	16	18	20
0.00	95	50	35	25	20	15	15	15	10	10	10	10	10	5	5
0.50	310	110	70	55	40	35	30	25	25	20	20	15	15	15	10
1.0		160	70	55	40	35	30	25	25	20	20	15	15	15	10
2.0			140	80	40	35	30	25	25	20	20	15	15	15	10
3.0				140	65	55	30	25	25	20	20	15	15	15	10
4.0					150	70	45	25	25	20	20	15	15	15	10
5.0						140	60	40	35	20	20	15	15	15	10
6.0							150	65	50	35	30	15	15	15	10
7.0								160	70	45	30	15	15	15	10
8.0									170	75	35	25	20	15	10
9.0										180	45	25	20	15	10
10.0											70	30	20	20	10

Appendix A: Table 2 Determination of Sample Size (Reliability = 80%)

Expected Deviation Rate (Percent)	Tolerable Deviation Rate (Percent)														
	1	2	3	4	5	6	7	8	9	10	12	14	16	18	20
0.00	170	80	55	40	35	30	25	20	20	20	15	15	10	10	10
0.50		150	100	75	60	50	45	40	35	30	25	25	20	20	15
1.0		280	100	75	60	50	45	40	35	30	25	25	20	20	15
2.0			340	140	85	50	45	40	35	30	25	25	20	20	15
3.0				400	160	95	60	55	35	30	25	25	20	20	15
4.0					450	150	95	70	50	45	25	25	20	20	15
5.0						500	180	100	60	55	35	30	20	20	15
6.0								190	100	70	45	30	30	20	15
7.0									200	120	55	40	30	25	15
8.0										230	75	50	35	25	25
9.0											130	55	45	30	25
10.0											240	80	50	30	30

Note: These tables are designed for one-sided tests. To determine the relevant table to use for two-sided estimation, double the one-sided test table indicated sampling risk. For example, the 95 percent reliability table implies a 5 percent sampling risk; doubling the sampling risk to 10 percent indicates that this table can also be used for a 90 percent reliability two-sided estimation sample.

Appendix A: Table 3   Determination of Sample Size (Reliability = 90%)

Expected Deviation Rate (Percent)	Tolerable Deviation Rate (Percent)														
	1	2	3	4	5	6	7	8	9	10	12	14	16	18	20
0.00	230	120	80	60	45	40	35	30	25	25	20	20	15	15	15
0.50		200	130	100	80	65	55	50	45	40	35	30	25	25	20
1.0		400	180	100	80	65	55	50	45	40	35	30	25	25	20
2.0				200	140	90	75	50	45	40	35	30	25	25	20
3.0					240	140	95	65	60	55	35	30	25	25	20
4.0						280	150	100	75	65	45	40	25	25	20
5.0							320	160	120	80	55	40	35	30	20
6.0								350	190	120	65	50	35	30	25
7.0									390	200	100	60	40	30	25
8.0										420	140	75	50	40	25
9.0											230	100	65	45	35
10.0											480	150	80	50	40

Appendix A: Table 4   Determination of Sample Size (Reliability = 95%)

Expected Deviation Rate (Percent)	Tolerable Deviation Rate (Percent)														
	1	2	3	4	5	6	7	8	9	10	12	14	16	18	20
0.00	300	150	100	75	60	50	45	40	35	30	25	20	20	20	15
0.50		320	160	120	95	80	70	60	55	50	40	35	30	25	25
1.0			260	160	95	80	70	60	55	50	40	35	30	25	25
2.0				300	190	130	90	80	70	50	40	35	30	25	25
3.0					370	200	130	95	85	65	55	35	30	25	25
4.0						430	230	150	100	90	65	45	40	25	25
5.0							480	240	160	120	75	55	40	35	30
6.0									270	180	100	65	50	35	30
7.0										300	130	85	55	45	40
8.0											200	100	75	50	40
9.0											350	150	90	65	45
10.0												220	120	70	50

Appendix B:
TABLES FOR EVALUATING SAMPLE RESULTS: ATTRIBUTES SAMPLING

Reliability Levels of 60, 80, 90, and 95 Percent

Note: Only upper deviation limits are obtainable using these tables.

Appendix B: Table 1 Evaluation of Results Based on Number of Observed Deviations (Reliability = 60%)

Sample Size	Achieved Upper Deviation Rate Limit (Percent)																
	1	2	3	4	5	6	7	8	9	10	12	14	16	18	20	25	30
5														0			
10									0						1		2
15						0						1			2		3
20					0					1			2			3	4
25				0				1			2			3	4	5	6
30				0			1			2		3		4	5	6	7
35			0			1			2		3		4	5	6	7	9
40			0			1		2			3	4	5		6	8	10
45		0			1		2			3	4	5		6	7	10	12
50		0			1		2		3		4	5	6	7	8	11	13
55		0				2		3		4	5	6	7	8	9	12	15
60		0		1		2	3		4		5	6	8	9	10	13	16
65		0		1	2		3		4	5	6	7	8	10	11	14	18
70		0	1			2?	3	4	5		7	8	9	11	12	16	19
75		0	1		2	3	4		5	6	7	9	10	12	13	17	20
80		0	1	2	3		4	5	6		8	9	11	12	14	18	22
85		0	1	2	3		4	5	6	7	8	10	11	13	15	19	24
90		0	1	2	3	4	5		6	7	9	11	13	14	16	21	25
95	0		1	2	3	4	5	6	7	8	9	12	13	15	17	22	26
100	0		1	2	3	4	5	6	7	8	10	12	14	16	18	23	28

110	0	1	2	3	4	5	6	7	8	9	11	14	16	18	20	25	31
120	0	1	2	3	4	6	7	8	9	10	12	15	17	19	22	28	34
130	0	1	2	3	4	6	7	8	10	11	14	16	19	21	24	30	37
140	0	1	3	4	5	7	8	9	11	12	15	17	20	23	26	33	40
150	0	1	3	4	5	7	9	10	11	13	16	19	22	25	28	35	43
160	0	2	3	5	6	8	9	11	12	14	17	20	24	26	30	38	45
170	0	2	3	5	7	8	10	12	13	15	19	22	25	29	32	40	48
180	0	2	4	5	7	9	11	13	14	16	19	23	26	30	34	42	51
190	0	2	4	6	8	9	11	13	15	17	21	25	28	32	36	45	54
200	1	2	4	6	8	10	12	14	16	18	22	26	30	34	37	47	58
210	1	3	5	7	9	11	13	15	17	19	23	27	32	36	39	50	61
220	1	3	5	7	9	11	14	15	18	20	24	28	33	37	41	52	64
230	1	3	5	7	10	12	14	16	18	21	26	30	34	39	43	55	67
240	1	3	5	8	10	13	15	17	20	22	26	32	36	41	45	58	70
250	1	3	6	8	10	13	16	18	20	23	28	32	37	42	47	60	73
260	1	3	6	8	11	13	16	19	21	24	29	34	39	45	49	63	76
270	1	4	6	9	11	14	17	20	22	25	30	35	41	46	51	65	79
280	1	4	7	9	12	15	17	20	23	26	32	37	43	48	54	68	82
290	1	4	7	10	12	16	18	21	24	27	32	39	44	49	56	70	85
300	1	4	7	10	13	16	19	22	25	28	33	40	45	51	58	73	88

Appendix B: Table 2 Evaluation of Results Based on Number of Observed Deviations (Reliability = 80%)

Sample Size		Achieved Upper Deviation Rate Limit (Percent)															
	1	2	3	4	5	6	7	8	9	10	12	14	16	18	20	25	30
5																	0
10													0				1
15											0				1		2
20								0					1			2	3
25							0				1			2		3	5
30											2	2	3	3	4	4	6
35					0				1	1	2	3		4	5	6	7
40				0			1				3		4	5	6	7	9
45				0		1				2	3		5	6	7	8	10
50				0					2		3	4				9	11
55			0		1	1		2		3	4	5	6	6	7	10	13
60			0				2		3		4	5	7	7	8	11	14
65			0				2		3		5	6	8	8	9	12	15
70			0				2	3		4	5	6	8	9	10	13	17
75			0		1	2		3	4		6	7		10	11	15	18
80		0		1		2	3	4	4	5	6	8	9	10	12	16	20
85		0		1	2		3	4		5	7	8	10	11	13	17	21
90		0		1	2	3	3	4	5	6	7	9	10	12	14	18	22
95		0		1	2	3	4	4	5	6	8	9	11	13	15	19	24
100		0	1		2	3	4	5	6	6	8	10	12	14	16	20	25

110		0	1	2	3		4	5	6	7	9	11	13	15	17	23	28
120		0	1	2	3	4	5	6	7	8	10	13	15	17	19	25	31
130		0	1	2	3	4	6	7	8	9	11	14	16	19	21	27	34
140		0	2	3	4	5	6	8	9	10	13	15	18	20	23	30	36
150		1	2	3	4	6	7	8	10	11	14	16	19	22	25	32	39
160	0	1	2	3	5	6	7	9	10	12	15	18	21	24	27	34	42
170	0	1	2	4	5	7	8	10	11	13	16	19	22	25	29	37	45
180	0	1	3	4	6	7	9	10	12	14	17	20	24	27	30	39	48
190	0	1	3	4	6	8	9	11	13	14	18	22	25	29	32	41	51
200	0	1	3	5	6	8	10	12	14	15	19	23	27	30	34	44	54
210	0	2	3	5	7	9	11	13	15	16	20	24	28	32	36	46	56
220	0	2	4	5	7	9	11	13	15	17	21	25	30	34	38	49	59
230	0	2	4	6	8	10	12	14	16	18	22	27	31	35	40	51	62
240	0	2	4	6	8	10	12	15	17	19	24	28	33	37	42	53	65
250	0	2	4	6	9	11	13	16	18	20	25	29	34	39	44	56	68
260	0	2	5	7	9	11	14	16	19	21	26	31	36	41	46	58	71
270	0	3	5	7	9	12	14	17	20	22	27	32	37	42	47	60	74
280	0	3	5	8	10	12	15	18	20	23	28	33	39	44	49	63	77
290	1	3	5	8	10	13	16	19	21	24	29	35	40	46	51	65	79
300	1	3	6	8	11	14	16	19	22	25	30	36	42	47	53	68	82

Appendix B: Table 3 Evaluation of Results Based on Number of Observed Deviations (Reliability = 90%)

Sample Size	Achieved Upper Deviation Rate Limit (Percent)																
	1	2	3	4	5	6	7	8	9	10	12	14	16	18	20	25	30
5																	
10																0	
15													0			1	
20											0				1	2	
25									0				1		2	3	4
30								0				1		2		4	5
35							0				1		2		3	5	6
40						0				1		2	3		4	6	7
45					0				1		2		3	4	5	7	9
50					0			1			2	3	4	5		8	10
55					0		1			2	3		4	5	6	9	11
60				0			1		2		3	4	5	6	7	10	13
65				0		1		2		3	4	5	6	7	8	11	14
70				0		1		2		3	4	5	6	8	9	12	15
75			0			1	2		3		4	6	7	8	10	13	16
80			0		1		2		3	4	5	6	8	9	10	14	18
85			0		1		2	3		4	5	7	8	10	11	15	19
90			0		1	2		3	4		6	7	9	11	12	16	20
95			0		1	2	3		4	5	6	8	10	11	13	17	22
100			0		1	2	3	4		5	7	9	10	12	14	19	23

110			0	1	2	3		4	5	6	8	10	12	14	16	21	26
120				1	2	3	4	5	6	7	9	11	13	15	17	23	29
130			1	2		3	4	6	7	8	10	12	15	17	19	25	31
140			1	2	3	4	5	6	7	9	11	13	16	18	21	27	34
150			1	2	3	4	6	7	8	9	12	15	17	20	23	30	37
160		0	1	2	4	5	6	8	9	10	13	16	19	22	25	32	40
170		0	1	3	4	5	7	8	10	11	14	17	20	23	26	34	42
180		0	2	3	4	6	7	9	11	12	15	18	22	25	28	37	45
190		0	2	3	5	6	8	10	11	13	16	20	23	26	30	39	48
200		0	2	4	5	7	8	10	12	14	17	21	24	28	32	41	51
210		1	2	4	6	7	9	11	13	15	18	22	26	30	34	44	54
220		1	3	4	6	8	10	12	14	15	19	23	27	31	35	46	56
230		1	3	5	6	8	10	12	14	16	20	25	29	33	37	48	59
240		1	3	5	7	9	11	13	15	17	21	26	30	35	39	50	62
250	0	1	3	5	7	9	11	14	16	18	23	27	32	36	41	53	65
260	0	2	4	6	8	10	12	15	17	19	24	28	33	38	43	55	68
270	0	2	4	6	8	10	13	15	18	20	25	30	35	40	45	57	70
280	0	2	4	6	8	11	13	16	18	21	26	31	36	41	47	60	73
290	0	2	4	7	9	11	14	17	19	22	27	32	37	43	48	62	76
300	0	2	4	7	9	12	14	17	20	22	28	33	39	45	50	64	79

Appendix B: Table 4 Evaluation of Results Based on Number of Observed Deviations (Reliability = 95%)

Sample Size	Achieved Upper Deviation Rate Limit (Percent)																
	1	2	3	4	5	6	7	8	9	10	12	14	16	18	20	25	30
5																	
10																	0
15															0		1
20												0				1	2
25											0			1		2	3
30										0			1		2	3	4
35									0			1		2		4	5
40								0			1		2		3	5	6
45							0				1	2		3	4	6	8
50						0				1		2	3	4	5	7	9
55						0			1		2	3	4		5	8	10
60					0			1			2	3	4	5	6	9	11
65					0			1		2	3	4	5	6	7	10	13
70					0		1		2		3	4	5	7	8	11	14
75				0			1		2		4	5	6	7	8	12	15
80				0		1		2		3	4	5	7	8	9	13	16
85				0		1		2	3		5	6	7	9	10	14	18
90				0		1	2		3	4	5	6	8	9	11	15	19
95				0	1		2	3		4	5	7	9	10	12	16	20
100			0		1		2	3	4		6	8	9	11	13	17	22

110	24	19	14	12	10	9	7	5	4		3	2	1		0		
120	27	21	16	14	12	10	8	6	5	4	3	2	1	1	0		
130	30	24	18	15	13	11	9	7	6	5	4	3	2	1	0		
140	32	26	19	17	14	12	10	7	6	5	4	3	2	1	0		
150	35	28	21	18	16	13	11	8	7	6	5	4	2	1	0	0	
160	38	30	23	20	17	14	12	9	8	7	5	4	3	2	1	0	
170	40	32	25	22	19	16	13	10	9	7	6	4	3	2	1	0	
180	43	35	26	23	20	17	14	11	9	8	6	5	3	2	1	0	
190	46	37	28	25	21	18	15	11	10	8	7	5	4	3	1	0	
200	48	39	30	26	23	19	16	12	11	9	7	6	4	3	1	0	
210	51	41	32	28	24	20	17	13	12	10	8	6	5	3	2	0	
220	54	44	33	29	25	22	18	14	12	10	8	7	5	3	2	1	
230	57	46	35	31	27	23	19	15	13	11	9	7	5	4	2	1	
240	59	48	37	33	28	24	20	16	14	12	10	8	6	4	2	1	
250	62	50	39	34	30	25	21	16	15	12	10	8	6	4	2	1	
260	65	53	41	36	31	26	22	17	15	13	11	9	7	5	3	1	
270	68	55	42	37	33	28	23	18	16	14	11	9	7	5	3	1	
280	71	57	44	39	34	29	24	19	17	14	12	10	7	5	3	1	
290	73	60	46	41	35	30	25	20	18	15	12	10	8	6	3	1	0
300	76	62	48	42	37	31	26	21	18	16	13	11	8	6	4	1	0

Appendix C:
TABLES FOR TWO-STAGE SEQUENTIAL SAMPLING PLANS: ATTRIBUTES SAMPLING

Reliability Levels of 80, 85, 90, and 95 Percent

Appendix C: Table 1   Two-Stage Sequential Sampling Plan (Reliability = 80%)

Tolerable Deviation Rate (Percent)	Initial Sample Size	Second-Stage Sample Size
10	17	22
9	19	24
8	21	30
7	24	36
6	29	36
5	35	43
4	46	45
3	62	59
2	97	77

Appendix C: Table 2   Two-Stage Sequential Sampling Plan (Reliability = 85%)

Tolerable Deviation Rate (Percent)	Initial Sample Size	Second-Stage Sample Size
10	20	22
9	22	26
8	25	29
7	29	31
6	34	37
5	41	44
4	54	45
3	71	65
2	113	79

Appendix C: Table 3   Two-Stage Sequential Sampling Plan (Reliability = 90%)

Tolerable Deviation Rate (Percent)	*Initial Sample Size*	*Second-Stage Sample Size*
10	23	29
9	26	30
8	30	30
7	35	32
6	41	38
5	51	39
4	64	49
3	89	56
2	133	87

Appendix C: Table 4   Two-Stage Sequential Sampling Plan (Reliability = 95%)

Tolerable Deviation Rate (Percent)	*Initial Sample Size*	*Second-Stage Sample Size*
10	31	23
9	34	29
8	39	30
7	45	33
6	53	38
5	65	42
4	84	46
3	113	60
2	169	94

Decision Rules for Two-Stage Sequential Sampling Plans

	No Deviations	*One Deviation*	*Two or More Deviations*
Initial sample	Stop—achieved goal	Go to next stage	Stop—failed
Second stage	Stop—achieved goal	Stop—failed	Stop—failed

11

Auditing in an EDP Environment

Changes in computer technology have been accompanied by changes in auditing standards. When the AICPA issued Statement on Auditing Standards (SAS) No. 3, *The Effects of EDP on the Auditor's Study and Evaluation of Internal Control*, in December 1974, it was still possible to consider the impact of computers on an audit in relative isolation. With the issuance of SAS No. 48, *The Effects of Computer Processing on the Examination of Financial Statements*, in July 1984, the profession integrated guidance on the effects of EDP (electronic data processing) on financial statement audits with other SASs, thereby formally acknowledging that computers had so permeated organizations that they must be considered throughout the audit. Subsequent SASs have continued to recognize that conclusion.

In early computerized systems that printed out all results of processing, the auditor's assurance about the accuracy of computer-generated data was frequently attained by obtaining detailed printouts (hardcopy) that included the calculations performed, data used, and all exceptions and rejections, and then reperforming the computerized procedures. Since this in essence bypassed the computer, it was called "auditing around the computer." Today, auditing this way is often impossible because of the large volume of transactions processed and the number of locations where processing may take place. Moreover, modern systems generally do not print out calculations in detail, and some systems do not generate all output in hardcopy form. (A common exception is microcomputer applications in small organizations, which in some cases still may print processing details.)

Using the computer itself in the audit, by testing general control procedures or using computer software to test the programmed procedures that carry out accounting and control activities, is today the usual method of conducting an audit. Originally called "auditing through the computer," this technique has become all but essential in modern processing systems. It entails audit strategy decisions about whether and to what extent to test control procedures, and about the nature, timing, and extent of substantive tests of computer-generated data. In addition, virtually all audit strategies in a computer environment present opportunities to increase audit efficiency by "auditing with the computer": Whether using the client's or the auditor's computer, the auditor can use computer software to perform many tests that would be too time-consuming and perhaps not even possible to do manually.

FEATURES OF COMPUTER ENVIRONMENTS

Computerized systems and their configurations vary widely from one computer environment to another. Even when the same type of mainframe from the same vendor is used, there is an almost infinite variety of combinations of types of peripheral devices, software options, telecommunications networks, and application software.

Computer Operations

To provide some background about different computer environments, an overview of computer processing concepts and terminology is presented here.

Detailed discussion is beyond the scope of this book and is available in works dealing specifically with EDP.

Hardware.   Computers basically consist of a central processing unit, internal storage (memory) and external storage, input/output devices, and other peripheral equipment. External storage can be on magnetic tape, disk, or both, depending on the system. Input/output devices consist mainly of terminals with screens and keyboards, and printers for hardcopy output. Other devices whose use is increasing in certain types of operations are scanners, point-of-sale registers, optical character readers, mark sense readers, and light guns. Other peripheral equipment includes telecommunications devices like modems, which translate digital computer signals into analog form for transmission over phone lines and retranslate them at the other end, as well as devices like multiplexors and controllers, which handle complex communications message requirements, directing the information to the appropriate part of the system or computer. The current trend—which can be expected to accelerate— is toward machines that communicate with each other and share data and programs via telecommunications and area networks. In many of these so-called paperless systems, such as those for telephone order entry, there is no printed documentation of transactions.

Software.   The programs that run the system and direct its operations are called the *system software*. System software includes the *operating system*, which directs internal operations and makes it possible for specific *application software programs* to be run. Among other components of system software in a modern system are *utilities*, which include report generators and powerful editors used to write or change programs; *telecommunications software; file and program access software;* and *data base management system software.*

Originally, software had to be created specifically for each application program, such as accounts receivable or payroll, to accomplish particular tasks. Most organizations still develop some custom-designed applications in-house. They are developed by EDP department staffs of system analysts and programmers, who use a standard system development methodology intended to ensure that applications are appropriate, are adequately controlled, and meet management and user needs.

Because the system development process is obviously expensive and time-consuming, however, outside vendors have developed standard applications, referred to as purchased systems or packaged software. Many organizations use these packages as an alternative to developing their own software. Purchased systems are normally sold with a maintenance agreement that provides program "fixes" as required to correct programming errors or add enhancements to the programs. To make these systems more efficient to use, vendors often build in numerous customizing features, called options, that allow users to tailor the software to their own needs without having to rewrite it.

Depending on the vendor, purchased systems may be available with or without source code. Source code is the series of instructions written so the programmer can understand them. They need to be "compiled," or translated, into machine language (object code) so that the computer can execute them. If the source code is not available to users, they cannot make changes to the programs easily. (Users can, however, change some program functions through other methods, such as "user exits," which allow the insertion of user programs, or selecting different options provided by the program.)

Data Base Management Systems.   Data base management systems (DBMS) eliminate much of the redundancy of data that exists when each program requires its own file structure. In a standard file structure, each program has data available to it in files specifically designed for that program. (A file consists of records, which in turn contain data fields or elements.) For example, in a payroll system, the payroll program would use an employee master file containing, for each employee, data fields for employee name, number, social security number, address, and pay rate. The personnel department would typically have another program, with its own file that duplicated much of the information held in the payroll system. In a DBMS, on the other hand, all data elements are held in a central data base and are called on as required by the particular application program. In the foregoing example, a "human resources data base" would contain elements used by the payroll, personnel, and other applicable departments.

Integrated Systems.   In today's environment, accounting systems are increasingly integrated with operational systems. These types of systems generate information used for both accounting and management decision-making purposes. An example is a manufacturer's accounting system that generates cost accounting information used for product pricing along with information for external financial reporting.

Organization of the EDP Department

The organization of the EDP department depends largely on the extent of computer processing, the number of employees, and the control techniques used. The department can range from one or two employees responsible for running a self-standing minicomputer to a large organization consisting of hundreds of people responsible for developing, maintaining, and executing applications on a multi-mainframe operation linked to a data telecommunications network.

Regardless of the size and complexity of the organization, there are a number of specific functions in an EDP installation.

Information systems management. Develop long-range plans and direct application development and computer operations.

System analysis. Design systems, prepare specifications for programmers, and serve as intermediary between users and programmers.

Programming. Develop logic, write computer programs, and prepare supporting documentation.

Technical support. Select, implement, and maintain system software, including operating systems, network software, DBMS, and so forth.

Data base administration (DBA). Design, implement, and maintain the data base in a DBMS.

Network management. Manage the operation of the organization's communication networks (including network utilization, routing, and problem management).

Computer operations. Operate computer in accordance with manually supplied and computer-generated instructions.

Data entry operations. Convert data into machine-readable form primarily using terminals or cathode ray tube (CRT) devices. Maintain and exercise control over the completeness, accuracy, and distribution of input and output.

Security administration. Control the security of the system, including the use of access controls and maintenance of user IDs and associated password files. (This function is normally found only in large installations.)

Tape library. Receive, maintain, and issue magnetic media files (data and programs) on tapes or disks; maintain systems libraries.

How duties are segregated within the EDP department is an important aspect of the control structure. To the extent possible, the aforementioned functions should be performed by different people, so that there is adequate separation of duties. For example, programmers should not have the ability to access programs actually in use. In general, the more sophisticated the system and the larger the department, the greater the opportunity to segregate incompatible functions. In small organizations, the same person may perform more than one function, which can present control problems with respect to incompatible duties, as, for example, when one person does almost all the work related to the operation of a departmental minicomputer.

Segregation of duties in computer environments, as in manual systems, also involves separating incompatible functions outside of the EDP department. This can be accomplished by permitting, normally via user IDs and passwords, user department operators access to only the functions required to perform their jobs. For example, if the payroll and personnel departments are among the users of a common data base, the payroll clerk should be able to access only the program that posts time sheets and enters paycheck-initiation transactions, while the appropriate personnel clerk should be able to access only the program that processes changes in pay status.

Supervisory control procedures in computerized systems are similar to those in noncomputerized systems. For example, in a user department, a responsible official should periodically determine that data rejected by the computer is being investigated as prescribed. Similarly, in the EDP department, a responsible manager should review and approve the adequacy of procedures for implementing and testing program changes. Supervisory control procedures can also be performed by the computer through its ability to match newly input information to preset tables or other files. Other supervisory tasks, such as recalculating invoices, are also performed by the computer; once appropriate formulas have been set up in the programs, and assuming that the programs are adequately controlled, the computer will do the calculations the same way every time.

Decentralized and Distributed Data Processing

The earliest EDP operations took place in centralized departments to which organizational users submitted requests for new and changed application systems and for job processing. Personnel in the EDP department designed, developed, operated, and maintained all of the organization's application systems. As the number of requests, together with the complexity of the systems, increased, however, many user departments sought alternatives to the centralized EDP function.

At the same time, technology advances made possible smaller, more powerful, and less expensive computer systems than the giant first-generation systems. Users began to buy and install these minicomputer systems throughout the organization, particularly at the departmental level. This was followed very quickly by a second phase of user computing resulting from the widespread availability and use of microcomputers. This form of computer use is referred to as decentralized or distributed data processing or computing. The most significant difference between decentralized computing and distributed computing is the extent of integration of the systems. Decentralized computing tends to be less integrated than distributed processing. In a decentralized environment, minicomputers and microcomputers generally operate independently of the centralized computer system. In a distributed system, there is usually a coordinating facility with responsibility for unifying the mainframe systems, minicomputers, and microcomputers, together with software, communications, and data base technology, into an organization-wide information system.

Distributed and decentralized environments have created new problems for both organizations and their auditors. For organizations, both the volume of requests for information and the amount of support required by users of these complex and sophisticated systems have increased dramatically. Other difficulties involve achieving compatibility of both hardware and software among different departments, conforming organizational and departmental standards, and establishing and implementing control structure policies and procedures. As noted later in this chapter, the existence of differing policies and procedures for different departments and applications may require the auditor to understand and test separate general control procedures for each application with audit relevance.

CONTROL PROCEDURES AND CONTROL OBJECTIVES IN COMPUTERIZED SYSTEMS

There are two types of control procedures associated with computerized systems: general control procedures, which for the most part apply to data processing as a whole, and control procedures that are applied to specific classes of transactions (such as cash collections from customers). The latter procedures are designed to ensure that all transactions are authorized and are processed and recorded completely and accurately; that the integrity of data on files is preserved; and that assets and related documents and records are protected from physical loss or theft and from unauthorized manipulation. Those control objectives and procedures for meeting them are discussed and illustrated in Chapter 7.

In computerized systems, processing is done by computer application programs, which are precise instructions to the computer to perform specific steps, referred to as *programmed procedures*, to achieve a particular task. There are two types of programmed procedures.

- *Programmed accounting procedures*, for example, calculating and producing sales invoices, updating master files, and generating data within the computer.
- *Programmed control procedures* that ensure the completeness, accuracy, and authorization of data being processed and stored, for example, matching sales orders against a master file containing credit information and reporting orders from customers not on the file or in excess of credit limits.

The consistency with which both programmed accounting and programmed control procedures process data is one of the benefits of the computer and is made possible in part by general control procedures. If the programmed accounting and control procedures are subject to adequate general control procedures, their performance should not vary unpredictably. Accordingly, random errors, which might occur in a manual accounting system, are virtually eliminated in a computerized system.

Control procedures designed to meet the control objectives for specific classes of transactions in a computerized system consist of a combination of programmed control procedures and manual procedures, called *user control procedures*. Programmed control procedures typically generate reports (known as exception reports) of instances when the computer, for one reason or another, is unable to complete the prescribed operation. The effectiveness of those programmed control procedures depends on two things. First, there must be adequate general control procedures to ensure the proper implementation, maintenance, and continued operation of the programmed procedures and that only authorized changes are made to programs and data. Otherwise, there is no assurance that the exception reports are accurate and complete. General control procedures are discussed extensively in this chapter. Second, a user control procedure, which commonly consists of the follow-up of items in exception reports, is also necessary. User control procedures are described and illustrated in Chapter 7.

For example, to ensure that only accurate data is entered into the system, the computer may be programmed to match cash receipts from customers to specific invoices in the open accounts receivable file, to print out an exception report of cash receipts that cannot be matched to specific invoices, and to create a file of unmatched cash receipts. The user control procedure consists of a person with the appropriate knowledge and authority investigating and following up on the exception report.

GENERAL CONTROL OBJECTIVES AND PROCEDURES

General control procedures are designed to ensure that the programmed (accounting and control) procedures within a computerized system are appropriately implemented, maintained, and operated and that only authorized changes are made to programs and data. Some auditors call general control procedures ''information technology control procedures'' because they believe that term better describes the purpose served by the procedures. This section describes those procedures and their objectives; a later section discusses methods of testing their effectiveness as a basis for reducing the assurance needed from substantive tests.

Overview of General Control Procedures

There are seven categories of general control procedures.

- *Implementation control procedures* are designed to ensure that programmed procedures for new systems or major enhancements to existing systems are effectively designed and implemented.
- *File conversion control procedures* are designed to ensure that when a significant new system is introduced or an existing system is modified, the conversion process does not give rise to data file errors.
- *Maintenance control procedures* are designed to ensure that changes to programmed procedures are effectively designed and implemented.
- *Computer operations control procedures* are designed to ensure the continuity of processing (that is, that the correct data files are used and recovery procedures are provided) and the consistent application of programmed procedures.
- *Data file security control procedures* are designed to prevent or detect unauthorized changes to stored data or the initiation of unauthorized transactions.
- *Program security control procedures* are designed to prevent or detect unauthorized amendments to programs.
- *System software control procedures* are designed to ensure that system software is effectively implemented, maintained, and protected from unauthorized changes.

The first four categories are necessary for the effective operation of programmed control procedures. The next two categories ensure that only properly approved changes are made to stored data and to programs. The last category relates to system functions and, therefore, can affect both programmed procedures and data files. System software procedures are particularly important because of their impact on the effectiveness of other control procedures. For example, the password verification procedures that permit access to data files are usually incorporated into system software. The circumstances when it would be appropriate for the auditor to test the different categories of general control procedures are discussed later in the chapter.

Implementation

Implementation control procedures help guard against financially significant errors in new applications. The procedures cover the authorization and design of new computer applications, testing of new application programs, and procedures for putting approved programs into use; they apply to both internally developed and vendor-supplied applications. In the latter situation, the principal concerns are the original selection of the package, any modifications required to the package, and the testing and implementation of the package in the client's environment.

System Design and Program Preparation. Control procedures for program preparation ensure that appropriate programmed procedures are designed and coded into computer language and that the appropriate user control procedures are designed as part of the system. General design requirements are converted into detailed system specifications. Once detailed specifications have been developed and approved in both the user and computer departments, which may be done in modules or for the system as a whole, programming can begin. The computer programs can be generated in a variety of ways, ranging from purchasing or customizing application software packages to writing programs in-house. In any event, the programs should be documented in enough detail to facilitate subsequent testing, appropriate future modifications, and training of personnel.

Program and System Testing. Testing is normally carried out in three distinct stages: program testing, system testing, and parallel running.

Program testing consists of verifying the logic of individual programs, usually through *desk checking* and computer processing of *test data*. Desk checking involves determining visually that the program coding is consistent with the program specifications; it is generally done by a programmer other than the one who wrote the code. Desk checking is normally performed in conjunction with computer processing of hypothetical test data. Test data is designed to cover all elements of data in all classes of transactions that are likely to be encountered and for which input specifications have been written.

System testing consists of determining that the programs are logically compatible with each other and do not have an adverse impact on the system as a whole. Processing test data is the principal technique used in system testing; adjustments and reruns are performed until all observed logic failures have been corrected. The user and system analysts are the principal parties involved in the system testing process; programmers primarily correct program errors.

Parallel running involves operating the system under conditions that approximate the anticipated "live" environment, while the old system (computer or manual) continues to operate. Results of operating the new system are compared with those of the old system, with appropriate follow-up of inconsistencies. Parallel running is a means of testing the logic, programming, and implementation of a complete system, including all user control procedures. One of its objectives is to confirm the system's ability to cope with actual conditions and volumes of transactions. Operating and user instructions may be reviewed and approved by a responsible official as part of the parallel running process, or this may be done as part of the final acceptance procedures.

Cataloguing.   Cataloguing is the process of incorporating computer programs into various program libraries, which may contain programs in source code, object code, or load module form. *Source code* or language refers to the high-level computer languages that programmers use (such as COBOL); *object code*, also known as object modules, is the output of the compiler, in machine code or language. Ordinarily, a program is written in source language form, which is then incorporated into a test source library. The program is subsequently compiled by the computer into an object module and catalogued into a test library. To be executable, the various object modules that make up a program are brought together in a process called link-editing. This process creates the *load module* that is actually used by the computer for program execution.

Program testing is performed using the program in a *test library*. After a program has been completely tested, the test source program is transferred to the production source library. The program in the production source library is used for cataloguing into the *production library*. This ensures that the production program is completely equivalent to the tested and approved source program.

It is important that cataloguing be effectively controlled. For example, it is preferable for programmers to have access to the test library only, and for testing and documentation to be satisfactorily completed before programs are incorporated into production libraries. At an appropriate cutoff point, a formal procedure transfers programs from test to production status.

File Conversion

Conversion of data files may be necessary when a computerized system is developed to replace a manual system or an existing computerized system, or an existing computerized system is significantly enhanced and the existing files need to be "rebuilt." To ensure that newly created or converted data files contain correct data, organizations typically develop a conversion plan, which generally covers

- Design of the conversion process.
- Documentation of any data conversion programs to be written.
- Techniques to be used to test the results of conversion (e.g., file balancing, one-to-one comparisons).
- Conversion timetable.
- Assignment of user and data processing responsibilities.

Data processing management involved in the process (e.g., the data base administrator and other programming project leaders) and user management (or its designee) review and approve the plan.

Normally, the conversion process is designed to ensure that

- Specifications for all master files and transaction files to be converted/created are identified.
- Specifications for new files are reviewed and approved by appropriate user and data processing management.
- Specifications for each new file are compared with those of existing files to determine the effect of any format changes to existing fields; new fields, if any, needed as a result of the new or modified system; and existing fields, if any, that will be eliminated from the converted files.
- Techniques are designed and responsibilities assigned to ensure that the newly created data files are complete and accurate.
- Data created for new files is appropriately reviewed and approved before being input to those files, e.g., one-for-one checks.

The final results of the conversion process are reviewed and approved by appropriate user and data processing management.

Maintenance

Maintenance control procedures cover the same areas as implementation procedures, but relate to program amendments rather than entirely new applications. Procedures ensure that amendments are properly designed, tested, approved, incorporated within the application, and updated to the live program file, and that change requests are handled appropriately.

Program changes occur frequently in most data processing installations. They vary in complexity, ranging from relatively simple changes in editing procedures to major overhauls of large systems. Control procedures for program changes are similar to those for new systems. Requests for changes are formalized and include enough details to facilitate authorization and to enable the changes to be designed. Testing of the changed program follows a process similar to that for new systems, and changes are appropriately approved before implementation.

Typically, maintenance policies and procedures require that

- All system change requests are properly approved and communicated to data processing, generally on a standard change request form.
- A cost–benefit analysis is performed to ensure efficient use of resources (personnel and hardware).
- Approved changes are tracked throughout the change process.
- The final design of changes is reviewed and approved by both user and data processing management.

- All changes, including those initiated within data processing, are subject to appropriate testing, and test results are reviewed and approved by user and data processing management.
- Implementation of tested changes is approved by the requestor.
- Data processing departments affected by the changes are notified, e.g., computer operations, data base administration.
- Documentation (such as operations runbooks, user manuals, program narratives, and system description) is prepared or updated.

Policies and procedures also ensure that an ''owner'' is defined for each system. An owner is the individual or department user of the system with the authority to request (or approve) changes in the system. System owners should be identified so that data processing management can ensure that changes are requested by the owner. In larger clients, because of the complexity and interrelationship of systems, a user committee reviews and coordinates changes. Once a request has been received and accepted by data processing, detailed specifications describing the requested change are developed by data processing personnel (e.g., programming, data base administration, or tele-communications specialists).

Users may inappropriately attempt to bypass formal change procedures by initiating program changes through direct contact with programmers. This can cause problems involving, for example, unauthorized changes, inappropriate installation dates, inadequate testing, and inconsistent application of accounting principles. In addition, EDP personnel may believe that there is no need to inform users of proposed program changes that are viewed as purely technical matters that users cannot comprehend and will not be affected by. Examples of such modifications are file reorganizations, changes from tape to disk, and optimizing restart procedures. All such changes should be appropriately communicated to users; although they may defer in-depth technical review to data processing management, they should at least be aware that the system is being modified so as to have an opportunity to determine whether output data is affected.

Computer Operations

Computer operations control procedures ensure the use of correct data files, including their correct version, and provide recovery procedures for processing failures; they also help ensure that programmed accounting and control procedures are consistently applied. Computer operations procedures cover both processing of data and computer department operations, and may be applied at a central location or at local installations.

Procedures to ensure the use of correct data files include software checking of information on files and manual checks of external file labels by operators. Control over recovery from processing failures requires that data is regularly copied as backup, that processing status at the time of failure can be established, and that proper recovery takes place. The consistent operation of programmed procedures is ensured by procedures that schedule jobs for processing, set them up, and execute them. Procedures also cover the actions of computer operators, such as supervision and review of their work. In on-line systems, data files normally are available to users at all times, so that relatively little operator intervention is required; in those systems, operations are controlled largely by the system software. In batch systems, jobs are grouped into job streams and are set up with the required files by operators. More operator intervention is required, and computer operations control procedures may be of greater concern.

Computer Processing Procedures.   The computer operations department or function usually controls the day-to-day functioning of data processing hardware and software. In many organizations, it is assisted by a production control department. Computer operations is responsible for the physical running of the computer system (e.g., mounting files and printer forms and making decisions about computer hardware, such as whether to discontinue using a device in the event of a failure). The production control department is responsible for job scheduling and setup.

Production control frequently uses a job scheduling system and a tape management system to control the submission of jobs to the computer and ensure that the correct files are used for those jobs. Production control normally provides standards (e.g., job classes, use of tape and disk storage devices, printer classes, routing of output) for developing or updating run instructions for new or modified systems. Those standards consider time constraints and processing sequences that apply to each system. Effective control procedures for implementing and modifying systems (discussed earlier) normally include review and approval of operating parameters and job schedules by application owners and production control or computer operations management.

In many data processing installations, job scheduling, setup, and execution are not formally controlled by software or a production control department; instead, they are controlled manually. In those environments, manual procedures should be supervised by computer operations supervisors or other computer operations management.

Backup and Recovery Procedures.   In the event of a computer failure, backup arrangements are needed so that the recovery process for production programs, system software, and data files does not introduce errors into the system. The principal techniques that may be employed are

- A facility for restarting at an intermediate stage of processing, for use if programs are intentionally or unintentionally terminated before their normal ending.
- A system to copy or store master files and associated transaction data, which makes it possible to restore files lost or damaged during disruption.
- Procedures to ensure that copies of operating instructions, run instructions, and other documentation are available if originals are lost.

- Formal instructions for resuming processing or transferring it to other locations, usually called a contingency plan.

Data File Security

Data file security control procedures are designed to protect data from unauthorized access that could result in their modification, disclosure, or destruction or that could inappropriately move assets, like cash or inventory, by manipulating data or processing unauthorized transactions. Data file security procedures are particularly important for master file data, since it is used repeatedly in processing transactions and may not be reviewed often enough to ensure timely identification of errors. Data file security control procedures are also necessary to protect files from accidental destruction or erasure. The extent of data file security needed depends on the sensitivity of the entity's data, characteristics of the related assets, and effectiveness of other control procedures.

Data file security control procedures usually involve techniques that restrict access to, use of, and ability to change data files to authorized users and ensure that the level of access is consistent with the users' responsibilities. The principal techniques are the use of software and physical security procedures. Access control software may entail the use of passwords, specialized security software, and tables that control the access rights of individuals. Where passwords are used, procedures are required to ensure that they are appropriately selected, kept secret, and regularly changed. Physical security procedures cover access to the computer room and terminals as well as the storage of data files held off-line. Data file security control procedures can enforce division of duties by limiting the functions or data to which specific users have access.

On-line environments provide greater opportunity for many users to gain access to data files and usually do not allow data processing to be adequately controlled by physical security procedures. Thus, system software is generally used to control data file security in on-line environments. Communications software and data base management packages often have password facilities. Security or access control software packages enhance the protection of data files.

Security procedures normally address such matters as

- The information classification scheme for information both stored on computers and located outside of data processing, including security categories (e.g., research, accounting, marketing) and security levels (e.g., top secret, confidential, internal use only, unclassified).
- The data in each information class and individuals or functions authorized to use it, and control and protection requirements.
- The types or classes of sensitive assets and the potential threats and protection requirements for each.
- The responsibilities of management, security administration, resource owners, computer operations, system users, and internal auditors.

- The consequences of noncompliance with policies and procedures.
- Any security implementation plan.

Where packaged application systems are used, data file access controls may be defined in option tables. Those tables may be maintained by user departments or by a security officer or administration function within data processing.

Program Security

In the absence of program security control procedures, the enterprise could be subject to the risk of defalcations or management fraud from unauthorized program changes. The risk of unauthorized amendment of programs is less where vendor-supplied packages are used and the user does not have access to the source code that would allow changes to the program. In on-line environments, users may be able to access program files, increasing the risk that unauthorized changes may be made to programs in order to misappropriate assets and modify reporting routines to conceal them. There is also a risk of unauthorized changes to options in purchased systems.

Features of system software are generally used to control program security in on-line environments. Communications software, data base management, and librarian packages commonly include password facilities. Librarian packages may also have other security features, such as the recording of program version numbers and the ability to secure production programs from alteration. Access control software packages are used to protect programs.

Program security control procedures may be similar to those used to achieve data file security or may be built into software used to maintain libraries of computer programs on file. Security procedures are also needed for system maintenance programs, for example, for correcting data files after a processing failure. These programs, commonly referred to as utility programs, can often make changes directly to programs or data, frequently without leaving any record of the changes.

System Software

System software control procedures ensure that system software is properly implemented, maintained, and protected from unauthorized changes. System software consists of various programs that direct computer functions and are not restricted to any one application. System software includes the operating system, utilities, sorts, compilers, file management systems, library management packages, time-sharing software, telecommunications software, job accounting software, data base management systems, and security software packages.

System software is typically acquired from computer or software vendors, rather than written by the user organization. Control procedures relate to selecting and implementing the appropriate software and options within it, including vendor-supplied amendments or "fixes," and to security and backup of system software. Control procedures for implementing system software are similar to those for packaged systems, except that the work is performed by the technical support group (i.e., system programmers), not application programmers. The "owners" are the management of various data processing functions, like the data base administrator, security administrator, and network or telecommunications administrator.

If an organization's technical support group develops some aspects of system software or adds functions to vendor-supplied system software (by making use of "exit" routines), appropriate system design procedures will be followed. When system software is supplied by a vendor, the user organization tests the integration of a particular package into the existing environment, including the selection of options and any subroutines added via exits by the technical support group.

Maintenance of system software deals primarily with changes supplied by the vendor. On rare occasions, the user may modify system software. All such modifications are controlled in much the same way as changes to application programs. Vendor-supplied system software is periodically modified by the vendor, and introduced as new programs or amendments to existing programs. New or amended system software is tested to ensure that it operates as intended within the organization's unique data processing environment. Tests of system software that interacts with application programs, such as the operating system, simulate the production environment. Normally, those tests involve running the system software with copies of proven application programs to identify anomalies associated with the modified system software.

In many organizations, neither the technical expertise nor the tools exist to make amendments to system software. This is often true of the operating system, which may be provided by the vendor in a low-level code like machine code or microcode, or in code built into the computer. In those circumstances the risk of unauthorized amendments to the system software is minimal. Where the technical expertise and tools do exist to change the system software, the organization establishes control procedures similar to those for the security of application programs. The technical support group is generally smaller than the application programming group, giving individual system programmers a greater opportunity to become familiar with a broader array of system software. The technical support group needs access to system software not only to perform routine maintenance but also when there are processing failures and other emergencies. Consequently, organizations normally enforce a division of duties to prevent technical support personnel from obtaining a detailed understanding of the applications processed and of user control procedures for key files and transactions in those applications. Also, the work of technical support staff is closely supervised.

COMPUTER FRAUD AND ABUSE

As computers become more sophisticated and pervasive, the potential for an entity to be harmed by computer fraud and abuse increases. While the distinctions are not always clear, computer fraud (or computer crime) usually refers to use of a computer to commit a crime; in computer abuse, the computer and related software are the objects of the crime. Instances of computer fraud and abuse, when discovered, frequently make sensational headlines; often the auditor is criticized for failing to detect fraud. Accordingly, auditors should be knowledgeable about control procedures to prevent computer fraud and abuse and about their responsibilities under GAAS to detect such acts.

Computer abuse encompasses the physical destruction and theft of computer hardware, software, or data and the unauthorized interception or alteration of software or data. Examples include sabotage of computers and software, unauthorized use of confidential records, unauthorized use of computer time for personal purposes, unauthorized alteration of data on file (such as student grades), the theft of portable computers, and the unauthorized copying of software.

Computer fraud involves using the computer to misappropriate assets (defalcations) or deliberately misstate an enterprise's financial statements (management fraud). Both types of fraud can be perpetrated by creating or altering computer programs and data on computer files or manipulating transaction data (altering, omitting, or creating unauthorized transactions), or both. For example,

- At a bank, a program was written to round downward to the nearest penny interest credited to depositors' accounts, accumulate the amounts rounded off, and credit them to the programmer's account—a case of a defalcation via unauthorized transactions generated by an unauthorized program.

- An employee of an insurance company who had clearance to process customer claims made unauthorized payments to himself and his children and then deleted the transactions from the files—a case of a defalcation by entering unauthorized transactions.

- Top management created nonexistent receivables and revenues by entering fictitious transactions; they then wrote a program to suppress the fictitious receivables when the auditor selected a sample from the accounts receivable file for the purpose of confirming them—a case of management fraud through entering fictitious transactions and creating a fraudulent program.

In most instances of computer fraud, it is clear that the fraud could have occurred in a manual system as well—particularly when the fraud was perpetrated by the inappropriate entry of transactions. Even many of the frauds involving the unauthorized creation or alteration of computer programs would be possible in manual systems, as, for example, crediting fractional cents of interest to an unauthorized account. In most instances, however, an enterprise uses a computer because of large transaction volumes. It is the combination of the existence of the computer and the large volumes of transactions that makes it possible for a person (or collusive group of people) to use the computer to assist in stealing assets or to intentionally misstate financial statements, and then to conceal those actions.

The incidence of defalcations can be reduced, at a price, through the effective design and operation of transaction processing and file control procedures and general control procedures relating to computer program and data file security. (As with any type of fraud, computer fraud can never be completely eliminated; even if it could, the cost of doing so would usually be far greater than the benefits derived.) Management fraud, however, whether perpetrated in a manual or computer environment, is less susceptible to prevention or detection by means of control procedures because of management's ability to override those procedures.

The auditor's responsibility for detecting computer fraud is the same as the responsibility for detecting other types of irregularities. Defalcations rarely result in material financial statement misstatements; management fraud, which typically is material to the financial statements, is often difficult to detect because it ordinarily involves control override and collusion. As discussed in Chapter 4, auditors have the responsibility to design their audits to provide reasonable assurance of detecting material fraud and to exercise due care and professional skepticism in performing them. They also have the responsibility under SAS No. 60, *Communication of Internal Control Structure Related Matters Noted in an Audit* (AU Section 325), to inform the client of significant deficiencies in the design or operation of the internal control structure—whether computer-related or otherwise—that come to their attention in the course of the audit.

AUDITING THROUGH AND WITH THE COMPUTER

To plan an effective and efficient audit, the auditor of an enterprise with a computerized accounting system needs to obtain, or update, and document the same kinds of information about the client's control structure as the auditor of an entity whose systems do not involve the use of EDP. Knowledge of the accounting system provides the auditor with information about the flow of significant classes of transactions through both manually operated and computerized elements of the system. That information, in turn, enables the auditor to identify the significant EDP accounting applications and understand such matters as the mode in which they operate (such as batch, on-line, or real-time), what accounting functions they perform (that is, the principal programmed accounting procedures), who operates them (including the relationships among users, operators, and programmers), how significant data used in processing those applications originates (for example, whether it is input through remote terminals or extracted from previously generated data files), the significant data files generated or updated by the processing, and information about reports produced—when and how they are produced, when and to whom they are distributed, and how they are used. All of that information generally enables the auditor to identify specific transaction processing, file, and asset protection control procedures that may prove useful in maximizing audit efficiency.

Information about the client's control environment relevant to the EDP department includes its organizational structure, the number of employees, and the extent of segregation of duties. The understanding of the control environment also helps the auditor assess the risk of computer fraud or abuse. As part of obtaining the understanding of the accounting system and control environment, the auditor also obtains some information about the client's general control procedures. Based on that information, the auditor considers what additional information is needed to plan the audit.

Audit Testing Plan

Audit objectives and the basis for the audit testing plan do not change because significant applications within the accounting system are computerized. As with manual systems, the auditor is concerned with whether particular audit objectives for individual accounts or groups of accounts can be achieved most efficiently by performing tests of controls as a basis for restricting substantive procedures, or by performing substantive procedures without significant reduction based on the effectiveness of the control structure. What does change when the accounting system is computerized are the points within the system where errors or irregularities can occur, the ways they can occur, and the ways they can be prevented or detected. Also, in a computerized environment the auditor may be able to use the computer to efficiently perform auditing procedures that would otherwise be prohibitively time-consuming and costly.

Audit strategy decisions in a computerized environment typically focus first on the effectiveness of general control procedures, because they ensure the proper implementation, maintenance, and operation of programmed accounting and programmed control procedures, and then on transaction processing and file control procedures. The auditor determines which categories of general control procedures to test by considering the risks associated with the different categories (risk of errors versus risk of irregularities), the programmed control procedures applied to transactions and files and what control objectives they relate to, and the likelihood that tests of controls will enable the auditor to assess control risk as low for specific control objectives.

The effectiveness of programmed control procedures relating to the completeness, accuracy, and authorization of transactions and files depends on the operation of general control procedures for implementation, file conversion, maintenance, and computer operations. Evidence that those programmed control procedures are effective may support a low assessment of control risk for the completeness, accuracy, and authorization transaction processing and file control objectives. The asset protection control objective is met, at least in part, by data file and program security general control procedures and by access control procedures that are part of system software, as well as by an appropriate division of duties. Evidence of the effectiveness of those procedures enables the auditor to assess control risk as low with respect to the protection of assets.

Typically in a computerized environment, one of the following audit testing plans results:

- The auditor tests all categories of general control procedures, and the results support the expected reduction in the assessed level of control risk for all relevant control objectives.

- The auditor's tests of general control procedures support the expected reduction in the assessed level of control risk for the completeness, accuracy, and authorization of transaction processing and files; however, the auditor determines that evidence of the effectiveness of certain categories of general control procedures, like those relating to program or data file security, is not available or not efficient to obtain. In this situation, the auditor assesses the risk of financial statement misstatements associated with those categories, by considering such factors as the susceptibility of relevant assets to theft, the sensitivity of stored data, and the adequacy and interrelationship of other relevant elements of the control structure, including the control environment, the accounting system, and other control procedures. Often, the auditor will not be able to conclude that the assessed level of control risk is low for asset protection; in that event, substantive procedures should be designed to provide the required assurance that related audit objectives have been achieved (principally the existence of assets and the classification of expenses and losses).
- The auditor determines that the general control procedures are not effective, and designs an audit testing plan that includes few tests of control procedures.

Transaction processing and file control procedures that depend on programmed control procedures are typically not tested unless the audit plan includes tests of related general control procedures. This is because obtaining evidence of the effectiveness of programmed control procedures by testing those procedures themselves is not likely to be efficient. In these circumstances, the auditor would obtain the necessary assurance from substantive tests instead. There may be some circumstances in which the auditor does not test general control procedures, but nevertheless wishes to test the effective operation of programmed accounting procedures directly. Those tests will be costly because of the sheer volume of such procedures in a typical computerized accounting system, although it might be possible to use software to facilitate the testing. Those tests are discussed later in the chapter.

Tests of Controls

The auditor's purpose in performing tests of controls, both of general control procedures and of user procedures, in EDP systems is the same as in manual systems, namely, to test the effectiveness of the control procedures as a basis for significantly restricting substantive tests. The same techniques are used in tests of controls regardless of whether the system is computerized or manual, that is, inquiry, observation, examination of evidence, and, where appropriate, reperformance. In computerized environments, however, the auditor may be able to use software to assist in performing the tests. Whenever the auditor uses the client's data files in performing tests, he or she should be sure the files are backed up so that the client's data will not be inadvertently lost or altered.

Testing General Control Procedures. Two current trends have affected the way the auditor approaches the testing of general control procedures. First, as noted earlier, many EDP functions are moving away from centralized systems toward decentralized or distributed data processing systems. Second, where large centralized systems still exist, their size and complexity have been increasing. While some general control procedures are still common to all applications, application-specific procedures have become more prevalent. For example, the applications for each major user may be supported by different system analysis and programming functions, which may be subject to different control procedures. In that situation, the auditor would have to test control procedures for applications in each of those user areas that have different functions and control procedures.

In some sophisticated computer environments, computer software can help the auditor test the client's general control procedures. For example, user procedures for reviewing and authorizing proposed changes to programs may be performed on-line without creating any tangible documentation. The auditor can use software to reperform such procedures. Although software can facilitate such tests of controls involving reperformance, the auditor should still consider carefully whether it might be more efficient to perform substantive tests than to reperform general control procedures.

Testing Control Procedures Applied to Classes of Transactions. As noted earlier, if the auditor intends to test control procedures related to classes of transactions as a basis for restricting substantive testing, he or she needs evidence that both relevant programmed control procedures and user control procedures operated effectively. Tests of user control procedures are described and illustrated in Chapter 8. Evidence about the effectiveness of programmed control procedures can be obtained either from tests of relevant general control procedures, as discussed earlier, or by seeking evidence about the effectiveness of the programmed procedures themselves. As already noted, however, testing programmed procedures is costly, and the auditor usually uses alternative means of obtaining evidence of their effectiveness.

Particularly in computerized systems where general control procedures may be less pervasive or sophisticated, or programmed accounting and control procedures are few, the auditor may be able to obtain indirect evidence about the effectiveness of control procedures applied to classes of transactions. Material misstatements that should have been prevented or detected by control procedures relating to the client's principal activities (such as sales, purchases, and receipt and disbursement of cash) may also be detected through management's use of the related data in managing the business. For example, material failures to bill for goods shipped or services rendered would generally come to management's attention through the adverse effect on profitability. Other misstatements affect relations with employees, customers, suppliers, or others. For instance, overbillings for goods shipped or services rendered would generally provoke unfavorable reactions from customers, including nonpayment of excess billings. The auditor may obtain evidence about whether such circumstances have arisen during the period by inquiring of client personnel, performing analytical procedures, or examining various management reports. The absence of such occurrences provides some evidence that the control procedures are effective.

After considering, in light of all relevant sources of evidence, whether a significant risk of material misstatement exists as a result of the failure of programmed accounting and control procedures to operate effectively, the auditor determines whether additional evidence is needed. If so, tests of specific programmed procedures may be necessary. Testing techniques using audit software are described briefly later in connection with substantive tests of programmed accounting procedures. Before undertaking such tests, however, the auditor should consider whether it would be more efficient to perform additional substantive tests directed at the relevant audit objective.

Substantive Tests Using Computer Software

In a computerized system, many substantive tests can be most efficiently performed using audit software on either the client's or the auditor's computer. Auditing with the computer can increase efficiency by mechanizing auditing procedures and enabling the auditor to test large numbers of transactions. Software is available or can be developed by the auditor to test transactions, master file and reference data, historical data, programs, activity logs—in fact, almost any information that is stored in a computerized system. The auditor can also perform various auditing procedures with the help of audit software designed specifically for that purpose. Auditors can use a microcomputer, a terminal connected to a large computer, or a micro-mainframe link in many phases of the audit—planning, engagement management, performing audit tests (including analytical procedures), and documenting the audit work.

The same software tools may be used in more than one testing technique; in certain circumstances these tools could also be used in performing tests of controls. Sometimes a combination of different types of software is required to meet a single audit objective. Audit software can assist in calculating, summarizing, selecting, sorting, and comparing data, and producing reports to the auditor's specifications. Sometimes, such as when generalized audit software packages (discussed later) are used, data can be accessed and processed by the same software tools. For example, the auditor can use software to examine all data on a file, to identify data that meets a particular condition (e.g., a total of debtors' balances that exceed their credit limits), and to print out selected data, like the results of tests or items selected for investigation. Figure 11.1 lists typical functions used by auditors in processing data.

Software tools that the auditor may use to access and process data include generalized audit software packages, application audit software packages, customized audit software, inquiry programs, and systems utility software and service aids.

Generalized Audit Software Packages. The most widely used computer-assisted audit techniques employ generalized software packages specifically designed for audit purposes. Audit tasks performed on client files include totaling a file, identifying exceptions, selecting items for manual review, and formatting reports. Generalized audit software packages help the auditor carry out those tasks on a variety of files at different installations. Their use

Figure 11.1   Common Audit Software Processing Functions

Function	*Example*
Total	Add invoice amounts on the accounts receivable open item file and agree to the control total.
Compute	Multiply inventory quantities by unit costs.
Sort } Summarize }	Sort the file into customer number sequence and summarize to obtain customers' outstanding balances.
Analyze	Produce a frequency distribution.
Create	Produce a file for later comparison with another file.
Select	Produce a list of customers whose balances outstanding over 90 days are greater than $10,000.
Sample	Statistically sample the file for customer accounts to be confirmed.
Compare	Compare the file created at the confirmation date with the file at the balance sheet date and print out accounts with large percentage changes.
Format reports	Print confirmation letters and working papers.

eliminates much of the work involved in writing individual computer programs to accomplish those functions.

To use audit software, the auditor defines what computer configuration the program is to be run on and which files to use. The program logic is controlled by simplified procedural statements or parameters. The packages normally have special functions to facilitate using the program to generate the kind of audit evidence and documentation desired. These include report formatting (page numbering, page breaking, column placement, and headings), totaling and subtotaling data, automatic production of processing statistics (number of records read and processed, and number of positive, negative, and zero-value records), and sorting and summarizing data.

Generalized audit software packages permit programs for specific applications to be developed in a relatively short time by people with somewhat limited programming skills. The use of generalized packages also reduces the auditor's reliance on the client's EDP staff, though client assistance is usually required to install the package and develop instructions to operate it. The main disadvantage of generalized packages is that there are usually limitations on the number and structure of files that can be accessed. Often the auditor can overcome those limitations by using a generalized audit software package in combination with customized software or utilities.

Application Audit Software Packages.   Certain auditing procedures and requirements are so similar from one audit to another that the same programs can be applied with only minor changes, even though the data files vary. Some auditing firms have developed application audit software packages to achieve common audit objectives in several areas, like accounts receivable, accounts payable, and payroll. For example, application audit software can be used to analyze the accounts receivable ledger by age, select items for audit testing, produce confirmation letters, and match subsequent collections received. To run the software, the auditor converts the data files into a compatible format, determines the appropriate parameters, and executes the software. Some audit tests are unique to certain industries and to applications within those industries; some firms have also developed packages for these specialized areas.

Customized Audit Software.   Although generalized and application software packages are useful in many situations, the auditor normally requires the ability to develop software for special needs beyond the capabilities of packaged software. For example, software packages may not be available for the client's computer, the output required may be very specialized, or the computations and data handling may be particularly intricate. In those circumstances, the auditor may use the computer languages available on the client's system to develop customized audit software. In addition, many generalized audit software packages allow additional routines written in computer languages to be integrated into the package, affording increased flexibility and wider applicability. If no compatible language is available, or if for other reasons it is impractical to integrate additional routines, an EDP audit specialist or a computer programmer can write programs to order.

Inquiry Programs.   When available, standard data inquiry (or interrogation) programs, which extract or display data without updating or otherwise changing it, can be an economical audit tool. Relatively easy-to-use interrogation methods exist for many smaller computers, and are often built into larger data base management systems. A disadvantage of using inquiry programs is that they are often unique to a particular computer or data base, which means that the auditor may have to read manuals and learn the particular program.

Systems Utility Software and Service Aids.   Systems utilities and service aids are provided by computer manufacturers and software vendors to perform limited, predefined tasks. Utilities and service aids are normally used to enhance system functioning or for programming. The auditor may use them to examine processing activity, interrogate data, and test programs and operational procedures. For example, one utility can copy and rearrange sequential files; another can extract particular records from one file and create a subset file for audit testing.

The auditor often needs utilities to set up and execute computerized auditing procedures. Some utilities may substitute for procedures that would otherwise be performed by generalized audit software or specially written programs. Most utilities come with a user manual that describes their functions. In smaller systems, utilities may allow the auditor access to many powerful, easy-to-use techniques. In larger systems, they may be much more difficult to use. Utilities are usually specific to a particular computer and operating system, so that the auditor must learn how to use separate ones for the different computers and systems that are audited.

Substantive Tests of Programmed Accounting Procedures

If the auditor needs evidence of the effective operation of programmed accounting procedures, it may be obtained by testing those procedures directly throughout the period, generally using various types of audit software. (In certain circumstances manual techniques may be appropriate; they are discussed later.) As noted earlier, however, testing specific programmed procedures is costly and the auditor usually chooses an alternative audit strategy. Therefore, only a brief description of some of the techniques used for testing client programs is presented here.

Flowcharting Programs. This software helps the auditor understand the programmed procedures by producing flowcharts and other documentation of the program being analyzed. The voluminous flowcharts produced, however, may contain more detail than is needed for that understanding. Lists of commands and data names in the program are also generated and are often helpful in program code analysis (described below).

Program Tracing and Mapping. These techniques involve processing test data through application programs and are used primarily by programmers when developing and testing programs. Program tracing identifies the actual steps executed; program mapping identifies any unexecuted program instructions. These techniques are only occasionally used by auditors because of the technical skills needed to analyze the results.

Program Code Analysis. This technique involves analyzing computer programs. Its main purpose is to confirm the existence of programmed procedures in a program or series of programs. Program code analysis consists of

- Identifying the program to be examined, by reference to the company's documentation.
- Selecting the form of code to be examined, which is normally the source code. The auditor must know the programming language and make sure that the source version examined is equivalent to the production program in use.
- Analyzing the selected coding. It is usually difficult to follow another person's coding, but adherence to standard programming methods may make this task a little easier. Software aids, such as flowcharting programs, can produce additional documentation. In subsequent periods, comparison programs can be used to indicate changes.

Test Data and Integrated Test Facility (ITF). The test data method tests the client's transaction processing control procedures. The audit software tools discussed earlier test actual client data; in the test data method, client programs are used to process test data. The output of the processing is then compared with predetermined results.

There are two methods of running test data.

- Test data can be processed using the company's operational programs, but separately from the company's data, and using either copies of master files or dummy files set up for testing purposes.

- Test data can be included in the company's regular data processing, with approval from a responsible official.

The latter method is referred to as an Integrated Test Facility (ITF). If specific records on the master files are reserved or created for this purpose and consistently processed during testing at regularly established intervals, an ITF is also referred to as a "Base Case System Evaluation."

Manual Testing. The auditor can use techniques for testing programmed procedures manually if adequate visible evidence is available. Data that must be tested to test the programmed procedures can be voluminous, however, making manual testing techniques impractical and inefficient. Although some visible evidence of the operation of programmed procedures is usually available, the results of processing are rarely printed out in detail (except in some microcomputer systems). Instead, totals and analyses are printed out without supporting details, thus rendering it impossible for the auditor to determine the correctness of a total or an analysis. Exception reports and rejection listings that are produced do not provide evidence that all items that should have been reported or rejected were properly treated. In those instances, the auditor may request and sometimes obtain reports generated specifically to meet audit needs.

Sometimes visible evidence not readily provided by the system can be recreated. Methods to achieve this are known collectively as "manual simulation techniques" and include

- Reassembling processed data into the same condition that existed when the programmed procedure was applied (e.g., reassembling batches of sales invoices to test the batch totals posted to the sales ledger control account).
- Using current data before processing by computer (e.g., testing the additions of batches before they are sent for processing, to determine that accurate batch totals are established to control subsequent processing).
- Selecting a small number of items from those submitted for processing and processing them in a separate run (e.g., splitting a batch into two batches, one large and one small, processing the small batch separately, and agreeing the resulting computer-produced total to manually precalculated results).
- Simulating a condition that will produce a report if the programmed procedure is working properly (e.g., altering a batch total to an incorrect figure so that the batch should be rejected, or withholding a document to see whether it is reported as missing); this approach requires careful planning and coordination with user departments.
- Requesting a special printout of items processed (e.g., a listing of sales invoices included in a sales total produced by the computer).

Manual tests cannot be performed if visible evidence of the operation of a programmed procedure neither exists nor can be produced, and the appropriate condition cannot be simulated. This often occurs in systems where transactions are entered directly through terminals without source documents.

Statistical Sampling Software

Statistical sampling applications, in both tests of controls and substantive tests, are particularly well suited to assistance from audit software. Using software reduces the need to make calculations manually and relieves the auditor of the need to understand fully some of the mathematical methods and concepts involved in sampling. In fact, many statistical sampling applications would be impractical without computer power.

A number of statistical sampling software packages are available to the auditor, some of which require almost no understanding of statistics. Most such packages support a limited number of statistical methodologies—usually those most frequently used by the accounting firm that developed the software. Other packages provide a wider selection of statistical methods, permitting the auditor to select the method best suited to the objective under consideration. Many of these packages can be used on microcomputers.

Two types of statistical sampling programs are generally available.

- Programs designed to develop strata boundaries, determine sample sizes, perform sample selection, and evaluate sampling results for variables sampling applications.
- Programs to calculate sample sizes and evaluate attributes sampling results.

Audit Documentation Software

Software packages are available that automate some of the labor-intensive tasks associated with auditing financial statements, including footing the trial balance and financial statements, ensuring the arithmetical accuracy and consistency of account groupings, and listing relevant financial statement ratios for subsequent analysis. Documentation programs can also be used to prepare opening and closing trial balances, lead schedules showing both current and prior-period information, financial statements, and other working papers. Software can be used to produce and format reports so they can be used as audit working papers. Auditors can use documentation software packages, instead of preparing working papers, to document the use of other audit software. The audit software packages—both for audit documentation and for the other purposes described in this chapter—are often designed to be used on the auditor's microcomputer at the client's office, a practice that is becoming increasingly common.

Analytical Procedures Software

Software can be used to calculate absolute dollar and percentage changes, ratios, and trends, and to highlight significant changes, enabling the auditor to concentrate on evaluating the differences and obtaining explanations for them. This software is available on microcomputers, or by using utilities or software packages on minicomputers and mainframes. Auditors are increasingly using computers to compare client data with industry data using public data bases and microcomputer software. Virtually all of the analytical techniques discussed in Chapter 9 can be performed using software.

AUDIT MANAGEMENT

Computers can contribute to efficient engagement management, particularly in planning, budgeting, and scheduling. Extremely time-consuming when performed manually, these tasks can be expedited considerably by software like calculation worksheets, or "spread sheets." Once a spread sheet is set up, the user can input and change data, conditions, and formulas, and the results are recalculated automatically. Software can facilitate the effective use of, and control over, audit resources by determining the cost of assigned staff and evaluating alternatives, allocating staff and available chargeable hours to assignments, and scheduling staff by client, tasks to be performed, expected utilization, and available hours.

Accounting firms also use computers in a number of other ways to enhance the efficiency of their practices. Some of these computer applications are

- *Word processing.* Many standard letters and documents can be maintained in word processing libraries, including engagement and representation letters, financial reports, audit programs, and audit reports.
- *Audit statistics.* In performing analytical procedures on clients' financial results, the auditor often makes comparisons with industry results. Industry statistics and key business ratios can be collected and maintained on computer files.
- *Electronic mail.* Electronic mail has the benefits of speed and ease of response. It can be sent by telecommunications systems to and from geographically dispersed locations, thereby improving communications within a firm.
- *Audit department accounting and management.* Many accounting firms have management information systems to record budgets and time charges, facilitate prompt billing and revenue collection, and produce management and exception reports, such as staff utilization rates and overdue accounts. In some firms this processing is done on a centralized basis. In the future, accounting firms will probably follow the trend in the business community toward decentralizing systems using mini- or microcomputers at the local level that process local data and then input results to, and retrieve reports from, the central processing site(s).

PART 3

Auditing Specific Cycles and Accounts

12

Auditing the Revenue Cycle

Revenue transactions that are completed within a relatively short time—when sale, delivery, and collection occur within a few weeks or months of each other—are the most common revenue transactions and are the subject of this chapter. The focus of the chapter is on revenues generated by an enterprise's principal operations; other chapters cover various types of ancillary revenues. For example, dividend and interest revenue is discussed in Chapter 17, "Auditing Investments," and rent revenue is discussed in Chapter 18, "Auditing Property, Plant, and Equipment."

ACCOUNTS RELATED TO THE REVENUE CYCLE

FASB Statement of Financial Accounting Concepts No. 6 (paragraphs 78 and 79) defines revenues and discusses their characteristics in business enterprises, as follows:

> Revenues are inflows or other enhancements of assets of an entity or settlements of its liabilities (or a combination of both) from delivering or producing goods, rendering services, or other activities that constitute the entity's ongoing major or central operations.

> Revenues represent actual or expected cash inflows (or the equivalent) that have occurred or will eventuate as a result of the enterprise's ongoing major or central operations. The assets increased by revenues may be of various kinds—for example, cash, claims against customers or clients, other goods or services received, or increased value of a product resulting from production. Similarly, the transactions and events from which revenues arise and the revenues themselves are in many forms and are called by various names—for example, output, deliveries, sales, fees, interest, dividends, royalties, and rent—depending on the kinds of operations involved and the way revenues are recognized.

Revenues are generally described more specifically in financial statements. For example, a manufacturing or retail enterprise calls revenue transactions "sales." On the other hand, revenues in a service organization may be referred to as fees, commissions, rents, royalties, tuition, dues, or more generally as "revenues" or "service revenues." In governmental or not-for-profit organizations, revenues may be referred to as grants or appropriations; in not-for-profit organizations, they may also be referred to as donations and contributions. Accounts related to ancillary revenue transactions include rents, dividends, interest (including lease finance income), by-product sales, and gains from the sale of nonproduct assets, like property.

Most companies have one or more major sources of revenues and several less significant types of miscellaneous revenues, commonly referred to as "other income." The term used for a given type of revenue usually depends on whether it is derived from one of the enterprise's principal business activities. For example, sales of transformers by an electrical supply company would be "sales," while such transactions would be "other income" to an electric utility. Conversely, interest and dividends from investments would be "other income" to almost all enterprises except investment companies, for which interest and dividends are a primary source of revenues.

If sales of products are the primary source of revenues, certain marketing and collection techniques are often used to increase sales and speed up the collection period. For example, returns may be allowed if the customer is not completely satisfied, or an allowance may be given if the goods are damaged; discounts may be available to customers who pay promptly. Management monitors such policies by establishing accounts for sales discounts, returns, and allowances. Additional techniques often used to increase sales include providing guarantees or warranties. Auditing the provisions or reserves for guarantees or warranties is discussed in Chapter 16, "Auditing Prepaid Expenses, Accrued Liabilities, and Risk Management."

Numerous balance sheet and income statement accounts are affected by transactions in the revenue cycle. The most significant of these is accounts receivable. Accounts receivable are generally short-term assets, often outstanding for little more than the amount of time needed for sellers and buyers to process transactions—shipping, billing, receiving, processing the invoice for payment, and processing and recording the cash receipt.

Accounts receivable that are completely and accurately recorded may not be fully collectible. Accordingly, the allowance for uncollectible accounts and related bad debt expense accounts are additional accounts in the revenue cycle. Accounts receivable, net of the allowance for uncollectible accounts, provides an estimate of the net realizable value of the receivables. Bad debt expense represents the amount charged to income in the current period for uncollectible accounts. (Other allowance accounts may be necessary if estimated discounts, returns, and allowances are material to the financial statements.)

The unearned revenue and deferred income accounts reflect various kinds of advance receipts for goods and services not yet delivered, such as prepayments from customers for goods to be delivered in the future, advance payments on transportation or entertainment ticket sales, and magazine subscriptions.

TYPICAL TRANSACTIONS, ACCOUNTING SYSTEMS, AND CONTROL PROCEDURES

The revenue cycle in most contemporary businesses can be divided into three typical classes of transactions.

- Sales of goods and services.
- Payments received for goods and services.
- Goods returned by and claims received from customers.

Sales of Goods and Services

The process of selling goods and services generally includes the following activities:

- Receiving and recording customers' orders.
- Authorizing credit terms and shipments.

- Confirming orders.
- Executing shipping orders for goods or work orders for the performance of services.
- Recording the shipments or services performed.

In considering the accounting system that processes revenue transactions and the control procedures applied to them, the auditor is interested mainly in procedures to ensure that all sales transactions that actually occurred are authorized and are recorded accurately; that is, that the control objectives of completeness, accuracy, and authorization of transaction processing and files are met. Those control objectives are closely related to the audit objectives of completeness, accuracy, and existence of revenue cycle accounts, particularly sales and accounts receivable. Other control procedures, while not directly related to those audit objectives, may also be of interest to the auditor. For example, the fact that credit checks are performed may provide evidence the auditor can use to evaluate whether the allowance for uncollectible accounts is adequate, which affects the valuation audit objective for accounts receivable.

The paragraphs that follow describe the various activities involved in the sale of goods, and the control procedures typically applied in processing the transactions. (Later sections discuss the audit relevance of those procedures.) Some of the activities described in this section also apply to sales of services, while others, like requisitioning, packing, and shipping, do not. To the extent that the processes are similar for both goods and services, the discussion of control procedures applies to sales of services as well.

Receiving and Recording Customers' Orders. For the selling enterprise, receipt of a customer's order, either by mail, telephone, or other electronic means, starts the revenue cycle. When customer orders are received, they may be logged in a sales order record or similar document, recorded on prenumbered forms, batched for further processing, or, increasingly, entered directly into a computer.

Typically in a computerized environment, an open order file is generated when orders are input. Completeness of input of orders may be ensured by numerical sequencing or controlling batch totals. Completeness of processing of sales orders is then controlled by subsequently matching shipments against open orders and deleting or flagging fully processed orders. In a manual system, completeness of processing of sales orders may be controlled by accounting for the numerical sequence of prenumbered sales order forms, maintaining a holding file of control copies of order forms, and periodically removing fully processed orders. Alternatively, the enterprise could use a sales order record on which orders processed are subsequently noted. In each case, the control procedure consists of periodic review of the sequencing, control totals, open order or holding file, or sales order record by a responsible person. Control procedures designed to ensure completeness of input of customer orders, for example, the use of batch controls, may also help ensure that orders were accurately input.

The objective of control procedures applied to customer orders when they are received is to ensure that all orders received are considered for shipment.

Although the absence or ineffectiveness of such control procedures could not result in financial statement misstatements, the auditor may still be interested in the procedures applied to sales orders before shipping orders (described below) are generated. Those procedures may indicate, for example, that management coordinates inventory requirements and production orders with product demand. They may also help ensure that all shipments are recorded; for example, the periodic review and follow-up of open orders should identify shipments that have not yet been recorded, as well as orders not yet shipped.

Authorizing Credit Terms and Shipments. Management establishes procedures to determine how much credit to extend to customers, communicates the information appropriately, revises it periodically, and monitors adherence to established credit limits. In some organizations that perform the credit approval function manually, customers' orders are sent to the credit department before they are recorded. In other entities, authorization takes place after orders have been recorded. Procedures for authorizing credit limits, other terms, and sales prices vary among companies, but certain practices are similar in most credit departments. Orders from repeat customers with a good record of payment, unless in excess of authorized credit limits, are usually routinely processed. Periodically, the credit department determines, by referring to published sources or requesting audited financial statements, that customers' financial condition has not deteriorated. The same means are used to ascertain new customers' creditworthiness. Many companies establish minimum sales order amounts before a credit check will be performed and credit extended. In any event, credit approval is usually evidenced in writing by the credit manager or other designated individual.

Where the authorization process is computerized, the input of sales orders generates a computer match of relevant customer information to master files of predetermined credit limits, other terms, and sales prices. If an order is in excess of the customer's limit or is for a customer not on the system, or if the sales terms or price is outside predetermined limits, a shipping or production order will not be generated and the sales order may not be accepted for further processing. Instead, an exception report will be produced for follow-up by a responsible individual. In some systems the computer also matches sales orders against an inventory master file to ascertain whether the goods are on hand to fill the order.

After all necessary approvals have been obtained, the shipment of goods or the production order is authorized. In a computerized system, when the goods are available for shipping, a shipping order is automatically generated. In a manual system, authorization may be noted on the sales order form or on a shipping order. The authorization process is usually subject to a supervisory control procedure, which in computerized systems covers the initial entry of and changes to predetermined credit limits, terms, and sales prices.

Confirming Orders. Inaccurately transcribed or lost orders can cause customer dissatisfaction and loss of revenues. To avoid errors or misunderstandings, many companies confirm orders with customers. This procedure may simply entail a telephone call or sending the customer a copy of the internally prepared sales order form or a computer-generated confirmation form. In many businesses, the substantial cost of changing or canceling an order after it has been processed makes the confirmation procedure a sound business practice; in other companies, however, order processing time is so short that confirming orders is not practicable.

Executing Shipping Orders.   The steps in executing an order for goods are usually requisitioning, packing, and shipping. The instructions for all of those steps may be prepared on one form, or several different forms may be used. The execution instructions may be generated either manually or by computer. If considerable work is involved in execution, such as fabrication to a customer's specifications, it may be necessary to prepare execution instructions in several stages. For items that are manufactured specifically for customers, work orders may be generated, either manually or by computer, and a file of open work orders maintained for follow-up. For other items, customers' orders may be requisitioned from finished goods inventory, from the factory by means of a production order, or from suppliers by means of a purchase order. The shipping orders are then usually matched against the inventory master file to determine whether the inventory exists to fill the order, or this match may have been done when the orders were received, as mentioned earlier.

In some organizations, a copy of the authorized sales order or a shipping order is used to instruct the various departments involved in physically executing shipments and to evidence the actual shipments. In other organizations, a "picking list" is generated, possibly by computer, and used by the warehouse or production department to gather and prepare orders for shipment. A packing slip or a bill of lading may be used by the shipping department in packing and shipping orders. Whatever form is used to document shipments, it will show the quantity shipped and the initials of the various people responsible for executing the shipment and the dates of their performance. Each department needs enough copies of the instructions to enable it to both advise other relevant departments of its action and retain evidence of performance in its own files.

Completeness of shipments (that is, the recording of all goods shipped) may be ensured by accounting for the numerical sequence of shipping orders or prenumbered bills of lading. An exception report listing outstanding shipping orders would identify authorized orders not yet input as shipped. In a computerized system, executed shipping orders are usually matched to the open order file to ensure that shipments input to the sales transaction file (and inventory master file) contain the quantities that were shipped. In a manual system, a holding file may be used; if execution involves a number of steps, a holding file is preferable because it affords ready access to information on uncompleted transactions. In many systems, it is useful to prepare and partially complete the invoice (described below) as part of preparing the execution instructions; the invoice can then serve as a holding file for the other execution steps. Sometimes invoices are not prepared until requisitioning, packing, and shipping have been completed; then a copy of the shipping order serves as a holding file. Either way, the control procedure consists of periodically matching notices of performance by each of the executing departments against the holding file to discover and investigate uncompleted transactions.

Recording Shipments. The recording of shipments generally initiates the formal recording of sales transactions for accounting purposes. In a computerized system, the input of executed shipping orders to the sales transaction file automatically generates a sales invoice. The control procedures of matching executed shipping orders to the open order file, as previously discussed, and of inputting executed shipping orders only when appropriate supporting documentation (for instance, initialed and dated shipping orders or supporting bills of lading) exists, are designed to ensure the complete and accurate recording of accounts receivable. In a manual system, invoices are authorized by a designated individual who ascertains that the supporting documents—sales and shipping orders and bills of lading, for example—exist and are appropriate.

Since invoices (and the sales transaction file in a computerized system) are the basis for recording sales and accounts receivable, control procedures to ensure that their processing is complete and accurate are imperative. Numerical sequencing is generally used for individual invoices; control totals are used for posting to the accounts receivable control account; and invoices or the sales transaction file is used for posting to the detailed accounts receivable listing (the accounts receivable subledger or subsidiary ledger). A typical control technique used to ensure the completeness of recorded sales transactions is periodic accounting for prenumbered shipping documents and sales invoices, with investigation of unmatched items by a person independent of the shipping and invoicing functions. Many computerized systems produce "missing item," or exception, reports of items like open shipping orders or missing bill of lading numbers, which are used for follow-up. Batch totals can also be used, for example, total units shipped and total units invoiced. Whether manual or automated, the investigation and resolution process is documented and periodically reviewed by supervisory personnel.

The final activity in a sales transaction is updating the general ledger accounts and the detailed accounts receivable listing. In computerized systems, there may be a matching procedure to ensure the completeness and accuracy of updating if the control account and detailed account are updated separately. It is also necessary to ensure that the accounts receivable control account and the detailed accounts receivable listing continue to be in agreement between postings, or transaction updates. A file control procedure commonly used to ensure this is the periodic comparison of the detailed listing with the general ledger control account by a person independent of the invoicing and cash receipts functions, with supervisory review of the comparison.

An inadequately designed accounting system or ineffective control procedures relating to invoicing and updating the accounts can result in critical misstatements. For example,

- Goods shipped but not invoiced could cause an understatement of revenues and accounts receivable.

- Unauthorized transactions could be recorded, causing a possibly uncollectible account.
- Errors on invoices could go undetected, causing an under- or overstatement of revenues and receivables.
- Errors in recording transactions in the detailed and control accounts could result in the misstatement of related balances. (Errors or delays in posting could also affect the collectibility of receivables.)

If customers detect errors, their confidence in the entity may be adversely affected.

Variations in Typical Sales Transactions. The activities described above are usually necessary, to the extent that they apply, in all sales transactions. Following are some common examples of variations in those activities.

- In over-the-counter retail sales, the above activities may be condensed into a short personal encounter. The customer orders orally, and the clerk accepts the order, reviewing authorized sales terms and often determining the customer's credit standing within the company or at a financial institution, like the issuer of a credit card, via a remote access computer terminal. The sales slip combines all the paperwork, sometimes including the stock withdrawal notice and possibly the reorder notice (or the tag removed from the goods may serve those purposes); the clerk physically executes the sale; the customer pays or the sales slip is forwarded to the billing department or the financial institution for invoicing. The control procedure consists of accounting for the prenumbered sales slips or the cash register tapes and following up on missing items.
- In contract sales, there may be requests for proposals, bid preparation, bidding, and extended contract negotiations.
- In providing continuing services, such as electric or telephone services, the activities are performed once for each customer and execution is continuous thereafter until the customer either cancels the service or fails to pay for it. The revenue process from rents, royalties, and interest is similar. A procedure for periodic reporting of the amount of service delivered is needed to initiate billing.
- In transportation services, billing and collection may come before physical execution and at a different time from the receipt, authorization, and confirmation of the order. A customer buys a ticket or a token and uses it at a later time.

Payments Received for Goods and Services

Payments received for goods and services generally include the following activities:

- Receiving the cash and depositing it in the bank.
- Comparing amounts remitted with recorded amounts.

- Authorizing discounts and allowances.
- Recording cash receipts, discounts, and allowances.

Receiving the Cash and Depositing It in the Bank.   Cash may be received by company personnel or directly by the bank. Asset protection is a significant control objective in the receipt stage. The procedures to accomplish this objective will differ depending on whether cash is received by the bank or by the company. Other control procedures applied to cash receipts are similar, regardless of where cash is received.

When cash is received by the company through the mail, it is usually in the form of checks; currency or checks may be received over the counter, by collectors, or by salespeople. Customer remittances received by the bank generally are through a lockbox or a wire transfer.

A lockbox system is a service offered by many banks to reduce cash transit time, thus increasing funds available to the company. Customers send their remittances to a post office box under control of the bank, which records the deposits and furnishes the company with the details. A lockbox provides improved protection of cash receipts because company personnel do not have access to them.

When funds are remitted by wire transfer, no currency or checks are involved. The customer provides details of the transfer (amount and bank account numbers) to its bank, which then executes the transfer. The receiving bank (the bank used by the company) notifies the company of the details of the transfer. Wire transfers are normally used only when large sums of money are being remitted. Cash transit time is significantly reduced; in fact, the funds normally are available for use by the company the same day the transfer is made. As with a lockbox, protection of cash receipts is improved because company personnel do not have access to them.

When cash is received through a lockbox or wire transfer, the bank provides some form of detail of the deposit. This may be remittance advices, statement stubs, or other correspondence from customers; alternatively, it may be a manual or computer-readable listing showing customers' names, amounts, and invoices being paid. This detail is used later to record cash receipts and for performing control procedures designed to ensure their complete and accurate processing.

Cash received by the company by mail is normally delivered from the mail room to an individual (e.g., a cashier) responsible for listing the receipts, endorsing checks, and preparing a deposit ticket. Listing (or, as it is frequently called, "prelisting") the cash receipts is the first step in establishing control over them. The listing usually includes names, amounts, and the invoices being paid (the customer's bill stub is commonly used for that purpose). Receipts over the counter may be listed on cash register tapes or counter sales slips prepared in the presence of customers; cash received from collectors or salespeople and not accompanied by listings is also listed upon receipt. Like the bank's detail of deposits, the company's cash receipts listing is used later to ensure the complete and accurate processing of cash receipts. Prenumbering counter sales slips, cashiers' receipts, and collectors' receipts and subsequently accounting for the numerical sequence help meet the transaction processing control objectives for cash receipts. Preparing the listing of receipts and accounting for the numerical sequence by an individual independent of other cash functions address asset protection, completeness, and accuracy of cash receipts.

Control procedures to ensure protection of cash received by the company include endorsing checks as soon as they are received and promptly depositing them in a bank account. Typically, an endorsement stamp including the notation "For Deposit Only" is used, and each day's cash receipts are deposited intact and without delay by an individual independent of other cash functions. Items not suitable for immediate deposit, like postdated checks or checks containing errors, typically are listed separately from the items ready for deposit, and later the two lists are reconciled with the deposit.

Often, cash is received from more than one source and at various times during the day. If more than one list or batch of cash receipts is prepared in a day, they usually are identified, for example, by batch number. Lists of receipts are totaled, usually at least daily, and the totals are compared with the corresponding deposit slip totals. If receipts flow from a number of sources, such as branch offices, collection departments, cash registers, lockboxes, and wire transfers, typically a control form or checklist is used to highlight missing entries and ensure the prompt reporting and inclusion of receipts from all locations daily.

Deposit or collection items charged back by a bank as uncollectible generally are delivered to and investigated by someone who has no responsibility for either handling or recording cash. Cash receipts of branch offices may be deposited in a bank account subject to withdrawal only by the main office.

Comparing Amounts Remitted with Recorded Amounts. This procedure, if done manually, is generally performed by the person responsible for maintaining the accounts receivable subsidiary ledger. In a computerized system, receipts may be matched against the accounts receivable detail file as they are input to ensure that the entity and its customer agree on the details of the invoice(s) being paid as well as the total amount. An exception report is then generated listing all cash receipts that could not be matched against an open invoice on the accounts receivable file. The comparison, whether performed manually or by computer, identifies credits taken for sales returns or allowances and whether they were authorized. The comparison also discloses whether discounts taken by customers were within the discount period, whether the receipt was applied to the right customer's account, and whether there are any potential disputes about amounts due. It also identifies cash receipts that were inaccurately input or that should not be applied against accounts receivable, for example, receipts from transactions outside the revenue cycle (such as the sale of a fixed asset). In addition, errors in the updating of sales to the accounts receivable file may be identified. For example, if certain sales were not updated to the accounts receivable file, investigation of the unmatched cash receipt would identify the error. Discrepancies, whether identified manually or by a computer match, are investigated and documentation of the resolution and any necessary corrections is reviewed by supervisory personnel.

Authorizing Discounts and Allowances.   Discounts and allowances represent noncash reductions of the recorded invoice and receivable amounts. Discounts taken by customers are reviewed to ascertain that they are within the stated terms and for the proper amount. In some companies, discounts are routine, and the approval and recording function is well systematized. In a computerized environment, the discount terms and amount may be matched against the invoice or a master file containing discount information, at the time the cash receipt is input. An exception report of unauthorized discounts taken is generated for follow-up, investigation, and necessary corrections.

Allowances, on the other hand, are less frequent, more difficult to ascertain, and often based on evaluations of customer complaints. Allowances are generally controlled by policies specifying who may authorize them and under what conditions. Forms and reporting procedures are used to establish prompt authorization, approval, and documentation of allowances. Investigation of uncollected receivables may reveal unrecorded allowances.

Nonroutine discounts and allowances taken by customers are usually approved by supervisory personnel independent of people who receive cash and maintain the accounts receivable subsidiary ledger. Documentation of approval is ordinarily noted on prenumbered credit memos whose numerical sequence is reviewed for missing numbers to ensure completeness of input.

Recording Cash Receipts, Discounts, and Allowances.   Cash receipts may be recorded before being compared with invoices, after any discounts or allowances taken have been approved, or at the same time as the comparison and identification of any discounts or allowances taken. In any event, the process of recording cash receipts is the same. In a manual system, cash received is generally entered by source (such as cash sale or payment from customer) in a cash receipts journal or other book of original entry that later serves as the basis for posting to the general ledger. The detailed lists prepared when the cash was received are used as the source documents for updating the subsidiary ledgers. In a computerized environment, the detailed listings are normally used as source documents for inputting cash receipts. If the bank provides details of lockbox receipts in machine-readable form, such as magnetic tape, inputting receipts may entail merely loading the tape onto the computer for processing. Typically a daily cash receipts report is generated, listing all receipts input. Once entered, the total cash receipts recorded for the day usually are reconciled to the original listings or batch totals and to authenticated duplicate deposit slips or other bank notices. This reconciliation, normally performed by an individual independent of those who enter the receipts, ensures that all cash receipts have been entered.

The final activity in processing payments for goods and services is updating the general ledger. In a manual system, the totals in the cash receipts journal and approved journal entries for discounts and allowances are posted to the general ledger periodically (usually monthly). When these transactions are processed by computer, the cash receipts file (which may also contain authorized discounts) is used to update the general ledger. The detailed accounts receivable file is relieved when the cash receipts and discounts are input and accepted for processing. Allowances and discounts, when not part of the routine transaction processing, are normally input separately and update the detailed accounts receivable file, if accepted for processing. Numerically sequenced credit memos are generated and the credit memo file is updated. This file is then used to update the general ledger.

Posting to the detailed accounts receivable ledger generally is performed by people independent of cash functions; the general ledger is ordinarily posted by computer or by someone other than the person who updates the accounts receivable subsidiary ledger or file. This segregation of duties meets both authorization and accuracy objectives; its effectiveness is typically ensured by periodic reconciliation of the general ledger to the detailed accounts receivable ledger. Periodic mailing of customer statements also helps ensure that all cash receipts, discounts, and allowances have been accurately recorded.

Goods Returned by and Claims Received from Customers

The third class of transactions in the revenue cycle is the processing of returns and claims. These transactions are often less well controlled than sales or cash receipts transactions: Returns and claims are likely to be sporadic and lacking in common characteristics. Accordingly, establishing control over them as early as possible enhances the achievement of the completeness, accuracy, and authorization control objectives. Since returned goods represent an asset to the company, many of the control procedures described in Chapter 13 for receiving goods are relevant.

Typically, goods returned by customers and the processing of claims are handled in the following steps:

- Receiving and accepting goods or claims.
- Preparing receiving reports.
- Reviewing claims.
- Authorizing credits.
- Preparing and mailing credit memos.
- Recording returns and claims.

Receiving and Accepting Goods or Claims.   The receiving department handles goods returned for credit. Returned goods may go through the same receiving routine as other receipts of goods (discussed in Chapter 13) or may be processed through a separate receiving area, inspection procedure, and paperwork system. In either case, counting, inspecting, and noting quantities and condition serve as a basis for later determining the credit to give the customer and whether the goods need repair or can be placed back in stock.

Preparing Receiving Reports.   Receiving reports typically are used for documenting and establishing control over goods returned. Generally, they are completed when goods are received. They are commonly prepared on prenumbered reports by the receiving department, which is independent of the shipping function. All pertinent data is recorded for later processing. If appropriate, reports may be completed in the presence of the customer to ensure that all customer complaints are recognized. The subsequent control procedure of accounting for the numerical sequence and investigating missing or duplicate receiving reports is performed by people independent of the shipping and receiving functions and is designed to ensure that all goods returned are recorded.

Reviewing Claims. After goods have been received and recorded by the receiving department, the related claims are reviewed by a customer service department that is independent of the receiving function. This procedure establishes the authenticity of claims and determines the amount of credit, if any, to be granted. Sometimes the customer service department prepares credit memos for approval by the credit, sales, and accounting departments. In other organizations, the results of the inspection and review are noted directly on the receiving reports and forwarded to the three departments.

Authorizing Credits. The sales department is generally responsible for final authorization of credits. This approval is based on receiving reports and careful independent and documented inspection of goods, and is evidenced on the receiving and inspection reports. Credit memos initiated by the sales department are usually independently reviewed.

Preparing and Mailing Credit Memos. Credit memos generally are prepared only on the basis of authorized receiving and inspection reports, by individuals (preferably in the sales department) other than those who receive cash and record accounts receivable. Credit memos are usually in numerical sequence, and quantities, terms, prices, and extensions are reviewed for accuracy before mailing, by someone other than the preparer. Listings of credit memos issued, containing all pertinent data, normally are prepared to support the appropriate journal entry and for posting the accounts receivable subsidiary ledger. In a computerized system, credits for returned goods may be processed in the same way as allowances. Approved receiving reports may be used as source documents for computing the credits. Numerically sequenced credit memos are generated, and the accounts receivable file and credit memo file updated.

Recording Returns and Claims. There is a natural inclination to delay the processing of returns and claims; periodic review of the open file of receiving reports is a useful control procedure for identifying unprocessed claims. Understanding the reason for returns may help management determine whether they are a symptom of a problem such as defective production or a malfunctioning order entry system. In addition, achievement of the completeness control objective is enhanced by accounting for the numerical sequence of recorded credit memos, with appropriate follow-up of duplicate or missing items.

DETERMINING THE AUDIT STRATEGY

The audit strategy for each account balance and class of transactions in the revenue cycle is based primarily on the auditor's assessment of inherent and control risk relating to specific audit objectives and on efficiency considerations.

Audit Objectives

The audit objectives applicable to the accounts in the revenue cycle are

Completeness
- Accounts receivable represent all amounts owed to the entity at the balance sheet date arising from sales transactions.
- Unearned revenues represent all amounts received for which shipment or services have not been rendered.
- All shipments or services rendered during the period covered by the financial statements and all returns or allowances provided are reflected in the financial statements.

Accuracy
- Sales transactions are based on correct prices and quantities and are accurately computed and classified in the appropriate general ledger and accounts receivable subsidiary ledger accounts.
- Unearned revenues represent the correct amount received for shipments or services to be rendered in future periods and are classified in the appropriate general ledger account.
- The accounts receivable subsidiary ledger is mathematically correct and agrees with the general ledger.

Existence/Occurrence
- Recorded accounts receivable represent amounts owed to the entity at the balance sheet date.
- Recorded sales transactions represent goods actually shipped or services actually rendered during the period covered by the financial statements.
- Unearned revenues represent amounts received by the entity for future sales transactions.

Cutoff
- Sales transactions, cash receipts, and returns and claims are recorded in the proper period.

Valuation
- Accounts receivable are stated at net realizable value (i.e., net of appropriate allowances for uncollectible accounts, discounts, returns, and similar items).

- Revenue is recognized only when appropriate accounting recognition and measurement criteria are met.

Rights and Obligations

- Accounts receivable are legal rights of the entity at the balance sheet date (i.e., customer accounts that have been sold or factored are excluded from the accounts receivable balance).
- Unearned revenues reflect the amounts received for which the entity is obligated to provide future shipments or services.

Presentation and Disclosure

- Accounts receivable, sales, and related accounts are properly described and classified in the financial statements.
- Accounts receivable pledged as collateral are properly disclosed.

The auditor achieves these objectives by performing substantive tests or a combination of substantive tests and tests of control structure policies and procedures. The auditor frequently tests an entity's control procedures to obtain evidence that they are designed and operating effectively as a basis for significantly reducing the assurance needed from substantive tests directed at the completeness, accuracy, and existence audit objectives. The auditor generally achieves the remaining audit objectives (with the exception of cutoff) by performing substantive tests, supplemented by the evidence obtained through assessing the entity's inherent risk conditions, control environment, and accounting system. For example, the auditor's awareness of an economic decline in an industry in which the entity has many customers may cause concern about the valuation audit objective for accounts receivable.

The auditor usually performs substantive tests to achieve the cutoff objective, because companies frequently do not establish control procedures related to cutoff. In some situations, however, management may implement special control procedures designed to achieve proper cutoff at year-end. The auditor may then decide to test those special control procedures in conjunction with other tests of control structure policies and procedures.

Risk Assessment

As discussed in Chapter 8, the auditor gathers or updates information about various aspects of the client and its business as a basis for assessing inherent and control risk.

Analytical Procedures. Analytical procedures frequently highlight relationships between accounts and risks not otherwise apparent during the risk assessment phase of the audit. As discussed in Chapter 8, analytical procedures are a required part of planning; their use at an early stage in the audit often results in more informed strategy decisions.

Analytical procedures can, for example, indicate trends in sales, returns, and collection of receivables that may assist the auditor in assessing risk.

Relationships among revenue accounts and between revenue and other accounts should be reviewed and compared with those of prior periods and those anticipated in budgets or forecasts. Those relationships include the ratios of accounts receivable to sales, various allowance accounts to sales, and cost of goods sold to sales. It may also be useful to relate sales of certain product lines to one another. The ratios and the balances in the accounts themselves are often compared from month to month and with the corresponding period of the prior year. Trends and fluctuations (seasonal and other) should be noted and explanations sought for unusual patterns. Sometimes sales can be related to units sold or produced and the trend of an ''average unit price'' examined.

The auditor should consider management's performance of analytical procedures as part of its reviews of reports and other internal documentation. The auditor may obtain an understanding of the reviews performed by management and consider using the results of those procedures, to the extent necessary, to supplement his or her own analytical procedures. Management typically reviews various internal sales and budgetary reports and data, such as the following:

- Actual sales compared with historical trends and budgets or forecasts.
- Actual gross margins compared with historical trends and budgets.
- Actual write-offs, credit memos, and other noncash reductions of receivables compared with budgets and historical information.
- Accounts receivable aging.
- Unfilled sales commitments.

Management's review of reports such as these may help identify material misstatements in the processing of sales transactions. For example, investigation of significant differences between reported sales and budgeted and historical sales could identify incomplete updating of shipments to the general ledger.

The way the client responds to the auditor's inquiries resulting from analytical procedures may give some indication of the quality of the client's control environment. For example, prompt, logical, and meaningful answers to questions about fluctuations in gross margins from the prior to the current year would provide some indication, in the absence of evidence to the contrary, that the company's management is ''in control'' and that the accounting system and control procedures appear to be functioning as intended. Analytical procedures, however, may also indicate trends, even in well-controlled companies, that may lead the auditor to extend substantive tests; for example, trends that raise questions about the collectibility of accounts receivable. Analytical procedures performed as substantive tests are discussed later in this chapter.

Control Risk. The auditor also is required, at a minimum, to obtain an understanding of the entity's control structure sufficient to plan the audit. This understanding is used to identify the types of misstatements that might occur and the risk of their occurring, and to design substantive tests. The understanding is obtained, or updated, by considering previous experience with the entity, reviewing prior-year audit results, interviewing client personnel, observing personnel as they perform their duties, reviewing client-prepared descriptions of policies and procedures, and inspecting documents and records. These procedures normally reveal information about all significant cycles and account balances.

In addition to information about the client's overall control environment, how transactions are processed (manually or by computer) and how sophisticated these systems are, and other general characteristics of the control structure, the auditor should consider the following types of information, as appropriate, related to the revenue cycle:

- The entity's main source(s) of revenues.
- The volume and dollar amount of sales and the number of customers it sells to.
- The usual terms of sales, which would determine when it is proper to record revenue.
- The usual credit and discount terms.
- The flow of revenue cycle transactions through the accounting system.

The auditor should also obtain an understanding of control procedures applied to sales orders, shipping documents, invoices, and cash collections, and the extent to which duties are segregated among the people performing those procedures. Based on all the above information, the auditor determines whether control structure policies and procedures for specific classes of transactions are appropriately designed and have been placed in operation.

In the course of obtaining the understanding of the control structure, the auditor may perform concurrent tests of controls (either incidental or planned) and thereby obtain evidence that control structure policies and procedures have been properly designed and are operating effectively. That evidence would enable the auditor to assess control risk at below the maximum for relevant audit objectives. For example, when inquiring about management's review of sales reports, the auditor may also observe personnel performing the review or examine reports or documents that provide evidence of it. If operating effectively, management's review provides some evidence with respect to the completeness and accuracy of sales. The auditor considers the level of detail reviewed and the likelihood that the reviewer would detect a material misstatement.

The auditor next considers whether he or she wishes to obtain additional evidence of the effectiveness of policies and procedures as a basis for a low assessment of control risk, and then whether such evidence is likely to be available and efficient to obtain. If so, the auditor would usually perform additional tests of controls for specific audit objectives—commonly, completeness, accuracy, and existence/occurrence of accounts receivable and sales.

Audit Testing Plan

As discussed in Chapter 5, the basic audit strategy decision the auditor makes for each significant account balance is whether to perform additional tests of controls to support a low assessed level of control risk for specific audit objectives, or to perform substantive tests directed at all relevant audit objectives, without significant restriction based on tests of controls.

Professional judgment is needed to assess risks and translate that assessment into the various decisions that determine the audit plan. The following two situations describe the testing decisions an auditor might make in developing an appropriate audit strategy for the revenue cycle.

The first situation is a small manufacturing company with a manual accounting system for sales and cash receipts. The volume of transactions is low. Customer orders are received by phone by the sales clerk, who prepares an order form containing the customer's name and address, item, quantity, and price. The sales clerk retains a copy of the order and forwards the original to the controller for credit approval. The sales clerk's copies of the orders are used to total the orders received each day. This information is used by the sales manager to track performance and anticipate sales volumes. The company does not have formal control procedures to ensure that all approved orders are shipped. It does not consider such procedures necessary because of the low volume of sales and the fact that there has never been a problem with lost orders.

The controller approves orders for shipment by initialling them. Unless the customer has a poor payment history or a large accounts receivable balance outstanding, credit is extended. The order is then forwarded to the warehouse for shipment. The warehouse employees prepare a numerically sequenced packing slip, and package and ship the goods. A copy of the packing slip, with the original order attached, is forwarded to the accounts receivable clerk in the accounting department. The clerk prepares an invoice (using numerically sequenced forms) and records the sale in the sales journal and accounts receivable subsidiary ledger. Periodically the clerk accounts for the numerical sequence of the packing slips to identify any shipments that were not invoiced. The invoice package (invoice, packing slip, and order) is reviewed by the controller before being mailed to the customer.

Customer remittances are received by mail. The mail is opened by the receptionist, who prepares the bank deposit slip and a listing (showing customer's name, invoice being paid, and amount) of the day's remittances, attaching the customer remittance advices. The deposit slip and checks are given to the controller, who makes the daily deposit. The listing, with the remittance advices, is given to the accounts receivable clerk, who records the remittances in the cash receipts journal and accounts receivable subsidiary ledger.

At the end of the month, the accounts receivable clerk summarizes the sales journal and cash receipts journal and prepares the monthly entries to the general ledger. The controller reviews the subsidiary ledgers and approves the general ledger entries. The controller's review consists of scanning the subsidiary ledgers to account for the numerical sequencing of invoices and determine that an entry was made each business day. An accounting clerk posts the general ledger entries and prepares the financial statements for the controller's review. This clerk also performs the monthly bank reconciliation and reconciles the accounts receivable subsidiary ledger to the general ledger; the controller then reviews the reconciliations. The sales and production managers review the financial statements and identify any unexpected results.

In this situation, the auditor, based on his or her understanding of the control structure and any concurrent tests of controls performed, would probably assess control risk at below the maximum and decide not to perform additional tests of controls. Substantive tests of details would be directed at all assertions. In addition to the substantive tests described later in the chapter, the auditor might need to perform additional tests with respect to the accuracy of accounts receivable and sales. Those tests might include tracing prices to approved price lists, determining that the account classifications are proper, and ascertaining that the posting to the subsidiary and general ledgers was done correctly. The tests of details would be performed as of year-end.

The above strategy decisions are based on the following factors:

- Low transaction volume, which makes substantive testing efficient.
- Manual accounting system, which increases the risk of random errors.
- Limited control procedures; for example, no control procedure that addresses accuracy of input, and no independent review to determine that all shipments have been approved by the controller.

The auditor's decision might have been different if the company had

- A higher volume of transactions.
- A computerized accounting system that used packaged software developed and maintained by third-party vendors.
- Increased segregation of duties, for example, if the person responsible for accounting for the numerical sequencing of packing slips and investigating missing items were independent from the clerk who recorded sales.
- Effective transaction processing and file control procedures; for example, matching of shipments to an open order file, investigation of unmatched items by accounting clerks, and investigation of long-outstanding orders by the sales department.

In those circumstances, the auditor might have decided to perform additional tests of control procedures to reduce the assurance needed from substantive tests for the completeness, accuracy, and possibly existence audit objectives.

In the second situation, the client is a large manufacturing company with a computerized accounting system for sales and cash receipts. The company has a large highly skilled EDP department with effective general control procedures and division of duties. The EDP department typically develops software internally, but sometimes modifies packaged software. Control procedures for implementing new systems, maintaining existing systems, and the operations functions are effective, as are program and data file security control procedures. (These general control procedures are discussed in detail in Chapter 11.) Control procedures applied to sales and cash receipts are designed to ensure that authorized transactions are completely and accurately input and updated.

In this situation, the auditor will likely have performed tests of controls concurrently with obtaining an understanding of the control structure. The auditor is also likely to consider it efficient to perform additional tests of controls relating to the completeness, accuracy, and authorization control objectives for sales and cash receipts transactions, as a basis for assessing control risk as low. If the additional tests of controls support a low assessment of control risk, substantive tests directed at the completeness, accuracy, and existence audit objectives could be reduced. (Except for the need to confirm some receivables as required by GAAS, they might even be limited to analytical procedures.) The auditor would be likely to perform any tests of details prior to year-end.

If the client did not have effective program and data file security control procedures, the auditor might revise the strategy to include more substantive tests directed at the existence/occurrence audit objective for accounts receivable and sales. Ineffective security control procedures increase the risk of unauthorized alterations to programs and data. The ability to manipulate data might make it possible for an employee who had access to cash receipts to misappropriate cash and conceal the defalcation.

ADDITIONAL TESTS OF CONTROLS

As discussed earlier, the auditor may have performed concurrent tests of controls while obtaining an understanding of control structure policies and procedures. Concurrent tests of controls often provide evidence to support an assessment of control risk at below the maximum for one or more audit objectives. However, concurrent tests of controls are generally directed mainly at policies and procedures that are part of the control environment and accounting system, as opposed to specific control procedures, and therefore usually relate to several audit objectives and affect several accounts. Thus, concurrent tests of controls are not enough to support a low assessment of control risk for specific audit objectives and account balances. To assess control risk as low for one or more audit objectives for some or all revenue cycle accounts, the auditor performs additional tests of controls. Such tests usually require substantial audit effort, and therefore the auditor generally performs them only when he or she believes they will significantly reduce the amount of substantive testing required.

The purpose of performing additional tests of individual control procedures is to obtain support for an assessment that all the control structure elements interacting together reduce to a low level the risk that control objectives will not be achieved. Specific control objectives and typical control procedures applicable to sales of goods and services and to payments received for them are described in Figures 12.1 and 12.2, respectively. The accounting system assumed to be in operation in the figures is a sophisticated computerized system. As discussed in Chapter 8, the tests of controls that the auditor would perform include an appropriate combination of inquiring about the client's control procedures, observing that the procedures have been placed in operation, and examining evidence that they are designed and operating effectively. Also as discussed in Chapter 8, reperformance may be used in tests of controls;

Figure 12.1 Sales of Goods and Services

	Control Objectives					
	Transaction Processing					
	Authorization	Completeness of Input	Accuracy of Input	Completeness and Accuracy of Updating[a]	File	Asset Protection
Specific Control Objectives	All recorded sales transactions represent actual shipments of goods or rendering of services to non-fictitious customers of the entity and are approved.	All sales transactions are input and accepted for processing.	Sales are correctly recorded as to amounts, quantities, dates, and customers; are recorded in the proper period; are accurately converted into computer-readable form; and are accurately input to the computer.	All sales transactions input and accepted for processing are accurately updated to the sales and accounts receivable data files.	The integrity of individual accounts receivable in the subsidiary ledger and the general ledger accounts receivable and sales accounts, after sales transactions have been accumulated in them, is preserved.	Only authorized personnel have access to accounts receivable records or data stored on them.
Typical Control Procedures	Reporting and resolving orders rejected because customers, prices, or credit or other terms were not	Accounting for the numerical sequence of shipping or work orders input to the computer.	Completeness of input control procedures for shipping or work orders also address the accuracy of in-	Comparing total sales input with the total updated to the sales and accounts receivable files.	Ensuring that the correct version of the file is being used for processing. Balancing of the subsidiary	Restricting access to accounts receivable files and files used in processing receivables.

390

contained on, or were outside the preestablished limits on, customer and price master files.

Approving changes to master files for customers, terms, credit limits, and sales prices.

Approving new customers on the files or changed customer information, such as shipping address or billing address.

Determining that a sales invoice was generated for each executed shipping or work order. Reporting and resolving missing, unmatched, or duplicate shipping orders or invoices by individuals independent of shipping functions.

Reporting and resolving long-outstanding items on the open shipping or work order file. Resolving reports of executed shipping and work orders rejected as not matching against the open file by individuals independent of shipping functions.

put for quantities and descriptions.

Mailing of customer statements, and investigating and resolving disputes or inquiries, by individuals independent of the invoicing function.

ledger (previous balance plus sales less receipts, compared with the current total). Reconciling the subsidiary ledger to the control account in the general ledger. Reporting and resolving discrepancies.

aCompleteness of updating and accuracy of updating have been combined in this figure for convenience, because typically the same control procedures apply to both objectives.

Figure 12.2 Payments Received for Goods and Services

	Control Objectives					
	Transaction Processing					
	Authorization	Completeness of Input	Accuracy of Input	Completeness and Accuracy of Updating[a]	File	Asset Protection
Specific Control Objectives	All cash receipts from customers are approved for application against specified invoices.	All payments received are input and accepted for processing.	Receipts are correctly recorded as to amounts, dates, and customers; are recorded in the proper period; are accurately converted into computer-readable form; and are accurately input to the computer.	All receipts input and accepted for processing are accurately updated to the cash receipts and accounts receivable data files.	The integrity of individual accounts receivable in the subsidiary ledger and the general ledger accounts receivable and cash accounts, after receipts have been updated to them, is preserved.	Only authorized personnel have access to receipts and accounts receivable records or data stored on them. Receipts are promptly deposited in the entity's bank account.
Typical Control Procedures	Reporting and resolving differences as to the appropriate invoice being paid. Reporting and	Prelisting of cash received. Comparing bank advice (e.g., validated deposit slip) with the total of	Reporting and resolving cash receipts not matched against an unpaid invoice on the accounts re-	Comparing total cash input with the totals updated to the cash receipts and accounts receivable files.	Same control procedures as described in Figure 12.1, "Sales of Goods and Services."	Receiving and prelisting cash by individuals independent of recording cash receipts. Restrictive en-

dorsement of checks on receipt.

Deposit of receipts intact daily.

Individuals involved in the receipt and deposit function are not authorized check signers.

Restricted access to accounts receivable files and files used in processing cash receipts.

Reconciling the bank statement to the general ledger cash account by personnel independent of receiving and recording cash receipts (and of accounts payable and cash disbursements functions).

ceivable subsidiary ledger by individuals independent of other receipt functions.

Mailing of customer statements, and investigating and resolving disputes or inquiries, by individuals independent of receiving or recording cash receipts, posting to the accounts receivable subsidiary ledger, or authorizing write-offs of receivables.

Investigation of past-due receivables by individuals independent of receiving or recording cash receipts.

the prelistings and the total receipts input, by individuals independent of receiving, prelisting, or recording cash receipts.

resolving differences as to the amount of the receipt and the amount of the invoice.

aCompleteness of updating and accuracy of updating have been combined in this figure for convenience, because typically the same control procedures apply to both objectives.

but if that becomes necessary, the auditor usually determines it is more efficient to perform substantive tests. In addition to testing control procedures specific to a particular transaction cycle, in order to assess control risk as low the auditor would also need evidence of the effectiveness of general control procedures. (General control procedures are discussed in Chapter 11.)

The third class of transactions in the revenue cycle, goods returned by and claims received from customers, is usually less significant than sales and payments received. Accordingly, additional tests of controls generally are not performed. If return transactions were significant, however, the auditor might perform additional tests of controls like the following:

Inquire about and observe

- Control procedures designed to ensure that all goods returned by customers are appropriately documented.
- Procedures for accounting for the numerical sequence of documents supporting goods returned by customers, claims made, and credit memos, including the way errors are investigated and resolved.
- Procedures for authorizing adjustments to the account.

Examine the following documents or reports to support inquiries and observations:

- Receiving reports.
- Credit memos.
- Exception reports for missing or duplicate items.

When performing tests of controls, the auditor should be aware of audit objectives other than completeness, accuracy, existence, and cutoff that may be affected by those tests. An audit objective frequently considered when testing controls in the revenue cycle is valuation. When tests of controls are performed, the auditor usually tests credit department approval procedures; the results of those tests help in evaluating the client's allowance for uncollectible accounts. For example, amounts due from sales made to potentially high-credit-risk customers close to year-end would be classified as "current" in the accounts receivable aged trial balance, which normally would not indicate a potential collection problem. In the absence of control procedures relating to granting credit, however, the auditor may consider it necessary to test the collectibility of "current" receivables. The auditor might do this by extending the review of collections in the post-balance-sheet period.

In evaluating the results of tests of controls (including tests of general control procedures), the auditor considers whether the control structure policies and procedures, taken as a whole, are appropriately designed to achieve the control objectives and are operating effectively. This will determine whether the expected assessment of control risk as low was attained for specific accounts and audit objectives and, thus, whether the auditor can significantly reduce substantive testing. Results differing from those anticipated when developing the audit testing plan require the auditor to reconsider the nature, timing, and extent of planned substantive tests—not only for revenue cycle accounts, but also for other accounts that may be affected. For example, ineffective control procedures to ensure completeness of recorded sales may also affect inventory and cost of sales.

SUBSTANTIVE TESTS

If the auditor has assessed control risk for some or all revenue cycle accounts as low for specific audit objectives, substantive tests addressing those audit objectives may, except for the need to confirm some accounts receivable, be limited to analytical procedures. The auditor will also consider whether evidence obtained from tests directed at other audit objectives is relevant to these audit objectives too. For example, the confirmation of accounts receivable is directed toward the existence audit objective, but provides some evidence about accuracy as well. Control risk is seldom assessed as low with respect to the cutoff, valuation, rights and obligations, and presentation and disclosure objectives, and therefore substantive tests of details are usually performed for these objectives.

Accounts Receivable

Before performing substantive tests directed toward the other audit objectives, the auditor should be reasonably assured that the accounts receivable trial balance contains all sales transactions that remain uncollected at year-end. If the results of tests of controls provide evidence about the completeness of the trial balance, substantive tests of the completeness of accounts receivable will generally be limited to analytical procedures, as discussed later in this chapter.

To achieve the cutoff objective, it is often more efficient for the auditor to perform substantive tests of details, particularly in the case of those companies that are not concerned about precise cutoffs on a month-to-month basis. Companies may, however, implement special control procedures at the end of the year (or possibly quarterly if quarterly earnings are published), which the auditor may decide to test. Also, control structure policies and procedures designed to ensure completeness of input and update may be effective in ensuring that transactions are recorded in the proper period. For example, the design of the accounting system itself may reduce control risk for cutoff.

Cutoff Tests of Shipments and Collections. Cutoff tests are intended to ascertain that all significant transactions have been recorded in the proper period. In the absence of control structure policies and procedures directed toward cutoff, the sooner accounts are closed after year-end, the greater the likelihood that there will be unrecorded sales invoices. Thus, examining files of unmatched shipping reports and unrecorded invoices, the sales journal, the cash receipts journal, and other relevant records for a period after year-end is an almost universal auditing procedure.

If the basic transaction documents are in numerical sequence, the auditor can note the number of the last shipping report and the last sales invoice recorded and also compare the date of the last entry in the cash receipts journal with the date those receipts were deposited in the bank. For clients that do not perform a wall-to-wall inventory at year-end, the auditor may examine perpetual inventory records, the sales journal, and the listing of unmatched shipping reports for evidence that goods sold and shipped before year-end have been removed from inventory. The auditor should apply the same procedures to obtain assurance that sales, shipments, and cash receipts applicable to the following year were not recorded in the year under audit. If the basic transaction documents are not prenumbered, it may be necessary to examine supporting documents for transactions with near-year-end dates and large amounts, selected from the sales journal, cash receipts journal, perpetual inventory records, and shipping reports both before and after the cutoff date to obtain sufficient evidence that the cutoff was properly made.

Cutoff tests of shipments are usually coordinated with the auditor's observation of the client's physical inventory count. When physical inventories are taken at a date other than year-end, it is important that shipment cutoff tests be made at the same date. Cutoff errors are compounded when perpetual inventory records and the general ledger inventory account are adjusted for differences between book and physical amounts (see Chapter 14, "Auditing the Production Cycle, Cost of Sales, and Inventory Balances").

Confirming Accounts Receivable. One of the most widely used substantive tests for determining the existence and, to a lesser extent, the accuracy of accounts receivable is direct communication by the auditor with customers, commonly referred to as "confirmation." Confirmation by the auditor of individual sales transactions or accounts receivable balances by direct communication with customers is one of only a few procedures that are designated as "generally accepted auditing procedures." Statement on Auditing Standards (SAS) No. 1 (AU Section 331.01 and .03) states

> Confirmation of receivables and observation of inventories are generally accepted auditing procedures. The independent auditor who issues an opinion when he has not employed them must bear in mind that he has the burden of justifying the opinion expressed.

> Confirmation of receivables requires direct communication with debtors either during or after the period under audit; the confirmation date, the method of requesting confirmations, and the number to be requested are determined by the independent auditor. Such matters as the effectiveness of internal control structure policies and procedures, the apparent possibility of disputes, inaccuracies or irregularities in the accounts, the probability that requests will receive consideration or that the debtor will be able to confirm the information requested, and the materiality of the amounts involved are factors to be considered by the auditor in selecting the information to be requested and the form of confirmation, as well as the extent and timing of his confirmation procedures.

Confirmation of receivables has been required by the profession since 1939, when Statement on Auditing Procedure No. 1 was adopted by the AICPA as a direct result of the McKesson & Robbins fraud. In the intervening years, confirmation has been the subject of extensive authoritative and other professional pronouncements. As discussed in Chapter 5, evidence obtained from third parties, such as confirmation of accounts receivable, is generally more reliable than evidence obtained from within the entity. However, confirmation is only one substantive procedure among several, just as substantive tests produce one kind of audit evidence among several.

Auditors should not blindly accept confirmation replies; they should be aware that many traditional auditing procedures, including confirming receivables, do not in all circumstances produce the assurance they were intended to provide. In its *Report, Conclusions, and Recommendations*, the Commission on Auditors' Responsibilities (Cohen Commission) pointed out that ''. . . in several cases, outsiders either ignored incorrect information that was clearly shown in confirmations or actively cooperated with management in giving incorrect confirmation'' (p. 40).

Moreover, while confirmation produces evidence about the existence and (to some extent) the accuracy of accounts receivable, other procedures are needed to establish their collectibility. The most direct evidence regarding collectibility of receivables is subsequent customer payments. Those payments also provide reliable evidence about existence and accuracy, because it is highly unlikely that a customer will pay a balance that is not owed or is overstated. Only the accuracy of the date the sale took place is not substantiated by a subsequent customer payment. Confirmation may, however, reveal the improper application of customer payments to older, disputed invoices, perhaps to conceal an unfavorable aging schedule. In practice, the auditor often uses a combination of confirmation, examination of subsequent customer payments, and other procedures to test the existence and accuracy of accounts receivable.

The auditor must make a decision regarding the confirmation date. If there were no deadline for the client to issue financial statements, confirming at year-end would be most effective. In today's business environment, however, there is usually a deadline, and accordingly the auditor often confirms receivables (and performs many other auditing procedures as well) at an earlier date. If early substantive testing is done, the auditor will have to obtain satisfaction that the risk of material misstatement occurring is low during the intervening period, as discussed in Chapter 9.

Substantive tests sometimes provide evidence about control structure policies and procedures, if errors or irregularities disclosed by those tests are investigated and found to result from a control deficiency or breakdown. Specifically, confirmation procedures may provide evidence of control structure effectiveness with respect to the revenue cycle. Accordingly, many auditors consider receivable confirmations as a source of evidence about the effectiveness of the control structure as well as a source of evidence about the existence and accuracy of accounts receivable.

Confirmation Procedures

Before selecting accounts for confirmation, the auditor should be sure the accounts receivable trial balance reconciles to the related control account.

Normally the client routinely compares general ledger control account balances with the totals of individual accounts receivable, investigates discrepancies between the two, and makes appropriate adjustments. The auditor should compare the accounts receivable trial balance with the general ledger account and test the arithmetical accuracy of the trial balance (which is often done using audit software) or should test general control procedures for evidence that the trial balance is mathematically accurate. Reasons for recurring discrepancies between the control account and subsidiary ledger should be investigated.

The paragraphs below describe the procedures involved in confirming receivables.

Selecting Accounts for Confirmation.   Depending on the audit testing plan and the results of tests of controls, the auditor should decide whether all or only part of the accounts should be confirmed and, if the latter, the basis for selecting them. Chapter 10 discusses various methods of sample selection. The selection should exclude debtors from whom replies to requests for confirmation cannot reasonably be expected, such as certain governmental agencies, foreign concerns, and some large industrial and commercial enterprises that use an open invoice or decentralized accounts payable processing system that makes confirmation impracticable.

An experienced auditor usually confirms accounts that appear unusual. Accounts with zero or credit balances should also be considered for confirmation. A credit balance suggests the possibility of an incorrect entry, especially if control structure policies and procedures are not effective.

Accounts and notes receivable that have been discounted or pledged should be confirmed with lenders, so that any unrecorded liability or contingency will be brought to the auditor's attention. This procedure helps the auditor achieve the audit objectives of rights and obligations, and presentation and disclosure. Confirming receivables with those they have been discounted or pledged with does not preclude an auditor from requesting confirmation from the debtors as well, particularly if the client is responsible for collections or the lender has recourse to the client.

To preserve the integrity of the confirmation process, the auditor should control the selection, preparation, mailing, and return of the confirmations. If the client does not wish statements or confirmation requests to be sent to certain debtors, the auditor should be satisfied that there is an adequate reason before agreeing to omit them. If such accounts are material, the auditor should use alternative procedures to obtain satisfaction that the accounts exist and are accurate. If the results of the alternative procedures are satisfactory, the client's request not to confirm directly would not be considered a scope limitation (discussed in Chapter 22).

In determining the sample size and selecting the specific accounts to be confirmed, the auditor should follow the guidance provided in Chapter 10. Guidance for extrapolating confirmation results to a conclusion about the total accounts receivable balance is also presented in that chapter.

Processing Confirmation Requests.   After selecting the accounts for confirmation, the auditor should observe the procedures below in processing the requests. They are applicable to both negative and positive confirmations (which are described and compared in later sections of this chapter).

- Names, addresses, and amounts shown on statements of accounts selected for confirmation or on the confirmation letters should be compared with the debtors' accounts and reviewed for reasonableness.
- The auditor should maintain control over confirmations until they are mailed; this does not preclude assistance from appropriate client personnel, under the auditor's supervision.
- Requests for confirmation, together with postage-paid return envelopes addressed to the auditor, should be mailed in envelopes showing the auditor's address as the return address. If the client objects to using the auditor's address, returns may be addressed to the client at a post office box controlled by the auditor; the post office should be directed to forward mail to the auditor after the box is surrendered.
- All requests should be mailed by the auditor; the client's mail room may be used for mechanical processing under the control of the auditor, who should deposit the completed requests at the post office.
- Undelivered requests returned by the post office should be investigated, corrected addresses obtained, and the requests remailed by the auditor.

The purpose of those procedures is not so much to protect against possible fraud on the part of the client (although that possibility is clearly implied) as to preserve the integrity of the confirmation procedure. The audit evidence obtained from confirmation is less reliable if there is the possibility of accidental or purposeful interference with direct communication with debtors; the auditor should take all reasonable steps to minimize that possibility.

Negative Confirmations. A negative confirmation is a request that a debtor communicate directly with the auditor only if the statement balance is considered in any way incorrect. It is most frequently used for clients with a large number of low-value accounts. Since debtors are asked to reply only if they wish to report differences, the auditor may conclude, in the absence of any reason to believe the contrary, that no reply signifies a debtor's acceptance of the balance.

It is important to impress on debtors the necessity for communicating directly with the auditor when discrepancies exist. If the auditor has reason to believe that the negative form of confirmation request will not receive consideration, sending out that form of confirmation request does not constitute compliance with generally accepted auditing standards. In that respect, SAS No. 1 (AU Section 331.05) states, in part,

> The negative form is useful particularly when the assessed level of control risk is low, when a large number of small balances are involved, and when the auditor has no reason to believe the persons receiving the requests are unlikely to give them consideration. If the negative rather than the positive form of confirmation is used, the number of requests sent or the extent of the other auditing procedures applied to the receivable balance should normally be greater in order for

the independent auditor to obtain the same degree of satisfaction with respect to the accounts receivable balance.

If statements of account are not ordinarily mailed at the time confirmations are requested, or if statements are not to be sent to debtors, the auditor may send a letter form of request. With appropriate changes of language to express the negative form, the positive confirmation letter shown in Figure 12.3 may be used.

If statements are sent to debtors, they may be rubber-stamped or have a sticker affixed reading somewhat as follows:

PLEASE EXAMINE THIS STATEMENT CAREFULLY.

If it is not correct, please write promptly, using the enclosed envelope and giving details of all differences, to our auditors,

[Name and Address of Auditors],

who are now making their periodic audit of our accounts.

Unless you promptly report a difference to our auditors, they will assume that you consider the statement to be correct.

Remittances should not be sent to the auditors.

It should be noted that the request is worded as coming from the client. Even though the auditor drafts the request, prepares it, and selects the accounts, all confirmation requests should be made in the client's name because the relationship exists between client and customer (or client and creditor, when liabilities are being confirmed) and information about it should not be given out to a third party without the client's authorization.

Depending on the circumstances of an engagement, negative confirmation requests may be supplemented by requests for positive confirmations, particularly of larger balances.

Positive Confirmations. A positive confirmation is a request that a debtor reply directly to the auditor stating whether the account balance is correct. Positive confirmations may be used for all accounts, a sample of accounts, or selected accounts, such as those with larger balances, those representing un-

Figure 12.3   Positive Confirmation Letter

[Name and Address of Debtor]

Dear Sirs:

In accordance with the request of our auditors [name and address of auditors], we ask that you kindly confirm to them your indebtedness to us at [date] which, according to our records, amounted to [amount].

If the amount shown is in agreement with your records, please so indicate by signing in the space provided below and return this letter directly to our auditors in the enclosed envelope. Your prompt compliance will facilitate the examination of our accounts.

If the amount is not in agreement with your records, please inform our auditors directly of the amount shown by your records, with full details of differences.

Remittances should not be sent to the auditors.

Very truly yours,

[Name of Client]

The above stated amount is correct as of [date].

[Debtor of Client]

[Title or Position]

usual or isolated transactions, or others for which an auditor needs greater specific assurance of existence and accuracy. The positive form of confirmation is called for if there are indications that a substantial number of accounts may be in dispute or inaccurate or if the individual receivable balances are unusually large or arise from sales to a few major customers. The request may be conveyed by a letter or directly on the statement by means of a rubber stamp or sticker. To facilitate replies, a postage-paid envelope addressed to the auditor should be enclosed.

Because the form of the request specifically asks for a reply, an auditor may not assume that failure to reply means the debtor agrees with the stated balance. Second requests should be sent, and sometimes third requests by registered mail. Replies to "positive" requests may be facilitated if the auditor furnishes the details of the individual items included in the balances, usually by providing a copy of the client's detailed customer statement. That may be particularly helpful if the debtor's accounting system does not readily permit identification of account balances. If the auditor fails to receive positive confirmation, alternative auditing procedures should be employed, as described later in the chapter.

It is impracticable for an auditor to determine the genuineness or authenticity of signatures on replies to confirmation requests. If the client has appropriate control structure policies and procedures, particularly with respect to the acceptance of customer orders, and if the auditor has considered the reasonableness of the addresses on the confirmations, signature authenticity is usually not a concern. If, however, the auditor has determined that the risk of material misstatement in a particular customer account is high, the client should be asked to request an officer of the debtor to sign the confirmation reply. The auditor may then wish to communicate with that officer by telephone or other means to corroborate the authenticity of the confirmation.

Experience has shown that a form of positive request, whether made by letter or a sticker affixed to the statement, that requires a minimum of effort on the part of the recipient produces more responses. The letter form, illustrated in Figure 12.3, is designed so that, when the amount shown agrees with the debtor's records, the individual need only sign in the space provided and return the letter in the envelope enclosed with the request.

If statements of account prepared by the client are to be used for positive confirmation requests, they may be sent in duplicate, with an appropriately worded request (often imprinted on the statement) that the debtor acknowledge the correctness of the statement by returning the duplicate, duly signed, directly to the auditor. A variation is the use of a monthly statement in which the balance and the name of the debtor appear in two places, separated by perforations. One part may be torn off, signed by the debtor, and returned directly to the auditor.

Confirmation Procedures as Affected by Certain Accounting Systems.   Replies to confirmation requests are sometimes difficult to obtain if a debtor's accounts payable processing is decentralized or uses an open invoice system, which is increasingly the case in a number of governmental departments and agencies as well as many large industrial and commercial enterprises. In an open invoice system, the debtor processes invoices individually and does not summarize them by vendor. Therefore, the debtor can identify whether or not an individual invoice has been paid, but cannot determine the total amount owed to any particular vendor. In many instances, however, such difficulties can be overcome with care and ingenuity; for example, an auditor may supply details of the balance to be confirmed, such as invoice dates, numbers (including customer purchase order numbers), and amounts, or may confirm specific transactions rather than an account balance.

The auditor can often make effective use of a client's computerized accounts receivable system. Sample selection can be programmed and the files of detail accounts searched automatically, lists and analyses can be prepared, and the confirmation request can be printed. General-purpose computer programs designed to aid in the confirmation process are available and are discussed in Chapter 11.

Exceptions to Confirmation Requests. Exceptions disclosed by the confirmation process should be carefully scrutinized by the auditor. The auditor should evaluate all exceptions and decide whether they represent isolated situations (such as a customer's not receiving goods, the client's not receiving a payment, or the wrong customer's being credited for a payment) or indicate a pattern of disputed sales or payments involving more than one customer. Debtors' responses indicating that payments were sent but not recorded by the client may signal misappropriations of cash and "lapping" of receivables (discussed below). If so, the situation should be thoroughly investigated to determine the amount of the misappropriation, and receivables should be reduced (since the client received the payment) and a loss recorded in the amount of the misappropriation. In addition, the auditor should bring the matter to management's attention and should consider its effect on his or her other auditing procedures.

In many instances, differences reported by debtors on accounts receivable confirmation requests do not have audit significance. Those differences are generally the result of either payments in transit at the confirmation date or delays in recording goods received by the debtor. The auditor should corroborate debtor assertions involving those kinds of differences by examining the cash receipts records and remittance advices for debtor payments received after the confirmation date to determine that the payments were for receivables existing at the confirmation date, and by examining bills of lading or other evidence of shipment. (Differences that are appropriately reconciled in this manner are not exceptions.) Those procedures are often performed on a sample basis. Other reported exceptions, usually involving small amounts, may result from disputes over allowances, discounts, shipping charges, or returned merchandise. These exceptions are usually neither material in amount nor indicative of serious deficiencies in the control structure. After the auditor has made a copy or other record for control purposes, investigation of replies may properly be turned over to a responsible client employee whose regular responsibilities do not involve cash, receivables, or credit functions. The auditor should review the employee's findings and, if considered necessary, perform additional procedures to obtain satisfaction about the balance.

Lapping

Lapping is a way of concealing a cash shortage by manipulating credits to the accounts receivable subsidiary ledger. To accomplish lapping, an employee must have access to incoming cash receipts, the cash receipts records, and the detailed accounts receivable records. Accordingly, if there is not appropriate segregation of duties, the auditor should consider the possibility of lapping and other irregularities.

Lapping is perpetrated in the following manner: An employee receives a customer's payment on an account receivable and misappropriates the cash, recording neither the cash receipt nor the reduction of the customer's account. Subsequent cash collections from another customer are later credited to the customer from whom the original collection was misappropriated, to prevent that customer's paid account from appearing as outstanding for more than a short time. Lapping is made easier when customers make periodic payments on their accounts, particularly in round amounts, rather than pay for specific invoices. Even if customers designate that remittances apply to specific invoices, the difference in amount between the second customer's remittance and the amount misappropriated from the first customer's remittance can be concealed by depositing additional cash if the subsequent payment is smaller or by making an additional credit to the first account, or even another account, if the subsequent payment is larger. Obviously, the lapping must continue indefinitely or until the cash shortage is replenished. Accordingly, the auditor should inquire about employees who are rarely absent from work or who do not take vacations that would require someone else to perform their work.

Control structure policies and procedures that should prevent or detect lapping include proper segregation of duties, required vacations for personnel responsible for handling cash and posting credits to customer accounts, mailing monthly statements to customers that show all activity in the accounts by dates, and reviewing entries to customers' accounts for unusual amounts.

The confirmation process, including careful attention to client explanations for delays in posting remittances when a customer states that the amount to be confirmed was paid before the confirmation date, should reveal lapping if it is present. If lapping is strongly suspected, the auditor may want to perform additional procedures. For example, comparing customer remittance advices with credits in the accounts receivable subsidiary ledger, individual amounts on deposit slips with individual amounts posted to the cash receipts records, and individual amounts in the cash receipts records with credits to individual customer accounts (in each case, scrutinizing the dates of the entry or posting) may also uncover lapping. The auditor should be aware, however, of the possibility of altered bank deposit slips and may wish to confirm the accuracy of individual deposit slips with banks.

Procedures in Lieu of Confirmation

If replies to confirmation requests cannot reasonably be expected or if the number and character of replies to positive confirmation requests are not satisfactory, the auditor should try to obtain satisfaction about the existence and accuracy of receivable balances by alternative procedures. These include examining relevant contracts, shipping documents, and subsequent cash receipts as evidence that the customer has received the shipment.

Tests for Valuation

To achieve the valuation audit objective, the auditor should review the collectibility of receivable balances to determine that the client's allowance for uncollectible accounts is adequate, that is, that receivables are stated at their net realizable value as of the balance sheet date. Before making the review, the auditor should determine whether the client's method of estimating the allowance is reasonable and consistent with prior years and, if so, whether any current business or economic conditions might make the method inappropriate in the current year. For example, if the client estimates an allowance for uncollectible accounts based on the historical relationship of write-offs to total sales (percent of sales method), a significant economic downturn may require a revision of the historical percentage. That same circumstance may also make it inappropriate to develop an allowance for uncollectible accounts by applying historical percentages to groupings of an aged trial balance. For example, usually only a small percentage of accounts receivable less than 30 days old become uncollectible; however, a large percentage of those balances may have to be considered in developing the allowance if the customer mix has changed in a time of economic distress.

Reviewing the Aged Trial Balance.   The usual starting point for an auditor's tests of valuation is an aged trial balance. The client should prepare periodic aging analyses as a routine procedure; if that is not done, the auditor should ask the client to prepare one. The auditor may be able to provide the client with a general-purpose computer program for aging accounts receivable. The auditor should compare the total shown on the analysis with the total receivables in the ledger and should obtain an understanding of how the aging was prepared. If it is produced by a computer software package, the auditor needs to know what options in the software the client uses. (This may be done during tests of controls.) Depending on the auditor's risk assessment, he or she may test to establish the accuracy of the analysis.

In reviewing an aging analysis, the most obvious aspect to evaluate is the number and dollar amount of overdue accounts. The auditor should probe more deeply than that, however, and scrutinize a number of accounts closely for evidence that might indicate collectibility problems. The auditor's purpose in inquiring into those matters is not to judge the collectibility of each individual account examined, but to gather evidence that the client's investigation and evaluation of individual accounts (usually performed by the credit manager) were adequate and that the overall allowance for uncollectible accounts is reasonable.

The auditor should review past-due receivable balances and other unusual balances with the credit manager to obtain information on which to base an opinion regarding their collectibility. Files of correspondence with collection agents and debtors should be examined. Past experience in collecting overdue accounts should be used as a guide in deciding the probable collectibility of current balances. Changes in the number and size of overdue accounts and possible changes in business conditions affecting collectibility should be discussed with the credit manager. As a result of those reviews and discussions, the auditor should understand the basis for the client's estimate of the allowance for uncollectible accounts and be able to judge whether the allowance is reasonable. Auditing accounting estimates is discussed further in Chapter 9.

Other Procedures. The auditor should also scan revenue and receivable transactions after the balance sheet date, including sales, cash receipts, discounts allowed, rebates, returns, and write-offs. Those transactions—or their absence or an unusual increase or decrease in them—may reveal abnormal conditions affecting valuation at the balance sheet date. Events after the close of the fiscal period are often the best proof of whether the receivable balances at the balance sheet date are actually what they purport to be. Approvals for notes and accounts receivable written off during the year should be examined.

Notes receivable, whether past due or current, may themselves signal doubtful collectibility if they were received for overdue accounts receivable. The origin of notes should be determined because current notes may sometimes represent renewals of matured notes. If usual trade practice is to obtain notes from debtors of poor credit standing, the collectibility of the notes should be considered in the same way as other receivables.

The collectibility of notes that collateral has been pledged against may depend on the value of the collateral. If the collectibility of significant collateralized notes is in question, the auditor may find it desirable to have an independent appraiser value the collateral.

The auditor should be particularly attentive to revenue transactions that the client has entered into that include contingent sales agreements, customer rights of return, repurchase agreements, or other ''special'' terms that call into question the collectibility of the receivable and even the entity's legal rights to the revenue. The possibility of misapplication of GAAP increases when those revenue transactions are with related parties. Many audit failures were caused by the auditor's not sufficiently understanding the nature of the client's business and the substance of transactions the enterprise entered into. Detecting unusual and complex revenue transactions is particularly difficult if management consciously withholds information from the auditor. Understanding the client's industry and the transactions the client enters into is an essential first step in determining the proper accounting for and reporting of these types of transactions.

The auditor should pay particular attention to large or unusual transactions recorded at or near year-end. The auditor may also scrutinize the appropriate journals for unusual entries, and should ask management whether transactions like those described above exist. Also, the auditor should perform analytical procedures in the overall review stage of the audit, as required by SAS No. 56, *Analytical Procedures* (AU Section 329). Generally, those are the same procedures (described earlier) as performed during the planning stage, but based on year-end data.

Tests of Rights and Obligations, and Presentation and Disclosure

Receivables from affiliates, directors, officers, and employees should be reviewed to determine that they have been properly authorized and are actually what they purport to be. If loans have been made over a long period of time, past experience often provides evidence of the debtors' intentions. It is good practice to review those receivable accounts even though they appear to have been settled before the balance sheet date, especially to see whether the loans were renewed after the balance sheet date. Receivables that in fact represent advances or loans should be segregated and so described. Disclosure on the balance sheet of receivables from affiliates, directors, officers, and employees does not reflect on the integrity of those debtors.

Proper presentation and disclosure of accounts receivable and sales also require that liens, security interests, and accounts receivable pledged as loan collateral be identified. Accordingly, the auditor should review debt and lease agreements; confirmation replies, particularly from financial institutions; and minutes of directors' meetings. The auditor should also inquire of management about those items.

Throughout the audit, the auditor should be alert for transactions or issues that affect the audit objectives of rights and obligations, and presentation and disclosure. The auditor considers all evidence related to other audit objectives in determining whether the recorded receivables are the legal rights of the entity and all necessary disclosures have been made. In particular, many of the "other procedures" (described above) used to test valuation also address these audit objectives.

Other Substantive Tests

In some circumstances, even though receivable balances have been confirmed, the auditor may consider it advisable to compare, on a test basis, billings, shipping documents, and other data with recorded transactions in accounts receivable for some period. (Those comparisons, if made for a period immediately before and after the fiscal year-end, also help determine that a proper sales cutoff was made. Improper cutoffs may result from errors or from intentional recording of sales in an improper period because of bonus arrangements, sales quotas, royalty agreements, income tax considerations, or other reasons.) Comparisons made on a test basis spread throughout the period help to achieve the completeness and accuracy objectives.

Substantive tests to provide assurance about the completeness of invoicing of goods shipped and recording of goods invoiced may consist primarily of analytical procedures applied to revenue cycle accounts, plus an analysis of the size and direction of adjustments to recorded inventory quantities as a result of the client's physical inventory count. Analytical procedures are helpful in providing assurance that sales and accounts receivable are neither understated nor overstated. Tests of the reasonableness of recorded sales and analytical comparisons of accounts and relationships may provide much assurance about completeness of sales and receivables. In addition, if there are few instances where perpetual inventory quantities must be reduced as a result of the physical count, the risk of unbilled or unrecorded receivables may be sufficiently reduced to the point where analytical procedures may provide most of any additional assurance needed about the completeness of recorded revenues and receivables.

The auditor usually examines credit memos issued during a period after the close of the fiscal year to determine that reported sales were not inflated by recording unauthorized sales in one year and issuing credit memos to eliminate them in the next year, and that proper provision has been made in the year under audit for any such credit memos and for applicable discounts, returns, and allowances. The auditor should be alert for sales under terms permitting customers to return unsold merchandise.

If the auditor finds that consigned goods are treated as sales and included in receivable balances, with a resulting anticipation of profits, the unsold goods in the hands of consignees (which should be confirmed) should be adjusted to the basis of like items in the merchandise inventory and reclassified as inventory. If the goods appear to be salable at an adequate margin of profit, related charges, such as freight paid by the consignor, may be added to the inventory costs.

The auditor should read sales contracts with selling agents and other agreements affecting receivables to become aware of matters such as title to accounts receivable, time of billings, method or time of payments, commissions, and special discounts or rebates.

The auditor should examine receivables other than trade accounts—such as debit balances in accounts payable, claims, and advances—by reviewing the recorded transactions and noting supporting evidence. Those accounts should be precisely identified to determine the extent of testing and to evaluate their collectibility and their classification in the balance sheet. The auditor should obtain confirmations by direct communication with debtors to the extent considered reasonable and practicable. Although those receivables may not be significant in amount, if they are not subject to adequate control structure policies and procedures, they may require relatively more extensive substantive testing than trade receivables.

The auditor should determine that drafts sent for collection are recorded in the accounts, either separately as drafts receivable or included in accounts receivable. The auditor should also inquire of the banks where drafts have been deposited for collection or from which loans or advances on account of foreign shipments have been obtained, to learn whether drafts have been pledged against loans or advances. Drafts in the hands of collection agents should be confirmed and their status determined as of the balance sheet date. Since the auditor cannot always use the usual confirmation procedures to substantiate receivable balances from foreign debtors, the existence of drafts may help to substantiate those balances.

Analytical procedures are particularly helpful in substantiating certain types of revenues. For example, the auditor can usually substantiate dues, tuition, and similar revenues rather easily by comparing receipts with membership or registration records. Sometimes the substantiation can be done on an overall basis: number of members or students multiplied by annual dues or tuition. At other times it is necessary to compare (usually on a test basis) individual items from the accounting records with the membership or registration rolls. In auditing revenues from services, there is often independently generated statistical data, such as numbers of rooms cleaned, beds made, meals served, and the like, that can be used to corroborate revenues.

AUDITING PROCEDURES: SPECIAL CONSIDERATIONS FOR PARTICULAR TYPES OF REVENUES

For the most part, the auditing procedures described so far in this chapter are adaptable to the great variety of circumstances encountered in practice. One auditing procedure may take on greater significance than another, or certain procedures may be used more extensively, but on the whole auditing procedures for many accounts in the revenue cycle are basically similar. Some of the more common revenue sources that require emphasis on particular procedures are the following:

- Cash sales.
- Interest, rents, and similar fixed payments for the use of property.
- Royalties, production payments, and similar variable revenues.
- Gifts and donations.
- Deferred income or unearned revenue.
- Revenues from long-term contracts.

Chapter 17 discusses auditing procedures for income from marketable securities and other investments.

Cash Sales

If cash sales are significant, asset protection control procedures are especially important. Cash sales are characteristic of relatively small unit value goods, which often are easily converted to cash and at the same time are difficult to keep under strict physical and accounting control. In many situations involving cash sales, segregating duties between access to merchandise and access to cash receipts is difficult, if not impossible, and enterprise management will often devise creative control procedures to compensate. Often, those procedures involve bringing the customer into the enterprise's control structure, possibly by creating incentives for the customer to demand a receipt for amounts paid (which is generated only when the sale is recorded) —perhaps to qualify for a prize or premium or to support a later merchandise return or exchange. Control over cash after it has been received and recorded is discussed in Chapter 15.

Interest, Rents, and Similar Fixed Payments for the Use of Property

Revenues from fixed payments can usually be substantiated fairly easily by an overall computation of amounts due and a comparison with amounts recorded. Usually, the client prepares a list of the properties, loans, and so on, and the related income; the auditor should test the list by examining leases, loan agreements, and similar contractual bases for revenues, noting and evaluating all special terms that have financial statement implications. The auditor may also assess control procedures applied to the receipt and recording of revenues, including measures for controlling and accounting for the vacancy rate in rental properties, and should note and evaluate delinquencies and arrearages and their implications for the realization of the related assets. Some or all significant loans receivable should be confirmed; the auditor may also wish to confirm leases and similar contractual obligations.

In particular, the auditor will be concerned about audit risk relating to revenue and cash flow from leased assets owned by a lessor. In obtaining an understanding of control structure policies and procedures and assessing control risk relating to leases, the auditor should focus on the completeness and accuracy of recorded revenue. This may require the auditor to evaluate how management arrived at the salvage value of leased property. For example, if a lessor leases a newly manufactured piece of equipment for a period of ten years, management may be required, depending on the equipment and the terms of the lease, to estimate the value of the equipment at the end of the ten years in order to properly record revenue from the transaction. In this situation, the auditor would need to know how management estimated salvage value and what factors it considered.

The auditor of the lessor is also concerned with the existence audit objective. Since the leased asset is not on the client's premises, the auditor is unable to determine its existence and condition by physical inspection. Most often the auditor will achieve the existence objective by direct confirmation with the lessee and by applying analytical procedures. The auditor should obtain evidence that the accounting classification, measurement, and disclosure requirements for lessors, as specified in Statement of Financial Accounting Standards No. 13 and related pronouncements (Accounting Standards Section L10), have been followed. Lease transactions are discussed in Chapter 18.

Royalties, Production Payments, and Similar Variable Revenues

Many kinds of revenues are based on a stipulated variable, such as production or sales. Usually, the buyer of a right subject to variable payments for its use is required to report to the seller from time to time the amount of the variable and the computation of the resulting payment. If the amount of revenue is not significant, most companies simply accept the payer's statement after a superficial scrutiny for reasonableness. In that event, the auditor can do much the same, by examining the agreement on which the payment is based, comparing receipts with those of the prior year, and possibly requesting confirmation that all amounts due have been reported and paid. If amounts are significant, contracts usually provide for an independent audit of the accounting for the variable, either by the seller's auditor or by an independent auditor acceptable to the seller. Satisfactory audit reports on the payments ordinarily provide reasonable assurance that the related revenues are complete. Such reports on parts of a financial statement are discussed and illustrated in Chapter 23.

Gifts and Donations

Accountability for donations can be a problem because they are rarely covered by contract and they lack a delivery of goods or services to provide evidence that the revenue is due. If gifts are received centrally—as in development offices of colleges, hospitals, museums, and similar institutions—reasonably effective control procedures can be established: properly supervised opening of mail and recording of receipts; segregation of duties among handling, acknowledging, and recording; and early accountability through means such as issuing prenumbered receipt forms that also serve as documentation for tax purposes. The auditor can test those policies and procedures in the same way as conventional cash receipts.

If donations are received by numerous volunteers—as in many agencies financed by "annual drives"—the control structure is likely to be ineffective because management may feel it is impolitic or impossible to ask volunteers to submit to control procedures. In those cases, the auditor may have to make it clear in the audit report that he or she cannot express an opinion that all donations were recorded, and that the report covers only "recorded receipts."

It is possible, however, to establish an adequate control structure for volunteer solicitations, as the methods used in many United Way drives have proven. Solicitation forms are prepared in advance, and their issuance to volunteers, processing, and return are controlled. The possibility of abuse is thus minimized though not eliminated. When those policies and procedures are in effect, the auditor can test them and usually obtain reasonable assurance that gift revenue is complete.

Deferred Income or Unearned Revenue

Sometimes the accounting system provides trial balances of detailed items supporting deferred income or unearned revenue balances, for example, students' advance payments of tuition. In those cases, the auditor can obtain the necessary assurance by reviewing the trial balance and comparing it with the control account, and examining individual items.

More often, transactions flowing through unearned revenue accounts are not controlled in detail. The input to the account may be on one basis—for example, ticket sales or subscription receipts—and the relief of the account may be on a different basis—a statistical measure of service delivered such as revenue per passenger mile or per issue delivered. In those cases, the client makes a periodic analysis or "inventory" of the account balance. That inventory consists of scrutinizing the detail of underlying data, for example, of subscription records or of transportation tickets subsequently "lifted." It can often be an extremely arduous and time-consuming effort, comparable in many ways to physically counting inventories. For that reason, the date selected is usually based on practicality and convenience, and seldom coincides with the fiscal year-end.

The auditor's observation of and participation in the analysis should be similar to the observation and testing of physical inventory procedures. The auditor should observe and test the client's procedures and evaluate the results. If control procedures appear adequate and the resulting adjustment of the account balance is small enough to indicate that the method of relieving the account is reasonably accurate, the auditor can be satisfied with applying analytical procedures to activity and balances between the test date and year-end.

Often, a client believes that an unearned revenue "inventory" is impossible or prohibitively expensive. For a transit company, for example, the unearned revenue balance represents tokens in the hands of the public, and there is no way—short of changing the token—to identify those bought before a given date. If the client cannot or will not substantiate the balance, neither can the auditor. The auditor can nevertheless usually obtain reasonable assurance that the balance is fairly stated in relation to the financial statements as a whole, by paying particular attention to tests of controls that provide evidence that all revenue commitments sold—tickets, tokens, subscriptions, and the like—are controlled and promptly recorded and that amounts transferred from unearned to earned revenue are accurately and consistently computed and well controlled, and by considering the relationship between the balance and the pattern of sales and service activity and investigating changes in the ratio. As long as transfers to revenue for estimates of lost and unused items are made on a conservative basis, the auditor can conclude that the amount is biased toward overstating the liability for service to be rendered.

Revenues from Long-Term Contracts

Audit evidence for revenues from long-term contracts is obtained from confirmations and the various means management uses to monitor and control fulfillment of contract terms and the allocation of revenues to fiscal periods. The client should provide the auditor with an analysis of each contract and the change orders that act as amendments. In many instances, an analysis prepared for management purposes will suffice, but in others an analysis will have to be prepared especially for audit purposes. Depending on the size and significance of the contracts, the auditor can compare the analysis with underlying data, including the contract itself, and review the accounting for costs incurred to date, the estimates of cost to complete each contract, and the amounts of revenue recorded in the period under audit. Such reviews should be done with operating personnel responsible for performance, as well as accounting and financial personnel.

Revenues from long-term contracts are usually accounted for by the percentage-of-completion method. Under that method, revenues and receivables are recognized in proportion to the degree of completion of a contract. Accordingly, the auditor's primary objective is to obtain evidence about the reasonableness of the client's estimate of the degree of completion of the project. The client's estimate may be made by relating costs incurred to date to the estimated total cost to complete the contract (the cost-to-cost method), by obtaining an architect's or engineer's estimate of the state of completion, or by physical measurement (usually accompanied by the auditor's observation) of the stage of completion, such as the number of production units completed. Further discussion of auditing accounting estimates is presented in Chapter 9.

After reviewing the client's documentation supporting the estimated total cost to complete a project, the auditor should compare the estimate with the contract price. If the estimated total cost to satisfy contract requirements exceeds the total contract price, a loss should usually be recognized. The auditor should also review the client's financial statement presentation, including disclosures, for conformity with the recommendations for long-term contracts found in the latest edition of the AICPA audit and accounting guide, *Construction Contractors*.

It is also usually necessary to test other accounts related to long-term contracts—such as progress billings and advance payments. Accordingly, the auditor should perform, as appropriate in the circumstances, the procedures related to billings, collections, and receivables that were discussed earlier in this chapter. Further discussion of auditing long-term contracts is presented in Chapter 28.

13

Auditing the Buying Cycle

This chapter covers the "buying cycle": the acquisition of goods and services in exchange for cash or promises to pay cash. The buying cycle is part of the larger "expenditure cycle" that comprises all transactions in which assets are produced or acquired, expenses are incurred, and payments are made to discharge liabilities incurred. Since the expenditure cycle is too broad to be covered in a single chapter and because it is usually more efficient to divide the cycle into more manageable segments when performing an audit, the expenditure cycle is discussed in several chapters. The discussion in this chapter is limited to auditing transactions involving purchases of and payments for goods and services generally, including human resources, and accounts related to those transactions. Expenditures that present specific auditing issues are covered elsewhere: Auditing the production of goods, cost of sales, and inventory balances is discussed in Chapter 14; prepayments and accruals, including pension expense, in Chapter 16; property, plant, and equipment and related accounts, in Chapter 18; income tax accounts, in Chapter 19; and loss contingencies, in Chapter 21.

ACCOUNTS RELATED TO THE BUYING CYCLE

Transactions that are part of the buying cycle affect numerous balance sheet and income statement accounts. The term "accounts payable" is used to describe specific amounts owed by an entity, usually arising from purchases of goods or services. It represents amounts due to suppliers of merchandise, materials, supplies, or services, and evidenced by vendors' invoices. Buying activities that generate accounts payable involve purchases of merchandise or raw materials and the incurring of selling, general, administrative, and other expenses.

Depending on their purpose, expenditures for payroll may be recorded as assets, expenses, or both. Amounts withheld from employees' gross pay for such items as federal and state income taxes and miscellaneous authorized deductions are recorded as agency obligations (amounts held in trust for third parties) until such time as the liabilities are paid. Similar obligations arise from payroll taxes and fringe benefits paid by employers. At the end of an accounting period, salaries and wages earned but not yet paid are recorded as an accrued payroll liability. Other related accruals must be recorded for certain compensated absences and rights to severance pay. Agency obligations and accrued liabilities are discussed in Chapter 16.

Selling expenses include expenditures for sales personnel salaries, commissions, and expenses, and other costs of selling goods and services, such as advertising, delivery, and sales department overhead. Also classified as selling expenses are warehousing costs for inventory pending sale, estimated losses from uncollectible accounts, and credit and collection expenses.

General and administrative expenses include executive salaries and costs associated with an enterprise's general offices and departments, corporate expenses such as business licenses and fees, costs of reports to stockholders, and legal and auditing fees. Charges related to the occupancy of buildings, like rent, depreciation, utilities, maintenance, taxes, and insurance, are usually allocated among manufacturing, selling, general, and administrative activities. Other expense accounts affected by transactions in the buying cycle include research and development, maintenance and repairs, and travel and entertainment.

TYPICAL TRANSACTIONS, ACCOUNTING SYSTEMS, AND CONTROL PROCEDURES

The procedures involved in buying goods and services in most contemporary businesses can be classified into three typical classes of transactions.

- Acquisition of goods and services.
- Payments made for goods and services.
- Goods returned to suppliers.

Conceptually, payrolls are part of the buying cycle, but the related control procedures are somewhat unique. Accordingly, two additional classes of transactions are often identified.

- Payroll processing.
- Payment of wages.

Acquisition of Goods and Services

The process of acquiring goods and services includes the following steps:

- Determining needs.
- Ordering.
- Receiving, inspecting, and accepting goods.
- Storing or using.
- Recording.

In considering the accounting system that processes buying transactions and the control procedures applied to them, the auditor is interested mainly in procedures to ensure that all purchase transactions that actually occurred are authorized and are recorded accurately; that is, that the control objectives of completeness, accuracy, and authorization for transaction processing and files are met. Those control objectives are closely related to the audit objectives of completeness, accuracy, and existence of buying cycle accounts, particularly purchases and accounts payable. Other control procedures, while not directly related to those audit objectives, may also be of interest to the auditor. For example, management reviews of open purchase orders may generate reports the auditor can use in evaluating whether there are unrealized losses on open purchase commitments, which affects the valuation audit objective.

The paragraphs that follow describe the various activities involved in the purchase of goods and services, and the control procedures typically applied in processing the transactions. (Later sections discuss the audit relevance of those procedures.)

Determining Needs.   The buying cycle starts when someone identifies a need, which may occur in several different ways. For example,

- Raw material inventory replenishment needs may be determined by a person or automatically when stock on hand reaches a reorder point or when a bill of materials for a job order is prepared. Some computerized systems may identify needs by reference to records of quantities on hand or production orders and simultaneously execute some of the steps in the buying process, for example, selecting vendors and preparing purchase orders. In certain sophisticated systems, raw material needs are identified and the order is placed with the vendor without any human intervention. The company's computer communicates directly with the vendor's computer.
- Needs for occasional goods and services are identified and described by the user, usually on a requisition form that is then approved by the person (who may be the same as the user) with authority over the user's department or the particular type of purchase.
- The need for some services that are provided on a recurring basis by the same vendor, such as utilities, telephone, periodicals, or maintenance services, is usually determined initially and thereafter provided continuously until the end of the contract period or until it is determined that the service is no longer needed or a different supplier is selected.
- Determining the need for specialized services, like insurance, advertising, and legal and auditing services, is ordinarily the responsibility of designated individuals.
- Needs for fixed assets are usually identified by a capital budgeting process.

Control procedures for requisitions typically include review and authorization by a responsible individual and accounting for the numerical sequence of prenumbered requisition forms. Those control procedures are designed to ensure that only necessary goods and services are ordered and that all items requisitioned are actually ordered. While the purpose of these procedures is more closely related to management's decision making than to financial statement assertions, the procedures may have an effect on certain financial statement accounts. For example, if review and authorization procedures for requisitions are absent or ineffective, inventory may become overstocked and eventually obsolete, thereby reducing its value.

Ordering.   In most large enterprises, trained purchasing agents rather than personnel from user departments determine sources, negotiate terms, and place orders. Vendor selection and monitoring can be important control procedures affecting both accounts payable and inventory. A separate purchasing function can provide cost savings to the company and enhance control over purchases by providing a division of duties.

Accumulating requisitions before purchase orders are placed requires specialized skills and experience to group items most efficiently, concentrate orders to obtain volume discounts while also maintaining multiple sources of supply, solicit bids effectively, negotiate schedules for vendor production and storage prior to delivery, and generally get the best possible prices and services. Absent or ineffective control procedures in this area are often difficult to quantify, because the cost of inefficient purchasing is generally not measurable, although a lack of effective control procedures usually results in an increase in the cost of items acquired.

When the purchasing department receives a requisition, typically it first determines that the amount and type of goods or services being requisitioned have been approved by an individual with the appropriate authority. The requisition then serves as the source document for inputting the order or, in a manual system, preparing the purchase order. In a computerized system, the requisition information may be input and matched against vendor, price, and (if applicable) inventory master files to assist in vendor selection, evaluating quoted prices, and determining the accuracy of product numbers or descriptions. After all of the specific information about the purchase, such as time and method of delivery, specifications for materials, and quantity and price, have been determined, a purchase order is generated and the open purchase order file is updated. The purchase order authorizes a vendor to deliver goods or services and bill on specified terms, and also authorizes the receiving department to accept the goods described. Since purchase orders authorize execution of transactions, control procedures for issuing them are generally in place. Typically, access to unissued purchase orders is restricted to prevent unauthorized personnel from initiating purchase transactions. Vendors may not be aware of or may not verify whether orders are placed by authorized individuals. While this may not have a financial statement impact, it could result in overstocking or the purchase of unnecessary items.

Prenumbering purchase orders and subsequently accounting for the numerical sequence help ensure that company personnel are aware of all open purchase commitments. That awareness is necessary to ensure that appropriate provisions for losses on purchase commitments are recorded.

Control procedures directed toward the accuracy and authorization of purchase orders typically include comparing them with requisition forms and reviewing them for approval by an authorized individual. These procedures are performed before orders are placed with vendors. An additional control procedure directed toward the accuracy of orders may be giving requisitioners copies of the purchase orders for them to review for conformity with their expectations. Purchase orders with small dollar amounts or routine characteristics may be subjected to a less detailed review.

Some specialized goods and services cannot be handled by a purchasing department because the technical and performance requirements are too specialized or in some cases cannot be specified in advance. For example, the purchase of property and casualty insurance generally requires an insurance risk analysis. This analysis and the subsequent negotiations with an independent insurance agent or broker require special skill and training. Such specialized purchases must be negotiated directly between representatives of the responsible department and the vendor. Bypassing the purchasing department is likely to be a persistent and sometimes highly sensitive problem for most companies because of the conflict between the need for control procedures that a centralized purchasing function can provide, and the desires of individual users, who may believe they can get better quality and service by dealing directly with vendors. Deciding where to draw the line between operating autonomy and centralized purchasing varies from company to company, but even in companies with highly centralized purchasing functions some specialized services are allowed to bypass them. In those situations, control procedures typically include requirements that agreements be in writing, goods be approved on receipt, and the user approves the invoices.

Receiving, Inspecting, and Accepting Goods.   In many enterprises the volume of receiving is so large that the receiving function is carried out in a specially organized department separate from the requisitioning, purchasing, and accounting departments. A separate receiving department enhances control over purchases by providing a division of duties.

The receiving function typically inspects goods for conformity with specifications on purchase orders. Quantities are verified by counting, weighing, or measuring. To improve the likelihood that receiving personnel will independently determine quantities, some systems provide for omitting quantities from the copy of the purchase order sent to the receiving department or, in a computerized system, restricting receiving personnel's access to quantity information on the open order file. The receivers also determine the quality of goods as far as possible, including whether or not there is shipping damage. Inspection of incoming goods is an essential control procedure for management's purposes. Laboratory or technical analysis of goods may be necessary in some cases to determine that their quality meets specifications. This requires specialized technical skills and is usually assigned to an appropriately staffed inspection department.

The purchasing and accounting departments are notified of the receipt and acceptance of shipments. Receiving personnel generally document receipts on a receiving report, a packing slip sent with the goods by the vendor, or a copy of the purchase order. The information provided includes vendor, date received, quantity and condition of goods received, and sometimes the carrier. The document is signed by whoever received the goods. In a computerized system, the receiver may input the information directly into the system, which then updates the open purchase order file, indicating that all or a portion of the order was received; generates a receiving report and an open receiving report file; and sometimes also updates the perpetual inventory file. Receipts that cannot be matched with an open purchase order may not be accepted by the receiving department; if they are accepted, they are reported on an exception report for investigation and follow-up, which are typically performed by accounting personnel. Whether prepared manually or by computer, receiving reports are generally prenumbered and their numerical sequence is subsequently accounted for. This control procedure is designed to ensure that goods received are reported completely and on a timely basis to prevent understatement of accounts payable and costs or inventory.

Services and some goods do not arrive through the receiving department but are received directly by users. While formal procedures may be prescribed for users to originate receiving reports, more often the vendor's invoice for the service or goods is forwarded to the user for approval and acknowledgment of receipt.

Storing or Using. Goods received through the receiving department are forwarded to the appropriate location for storage or use. Control procedures for storing purchased goods and issuing them to production are covered in Chapter 14, ''Auditing the Production Cycle, Cost of Sales, and Inventory Balances.''

Recording. An asset or expense and the related liability are most often recorded by people independent of the ordering and receiving functions on the basis of a vendor's invoice that has been matched to an approved purchase order, and of evidence that goods were received or services performed. In some computerized systems, perpetual inventory records are posted when the receiving department inputs the receipt; alternatively, the accounting department may post the inventory records using a copy of the receiving report. Receiving reports not matched with invoices at the end of a period should generate an entry to record a liability for goods received but not billed.

Failure to apply control procedures to vendors' invoices as soon as they are received is a common control structure deficiency, particularly if many invoices must be routed for approval to operating personnel whose main interests are directed elsewhere. The resulting delay in recording invoices may, depending on the accounting system and related control procedures, cause accounts payable and the related asset or expense accounts to be misstated and may result in the loss of discounts for prompt payment. (A large number of unmatched invoices or receiving reports that have not been approved and recorded may indicate deficiencies, breakdowns, or delays in the procedures for processing and approving invoices.)

In a manual system, invoices may be listed in a log upon receipt and the log subsequently reviewed for invoices that were not returned to the accounting department for processing. In a computerized system, invoices may not be specifically approved, but may be recorded based on the authorization of the related purchase orders and on evidence that receiving reports are properly matched to purchase orders. The invoices would then be matched to the open receiving report file; invoices that did not match would be reported on an exception report and updated to a temporary file of unmatched invoices.

Once invoices have been authorized for recording, the transactions are recorded in a manual or computerized purchases journal and are then summarized and posted. Before recording transactions in a manual system, a clerk usually recomputes the calculations on the invoices and compares them with amounts on the purchase orders. The account distribution is reviewed and entered (sometimes an initial account distribution is noted on the purchase order) to prevent transactions from being misclassified. Cutoff procedures to ensure that invoices are recorded in the proper period include reviewing the receiving report file, with attention to the dates goods were received.

The process of authorizing invoices for recording may be reviewed and approved by supervisors. Alternatively, invoices may be approved by supervisors when checks for payment are prepared or when they are signed. Supervisory review and approval are sometimes performed on only a representative sample of vendors' invoices or on specific types of invoices, most commonly if the entity has a large volume of low-dollar-value transactions and effective control procedures.

File control procedures consist primarily of supervising reconciliations of accounts payable subsidiary ledgers to control accounts. If the entity does not maintain accounts payable subsidiary ledgers, as is the case in some manual systems, the reconciliation of total open (unpaid) invoices to the accounts payable control account is subjected to supervisory review. The resolution of errors detected by the reconciliation and review processes is also adequately supervised. Segregating the duties of those who approve invoices, post the detailed inventory and accounts payable records, maintain control accounts, perform the reconciliations and reviews, and resolve errors also enhances the effectiveness of control procedures.

Payments Made for Goods and Services

Control procedures relating to the cash disbursements process—the second transaction class in the buying cycle—are intended to ensure that no unauthorized payments are made, that accurate records are made of each payment, and that unclaimed checks are adequately identified, controlled, and ultimately voided. Other procedures, more closely related to management decision making than to financial statement assertions, are designed to ensure that all liabilities are paid in ways that meet cash flow and vendor relationship objectives, including taking all available discounts for timely payment.

To prevent unauthorized payments, approvals are required for all requests for payment, and invoices and receiving documents are canceled after the related checks have been signed, so that those documents cannot be submitted for processing again. Control procedures to accomplish those objectives may be manual or computerized, and are enhanced if there is division of duties between those who prepare checks and those who originate requests for payment. The check signer should have evidence, at the time the check is signed, that the payment has been authorized. Computerized systems may prevent checks from being printed unless the invoice matches the appropriate purchase files. Asset protection control procedures require the signer to mail or handle signed checks in a way that makes them inaccessible to the people who authorize or process payments; unissued checks are safeguarded, and spoiled checks are mutilated or otherwise controlled.

If the number of employees is limited and the same person performs duties that are incompatible from a strict internal control viewpoint, some measure of control can be achieved by involving the supervisor in the processing. For example, sometimes the same person records payments to vendors and draws the checks. In this situation, the supervisor who signs the checks might require that all supporting evidence accompany the checks presented for signature and might assign someone other than the processor to cancel the supporting documents and mail the checks directly to the vendors.

Checks are drawn specifically to the order of the creditors being paid or to custodians of imprest funds being reimbursed, not to "cash" or "bearer." Drawing checks to the order of a specific entity or individual limits their negotiability and provides an acknowledgment of receipt through payees' endorsements.

Countersignatures are an effective control procedure only if each signer makes an independent examination of checks and supporting documents. Although a countersignature affixed with proper understanding and discharge of assigned responsibility provides effective control, signature by a single employee after careful examination of supporting documents offers greater protection than superficial countersignatures, which create an illusion of control and could result in reliance by one person on functions not performed by another.

Control procedures to ensure that all acknowledged liabilities are paid in time to take advantage of cash discounts, promote good relations with suppliers, and maintain the enterprise's credit rating are more closely related to management's decision making than to financial statement assertions. Timely payments are ensured by periodic reviews of files of unmatched receiving reports and invoices and by the aging of open accounts payable.

Complete and accurate recording of payments is controlled by prenumbering checks, maintaining a detailed check register, accounting for the numerical sequence of checks entered in the register, and comparing paid checks returned by the bank with the check register as part of the periodic reconciliation of cash in banks. After appropriate inquiry into the reasons for long-outstanding checks, payment is stopped at the bank and the accounts are adjusted either to reverse the original entries or to record the items in a separate liability account.

Supervision of the cash disbursements process is provided by the check signer's review of supporting documentation, the review of bank reconciliations, and the reconciliation and review of the accounts payable trial balance.

Goods Returned to Suppliers

Every credit due an enterprise because goods are returned or an allowance is negotiated is an asset equivalent to a receivable, although its recording is usually different, as discussed below. It is important, therefore, that these claims be adequately controlled, even though they are likely to be nonroutine and infrequent. Many companies also have policies and procedures for processing their own internally generated debit memos.

Returns for credit must be prepared for shipment to the vendor; the shipping department usually has procedures for notifying the accounts payable and purchasing departments at the time items are returned. Policies and procedures similar to those used for sales can be used, for example, requiring all shipping documents and supporting materials to be accompanied by a numerically controlled debit memo, usually prepared by the purchasing department and recorded in a debit memo journal by the accounting department. (Chapter 12, "Auditing the Revenue Cycle," discusses those policies and procedures.) Control of freight claims can usually be achieved in a similar manner.

When a credit memo is received from a vendor, it is matched to the related debit memo, if any, shipping documents, or other relevant internally generated documents. Quantities returned, prices, dates, vendor's name, extensions, and footings are compared by personnel independent of the purchasing, shipping, and inventory control functions. If companies have formal debit memo procedures, credits and claims are often deducted immediately from the next vendor payment without waiting for a vendor credit memo.

Claims for allowances, adjustments, and occasional returns that are not subject to the above procedures are subject to some procedure for notifying the accounting and purchasing departments of a dispute or claim due. Since there are no positive means for controlling compliance with that type of procedure, knowledgeable personnel throughout the company are periodically asked about the existence of outstanding claims or allowances.

Even though they represent a valid asset, vendor credit memos or internally generated debit memos are usually not recorded as receivables, but rather are recorded as reductions of the payable to the vendor because a legal right of offset ordinarily exists in such instances. If this offsetting results in a debit balance in a vendor payable account, the debit balance may be recorded as a receivable. Vendor debit balances are usually not reclassified unless the total amount of such accounts is material. If they are reclassified because they are material, it is necessary to consider appropriate allowances for collectibility, because the debit balances may arise from deposits with vendors who no longer do business with the company.

Payroll Processing

Payroll processing is the one function most likely to have similar characteristics from one entity to another, which is one reason that payroll processing is the service most commonly offered by data processing service organizations. Over the years, payroll transaction processing has become increasingly systematized and generally well controlled. The typical payroll transaction is distinguished from other buying cycle transactions by the withholding of amounts to cover various types of employee obligations (for example, taxes and insurance premiums) and by different control procedures.

Payroll processing includes

- Authorizing employment.
- Recording time worked or output produced.
- Calculating gross pay and deductions.

Authorizing Employment. Documents authorizing employment are prepared independently of the prospective employee's immediate supervisor and those responsible for preparing the payroll. Preferred practice is to lodge that responsibility in the personnel department, which, in the formal hiring process, creates records authorizing employment, the rate of pay, and payroll deductions. The personnel department also prepares pay rate changes and employee termination notices.

The employment records contain data of a permanent or semipermanent nature, which is referred to as "standing data." Standing data, such as employee name, social security number, rate of pay, authorized deductions, and tax exemptions, is used for calculating gross pay and deductions each time a payroll is processed. Consequently, errors in standing data are usually more significant than errors in data relating to a single pay period (referred to as "transaction data"), such as hours worked. The completeness, accuracy, and authorization of standing data, which is not changed frequently, should be controlled by periodic review by the personnel department of recorded payroll standing data and of changes thereto.

Recording Time Worked or Output Produced.   Evidence of performance of services (including overtime) is produced in the form of time reports or clock cards, which should be controlled by supervisory review and approval. If pay is based on production quantity rather than time, as with piecework or commissions, the quantity should be similarly approved and reconciled to recorded production or sales data.

Calculating Gross Pay and Deductions.   Calculating gross pay and deductions involves matching the transaction data (that is, the records of time or output for the payroll period) and standing data for each employee. The computation of pay may be simple or exceedingly complex; it may be done manually or by computer. In a manual system, control procedures consist of reviewing the payroll journal and recalculating the gross pay (including the rates used) if part or all of the payroll is calculated on an hourly rather than a straight salary basis, or using control totals derived from a separate calculation of the aggregate payroll amount. In either event, the payroll should be approved by a responsible official based on evidence that control procedures have been performed. Where payrolls are calculated by a computer program, a responsible official reviews the gross payroll and deductions for reasonableness and approves the amounts. The self-interest of employees and their ready access to the personnel department also act to limit the risk of underpayment. Normally the risk of overpayment is reduced by specifying the maximum amount of a payroll check or establishing payroll grade levels with maximum salaries for each level. Control is also facilitated by comparing payroll costs with standards or budgets or by reconciling payroll costs to production cost or job order records.

Accounting distribution for financial statement purposes is ordinarily not difficult to control because the wages of most employees are charged to the same account from one period to another. Detailed cost accounting systems may call for distributing the total amount among cost centers; in those cases, control over the completeness of the distribution is usually exercised by comparing the amount distributed with the total payroll. The accuracy of the distribution is ensured by investigating differences revealed by variance analyses.

The computation of payroll deductions is governed either by statute (in the case of payroll taxes) or contract (union agreement, group insurance contract, or agency agreements with charitable organizations or credit unions). The authorization to deduct amounts from an employee's pay is given by the individual in writing and is ordinarily obtained and maintained by the personnel department. Cumulative records of deductions are required for each employee. Control procedures for payments of withheld amounts are similar to those for payments of recorded accounts payable.

As previously noted, many companies contract with a data processing service organization for the actual calculation of gross pay and deductions, based on appropriately approved standing and transaction data. If this is done, the output from the service bureau should be reviewed in the same manner as discussed earlier. (See Chapter 6 for a discussion of the auditor's responsibilities in this situation.)

In most organizations, the recognized advantages of segregation of duties in payroll processing are not difficult to achieve. The duties of the personnel and accounting departments are separated, and the person who approves time records is independent of both departments. All of those functions are separate from the handling of payroll checks or cash, as discussed below.

Payment of Wages

Payment of the net payroll amount may be accomplished by check, direct deposit into the employee's bank account, or, in increasingly rare instances, cash payment. Approval of payroll checks, which are often prepared as an integral part of the payroll calculation, usually includes comparing the total of all checks with the total of the payroll summary. Segregation of duties related to payroll disbursements made by check should be the same as for other cash disbursements. It is especially important to segregate duties if the checks are distributed rather than mailed. For example, employees' checks should be distributed by people who do not have responsibility for preparing or approving the payroll.[1]

Unclaimed wages are listed at once, safeguarded, investigated with the personnel department to determine the existence of the employees, and returned to cash if unclaimed within a short time.

DETERMINING THE AUDIT STRATEGY

The audit strategy for each account balance and class of transactions in the buying cycle is based primarily on the auditor's assessment of inherent and

---

[1]Internal auditors may observe a payroll distribution to provide assurance that payments are not made to nonexistent personnel. At one time, it was not uncommon for external auditors to perform the same test, but, except for special "fraud audits," it is rarely done today.

control risk relating to the specific audit objectives and on efficiency considerations.

Audit Objectives

The audit objectives applicable to accounts in the buying cycle are

Completeness
- Accounts payable represent all amounts owed by the entity at the balance sheet date with respect to the purchase of goods or services.
- All goods or services received, less goods returned, during the period covered by the financial statements are reflected in the financial statements.
- All employee wages for services performed during the period covered by the financial statements are reflected in the financial statements; accrued payroll represents all amounts owed to employees at the balance sheet date.

Accuracy
- Purchase transactions are based on correct prices and quantities and are accurately computed and classified in the appropriate general ledger and accounts payable subsidiary ledger accounts.
- Invoice summarizations and postings to the accounts payable subsidiary ledger and purchases account are correct.
- The accounts payable subsidiary ledger is mathematically correct and agrees with the general ledger.
- All payroll amounts are based on correct wage rates and hours, and are accurately computed, summarized, and classified in the appropriate general ledger accounts.

Existence/Occurrence
- Recorded accounts payable represent amounts owed by the entity at the balance sheet date.
- Recorded purchase transactions represent goods or services actually received during the period covered by the financial statements.
- Recorded payroll transactions represent wages for services actually performed during the period covered by the financial statements.

Cutoff
- Purchase transactions, accounts payable, returns, and payroll transactions are recorded in the proper period.

Valuation
- Accounts payable and accrued payroll are stated at the correct amount the entity owes.

- All expenses and losses applicable to the period have been recognized, including unrealized losses on unfavorable purchase commitments.

Rights and Obligations

- Accounts payable and accrued payroll are legal obligations of the entity at the balance sheet date.

Presentation and Disclosure

- Accounts payable, accrued payroll, and expenses are properly described and classified in the financial statements.
- Loss contingencies related to purchase commitments are properly disclosed.

The auditor achieves these objectives by performing substantive tests or a combination of substantive tests and tests of control structure policies and procedures. The auditor often tests an entity's control procedures to obtain evidence that they are designed and operating effectively as a basis for significantly reducing the assurance needed from substantive tests directed at the completeness, accuracy, and existence audit objectives. The auditor generally achieves the remaining audit objectives (with the exception of cutoff) by performing substantive tests, supplemented by the evidence obtained through assessing the entity's inherent risk conditions, control environment, and accounting system. For example, the auditor's awareness of fluctuations in foreign currency exchange rates may cause concern about the valuation audit objective for accounts payable denominated in foreign currencies.

The auditor usually finds it efficient to perform substantive tests to achieve the cutoff objective, particularly if the client has not established control procedures related to cutoff. If management has implemented special control procedures designed to achieve proper cutoff at year-end, the auditor may decide to test those special control procedures in conjunction with other tests of control structure policies and procedures.

Liabilities are more likely to be understated or omitted from the accounts than overstated because the account balances consist of items that have been scrutinized and acknowledged before being recorded, and any inclination to improve financial statement presentation may be reflected in that process. Therefore, auditing procedures in the buying cycle concentrate heavily on seeking evidence of omitted or understated liabilities, although the possibility of overstatement is not ignored.

Risk Assessment

As discussed in Chapter 8, the auditor gathers or updates information about various aspects of the client and its business as a basis for assessing inherent and control risk.

Analytical Procedures.   Analytical procedures frequently highlight relationships between accounts and risks not otherwise apparent during the risk assessment phase of the audit. As discussed in Chapter 8, analytical procedures are a required part of planning; their use at an early stage in the audit often results in more informed strategy decisions.

Analytical procedures can, for example, indicate trends in expenses that may assist the auditor in assessing risk. Relationships among expense accounts and between expense and other accounts should be reviewed and compared with those of prior periods and those anticipated in budgets or forecasts. The account balances themselves are often compared from month to month and with the corresponding period of the prior year. Trends and fluctuations (seasonal and other) should be noted and explanations sought for unusual patterns.

The auditor should consider management's performance of analytical procedures as part of its reviews of reports and other internal documentation. The auditor may consider using the results of those procedures, to the extent appropriate, to supplement his or her own analytical procedures.

Management typically reviews various internal expense and budgetary reports and data, such as the following:

- Actual gross profit compared with historical trends and budgets or forecasts.
- Actual expenses, including payroll, compared with historical trends and budgets.
- Trends of returns and debit memos.
- Accounts payable aging.
- Open purchase commitments.

Management's review of reports like these may help identify material misstatements in the processing of purchase transactions. For example, investigation of significant differences between reported expenses and budgeted and historical expenses could identify incomplete updating of invoices to the general ledger.

The way the client responds to the auditor's inquiries resulting from analytical procedures may give some indication of the quality of the client's control environment. For example, prompt, logical, and meaningful answers to questions about differences between current-year expenses and budgeted amounts as of an interim date or corresponding prior-year amounts would provide some indication, in the absence of evidence to the contrary, that the company's management is "in control" and that the accounting system and control procedures appear to be functioning as intended. Analytical procedures, however, may also indicate trends, even in well-controlled companies, that may lead the auditor to extend substantive tests. Analytical procedures performed as substantive tests are discussed later in this chapter.

Control Risk. The auditor also is required, at a minimum, to obtain an understanding of the entity's control structure sufficient to plan the audit. This understanding is used to identify the types of misstatements that might occur and the risk of their occurring, and to design substantive tests. The understanding is obtained, or updated, by considering previous experience with the entity, reviewing prior-year audit results, interviewing client personnel, observing personnel as they perform their duties, reviewing client-prepared descriptions of policies and procedures, and inspecting documents and records. These procedures normally reveal information about all significant cycles and account balances.

In addition to information about the client's overall control environment, how transactions are processed (manually or by computer) and how sophisticated these systems are, and other general characteristics of the control structure, the auditor should consider the following types of information, as appropriate, related to the buying cycle:

- The volume, dollar amount, and types of purchases, and the number of vendors the entity buys from.
- The flow of buying cycle transactions through the accounting system.

The auditor should also obtain an understanding of control procedures applied to purchase orders, receiving documents, invoices, and cash disbursements, and the extent to which duties are segregated among the people performing those procedures. Based on all the above information, the auditor determines whether control structure policies and procedures for specific classes of transactions are appropriately designed and have been placed in operation.

In the course of obtaining the understanding of the control structure, the auditor may perform concurrent tests of controls (either incidental or planned) and thereby obtain evidence that control structure policies and procedures have been properly designed and are operating effectively. That evidence would enable the auditor to assess control risk at below the maximum for relevant audit objectives. For example, when inquiring about management's review of reported expenses, the auditor may also observe personnel performing the review or examine reports or documents that provide evidence of it. If operating effectively, management's review provides some evidence with respect to the completeness and accuracy of expenses. The auditor considers the level of detail reviewed and the likelihood that the reviewer would detect a material misstatement.

The auditor next considers whether he or she wishes to obtain additional evidence of the effectiveness of policies and procedures as a basis for a low assessment of control risk, and then whether such evidence is likely to be available and efficient to obtain. If so, the auditor would usually perform additional tests of controls for specific audit objectives—commonly, completeness, accuracy, and existence/occurrence of accounts payable, purchases, and accrued payroll.

Audit Testing Plan

As discussed in Chapter 5, the basic audit strategy decision the auditor makes for each significant account balance is whether to perform additional tests of controls to support a low assessed level of control risk for specific audit objectives, or to perform substantive tests directed at all relevant audit objectives, without significant restriction based on tests of controls.

Professional judgment is needed to assess risks and translate that assessment into the various decisions that determine the audit plan. The following two situations describe the testing decisions an auditor might make in developing an appropriate audit strategy for the buying cycle.

The first situation is a small manufacturing company with a manual accounting system for purchases and cash disbursements. The volume of transactions is low. The user determines the need to purchase goods or services; for example, the production supervisor determines that the supply of a particular part is low. The user prepares a purchase order, including the item, quantity, vendor, shipping terms, and price. The user determines this information by calling various vendors for quotes. The purchase orders are prenumbered, but the numbers are not accounted for since many individuals have access to and use the forms.

Purchase orders are approved by appropriate individuals in the various departments. For example, the production manager would approve the production supervisor's order. Various individuals have the authority to purchase items up to certain dollar amounts. Frequently, the user obtains verbal approval for orders. For example, the production supervisor may tell the production manager that certain items are needed and, based on vendors' quotes, will cost $X. The manager gives the supervisor verbal approval to order the items. The supervisor places the order over the phone. Later, the supervisor completes a purchase order for the manager to sign. Sometimes purchase orders are not completed because the user simply forgets to do so.

Inventory items are received by the production department at the receiving dock, and items like supplies are received by the receptionist. A copy of the purchase order is given to the receiving dock personnel or the receptionist. Typically, the purchase order copy is used only if there is some question about who ordered the goods or if there is no packing slip with the merchandise. The individual receiving the goods counts the items received and indicates the quantity on the packing slip or purchase order copy and signs it. The person who ordered the goods is then notified that they are in, and the packing slip or purchase order copy is forwarded to the accounting department.

The packing slip or purchase order is filed in an open receiving order file until the invoice is received. The accounting clerk then matches the invoice to the packing slip or purchase order and forwards them both to the appropriate individual for approval. If the invoice cannot be matched to a packing slip or purchase order, the accounting clerk tries to identify the person who ordered the goods to determine whether they were received, and then forwards the invoice package to that person for approval.

When approved invoice packages are returned to the accounting clerk, they are filed by expected payment date, but the purchases are not recorded. Each week, the accounting clerk pulls the invoices to be paid that week, types the checks, and lists the account distribution on the invoices. The checks and the invoice packages are then given to the controller for review and signature. The checks and any items to be sent with them (for example, a copy of the invoice or remittance advice) are given to the receptionist to mail. The check copies and the invoice packages are returned to the accounting clerk, who then records the purchases and the cash disbursements in the check register and files the check copies and the invoice packages.

At the end of the month, the accounting clerk totals the check register and posts the monthly entry to the ledger. The clerk also totals the unpaid invoices and prepares an entry to record the liability for unpaid purchases and the related expense or inventory. (This entry is reversed at the beginning of the following month.) The controller approves all entries before the accounting clerk posts them to the ledger.

The accounting clerk also performs the monthly reconciliations and prepares the financial statements. The financial statements are reviewed by management, and any unexpected results are investigated.

The accounting system for payroll in this company would be similar to that for purchases in general. Gross pay, net pay, and withholdings are calculated manually. The postings to the general ledger are similar to those for purchases, except that the amounts come from the payroll journal and the processing and recording are done by the payroll clerk.

In this situation, the auditor, based on his or her understanding of the control structure and any concurrent tests of controls performed, would probably assess control risk at below the maximum and decide not to perform additional tests of controls. Substantive tests of details would be directed at all assertions. In addition to the substantive tests described later in the chapter, the auditor might need to perform additional tests with respect to the accuracy of accounts payable, accrued payroll, and purchases. Those tests might include determining that the account distributions are proper and that the posting to the subsidiary and general ledgers was done correctly. The tests of details would be performed as of year-end.

The above strategy decisions are based on the following factors:

- Low transaction volume, which makes substantive testing efficient.
- Manual accounting system, which increases the risk of random errors.
- Ineffective division of duties.
- Limited control procedures; for example, there is no review of the invoice package before it is given to the controller, and the invoice package is not canceled or stamped ''paid'' after the controller signs the check.

The auditor's decision might have been different if the company had

- A higher volume of transactions.
- A computerized accounting system that used packaged software developed and maintained by third-party vendors.
- Increased segregation of duties, for example, if the person responsible for matching invoices to the packing slips or purchase orders and investigat-

ing missing orders were independent from the person who recorded payments, typed checks, and performed reconciliations.

- Effective transaction processing and file control procedures, for example, accounting for the numerical sequence of purchase orders, matching of purchases to receiving reports and purchase orders, investigation of unmatched items by accounting clerks, and investigation of long-outstanding orders by the production department.

In those circumstances, the auditor might have decided to perform additional tests of control procedures to reduce the assurance needed from substantive tests for the completeness, accuracy, and existence/occurrence audit objectives.

In the second situation, the client is a large manufacturing company with a computerized accounting system for purchases and cash disbursements. The company has a large, highly skilled EDP department with effective general control procedures and division of duties. The EDP department typically develops software internally, but sometimes modifies packaged software. Control procedures for implementing new systems, maintaining existing systems, and the operations functions are effective, as are program and data file security control procedures. (These general control procedures are discussed in detail in Chapter 11.) Control procedures applied to purchases and cash disbursements are designed to ensure that authorized transactions are completely and accurately input and updated.

In this situation, the auditor will likely have performed tests of controls concurrently with obtaining an understanding of the control structure. The auditor is also likely to consider it efficient to perform additional tests of controls relating to the completeness, accuracy, and authorization control objectives for purchase and cash disbursements transactions, as a basis for assessing control risk as low. If the additional tests of controls support a low assessment of control risk, substantive tests directed at the completeness, accuracy, and existence/occurrence audit objectives could be reduced. They might even be limited to analytical procedures. The auditor would be likely to perform any tests of details prior to year-end.

If the client did not have effective program and data file security control procedures, the auditor might revise the strategy to include more substantive tests directed at the existence audit objective for accounts payable. Ineffective security control procedures increase the risk of unauthorized alterations to programs and data. The ability to manipulate accounts payable data might make it possible for an employee to initiate payment of a check to himself or herself and conceal the defalcation.

ADDITIONAL TESTS OF CONTROLS

As discussed earlier, the auditor may have performed concurrent tests of controls while obtaining an understanding of control structure policies and procedures. Concurrent tests of controls often provide evidence to support an assessment of control risk at below the maximum for one or more audit objectives. However, concurrent tests of controls are generally directed mainly at policies and procedures that are part of the control environment and accounting system, as opposed to specific control procedures, and therefore usually relate to several audit objectives and affect several accounts. Thus, concurrent tests of controls are not enough to support a low assessment of control risk for specific audit objectives and account balances. To assess control risk as low for one or more audit objectives for some or all buying cycle accounts, the auditor performs additional tests of controls. Such tests usually require substantial audit effort, and therefore the auditor generally performs them when he or she believes they will significantly reduce the amount of substantive testing required.

The purpose of performing tests of individual control procedures is to obtain support for an assessment that all the control structure elements interacting together reduce to a low level the risk that control objectives will not be achieved. Specific control objectives and typical control procedures applicable to acquisitions of goods and services, payments made for them, and calculating and recording payroll are described in Figures 13.1, 13.2, and 13.3, respectively. The accounting system assumed to be in operation in the figures is a sophisticated computerized system. As discussed in Chapter 8, the tests of controls the auditor would perform include an appropriate combination of inquiring about the client's control procedures, observing that the procedures have been placed in operation, and examining evidence that they are designed and operating effectively. Also as discussed in Chapter 8, reperformance may be used in tests of controls; but if that becomes necessary, the auditor usually determines it is more efficient to perform substantive tests. In addition to testing control procedures specific to a particular transaction cycle, in order to assess control risk as low the auditor would also need evidence of the effectiveness of general control procedures.

In evaluating the results of tests of controls (including tests of general control procedures), the auditor considers whether the control structure policies and procedures, taken as a whole, are appropriately designed to achieve the control objectives and are operating effectively. This will determine whether the expected assessment of control risk as low was attained for specific accounts and audit objectives and, thus, whether the auditor can significantly reduce substantive testing. Results differing from those anticipated when developing the audit testing plan require the auditor to reconsider the nature, timing, and extent of planned substantive tests—not only for buying cycle accounts, but also for other accounts that may be affected. For example, ineffective control procedures to ensure completeness of recorded purchases may also affect inventory and cost of sales.

SUBSTANTIVE TESTS

If the auditor has assessed control risk for some or all buying cycle accounts as low for specific audit objectives, substantive tests addressing those audit objectives may be limited to analytical procedures. This is more likely to be done for expense and payroll accounts than for accounts payable and other liability accounts. The auditor will also consider whether evidence obtained from tests directed at other audit objectives is relevant to these audit objectives too. For example, tracing accounts payable to supporting documentation is directed toward the accuracy audit objective, but provides some evidence about existence as well. Control risk is seldom assessed as low with respect to the cutoff, valuation, rights and obligations, and presentation and disclosure objectives, and therefore substantive tests of details are usually performed for these objectives.

Accounts Payable

Before performing substantive tests directed toward the other audit objectives, the auditor should be reasonably assured that the accounts payable trial balance contains all purchase transactions that remain unpaid at year-end. Evidence about the completeness of the trial balance is often provided largely by the results of tests of controls.

To achieve the cutoff objective, it is usually more efficient for the auditor to perform substantive tests of details, particularly in the case of those companies that are not concerned about precise cutoff on a month-to-month basis. Companies may, however, implement special control procedures at the end of the year, which the auditor may decide to test. Also, control structure policies and procedures designed to ensure completeness of input and update may be effective in ensuring that transactions are recorded in the proper period. For example, the design of the accounting system itself may reduce control risk for cutoff.

Cutoff tests are intended to ascertain that all significant transactions have been recorded in the proper period. In the absence of control structure policies and procedures directed toward cutoff, the sooner the accounts are closed after year-end, the greater the likelihood that there will be unrecorded vendors' invoices. Thus, examining files of unmatched receiving reports and unre- corded invoices, the purchases journal, and the cash disbursements journal, and other relevant records for a period after year-end is an almost universal auditing procedure. (Cutoff tests of the receipt of goods and recording of inventory are usually coordinated with the auditor's observation of the client's physical inventory count; those tests are discussed in Chapter 14.)

If the basic transaction documents are in numerical sequence, the auditor can note the number of the last receiving report, and the last check issued (or other basic transaction documents) prior to year-end. The auditor can exam- ine perpetual inventory records, the year-end accounts payable trial balance, and the listing of unmatched receiving reports to determine whether goods received at or near year-end are included. Similarly, the last check issued can be traced to the cash disbursements records and the list of outstanding checks in the bank reconciliation. The auditor should apply the same procedures to obtain assurance that receipts and invoices applicable to the following year were not recorded in the current year. If the basic transaction documents are not prenumbered, it may be necessary to examine relevant documents, with emphasis on transaction dates and large amounts, selected from the various

Figure 13.1 Acquisitions of Goods and Services

	Control Objectives					
	Transaction Processing					
	Authorization	Completeness of Input	Accuracy of Input	Completeness and Accuracy of Updating[a]	File	Asset Protection
Specific Control Objectives	All recorded purchase transactions represent actual receipts of goods and services and are approved.	All purchase transactions are input and accepted for processing.	Purchases are correctly recorded as to amounts, quantities, dates, vendors, and general ledger account; are recorded in the proper period; are accurately converted into computer-readable form; and are accurately input to the computer.	All purchase transactions input and accepted for processing are accurately updated to the general ledger and accounts payable data files.	The integrity of individual accounts payable in the subsidiary ledger and the general ledger accounts, after purchase transactions have been accumulated in them, is preserved.	Only authorized personnel have access to accounts payable records and data stored on them.
Typical Control Procedures	Approval of requisitions and purchase orders. Matching invoices for goods and services received to receiving reports and purchase orders by indi-	Accounting for the numerical sequence of requisitions and purchase orders input to the computer. Reporting and resolving missing or duplicate items by indi-	Counting, where appropriate, and inspecting goods received, by personnel independent of purchasing and accounting functions. Completeness	Comparing total purchases input with the total updated to the purchases and accounts payable files.	Ensuring that the correct version of the file is being used for processing. Balancing of the subsidiary ledger (previous balance plus purchases less payments,	Restricting access to accounts payable files and files used in processing payables.

viduals independent of purchasing and receiving functions.

Reporting and resolving invoices and receiving reports that do not match against approved purchase orders.

viduals independent of receiving and purchasing functions.

Reporting and resolving long-outstanding items on the aged open purchase order file, and receipts and invoices rejected as not matching against the open purchase order file.

Accounting for the numerical sequence of receiving reports.

Reporting and resolving missing or duplicate items by individuals independent of receiving and cash disbursements functions.

of input control procedures for purchase orders also address the accuracy of input for vendor, prices, and descriptions; completeness of input procedures for receiving reports also address the accuracy of input for date, quantities, and descriptions.

Reporting and resolving unmatched items by individuals independent of receiving and purchasing functions.

Review of account classifications.

compared with the current total).

Reconciling the subsidiary ledger to the control account in the general ledger; reporting and resolving discrepancies.

aCompleteness of updating and accuracy of updating have been combined in this figure for convenience, because typically the same control procedures apply to both objectives.

Figure 13.2 Payments Made for Goods and Services

| | Control Objectives | | | | | |
| | Transaction Processing | | | | | |
	Authorization	*Completeness of Input*	*Accuracy of Input*	*Completeness and Accuracy of Updating*[a]	*File*	*Asset Protection*
Specific Control Objectives	All recorded cash disbursements are for actual purchases of goods and services and are approved.	All payments made are input and accepted for processing.	Disbursements are correctly recorded as to amounts, dates, and payees; are recorded in the proper period; are accurately converted into computer-readable form; and are accurately input to the computer.	All disbursements input and accepted for processing are accurately updated to the cash disbursements and accounts payable data files.	The integrity of individual accounts payable in the subsidiary ledger and the general ledger accounts, after purchase transactions have been updated to them, is preserved.	Only authorized personnel have access to cash, unissued checks, and accounts payable files or data stored on them.
Typical Control Procedures	Approving payment (before checks are signed) by	Accounting for the numerical sequence of checks, both	Matching disbursements records against accounts	Comparing total disbursements input with the totals	Same control procedures as described in Figure 13.1,	Mailing of checks by individuals independent of

officials independent of purchasing, receiving, and accounts payable functions. Examination by signatory, at time of signing checks, of supporting documentation (e.g., invoices, receiving reports, purchase orders). Canceling supporting documentation to prevent resubmission for payment.

used and unused. Reporting and investigating missing or duplicate checks. Reporting and investigating long-outstanding checks by individuals independent of accounts payable and cash disbursements functions.

payable/open invoice files. Reporting and resolving differences by individuals independent of accounts payable and cash disbursements functions.

updated to the cash disbursements and accounts payable files.

"Acquisitions of Goods and Services." Reconciling the bank statement to the general ledger cash account by personnel independent of accounts payable and cash disbursements functions (and receiving and recording cash receipts).

recording accounts payable. Authorized check signers are independent of cash receipts functions. Physically protecting mechanical check signers and signature plates. Restricting access to accounts payable files and files used in processing cash disbursements.

aCompleteness of updating and accuracy of updating have been combined in this figure for convenience, because typically the same control procedures apply to both objectives.

Figure 13.3 Calculating and Recording Payroll

	Control Objectives				
	Transaction Processing				
	Authorization	*Completeness of Input*	*Accuracy of Input*	*Completeness and Accuracy of Updating*[a]	*File*	*Asset Protection*
Specific Control Objectives	All recorded transactions for employee wages are for actual services performed and are approved.	All employee wages for services performed are input and accepted for processing.	Employee wages are correctly recorded as to wage rate, hours, and time period; are properly calculated as to gross wages, withholdings, and net pay; are recorded to the correct general ledger accounts; are accurately converted into machine-readable form; and are accurately input to the computer.	All employee wage transactions input and accepted for processing are accurately updated to the payroll register and individual payroll files.	The integrity of the individual employee payroll records and the payroll summary and general ledger accounts for payroll withholdings is preserved.	Only authorized personnel have access to payroll files and data stored on them.

Typical Control Procedures					
Approving changes to master files for wage and salary rates. Approving changes to master files for new employees and deleted employees. Approving processing of pay for employees with hours in excess of a predetermined limit.	Comparing total hours (in batch form) with total hours input to the computer. Reporting and investigating employees on master file for whom no hours worked have been input.	Completeness of input control procedures for total hours also addresses the accuracy of input. Matching employee data to comparable master file data—employee name, number, and so on. Reporting and investigating mismatched items. Reporting hours worked in excess of a predetermined limit.	Comparing total hours and number of employees input with the totals updated to the payroll register.	Ensuring that the correct version of the file is being used for processing. Reconciling the employee subsidiary ledger to the control accounts in the general ledger; reporting and resolving discrepancies.	Restricting access to payroll files and data stored on them. Distribution of checks by persons independent of recording and approving the payroll. Physically protecting mechanical check signers and signature plates.

aCompleteness of updating and accuracy of updating have been combined in this figure for convenience, because typically the same control procedures apply to both objectives.

sources both before and after the cutoff date to obtain sufficient evidence that the cutoff was properly made.

Confirmation of accounts payable balances does not have the widespread acceptance as a substantive test that confirmation of accounts receivable has. Evidence about the existence of payables is usually obtained through tests of control procedures for ordering and receiving goods and for recording invoices, through analytical procedures, and through the substantive tests discussed below; only rarely is confirmation an effective or efficient means of obtaining the necessary assurance that accounts payable have been properly authorized and recorded. Reviewing purchase and disbursement records subsequent to year-end (commonly referred to as unrecorded liability tests) addresses the completeness of payables. (Confirming a few payables as a test of controls, however, may provide the auditor with useful evidence about the effective operation of control policies and procedures directed toward the completeness, accuracy, and proper cutoff of purchases from and disbursements to vendors.) Confirmation (as a substantive test) may be called for if there are deficiencies in control procedures or if the results of other substantive tests indicate that payables may be incomplete or otherwise misstated. If undertaken, the confirmation procedure is like that described in Chapter 12 for confirming accounts receivable, except that an additional step of circularizing known suppliers with zero balances may be included. In extreme situations, if the auditor is still not satisfied as to possible unrecorded liabilities or the accuracy of recorded balances, the client may be requested to deliver the mail, unopened, to the auditor daily for a reasonable period after year-end, so that the auditor can search for vendors' invoices and statements applicable to the year under audit.

Substantive tests directed at the existence and accuracy of recorded accounts payable normally consist of

- Tracing selected entries in the accounts payable subsidiary ledger or trial balance to subsequent cash disbursements or other supporting documents, such as vendors' invoices; examining evidence that the client has matched all invoices to purchase orders and receiving reports; and reperforming the matching procedure (on a test basis if appropriate) to determine that all aspects of the transaction appear reasonable (e.g., that suppliers' invoices are addressed to the client).

- Tracing to appropriate supporting documentation, adjusting items in the client's reconciliation of the subsidiary ledger to the control account. The auditor should also test the mathematical accuracy of the client's accounts payable subsidiary ledger or trial balance and the reconciliation.

- Investigating the underlying causes of debit balances in accounts payable. They may represent overpayments; if so, the auditor should consider whether they are collectible. They may also represent purchases that were not recorded but were nevertheless paid; in that event, the auditor should ascertain why the purchases were not recorded.

Losses from purchase commitments may arise in connection with commodity purchases, forward transactions, or purchase commitments in excess of short-term requirements. If material losses could arise from unfulfilled purchase commitments, the commitments should be identified and the auditor should assess the potential need for a loss provision. This may be accomplished by examining open purchase order records, inquiring of employees who make purchase commitments, or requesting major suppliers to provide details of any purchase commitments outstanding as of year-end. If the auditor is uncertain whether all commitments have been identified, it may be appropriate to review suppliers' invoices and receiving reports for a period after year-end for evidence of purchases above prevailing prices or in quantities in excess of current requirements (by reviewing perpetual inventory records for evidence of goods that are slow-moving or obsolete), which may indicate unfavorable purchase commitments at year-end. Also, since major purchase commitments generally require the approval of the board of directors, examination of minutes of board meetings may help the auditor discover such purchase commitments. Chapter 21 illustrates the statement about purchase commitments that should be included in the client's representation letter.

Salaries, Wages, and Payroll Taxes

Substantive tests directed at the completeness and accuracy of accrued payroll and related liabilities consist primarily of analytical procedures and examining the subsequent payment of the liability in the following year. The auditor should obtain an analysis of accrued salaries and wages and test its mathematical accuracy; totals should be agreed to the payroll records. If the company has recorded an estimate (e.g., proration of the payroll for the overlapping period) rather than an exact computation, the appropriateness and consistency with prior years of the method of estimating should be ascertained. The auditor should also review the general ledger accounts relating to payroll expense. Analytical procedures can be helpful in this regard; for instance, the number of employees and the average salary per employee can be compared with the prior year. Any material unusual entries, unusual fluctuations in normal recurring entries in the payroll summaries, and payroll amounts capitalized in fixed asset accounts should be investigated. Substantive tests of details are normally not performed on payroll expense account balances unless control structure policies and procedures are extremely ineffective or the results of other procedures, primarily analytical procedures, indicate the need for additional assurance from detail testing.

Based on materiality and risk assessment, the auditor may examine subsequent payments of agency obligations. Comparing current year-end balances with those of the prior year may indicate unusual items. For accounts like unclaimed wages, the auditor should examine and test a trial balance reconciling the details to a control account and should scrutinize the underlying details for unusual items. If old unclaimed wages have been written off, potential liability under state escheat or unclaimed property laws should be considered.

Accrued commissions should be substantiated by examining sales reports submitted by sales personnel, commission schedules, and contracts with sales personnel. If accrued commissions are significant, the auditor should consider confirming amounts due and commissions earned during the year directly with sales personnel. The overall reasonableness of commission expense for the year may be tested by multiplying commission rates by sales.

The year-end liability for vacation pay, sick pay, and other compensated absences should be reviewed for compliance with Statement of Financial Accounting Standards (SFAS) No. 43 (Accounting Standards Section C44). If vacation periods are based on length of service, normally the client prepares a detailed computation of the accrued liability. The auditor should review the method used and the computation to determine that the amount accrued is appropriate.

A published statement of company policy may create liabilities for rights that accrue to employees even without formal labor contracts. Opinion of counsel may sometimes be necessary to determine whether there is a legal liability at the balance sheet date. Contracts and policies of that nature do not always clearly indicate whether employees' rights accrue ratably over a period or come into existence in their entirety at a specific date. The auditor must also be alert for possible liabilities arising from employee benefits so customary as to constitute an implied promise. Sick pay, severance pay, and some kinds of bonuses and pensions are examples.

Costs and Expenses

Audit evidence with respect to the income statement is based mainly on auditing procedures applied to balance sheet accounts, correlation of amounts on the income statement with balances on the balance sheet, analytical procedures such as the review of performance indicators, and, where applicable, tests of controls. If control risk has not been assessed as low, procedures like correlating income statement amounts with balances in the balance sheet become more important. Many income statement items can be correlated with balance sheet accounts, such as interest with loan balances. In addition, the auditor can assess the reasonableness of the amounts, for example, by comparing the percentage of selling, general, and administrative expenses in relation to sales from period to period. In computerized systems, computer software can facilitate these tests.

When the procedures outlined above have been completed, there may still be income statement accounts the auditor needs further assurance about. Tests should be designed to provide such assurance, normally in one of the following forms:

- If further assurance is needed about the occurrence or accuracy of specific expense accounts (like travel expense or maintenance expense), the auditor should request or prepare an analysis of the account in question or, at least, of the material items in it, and examine supporting documentation for enough items to gain assurance that there is no material misstatement. For example, an auditor may obtain a list of employees with expense accounts and make appropriate tests to determine whether all expenses have been reported and recorded in the accounts in the proper period, and may test related post-balance-sheet entries to determine whether a proper cutoff was made.

- If the auditor is concerned about the possibility of misstatement associated with a particular type of transaction rather than with particular account balances (as might be the case when control structure policies and procedures relating to certain types of payments are ineffective), the areas in the expense accounts that might be affected should be isolated. For example, if certain payments are supported by receiving reports and other payments are not, the auditor need perform substantive tests only for the payments that are not supported by receiving reports. In this situation, the auditor would select a sufficient number of accounts that might be misstated and examine them to the extent necessary to obtain assurance that no material misstatement had occurred.

Other Auditing Procedures

In addition to the specific substantive tests described above, the auditor typically performs procedures designed to detect other unrecorded liabilities, like insurance claims and other loss contingencies, as well as receives a letter of representation from management and a letter from the company's counsel. Those topics are covered in detail in Chapter 21. The remainder of this section describes other procedures the auditor should perform to detect unrecorded liabilities.

The auditor should read minutes of meetings of stockholders, directors, and appropriate committees for the period under audit and up to the date of the audit report. Those minutes may reveal contracts, commitments, and other matters requiring investigation. The auditor should also examine contracts, loan agreements, leases, correspondence from taxing or other governmental agencies, and similar documents. Reviewing such documents may disclose unrecorded liabilities as of the balance sheet date.

One of the auditor's most difficult tasks is identifying liabilities for which no direct reference appears in the accounts. Clues to those obligations may be discovered in unexpected places, and the auditor should be constantly alert for them. For example,

- The auditor should review responses to bank confirmation requests in addition to analyzing interest expense to determine if there are any unrecorded bank loans.
- Responses to requests for confirmation of bank loans may list as collateral securities or other assets that do not appear in the records. They may be borrowed from affiliated companies or others.
- Manufacturers of machinery and equipment often sell their products at prices that include cost of installation. The auditor should determine that the estimated cost of completing the installation of equipment sold has been recorded in the same period as the sale of the equipment.

In a decentralized environment, the possibility of unrecorded liabilities may be more significant than in a centralized environment and may warrant a procedure for formal inquiry of department heads, supervisors, and other responsible officials regarding knowledge of unprocessed invoices, unrecorded commitments, or contingent liabilities. This procedure may apply in a loosely controlled centralized environment as well.

The auditor should take a broad look at the client's operations to determine whether all types of expenses and the related liabilities, if any, that are expected have been recorded and appear to be reasonable. Familiarity with the client's operations should disclose whether such items as royalties, commissions, interest, consignments, and the myriad of taxes most businesses are subject to have been properly recorded.

The search for unrecorded liabilities cannot, of course, bring to light liabilities that have been deliberately withheld from the auditor's attention. The auditor's responsibility regarding irregularities and illegal acts is discussed in Chapter 4. The receipt of a client representation letter, as discussed in Chapter 21, does not relieve the auditor of professional responsibilities in this area.

Finally, transactions with affiliated entities often are not conducted on the same basis as transactions with outsiders; thus, they deserve special attention from the auditor. For example, charges for services rendered may not be billed on a timely basis. Whenever feasible, the auditor should review a reconciliation of the amount due to or from an affiliate by reference to both sets of records. If this cannot be done, the balance should be confirmed.

14

Auditing the Production Cycle, Cost of Sales, and Inventory Balances

The production cycle and inventories are often among the most significant and difficult areas in auditing. Service-based enterprises as well as manufacturers, retailers, and wholesalers maintain significant amounts of inventory. The auditor's primary objective in this area is to gather evidence to support management's assertions about the existence, ownership, pricing, and valuation of inventory.

Since the production cycle is normally associated with manufacturing enterprises, this chapter is written primarily from that perspective. Much of the discussion in the chapter, however, applies to other types of enterprises as well, like retailers and wholesalers that purchase and hold inventory for future sale, and various types of service organizations that consume inventory in the process of generating revenues.

ACCOUNTS RELATED TO THE PRODUCTION CYCLE

The production cycle deals with tangible personal property manufactured for sale in the ordinary course of business. The term "inventory" is used to refer to items held for sale, in process of production, or to be converted or consumed in the production of goods or services. Inventory is usually characterized as either merchandise, raw materials, work in process, or finished goods. Merchandise refers to goods acquired for resale by dealers, who incur little or no additional cost preparing them for resale. Raw materials are items or commodities converted or consumed in the production process. Work in process represents products in intermediate stages of production. Finished goods represent the end products of the manufacturing process. Both finished goods and work in process normally have material, labor, and overhead components. The classification of inventory depends on the entity holding it and the nature of its operations. For example, coil steel is a finished product to a steel mill, but a raw material to an appliance manufacturer.

Cost of sales (also called cost of goods sold) includes all costs directly associated with purchasing and producing goods sold. Material costs assignable to inventory include merchandise, raw materials, and component parts used in the production process or purchased for resale, net of purchase returns, discounts, and other allowances. All direct costs incurred in the purchasing process, like inbound transportation (freight in), duties and taxes, and warehousing, are also included. In complex procurement systems that are expensive to operate, a separate purchasing overhead account may be maintained and included in material costs.

Other costs associated with production include direct labor and related costs, like employee fringe benefits, and manufacturing overhead. Manufacturing overhead comprises costs that cannot be directly assigned to specific units of production but are nonetheless directly associated with the production process, for example, indirect labor, supervision, occupancy costs, utilities, repairs and maintenance, and depreciation. Operating supplies and other materials that do not become parts of products, like oils for lubricating machinery, normally are also included in overhead.

Cost of sales may include additional items such as losses from writing inventories down to market value, royalties paid for the right to manufacture a product or use a patented process or equipment, and amortization of pre-production and tooling costs. Cost of sales is often reduced by sales of by-products and the disposal value of scrap. Estimated costs of warranties, guarantees, and other commitments for future expenditures are usually included in cost of sales, although sometimes they are included in other expense categories.

The term "operating expenses" is sometimes used to describe costs and expenses incurred in generating revenues from the sale of services.

TYPICAL TRANSACTIONS, ACCOUNTING SYSTEMS, AND CONTROL PROCEDURES

There are essentially two major kinds of cost accounting systems—a job order system, in which goods are made in the quantities and to the specifications called for by a particular order, and a process system, in which goods are produced repetitively according to a schedule. The number of classes of transactions in the production cycle of either system depends on the complexity of the production process. Among the transactions typically found in a production cycle are issuing raw materials for use in production, allocating labor and overhead costs, computing piecework and incentive pay, receiving materials directly into production, processing customers' materials, and transferring completed products to inventory. The production cycle also includes policies and procedures for storing raw materials, component parts, and finished goods, and for shipping goods produced.

There are virtually unlimited combinations and sequences that may occur in connection with producing goods for sale and storing raw materials and finished goods. The operating, accounting, and control procedures associated with production appear in many forms because of the technological diversity of modern manufacturing operations. The discussion in this chapter of typical transactions, accounting systems, and control procedures provides only a generalized suggestion of the kinds of conditions that may be encountered in the three major transaction classes in the production cycle.

- Producing goods for sale.
- Storing raw materials (including component parts) and finished goods.
- Shipping goods produced.

Producing Goods for Sale

The process of producing goods for sale generally includes the following activities:

- Identifying production needs, and planning and scheduling production.
- Producing goods.

- Accounting for production costs.
- Accounting for work in process.

In considering the accounting system through which production transactions are processed and the control procedures applied to them, the auditor is interested primarily in procedures to ensure that incurred production costs are authorized and are accurately recorded and accumulated; that is, that the control objectives of completeness, accuracy, and authorization of transaction processing and files are met. Those control objectives are closely related to the audit objectives of completeness, accuracy, and existence of accounts that are part of the production cycle—most significantly, raw materials, work-in-process, and finished goods inventories, and cost of sales. Other control procedures, while not directly related to those audit objectives, may also be of interest to the auditor. For example, the fact that production is carefully planned to meet anticipated sales may provide evidence the auditor can use in evaluating the adequacy of the allowance for obsolete inventory, which affects the valuation audit objective relating to inventory.

Control procedures for the production process are also important to management because errors in production and inventory data can result in wrong decisions. For example, inaccurate inventory records can result in poor purchasing or production planning decisions. Overstocking can lead to higher inventory carrying costs and a greater risk of obsolescence; understocking can lead to stock-outs, production downtime, and lost sales. Effective procedures to control inventory levels also reduce the probability of errors in accounting data and other data used by management in running the business, thereby contributing to operating effectiveness.

Identifying Production Needs, and Planning and Scheduling Production.   In a process system that produces finished goods inventory, identifying production needs may be an integral part of the system and may be accomplished by evaluating existing inventory levels in relation to sales projections. The need may be signaled by a periodic matching of physical or recorded inventory levels against a predetermined minimum. Computerized inventory records offer the opportunity for sophisticated forecasting and modeling computations.

After a need has been identified, a production requisition is initiated, which, after review and approval, becomes the authorization to produce. Product specifications and time and cost estimates are usually developed as part of the production planning and scheduling process. In particular, cost estimates give management a basis for informed scrutiny of actual costs. The result of planning and scheduling is a production order—the detailed execution instructions listing the operations and the desired results.

Poor product specifications (as well as poor inspection procedures) can cause rework, unsalable goods, or returned merchandise. Poor estimates and poor scheduling can give rise to excess cost in inventory, especially overruns on contracts. An auditor who understands the role of planning and scheduling in the production process will be able to more effectively assess the inherent and control risks associated with inventory and cost of sales.

Producing Goods.   Raw materials may be moved into the production process on the basis of a document (like an authorized bill of materials supporting an approved production order, an approved materials requisition, or a report of production orders scheduled to start), or electronically when an authorized production order is entered into the system. In either event, an appropriately authorized document or file should be created to account for the movement of materials, for both operational and accounting purposes. Often these documents or files may serve as authorization to update the perpetual inventory records for issues of materials to production. The documents, which are usually prenumbered, are accounted for or open files are reviewed periodically as part of procedures to ascertain that all transactions have been processed and recorded. If material is ordered directly for production, the production order, sometimes supported by an accompanying purchase order, alerts those concerned to the expected delivery date.

Setup time for machines used in the production process may or may not be accounted for separately, depending on management's informational needs. Tools and dies are sometimes charged as direct costs, particularly in job order production systems in which tools are likely to have been designed especially for a particular order and sometimes are paid for by the customer. Most often, though, tools and dies are capitalized because they can be reused on other work or production runs at other times. Usually, documents are prepared to record these processing steps: a time report or job ticket for the setup time and an issues slip or production order for the tool requirements. The documents are then reviewed and approved by supervisory personnel.

Measuring production quantities is a problem in a great many operations. Both production managers and cost accountants want accurate production counts, but in many cases the large number of units, the inaccuracy of measuring devices, and the problems of distinguishing between acceptable and unacceptable units make it difficult or uneconomical to measure production precisely.

Production is often inspected at several stages and levels. Operators inspect for signs of problems as they complete their work; supervisors may inspect output on a test basis. There may be specialists in quality control, or it may be necessary to employ the special skills and equipment of a laboratory to test the quality of production. Control procedures related to measuring and inspecting production output provide evidence of the salability of the inventory and the level of warranty costs that may be incurred after the sale.

Accounting for Production Costs.   The accounting aspects of the production cycle are manifested in the entity's cost accounting system. Cost accounting systems employed by manufacturing concerns vary widely, and range from very simple systems, which account for ending inventory balances annually, to very well-developed standard cost systems, which account for all materials handling, production in process. and completed production, and generate analyses of related variances from predetermined standard costs. A well-developed cost system should provide the details of transfers between raw materials and work in process and between work in process and finished goods, and of the distribution and accumulation of material, labor, and overhead costs by cost centers, job orders, or production runs.

Depending on the structure of the cost accounting system, raw materials may be charged to a job order or to a materials usage account in a process system. If a standard cost system is used, materials may be charged to production at standard quantities and prices, with resulting variances between standard and actual costs subsequently allocated to inventory and cost of sales.

Issues of raw materials may be recorded from a report of production orders scheduled to start, which is compared with production orders reported as actually started, or from raw materials storeroom issue slips whose numerical sequence is accounted for. Occasionally, especially in computerized systems, raw materials usage may be measured by periodically—usually monthly— pricing the ending raw materials inventory and adjusting the account balance through a charge to production.

The total cost of production payroll is accounted for through the buying cycle (covered in Chapter 13). Payroll costs are distributed to detailed cost accounts from payroll records or production reports. The aggregate labor cost distributed to production or other expense accounts is reconciled to a control total from the payroll records to ensure that all labor costs have been allocated to either job order or departmental expense accounts. The system may provide detailed accounts for idle time, waiting time, setup time, cleanup time, rework time, and so on. When a standard cost system is used, production labor is computed at standard rates and hours and, by comparison with actual costs, labor rate and efficiency variances are produced.

Many different kinds of costs enter into overhead, and they are accumulated in descriptive accounts as charges originate. The basis for charging overhead to job orders, departments, or work-in-process inventory is usually some measure of activity, such as direct labor hours or dollars. There are likely to be different overhead rates for different departments, based on accounting or engineering studies. Entries to record overhead absorption may be originated as a separate accounting procedure, but most often they are integrated with entries for the data—payroll or materials usage—on which the absorption rate is based.

In a standard cost system, overhead may be charged through several intermediate accounts before eventually ending up in work in process, finished goods, and cost of sales to produce price, efficiency, and volume variances for management purposes. Overabsorbed overhead is removed from inventories to prevent stating them in excess of actual cost; underabsorbed overhead is generally allocated to inventories, unless it arises from costs that are written off as incurred. Some companies establish and allocate separate overheads for materials handling (purchasing, receiving, inspecting, and storing), as distinguished from manufacturing overhead, when those costs are significant.

Production rejected as a result of inspection is reported for cost accounting purposes. Sometimes the time spent reworking faulty items to meet specifications is also reported separately. Minimizing the amount of scrap and rework is an important management objective; identifying and accounting for the cost of scrap and rework help achieve that objective. Once scrap has been created, it is subject to custodial procedures and disposed of in a way that maximizes cost recovery and thereby minimizes production costs. Cost accounting is improved if scrap is identified with the operations or products creating it, but that is often impossible. Control procedures for gathering, protecting, weighing, recording, storing, and disposing of scrap are sometimes as important as those for other assets.

Accounting for Work in Process.   Movement of production between departments during the manufacturing process is reported for operational purposes, but may or may not be recorded for accounting purposes. Work in process is credited and finished goods are charged when production is complete, on the basis of completed production orders, inspection reports, or finished goods receiving tickets that have been authorized. In addition, most entities have procedures for documenting evidence of inspection according to quality control standards.

Physical inventory counts of work in process are often difficult because a great many items in many different stages of completion must be identified. Goods may be scattered or in hoppers, vats, or pipelines where access, observation, or measurement is difficult, or they may be in the hands of outside processors. Adequate production management, however, requires that someone know the location and stage of completion of each item. The more difficult controlling production is, the more essential it is to have a means of ensuring that excess or "lost" costs do not build up in the work-in-process account.

Storing Raw Materials and Finished Goods

Raw materials and component parts are accounted for and controlled from the time of their receipt through their use in the manufacturing process. Procedures for accomplishing this include protecting the inventory by restricting access to it to authorized personnel, issuing materials to production only upon proper authorization, crediting the perpetual inventory records for issuances to production, and periodically counting materials on hand and agreeing the results to those records. Procedures relating to receiving raw materials and updating perpetual inventory records are covered in Chapter 13, "Auditing the Buying Cycle." Procedures relating to issuing raw materials to production were discussed above.

After production has been completed and has passed final inspection, it goes either to a warehouse or to a storage area to await shipment to customers. The notice to production management may be a copy of the completed production order, or it may be an inspection report or a warehouse receiving report. The completeness of charges to finished goods is controlled by accounting for the numerical sequence of production or receiving reports.

The primary control procedures for inventories in most companies are physical counts of quantities on hand and periodic reconciliations to perpetual inventory records or general ledger balances. Perpetual inventory records of varying degrees of sophistication are found in practice. Some companies maintain perpetual records that reflect both inventory quantities and costs;

others keep perpetual records in quantities only. Companies with simple operations and relatively few inventory items frequently do not maintain perpetual records at all.

Physical inventories are part of an effective internal control structure. In entities with an effective control structure, a physical inventory is taken at least annually and sometimes more often, depending on the type of business and the nature of the inventory. The term "physical inventory" includes not only physically counting items but also translating the quantities into dollars, summarizing the dollars, and comparing the results with the accounts. A complete count of the inventory of a company, plant, or department may be made at one time while operations are suspended (sometimes referred to as a wall-to-wall inventory) or, if perpetual inventory records are maintained and other conditions are satisfactory, periodic counts of selected items may be made at various times during the year (known as a cycle count inventory). In the latter instance, all items in the inventory are generally counted at least once each year. Sometimes both types of inventory-taking are used. Since the two methods involve somewhat different techniques, they are discussed separately below.

Inventories Taken at One Time.   Taking a complete inventory requires the cooperation of production, accounting, and storekeeping personnel since it often involves suspending or significantly reducing production, shipping, and receiving operations, and physically rearranging inventory to facilitate counting. Often an "inventory committee" is organized, consisting of management representatives of production departments, the controller's office, the general or cost accounting department, the shipping and receiving departments, and the internal audit department, and the independent auditors. It is usually desirable for someone from production management to assume responsibility for rearranging the inventory and making available employees who are familiar with it to assist in the physical inventory procedures.

A physical inventory may be taken during the vacation period for factory employees, when production is stopped for some other reason, at a time when inventories are at a low level, at year-end, or at a convenient month-end prior to the balance sheet date. Inventory-taking before the balance sheet date is advisable, however, only if there are adequate procedures to safeguard the inventory and to control and document inventory movements between the physical inventory and balance sheet dates.

The counts may be made by production, clerical, or accounting personnel; storekeepers; internal auditors; or an outside inventory service. Count teams often include at least one individual from the production department. Such an arrangement provides an added degree of control while utilizing the production department employee's familiarity with the inventory. However the initial counting is organized, the counts are verified. Some companies have a complete recount by independent teams. Others assign production supervisors or internal auditors to make random test counts. These test counts are documented to provide adequate evidence of their performance and to establish responsibility for them.

An almost invariable requirement for a good physical inventory is preparing a written program in advance. An effective program includes instructions about how to

1. Physically arrange the inventory in a way that simplifies the counts.
2. Identify and describe the inventory properly, including stage of completion and condition, when appropriate.
3. Segregate or properly identify slow-moving, obsolete, or damaged goods.
4. Identify and list inventory belonging to others.
5. Numerically control inventory tags or sheets.
6. Record and verify individual counts.
7. Obtain a proper cutoff of receipts and shipments and interdepartmental movements, and the related documentation.
8. Determine and list goods in the hands of others.
9. Correct errors discovered as a result of the counts.

In addition to instructions for controlling and recording the inventory, the program would include instructions to the accounting department for summarizing quantities, costing (pricing), extending (multiplying quantity by price), and summarizing the priced inventory. Special procedures may be required for consignments in or out, goods in transit, and goods in public warehouses or at branches. Adequate supervision helps to ensure that procedures for arranging and counting the inventory, pricing, and summarizing the counts are properly followed.

The mechanics of counting vary. Seldom, if ever, can all individual items in an inventory be seen and counted; often they are in the packages or cartons they were purchased or are to be shipped in, or are located in bins or stockpiles in large numbers that cannot be physically weighed or counted. General practice is to count a reasonable number of items; some packages are opened and some items inspected, particularly if there are any unusual circumstances.

Differences between physical and recorded inventories are investigated, and the possibility of leakage or pilferage needs to be considered. The records may be right and the count wrong; significant adjustments are not made without a thorough investigation.

Cycle Counts.   Instead of a wall-to-wall inventory, cycle counts may be made throughout the year if there are adequate perpetual inventory records and control procedures for physical inventory movements and cutoff. Procedures used in making periodic counts differ from those for inventories taken at one time. Rather than large numbers of production and other personnel rearranging and counting all the inventory in a plant, periodic counts are usually made by relatively small groups of employees who are independent of the accounting function and who soon become expert at counting inventories.

Cycle count results are reported to accounting personnel and compared with the perpetual inventory records. Discrepancies between them are identified, investigated, and resolved. Discrepancies may result from improper physical counts, clerical errors, cutoff problems, and improper inputting of transactions. Identifying and correcting the causes of discrepancies are important aspects of a cycle counting system. Procedures to ensure the accuracy of cycle counts are similar to those used in wall-to-wall counts. When periodic counts are made and found to be reliable, the perpetual records may serve as the equivalent of a complete physical inventory and are priced, extended, and summarized for comparison with general ledger accounts at or near year-end.

Inventories in Public Warehouses.   Control procedures generally include a preliminary investigation and continuing evaluation of the performance of the custodian. Statement on Auditing Standards (SAS) No. 1, as amended by SAS No. 43 (AU Section 901.26–.27), suggests the following procedures:

Consideration of the business reputation and financial standing of the warehouseman.

Inspection of the physical facilities.

Inquiries as to the warehouseman's internal control structure policies and procedures and whether the warehouseman holds goods for his own account.

Inquiries as to type and adequacy of the warehouseman's insurance.

Inquiries as to government or other licensing and bonding requirements and the nature, extent, and results of any inspection by government or other agencies.

Review of the warehouseman's financial statements and related reports of independent auditors.

Review and update [of] the information developed from the investigation described above.

Physical counts (or test counts) of the goods, wherever practicable and reasonable (may not be practicable in the case of fungible goods).

Reconcilement of quantities shown on statements received from the warehouseman with the owner's records.

Other Inventories Not on the Premises.   Other inventories not on the premises normally include inventories on consignment, in the hands of processors or suppliers, and at branches. Those classifications of inventory are carried in separate accounts supported by perpetual records. Control procedures may include review of monthly inventory and activity reports, confirmation, and periodic physical counts. Control procedures for receipts and shipments are similar to those for inventory on the premises, even though shipments may be on memorandum only. To avoid possible duplication, special attention is given to goods in transit.

Inventories Belonging to Others.   Many companies receive material purchased by their customers, process it in various ways, and hold it pending further instructions. All inventory belonging to others needs to be clearly identified and physically segregated to avoid erroneously including it in the client's inventory counts. If the amount is significant and the activity frequent, perpetual records are maintained. Records of the property of others are generally maintained carefully, particularly if the items are similar to or commingled with inventory the client owns. The items are also counted to establish accountability to the owner.

Items Charged Off, But Physically on Hand.   Frequently, certain types of supplies, such as small tools, are charged to expense as purchased or classified as prepaid expenses. Those items are kept under physical protection; unissued items are subject to requisitioning procedures similar to those for other inventories. Items of doubtful value written off, but on hand, are segregated and protected until they are disposed of. Scrap and defective items that can be utilized in some manner or sold as seconds are subject to similar control procedures. Periodic physical inventories of such items are taken.

Shipping Goods Produced

When finished goods are shipped to customers, the transfer of costs from the finished goods account to cost of sales (if the detailed perpetual records reflect both inventory quantities and costs) is based on executed shipping orders. The process of executing orders and recording shipments and related control procedures are described in Chapter 12, "Auditing the Revenue Cycle." As discussed there, the complete and accurate recording of accounts receivable and sales is ensured by requiring appropriate supporting documentation before executed shipping orders are input to the sales transaction file. Simultaneously inputting those orders to the cost of sales transaction file (if perpetual records reflect both inventory quantities and costs) ensures the complete recording of charges to cost of sales and the reduction of finished goods inventory. Periodically, the detailed perpetual inventory records are adjusted to agree with physical counts, are costed (if only unit records are kept) and aggregated, and any difference between their total and the control account balance is charged to cost of sales. Significant or recurring differences are investigated to determine their causes, and corrective action is taken as necessary.

DETERMINING THE AUDIT STRATEGY

The audit strategy for each account balance and class of transactions in the production cycle is based primarily on the auditor's assessment of inherent and control risk relating to specific audit objectives and on efficiency considerations.

Audit Objectives

The audit objectives applicable to the production cycle and inventories are as follows:

Completeness
- Inventories represent all raw materials, work in process, and finished goods that the enterprise owns, including those on hand, in transit, or on the premises of others.
- All shipments (and returns) of goods during the period covered by the financial statements are reflected in cost of sales.

Accuracy
- The detailed perpetual inventory records are mathematically correct and agree with the general ledger inventory control account.
- Costs associated with inventories have been properly classified and accumulated.
- Cost of sales is based on correct costs and quantities, is properly summarized and posted to the costs of sales and inventory control accounts, and, if appropriate, is credited in the perpetual inventory records.

Existence/Occurrence
- Recorded inventories physically exist in salable condition and represent property held for sale in the ordinary course of business.
- Recorded cost of sales represents goods actually shipped during the period covered by the financial statements.

Cutoff
- Production costs incurred and charged to work in process, transfers to finished goods, and cost of sales (and returns) are recorded in the proper period.

Valuation
- Costs associated with inventory and cost of sales are determined and accumulated using generally accepted accounting principles consistently applied.
- Inventories (including slow-moving and obsolete items) are stated at not more than their net realizable value.

Rights and Obligations
- The entity has legal title or ownership rights to the inventory; inventory excludes goods that are the property of others or have been billed to customers.

Presentation and Disclosure
- Inventories and cost of sales are properly described and classified in the financial statements.
- All encumbrances against inventory are adequately disclosed.

The auditor achieves these objectives by performing substantive tests or a combination of substantive tests and tests of control structure policies and procedures. The auditor frequently tests an entity's control procedures to obtain evidence of the effectiveness of their design and operation as a basis for significantly reducing the assurance needed from substantive tests directed at the completeness, accuracy, and existence objectives. The cutoff objective for cost of sales is typically achieved concurrently with the cutoff objective for sales, as described in Chapter 12. The auditor generally achieves the remaining audit objectives by performing substantive tests, supplemented by the evidence obtained through assessing the entity's inherent risk conditions, control environment, and accounting system. For example, the auditor's awareness of an economic decline in the client's industry may cause concern about the salability of inventory and hence its valuation.

Risk Assessment

As discussed in Chapter 8, the auditor gathers or updates information about the client and its business as a basis for assessing inherent and control risk. The audit risks associated with inventories vary based on the nature of an enterprise's inventory and its materiality to the financial statements. For example, there is a high level of inherent risk associated with inventories like precious metals or gems that have relatively high value and can be easily converted to cash. Accordingly, such inventories require more effective control procedures. Or, in estimating net realizable value, there is a higher level of risk associated with a product that must meet very strict technical standards or composition requirements than with a commodity that is generally acceptable to many potential users.

Analytical Procedures. Analytical procedures often highlight relationships between accounts and reveal risks not otherwise apparent during the risk assessment phase of the audit. As discussed in Chapter 8, analytical procedures are a required part of audit planning. Their use at an early stage in the audit often results in more informed strategy decisions.

Analytical procedures can, for example, indicate trends that may help the auditor assess risk. Such trends may involve

- The relationship among the components of production cost.
- Production usage and price variances.
- Finished goods inventory turnover (the ratio of cost of sales to average finished goods inventory).

The auditor should review those relationships and compare them with those of prior periods and those anticipated in budgets or forecasts. The ratios and the account balances themselves are often compared from month to month and with the corresponding period of the prior year. The auditor should note trends and fluctuations (seasonal and other) and seek explanations for unusual patterns.

The auditor should consider management's performance of analytical procedures as part of its reviews of reports and other internal documentation. The auditor may consider using the results of those procedures, to the extent necessary, to supplement his or her own analytical procedures. Management typically reviews various internal production and inventory reports and data, like the following:

- Actual production and inventory levels in relation to historical trends and budgets or forecasts.
- Material, labor, and overhead standard cost variances.
- Actual gross margins compared with historical trends and budgets.
- Write-offs of obsolete and otherwise unsalable inventory and other write-downs compared with budgets and historical data.
- Trends in inventory turnover.

Management's review of reports such as these may help identify material misstatements in processing or recording production costs or cost of sales. For example, investigating significant differences between reported and budgeted production costs could identify incomplete recording of production costs in the general ledger.

The way the client responds to the auditor's inquiries resulting from analytical procedures may give some indication of the quality of the client's control environment. For example, prompt, logical, and meaningful answers to questions about fluctuations in inventory turnover ratios from the prior to the current year would provide some indication, in the absence of evidence to the contrary, that the company's management is "in control" and that the accounting system and control procedures appear to be functioning as intended. Analytical procedures, however, may also indicate trends, even in well-controlled companies, that may lead the auditor to extend substantive tests; for example, trends that raise questions about the realizability of recorded inventory values. Analytical procedures performed as substantive tests are discussed later in this chapter.

Control Risk. The auditor also is required, at a minimum, to obtain an understanding of the entity's control structure sufficient to plan the audit. This understanding is used to identify the types of misstatements that might occur and the risk of their occurring, and to design substantive tests. The understanding is obtained or updated by considering previous experience with the entity, reviewing prior-year audit results, interviewing client personnel, observing personnel as they perform their duties, reviewing client-prepared descriptions of policies and procedures, and inspecting documents and records. These procedures normally reveal information about all significant cycles and account balances.

In addition to information regarding the client's overall control environment, the predominant means of processing transactions (manually or by computer) and the level of its sophistication, and other general characteristics of the control structure, the auditor should consider the following types of information, as appropriate, related to the production cycle:

- Liquidity of the inventory, that is, how easily it can be converted into cash.

- Number of items in the inventory.
- What judgments enter into the inventory valuation (e.g., judgments about inventory obsolescence).
- Susceptibility of major products to technological obsolescence, spoilage, or changes in demand.
- Availability of materials critical to the production process, number of vendors able to supply such materials, price stability of the materials, and ability of the client to pass along price increases to its customers.
- Historical trends of applicable inventory turnover ratios, net realizable value, and inventory obsolescence problems.
- The cost accounting system in use and how well it reflects the actual production process and how it reports the production costs incurred, the application of overhead, and the transfer of production costs to finished goods inventory and cost of sales.
- The accounting methods used to value inventory.
- Current-year production cost variances from standards or budgets.

The auditor should also obtain an understanding of control procedures applied to producing and shipping goods and storing raw materials and finished goods inventories, and how duties are segregated in performing those procedures. Based on this information, the auditor determines whether control structure policies and procedures for specific classes of transactions are appropriately designed and have been placed in operation.

In the course of obtaining the understanding of the control structure, the auditor may perform concurrent tests of controls (either incidental or planned) and thereby obtain evidence that control structure policies and procedures have been properly designed and are operating effectively. That evidence would enable the auditor to assess control risk at below the maximum for relevant audit objectives. For example, when inquiring about management's review of production reports, the auditor may also observe the performance of the review or examine reports or documents that provide evidence of the review. If operating effectively, management's review provides some evidence with respect to the completeness and accuracy of costs charged to production. The auditor considers the level of detail reviewed and whether the individual performing the review would be likely to detect a material misstatement.

The auditor next considers whether he or she wishes to obtain additional evidence of the effectiveness of policies and procedures as a basis for a low assessment of control risk, and then whether such evidence is likely to be available and efficient to obtain. If so, the auditor would usually perform additional tests of controls for specific audit objectives—commonly, completeness, accuracy, and existence/occurrence of inventory, cost of sales, and production costs.

Audit Testing Plan

As discussed in Chapter 5, the basic audit strategy decision the auditor makes for each significant account balance is whether to perform additional tests of controls to support a low assessed level of control risk for specific audit objectives, or to perform substantive tests directed at all relevant audit objectives without significant restriction based on tests of controls. Factors affecting that decision are described below.

Whether to perform additional tests of controls in the production cycle should be determined separately for each transaction class, for each segment of the inventory (raw materials, work in process, and finished goods), and for the price and quantity components of inventory values. For example, the auditor may decide to obtain assurance about the quantity of items on hand by observing and testing the physical count of the items. The auditor may decide, however, that control procedures for pricing the inventory are effective enough to warrant testing them, and that it would be efficient to do so.

Although audit strategy decisions must always be tailored to specific client circumstances, it is possible to make some general observations about what conditions might lead the auditor to either perform or not perform additional tests of controls. Such tests are likely to be effective and efficient if the assessment of inherent risk and the understanding of the control structure, including any concurrent tests of controls performed, indicated that the client had

- Effective production planning, budgeting, and management information systems.
- Effective general control procedures as well as transaction processing and file control procedures for production and inventory.
- Adequate segregation of duties between personnel who produce and store inventory and those responsible for the related accounting, and between personnel who store inventory and those responsible for receiving and shipping.
- Adequate asset protection control procedures for all significant inventories.
- A policy of taking physical inventories regularly to ensure the existence, accuracy, and salable condition of recorded inventories.
- An effective accounting system and related control procedures for accumulating all production costs and properly allocating them to inventory.
- Adequate control procedures to ensure proper cutoffs in the receiving and shipping departments.

Moreover, the auditor would probably be able to perform a significant portion of substantive testing before the balance sheet date, provided that activity during the period between early substantive testing and year-end could be adequately tested. For example, it might be more difficult to test activity during the intervening period for a large number of low-cost items than for a small number of high-cost items. Early testing may be particularly efficient if the client desires the audit report relatively close to year-end, since substantive procedures for inventory balances are often fairly extensive.

On the other hand, in the absence of the above effective control structure factors, or if the auditor's inherent risk assessment suggests the client may have potential motives for overstating inventories, the audit strategy should emphasize substantive testing, probably as of the balance sheet date.

The auditor's assessment of control risk, along with the results of early substantive testing and the length of time between those tests and year-end, will also affect how the auditor obtains the necessary assurance as to the year-end inventory balance if the client takes its physical inventory before year-end or uses cycle counting procedures. The required low level of audit risk can be achieved through an appropriate combination of procedures, including tests of supervisory procedures and special procedures implemented by the client for the intervening period; reviews of the client's method of calculating ending inventory and cost of sales if inventory activity is not recorded on a perpetual basis; reviews of production and sales reports generated for management decision-making purposes; analytical procedures; and tests of details of purchase, sale, and production activity during the intervening period.

ADDITIONAL TESTS OF CONTROLS

As discussed earlier, the auditor may have performed concurrent tests of controls while obtaining an understanding of control structure policies and procedures. Concurrent tests of controls often provide evidence to support an assessment of control risk at below the maximum for one or more audit objectives. However, concurrent tests of controls are generally directed mainly at policies and procedures that are part of the control environment and accounting system, as opposed to specific control procedures, and therefore usually relate to several audit objectives and affect several accounts. Accordingly, tests of controls performed concurrently with obtaining the understanding of the control structure are not sufficient to support a low assessment of control risk for specific audit objectives and account balances. To assess control risk as low for one or more audit objectives for some or all production cycle accounts, the auditor performs additional tests of controls. Such tests usually require substantial audit effort, and therefore the auditor generally performs them only when he or she believes they will significantly reduce the amount of substantive testing required. This principle is particularly applicable to inventories, because the minimum substantive testing necessary to achieve the existence and accuracy (pricing) audit objectives is often extensive.

The purpose of performing additional tests of individual control procedures is to obtain support for an assessment that all the control structure elements interacting together reduce to a low level the risk that control objectives will not be achieved. Specific control objectives and typical control procedures applicable to producing goods for sale and storing inventory are described in Figure 14.1. The accounting system assumed to be in operation in the figure is a sophisticated computerized system. As discussed in Chapter 8, the tests of controls that the auditor would perform include an appropriate combination of inquiring about the client's control procedures, observing that the procedures have been placed in operation, and examining evidence that they are designed and operating effectively. Also as discussed in Chapter 8, reperformance may be used in tests of controls; but if that becomes necessary, the auditor usually determines it is more efficient to perform substantive tests. In addition to testing control procedures specific to a particular transaction cycle, in order to assess control risk as low the auditor would also need evidence of the effectiveness of general control procedures. (General control procedures are discussed in Chapter 11.)

When performing tests of controls, the auditor should be aware of audit objectives other than completeness, accuracy, existence, and cutoff that may be affected by those tests. For example, the auditor frequently considers the valuation objective when testing controls in the production cycle. Tests of the client's procedures for pricing inventory components used in production are performed primarily to obtain evidence of the accuracy of the costs. The results of those tests, however, will also help the auditor determine whether the inventory is valued in accordance with the entity's inventory pricing method. For example, if the entity uses the FIFO method of pricing inventory, the auditor could determine from testing the procedures used in charging costs during the various stages of production whether finished goods are valued according to the FIFO assumption.

The underlying data supporting inventory valuation is derived mainly from the buying cycle, described in Chapter 13. If tests of controls for purchase and payroll transactions produce evidence that related accounting data is reliable, it can be relied on for inventory valuation purposes as well, often with little additional testing. This is particularly true if tests of controls in the buying cycle are planned and performed with production cycle audit objectives in mind as well. For example, tests of controls of payroll can easily be expanded to include the distribution of labor costs to specific production lots or units in the perpetual inventory records. This may provide evidence about the accuracy of unit costs reflected in the perpetual inventory records as a basis for pricing the inventory.

Highly developed cost systems often generate data that provides the details of

- Transfers between raw materials and work in process and between work in process and finished goods.
- Distribution of material, labor, and overhead expenses to cost centers, job orders, or production runs.
- Stages of completion of work in process.
- Variance accounts (in the case of standard cost systems) identifying differences between actual and standard.
- Differences between actual and budgeted costs.

An effective cost accounting system usually generates reports that analyze and explain standard cost variances or differences between actual and budgeted amounts. If management reviews these reports, the auditor may test the accuracy of the analyses and review management's explanations for variances.

In evaluating the results of tests of controls (including tests of general control procedures), the auditor considers whether the control structure policies and

Figure 14.1 Producing Goods for Sale and Storing Inventory

		Control Objectives				
		Transaction Processing				
Specific Control Objectives	*Authorization*	*Completeness of Input*	*Accuracy of Input*	*Completeness and Accuracy of Updating[a]*	*File*	*Asset Protection*
	All recorded production costs and transfers of production within work in process and to finished goods represent actual activity and are approved.	All production costs (materials, labor, and overhead) and transfers to and from work in process are input and accepted for processing.	Charges to production for materials, labor, and overhead, and transfers within work in process and transfers of completed production to finished goods are correctly recorded in the proper period as to quantities, descriptions, amounts, and dates in the general ledger control accounts and perpetual inventory records; are accurately converted into computer-readable form; and are accu-	All production costs and transfers input and accepted for processing are accurately updated to the work-in-process and finished goods data files.	The integrity of the perpetual inventory records and the general ledger inventory accounts, after production costs have been accumulated and transferred, is preserved.	Only authorized personnel have access to raw materials, work-in-process, and finished goods inventories and the related accounting records or data stored on them.

Typical Control Procedures				
Approval of materials, labor, and overhead charged to production, including determination of standard costs and overhead application rates, and of transfers within work in process and to finished goods. Review of materials requisitions and labor distribution by department and/or job number. Approval of changes to standard costs and overhead application rates. Approval of new products on the files.	Accounting for the numerical sequence of requisitions of materials and component parts issued to and returned from production. Reporting and resolving missing or duplicate (unmatched) items by people independent of the materials handling function. Reconciliation of records of labor and overhead charges to payrolls and overhead cost incurred, including reporting and resolving differences. Accounting for the numerical sequence of	rately input to the computer. Completeness of input control procedures for missing or duplicate materials requisitions, records of labor and overhead charges, and transfers within work in process and to finished goods also address the accuracy of input for the fields matched or reconciled. Counting work-in-process and finished goods inventories and reconciling to the perpetual records. Review of period-end cutoff procedures by personnel other than those who	Comparing total costs input with the total updated to the work-in-process and finished goods files.	Ensuring that the correct version of the file is being used for processing. Balancing of the raw materials, work-in-process, and finished goods records (previous balance plus additions less transfers out, compared with the current total). Counting raw materials, work-in-process, and finished goods inventories and adjusting the perpetual records. Reconciling the perpetual records to the general ledger control accounts and ap-	Adequate physical control procedures to prevent unauthorized access to inventories and related documents (requisitions, production reports) and inventory files and files used in processing production activity.

(Continued)

Figure 14.1   Continued

Control Objectives

	Transaction Processing		Completeness and Accuracy of Updating[a]		
	Authorization	Completeness of Input	Accuracy of Input	File	Asset Protection
Typical Control Procedures (Continued)		production reports or other records of finished production and transfers within work in process; reconciliation of those reports to quantities recorded, including investigation and resolution of missing documents and differences. Review and approval of monthly summarizing entries.	maintain related perpetual inventory or other accounting records or safeguard inventories. Reporting adjustments to the perpetual inventory records as a result of inventory counts. Reporting and resolving production costs and inventory transfers recorded in the wrong period.	proving adjustments, by personnel other than those responsible for maintaining related perpetual records or for safeguarding inventories.	

[a] Completeness of updating and accuracy of updating have been combined in this figure for convenience, because typically the same control procedures apply to both objectives.

procedures, taken as a whole, are appropriately designed to achieve the control objectives and are operating effectively. This will determine whether the auditor can achieve the expected reduction in the assessed level of control risk for specific accounts and audit objectives and, thus, whether the auditor can significantly reduce substantive testing. Results differing from those anticipated require the auditor to reconsider the nature, timing, and extent of planned substantive tests. The auditor should reconsider the planned substantive tests not only for production cycle accounts, but also for other accounts that may be affected. For example, ineffective control procedures to ensure completeness of recorded shipments to customers may affect sales revenue as well as inventory and cost of sales.

SUBSTANTIVE TESTS

If the auditor has assessed control risk for some or all production cycle accounts as low for the audit objectives of completeness, accuracy, and existence, substantive tests addressing those audit objectives may, except for the need to observe physical inventory counts, be limited to analytical procedures. The auditor will also consider the relevance to those audit objectives of evidence obtained from tests directed at other audit objectives and other accounts. For example, tests that provide evidence of the completeness of accounts payable also provide some evidence about the existence and accuracy of raw materials inventory. The auditor seldom assesses control risk as low for the cutoff, valuation, rights and obligations, and presentation and disclosure objectives, and therefore generally performs substantive tests of details for these objectives. (As noted earlier, cutoff tests for cost of sales are typically performed concurrently with cutoff tests for sales.)

Observation of Physical Inventories

Since the *McKesson & Robbins* case precipitated the issue in 1939, the observation of physical inventories has been a required auditing procedure and one of the principal substantive tests of inventories. For a long time after 1939, auditors were expected to make voluminous and extensive test counts, sometimes virtually taking the physical inventory side-by-side with client personnel. In recent years, the emphasis has shifted to observation and testing of the client's procedures for physical counts of inventories. In any event, both auditor and client should keep in mind that the client is responsible for inventory quantities; the auditor's responsibility is to observe and evaluate the client's procedures and results.

The official position of the profession is now stated in SAS No. 1 (AU Section 331.09), as follows:

> It is ordinarily necessary for the independent auditor to be present at the time of count and, by suitable observation, tests, and inquiries, satisfy himself respecting the effectiveness of the methods of inventory-taking and the measure of reliance which may be placed upon the client's representations about the quantities and physical condition of the inventories.

AU Section 331.12 goes on to state

> When the independent auditor has not satisfied himself as to inventories in the possession of the client through the procedures [of a physical count], tests of the accounting records alone will not be sufficient for him to become satisfied as to quantities; it will always be necessary for the auditor to make, or observe, some physical counts of the inventory and apply appropriate tests of intervening transactions.

Planning the Inventory Observation.   The client has the primary responsibility for planning and taking the physical inventory. Because of the auditor's participation, however, the planning should be a joint effort. The client and auditor should agree on the timing of the inventory after considering the following factors: The inventory should be counted at year-end if it is subject to significant volatility of movement or quantities, or if the control procedures for accounting for movement are ineffective. If those procedures are effective, the count can be taken before year-end or, if the client uses cycle counts, on a staggered basis throughout the year; if the inventory is taken at one time, both client and auditor usually prefer a month in the last quarter of the fiscal year. Unless the client has effective control procedures that address proper cutoff, the auditor should discourage the client from taking inventories of different departments (especially sequential work-in-process departments) over a period of several days, because double-counting of inventory could result. Alternative control procedures to prevent double-counting are rarely cost-effective.

The auditor should review and comment on the written instructions or memorandum of inventory plans. Often the client executive responsible for the inventory holds one or more instructional meetings with those who are to supervise the inventory-taking. The auditor's presence at the meetings usually facilitates the plans for observing the inventory.

The need for a large number of auditors to be present is naturally greater if a complete physical inventory is taken at one time than if cycle counts or staggered inventories are taken. Audit staffing requirements must be determined based on the timing of inventories at various locations, the difficulty of observing them, and the number of counting teams the client provides.

Observing the Physical Inventory.   The auditor must keep in mind the objectives of observing a physical inventory: to ascertain that the inventory exists and to observe that the count and description of the inventory and its condition are accurate and properly recorded. An auditor is neither a taker of inventory nor an expert appraiser of inventory quality, quantities, or condition; nonetheless, he or she cannot neglect the intelligent application of common sense. Well-arranged inventory is more likely to be accurately counted than is poorly arranged inventory. Signs of age and neglect are often obvious, for example, dust on cartons or rust and corrosion of containers, and they naturally raise questions about the inventory's usefulness and salability. The condition of the inventory is particularly important if the product must meet strict technical specifications. For example, in the aerospace industry, a metal part may have to possess specific size, weight, and shape characteristics, as well as conform to standards for a particular alloy mix. Failure to meet the specifications in the smallest way can mean that the part should be valued as scrap. Before observing the inventory, the auditor should know enough about the client's business to be able to recognize, at least in broad terms, the product under observation and the measures appropriate to determining its quality and condition. Thus, an auditor should spend some time examining the inventory being counted; however, the client, and everyone else concerned, should recognize that the auditor is not acting as an expert appraiser.

The auditor should spend most of the time observing the client's procedures in operation. The diligence of the counting teams should be noted: how carefully they count, weigh, and measure; how well they identify and describe the inventory; what methods they use to make sure no items are omitted or duplicated. The auditor should also observe whether supervisory personnel are present, how planned recounting procedures are executed, whether cutoff procedures are performed, how inventory count documents are controlled, how individual areas or departments are controlled and "cleared," and whether instructions are followed.

The auditor should make some test counts, both to confirm the accuracy of the client's counting and to record corroborative evidence of the existence of the inventory for later tracing to the inventory summarization. Recorded client counts should be selected and reperformed to test their accuracy; in addition, inventory items should be selected and independently counted and compared with quantities recorded by the client. This provides evidence that all items on hand are accurately included in the client's recorded counts.

The auditor must use judgment in determining how many test counts to perform. In the absence of specific reasons to do otherwise, the auditor usually performs a small number of test counts in relation to the total number of items in the inventory. If the auditor's counts disclose an unacceptable number of errors in a particular location, the client would ordinarily recount the inventory. The auditor should record the test counts for subsequent tracing to the inventory summarization.

Client inventory counts are commonly recorded at least in duplicate, with one copy retained at the scene of the count and another gathered for summarization. The client normally controls the summarization process, and the auditor makes notations of tag or count sheet numbers or other control data on a test basis for later tracing to summarized records to provide corroborative evidence that the process was adequately controlled, that is, that all tags or count sheets were accounted for and none was added later.

As part of the review of plans and observation of the physical inventory procedures, the auditor should note and evaluate the procedures followed in separately identifying and counting items moved from place to place (such as from department to department or from receiving area to storage area) and goods on hand belonging to others, such as consignments, bailments, goods on approval, and property of customers returned for repair or held awaiting delivery instructions. All items belonging to others should be counted and recorded separately, both because they should be subject to control and to preclude their mistaken or purposeful substitution for the client's inventory.

Adequately identifying work in process, especially its stage of completion, is likely to be difficult and may be impossible without a bill of materials or similar document. Production or operating personnel must be able to identify items in process and their condition or stage of completion in order to control the production process, and so they should be able to do so for physical count purposes as well. If they cannot, the auditor may find any of a number of practical ways to deal with the problems of identifying and valuing work in process. On the basis of experience and common sense, the auditor can make assumptions that clearly cannot be materially in error: Goods in a given department can be assumed to have passed through an average stage of completion; the variety of goods in a given department can be assumed to be of an average size, formula, or character; tote boxes, bales, or coils can be assumed to be of an average weight.

Cycle Counts.   All procedures applicable to wall-to-wall physical inventory observation can be readily adapted to cycle count observation. The auditor can review the cycle counting schedules, plans, and instructions, and observe the physical arrangement and condition of the inventory, and the diligence and proficiency of the inventory count teams in counting and identifying inventory, controlling records of test counts, preventing omissions or duplications, and identifying and segregating slow-moving, obsolete, or damaged goods. Because the entire inventory is not being counted at one time, the auditor must take steps to ensure that the items counted are properly identified. The auditor can make a few test counts either independently or with the count teams and can observe and, if desired, participate in reconciling the counts to perpetual records and investigating differences.

Effective cycle counting depends on effective control procedures for inventory quantities and timely recording throughout the production process. Having tested the effectiveness of the client's procedures for controlling inventory quantities and related cycle counting, the auditor can choose to observe and test physical inventory procedures at any convenient time, including, if necessary, before or after the period under audit.

The auditor also needs evidence that the cycle counting procedures observed were functioning before and can be expected to function after they were observed and that they are applied to substantially all inventory items. A formal schedule of counts and specific assignments (covering both personnel to perform the counts and supervisory responsibility) is preferable. Many companies, however, operate under a loose policy of "counting all items at least once a year" and assign the counting to the stockkeepers to do as time allows. In those instances, the auditor can review work sheets, entries in the perpetual inventory records, and other evidence of the regularity of test counting, and can evaluate the results. Evidence of proper count procedures includes frequent counting; absence of substantial differences between counts and records over a period of time; adequate cutoff of receipts, shipments, and transfers (at the date of each count); quality of investigation of differences that occur (including segregation of duties between personnel performing initial counts and those investigating differences); and quality of storeroom housekeeping and inventory identification.

Difficult Inventories. Certain types of material—for example, logs in a river, piles of coal and scrap metal, vats of chemicals—by their nature may be difficult to count, and an auditor may have to use ingenuity to substantiate quantities on hand. Measurement of a pile of metals may be difficult for a number of reasons: The pile may have sunk into the ground to an unknown depth; the metals may be of varying weights, precluding the use of an average; or the pile may be of uneven density. The quality of chemicals and similar materials may be impossible to determine without specialized knowledge, and the auditor may find it necessary to draw samples from various levels of holding tanks and send them for independent analysis. Irregularities have been perpetrated by substituting water for materials stored in tanks.

Clients sometimes use photographic surveys, engineering studies, and similar specialized techniques to take physical inventories, and an auditor can observe how carefully they are conducted. In such situations, the auditor should consider the need for an expert or specialist to help take or evaluate the inventory. Guidance on the use of specialists is contained in Chapter 6.

In some circumstances, the auditor may be guided by the client's system of handling receipts and disbursements from the piles. For example, the client may use a pile rotation or exhaustion system, in which material received is placed in other piles until a pile is exhausted, at which time errors in the accounts are disclosed. If the pile rotation system functions satisfactorily, the auditor may be willing to consider the accounting records, to a certain extent, as a source of evidence.

Alternative Procedures If Observation of Physical Inventories Is Not Practicable. The auditor should not decide lightly that observation of inventories is impracticable or impossible. If the client does not or cannot take a physical inventory, however, or if the auditor cannot be present at the inventory-taking, the auditor may be able to form an opinion regarding the reasonableness of inventory quantities by applying alternative procedures. Those alternative procedures fall into the following two basic categories:

Examining other physical evidence that may be tantamount to observing physical inventories.
Substantiating inventories through further examination of accounting documents and records.

As an example of the first category, if the auditor is engaged after the physical inventory has been taken, subsequent physical tests (before or after year-end) may be a satisfactory substitute for observing the inventory-taking. The auditor may also examine written instructions for the inventory-taking, review the original tags or sheets, and make suitable tests of the summarization.

Governmental or production requirements may prohibit interrupting production to take inventory. If work-in-process inventory cannot be taken in the customary way for that or any other reason, the auditor may have to find a reasonable alternative way to obtain the necessary evidence.

In any event, the auditor must examine or observe some physical evidence of the existence of the inventory and make appropriate tests of intervening transactions or control procedures applied to them. If, on the basis of those tests, the auditor is satisfied that inventories are fairly stated, he or she is in a position to express an unqualified opinion. On the other hand, there may be no practicable substitute for observation of inventory-taking, and an auditor may have to express a qualified opinion or disclaimer, depending on the materiality of the inventories and on whether the failure to observe was unavoidable or resulted from management's decision to limit the scope of the audit.

Sometimes procedures for substantiating inventories must be based on examining other accounting documents and records. For example, in an initial audit, the auditor generally will not have observed the physical inventory at the previous year-end, which is a principal factor in determining cost of sales for the current year. If reputable independent accountants expressed an unqualified opinion on the prior-year statements, a successor auditor may accept that opinion and perhaps merely review the predecessor auditor's working papers supporting the prior-year balances. If no audit was made for the preceding year, the auditor may have no alternative but to substantially expand the tests of accounting records to attempt to obtain reasonable assurance about the beginning inventories in order to be able to express an opinion on the current year's results of operations.

Those expanded tests may include a detailed examination of physical inventory sheets and summaries, including review and testing of cutoff data, examination of perpetual inventory records and production records, and review of individual product and overall gross profit percentages. In connection with the latter procedures, cost accumulations for selected inventory items should be tested and significant changes in unit costs directly traced to factors such as technological changes, mass buying economies and freight rate "breaks," changes in labor costs, and changes in overhead rates. Changes in gross profit percentages should be further related to changes in unit sales prices and changes in the profitability of the sales mix, if applicable.

An auditor who is unable to form an opinion on the opening inventory may decide to qualify the audit opinion or disclaim an opinion with respect to results of operations for the year under audit.

Initial audits involving filings with the Securities and Exchange Commission present problems because audited income statements are required for three years. Despite the inherent difficulties in reporting on inventories of earlier years, the auditor must obtain reasonable assurance about the prior years' inventories through appropriate alternative auditing procedures if an unqualified opinion is to be issued.

Testing Ownership and Cutoff

The auditor must determine that the client holds title to the inventories. In many cases, this is relatively straightforward. Theoretically, the accounting for purchases and sales in transit at year-end is determined by the FOB terms (shipping point or destination), which determine title. Unless financial statements would otherwise be misleading, however, the legal test of title is often disregarded based on materiality considerations: Purchases are generally recorded when received, and sales when shipped.

The primary focus for determining ownership is on proper control of receiving and shipping activities and cutoffs at year-end and, if different, at the physical inventory date. Control over sales cutoff at an early physical inventory date is particularly important because sales cutoff errors at that date—as compared with year-end—are compounded when perpetual inventory records and control account balances are adjusted for differences between recorded and physical inventory. Since cutoff errors correct themselves in the following period when the sales and cost of sales are recorded in the normal course of transaction processing, a reduction of inventory and increase in cost of sales, if goods were shipped before the physical count but not recorded until after the physical count, will be recorded twice. The effect in that situation is to misstate gross profit by the full cost of the inventory involved in the cutoff error. On the other hand, a sales cutoff error at year-end (when the physical inventory has been taken at an earlier date) will result in a misstatement of gross profit only to the extent of the gross profit on the sale.[1]

At the time of the inventory observation, the auditor should visit the receiving and shipping departments, record the last receiving and shipping document numbers, and ascertain that each department has been informed that no receipts after or shipments before the cutoff date should be included in inventory. The auditor should review the records of those departments after the inventory date and compare the last receiving and shipping numbers with accounting department records to ensure that a proper cutoff was achieved. Special care should be taken to control the movement of inventory when manufacturing operations are not suspended during the physical inventory.

If there are consignment inventories, inventories in public warehouses, or customer inventories, those procedures must be expanded. Inventory held by others should be substantiated by direct confirmation in writing with the custodians. If such inventory is material, the auditor should apply one or more of the following procedures, in accordance with SAS No. 1, as amended by SAS No. 43 (AU Section 331.14), to obtain reasonable assurance with respect to the existence of the inventory:

a. Test the owner's procedures for investigating the warehouseman and evaluating the warehouseman's performance.

b. Obtain an independent accountant's report on the warehouseman's control procedures relevant to custody of goods and, if applicable, pledging of receipts, or apply alternative procedures at the warehouse to gain reasonable assurance that information received from the warehouseman is reliable.

c. Observe physical counts of the goods, if practicable and reasonable.

d. If warehouse receipts have been pledged as collateral, confirm with lenders pertinent details of the pledged receipts (on a test basis, if appropriate).

---

[1]Cutoff errors involving receipt of goods at the physical inventory date also misstate gross profit by the full cost of the inventory involved; cutoff errors involving receipt of goods at year-end (when the physical inventory has been taken at an earlier date) have no effect on gross profit, except in the rare situation in which the merchandise was also sold.

If merchandise is billed to customers and held for them, care must be exercised to exclude that merchandise from inventory and to determine that the customers have authorized billing before delivery. Goods belonging to customers or others should be counted and, if significant in amount, should be confirmed with their owners. The auditor should be alert to the possibility of such goods and should make certain that the client has a system for controlling the goods and that they are properly identified and segregated.

The auditor should also be alert for liens and encumbrances against the inventories. These are normally evident from reading minutes and agreements, or as a result of confirmations with lenders relating to loans or loan agreements. It may be necessary to investigate whether additional liens and encumbrances have been filed with state or local governmental authorities.

Inventory Costing and Summarization

Inventory costing and summarization may be based on the physical inventory results or the perpetual inventory records (if those records have been determined to be reliable); in either case, the results are compared with the recorded amounts. The procedures performed in testing the summarization of the physical inventory quantities are as follows:

1. The inventory tags are tested to determine that all tags used for the physical counts and only those tags are included in the physical inventory summaries. The auditor should also ascertain that tags that were voided during the physical count have been properly accounted for. If count sheets were used for recording physical inventory results, the auditor should ascertain that unused spaces have not been filled in after the physical count was completed.

2. The inventory summaries are compared with the auditor's record of counts and with the client's count sheets or tags; conversions and summarizations of units are tested.

3. Quantities are compared with perpetual records, if they exist, on a test basis, and differences and client dispositions are reviewed; this is particularly important when inventories are taken prior to year-end and perpetual records will be the basis for year-end inventory valuation.

4. Cutoff procedures are tested.

5. Customers' materials on hand and client's inventories in the hands of others are reviewed and confirmed.

6. Raw materials, labor, and overhead costs to be applied to inventories are tested to determine that they are reasonably computed in accordance with an acceptable and consistent accounting method.

7. The multiplication of prices and inventory quantities and the resulting footings and summarizations are tested.

How extensively the auditor performs each of the above procedures depends on the auditor's knowledge of and experience with the client, information obtained when observing the physical inventory count, understanding of the control structure, and the results of any tests of controls performed. Errors noted when testing the summarization should be given particular consideration in assessing whether client procedures are effective and whether additional testing is necessary.

In testing the costing of merchandise inventories and inventories of simple manufacturing operations, the auditor can often relate costs directly to specific vendor invoices and labor summaries. For example, for merchandising operations in which goods are purchased for resale, the cost of inventory can be determined by reference to appropriate purchase invoices. In simple manufacturing operations, the allocation of material costs, direct labor, and overhead to inventory may be straightforward. For such operations, it may be most efficient to substantively test the assigned costs.

In more complex manufacturing operations, evaluating material, labor, and overhead allocations may be more difficult. An example is the manufacturing operation of a steel mill where the raw materials ore, coal, and limestone are converted into finished steel. Allocating costs is less objective and requires an understanding of process costing and an in-depth knowledge of the manufacturing process. It may be difficult for the auditor to obtain satisfaction regarding the costing of inventory without obtaining some evidence that the client's procedures for product costing and tracking inventory through the various stages of completion are effective.

Accountants have long recognized the conceptual problems associated with allocating overhead to work in process based on activity such as direct labor hours or dollars. Changes in the manufacturing environment—in particular increased automation and computerization, reduced levels of inventories of raw materials and component parts through the use of just-in-time techniques, and direct labor becoming a smaller portion of production costs—have called into question the appropriateness of commonly used overhead allocation bases. Some enterprises have considered new techniques to generate cost accounting data that both better reflects the results of management's decisions and produces financial statements acceptable for financial reporting. The auditor should consider the client's overhead allocation methods to ensure that they generate inventory and cost of sales values that are in conformity with GAAP appropriate to the enterprise's circumstances, and that those methods are not merely routine or mechanical applications of traditional techniques that do not reflect the enterprise's manufacturing environment.

The accounting method used to price inventory also affects the substantive tests to be performed. The differences in the procedures used under different valuation methods relate mainly to the sources of cost information and the mechanics of the pricing calculations. For example, pricing tests of inventory valued on a FIFO basis normally include a comparison of costs to most recent invoice prices for purchased merchandise and most recent unit production costs for manufactured goods. Pricing tests of LIFO inventories normally include procedures to test consistency of base-year prices between years, comparisons of base-year costs for new items with current-year costs, recalculation of indices used to value current-year LIFO increments, and an overall review of the accuracy of the LIFO application.

LIFO presents opportunities, not available under other inventory costing methods, for the client to manage earnings. Those opportunities often involve transactions, usually entered into near year-end, that would charge portions of the beginning inventory to cost of sales or, depending on management's reporting objectives, prevent a liquidation of the beginning inventory from being charged to cost of sales. Management could accomplish these income-managing objectives by entering into accommodation purchases or sales that, pursuant to an undisclosed resale agreement, would later be reversed. The auditor should be alert to the possibility of such transactions, which may be discovered by scanning the records for unusual transactions early in the next accounting period, particularly transactions with known related parties.

Inventory Valuation

Generally accepted accounting principles require that inventories be reported at the lower of historical cost (using an acceptable flow-of-cost assumption) or market (current replacement cost by either purchase or production), except that the carrying value should not exceed net realizable value (estimated selling price minus costs of completion and disposal) or be lower than net realizable value reduced by the normal profit margin. (Net realizable value is frequently referred to as the ''ceiling,'' and net realizable value reduced by the normal profit margin is frequently referred to as the ''floor.'') To achieve the valuation objective for inventories, the auditor should test the inventory costing as indicated above, and should also

- Review and test procedures for identifying obsolete or slow-moving items.
- Review the costing of damaged or obsolete items to determine that the assigned value does not exceed net realizable value.
- Review and test the determination of market prices to determine whether market is lower than cost.

In reviewing for obsolete items in inventory, the auditor should consider not only finished goods but also work in process and raw materials that will eventually become finished goods. The auditor may compare quantities with those in previous inventories on a test basis to identify slow-moving items or abnormally large or small balances. Comparing inventory quantities with sales forecasts is an effective test for obsolete items. Reviews of usage records can provide further indications of slow-moving items. If the client does not maintain perpetual records, the auditor may examine purchase orders or production orders to determine how recently certain items of inventory were acquired. Many companies have formulas or rules of thumb that translate overall judgments on obsolete inventory into practical detailed applications, like all items over a year's supply, all items that have not moved within six months, or all items bearing certain identifying numbers with regard to date or class of product. The auditor must review whether the rules are realistic and comprehensive enough as well as whether they are fully and accurately applied. In addition to reviewing and testing the client's rules, the auditor must evaluate, based on an understanding of the client's business, whether, for each segment of the inventory, market conditions might raise questions about its realizability in the normal course of operations. The auditor may also inquire of sales and marketing executives about the salability of the inventories. Past experience can be the best guide to the net realizable value of items that must be disposed of at salvage prices. When certain finished goods are declared obsolete (or severe markdowns are required), related raw materials and work-in-process inventories (unless usable for other products) may also need to be written down.

Testing the client's application of the lower of cost or market principle is one of the more difficult and subjective aspects of the audit. In most situations, the auditor's assessment of inherent risk is particularly important in determining the extent of substantive testing. For example, if the risk of defective production or of the acceptance of incoming shipments of defective merchandise is high, the auditor may need to expand testing of the condition of inventories. Companies usually apply the lower of cost or market test on an exception basis when a problem is identified. Accordingly, the auditor has limited opportunity to test control procedures in this area. The greater audit risk is that not all problems have been identified, not that an identified problem may lead to a misstatement in the financial statements.

The auditor should test the client's calculation of net realizable value of individual or major groups of products. Estimated selling prices may be compared with recent sales invoices—or preferably with the latest customer orders—and evaluated for possible trends in prices. Estimated costs of completion and disposal may be tested for reasonableness by an overall computation. The auditor ordinarily need not determine the value of inventory at reproduction or replacement costs if there is acceptable evidence that, for individual or groups of products, the range between net realizable value and the market floor is not great. If necessary, however, the auditor may test replacement costs by reference to cost records, current invoices, or purchase contracts. Reproduction costs may be tested in a similar manner, supplemented by discussions with production and accounting employees.

Auditing Cost of Sales

In planning the audit, the auditor often views the income statement as the residual effect of changes in the balance sheet. The primary focus is on auditing balance sheet accounts at the beginning and end of the year. The audit opinion on results of operations, however, requires that the auditor perform auditing procedures to obtain satisfaction that transactions are properly accounted for and classified in the income statement.

Substantive tests of cost of sales are usually limited for two reasons. First, the audit plan is likely to include tests of controls in the production cycle. Second, if the auditor performs substantive tests of the beginning and ending inventory balances and obtains evidence about the completeness, accuracy, and authorization of purchases of goods and services (including their proper classification) by testing controls that are part of the buying cycle, he or she has significant amounts of evidence about the "residual" cost of sales figure. Accordingly, substantive tests of cost of sales can normally be limited to analytical procedures that test the proper classification of costs by focusing on expected or traditional relationships among various components of cost of sales and obtaining explanations for fluctuations in expense account balances. Often overhead and other variances are also analyzed as part of substantive tests of cost of sales. Typical analytical procedures are discussed later in this section.

If results of the above procedures indicate that additional evidence is needed to support the cost of sales balance, the auditor may also examine selected invoices for material and overhead costs and test the allocation of payroll costs, together with testing the summarization of detailed amounts in the account balances that enter into cost of sales. The auditor would probably perform analytical procedures as well.

Purchase Commitments

Losses from purchase commitments may arise in connection with commodity purchases, forward transactions, or purchase commitments in excess of short-term requirements. If material losses could arise from unfulfilled purchase commitments, the auditor should identify the commitments and assess the potential need for a loss provision. This may be accomplished by examining open purchase order records, inquiring of employees who make purchase commitments, or requesting major suppliers to provide details of any purchase commitments outstanding at year-end. If there is doubt regarding whether all commitments have been identified, it may be appropriate to review suppliers' invoices and receiving reports for a period after year-end for evidence of purchases above prevailing prices or in quantities exceeding current requirements (by reviewing perpetual inventory records for evidence of goods that are slow-moving or obsolete), which may indicate unfavorable purchase commitments at year-end. Also, since major purchase commitments generally require the approval of the board of directors, examining minutes of board meetings may be helpful in discovering such commitments. Chapter 21 contains a discussion of the statements about purchase commitments that should be included in the client's representation letter.

Analytical Procedures

Auditing inventories challenges an auditor's knowledge and analytical skills more than almost any other audit activity. The better the auditor understands the client's business, its operating problems, and the market and other economic conditions it operates in, the greater the ability to determine that the inventory is fairly stated in conformity with generally accepted accounting principles. That understanding can be applied to specific judgments in designing analytical procedures.

Both internal and external data is abundantly available for designing and testing statistical, ratio, and other kinds of analyses. The auditor should make every effort to use analytical procedures unique to the client, but only on the basis of a thorough understanding. The following paragraphs describe only those analytical procedures that are likely to apply to most inventories.

If standard cost systems or budgetary systems produce variance reports, the system has, in effect, performed a large part of the analytical procedure by identifying the variances. The auditor can then read the variance reports carefully and analyze reasons for variances. If variances are small, the auditor can infer that standards approximate actual costs and can significantly reduce price testing.

The auditor may compare purchases, usage reports, and production costs from month to month, and investigate and obtain explanations for fluctuations. Significant ratios may be computed and compared from month to month and with the prior year. The ratios of cost of sales to inventory and to sales (or profit margin) are universally considered informative. They must be used with caution in a period of changing prices, however, as results under FIFO will differ, perhaps significantly, from those under LIFO. In a great many industries, the computation of the ratio of total units to total value—that is, average unit cost—is valid and informative, but if the "mix" of unit costs is likely to vary substantially, explaining fluctuations in average unit costs may not be cost effective. If they are valid, average unit costs can be computed for sales, purchases, and inventory balances.

If available, sales forecasts and marketing plans can provide important information about salability and net realizable value of inventories. For example, marketing plans for a "new line" can effectively render obsolete an inventory that otherwise appears salable at normal profit margins. Sales forecasts and marketing plans, however, are often not well organized or in written form, and thus the auditor must take care not to waste time searching for material that is nonexistent or inconclusive. An auditor who has an adequate understanding of the client will know what to expect and of whom to inquire.

Analytical procedures must be particularly intensive between an interim inventory date and year-end. Often the audit effort during this period is directed primarily toward tests of controls, with minimal substantive testing of intervening activity or the year-end balance. Analytical procedures provide an excellent means of identifying changes in conditions that may require additional substantive tests or, in conjunction with the results of related tests of controls and other substantive tests, of providing the needed assurance regarding the year-end balances.

Management Representation Letter

It is standard practice for the auditor to request management to include certain matters relating to inventory in the representation letter. The focus of the letter is on judgments made by management in the financial accounting process; the letter includes representations relating to agreements to repurchase inventory or the absence thereof, net realizable value judgments, pledging of assets, and the nature of significant inventory purchase commitments. Management representation letters are discussed in Chapter 21.

15

Auditing Cash and Cash Equivalents

In auditing cash and cash equivalents, the auditor must exercise judgment to select and apply auditing procedures to determine that cash and cash equivalents are not materially misstated in relation to the financial statements taken as a whole.

FINANCIAL STATEMENT PRESENTATION

Many enterprises use sophisticated cash management techniques to accelerate cash inflows, slow cash outflows, invest excess funds, and reduce costly borrowing. The increased attention being focused on cash management has raised questions about the appropriate balance sheet treatment of cash equivalents, bank overdrafts, outstanding checks and drafts, and restricted cash balances.

Cash Equivalents

Unless otherwise stated, the cash caption on the balance sheet should include cash on hand and balances with financial institutions that are immediately available for any purpose, and cash equivalents. Statement of Financial Accounting Standards No. 95, *Statement of Cash Flows* (Accounting Standards Section C25), defines cash equivalents as short-term, highly liquid investments that are readily convertible to known amounts of cash and are so near their maturity (generally within three months) at the date of purchase that they present an insignificant risk of changes in value because of changes in interest rates. Examples of cash equivalents are money market funds, time deposits, commercial paper, certificates of deposit, and similar types of deposits. The company's policy for determining which items are treated as cash equivalents should be disclosed, either parenthetically or in the notes. Other temporary investments that because of size or maturity are not considered readily available should not be included as cash equivalents.

Bank Overdrafts

There are two types of bank overdrafts.

> *Book*—in which checks have been issued for more than the book balance in the account on which they were drawn but, because of outstanding checks, the bank's records show a positive balance.
>
> *Actual*—in which the bank has paid out more funds than are in the account.

If an actual overdraft is the bank's method of temporarily lending funds to a company, the overdraft should *not* be offset against other cash balances (with either the same or a different bank), but should be classified as a liability.

For financial statement purposes, overdrafts are determined based on book balances. Book overdrafts may be offset against positive book balances that are not legally restricted or subject to exchange restrictions. A book overdraft in one bank account may be properly offset by a positive book balance in an account with the same or another bank. Any portion of a book overdraft that exceeds the positive balances in other cash accounts should be classified as a liability.

Outstanding Checks and Drafts

Checks that have not been released at the end of an accounting period should not be considered outstanding, that is, should not be deducted from the cash balance. Drafts payable on demand that have been issued and are outstanding at the end of an accounting period should be netted against the cash balance because they are similar in substance to outstanding checks. However, the legal distinctions between drafts and checks make it also acceptable to present drafts payable as liabilities, with disclosure of the amount.

Restricted Cash

Cash sometimes includes balances with trustees, such as sinking funds, or other amounts not immediately available, for example, those restricted to uses other than current operations, designated for acquisition or construction of noncurrent assets, or segregated for the liquidation of long-term debt. Restrictions are considered effective if the company clearly intends to observe them, even though the funds are not actually set aside in special bank accounts. The facts pertaining to those balances should be adequately disclosed, and the amounts should be properly classified as current or noncurrent.

Enterprises often maintain compensating balances with banks to support their outstanding borrowings or to ensure future credit availability. Balances maintained under agreements that contractually restrict the use of the funds should be segregated on the balance sheet and classified as current or noncurrent depending on whether the related debt is short- or long-term. In addition, the Securities and Exchange Commission requires additional disclosures of compensating balances[1] maintained under formal and informal arrangements.

AUDIT OBJECTIVES

The objectives of auditing cash and cash equivalents are to obtain reasonable assurance that

- Recorded cash, on hand and in financial institutions, and cash equivalents exist, and are accurate and complete, and the client has legal title to them at the balance sheet date.

---

[1]SEC Accounting Series Release No. 148 defines compensating balances as "that portion of any demand deposit (or any time deposit or certificate of deposit) maintained by a corporation which constitutes support for existing borrowing arrangements of the corporation with a lending institution. Such arrangements would include both outstanding borrowings and the assurance of future credit availability."

- All items properly included as part of cash are realizable in the amounts stated; for example, foreign currency on hand or on deposit in foreign countries is properly valued.

- Cash restricted as to availability or use is properly identified and disclosed.

- Cash equivalents pledged as collateral or otherwise restricted are appropriately identified and disclosed.

- Cash receipts, disbursements, and transfers between bank accounts are recorded in the proper period.

Meeting the cutoff objective with respect to cash receipts from customers and disbursements to vendors is important to prevent end-of-period "window dressing" of working capital accounts. Recording bank transfers in the wrong period could be indicative of a defalcation, as discussed under "Bank Transfer Schedule" later in this chapter.

CASH TRANSACTIONS AND INTERNAL CONTROL STRUCTURE POLICIES AND PROCEDURES

The balance in the cash account results from cash receipts and cash disbursements. The principal source of cash receipts is collections from customers; those transactions are part of the revenue cycle, which was discussed in depth in Chapter 12. Other sources of cash are the issuance of debt and equity (Chapter 20); the sale of property, plant, and equipment (Chapter 18); and revenues from investments (Chapter 17). The principal use of cash is to pay for purchases of goods and services, which are part of the buying cycle, discussed in Chapter 13. Other uses of cash are to purchase property, plant, and equipment (Chapter 18); repay long-term borrowing and acquire treasury stock (Chapter 20); and pay interest and dividends (Chapter 20). Purchases and sales of securities, either as part of the enterprise's cash management procedures (described below) or to accomplish other objectives, also can represent significant uses and sources of cash. Lastly, cash receipts and disbursements may be generated by nonrecurring transactions, such as the sale of a segment of the business.

Management ordinarily institutes appropriate policies and procedures in each of the three elements of the control structure to address the completeness, accuracy, and authorization of cash transactions, as well as appropriate segregation of duties and asset protection control procedures with respect to cash transactions. Those policies and procedures are described in the chapters noted above and are not repeated here. Management generally also institutes policies and procedures to achieve the file control objective, that is, to ensure the completeness, accuracy, and authorization of the cash balance after transactions have been posted to a manual ledger or entered in a computer file, and to safeguard cash once it has been recorded. Segregation of duties and asset protection control procedures (both custodial control procedures and timely bank reconciliations) are particularly significant because cash represents the highest form of liquidity and is so easily transferable. The remainder of this section focuses on those policies and procedures.

Disbursements of Currency

Disbursements made in currency from petty cash funds are normally for advances, freight bills, and other minor expenditures. Sometimes wages and salaries are paid in currency. Asset protection of funds used for currency disbursements is usually achieved by keeping the relevant fund (or funds) on an imprest system under which the sum of unexpended cash and paid vouchers equals the fixed amount in the fund. Imprest bank accounts are sometimes used like petty cash funds, for payroll and branch office local expenditures.

Reconciliation of Bank Accounts and Cash Transactions

Periodic reconciliations of cash receipts and disbursements to amounts shown on bank statements are key control procedures to meet the asset protection objective for cash. The reconciliation procedure will be more effective if, in addition to reconciling the balances, the detailed items listed on the bank statement are reconciled to the detailed items recorded in the accounts during the period covered by the bank statement. The latter step ensures that all items recorded in the accounts, including offsetting items within receipts or disbursements, are also recorded on the bank statement and vice versa. The preferred reconciliation procedure is the "proof of cash," which is described in detail later in this chapter.

Segregation of Duties

Effective segregation of duties requires that the person responsible for reconciling bank balances to account balances not have functions relating to cash receipts, cash disbursements, or preparing or approving vouchers for payment. It also requires that the person performing the reconciliation obtain the bank statements directly from the bank and make specific comparisons, like comparing paid checks and other debits and credits listed on the bank statement with entries in the accounts, examining checks for signatures and endorsements, and reconciling bank transfers.

Cash Management

Enterprises have certain objectives for managing their cash. A universal objective is to generate maximum earnings, consistent with the risks involved, by investing or otherwise using cash, including concentrating it in deposits that "earn" the most in banking relations and bankers' services. Management's use of the cash records to monitor its cash management strategies may also contribute toward meeting other control objectives for cash.

A principal tool of cash management is cash forecasting and budgeting, that is, trying to plan, in as much detail and as far ahead as possible, what receipts can be expected and what disbursements will be required. The objective is to schedule as precisely as possible the amount and timing of borrowings and of cash available for temporary investments. Doing this requires accurate daily calculations of balances, transfers, and commitments, which often leads to effective policies and procedures relating to cash. Variations from budget are reported to and closely scrutinized by a cash manager; if the manager is independent of the handling of and accounting for cash, these reviews may be an effective part of the control environment.

Good cash management requires policies and procedures for (1) evaluating the risk and return of different kinds of cash equivalents and temporary investments, and (2) making the actual investment decisions. The treasury function in many enterprises has become increasingly sophisticated in response to the rapidly growing number of complex financial instruments for investing available cash for periods ranging from overnight to several months. The risks and returns associated with those instruments vary widely and may be difficult to understand and analyze. (See Chapter 39 for a further discussion of financial instruments.) Management must understand the risks and returns, however, both to make informed investment decisions and to apply appropriate accounting measurement and disclosure principles. Finally, treasury management also entails decisions about who should authorize and execute cash management transactions. Sometimes the transactions are initiated automatically, for example, by overnight sweeps of cash balances into money market instruments; sometimes they are discretionary on the part of cash managers; and sometimes authorization by senior-level management is required.

Another objective of effective cash management is to bring receipts under managerial control as quickly as possible, which depends on fast and accurate processing, including daily bank deposits, lockbox systems, wire transfers, and one-way depository bank accounts. Effective cash management also calls for close attention to invoices in process to make sure payments are timed to use cash resources most effectively.

AUDIT TESTING PLAN

The remainder of this chapter is based on the assumption that the auditor, through the appropriate combination of risk assessment activities and substantive tests, will have reduced audit risk to an appropriately low level with regard to cash receipts from customers, cash disbursements to vendors, cash transactions related to cash management,[2] and other cash transactions. Accordingly, the following discussions of the audit testing plan and substantive tests are limited to auditing the balance in the cash account on the balance sheet.

Assessing Inherent Risk and Considering Materiality

Because cash and cash equivalents are so liquid and transferable, the risk of theft is greater than for any other asset. Accordingly, the auditor focuses on

---

[2]Auditing procedures for investments, discussed in Chapter 17, may be appropriate for auditing certain cash equivalents.

how responsive the client's control structure policies and procedures, particularly relating to asset protection and segregation of duties, are to that inherent risk characteristic.

Failure to detect cash defalcations is, at a minimum, frequently a source of embarrassment to the auditor. Often, it may be the basis for litigation, particularly if it involves material fraud that a plaintiff contends should have been detected by an auditor following a testing plan that gave appropriate consideration to the inherent risk associated with cash and the client's response to that risk. Cash defalcations may result in nonexistent assets being reported on the balance sheet, which would be the case if a theft was not concealed and the cash account not reduced by the amount stolen. Often, however, cash defalcations are concealed by unauthorized charges to income statement accounts, resulting in an appropriate balance sheet presentation for cash, but an income statement containing misclassified or fictitious expenses, along with possibly deficient disclosures.

In considering materiality, the auditor should determine the volume and value of cash transactions and the locations and approximate amounts of all cash funds, bank accounts, cash equivalents, and other negotiable assets. (The auditor also should inquire whether cash or securities in the possession of the client include property of other organizations, such as an employees' association, or company property not recorded in the accounts, such as unclaimed wages and employees' savings.) This information will reveal the actual size of the cash account and enable the auditor to assess its significance in relation to the client's financial position.

Assessing Control Risk

The auditor ordinarily will have gained an understanding of how well duties involving recording and handling cash are segregated, as well as other aspects of the control structure relating to cash transactions, when auditing the revenue and buying cycles. The auditor now needs to assess whether the client has effective asset protection control procedures and segregation of duties to safeguard cash balances, and has established effective policies and procedures—mainly reconciliations—to meet the file control objective relating to cash.

The nature, timing, and extent of substantive tests of cash and cash equivalents are strongly influenced by the auditor's assessment of inherent and control risk. For example, the auditor may merely review the client's bank reconciliations, rather than perform one or more reconciliations, if he or she has obtained evidence that bank reconciliations are performed regularly and there is proper segregation of duties within the various cash functions. The effectiveness of control procedures also affects the timing of substantive tests. For example, public companies often have early earnings release dates, so that the auditor may wish to perform early substantive tests of cash. If segregation of duties and asset protection control procedures have been tested and found adequate, they may provide evidence that the control objectives are met in the period between the early testing date and year-end. When performing substantive tests before the balance sheet date, the auditor should consider the factors discussed under "Timing of Tests of Details" in Chapter 9.

Other control structure policies and procedures may affect the nature and extent of substantive tests. For example, management personnel or the internal auditors may receive monthly bank statements directly from the banks, review the statements for unusual transactions, and examine the signatures on the returned checks. Those procedures provide the auditor with additional evidence of the effectiveness of the control structure regarding cash.

In the past, many auditors spent an inordinate amount of time applying detailed auditing procedures to cash—for example, reviewing or reperforming bank reconciliations at one or more dates, performing one or more independent reconciliations, and examining every cash receipt and disbursement and supporting documents for one or more months. If control structure policies and procedures relating to cash are not designed and operating effectively, such detailed auditing procedures may be necessary to provide reasonable assurance about the cash account. Over the years, however, those procedures have increasingly taken on the character of extended rather than routine auditing procedures, and are performed only if the auditor suspects a material misstatement of the cash balance and is unable to obtain sufficient evidence by other means to either affirm or allay that suspicion.

SUBSTANTIVE TESTS

This section describes substantive tests for auditing cash balances.[3] To the extent called for as a result of the assessment of inherent and control risks, the auditor typically obtains the necessary assurance about cash receipts and disbursements by tracing the following to the cash account, on a test basis if appropriate: receipts from customers and disbursements to vendors, receipts and disbursements from transactions involving cash equivalents and investments, sales of fixed assets, debt and equity transactions, and other nonrecurring transactions. Often this is done in conjunction with auditing the other accounts affected by cash transactions, for example, long-term debt. The tests that remain to be performed are related to the cash balance, and fall into the following categories:

- Testing completeness, accuracy, and existence of ending balances.
  - •• Confirming balances and other information with banks and other financial institutions.
  - •• Preparing, reviewing, or testing bank reconciliations.
  - •• Cash counts.
- Testing bank transfer cutoff.
- Reviewing restrictions on cash balances and related disclosures.

Analytical procedures that can be applied to cash and cash equivalents are limited, primarily because those accounts have few relationships with other

---

[3]As noted earlier, auditing procedures for investments, discussed in Chapter 17, may be appropriate for auditing certain cash equivalents.

accounts. Scanning the cash records for unusual transactions or adjustments to cash may uncover misstatements that might otherwise be overlooked. Other analytical procedures, however, would generally not be helpful in identifying significant risks related to cash or in flagging potential misstatements in cash or cash equivalents.

Confirming Bank Balances and Other Information

Bank Balances.   The auditor should ordinarily confirm balances at year-end by direct correspondence with all banks the client has conducted business with during the year, regardless of whether all year-end reconciliations are reviewed or tested. Usual practice is to confirm all bank accounts open at any time during the year under audit. In the past, auditors ordinarily requested confirmations of bank balances and various aspects of indebtedness to banks by using a standard confirmation form, appropriately signed by the client, approved by the AICPA and the Bank Administration Institute; some auditors still use this form. With the increase in the number of services provided by banks and the number of different people in positions to confirm various items (in both banks and other financial institutions), the practicality of using a form that combines a number of requests for confirmation has become questionable. At the time of this writing, the AICPA is considering revisions to the standard form that would make it appropriate only for confirming bank balances. Indebtedness and various other matters, such as requirements to maintain compensating balances, would be confirmed by separate communications to officials of banks and other financial institutions, as discussed below.

When a bank confirmation form is used, an original and a duplicate are mailed to the bank; one copy is intended to be signed by the bank and returned to the auditor, and the other retained by the bank. Because of increased mechanization of bank accounting, the confirmation procedure can be expedited if the bank receives the confirmation request before the confirmation date and at least two weeks before a reply is required. The exact names and account numbers of the accounts to be confirmed should be specified.

Indebtedness, Compensating Balances, and Other Arrangements.   Banks may have arrangements with or provide services to the client other than maintaining deposits or granting loans. For example, banks may require borrowers to keep certain amounts on deposit (compensating balances) as a condition for a loan. Banks may also hold, as agent or trustee, securities or other items in safekeeping or for collection for the account of the client. Other arrangements—such as oral and written guarantees, commitments to buy foreign currencies, repurchase or reverse repurchase agreements, and letters of credit and lines of credit—may create contingent liabilities.

Auditors typically confirm client indebtedness to banks and other financial institutions, as well as related financial arrangements such as compensating balances, by requesting the client to send confirmation requests to specific officials of those institutions who are knowledgeable about the transactions or arrangements. Thus, the auditor might ask the client to address letters to a number of bank officials asking for information about various debt and other arrangements, like automatic investment services, bank acceptances, cash management services, commitments to purchase foreign currencies and U.S. dollar exchange, repurchase or reverse repurchase transactions, lines of credit, letters of credit, futures and forward contracts, interest rate or loan swaps, loan agreements and related covenants, and standby contracts and other option arrangements.

Other Balances.   Commonly, confirmation of cash on hand is requested from other custodians of funds; often the request to confirm the fund balance is combined with a request to notify the auditor of any unrecorded expenses.

Bank Reconciliations

As noted earlier, the client's reconciliation of bank accounts, and the appropriate division of duties with respect to cash balances and transactions, are key control procedures. The auditor's assessment of how effective the client's reconciliations are determines the nature, timing, and extent of many of the substantive tests of cash. The adequacy of the accounting system, the competence of employees doing the reconciliations, and the segregation of duties are the major factors in that assessment. The more effective the auditor finds the client's reconciliations to be, that is, the lower the assessed level of control risk, the less detailed the auditor's reconciliation procedures have to be. Those procedures may range from simply reviewing the client's reconciliations at year-end, if control risk has been assessed as low, to performing independent reconciliations covering the entire year using the proof of cash form (discussed later). Generally, performing proof of cash reconciliations for the entire year is considered necessary only in special situations, such as when a defalcation is believed to have occurred. Between those two extremes, the auditor may review and test the client's reconciliations, or may perform independent reconciliations at year-end (either using the proof of cash form or not). The various audit approaches to bank reconciliations are described below.

Review of Client's Reconciliations.   If the auditor has assessed control risk as low, then merely reviewing the client's reconciliations at year-end may be appropriate. The steps in reviewing a client's bank reconciliation are

1. Obtain copies of the client's bank reconciliations and establish their mathematical accuracy.
2. Reconcile the total of the bank balances on the reconciliations to the general ledger balance. This will generally require using a summary of the individual cash account balances in the general ledger account.
3. Scan the bank reconciliation for significant unusual reconciling items and adjustments, and obtain evidence to support them by inquiry or examination of appropriate documents.

Review and Test of Client's Reconciliations.   In addition to the review procedures described above, the auditor may decide to test the client's reconciliations. The tests may be performed at an interim date, if the auditor has assessed that the client's reconciliations are subject to effective supervisory control procedures. If supervision during the intervening period is not considered effective, the auditor would probably perform the tests at year-end. If he or she has determined that segregation of duties and asset protection control procedures are effective, the extent of testing of reconciliations may be limited. In addition, depending on these same considerations, the auditor might ask the client to request the bank to send directly to the auditor a bank statement and related canceled checks for the "cutoff period" (usually a week or two immediately following the balance sheet date) or for the following month. Alternatively, the auditor may use the client's bank statement for the following month, if the reconciliation is tested at an interim date.

In addition to steps 1 and 2 above, the procedures below are typically performed in testing the client's reconciliations. These procedures assume that the testing is performed as of the balance sheet date and that cutoff statements for a reasonable period after the balance sheet date are obtained from the bank.

1. Determine that paid checks, deposits, and debit and credit advices appearing on the cutoff bank statements and issued on or before the balance sheet date appear on the year-end reconciliations.

2. Trace to the cash disbursements records outstanding checks listed on bank reconciliations but not returned with the cutoff statements.

3. Trace deposits in transit on the bank reconciliations to the cutoff bank statements and the cash receipts records, and determine whether there are any unusual delays between the date received per the books and the date deposited per the bank statements.

4. Trace other reconciling items to supporting documentation and entries in the cash records.

5. Investigate old or unusual reconciling items. If checks remain uncashed after a specified period of time, the reason should be determined and the amounts either restored to the cash account or disposed of according to state escheat law.

6. Determine the exact nature of items on the year-end bank statements not accounted for by the reconciliation procedures, such as debits or credits followed by offsetting entries of identical amounts that appear to be, or are represented by the client to be, bank errors and corrections not so coded. If information in the client's records is inadequate, clarification should be requested from the bank. In these circumstances, the auditor should consider performing a "proof of cash" reconciliation (described below) if the client's reconciliation process does not include one.

Some companies experiencing cash flow difficulties follow a practice of preparing, recording, and then "holding" checks and releasing them as cash balances become available. The client may believe it is easier to "hold" the checks than to void them and replace them when cash becomes available. Although clients should be urged to prepare checks only when they can be released, the auditor may encounter this situation when checks are routinely prepared by computer at the time invoices are processed based on predetermined invoice due dates. Accordingly, the auditor should inquire whether any checks drawn before year-end were released after year-end and should consider obtaining the numbers of the last checks written for the current fiscal year. If the amount of "held" checks is potentially significant at the balance sheet date, the auditor should plan to examine them at that date and subsequently determine that the amount of such checks has been reinstated by appropriate adjusting entries in the cash account (and related liability accounts) at that date.

Independent "Proof of Cash" Reconciliations.   A proof of cash reconciliation (also known as a "four-column reconciliation") summarizes and controls the examination of cash records for a selected period. An advantage of the proof of cash is that it provides a reconciliation of balances at the beginning and end of the period and, with little additional effort, also reconciles transactions recorded in the accounts during the period to those reflected on the bank statement. An auditor preparing a proof of cash is thus able to "prove" the propriety of recorded transactions in the accounts to an independent source (the bank statement). Any other audit tests applied to the receipts, disbursements, or balances can also be described on the form. A proof of cash working paper is illustrated in Figure 15.1.

A proof of cash reconciliation involves performing the steps described above for reviewing and testing the client's reconciliations (which may or may not be in the form of a proof of cash), plus the procedures described below. Procedures already performed need not be performed again.

1. Enter the totals from the bank statement on the proof of cash form.
2. Obtain the client's reconciliation as of the close of the preceding period and compare balances shown on that reconciliation with the corresponding amounts shown by the accounts and the bank statement; substantiate outstanding checks at the close of the preceding period by examining paid checks returned by the bank in the current period and investigating any still outstanding; and substantiate deposits in transit and other reconciling items at the close of the preceding period by referring to the current bank statement, bank notifications of charges and credits, and other supporting documents.
3. Compare daily totals of recorded cash receipts shown in the cash journal with daily deposits appearing on the bank statement. If there are time lags between the receipt, recording, and depositing of collections, investigate any that appear unreasonable in light of the company's usual practices. (Delay in depositing receipts constitutes inefficient cash management and exposes cash items on hand to risk of loss or misuse, such as "lapping" collections of accounts receivable—a method of continuously concealing a defalcation by crediting later collections to accounts whose collections were not previously recorded.) Enter unmatched cash receipts items or deposit items on the proof of cash form.
4. Compare paid checks returned with the bank statement with the disbursements records for check number, date, payee, and amount. The

Figure 15.1   Proof of Cash

Date Prepared: _1/26/9-_
Prepared By:
  a) C&L   _PLD_
  b) Client and
     Examined By _____
Reviewed By:
  C&L Sr Sup _SAC_

XYZ Corporation
Proof of Cash - Month of December
12/31/9 -

	Balance Beginning of period	Receipts	Disbursements	Balance End of period
Per bank statement	$31268 A	$42687 A	$46560 A	$27395 C A
Deposits in transit:				
Beginning	1000 T	(1000)		
End		2000		2000 T
Outstanding checks:				
Beginning	(3917)		(2817) ∅	(1100) y
End			3460	(3460) ∅
Unrecorded charges and credits:				
Collection from customer				
on note, credited by				
bank during period,				
entered on books after				
end of period		(2078)		(2078) CM
Per Books	$28351 A	$41609 A	$47203 A	22757 A
	✓	✓	✓	✓
Audit adjusting entry #1:				
Collection of customer note				2078
Per books as adjusted				$24835
				✓

Legend of audit procedures:
✓ = Footed & cross-footed
A = Agreed with amounts shown on bank statement/books
C = Balance confirmed with bank; see bank confirmation on W/P —
T = Traced to subsequent bank statement
∅ = Checks cleared on subsequent bank statement
y = Check #895 dated 11/27/9- for $1,100 is still outstanding
   Examined purchase order, receiving report and vendor
   invoice. The purchase made and paid by this check appears
   proper. No adjusting entry proposed
CM = Examined bank credit memo

comparison determines not only which checks have not cleared the bank during the period but also that dates, payees, and amounts of disbursements as shown by the paid checks agree with recorded disbursements. List checks outstanding at the end of the period, foot the list, and enter the total on the proof of cash form.

5. Account for all checks issued in the sequence between the first and last checks drawn on the bank account during the period.

6. Determine that the reconciliation foots and cross-foots. All items appearing in either of the balance columns and bank errors corrected in the same period must also appear appropriately in either the receipts or disbursements column (as additions or subtractions) so that both activity and balances are reconciled. A later entry in the accounts that apparently offsets an item in a reconciliation is not necessarily proof of its correctness. The propriety of reconciling items or adjusting entries is not established merely by the fact that including them makes it possible to reconcile the balances.

7. Compare deposits in transit and outstanding checks revealed by the reconciliation with a subsequent bank statement and accompanying paid checks. Substantiate checks outstanding at the date of the reconciliation that are not returned with the subsequent bank statement, if material in amount, by referring to properly approved vouchers or other available documents.

As noted earlier, the auditor may, in special situations, consider it necessary to perform proof of cash reconciliations throughout the year. In that event, following up reconciling items (step 7 above) would ordinarily not be required, because the client's procedures in that area would have been tested in step 2.

Count of Cash on Hand

Cash funds on hand, normally constituting one or more petty cash funds, are seldom significant in relation to the overall cash balance, except in retail operations. Therefore, auditors generally do not perform substantive tests of the year-end balance of cash on hand. They may nevertheless wish to perform tests of control procedures relating to the day-to-day operation of cash funds to obtain evidence that the activity in the funds has been authorized and is completely and accurately recorded. Ineffective control procedures could result in improperly classified expenses in the income statement.

Some circumstances require physical counting of currency and other cash items on hand. If cash funds on hand and undeposited receipts are significant in relation to the overall cash balance, and if control procedures are ineffective, there may be no alternative to a year-end cash count. If the auditor concludes that a cash count is required, it should be coordinated with the examination or confirmation of negotiable assets such as marketable securities, notes receivable, and collateral held as security for loans to others. In addition, the auditor should take appropriate steps to ensure that a cash shortage at a particular location cannot be concealed by the conversion of negotiable assets or the transfer of cash from another location. If simultaneous physical examination of negotiable assets on hand is not practicable, the auditor should establish control over all such assets to avoid the possibility of a shortage in one group being covered up by other assets already examined. Less active negotiable assets—such as notes receivable and marketable securities—may be counted in advance and placed under seal until all counts are completed. Occasionally it is necessary to permit movement of assets under seal; the auditor should control and record all such transactions. Totals of funds and other negotiable assets counted or confirmed should be reconciled to general ledger controlling accounts as of the date of the examination.

An auditor should not assume responsibility for custody of cash or negotiable assets in a physical count, but should insist on continuous attendance by a representative of the client while those assets are being examined. After the count has been completed, the client's representative should be asked to acknowledge its accuracy. Auditors should never count funds in the absence (even if temporary) of the custodian, and should always obtain a written acknowledgment from the client's representative that the funds have been returned intact. If the count discloses an overage or shortage in the fund, the auditor should ask for a recount and acknowledgment by the client's representative of the accuracy of the count.

Bank Transfer Schedule

To ensure there has been a proper cutoff at year-end, the auditor should determine whether significant transfers of funds occurred among the client's various bank accounts near the balance sheet date. All transfers of funds within the organization should be considered—whether among branches, divisions, or affiliates—to make sure that cash is not "double counted" in two or more bank accounts and that "kiting" (explained below) has not occurred. The auditor should determine (1) that each transaction represented as a transfer is in fact an authorized transfer; (2) that debits and credits representing transfers of cash are recorded in the same period; and (3) that the funds are actually deposited in the receiving bank in the appropriate period.

Kiting is a way of concealing a cash shortage caused by a defalcation, such as misappropriating cash receipts, that was perpetrated previously. It involves the careful and deliberate use of the "float" (the time necessary for a check to clear the bank it was drawn on). Kiting is effected by drawing a check on one bank, depositing it in another bank just before year-end so that the deposit appears on the bank statement, and not recording the transfer in the cash receipts or cash disbursements journals until after year-end. The float period will cause the check not to clear the bank it was drawn on until after year-end, and the amount transferred is included in the balances of both bank accounts. Since the transfer is not recorded as a receipt or a disbursement until the following year, it will not appear as an outstanding check or a deposit in transit on the reconciliation of either bank account. The effect is to increase receipts per the bank statement; if the misappropriation of cash receipts and the kiting take place in the same period, receipts per the bank statement will agree with receipts per the cash receipts journal at the date of the bank reconciliation. (If the misappropriation of cash receipts takes place in the period before the kiting, a proof of cash may also reveal the kiting.) Kiting requires that the transfer process be repeated continually until the misappropriated funds have been restored.[4]

A bank transfer schedule is an efficient and effective tool that assists the auditor in determining that all transfers of funds among bank accounts near the balance sheet date are recorded in the books in the proper accounting period, that cash has not been double-counted, and that there is no apparent kiting. The schedule should indicate, for each transfer, the date the check effecting the transfer was recorded as a cash disbursement, the date it was recorded as a cash receipt, the date it cleared the bank it was drawn on, and the date it cleared the bank it was deposited in. The list of bank transfers should be compiled from both originating documents (paid checks or bank advices) returned with the subsequent bank statement and the client's cash receipts and disbursements records. A bank transfer schedule is illustrated in Figure 15.2.

The dates on the bank transfer schedule should be obtained from the cash records and the dates on the check showing when it was received by the bank it was deposited in and when it was canceled by the bank it was drawn on. The date the check was recorded as a disbursement should be compared with the date it was recorded as a receipt; the dates should be the same. If they are not and the entries are in different fiscal years, an adjusting entry may be necessary to prevent double-counting of cash, depending on the offsetting debit or credit to the entry that was made in the year being audited. Then, for each transfer, the bank dates (paid and cleared) should be compared with the corresponding dates the transaction was recorded in the books (received and disbursed). If those dates are in different accounting periods, the transfer should appear on the bank reconciliation as a reconciling item—an outstanding check if the check cleared the disbursing bank in a later period than it was recorded, and a deposit in transit if it cleared the receiving bank in a later period than the receipt was recorded. Lastly, unusually long time lags between dates recorded and dates cleared should be investigated for possible holding of checks at year-end—a cutoff problem.

In Figure 15.2, there are no double-counting problems with the transfers involving checks A, B, and E because the transfer out of one bank account was recorded in the same period as the transfer into the other bank account. Transfers A and B should appear as outstanding checks on the reconciliation of the disbursing bank's account. Transfer B should also appear as a deposit in transit on the reconciliation of the receiving bank's account. Transfer E should not affect either the books or the reconciliations, because it occurred in the following year and all dates are in the same accounting period.

The other transfers in the figure require further analysis. Transfer C should appear on the reconciliation of the disbursing bank's account as an outstanding check at December 31, 1989. If it does, the balance per the books will not be in error. If it does not, the total of outstanding checks will be understated and the

[4]Banks and other financial institutions use the term "kiting" in a wider sense, to include writing checks against inadequate funds with the intent of depositing sufficient funds later, but before the checks clear the bank.

Figure 15.2   Bank Transfer Schedule

Check Number	Disbursement (Transfer Out)		Receipt (Transfer In)	
	Date Recorded in Books	Date Paid by Bank	Date Recorded in Books	Date Received by Bank
A	12/28/89	01/03/90	12/28/89	12/29/89
B	12/29/89	01/05/90	12/29/89	01/03/90
C	12/29/89	01/03/90	01/02/90	01/02/90
D	01/02/90	01/05/90	01/02/90	12/29/89
E	01/04/90	01/10/90	01/04/90	01/08/90

balance per the books will be overstated, possibly covering up an unrecorded check drawn on that account that already cleared the bank.

Transfer D is an example of possible kiting. That transfer should appear as an outstanding check on the reconciliation of the disbursing bank's account; it should also appear as a recording error (an omitted disbursement) on the reconciliation. If kiting were taking place, it is unlikely that the preparer of the reconciliation would be aware that a check was outstanding that should be included on the outstanding check list; nor would the person doing the kiting call the "recording error" to anyone's attention. The funds transferred would thus be counted twice—once in the bank account the check was drawn on and once again in the account it was deposited in. Transfer D would result in a misstatement, though not from kiting, if the delay in recording was the result of an oversight or an attempt to conceal an overdraft at the bank.

Reviewing Cash Restrictions and Related Disclosures

The auditor should review the evidence previously obtained and, if necessary, perform further procedures to ensure that all appropriate disclosures related to cash have been made. Bank confirmations, responses to inquiry letters, loan agreements, minutes of board of directors' meetings, and bond indentures may indicate restrictions on the availability or use of cash that should be disclosed. Inquiries of client management may also indicate the need for disclosures of cash balances that are restricted or the property of others. (If the latter, the related liability should be recorded.) If the entity has substantial funds in other countries or in foreign currencies, the auditor should determine whether there are any restrictions on their availability and that appropriate disclosures have been made.

16

Auditing Prepaid Expenses, Accrued Liabilities, and Risk Management

Prepaid expenses are assets, most often in the form of services (but sometimes for goods such as stationery and supplies), that have been acquired as part of the buying cycle but that apply to future periods or to the production of future revenues—for example, unexpired insurance, rent paid in advance, and prepaid taxes other than those on income. There is little conceptual difference between prepayments and assets like inventories, plant and equipment, and intangibles: All are expected to benefit future periods. Prepayments are often assumed to be less readily realizable than inventory or equipment, but there are significant exceptions; it may be easier to realize cash from the contractual right to cancel an insurance policy than on a custom-built, single-purpose structure.

The distinction between prepaid expenses and deferred charges is based mainly on whether the asset is current or noncurrent. How precisely that distinction is made depends on custom and materiality considerations. Prepaid insurance, for example, and many types of deposits do not expire and are not realized within one year or the enterprise's operating cycle, but are traditionally classified as current. The prepaid expense account is seldom material to the financial statements, and noncurrent items that are not material are included in prepaid expenses for convenience. If deferred costs (such as debt issuance costs) are material and will expire over several years, they are properly classified as noncurrent deferred charges.

Accrued liabilities, often referred to as accrued expenses, are items for which a service or benefit has been received and for which the related liability is acknowledged and reasonably determinable, but that are not yet payable (either because of the terms of the commitment or because the invoice has not been received). Most accrued liabilities accrue with the passage of time—for example, interest, rent, and property taxes—or with some service or activity, for example, payrolls, vacation pay, royalties, sales commissions, and payroll taxes. Deferred credits (such as unearned revenue and deferred income accounts) result from the receipt of revenues in advance of the related delivery of goods or services and are discussed in Chapter 12.

Agency obligations, such as payroll withholdings and deductions, are funds collected for others for which accountability must be maintained until the funds are turned over at the required time to the agency for whom they are held in trust. Those obligations result from transactions that are part of the buying cycle, discussed in Chapter 13, and the revenue cycle, discussed in Chapter 12.

Many similarities exist among prepaid expenses, accrued liabilities, and agency obligations and among the underlying transactions that affect these accounts. For example, similar types of transactions may result in prepaid insurance or accrued insurance expense; the same is true for rent and property taxes. Items such as insurance premiums and various deposits are often held as agency obligations. All three categories of accounts are frequently subjected to similar types of control structure policies and procedures, and the general audit approach employed is also similar.

AUDIT OBJECTIVES

The auditor should approach prepaid assets and accrued liabilities with the view that liabilities are more likely to be understated or omitted from the accounts than overstated and, conversely, assets are more likely to be overstated than understated. Therefore, audit objectives should focus on ascertaining that prepaid assets are not overstated and that accrued liabilities are not understated, but without ignoring the possibility that the opposite may occur.

In specifying audit objectives for prepaid expenses, the auditor should focus on obtaining reasonable assurance that

- All amounts reported as assets were acquired in authorized transactions and were properly recorded at the time of acquisition.
- The balance of the expenditure carried forward can be reasonably expected to be recovered from future income.
- The basis of amortization is reasonable and consistent with prior years and the related expenses are properly classified.

Principal audit objectives related to accrued expenses and other liabilities are to obtain reasonable assurance that

- All material accrued expenses, agency obligations, and other liabilities existing at the balance sheet date have been recorded and properly measured.
- The amounts recorded for accrued expenses, agency obligations, and other liabilities have been authorized and are properly measured.
- Related expenses have been recognized and properly measured on a consistent basis.

INTERNAL CONTROL STRUCTURE POLICIES AND PROCEDURES

Chapter 13 discusses the acquisition of goods and services and the control structure policies and procedures to which such expenditures are usually subjected. The transactions that give rise to prepayments and accruals originate and generally are processed and controlled in the same way as transactions for other goods and services.

Control procedures are applied to prepaid expenses, accrued liabilities, agency accounts, and other liabilities to ensure timely recording of the required entries. Those procedures are necessary because of the method of procuring many prepaid and accrued expense items. Recurring services such as utilities and rents, after initial identification, are provided continuously without further request. Specialized services, such as insurance, legal, advertising, and auditing services, also are frequently rendered on an ongoing basis. Real estate and property taxes are assessed and paid according to the taxing authority's fiscal year, and must be properly allocated to the enterprise's interim accounting periods. Accordingly, reminder lists—calendars or tickler files to alert those responsible to payment due dates—are usually maintained. Systematic recording of accruals and amortization is best ensured by making standard monthly journal entries, approved by appropriate personnel.

After a prepaid expense has been recorded, further monitoring is required to ensure that it is amortized properly and that the unamortized balance does not exceed the value of the future benefit. If the expenditure was initially charged directly to an expense account, the appropriate amount (i.e., that portion deemed applicable to future periods) is removed from the expense account at the end of each accounting period and set up as an asset.

Control procedures for prepayments, accruals, and the related expense accounts frequently include maintaining detailed files for expenditures like insurance, rent, and commissions, or schedules that are cross-referenced to the related supporting documents and contain pertinent information like cost, starting date, period covered, and amount to be expensed or accrued each period. The account balances and amortization computations are subjected to periodic supervisory procedures. Some liability and agency accounts are treated as part of the buying cycle and are subjected to related control structure policies and procedures. That may be the case for payroll withholdings, customers' deposits, and commissions payable.

AUDIT TESTING PLAN

The auditor may obtain the required understanding of the control structure with respect to prepaid and accrued accounts as part of auditing the buying cycle. Although the assessment of control risk for these accounts is strongly influenced by the level of control risk assessed for the buying cycle, the audit strategy for the prepaid and accrued accounts usually emphasizes substantive tests of year-end account balances, largely because of efficiency considerations. In this regard, Statement on Auditing Standards (SAS) No. 55, *Consideration of the Internal Control Structure in a Financial Statement Audit* (AU Section 319), recognizes that "audit planning does not require an understanding of the control procedures related to each account balance, transaction class, and disclosure component in the financial statements or to every assertion relevant to those components." Also, a single test may serve to both substantiate a prepaid or an accrued account balance and test the related control procedures. Moreover, since substantive tests of balance sheet accounts at the beginning and end of a period also tend to provide assurance about the related expense accounts, it is both conceptually sound and efficient for the auditor to focus on substantive testing of the balance sheet accounts.

In determining the testing plan for prepaid and accrued accounts, the auditor considers the nature and materiality of the specific accounts and the desired timing of their examination, and the assessment of inherent risk. The auditor might perform tests of controls relating to prepayments and accruals on an engagement involving an extremely fast year-end report release or publication of financial data by a large, well-controlled corporation. Those tests would focus on file control procedures addressing the accuracy and authorization of prepayments, and the completeness of accruals.

In determining which substantive tests to apply to prepaid and accrued accounts, the auditor should focus attention on the larger items, for which a possible misstatement of the ending balance would be more likely to have a significant impact on results of operations (and possibly on financial position). For accrued liabilities, substantive tests must also focus on seeking evidence that all items have been recorded and are not understated.

The auditor often reviews and analyzes the composition of prepaid expenses and accrued liabilities at an interim date. It is ordinarily more efficient, however, to perform other substantive tests of prepaid expenses and accrued liabilities at the balance sheet date, unless there are year-end time constraints that make early testing desirable. Early substantive testing requires the auditor to consider alternative means of obtaining the necessary audit assurance at the balance sheet date. In many cases, this is accomplished by updating the substantive tests performed at an interim date. In other situations, the auditor performs tests of controls during the intervening period. Even in these cases, however, the auditor would be likely, at a minimum, to review the year-end account balances for reasonableness.

In determining the extent of substantive tests, the auditor should consider the inherent risk that the account may be materially misstated or may have been affected by irregular transactions. Two key aspects of this risk are how liquid an asset is and the extent to which judgment enters into determining the account balance. Since prepayments by their nature are not particularly liquid, this is usually not a significant factor. Neither is judgment, except with respect to provisions for loss contingencies (discussed in Chapter 21). Very little judgment is required for many of the expenses that are amortized or accrued on a time basis, such as rent, insurance, and interest.

The materiality of prepaid and accrued liability accounts may also be a significant consideration in determining the extent of substantive tests. Many prepaid and accrued accounts are insignificant, and an auditor may consider it sufficient simply to compare the balance with the corresponding balance in the prior period and scan the activity during the period. On the other hand, since auditing prepaid and accrued accounts often affords insight into certain control structure policies and procedures in the buying cycle and therefore may contribute to an auditor's understanding of the control structure, some auditors scrutinize individual accrued and prepaid accounts even though the balances are insignificant.

Furthermore, while an individual prepaid account may not be significant to the balance sheet, an understanding of the content of the account may alert the auditor to a potential misstatement that could have a material effect on the financial statements. This is especially true of the prepaid insurance account. An understanding of the manner in which the client manages risk, in particular the types of insurance coverage it maintains, may make the auditor aware of uninsured risks or unrecorded liabilities. A discussion of risk management appears at the end of this chapter.

SUBSTANTIVE TESTS

Substantive testing usually consists of examining the contractual, statutory, or other basis for prepaid expenses or accrued liabilities; ascertaining that the method of calculating periodic amortization or accrual is appropriate; and recomputing the amortization or accrual and the balance as of the dates selected for testing (either interim or year-end). For many accrued liabilities and some prepaid expenses, the accrual or prepayment is based on an estimate of a liability or a future benefit that cannot be determined precisely. In that case, the basis and rationale for the estimate should be reviewed, compared with prior experience, and evaluated in the light of related circumstances. The related expense account is usually audited (at least in part) in connection with the aforementioned amortization or accrual.

The balances of agency accounts should be supported by trial balances of the detailed amounts. Based on materiality and risk assessment, the auditor should consider the need for substantive tests directed at the completeness and accuracy of agency accounts.

In many cases, analytical procedures are the only type of substantive tests performed on prepaid and accrued accounts. Balances in those and related expense accounts should be compared with the prior-year balance sheet and income statement amounts. The underlying causes of trends, fluctuations, and unusual transactions noted should be understood thoroughly and evaluated for their implications for other accounts.

If they exist, variance reports and analyses of actual costs and expenses compared with budgeted amounts may be examined. The auditor should critically evaluate explanations of variances, both for their adequacy and for evidence they may provide about the accuracy and authorization of the accounts.

In a stable business, predictable relationships often exist among certain accounts, and changes in those relationships may signal conditions requiring accounting recognition. The auditor should compute pertinent ratios and compare them with corresponding ones for prior periods. For example, comparing selling expense with sales might lead the auditor to discover sales commissions that should be but were not accrued. Unexplained changes in ratios involving revenue and expense accounts may indicate possible misstatements of related prepayments and accruals.

Analytical procedures applied to related expense accounts can provide additional assurance about the reasonableness of prepayments and accruals. The auditor may review expense account activity for missing or unusual entries that may indicate unrecorded liabilities or the failure to amortize prepayments. Substantive tests of details are normally not performed on expense account balances unless the control structure is extremely ineffective or the auditor wants additional assurance in high-risk or sensitive areas (such as legal expense).

Control risk for prepaid assets and accrued liabilities is not usually assessed as low; therefore the auditor should perform substantive testing beyond analytical procedures. Substantive tests of specific prepaid and accrued accounts are discussed in the following section of the chapter.

Substantive Tests of Specific Accounts

Prepaid Insurance.   Most well-controlled companies maintain an insurance register that indicates, for each policy, the insurance company, policy number, type and amount of coverage, policy dates, premium, prepayments, expense for the period, and any coinsurance provision. From this register or from the insurance policies themselves, a schedule of prepaid insurance should be prepared, preferably by the client's staff. The auditor should test the data shown on the schedule and examine insurance policies and vouchers supporting premiums. In addition, the auditor should note beneficiaries and evidence of liens on the insured property.

If original insurance policies are not available for inspection, the auditor should determine the reason. Since lenders often retain insurance policies on property that collateralizes loans, the absence of policies may indicate the existence of liens on the property. The auditor should request the client to obtain the policies (or copies of them) and should examine them. Depending on his or her assessment of control risk, the auditor may request confirmations from the insurance companies or brokers.

Prepaid liability and compensation insurance, if premiums are based on payrolls, may be compared with payrolls to determine that charges to expense appear proper. Premiums due may exceed advance payments so that at the end of a period there may be a liability rather than a prepayment. Total prepaid insurance per the insurance register or schedule of prepaid insurance should be compared with the general ledger.

An auditor is usually not an expert in determining insurable values and has no responsibility for management's decisions concerning insuring risks and coverage, but may render helpful service to the client by calling attention to differences among the amount of coverage, the insurable value (if available), and the recorded amount of insured property.

Prepaid and Accrued Property Taxes.   The auditor should determine that the amount of prepaid taxes is actually an expense applicable to future periods, and should refer to local tax bills and laws because state and local tax statutes vary widely in their proration provisions. The related expense account should be examined closely and compared with prior years' accounts. Since taxes are generally computed by multiplying a base by a rate, the auditor can analyze the two components and seek explanations for fluctuations.

Prepaid and Accrued Commissions.   The auditor should investigate whether prepaid or accrued commissions are proper. If commission expense is material, the auditor may wish to examine contracts with salespeople or obtain from management an authoritative statement of the employment terms. He or she may review sales reports, commission records, or other evidence of commissions earned, or may trace amounts in sales reports to commission records and cash records. If there are many salespeople, the auditor may, depending on the risk assessment, limit the examination to only a few accounts or to the entries for only a limited period. Transactions in the last month of the period may be reviewed to determine that commissions have been allocated to the proper period. The auditor should be satisfied that prepayments will be matched with revenues of future periods and are not current-period compensation. If amounts are significant, the auditor should consider confirming directly with salespeople the amounts due them and the commissions they earned during the year, and should test—for example, by applying commission rates against sales—the overall reasonableness of commission expense for the year. If there is a subsidiary ledger for prepaid or accrued commission accounts, the auditor should compare the balance of the general ledger account with the trial balance of the subsidiary ledger and investigate differences.

Travel and Entertainment Advances.   Advances to employees for expenses may be tested by examining cash disbursements, expense reports, and cash receipts. If employees are advanced amounts as working funds on an imprest basis, the auditor may examine reimbursements in the month following the end of the period to determine whether material expenditures prior to the end of the period have been reimbursed. The auditor may review related entries after period-end to determine whether any should have been recorded in the period under audit. Advances may be confirmed by correspondence with employees. The general ledger account should be compared with the subsidiary ledger and differences investigated; the individual balances may be aged and long outstanding balances scrutinized. The auditor should identify unusual advances to officers and examine evidence that they were authorized.

Accrued Professional Fees.   The auditor should consider including in the audit inquiry letters to lawyers a request for the amounts of unpaid or unbilled charges, which can then be compared with the recorded liability.

Bonuses and Profit-Sharing Plans.   Amounts due officers and employees under profit-sharing plans become a liability in the period during which the profits are earned. The auditor should determine that the liability is computed in accordance with the authorization and the plans in effect. If the exact amount of the liability cannot be determined until a later date, it must be estimated at the balance sheet date.

Unpaid Dividends.   The auditor should recompute the liability for cash dividends declared but unpaid at the balance sheet date by multiplying the number of shares outstanding at the date of record by the rate of the dividend declared.

Frequently stockholders cannot be reached and dividend checks may be returned by the post office. The liability for unclaimed dividends may remain undischarged for some time, and the auditor may examine evidence to support charges and credits to the account.

Many large corporations, particularly those that have numerous stockholders or bondholders, turn over to fiscal agents the details of dividend or bond interest payments. Under those arrangements, the corporations usually consider their dividend or interest obligations discharged when they deposit the amount of the aggregate required payments with the fiscal agent. In those circumstances, the auditor is not concerned with unpaid dividend checks or uncashed bond coupons, which become obligations of the agent.

Compensated Absences.   Statement of Financial Accounting Standards (SFAS) No. 43, *Accounting for Compensated Absences* (Accounting Standards Section C44), requires that a liability be accrued for vacation benefits earned but not yet taken by employees. SFAS No. 43 generally does not, however, require a liability to be accrued for nonvesting sick pay, holidays, and other similar benefits until employees are actually absent.

The auditor should determine the method used by the client to accrue vacation pay and accumulated vested sick pay, consider whether the method is appropriate and consistent with prior years, and recompute or test the recorded amounts. If vacation periods are based on length of service, the client normally prepares a detailed computation of the accrued liability. The auditor should review the computation method used and test the accuracy of the computation. If a detailed computation is not available for testing, the auditor should estimate the amount of the accrual on an overall basis.

Royalties Payable.   In evaluating the amount of royalties payable, the auditor should examine royalty and licensing contracts and extract important provisions for the permanent files. He or she should try to determine from a royalty contract whether the payments are actually royalties or whether, in fact, they represent payments for the purchase of a patent or other asset covered by the agreement. If the contract is in reality a purchase agreement, the asset and liability should be recognized at the date of the contract, and depreciation or amortization of the asset should be charged to expense. If provisions of a royalty contract are not clear, the auditor should request a legal interpretation of ambiguous provisions.

Many contracts provide for a minimum royalty payment regardless of whether a liability for royalties accrues on a unit basis. If royalty payments are based on sales, the auditor may compare computations with recorded sales; statements of royalties due may be tested to substantiate recorded amounts. If royalty payments are based on the quantity or value of goods produced, rather than on sales, the auditor should review documents on file supporting amounts accrued and test the underlying data. If accounting records are not kept in sufficient detail to furnish the required information, it may be necessary to analyze production records.

If lessors or vendors possess the only data on which royalties are based, statements of liability under royalty agreements may be secured from them. A request for confirmation may produce evidence of important differences in interpretation of contract provisions.

Provisions for Warranty Costs.   Through inquiry and reading contracts and similar documents, the auditor should obtain an understanding of the client's warranty policies as a first step in evaluating whether the estimated liability for warranty claims is adequate. Auditing procedures in this area commonly include examining documentation supporting open warranty claims, reviewing claims settled after the balance sheet date, and considering past activity in the account in the light of relevant changes (such as new products or changes in warranty periods)—all for the purpose of determining whether the estimated liability at the balance sheet date is adequate. The auditor should also apply the procedures discussed under ''Auditing Accounting Estimates'' in Chapter 9.

Suspense Debits and Credits.   Every chart of accounts contains a place for debit and credit items whose final accounting has not been determined. The person responsible may not have decided which expense account should be charged; the job order, cost center, or subaccount may not have been opened yet; or there may be some other unresolved question about the handling or propriety of the item. Although most suspense debit and credit accounts may be quite active during the year, all material issues should be resolved by year-end. The auditor should understand the nature of suspense items and how they arose, since their existence, even at an interim date, could indicate a deficiency in the client's control structure.

The auditor may want to test balances at an interim date, however, and inquire into the disposition of items. This may contribute considerably to understanding the kinds of accounting problems that can occur and their implications for the auditor's risk assessment. In the rare instance of balances remaining at the end of the year, the auditor should age the items and inquire into the reasons why the proper distribution has not been determined. Particularly in the case of suspense debits, a client commonly and understandably often wishes to carry in the balance sheet disputed items that someone in management ''just doesn't want to give up on.'' If those debits are significant, the auditor needs evidence that they are likely to have a realizable value or to benefit future operations, and are therefore properly classified as assets.

Accrued Pension Costs.   To ascertain that the liability for pension costs and the related expense have been determined in conformity with generally accepted accounting principles (GAAP), as set forth in SFAS No. 87, *Employers' Accounting for Pensions* (Accounting Standards Section P16), the auditor must understand the contractual and other arrangements giving rise to pension costs and be aware of the requirements of the Employee Retirement Income Security Act of 1974 (ERISA).[1] SFAS No. 87 prescribes precisely the way to calculate pension costs. The significance of pension costs to most companies, and the effect of a possible misstatement of them on the financial statements, often calls for substantive testing. The extent of testing will depend on the auditor's risk assessment and on materiality considerations.

Many of the basic calculations required by SFAS No. 87 are actuarial calculations that should be considered the work of a specialist, and the auditor should apply the provisions of SAS No. 11, *Using the Work of a Specialist* (AU Section 336), in auditing those amounts. This does not require the auditor to reperform the actuary's calculations. Rather, the auditor needs to be satisfied

[1]Auditing pension plans is the subject of Chapter 36.

that the methods and assumptions the actuary used are in conformity with GAAP. It is particularly important for the auditor to understand the reasons for fluctuations in pension information from one period to the next, for example, changes in the settlement rate assumption, the methods and time periods for amortizing gains and losses, prior service cost, and the transition amount.

Under SAS No. 11, the auditor should reach an understanding with the client and the actuary about the nature of the actuary's work. This understanding should cover

- The objectives and scope of the actuary's work.
- The actuary's representations regarding his or her relationship, if any, to the client.
- The methods and assumptions to be used.
- A comparison of those methods and assumptions with the ones used in the preceding period.
- The actuary's understanding of how the auditor will use the actuary's findings to corroborate the representations in the financial statements.
- The form and content of the actuary's report needed by the auditor.

SAS No. 11 requires the auditor to evaluate the actuary's qualifications, reputation, and relationship (if any) to the client. The auditor is also required to make appropriate tests of the accounting data the client provided to the actuary.

In examining actuarially determined amounts, the auditor should be satisfied that the actuary's methods and assumptions conform with the provisions of SFAS No. 87. The auditor should not rely on an actuary's conclusion about whether the actuarially computed amounts conform with GAAP; such a conclusion requires a skilled and experience-based knowledge of accounting principles. The auditor should inquire of the client or the actuary about unusual or unexpected shifts from the prior period in components of pension cost or benefit obligation. Analytical techniques can be effective audit tools, when performed with an appropriate understanding of the methodologies prescribed in SFAS No. 87, the client's activities, and the characteristics of the client's work force.

Other suggested procedures are set forth below. They are not intended to be all inclusive or to apply to all situations. Selecting auditing procedures appropriate for a particular situation is a matter of judgment.

- Identify the client's pension plans, and obtain an understanding of the nature, coverage, and other relevant matters pertaining to each plan.
- Compare pension cost and related balance sheet and disclosure amounts and other information with the prior year for reasonableness and changes affecting comparability. Trace amounts to the actuary's report and to any supporting schedules or working papers used in connection with other auditing procedures.

- Evaluate compliance with ERISA (see below).
- Determine whether plan asset and obligation amounts have been computed as of the measurement date and whether plan assets have been measured at their fair value.
- Examine the client's records to determine that the basic data (e.g., size, age, and sex distribution of the work force) used by the actuary is appropriate and that employees ultimately entitled to participate in the plan have been included in the actuarial calculations. Trace (normally in summary form) the employee data tested to the actuary's report or confirm it directly with the actuary.
- Review the actuary's report to determine whether all plan terms have been properly reflected in it and that the actuarial cost method is appropriate.
- Determine whether pension cost and related amounts have been computed on a consistent basis and recognized and disclosed in conformity with GAAP.
- Review the period from the measurement date to the company's year-end (and beyond, to the extent necessary) to determine whether any significant events (e.g., changes in plan provisions) have occurred that would materially affect the computation of the provision for pension costs. If such events have occurred, consult with the actuary and obtain an estimate of the dollar effect on the provision.

Auditing Insured Plans.   The auditor needs to determine the nature of the arrangement between the employer and the insurance company. In some arrangements, an insurance company unconditionally undertakes a legal obligation to provide specified benefits to specific individuals in return for a fixed consideration or premium. For example, the insurance company sells a non-participating annuity and assumes the risks and rewards associated with the benefit obligation and the assets transferred. On the other hand, in participating annuity arrangements, the employer participates in the experience of the insurance company, whereby the insurance company typically pays dividends to the purchaser, effectively reducing the employer's cost. Many variations of such contracts exist.

Auditing procedures for annuity contracts normally involve examining the contract or insurance company dividend and premium statements. If the annuity is a participating annuity, the participation right should be recognized, at cost, as an asset at its inception. The cost is determined by comparing the participating annuity contract with equivalent contracts without participation rights. In subsequent periods, the auditor should ascertain whether fair value can be reasonably determined and, if it cannot, should review the method used to amortize the cost of the participation right.

ERISA Related Procedures.   In reading minutes of meetings of the company's board of directors and pertinent committees, and in performing other auditing procedures, the auditor should be alert to any evidence that a pension plan may potentially be terminated. In addition, the auditor may wish to inquire of management about the possibility of a plan termination. If there is more than a remote possibility, the auditor should ensure that appropriate entries are recorded or disclosures made in the financial statements.

The auditor should obtain evidence that the client is in compliance with ERISA (the Act), since noncompliance may have an impact on the financial statements. In addition to funding requirements, the Act requires compliance in the areas of plan design, reporting and disclosure, fiduciary responsibilities, and record keeping. Determining compliance with the Act is a legal matter, and the auditor therefore customarily relies on inquiries of the actuary, plan trustees, and the client's and the plan's legal counsel for those determinations, as well as obtaining a representation from the client as part of the client representation letter.

CONSIDERING THE CLIENT'S RISK MANAGEMENT

All enterprises face risks in achieving their goals. Profits—or, in a nonbusiness environment, the achievement of other operating objectives—are the result, at least in part, of the assumption of those risks. Risk results from the chance that enterprise activities (financial, production, marketing) will not turn out as planned. Sound management entails assessing risks, deciding which ones to assume, and then instituting policies and procedures to control and reduce those risks as much as possible.

Among the risks that enterprises face are losses of assets from casualties or theft and the incurrence of liabilities as the result of injury to individuals, damage to their business or property, or damage to the environment. For example, a company's premises or property may be vandalized or destroyed by fire; its products may malfunction, causing financial hardships to customers; its employees may injure themselves at work. Some of those risks may expose the company to potentially bankrupting loss of business or assets or incurrence of liabilities. A major concern of the auditor is management's policies and procedures for identifying the occurrence of an event that requires recording a liability for an estimated loss in accordance with SFAS No. 5, *Accounting for Contingencies* (Accounting Standards Section C59). Most entities, either formally or informally, analyze their exposure to such risks and decide which they are willing to accept, which they are not, and the most appropriate means of avoiding or transferring risks in the latter group. In addition, enterprises have potential exposure from unintentional violations of laws or regulations, such as those regarding occupational safety and health, the environment, or equal employment. The auditor should be aware that such violations could also create the need to record a liability.

Companies that choose to deal with the analysis of risk on a formal basis usually establish a risk management function that is responsible for designing an insurance program flexible enough to take into consideration changing conditions and circumstances in the company's business operations. Through effective coordination with management, the risk management function identifies risks and potential loss exposures facing the company and designs ways to manage them. Purchasing insurance coverage through insurance underwriters is the most common practice. One alternative is the establishment of self-insurance trusts from which claims are paid, and another is to self-insure without the establishment of a trust or other means of segregating assets.

Insurance programs relate, in some way, to almost every phase of a company's operations. Thus, the risk management function—or insurance group, as it is sometimes called—coordinates its activities with managers throughout the company to determine the types and amounts of coverage. The insurance group's records need to be current and reflect all appropriate information to ensure that all material risks are considered. The insurance group also reviews billings received for accuracy of rates charged and the coverage provided.

Management should periodically reevaluate the appropriateness of the enterprise's risk management policies, considering changes in the company's operations, such as the opening of new plant facilities, that may necessitate changes in insurance coverage. These are various ways in which risk may be managed, and the auditor should understand the methods the client uses. The remainder of this section discusses several key concepts in risk management.

Self-insurance (sometimes referred to as ''no insurance'') is a method of risk management in which the enterprise retains some risk of loss rather than pay a third party (i.e., an insurance company) to assume the risk. The amount of risk that a company retains will vary depending on the nature of the risk and other considerations, such as the cost of insurance versus the monetary exposure if a loss had to be absorbed. Self-insurance may be combined with purchased insurance; for example, a company may opt to self-insure small losses and purchase insurance (umbrella coverage) to protect against major losses.

A captive insurance company is an entity created and controlled by a parent entity for the main purpose of providing insurance for the parent. If risk is underwritten through this device, the auditor should understand the specialized accounting and auditing issues associated with a captive insurance company, and consider performing some or all of the following procedures:

- Assess the economic viability of the insurance captive.
- Review its audited financial statements and actuarial loss reserve certifications.
- Determine whether the captive underwrites insurance for third parties (e.g., reinsurers and other insurance providers). If so, review agreements to ensure the propriety of coverage limits, periods covered, and premium and loss activity.
- Determine that the captive has the proper legal status in the country of its domicile.
- Assess the appropriateness of the captive's reserves for estimated losses from asserted and unasserted claims, ensuring that reserves are consistent with industry practices.

In retrospectively rated policies, an estimated or deposit premium is paid to the insurance company at the inception of the contract period. The deposit premium consists of a minimum premium plus an amount for estimated claims. During the term of the policy, the deposit premium is adjusted, subject to any minimum and maximum premium limitations of the contract, based on the insured's claims experience. Auditors normally review retrospectively rated policy agreements, noting specific terms that affect premium adjustments (such as experience and claims periods and the methodology for calculating adjustments) to determine whether an additional premium liability should be recorded at the balance sheet date.

Claims-made insurance is a type of insurance that covers damage claims presented to the insurance company during the policy period. This form of coverage differs from the more traditional, occurrence-based coverage, which covers damages that occur (regardless of when the claims are presented for reimbursement) during the policy period. The major difference between the two versions of liability coverage is the event that activates or triggers the coverage. If a claims-made policy is not continually renewed or if "tail coverage" (that is, coverage for future periods) is not obtained when the policy is discontinued, a company will be uninsured for claims reported to the insurance company after the termination of the policy, regardless of when the incidents occurred. Accordingly, the client may need to accrue a liability at the balance sheet date for incurred but not reported claims that will be reported after the claims-made policy expires.

The auditor should also determine whether additional accruals for losses or unpaid deductibles are necessary as a result, for example, of cancellation of policies previously in force or changes in deductibles for new types of coverage.

17

Auditing Investments*

*Auditing investment companies is covered in Chapter 33.

"Investments" is a broad term used to describe nonoperating, income-producing assets of a commercial or industrial enterprise that are held either as a means of using excess cash or to accomplish some special purpose. The term "securities" is commonly used interchangeably with investments, as it is in this chapter. Often, the description of investment assets in the financial statements gives further insight into the specific reasons they are held. Readers of financial statements should look at classifications, descriptions in captions, and descriptive notes to determine the nature and purpose of a company's investments in securities.

"Short-term investments" usually consist of marketable securities acquired for income-producing purposes by temporarily using excess cash. In a classified balance sheet, short-term investments are classified as current. The term "investments" without any modifier often identifies assets held for long-term yield and market appreciation and consequently classified as noncurrent assets. Balance sheets of banks, insurance companies, investment companies, and securities and commodities broker-dealers (which are discussed in Chapters 26, 32, 33, and 39, respectively) customarily do not classify assets as current or noncurrent.

The phrase "marketable securities" indicates a high degree of liquidity, that is, securities for which an organized and active market exists. Such securities may be held in either a current or long-term investment account and may consist of equity or other securities. It is important to identify marketable equity securities, since they are required by Statement of Financial Accounting Standards (SFAS) No. 12, *Accounting for Certain Marketable Securities* (Accounting Standards Section I89), to be carried in the financial statements at the lower of aggregate cost or market. Paragraphs 7(a) and 7(b) of SFAS No. 12 (paragraphs .403 and .404 of the Glossary to Section I89) provide the following definitions:

> *Equity security* encompasses any instrument representing ownership shares (e.g., common, preferred, and other capital stock), or the right to acquire (e.g., warrants, rights, and call options) or dispose of (e.g., put options) ownership shares in an enterprise at fixed or determinable prices. The term does not encompass preferred stock that by its terms either must be redeemed by the issuing enterprise or is redeemable at the option of the investor, nor does it include treasury stock or convertible bonds.

> *Marketable*, as applied to an equity security, means an equity security as to which sales prices or bid and ask prices are currently available on a national securities exchange (i.e., those registered with the Securities and Exchange Commission) or in the over-the-counter market. In the over-the-counter market, an equity security shall be considered marketable when a quotation is publicly reported by the National Association of Securities Dealers Automatic Quotations System or by the National Quotations Bureau Inc. (provided, in the latter case, that quotations are available from at least three dealers). Equity securities traded in foreign markets shall be considered marketable when such markets are of a breadth and scope comparable to those referred to above. Restricted stock does not meet this definition.

"Long-term investments," "investments in affiliates," or "investments" may also represent holdings of securities for purposes of control, affiliation, or financing of enterprises related to the investing company's operations. Those investments, which are classified as noncurrent assets, may require using the equity method of accounting. Sinking funds, building funds, and other funds accumulated for special purposes may consist of investments in securities and are classified as noncurrent assets.

Income statement accounts related to investments are generally "interest revenue" (including amortization of premium and discount, as appropriate), "dividend revenue," "realized gain or loss on sale of securities," "unrealized gain or loss from holding marketable equity securities," and "earnings or losses from investments accounted for by the equity method." Market value adjustments made for long-term marketable equity securities are reflected in the equity section of the balance sheet and not on the income statement.

AUDIT OBJECTIVES

The auditor should design tests to provide reasonable assurance that

- Investments exist and the client has legal title to them at the balance sheet date. Establishing the existence (in either certificate form, electronic or "book entry" form, or a custodial account) and ownership of investments is paramount to the audit process, particularly because many securities are readily negotiable.
- All investments owned by the client at the balance sheet date are included in the investment accounts.
- The values at which investments are carried in the financial statements are appropriate and are adequately disclosed.
- The investments are properly classified between current and noncurrent components.
- Investments pledged as collateral or otherwise restricted are appropriately identified and disclosed.
- Income from investments, including gains and losses on sales and adjustments in valuation allowances, is appropriately reflected in the financial statements.

The nature, timing, and extent of substantive tests that the auditor applies to achieve those objectives, as well as tests of controls, are discussed later in this chapter. The auditor should be familiar with the key accounting measurement and disclosure concepts related to investments, as discussed in the following paragraphs.

Carrying Value

The value at which investments are carried in the financial statements varies with the type of investment and any specialized industry practices. The following is a synopsis of different bases for carrying values.

Lower of Cost or Market. Marketable equity securities, whether classified as current or noncurrent, are carried at the lower of aggregate cost or market. The financial reporting of market value adjustments differs significantly, however, depending on the balance sheet classification. If aggregate market is below aggregate cost for investments classified as current, a valuation allowance account should be established for the difference. Changes in the valuation allowance account should be reflected in income. On the other hand, if securities are classified as noncurrent, the charge is to the equity section of the balance sheet. Subsequent adjustments (recoveries or further declines) should be recorded in the same way. These adjustments to carrying value result in temporary differences between accounting and taxable income.

Equity. Under the equity method, an investment is recorded at cost at the date of acquisition and is then adjusted each period for the investor's appropriate share of earnings, losses, and other changes in stockholders' equity of the investee corporation. The investor's share of earnings and losses should be adjusted for the amortization of the difference between cost and the investor's share of the underlying book value at the acquisition date. If the investor is not obligated to make further advances or investments, the carrying value of the investment should not be reduced below zero as a result of investee losses. The equity method is appropriate for accounting for investments in common stock of unconsolidated subsidiaries, corporate joint ventures, and other investments of 50 percent or less of the voting stock of the investee corporation if the investor has the ability to exercise "significant influence" over operating and financial policies of the investee. According to Accounting Principles Board (APB) Opinion No. 18, *Equity Method of Accounting for Investments in Common Stock* (Accounting Standards Section I82.104), an investment of 20 percent or more of the voting stock of an investee should lead to a presumption that, in the absence of evidence to the contrary, an investor has the ability to exercise significant influence over an investee. If it is clear that the investor exercises significant influence, the equity method is required even if less than 20 percent is owned.

Cost (or Amortized Cost). Cost is the amount paid for an investment at the date of acquisition and includes such items as commissions and fees, but not accrued interest paid at acquisition. If securities are received as gifts (which occurs most commonly in not-for-profit institutions), cost is the fair value as of the date of the gift.

Debt securities are normally acquired at a premium or discount, depending on the stated rate on the bond compared with the market rate at the date of acquisition. The premium or discount should be amortized over the remaining life of the investment, using the effective interest method. For debt securities classified as current assets, entities may elect not to amortize bond premium or discount, based on materiality. Investments in debt securities classified as either current or noncurrent assets are generally carried at either cost or amortized cost, unless there is a decline in value that is other than temporary. In addition, some entities have adopted the lower of cost or market method for all marketable nonequity securities classified as current assets. Some specialized industries (such as investment companies and banks' trading accounts) carry all investments in securities at market value, or fair value in the absence of quoted market values.

Generally, securities carried on the cost method should be adjusted to a lower market value only if there is evidence that the decline in value is other than temporary. An auditing interpretation of Section 332, *Long-Term Investments*, of Statement on Auditing Standards (SAS) No. 1 (AU Section 9332.03) provides some guidance on evidential matter about the carrying amount of marketable securities. As that interpretation indicates, the distinction between temporary and persistent (nontemporary) declines in value is largely undefined in the accounting and auditing literature.[1]

The distinction was considered by the SEC staff in 1985, however, with respect to write-downs of noncurrent marketable equity securities. Staff Accounting Bulletin (SAB) No. 59 cautioned that "other than temporary" should not be interpreted to mean "permanent" and stated that "unless evidence exists to support a realizable value equal to or greater than the carrying value of the investment, a write-down accounted for as a realized loss should be recorded." The SAB included examples of factors that should be considered in evaluating whether a decline is other than temporary: the length of time and the extent to which market value has been less than cost, the financial condition and near-term prospects of the issuer, and the intent and ability of the holder to retain its investment long enough for any anticipated recovery in market value to occur. The conditions of paragraph 8 of SFAS No. 5, *Accounting for Contingencies* (Accounting Standards Section C59.105), may also be applicable; that is, a nontemporary impairment should be considered to have occurred when it is probable that the asset was impaired at the date of the financial statements and the loss can be reasonably estimated.

Income from Investments

The auditor is concerned primarily with the following accounts related to income from investments.

Interest and Dividend Revenue.   Interest income should be accrued to the balance sheet date; dividends should be recorded on the "ex-dividend" date. As mentioned earlier, bond premium and discount on investments in debt securities classified as noncurrent should be amortized to the maturity date of the issue, using the effective interest method.

Realized Gains or Losses.   Realized gains or losses are recorded when securities are sold or, in certain cases, when they are exchanged for other

---

[1] In 1988, the FASB added a project on impairment of assets to its agenda; the project is expected to focus initially on long-lived physical assets and include consideration of identifiable intangible assets. See the discussion of declines in carrying value of assets generally in *Survey of Present Practices for Recognizing Revenues, Expenses, Gains, and Losses*, by Henry R. Jaenicke (Stamford, CT: Financial Accounting Standards Board, 1981), pp. 147-156.

securities. The gain or loss is computed by deducting the carrying amount and costs of disposal from the proceeds, reduced by accrued interest or declared dividends, if any. If only part of an investment in a security is sold, cost is usually apportioned on the basis of average cost, first-in, first-out, or identification of the cost of specific certificates. The method selected should be consistently followed.

The average cost method has the merit of recognizing the fungible character of different lots of the same security and is generally considered preferable to the other two methods. The identified cost method allows considerable choice in the amount of gain or loss to be recognized if different lots of a security were purchased at different prices.

The average cost method cannot be used for federal income tax purposes under current regulations. Either specific identification or the first-in, first-out method must be used. If the average cost method is used for financial statement reporting of sales of partial holdings, a difference arises between the book basis and tax basis of both the securities sold and the remaining holdings. Deferred tax accounting is necessary, and memorandum records of tax cost must be maintained.

Earnings or Losses from Investments Accounted for by the Equity Method. The mechanics of the equity method can be handled in either of two ways. The simpler way is to credit dividends received to the investment account and to adjust the investment periodically by the investor's appropriate share of the earnings or losses for the period, recording income or loss from the investment. However, since it is necessary to account for distributed earnings separately from equity in undistributed earnings for various reasons (e.g., SEC and federal income tax reporting), dividends received are commonly credited to an income account and the investment account is adjusted only for the net change in underlying equity (after adjustments equivalent to those made for consolidations).

Disclosures

The necessary disclosures may be made either in the body of the financial statements or in the accompanying notes. The required disclosures are

- Aggregate cost and aggregate market value, and which is the carrying amount.
- Valuation allowance, deducted from related investment.
- Investments pledged as collateral or otherwise restricted.
- For marketable equity securities
  - •• Gross unrealized gains and gross unrealized losses in the investment portfolio (segregated between current and noncurrent) for the latest balance sheet presented.
  - •• Net realized gain or loss recognized in the income statement (and the basis on which cost was determined for securities sold) for each income statement presented.

- •• Amount of the change in the valuation allowance included in the equity section of the balance sheet and in the income statement for each year for which an income statement is presented.

- •• Significant net realized and net unrealized gains and losses arising after the date of the financial statements but prior to their issuance. (In determining significance, the authors believe gains and losses related to securities classified as current should be considered in relation to net income, while gains and losses related to securities classified as noncurrent should be determined in relation to total stockholders' equity.)

(The SEC also requires registrants to disclose the nature and extent of repurchase and reverse repurchase securities transactions entered into and the degree of risk involved. At the time of this writing, the FASB is considering disclosure requirements for financial instruments generally.)

INVESTMENT TRANSACTIONS AND INTERNAL CONTROL STRUCTURE POLICIES AND PROCEDURES

The steps involved in investment activity by industrial and commercial companies are more likely to be similar from one company to another than in many other areas of business operations. They are often rather formal and well organized, whether the purpose is short-term investment of temporary excess cash, long-term investment, or investment for purposes of affiliation or control. The activity begins with selection and authorization of an investment; subsequent steps are acquisition, safeguarding, accounting for income, appraisal, and disposition.

Management normally is aware of the amounts of funds available for investment as well as the future need for funds. In addition, many of the control procedures for investment activities are administered directly by management.

Selection and Authorization

If the investment activity is not significant, the selection and authorization of investments are generally specifically delegated to an executive officer, often the treasurer. If the activity is significant, it is usually overseen by top officers or by the board of directors itself, although investment transactions may be initiated automatically, for example, by overnight sweeps of cash balances into money market instruments, or by portfolio managers who operate discretionary accounts. Often an investment committee of officers or directors employs an investment advisor to whom it delegates the authority to make specific decisions about investment acquisitions and dispositions. Ultimately, however, the responsibility for investment decisions rests with management.

Control procedures for selecting investments include authorization by the board, either for specific investments or in the form of a general authorization to an officer or advisor to make investment decisions, and high-level management review and explicit approval of specific investment decisions before they are executed.

Acquisition

Control structure policies and procedures that are part of the acquisition process in general, for example, authorization for the disbursement of funds, are discussed in Chapter 13. The following discussion relates to additional policies and procedures that are specific to the acquisition of investments.

Investments in marketable securities are often acquired through financial institutions that deal in formal markets. Typically the control mechanism consists of some form of approved acquisition list, which may include maximum prices or minimum yields. In an effective control structure, the approved list would reflect the client's assessment of the risks inherent in various types of securities and the returns they generate. Acquisitions of investments in other than marketable securities are almost always unique events, even if a fairly large number of units is acquired at one time, such as acquisitions of real estate for an endowment fund or investment portfolio. Selecting investments and negotiating acquisition terms are likely to be delegated to an investment specialist; high-level management review and approval are required before investment decisions are executed.

Safeguarding Investments

Physical protection of securities is vital because many marketable securities are readily negotiable; moreover, documents evidencing legal ownership have value even if securities are not readily negotiable. Therefore, restricted access and segregation of duties are particularly important aspects of the control structure for investments. Securities are generally kept in a vault or safe deposit box, or entrusted to a financial institution for safekeeping. The custodian and other personnel who have access to the securities would be independent of the functions of authorizing investment transactions, keeping investment records, handling cash, and maintaining the general ledger; preferably each of those employees would be independent of all the others.

If securities are kept in a safe deposit box, the number of people with authorized access is kept to a minimum, but it is preferable for two people to be present whenever the box is opened. A safe deposit box is an effective means of protection because a bank's provisions for physical security and procedures for restricting and controlling access to the vault are normally more extensive than most commercial and industrial organizations are able to maintain.

Other control procedures for investments generally include periodically inspecting and counting securities for which delivery has been taken, and reconciling and investigating differences. Those procedures are performed by people other than those responsible for authorizing and executing transactions and maintaining custody of the securities. Even if securities have been entrusted to a financial institution for safekeeping, or exist in electronic notation (book entry) form, the entity still needs to maintain records of transactions and balances and to periodically reconcile the records with those of the custodian.

Accounting for Income

Chapter 12 discusses control procedures for incoming receipts; those procedures are applicable to the processing of income from dividends and interest received directly by an entity.

Accounting for income from publicly traded marketable securities is usually straightforward: Interest is accrued periodically and dividends are recorded as received (or when the shares first trade "ex-dividend"). Published records of interest, dividends, and other distributions are compared with recorded income periodically to ensure that all income has been received on a timely basis. That procedure is more effective if it is exercised by a person other than those responsible for initially recording investments and cash receipts from investment income. If an investment is accounted for on the equity method, copies of financial statements of the investee are needed to determine the appropriate earnings or losses to record.

Valuation of Investments

Periodic valuation of investments is necessary for management decision-making purposes; it is also required so that market or fair value can be determined for financial statement purposes. If investments are few, relatively short-term, and not significant to a company's operations, the valuation process is sometimes performed informally by the officer responsible for investments. If investments are significant, the valuation should be formally executed and documented. The frequency of valuation depends on the amount of investment activity and how often financial statements are issued. (Some active investment portfolios are under virtually continual valuation.)

Disposition

Dispositions of investments are usually subject to the same procedures as acquisitions. Control procedures for the receipt and processing of proceeds from dispositions are discussed in Chapter 12.

Records of Investments

An investment ledger is desirable regardless of the size of a portfolio. The ledger generally contains an account for each investment, which is described completely: full title of the issue; number of shares or face value; certificate numbers (if the enterprise takes delivery of the securities); interest or dividend rate; maturities or other features such as call, conversion, or collateral; cost; and required amortization of premium or discount. If the tax basis is different from the book basis, the former may also be noted in the investment ledger account. The detail of the investment ledger is reconciled periodically to the general ledger control account.

Some investments, such as mortgages, are supported by a permanent file of documents controlled by a checklist: for example, note (bond) receivable, mortgage, record of registering the mortgage, insurance policies, and tax bills.

AUDIT TESTING PLAN

The investment portfolio of many industrial and commercial companies is not significant to the financial statements, and efficiency considerations often lead the auditor to adopt a testing plan that emphasizes substantive testing. In some situations, however, the auditor may choose to perform tests of controls as a basis for reducing the assurance needed from substantive tests. That strategy decision partly reflects the auditor's assessment of the inherent risk characteristics associated with the particular types of investments the client has.

Assessing those risks, which have both accounting and auditing implications, is especially important if the client's investment portfolio includes sophisticated, complex financial instruments whose terms and risks may not be widely understood. All investments contain elements of business risk, market risk, credit risk, and the risk of intentional or unintentional loss of securities (collateral risk).

- Business risk relates to the possibility that the investor will misunderstand the terms and the underlying economic substance of an investment, including the expected return. This can result in incorrect pricing of securities, inappropriate accounting for investment income, or unrealistic expectations about the marketability or liquidity of an investment.
- Market risk is the risk that changes in security prices may affect the investor's ability to continue to finance an investment made with borrowed funds, thus forcing the investment to be liquidated sooner than intended.
- Credit risk is the risk of default, either by the issuer of the securities or by the financial institution that holds securities as a custodian or has entered into a commitment to deliver securities some time in the future. Credit risk and market risk are interrelated; adverse price fluctuations may create losses that preclude a debtor or other obligor from honoring its commitments.
- Collateral risk is the risk that the custodian of securities in which the client has not perfected a security interest may not be able to deliver the securities.

The decision whether to perform tests of controls also reflects the auditor's understanding and assessment of control structure policies and procedures the client has created in response to those risks. Those policies and procedures should (1) ensure that the personnel authorized to enter into investment transactions are competent, (2) require that written contracts specify the rights and obligations inherent in the investment transaction, (3) establish trading limits, (4) require reviews of investment transactions by competent personnel, and (5) require periodic evaluation of credit, market, and collateral risk.

As mentioned earlier, many of the control procedures for investments are exercised directly by management. While management's close attention to investment transactions can be an effective factor in the control structure, the auditor must be alert for potential abuses and override of policies and procedures. Other key aspects of the control structure are asset protection policies and procedures and segregation of duties. These will usually be the focus of tests of controls, if the auditor does decide to perform them. In addition, the auditor may obtain evidence of the effectiveness of certain control procedures (such as those relating to depositing incoming receipts or disbursing funds) in connection with auditing the revenue and buying cycles, as discussed in Chapters 12 and 13.

Tests of controls of investment activity may also focus on the acquisition or disposal of investments. For example, the auditor may perform tests of controls of authorization of investment transactions and safeguarding of investments to obtain evidence that recorded investments exist and are owned at the balance sheet date. If those control procedures are found to be in place and operating effectively, the auditor may decide to reduce year-end confirmations (see below) or to perform them before year-end. Conversely, if those procedures are absent or ineffective, the auditor may need to revise the audit testing plan and perform 100 percent confirmation at year-end. The auditor may also test control procedures for recording investment income to obtain evidence of its accuracy.

SUBSTANTIVE TESTS

This section discusses tests of existence, ownership, accuracy, and completeness; carrying values; investment income; and classification and presentation. It concludes with tests related to investments in sophisticated financial instruments.

Existence, Ownership, Accuracy, and Completeness

Evidence of the existence and ownership of investments, as well as some assurance about the accuracy and completeness of the investment accounts, is normally obtained by confirmation or inspection. The auditor should agree the securities confirmed or inspected to the client's detailed records. Whether these procedures are performed at year-end or at an interim date will be based on the auditor's assessment of control risk and on efficiency considerations.

Counting Securities.   Most industrial and commercial companies do not own numerous securities, and physical inspection is not difficult. The auditor usually obtains a list of securities supporting the general ledger balance at the date of the count and arranges to visit the place where the securities are kept, accompanied by the custodian.

The list of securities owned (and those held as collateral or for safekeeping) at the date of the count is prepared from the security records and includes aggregate principal amount of bonds and notes; number of shares of stock; denomination of bonds or par value, if any, of stocks; maturity dates of bonds; and interest and preferred stock dividend rates. If available, information about the location of the securities is usually included on the list. The auditor examines the securities and compares them with the list. This process normally provides the auditor with evidence about the control structure; for example, an accurate security list, proper endorsement or evidence of ownership on the securities, proper division of duties between custodian and record keeper, adequate physical safeguards (such as use of a bank's safe deposit vault), and requirements that two people be present for access to the securities are all indications of an effective control structure.

Generally, the auditor should count the securities at the balance sheet date; if it is done at another date, the vault or safe deposit box should be sealed during the intervening period. Banks ordinarily seal a safe deposit box on a client's request and subsequently confirm to the auditor that no access to the box was granted during the specified period. Securities should be counted simultaneously with cash and other negotiable assets. A count is considered "simultaneous" if the securities are sealed or otherwise controlled until all negotiable assets have been examined.

The auditor should maintain control over the securities from the start of the count until it has been completed, the results have been compared with the list of securities, and all exceptions have been investigated to the extent possible at the time. Responsible officers and employees of the client should be present during the count to reduce the possibility of later questions about the handling of securities, and should acknowledge, in writing, the return of the securities intact upon conclusion of the count.

In the process of counting the securities, the auditor should also examine them. Although auditors are not qualified to assume responsibility for the genuineness or authenticity of certificates or instruments representing investments, they should be alert to the possibility of forged certificates. If any certificates appear to be unusual and if the auditor is unable to establish their authenticity by examining purchase documents, income records, or similar items, the security should be confirmed with the issuer or transfer agent.

Insurance companies and similar institutional investors often have in their portfolios registered instruments in large denominations that may have been reduced below face amount by partial payments. The auditor should confirm the amount of those instruments outstanding with the issuer, if it appears they do not have to be presented to the issuer or an agent for endorsement or reissue at the time a partial payment is received.

The auditor should note that stock certificates and registered bonds are in the name of the client or an accredited nominee or, if they are not, that certificates are appropriately endorsed or accompanied by powers of attorney. Bonds with interest coupons should be examined to determine that coupons not yet due have not been detached. If coupons presently coming due are not attached to the bonds, the auditor should ask where they are and either inspect them or confirm them with the holders. Likewise, explanations should be obtained and evaluated for any coupons past due that are attached and have not been presented for payment. Interest in default should be noted in the working papers for consideration in connection with the audit of accrued income and carrying amounts of investments.

The auditor should investigate reasons for differences between the count and the list of securities. Certain types of differences are normal and expected, for example, securities held by others and securities in transit. The holders of securities in other locations should be identified and requests for confirmation sent. In-transit items should be related to recent transactions; outgoing in-transit items should be confirmed with recipients. Securities received by the client through the mail for a few days following the date of the count should be examined to substantiate items in transit. Once the auditor is satisfied that all items on the security list have been counted or their location elsewhere has been confirmed and all differences have been reconciled, he or she may "release" control over securities.

The auditor should not overlook the possibility of substitutions. If, for example, examinations are being made of one or more trust accounts handled by the same trustee, securities in all accounts should be counted at the same time. Similarly, if different auditors are employed to examine several accounts, they should make their counts simultaneously. Otherwise, material shortages may be concealed by temporary transfers from accounts whose securities are not being counted. If a client is reluctant to permit an auditor to count securities of other accounts or is unwilling or unable to arrange for a simultaneous count by all auditors concerned, the auditor may identify securities owned by the client by accounting for certificate numbers of stocks and bonds; however, that procedure is difficult and time-consuming for a large portfolio with numerous purchases and sales. Securities owned or held as collateral or for safekeeping should also be counted simultaneously with cash funds and cash equivalents, undeposited receipts, notes receivable, and other negotiable assets if there is a possibility of substitution of one item for another.

Counts of Large Portfolios.   If an investment portfolio is relatively large and active (as in banks, insurance companies, investment companies, and stock brokerages), the count of securities may be a major undertaking requiring extensive planning, precise execution, and a large staff of auditors. The following matters should be considered in conjunction with those applicable to counts of small portfolios.

In counts of large portfolios, the auditor should make every effort to plan the count most expeditiously and also to institute the necessary controls with minimum inconvenience to the client. Especially if a "surprise" count is made without prior notice to the client, the auditor must ascertain the location of all securities, establish controls at various points necessary to record movements of securities, and plan the sequence of the count.

A properly controlled plan may consist of stationing an auditor—the "control" auditor—at each location to observe and record movements of securities, while other auditors perform the actual count. Bags, boxes, safes, or whole rooms may be sealed to be counted later. (The purpose of seals is to provide assurance to the auditor that no one has had access to the sealed items.)

If securities must be moved before the count is completed, the control auditor should observe the withdrawal or deposit, determine the reason for withdrawals, and record the transactions in the working papers. If securities that have already been counted must be removed to be mailed to correspondents, brokers, transfer agents, or others, they should be recorded and controlled until they are turned over to the postal authorities. Relatively inactive securities may be counted and placed under seal in advance of the main count or may be placed under seal and counted after the more active items have been examined.

The usual counting procedure is for the control auditor to release batches of securities to the counting auditors, keeping a record of batches released. The counting auditors count each issue of securities and call off the count to an auditor holding the security list. If the count and the list do not agree, the issue is recounted, sometimes by a different person, until the count agrees with the listed amount or it is determined that a difference exists.

Confirmation of Securities Not on Hand.   Items on the list of securities owned at the count date but not counted should be confirmed with the holders. If a client's entire portfolio is held by a custodian, confirmation procedures usually take the place of the security count.

Items not on hand ordinarily include securities held by banks as collateral for loans, securities left with broker-dealers as custodians for safekeeping, securities with transfer agents, securities that exist on computerized files in "book entry" form, and, if the client is a broker-dealer, items with other brokers on loan or awaiting delivery. The auditor should determine the location of those securities at the examination date, the appropriate responsible person acting as custodian, and the reasons they are held by the custodian. (If the securities are held by people or organizations unknown to the auditor, he or she may consider it necessary to inspect them physically rather than confirm them.) In examining the accounts of financial institutions, the auditor should also confirm contracts for the purchase or sale of securities on a "when issued" basis.

If the client's entire portfolio of securities is held in custody by a well-known, reliable financial institution independent of the client, the custodian should be requested to furnish directly to the auditor a list of securities held for the client at the examination date. The confirmation request should also ask whether the client has clear title to the securities. The auditor should compare the list with the client's security records and account for differences noted. It is sometimes desirable to corroborate the custodian's confirmation by counting the securities, for example, if the portfolio is large in relation to the custodian's assets or if the auditor seeks assurance about the adequacy of the custodian's procedures. A letter from the custodian's auditor addressing its internal control structure can also provide that assurance. Joint counts with other auditors having a similar interest are possible. (See the discussion in Chapter 6 of the auditor's responsibilities under SAS No. 44, *Special-Purpose Reports on Internal Accounting Control at Service Organizations* [AU Section 324].)

If securities are in the custody of an affiliate or are under the control of a person or group of people who take an active part in the management of the client, the auditor is not justified in relying solely on written confirmation from the custodian. Instead, the auditing procedures outlined above for counting securities under the client's control should be followed.

Tests of Carrying Values

Cost of securities purchased and proceeds from securities sold are normally supported by brokers' advices. The auditor should examine these documents to substantiate the basis for initially recording those transactions. Additionally, the auditor should review the client's method of determining cost (first in, first out, average, or specific identification) of securities sold and ascertain that it is consistent during the year and with prior years.

The auditor should test the client's identification of marketable equity securities that are required to be carried at the lower of aggregate cost or market and should determine that market values have been appropriately applied to those securities. Normally, this is accomplished by comparing values with published sources. The auditor should also determine that any necessary valuation allowance adjustment is properly reflected in the financial statements. The client's support for fair values of investments that are determined on a basis other than published values should be tested for propriety and consistency. The auditor should be alert to any indication that declines in market value below cost may be other than temporary.

The auditor should consider evidence related to the degree of influence or control the client can exercise over an investee, to evaluate whether the equity method of accounting or consolidation is appropriate in the circumstances. In addition, the auditor should exercise appropriate professional care to ensure that transactions involving investments are accounted for in accordance with their substance, regardless of their form.

If there are investments accounted for by the equity method and if the investee enterprise is audited by other auditors, the auditor will have to use the report of the investee's auditors to be able to report on the client investor's equity in the investee's underlying net assets and its share of the investee's earnings or losses and other transactions. This places the auditor in the position of a principal auditor who is using the work and reports of other auditors. The work and reports of other auditors may also serve as evidence with respect to investments carried on the cost basis or at the lower of cost or market, which would similarly place the auditor in the position of a principal auditor. The procedures to be followed in those instances are discussed in Chapter 6; reporting aspects of using the work and reports of other auditors are discussed in Chapter 22.

For investments accounted for by the equity method, the investor's share of the investee's results of operations should be based on data from the investee's most recent reliable financial statements, which may be audited year-end statements or unaudited interim statements. If audited statements are used and there is a time lag, for example, three months, between the reporting dates of the investor and the investee, the lag should be consistent from year to year. If the most recent reliable financial statements of the investee are unaudited interim statements as of the same date as the investor's year-end, the auditor should apply auditing procedures to those statements in light of the materiality of the investment in relation to the investor's financial statements. If audited financial statements of the investee cannot be obtained, which may happen particularly for foreign investees, a scope limitation is present that, depending on materiality, could result in a qualified opinion or a disclaimer. See the discussion and examples of scope limitations in Chapter 22.

The auditor should read available interim financial statements of the investee and inquire of the investor about events and transactions of the investee between the date of its financial statements and the date of the audit report on the investor's financial statements. Through such inquiries, the auditor should also ascertain that the investor is aware of any material events or transactions subsequent to the date of the investee's financial statements.

Tests of Investment Income

The auditor should determine that all income earned has been appropriately recorded and either collected or recognized as a receivable, and that all accrued income receivable has in fact been earned. The auditor usually obtains evidence about investment income and collection dates by referring to dates of purchase and disposal of investments, interest rates, and published dividend records. Interest should not be accrued on debt securities unless its collectibility is probable; previously accrued interest in arrears should be evaluated for collectibility and written off if it does not appear probable that it will be collected.

In testing income from investments, the auditor can often perform analytical procedures, for example, analyzing the rate of return or gross investment income on a month-to-month or quarter-to-quarter basis, or comparing income with budgeted or prior-year data. Fluctuations in investment income that do not conform to the auditor's expectations would indicate that recorded investments might not exist or that investments exist that have not been recorded. (Analytical procedures, however, are generally not relevant for achieving other audit objectives with respect to investments.)

Tests of Classification and Presentation

If the balance sheet is classified, the auditor should determine that the investments are properly classified between the current and noncurrent categories. The auditor should also ascertain that the financial statements contain all required disclosures regarding investment carrying values and realized and unrealized gains and losses. In addition, minutes, confirmation replies, loan agreements, bond indentures, and other appropriate documents should be reviewed to determine whether investments have been pledged as collateral or whether there is evidence of commitments to acquire or dispose of investments, both of which may require disclosures.

Financial statement classification of investments depends largely on management's objectives and intentions. The auditor can ascertain management's objectives through inquiry and by reviewing minutes of meetings of the board of directors and its investment committee. It may be desirable to include a statement of management's intent in the client representation letter (discussed in Chapter 21). To evaluate management's representations about its intentions, the auditor should consider whether they are reasonable in light of the enterprise's financial position, working capital requirements, debt agreements, and other contractual obligations. For example, the client's needs may indicate a reasonable presumption that marketable securities will have to be sold to meet operating requirements and that therefore they should be classified as current assets.

Tests Related to Investments in Sophisticated Financial Instruments

More and more, enterprises are managing their available cash in ways that try to achieve the highest rates of return for a given level of acceptable risk. One result has been the increasing use of innovative, sophisticated, and often complex financial instruments to generate investment income. The proliferation and relatively short "shelf lives" of such investments make describing all of them and providing guidance for auditing them a most formidable task—far beyond the scope of this book.

The guidance that follows is, therefore, extremely "generic." It applies to all investments and should be considered in addition to the procedures discussed earlier in this chapter. The suggested guidance should, of course, be tailored to risks associated with the specific types of investments being audited. (Guidance on auditing some of these kinds of investments is also presented in Chapter 39, "Auditing Securities and Commodities Broker-Dealers.") The auditor should always consider the substance of the transaction, not its form, and should consult with experts, as appropriate in the circumstances.

1. Review the client's records for transactions involving purchases and sales of investments in financial instruments of all types.
2. Develop an understanding of the nature of each financial instrument the client has invested in.
3. Determine the appropriate accounting measurement and recognition principles for each type of instrument.
4. Assess the risks associated with each instrument and evaluate how those risks affect the realizability of the investment. Those risks include (a) the risk that the issuer of the instrument or the counterparty to the investment transaction will be unable to make payment or otherwise complete the transaction at its scheduled maturity, and (b) the risk that fluctuations in interest rates may reduce the underlying value of the investment.
5. Evaluate the appropriateness of the financial statement classification and disclosure of investment transactions and the degree of risk involved in them.
6. Count or confirm securities delivered to the client or its agent, as appropriate.

7. Determine where securities not transferred to the investor or its agent are being held and confirm their existence and the custodian's legal obligation to the investor.

8. Consider whether it is desirable to (a) obtain a report from the custodian's auditor evaluating the custodian's internal control structure with respect to securities held in safekeeping, (b) request that specific tests be performed by that auditor, or (c) personally perform such tests.

18

Auditing Property, Plant, and Equipment

Most businesses use property, plant, and equipment in the process of generating revenues. The term "property, plant, and equipment" generally refers to noncurrent tangible assets, including those held under capital leases, used by a business to create and distribute its goods and services. The term "fixed assets" is also used (although not as much as in the past) to describe the property, plant, and equipment accounts. Related accounts that are audited in the same manner as property, plant, and equipment are leasehold improvements and construction in progress.

Many businesses also incur expenditures for the acquisition of noncurrent intangible assets. Some "intangible assets" are specifically identifiable, for example, patents, franchises, and trademarks, and have lives established by law, regulation, or contract. Other intangible assets cannot be specifically identified. The most common unidentifiable intangible asset is typically called "goodwill," which is the excess of the purchase price paid for a business over the sum of its identifiable net assets. Certain other expenditures are recorded as intangible assets or "deferred charges" because the expenditures are considered to benefit future operations and are not regarded as current expenses or losses.

Accounting principles require the cost of plant and equipment and intangible assets to be allocated on a rational and systematic basis over the periods benefited. Various depreciation or amortization methods are utilized to allocate the net cost of an asset (acquisition cost less estimated recoverable salvage value) over the period of benefit.

Expenditures to maintain or improve property, plant, and equipment are normal following their acquisition. A major audit consideration is whether such expenditures should be accounted for as expenses of the current period or reflected on the balance sheet as either an addition to the cost of the asset or a reduction of the related accumulated depreciation. As a general rule, an expenditure should be capitalized if it benefits future periods by extending the useful or productive life of the asset. The distinction between the two categories of expenditures frequently is not clear-cut. Enterprises usually have stated policies defining which expenditures are to be capitalized, and the auditor must exercise judgment in determining whether the policies are appropriate and are being complied with.

This chapter presents the objectives of auditing property, plant, and equipment and intangible assets and deferred charges, and describes typical transactions and control structure policies and procedures. Control structure policies and procedures applied to purchases and cash disbursements and related tests of controls and substantive tests were covered as part of the buying cycle in Chapter 13. Many of the control procedures for ordering, receiving, paying for, and recording property, plant, and equipment purchases may be similar to those for purchases in general. This chapter focuses on control procedures normally not associated with the buying cycle, for example, those relating to the completeness, accuracy, and authorization of files containing property, plant, and equipment balances; to the protection of assets; and to authorization for acquisitions and sales of assets. The chapter also discusses the audit testing plan for property, plant, and equipment and other noncurrent asset accounts, based on the auditor's risk assessment; that is followed by specific substantive tests that may be used in auditing property transactions and related account balances.

AUDIT OBJECTIVES

Property, Plant, and Equipment

The objectives of auditing property, plant, and equipment and related accounts are to obtain reasonable assurance that

- Property, plant, and equipment recorded in the accounts exist and are owned or leased under capital leases[1] by the company.
- All additions to and disposals of property, plant, and equipment have been properly authorized and accurately recorded.
- No material items were charged to expense that should have been capitalized.
- The cost or other basis of initially recording property, plant, and equipment is appropriate.
- Appropriate methods of depreciation have been properly applied, on a basis consistent with the previous year, to all items of property, plant, and equipment that should be depreciated.
- The carrying value of property, plant, and equipment is appropriate in periods subsequent to acquisition, considering such factors as utilization, geographic location, laws and regulations, and technological changes.
- Property, plant, and equipment pledged as collateral are identified and disclosed, along with other necessary disclosures.

The auditor may meet some of these objectives through procedures performed in connection with other aspects of the audit or tests of other accounts. For example, the pledging of property, plant, and equipment is generally discovered through reading and analyzing loan documents and minutes of meetings of the board of directors or other management groups. Property acquired under capital leases may be determined by reading minutes and analyzing lease or rental expense accounts. Similarly, the auditor may determine the continued existence of recorded property, plant, and equipment (though often not specifically or explicitly) as he or she moves about the facilities in the course of observing physical inventories and performing other audit tasks.

Other objectives are achieved through specific tests of controls and substantive tests of balances. For example, the auditor may perform tests of controls of additions and disposals or retirements of property, plant, and equipment, and may examine appropriate documents for selected additions and retirements. Similarly, auditors often review charges to repair and maintenance accounts

---

[1]Audit objectives relating specifically to leased assets are discussed under "Capital Leases."

for items that should have been capitalized, and test the calculation and summarization of depreciation.

Determining the cost or other basis of recording property, plant, and equipment usually presents few problems, because most assets are acquired individually in short-term credit transactions. The auditor must exercise judgment, however, about the appropriate cost in situations involving business combinations, self-constructed assets, capitalized leases, and nonmonetary transactions. While they are not usually a major audit concern, the auditor must be alert for changes in laws or general business conditions that might make it impossible to recover the remaining costs of property through revenue generated or outright sale. Also, the auditor should be aware of conditions that might require reevaluation of the remaining depreciable lives of property, plant, and equipment.

Intangible Assets and Deferred Charges

The audit objectives relating to intangible assets and deferred charges are to obtain evidence that

- Recorded intangible assets exist and are owned by the company, and the recorded amounts represent appropriate valuations.
- Intangible assets are being amortized on a consistent basis over the estimated periods of benefit.
- Adequate provision has been made for any permanent decline in value.
- Deferred charges represent expenditures that are appropriately deferred to future periods.
- The basis for amortizing deferred charges is reasonable.
- Appropriate disclosures have been made regarding intangibles and deferred charges.

These objectives are similar to those for property, plant, and equipment, as discussed earlier. Auditing intangible assets and deferred charges is often uncomplicated because of the limited number of transactions generally found in these accounts, and accordingly is given relatively little attention in this chapter. The auditor should, however, determine that the carrying value of those assets can be fully recovered, that there has not been a permanent impairment of their value, and that the remaining period of amortization is appropriate.

TYPICAL TRANSACTIONS AND INTERNAL CONTROL STRUCTURE POLICIES AND PROCEDURES

Authorization of Expenditures

The acquisition of property usually requires a major use of funds, and the capital budget for property acquisitions often is approved by the board of directors. Some companies use well-developed techniques of capital budgeting to evaluate the economic feasibility of proposed acquisitions, both large and small. Other companies are less formal and more subjective and judgmental in their analysis. The extent of economic justification required depends on the management style and preferences of those responsible for authorizing acquisitions of property; usually those preferences are formally expressed in company policy.

A company's policies and procedures governing property acquisitions are generally well defined. Usually the procedures call for a formal written request and specify the extent of economic justification that must accompany it, including the reasons for the expenditure and the estimated amount. This information is necessary to give those who authorize expenditures a meaningful basis for evaluating them. In most organizations, purchases are initiated only on the basis of appropriate authorizations. Often the procedures provide for several levels of authorization, which may be set based on predetermined amounts; the larger the expenditure, the higher the level at which it is authorized.

Expenditures may be authorized on an ad hoc basis as requests are received, but it is preferable to compile them in a capital budget for formal review and approval. Sometimes a capital budget enumerates specific acquisitions, but most often it has to be prepared far in advance and thus necessarily consists of estimates or aggregates of probable acquisitions. When a capital budget has been approved, it becomes the authorization for the purchasing or other department to execute acquisition transactions. Thereafter, specific transactions are authorized by the people responsible for the various segments of the capital budget.

Documents authorizing acquisitions are typically subject to numerical control. Records of purchase commitments are usually also maintained. Written records are necessary to determine that transactions are executed in accordance with the authorization. One common system is to assign a "construction work order" number or "appropriation" number to each authorization, even if no construction is involved. Often, control totals of "commitments" and "construction work in progress" are supported by holding files of open work orders, which can be reconciled periodically to the control total.

Actual expenditures for property, plant, and equipment and other noncurrent assets are compared with the authorized requests; approval by the person who originally approved the estimated expenditure is required for expenditures that exceed amounts initially authorized. Control is further enhanced if approvals are obtained before overruns are incurred and if the accounting treatment of overruns is also approved.

If an expenditure is for the replacement of an existing asset, control structure policies and procedures are needed to ensure that the related retirement or disposal is accurately recorded. A procedure for identifying assets that are no longer in use or are being replaced helps ensure that assets disposed of or no longer in use are properly recorded as retirements. For example, a company's procedures might require that all accounting entries related to a capital project be summarized and approved each quarter; the approval process might include comparing the summarization with the written approval for the replacement, which would detect a failure to record a retirement. Other control procedures for property, plant, and equipment expenditures, such as recording vendors' invoices, preparing and signing checks, and recording them in the general ledger, are normally the same as for other purchases.

As part of authorizing expenditures, a designated official should approve the allocation between the asset accounts and current operations. The allocation should be based on the account classification in the approved written request. Account classifications of expenditures should be reviewed by someone independent of the person who prepared the initial coding.

Receipt and Installation

Routine or recurring acquisitions are usually processed through the normal purchasing procedures and are subject to the control structure policies and procedures described in Chapter 13 in connection with purchases in general. Larger or technically specialized acquisitions may be handled by specialists in engineering or contract negotiation. In either event, control procedures are applied to receipts of property, plant, and equipment to ensure that purchases are recorded in the general ledger and in the detailed property records. Control procedures for returned property, review and approval of invoices and related documentation, and authorization control procedures for entries in the detailed property records are as important in property purchases as in purchases of inventory or services.

Acquisitions that are complex or specialized enough to be the responsibility of a separate department are generally subject to specialized control procedures. Control over large-scale procurement has become a highly developed art over the last several decades, and "procurement" or "contract management" has become a profession in its own right. This discussion can only touch in the most general way on the kinds of control procedures that may be found in practice.

A contract, including all specifications, is usually reviewed for completeness; the more detailed the initial specifications, the less the risk of costly unforeseen variations. The range of tolerable deviation from the specified standards is spelled out, and the time of delivery and quality of performance are specified. Since higher quality or closer tolerances are almost always more costly, contracts are best reviewed by a team comprising different skills and points of view: purchasing specialists, engineers, production personnel, lawyers, and cost accountants.

During construction, acquisition, or installation, a specified employee supervises step-by-step compliance by the contractor with the terms of the contract. Sometimes the supervision can be supplied by an outside specialist, like an architect; other projects may require the full-time attention of one or more of the purchaser's executives or employees. Formal procedures generally exist for testing and accepting an acquisition, and compliance with them is documented and reviewed before the acquisition is legally accepted and final payment made.

Costs of acquisitions are accumulated in work order ledgers containing information relative to purchases, payments to contractors, and "in-house" labor and overhead. Accumulated costs are balanced to the control account periodically and compared with the authorized expenditure.

Acquisitions of small dollar value items, with a cost of less than $200, for example, may be routinely expensed even though the item is properly capitalizable. Such a policy is followed to reduce the clerical effort involved in maintaining detailed records for many small dollar value items. Materiality, however, should be determined on the basis of the aggregate of these small dollar items. Otherwise, a department that is authorized to purchase and expense components below the $200 limit could purchase components as replacement parts and use them to construct an asset at a cost of $2000 that would not have been approved.

Existence of Assets

Assets representing the balances included in the detailed property records are generally inspected periodically, and, if appropriate, documents of title are examined at reasonable intervals. These procedures will be more effective if they are carried out by people other than those who have custody of the assets, maintain the detailed records, and have custody of the documents of title. Typically, assets that are highly susceptible to theft, loss, or abnormal damage are physically inspected at least annually. Inspection of other assets on a periodic basis may be adequate unless there is an unusual amount of activity in the property accounts and the individual assets are replaced frequently.

Periodic physical inspection of individual assets by client personnel is an effective means of avoiding misstatement of the property accounts by including assets that have disappeared or become unusable, or excluding items on hand but not recorded. The inspection entails determining both the existence of the asset and whether it is in current use and good condition.

Property, Plant, and Equipment Records

Property, plant, and equipment control accounts are usually supported by subsidiary ledgers for the following classifications of assets: land; buildings; leasehold improvements; machinery and equipment; furniture and fixtures; office equipment; motor vehicles; property, plant, and equipment leased or loaned to or from third parties; other property, plant, and equipment; and other noncurrent assets. Each subsidiary ledger consists of a detailed record for each asset in that class; records are kept for all items in use, including fully depreciated assets. The record for each item usually includes a description of the asset, its location in the plant, date of purchase or construction, identifying (voucher or work order) number, cost, depreciation or amortization method, salvage value, depreciation or amortization for the period, and accumulated depreciation or amortization. Often those records also show maintenance and repair history. Supporting documentation for interest capitalized as part of the cost of assets would also be retained.

The subsidiary ledgers need to have sufficient information for individual assets to be identified, and their cost and accumulated depreciation or amortization to be reconciled to the respective control accounts. One means of doing this is by marking the assets with identifying numbers and recording the numbers. Alternatively, the accounting records may contain detailed descriptions of the individual assets, including, for example, manufacturer's serial numbers, which would allow ready identification of specific assets.

The subsidiary ledgers are updated regularly for the cost of additions and disposals and depreciation for the period, and are reconciled to the general ledger control accounts at least annually. Differences disclosed by the reconciliations are investigated, and the results are reviewed and approved by a designated official before any adjustments are made.

Detailed records for property leased to or from other entities are also maintained. Those records include description, location, identifying number, and owner, and provide a complete record of leased assets. In the case of assets leased from others, the records allow the company to distinguish such assets from assets it owns. In addition, records for leased property contain details of purchase options, renewal options, implicit interest rates, fair values of the items being leased, and other information necessary to account for the leases properly. Copies or extracts of lease agreements—both those of the company as lessee and those of the company as lessor—are normally retained with the company's property records.

Records of Use, Maintenance, and Repairs

Records are kept of the use and maintenance history of equipment. The amount of use affects the amount of maintenance needed, and the maintenance history indicates the kinds of repairs that may be expected and how much maintenance costs increase as the equipment is used. In some industries, regulatory agencies require usage, maintenance, and repair records to be kept. Rentals for many kinds of leased property are based partly on the amount of use (e.g., mileage for automobiles, units produced for machines, or hours of service for computers). Usage records that serve accounting purposes should be carefully maintained and controlled.

Accounting records and control procedures related to use of equipment are usually very simple. Generally, they include policies for rates and methods of depreciation, depletion, and amortization; forms or schedules for computing data for entries and often a standard journal entry for recording them; and procedures for periodically reconciling the subsidiary ledgers to control accounts, reviewing differences, and adjusting recorded amounts.

Disposition of Property, Plant, and Equipment

Control structure policies and procedures for dispositions of property, plant, and equipment are important to all businesses, not only to preserve accurate records but also to make sure that assets are safeguarded and residual and salvage values effectively realized. Policies and procedures relating to disposition often do not receive the attention they deserve. Some managements believe that disposals are infrequent occurrences and can be accounted for on an ad hoc basis. Others believe that accumulating depreciation takes care of accounting for expiration of the value of the asset whether it remains on hand or not, and that therefore precise record keeping is not important. Approaches such as these fail to recognize that assets can be misappropriated, not only physically but also through the manipulation of records. A more appropriate approach is to recognize that control procedures are important because many costly items of property, plant, and equipment are desirable, easily moved, and readily marketable.

Perhaps the best control procedures over dispositions are a work order system to document and account for retirements, restricted access to the property, and division of duties between those responsible for assets; those authorized to move, remove, or otherwise work on them; and those authorized to approve construction or removal work orders. Those procedures would prevent the person responsible for property from releasing it without a properly authorized work order. Retirement work orders would be reviewed by a plant engineer or someone similarly responsible and knowledgeable, who would evaluate the reason given for the disposition, the estimated cost of removal, and the estimated recovery for scrap or salvage.

As with major acquisitions, significant dispositions of property are approved by an appropriate level of management. Dollar guidelines may be established for the level of management required to authorize a disposition. Very large dispositions, for example, an operating plant, major product line, or large pieces of property or machinery, may require approval by the board of directors. The policy governing disposals of property, plant, and equipment is included in the company's overall property accounting policy. A frequently encountered intermediate stage of control between little or none at all and a well-systematized and disciplined system consists of a written policy calling for documentation of removals and dispositions. That policy would be supported by detailed records of assets on hand and comparisons of the records with periodic inventories, at least for movable and salable items.

Intangible Assets and Deferred Charges

An entity's control structure policies and procedures for intangible assets and deferred charges are normally similar to those for tangible property. Effective policies and procedures relating to intangible assets and deferred charges generally include

- A policy specifying the kinds of expenditures that are deferrable, and amortization methods and rates.
- Proper authorization of related entries.
- Periodic reviews of balances, realizable values, and deferral policy by responsible officials.

AUDIT TESTING PLAN

Understanding the Control Structure

As discussed in Chapter 8, the auditor is required by professional standards to obtain an understanding of the control structure as a basis for developing the audit testing plan. Among the most important procedures performed to understand the control structure are learning about the client's operations and economic environment, and correlating developments in those areas with activity in the property accounts. The auditor should be sure to understand the business reasons for additions and retirements and whether trends in operations or in the environment are likely to affect the values at which property is carried in the accounts.

The auditor should visit and tour the company's main plants perhaps once a year and smaller plants less frequently. One among several reasons for making a tour is to observe the existence and condition of the plant. Other evidence of matters affecting the property accounts can be found in the minutes of directors' and executive committee meetings. The auditor should also routinely inquire of company personnel about past or prospective changes in operations that might affect the property accounts. In addition, the auditor needs an understanding of the flow of transactions involving changes in the property, plant, and equipment accounts.

Further, the auditor should consider the general business environment of the entity and the nature of its property. In certain circumstances it may be appropriate to extend or otherwise amend the planned substantive procedures. For instance,

- If the auditor has reason to think that management may be attempting to inflate profits and thus may have capitalized items that should have been expensed, the auditor should pay particular attention to scrutinizing property, plant, and equipment additions for such items.
- If the entity's equipment is both mobile and readily marketable and hence could easily be misappropriated, the auditor should focus particularly on the authorization of disposals and substantiating the existence of items.
- If the client had, for the first time, construction in progress and had not designed a proper cost accumulation system, the auditor should extend procedures.

Analytical Procedures

The auditor should compare the total amount of additions with budgeted amounts and, in light of what is known about the business, identify major individual additions and disposals, review gains and losses on disposals, and review the reasonableness of the depreciation expense for the year. Balances of asset, accumulated depreciation and amortization, and related expense accounts should be compared with the prior year and, if possible, month to month to identify fluctuations and unusual entries requiring explanation. In some specialized industries, it may be possible to correlate income with the related asset. These analytical procedures may indicate areas that should be inquired about further, and may possibly indicate the need to modify planned substantive tests.

Assessing Control Risk

Most companies do not have a large volume of transactions in their property accounts, and most transactions are of high dollar value. Thus, the auditor can generally obtain evidence about the existence of particular assets from informal walk-throughs of client facilities or from observing and testing the client's fixed asset physical inventory counts. Because of the permanent nature of the assets, there is less likelihood of unrecorded transactions remaining undetected.

Property, plant, and equipment are recorded and carried in the financial statements at amounts equal to the costs identified with specific assets; net realizable values of productive assets are normally not relevant to the values at which assets are carried. After acquisition and recognition as an asset, the cost of property, plant, and equipment enters into the determination of periodic income through depreciation. A misstatement of income resulting from the property accounts would normally occur only through depreciation errors (including unrecognized premature obsolescence) or misclassification of expenditures between the asset account and the repairs and maintenance account.

Other noncurrent asset accounts such as deferred charges also generally have few transactions, and charges to income are normally made by periodic computations of amortization. Evaluating the carrying value of deferred charges and the benefit to future periods is frequently highly judgmental and therefore requires particular attention by the auditor.

The auditor may have obtained some evidence of the effectiveness of policies and procedures relating to property transactions from tests of controls performed concurrently with developing an understanding of the control structure. To reduce substantive tests significantly, however, the auditor would have to perform additional tests of controls to obtain evidence to support a low assessment of control risk. In the property accounts, it is generally more efficient to use an audit testing plan that emphasizes substantive tests. Exceptions occur in highly capital-intensive companies that have a large volume of property transactions. For example, utilities generally have an effective accounting system for processing and recording property transactions, most of which are for the acquisition or repair of utility properties. In any event, the auditor considers the assessed level of control risk and the assessment of inherent risk conditions in developing the audit testing plan.

The auditor's decision whether or not to perform additional tests of controls is based on which strategy would be more efficient. The auditor may decide, for example, that performing mainly substantive tests would be more efficient, even if it is likely that control risk could be assessed as low. Such a conclusion might be appropriate if few assets are involved and they are generally high-value items, as commonly occurs. In those instances, the time required to perform tests of controls might be greater than the time required to substantively test the account balances. Or, if the property accounts are relatively immaterial, only limited substantive testing may be appropriate.

In other circumstances, such as a large company with a centralized property department to control all aspects of acquisition, disposal, and record keeping, the auditor may decide that performing additional tests of controls is likely to be efficient. Previous chapters discussed tests of controls of other purchase and sales transactions; many of those tests will provide the auditor with evidence about the effectiveness of control structure policies and procedures pertaining to certain aspects of property, plant, and equipment and other noncurrent asset transactions as well. However, control structure policies and procedures relating to the purchase or sale of property, plant, and equipment often differ from those for other purchase and sales transactions. For example, different authorization procedures may be required, such as approval by the board of directors, or different procedures for verifying the receipt of equipment may be prescribed, for example, examination by the engineering department. Also, certain control procedures, such as those related to disposals or retirements, are often unique to the property accounts and may not be covered by tests of controls in the revenue and buying cycles.

The paragraphs that follow describe some of the tests of controls that may be performed if the auditor decides to test the effectiveness of the control structure as it relates to the property accounts.

Tests of controls may be performed to provide evidence of the effectiveness of the company's control procedures for ensuring that all expenditures have been authorized. If only purchases over a predetermined amount require written authorization, the auditor should evaluate whether the specified amount is reasonable; if it is too high, material unauthorized expenditures could occur. The auditor should examine selected authorizations to determine whether adequate details are provided to those who approve expenditures to allow them to make reasonable judgments. The auditor might also test the client's supervisory review of the account classifications of expenditures. To obtain evidence that disposals were appropriately accounted for, the auditor might test the client's procedures to ensure that all retirements are recorded. Testing the client's procedures for accumulating costs and comparing them with the authorized expenditures will also provide evidence that recorded acquisitions were properly authorized and are accurate.

Tests of controls with respect to physical protection of assets generally include observation and examining documents such as reports on the results of a physical inspection, including evidence of appropriate adjustments to the accounting records. The auditor might also observe part or all of the client's physical inspection and examine signatures or initials of the person who independently supervised the inspection. If there are confirmations or other correspondence regarding title documents, the auditor should also examine this documentation.

Tests of controls may include examining documents and records to determine whether the descriptions or the identification system used in the property records is adequate. Records of leased assets should also be examined to determine that they are adequate. In addition, the auditor may reperform the client's reconciliation of the subsidiary ledgers to the general ledger and examine evidence of the appropriate review and approval of differences.

If additional tests of controls support a low assessment of control risk, substantive tests can be reduced significantly. In those circumstances, substantive tests of changes in the property, plant, and equipment accounts during the year are normally restricted to

- Reperforming or reviewing the control account reconciliation.
- Testing major additions and disposals for authorization and accuracy.
- Reviewing the reasonableness of the depreciation calculation for the year and the consistency of the method used.

If a company's control structure with respect to expenditures for other noncurrent assets appears to be effective, and if policies and procedures for recording and retaining such assets are reviewed periodically, the auditor may be able to perform tests of controls to obtain evidence of their effectiveness. Such tests of controls might include inspecting reports or other records evidencing the review of intangible assets and deferred charges by a responsible official.

In deciding the audit testing plan for intangible assets and deferred charges, the auditor should recognize that judgments about whether to defer costs to future periods, what amortization periods are appropriate, and how to determine realizable values are all highly subjective. For this reason, the auditor needs to evaluate the environment in which decisions about recording such assets are made, and whether those matters are reviewed at an appropriate level. In particular, the auditor should be satisfied that expenditures that should properly be expensed currently are not deferred to future periods to improve the profit position of a company experiencing an economic downturn, and that the reverse does not occur as a means of "normalizing" or minimizing income to achieve other enterprise objectives.

Even when the audit strategy is to emphasize substantive tests of the property and intangible asset accounts, the nature, timing, and extent of those tests are directly related to the auditor's understanding of the control structure and assessment of control risk.

Substantive Testing at Interim Dates

There are many occasions when staffing efficiency, reporting deadlines, or other factors prompt the auditor to perform substantive tests of property and other noncurrent asset accounts before year-end. Early testing may be appropriate, if the company has effective control procedures for transaction processing during the period between the early testing date and year-end. The auditor should also pay particular attention to control procedures relating to asset protection and, in some circumstances, to segregation of duties. On the other hand, substantive tests are likely to be performed at year-end if relevant aspects of the control structure are not effective (e.g., the detailed property or depreciation records are not adequately maintained).

Even if the auditor decides to perform substantive tests at year-end, as often happens when property, plant, and equipment comprise a few items of high individual value, it is often desirable to complete some of the work before year-end. For instance, purchases and dispositions of property, plant, and equipment during the first ten months of the year could be tested before year-end and the details recorded on a working paper for completion and assessment at year-end. Much of the testing of other noncurrent assets, such as deferred charges, generally can be performed before year-end because the account balances frequently are adjusted only for periodic amortization. In those instances, only an evaluation of the carrying value of the asset may be required at year-end. Chapter 9 discusses more fully the factors that should enter into decisions about early substantive testing.

SUBSTANTIVE TESTS

Many of the substantive tests described below can be traced to a "Summary of Property, Plant, & Equipment & Accumulated Depreciation," frequently referred to as a "lead schedule," an example of which is shown in Figure 18.1. Similar schedules may be prepared for intangible assets and deferred charges.

Examination of Opening Balances and Prior Year's Transactions

If financial statements are being audited for the first time, the auditor must decide to what extent it is necessary to examine property and other noncurrent asset accounts before the beginning of the year or years under audit. Since assets acquired in prior years and related accumulated depreciation are likely to be significant in the current balance sheet and income statement, the auditor must have a basis for believing that both are fairly stated in conformity with generally accepted accounting principles (GAAP).

If financial statements for earlier years have been audited and reported on by independent auditors, reviewing the other auditors' working papers and the client's records should be sufficient to provide the necessary understanding of the accounting principles, policies, and methods employed. In some cases—for example, if no audit was made in earlier years or if the successor auditor does not choose to rely on the predecessor auditor's work—the successor auditor's work should be a combination of analytical procedures and substantive tests of details. Available property records should be reviewed in enough depth to give the auditor an understanding of the accounting principles used and the consistency with which they were applied. The auditor may prepare or obtain analyses summarizing the annual changes in the asset and depreciation accounts and may examine evidence to support major additions and reductions. In particular, unusual items should be investigated to learn of revaluations or other major adjustments. The auditor should pay particular attention to property acquired by issuing common stock or exchanging other property. In an initial engagement, numerous historical analyses—such as of long-term debt, capital stock, additional paid-in capital, retained earnings, and minutes of directors' meetings—are made. The auditor should be alert for matters in those analyses that affect property, plant, and equipment and other noncurrent asset accounts.

Existence and Ownership of Assets

In an initial engagement, the auditor should seek evidence that tangible and intangible assets exist and are, in fact, the property of the company. If a company's record keeping is adequate, deeds, purchase contracts, and other evidence of ownership will be on file and retrievable. Sometimes, however, those documents get mislaid over the years as successive generations of management come and go and files are moved, rearranged, or culled. If no other evidence can be found, the auditor can ask management to seek representations from counsel concerning legal title to properties.

Figure 18.1   Property, Plant, and Equipment Lead Schedule

Date Prepared 1/23/8—
Prepared by
a) C & L
b) Client and
Examined by δ
Reviewed by
C & L SR/SUP HRJ

ACE Enterprises Inc.
Summary of Property, Plant, & Equipment & Accumulated Depreciation
12/31/8—

Classification	Balance at Beginning of period	Additions	Disposals	Other	Balance at End of period
Cost	Ⓐ	Ⓑ Ⓒ	Ⓓ	Ⓔ	TB
Buildings	10745986 43	98723 66	9161 31 Ⓕ	(334783)	10832200 95
Machinery & Equipment	2088816 57	337937 01	1962 22 Ⓖ		2424791 36 TB
Furniture & Fixtures	580770 6	66849 1		334783	6810980 TB
	12892880 06	4433455 8	111123 53	— o —	13325102 11 ☑
	☑	☑	☑	☑	
Accumulated Depreciation	Ⓐ	Ⓗ	Ⓕ	Ⓔ	Ⓐ
Buildings	3007975 34	214929 27	9161 31	(16735)	3213575 95 TB
Machinery & Equipment	743567 95	1045495 7	1758 46 Ⓖ		846359 06 TB
Furniture & Fixtures	185211 8	59273 3		167 35	246158 6 TB
	3770064 47	3254061 7	10919 77	— o —	4089455087 ☑
	☑	☑	☑	☑	☑

Legend

ℐ = Traced to prior year work papers

☑ = Footed & cross-footed

TB = Agreed to trial balance

Ⓐ = Agreed to fixed asset subsidiary ledger

Ⓑ = Supported by detail listing of fixed asset additions. See
　　work papers —— to —— where additions were vouched

Ⓒ = See w/p —— For calculation of investment tax credit

Ⓓ = See w/p —— For calculation of investment tax credit recapture

Ⓔ = Reclassification for light fixtures erroneously classified as building

Ⓕ = Write off obsolete and scrapped items

Ⓖ = Sale of miscellaneous M & E - No further audit work deemed necessary

Ⓗ = See w/p's —— To —— where reasonableness of client's
　　calculation of depreciation was tested using the firm's
　　computer audit program for estimating depreciation

On subsequent audits, tests directed at the existence and ownership of property, plant, and equipment, and intangible assets and deferred charges normally consist of reviewing the company's procedures for maintaining detailed records and for periodically comparing those records with the assets themselves, and examining selected additions, disposals, and allocations during the year. If the company's detailed records are accurate, and if the auditor has performed tests of the client's physical inspections and control procedures related to existence and ownership of property, plant, and equipment, substantive procedures can be limited to reviews of selected major additions and disposals and periodic allocations.

If the company periodically compares its detailed records with the actual assets but the auditor has not performed tests of those procedures, the procedures set forth below should be carried out as of the date selected for testing.

- Review the company's procedures for conducting the physical inspection and comparison.
- Consider whether to observe those procedures.
- Review the actions taken to investigate discrepancies disclosed and to propose necessary adjustments to the records.

The auditor should determine that the company's comparison of assets with records is performed by a person who is independent of the custody of the assets and of maintaining the detailed property records. If the comparison is performed by a person who has custodial responsibility for or other access to the assets, the auditor should consider testing the client's comparison more extensively.

The comparison of the accounting records with the assets themselves should also be used to determine whether the carrying value of property, plant, and equipment requires adjustment because the assets are no longer in use or in good condition. The auditor should review the comparison to determine if obsolete or damaged assets on hand have been included and whether these assets are carried at an amount in excess of what can be recovered through revenue generated or outright sale.

If the company does not compare assets with the accounting records, the auditor should consider requesting the client to perform a complete or partial comparison, depending on such factors as susceptibility to loss, theft, or destruction. Alternatively, the auditor may make the comparison, although that may be a very inefficient use of audit time. If equipment is easily damaged, lost, stolen, or subject to personal use, such as in the case of small tools, the auditor should determine if the depreciation rate used by the company considers those factors and, if not, should consider physically inspecting such assets, if material.

In many instances, the auditor may obtain evidence of the existence and condition of a major portion of the company's property, plant, and equipment through observation during physical inventory observations or routine plant tours. Other evidence may also be available regarding the existence of major property items; for example, continued sales of specific products provide evidence that the assets used to produce the products are still in existence and operating effectively. Conversely, discontinuance of a product or product line should raise questions as to the carrying value of the related production facilities. Continued full occupancy of a hotel facility, for example, might also provide evidence regarding the existence and condition of the furniture and equipment used in the facility and might preclude the need for an annual physical inspection of those assets. The auditor should consider, however, the risk of material misstatements arising in the property accounts if incorrect conclusions are drawn.

In selecting procedures for substantiating the existence and ownership of real property, if transactions are usually few and of high value, the auditor should consider inspecting documents of title (or confirming that such documents are held by proper custodians—normally banks or other lending institutions) for all or a substantial proportion of the properties, to ascertain that the company has valid title and that the assets have not been pledged. In addition, the auditor may examine title insurance policies, confirm with title insurance companies, or, in some cases, examine recorded deeds. Schedules of property covered by casualty insurance policies may be compared with recorded assets, as may schedules used for property tax records. Documentation and confirmations relating to notes payable and long-term debt should be reviewed for indications of assets that have been pledged as collateral. These procedures are normally performed at the balance sheet date.

Acquisition of Assets

Substantive tests of property, plant, and equipment additions normally include the following (the extent of testing depends on the assessed level of control risk):

- Examining properly authorized agreements, architects' certificates, deeds, invoices, and other documents. For a purchase of land and buildings as a complete unit, the auditor should test the purchase price by comparing the data with the purchase agreement.
- Examining work orders and other supporting documentation for the company's own materials and labor. The auditor should review the percentage added for overhead to ensure that only factory overhead, as appropriate, has been allocated to the addition.
- Reviewing the minutes of meetings of the board of directors or other committees to determine whether major additions were appropriately authorized.

Evaluating whether additions were appropriately approved should be based on the auditor's understanding of the authorization procedures and the level of the individuals authorized to approve acquisitions. If written authorizations are not obtained, unneeded assets may be acquired or portions of cost overruns that should be expensed may be capitalized. The approval process may not be adequate if authorizations do not include the reason for the expenditure, the estimated amount, the allocation between capital expenditures and charges to current operations, and procedures for comparing estimated amounts with actual expenditures. If these are lacking, the auditor should consider expanding the substantive tests, for example, by reviewing with senior company officials the usefulness of assets acquired during the year or reasons for budget overruns, to obtain satisfaction that the recorded additions are appropriate.

Disposition of Assets

The auditor should test entries removing assets from the accounts by examining evidence of approval, comparing acquisition cost with underlying records, recomputing accumulated depreciation and the resulting gain or loss, and evaluating the reasonableness of removal costs and recovery from scrap or salvage. If there is a properly controlled work order system or if numerous assets are disposed of at the same time, as in the case of a sale or an abandonment of a plant, the auditor can usually test the entries using a sample of the individual transactions.

As with acquisitions of assets, the auditor should also be familiar with the company's procedures for recording dispositions and with the levels of the people who approve them. If the company's procedures for recording new assets that replace existing assets do not identify the related retirement or disposal, the auditor may need to expand the testing of asset dispositions. The auditor should review additions for the year to determine if they are replacements for other assets and, if so, should ascertain that the replaced asset has been correctly accounted for. Also, miscellaneous income accounts should be reviewed for evidence of sales or disposals of assets.

Classification of Expenditures

If tests of controls provide evidence that control procedures for classifying expenditures between capital expenditures and current-period expenses are effective, the auditor may limit testing of classifications to scanning the charges to repair and maintenance accounts for significant or unusual items, reviewing fluctuations, and other substantive tests of additions. Ordinarily, however, the auditor will perform further substantive tests, on at least a limited basis, even if control risk has been assessed as low. Those tests may include

- Reviewing capitalizations, disposals, and repair and maintenance expense for reasonableness in relation to budgets and to the previous year, and obtaining explanations for any large or unusual fluctuations.
- Reviewing whether all major additions and disposals during the year are properly classified.
- Reviewing significant charges to repair and maintenance expense.

The auditor might vary the extent of these tests depending on whether the classification of expenditures is approved by a designated official.

As noted earlier in this chapter, a company may routinely expense the cost of small-dollar items to reduce the clerical effort involved in maintaining detailed asset records. In reviewing charges to repair and maintenance accounts, the auditor should consider whether such items in the aggregate could have a material effect on the financial statements. Also, the auditor must recognize that determining whether an expenditure should be capitalized or charged to current operations may be subjective and highly judgmental. Even in a company with effective control structure policies and procedures, differences of opinion may arise over the nature and proper recording of a particular expenditure.

Carrying Values

Property, plant, and equipment are typically carried on the balance sheet at cost, which includes all expenditures necessary to make an asset ready for its intended use, including freight and taxes. Determining whether the client has appropriately capitalized costs requires the auditor to have extensive expertise in evaluating accounting principles selected and applied to asset acquisitions.

The auditor is concerned with recoverable value of noncurrent assets only in considering whether there has been a material permanent decline in value. Depreciable assets are, in effect, "realized" in the normal course of business by charging depreciation to income, and thus provision for a decline in value may be necessary only if future income from an asset is unlikely to equal or exceed its carrying value. This can normally be calculated only for a complete production unit or similar group of assets.

A change in general business conditions or in the area where property is located may indicate that carrying values may not be fully recoverable. On occasion, adverse conditions are so prevalent as to be obvious: idle plant or excess capacity; a depressed or deteriorating neighborhood, region, or industry; continuing losses. More often, however, the concept of a permanent decline in value is difficult to apply in practice because the existing accounting literature does not provide specific authoritative guidance on accounting for the inability to fully recover the carrying values of long-lived assets. As indicated by current practice, the existing literature is being interpreted as permitting or requiring write-downs of long-lived assets to estimated recoverable value only in rare situations. Thus, a loss should be recognized only when it becomes obvious that the remaining net book value of property cannot be recovered through sale or use. Once a write-down has been made, it is generally not acceptable to write the asset back up to reflect an increase in value, unless an asset previously expected to be sold or abandoned is subsequently put back into use. Other indications of potential inability to recover carrying values may be dramatic changes in the way an asset is used, changes in laws regulating environmental matters, a forecast of long-term losses from operations, and costs exceeding original expectations for acquiring or constructing an asset. In November 1988, the Financial Accounting Standards Board added a project to its agenda dealing with reporting and accounting for the impairment of long-lived assets.

If property previously used in operations is expected to be sold, its carrying amount should be written down to, but not below, net realizable value. The auditor must evaluate the circumstances surrounding the intended sale of significant assets or plant, to determine that the distinction required by Accounting Principles Board (APB) Opinion No. 30 (Accounting Standards Section I13) between a disposal of a segment of a business and the sale of significant assets has been properly made. If the transaction is accounted for as the disposal of a segment of a business, the auditor should also review the treatment of expected operating income or losses from the measurement date to the disposal date. If expected income is used to offset other losses on the disposal, the auditor must take particular care in evaluating the methods and assumptions used to calculate the income amount. Finally, the auditor should consider whether the client's evaluation of the carrying value of specific productive assets or segments has implications for evaluating the enterprise as a "going concern," as indicated by SAS No. 59 (AU Section 341) and discussed further in Chapter 22.

Appraisal values are not generally accepted as a basis for carrying values of property; however, there are exceptions, such as reorganizations, quasi-reorganizations, the allocation of a basket purchase price, and other occasions when the consideration given to acquire assets has no objectively determinable value, for example, a purchase of assets for common stock that has no readily determinable fair value. Appraisal values are also used for determining carrying amounts of donated property, assets acquired in certain nonmonetary transactions, and troubled debt restructurings. Property, plant, and equipment acquired in a transaction that must be accounted for by the purchase method are valued at fair value at the date of acquisition. Often the amounts are determined by an appraisal performed at that time.

The appraisal is usually performed by an independent appraiser. The auditor should obtain satisfaction concerning the professional qualifications and reputation of the appraiser by inquiry or other procedures, as appropriate. The auditor should also obtain an understanding of the methods or assumptions the appraiser used to determine the assigned values, as required by SAS No. 11, *Using the Work of a Specialist* (AU Section 336). Based on knowledge of the client's business and industry, the auditor should determine whether the values the appraiser assigned are appropriate for use in the financial statements. (Appraisal reports on the value of assets are among the most subjective and sensitive specialist reports that an auditor uses. SAS No. 11, discussed in Chapter 6, provides guidance on the auditor's use of the work of a specialist.) In applying SAS No. 11 to the work of a real estate appraiser, the auditor may consider the guidance in the AICPA audit and accounting guide, *Guide for the Use of Real Estate Appraisal Information*. This guide also helps the auditor understand the real estate appraisal process and how to use real estate appraisal information. While the majority of items purchased may be for use on an ongoing basis, management may intend to hold other items for resale or to use them only temporarily. In that case, the auditor should ensure that the assigned values do not exceed net realizable values.

Capital Leases

The discussion so far in this chapter has generally centered around transactions in which property, plant, and equipment are acquired by outright purchase. Increasingly, however, the rights to such assets are obtained through lease transactions, and these have grown in sophistication and complexity in recent years, as has the accounting for them. Although much of this chapter is equally applicable to purchased and leased assets, the auditor should take into consideration the unique aspects of lease transactions. Detailed coverage of the various types of lease transactions and related accounting standards, however, is beyond the scope of this book.

In most companies, control structure policies and procedures relating to the acquisition of property apply equally to purchases and leases. For example, a requirement for approval at a certain level for purchases of property over a specified amount typically applies to leases as well. If such a policy does not exist, the auditor should take this into consideration when obtaining an understanding of the control environment and assessing risk.

For the auditor, the most important differences between purchase and lease transactions are those that deal with the audit objectives of rights and obligations, valuation, and presentation and disclosure. In a purchase transaction, the company acquires title to the property and generally is not restricted in how it may use the property. In a lease transaction, the company does not own the property and may use it only in the manner specified in the lease agreement. For example, the lessee may be precluded by terms of the lease agreement from improving, modifying, or moving the property. In addition, the lessee will have use of the property only as long as the requirements of the lease agreement are met. Typically, the lessee has an obligation to make timely payments to the lessor, maintain the property, and, in many cases, pay taxes and insurance. In planning the engagement, the auditor should consider procedures that will identify material leases and provide assurance that the lessee is fulfilling its obligations under the agreement.

Obtaining assurance about proper valuation under GAAP and presentation and disclosure of lease transactions is more difficult. To properly evaluate the lessee's choice of accounting measurement and disclosure principles, the auditor needs to understand the lease transaction and the appropriate accounting treatment. In some instances, the client's documentation may not be sufficient for the auditor to evaluate the transaction. For example, the auditor may not be able to determine from the client's records the interest rates implicit in the lease. In these instances, the auditor should arrange with the client to obtain the necessary information directly from the lessor.

The specific measurement and disclosure requirements for accounting for leases are described in Statement of Financial Accounting Standards (SFAS) No. 13, *Accounting for Leases*, and related pronouncements (Accounting Standards Section L10). In general, lease transactions that have specified characteristics (capital leases) are required to be recorded by the lessee as if the lease resulted in acquiring property and incurring long-term debt. Assets acquired under capital leases are subject to the same accounting rules as other property, and the audit objectives related to assets acquired under capital leases are identical to those for other property, plant, and equipment accounts.

Because an entity may have lease obligations that do not meet the capitalization criteria, or may not have identified all leases that meet the criteria, the auditor must be familiar with those criteria and design auditing procedures to ensure that lease transactions have been properly classified. Analysis of lease expense accounts will generally help the auditor identify significant leasing transactions. The auditor should ordinarily examine records of leased assets, lease agreements, and other data related to leases capitalized during the period, to determine that they were properly classified and valued. Documents supporting rentals classified as operating leases should also be reviewed to determine that they, too, were properly classified. Auditing procedures frequently required to evaluate the financial statement presentation of capital leases include reviewing the terms of individual leases; determining and evaluating the fair value, residual value, and estimated economic life of leased property; evaluating interest rate assumptions; and analyzing income tax considerations.

Because of the almost unlimited variety of leasing transactions, the complexity of lease computations, and the judgmental factors involved in assessing whether the audit evidence is appropriate, the auditor's review of leases may require more judgment than substantive tests of other property, plant, and equipment accounts. Often, the auditor of a lessee is presented with information obtained from the lessor and purporting to support classification as an operating lease. The auditor should independently determine the classification in light of the facts and circumstances of the particular client. The auditor may need to use the services of specialists to review the fair value of property and estimated residual value under lease agreements. Finally, some leasing transactions are so complicated that often the auditor must look at a series of transactions and agreements to determine their economic substance—a process requiring much more judgment and experience than simply applying the criteria of SFAS No. 13.

Constructed Assets—Interest Capitalization

The historical cost of acquiring an asset includes the costs of bringing it to the condition and location of its intended use. If that will take time, SFAS No. 34, paragraph 6 (Accounting Standards Section I67.102), states that the related interest cost incurred during that period is a part of the historical cost of acquiring the asset.

In evaluating the amounts of interest capitalized, the auditor must determine that

- Interest cost is being incurred.
- The interest rate used is proper.
- The average expenditures on which interest is capitalized have required the payment of cash, transfer of assets, or creation of a liability on which interest costs are incurred.
- The activities necessary to get the asset ready for its intended use have been in progress throughout the period for which interest is capitalized.

Determining the proper rate to use for capitalization can be simple if the expenditures are financed by a specific borrowing incurred for that purpose or by a specific working capital line of credit. If the expenditures are financed by an outside party that is constructing the asset, the auditor should determine whether the stated interest rate is the appropriate interest rate as specified by APB Opinion No. 21 (Accounting Standards Section I69); if it is not, the need for imputing interest at a fair rate should be considered. If specific borrowings cannot be identified, the auditor must use judgment in reviewing and testing the client's determination of the appropriate weighted average interest rate, using the guidelines of SFAS No. 34. In making this judgment, the auditor should keep in mind that the objective is a reasonable measure of the interest cost incurred in acquiring the asset that otherwise would have been avoided. For example, the auditor may exclude certain borrowings that have been outstanding for a long time and bear interest at a rate not in line with current market conditions, like industrial bond issues relating to other assets.

Capitalization rates are to be applied to expenditures that have required the payment of cash, transfer of assets, or recognition of a liability on which interest is incurred. As a practical matter, monthly capitalized costs of an asset under construction are often used as an approximation of actual expenditures, unless the difference is material. In evaluating the reasonableness of this practice, the auditor might want to consider the company's average time to liquidate trade payables. If the asset is being constructed by outsiders, the auditor should be alert for material retainages withheld from progress payments until construction is completed.

Often the auditor can determine that activities necessary to get the asset ready for its intended use are in progress by observing a steady stream of expenditures over the construction period. The term "activities" is construed broadly to include all steps required to prepare the asset for its intended use, including administrative and technical activities during the preconstruction stage. Brief interruptions in activities, externally imposed interruptions, and delays inherent in the acquisition process do not require cessation of interest capitalization.

The capitalization period ends when the asset is substantially complete and ready for its intended use. The auditor should be aware that in a complex construction project, certain segments may be completed and become productive before completion of the entire project.

Other costs incurred on constructed assets that are properly capitalizable include costs to modify an asset for its intended use and costs of operating machinery during the testing phase of installation. Any revenue received from the sale of salvage materials or test production should reduce the capitalized costs. Interest income, however, should not be offset against capitalized costs except in the specific situation allowed by SFAS No. 62 (Accounting Standards Section I67.116A–B).

Depreciation and Salvage Values

Substantive testing of depreciation accounts should start with a review of the company's methods and policies. Policies preferably should be systematically documented, but if they are not, they can be inferred from the computations and work sheets of prior and current years. Depreciation rates, salvage values, and useful lives may be compared with those in general use by similar enterprises. Computations of depreciation expense should be tested, which in many cases may be accomplished by making approximations on an overall basis.

The auditor should consider the reasonableness of useful lives and whether known factors require reducing or extending the lives of any categories of plant assets. This can be accomplished by observing the pattern of gains and losses on disposition; consistent gains or consistent losses could suggest that the lives used are too short or too long or that salvage values used are inappropriate. For assets depreciated on the composite method, the auditor should review the relationship of the balances of allowance accounts to those of asset accounts. Ratios are, of course, affected by the pattern of additions, but after an auditor allows for unusually high or low additions in certain years, a significant upward or downward trend in the ratio of an allowance account to a related asset account should indicate whether useful lives are too short or too long. If either seems possible, an analysis of actual useful lives is called for.

The auditor should also be aware of changing business conditions that might suggest the client should revise the estimated remaining lives of assets upward or downward for purposes of future depreciation charges. For example, leasehold improvements are depreciated over the estimated useful life of the improvements or over the original term of the lease, whichever is shorter, without regard to renewal options until those options are actually exercised or it becomes obvious they will be exercised. Significant expenditures for additional improvements with a life considerably longer than the remaining original lease might indicate management's intention to exercise a renewal option. Conversely, the auditor might learn that management intends to replace within the next two years computer equipment with a remaining depreciable life of four years. In these situations, the auditor must assess management's justification for changing or not changing the remaining depreciable life.

In practice, estimated lives, salvage values, and depreciation methods are not commonly reviewed, by either clients or auditors. Once established for particular assets, these items are usually left unchanged unless events or circumstances arise that call them into question. Auditors usually do not have the expertise to evaluate the remaining life of an asset and generally rely on other experts when necessary. Formal, in-depth reviews are usually made only for tax purposes, as part of acquisition reviews, or in industries in which depreciation has a significant effect on earnings, such as equipment leasing. The auditor's risk assessment process should include determining whether such an evaluation is appropriate.

If the reasonableness of the depreciation charges cannot be determined by making approximations on an overall basis for each class of assets, the auditor should test the individual computations and the balances in the subsidiary ledgers, compare the totals with the control account, and investigate any difference at year-end.

Other Substantive Tests

Among the most important of an auditor's procedures are reviewing his or her knowledge of the client's operations and business environment and correlating developments in those areas with activity in the property accounts. The auditor should be sure to understand the business reasons for additions and retirements and whether trends in operations or in the industry are likely to affect the values of property carried in the accounts. The auditor can perform several other procedures to gather additional evidence about the property accounts. For example, the auditor should

- Visit and tour the company's main plants probably once a year and smaller plants less frequently. One among several reasons for making a tour is to observe the existence and condition of the plant.
- Examine the minutes of directors' meetings and executive committee meetings for other evidence of matters affecting the property accounts.
- Review documentation and confirmations relating to notes payable and long-term debt for indications of assets that have been pledged as collateral.
- If there were any foreign currency transactions during the year or balances at year-end, determine whether they were translated at appropriate rates.
- If the company has several departments, subsidiaries, or affiliates, determine whether profits on transfers or sales within the group have been recognized that should be eliminated from the property accounts.
- Routinely inquire of company personnel encountered in the course of the audit about past or prospective changes in the operations that might affect the property accounts.
- Compare balances of asset, allowance, and expense accounts with the prior year and, if possible, month to month to identify fluctuations and unusual entries calling for inquiry and explanation.

Intangible Assets

Substantiating the valuation of intangible assets requires extensive judgment on the auditor's part. Documentation for an account balance seldom provides conclusive evidence of value. The following table illustrates some common types of intangible assets, bases for determining cost, and typical amortization periods[2]:

Asset	Basis for Determining Cost	Amortization Period
Patents	Cost of purchased patents; legal costs incurred in connection with successfully defending a patent suit. (Costs of developing patents internally are generally expensed as incurred.)	Estimated period of benefit or 17 years (the legal life of a patent), whichever is less.

[2]APB Opinion No. 17, which was issued in 1970, established that the amortization period for intangible assets should not exceed 40 years. Recently, questions have been raised about whether this period should be shortened.

Asset	Basis for Determining Cost	Amortization Period
Copyrights	Expenditures for government fees, attorneys' fees, and expenses. (As with patents, research and development costs involved should be expensed as incurred.)	Estimated period of benefit or life of author plus 50 years (the legal life of a copyright), whichever is less.
Trademarks, brands, and trade names	Expenditures for attorneys' fees, registration fees, and other expenditures identifiable with acquisition.	Estimated period of use, but not more than 40 years.
Franchises	Purchase price, including legal fees and similar costs.	Estimated period of benefit, but not more than 40 years.
Covenants not to compete	Purchase price or allocated purchase price in the case of a business combination.	Specified term of the covenant, but not more than 40 years.
Goodwill acquired	The excess of cost of the acquired company over the sum of the amounts assigned to identifiable assets (tangible and intangible) acquired less liabilities assumed.	Estimated period of benefit, but not more than 40 years.
Intangibles generally	Cost of intangible assets acquired from others. (Costs to develop intangible assets that are not specifically identifiable are expensed as incurred.)	Estimated period of benefit, but not more than 40 years.

When an intangible asset is capitalized and is to be written off against income of future years, the auditor should determine whether it is reasonable to assume the income will be earned. This may include, for example, the following procedures:

- Reviewing marketing forecasts and other management plans, which the auditor should assess to ensure they are not unrealistically optimistic and to determine that it appears the resources needed to finance the plans will be available.

- Discussing those forecasts and plans with management. If relevant, the auditor should obtain formal representation that the forecasts of future income have been prepared with due care.

- Considering whether income equal to amounts of intangible assets capitalized in past years has materialized.

In assessing the future benefits expected to be derived from the assets, the auditor should consider the possibility that the benefits will not materialize because of

- The operation of law (e.g., expiration of a patent).
- The termination of or change in a contract (e.g., a license agreement).
- Changes in the client's circumstances (e.g., the disposal of part of its business).
- Obsolescence (e.g., a patent on a product may have little or no future benefit when a better or more advanced product has been developed).

In addition, it may occasionally be desirable to confirm the existence of material intangible assets by direct correspondence with attorneys or grantors of royalties, licenses, franchises, copyrights, or patents. Normally it is not possible to confirm or otherwise substantiate title to goodwill, although the auditor should ascertain that the business to which the goodwill relates is still active and operating well enough to warrant continued valuation of the goodwill at its recorded amount.

Income Tax Considerations

In planning and performing auditing procedures for the property, plant, and equipment and other noncurrent asset accounts, the auditor must take into consideration the interrelationship of those accounts and various income tax accounts. Many amounts used in determining periodic income tax accruals and deferred taxes are computed from the property and other noncurrent asset records.

The Tax Reform Act of 1986 modified the Accelerated Cost Recovery System (ACRS) established by the Economic Recovery Tax Act of 1981. Generally accepted accounting principles require that plant and equipment be depreciated over their expected useful lives. The useful life categories provided under the ACRS guidelines, however, generally do not conform with the actual expected useful lives of the assets they apply to. If the effect of the difference between depreciation based on ACRS lives and depreciation based on actual expected lives on current or future financial statements is material, using ACRS depreciation for financial reporting purposes is not acceptable. For many businesses, this necessitates a second set of depreciation records for income tax purposes.

With the passage of the Tax Reform Act of 1986, a corporate alternative minimum tax (AMT) was introduced. In determining the AMT income, depreciation calculations are made under the Alternative Depreciation System and then additional depreciation calculations are required to determine AMT income. Thus, companies may be required to maintain as many as four sets of depreciation records (i.e., financial reporting, regular tax, and two for AMT) and possibly more, depending on whether a company is subject to taxation in other jurisdictions.

Interest capitalization policies and the treatment of lease payments may also be different for financial reporting and income tax purposes. As stated above, SFAS No. 34 (Accounting Standards Section I67) requires that interest be capitalized during the acquisition period as part of the historical cost of acquiring certain property, plant, and equipment. The amount of interest capitalized for income tax purposes, however, will probably be different from that used for financial reporting, resulting in different book and tax bases for individual assets. Also, certain leasing transactions are recorded for financial statement purposes as assets acquired under capital leases, while for income tax purposes they may be treated as operating leases.

For transactions that result in different accounting for financial statement and income tax purposes, the auditor must identify the differences and consider them in planning the audit. The relationship of the property accounts to the income tax accounts generally requires close coordination of auditing procedures in the two areas. In reviewing the temporary differences between book and tax bases, the auditor may need to perform separate tests to substantiate the tax basis balances as well as the financial statement balances.

19

Auditing Income Taxes

Income tax differs from other costs and expenses because it is largely a dependent variable, based on revenue received and costs and expenses incurred by an enterprise. Management often has the ability to control the timing and amount of tax payments by controlling the related underlying transactions, particularly in closely held enterprises where minimizing taxes currently payable is often a significant management objective.

The issues associated with accounting for income taxes fall principally into two broad categories: determining the tax provision in the income statement and the timing of its payment. Those two issues complicate presentation of the current tax liability and deferred tax accounts on the balance sheet and the expense on the income statement. The actual liability is difficult to determine because of the complexities of federal and state tax statutes and regulations. The accounting is further complicated by the number and variety of differences between generally accepted accounting principles (GAAP) and the treatment permitted or required by tax laws and related rulings and regulations of the various taxing jurisdictions an entity is subject to. For multinational companies, income taxes levied in foreign countries under the laws and regulations of those countries must also be evaluated to determine their treatment under U.S. accounting pronouncements.

Accounting for income taxes is currently governed mainly by either Accounting Principles Board (APB) Opinion No. 11, *Accounting for Income Taxes* (Accounting Standards Sections I24, I28, I32, and I37, found in Appendix E of the *Current Text* of FASB Accounting Standards),[1] or Statement of Financial Accounting Standards (SFAS) No. 96, *Accounting for Income Taxes* (Accounting Standards Section I25). When originally issued, SFAS No. 96 was to be effective for fiscal years beginning after December 15, 1988. The effective date was amended by SFAS No. 100, *Accounting for Income Taxes—Deferral of the Effective Date of FASB Statement No. 96*, to fiscal years beginning after December 15, 1989.

In December 1989, the Financial Accounting Standards Board (FASB) voted to further defer the effective date of SFAS No. 96 to fiscal years beginning after December 15, 1991. Companies that have already adopted SFAS No. 96 may not revert to APB Opinion No. 11.

At the time of this writing, the FASB continues to explore possible amendments to SFAS No. 96. Because of the uncertainty surrounding such amendments, this chapter does not discuss accounting principles related to income taxes. An overview of accounting principles for income taxes will be published in an update supplement after those uncertainties have been resolved.

AUDIT OBJECTIVES

The objectives in auditing income tax accounts are to obtain reasonable assurance that all tax liabilities (or refunds receivable), tax provisions, and

---

[1] In addition to Opinion No. 11, Opinion Nos. 23, 24, 25, and 28 also deal with accounting for income taxes.

deferred tax accounts are included in the financial statements; that they are properly measured, classified, and described; and that all necessary disclosures are made in the financial statements. The basic auditing procedures are to test the accuracy of the computation of the current and deferred tax liability or asset accounts and the charge or credit to expense for the period. This requires that the auditor determine that the underlying data is complete and accurate. The amounts involved are likely to be significant, and the issues affecting them numerous, complex, and often debatable. The discussion that follows suggests some of the specific objectives the auditor must meet in auditing income taxes.

In addition to obtaining reasonable assurance that the tax liability accounts accurately reflect the company's current tax obligations (including interest and penalty charges, which should be accounted for separately from the tax expense and liability accounts), the auditor must determine that probable loss contingencies that are reasonably estimable are provided for. Such contingencies may result from existing disagreements with taxing authorities or from the possibility that future disagreements may arise over positions taken by a company in its current tax return that may be interpreted differently by the Internal Revenue Service (IRS). Guidance for dealing with contingencies of this nature is contained in SFAS No. 5, *Accounting for Contingencies* (Accounting Standards Section C59). Further, the auditor should obtain reasonable assurance that deferred tax liabilities and assets are properly classified as to current and noncurrent amounts. The auditor should also determine that the total tax provision in the income statement is properly classified as to currently payable and deferred amounts. In addition, the auditor must ascertain that the tax effects of extraordinary items, discontinued operations, and changes in accounting principles have been properly calculated and reflected in the income statement.

Required disclosures relating to income taxes contain information of particular interest to financial statement users. Those disclosures include the nature of and changes in the composition of deferred taxes, variations from statutory tax rates (including treatment of investment tax credits), operating loss and tax credit carryforwards, and information about tax aspects of subsidiaries or investments. The auditor must also be satisfied that tax exposures not provided for in the financial statements but requiring disclosure under SFAS No. 5 are properly set forth in the notes to the financial statements. In addition, public companies are subject to specific disclosure requirements of the Securities and Exchange Commission.

The efficiency of the audit of income tax accounts can be enhanced by collecting, in the course of examining other accounts, data that may be useful in examining the tax accrual. Examples include collecting tax depreciation data when auditing fixed asset accounts, and gathering officer compensation data when testing the payroll accounts. The auditor should analyze significant nonrecurring transactions to determine their impact on the tax accrual. Equally important from a client service standpoint, the auditor should be alert to tax planning and tax savings opportunities, and can help the client plan transactions to result in the most favorable tax treatment.

INCOME TAX TRANSACTIONS AND INTERNAL CONTROL STRUCTURE POLICIES AND PROCEDURES

Typical Transactions

The tax transaction cycle consists of obtaining and summarizing the appropriate data, calculating the income tax effects, and disbursing the required tax payments at the appropriate time. Most tax compliance systems are organized according to the timing requirements of taxing authorities. A reminder list, often called a "tax calendar," helps control the filing of required tax returns and the timing of payments. Tax amounts are usually computed by a tax specialist and then authorized by a financial officer. The appropriate determination and recording of income tax expense and the related balance sheet accounts depend on proper recognition of the tax consequences of transactions for financial statement purposes, which may differ in many instances from the consequences reported on the tax returns. Control structure policies and procedures for income tax matters, therefore, may be sophisticated and complex.

Internal Control Structure

Even though the audit testing plan for income tax accounts usually emphasizes substantive testing, it is important to recognize that a separate tax transaction cycle and related control structure policies and procedures exist in most enterprises. It is the auditor's responsibility to obtain an understanding of the control structure relating to tax transactions and to identify situations where tests of controls might be appropriate. The three key functions that usually have control structure policies and procedures are tax planning, compliance, and recording. If policies and procedures are tested and found to be effective, the auditor may be able to adjust the timing and extent of substantive tests.

Tax Planning. Adequate control of income tax expense requires extensive advance planning. This begins with management's setting financial objectives for a given period and considering the effect of taxes on those goals. Then tax transactions are scheduled and specific decisions made to minimize the tax liability and plan for the consequent cash disbursements. Cash flow implications significantly influence tax planning in many cases.

Tax planning is facilitated and in part controlled by checklists of compliance requirements (due dates, elections to be made, information requirements, legislative activity, and the like), alternatives and opportunities, and open issues. It is particularly important for companies to keep records of past decisions having future tax implications. In making decisions about the tax treatments of transactions, companies need to consider not only future business plans but also the ongoing tax implications of past elections and differences between accounting and tax recording of transactions.

Tax specialists, both employees of the company and external consultants and auditors, are usually involved in the planning effort. They maintain reminder lists or checklists of tax savings opportunities, which are used to ensure that the company properly avails itself of deductions, exemptions, deferrals, and elections permitted by the law. Tax savings opportunities are reviewed and the checklists prepared, usually early in the client's fiscal year, and definitely before year-end.

Tax Compliance. Control over compliance with taxation requirements is necessary both to minimize liability for taxes and for accounting purposes, especially when a company is subject to multiple taxing jurisdictions. Many companies have designed and established well-controlled compliance systems in recognition of this fact.

The actual preparation of tax returns and compliance with tax laws may be a full-time task for a staff of specialists in a large company, or it may be delegated to an outside professional, like a certified public accountant, lawyer, or tax specialist. Smaller companies generally rely on outside professionals for tax services. Gathering the necessary information, planning and preparing returns, and payment of tax are generally systematized, subject to supervisory control procedures, and overseen by a financial officer of the company, who also reviews the details supporting the financial statement balances.

Recording Tax Transactions. Once taxes have been appropriately planned, statutory compliance determined, and payments either disbursed or estimated, the company must record tax transactions. Recording taxes is complicated by differences in recognizing transactions for accounting purposes and for tax purposes and by the estimation process that is part of determining the tax liability. Therefore, effective procedures for controlling entries to tax accounts are essential. All tax liability and asset accounts should be reconciled periodically to underlying detailed schedules or subsidiary ledgers. The current and deferred liability and asset accounts should be supported by appropriate computations.

To evaluate the appropriateness of the income tax liability, the company's tax specialist may prepare an analysis of the alternatives and uncertainties that might affect the liability for the current and prior years. That analysis may then be discussed with the auditor and one or more external tax specialists. Once the alternatives and uncertainties have been sufficiently explored and understood, management is in a position to determine the amount of accrued tax liability that most reasonably represents their probable outcome, consistent with the guidance provided in SFAS No. 5.

The responsibility for authorizing entries in the various income tax accounts should be delegated to one official. Because of differences in recording transactions for accounting and tax purposes, confusion often arises about the amounts and timely recording of monthly tax entries. The responsibility may rest with either an accountant or a tax specialist; there is no universal preference. The key point is that all entries are reviewed, reconciled, and controlled monthly in a consistent manner.

AUDIT TESTING PLAN

Risk Characteristics

Income tax has long been one of the most significant items in financial statements. Most often the expense and the current and deferred liability are material to fair presentation of the financial statements. Thus, a misstatement of tax accounts may result in a material misstatement of the financial statements taken as a whole. Misstatements of income taxes can result from the incorrect calculation of taxable income, which affects the tax provision and net income, or from the inappropriate treatment of temporary differences, which affects the balance sheet classification of the tax liability but not the tax provision or net income. In determining an appropriate audit testing plan for income taxes, the auditor must assess the inherent and control risk associated with the tax accounts.

Income tax recorded in the accounts is always an estimate—or more properly the sum of a large number of estimates. For purposes of timely preparation of financial statements, estimates of amounts that will ultimately be reflected in the tax returns usually must be made before the returns themselves are prepared. Also, revenue agents' examinations often extend over several years, and informal and formal discussions of the resulting findings over several more years. It is common to have a number of taxable years "open" for review at one time. Meanwhile, judgments have to be made at least annually of the adequacy of the current and deferred tax liability. Companies must make those judgments with great care and attention to detail, often with assistance from their auditors and tax counsel.

Lastly, the appropriate tax treatment of many transactions is simply not clear, particularly because of the numerous changes in the tax laws and regulations in recent years and the proliferation of court decisions affecting the interpretation of those laws. In making the necessary estimates in the face of all these uncertainties, some managements take an "aggressive" stance, while others are more "conservative." An aggressive position regarding tax estimates does not necessarily suggest questionable business ethics or a desire to portray the enterprise in an unrealistically favorable light; rather, it may reflect sound business judgment—a desire to postpone cash outflows as long as legally possible. However, the risk of the auditor's issuing an incorrect opinion may be increased by management's aggressiveness in this area.

Designing an Appropriate Audit Testing Plan

As previously noted, taxes are usually audited through substantive tests; however, some control structures may be effective enough to allow the auditor to limit substantive tests or to perform certain substantive tests at an interim date. How much the auditor can limit substantive tests depends on the assessment of inherent and control risk. In particular, the following attributes of the control structure may enable the auditor to reduce substantive tests:

- Reconciliation of tax account balances to supporting detail (like tax returns and summaries of differences between taxable income and accounting income).
- Supervision of those reconciliations and the supporting detail.
- Management reviews of tax-related matters, as described below.

Other factors that typically indicate the presence of effective policies and procedures are

- Assigning responsibility for tax planning, return preparation, and follow-up to competent officials.
- If subsidiaries maintain separate tax departments, coordination among them with respect to overall corporate planning.
- A satisfactory system of reporting by branches, divisions, or subsidiaries.
- A practice of obtaining competent outside advice, as warranted, on significant tax questions before and after major transactions are entered into.
- Well-prepared and readily accessible historical tax material.
- Maintaining records of adequate follow-up of due dates, payment dates, claims for refund, revenue agent adjustments, and coordination of federal and state taxes.

There are several reasons why a substantive testing approach to income tax accounts is usually taken. First, transactions in the tax accounts are not numerous and each one may be significant. The auditor may decide to substantively test each significant account balance and not perform tests of controls at all. In addition to being effective, in most instances this approach is also most efficient. Second, most significant tax decisions require a high degree of subjective analysis. The thought processes and research required to determine the appropriate accounting are difficult to test and often would need to be duplicated, at least in part, by the auditor. Finally, as required by APB Opinion No. 28, *Interim Financial Reporting* (Accounting Standards Section I73), the recording of tax expense, liabilities, and deferred taxes throughout the year is based on an estimate of the effective tax rate expected to apply for the full year. At year-end, final tax estimates are recorded based on actual results. The year-end determination logically becomes the focal point for testing tax account balances.

As noted earlier, the effectiveness of a company's control structure may have an impact on the extent and timing of substantive tests. Additionally, even if control procedures have not been tested, it may be appropriate for the auditor to perform some substantive tests before year-end, especially reconciling the prior-year tax return to the opening tax liability accounts, reviewing revenue agents' examinations, and examining records of estimated tax payments. On the other hand, identifying and testing differences between taxable income and accounting income are more likely to be done early only if control procedures are effective.

The existence of management reviews of income taxes may also affect the audit strategy. If the tax aspects of transactions are well planned and periodically monitored by qualified personnel (such as through reviews of effective tax rates and comparisons with budgets), and if those procedures can be assessed as adequate, this may allow the auditor to decrease emphasis on identifying the tax implications of transactions. On the other hand, the auditor would probably increase substantive testing if management did not employ a tax specialist, but focused on taxes only when preparing tax returns.

SUBSTANTIVE TESTS

The auditor should review the tax returns and related correspondence for all "open" years (for a recurring engagement this means reviewing the most recent year and updating the understanding of earlier years). Often the review can be combined with the auditor's participation in the preparation of the prior year's tax return or the technical review of the client's preparation. If a revenue agent's examination is in process, the auditor should request from the client reports and memorandums related to the examination and should review and evaluate any issues set forth in them. The auditor should also ask the client about any other adjustments proposed by the agent. The auditor should determine whether the status of "open" tax years has been affected by extensions of the statute of limitations granted by the client.

An auditor is expected to have sufficient knowledge of the major taxing statutes to be able to evaluate the accrued liabilities for the various taxes a company is subject to. Accordingly, on a recurring engagement, the auditor must review changes in the tax laws and regulations and court decisions since the preceding audit and consider whether they apply to the company. It is extremely important that the auditor have sufficient expertise in tax matters to resolve all questions that arise; how much a tax specialist needs to be involved in the audit varies with the circumstances.

Summary Account Analysis

As the starting point in the audit of the tax accounts and to provide an orderly framework for testing, the auditor usually requests analyses of the tax accounts for the year. The analyses may be prepared as of an interim date and later updated to year-end, and should show, for each kind of tax (including each type of deferred tax) and for each year still "open," the beginning balance, accruals, payments, transfers or adjustments, and the ending balance.

The auditor can then review the analyses, examine documents supporting transactions (to determine their existence or occurrence), and determine that prior-year overpayments and underpayments are properly identified (completeness), that deferred taxes are properly identified and computed (completeness and valuation), and that amounts currently payable are identified and scheduled for payment on the due dates (completeness and presentation). The appropriateness of the tax and accounting principles used and the mechanics of their application should also be substantiated (valuation). The level of detail the auditor examines in support of account balances and the extent to which normal business transactions (generated from other transaction cycles) are reviewed will depend on the auditor's assessment of inherent and control risk and the materiality of the accounts.

Often the auditor obtains or prepares a comparative summary of income and other tax account balances, ascertains that the summary is mathematically accurate, agrees the totals to the general ledger trial balance and the previous year's working papers, and traces significant reconciling items to supporting documentation.

Income Tax Payments and Refunds

Tax payments should be tested by examining assessment notices, correspondence with taxing authorities, canceled checks, and receipts, if available. The auditor should ascertain whether appropriate estimated taxes were paid during the year; support for refunds received should also be examined. In addition, the auditor should determine that the client reviewed assessments before making payments and that the payments were made on the due dates. If interest has been charged for late payment of tax, the period of charge should be ascertained and the calculations reviewed. The auditor should also compare taxes payable or refundable as shown on the tax returns filed for the previous year with the amounts recorded for that year and ascertain that any necessary accounting adjustments have been made. A schedule of carryover items from prior years should be prepared and the current impact of the items considered.

Income Tax Expense, Deferred Taxes, and Related Disclosures

The auditor should obtain or prepare a schedule showing the computation of the tax provision. The current and deferred tax liability accounts should be tested against the current and deferred tax computation. As mentioned earlier, it is normally efficient to gather the information required to prepare or review tax computations during the course of audit work on other accounts. Such information includes differences in tax and financial statement bases of many asset and liability accounts. For example, basis differences can be assembled when reviewing book and tax depreciation during the audit of fixed assets. Tax credits (such as foreign tax credits) and deductions (such as accelerated depreciation) based on special provisions of the law should be scrutinized and tested for compliance with the Internal Revenue Code. The auditor should test the mathematical accuracy of the schedule and determine that it includes consideration of all matters affecting the computation of income taxes currently payable or refundable. Beginning and ending balances should be traced to the summary of income taxes payable, and significant reconciling items should be traced to supporting documentation.

The schedule supporting the tax calculations should include a reconciliation of accounting income to taxable income; differences should be individually identified. The auditor should be particularly concerned about permanent differences, because of their direct effect on the amounts included in the provision for income taxes. In addition, if differences are significant, the auditor may review their nature and amounts for propriety and consistency with the prior year, agree amounts to supporting documentation in the working papers, and determine that the differences are accounted for properly.

The auditor should determine that the client has complied with requirements related to special tax status that may have been claimed. For example, favorable tax treatment may be available to certain entities, like real estate investment trusts, financial institutions, S Corporations, regulated investment companies, and Foreign Sales Corporations (FSCs). If the client claims status as one of those or similar types of enterprises, the auditor should ascertain that the client has in fact met the relevant eligibility requirements. Similarly, the auditor should test for compliance with federal tax documentation requirements regarding travel and entertainment expenditures, expenditures for charitable purposes, and other similar deductions.

In addition, the auditor should inquire about the status of all IRS examinations, examine revenue agents' reports for their effect on the prior and current years' tax provisions and financial statements (including necessary disclosures), and review the status of all tax disagreements. Adjustments to tax provisions for a previous year determined as a result of examinations by taxing authorities should be tested by examining the previous year's computations and any related correspondence.

The auditor must evaluate the adequacy of financial statement disclosures relating to income taxes as well as the propriety of the principles used to recognize and measure income taxes. Disclosures of accounting changes and significant uncertainties related to tax issues (discussed below) may be particularly sensitive matters. In addition, auditors of public companies must consider SEC disclosure requirements.

Estimated and Contingent Liabilities

It is often necessary to provide in the accounts for possible additional liability that might result from revenue agents' examinations of the current year's and prior years' returns. Although such liability may not become payable for a long time, it should be included in the tax liability and the provision for income taxes in the income statement, in accordance with SFAS No. 5. Prior-year estimates of tax provisions should be reassessed based on recent IRS or court decisions or interpretations. The amount of any "cushion" should be supported by a detailed listing of possible tax questions and potential liabilities. The auditor should evaluate the propriety of contingent amounts and assess the adequacy of the tax accrual in light of all pending tax matters.

The auditor, by exercising judgment and consulting tax specialists, must reach a conclusion about each of the issues affecting the tax liability. While the function of a tax specialist may end with the estimate of the liability, the auditor's responsibility goes further. The auditor must evaluate the adequacy of the evidence supporting the decisions made—whether any data or matters affecting taxes have been overlooked and whether the evidence is adequate in the circumstances. If the treatment and disclosure of taxes in the financial statements depend significantly on the intentions of management, it is generally appropriate to obtain written representation of those intentions in the client representation letter. For example, evidence of management's intentions may be needed to support a decision to provide or not to provide for taxes on the undistributed earnings of subsidiaries. Also, evidence must be present to support the tax basis of assets purchased in an acquisition in which the purchase price must be allocated.

The auditor's need to obtain sufficient competent evidence to support the income tax accrual has several implications. First, a mere statement of management's intentions that might affect the tax accrual is insufficient evidence. Management must have specific plans that the auditor can evaluate to determine that they are reasonable and feasible. Second, client restrictions that limit the auditor's access to information necessary to audit the tax accrual, possibly out of concern over IRS access to tax accrual working papers, may constitute a scope limitation and affect the auditor's ability to issue an unqualified opinion. (See an auditing interpretation of Section 326, *Evidential Matter* [AU Section 9326.06–.12], and the further discussion of IRS access to tax accrual working papers in Chapter 3.) Third, the opinion of the client's outside or in-house legal counsel on the adequacy of the tax accrual is not sufficient competent evidence to support an opinion on the financial statements. According to the auditing interpretation of Section 326 (AU Section 9326.13–.17), the auditor should not rely on a specialist in another discipline if the auditor possesses the necessary competence to assess the matter.

The auditor should consider the working paper documentation necessary to support the portion of the tax accrual that relates to contingent items. The working papers should contain sufficient documentation to demonstrate compliance with generally accepted auditing standards and that the tax accrual was prepared in conformity with GAAP. As a minimum, the working papers should document the scope of the work the auditor performed and the conclusion reached regarding the adequacy of the tax accrual and should identify issues involving risk and exposure and the related dollar amounts. The auditor's professional judgment must determine the level of documentation of the tax accrual, including the accrual for contingencies, based on the facts and circumstances of the particular situation.

Documentation of the provision for income taxes has become a particularly sensitive area as a result of the 1984 U.S. Supreme Court ruling that an entity's tax accrual working papers prepared by independent auditors may be subject to Internal Revenue Service (IRS) summonses.[2] Guidelines subsequently issued by the IRS, however, allow auditors' tax accrual working papers to be subpoenaed only if the relevant information is not available from client records. Since there is no such restriction with regard to other working papers, the authors believe that tax accrual working papers should not be included with or filed with tax return or tax planning working papers. Each of the three sets

---

[2]*United States* v. *Arthur Young & Company*, 465 U.S. 805 (1984).

of working papers should contain documentation appropriate to the purpose of the working papers, and cross-referencing between sets of working papers should be avoided.

State and Local Taxes

Accruals for state and local income taxes (including franchise taxes based on income) are reviewed in much the same way as federal income tax accruals. The auditor should obtain or prepare an analysis for the year of deferred and accrued state and local income taxes, showing the computation of the provisions for the current year. He or she should test the mathematical accuracy of the analysis and trace applicable amounts to the general ledger, trial balance, and prior year's working papers. Significant reconciling items should be traced to supporting documentation. Support for payments made and refunds received during the year should be examined. The auditor should also compare the liability per the returns filed for the preceding year, the estimated liability recorded for that year, and the payments made to discharge that liability; evaluate the reasons for any differences; and determine that they have been appropriately accounted for. All state and local tax examinations should be reviewed, and the auditor should determine that appropriate provisions have been made for unresolved assessments.

20

Auditing Debt and Equity

The traditional distinction between debt and equity is clear in most businesses. Equity arises from owners' invested funds plus earnings retained and reinvested; debt is the result of borrowing funds for specific periods, both short and long term, although the individual loans are often renewed indefinitely. The distinctions among debt, equity, and other financing arrangements are often blurred, however. It is more realistic to view various debt, equity, lease, and other contractual arrangements as an array of alternatives that financial managers use to enhance the company's earnings record as well as its financial strength. Common stock is as much a financing instrument as bank loans, and convertible debt may have as many equity characteristics as preferred stock. Financial managers may adjust the legal characteristics of an instrument, whether formally designated as debt or equity, to achieve a desired (or required) balance between protecting principal and income and sharing the risks and rewards of ownership. Financial instruments may be designed to reconcile an enterprise's need for financial resources at minimal cost with investors' preferences for safety and rewards. The result is a virtually continuous spectrum of financing instruments, ranging from straight borrowing to borrowing with equity features, borrowing with variable income features, stock with preferences as to income and principal, common stock, and even promises of future stock. The Securities and Exchange Commission (SEC) and the Internal Revenue Service have from time to time addressed the distinctions among debt, equity, and other financing arrangements, and the subject continues to be of interest to those agencies and to auditors and users of financial statements.

The amount, type, and classification of financing appearing in a company's balance sheet are of concern to investors, lenders, bond rating agencies, and others who influence the supply of financial resources. It is therefore important to financial management. Over the years, a great deal of ingenuity has gone into designing financing that looks like something else, like disguising what were actually asset acquisitions as off-balance-sheet operating lease transactions. The Financial Accounting Standards Board (FASB) and its Emerging Issues Task Force (EITF) have since addressed many of those transactions, but auditors must constantly be alert to discern the substance of each transaction. If form is allowed to rule over substance, one or more audit objectives may not be achieved.

The description of financing instruments and their purposes is limited in this chapter to what is necessary to explain audit considerations. The discussions of transactions and accounts will center around the basic, most common debt and equity instruments. Other instruments representing variations or hybrids will be discussed only if special auditing procedures should be considered as a result of peculiarities in accounting principles, presentation and disclosure, or tax treatment.

Transactions and accounts related to debt and equity include lessee accounting for capital leases, interest expense, debt discount and premium, early extinguishment of debt (including gain or loss thereon), debt defeasance (and "in substance" defeasance), troubled debt restructuring, product financing arrangements, cash and stock dividends, stock splits, stock warrants, options and purchase plans, and treasury stock transactions. Many of these transactions and accounts involve special accounting measurement, presentation, and disclosure principles that require particular audit attention. Other matters with audit implications include short-term debt expected to be refinanced, debt covenants and security, compensating balance arrangements, debt conversion features, mandatory stock redemption requirements, and stock conversion features.

AUDIT OBJECTIVES

The auditor's objectives in examining debt and equity transactions and accounts are to obtain reasonable assurance that

- All obligations for notes payable, long-term debt, and capitalized leases and all equity accounts have been properly valued, classified, described, and disclosed.
- All off-balance-sheet obligations have been identified and considered (e.g., operating leases, product financing arrangements, take-or-pay contracts, and throughput contracts).
- All liability and equity transactions, accounts, and changes therein have been properly authorized and are obligations of the entity or ownership rights in the entity.
- Interest, discounts, premiums, dividends, and other debt-related and equity-related transactions and accounts have been properly valued, classified, described, and disclosed.
- All terms, requirements, instructions, commitments, and other debt-related and equity-related matters have been identified, complied with, and disclosed, as appropriate.

Of course, the application of these broad audit objectives to specific accounts varies depending on the nature of the debt and equity instruments and the related accounts. Most of the audit objectives listed above are self-explanatory; however, two issues related to classification and disclosure merit further comment.

The question of whether particular assets and liabilities may be offset or "netted" usually arises when an asset is held for the purpose of settling a specific liability or when a debt is incurred to finance a specific asset. As a general rule, assets and liabilities should not be offset unless they are exclusively related to each other: Assets can be used for other purposes, and debts are a lien on all assets as well as those specifically pledged. Furthermore, paragraph 7 of Accounting Principles Board (APB) Opinion No. 10 states that "it is a general principle of accounting that the offsetting of assets and liabilities in the balance sheet is improper except where a right of setoff exists." FASB Technical Bulletin (FTB) No. 88-2, *Definition of a Right of Setoff*, defines the term "right of setoff" as a debtor's legal right, by contract or otherwise, to discharge all or a portion of the debt owed to another party by applying against the debt an amount that the other party owes to the debtor. A right of setoff exists only when all of the following conditions are met:

- Each of two parties owes the other determinable amounts.
- The reporting party has the right to set off the amount owed with the amount owed by the other party.
- The reporting party intends to set off the debt.
- The right of setoff is legally enforceable.

Various commitments are customarily given and received in negotiating long-term financing and are included in formal debt covenants. Typical debt covenants include agreements to maintain a minimum level of working capital or net assets; to maintain adequate insurance; to maintain property, sometimes through specified additions to maintenance funds; to restrict dividends; not to pledge or mortgage certain property or to restrict the use of proceeds from its sale; to restrict leasing, borrowing, mergers, and the issuance or repurchase of other types of securities; to restrict the use of the proceeds from issuing the debt; to accumulate funds for repayment through a sinking fund; and to render reports and financial statements on specified dates. Such covenants are intended to protect the interests of securityholders, and failure to comply may be an event of default, which may give the securityholders the right to demand immediate repayment and perhaps other rights as well. Such covenants may also be important factors in encouraging or inhibiting changes in financial structure, selecting accounting principles, and adopting new accounting principles.

FINANCING TRANSACTIONS AND INTERNAL CONTROL STRUCTURE POLICIES AND PROCEDURES

Financing transactions are likely to be relatively simple. Often, authorizing a transaction, executing it, and recording it each involve only one step. The preparation for authorization and execution, however, may be lengthy and complex; the study of whether to enter into a long-term financing transaction may take months, and once it has been decided on, the time expended by lawyers, accountants, investment bankers, and the company's personnel in preparing to execute the transaction may be tremendous.

Since an enterprise's financing activities entail issuing legal obligations—both debt and equity—in exchange for cash or other property, control over authorization for issuance is critical. In almost all enterprises, the board of directors specifically and explicitly authorizes financing transactions. In fact, many legal jurisdictions, investment bankers, and institutional investors require board authorization. The board may authorize a type of financing and a maximum amount in general terms and then delegate to a financial officer the authority to execute the details, but the significance of financing transactions requires that the board assume direct and explicit responsibility for their authorization. The importance of the need for financing and the commitments made to obtain it ensure close attention by top management.

In the typical business that executes no more than half a dozen financing transactions in a year, control structure policies and procedures consist of a detailed review of transactions before they are executed and follow-up by the authorizing board or chief financial officer. In other companies the volume of activity may be greater, and a formalized accounting system and control procedures may exist. The company may act as its own registrar of bonds and stock, and may disburse its own interest and dividends. Alternatively, the volume of activity may be great enough to justify using a registrar, transfer agent, and paying agent. If the volume of transactions is large enough, authorizing transactions and issuing instruments may be systematized. For example, new stock certificates may be issued routinely on receipt of cash or a corresponding number of old certificates. Control totals are computed for instruments issued and recorded, and the propriety of each transaction is subject to supervisory review. In view of the relatively high value and negotiability of many financing instruments, the expensive control procedure of detailed review of each transaction is often considered worthwhile. Whether or not that review is performed, close supervision of transaction activity and control procedures is essential.

Some companies have developed variations of the basic financing transaction to serve particular purposes. These variations include dividend reinvestment plans, in which dividends may be accumulated for a stockholder's account and additional shares purchased from the funds; "certificateless" plans, in which the cumbersome handling of certificates is replaced by records on a file; and plans for purchase of stock on an installment basis. Each of them, however voluminous the related data, involves a relatively simple accounting system. An account is maintained (either manually or by computer) for each participating stockholder; additions and reductions are authorized, recorded in a journal or other book of original entry, and posted to the accounts; the accounts are periodically reconciled to the control account; and statements of the accounts are sent to stockholders.

The authorization and issuing of financing instruments are documented, both by executing the instrument itself and by initiating a record of it, for example, a register listing each item issued. Reacquired instruments are canceled and appropriately filed; the canceled instrument serves as documentation of reacquisition. Subsidiary ledgers are reconciled periodically to control accounts; the reconciliations account for all unissued, issued, and canceled financing instruments.

Issuing securities to the public is highly regulated by the SEC pursuant to the Securities Act of 1933 and by the "Blue Sky" laws of the various states. Subsequent securities trading is also regulated by the SEC under the Securities Exchange Act of 1934 and by the various stock exchanges. Monitoring compliance with the various regulations is primarily a legal function and normally is supervised by legal counsel. The company's accounting department and its independent auditors, however, perform vital roles in preparing and auditing financial statements and other data required to comply with the regulations.

Interest payments are authorized in the broad sense by the terms of the financing instrument; specific payments are approved by a responsible officer. Dividends must be formally declared by the board of directors. Usually, the total interest installment or total dividend is deposited in an imprest fund, and disbursements are then subject to the same control procedures as other cash disbursements. If interest is paid by redeeming coupons detached from bonds, the coupons received are canceled and retained.

Interest and dividends unclaimed for a reasonable period are accounted for according to state law, which may permit writing them off by reversing the original accounting entry or may require that they be turned over to the state or continue to be carried as a liability. In either case, unclaimed items are identified and removed from the active accounts.

Reacquired financing instruments are generally subject to the same control procedures as negotiable instruments held as assets: They are kept under restricted access, counted periodically, and reconciled to a control account. Physical movement into or out of the "treasury" is also controlled by limiting access to authorized individuals.

The detailed task of accounting for and controlling ledgers of bondholders and stockholders and paying interest and dividends is most often delegated to independent registrars and transfer agents. The independent agents take over the control operations, but the company's responsibility remains unchanged. Therefore, if independent agents are used, the company maintains control accounts, requests periodic reports from the agents, and compares the reports with the accounts.

Control procedures for warrants and options are similar to those for the financing instruments themselves: careful authorization, restricted access to unexecuted documents, a record of activity, a ledger of outstanding balances, and periodic reconciliation of the ledger to control accounts.

Control procedures to ensure that all rental payments required under leases are made consist of reminder lists, often in the form of a register of leases by payment due date. The information required for financial disclosures may be incorporated in the lease register or maintained separately in the department responsible for leases.

Compliance with commitments made in connection with financing is most commonly controlled by a reminder list, which is often maintained by the office of the treasurer, the official most likely to be responsible for financing activity. It may also be found in the office of the secretary, the office of legal counsel, or the controller's department.

Most transactions affecting retained earnings and paid-in capital accounts occur as an integral part of some other major transaction: stock issues, retirements or conversions, or dividend payments. Accordingly, the key control procedures are those applied to the major transaction. An event giving rise to any other kind of entry in these accounts would be unusual and would call for authorization by the board of directors.

AUDIT TESTING PLAN

Terms of Engagement

Additional responsibilities beyond performing the audit in accordance with generally accepted auditing standards may arise from client requests or because the enterprise is required to conform with special requirements. This might apply when an entity has equity securities that are subject to regulatory requirements or debt securities requiring compliance with covenants and restrictions.

The audit strategy may also be affected by the client's timetable for releasing the financial statements. For example, the need to complete the audit early may necessitate a different audit strategy than would have been selected without the time constraint. Timing of substantive tests is discussed in Chapter 9.

Nature of Business and Related Risks

The auditor needs a sufficient understanding of the client's industry and business and its control structure to determine the audit testing plan. Of particular importance are the level of the client's debt and equity financing activity and the individuals responsible for, and procedures governing, the issuance of debt and equity instruments and the execution of leases and other financing arrangements.

Another factor relevant to determining the audit plan is the auditor's assessment of inherent risk. Inherent risk relates to how liquid the items are, how much judgment is exercised in recording transactions, the size of individual transactions, and the relative significance of the debt and equity accounts. This assessment should take into account any audit risks identified in considering the client's business, the nature and volume of debt and equity transactions, and the size of the account balances.

Assessing Control Risk

Because of the significance of debt and equity accounts to an enterprise, they are usually closely monitored by management. In assessing control risk, the auditor should consider the effect of management's close attention to debt and equity transactions and accounts. In practice, however, since all the transactions for a year can often be examined fairly easily, it is frequently not efficient for the auditor to perform tests of controls. In these circumstances, the auditor's basis for the opinion comes from the detailed examination of transactions. On the other hand, in situations where financing activity is extensive, the auditor may consider it efficient to perform tests of controls to attain a low assessed level of control risk and restrict tests of details.

SUBSTANTIVE TESTS

The following discussion applies to all kinds of financing transactions unless clearly inapplicable in the context or specified in the discussion. A convenient way to document substantive tests of the various kinds of financing transactions and accounts is an account analysis working paper, that is, a list of the notes, debt issues, or equities outstanding at the beginning of a period, and the additions, reductions, and outstanding amounts at the end of the period. Often the list can be carried forward from year to year if changes are infrequent. It may incorporate all pertinent information about the financing instruments, or that information may be summarized separately. The auditor should compare the list with the accounts and reconcile the total to the general ledger. The list can also be used to document other audit tests performed.

Tests of Details

Tests of details of debt and equity transactions and balances consist of obtaining confirmations from third parties, reperforming computations, and examining documents and records. The following are some examples:

Confirmations—debt payable and terms with holder; outstanding stock with holder and registrar; authorized stock with the Secretary of State of the state in which the entity is incorporated; treasury stock with safekeeping agent; and dividend and interest payments with disbursing agent.

Reperformance of computations—debt discount or premium, interest, gains or losses on debt extinguishment, stock issuances and purchases, and dividends.

Examining documents and records—debt and stock issuances and retirements, and interest and dividend payments to registrar; unissued debt and stock instruments (as partial substantiation of the completeness of recorded outstanding instruments).

Analytical Procedures

The most basic analytical procedures performed on debt and equity accounts are reasonableness tests of the amount of dividends paid, calculated by multiplying the number of shares outstanding on the dividend declaration date by the per share amount of the dividend, and of interest paid on bonds, calculated by multiplying the amount of debt outstanding by the stated interest rate. In addition, the auditor may analyze fluctuations in account balances compared with budgets, amounts for the prior year(s), amounts subjected to substantive tests at an interim date, and any other appropriate base figures, and evaluate the results for reasonableness in relation to other financial information and his or her knowledge of the client's business.

Extent of Tests

The extent of substantive testing depends on a number of factors, the most important of which generally are the assessed level of control risk, the nature and materiality of account balances, and the degree to which account balances are interrelated.

As noted previously, it is generally efficient to audit debt and equity transactions and accounts through substantive tests. In these circumstances, the extent of substantive testing is greater than if a low assessed level of control risk had been attained through tests of controls.

Generally, debt and equity accounts are material and are not directly related to other accounts, although there are some relationships between debt and asset levels, debt and interest expense, and equity and dividends. Although recording debt and equity transactions normally requires little judgment, the instruments are generally easily transferable, and transactions are material. Typically, these factors call for increased testing unless the current-period transactions are minimal. If there is little activity in accounts that were audited in the prior year, the auditor can reduce the testing.

Other Procedures

Other procedures of a more general nature include reading articles of incorporation and minutes of meetings of the board of directors and its committees, and obtaining letters from lawyers about legal matters and letters of representation from clients. The latter two topics are discussed in Chapter 21.

Minutes of Meetings. Reading the minutes of meetings of the board of directors and its committees enables the auditor to examine the board's approval of significant financing activities and to determine whether decisions affecting the financial statements (including required disclosures) have been dealt with properly. The auditor should be satisfied that copies of minutes of all meetings held during the period have been obtained as well as copies or drafts of minutes of all meetings held from the date of the financial statements through the end of field work.

Articles of Incorporation. The articles of incorporation contain information about the classes of stock the enterprise is empowered to issue and the number of authorized shares in each class. Once this information is obtained, it can be kept in a permanent file; the articles of incorporation need not be read each year.

Common Substantive Tests of Debt and Equity Accounts

The auditor should trace authorization for all types of financing to a vote of the board of directors. If the directors have delegated authority for the details of financing, individual transactions should be traced to the authorizing officer's signature.

The auditor should read financing instruments carefully to be sure that the financing is properly classified and described in the financial statements. The instruments should be examined for commitments, which often accompany financing arrangements, and evidence of rights given or received, which might require accounting recognition and/or disclosure. For example, specific SEC rules govern the classification of preferred stock with mandatory redemption requirements or whose redemption is outside the control of the issuer. Regulation S-X, Rule 5-02-28, requires such stock to be included under a separate caption outside the stockholders' equity section of the balance sheet. Often an instrument is designed to achieve a desired accounting and tax result; it is good practice for clients to seek the auditor's interpretation of accounting and disclosure implications of financing instruments before they are executed. Once the accounting and disclosure implications have been analyzed and understood, it is usually possible to set up a worksheet that can be carried forward from year to year for computing and documenting compliance with pertinent commitments and covenants.

If financing is in the form of a lease, the terms must be evaluated to determine whether it should be accounted for as an operating or a capital lease. If leases are capitalized, the auditor should test computations of the carrying amounts of assets and debt, and compare the terms with the underlying lease contract. Chapter 18 discusses lease transactions.

The auditor should trace the recording of cash receipts and payments from financing and related activities into the accounts and compare those transactions with the authorization and terms of the instrument for timing and amount. Paid notes should be examined for evidence of proper authorization, documentation, and cancellation; the mathematical accuracy of interest expense, accrued interest, and dividends declared should be tested; in some circumstances, the auditor may recompute the amounts.

The auditor often confirms outstanding balances, usually at year-end, with holders of notes and issuers of lines of credit, trustees under bond and debenture indentures, and registrars and transfer agents for stock issues. Authorized stock often must be recorded with the Secretary of State in the state of incorporation, and the auditor may request confirmation from that office. Treasury stock should be confirmed with the custodian, or, if there is no custodian, the auditor should examine the certificates in the presence of client personnel.

If several types of financing are outstanding, the auditor should compare transactions in each with restrictions and provisions of the others. Dividend payments may be restricted by bond and note indentures; dividends on common stock may be affected by the rights of preferred stockholders or their rights may change with changes in capital structure or retained earnings accounts; certain transactions may require the consent of holders of senior securities, and so on. It is essential that the client determine and the auditor review the restrictive provisions of the various agreements and determine whether disclosure in the financial statements is appropriate.

The client's reconciliation of detailed stock ledgers to the control account should be reviewed and tested. Accounting for unissued, issued, and canceled certificates should be similarly tested.

The auditor may reperform computations of shares reserved for issuance on exercise of options and warrants or conversion of convertible securities and of the basis for valuing stock dividends and splits. In testing those computations, the auditor should pay close attention to the interrelated effects of one issue on another and on the total amount of each issue authorized and outstanding. The accuracy of accounting for warrants, options, and conversion privileges exercised can often be reviewed by an overall computation based on the terms of the related instruments.

If the interest rate of a financing instrument is not clearly the going market rate for that type of instrument at time of issuance, the auditor should evaluate the reasonableness of the interest rate in terms of the requirements of APB Opinion No. 21, *Interest on Receivables and Payables* (Accounting Standards Section 169), and document the evaluation in the working papers. If the interest rate must be imputed, the documentation for the imputed rate may be carried forward from year to year.

If a financing instrument is issued for property other than cash, the auditor should review the terms of the transaction, basis for recording, and evidence of approval by the board of directors. Usually, a transaction of that kind is significant enough for the auditor to have been involved in the client's planning of the transaction. In that event, there is ample opportunity for the auditor to suggest the appropriate basis for recording the property received and the kind of documentation that should be retained to support it.

Debt Covenant Violations. Debt agreements often contain covenants or provisions requiring the borrower to meet certain standards (e.g., specified levels of working capital and income) and to provide the lender with periodic information. These provisions are referred to as positive covenants. Positive covenants may also require the borrower to provide the lender with periodic financial statements, market values of pledged properties, or other internally generated reports. In addition, the borrower is often required to comply with various negative covenants (like limitations on capital expenditures, officers' salaries, and dividends) and to present its financial statements in accordance with generally accepted accounting principles (GAAP). Some debt agreements may contain cross-default provisions, which could result in acceleration of the lender's right of repayment because of default under or violation of other agreements. Violations of covenants or provisions, unless waived by the lender, usually require the borrower to classify the debt obligation as a current liability.

Furthermore, some long-term debt agreements may include subjective acceleration clauses. These clauses typically state that the lender may accelerate the scheduled maturities of the obligation under conditions that are not objectively determinable. For example, a clause of this nature may state that if a material adverse change occurs in the borrower's financial condition or operations, the full amount of the obligation will become due on demand. In these circumstances, if the borrower incurs significant losses or experiences liquidity problems, the obligation should probably be classified as a current liability, because the borrower would be deemed to be in violation of this covenant. The auditor should consider consulting legal counsel in this situation. Guidance with respect to subjective acceleration clauses is provided in FTB No. 79-3, *Subjective Acceleration Clauses in Long-Term Debt Agreements* (Accounting Standards Section B05.501–.503).

As previously mentioned, long-term debt obligations that will become callable by the lender or due on demand because of the borrower's violation of a debt covenant or provision at the balance sheet date, or because of failure to cure the violation within a specified grace period, may need to be classified as current liabilities. Guidance in this area is contained in Statement of Financial Accounting Standards (SFAS) No. 78, *Classification of Obligations That Are*

Callable by the Creditor, and FTB No. 79-3 (Accounting Standards Section B05); and EITF Issue No. 86-30, ''Classification of Obligations When a Violation Is Waived by the Creditor.''

The auditor should test for compliance with debt covenants at all applicable dates during the year (recognizing, of course, the effect of any grace periods within which a violation could be cured). For example, some debt covenants may require the borrower to maintain a minimum amount of working capital at the end of each specified interim period as well as at year-end. In addition, some debt covenants may be applicable to a party other than the borrower. For example, the borrower may be a subsidiary whose debt agreement contains covenants requiring the parent company to maintain a minimum net worth or restricting transactions between the parent and subsidiary. In these instances, the auditor should obtain written representation from the parent company and its auditor that the applicable debt covenants have been complied with. If provisions or covenants of debt agreements are unclear, the auditor should ask the client to request the lenders to provide a written interpretation of the item or items in question.

Initial Audits. In an initial audit, the auditor should review the corporation's charter or certificate of incorporation, bylaws, and all pertinent amendments. How extensively the auditor reviews prior years' minutes of meetings of the board of directors and stockholders, other documents, and capital stock accounts depends on the circumstances and whether the financial statements were previously audited.

The auditor should also analyze the additional paid-in capital and retained earnings accounts from the corporation's inception to determine whether all entries were in conformity with GAAP then prevailing. If, however, previous audits have been made, the procedures may be limited to a review of analyses made by the predecessor auditors. Entries in those accounts should also be reviewed for consistency of treatment from year to year. The analyses of additional paid-in capital accounts should segregate the balances by classes of stock outstanding.

Permanent Files. The auditor should include in the permanent working paper files information about the kinds of stock authorized, the number of shares of each class authorized, par or stated values, provisions concerning dividend rates, redemption values, priority rights to dividends and in liquidation, cumulative or noncumulative rights to dividends, participation or conversion privileges, and other pertinent data. The auditor should also retain the analyses of additional paid-in capital and retained earnings in the permanent files so that changes in the current year may be readily compared with those in previous years.

Tests Unique to Stockholders' Equity Accounts. Since analyses of stockholders' equity accounts appear in the financial statements and are subject to detailed scrutiny by security analysts and others, the auditor should ordinarily perform detailed substantive tests of changes in those accounts. Some entries, like appropriations of retained earnings, are simply traced to the authorization by the board of directors. Other entries summarize a large volume of individual transactions and can be tested by means of an overall computation based on the authorizing instrument or vote of the directors. Still other entries—the most common example is the exercise of stock options that were granted in the past at various times and prices—are an aggregation of unique transactions and are best audited by examining the underlying authorization of the transactions and reperforming the calculations, as well as reconciling beginning and ending balances with the activity for the year. Each type of entry should be evaluated for compliance with loan agreements or other restrictive covenants or commitments.

The auditor should review the terms of outstanding stock subscriptions and perform enough tests of activity and balances to obtain reasonable assurance that they are being complied with. Outstanding stock subscriptions receivable preferably should be confirmed. Such receivables (whether for shares already issued or to be issued) typically are deducted from capital stock issued or subscribed, as appropriate, and additional paid-in capital; this accounting is required for SEC registrants.

Tests Unique to Dividends.   The auditor should determine whether cash dividends, stock dividends and splits (including reverse splits), dividends payable in scrip, and dividends payable in assets other than cash have been properly accounted for. One of an auditor's responsibilities is to form an opinion on whether the intentions of the board, as indicated in the resolutions authorizing dividends, are properly reflected in the financial statements.

In making the above determinations, the auditor must be aware of the distinction between stock dividends and stock splits. Accounting Research Bulletin (ARB) No. 43, Chapter 7B (Accounting Standards Section C20), provides guidance on the appropriate accounting. Generally, a distribution of less than 20 to 25 percent of the previously outstanding shares should be accounted for as a stock dividend by transferring an amount equal to the fair value of the stock dividend from retained earnings to the appropriate paid-in capital accounts. The New York Stock Exchange (*Company Manual*, Section A 13) specifically requires distributions of less than 25 percent to be accounted for as stock dividends. A distribution exceeding 20 to 25 percent of the previously outstanding shares should be accounted for as a stock split, and does not affect retained earnings, except as specified by state laws.

In the authors' opinion, the time to determine the fair value of the stock dividend shares and to make the appropriate transfer from retained earnings is the date the stock dividend is declared rather than the ex-dividend date or payment date. To compute the fair value of the shares to be issued, consideration may be given to the dilutive effect of the additional shares on market value. One way to recognize the dilutive effect is to divide the market value of a present share by 1 plus the stock dividend percentage to obtain the fair value of each share to be issued in the stock dividend. An alternative is to request the client to obtain an investment banker's opinion of fair value appropriate for the stock dividend.

Covenants of debentures and other debt instruments often restrict the payment of cash dividends in some way (e.g., to earnings subsequent to the date of the instrument). The auditor should ascertain that dividend declarations do not exceed the amount of retained earnings available for dividends, and that the amount of unrestricted retained earnings has been properly calculated in accordance with the debt covenants or other restrictions and has been appropriately disclosed.

Holders of noncumulative preferred stock ordinarily have no claim to dividends in a year when the amount of the dividends has not been earned, except possibly when dividends earned in a prior year have been improperly withheld. Dividends paid on common stock may have encroached on the rights of holders of noncumulative preferred stock. An auditor who discovers that situation should bring the matter to the attention of appropriate client personnel and suggest that counsel be consulted about a possible liability to holders of noncumulative preferred stock.

In the event of a stock dividend or split, the auditor must ascertain that the capital stock authorization is not exceeded and that consideration has been given to shares reserved for stock options and conversions of other issues.

Partnership Capital

In auditing partnership financial statements, the auditor should read the partnership agreement. Ordinarily those agreements not only show the basis for sharing profits and losses but also often call for special allocations of different components of net income (like cash flows and depreciation) or contain provisions about fixed amounts of capital to be maintained by the various partners, loans by partners in certain circumstances, interest on partners' capital and loans, limitations on withdrawals, and similar matters. The auditor should analyze and substantiate changes in partnership capital between balance sheet dates and determine whether allocations and computations are in accordance with the partnership agreement.

Some partnerships conduct business without written partnership agreements. In those circumstances, the auditor should inquire whether the partners understand the bases on which the accounts are kept, particularly with respect to distributions of profits and losses and interest on partners' capital. If there are few partners, it may be appropriate to ask all partners to sign the financial statements on which the partners' accounts appear or, alternatively, to confirm the balances in their accounts. The required client representation letter (discussed in Chapter 21) may serve in lieu of those procedures.

PART 4

Completing the Work and Reporting the Results

21

Completing the Audit

This chapter deals with auditing procedures and considerations that are part of the completion phase of an audit but are not related to specific transaction cycles or accounts. The completion phase takes place primarily after the balance sheet date. These procedures entail many subjective decisions requiring judgment and experience, and thus are usually performed by the senior members of the engagement team.

The judgments made during this phase of an audit are often crucial to the ultimate outcome of the engagement. Accordingly, the procedures employed should reflect the auditor's assessment of the risks associated with the business and the financial statements. The procedures covered in this chapter often bring to light matters that are of major concern in forming an opinion on the financial statements.

PROCEDURES PERFORMED AT THE CONCLUSION OF THE AUDIT

Analytical Procedures

As noted in Chapter 9, Statement on Auditing Standards (SAS) No. 56, *Analytical Procedures* (AU Section 329), requires the auditor to perform analytical procedures as a final review of the financial statements at or near the end of the audit. The objective of analytical procedures used at this stage is to help the auditor assess the conclusions reached during the audit and form an opinion on the financial statements. The final review generally includes reading the statements and notes, and considering (a) whether the information and explanations gathered in response to unusual or unexpected balances or relationships previously identified are adequate, and (b) whether there are unusual or unexpected balances or relationships that were not previously identified. The auditor may use a variety of analytical procedures (as described in Chapter 9) in making this overall review. Those procedures may provide added evidence that the financial statements are not materially misstated because of undetected errors or irregularities; or, they may indicate the need for additional auditing procedures before the report on the financial statements is issued.

Reading Minutes of Meetings

Reading the minutes of meetings of the board of directors and its important committees enables the auditor to examine the board's approval of management's significant actions and to determine whether significant decisions that affect the financial statements or require disclosure in the notes have been appropriately reflected. Often the auditor reads minutes of meetings shortly after the meetings or during the early stage of the year-end field work. This allows the auditor to amend the audit testing plan, if necessary, for actions taken by the board or a board committee. For example, the board's authorizing the disposal of a segment of the business could significantly affect the audit testing plan. The auditor should be satisfied that copies of minutes of all meetings held during the period have been provided, including meetings held after year-end but before the date of the audit report. If minutes were not prepared and approved for meetings held shortly before the date of the audit report, the auditor should inquire of the secretary of the board or the committee about actions taken. This inquiry should be documented in the working papers.

Tests for Contingent Liabilities

A contingency may be defined as an existing condition, situation, or set of circumstances involving uncertainty as to possible gain (gain contingency) or loss (loss contingency) that will be resolved when one or more future events occur or fail to occur.

Accounting Overview. Contingencies that might result in gains, such as claims against others for patent infringement, usually are not recorded until realized. They should be adequately disclosed in the notes to the financial statements; however, misleading implications as to the likelihood of their realization should be avoided.

In many cases, the existence of a loss contingency results in a charge to income and the recording of a liability, for example, a probable loss resulting from the guarantee of the indebtedness of others or an obligation relating to a product warranty or defect. In other cases, such as a probable loss from uncollectible receivables, the existence of a loss contingency results in the write-down of an asset (often by means of an allowance account) and a charge to income. Still other loss contingencies result only in financial statement disclosure; an example would be litigation whose outcome is uncertain. (Loss contingencies arising from litigation, claims, and assessments are discussed in detail in the next section of this chapter.) Lastly, some loss contingencies need not be either accrued (recorded) or disclosed, for example, the uninsured risk of property loss or damage from fire or other hazards. The following table summarizes the proper financial accounting and reporting for material loss contingencies.[1]

	Amount of Loss Can Be Reasonably Estimated	
Likelihood of Occurrence	*Yes*	*No*
Probable	Accrue; consider need to disclose	Disclose
Reasonably possible	Disclose	Disclose
Remote	Not accrued or disclosed	

---

[1]Explanatory paragraphs in the auditor's report because of potential losses arising from uncertainties are discussed in Chapter 22.

Paragraph 3 of Statement of Financial Accounting Standards (SFAS) No. 5, *Accounting for Contingencies* (Accounting Standards Section C59.104), defines the ranges of likelihood of occurrence, as follows:

- *Probable*. The future event or events are likely to occur.
- *Reasonably possible*. The chance of the future event or events occurring is more than remote but less than likely.
- *Remote*. The chance of the future event or events occurring is slight.

When a material loss contingency involves an *unasserted* claim or assessment, disclosure is not required if there is no evidence that the assertion of a claim is probable. If it is considered probable that the claim will be asserted and there is a reasonable possibility that the outcome will be unfavorable, disclosure is required.

Auditing Procedures.   Auditing loss contingencies is one of the most difficult aspects of many audits, and the variety of conditions encountered makes it impossible to describe the auditor's task definitively. Even in the best and most responsibly managed companies, a loss contingency requiring evaluation can be overlooked. Following is a description of the kinds of procedures the auditor usually undertakes to identify material loss contingencies.

The auditor should be alert for possible contingent liabilities while performing tests for unrecorded liabilities, described in Chapter 13. For example, when inspecting the minute books, contracts, and other documents, the auditor should be alert for matters indicating contingencies to be investigated. When inquiring of management about the existence of unrecorded liabilities, the auditor should also consider the possibility of loss contingencies. Management's statement about loss contingencies should be included in the representation letter, discussed later.

An entity may have contingent liabilities for accounts receivable it has discounted, with recourse, with banks or other financial institutions. The auditor should be alert when performing other auditing procedures for indications of such transactions, for example, interest payments unrelated to recorded debt obligations, and should investigate them. An entity may also have guaranteed payment of the indebtedness of another entity, which may be an affiliate or a subsidiary or may be unrelated to the guarantor entity. The auditor should review the representation letter from management and corporate minutes and contractual arrangements, and inquire of officials of the guarantor about such contingent liabilities.

Although it is customary to insure against liability for damages claimed by employees and the public, insurance policies usually do not cover unlimited liabilities and not all companies carry adequate insurance against all potential claims. Furthermore, unusual claims for damages may arise from alleged breach of contract, failure to deliver goods, antitrust violations, existence of foreign substances in a company's product, and other causes. The auditor should inquire about possible liabilities of that general character. Possible sources of information include the client's inside and outside attorneys and its risk manager, risk consultants, and insurance agents or brokers who provide insurance coverage.

Some claims may not be referred to the client's counsel. For example, salespeople may claim commissions in excess of those paid or accrued, or employees who have been dismissed may claim salaries or other compensation for uncompleted terms of service. Often, those claims are handled as purely administrative matters and may not be referred to counsel unless they are substantial in amount. If the auditor learns of a possible material loss contingency from those types of claims, he or she should obtain the opinion of the client's counsel with respect to the possible liability. (See "Lawyers' Letters," below.)

Occasionally a company disputes a claim, resorts to litigation, and has a judgment entered against it. If the case is appealed and a bond is given pending final decision, execution of the judgment may be stayed and the judgment not entered in the accounts. The auditor should obtain the opinion of the client's counsel in these areas.

Auditors ordinarily must perform additional procedures to obtain sufficient competent evidential matter concerning litigation, claims, and assessments. Those procedures are discussed below.

LAWYERS' LETTERS

With respect to one particular group of loss contingencies— litigation, claims, and assessments—the auditor is required by paragraph 4 of Statement on Auditing Standards No. 12, *Inquiry of a Client's Lawyer Concerning Litigation, Claims, and Assessments* (AU Section 337.04), to obtain evidential matter related to the following factors:

a. The existence of a condition, situation, or set of circumstances indicating an uncertainty as to the possible loss to an entity arising from litigation, claims, and assessments.
b. The period in which the underlying cause for legal action occurred.
c. The probability of an unfavorable outcome.
d. The amount or range of potential loss.

The term "litigation, claims, and assessments" includes both pending and threatened litigation, claims, and assessments and unasserted claims and assessments.

Auditing Procedures

Management is responsible for adopting policies and procedures to identify, evaluate, and account for litigation, claims, and assessments. Accordingly, the auditor's procedures with respect to such matters should include

- Inquiring of management about its policies and procedures for identifying, evaluating, and accounting for litigation, claims, and assessments.
- Near the completion of field work, obtaining from management a description and evaluation of litigation, claims, and assessments as of the balance sheet date and during the period from the balance sheet date to the date the information is furnished.
- Examining documents related to litigation, claims, and assessments, including correspondence and invoices from lawyers.
- Requesting management to send a letter of audit inquiry to lawyers who were consulted concerning litigation, claims, and assessments.
- Obtaining assurance from management—preferably in the representation letter, discussed below—that all contingencies, including litigation, claims, and assessments, required to be disclosed by SFAS No. 5 have been disclosed and that all unasserted claims that counsel has advised management are probable of assertion and must be disclosed in accordance with SFAS No. 5 have been disclosed.

Procedures undertaken for different purposes, for example, reading minutes, contracts, agreements, leases, and correspondence with taxing authorities, may also disclose the existence of litigation, claims, and assessments.

Inquiry of a Client's Lawyer

The auditor can readily ascertain the existence of litigation, claims, and assessments when provisions for losses are recorded in the accounts. Also, while making routine audit inquiries and performing tests for unrecorded and contingent liabilities, the auditor may become aware of events that are likely to give or have given rise to litigation, claims, or assessments. Certain events, however, such as patent infringement or price fixing, may be more difficult to detect in an audit. As noted in SAS No. 54, *Illegal Acts by Clients* (AU Section 317.06), many laws or regulations "relate more to an entity's operating aspects than to its financial and accounting aspects, and their financial statement effect is indirect. An auditor ordinarily does not have sufficient basis for recognizing possible violations of such laws and regulations."

SAS No. 12 was issued in January 1976. At about the same time, the American Bar Association (ABA) issued a "Statement of Policy Regarding Lawyers' Responses to Auditors' Requests for Information," which is reproduced in Appendix C to SAS No. 12. These professional standards require the auditor, client, and lawyer all to become involved in determining which litigation, claims, and assessments need to be disclosed. As can be seen from the specimen letters of audit inquiry that appear in Appendix A to SAS No. 12 and in an interpretation of that SAS (AU Section 9337.10–.14), management is the primary source of information concerning litigation, claims, and assessments; the lawyer is expected to corroborate the completeness of the information supplied by management regarding pending or threatened litigation, claims, and assessments.

Specifically, SAS No. 12 (AU Section 337.09) requires, among other things, the following to be included in the client's letter of audit inquiry to the lawyer:

- A list prepared by management (or a request by management that the lawyer prepare a list) that describes and evaluates pending or threatened litigation, claims, and assessments with respect to which the lawyer has been engaged. When the list is prepared by the client, the lawyer's response should state that the list is complete (or identify any omissions) and comment on the client's evaluation.

- A list prepared by management (the lawyer will not prepare this list) that describes and evaluates unasserted claims, if any, that management considers to be probable of assertion, and that, if asserted, would have at least a reasonable possibility of an unfavorable outcome, with respect to which the lawyer has been engaged. The lawyer's response will not comment on the completeness of the list, but should comment on the client's descriptions and evaluations.

The lawyer should be informed in the client's letter of audit inquiry or, with the client's permission, in a separate letter from the auditor (illustrated in Figure 21.1), of management's assurance to the auditor concerning unasserted claims and assessments.

If the lawyer has formed a professional conclusion that the client should

Figure 21.1   Specimen Letter to Inform Lawyer of Management's Assurance, When Not Included in Client's Letter of Audit Inquiry

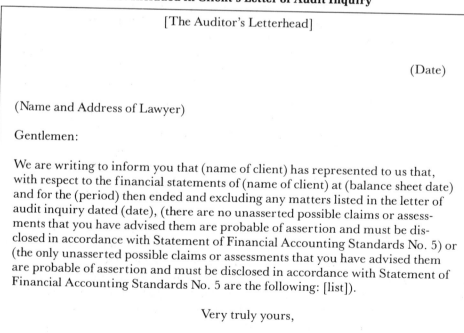

[The Auditor's Letterhead]

(Date)

(Name and Address of Lawyer)

Gentlemen:

We are writing to inform you that (name of client) has represented to us that, with respect to the financial statements of (name of client) at (balance sheet date) and for the (period) then ended and excluding any matters listed in the letter of audit inquiry dated (date), (there are no unasserted possible claims or assessments that you have advised them are probable of assertion and must be disclosed in accordance with Statement of Financial Accounting Standards No. 5) or (the only unasserted possible claims or assessments that you have advised them are probable of assertion and must be disclosed in accordance with Statement of Financial Accounting Standards No. 5 are the following: [list]).

Very truly yours,

(The Auditor's Firm)

consider disclosure of an unasserted possible claim or assessment, the lawyer will, as a matter of professional responsibility to the client, consult with the client concerning the applicable requirements of SFAS No. 5. While the lawyer will not comment on the completeness of the client's list of unasserted claims, he or she will, at the client's request, confirm to the auditor this professional responsibility to the client.

Inquiries generally should be sent to all lawyers who have devoted substantive attention to a matter on behalf of the client in the form of legal consultation or representation. The client may not wish, however, to send a letter to a lawyer whose only relationship with the client was representation in a case that was closed during the year or to lawyers handling routine matters such as collection of overdue accounts. If the auditor is satisfied either that the case is closed and other auditing procedures do not indicate the lawyer was involved in other matters, or that lawyers were involved in routine matters only, the auditor may accede to the client's request.

If the lawyer disclaims responsibility for informing the auditor of any changes in the information reported to the auditor from the date of the response to the date of the auditor's report, it may be necessary to send a supplemental letter of audit inquiry. Factors to be considered in determining the need for a supplemental letter of audit inquiry include the length of time between the date of the response and the date of the auditor's report, the number and significance of matters included in the lawyer's response, the probability of more current developments related to matters included in the lawyer's response, and the reliability of the client's policies and procedures for identifying, evaluating, and accounting for litigation, claims, and assessments. The auditor may determine that a supplemental letter of inquiry is not required, even though the lawyer's response is dated considerably earlier than the auditor's report. In those circumstances, the auditor should ordinarily arrange for an oral update and should document it in the working papers.

The specimen letters of audit inquiry in Appendix A to SAS No. 12 and in the related interpretation include a "response date" that, combined with proper timing in mailing letters of audit inquiry, is intended to minimize the need for supplemental letters of audit inquiry. Letters of audit inquiry should be mailed at a date that provides the lawyer sufficient time to meet the response date (two weeks is ordinarily sufficient time). The response date should allow sufficient time prior to the date of the audit report for the auditor to evaluate the response and make supplemental inquiries, if necessary.

Acceptable responses from lawyers to letters of audit inquiry and the procedures outlined above and in SAS No. 12 will usually provide sufficient competent evidential matter to satisfy the auditor concerning the accounting for and reporting of litigation, claims, and assessments. The auditor should also investigate, however, to the extent deemed appropriate in the circumstances, any information gained in the course of the engagement that indicates there may be material litigation, claims, and assessments that have not been disclosed by the client or the lawyer.

Acceptable Limitations on the Scope of Lawyers' Responses.   Several types of limitations on the scope of a lawyer's response to a letter of audit inquiry are acceptable. These limitations, which the lawyer may indicate in the response by either a direct statement or a reference to the ABA Statement of Policy, include

- Limiting the response to matters to which the lawyer has devoted substantive attention on behalf of the client in the form of legal consultation or representation.
- When the letter of inquiry is addressed to a law firm, excluding matters that have been communicated to an individual member or employee of the firm by reason of that individual's serving in the capacity of director or officer of the client.
- Limiting the response to matters that are considered, individually or collectively, to be material to the client's financial statements (see the discussion below of the need to provide the lawyer with materiality guidelines).
- Disclaiming any undertaking to advise the auditor of changes in the status of litigation, claims, and assessments since the date the lawyer began internal review procedures for purposes of preparing the response.

Sometimes a response from a lawyer contains the phrase "not material" or "would not have a material effect on the financial condition of the company or the results of its operations." Responses containing these or similar phrases are acceptable and do not constitute an audit scope limitation if the response itself provides data sufficient for the auditor to evaluate the lawyer's conclusion. Such responses are also acceptable if materiality guidelines for the lawyer's use on both an individual item and an aggregate basis were included in the letter of audit inquiry from management, as the authors believe should be done. The auditor should be satisfied with the materiality guidelines provided to the client's lawyer. A materiality guideline in the inquiry letter might read as follows: "This request is limited to contingencies amounting to $XXX individually or items involving lesser amounts that exceed $XXX in the aggregate."

Evaluating Lawyers' Responses.   In evaluating responses from lawyers, the auditor should consider whether there is any reason to doubt their professional qualifications and reputation. If, as will often be the case, the auditor is familiar with the lawyer's professional reputation, there would be no need to make specific inquiries in this regard. An auditor who is not familiar with a lawyer representing the client in what appears to be a significant case may wish to inquire as to the lawyer's professional background, reputation, and standing in the legal and financial community and to consider information available in such legal publications as the *Martindale–Hubbell Law Directory*. Once satisfied in this regard, the auditor can accept the lawyer's opinion regarding a legal matter, unless it appears to be unreasonable.

The lawyer's response should be read in its totality to ascertain its overall responsiveness to the letter of audit inquiry and to determine whether it conflicts with information otherwise known to the auditor. The language used in responses from lawyers takes many forms, and definitive guidance does not exist on the effect of the language used on the type of opinion the auditor may express. Certain responses, however, ordinarily permit an unqualified opinion, while others may preclude an unqualified opinion.

Responses Permitting a Standard Unqualified Opinion.   Responses from lawyers that enable the auditor to render a standard unqualified opinion usually (a) indicate a high probability of a favorable outcome or that the matters in question are not material, and (b) do not indicate that the lawyer has not made a reasonable investigation of the case. The following examples of actual language from lawyers' letters would permit the auditor to render a standard unqualified opinion:

- It is our opinion that if the matter is litigated, it will be successfully defended on behalf of the Company.
- We believe plaintiff's assertions to be without merit.
- In connection with your audit of the financial statements of the Company, please be advised that to the best of our knowledge and belief, there were no material pending claims in which the Company was involved as of (date).
- The possibility of unfavorable outcome is remote (slight).

Responses Leading to an Explanatory Paragraph Because of an Uncertainty. If because of inherent uncertainties a lawyer is unable to indicate whether an unfavorable outcome of material litigation, claims, or assessments is likely or to estimate the amount or range of potential loss, the auditor will ordinarily conclude that an explanatory paragraph should be added to the auditor's report because of a matter involving an uncertainty (SAS No. 12 [AU Section 337.14]). The lawyer may not be able to respond because the factors influencing the likelihood of an unfavorable outcome are not within the competence of lawyers to judge, historical experience of the entity in similar litigation or the experience of other entities may not be relevant or available, or the amount or range of possible loss may vary widely at different stages of litigation. The following examples of actual language from lawyers' letters would, if related to material items that are not remedied, result in an explanatory paragraph (following the opinion paragraph) in the auditor's report:

- No demand for monetary damages has been made in the complaint. Consequently, I am unable to give an estimate as to potential loss.
- In the case of nonpersonal injury claims, the Company should be contacted for further information regarding such claims. Our substantive attention to the claims set forth in the exhibits hereto has been limited either to coordinating activities and communication between the Company and its risk managers or to a lesser extent facilitating communications between the Company and the various claimants.

In the latter example, the lawyer did not feel that the factors influencing the likelihood of unfavorable outcomes were within his competence to judge. The company then employed a specialist to determine the likelihood of unfavorable outcomes and amounts or ranges of possible losses. The auditor was able to conclude that the specialist's findings were suitable for corroborating the information related to these claims in the financial statements, and a standard unqualified opinion was issued. Generally accepted auditing standards for using the work of a specialist are discussed in Chapter 6.

Responses from lawyers that the auditor initially believes may result in an explanatory paragraph in the opinion may in some instances be resolved to the extent that an explanatory paragraph is not necessary. Sometimes discussion with the client may clarify the matter or provide additional evidence that the auditor deems adequate. In other instances, information may have been withheld that the client can persuade the lawyer to furnish. In still other instances, the client may authorize the lawyer to investigate the matter more thoroughly, which could lead to a change in the lawyer's evaluation. Occasionally the apparent problem is the lawyer's choice of language and can be remedied by the lawyer's revising the letter.

Lawyers sometimes use language that is not sufficiently clear as to the likelihood of a favorable outcome. Examples of that kind of language are provided in an interpretation of SAS No. 12 (AU Section 9337.22), as follows:

- This action involves unique characteristics wherein authoritative legal precedents do not seem to exist. We believe that the plaintiff will have serious problems establishing the company's liability under the act; nevertheless, if the plaintiff is successful, the award may be substantial.

- It is our opinion that the company will be able to assert meritorious defenses to this action. (The term "meritorious defenses" indicates that the company's defenses will not be summarily dismissed by the court; it does not necessarily indicate counsel's opinion that the company will prevail.)

- We believe the action can be settled for less than the damages claimed.

- We are unable to express an opinion as to the merits of the litigation at this time. The company believes there is absolutely no merit to the litigation. (If the client's counsel, with the benefit of all relevant information, is unable to conclude that the likelihood of an unfavorable outcome is "remote," it is unlikely that management would be able to form a judgment to that effect.)

- In our opinion, the company has a substantial chance of prevailing in this action. (A "substantial chance," a "reasonable opportunity," and similar terms indicate more uncertainty than an opinion that the company will prevail.)

The interpretation states that an auditor who is uncertain about the meaning of a lawyer's evaluation should request clarification either in a follow-up letter or in a conference with the lawyer and client, which should be appropriately documented. If the lawyer is still unable to give, either in writing or orally, an unequivocal evaluation of the likelihood of an unfavorable outcome, the auditor should consider the effect of the resulting uncertainty on the audit report.

Responses Resulting in Scope Limitations.   Responses that indicate or imply that the lawyer is withholding information should ordinarily, if not remedied, be considered an audit scope limitation (SAS No. 58, *Reports on Audited Financial Statements* [AU Section 508.40–.41]). For example, the lawyer may state that the reply is limited because of the policy of the law firm or the impracticability of reviewing the files, or for reasons not given. Normally, such limitations would be considered significant, since the auditor usually cannot evaluate the effect of withheld information.

A response indicating that the newness of a case precludes evaluating it does not provide sufficient evidence to support an unqualified opinion. The following examples of actual language from lawyers' letters would, if related to material items that are not resolved, constitute limitations on the scope of the engagement, requiring modification of the scope paragraph of the audit report, a separate paragraph (preceding the opinion paragraph) describing the limitation, and a qualified opinion:

- The claim has been received by this office only recently, and is being investigated. At this time it is not possible to predict the outcome of the litigation.
- This suit for declaratory judgment by the plaintiff presents some risk for the Bank depending upon the values assigned to parcels of realty transferred to the Bank to reduce a preexisting debt owed by the plaintiff to the Bank. We have not been supplied with sufficient information to determine whether a deficiency existed which warranted the note and mortgage obtained from the plaintiff. At present, we can only assume that the Bank was justified in obtaining this obligation.

Inside Counsel.   The duties of an inside counsel may vary from handling specialized litigation to acting as general counsel with supervisory authority in all legal matters, including the selection of outside counsel to represent or advise the client on specific matters.

If inside counsel acts as general counsel, evidential matter gathered by and obtained from inside counsel may provide the necessary corroboration for the auditor. Letters of audit inquiry to outside counsel may be appropriate if inside general counsel has retained outside counsel to represent or advise the client on certain matters. Information provided by inside counsel is not a substitute for information that outside counsel refuses to furnish.

Changes or Resignations of Lawyers.   The legal profession's Code of Professional Responsibility requires that, in some circumstances, lawyers must resign if the client has disregarded their advice concerning financial accounting for and reporting of litigation, claims, and assessments. The auditor should be alert for such circumstances and should ensure that he or she understands the reasons for the change or resignation of lawyers, and should also consider the implications for financial statement disclosures concerning litigation, claims, and assessments.

CLIENT REPRESENTATIONS

The auditor is required by SAS No. 19, *Client Representations* (AU Section 333), to obtain a representation letter from management confirming that they are responsible for the financial statements and have made all pertinent information available to the auditor, and stating their belief in the accuracy and completeness of that information. The representation letter provides written evidence that the auditor has made certain inquiries of management; ordinarily it documents oral responses given to the auditor, thus reducing the possibility of errors or misunderstandings. A representation letter is one kind of competent evidence, but it is not sufficient in itself to provide the auditor with a reasonable basis for forming an opinion.

Written Representations

The representation letter illustrated in Figure 21.2 incorporates the written representations that the auditor should ordinarily obtain. The letter should be modified to meet the circumstances of the particular engagement and the nature and basis of presentation of the financial statements. For example, if the auditor is reporting on consolidated financial statements, the written representations obtained from the parent company's management should specify that they pertain to the consolidated financial statements. If the auditor is reporting on the parent company's separate financial statements as well, the letter should also extend to them. Representation letters in compliance audits (see Chapter 25) may cover matters relating to laws and regulations affecting the company.

Written representations relating to management's knowledge or intent should be obtained when the auditor believes they are necessary to complement other auditing procedures. For example, even if the auditor has performed tests for unrecorded liabilities and has not detected any, written representation should be obtained to document that management has no knowledge of any liabilities that have not been recorded. Liabilities known to management but not accrued, through oversight, might be brought to the auditor's attention in this manner. Such a written representation, however, does not relieve the auditor of responsibility for planning the audit to identify material unrecorded liabilities. Information may be unintentionally overlooked or intentionally withheld from the auditor. Accordingly, the auditor must still perform all the usual tests to corroborate representations made by management.

In some cases, evidential matter to corroborate written representations is limited. For example, income taxes may not be provided for undistributed income of a subsidiary because management of the parent company represents that it intends to permanently reinvest that income, but the auditor may not be able to obtain sufficient information through other auditing procedures to corroborate that intent. Unless the auditor obtains evidential matter to the

Figure 21.2   Illustrative Client Representation Letter

[Client's Letterhead]

[Date—no earlier than date of auditor's report, but no later than report release date]

[To Independent Auditor]

In connection with your audit of the [consolidated] financial statements of [name of client] as of [date] and for the [period of audit] for the purpose of expressing an opinion as to whether such financial statements present fairly, in all material respects, the financial position, results of operations, and cash flows of [name of client] in conformity with generally accepted accounting principles [other comprehensive basis of accounting], we confirm, to the best of our knowledge and belief, as of __/ __/ __, the date of your report, the following representations made to you during your audit. [The client may specify the materiality limits agreed on as follows: Certain representations in this letter are described as being limited to those matters that may have a material effect on the financial statements. As used here, the term "material" means any item or group of similar items involving potential amounts of more than $_____ (or __% of assets, liabilities, shareholders' equity, or net income).]

1. We are responsible for the fair presentation in the [consolidated] financial statements of financial position, results of operations, and cash flows in conformity with generally accepted accounting principles [or other comprehensive basis of accounting].

2. We have made available to you all financial and accounting records and related data and all minutes of the meetings of shareholders, directors, and committees of directors [or summaries of actions of recent meetings for which minutes have not yet been prepared]. The most recent meetings held were: [state by group and date]. We are not aware of any accounts, transactions, or material agreements not fairly described and properly recorded in the financial and accounting records underlying the financial statements.

3. We are not aware of (a) any irregularities involving management or those employees who have significant roles in the internal control structure, or any irregularities involving other employees that could have a material effect on the financial statements, or (b) any violations or possible violations of laws or regulations whose effects should be considered for disclosure in the financial statements or as a basis for recording a loss contingency. (We understand the term "irregularities" to mean those matters described in Statement on Auditing Standards No. 53.) There have been no communications from regulatory agencies concerning noncompliance with or deficiencies in financial reporting practices that could have a material effect on the financial statements. The company has complied with all aspects of contractual agreements that would have a material effect on the financial statements in the event of noncompliance [state exceptions, if any].

Figure 21.2 *Continued*

4. All cash and bank accounts and all other properties and assets of the company of which we are aware are included in the financial statements at [balance sheet date]. The company has satisfactory title to all owned assets [state exceptions, if any], and all liens, encumbrances, or security interests having any important consequence on any asset of the company are disclosed in the statements or notes thereto.

5. The receivables in the aggregate gross amount of $_____ at [balance sheet date] represent bona fide claims against debtors for sales or other charges arising on or before that date and are not subject to discount except for normal cash discounts. These receivables do not include any amounts that are collectible after one year [state exceptions, if any]. The amount of $_____ carried as an allowance for uncollectible accounts is sufficient to provide for any losses that may be sustained on realization of the receivables.

6. Inventories at [balance sheet date] in the aggregate amount of $_____ are stated at the lower of cost or market, cost being determined on the basis of [LIFO, FIFO, or other] and consistently with the prior year, and provision was made to reduce all slow-moving, obsolete, or unusable inventories to their estimated net realizable values. Inventory quantities at [balance sheet date] were determined from the company's perpetual inventory records, which have been adjusted on the basis of physical inventories taken by competent employees at [date of physical inventory or various times during the year]. Liability, if unpaid, for all items included in inventories is recorded at [balance sheet date], and all quantities billed to customers at that date are excluded from the inventory balances.

7. All liabilities of the company of which we are aware are included in the financial statements at [balance sheet date]. There are no other material liabilities or gain or loss contingencies that are required to be accrued or disclosed by Statement of Financial Accounting Standards No. 5 and no unasserted claims or assessments that our legal counsel has advised us are probable of assertion and must be disclosed in accordance with that Statement.

8. Commitments for future purchases are for quantities not in excess of anticipated requirements and at prices that will not result in loss. Provision has been made for any material loss to be sustained in the fulfillment of, or from the inability to fulfill, any sales commitments.

9. We have no plans or intentions that may materially affect the carrying value or classification of assets and liabilities.

10. The financial statements and related notes include all disclosures necessary for a fair presentation of the financial position, results of operations, and cash flows of the company in conformity with generally accepted accounting principles, and disclosures otherwise required to be included therein by the laws and regulations to which the company is

Figure 21.2 *Continued*

subject. The following have been properly recorded or disclosed in the financial statements[a]:

a. Related party transactions and related amounts receivable or payable, including sales, purchases, loans, transfers, leasing arrangements, and guarantees. (We understand the term "related party" to include those entities described in Statement of Financial Accounting Standards No. 57.)

b. Capital stock repurchase options or agreements or capital stock reserved for options, warrants, conversions, or other requirements.

c. Arrangements with financial institutions involving compensating balances, arrangements involving restrictions on cash balances and lines of credit, or similar arrangements.

d. Guarantees, whether written or oral, under which the company is contingently liable to a bank or other lending institution.

[Add special-purpose representations that may be required in this letter in certain circumstances.]

No matters or occurrences have come to our attention up to the date of this letter that would materially affect the financial statements and related disclosures for the year ended [balance sheet date] or, although not affecting such financial statements or disclosures, have caused or are likely to cause any material change, adverse or otherwise, in the financial position, results of operations, or cash flows of the company.

_____
[Name and title of chief executive officer]

_____
[Name and title of chief financial officer]

[a]If any of the following items are not applicable, the letter should include a separate caption with the introduction "There are no . . ."

contrary, he or she may rely on the truthfulness of management's representations, as discussed in SAS No. 53, *The Auditor's Responsibility to Detect and Report Errors and Irregularities* (AU Section 316.17).

Materiality. Paragraph 5 of SAS No. 19 (AU Section 333.05) states that "management's representations may be limited to matters that are considered either individually or collectively material to the financial statements, provided management and the auditor have reached an understanding on the limits of materiality for this purpose.'' The limits of materiality may differ in different circumstances, for example, amounts that affect only the balance sheet versus amounts that affect income. The auditor may wish to request management to specify in the representation letter the materiality limits agreed on, as shown in the letter in Figure 21.2.

Definitions.   Certain terms used in the letter in Figure 21.2 are defined in the authoritative literature, for example, irregularities (SAS No. 53 [AU Section 316.02–.03]), related party transactions (SFAS No. 57 [Accounting Standards Section R36.101]), and contingencies (SFAS No. 5 [Accounting Standards Section C59.101]). The auditor may wish to furnish the applicable literature to the client and request that management acknowledge in the representation letter that they have received it.

Dating and Signing.   The representation letter should be addressed to the auditor and should be dated no earlier than the date of the auditor's report (discussed later), but no later than the report release date. In any event, the letter should include a statement that management has made the representations as of the date of the auditor's report. If there is an inordinate delay in issuing the report, the auditor should consider asking management to update its written representations.

Representation letters should ordinarily be signed by both the chief executive and chief financial officers. Other members of management may sign the letter instead, however, if the auditor is satisfied that they are responsible for and knowledgeable about the matters covered by the representations. A chief executive officer who does not participate in making accounting decisions may express an unwillingness to sign the standard representation letter. A separate letter indicating reliance on the chief financial officer's representations, and no contrary knowledge, would be acceptable.

Scope Limitations.   In rare instances, management may refuse to furnish a written representation that the auditor believes is essential or may refuse to sign the representation letter. SAS No. 19 (AU Section 333.11) notes that either refusal constitutes a limitation on the scope of the audit sufficient to preclude an unqualified opinion (SAS No. 58 [AU Section 508.40–.41]). An auditor must consider whether management's refusal to furnish a written representation affects the reliability of their other representations. Executives are expected to understand their legal and ethical responsibilities for financial statement representations. Thus, they should also understand that the representation letter only specifies some of those responsibilities but does not increase them. Refusal to sign the letter must be taken as a signal either of withheld evidence or of inadequately understood responsibilities; either destroys the basis for an unqualified opinion.

Representations from Others. In certain circumstances, the auditor may want to obtain representation letters from persons other than the client's management. For example, an auditor of a subsidiary but not of its parent company may want to obtain representations from management or the auditor of the parent company regarding information that might require adjustment or disclosure in the subsidiary's financial statements.

Refusal by the parent company or principal auditor to furnish the written representations the secondary auditor believes are essential to the audit of the subsidiary constitutes a scope limitation, as described above. A representation letter from the parent company to a secondary auditor is illustrated in Figure 21.3.

**Figure 21.3   Illustrative Representation Letter
from Parent Company to Secondary Auditor**

[Date—no earlier than date of auditor's report, but no later than report release date]

[Name and Address of Secondary Auditor]

Gentlemen:

We understand you will be reporting on your audit of the financial statements of [name of subsidiary] as of [date] and for the [period of audit]. This is to advise you that, to the best of our knowledge and belief, there are no related party transactions, including accounts receivable or payable, sales, purchases, loans, transfers, leasing arrangements, and guarantees, either recorded in the books and records of [name of parent company] or not recorded in them (such as loan guarantees), that should be considered for possible adjustment or disclosure in the financial statements of [name of subsidiary] as of [date] and for the [period of audit], except as follows:

a. Amounts receivable [payable] at [date] _____

b. Guarantees of amounts receivable [payable] at [date] _____

c. Sales [purchases] for the [period of audit] _____

d. Rental income [expense] for the [period of audit] _____

[Add other representations that may be required in this letter in certain circumstances.]

_____
[Name and title of chief financial officer of parent company]

Representations in Other Than Audit Engagements

AICPA professional standards currently require CPAs to obtain written client representations when performing attestation services, including certain prospective financial information engagements, as discussed in Chapter 24. In addition, it is good practice to obtain written representations from clients when performing other services, such as reviews of annual financial statements or limited reviews of interim financial information. Generally, the guidance for written audit representations can be appropriately modified for nonaudit services.

SUMMARIZING AND EVALUATING THE AUDIT FINDINGS

The discussion of materiality in Chapter 6 noted that auditors frequently maintain a summary of the misstatements found in the course of the various procedures performed throughout the audit. Misstatements may result from either errors or irregularities, as defined in Chapter 4. Thus, misstatements include unintentional mistakes, unreasonable accounting estimates, intentional misrepresentations, and intentional or unintentional misapplications of GAAP. Ordinarily, management makes adjustments for some items, leaving the unadjusted differences to be evaluated by the auditor.[2] Normally the summary includes items arising in the current year, but, as discussed below, it may also include waived adjustments from prior years' audits that have an effect on the current year's financial statements.

The summary serves as the central means of evaluating whether the evidence examined by the auditor supports the conclusion that the financial statements are presented fairly, in all material respects, in conformity with generally accepted accounting principles. The auditor should be sure that the items on the summary, either individually or in the aggregate, do not cause the financial statements to be materially misstated. If they do, either the financial statements will have to be revised by the client, or the auditor will have to express a qualified opinion or an adverse opinion because of departures from GAAP. Usually the auditor and the client are able to reach agreement so that a qualified or an adverse opinion is not necessary.

Categories of Misstatements to Be Evaluated

Authoritative auditing literature addresses the auditor's consideration of misstatements. SAS No. 39, *Auditing Sampling* (AU Section 350.30), requires the auditor to consider "projected misstatement results for all audit sampling applications and all known misstatements from nonsampling applications" in the aggregate in evaluating whether the financial statements as a whole may be materially misstated. Projected misstatement is discussed in Chapter 10. SAS

---

[2]The auditor's responsibilities when a potential audit adjustment is or may be an irregularity are described in Chapter 4. The discussion here is limited to considering whether an audit adjustment is necessary.

No. 47, *Audit Risk and Materiality in Conducting an Audit* (AU Section 312.27), expands on this concept by stating that "the auditor should aggregate misstatements that the entity has not corrected in a way that enables him to consider whether, in relation to individual amounts, subtotals, or totals in the financial statements, they materially misstate the financial statements taken as a whole." With regard to the amounts to be aggregated, SAS No. 47 states

> The aggregation of misstatements should include the auditor's best estimate of the total misstatements in the account balances or classes of transactions that he has examined (hereafter referred to as likely misstatement), not just the amount of misstatements he specifically identifies (hereafter referred to as known misstatement). . . . Projected misstatement [from audit sampling, if used], along with the results of other substantive tests, contributes to the auditor's assessment of likely misstatement in the balance or class. (para. 28)

As defined in SAS No. 47, likely misstatement includes unreasonable differences between accounting estimates as determined by the client and the amounts supported by audit evidence. SAS No. 47 states

> Since no one accounting estimate can be considered accurate with certainty, the auditor recognizes that a difference between an estimated amount best supported by the audit evidence and the estimated amount included in the financial statements may be reasonable, and such difference would not be considered to be a likely misstatement. However, if the auditor believes the estimated amount included in the financial statements is unreasonable, he should treat the difference between that estimate and the closest reasonable estimate as a likely misstatement and aggregate it with other likely misstatements. (para. 29)

Preparing and Using the Summary

The exact form of the summary used to aggregate misstatements, and even what it is called, varies in practice. Its complexity depends on the complexity of the engagement (e.g., extensive subsidiary operations may require a more complex format) and circumstances (e.g., if significant misstatements are expected or many accounts are considered potentially troublesome, a more structured, formal format may be required). Additionally, professional standards may require specific documentation.

In general, the summary is a multiple-column work sheet. In the extreme left columns, the auditor records the nature of misstatements identified, for example, descriptions of known misstatements from nonsampling procedures and projected misstatements from sampling procedures in the inventory accounts. The amount in question is then "spread" to show its impact on assets, liabilities and owners' equity, and income, such as a failure to record on a timely basis $10,000 of inventory received before year-end that might result in a $10,000 understatement of assets and a $10,000 understatement of liabilities.

A single document that summarizes and accumulates misstatements identified in the various accounts, such as receivables and payables, makes it easier for the auditor to evaluate the overall audit findings. For example, a review of

Summary of Adjustments

Figure 21.4 Summary of Adjustments

Client: PSR Corporation
Year End: 12/31/90

Prepared by/Date: R.B. 2/28/91
Reviewed by/Date: m.C. 3/2/91

Working Paper Ref.	DESCRIPTION OF ADJUSTMENT NEEDED	BALANCE SHEET IMPACT — Assets Non-current	Assets Current	Liabilities Current	Liabilities Non-current	Equity	PRETAX INCOME STATEMENT IMPACT — Known Mis-statements[1]	Projected[2]	Estimated[3]	Total
53.2	Additional provision for uncollectible accounts		(39,000)						39,000	39,000
53.25	Sales invoice pricing misstatements (underbillings)		34,000					(34,000)		(34,000)
55.2	Physical inventory count adjustments		38,000				(38,000)			(38,000)
55.2	Inventory pricing misstatements		76,000					(76,000)		(76,000)
71.2	Unrecorded liabilities adjustments (invoices received after cutoff date)		47,000	(67,000)			20,000			20,000
72.25	Warranty accruals understatement			(50,000)					50,000	50,000
	TOTAL PRETAX UNADJUSTED MISSTATEMENTS		156,000	(117,000)		(39,000)	(18,000)	(110,000)	89,000	(39,000)(A)
	TAX EFFECTS:									
	Estimated tax impact of unadjusted misstatements			(14,000)		14,000	6,000	38,000	(30,000)	14,000
	TOTAL AFTER-TAX UNADJUSTED MISSTATEMENTS		156,000(B)	(131,000)(B)		(25,000)(B)	(12,000)	(72,000)	59,000	(25,000)(B)
	BALANCE SHEET AMOUNTS	22,438,000(C)	11,193,000(C)	5,780,000 (C)	10,354,000(C)	17,497,000 (C)				
	PERCENTAGE OF MISSTATEMENTS TO BALANCE SHEET AMOUNTS (B)÷(C)		1.4%	2.3%	%	.1%				

PRETAX INCOME 3,671,000 (D)
PERCENTAGE OF PRETAX MISSTATEMENTS TO PRETAX INCOME (A)÷(D) 1.1%
AFTER-TAX INCOME 2,569,000 (E)
PERCENTAGE OF AFTER-TAX MISSTATEMENTS TO AFTER-TAX INCOME (B)÷(E) 1.0%

[1] Misstatements specifically identified in nonsampling applications.
[2] Misstatements relating to the application of audit sampling techniques (includes known misstatements identified in samples examined).
[3] Misstatements determined by the difference between the client's accounting estimate and the closest reasonable amount supported by the audit evidence.

the summary may reveal that individually immaterial misstatements taken together have a material impact on income or some other financial statement element. The summary is helpful in comparing the results of auditing procedures with materiality at the account level, for major groups of accounts (such as current assets), and for the financial statements as a whole. Figure 21.4 illustrates a summary of adjustments.

Aggregating and Netting

The issue of aggregating and netting misstated amounts in the final evaluation of audit evidence is complicated and somewhat controversial. The controversy centers around the appropriateness of netting or offsetting certain misstatements.

In aggregating misstatements affecting the income statement or balance sheet, likely misstatements relating to each line item are considered together to determine whether the line item is not materially misstated. The more "cushion" that exists between the total of likely misstatements and a larger amount that the auditor considers "material" for the line item, the higher the auditor's level of assurance that the item is not materially misstated.

One technique used in practice is to aggregate misstatements within groupings of financial statement components and to assess materiality at that level and at each successively higher logical subdivision of the financial statements. For example, in assessing the fair presentation of assets, the results of the audit of cash and short-term liquid assets might be aggregated to determine whether the sum of those assets, which enters into the computation of the "quick ratio," is reasonable. Other current assets such as accounts receivable might then be added and another assessment made at the current asset level. Finally, these results would be combined with a similar series of aggregations for noncurrent assets to evaluate reported assets in total. The auditor's objective is to obtain reasonable assurance that neither the line item itself, subtotals or important ratios of which the line item is a component, or the financial statements as a whole are materially misstated.

The way items are added together or offset against each other can significantly affect evaluations of materiality. Some items or events are more significant than others, implying that they should be evaluated individually while others may be evaluated in groups. For example, many auditors consider it inappropriate to aggregate or offset an individually immaterial overstatement of cash with a misstatement in an unrelated account. The inherent risk associated with the cash account, as well as the potential for determining its value precisely, often precludes an auditor from treating misstatements of cash in the same manner as misstatements in other accounts. Immaterial inventory misstatements and immaterial receivable misstatements, however, are often offset in determining whether the financial statements as a whole may be materially misstated.

Netting separate items to determine the amount to be compared with materiality raises several questions. Is it acceptable, for example, to net the effect of an error against the effect of a change in accounting principle? Clearly, the answer is no. APB Opinion No. 20, paragraph 38 (Accounting

Standards Section A06.133), requires that materiality be considered for the separate effects of each accounting change. Also, netting individually material items to obtain an immaterial total would result in inadequate financial statement disclosure. It is acceptable, however, to net immaterial misstatements in a particular component of financial statements or in related accounts.

Quantitative Aspects of Materiality Judgments

The question of how large a "difference" must be before it is material has never been definitively answered in the accounting and auditing literature. Many auditors have developed rules of thumb for setting materiality thresholds, such as some percentage of one or more financial statement totals. Net income is a commonly cited base for assessing materiality, but there are others, such as total assets, equities, or revenues, as well as trends in each of these. As long as investors continue to pay attention to net income in their investment assessments, however, an audit standard of materiality based on net income (or the trend of net income) is likely to be widely used.

A commonly used figure for materiality is 5 percent of the chosen base. That is, if the item is within 5 percent of what it might otherwise be, the difference may be immaterial. Obviously, any rule of thumb, such as 5 percent, must be used with a great deal of caution and careful judgment. Qualitative considerations, as discussed below, can render such a range too broad. Most studies of the subject have generally concluded that a single dollar amount or percentage is not appropriate in all situations. Five to ten percent of net income is frequently used, but is affected in individual cases by nonquantitative criteria. Some examples of quantitative criteria for significance or materiality that have been used by professional and regulatory standard-setting bodies are cited in Table 1 in Appendix C to FASB Statement of Financial Accounting Concepts No. 2. In addition, many auditors assign greater significance to differences that change the client's trend of earnings than to those that do not.

Having established that there may be more than one level of materiality—for example, one level for income statement effects and a higher level in absolute terms for balance sheet effects—the auditor should recognize that a misstatement that affects both statements should be compared with the smaller materiality level in determining whether the misstatement requires correction or can be "waived" as immaterial. For example, a misstated accrual may not materially affect the balance sheet, but may materially affect reported expenses and consequently net income. In that situation, the lower income statement threshold would determine materiality. Misclassifications that affect only balance sheet accounts would be material if they exceeded the balance sheet materiality threshold.

Qualitative Considerations in Assessing Materiality

The types of misstatements found may influence the auditor's evaluation of the audit results. Paragraph 22 of SAS No. 53 (AU Section 316.22) states that the auditor should consider whether misstatements are the result of errors or of irregularities. Because irregularities are intentional, their implications for the audit extend beyond their direct monetary effect, and the auditor must consider those implications in evaluating the audit results. Chapter 4 discusses actions the auditor should take, including disclosures, when an irregularity may have a material effect on the financial statements.

In many cases, known misstatements in an account discovered by applying either sampling or nonsampling procedures are corrected in the accounts and entail no further consideration. Misstatements that arise from projecting the results of a sample to the population are more difficult to deal with. While projected misstatements should be included on the summary of adjustments, correcting the financial statements for them is difficult in practice, since sampling does not help identify all of the specific components, such as the individual accounts receivable, that may be misstated. Additionally, according to sampling theory, the projected misstatement is not the "true" misstatement, but only a presumably close approximation. Therefore, correcting the financial statements for nonspecific "projected" misstatements may create a risk that actual misstatements will be introduced into the financial statements. Sample results may be used, however, to identify aspects of an account (e.g., inventory) that deserve special attention by the client, such as repricing or recounting. If such procedures are performed, the auditor will need to adjust the projected misstatement amount based on the results of the procedures.

Evaluating some types of misstatements involves distinguishing between "hard" and "soft" misstatements and properly characterizing the "soft" ones. A mathematical mistake, omission of a segment of inventory from the total inventory, or an accounting principle misapplication, whether discovered by sampling or nonsampling procedures, may be referred to as a "hard" misstatement. In these cases, the auditor knows there is a problem and can calculate the misstatement. If potential misstatements are based on judgments or estimates that cannot be calculated precisely but must be estimated, they are described as "soft."

Accounting and auditing are not exact sciences, and much judgment often goes into developing the account balances presented in the financial statements. The auditor must evaluate accounts, such as the allowance for uncollectible accounts receivable and liability for product warranties, that are based on estimates and are not subject to absolute determination. (The auditor's responsibility to evaluate management's estimates is discussed in Chapter 9.) Using methods that are appropriate in the circumstances but are not exactly the same ones the client used, the auditor may develop an estimate that differs from the client's. The auditor should develop such estimates carefully and compare them with the client's estimates to determine whether the client's estimates are reasonable. Those considered unreasonable should be included with other likely misstatements and evaluated, and those deemed to be reasonable should be excluded from likely misstatement.

Sometimes the auditor may not be able to arrive at a single estimated amount, but may establish a range of "reasonableness"; if the client's estimate falls within that range, it does not belong on the summary. If the client's estimate falls outside that range, the auditor should enter an item representing the difference between the client's estimate and the nearest point in the range.

For example, if a client established a product warranty liability for $150,000 and the auditor, by analyzing past trends and the experience of other companies in similar circumstances, established a reasonable range of product warranty liability of between $200,000 and $300,000, the auditor might include on the summary $50,000 ($200,000 – $150,000) for possible adjustment by the client. This would be a ''soft'' misstatement; only if the auditor knew the liability must exceed $200,000 could the difference in estimates be called a ''hard'' or ''known'' misstatement.

The Commission on Auditors' Responsibilities noted that ''the auditor may make many separate evaluations of the appropriateness of accounting principles selected and estimates made by management. On viewing the financial statements as a whole, the auditor may find that most or all of the selections or estimates made by management had the effect of increasing (or decreasing) earnings and that the overall result is a misleading picture of the entity's earning power or liquidity'' (page 21). SAS No. 47, *Audit Risk and Materiality in Conducting an Audit* (AU Section 312.29), addresses that possibility, and suggests that ''the auditor should also consider whether the difference between estimates best supported by the audit evidence and the estimates included in the financial statements, which are individually reasonable, indicate a possible bias on the part of the entity's management. For example, if each accounting estimate included in the financial statements was individually reasonable, but the effect of the difference between each estimate and the estimate best supported by the audit evidence was to increase income, the auditor should reconsider the estimates taken as a whole.''

Other qualitative factors may also influence the auditor's response to likely misstatements in the financial statements. These factors may warrant consideration that goes beyond the quantitative significance of the misstatements. Following are examples of factors that may cause the auditor greater concern and prompt other reactions than the quantitative amounts themselves might indicate:

- *Business conditions.* For example, in a weak economy or in a company with a weak financial condition, materiality is sometimes given special emphasis since the company's future may rest on investors' and creditors' evaluations of the current financial position and recent trends.
- *Contractual arrangements.* Debt covenants, buy–sell agreements, and union contracts may be geared to various financial statement elements or relationships (such as the current ratio).
- *Cause of the misstatement.* Misapplications of GAAP (e.g., recording a purchase of a business as a pooling of interests or failing to accrue vacation pay or product warranties) may have possible long-term effects the auditor should assess, since correcting the misstatement later may erode investors' confidence in the company's financial reporting.
- *Situations in which the ''investor-based'' materiality rule is difficult to apply.* For entities such as privately owned companies, trusts, and others, the auditor may need to consider who are the likely users of the financial statements and what their interests are, and designate a materiality level appropriate

for their needs. Special user needs may tighten customary materiality standards.

- *Susceptibility of an account to misstatement.* Misstatements in the cash and capital accounts are generally unexpected and may warrant further investigation if discovered. The susceptibility of cash and other liquid assets to misuse or misappropriation should naturally heighten auditor concern about likely misstatements in these accounts.

- *Trends in financial statement components.* While it may be unrealistic to use a materiality standard as tight as a small fraction of the yearly change in net income or other financial statement components, longer-range trends or averages of balances or components (e.g., "normal income") may serve as useful signals that users react to. Consequently, auditors should be sensitive to departures from trends or normal expectations. Additionally, in a company with a stable earnings history, smaller variations in cash flow, income, or other financial statement components may have more impact than in a less stable business environment where wider fluctuations are more common.

Treatment of Prior-Year Waived Adjustments

An issue that often arises in assessing materiality is the treatment in the current year of prior-year waived adjustments. For example, the auditor may have waived a known overstatement of $10,000 in ending inventory and income in 1989, caused perhaps by errors in pricing the inventory, on the grounds that the misstatement was not material. The overstatement of the 1989 ending inventory and income will flow through to 1990 income as an overstatement of cost of sales and an understatement of income. The issue in this case is this: In considering misstatements affecting income in the 1990 financial statements, should the auditor include the $10,000 understatement of 1990 income caused by the waived adjustment of the 1989 misstatement?

Some auditors believe that prior-year waived adjustments should be ignored in considering likely misstatements in the current year; in effect, the "correct" beginning 1990 inventory in the above example is the 1989 ending inventory, with the misstatement in it. Since it was waived, those auditors treat the misstatement as not existing after 1989 and consider that 1990 starts with a "clean slate." Other auditors believe that the reversal in 1990 of the 1989 misstatement should be considered in assessing likely misstatements in 1990.

The issue becomes even more complex when unadjusted misstatements, instead of reversing in the following year as in the above example, build up. Assume that the auditor determines that the estimated warranty liability at the end of 1989 and warranty expense for 1989 are understated by $15,000 because an unreasonable estimate was made by the client. The auditor waived the adjustment because the amount was not material to either the balance sheet or the income statement. In the course of the audit of the 1990 financial statements, the auditor determines that the estimated warranty liability at December 31, 1990, is understated by $35,000—an additional $20,000. In assessing the materiality of the misstatement, the auditor may determine that neither the $35,000 cumulative misstatement on the balance sheet nor the $20,000 impact on current-year income is material and again waive the adjustment. This may continue for several years. At some point, the accumulated misstatement on the balance sheet will become material, and an adjustment will be needed if the financial statements are to be presented fairly in conformity with GAAP. The resulting adjustment may be so large that it will produce a material misstatement in that year's income statement.

SAS No. 47 provides only the broadest guidance on this topic, stating merely that "if the auditor believes that there is an unacceptably high risk that the current period's financial statements may be materially misstated when those prior-period likely misstatements that affect the current period's financial statements are considered along with likely misstatements arising in the current period, he should include in aggregate likely misstatement the effect on the current period's financial statements of those prior-period likely misstatements" (AU Section 312.30). It does not, however, state how the auditor should include the effect in likely misstatement, and accordingly does not resolve the issues discussed here.

The auditor must plan properly to ensure that sufficient auditing procedures are performed in the various accounts so that he or she can draw appropriate audit conclusions. If there has been a buildup of misstatements in an account from prior years, the auditor may have to do more work to refine the estimate of the present misstatement in the account. More audit work may also be necessary to prevent a materially misstated balance from going undetected. Of course, assessing at the planning stage whether an immaterially misstated account balance from prior years will no longer be misstated, remain similarly misstated, or become misstated in the opposite direction in the current period is difficult. Thus, the auditor's experience with the client, assessment of the possible level of misstatement in the account, and the nature of the account all influence the testing plan for the current period.

Resolving Material Differences

Occasionally, the auditor will conclude after reviewing the summary that one or more financial statement components are materially misstated or cause the income statement or balance sheet in the aggregate to be materially misstated. The auditor then needs to discuss the items in question with the client's management. Management may be able to produce further evidence to justify the initial treatment of some items or may agree to record some of the discovered misstatements in the accounts and to disclose more about the nature of and assumptions used in creating subjectively developed estimates that may be in dispute. The discussions continue until enough items are resolved so that the auditor can conclude that the remaining items do not adversely affect the fair presentation of the financial statements.

Depending on the size and complexity of an organization, the auditor may have to take up each item on the summary with several levels of management. The first consultation, of course, is with the individual directly responsible, who must supply all the facts. Additional conferences may include a supervisor and sometimes a plant or division controller. Often the deciding conference includes top management—the financial vice president and chief executive. If discussions reach that level, two subjects should be probed: how to resolve the current problems so that an unqualified opinion can be given, and how to prevent similar problems from growing to such magnitude in the future. In these conferences, auditors must be careful not to allow factors such as pressing deadlines, heated arguments, or client dissatisfaction to influence them or to compromise their professional objectivity. Diplomacy and tact and an attitude of constructive assistance are obviously important in such situations. Early and thorough consideration of potential problems is the best way to avoid actual problems that may lead to qualified or adverse opinions. In some situations, however, such opinions may be the only appropriate response to a client's unwillingness to correct material financial statement misstatements.

WORKING PAPER REVIEW

Paragraph 11 of SAS No. 22, *Planning and Supervision* (AU Section 311.13), states that "the work performed by each assistant should be reviewed to determine whether it was adequately performed and to evaluate whether the results are consistent with the conclusions to be presented in the auditor's report."

Key Engagement Matters

To facilitate the review process, the audit personnel in charge of the field work should document significant matters relating to the engagement and bring them to the attention of the partner in charge of the engagement. Key engagement matters include, but are not limited to, the following:

1. Significant questions involving accounting principles and auditing procedures, or failure to comply with regulatory requirements, even when the person in charge of the field work is satisfied that the matter has been disposed of properly.
2. Incomplete audit steps or unresolved questions.
3. Matters of significance noted in the previous year's engagement and their disposition.
4. Resolved or unresolved disagreements with the client on accounting and auditing matters.
5. Any information, not otherwise obvious, that should be considered in evaluating the results of the audit or in discussing the financial statements with the client.

It is desirable to address significant matters in one section of the working papers. Those matters may be summarized in the lead working paper binder, with cross-references to the related working papers that contain the details.

Types of Reviews

Generally, two types of reviews of working papers and procedures are performed on audit engagements.

- A review of the completed working papers by the person in charge of the field work to evaluate the audit results and ascertain that all appropriate auditing procedures have been applied.
- A review of the auditing procedures by an individual who did not participate in the field work. This review provides an objective assessment of the procedures applied during the field work and their results, which form the basis of the audit opinion.

The person in charge of the field work is responsible for reviewing all completed working papers to determine that

1. All appropriate auditing procedures have been completed and that the nature and extent of the work performed have been adequately documented in the working papers.
2. The requirements of the audit program were adhered to.
3. The working papers are relevant, clearly presented, orderly, and self-explanatory.
4. All exceptions have been appropriately cleared and documented.

The second review is the responsibility of the partner, who exercises overall supervision but does not usually perform the detailed auditing procedures. Depending on the structure of the audit team, the partner may delegate a portion of the review to a manager who was not involved in preparing the working papers. The partner would then ordinarily focus primarily on the key engagement matters and any areas in which there is a high risk of material misstatement, taking into consideration the dollar amounts involved, the complexity of the problems, and the internal control structure.

The purpose of the review of the working papers and audit program is to ensure that the procedures used are adequate and appropriate, that they have been performed properly, that they generated sufficient evidence to support the auditor's conclusions, that the conclusions reached are objective and logical, and that there is a properly documented basis for an informed opinion. The reviewer must evaluate the completeness of the audit program—including changes made to reflect changes in audit strategy in the course of the audit—in light of the results of the tests, the quality of the work performed by assistants, the quality of management's judgments and decisions, and the adequacy of both the work performed and its documentation by the assistants. The exacting but inconclusive nature of most audit tasks makes it imperative that every piece of work be reviewed for completeness and logic by another qualified professional.

Whatever other purposes the review may have, its primary purpose must be to make sure that the logic of the audit is complete and properly documented.

The logic calls for evidence in the working papers that the control structure was understood and inherent and control risks were assessed, and, if appropriate, tests of controls were performed; the understanding and assessment were translated into a program of substantive tests; the results of those tests either corroborated the assertions embodied in the financial statement components or led to a rational exploration of differences; and the results support each item in the financial statements.

The reviewer should be satisfied that the working papers have been integrated with the final financial statements. That is, the reviewer should ascertain that each account analysis in the working papers agrees with the corresponding amount shown on the trial balance, and that those amounts are reconcilable to the amounts shown on the financial statements. Amounts or other data appearing on the financial statements but not reflected on the trial balance (e.g., footnote or supplementary information) must also be agreed to the related working papers.

Regardless of what duties the partner delegates to a manager, the partner should review the auditor's report, related financial statements, and, where applicable, the entire text of the published report. The partner should consider each of the key engagement matters and ensure that the decision reached as to its disposition is appropriate.

Review by a Concurring Partner

Many accounting firms require that all financial statements be reviewed by a concurring (sometimes referred to as a second) partner before the audit report is released. Other firms limit this requirement to audits of specified entities, for example, entities in specialized industries and publicly owned entities.[3] In this review, the concurring partner should be particularly concerned that matters of importance have been appropriately dealt with and that the financial statements and audit report comply with professional standards and firm policies. The concurring partner should discuss with the partner in charge of the engagement questions regarding the consistent application of GAAP, auditing standards, or auditing procedures. The concurring partner may also consider it advisable to review certain working papers. If a concurring-partner review is required, the auditor's report should not be signed until all questions raised by the concurring partner have been disposed of properly.

Aids for Reviewers

The review process is so critical that accounting firms are constantly seeking ways to help reviewers by providing aids such as engagement control checklists, standardized procedures, and policy bulletins. In providing such aids to the reviewer, accounting firms must try to guard against routinized performance of a highly judgmental task. The quality of the review, and therefore of the audit, rests on the professional diligence and sense of responsibility of the

[3]As indicated in Chapter 3, second-partner reviews are required on SEC engagements if the auditor is a member of the SEC Practice Section of the AICPA Division for CPA Firms.

reviewer. Although guided and supported by aids such as those mentioned above, the reviewer cannot and should not be relieved of the responsibility for understanding all that is needed to be able to form an appropriate opinion on the financial statements.

Timing of the Review Process

For the sake of both audit efficiency and good client relations, potentially material issues must be raised at the earliest possible stage. More time for consideration by the partner on the engagement and the client is thus available than if the review is postponed until the final stages of the audit when the report deadline is near.

The real substance of an audit is planning it intelligently and logically, executing it diligently and perceptively, and supervising it so that the review is continuous and active. If an audit is properly planned, executed, and supervised, the working paper review becomes the final control over a result already accomplished—a means of determining that all items of significance have been considered in reaching an audit conclusion.

In practice, the review process rarely works as smoothly as it does in theory. There are delays by client personnel, unexpected auditing or accounting problems, an assistant who falls ill or cannot complete the assignment on time, and innumerable other possible complications. Increasing public pressure for the fastest possible release of significant information causes deadlines to be drawn constantly tighter. The risk of oversight or misjudgment is greatest under the pressure of a deadline. Experienced auditors learn to resist those problems and pressures, and make sure they review an integrated set of financial statements supported by coherent working papers before committing themselves, explicitly or implicitly, to an opinion on the financial statements or to approving release of information drawn from them.

Documentation of Significant Review Findings

During the various working paper reviews, questions usually arise concerning significant unresolved matters. Those questions are commonly referred to as "review notes." They often involve the appropriateness of accounting principles, auditing procedures used, or compliance with regulatory requirements, and call for further investigation. Some auditors require that the review notes become part of the audit working papers and that a clear and precise record be maintained of how such questions were resolved, including, among other things, such matters as the following (if applicable):

- The additional auditing procedures performed.
- The individuals with whom the matter was discussed.
- The conclusions arrived at and supporting rationale.

Other auditors believe that matters identified in review notes should be adequately disposed of by changes or additions to appropriate working papers and the review notes destroyed.

REVIEW OF FINANCIAL STATEMENTS FOR APPROPRIATE DISCLOSURE

The third generally accepted auditing standard applicable to reporting is

Informative disclosures in the financial statements are to be regarded as reasonably adequate unless otherwise stated in the report. (SAS No. 1 [AU Section 150.02])

SAS No. 32, *Adequacy of Disclosure in Financial Statements* (AU Section 431), discusses this standard in very general terms. Essentially, material matters regarding the financial statements are to be disclosed in the financial statements or notes; if they are not, the auditor should express a qualified or an adverse opinion and should, if practicable, provide the information in the auditor's report. The auditor's reporting responsibilities with regard to inadequate disclosures are discussed in Chapter 22.

With the proliferation of accounting standards in recent years, many auditors, including sole practitioners, have adopted checklists as a means of enhancing overall quality control and furthering staff development. Disclosure checklists can deal adequately with specifically required disclosures and serve as a "memory jogger"; they can, if properly prepared, also assist the auditor in meeting the standard of informative disclosure. Of course, an auditor's level of skill and judgment and the knowledge of the client's affairs obtained during the audit are the ultimate resources available to meet the disclosure standard.

Some auditors have developed separate disclosure checklists for companies subject to SEC reporting requirements and those that are not. Further, separate checklists may be prepared for certain specialized industries, such as banking, insurance, government units, and colleges and universities. A typical arrangement would be to have a series of questions covering all aspects of the financial statements in one column; specific references to the relevant authoritative pronouncement or the auditing firm's preferences in another column (by necessity, the requirements can only be generally stated in the checklist, but the references can make it easier to prepare and review the document); and an indication, in a third column, of whether the item is applicable, and, if so, whether it has been complied with. Space should be allowed for notes or calculations of amounts to demonstrate how materiality considerations entered into disclosure decisions. A completed checklist for an audit can document in one place all reporting and disclosure considerations.

If checklists are used by an auditing firm, it is desirable that a clear statement be appended setting forth the firm's policy on whether they are mandatory for all engagements or only for certain specified engagements, or simply to be used as practice aids. Disclosure checklists should be updated periodically and should also indicate the date produced so that authoritative pronouncements after that date will be considered.

SUBSEQUENT EVENTS

Types of Subsequent Events

Subsequent events are defined in Section 560 of SAS No. 1 (AU Sections 560.01–.09) as events or transactions that "occur subsequent to the balance-sheet date, but prior to the issuance of the financial statements and auditor's report, that have a material effect on the financial statements and therefore require adjustment or disclosure in the statements."[4] Subsequent events that occur after the balance sheet date but before the issuance of the financial statements and the auditor's report fall into two categories: those that require adjustment of account balances (and consequently are reflected on the face of the financial statements) and those that should not be recorded but should be disclosed in the financial statements.

The first category of subsequent event is succinctly described in SAS No. 1 (AU Section 560.03), as follows:

> Those events that provide additional evidence with respect to conditions that existed at the date of the balance sheet and affect the estimates inherent in the process of preparing financial statements. All information that becomes available prior to the issuance of the financial statements should be used by management in its evaluation of the conditions on which the estimates were based. The financial statements should be adjusted for any changes in estimates resulting from the use of such evidence.

The second type of subsequent event is one that provides evidence about conditions that did not exist at the balance sheet date but arose afterwards. These events should be reflected in the financial statements of the year in which they occurred, and should not result in adjustment of the statements of the year being reported on. Some of these events, however, may be significant enough that, if they are not disclosed, the prior-year financial statements would be misleading. They include all transactions and other events and circumstances having significant financial impact. Some examples given in SAS No. 1 are issuance of debt or stock, acquisition of a business, and casualty losses.

Occasionally, an event of that type may be so significant that the auditor's report should call attention to it in an explanatory paragraph. Sometimes adequate disclosure can be made only by means of pro forma data giving effect to the event as if it had occurred at the balance sheet date; major acquisitions, mergers, and recapitalizations are examples.

Section 560 of SAS No. 1 illustrates the distinction between events that reveal or clarify conditions existing at the balance sheet date and those that

---

[4]The distinction between the discovery of subsequent events before the financial statements are issued and the later discovery of facts that existed at the date of the auditor's report is significant. The latter is discussed in Chapter 22.

represent new conditions. The illustration used is a receivable found to be uncollectible after year-end because of a customer's bankruptcy subsequent to that date. This event is in the first category (requiring adjustment of the gross receivable and possibly recalculation of bad debt expense and the allowance for uncollectible accounts) because the debtor's poor financial condition existed at the balance sheet date. A similar receivable found to be uncollectible because of a disaster occurring to the debtor after the balance sheet date is a new condition and falls in the second category, requiring disclosure in the notes to the financial statements rather than adjustment of the accounts. The SAS notes that making the distinction requires ''the exercise of judgment and knowledge of the facts and circumstances'' (AU Section 560.04).

The distinction is often a fine one and the judgment difficult to make. For example, deteriorating market conditions subsequent to year-end could be a new condition that merely requires disclosure, or it could be evidence of a condition that was inherent in the inventory at year-end, which calls for adjusting it to net realizable value. Similarly, a subsequent event that reveals that estimated expenses are insufficient because of conditions occurring after the balance sheet date should be disclosed. On the other hand, if the reason for the insufficiency is newly discovered evidence of conditions that existed at the balance sheet date, that evidence should be reflected in the expense and related asset or liability accounts on the face of the statements.

There is a third type of subsequent event—one occurring after year-end that requires neither adjustment nor disclosure in the financial statements. Events that do not affect the interpretation of financial statements should not be disclosed because describing them in notes could cause misleading or confusing inferences. Since every event may have a financial impact, it is often extremely difficult to distinguish between events that should and those that should not be disclosed in the financial statements. Strikes, changes in customers or management, and new contracts and agreements are examples of events that ordinarily should not be disclosed in the financial statements, although management may have a responsibility to make public disclosure apart from the financial statements. If the events occur before the annual report to shareholders is printed, the president's letter is often used as a convenient method of communication.

Auditor's Responsibility for Subsequent Events

The auditor's responsibility for subsequent events depends on whether they occurred before or after the date of the auditor's report (discussed below). The auditor's responsibility for events occurring in the period between the client's year-end and the audit report date (called the subsequent period) is defined in Section 560 of SAS No. 1. Auditors have no responsibility to seek any additional evidence in the period (typically a rather short time) between the date of the auditor's report and the date the financial statements and auditor's report are issued. Nevertheless, many auditors believe that while they have no responsibility to seek additional evidence during that period, they do have a responsibility not to ignore information that comes to their attention.

Auditing Procedures in the Subsequent Period

Paragraphs 10–12 of Section 560 of SAS No. 1 (AU Section 560.10–.12) define the auditor's responsibility to determine whether relevant subsequent events have occurred and discuss auditing procedures performed in the subsequent period. That work generally falls into two major categories—procedures performed for the purpose of keeping current with respect to events occurring in the subsequent period, and completion of auditing procedures performed for other purposes.

The latter category consists of substantive tests and other auditing procedures that involve reviewing transactions occurring in the subsequent period as part of the audit of year-end account balances. These procedures, which have been discussed earlier in this book, include tests of the client's cash cutoffs and sales and purchase cutoffs, and reviews of collections and payments after year-end. As previously noted, however, the auditor has no responsibility to carry out any auditing procedures for the period after the report date.

The procedures for keeping current with respect to events occurring in the subsequent period are specified in AU Section 560.12 and may be summarized as follows:

Read all available information relating to the client's financial affairs: interim financial statements; minutes of meetings of stockholders, directors, and any appropriate committees; pertinent variance and other management reports, and the like. An auditor who understands the client knows which areas are sensitive or volatile and what information about them is likely to be available.

Make inquiries—the more specific the better—about such things as financing activities, unusual entries or adjustments in the accounts, and potential problems discovered during the audit. An auditor who has developed a close working relationship with the client can make those inquiries easily and expeditiously.

Inquire of client's legal counsel concerning litigation, claims, and assessments.

Obtain a letter of representation from client officers describing subsequent events or disclaiming knowledge of any.

In addition, as part of the subsequent-period review, the auditor may compare the latest available interim financial statements with the financial statements being reported on, as well as making other comparisons considered appropriate in the circumstances.

It is sometimes necessary in the subsequent period to perform analytical procedures or other substantive tests in a recognized problem area. Usually, their purpose is to form an opinion on whether a client has measured the impact of a subsequent event reasonably, for example, the impact of a decision to discontinue a line of business made subsequent to year-end. Sometimes, however, tests are required to satisfy the auditor that a possible subsequent event did not occur; an example is tests of the net realizable value of inventories due to changed market conditions subsequent to year-end.

Dating the Report

SAS No. 1 (AU Section 530.01) states that the auditor's report generally should be dated the date when the audit field work is completed, that is, when the auditor has completed substantially all the tests of the accounting records and all other auditing procedures considered necessary in the circumstances of the particular engagement. Matters that may require follow-up with the client, particularly if performed off the client's premises, generally do not affect the date of the auditor's report.

The date of the auditor's report establishes the end of the subsequent period—the period during which an auditor has responsibility for events occurring after the client's year-end—unless the auditor agrees or is required to perform additional procedures, as for example, in filings with the SEC under the Securities Act of 1933, discussed later in this chapter. The higher levels of responsibility that auditors are now being held to, the increased demands of users for reliable financial information, and the fact that the report date signifies the end of the period of the auditor's responsibility for that information have all imparted greater significance to the date of the auditor's report.

The report date is seldom the last day the auditors are on the client's premises. Ancillary matters often require the audit team's presence after the completion of field work. For example, various regulatory reports, covenant letters, and communications to management may have to be prepared or completed. Separate audits may be required for employee benefit plans or related foundations.

A report date about 25 to 45 days after the end of the fiscal year is common for publicly held commercial and manufacturing companies; 15 to 20 days is usual for commercial banks. It then may take several weeks for the published annual report containing the financial statements to be prepared, printed, and mailed, but the auditor's report carries the date on which agreement on the financial statements was reached (unless new information is incorporated in the statements—see the discussion under "Dual Dating," below).

Audit Planning Considerations. If an audit report must be issued within two or three weeks of year-end, the amount of auditing that can take place after year-end is obviously limited. Thus, much of the auditor's work must be essentially completed by year-end. This usually requires that the client have an effective internal control structure and always requires careful planning by the auditor. As indicated in Chapter 9, there are several strategies under which an auditor can perform substantive tests before the balance sheet date and have a reasonable basis for "rolling forward" conclusions from those tests to the balance sheet date.

Many companies, however, cannot or do not choose to seek such early publication of their financial statements. Also, depending on risk assessment, the auditor may find it necessary to perform much of the substantive testing after the balance sheet date, or problems may be encountered in making necessary valuations, estimates, and judgments. It may take 8 to 12 weeks, or even longer, for the audit to be completed. During that time, the auditor must "keep current" with client affairs so as to have a basis for an opinion that subsequent events are properly reflected or disclosed in the financial statements.

Dual Dating.   As described earlier, subsequent events that occur after the date of the auditor's report but before the report is issued and that come to the auditor's attention may require adjustment or disclosure in the financial statements. If such an event is disclosed, the auditor can either redate the report as of the date of that event or use "dual dating." In practice, unless the time period is very short, dual dating is more common because of the additional work (discussed above) necessary for the extended period if the report is redated.

An auditor may be required or requested to reissue a report after it was first issued. If the auditor is aware of subsequent events that occurred after the date of the original report, several alternatives are possible. For events that require adjustment of the previously issued financial statements, the report should be dual dated. For events that require disclosure only, the auditor may dual date the report, or the disclosure may be included in an additional (usually the last) note to the financial statements that is labeled "unaudited." When dual dating is used, it usually appears as "January 25, 19X9, except as to Note ___, for which the date is March 1, 19X9."

The Securities Act of 1933

Auditors' SEC practice is dealt with in entire volumes and is beyond the scope of this work. As mentioned in SAS No. 37, *Filings Under Federal Securities Statutes* (AU Section 711.02), "the accountant's responsibility, generally [when reporting on financial statements included in a filing with the SEC], is in substance no different from that involved in other types of reporting." A critical consideration in a 1933 Act filing, however, is that the independent auditor's responsibility with respect to subsequent events extends *to the effective date* of the registration statement and does not terminate at the date of the audit report. This situation results from Section 11(a) of the 1933 Act, which provides for substantial liabilities to those involved in the preparation of a registration statement found to contain untrue statements or material omissions. As pointed out in SAS No. 37 (AU Section 711.10), "To sustain the burden of proof that he has made a 'reasonable investigation,' . . . as required under the Securities Act of 1933, an auditor should extend his procedures with respect to subsequent events from the date of his audit report up to the effective date or as close thereto as is reasonable and practicable in the circumstances."

Subsequent Event Procedures for Keeping Current.   The procedures already discussed for keeping current with respect to subsequent events through the date of the auditor's report should be extended to the effective date of the registration statement. In addition, the auditor generally should read the entire prospectus and other pertinent sections of the registration statement.

Letters for Underwriters. The procedures for keeping current that were discussed above are separate and distinct from any procedures that may be required by underwriters in connection with a 1933 Act filing, even though they may frequently be performed at the same time. Letters for underwriters, commonly called "comfort letters," are the subject of SAS No. 49, *Letters for Underwriters* (AU Section 634), and are discussed in Chapter 23.

ADMINISTRATIVE WRAP-UP

After the audit has been completed and the working papers have been reviewed and filed, there are both technical and administrative loose ends to wrap up. Special reports, tax returns, and similar matters are likely to have due dates that act as a professional discipline, but it is easy to let administrative matters slide. Tight administrative controls are necessary to prevent that from happening.

Time analyses must be completed and budget variances analyzed. Billings must be prepared and processed. The audit program should be revised in preliminary preparation for the next year's engagement. Ideally, the next year's engagement should be planned with the client as part of the current wrapping-up process. On many well-organized engagements, the end of one engagement constitutes the beginning of the next.

COMMUNICATION WITH AUDIT COMMITTEES

Auditors usually acquire information in the course of an audit that may help the audit committee of the board of directors meet its responsibility for overseeing the entity's financial reporting process, including the audit itself. Various Statements on Auditing Standards require the auditor to communicate certain matters to the audit committee, or to determine that management has appropriately reported them. Those matters include material errors and irregularities, illegal acts, and significant deficiencies in the design or operation of the internal control structure that the auditor became aware of in the course of the audit, including deficiencies related to the preparation of interim financial information. The SEC Practice Section of the AICPA Division for CPA Firms requires the auditor to communicate to the audit committee fees received for management advisory services.

SAS No. 61, *Communication With Audit Committees* (AU Section 380), requires the auditor to determine that certain additional matters related to the conduct of an audit are communicated to those who have responsibility for financial reporting; generally, this means the audit committee. The required communications are applicable to all SEC engagements (as defined in Chapter 3) and to other entities that have an audit committee or equivalent group with formally designated oversight of the financial reporting process. Among the items that should be communicated are

- The level of responsibility the auditor assumes under GAAS for the financial statements and for considering the entity's internal control structure.

- Significant accounting policies that the entity has selected for new or unusual transactions, and changes in those policies.

- The process management used to formulate particularly sensitive accounting estimates, and the basis for the auditor's conclusion that they were reasonable.

- Significant adjustments to the financial statements that resulted from the audit and that have a significant effect on the entity's financial reporting process.

- The auditor's responsibility for other information in documents, such as annual reports to shareholders, containing audited financial statements (see the discussion in the section, "Material Inconsistency Between Financial Statements and Other Information Reported by Management," in Chapter 22).

- Disagreements with management over the application of accounting principles, the scope of the audit, and the wording of the auditor's report.

- The auditor's views on auditing and accounting matters that management consulted other auditors about (see the discussions in Chapters 3 and 23).

- Major issues regarding the application of accounting principles and auditing standards that the auditor and management discussed in connection with the auditor's initial or recurring retention.

- Serious difficulties encountered in dealing with management related to the performance of the audit, such as unreasonable delays in permitting the start of the audit or in providing needed information, unreasonable timetables, or not making needed client personnel available.

As noted earlier, these matters may be communicated either by the auditor or by management, but the communications must be timely. Some matters should logically be discussed with the audit committee before the auditor's report is drafted, because the discussion may help the auditor form the appropriate conclusion about the financial statements. Others could occur after the report has been issued. The communication of recurring matters need not be repeated every year.

22

The Auditor's Report

An auditor's report is the formal result of all the effort that goes into an audit. There are many other results—for example, the direct and indirect impact of audits on the control, accountability, and public reporting practices of companies—and some people maintain that these are more significant, but the report is the specific, identifiable focal point for the auditor and for all those who rely on the audit.

This chapter covers the standard report (often called an unqualified or "clean" report or opinion), matters that require explicit attention in issuing a report, and the handling of variations from the standard report. Those variations fall into two categories—*explanatory language* in the standard report that does not constitute a qualified opinion, and *departures* from the standard report to express other than an unqualified opinion. The three types of departures from unqualified opinions—qualified opinions, adverse opinions, and disclaimers of opinion—what each conveys, and the circumstances in which each is appropriate are examined in detail, with illustrations. The chapter also includes a discussion of the auditor's responsibilities after the report date.

STANDARD REPORTS

The auditor's report that appears in Figure 22.1 indicates the wording of the standard report prescribed by SAS No. 58, *Reports on Audited Financial Statements* (AU Section 508), issued in 1988.

Organization and Wording

The following paragraphs explain the language used in the standard report and its organization.

Title. The title should include the word "independent," as in the phrase "Independent Auditor's Report." This is intended to remind the reader of the credibility an audit adds to the financial statements because of the auditor's independence.

Introductory Paragraph. The opening paragraph of the report identifies the financial statements that were audited and states that management is responsible for them.[1] The auditor's responsibility is to give an opinion on those statements based on the results of the audit. The phrase "we have audited" implies that the auditor is providing the highest level of assurance that can be

---

[1]Many publicly traded companies include reports by management in their financial statements. Those reports usually contain a statement of management's responsibility for the financial statements. An auditing interpretation of SAS No. 58 (AU Section 9508.51) indicates that the statement about management's responsibility for the financial statements that appears in the introductory paragraph of the auditor's standard report should not be further elaborated on nor should it refer to a management report. Such modifications of the auditor's report might lead to unwarranted assumptions that the auditor was providing assurance about representations made by management about its responsibility for financial reporting, internal control, and other matters that might be discussed in the management report. Management reports are discussed further in Chapter 23.

Figure 22.1   Auditor's Standard Report

Report of Independent Accountants

To the Stockholders and Board of Directors of NYNEX Corporation:

We have audited the accompanying consolidated balance sheets of NYNEX Corporation and its subsidiaries as of December 31, 1988 and 1987, and related consolidated statements of income, changes in stockholders' equity, and cash flows for each of the three years in the period ended December 31, 1988. These consolidated financial statements are the responsibility of NYNEX Corporation's management. Our responsibility is to express an opinion on these consolidated financial statements based on our audits.

We conducted our audits in accordance with generally accepted auditing standards. Those standards require that we plan and perform the audit to obtain reasonable assurance about whether the consolidated financial statements are free of material misstatement. An audit includes examining, on a test basis, evidence supporting the amounts and disclosures in the consolidated financial statements. An audit also includes assessing the accounting principles used and significant estimates made by management, as well as evaluating the overall consolidated financial statement presentation. We believe that our audits provide a reasonable basis for our opinion.

In our opinion, the consolidated financial statements referred to above present fairly, in all material respects, the consolidated financial position of NYNEX Corporation and its subsidiaries as of December 31, 1988 and 1987, and the results of their operations and their cash flows for each of the three years in the period ended December 31, 1988, in conformity with generally accepted accounting principles.

Coopers & Lybrand

New York, New York
February 7, 1989

given. (Lower levels of assurance can be provided in other types of engagements, such as "reviews.") The introductory paragraph also specifies the dates of and periods covered by the financial statements that were audited.

It is important that the reader of the document in which the financial statements appear know precisely what is covered by the auditor's report and, by inference, what is not. Since an annual report or prospectus contains much more than the financial statements, the reader must be told specifically what has been audited (the financial statements and the related notes that are, as stated on each page of the body of the financial statements, an "integral part of the financial statements") and what, by implication, has not been audited, such as the letter from the president and chairman of the board, financial ratios, and information about stock prices.

Scope Paragraph. The scope paragraph describes the auditor's basis for forming the opinion on the financial statements. Telling the reader that the audit was conducted in accordance with generally accepted auditing standards is the equivalent of saying that the auditor has complied with the standards established by the auditing profession for performing an audit. The auditor's objective in performing an audit is to gather enough evidence to enable him or her to provide *reasonable* assurance, but not a guarantee, that the financial statements do not contain material misstatements. (A misstatement is considered material if it is probable that the judgment of a reasonable person relying on the financial statements would have been changed or influenced by the misstatement.)

The scope paragraph includes a thumbnail sketch of what an audit entails. It notes that evidence about the accounting measurements and disclosures in the financial statements was obtained only on a test basis. To do otherwise would be economically prohibitive and would entail costs that society as a whole would not be willing to pay. The report specifically states that assessing the client's accounting principles, the estimates that are part of the financial statements, and the overall financial statement presentation are key elements of an audit. Last, the auditor explicitly states that the evidence obtained and evaluated in the course of the audit was sufficient to support the opinion given.

Opinion Paragraph. The opinion paragraph of the auditor's report—usually the third, and final, paragraph—states the auditor's conclusions reached from the work performed. The auditor's opinion represents a judgment made after evaluating evidence about the assertions implicit in the financial statements; the phrase "in our opinion" is intended to convey this element of judgment, as opposed to a statement of fact. (As discussed later, in some cases the auditor may be unable to form an opinion.)

The conclusion the auditor reaches in most audits of financial statements is that the financial statements "present fairly . . . in conformity with generally accepted accounting principles."[2] The opinion illustrated here is technically called an unqualified opinion—that is, it is not qualified by any exceptions. A

[2]Note that the illustrative opinion is about the financial statements, not about individual account balances. The auditor may express an opinion about specific accounts, rather than about the financial statements taken as a whole, in a "special report," which is discussed in Chapter 23.

less technical term for an unqualified opinion is a "clean" opinion. Although authoritative AICPA literature describes other types of opinions (qualified opinions, adverse opinions, and disclaimers of opinion), the usual expectation is that the auditor will be able to render a positive, unqualified opinion. Anything less is usually undesirable, and often unacceptable either to the client or to regulatory bodies. Users of financial statements are best served if the client's financial statements do "present fairly . . . in conformity with generally accepted accounting principles." Thus, auditors have a responsibility to both the public and their clients to assist clients in receiving an unqualified opinion by seeking to improve their financial reporting practices, when that may be necessary.

Until 1988, generally accepted auditing standards required a reference to consistency in the auditor's report. That requirement was eliminated by SAS No. 58, which requires the auditor to report only a *lack* of consistency in the application of GAAP.

History of the Standard Report

The wording of the auditor's report went through several changes before the present-day report was adopted in 1988. In the early 1920s, a typical audit report (covering a single year) was worded as follows:

We have audited the accounts and records of the XYZ Company for the fiscal year ended March 31, 1920, and hereby Certify that, in our opinion, the annexed Balance Sheet correctly reflects the financial condition of the Company at March 31, 1920, subject to the liability for Federal Income and Profits Taxes accrued at that date.

It should be noted that this report refers to an audit of the "accounts and records" as opposed to the financial statements and that the auditors "certified" the balance sheet as being "correct." By the early 1930s, the accounting profession had come to the realization that it would be unwise to continue to use the word "certify" or similar words in the audit opinion. The word "certify" gives the reader the incorrect impression that the contents of the audited financial statements are subject to precise measurements and that the auditor could guarantee the exactness of the data in those statements.

Changes to the report in the 1930s deleted the word "certify" and introduced two new concepts: consistency of application of accepted accounting principles and fair presentation. Also, the scope paragraph of the report clarified the extent of the examination and included a specific reference to the review of internal control.

The SEC stated in 1941 that the auditor must indicate whether the examination was made in accordance with "generally accepted auditing standards" and whether all procedures that were deemed necessary were carried out. As a result, the AICPA promptly initiated a change in the wording of the audit report. The 1941 audit report follows:

We have examined the balance sheet of the XYZ Company as of February 28, 1941, and the statements of income and surplus for the fiscal year then ended, have reviewed the system of internal control and the accounting procedures of the company and, without making a detailed audit of the transactions, have examined or tested accounting records of the company and other supporting evidence, by methods and to the extent we deemed appropriate. Our examination was made in accordance with generally accepted auditing standards applicable in the circumstances and included all procedures which we considered necessary.

In our opinion, the accompanying balance sheet and related statements of income and surplus present fairly the position of the XYZ Company at February 28, 1941, and the results of its operations for the fiscal year, in conformity with generally accepted accounting principles applied on a basis consistent with that of the preceding year.

In 1944, further modifications were made, such as deleting mention of some of the specific procedures carried out by the auditor. This change was based on the recognition that "generally accepted auditing standards" encompassed the stated auditing procedures, therefore making the enumeration redundant. Minor modifications were made in 1948, and for the next 40 years the report read essentially as follows:

We have examined the balance sheet of X Company as of December 31, 19XX, and the related statements of income and retained earnings and changes in financial position for the year then ended. Our examination was made in accordance with generally accepted auditing standards and, accordingly, included such tests of the accounting records and such other auditing procedures as we considered necessary in the circumstances.

In our opinion, the financial statements referred to above present fairly the financial position of X Company at December 31, 19XX, and the results of its operations and the changes in its financial position for the year then ended, in conformity with generally accepted accounting principles applied on a basis consistent with that of the preceding year.

The Meaning of Fair Presentation in Conformity with GAAP

The first standard of reporting states

The report shall state whether the financial statements are presented in accordance with generally accepted accounting principles.

Generally accepted accounting principles provide a consistent frame of reference against which each of management's assertions that are implicit in the financial statements can be evaluated. Obviously, an auditor must be thoroughly familiar with generally accepted accounting principles to comply responsibly with this standard. The literature is vast on accounting principles and the meaning of "generally accepted." Nevertheless, the accounting profession has been criticized for failure to promulgate GAAP that would provide even more detailed guidance.

Despite acknowledged deficiencies in generally accepted accounting principles, aggravated by some misunderstanding by nonaccountants, the phrase is generally understood by practitioners and many users of the report as well.

Paragraph 138 of APB Statement No. 4, *Basic Concepts and Accounting Principles Underlying Financial Statements of Business Enterprises*, defines generally accepted accounting principles as "the conventions, rules, and procedures necessary to define accepted accounting practice at a particular time." The Commission on Auditors' Responsibilities (Cohen Commission) noted that generally accepted accounting principles

> Are not limited to the principles in pronouncements of authoritative bodies such as the Financial Accounting Standards Board (FASB). They also include practices that have achieved acceptance through common usage as well as principles in nonauthoritative pronouncements of bodies of recognized stature such as the Accounting Standards Division of the American Institute of Certified Public Accountants. Too narrow a view of the scope of those principles by auditors and preparers has contributed to the criticism of both generally accepted accounting principles and auditors. (p. 15)

SAS No. 5, *The Meaning of "Present Fairly in Conformity With Generally Accepted Accounting Principles" in the Independent Auditor's Report*, as amended (AU Section 411), also suggests that in addition to the accounting principles covered by Rule 203 of the AICPA Code of Professional Conduct (FASB Statements, FASB Interpretations, APB Opinions, AICPA Accounting Research Bulletins, and Statements and Interpretations of the Governmental Accounting Standards Board [GASB]), there are other possible sources of GAAP. These other sources include AICPA industry audit and accounting guides and Statements of Position, FASB and GASB Technical Bulletins, AICPA Accounting Interpretations, prevalent industry accounting practices, and other accounting literature, such as APB Statements, AICPA Issues Papers and Practice Bulletins, minutes of the FASB Emerging Issues Task Force, FASB and GASB Concepts Statements, and Statements of the International Accounting Standards Committee, as well as accounting textbooks and articles. SAS No. 5 also notes that

> On occasion, established accounting principles may not exist for recording and presenting a specific event or transaction because of developments such as new legislation or the evolution of a new type of business transaction. In certain instances, it may be possible to account for the event or transaction on the basis of its substance by selecting an accounting principle that appears appropriate when applied in a manner similar to the application of an established principle to an analogous event or transaction.

Accountants generally agree that, unlike Newton's laws in physics, the accounting principles referred to in the first standard of reporting and in the auditor's opinion are not fundamental truths or comprehensive laws from which the details of practice are derived. As a result, accountants over the years have wrestled with specific situations arising in practice and have developed and adopted numerous rules, conventions, and doctrines, which are now called principles. Some of those principles have been promulgated formally by an authoritative body of the profession (such as the FASB, the GASB, or the APB) or by the SEC, but often they represent a consensus of professional bodies, prominent writers, and eminent practitioners. As suggested earlier, all of those accepted conventions constitute the body of GAAP.

There have been efforts to expand the first reporting standard to require auditors to report on "fairness" separately from GAAP. The reason for these attempts is a belief in some quarters that it is possible to prepare financial statements that conform with GAAP but that nevertheless are not presented fairly and may in fact be misleading. Unfortunately, there has been some basis for that view in the past, principally because some preparers and auditors took a much narrower view of what constitutes GAAP than was explained earlier. SAS No. 5 (AU Section 411) clarified the situation by setting forth what the term "generally accepted accounting principles" encompassed (essentially, what was described earlier), and by noting that the auditor's judgment concerning the fairness of financial statement presentation should be applied within that frame of reference. Clearly, "fairness" is too loose a term to be practical or useful unless it is defined within a specific frame of reference, that is, GAAP. Some auditors believe that the word "fairly" should be removed from the auditor's opinion; that proposal has met strong resistance, particularly from the SEC.

The SAS also enumerated the various judgments that the auditor must make before rendering an unqualified opinion. The auditor's positive opinion about fair presentation in conformity with generally accepted accounting principles implies a belief that the financial statements have the following qualities:

1. The accounting principles selected and applied have general acceptance;
2. The accounting principles are appropriate in the circumstances;
3. The financial statements, including the related notes, are informative on matters that may affect their use, understanding, and interpretation;
4. The information presented in the financial statements is classified and summarized in a reasonable manner, that is, neither too detailed nor too condensed; and
5. The financial statements reflect the underlying events and transactions in a manner that presents financial position, results of operations, and cash flows stated within a range of acceptable limits—that is, limits that are reasonable and practicable to attain in financial statements. (SAS No. 5 [AU Section 411.04])

Routine Variations in the Standard Report

Routine variations in the wording of the standard report include the party or parties to whom it is addressed, the identification of the statements reported on, the period(s) covered, and the date of the report. An auditor should not alter the standard report unless there are problems or unusual conditions to be highlighted—and then the alterations should follow the carefully drawn rules referred to in the following sections of this chapter—because any departure from the standard words is usually regarded as some sort of warning to the reader.

Addressing the Report.   The report may be addressed to the client company itself or to its board of directors or stockholders. The authors believe auditors have a responsibility to the owners of a business enterprise and therefore that the report should be addressed to the stockholders, board of directors and stockholders, partners, or proprietor. The authors also believe reports generally should not be addressed solely to the board of directors, unless the company is closely held. An auditor's ultimate responsibility is to the stockholders rather than to the company or its management.

Sometimes an auditor is retained to audit the financial statements of a nonclient company on behalf of a client. In that case, the report should be addressed to the client and not to the company being audited or its directors or stockholders (but see the discussion about confidentiality in Chapter 3, concerning the necessity for making sure that all parties involved understand the auditor's responsibility).

Identifying the Statements.   The statements should be clearly identified, usually in the introductory paragraph. The exact name of the company should be used and the statements audited should be enumerated. Generally, these are the balance sheet, the statement of income and retained earnings, and the statement of cash flows. If any other statements are covered by the report, they should also be enumerated; for example, some companies present a separate statement of changes in stockholders' equity accounts. Sometimes it is more convenient to refer to an accompanying list or table of contents that enumerates the statements, in which case the first sentence of the scope paragraph would read as follows: "We have audited the financial statements of X Company listed in the accompanying table of contents." The enumeration of the statements need not be repeated in the opinion paragraph.

Periods Covered.   The periods reported on should also be specified. In annual reports it is common to report on two years for comparative purposes. Companies whose securities are registered with the SEC are, however, required to present audited comparative income statements and statements of cash flows for three years and balance sheets for two years. A continuing auditor should update his or her report on the individual financial statements of the one or more prior periods presented on a comparative basis with those of the current period by referring to those statements in the introductory and opinion paragraphs.[3]

Dating the Report.   Inevitably, an auditor's report is issued on a date later than the end of the period being reported on because it takes time to close the books, prepare financial statements, and complete final auditing procedures. The selection of the appropriate date is discussed in Chapter 21.

[3]SAS No. 58 states in a footnote to paragraph 74 (AU Section 508.74)

> An updated report on prior-period financial statements should be distinguished from a reissuance of a previous report . . . since in issuing an updated report the continuing auditor considers information that he has become aware of during his audit of the current-period financial statements . . . and because an updated report is issued in conjunction with the auditor's report on the current-period financial statements.

See also the discussion later in this chapter, "Different Reports on Comparative Financial Statements Presented."

EXPLANATORY LANGUAGE ADDED TO THE STANDARD REPORT

There are several circumstances that while not affecting the auditor's unqualified opinion may require that the auditor add an explanatory paragraph (or other explanatory language) to the standard report. Those circumstances are discussed in the following paragraphs.

Opinion Based in Part on Report of Another Auditor

Chapter 6 discusses audit planning considerations when part of an engagement is carried out by another auditor. The auditor who serves as the principal auditor may decide not to refer to that circumstance in the report, thus assuming responsibility for the work of the other auditor. If the principal auditor does refer to the work of the other auditor, the standard report is expanded to indicate the division of responsibility and the magnitude of the portion of the financial statements audited by the other auditor. Normally, this is done by noting the percentage or dollar amount of total assets and total revenues audited by the other auditor. Sometimes, other appropriate criteria, such as the percentage of net income, may be used. The other auditor usually is not named. When other auditors are named, their express permission must be obtained and their reports must be presented together with that of the principal auditor.

If the other auditor's report contains explanatory language or a departure from an unqualified opinion (see the later discussion), the principal auditor should decide whether the cause of the explanatory language or departure is of such a nature and significance, in relation to the financial statements the principal auditor is reporting on, that it requires explanatory language or a departure from an unqualified opinion in the principal auditor's report. If the subject of the explanatory language or departure is not material to the overall financial statements, and if the other auditor's report is not presented, the principal auditor need not refer to the explanatory language or departure. If the other auditor's report is presented, the principal auditor may nevertheless wish to make reference to the explanatory language or departure and its disposition.

An example of an unqualified report (on comparative financial statements) in which the work of another auditor has been used and is referred to follows[4]:

> We have audited the consolidated balance sheets of ABC Company as of December 31, 19X2 and 19X1, and the related consolidated statements of income, retained earnings, and cash flows for the years then ended. These financial statements are the responsibility of the Company's management. Our responsibility is to express an opinion on these financial statements based on our audits.

---

[4]SAS No. 58 (AU Section 508.08) specifies that a title that includes the word "independent" is one of the basic elements of the standard audit report. The illustrative standard reports in AU Section 508 use the title "Independent Auditor's Report." This and subsequent illustrative audit reports present only the body of the report and omit the title, as well as the date of the report and signature of the auditor's firm.

We did not audit the financial statements of B Company, a wholly-owned subsidiary, which statements reflect total assets of $ _____ and $ _____ as of December 31, 19X2 and 19X1, respectively, and total revenues of $ _____ and $ _____ for the years then ended. Those statements were audited by other auditors whose report has been furnished to us, and our opinion, insofar as it relates to the amounts included for B Company, is based solely on the report of the other auditors.

We conducted our audits in accordance with generally accepted auditing standards. Those standards require that we plan and perform the audit to obtain reasonable assurance about whether the financial statements are free of material misstatement. An audit includes examining, on a test basis, evidence supporting the amounts and disclosures in the financial statements. An audit also includes assessing the accounting principles used and significant estimates made by management, as well as evaluating the overall financial statement presentation. We believe that our audits and the report of other auditors provide a reasonable basis for our opinion.

In our opinion, based on our audits and the report of other auditors, the consolidated financial statements referred to above present fairly, in all material respects, the financial position of ABC Company as of December 31, 19X2 and 19X1, and the results of its operations and its cash flows for the years then ended in conformity with generally accepted accounting principles.

The disclosure is lengthy and somewhat awkward and much expanded from reporting practice of some years ago when it was customary only to state that part of the engagement had been carried out by other auditors. Employing more than one auditor is an acceptable practice, but inevitably results in divided responsibility and risk of misunderstanding or omission. The practice is sometimes followed, however, to take advantage of specialized expertise or when the principal auditor is not located in areas served by other auditors. Chapter 6 includes a discussion of additional procedures the principal auditor may follow when the work of other auditors is used.

Also as discussed in Chapter 6, an auditor may obtain and use a report by another auditor on internal control at a service organization that is used by the client to execute or record certain transactions or to process certain data. The auditor's report on the financial statements should not refer to the report of the auditor who reported on the service organization's internal control. As stated in AU Section 324.24, "The service [organization's] auditor's report is used in the audit, but the service [organization's] auditor is not responsible for examining a portion of the financial statements. . . . Thus, there cannot be a meaningful indication of a division of responsibility for the financial statements."

Departures from a Promulgated Accounting Principle with Which an Auditor Agrees

Since 1964, members of the AICPA have been expected to treat departures from accounting principles promulgated in the Opinions of the APB and in the predecessor Accounting Research Bulletins as departures from GAAP, leading to a qualified or an adverse opinion. That expectation is now incorporated in

Rule 203 of the AICPA Code of Professional Conduct and the related interpretations; it also applies to the pronouncements of the FASB and the GASB. It is covered as a special case in paragraphs 14 and 15 of SAS No. 58 (AU Section 508.14–.15).

In rare and unusual circumstances, a departure from an accounting principle promulgated by the APB, the FASB, or the GASB may be required to present a particular transaction or other event or circumstance in a manner that is not misleading. If the auditor and client agree that a certain treatment that departs from such a promulgated principle is required in order to make the statements not misleading, it is permissible for the financial statements to reflect the departure, provided the departure and its effect are disclosed both in a note to the financial statements and in the auditor's report. The reason for believing that the departure from a promulgated standard is justified should be stated, and the auditor should then express an unqualified opinion.

Although the kind of "unusual circumstances" referred to herein might conceivably exist in which the literal application of a pronouncement covered by Rule 203 would have the effect of making the financial statements misleading, instances of this kind arise only very rarely. Consequently, this type of opinion modification is rare and a recent example of it could not be located. The best-known example of that circumstance dates back to a report on a company's financial statements for the year ended December 31, 1973. An explanatory paragraph therein read as follows:

> In October, 1973, the Company extinguished a substantial amount of debt through a direct exchange of new equity securities. Application of Opinion No. 26 of the Accounting Principles Board to this exchange requires that the excess of the debt extinguished over the present value of the new securities should be recognized as a gain in the period in which the extinguishment occurred. While it is not practicable to determine the present value of the new equity securities issued, such value is at least $2,000,000 less than the face amount of the debt extinguished. It is the opinion of the Company's Management, an opinion with which we agree, that no realization of a gain occurred in this exchange (Note 1), and therefore, no recognition of the excess of the debt extinguished over the present value of the new securities has been made in these financial statements.

Note 1 read (in part) as follows:

> *Extinguishment of Debt*: In October, 1973, the Company issued 50,000 shares of 6% Prior Preferred Shares, par value $100, in exchange for the outstanding $5,000,000 of 6% senior subordinated notes. It also issued 18,040 shares of convertible $6 Serial Preference Shares, Series A, stated value $100 a share, in exchange for $1,300,000 and $504,000 of outstanding 6% convertible subordinated debentures and 5 3/4% convertible subordinated debentures, respectively. The Company expensed the unamortized balance (approximately $148,000) of the deferred financing costs associated with the issuance of each of the three classes of subordinated debt to the extent that such unamortized balances were allocable to the debt so extinguished.

> Opinion No. 26 of the Accounting Principles Board of the American Institute of CPA's states that the excess of the carrying amount of the extinguished debt over the present value of the new securities issued should be recognized as a gain in

the statement of operations of the period in which the extinguishment occurred. While it is not practicable to determine the present value of the new equity securities issued, such value is at least $2,000,000 less than the face amount of the debt extinguished. However, the terms and provisions of these new equity securities [which included a mandatory redemption provision] are substantially similar to those of the debt securities extinguished, both on the basis of the Company's continuing operations and in the event of liquidation. It is the opinion of the management, therefore, that no gain as a result of this exchange has been realized or should be recognized in the financial statements.

The auditors believed that the financial statements *were* presented fairly in conformity with GAAP, which would not have been the case if APB Opinion No. 26 had been followed. In this instance, the auditors did not, in the opinion paragraph, qualify the opinion as a result of the described departure from a promulgated accounting principle.

Predecessor Auditor's Report Not Presented

When comparative financial statements are presented and the prior year's statements were audited by another auditor, the successor auditor and the client have two options concerning the auditor's report. Under the first option, the client could make arrangements with the predecessor auditor to reissue the report on the financial statements of the prior period, provided the predecessor auditor performs the procedures described in paragraph 80 of SAS No. 58 (AU Section 508.80). Paragraph 80 requires that before reissuing a previously issued report, a predecessor auditor should consider whether the previous opinion is still appropriate. To do that,

A predecessor auditor should (a) read the financial statements of the current period, (b) compare the prior-period financial statements that he reported on with the financial statements to be presented for comparative purposes, and (c) obtain a letter of representations from the successor auditor.

The predecessor auditor should not refer in the reissued report to the report of the successor auditor. The successor auditor should report only on the current year's financial statements.

Under the second option, the predecessor auditor's report is not presented.[5] In this case, pursuant to paragraph 83 of SAS No. 58 (AU Section 508.83),

The successor auditor should indicate in the introductory paragraph of his report (a) that the financial statements of the prior period were audited by another auditor, (b) the date of his report, (c) the type of report issued by the predecessor auditor, and (d) if the report was other than a standard report, the substantive reasons therefor.

---

[5]SEC proxy Rule 14c-3 permits the separate report of the predecessor auditor to be omitted in the annual report to securityholders, provided the registrant has obtained a reissued report from the predecessor auditor. The separate report of the predecessor auditor is, however, required in filings with the Commission.

An example of a successor auditor's report when the predecessor auditor's report is not presented follows:

> We have audited the balance sheet of ABC Company as of December 31, 19X2, and the related statements of income, retained earnings, and cash flows for the year then ended. These financial statements are the responsibility of the Company's management. Our responsibility is to express an opinion on these financial statements based on our audit. The financial statements of ABC Company as of December 31, 19X1, were audited by other auditors whose report dated March 31, 19X2, expressed an unqualified opinion on those statements.
>
> [*Same second paragraph as the standard report*]
>
> In our opinion, the 19X2 financial statements referred to above present fairly, in all material respects, the financial position of ABC Company as of December 31, 19X2, and the results of its operations and its cash flows for the year then ended in conformity with generally accepted accounting principles.

If the predecessor auditor's report was other than a standard report, the successor auditor should describe the nature of and reasons for any explanatory paragraphs or opinion qualifications.

Report on a Balance Sheet Only

In certain instances, an auditor may be asked to report only on a client's balance sheet, rather than on all of the financial statements. This may occur in filings under debt or credit agreements. The following is an example (from AU Section 508.48) of a report on a balance sheet only:

> We have audited the accompanying balance sheet of X Company as of December 31, 19XX. This financial statement is the responsibility of the Company's management. Our responsibility is to express an opinion on this financial statement based on our audit.
>
> We conducted our audit in accordance with generally accepted auditing standards. Those standards require that we plan and perform the audit to obtain reasonable assurance about whether the balance sheet is free of material misstatement. An audit includes examining, on a test basis, evidence supporting the amounts and disclosures in the balance sheet. An audit also includes assessing the accounting principles used and significant estimates made by management, as well as evaluating the overall balance sheet presentation. We believe that our audit of the balance sheet provides a reasonable basis for our opinion.
>
> In our opinion, the balance sheet referred to above presents fairly, in all material respects, the financial position of X Company as of December 31, 19XX, in conformity with generally accepted accounting principles.

Material Inconsistency Between Financial Statements and Other Information Reported by Management

An enterprise may publish a document, such as an annual report, that contains information in addition to audited financial statements and the auditor's report. That information, which is referred to in professional pronouncements (SAS No. 8, *Other Information in Documents Containing Audited Financial Statements* [AU Section 550]) as "other information," includes such items as a ten-year financial summary and an analysis of financial data in the president's letter. It also includes management's discussion and analysis of operations (for the three most recent years) and of changes in financial position and liquidity (during the two most recent years), as required of enterprises whose securities are registered with the SEC. In addition, an auditing interpretation (AU Section 9550.01–.06) indicates that statements made in a report by management on the entity's internal control structure are "other information" covered by SAS No. 8.

The auditor has no responsibility to corroborate "other information," but SAS No. 8 specifies that the auditor does have a responsibility to read it and consider whether it is materially inconsistent with information appearing in the financial statements. If it is, the auditor should request the client to revise the other information. If the other information is not revised to eliminate the inconsistency, the auditor should consider whether to withhold the audit report, withdraw from the engagement, or include an explanatory paragraph describing the inconsistency.[6] The auditor's opinion would still be unqualified, since the deficiency would not be in the audited financial statements. Such instances are, as might be expected, extremely rare, since even management that is prone to "puffery" of its accomplishments is likely to retreat in the face of the possibility of an explanatory comment in the auditor's report.

Another problem arises when the auditor, on reading the other information, determines (on the basis of knowledge obtained in the course of the audit) that there is a material misstatement of fact that is not related to information in the audited financial statements. Beyond suggesting that the auditor consult others, including legal counsel, and notify the client, the authoritative literature provides scant guidance; nor does the literature require the auditor to disclose the misstatement. The Cohen Commission recommended (page 69) that the auditor be required to read the other information to ensure that it is not inconsistent with *anything* the auditor knows, as a result of the audit, about the company and its operations and that the auditor modify the report to describe the misstatement if management does not correct it. At the date of this writing, no professional standard-setting body has acted on this recommendation.

Supplementary Information Required by FASB or GASB Pronouncements

Supplementary information required by the FASB or the GASB differs from other types of information outside the basic financial statements. This is because the FASB or the GASB considers the information an essential part of the financial reporting of certain entities and has, therefore, established guidelines for the measurement and presentation of the information. For this reason, the AICPA has established limited procedures to be applied by the

---

[6]As discussed in Chapter 23, an explanatory paragraph is also required if selected quarterly financial data required by SEC Regulation S-K has been omitted by the client or has not been reviewed by the auditor.

auditor to this information. The limited procedures, found in AU Section 558, *Required Supplementary Information*, can be summarized as follows:

- Inquire of management as to any significant assumptions or interpretations underlying the measurement or presentation, whether the methods of measurement and presentation are within guidelines prescribed by the FASB or the GASB, whether the assumptions or methods have changed from those used in the prior period, and the reasons for any such changes.
- Compare the information for consistency with the audited financial statements, other knowledge obtained during the audit of the financial statements, and management's responses to the specific inquiries.
- Consider whether specific written representations on the information should be obtained from management.
- Make additional inquiries based on the results of the foregoing if the auditor believes that the measurement or presentation of the information may be inappropriate.

At the time of this writing, the only supplementary information required by the FASB or the GASB is oil and gas reserve information (SFAS No. 69, *Disclosures about Oil and Gas Producing Activities*) and ten-year historical trend pension information by public employee retirement systems and state and local governmental employers (GASB Statement No. 5, *Disclosure of Pension Information by Public Employee Retirement Systems and State and Local Government Employers*).

AU Section 558 specifies reporting guidelines, based on the performance of the limited procedures listed above, for FASB- or GASB-required information. If the information is presented in a note to the financial statements, it should be marked as ''unaudited'' or the auditor should expand the standard audit report to disclaim an opinion on the information. If the information appears outside the financial statements and the entity indicates that the auditor has performed procedures and does not also indicate that the auditor does not express an opinion on the information, the auditor should disclaim an opinion on the information. (If the required information has been audited, the auditor should follow the reporting guidance in SAS No. 42, *Reporting on Condensed Financial Statements and Selected Financial Data* [AU Section 552].) In addition, AU Section 558.08 provides only for exception reporting; that is, the auditor is required to report, in an additional explanatory paragraph (a) deficiencies in or the omission of such information, (b) an inability to complete the prescribed limited procedures, or (c) the inability to remove substantial doubts about whether the supplementary information conforms to prescribed guidelines.

Uncertainties

Management is expected to evaluate and reach a reasoned conclusion on all matters materially affecting financial position and results of operations, and an auditor is expected to review and form an opinion on those conclusions.

Sometimes, however, the financial statements are affected by uncertainties concerning future events, such as a lawsuit whose outcome cannot be reasonably estimated by either management or the auditor. Such uncertainties may give rise to explanatory paragraphs in the auditor's report, or possibly even to disclaimers when the uncertainties are pervasive (see discussion of disclaimers later in this chapter).

SFAS No. 5 (Accounting Standards Section C59.104) requires that potential losses due to uncertainties be classified as "probable," "reasonably possible," or "remote." If a loss is probable, management must provide for it in the financial statements, either by accruing it if the amount is susceptible to reasonable determination or by disclosing it if the amount cannot be reasonably estimated. No explanatory language is needed in the auditor's standard report if the auditor agrees that the provision or disclosure is appropriate; if the amount cannot be reasonably estimated, however, the auditor should add an explanatory paragraph to the report because of the uncertainty. Likewise, a "remote" uncertainty would not require an explanatory paragraph in the standard report. If a material loss is "reasonably possible," however, management is required to disclose the uncertainty in the notes to the financial statements, including an estimate of the amount, and the auditor would normally add an explanatory paragraph to the report.

For instance, if the outcome of a matter having an impact on the financial statements depends on the decisions of others, it may be impossible for management and the auditor to reach a valid conclusion about it because competent evidential matter simply does not exist. The most common events of that kind are lawsuits and tax disputes. The mere existence of an unresolved question does not relieve management or the auditor of the responsibility for forming a judgment about the outcome, if at all possible; for many disputed tax issues, for example, the outcome can be reasonably determined by an informed analysis. In some cases, however, the best possible efforts result in a judgment that no valid conclusion can be formed. In that event, the auditor should describe the uncertainty in a separate explanatory paragraph following the opinion paragraph of the report, along with an indication that its outcome cannot presently be determined. The separate paragraph may be shortened to refer to disclosures made in a note to the financial statements.

SAS No. 58 (AU Section 508.32) gives an example of the wording of a report containing an explanatory paragraph describing an uncertainty affecting the financial statements.

[Separate paragraph following the opinion paragraph]

As discussed in Note X to the financial statements, the Company is a defendant in a lawsuit alleging infringement of certain patent rights and claiming royalties and punitive damages. The Company has filed a counteraction, and preliminary hearings and discovery proceedings on both actions are in progress. The ultimate outcome of the litigation cannot presently be determined. Accordingly, no provision for any liability that may result upon adjudication has been made in the accompanying financial statements.

The Likelihood and Materiality of Uncertainties.   The auditor must use professional judgment in considering whether a loss resulting from the resolution of an uncertainty is sufficiently likely and material to require adding an explanatory paragraph in the report.

If the likelihood of a material loss is only remote, no explanatory paragraph would be necessary. If it is probable (likely) that a material loss will occur, but management cannot make a reasonable estimate of the amount or range of the potential loss and thus cannot accrue the loss in the financial statements, the auditor should add an explanatory paragraph. If the chance of a material loss is ''reasonably possible'' (that is, more than remote but less than probable), whether or not an explanatory paragraph should be added depends on the likelihood of the loss occurring (for example, whether that likelihood is closer to remote or to probable) and on by how much the possible loss exceeds the auditor's materiality threshold.

SAS No. 58 (AU Section 508.28–.30) offers the following guidance regarding materiality considerations in situations where uncertainties exist:

> Materiality judgments involving uncertainties are made in light of the surrounding circumstances. Some uncertainties relate primarily to financial position, while others more closely relate to results of operations or cash flows. Thus, for purposes of evaluating the materiality of a possible loss, the auditor should consider which, if any, of the financial statements is the more appropriate base in the circumstances.

> Some uncertainties are unusual in nature or infrequent in occurrence and thus more closely related to financial position than to normal, recurring operations (for example, litigation relating to alleged violations of antitrust or securities laws). In such instances, the auditor should consider the possible loss in relation to shareholder's equity and other relevant balance sheet components such as total assets, total liabilities, current assets, and current liabilities.

> In other instances, the nature of an uncertainty may be more closely related to normal, recurring operations (for example, litigation with a party to a royalty agreement concerning whether a royalty fee should be paid on certain revenues). In such circumstances, the auditor should consider the possible loss in relation to relevant income statement components such as income from continuing operations.

Going Concern.   One specific type of uncertainty the auditor must consider is the client's continued existence as a ''going concern.'' An entity is a going concern when it has the ability to continue in operation and meet its obligations. The concept that financial statements are prepared on the basis of a going concern is one of the basic tenets of financial accounting. Because the going concern assumption is so basic, the standard auditor's report does not make reference to it.

When the entity can continue in operation and meet its obligations only by selling substantial amounts of its assets outside the ordinary course of business or by its creditors' willingness to forgive or restructure its debt, such circumstances should raise doubts about whether the enterprise is a going concern. Doubts about the entity's continued existence should also raise questions about realizable value of assets, the order of payment of liabilities, the proper classification and carrying amounts of both, and the appropriateness of necessary financial statement disclosures. If the auditor concludes there is substantial doubt about the entity's ability to continue as a going concern for a reasonable period of time (not to exceed one year from the date of the financial statements), he or she should determine that this is appropriately disclosed in the financial statements and should include an explanatory paragraph in the auditor's report to reflect that conclusion.

SAS No. 59, *The Auditor's Consideration of an Entity's Ability to Continue as a Going Concern* (AU Section 341), provides guidance to the auditor for meeting an explicit responsibility to evaluate whether there is substantial doubt about the entity's ability to continue as a going concern for a reasonable period of time. This is done through the following steps:

1. *Consider whether the results of procedures performed in planning, gathering evidence relative to the various audit objectives, and completing the audit identify conditions and events that, when considered in the aggregate, indicate there could be substantial doubt about the entity's ability to continue as a going concern for a reasonable period of time.*

In a properly planned audit, it should not be necessary to design auditing procedures specifically directed at the going concern issue. The results of auditing procedures designed and performed to achieve other audit objectives should be sufficient for that purpose. For example, conditions and events that could raise doubts may be identified through some of the following procedures: analytical procedures; review of subsequent events; review of compliance with the terms of debt and loan agreements; reading of minutes of meetings of stockholders, board of directors, and important committees of the board; inquiry of the entity's lawyers about litigation, claims, and assessments; and confirmation with related and third parties of the details of arrangements to provide or maintain financial support.

In considering the evidence provided by those procedures, it may be necessary for the auditor to obtain additional information about conditions and events identified that could create substantial doubt about the entity's ability to continue as a going concern. Their significance will depend on the circumstances. SAS No. 59 (AU Section 341.06) gives the following examples of such conditions and events, some of which are interrelated:

Negative trends—for example, recurring operating losses, working capital deficiencies, negative cash flows from operating activities, adverse key financial ratios.

Other indications of possible financial difficulties—for example, default on loan or similar agreements, arrearages in dividends, denial of usual trade credit from suppliers, restructuring of debt, noncompliance with statutory capital requirements, need to seek new sources or methods of financing or to dispose of substantial assets.

Internal matters—for example, work stoppages or other labor difficulties, substantial dependence on the success of a particular project, uneconomic long-term commitments, need to significantly revise operations.

External matters that have occurred—for example, legal proceedings, legislation, or similar matters that might jeopardize an entity's ability to operate; loss of a key franchise, license, or patent; loss of a principal customer or supplier; uninsured or underinsured catastrophe such as a drought, earthquake, or flood.

2. *If substantial doubt exists about the entity's ability to continue as a going concern for a reasonable period of time, obtain information about management's plans that are intended to mitigate the adverse effects of the conditions or events that gave rise to the doubt, and assess the likelihood that such plans can be effectively implemented.*

Those plans might include plans to dispose of assets, reduce or delay expenditures, borrow money or restructure debt, or increase ownership equity. In evaluating those plans, the auditor should consider whether there is adequate evidence supporting management's ability to carry out the plans. For example, plans to dispose of assets could be difficult or impossible to accomplish if there are restrictive covenants in loan agreements limiting such disposals. When prospective financial information is particularly significant to management's plans, the auditor should request management to provide that information and should consider whether there is adequate support for the significant assumptions underlying it.

3. *After evaluating management's plans, conclude whether substantial doubt exists about the entity's ability to continue as a going concern for a reasonable period of time.*

If the auditor concludes there *is* substantial doubt, he or she should then consider the adequacy of financial statement disclosure about the entity's possible inability to continue as a going concern *and include an explanatory paragraph* (following the opinion paragraph) in the audit report to reflect that conclusion. (If the entity's disclosures with respect to its ability to continue as a going concern are inadequate, a departure from generally accepted accounting principles exists and would result in either a qualified or an adverse opinion, as explained later in this chapter.) An example of such a paragraph from SAS No. 59 (AU Section 341.13) follows:

> The accompanying financial statements have been prepared assuming that the Company will continue as a going concern. As discussed in Note X to the financial statements, the Company has suffered recurring losses from operations and has a net capital deficiency that raise substantial doubt about its ability to continue as a going concern. Management's plans in regard to these matters are also described in Note X. The financial statements do not include any adjustments that might result from the outcome of this uncertainty.[7]

---

[7]SAS No. 59 provides the following guidance when substantial doubt that formerly existed no longer exists:

> If substantial doubt about the entity's ability to continue as a going concern for a reasonable period of time existed at the date of prior period financial statements that are presented on a comparative basis, and that doubt has been removed in the current period, the explanatory paragraph included in the auditor's report (following the opinion paragraph) on the financial statements of the prior period should not be repeated.

Financial statement disclosures about the entity's ability to continue as a going concern might include the following information (as described in SAS No. 59 [AU Section 341.10]):

- Pertinent conditions and events giving rise to the assessment of substantial doubt about the entity's ability to continue as a going concern for a reasonable period of time.
- The possible effects of such conditions and events.
- Management's evaluation of the significance of those conditions and events and any mitigating factors.
- Possible discontinuance of operations.
- Management's plans (including relevant prospective financial information).
- Information about the recoverability or classification of recorded asset amounts or the amounts or classification of liabilities. . . .

If, after considering management's plans, substantial doubt about the entity's ability to continue as a going concern does *not* exist, the auditor should still consider whether the principal conditions and events that initially generated the doubt need to be disclosed. The consideration of disclosure should include the possible effects of those conditions and events and any mitigating factors, including management's plans.

SAS No. 59 (AU Section 341.04) notes that

> The auditor is not responsible for predicting future conditions or events. The fact that the entity may cease to exist as a going concern subsequent to receiving a report from the auditor that does not refer to substantial doubt, even within one year following the date of the financial statements, does not, in itself, indicate inadequate performance by the auditor. Accordingly, the absence of reference to substantial doubt in an auditor's report should not be viewed as providing assurance as to an entity's ability to continue as a going concern.

Operating in Bankruptcy or Liquidation.   Companies that continue operations while in bankruptcy and prepare financial statements on a "going concern basis" are also subject to the requirements of SAS No. 59. In that situation, the financial statements would ordinarily include extensive disclosures about the enterprise's legal status, and the auditor's report would ordinarily contain an explanatory paragraph conveying the existence of substantial doubt about the entity's ability to continue as a going concern and referring the reader to the disclosures in the financial statements. If the enterprise is in liquidation, or if liquidation appears probable, a liquidation basis of accounting would be considered GAAP. If the liquidation basis of accounting has been properly applied and adequate disclosures made, the auditor's report should be unqualified, with the addition of explanatory language stating that the entity is being liquidated. An auditing interpretation (AU Section 9508.33–.38) provides reporting guidance in this situation.

Lack of Consistency

The second standard of reporting is

> The report shall identify those circumstances in which . . . [generally accepted accounting] principles have not been consistently observed in the current period in relation to the preceding period.

The consistency standard requires an auditor to inform readers in the report if GAAP have not been applied consistently from period to period; consistency within a period and between periods is presumed unless otherwise disclosed. The objective is to ensure that changes in accounting principles that materially affect the comparability of financial statements between periods are highlighted in the auditor's report as well as in the financial statements.

Of course, factors other than consistent application of accounting principles also affect the comparability of financial statements between periods. For example, changed conditions that necessitate changes in accounting and changed conditions that are unrelated to accounting may exist. The effect of those other factors normally requires disclosure in the financial statements (covered by the third standard of reporting) but not explanatory language in the auditor's report. In requiring other effects on comparability to be disclosed only under the more general third standard, the profession has singled out the consistency of accounting principles for separate attention. The reason for the different treatment lies in the nature of alternative accounting principles: Alternatives that are considered generally accepted may in some cases be substituted one for another, thus changing accounting results without any change in the underlying economic substance—a sound and sometimes necessary practice that is obviously susceptible to abuse.

Changes in accounting principles occur fairly often. Companies from time to time change managements, operating philosophies, or judgments about which accounting principles are most appropriate for the company. Also, authoritative FASB and GASB pronouncements may change the way that various transactions or other events and circumstances are to be measured or reported.

Any significant change in accounting principle or method of applying a principle must be referred to in the auditor's report in an explanatory paragraph (following the opinion paragraph). That paragraph should identify the change and refer to the note in the financial statements that discusses the change. An example of an appropriate explanatory paragraph would be[8]

---

[8]SAS No. 58 (AU Section 508.36) notes that

> The addition of this explanatory paragraph in the auditor's report is required in reports on financial statements of subsequent years as long as the year of the change is presented and reported on. However, if the accounting change is accounted for by retroactive restatement of the financial statements affected, the additional paragraph is required only in the year of the change since, in subsequent years, all periods presented will be comparable.

An explanatory paragraph is also not required when a change in accounting principle that does not require a cumulative effect adjustment is made at the beginning of the earliest year presented and reported on.

As discussed in Note X to the financial statements, the Company changed its method of computing depreciation in 19X2.

The auditor's concurrence with a change is implicit unless he or she takes exception to it in the opinion.

Accounting Principles Board Opinion No. 20, *Accounting Changes* (Accounting Standards Sections A06 and A35), provides standards for accounting for and disclosing accounting changes in financial statements. Section 420, "Consistency of Application of Generally Accepted Accounting Principles," of SAS No. 1 (AU Section 420) provides guidelines for determining which accounting changes affect consistency and, therefore, require an explanatory paragraph in the auditor's report.

Identifying Changes in Accounting Principles.   Both the Opinion and SAS No. 1 distinguish changes in accounting principles from changes in accounting estimates or changes in the reporting entity. The three kinds of changes, called collectively "accounting changes," are further distinguished from other factors affecting the comparability of financial statements between periods, including errors in previously issued statements, changes in statement classification, initial adoption of an accounting principle to recognize an event occurring for the first time, and adoption or modification of an accounting principle necessitated by transactions that are clearly different in substance from previous transactions. Of all classes mentioned, only changes in accounting principles and, sometimes, changes in the reporting entity require an explanatory paragraph in an auditor's report under the second standard of reporting. Of course, the others may have to be either disclosed or commented on under the third standard of reporting.

Justification for Changes in Accounting Principles.   An important advance in disclosure standards was the requirement in APB Opinion No. 20 (Accounting Standards Section A06), issued in 1971, that a change in accounting principle be justified by a clear explanation by management of why the newly adopted principle is preferable and that the justification be disclosed in the financial statements. Requiring that changes in accounting principles be justified was a significant step toward expecting issuers of financial statements to explain the "why" of their accounting as well as the "what." It should be noted, however, that while Opinion No. 20 prescribes that a note to the financial statements explain clearly why a newly adopted accounting principle is preferable, the authoritative literature of the profession does not explicitly require the auditor to be satisfied as to that preferability. The authoritative literature requires only that the auditor determine that a reasonable justification of preferability was properly disclosed. The SEC, however, requires the auditor to submit a "preferability letter" stating that the auditor is satisfied with the justification provided by the company when an accounting change has been made. An illustrative preferability letter is shown in Chapter 23.

Emphasis of a Matter

The foregoing discussion of explanatory language added to the standard report covered situations in which such language is required. Although it does not occur often, sometimes the auditor wishes to emphasize a matter regarding the financial statements, even though he or she is expressing an unqualified opinion. SAS No. 58 (AU Section 508.37) states: "For example, he may wish to emphasize that the entity is a component of a larger business enterprise or that it has had significant transactions with related parties, or he may wish to emphasize an unusually important subsequent event or an accounting matter affecting the comparability of the financial statements with those of the preceding period." Such explanatory language should be presented in a separate paragraph of the auditor's report. The opinion paragraph should not refer to the explanatory paragraph.

DEPARTURES FROM UNQUALIFIED OPINIONS

The fourth standard of reporting (AU Section 150.02) reads as follows:

> The report shall either contain an expression of opinion regarding the financial statements, taken as a whole, or an assertion to the effect that an opinion cannot be expressed. When an overall opinion cannot be expressed, the reasons therefor should be stated. In all cases where an auditor's name is associated with financial statements, the report should contain a clear-cut indication of the character of the auditor's work and the degree of responsibility the auditor is taking.

The standardized language of the unqualified report fosters precision in meeting this standard. The professional literature, both at the time of publication of the fourth standard of reporting and since then, has attempted to provide similar precision in describing departures from the standard report. Authoritative pronouncements on the fourth standard of reporting, including SAS No. 58, are set forth in AU Section 500 of *AICPA Professional Standards*.

There are two kinds of problems to overcome in achieving adequate precision and clarity of communication. First is the problem of trying to find a limited number of precisely defined qualifying or limiting phrases that will cover all possible situations. For professional auditors who have studied and understand the meaning and usage of the common qualifying phrases that have been developed, the effort has been largely successful. New conditions keep appearing, however, and when they do a period of uncertainty ensues while auditors experiment and decide whether the new conditions can be covered by an existing type of qualification or a new phrase is required.

The second problem is communicating to the public the meaning of the qualifying phrases and the distinctions between them. The meaning of a highly stylized phrase can be understood and agreed on by practitioners, but it is useless unless it is equally recognized and understood by most readers. SAS No. 58 (AU Section 508.39) calls for explaining all departures from an unqualified opinion in one or more separate paragraphs preceding the opinion paragraph. Doing so clearly highlights the departures and provides an unmistakable place for full description, improving both disclosure and communication.

SAS No. 58 classifies departures from the standard unqualified report, sometimes referred to as a "clean" opinion, as qualified opinions, adverse opinions, and disclaimers of opinion. These departures are discussed in the following paragraphs.

Qualified Opinions

There are two basic reasons for qualifying an opinion: limitations on the scope of the audit and departures from GAAP.

Scope Limitations. An audit can be limited by circumstances beyond the client's control that preclude the auditor from employing the auditing procedures that would otherwise be considered necessary, or it can be limited by client-imposed restrictions.

Circumstances Precluding Necessary Auditing Procedures. Sometimes an auditor is not able to carry out procedures that customarily are considered necessary in the circumstances as a basis for rendering an unqualified opinion. In most instances, the auditor is able to design and perform alternative procedures that provide sufficient assurance that the relevant audit objectives have been achieved. The most common instances in which the auditor might not be able to perform alternative procedures are when conditions make it impracticable or impossible to confirm accounts receivable or observe inventories. Other examples of such scope limitations involve noncontrolling investments in affiliated companies, when the auditor is unable to either (1) obtain audited financial statements of an investee or apply auditing procedures to unaudited financial statements of an investee, or (2) examine sufficient evidence that unrealized profits and losses resulting from transactions between the investor and the investee have been eliminated.

If an auditor cannot obtain satisfaction by means of alternative auditing procedures when circumstances preclude conventional procedures, the auditor should describe the problem and modify the standard report. If the auditor decides to express a qualified opinion (rather than disclaim an opinion), the problem should be described in a separate paragraph and referred to in both the scope paragraph and the opinion paragraph.

A scope limitation should always be described entirely within the auditor's report, in contrast to the treatment of qualifications related to information presented in the financial statements, which are usually described in a note to the statements and only referred to in the report. That is because a qualification based on a scope limitation arises from the auditor's activities, and limitations on them, not from the financial statements themselves, which are the representations of management. The qualification itself should be stated in terms of the scope limitation. SAS No. 58 (AU Section 508.44) presents an example regarding an investment in a foreign affiliate (the example assumes that the effects of the scope limitation do not cause the auditor to conclude that a disclaimer of opinion is appropriate).

[*Same first paragraph as the standard report*]

Except as discussed in the following paragraph, we conducted our audits in accordance with generally accepted auditing standards. Those standards require that we plan and perform the audit to obtain reasonable assurance about whether the financial statements are free of material misstatement. An audit includes examining, on a test basis, evidence supporting the amounts and disclosures in the financial statements. An audit also includes assessing the accounting principles used and significant estimates made by management, as well as evaluating the overall financial statement presentation. We believe that our audits provide a reasonable basis for our opinion.

We were unable to obtain audited financial statements supporting the Company's investment in a foreign affiliate stated at \$ _____ and \$ _____ at December 31, 19X2 and 19X1, respectively, or its equity in earnings of that affiliate of \$ _____ and \$ _____, which is included in net income for the years then ended as described in Note X to the financial statements; nor were we able to satisfy ourselves as to the carrying value of the investment in the foreign affiliate or the equity in its earnings by other auditing procedures.

In our opinion, except for the effects of such adjustments, if any, as might have been determined to be necessary had we been able to examine evidence regarding the foreign affiliate investment and earnings, the financial statements referred to in the first paragraph above present fairly, in all material respects, the financial position of X Company as of December 31, 19X2 and 19X1, and the results of its operations and its cash flows for the years then ended in conformity with generally accepted accounting principles.

Client-Imposed Restrictions.   The most common client-imposed restrictions are limitations preventing observation of physical inventories, confirmation of accounts receivable, or examination of a significant subsidiary. Usually, if scope is limited by client-imposed restrictions, an auditor should disclaim an opinion (see later discussion) because the client's election to limit the auditor's scope implies also an election to limit the auditor's responsibility. On rare occasions, if a client-imposed scope limitation applies to an isolated transaction or a single account, a qualified opinion may be acceptable.

Departures from GAAP.   The standard report makes the positive assertion that the financial statements are presented in conformity with generally accepted accounting principles; thus, any departures from GAAP must be noted as "exceptions" to that assertion. Such departures are rare in practice because most companies believe that an auditor's opinion qualified because of a departure from GAAP carries intolerable implications, and so they use accounting principles that are generally accepted. Also, only rarely are such qualified opinions acceptable in SEC filings. Nevertheless, instances of departures sometimes occur; the most common ones are described and examples presented in the following paragraphs.

Departures from Measurement Principles. SAS No. 58 (AU Section 508.53) gives the following example of an auditor's report that is qualified because of the use of an accounting principle that is at variance with GAAP:

[Same first and second paragraphs as the standard report]

The Company has excluded, from property and debt in the accompanying balance sheets, certain lease obligations that, in our opinion, should be capitalized in order to conform with generally accepted accounting principles. If these lease obligations were capitalized, property would be increased by $ _____ and $ _____, long-term debt by $ _____ and $ _____, and retained earnings by $ _____ and $ _____ as of December 31, 19X2 and 19X1, respectively. Additionally, net income would be increased (decreased) by $ _____ and $ _____ and earnings per share would be increased (decreased) by $ _____ and $ _____, respectively, for the years then ended.

In our opinion, except for the effects of not capitalizing certain lease obligations as discussed in the preceding paragraph, the financial statements referred to above present fairly, in all material respects, the financial position of X Company as of December 31, 19X2 and 19X1, and the results of its operations and its cash flows for the years then ended in conformity with generally accepted accounting principles.

If the pertinent facts are disclosed in the notes to the financial statements, the separate paragraph preceding the opinion paragraph would read as follows:

As more fully described in Note X to the financial statements, the Company has excluded certain lease obligations from property and debt in the accompanying balance sheets. In our opinion, generally accepted accounting principles require that such obligations be included in the balance sheets.

Departures from Disclosure Principles. Under the third standard of reporting (AU Section 150.02),

Informative disclosures in the financial statements are to be regarded as reasonably adequate unless otherwise stated in the report.

SAS No. 32, *Adequacy of Disclosure in Financial Statements* (AU Section 431), is general about what constitutes informative disclosures. Some specific disclosures required in financial statements are contained in various pronouncements that constitute GAAP, for example, Statements of the FASB and the GASB, Opinions of the Accounting Principles Board, and Accounting Research Bulletins. Specific industry disclosures are often called for in AICPA industry audit and accounting guides. Those pronouncements, however, cover only the topics addressed, and not the vast area of financial information on which no pronouncement has been issued. Identifying matters of potential interest to financial statement users, deciding whether and how they should be disclosed, and then demonstrating the appropriateness of the conclusion to the client place great demands on an auditor's skill and judgment.

The intent of the third standard of reporting is to establish that issuers of financial statements and auditors have a responsibility to ensure that disclosures are adequate, regardless of whether a requirement, convention, or precedent covers the matter. Some issuers of financial statements, however, take the approach of "no rule, no disclosure." Court cases and items appearing in the press indicate that a disclosure policy based on this attitude is dangerous, not to mention its not being in the public interest. Deciding what should be disclosed beyond what is specifically required in authoritative pronouncements, however, requires a balancing of diverse interests. On the one hand, management may believe that certain disclosures are likely to result in a competitive disadvantage or other detriment to the company or its stockholders. On the other hand, directors, management, auditors, and their legal counsel need to consider the possibility that a detrimental disclosure not made may be a basis for litigation in the wake of subsequent difficulties, even if the cause of the difficulties is completely unrelated to the undisclosed matter.

Disclosure is never a substitute for the proper recognition and measurement of transactions and other events and circumstances in conformity with GAAP. In practice, a temptation on the part of issuers and auditors sometimes exists to resolve a difficult problem by presenting information in a footnote rather than by adjusting the financial statements. For example, a contingency that is likely to occur and for which an estimate of loss is known must be accrued in the financial statements according to GAAP; mere disclosure of such an item is not an acceptable alternative.

An auditor who believes that disclosures in the financial statements are inadequate is required to so state and to make the necessary disclosures in the auditor's report, if it is practicable to do so and unless the omission from the auditor's report is recognized as appropriate in a specific SAS. Since most clients choose to make the necessary disclosures rather than to have them appear in the auditor's report, this type of disclosure in an auditor's report is extremely rare. SAS No. 58 (AU Section 508.56) contains the following example of a report qualified for inadequate disclosure:

[*Same first and second paragraphs as the standard report*]

The Company's financial statements do not disclose [*describe the nature of the omitted disclosures*]. In our opinion, disclosure of this information is required by generally accepted accounting principles.

In our opinion, except for the omission of the information discussed in the preceding paragraph, . . .

There are two exceptions to the requirement that when informative disclosures are omitted from the financial statements, the auditor should make the necessary disclosures in the auditor's report. The two exceptions, specifically sanctioned in the SASs (AU Sections 435.10 and 508.58), pertain to omitted segment information that is required by GAAP and to the statement of cash flows. The auditor should qualify the report if an entity declines to present the necessary segment information or a statement of cash flows, but the auditor is not required to provide the omitted segment information or to prepare the statement of cash flows and include it in the report.

An example of a report qualified because of the absence of a statement of cash flows follows:

> We have audited the accompanying balance sheets of X Company as of December 31, 19X2 and 19X1, and the related statements of income and retained earnings for the years then ended. These financial statements are the responsibility of the Company's management. Our responsibility is to express an opinion on these financial statements based on our audit.
>
> [*Same second paragraph as the standard report*]
>
> The Company declined to present a statement of cash flows for the years ended December 31, 19X2 and 19X1. Presentation of such statement summarizing the Company's operating, investing, and financing activities is required by generally accepted accounting principles.
>
> In our opinion, except that the omission of a statement of cash flows results in an incomplete presentation as explained in the preceding paragraph, the financial statements referred to above present fairly, in all material respects, the financial position of X Company as of December 31, 19X2 and 19X1, and the results of its operations for the years then ended in conformity with generally accepted accounting principles.

Departures Related to Accounting Changes. SAS No. 58 requires the auditor to evaluate a change in accounting principle to be satisfied that (a) the newly adopted accounting principle is GAAP, (b) the method of accounting for the effect of the change is in conformity with GAAP, and (c) management's justification for the change is reasonable. APB Opinion No. 20, paragraph 16 (Accounting Standards Section A06.112), states

> The presumption that an entity should not change an accounting principle may be overcome only if the enterprise justifies the use of an alternative acceptable accounting principle on the basis that it is preferable.

If management has not provided reasonable justification for the change, or if the change does not meet both of the other conditions mentioned above, the auditor should express a qualified opinion or, if the effect of the change is sufficiently material, express an adverse opinion on the financial statements.

AU Section 508.61 contains an example of a report qualified because management has not provided reasonable justification for a change in accounting principles.

> [*Same first and second paragraphs as the standard report*]
>
> As disclosed in Note X to the financial statements, the Company adopted, in 19X2, the first-in, first-out method of accounting for its inventories, whereas it previously used the last-in, first-out method. Although use of the first-in, first-out method is in conformity with generally accepted accounting principles, in

our opinion the Company has not provided reasonable justification for making this change as required by generally accepted accounting principles.[9]

In our opinion, except for the change in accounting principle discussed in the preceding paragraph, the financial statements referred to above present fairly, in all material respects, the financial position of X Company as of December 31, 19X2 and 19X1, and the results of its operations and its cash flows for the years then ended in conformity with generally accepted accounting principles.

Accounting changes that result in qualified or adverse opinions should also trigger similar opinions in future years as long as the change continues to have a material effect on either the financial statements of subsequent years or the financial statements of the year of the change when presented for comparative purposes. For example, as indicated by SAS No. 58 (AU Section 508.63–.66):

- If the financial statements for the year of such change are presented and reported on with a subsequent year's financial statements, the auditor's report should disclose his reservations with respect to the statements for the year of change.
- If an entity has adopted an accounting principle that is not a generally accepted accounting principle, its continued use might have a material effect on the statements of a subsequent year on which the auditor is reporting. In this situation, the independent auditor should express either a qualified opinion or an adverse opinion, depending on the materiality of the departure in relation to the statements of the subsequent year.
- If an entity accounts for the effect of a change prospectively when generally accepted accounting principles require restatement or the inclusion of the cumulative effect of the change in the year of change, a subsequent year's financial statements could improperly include a charge or credit that is material to those statements. This situation also requires that the auditor express a qualified or an adverse opinion.
- If management has not provided reasonable justification for a change in accounting principles, . . . the auditor's opinion should continue to express his exception with respect to the financial statements for the year of change as long as they are presented and reported on. However, the auditor's exception relates to the accounting change and does not affect the status of a newly adopted principle as a generally accepted accounting principle. Accordingly, while expressing an exception for the year of change, the independent auditor's opinion regarding the subsequent years' statements need not express an exception to the use of the newly adopted principle.

Adverse Opinions

An adverse opinion expresses a belief that financial statements are not presented fairly in conformity with generally accepted accounting principles or

---

[9]Because this paragraph contains all of the information required in an explanatory paragraph on consistency, a separate explanatory paragraph (following the opinion paragraph) is not necessary in this instance.

otherwise do not present fairly what they purport to present. It is required when an auditor believes that one or more departures from GAAP are sufficiently material to make the statements as a whole misleading. The auditor cannot sidestep an adverse opinion by disclaiming an opinion.

When an adverse opinion is issued, the opinion paragraph should include a reference to a separate paragraph in the auditor's report that discloses all the reasons for the adverse opinion, including any reservations the auditor may have regarding fair presentation in conformity with GAAP other than those that gave rise to the adverse opinion. The separate paragraph (or paragraphs, if appropriate) should also disclose the effects of the departures from GAAP on the financial statements, or state that such a determination is not possible.

Adverse opinions are rare. It is obviously better for all concerned to correct the conditions before such an opinion is issued, and it is usually within the client's power to correct them. Adverse opinions are sometimes issued on financial statements showing appraised values of property. Occasionally, an adverse opinion is issued on the financial statements of a regulated company that are prepared in accordance with a basis of accounting prescribed by a governmental agency and are presented other than in filings with the agency. In that situation, AU Section 544 indicates that the auditor generally should issue either a qualified or an adverse opinion, depending on the materiality of the departures from GAAP, and also, in an additional paragraph of the report, express an opinion on whether the financial statements are presented in conformity with the prescribed basis of accounting.

An example of an adverse opinion, taken from SAS No. 58 (AU Section 508.69), follows:

[Same first and second paragraphs as the standard report]

As discussed in Note X to the financial statements, the Company carries its property, plant and equipment accounts at appraisal values, and provides depreciation on the basis of such values. Further, the Company does not provide for income taxes with respect to differences between financial income and taxable income arising because of the use, for income tax purposes, of the installment method of reporting gross profit from certain types of sales. Generally accepted accounting principles require that property, plant and equipment be stated at an amount not in excess of cost, reduced by depreciation based on such amount, and that deferred income taxes be provided.

Because of the departures from generally accepted accounting principles identified above, as of December 31, 19X2 and 19X1, inventories have been increased $ _____ and $ _____ by inclusion in manufacturing overhead of depreciation in excess of that based on cost; property, plant and equipment, less accumulated depreciation, is carried at $ _____ and $ _____ in excess of an amount based on the cost to the Company; and deferred income taxes of $ _____ and $ _____ have not been recorded; resulting in an increase of $ _____ and $ _____ in retained earnings and in appraisal surplus of $ _____ and $ _____, respectively. For the years ended December 31, 19X2 and 19X1, cost of goods sold has been increased $ _____ and $ _____, respectively, because of the effects of the depreciation accounting referred to above and deferred income taxes of $ _____ and $ _____

have not been provided, resulting in an increase in net income of $ _____ and $ _____, respectively.

In our opinion, because of the effects of the matters discussed in the preceding paragraphs, the financial statements referred to above do not present fairly, in conformity with generally accepted accounting principles, the financial position of X Company as of December 31, 19X2 and 19X1, or the results of its operations or its cash flows for the years then ended.

Disclaimers of Opinion

If an auditor does not have enough evidence to form an opinion, the appropriate form of report is a disclaimer of opinion. A disclaimer can result from an inability to obtain sufficient competent evidential matter because the scope of the audit was seriously limited. In addition, while SAS No. 58 indicates that the addition of an explanatory paragraph to the auditor's report serves adequately to inform financial statement users when there are uncertainties, an auditor may nevertheless decide to decline to express an opinion in some cases involving uncertainties.

SAS No. 58 (AU Section 508.71) states that the reasons for a disclaimer must be given in a separate paragraph of the report. The auditor is also required to disclose in a separate paragraph any reservations about fair presentation in conformity with GAAP. It would be misleading for an auditor to issue a disclaimer if a basis for an adverse or a qualified opinion existed. Adverse opinions and disclaimers of opinion are never interchangeable, nor can an auditor's report contain both an adverse opinion and a disclaimer of opinion. A report may, however, contain an opinion that is qualified for more than one reason. For example, an opinion may be qualified because of a scope limitation and because of a departure from GAAP.

An example of a report (AU Section 508.71) disclaiming an opinion resulting from a scope limitation follows:

We were engaged to audit the accompanying balance sheets of X Company as of December 31, 19X2 and 19X1, and the related statements of income, retained earnings, and cash flows for the years then ended. These financial statements are the responsibility of the Company's management.

[*Second paragraph of standard report should be omitted.*]

The Company did not make a count of its physical inventory in 19X2 or 19X1, stated in the accompanying financial statements at $ _____ as of December 31, 19X2, and at $ _____ as of December 31, 19X1. Further, evidence supporting the cost of property and equipment acquired prior to December 31, 19X1, is no longer available. The Company's records do not permit the application of other auditing procedures to inventories or property and equipment.

Since the Company did not take physical inventories and we were not able to apply other auditing procedures to satisfy ourselves as to inventory quantities and the cost of property and equipment, the scope of our work was not sufficient to enable us to express, and we do not express, an opinion on these financial statements.

Note that, as required in a footnote to AU Section 508.72,

> The wording in the first paragraph of the auditor's standard report is changed in a disclaimer of opinion because of a scope limitation. The first sentence now states that ''we were engaged to audit'' rather than ''we have audited'' since, because of the scope limitation, the auditor was not able to perform an audit in accordance with generally accepted auditing standards. In addition, the last sentence of the first paragraph is also deleted, because of the scope limitation, to eliminate the reference to the auditor's responsibility to express an opinion.

The most frequently encountered examples of disclaimers because of scope limitations arise in initial engagements for new clients. In those circumstances, an auditor may begin work well after the beginning of the year under audit. If the opening inventory has a material effect on income for the year (as it usually does in most manufacturing and commercial enterprises), an auditor must gather evidence on which to base an opinion on the opening inventory in order to issue an unqualified opinion. If this is not possible, which often occurs, the auditor should, in the authors' opinion, disclaim an opinion on the income statement and statement of cash flows. When the auditor is able to form an opinion on the opening inventory—which ordinarily happens when another reputable auditor is succeeded—there is no need to cover the point in the report. (Chapter 14 discusses appropriate auditing procedures in this situation.)

As an alternative, the auditor could be asked to report on the balance sheet only. Such an engagement does not involve a scope limitation if the auditor's access to information is not limited and if the auditor applies all procedures appropriate in the circumstances. An example of a report on a balance-sheet-only audit was presented on page 645. (That report assumed that the auditor was satisfied as to the consistent application of GAAP.) If an income statement and statement of cash flows accompany the balance sheet, a disclaimer on them will be required.

While an auditor must stand ready to serve a client in any way appropriate, limited reporting engagements in which only a balance sheet is presented may not best meet the client's needs. Engagements likely to lead to a disclaimer on the income statement and statement of cash flows when a full set of financial statements is presented (other than when the auditor is appointed after year-end) should be approached reluctantly because of the risk that incorrect inferences about the auditor's responsibilities will be drawn by the client and other users. Consideration should be given to whether a client's needs can be better served by a review of financial statements performed in accordance with SSARS No. 1 or by designing a special engagement in which responsibilities can be spelled out explicitly. Various special reports are discussed in Chapter 23.

Piecemeal Opinions

Piecemeal opinions (opinions on certain identified financial statement items) are prohibited by SAS No. 58. A piecemeal opinion is the complement of a qualified opinion: That is, a qualified opinion gives an opinion on the financial statements as a whole and makes exceptions for certain items, whereas a piecemeal opinion disclaims or is adverse on the financial statements as a whole and gives an opinion on certain items. In the past, piecemeal opinions were not uncommon, but they presented so many problems that they are now prohibited.

SAS No. 58 (AU Section 508.73) states as a reason that "piecemeal opinions tend to overshadow or contradict a disclaimer of opinion or an adverse opinion." In addition, piecemeal opinions took specific items out of the context of the financial statements as a whole, thus implying a greater degree of precision about those items under conditions that usually entailed a lesser degree of certainty. Also, the defect in the financial statements as a whole that caused the disclaimer or adverse opinion tended to destroy or call into question the interrelated, corroborative nature of accounts on which the audit logic depended. When all of these deficiencies were balanced against the limited usefulness of piecemeal opinions, the profession was well advised to abandon them.

Adverse Opinions Versus Disclaimers

There is a fundamental difference between departures from GAAP, which affect the quality of the financial statements, and scope limitations, which affect the sufficiency and competence of audit evidence. Departures from GAAP call for a qualified opinion because of the auditor's reservations about the quality of the financial statements. If departures from GAAP become so great as to make the financial statements useless, an adverse opinion is called for. On the other hand, scope limitations affect the degree of assurance contained in the opinion, whether the limitations are client imposed or the result of circumstances, and call for a qualification in both the scope and opinion paragraphs. If scope limitations are so pervasive that the auditor cannot form an opinion, a disclaimer of opinion may be called for. The following tabulation helps keep in perspective the distinctions among qualified opinions, adverse opinions, and disclaimers of opinion.

Condition	Degree of Materiality or Pervasiveness	
	Less	*More*
Departures from GAAP	Qualified opinion	Adverse opinion
Scope limitations	Qualified opinion	Disclaimer of opinion

Distinguishing Among Situations Involving Scope Limitations, Uncertainties, and Departures from GAAP

Distinguishing between situations that require an explanatory paragraph because of an uncertainty and those that require departures from an unqualified opinion because of a scope limitation or a departure from GAAP can sometimes be difficult.

SAS No. 58 (AU Section 508.18) notes that

> A matter involving an uncertainty is one that is expected to be resolved at a future date, at which time sufficient evidential matter concerning its outcome would be expected to become available. A qualification or disclaimer of opinion because of a scope limitation is appropriate when sufficient evidential matter does or did exist but was not available to the auditor for reasons such as management's record retention policies or a restriction imposed by management.

Departures from generally accepted accounting principles involving uncertainties usually involve inadequate disclosure of the uncertainty, the use of inappropriate accounting principles in making accounting estimates, or unreasonable accounting estimates themselves. These situations would require a qualified or an adverse opinion because of a departure from GAAP.

To distinguish among the various types of auditors' reports that are possible in situations involving uncertainties, consider the following example. As discussed in Chapter 21, SAS No. 12, *Inquiry of a Client's Lawyer Concerning Litigation, Claims, and Assessments* (AU Section 337), requires the auditor to obtain corroborating evidence from the client's legal counsel about the completeness of the information supplied by management regarding pending or threatened litigation, claims, and assessments. If the client refuses to request its lawyer to communicate with the auditor, or if the lawyer refuses to furnish information concerning the likelihood of an unfavorable outcome of material litigation, claims, or assessments, an audit scope limitation exists that would, depending on the potential materiality of the unresolved items, lead to a scope qualification or a disclaimer of opinion, along with a separate explanatory paragraph preceding the opinion or disclaimer. If the lawyer is unable to respond concerning the likelihood of an unfavorable outcome of the uncertainty or the amount or range of potential loss, an uncertainty exists that would lead to an explanatory paragraph, assuming that the uncertainty is appropriately disclosed in the notes to the financial statements. If, however, after both the client and the lawyer acknowledge the uncertainty, the client refuses to make the appropriate disclosures, a qualified or an adverse opinion because of a GAAP departure (along with a separate explanatory paragraph preceding the opinion paragraph) would be required. In practice, distinguishing among these three situations is not always easy.

Different Reports on Comparative Financial Statements Presented

An auditor may express a qualified or an adverse opinion, disclaim an opinion, or include an explanatory paragraph with respect to one or more financial statements of one or more periods presented and issue a different report on the other financial statements presented. Following is an example of a report (AU Section 508.76) on comparative financial statements, consisting of a standard report on the current-year financial statements with a disclaimer of opinion on the prior-year statements of income, retained earnings, and cash flows:

[*Same first paragraph as the standard report*]

Except as explained in the following paragraph, we conducted our audits in accordance with generally accepted auditing standards. Those standards require that we plan and perform our audit to obtain reasonable assurance about whether the financial statements are free of material misstatement. An audit includes examining, on a test basis, evidence supporting the amounts and disclosures in the financial statements. An audit also includes assessing the accounting principles used and significant estimates made by management, as well as evaluating the overall financial statement presentation. We believe that our audits provide a reasonable basis for our opinion.

We did not observe the taking of the physical inventory as of December 31, 19X0, since that date was prior to our appointment as auditors for the Company, and we were unable to satisfy ourselves regarding inventory quantities by means of other auditing procedures. Inventory amounts as of December 31, 19X0, enter into the determination of net income and cash flows for the year ended December 31, 19X1.

Because of the matter discussed in the preceding paragraph, the scope of our work was not sufficient to enable us to express, and we do not express, an opinion on the results of operations and cash flows for the year ended December 31, 19X1.

In our opinion, the balance sheets of ABC Company as of December 31, 19X2 and 19X1, and the related statements of income, retained earnings, and cash flows for the year ended December 31, 19X2, present fairly, in all material respects, the financial position of ABC Company as of December 31, 19X2 and 19X1, and the results of its operations and its cash flows for the year ended December 31, 19X2, in conformity with generally accepted accounting principles.

SAS No. 58 also provides guidance for situations when an auditor becomes aware, during the current audit, of circumstances or events that affect the financial statements of a prior period. For example, the subsequent restatement of prior-period financial statements on which the auditor had issued a qualified or an adverse opinion would cause the auditor to express an unqualified opinion in an updated report on the financial statements of the prior period. In these circumstances, SAS No. 58 (AU Section 508.78) requires that all the substantive reasons for the different opinion be disclosed in a separate explanatory paragraph(s) preceding the opinion paragraph of the report. According to SAS No. 58, the explanatory paragraph should include

(a) the date of the auditor's previous report, (b) the type of opinion previously expressed, (c) the circumstances or events that caused the auditor to express a different opinion, and (d) that the auditor's updated opinion on the financial statements of the prior period is different from his previous opinion on those statements.

SUMMARY: PRINCIPAL VARIATIONS FROM STANDARD REPORTS

Figure 22.2 summarizes the principal causes of variations from the standard, unqualified report and how they affect the report. In deciding whether a variation from the standard, unqualified report is appropriate, the auditor considers the materiality of the condition or circumstance in question. A materiality test must be applied in determining not only whether to depart from a standard, unqualified opinion but also whether the appropriate variation is to include explanatory language or to issue a qualified opinion on the one hand or to issue an adverse opinion or a disclaimer of opinion on the other. As noted earlier, a departure from GAAP that is sufficiently material could lead to an adverse opinion, and scope limitations that are sufficiently material could lead to a disclaimer of opinion.

Authoritative auditing literature provides scant guidance for deciding whether the effects of a particular condition or circumstance are sufficiently material to require explanatory language, a qualified opinion, or either an adverse opinion or a disclaimer. Paragraph 50 of SAS No. 58 suggests several factors to be considered in determining the materiality of the effects of a departure from GAAP, namely, the dollar magnitude of the effects, the significance of an item to a particular enterprise, the pervasiveness of the misstatement, and the impact of the misstatement on the financial statements taken as a whole. As previously noted, paragraphs 28–30 of SAS No. 58 provide some guidance regarding materiality considerations when uncertainties exist. There is no guidance in the authoritative literature concerning scope limitations.

RESPONSIBILITIES AFTER THE REPORT DATE

Discovery of Information After the Report Date

Chapter 21 discusses an auditor's responsibility to obtain knowledge about subsequent events up to certain dates. Clearly, the auditor is not obligated to "keep current" indefinitely; as explained in Chapter 21, the responsibility ends with the issuance of the financial statements and the auditor's report, with the exception of a 1933 Act filing with the SEC. In that situation, the responsibility extends to the effective date of the registration statement.

After the financial statements and audit report have been issued, however, an auditor may become aware of new information regarding the client. If the new information refers to a condition that did not exist at the date of the audit report, or if it refers to final resolutions of contingencies or other matters disclosed in the financial statements or the auditor's report, the auditor has no further obligation. The new information may, however, relate to facts existing at the date of the audit report that might have affected the financial statements or auditor's report had the auditor been aware of them. For example, the auditor may learn on April 14, 19X2, after the financial statements for 19X1 were issued, that a large receivable on the December 31, 19X1, balance sheet believed at that date to be collectible was in fact uncollectible because the

Figure 22.2   Summary of Principal Variations from Standard Reports

Type of Variation	*Report Treatment*
Situations Requiring Unqualified Opinions with Explanatory Language	
Opinion based in part on report of another auditor	Add explanatory language in the introductory and opinion paragraphs.
Departure from an authoritative pronouncement with which the auditor agrees	Add an explanatory paragraph describing and justifying the departure.
Predecessor auditor's reports on prior year's comparative statements not presented	Add explanatory language in the introductory paragraph.
Report on a balance sheet only	Refer only to balance sheet in introductory, scope, and opinion paragraphs.
Material inconsistency between financial statements and other information reported by management	Add an explanatory paragraph describing the inconsistency. (The auditor should also consider withholding the audit report or withdrawing from the engagement.)
Exceptions regarding supplementary information required by FASB or GASB	Add an explanatory paragraph describing the circumstances.
Existence of a material uncertainty affecting the financial statements	Add an explanatory paragraph after the opinion paragraph (disclaimer of opinion is permissible but not required).
Lack of consistency in application of accounting principles	Add an explanatory paragraph after the opinion paragraph.
Auditor wishes to emphasize a matter	Add an explanatory paragraph.
Situations Requiring Departures from Unqualified Opinions	
Scope limitation	Qualify the scope paragraph ("except as"); describe the scope limitation in a separate paragraph preceding the opinion paragraph; qualify the opinion ("except for") or disclaim an opinion, depending on circumstances and materiality.
Departure from GAAP	Describe the departure in a separate paragraph preceding the opinion paragraph; qualify the opinion ("except for") or give an adverse opinion, depending on materiality.

customer had declared bankruptcy on December 5, 19X1. In those circumstances, the auditor is obligated to pursue the matter. According to an auditing interpretation (AU Section 9561.01), that obligation exists even if the auditor has resigned or has been discharged.

While the distinction between the two kinds of new information is conceptually clear, in practice it is often difficult to tell, at least initially, whether the new information refers to a new condition or a preexisting one. The new information is often fragmentary, hearsay, or otherwise suspect, and may come from inside or outside the entity. Regardless of its source, the auditor should ordinarily discuss the information with the client and request that the client make any necessary investigations. There may be situations in which the auditor may find it desirable to seek the advice of legal counsel.

SAS No. 1 (AU Section 561) provides guidance to the auditor on subsequent steps to be taken. If the client cooperates and the information is found to be reliable and to have existed at the date of the auditor's report, the client should be advised to disclose the newly discovered facts and their effect on the financial statements by issuing revised financial statements and auditor's report. The reasons for the revisions should be described in a note to the financial statements and referred to in the auditor's report. An auditor's report accompanying revised financial statements would read (in part) as follows: "In our opinion, the financial statements referred to above, revised as described in Note X, present fairly. . . ." If financial statements for a subsequent period are about to be issued, the revision may be incorporated in those statements, as long as disclosure of the revision is not thereby unduly delayed. The auditor's report on the comparative financial statements need not refer to the revision provided there is appropriate disclosure. The auditor may, however, include an explanatory paragraph to emphasize the revision.

Sometimes, determining the effect on the financial statements requires prolonged investigation, or the information is so significant that no delay is tolerable. In those circumstances, the client should notify all persons likely to be relying on the financial statements of the problem under investigation. Usually, that would include stockholders, banks, and, for publicly held companies, the SEC, stock exchanges, regulatory agencies, and the press.

If the client's management refuses to make the appropriate disclosures, the auditor should obtain the advice of legal counsel and should notify each member of the client's board of directors of that refusal and of the subsequent steps the auditor will take to prevent future reliance on the audit report. Unless the auditor's counsel recommends otherwise, the auditor should notify the client that the auditor's report is no longer to be associated with the financial statements. In addition, the auditor should notify the SEC, stock exchanges, and any other regulatory agencies involved of the situation and the withdrawal of the report and request that steps be taken to accomplish the necessary public disclosure (usually this notification is made public at once). The auditor should also notify in writing any others who are known to be currently relying or who are likely to rely on the financial statements and the related auditor's report. The public disclosure following notification of the SEC is intended to take care of all unknown interested parties.

The disclosures made by the auditor to regulatory agencies and other parties should, if possible, describe the information and its effect on the financial statements and the auditor's report. The description should be precise and factual and should avoid references to conduct, motives, and the like. SAS No. 1 (AU Section 561.09) describes the appropriate disclosure if precise and factual information is not available, as follows:

If the client has not cooperated and as a result the auditor is unable to conduct a satisfactory investigation of the information, his disclosure need not detail the specific information but can merely indicate that information has come to his attention which his client has not cooperated in attempting to substantiate and that, if the information is true, the auditor believes that his report must no longer be relied upon or be associated with the financial statements. No such disclosure should be made unless the auditor believes that the financial statements are likely to be misleading and that his report should not be relied on.

Consideration of Omitted Procedures After the Report Date

The auditor may, subsequent to issuing an audit report, conclude that one or more auditing procedures considered necessary in the circumstances were omitted during the audit. For example, as part of its internal quality review program, a CPA firm may discover that no physical inspection was performed of a significant quantity of a client's inventory stored at a remote location. The actions to be taken by the auditor in this and similar situations vary depending on the circumstances, and the auditor should be guided by the advice of legal counsel. SAS No. 46, *Consideration of Omitted Procedures After the Report Date* (AU Section 390), provides guidance in this area.

The auditor should, as a first step, assess the importance of the omitted procedure in relation to his or her ability to support the previously issued opinion. On further investigation (such as, for example, review of working papers and inquiry of members of the engagement team), the auditor may decide that other procedures that were performed compensated adequately for the omitted procedure. In this instance, the auditor usually does not take any further steps. If, however, the auditor concludes that the omission of the auditing procedure significantly impairs his or her ability to support the previously issued opinion and believes there are persons currently relying or likely to rely on the report, additional procedures necessary to provide an adequate basis for the opinion issued should be performed promptly. Those procedures may be the omitted procedure or appropriate alternatives designed to compensate adequately for it.

The performance of those procedures may disclose facts that existed at the date of the audit report that would have affected the opinion rendered had the auditor been aware of them at the time. In such circumstances, the auditor should follow the steps outlined in the preceding section of this chapter.

Situations may arise, however, when because of the passage of time or other reasons, the auditor is unable to perform the previously omitted or alternative procedures. In such instances, the auditor should seek the advice of legal counsel before deciding on the appropriate course of action. In any event, strong consideration should be given to notifying the client regarding the problem and the proposed action.

23

Special Reporting Situations

The increased sophistication of our society and of the business environment, coupled with a better understanding by the public of auditors' skills and experience, has created a demand for a variety of services far beyond audits of financial statements. The work accountants in public practice may be asked to perform, the diversity of resulting reports and letters that may be issued, and the reporting problems these create are literally infinite. Standard-setters have tried to keep pace with this explosion in the demand for special services. Their efforts are reflected in the series of attestation standards as well as in the Statements on Auditing Standards and Statements on Standards for Accounting and Review Services. The latter two series of statements address a number of special reporting situations and nonaudit services—among them compilations, reviews, interim reviews, a variety of special reports, reporting on information accompanying basic financial statements, reports on internal control, reports on compliance with contractual agreements, and letters for underwriters. Both the procedures employed in providing those and other services and the reports issued are discussed in this chapter. Attestation services, including those in connection with prospective financial information, are described in Chapter 24; compliance audits are covered in depth in Chapter 25.

The professional standards discussed in Chapter 3 apply with equal rigor to all work performed by a CPA—the only exception is the practical irrelevance of some of them in some special reporting situations. AU Section 150.06 states, for example, that the "ten generally accepted standards, to the extent that they are relevant in the circumstances, apply to all other services covered by Statements on Auditing Standards unless the Statement specifies otherwise." The general standards—adequate training and proficiency, independence of mental attitude, and due care in the performance of the work—are all clearly applicable in every professional effort. Of the standards of field work, the first and third—planning and supervision of field work and sufficiency and competency of evidential matter as a basis for an opinion—also apply universally. The second standard—a sufficient understanding of the internal control structure—is generally, though not universally, applicable. Whenever a professional report involves business activities, the auditor must obtain an understanding of the applicable control structure policies and procedures to make adequate professional judgments. Some reports, however, such as those on an entity's compliance with aspects of contractual agreements, do not necessarily involve its internal control structure. The standards of reporting are more specific and therefore cannot be as universally applied. The first standard— adherence to generally accepted accounting principles (GAAP)—obviously applies only to financial statements that purport to present financial position and results of operations and to items derived from those statements. The second standard, consistency, applies whenever a report addresses conformity with GAAP. The third and fourth standards—adequacy of informative disclosures and the requirement for a clear-cut indication of the degree of responsibility the auditor is taking—while stated in terms of financial statements, should be viewed as generally applicable to every report the auditor writes.

This chapter covers the types of special reports and special reporting problems most commonly encountered in practice. Some of the special reporting problems addressed in this chapter arise because nonaudit engagements do not require obtaining sufficient competent evidence to provide the relatively high level of assurance an audit opinion demands. In those situations, both the professional literature and this chapter refer to a person who undertakes the engagement and issues a report as an "accountant," a "certified public accountant" (CPA), or a "practitioner." The term "auditor" is reserved for a person who undertakes to perform an audit in accordance with generally accepted auditing standards (GAAS) and expresses an opinion based on the results of that audit.

NONAUDITS, COMPILATIONS, AND REVIEWS

Direct Association with Financial Data

When a practitioner is directly involved with financial data, he or she has a duty to clearly indicate the character of the work done and the degree of responsibility taken. The practitioner's objective is to prevent readers from misinterpreting his or her role and association with the data. In that regard, SAS No. 26 (AU Section 504.03) provides that "when an accountant submits to his client or others financial statements that he has prepared or assisted in preparing, he is deemed to be associated even though the accountant does not append his name to the statements."

A practitioner is directly involved with financial data whenever he or she is engaged to perform a compilation, review, or audit. The level of assurance provided by these services ranges from no assurance on compiled statements, to limited or moderate assurance on reviews, to high assurance on audits. Also, as discussed in a later section of this chapter, the practitioner is directly involved with financial data when he or she is engaged to apply agreed-upon procedures to specified elements, accounts, or items of a financial statement. In this type of engagement, the practitioner's assurance is limited to findings based on the specified procedures and does not extend to the financial statement taken as a whole. For each of these types of engagements, there is a standard reporting format that conveys the appropriate level of assurance. Reporting on audited financial statements was discussed extensively in Chapter 22. Reporting on compilations, reviews, and agreed-upon procedures engagements is discussed later in this chapter.

Indirect Association with Financial Data

Practitioners may be indirectly associated with financial data by virtue of special services provided to clients. These services can range from merely typing financial statements to various types of accounting services such as preparing a trial balance or assisting in adjusting the accounts. When a practitioner is indirectly associated with financial data, he or she needs to be aware that third parties may infer an unwarranted level of assurance based on knowledge of the practitioner's involvement. Because of this, the profession has provided guidance in some areas where a practitioner may be indirectly associated with financial data.

A client may ask the accountant merely to type or reproduce financial statements that the accountant has not otherwise prepared or assisted in preparing. Paragraph 7 of Statement on Standards for Accounting and Review Services (SSARS) No. 1 (AR Section 100.07) prohibits an accountant from rendering such a service for a *nonpublic* entity.[1]

A form of indirect association with financial statements of a nonpublic company that was permitted at one time but is now generally prohibited is referred to as a "plain paper" engagement. This is an engagement to prepare and submit to the client, for management's use only, financial statements without any accompanying report or other direct association of the CPA and without meeting the requirements for a compilation service (discussed below). In September 1989, the Accounting and Review Services Committee of the AICPA decided to continue the prohibition of plain paper engagements and rejected a proposal to allow CPAs to submit interim financial statements to nonpublic entities without issuing a compilation, review, or other report.

Unwarranted Representation

An accountant may become aware that his or her name is to be included in a client-prepared written communication containing financial statements that have not been audited, reviewed, or compiled. In that event, the accountant should make sure that either (a) the name is not included in the communication or (b) the financial statements are accompanied by a notation that the accountant has not audited, reviewed, or compiled them and thus does not assume any responsibility or express an opinion on them. If the client does not comply, the accountant should advise the client that consent to use his or her name is not given. The accountant should also consider what other actions might be appropriate, including consulting with an attorney.

On the other hand, if an auditor is identified by a financial reporting service as being a company's independent auditor in association with condensed financial data (discussed later in this chapter) produced by the reporting service, the auditor is not deemed to be associated, because neither the auditor nor the client has the ability to require the reporting service to withhold what is, in fact, public information.

Personal Financial Statements in a Financial Plan

Personal financial statements included in written personal financial plans prepared by an accountant are exempt from the requirements of SSARS No. 1 (AR Section 100), provided the accountant establishes an understanding with the client that the financial statements will be used solely to assist the client and

---

[1]SSARS No. 1 defines "nonpublic entity" in paragraph 4 (AR Section 100.04) as follows: "A nonpublic entity is any entity other than (a) one whose securities trade in a public market either on a stock exchange (domestic or foreign) or in the over-the-counter market, including securities quoted only locally or regionally, (b) one that makes a filing with a regulatory agency in preparation for the sale of any class of its securities in a public market, or (c) a subsidiary, corporate joint venture, or other entity controlled by an entity covered by (a) or (b)."

the client's advisors in developing the client's personal goals and objectives. SSARS No. 6 (AR Section 600.04–.05) specifies the content of a report on financial statements contained in a personal financial plan. The SSARS contains the following illustrative report:

> The accompanying Statement of Financial Condition of X, as of December 31, 19XX, was prepared solely to help you develop your personal financial plan. Accordingly, it may be incomplete or contain other departures from generally accepted accounting principles and should not be used to obtain credit or for any purposes other than developing your financial plan. We have not audited, reviewed, or compiled the statement.

Compilations of Financial Statements

Financial statements are considered unaudited if the accountant has not applied auditing procedures that are sufficient to permit the expression of an opinion on them, as described in Chapter 22.

The Accounting and Review Services Committee has established a level of professional service for nonpublic companies called a compilation. This service involves presenting information, consisting of management's representations in the form of financial statements, without expressing any assurance on them. The accountant is not required to make inquiries or perform other procedures to corroborate or review the information supplied by the client. The accountant does, however, have certain other duties and responsibilities, specified in SSARS No. 1 (AR Section 100), because of this direct association with the financial statements.

Compilation Procedures.   At the outset, the accountant should establish an understanding, preferably in writing, with the client as to the nature and limitations of the service to be performed, and the type of report to be rendered. Before beginning the work, the accountant should have or acquire a knowledge of the accounting principles and practices of the client's industry and a general understanding of the nature of the client's business transactions, the form of its accounting records, the qualifications of its accounting personnel, the accounting basis used, and the form and content of the financial statements.[2] The accountant should read the financial statements to see if they are free from obvious material errors, such as arithmetical or clerical mistakes, misapplication of accounting principles, and inadequate disclosures.

The accountant should discuss with the client any items of concern that arise from performing the foregoing procedures. The client should be asked to revise the financial statements, as appropriate; if the client does not comply, the accountant should modify the report. At the extreme, the accountant

---

[2]SSARS No. 4, *Communications Between Predecessor and Successor Accountants* (AR Section 400), provides guidance on inquiries of a predecessor by a successor accountant regarding acceptance of an engagement and to facilitate the conduct of that engagement.

should withdraw from the engagement if modifying the report is not adequate to communicate the deficiencies.

Form of Reporting. The accountant's report on a compilation engagement explicitly disclaims an opinion and gives no other form of assurance about the financial statements. The standard form of compilation report, as suggested in SSARS No. 5, *Reporting on Compiled Financial Statements* (AR Section 500), for a nonpublic company follows:

> We have compiled the accompanying balance sheet of XYZ Company as of December 31, 19XX, and the related statements of income, retained earnings, and cash flows for the year then ended, in accordance with standards established by the American Institute of Certified Public Accountants.

> A compilation is limited to presenting in the form of financial statements information that is the representation of management (owners). We have not audited or reviewed the accompanying financial statements and, accordingly, do not express an opinion or any other form of assurance on them.

The accountant's report should be dated as of the date the compilation was completed. Each page of the financial statements should include a reference such as "See Accountant's Compilation Report." If substantially all disclosures are omitted, the accountant's report should highlight this fact to alert users of the financial statements.[3]

Reviews of Financial Statements

A review of financial statements, as described in SSARS No. 1 (AR Section 100), involves inquiry and analytical procedures intended to provide the accountant with a reasonable basis for expressing limited assurance that there are no material modifications that should be made to the financial statements in order for them to be in conformity with GAAP or some other comprehensive basis of accounting.[4] Paragraph 4 of SSARS No. 1 (AR Section 100.04) compares a review with a compilation and an audit, as follows:

> The objective of a review differs significantly from the objective of a compilation. The inquiry and analytical procedures performed in a review should provide the accountant with a reasonable basis for expressing limited assurance that there are no material modifications that should be made to the financial statements. No expression of assurance is contemplated in a compilation.

---

[3]SSARS No. 3, *Compilation Reports on Financial Statements Included in Certain Prescribed Forms* (AR Section 300), provides additional guidance for accountants who are asked to compile financial statements included in a prescribed form that calls for departures from GAAP.

[4]Comprehensive bases of accounting other than GAAP are described and discussed later in this chapter. Hereafter, reference to GAAP in this section of the chapter includes, where applicable, another comprehensive basis of accounting.

The objective of a review also differs significantly from the objective of an audit of financial statements in accordance with generally accepted auditing standards. The objective of an audit is to provide a reasonable basis for expressing an opinion regarding the financial statements taken as a whole. A review does not provide a basis for the expression of such an opinion because a review does not contemplate obtaining an understanding of the internal control structure or assessing control risk, tests of accounting records and of responses to inquiries by obtaining corroborating evidential matter through inspection, observation or confirmation, and certain other procedures ordinarily performed during an audit. A review may bring to the accountant's attention significant matters affecting the financial statements, but it does not provide assurance that the accountant will become aware of all significant matters that would be disclosed in an audit.

As in the case of compilations, reviews (as discussed in AR Section 100) may be performed only for nonpublic entities.

Review Procedures.   In a review engagement, either the accountant or the client prepares the financial statements from the entity's records. As with a compilation engagement, the accountant should have or acquire a knowledge of the client's industry and business. If the client prepares the financial statements, the accountant should ascertain that they are supported by formal accounting records.

The accountant should ordinarily make inquiries about

- The entity's accounting principles, practices, and methods of applying them.
- Procedures for recording, classifying, and summarizing transactions and accumulating information for financial statement disclosures.
- Actions taken at meetings (such as of stockholders or the board of directors) that could affect the financial statements.
- Whether the financial statements have been prepared in conformity with GAAP consistently applied.
- Changes in business activities or accounting principles and practices.
- Subsequent events that could have a material effect on the financial statements.
- Matters on which questions have arisen during the conduct of the review.

Some accountants may find it helpful in making inquiries to use a checklist covering the general areas to ensure that important questions are not overlooked.

The analytical procedures to be performed should be designed to identify relationships between account balances, and other fluctuations that appear unusual because they do not conform to a predictable pattern (e.g., changes in sales and in accounts receivable and expenses that ordinarily fluctuate with sales). The accountant should also make comparisons with prior-period financial statements and with budgets and forecasts, if any.

If other accountants have been engaged to audit or review the financial statements of significant components of the reporting entity, its subsidiaries, or other investees, the principal accountant should obtain reports from the other accountants as a basis, in part, for his or her report on the review of the reporting entity's financial statements. SSARS No. 1 also suggests that the accountant may wish to obtain a representation letter from the client to confirm the oral representations made in the course of the review. Although such a letter from the client is optional, in the authors' opinion it is highly desirable as a means of reducing the possibility of misunderstanding and of documenting some of the more important inquiries.

Based on the results of the review, the accountant should consider whether the financial statements appear to conform with GAAP. Material departures from GAAP should cause the accountant to modify the standard review report, unless the financial statements are revised. If modifying the report is not adequate to indicate the deficiencies in the financial statements taken as a whole, the accountant may have to withdraw from the engagement.

Form of Reporting.   The accountant's report on reviewed financial statements expresses limited assurance. The opinion is in the form of "negative assurance" that the accountant is not aware of any material modifications that should be made to the financial statements in order for them to be in conformity with GAAP. The standard form of review report to be issued, as specified in SSARS No. 1 (AR Section 100.35), follows:

> We have reviewed the accompanying balance sheet of XYZ Company as of December 31, 19XX, and the related statements of income, retained earnings, and cash flows for the year then ended, in accordance with standards established by the American Institute of Certified Public Accountants. All information included in these financial statements is the representation of the management (owners) of XYZ Company.
>
> A review consists principally of inquiries of company personnel and analytical procedures applied to financial data. It is substantially less in scope than an audit in accordance with generally accepted auditing standards, the objective of which is the expression of an opinion regarding the financial statements taken as a whole. Accordingly, we do not express such an opinion.
>
> Based on our review, we are not aware of any material modifications that should be made to the accompanying financial statements in order for them to be in conformity with generally accepted accounting principles.

The accountant's report should be dated as of the date the review was completed. Each page of the financial statements should include a reference such as "See Accountant's Review Report."[5]

---

[5]SSARS No. 2, *Reporting on Comparative Financial Statements* (AR Section 200), provides guidance for reporting on comparative financial statements of a nonpublic entity when financial statements of one or more periods presented have been compiled or reviewed.

Reporting When the Accountant Is Not Independent

Lack of independence precludes an accountant from issuing a review report. The accountant may, however, issue a report on a compilation engagement for a nonpublic company with respect to which the accountant is not independent, provided the report includes language specifically stating the lack of independence. The reason for lack of independence should not be described.

INTERIM REVIEWS

A public accountant may be requested to perform a preissuance review of interim financial information for a client for a number of reasons. The client may wish to include a representation that the information has been reviewed in a document issued to stockholders or third parties or in Form 10-Q, a quarterly report required to be submitted to the SEC pursuant to Section 13 or 15(d) of the Securities Exchange Act of 1934. Such representation may also be included or incorporated by reference in a registration statement.

Larger, more widely traded companies meeting specified criteria are also required by Item 302(a) of SEC Regulation S-K to include selected quarterly financial data in their annual reports or other documents filed with the SEC that contain audited financial statements. The selected quarterly financial data is required to be reviewed, on either a preissuance or retrospective basis. Other entities may voluntarily include similar information in documents containing audited financial statements. In the latter instance, the interim financial information may or may not have been reviewed. It is unlikely that an entity not required to include that information would do so without having it reviewed, since that would give rise to an expansion of the auditor's report. (See the discussion on page 685.)

Companies that include quarterly financial information with their audited annual financial statements may want their accountants to review the information periodically throughout the year, rather than retrospectively at year-end. There are a number of tangible benefits to this approach. First, a preissuance review helps bring accounting problems to light early enough to avoid year-end "surprises." Second, there may be some offsetting reductions in the audit fee for the year because, even though the review does not entail actual audit tests, it involves procedures that, if the work is coordinated, the auditor can utilize in performing the audit. Finally, it may prevent the need to publish at year-end quarterly financial information that differs from amounts previously reported during the year.

The National Commission on Fraudulent Financial Reporting (Treadway Commission) recommended that "the SEC should require independent public accountants to review quarterly financial data of all public companies before release to the public." At the time of this writing, the SEC staff has issued a concepts release on timely reviews of interim financial information. This release asks for comments on whether the SEC should propose a requirement that (1) interim financial data of registrants be reviewed by independent accountants before it is filed with the SEC, and (2) a report issued by the independent accountant be included in the registrant's Form 10-Q and any registration statements that include the interim financial information.

Objective of Reviews of Interim Financial Information

A review of interim financial information is intended to provide the accountant with a basis for reporting whether material modifications should be made to such information in order for it to conform with GAAP. The accountant does this by applying a knowledge of financial reporting practices to significant accounting matters that come to his or her attention through inquiries and analytical procedures.

Nature of Reviews

SAS No. 36, *Review of Interim Financial Information* (AU Section 722), sets forth the procedures established by the profession for a review of interim financial information. Those procedures are similar to the procedures previously discussed for a review engagement, with one main exception. In an engagement to review interim financial information, as contrasted with an ordinary review engagement, the accountant should normally obtain written representations from management stating its responsibility for the financial information, completeness of minutes, subsequent events, and other matters for which the accountant believes written representations are appropriate in the circumstances.

Information may come to the accountant's attention that raises questions about whether the unaudited interim information departs from GAAP with respect to litigation, claims, or assessments. According to an auditing interpretation of AU Section 722, if the accountant believes the client's lawyer may have information concerning that possibility, the accountant should inquire of the lawyer, even though a review of interim financial information does not require corroborative evidential matter for responses to inquiries.

Timing of Reviews

The timing of procedures to be performed depends largely on whether the accountant has been engaged to perform a preissuance (or ''timely'') review of the interim financial information or a retrospective review.

While adequate planning by the accountant is essential to the timely completion of a preissuance review, the most critical element is the client's interim reporting system. It must permit the preparation of reliable interim financial information; otherwise, the scope of the accountant's engagement may be restricted. In addition, the client's interim financial control procedures should be adequate so that a preissuance review is not unduly expensive or time-consuming.

On the other hand, if a review is done retrospectively, there must be sufficient documentation, including the rationale for conclusions reached during the year, available for the accountant's purpose. For example, the accountant may review the client's documentation in deciding whether an adjustment arising in a later quarter of the year is a change in estimate or correction of an error.

Extent of Reviews

The extent to which the accountant makes inquiries and performs analytical procedures on the financial information to be reported on depends on a number of considerations. First, the accountant needs a knowledge of the client's accounting and reporting practices, as well as its control structure policies and procedures, as a practical basis for the inquiry and other procedures. The accountant ordinarily acquires this knowledge as a result of having audited the client's previous annual financial statements. Knowledge of deficiencies in control structure policies and procedures, accounting changes, and changes in the nature or volume of the client's business activities; the issuance of new accounting pronouncements; and questions raised during the review all may prompt the accountant to make more extensive inquiries or to employ other procedures to assess interim financial information.

If there appear to be deficiencies in the client's control structure policies and procedures that prevent the preparation of interim financial information in conformity with GAAP, and, as a result, the accountant cannot effectively apply his or her knowledge of financial reporting practices to the interim financial information, the accountant should consider whether there is a restriction on the scope of the engagement sufficient to preclude completing the review. Furthermore, the accountant should inform senior management and the board of directors (or its audit committee) of these circumstances.

There are also a number of practical considerations that affect the extent of review procedures. Examples are selecting locations to be visited if the accounting records are maintained at multiple client locations, and acquiring the necessary "knowledge" if there has been a change in auditors and the current accountant does not have an audit base to work from. These are special matters that the accountant should consider in determining the review strategy.

Reporting Standards

An accountant may address a report on interim financial information to the company, its board of directors, or its stockholders. The report should be dated as of the date the review was completed and is similar to a review report, as previously discussed. The standard form of interim review report presented in AU Section 722.18 follows:

> We have made a review of (describe the information or statements reviewed) of ABC Company and consolidated subsidiaries as of September 30, 19X1, and for the three-month and nine-month periods then ended, in accordance with standards established by the American Institute of Certified Public Accountants.
>
> A review of interim financial information consists principally of obtaining an understanding of the system for the preparation of interim financial information, applying analytical procedures to financial data, and making inquiries of persons responsible for financial and accounting matters. It is substantially less

in scope than an audit conducted in accordance with generally accepted auditing standards, the objective of which is the expression of an opinion regarding the financial statements taken as a whole. Accordingly, we do not express such an opinion.

Based on our review, we are not aware of any material modifications that should be made to the accompanying financial (information or statements) for them to be in conformity with generally accepted accounting principles.

Each page of the interim financial information should be marked as "unaudited."

When an accountant requires reports from other accountants as a basis, in part, for a report on a review of consolidated interim financial information, the accountant may refer in the report to the reports of the other accountants to indicate a division of responsibility for performance of the review.

Modifications to the Standard Review Report. Since an accountant reporting on a review of interim financial information is not expressing an opinion on audited financial statements, the circumstances that require modifying the standard review report are somewhat different than for an audit report. The accountant should modify the standard review report only if the interim financial information departs from GAAP. Such departures include inadequate disclosure, as well as changes in accounting principles that are not in conformity with GAAP. A lack of consistency in the application of GAAP, however, would not cause the accountant to modify the standard review report as long as the lack of consistency was adequately disclosed in the interim financial information.

Interim Financial Information Presented in Annual Reports to Shareholders.
Selected quarterly financial data may be presented in a note to the audited financial statements or as supplementary information outside the audited financial statements. If such information is presented in a note to the audited financial statements, the information should be marked as "unaudited." If it is included in an annual report to shareholders, either voluntarily or as required by Item 302(a) of SEC Regulation S-K, there is a presumption in the absence of an indication to the contrary that the data has been reviewed in accordance with the established professional standards previously discussed. Because of this presumption, if an accountant has reviewed the data, the audit report on the annual financial statements ordinarily need not be modified, nor does the accountant have to report separately on the review.

If the selected quarterly financial data is required by Item 302(a) of Regulation S-K, the auditor's report on the annual financial statements should be expanded if such information is omitted, is not appropriately marked as "unaudited" (when presented in a note to the audited financial statements), has not been reviewed, does not appear to be presented in conformity with GAAP, or includes an indication that a review was made but fails to state that "the review is substantially less in scope than an audit conducted in accordance with generally accepted auditing standards, the objective of which is an expression of opinion regarding the financial statements taken as a whole, and accordingly, no such opinion is expressed" (AU Section 722.30).[6] If selected quarterly financial data that has not been reviewed is voluntarily presented, expanding the auditor's report on the annual financial statements would be called for if the entity does not indicate that the data has not been reviewed.

SEC Filings. If the client includes a representation in a Form 10-Q that an accountant has reviewed interim financial information set forth in that document, the accountant should request that the review report be included.

An accountant's report based on a review of interim financial information also may be presented or incorporated by reference in a registration statement. In that event, the prospectus should discuss the independent accountant's involvement and the legal status of the review report. The discussion should make it clear that, under SEC rules, the accountant's statutory responsibility as to liability for the report does not extend to the effective date of the registration statement. Suitable wording for this purpose is included in SAS No. 37, *Filings Under Federal Securities Statutes*, paragraph 9 (AU Section 711.09).

SPECIAL REPORTS

An auditor may be asked to audit and report on financial information other than financial statements prepared in conformity with GAAP. This section covers auditors' reports issued in connection with financial statements prepared on a basis of accounting other than GAAP and in connection with parts of a financial statement. It also discusses reports on client compliance with aspects of contracts or regulations and reports involving financial information presented on prescribed forms requiring a prescribed form of auditor's report.

Non-GAAP Financial Statements

Statement of Financial Accounting Concepts (SFAC) No. 1, *Objectives of Financial Reporting by Business Enterprises* (Accounting Standards Section CON1), issued by the Financial Accounting Standards Board (FASB), states that "information about enterprise earnings and its components measured by accrual accounting generally provides a better indication of enterprise performance than information about current cash receipts and payments" (para. 44). Stated another way, the accrual basis is generally necessary to measure financial position and results of operations in conformity with GAAP. Other comprehensive bases of accounting, such as the cash or modified accrual basis, the income tax basis, and statutory bases that meet reporting requirements of a governmental regulatory agency, ordinarily do not accomplish that objective. Nevertheless, there are some organizations that believe they do not need

---

[6]Under its present rules, it is unlikely the SEC would accept any expansion of the auditor's report in this regard. A possible exception might be if the auditor could not review the selected quarterly financial data in the annual report because the company's system for preparing interim financial information did not provide an adequate basis for making such a review. In that case, however, there is a possibility that the client might be in violation of the "accounting standards" provisions of the Foreign Corrupt Practices Act, as discussed in Chapter 7.

financial statements based on GAAP or that non-GAAP financial statements would be more informative in a particular situation. Those organizations that do not find the extra effort and cost to prepare accrual basis statements worthwhile believe they are better served by a comprehensive basis of accounting other than GAAP. Typical of these organizations are some not-for-profit entities, certain nonpublic companies, regulated companies that must file financial statements based on accounting principles prescribed by a government regulatory agency, and entities formed for special purposes, such as certain partnerships and joint ventures. A special report containing an unqualified opinion on financial statements prepared in accordance with a comprehensive basis of accounting other than GAAP is a useful, practical alternative for companies that prepare statements on such a basis and wish an audit.

Definition.   SAS No. 62, *Special Reports*, paragraph 4 (AU Section 623.04), defines a comprehensive basis of accounting other than GAAP as one of the following:

- A basis of accounting that the reporting entity uses to comply with the requirements or financial reporting provisions of a governmental regulatory agency to whose jurisdiction the entity is subject.
- A basis of accounting that the reporting entity uses or expects to use to file its income tax return for the period covered by the financial statements.
- The cash receipts and disbursements basis of accounting, and modifications of the cash basis having substantial support, such as recording depreciation on fixed assets or accruing income taxes.
- A definite set of criteria having substantial support that is applied to all material items appearing in financial statements, such as the price-level basis of accounting.

Forms of Reporting.   The key element of a special report on a comprehensive basis of accounting other than GAAP is a paragraph stating what the basis of presentation is and that it is a comprehensive basis of accounting other than GAAP. The paragraph also refers to a note to the financial statements that describes the basis of presentation and how it differs from GAAP. (These differences need not be quantified, however.)

The financial statements should be titled using terms that are not generally associated with financial statements intended to present financial position, results of operations, or cash flows in conformity with GAAP. For example, "statement of assets and liabilities arising from cash transactions" should be used instead of "balance sheet." If the financial statements are not suitably titled, the auditor should disclose his or her reservations in an explanatory paragraph of the report and qualify the opinion.

If the financial statements are prepared in conformity with the requirements or financial reporting provisions of a governmental regulatory agency solely for filing with that agency, the auditor should include a paragraph that restricts the distribution of the report to those within the entity and the regulatory agency. The only exceptions to this restriction on distribution are situations where an AICPA audit or accounting guide or auditing interpretation recognizes additional distribution as appropriate. The fact that by law or regulation the auditor's report may be made a matter of public record is not relevant.

Furthermore, AU Section 544 provides reporting guidance when a regulated company issues to the public the same financial statements that it files with the appropriate regulatory agency (where the basis of accounting complies with the regulatory agency's requirements but differs from GAAP). In this situation, except when such reporting is recognized as appropriate by an AICPA audit or accounting guide or auditing interpretation, the auditor's report on the financial statements should contain two opinions, one modified as appropriate because of the departures from GAAP and the other expressing an opinion on whether the financial statements are presented in conformity with the regulatory agency's basis of accounting.

In all other situations, if the financial statements do not meet the definition of a presentation in conformity with a comprehensive basis of accounting other than GAAP, the auditor should issue the standard form of report (see Chapter 22), modified, as appropriate, for the departures from GAAP.

Illustrations of reports on financial statements prepared in accordance with a comprehensive basis of accounting other than GAAP can be found in SAS No. 62 (AU Section 623.08). One example, that of a report on financial statements prepared on the entity's income tax basis, follows[7]:

> We have audited the accompanying statements of assets, liabilities, and capital—income tax basis of ABC Partnership as of December 31, 19X2 and 19X1, and the related statements of revenue and expenses—income tax basis and of changes in partners' capital accounts—income tax basis for the years then ended. These financial statements are the responsibility of the Partnership's management. Our responsibility is to express an opinion on these financial statements based on our audits.
>
> [*Standard scope paragraph*]
>
> As described in Note X, these financial statements were prepared on the basis of accounting the Partnership uses for income tax purposes, which is a comprehensive basis of accounting other than generally accepted accounting principles.
>
> In our opinion, the financial statements referred to above present fairly, in all material respects, the assets, liabilities, and capital of ABC Partnership as of December 31, 19X2 and 19X1, and its revenue and expenses and changes in partners' capital accounts for the years then ended, on the basis of accounting described in Note X.

---

[7]SAS No. 58 (AU Section 508.08) specifies that a title that includes the word "independent" is one of the basic elements of the standard audit report. The illustrative standard reports in AU Section 508 use the title "Independent Auditor's Report." This and subsequent illustrative audit reports present only the body of the report and omit the title, as well as the date of the report and signature of the auditor's firm.

Reports on Parts of a Financial Statement

An auditor may be engaged to audit and express an opinion on one or more specified elements, accounts, or items of a financial statement.[8] The audit might be performed as a separate engagement or, more commonly, in conjunction with an audit of financial statements taken as a whole. For example, the report might be on the amount of sales for the purpose of computing rentals, royalties, a profit participation, or the adequacy of a provision for income taxes in financial statements. SAS No. 62 (AU Section 623) provides guidance on these kinds of engagements.

Applicability of GAAP.   The auditor's report should not address GAAP unless the elements, accounts, or items the auditor is reporting on are prepared in conformity with GAAP. For example, GAAP normally would not be applicable to items prepared in accordance with the provisions of a contract, law, or government regulation.

Materiality.   Since the auditor expresses an opinion on each specified element, account, or item of a financial statement covered by the report, the measurement of materiality should be related to each individual element, account, or item rather than to the aggregate thereof or to the financial statements taken as a whole. Thus, an audit of only specified parts of a set of financial statements is usually more extensive than an audit of those same parts if they are included in a full set of audited financial statements. Items that are interrelated with those the auditor has been engaged to express an opinion on must also be considered. Examples of interrelated financial statement elements are sales and receivables, inventories and payables, and property, plant, and equipment, and depreciation.

Forms of Reporting.   As noted in Chapter 22, piecemeal opinions are not permitted, since they are considered to overshadow or contradict a disclaimer of opinion or an adverse opinion. Thus, the auditor must be careful to avoid expressing an opinion on specified elements, accounts, or items of a financial statement that is tantamount to a piecemeal opinion, if the audit of the financial statements as a whole resulted in an adverse opinion or a disclaimer. That generally would not be a concern if the special report did not cover a major portion of the financial statement elements, accounts, or items and did not accompany the entity's financial statements.

If the specified elements, accounts, or items are prepared in accordance with the requirements or financial reporting provisions of a contract or agreement that results in a presentation not in conformity with GAAP or other

---

[8]In a different type of engagement, discussed later in this section of the chapter, an accountant may be engaged to apply agreed-upon procedures to specified elements, accounts, or items of a financial statement. An accountant may also be asked to provide a review of one or more specified elements, accounts, or items of a financial statement. For that type of engagement, the auditor should refer to the attestation standards (AT Section 100).

comprehensive basis of accounting, the auditor's report should contain a paragraph restricting distribution of the report to those within the entity and parties to the contract or agreement. As previously discussed, a similar paragraph restricting distribution is required if the presentation is prepared on a basis prescribed by a governmental regulatory agency solely for filing with that agency.

The form of report depends on the purpose of the audit and the elements, accounts, or items audited. Although the form of report varies, there are characteristics common to all reports on specified elements, accounts, or items. Illustrations of reports of this type follow; other examples are presented in SAS No. 62 (AU Section 623.18).

Report Relating to Royalties

We have audited the accompanying schedule of royalties applicable to engine production of the Q Division of XYZ Corporation for the year ended December 31 19X2, under the terms of a license agreement dated May 14, 19XX, between ABC Company and XYZ Corporation. This schedule is the responsibility of XYZ Corporation's management. Our responsibility is to express an opinion on this schedule based on our audit.

We conducted our audit in accordance with generally accepted auditing standards. Those standards require that we plan and perform the audit to obtain reasonable assurance about whether the schedule of royalties is free of material misstatement. An audit includes examining, on a test basis, evidence supporting the amounts and disclosures in the schedule. An audit also includes assessing the accounting principles used and significant estimates made by management, as well as evaluating the overall schedule presentation. We believe that our audit provides a reasonable basis for our opinion.

We have been informed that, under XYZ Corporation's interpretation of the agreement referred to in the first paragraph, royalties were based on the number of engines produced after giving effect to a reduction for production retirements that were scrapped, but without a reduction for field returns that were scrapped, even though the field returns were replaced with new engines without charge to customers.

In our opinion, the schedule of royalties referred to above presents fairly, in all material respects, the number of engines produced by the Q Division of XYZ Corporation during the year ended December 31, 19X2, and the amount of royalties applicable thereto, under the license agreement referred to above.

This report is intended solely for the information and use of the boards of directors and managements of XYZ Corporation and ABC Company and should not be used for any other purpose.

Report on Federal and State Income Taxes
Included in Financial Statements

We have audited, in accordance with generally accepted auditing standards, the financial statements of XYZ Company, Inc., for the year ended June 30, 19XX, and have issued our report thereon dated August 15, 19XX. We have also audited the current and deferred provision for the Company's federal and state income taxes for the year ended June 30, 19XX, included in those financial statements, and the related asset and liability tax accounts as of June 30, 19XX. This income tax information is the responsibility of the Company's management. Our responsibility is to express an opinion on it based on our audit.

We conducted our audit of the income tax information in accordance with generally accepted auditing standards. Those standards require that we plan and perform the audit to obtain reasonable assurance about whether the federal and state income tax accounts are free of material misstatement. An audit includes examining, on a test basis, evidence supporting the amounts and disclosures related to the federal and state income tax accounts. An audit also includes assessing the accounting principles used and significant estimates made by management, as well as evaluating the overall presentation of the federal and state income tax accounts. We believe that our audit provides a reasonable basis for our opinion.

In our opinion, the Company has paid or, in all material respects, made adequate provision in the financial statements referred to above for the payment of all federal and state income taxes and for related deferred income taxes that could be reasonably estimated at the time of our audit of the financial statements of XYZ Company, Inc., for the year ended June 30, 19XX.

Evaluating the reasonableness of a provision for income taxes requires broad knowledge of a company's business transactions and of the content of many individual accounts. For that reason, a report on the adequacy of a provision for income taxes in financial statements should not be issued unless the auditor has audited the complete financial statements in which the provision appears. Similarly, the auditor should have audited the complete financial statements before issuing an opinion on a specified element, account, or item based on an entity's net income or equity.

Applying Agreed-Upon Procedures to Specified Elements, Accounts, or Items of a Financial Statement. An accountant may be asked to apply agreed-upon procedures to one or more specified elements, accounts, or items of a financial statement that are not sufficient to allow expressing an opinion on them. Even though the scope of the engagement is limited, the accountant may accept such an engagement provided the parties involved have a clear understanding of the procedures to be performed, and distribution of the accountant's report is restricted to the named parties involved. There are a number of ways the accountant can obtain satisfaction that all parties involved know and agree on what is to be done. They range from meeting with the parties involved to discuss the procedures to be applied, to supplying a draft of the report to such parties with a request for comments before the report is issued. SAS No. 35, *Special Reports—Applying Agreed-Upon Procedures to Specified Elements, Accounts, or Items of a Financial Statement* (AU Section 622), provides guidance for these engagements.

The content of the accountant's report on the results of applying agreed-upon procedures varies with the circumstances. Certain characteristics, however, are common to all such reports. The report should identify the specified elements, accounts, or items to which the agreed-upon procedures were applied; enumerate the procedures performed; state the accountant's findings; specify the intended distribution of the report; state that the report relates only to the elements, accounts, or items specified and does not extend to the entity's financial statements taken as a whole; and disclaim an opinion with respect to such elements, accounts, or items. Distribution of the report is restricted to parties that have a clear understanding of the procedures performed. If the accountant has no adjustments to propose, negative assurance may be expressed to that effect. The negative assurance and disclaimer are illustrated below.

> Because the above procedures do not constitute an audit conducted in accordance with generally accepted auditing standards, we do not express an opinion on any of the accounts or items referred to above. In connection with the procedures referred to above, no matters came to our attention that caused us to believe that the specified accounts or items should be adjusted. Had we performed additional procedures or had we conducted an audit of the financial statements in accordance with generally accepted auditing standards, matters might have come to our attention that would have been reported to you. This report relates only to the accounts and items specified above and does not extend to any financial statements of Y Company, Inc., taken as a whole. (AU Section 622.06)

Reports on Compliance with Aspects of Contractual Agreements or Regulatory Requirements

Determining a client's compliance with contractual agreements or regulatory requirements is integral to an audit of financial statements. If noncompliance with contracts or statutes could have a material effect on a client's financial statements, the auditor should determine the extent of compliance with them. For example, an auditor should determine that the client has conformed with the restrictive covenants in a long-term bond agreement, since a violation of those covenants could make the entire issue due and payable at the lender's option and require the debt to be classified as a current rather than a long-term liability. Companies may be required by a contractual agreement or regulatory agency to furnish a report on compliance with aspects of the agreement or regulatory requirements. For example, a loan agreement may call for assurance from an independent auditor that the borrower has complied with covenants in the agreement relating to accounting or auditing matters, or a state regulatory agency may require assurance that the enterprise has complied with certain accounting provisions specified by the agency. This section discusses engagements where the auditor has been requested to provide explicit assurance about the client's compliance with contractual agreements or regulatory requirements.

SAS No. 62 (AU Section 623) provides guidance on reports on compliance with aspects of contractual agreements or regulatory requirements related to audited financial statements. Special reports of this type should be issued only if the auditor has audited the financial statements to which the contractual agreement or regulatory requirements relate.[9] The report usually contains negative assurance relative to the applicable covenants of the agreement or the applicable regulatory requirements, and a statement that the audit of the financial statements was not directed primarily toward obtaining knowledge about compliance. Furthermore, since the matters the auditor is reporting on are set forth in a document that generally would not be publicly available, the auditor's report should contain a paragraph restricting distribution to those within the entity and the parties to the contract or agreement or for filing with any applicable regulatory agency. The report on compliance may be given in a separate report or in one or more paragraphs following the opinion paragraph of the auditor's report accompanying the financial statements. An example of a separate report on compliance is presented below.

Report on Compliance with Contractual Provisions

We have audited, in accordance with generally accepted auditing standards, the balance sheet of XYZ Company as of December 31, 19X2, and the related statements of income, retained earnings, and cash flows for the year then ended, and have issued our report thereon dated February 16, 19X3.

In connection with our audit, nothing came to our attention that caused us to believe that the Company failed to comply with the terms, covenants, provisions, or conditions of sections XX to XX, inclusive, of the Indenture dated July 21, 19X0, with ABC Bank insofar as they relate to accounting matters. However, our audit was not directed primarily toward obtaining knowledge of such non-compliance.

This report is intended solely for the information and use of the boards of directors and managements of XYZ Company and ABC Bank and should not be used for any other purpose.

An auditor may also be engaged to provide assurance on compliance with contractual agreements or regulatory requirements relating to matters that have not been subjected to the auditing procedures applied in the audit of the financial statements. In those circumstances, the auditor should follow the guidance in the attestation standards, which are discussed in Chapter 24. When an auditor is engaged by a governmental entity or other recipient of governmental financial assistance to test compliance with the *Government Auditing Standards* (Yellow Book) issued by the Comptroller General of the United States, he or she should follow the performance and reporting guidance contained in SAS No. 63, *Compliance Auditing Applicable to Governmental Entities and Other Recipients of Governmental Financial Assistance*, which is discussed in Chapter 25.

Finally, an auditor may be engaged to audit and express an opinion on special-purpose financial statements prepared to comply with a contractual agreement or regulatory provisions. Those presentations are typically prepared on a basis of accounting that results in either (1) an incomplete presenta-

---

[9]However, as noted later in this section, a similar report may be issued under the attestation standards.

tion of an entity's historical financial position or results of operations (although the presentation is otherwise in conformity with GAAP or another comprehensive basis of accounting), or (2) a presentation that is not in conformity with GAAP or another comprehensive basis of accounting. Illustrations of reports on these types of financial presentations are provided in SAS No. 62.

Reports on Prescribed Forms

Printed forms or schedules designed for filing with various bodies sometimes prescribe the wording of the auditor's report. The prescribed wording may call for statements by the auditor that do not conform with the applicable professional reporting standards. In those instances, the auditor should either reword the prescribed report language or replace it with a separate report on the financial information presented in the prescribed forms or schedules.[10]

REPORTING ON INFORMATION ACCOMPANYING BASIC FINANCIAL STATEMENTS

Information such as additional details or explanations of items in the basic financial statements, historical summaries of items extracted from the basic financial statements, and other material, some of which may be from sources outside the accounting system or outside the entity, may be presented in a document, like an annual report, that also includes basic audited financial statements. That information is not considered necessary for the fair presentation of financial position, results of operations, or cash flows in conformity with GAAP.

Such additional information, often referred to as "other information," may be included in a *client-prepared document* like the annual report to shareholders. Alternatively, additional information could be included in an *auditor-submitted document*. For example, the auditor could present the client with a document bound in the CPA's own cover and including not only the basic financial statements and auditor's report, but also a schedule of general and administrative expenses. The auditor's responsibility for additional information in auditor-submitted documents is discussed later in this section.

Additional Information in Client-Prepared Documents

The auditor's responsibility for other information included in a client-prepared document is set forth in SAS No. 8 (AU Section 550) and is discussed in Chapter 22. That chapter also discusses a specific type of other information for which AU Section 558 prescribes additional performance and exception reporting responsibilities. That type of information is supplementary infor-

---

[10]Guidance on compilation reports issued by an accountant on financial statements included in prescribed forms is provided in SSARS No. 3, *Compilation Reports on Financial Statements Included in Certain Prescribed Forms* (AR Section 300).

mation *required* by FASB or GASB pronouncements. Some entities may *voluntarily* include in documents containing audited financial statements, certain supplementary information that is required by the FASB or the GASB to be presented by other entities. In that situation, the additional responsibilities set forth in AU Section 558 do *not* apply, provided it is clear that the information is not covered by the auditor's report. This may be accomplished by a statement by the entity that the auditor has not applied any procedures to the information or by the auditor's including in the report a disclaimer on the information.

Additional Information in Auditor-Submitted Documents

The auditor may be requested to include a variety of material in addition to the basic financial statements in a document submitted to the client. For example, the document might include details of the subaccounts composing financial statement captions, statistical data, consolidating data, explanatory comments, financial analyses, possibly some operational data, and occasionally a description of the auditing procedures applied to specific items in the financial statements. The account details, analytical comment, and audit scope explanations might be combined under appropriate account headings, or these subjects might be separated and presented in different sections of the document.

The auditor has a responsibility to report—by a disclaimer or otherwise—on all information in a document containing audited financial statements that is submitted to the client. The auditor is not obligated, however, to apply auditing procedures to information presented outside the basic financial statements in such a document; in that event, the auditor should disclaim an opinion on the additional information. Alternatively, the auditor may choose to modify or redirect certain of the procedures applied in the audit so as to be able to express an opinion on the accompanying information rather than disclaim an opinion on it. SAS No. 29, *Reporting on Information Accompanying the Basic Financial Statements in Auditor-Submitted Documents* (AU Section 551), contains reporting guidelines, as well as examples, for information accompanying the basic financial statements in an auditor-submitted document. The auditor's report on the accompanying information may be either added to the standard report on the basic financial statements or presented separately. In either case, the report should

- State that the audit has been conducted for the purpose of forming an opinion on the basic financial statements taken as a whole.
- Identify the accompanying information.
- State that the accompanying information is presented for purposes of additional analysis and is not a required part of the basic financial statements.
- Include either an opinion on whether the accompanying information is fairly stated in all material respects in relation to the basic financial statements taken as a whole or a disclaimer of opinion, depending on whether the information has been subjected to the auditing procedures applied in the audit of the basic financial statements. (The auditor may

express an opinion on a portion of the accompanying information and disclaim an opinion on the remainder.)

For purposes of reporting in this manner, the measurement of materiality is the same as in forming an opinion on the basic financial statements taken as a whole. Accordingly, the auditor need not apply procedures as extensive as would be necessary to express an opinion on a separate presentation of the information, as would be true for a report on parts of a financial statement, as described earlier in this chapter.

Consolidating Information

The auditor may be requested to submit to the client consolidating or combining financial statements with the basic consolidated financial statements. The consolidating or combining financial statements are usually presented in tabular form showing the accounts for each of the companies entering into the consolidated financial statements, together with the necessary eliminations and reclassifications. Usually the auditor is not engaged to report on each of the consolidated subsidiaries separately and thus does not specifically audit each subsidiary. The auditor's report should make clear the limits of responsibility taken for the individual company amounts. In this instance, the paragraph in the auditor's report relating to the consolidating information might read as follows, based on the guidance in SAS No. 29 (AU Section 551.18):

> Our audit was conducted for the purpose of forming an opinion on the consolidated financial statements taken as a whole. The consolidating information is presented for purposes of additional analysis of the consolidated financial statements rather than to present the financial position, results of operations, and cash flows of the individual companies. The consolidating information has been subjected to the auditing procedures applied in the audit of the consolidated financial statements and, in our opinion, is fairly stated in all material respects in relation to the consolidated financial statements taken as a whole.

On the rare occasion when an auditor conducts an audit of each of the companies, an opinion on each should be issued, referring to the companies by name or collectively. In that instance, the auditor's reporting responsibilities for the separate financial statements are the same as for the consolidated financial statements.

Condensed Financial Statements and Selected Financial Data

Condensed financial statements derived from audited financial statements may be included by a public entity in a client-prepared document, for example, an SEC filing on Form 10-Q in which condensed balance sheets are presented on a comparative basis with condensed interim financial information as of a subsequent date that is accompanied by an auditor's review report. In that case, the auditor should report on the condensed financial statements of each period in a manner appropriate for the type of service provided in that period. SAS No. 42, *Reporting on Condensed Financial Statements and Selected Financial Data* (AU Section 552), provides the following example of such reporting in filings on Form 10-Q:

> We have made a review of the condensed consolidated balance sheet of ABC Company and subsidiaries as of March 31, 19X1, and the related condensed consolidated statements of income and cash flows for the three-month periods ended March 31, 19X1 and 19X0, in accordance with standards established by the American Institute of Certified Public Accountants.
>
> A review of interim financial information consists principally of obtaining an understanding of the system for the preparation of interim financial information, applying analytical procedures to financial data, and making inquiries of persons responsible for financial and accounting matters. It is substantially less in scope than an audit in accordance with generally accepted auditing standards, the objective of which is the expression of an opinion regarding the financial statements taken as a whole. Accordingly, we do not express such an opinion.
>
> Based on our review, we are not aware of any material modifications that should be made to the condensed consolidated financial statements referred to above for them to be in conformity with generally accepted accounting principles.
>
> We have previously audited, in accordance with generally accepted auditing standards, the consolidated balance sheet as of December 31, 19X0, and the related consolidated statements of income, retained earnings, and cash flows for the year then ended (not presented herein); and in our report dated February 15, 19X1, we expressed an unqualified opinion on those consolidated financial statements. In our opinion, the information set forth in the accompanying condensed consolidated balance sheet as of December 31, 19X0, is fairly stated, in all material respects, in relation to the consolidated balance sheet from which it has been derived. (AU Section 552.08)

If, in a client-prepared document containing condensed financial statements identified as being derived from audited financial statements, a nonpublic entity names its auditor without including the audited financial statements, the auditor should request the client to remove the auditor's name from the document. If the client does not comply, the auditor should ordinarily express an adverse opinion on the condensed financial statements because of inadequate disclosure and should request the client to include the report in the document. The auditor's report should not provide the disclosure. This requirement is intended to discourage nonpublic entities from substituting condensed financial statements for complete audited financial statements in a client-prepared document.

An auditor may also be engaged to report on selected financial data included in a client-prepared document that contains audited financial statements (or, for a public entity, that incorporates such statements by reference to information filed with a regulatory agency). The auditor's report should be limited to data derived from the audited financial statements. As in a report on condensed financial statements, it is appropriate to use wording indicating that the information is fairly stated in all material respects in relation to the financial statements from which it has been derived. SAS No. 42 (AU Section 552.10) contains the following example of an auditor's report on selected financial data for a five-year period in a client-prepared document that includes audited financial statements:

> We have audited the consolidated balance sheets of ABC Company and subsidiaries as of December 31, 19X5 and 19X4, and the related consolidated statements of income, retained earnings, and cash flows for each of the three years in the period ended December 31, 19X5. These financial statements are the responsibility of the Company's management. Our responsibility is to express an opinion on these financial statements based on our audits.
>
> [*Standard scope paragraph*]
>
> In our opinion, the consolidated financial statements referred to above present fairly, in all material respects, the financial position of the ABC Company and subsidiaries as of December 31, 19X5 and 19X4, and the results of their operations and their cash flows for each of the three years in the period ended December 31, 19X5, in conformity with generally accepted accounting principles.
>
> We have also previously audited, in accordance with generally accepted auditing standards, the consolidated balance sheets as of December 31, 19X3, 19X2, and 19X1, and the related statements of income, retained earnings, and cash flows for the years ended December 31, 19X2 and 19X1 (none of which are presented herein); and we expressed unqualified opinions on those consolidated financial statements.
>
> In our opinion, the information set forth in the selected financial data for each of the five years in the period ended December 31, 19X5, appearing on page xx, is fairly stated, in all material respects, in relation to the consolidated financial statements from which it has been derived.

REPORTING ON FINANCIAL STATEMENTS PREPARED FOR USE IN OTHER COUNTRIES

An auditor may be engaged to report on the financial statements of a U.S. entity (i.e., an entity that is organized or domiciled in the United States) that have been prepared in conformity with accounting principles generally accepted in another country. For example, the financial statements of a U.S. entity may be prepared for inclusion in the consolidated financial statements of a foreign parent company. SAS No. 51, *Reporting on Financial Statements Prepared for Use in Other Countries* (AU Section 534), provides performance and reporting standards for such engagements.

When auditing the financial statements of a U.S. entity prepared in conformity with accounting principles generally accepted in another country, the auditor should comply with both the general and field work standards of U.S. generally accepted auditing standards. The auditor should also comply with the general and field work standards of the other country, if asked to apply the auditing standards of that country. In engagements of this nature, the auditor should have an adequate understanding of the accounting principles generally accepted in the other country. The auditor can usually obtain this knowledge by reading the professional literature or statutes describing accounting principles generally accepted in the particular country.

Illustrations of various reports on financial statements prepared for use in other countries are provided in AU Section 534.

REPORTS ON INTERNAL CONTROL

Management Reporting on the Internal Control Structure

Financial statement users have become increasingly interested in the effectiveness of an entity's internal control structure since passage of the Foreign Corrupt Practices Act of 1977 (FCPA) (see Chapter 7) and the events that led to it. In the 1970s, both the Commission on Auditors' Responsibilities (Cohen Commission) and the Financial Executives Institute endorsed the publication of a report by enterprise management on, among other matters, the enterprise's internal control. The Cohen Commission further recommended that both management and the auditor should report separately to shareholders on their assessment of the control structure. In 1979, the SEC proposed a rule that would have required the management of publicly held companies to include a statement on the adequacy of internal controls in annual reports to the Commission, proxy material, and reports to shareholders. The proposed rule also would have required independent public accountants to review the internal controls and report on them. Although the SEC formally withdrew the proposal, it urged the private sector to develop disclosure practices voluntarily and also urged auditor association with the voluntary management reports. In response to these developments, numerous public companies included a report of management in their annual report to shareholders. An example of a management report taken from the 1988 annual report to shareholders of American Telephone and Telegraph Company, signed by both the chairman of the board and the chief financial officer, is found in Figure 23.1.

In its 1987 report, the Treadway Commission recommended that the auditor's standard report should be revised to describe the independent public accountant's work with respect to understanding and evaluating the control structure. In 1988, the Auditing Standards Board (ASB) formed a task force to consider whether the auditor could attest to management's assertions about an entity's internal control structure. Specifically, this task force was charged with developing language that would describe in the auditor's standard report the auditor's responsibilities with respect to an entity's internal control structure as part of conducting a financial statement audit. This task force was also to consider developing an attestation standard for engagements where an accountant is requested to express either positive or negative assurance on management's assertions about the effectiveness of the entity's internal control structure. In response to the Treadway Commission report, the Financial Executives Research Foundation has appointed Coopers & Lybrand to conduct a study to develop a framework of internal control, including a definition, description of its elements, and criteria as to what constitutes an effective

Figure 23.1 Report of Management

Report of Management

The accompanying financial statements, which consolidate the accounts of American Telephone and Telegraph Company and its subsidiaries, have been prepared in conformity with generally accepted accounting principles.

The integrity and the objectivity of the data in these financial statements, including estimates and judgments relating to matters not concluded by year-end, are the responsibility of management as is all other information included in this Annual Report unless indicated otherwise. To this end, management maintains a system of internal controls. Our internal auditors monitor compliance with it in connection with an annual plan of internal audits. The system of internal controls, on an ongoing basis, is reviewed, evaluated and revised as necessary in view of the results of constant management oversight, internal and independent audits, changes in the Company's business, and other conditions and changes. Management believes that the Company's internal control system, taken as a whole, provides reasonable assurance that (1) financial records are adequate and can be relied upon to permit the preparation of financial statements in conformity with generally accepted accounting principles and (2) access to assets occurs only in accordance with management's authorizations. Recorded assets are compared with existing assets at reasonable intervals and appropriate action is taken with respect to any differences. As a part of the system of internal controls, management establishes organization structures, carefully selects key personnel to provide an appropriate division of responsibility, and uses informational programs designed to assure that its policies, standards, and managerial authorities are understood throughout the organization.

These financial statements have been audited by Coopers & Lybrand, Independent Certified Public Accountants. Their audits are conducted in accordance with generally accepted auditing standards and include selective tests of transactions and a review of internal controls.

The Audit Committee of the Board of Directors, which is composed of Directors who are not employees, meets periodically with management, the internal auditors, and the independent auditors to review the manner in which they are performing their responsibilities and to carry out its oversight role with respect to auditing, internal controls, and financial reporting matters. Both the internal auditors and the independent auditors periodically meet alone with the Audit Committee and have access to the Audit Committee, and its individual members, at any time.

Morris Tanenbaum
Vice Chairman and Chief Financial Officer

Robert E. Allen
Chairman of the Board and Chief Executive Officer

system, along with implementation guidelines for designing, evaluating, and monitoring internal control systems.

Also in 1988, the SEC issued proposed rules (which at the time of this writing have not been adopted) requiring registrants to include a report of management's responsibilities in annual reports to shareholders and annual filings with the SEC. This management report would describe management's responsibilities for the preparation of financial statements in accordance with GAAP, for determining the estimates and judgments used therein, and for preparing other financial information included in the annual report. The management report would also describe management's responsibilities for establishing and maintaining an internal control structure and would include an assessment of the effectiveness of the structure. In addition, management would state how it responded to significant recommendations on the internal control structure made by both the internal and external auditors. Unlike the SEC's 1979 proposal, these proposed rules would not include explicit reporting by the entity's external auditors; they would, however, direct the auditor to consider the requirements of SAS No. 8.

Providing Assurance on the Internal Control Structure

Generally, members of audit committees want to be informed about deficiencies in the internal control structure. As discussed in Chapter 8, auditors are required to communicate to the audit committee (or its equivalent) matters coming to their attention in the course of the audit that represent material weaknesses or other reportable conditions. Sometimes, however, audit committee members, as well as members of management, want more information and request auditors to provide assurance on an entity's internal control structure.

SAS No. 30, *Reporting on Internal Accounting Control*[11] (AU Section 642), provides guidance to auditors in connection with engagements to express an opinion on an entity's internal control structure, or a part thereof, and similar types of engagements. The scope of such an engagement is more extensive than that in a financial statement audit, although some of the procedures are similar. Paragraphs 13–34 of SAS No. 30 (AU Section 642.13–.34) specify that engagements under that standard involve planning the scope of the engagement, reviewing the design of the internal control structure, performing tests of controls, and evaluating the results.

AU Section 642 also specifies the forms of reporting on the internal control structure for various types of engagements. The main elements of the standard report expressing an unqualified opinion on an entity's internal control structure are

- A description of the scope of the engagement.
- The date to which the opinion relates.

[11]The terminology and concepts in SAS No. 30 have not been conformed to those in SAS Nos. 53 through 61 at the time of this writing. An ASB task force is considering substantive amendments to SAS No. 30.

- A statement that establishing and maintaining the internal control structure are the responsibility of management.
- A brief explanation of the broad objectives and inherent limitations of an internal control structure.
- The auditor's opinion on whether the entity's control structure policies and procedures meet the objectives of an internal control structure pertaining to preventing or detecting errors or irregularities that would be material to the financial statements (material weaknesses).

If the auditor's procedures disclose conditions that, individually or in combination, result in one or more material weaknesses, the auditor's report should be modified to describe the material weaknesses, the general nature of potential errors or irregularities that might occur as a result of the weaknesses, and whether the weaknesses arose from a lack of control structure policies and procedures or a breakdown in adhering to specific control procedures. If the auditor issues the opinion on the internal control structure in conjunction with or as part of an audit of the entity's financial statements, the report should state that the material weaknesses were considered in determining what audit tests to apply in conducting the financial statement audit.

Reports on Internal Control at Service Organizations

Service organizations may record transactions, process related data, or even execute and account for transactions on behalf of others. Companies that provide such services include, for example, trust departments of banks (which invest and hold securities for others), computer service centers (which process data for others), and securities depositories (which hold and account for securities for others). A service organization may seek a special-purpose report from an auditor on the design of its internal control structure or on both the design of the structure and the tests directed at specified control objectives. SAS No. 44, *Special-Purpose Reports on Internal Accounting Control at Service Organizations*[12] (AU Section 324), provides guidance on the responsibilities of an auditor who issues that type of special-purpose report. Those reports are frequently used by auditors of the enterprises whose transactions are executed or processed by the service organization (see the discussion in Chapter 6); the SAS also provides guidance on the auditor's decision to obtain a report on the internal control structure at a service organization and on considerations in using that type of report.

OPINIONS ON ACCOUNTING PRINCIPLES

An auditor is often requested to give a formal opinion on an accepted or preferred method of accounting, either for a hypothetical situation or for a

---

[12]The terminology and concepts in SAS No. 44 (AU Section 324) have not been conformed to those in SAS Nos. 53 through 61 at the time of this writing. An ASB task force is considering substantive amendments to SAS No. 44.

specific proposed or completed transaction. Notable examples of this type of opinion are the reports required by the SEC when a company changes an accounting principle, and by the New York Stock Exchange (NYSE) in connection with the accounting for a business combination as a pooling of interests.

Preferability Letters

Paragraph 16 of Accounting Principles Board (APB) Opinion No. 20, *Accounting Changes* (Accounting Standards Section A06.112), requires enterprise management to justify using an alternative accounting principle on the basis that it is preferable. The SEC requires companies subject to its reporting regulations that make a discretionary accounting change to obtain concurrence from their independent public accountants that the change is to a principle that is preferable in the circumstances.[13] The accountant's concurrence is required to be set forth in a "preferability letter" accompanying the first Form 10-Q filed after the discretionary accounting change.[14] The requirements are also applicable to Form 10-K if a discretionary accounting change is made in the fourth quarter of a company's fiscal year. Furthermore, as discussed in Chapter 21, the auditor should determine that the audit committee is informed about the initial selection of and changes in all significant accounting policies and their application.

The auditor's evaluation of the justification for a discretionary accounting change depends on the facts and circumstances of the specific situation. Possible justifications for discretionary accounting changes include

- Change to the preferred method where preferability among alternatives is expressed in authoritative pronouncements by organizations like the AICPA Accounting Standards Executive Committee on specialized accounting principles and practices.
- Change to the method of accounting prevalent in a particular industry.
- Change to reflect new circumstances (such as a change in depreciation methods to reflect the introduction of new types of equipment or new production processes).
- Change where preferability is based solely on elements of business judgment and business planning that do not fit into the aforementioned categories.

The auditor should carefully review the reasonableness of the client's justification for a change. This requires considering the client's business as well as

---

[13]Paragraph 29 of APB Opinion No. 20 (Accounting Standards Section A06.125) provides for a one-time exemption for accounting changes when a company makes an initial public offering of its shares; in that situation, the company is allowed to restate retroactively financial statements for all prior periods presented. The SEC also permits first-time registrants to change their accounting methods without filing a preferability letter.

[14]Changes necessitated by new authoritative pronouncements do not require preferability letters. The auditor should, of course, evaluate how the client has applied a new pronouncement to meet its particular facts and circumstances.

industry conditions, and the recent history of the client's changes applicable to the same circumstances. If the justification for the change is based on a desire to conform with industry practice, the auditor should corroborate the client's position that the new accounting method is prevalent in the industry. Citing one or two instances of its use in a large industry would not necessarily indicate that the new method is prevalent in the industry.

The SEC has indicated the auditor may rely, and express that reliance in the preferability letter, on management's determination of the elements of business judgment and business planning that affected the decision to make the accounting change. Examples of this may include management's expectations of the effect of general economic trends on the business, and planned changes in products or marketing methods to meet expected changes in demand. Although the auditor's judgments should not replace management's judgments, the auditor must conclude that management's judgments are not unreasonable.

The staff of the SEC has informally indicated that a preferability letter is also required if a change in accounting is described in a document, even if the effect of the change is not material in the current period. For example, a preferability letter would be required if a change in accounting was described in management's discussion and analysis but, because of immateriality, was not disclosed in the financial statements.

An example of an auditor's preferability letter to a client for filing with the SEC on an accounting change follows:

> We are providing this letter to you for inclusion as an exhibit to your Form 10-Q filing pursuant to Item 601 of Regulation S-K.
>
> We have read management's justification for the change in accounting from the _____ method to the _____ method contained in the Company's Form 10-Q for the quarter ended _____. Based on our reading of the data and discussions with Company officials of the business judgment and business planning factors relating to the change, we believe management's justification to be reasonable. Accordingly (in reliance on management's determination as regards elements of business judgment and business planning), we concur that the newly adopted accounting principle described above is preferable in the Company's circumstances to the method previously applied. [Note: The phrase in parentheses should be deleted if the auditor is not relying on management's determination in that regard in deciding on concurrence with the preferability of the accounting change.]
>
> We have not audited any financial statements of ABC Corp. as of any date or for any period subsequent to _____ nor have we audited the application of the change in accounting principle disclosed in Form 10-Q of ABC Corp. for the three months ended _____; accordingly, our comments are subject to revision on completion of an audit of the financial statements that include the accounting change.

If the letter is to be filed with Form 10-K, the form references should be changed and the third paragraph omitted.

Pooling Letters

Since the adoption of APB Opinion No. 16, *Business Combinations* (Accounting Standards Section B50), the NYSE has requested each company listing shares to be issued in a business combination accounted for as a pooling of interests to furnish the Exchange with a letter setting forth the requirements for pooling of interests accounting and indicating that the contemplated transaction meets each of those requirements. The NYSE requires that the other party to the business combination assent to the letter as an indication of its agreement with the specified terms of the transaction. In addition, the NYSE asks that the auditors of the corporation issuing stock in the transaction also furnish a letter to the Exchange indicating that they have reviewed the transaction and expressing their opinion that the combination meets the requirements for pooling accounting set forth in Opinion No. 16.

Before furnishing a "pooling letter" to the Exchange, the auditor should obtain copies of the full executed agreements and any other pertinent documents, together with an executed copy of the company's letter to the NYSE pertinent to the transaction. An example of a pooling letter from the auditor to the NYSE follows:

> We have read the Agreement and Plan of Reorganization between ABC Corporation and XYZ Corporation along with information and representations submitted to us by the companies, and the accompanying Letter of Compliance with Pooling of Interests Criteria. This Agreement is to be consummated through the issuance of (number) shares of ABC Corporation common stock on or about (date).

> In our opinion, based upon the information presented to us as of (date), this combination conforms in substance with the principles, guides, rules, and criteria of APB Opinion No. 16, and we concur in the treatment of this combination as a pooling of interests.

REPORTS ON THE APPLICATION OF ACCOUNTING PRINCIPLES

The preceding section of this chapter considered instances where a client asks an auditor to give an opinion on the appropriate accounting for recording a hypothetical, proposed, or consummated transaction. An accountant (the "reporting accountant") may also be asked by a nonaudit client (the "requestor") to give a similar opinion on the application of accounting principles. The requestor may be, among others, an investment banker that has created a new type of financial product and wants to include an opinion from the reporting accountant (sometimes called a "generic letter") in its promotional material, an investment banker representing another auditor's client that is contemplating a specific transaction, or another auditor's (the "continuing accountant") client seeking a "second opinion" on a proposed or consummated transaction. The requestor may have only the purest motives for seeking the advice of a CPA other than its own auditor, perhaps based on a belief that its auditor lacks the expertise to evaluate the appropriate accounting for a new financial product. Or the requestor may be "opinion shopping," seeking an opinion that can be used to intimidate its auditor to accede to its preferences or risk losing the engagement.

The profession has long been concerned with opinion shopping and has tried to prevent it. SAS No. 50, *Reports on the Application of Accounting Principles* (AU Section 625), specifies standards, for both performance and reporting, that should be followed by the reporting accountant when providing advice (either written or oral) on accounting matters or on the appropriate type of opinion on an entity's financial statements. The performance standards include a requirement that the reporting accountant seek permission from the requestor to consult with the continuing accountant and ask the requestor to authorize the continuing accountant to respond fully to the reporting accountant's inquiries. That requirement serves two purposes. The first, not explicitly stated in the SAS, is to discourage opinion shopping. The second is to provide the reporting accountant with information that the continuing accountant may have and that might not otherwise be available.

A written report giving advice on accounting matters or on the appropriate type of opinion would usually contain the items described in AU Section 625.08. An illustrative format for a report on the application of GAAP to a specific or hypothetical transaction follows:

Introduction

We have been engaged to report on the appropriate application of generally accepted accounting principles to the specific (hypothetical) transaction described below. This report is being issued to the ABC Company (XYZ Intermediaries) for assistance in evaluating accounting principles for the described specific (hypothetical) transaction. Our engagement has been conducted in accordance with standards established by the American Institute of Certified Public Accountants.

Description of Transaction

The facts, circumstances, and assumptions relevant to the specific (hypothetical) transaction as provided to us by the management of the ABC Company (XYZ Intermediaries) are as follows:

Appropriate Accounting Principles

[*Text discussing principles*]

Concluding Comments

The ultimate responsibility for the decision on the appropriate application of generally accepted accounting principles for an actual transaction rests with the preparers of financial statements, who should consult with their continuing accountants. Our judgment on the appropriate application of generally accepted accounting principles for the described specific (hypothetical) transaction is based solely on the facts provided to us as described above; should these facts and circumstances differ, our conclusion may change.

As discussed in Chapter 21, if an entity's auditor is aware that its management has consulted with other accountants (i.e., reporting accountants) about the application of accounting principles or the rendering of an opinion on the entity's financial statements, the auditor should communicate his or her views about the subject of the consultation to the audit committee.

SAS No. 50 is not applicable when an independent accountant (1) is engaged to report on financial statements, (2) assists in litigation involving accounting matters or appears as an ''expert'' witness in connection with such litigation, or (3) provides professional advice to another accountant in public practice.

MATTERS RELATING TO SOLVENCY

In certain secured financing transactions, particularly those in which owners' equity is significantly depleted, such as a leveraged buyout, the lenders may request written assurance from an accountant regarding the borrower's solvency, assuming the consummation of the transaction. The lenders are concerned that the financing not be considered a fraudulent conveyance under the Federal Bankruptcy Code and related state statutes. That would occur if the borrower was rendered insolvent as a result of the financing transaction, had unreasonably small capital after the transaction, or did not have the ability to pay its debts as they matured. Each of these situations is subject to legal interpretation.

In 1984, the AICPA issued an auditing interpretation stating that an auditor may issue a report on solvency provided that terms used in the financing agreement, such as ''debt,'' ''property,'' and ''fair value,'' were defined in reasonable detail so that they were ''susceptible to objective application.'' However, in 1988, the AICPA reconsidered reporting on solvency, this time from the perspective of the attestation standards, and came to a different conclusion. In an attestation interpretation entitled ''Responding to Requests for Reports on Matters Relating to Solvency'' (AT Section 9100.28–.41), the AICPA concluded that because matters relating to solvency, unreasonably small capital, and ability to pay debts as they mature

> are not clearly defined in an accounting sense, and are therefore subject to varying interpretations, they do not provide the accountant with the reasonable criteria required to evaluate the assertion under the third general attestation standard [see Chapter 24]. In addition, lenders are concerned with legal issues on matters relating to solvency and the accountant is generally unable to evaluate or provide assurance on these matters of legal interpretation. Therefore, accountants are precluded from giving any form of assurance on matters relating to solvency or any financial presentation of matters relating to solvency. (AT Section 9100.32)

LETTERS FOR UNDERWRITERS

The SEC's requirements for disclosures to be made in prospectuses and registration statements are complicated and periodically undergo significant changes. Accordingly, all parties to an SEC filing go to great lengths to ensure that the contents of those filings comply with the applicable requirements. In particular, as part of their "due diligence" duties, underwriters have had a long-standing practice of seeking specific assurance from lawyers and accountants that the SEC rules and regulations have been complied with. A common practice for underwriters has long been to seek "comfort" from an auditor on financial information in registration statements that is not covered by the auditor's report and on events subsequent to the report date.

As public expectations have grown and been reflected in legal and other attacks on those associated with disclosures, underwriters and their counsel have sought to obtain more and more "comfort" from auditors, which is formally expressed in a letter called a comfort letter. (Some lawyers still use the phrase common in earlier, more austere times: "cold comfort" letter.) While the comfort letter may originally have been an informal or semiformal helpful gesture on the part of an auditor, it is now a significant formal communication. In drafting comfort letters, formally called "letters for underwriters," auditors must therefore be especially careful not to assume unwarranted responsibility, either explicitly or implicitly.

SAS No. 49, *Letters for Underwriters*[15] (AU Section 634), provides guidelines intended to minimize misunderstandings in connection with comfort letters. The importance attached to comfort letters is reflected in the length and details of the numerous paragraphs in the Statement. It covers the kinds of matters that may properly be commented on by auditors in comfort letters and how the matters should be phrased, suggests forms of letters and how to prepare them, and recommends ways of reducing or avoiding misunderstanding about responsibility. Auditors who are asked to prepare letters for underwriters should become thoroughly familiar with SAS No. 49. While the following paragraphs summarize and paraphrase the SAS, the treatment in this book is not intended to serve as a substitute for a thorough understanding of the Statement.

Comfort letters are required not by the SEC but by underwriters as part of meeting their due diligence responsibilities; the letters are not "filed" with the SEC. Underwriting agreements usually set forth the requirement for and scope of a comfort letter. As soon as an underwriting is planned, the auditor, underwriter, and client meet to discuss the comfort letter. All parties usually recognize their respective objectives and welcome such a conference. The underwriter wants to have as much comfort as possible, the client is concerned with avoiding unnecessary problems and delays in the underwriting, and the auditor must determine whether he or she can provide the comfort called for by the underwriting agreement. Furthermore, an auditor who understands the client in the breadth and depth presumed throughout this book can usually

---

[15]At the time of this writing, an ASB task force is reconsidering the guidance in SAS No. 49, which was issued in 1984, because of possible inconsistencies between it and the attestation standards, issued in 1986, as well as possible practice problems in applying SAS No. 49.

benefit both the underwriter and the client by clarifying what is possible and what is not possible. An early conference often results in timely recognition of desirable clarifying changes both in the registration statement itself and in the underwriting agreement.

The auditor should obtain a copy of the underwriting agreement as soon as it is in draft form. After reading the draft agreement, the auditor may wish to draft the comfort letter. The purpose of the draft letter is to inform all parties what they may expect, provide an opportunity to discuss and change contemplated procedures, and enhance a smooth execution of the subsequent steps in the underwriting.

Preparing and reviewing the draft comfort letter also gives the auditor the opportunity to emphasize that responsibility for the sufficiency of procedures carried out in the comfort review is the underwriter's, not the auditor's. The auditor's purpose is to preclude allegations in support of a claim against the auditor that the underwriter relied on the auditor for the sufficiency of the procedures if they subsequently appear to have been insufficient. An auditor must take great care to make clear to all parties that a CPA may advise on procedures but may not assume responsibility for adequacy or sufficiency.

Dating the Letter

A comfort letter usually is requested at or shortly before the "effective date" of the registration statement. Underwriting agreements generally specify the date, often referred to as the "cutoff date," through which procedures specified in the letter are to be performed (perhaps five business days before the effective date). The letter should make clear that the period between the cutoff date and the date of the letter is not covered by the procedures and disclosures set forth in the letter. The comfort letter usually is updated to a new cutoff date at or shortly before the "closing date" (the date the securities are to be delivered to the underwriter in exchange for the proceeds of the offering) or to several closing dates, as might happen when securities are issued under a shelf registration.[16]

Addressee

The underwriting agreement often specifies to whom the letter should be addressed. Sometimes it is addressed to the lead underwriter, sometimes to the client, and sometimes to both. An auditor should not agree to address the letter to anyone else without first consulting legal counsel. If the lead underwriter has not been named (as may be the case in a shelf registration), the auditor may write a draft comfort letter with no addressee indicated, but should not furnish a letter in final form until the underwriter has been named; only the underwriter can determine the procedures that will be necessary for his or her purposes.

---

[16]Rule 415 of the 1933 Act permits, in certain circumstances, the registration of securities to be offered on a delayed or continuous basis over an extended period of time—known as a shelf registration.

Contents of the Letter

Comfort letters generally cover some or all of the following: the auditor's independence; the conformity, in all material respects, of the audited financial statements and schedules in the registration statement with the applicable accounting requirements of the Securities Act of 1933 and the SEC's published rules and regulations; unaudited financial statements, condensed financial statements, capsule information, or pro forma financial information; changes in selected financial statement items during the period after the latest statements contained in the filing; tables, statistics, and other financial information; and an understanding about the restricted circulation of the letter. The auditor's letter usually "tracks" the underwriting agreement precisely. The following paragraphs taken from AU Section 634.49–.61, illustrate a typical comfort letter. They need not be presented in the same order in an actual letter.

Introductory Paragraph.   A typical introductory paragraph is as follows:

June 30, 19X2

(Addressee)
Gentlemen:

We have audited the consolidated balance sheets of X Company (the company) and subsidiaries as of December 31, 19X5 and 19X4, and the consolidated statements of income, retained earnings, and cash flows for each of the three years in the period ended December 31, 19X5, and the related financial statement schedules included in the registration statement (No. _____) on Form _____ filed by the company under the Securities Act of 1933 (the Act); our reports with respect thereto are also included in that registration statement. The registration statement, as amended on [date], is herein referred to as the registration statement.

Auditors may refer to the fact that they have issued reports on other financial information. For example, if the auditor refers to the fact that a review of interim financial information was performed, an additional paragraph, such as the following, may be added:

Also, we have made a review of the unaudited condensed interim financial statements for the three-month periods ended March 31, 19X6 and 19X5, as indicated in our report dated May 15, 19X6, which is included in the registration statement.

Similar reference may be made to reports issued on condensed financial statements derived from audited financial statements, selected financial data, and pro forma financial information (or a financial forecast filed in lieu of a pro forma condensed income statement).

Independence.   It is customary to make an assertion about independence, substantially as follows:

We are independent certified public accountants with respect to X Company, within the meaning of the Act and the applicable published rules and regulations thereunder.

When the auditor reports on a predecessor company rather than the registrant named in the registration statement and is no longer associated and therefore does not need to be independent currently, the assertion begins along the following lines:

As of [date of the predecessor auditor's report] and during the period covered by the financial statements on which we reported, we were independent . . .

Compliance.   It is also customary to require comfort on compliance with SEC requirements as to form, which may be expressed as follows:

In our opinion, the consolidated financial statements and schedules audited by us and included or incorporated by reference in the registration statement comply in form in all material respects with the applicable accounting requirements of the Act and the related published rules and regulations.

In the rare case of a material departure from the published requirements, either the paragraph would include the phrase ''except as disclosed in the registration statement'' or the departure would be disclosed in the letter. Normally, a departure would not be considered unless representatives of the SEC had agreed to it in advance; in that event, the agreement should be mentioned in the comfort letter.

Unaudited Information.   AU Section 634 contains a number of guidelines for commenting in comfort letters on unaudited condensed interim financial statements, capsule information, pro forma financial information, and subsequent changes. The guidelines and illustrative comments follow.

Negative Assurance.   Comments on unaudited condensed financial statements, capsule information, and subsequent changes or decreases in specified financial statement items should be limited to negative assurance because that information has not been audited in accordance with generally accepted auditing standards. The following is an example of negative assurance:

Nothing came to our attention as a result of the foregoing procedures, however, that caused us to believe that:

a. (i) The unaudited consolidated condensed financial statements described in [cite paragraph number], included in the registration statement, do not comply in form in all material respects with the applicable accounting requirements of the Act and the related published rules and regulations and (ii) the unaudited consolidated condensed financial statements are not in conformity with generally accepted accounting principles applied on a basis substantially consistent with that of the audited consolidated financial statements; or

b. (i) At May 31, 19X6, there was any change in the capital stock or long-term debt of the company and subsidiaries consolidated or any decreases in consolidated net current assets or net assets as compared with amounts shown in the March 31, 19X6, unaudited consolidated condensed balance sheet included in the registration statement; or (ii) for the period from April 1, 19X6, to May 31, 19X6, there were any decreases, as compared with the corresponding period in the preceding year, in consolidated net sales or in the total or per share amounts of income before extraordinary items or of net income, except in all instances for changes or decreases that the registration statement discloses have occurred or may occur.

Enumerating Procedures.   The limited procedures carried out by the auditor, which should have been agreed on in advance, as described above, should be set forth in the letter. The following is an example:

For purposes of this letter we have read the 19X6 minutes of meetings of the stockholders, the board of directors, and [include other appropriate committees, if any] of the company and its subsidiaries as set forth in the minute books at June 25, 19X6, officials of the company having advised us that the minutes of all such meetings through that date were set forth therein; and we have carried out other procedures to June 25, 19X6 (our work did not extend to the period from June 26, 19X6, to June 30, 19X6, inclusive), as follows:

a. With respect to the three-month periods ended March 31, 19X6 and 19X5, we have

   (i) Read the unaudited consolidated condensed balance sheet as of March 31, 19X6, and unaudited consolidated condensed statements of income, retained earnings, and cash flows for the three-month periods ended March 31, 19X6 and 19X5, included in the registration statement; and

   (ii) Made inquiries of certain officials of the company who have responsibility for financial and accounting matters regarding (1) whether the unaudited consolidated condensed financial statements referred to in a(i) comply in form in all material respects with the applicable accounting requirements of the Act and the related published rules and regulations and (2) whether those unaudited consolidated condensed financial statements are in conformity with generally accepted accounting principles applied on a basis substantially consistent with that of the audited consolidated financial statements included in the registration statement.

b. With respect to the period from April 1, 19X6 to May 31, 19X6, we have

   (i) Read the unaudited consolidated financial statements of the company and subsidiaries for April and May of both 19X5 and 19X6 furnished us by the company, officials of the company having advised us that no such financial statements as of any date or for any period subsequent to May 31, 19X6 were available; and

   (ii) Made inquiries of certain officials of the company who have responsibility for financial and accounting matters regarding whether the unaudited financial statements referred to in b(i) are stated on a basis substantially consistent with that of the audited financial statements included in the registration statement.

The foregoing procedures do not constitute an audit conducted in accordance with generally accepted auditing standards. Also, they would not necessarily reveal matters of significance with respect to the comments in the following paragraph. [See the paragraph illustrated above under "Negative Assurance" for the "following paragraph" referred to.] Accordingly, we make no representations regarding the sufficiency of the foregoing procedures for your purposes.

As mentioned above, company officials have advised us that no consolidated financial statements as of any date or for any period subsequent to May 31, 19X6, are available; accordingly, the procedures carried out by us with respect to changes in financial statement items after May 31, 19X6, have, of necessity, been even more limited than those with respect to the periods referred to in the preceding paragraph. We have made inquiries of certain company officials who have responsibility for financial and accounting matters regarding whether (i) there was any change at June 25, 19X6, in the capital stock or long-term debt of the company and subsidiaries consolidated or any decreases in consolidated net current assets or net assets as compared with amounts shown on the March 31, 19X6, unaudited consolidated condensed balance sheet included in the registration statement or (ii) for the period from April 1, 19X6, to June 25, 19X6, there were any decreases, as compared with the corresponding period in the preceding year, in consolidated net sales or in the total or per share amounts of income before extraordinary items or of net income. On the basis of these inquiries and our reading of the minutes as described in the preceding paragraph, nothing came to our attention that caused us to believe that there was any such change or decrease, except in all instances for changes or decreases that the registration statement discloses have occurred or may occur.

Precise Terminology.   Terms of uncertain meaning, such as "general review," "limited review," "check," or "test," should not be used to describe the work unless they are defined in the letter. Terms not defined should be precise enough to preclude misunderstanding: for example, "read" or "compare" instead of "general review."

Specific Identification.   The unaudited condensed financial statements the letter refers to should be specifically and explicitly identified and the auditor's responsibility with respect to each item should be clearly stated. The following is an example:

We have not audited any financial statements of the company as of any date or for any period subsequent to December 31, 19X5; although we have conducted an audit for the year ended December 31, 19X5, the purpose (and therefore the scope) of the audit was to enable us to express our opinion on the consolidated financial statements as of December 31, 19X5, and for the year then ended, but not on the financial statements for any interim period within that year. Therefore, we are unable to and do not express any opinion on the unaudited consolidated condensed balance sheet as of March 31, 19X6, and unaudited consolidated condensed statements of income, retained earnings, and cash flows for the three-month periods ended March 31, 19X6 and 19X5, included in the registration statement, or on the financial position, results of operations, or cash flows as of any date or for any period subsequent to December 31, 19X5.

Importance of an Audit Base. Negative assurance with respect to un-audited condensed financial statements, capsule information, or subsequent changes or decreases should be given only if the auditor has obtained knowledge of the client's accounting and financial reporting practices and its control structure policies and procedures relating to the preparation of financial statements. This understanding provides a practical basis for the auditor's inquiries or procedures and ordinarily is obtained by auditing the client's financial statements for one or more years. If the auditor has not conducted such an audit, he or she should consider whether, in the particular circumstances, sufficient knowledge of these matters can be acquired to properly perform the inquiries and procedures requested by the underwriter.

Subsequent Changes. The procedures followed for interim periods may not disclose changes in capital stock or long-term debt or decreases in specified financial statement items, inconsistencies in the application of GAAP, instances of noncompliance as to form with accounting requirements of the SEC, or other matters about which negative assurance is requested. An appropriate way of making this clear is shown in the caveat included in the illustrative paragraphs under "Enumerating Procedures," above.

Working Papers. Obviously, working papers should be prepared to support the assertions made in the comfort letter and to document the procedures followed.

Other Considerations. A comfort letter should not repeat the standard opinion or give negative assurance on it because doing so would obscure the relative responsibilities for subsequent events and could give rise to misunderstandings. The letter also should not give negative assurance about "adverse changes"—a phrase formerly in common use—because the term is too broad and imprecise. The letter should refer to changes (either increases or decreases) in specified items, as illustrated under "Negative Assurance," above.

It is essential that terms be defined as precisely as possible and that everything feasible be done to make sure that all parties understand the terms. The "change period" to be covered by the comfort letter and the financial statement items to be covered should be specified. What constitutes a change should be defined, including what period or date is to be compared with what earlier period or date. Comments on changes in capital stock or long-term debt and decreases in other specified financial statement items should be limited to changes or decreases not disclosed in the registration statement. The comfort letter should not include a general statement that, as a result of carrying out the specified procedures, nothing else came to the auditor's attention that would be of interest to the underwriter, because there is no way for the auditor to anticipate what other matters might be of interest to an underwriter.

When other auditors have audited a portion of the accounts (e.g., significant divisions, branches, or subsidiaries), usually they are asked for comfort letters that duplicate as closely as possible the one the principal auditor is to issue. The principal auditor's comfort letter then states that he or she has read the letters of the other auditors and has not performed any procedures other than reading those letters.

The auditor may discover matters that require mention in the final comfort letter but that are not mentioned in the draft letter. Those matters should be discussed with the client and considered for disclosure in the registration statement. If disclosure will not be made, the auditor should inform the client that the matters will be mentioned in the comfort letter and should suggest that the client notify the underwriter promptly. As a general rule, the auditor should be present when such matters are discussed by the client and underwriter.

Tables, Statistics, and Other Financial Information. Some underwriters would like an auditor to give comfort on every numerical figure appearing in a registration statement. Many of those figures, however, are beyond the professional competence of an auditor to comment on. It is appropriate for an auditor to comment on information expressed in dollars or in percentages derived from dollar amounts and on other quantitative information obtained from accounting records by analysis or computation. Auditors should not comment on matters involving the exercise of management judgment, like explanations of the reasons for changes in income or operating ratios. Nor should they comment on matters that are not subject to internal control structure policies and procedures, like square footage of facilities and backlog information. As with all other comments, the procedures followed by the auditor in support of comments on tables, statistics, and other financial information should be set out clearly in the letter and agreed on in advance. They should also be accompanied by a disclaimer of responsibility for their sufficiency.

The expression ''present fairly'' should not be used in comments concerning tables, statistics, and other financial information. As discussed more fully in Chapter 22, ''present fairly'' is meaningful only in relation to a specific frame of reference—which, for an auditor, usually is conformity with generally accepted accounting principles. Without that qualifying phrase, ''present fairly'' is too broad and imprecise and is likely to give rise to misunderstandings.

Concluding Paragraph. To avoid the possibility of misunderstanding about the purpose and intended use of the comfort letter, it is customary to conclude the letter with a paragraph along the following lines:

> This letter is solely for the information of the addressees and to assist the underwriters in conducting and documenting their investigation of the affairs of the company in connection with the offering of the securities covered by the registration statement, and it is not to be used, circulated, quoted, or otherwise referred to within or without the underwriting group for any other purpose, including, but not limited to, the registration, purchase, or sale of securities, nor is it to be filed with or referred to in whole or in part in the registration statement or any other document, except that reference may be made to it in the underwriting agreement or in any list of closing documents pertaining to the offering of the securities covered by the registration statement.

24

Attestation Engagements

In recent years, clients have increasingly requested accountants to express opinions about various representations unrelated to an audit of historical financial statements. CPAs were usually able to seek guidance by referring to AICPA auditing pronouncements or by applying the concepts underlying them. As the range of requests for attest services expanded, it became increasingly difficult to look to the existing standards for guidance, and the need for new standards that would be responsive to the changing environment became apparent.

Consequently, attestation standards were developed to establish a broad framework for addressing engagements to provide assurance on a wide variety of client assertions. The standards set boundaries around the types of attest services a CPA in the practice of public accounting (referred to hereafter as a practitioner) may perform, and also provide a guide for the AICPA in promulgating future interpretive pronouncements.

Statement on Standards for Attestation Engagements (SSAE), *Attestation Standards* (AT Section 100) (the Statement), was issued jointly by the Auditing Standards Board and the Accounting and Review Services Committee in 1986. In December 1987, the Management Advisory Services (MAS) Executive Committee issued an SSAE, *Attest Services Related to MAS Engagements* (AT Section 100.71–.76), which effectively extended the applicability of the attestation standards to MAS services. Two other statements have been issued that rely on the attestation standards for their authority. *Reporting on Pro Forma Financial Information* (AT Section 300) was issued in 1988; it provides interpretive guidance based on the standards. The other statement, *Financial Forecasts and Projections* (AT Section 200), was actually issued shortly before the first SSAE, but it too draws on the attestation standards as a basis for its interpretive guidance. In addition, two interpretations of the attestation standards have been issued. All of those pronouncements are discussed in this chapter.

ATTESTATION STANDARDS

Definitions

The Statement (AT Section 100.01) defines an attest engagement as "one in which a practitioner is engaged to issue or does issue a written communication that expresses a conclusion about the reliability of a written assertion that is the responsibility of another party." The definition uses the term "practitioner," which according to the Statement includes not only CPAs but full- or part-time employees of a public accounting firm. Thus, an employee of a CPA firm who is not a CPA, such as a management advisory services consultant, is required to comply with the provisions of the Statement if the engagement meets the definition of an attest engagement.

Services Covered by Standards

Attest engagements might include examining or reviewing, and reporting on

- Descriptions of an entity's internal control structure.
- Descriptions of computer software products to be marketed.

- Investment performance statistics.
- Antitrust case data.
- Insurance claims data.
- Labor data for union contract negotiation.
- Audience and circulation data for broadcasters and publishers.
- Occupancy, enrollment, and attendance data for universities.
- Cost justification for a utility rate increase.
- Productivity indicators.
- Pension plan obligations of a target company in a buy–sell agreement.

By contrast, the following professional services typically provided by practitioners are *not* attest engagements:

- Management consulting engagements in which the practitioner provides advice or recommendations to a client.
- Engagements in which the practitioner is engaged to advocate a client's position—for example, concerning tax matters being reviewed by the Internal Revenue Service.
- Tax engagements in which a practitioner prepares tax returns or provides tax advice.
- Engagements in which the practitioner compiles financial statements, because he or she is not required to examine or review evidence supporting the information furnished by the client and does not express any conclusion on its reliability.
- Engagements in which the practitioner's role is solely to assist the client—such as preparing information other than financial statements.
- Engagements in which a practitioner is engaged to testify as an expert witness in accounting, auditing, taxation, or other matters, given certain stipulated facts.
- Engagements in which a practitioner provides an expert opinion on certain points of principle, such as the application of tax laws or accounting standards, given specific facts provided by another party. (In this type of engagement, the expert opinion must not express a conclusion about the reliability of the facts provided by the other party.)

The distinguishing characteristic of the above services that are not attest engagements is that the services involve providing advice, recommendations, or assistance to a client on the basis of a practitioner's experience and expertise in a particular area. They do not require the practitioner to express a conclusion about an assertion.

Standards for Attestation Engagements

The Statement's introduction describes the 11 attestation standards as "a natural extension of the ten generally accepted auditing standards. Like the auditing standards, the attestation standards deal with the need for technical competence, independence in mental attitude, due professional care, adequate planning and supervision, sufficient evidence, and appropriate reporting; however, they are much broader in scope." The attestation standards needed to be broader in scope than the ten generally accepted auditing standards, because of the distinction between an audit engagement and an attest engagement. In its most basic form, auditing is concerned only with an enterprise's historical financial statements measured against a set of criteria known as generally accepted accounting principles. Because of the range of services that might qualify as an attest engagement, however, it is not possible to establish a single set of criteria for only one kind of assertion. In one instance, the attestor may be asked to express a conclusion about the reliability of audit software, and in the next instance, the conclusion may relate to whether management's assumptions provide a reasonable basis for a financial forecast.

In adopting the Statement, the AICPA pointed out that the attestation standards did not supersede any existing standards. That is, the practitioner should first look to Statements on Auditing Standards or Statements on Standards for Accounting and Review Services for guidance, before looking to the attestation standards.

In practice, this frequently creates a dilemma—caused less by the attestation standards than by the auditing standards. When the ten generally accepted auditing standards were developed, the drafters undoubtedly had in mind a set of standards that would serve the attest function as it applied to historical financial statements. However, over time, the standards were interpreted broadly to include services that were not originally contemplated and that fall more logically under the umbrella of attestation. For example, it is difficult to understand how an engagement to apply agreed-upon procedures can measure up to *each* of the ten auditing standards, such as the standard that calls for obtaining an understanding of the internal control structure, yet such an engagement fits comfortably into the attestation standards, which do not require an understanding of the control structure.

The problem of which set of standards applies is caused by inconsistencies between the sets of standards and the fact that auditing standards were interpreted over the years in ways that broadened their original scope. The AICPA recognized this and has indicated its intention to resolve these inconsistencies. In the meantime, practitioners should refer to the attestation standards only after considering other available guidance. Figure 24.1 shows the 11 attestation standards and compares them with the 10 auditing standards.

Some of the attestation standards are analogous to the auditing standards and related interpretations. For example, the third attestation standard of reporting, "The report shall state all of the practitioner's significant reservations about the engagement and the presentation of the assertion," is little different from the following statement from Statement on Auditing Standards (SAS) No. 58 (AU Section 508.39): "When the auditor expresses a qualified opinion, he should disclose all of the substantive reasons in . . . his report." Similarly, the fourth attestation standard of reporting, which limits the distribution of an agreed-upon procedures report to the parties who have agreed to the procedures, is no different from AU Section 622.01, which states

Figure 24.1   Attestation Standards Compared with Generally Accepted Auditing Standards

Attestation Standards	*Generally Accepted Auditing Standards*

General Standards

1. The engagement shall be performed by a practitioner or practitioners having adequate technical training and proficiency in the attest function.	1. The audit is to be performed by a person or persons having adequate technical training and proficiency as an auditor.
2. The engagement shall be performed by a practitioner or practitioners having adequate knowledge in the subject matter of the assertion.	
3. The practitioner shall perform an engagement only if he or she has reason to believe that the following two conditions exist: • The assertion is capable of evaluation against reasonable criteria that either have been established by a recognized body or are stated in the presentation of the assertion in a sufficiently clear and comprehensive manner for a knowledgeable reader to be able to understand them. • The assertion is capable of reasonably consistent estimation or measurement using such criteria.	
4. In all matters relating to the engagement, an independence in mental attitude shall be maintained by the practitioner or practitioners.	2. In all matters relating to the assignment, an independence in mental attitude is to be maintained by the auditor or auditors.
5. Due professional care shall be exercised in the performance of the engagement.	3. Due professional care is to be exercised in the performance of the audit and the preparation of the report.

Standards of Fieldwork

1. The work shall be adequately planned and assistants, if any, shall be properly supervised.	1. The work is to be adequately planned and assistants, if any, are to be properly supervised.
	2. A sufficient understanding of the internal control structure is to be obtained to plan the audit and to determine the nature, timing, and extent of tests to be performed.
2. Sufficient evidence shall be obtained to provide a reasonable basis for the conclusion that is expressed in the report.	3. Sufficient competent evidential matter is to be obtained through inspection, observation, inquiries, and confirmations to afford a reasonable basis

Figure 24.1 **Continued**

Attestation Standards	*Generally Accepted Auditing Standards*
	for an opinion regarding the financial statements under audit.

Standards of Reporting

Attestation Standards	*Generally Accepted Auditing Standards*
1. The report shall identify the assertion being reported on and state the character of the engagement.	
2. The report shall state the practitioner's conclusion about whether the assertion is presented in conformity with the established or stated criteria against which it was measured.	1. The report shall state whether the financial statements are presented in accordance with generally accepted accounting principles.
	2. The report shall identify those circumstances in which such principles have not been consistently observed in the current period in relation to the preceding period.
	3. Informative disclosures in the financial statements are to be regarded as reasonably adequate unless otherwise stated in the report.
3. The report shall state all of the practitioner's significant reservations about the engagement and the presentation of the assertion.	4. The report shall either contain an expression of opinion regarding the financial statements, taken as a whole, or an assertion to the effect than an opinion cannot be expressed. When an overall opinion cannot be expressed, the reasons therefor should be stated. In all cases where an auditor's name is associated with financial statements, the report should contain a clear-cut indication of the character of the auditor's work and the degree of responsibility the auditor is taking.
4. The report on an engagement to evaluate an assertion that has been prepared in conformity with agreed-upon criteria or on an engagement to apply agreed-upon procedures should contain a statement limiting its use to the parties who have agreed upon such criteria or procedures.	

Source: Adapted from Statement on Standards for Attestation Engagements, *Attestation Standards* (AT Section 100.77).

An accountant may accept an engagement in which the scope is limited to applying to one or more specified elements, accounts, or items of a financial statement agreed-upon procedures that are not sufficient to enable him to express an opinion on the specified elements, accounts, or items, provided (a) the parties involved have a clear understanding of the procedures to be performed and (b) distribution of the report is to be restricted to named parties involved.

Other attestation standards, however, are based on concepts that differ from their counterparts in an auditing environment. These concepts are explained in the remainder of this section of the chapter.

Independence in Attest Engagements.   The Statement (AT Section 100.23) notes that "practitioners performing an attest service should not only be independent in fact, but also should avoid situations that may impair the appearance of independence." All personnel assigned to the engagement, as well as those to whom members of the engagement team report or with whom they consult, are required to be independent of the client. This contrasts with an audit engagement, where the CPA firm as a whole is required to be independent of the client. Chapter 3 discusses in detail matters relating to independence, including a proposed interpretation under Rule 101 dealing with independence and attest engagements.

The Need for Reasonable Criteria.   AT Section 100.12 states that "the attest function should be performed only when it can be effective and useful. Practitioners should have a reasonable basis for believing that a meaningful conclusion can be provided on an assertion." This means that the assertion cannot be so subjective that it is meaningless or possibly misleading. To meet this condition, *reasonable criteria* should exist that competent persons could use to reach substantially similar estimates or measurements, though not necessarily the same conclusion. For example, attesting to a software product characterized as the "best" or attesting to the competence of management would not meet this condition for an attest function, since it is unlikely that reasonable criteria exist against which "best" and "competent" can be consistently measured. This condition applies equally to providing positive and negative assurance (discussed later).

The SSAE (AT Section 100.15) defines reasonable criteria as "those that yield useful information." They may be criteria established by a recognized body such as the FASB or GASB, which are authoritative and therefore need only be referred to in the presentation of the assertion. (These are referred to as *established criteria*.) The absence of established criteria for estimating or measuring an assertion, however, does not prevent a practitioner from accepting an attest engagement. The main consideration is whether the criteria used are reasonable. Other criteria, such as standards prepared by an industry association, even though they do not have authoritative support, may also pass the "reasonableness" test. If the assertion is to be evaluated against the latter type of criteria, they must be stated in the presentation of the assertion, as indicated by the third general attestation standard. (These are referred to as *stated criteria*.) Still other criteria are reasonable for evaluating an assertion, but only by a limited number of specified users who participated in establishing the criteria. (These are referred to as *agreed-upon criteria*.)

Engagement Planning and Performance.   Planning an attest engagement involves developing an overall strategy and designing a program of procedures that is consistent with the level of assurance to be provided. When planning those procedures, the practitioner considers a number of factors, including the nature and complexity of the assertions, the criteria against which the assertions will be evaluated, preliminary judgments about materiality, the anticipated level of attestation risk related to the assertions, and the level of assurance that the practitioner has been engaged to provide in the attest report.

Attestation risk, which is similar to the concept of audit risk as described in SAS No. 47, *Audit Risk and Materiality in Conducting an Audit* (AU Section 312), is the risk that the practitioner may unknowingly fail to appropriately modify his or her attest report on an assertion that is materially misstated. The level of attestation risk the practitioner is willing to accept varies inversely with the level of assurance the practitioner plans to provide on the presentation of assertions. In an attest engagement designed to provide the highest level of assurance (an "examination"), the practitioner should plan and perform procedures to generate sufficient evidence to limit attestation risk to an appropriately low level for the high level of assurance that may be imparted. Those procedures generally involve search and verification (for example, inspection, confirmation, and observation) as well as internal inquiries and comparisons of internal information. In a limited assurance engagement (a "review"), the practitioner's objective is to accumulate sufficient evidence to limit attestation risk to a moderate level. This can ordinarily be achieved by internal inquiries and analytical procedures.

A report for public distribution on an attest service may be based on either an examination or a review. The high level of assurance provided in a report on an examination is referred to as positive assurance; in a report on a review, the moderate level of assurance expressed is in the form of negative assurance.

Reports on Attest Engagements

Two levels of assurance may be provided in a report for public distribution when an attest service is performed: positive assurance on the basis of an examination, and negative assurance on the basis of a review. When expressing positive assurance, the practitioner states a conclusion about whether the assertions are presented in conformity with established or stated criteria. In providing negative assurance, the practitioner states only whether information has come to his or her attention that indicates the assertions are not presented in conformity with those criteria.

Reports expressing positive assurance based on an examination or negative assurance based on a review may be issued for general distribution, provided the assertions on which the auditor provides assurance are based on established or stated criteria. Examination and review reports may also be based on specified criteria agreed upon by the asserter and the user(s); in that event, use of the report is limited to those parties, because other parties may not understand the criteria or the assurance expressed in the report. For example, the assertion may be based on contractual terms known only by the specified users who participated in negotiating the contract.

When the presentation of assertions has been prepared in conformity with specified criteria agreed to by the asserter and the user, the report should contain

a. A statement limiting use of the report to the specified parties.
b. An indication, when applicable, that the presentation of assertions differs materially from what would have been presented if criteria for the presentation of such assertions for general distribution had been fol-

lowed. (For example, financial information prepared in accordance with criteria specified in a contract may differ materially from information prepared in conformity with generally accepted accounting principles [GAAP].)

A practitioner may also perform attest services based on agreed-upon procedures; in those services, the reports are also restricted to the parties that agreed to the procedures. The report in an agreed-upon procedures engagement may be in the form of a summary of findings, negative assurance, or both.

An overview of each of the three attest services (including examples of reports) follows.

Examination. When expressing a positive opinion, the practitioner should clearly state whether, in his or her opinion, the presentation of assertions is in conformity with established or stated criteria. Examination reports may be qualified or modified for some aspect of the presentation or the engagement. In addition, they may emphasize certain matters relating to the attest engagement or the presentation of assertions. The following is an illustrative examination report that expresses an unqualified opinion on a presentation of assertions:

We have examined the accompanying Statement of Investment Performance Statistics of XYZ Fund for the year ended December 31, 19X1. Our examination was made in accordance with standards established by the American Institute of Certified Public Accountants and, accordingly, included such procedures as we considered necessary in the circumstances.

[*Additional paragraph(s) may be added to emphasize certain matters relating to the attest engagement or the presentation of assertions.*]

In our opinion, the Statement of Investment Performance Statistics referred to above presents the investment performance of XYZ Fund for the year ended December 31, 19X1, in conformity with the measurement and disclosure criteria set forth in Note 1.

Review. In providing negative assurance, the practitioner's conclusion should state whether any information came to his or her attention on the basis of the work performed that indicates the assertions are not presented in all material respects in conformity with established or stated criteria. The following illustrative review report expresses negative assurance where no exceptions have been found:

We have reviewed the accompanying Statement of Investment Performance Statistics of XYZ Fund for the year ended December 31, 19X1. Our review was conducted in accordance with standards established by the American Institute of Certified Public Accountants.

A review is substantially less in scope than an examination, the objective of which is the expression of an opinion on the Statement of Investment Performance Statistics. Accordingly, we do not express such an opinion.

[Additional paragraph(s) may be added to emphasize certain matters relating to the attest engagement or the presentation of assertions.]

Based on our review, nothing came to our attention that caused us to believe that the accompanying Statement of Investment Performance Statistics is not presented in conformity with the measurement and disclosure criteria set forth in Note 1.

Agreed-Upon Procedures. A practitioner's conclusion on the results of applying agreed-upon procedures to a presentation of assertions should be in the form of a summary of findings, negative assurance, or both. The level of assurance provided in a report on the application of agreed-upon procedures depends on the nature and scope of the practitioner's procedures as agreed to by the specified parties to whom the report is restricted. Furthermore, such parties must understand that they take responsibility for the adequacy of the attest procedures (and, therefore, the amount of assurance provided) for their purposes.

Following is an illustrative agreed-upon procedures report that enumerates the procedures performed and includes both a summary of findings and negative assurance. Either the summary of findings, if no exceptions are found, or negative assurance could be omitted.

To ABC Inc. and XYZ Fund

We have applied the procedures enumerated below to the accompanying Statement of Investment Performance Statistics of XYZ Fund for the year ended December 31, 19X1. These procedures, which were agreed to by ABC Inc. and XYZ Fund, were performed solely to assist you in evaluating the investment performance of XYZ Fund. This report is intended solely for your information and should not be used by those who did not participate in determining the procedures.

[Include paragraph enumerating procedures and findings.]

These agreed-upon procedures are substantially less in scope than an examination, the objective of which is the expression of an opinion on the Statement of Investment Performance Statistics. Accordingly, we do not express such an opinion.

Based on the application of the procedures referred to above, nothing came to our attention that caused us to believe that the accompanying Statement of Investment Performance Statistics is not presented in conformity with the measurement and disclosure criteria set forth in Note 1. Had we performed additional procedures or had we made an examination of the Statement of Investment Performance Statistics, other matters might have come to our attention that would have been reported to you.

Modifications to Standard Report. If the practitioner has any reservations about the engagement or the presentation of assertions (e.g., restrictions on the scope of the engagement or concerns about conformity of the presentation with stated criteria), the report should be modified. A detailed discussion of modified reports is included in the Statement.

Interpretations of Attestation Standards

Two interpretations of the attestation standards have been issued that indicate how the standards may be used.

- *Defense Industry Questionnaire on Business Ethics and Conduct* (AT Section 9100.1–.27) provides guidance for engagements to express a conclusion about the appropriateness of management's responses to a defense industry questionnaire covering certain principles of business ethics and conduct. The interpretation contains guidance for this type of engagement, illustrative procedures that an attestor may apply, and illustrative reports.

The questions in the questionnaire and accompanying responses constitute the written assertions of the defense contractor.

The practitioner's procedures are designed to obtain evidence that the defense contractor has designed and placed in operation policies and programs that conform to the criteria in the questionnaire in a manner that supports the responses to the questions, and that those policies and programs operated during the period covered by the defense contractor's assertions. The practitioner does not, however, provide assurance about the effectiveness of those policies and programs in ensuring compliance with the contractor's code of business ethics and conduct or about whether the contractor and its employees have complied with federal procurement laws.

- *Responding to Requests for Reports on Matters Relating to Solvency* (AT Section 9100.28–.41) discusses services the practitioner may perform in connection with a financing arrangement. Lenders, as a condition to the closing of certain secured financings in connection with leveraged buyouts, recapitalizations, and certain other transactions, have sometimes requested written assurance from an accountant regarding the prospective borrower's solvency and related matters. Such services were previously permitted under an interpretation of AU Section 504, "Association With Financial Statements." That interpretation concluded that if there was agreement on the meaning of the terms "fair value," "property," and "debt," the independent accountant could report, based on an examination made in accordance with GAAS, on a statement that presented the excess of a borrower's property at fair value over the total amount of its debt. However, when viewed from the perspective of the attestation standards, matters relating to solvency are subject to varying interpretations of the Federal Bankruptcy Code and various state fraudulent conveyance and transfer statutes. Accordingly, the accountant cannot find reasonable criteria to evaluate the assertions against. For that reason, the interpretation based on AU Section 504 was withdrawn, and practitioners are prohibited from providing assurance with respect to "matters relating to solvency."

PRO FORMA FINANCIAL INFORMATION

Pro forma financial information presents the significant effects on historical financial information of "what might have been," had a consummated or proposed transaction or event occurred at an earlier date. It is commonly used to show the effects of

- Business combinations.
- Changes in capitalization.
- Dispositions of a significant portion of a business.
- Changes in the form of a business organization or in its status as an autonomous entity.
- Proposed sales of securities and the application of the proceeds.

Pro forma financial information is sometimes included in prospectuses, proxy statements, and other public documents, and more often in less widely circulated, special-purpose statements. It is frequently the only way to illustrate the effects of a particular contemplated transaction. An important business decision may be impossible to describe intelligibly without the use of pro forma data.

In September 1988, the Auditing Standards Board issued an SSAE on *Reporting on Pro Forma Financial Information* (AT Section 300). It provides guidance to a practitioner who is engaged to examine or review and to report on pro forma financial information. Although this SSAE provides standards only for examinations and reviews of pro forma financial information, it notes that practitioners may apply agreed-upon procedures to such information in accordance with the SSAE on *Attestation Standards*, provided the resulting report is restricted to the parties that agreed to the procedures.

The SSAE on pro forma information does not address those circumstances when, for purposes of a more meaningful presentation, a transaction consummated after the balance sheet date is reflected in the historical financial statements, such as a revision of debt maturities or of earnings per share calculations for a stock split. It also does not cover pro forma financial information that the practitioner is not engaged to report on and that is presented outside the basic financial statements, but within the same document. SAS No. 8, *Other Information in Documents Containing Audited Financial Statements* (AU Section 550), and SAS No. 37, *Filings Under Federal Securities Statutes* (AU Section 711), describe the practitioner's responsibilities in those circumstances.

Components of Pro Forma Financial Information

Pro forma financial information includes historical financial information and pro forma adjustments that are applied to the historical data to show the effect of the proposed transaction or event. The historical information, adjustments, and resulting pro forma amounts are commonly presented in columnar form.

Pro forma adjustments are based on assumptions reflecting, to the best of management's knowledge and belief, the conditions it expects would have existed and the course of action it would have taken had the proposed transaction or event occurred at an earlier date. Assumptions typically included in a presentation of pro forma financial information are

- Bank borrowings and related interest rates.
- Fixed asset purchases and disposals.
- Business combinations and divestitures, including cash layouts and proceeds, respectively.

Criteria for Reporting

There are three conditions that must be met for a practitioner to examine or review, and report on, pro forma financial information.

- The document containing the pro forma financial information should include (or incorporate by reference) complete historical financial statements of the entity or entities for the most recent year. When pro forma financial information is presented for an interim period, the document should include historical financial information for that interim period. This facilitates comparisons of the effects of the proposed transaction or event with historical results. If pro forma financial information is presented in connection with a proposed business combination, appropriate historical financial information for the significant constituents of the combined entity should be included in the document.
- The historical financial statements on which the pro forma financial information is based must have been audited or reviewed. The level of assurance that may be provided on the pro forma financial information as of a particular date or for a particular period cannot exceed the level of assurance provided on the accompanying historical financial information. For example, if the underlying historical financial statements of the entity have been audited at year-end and reviewed at an interim date, the practitioner may perform an examination or a review of the year-end pro forma financial information, but is limited to performing a review of the interim pro forma financial information.
- The practitioner should have an appropriate level of knowledge of the accounting and financial reporting practices of the entity or entities. This knowledge may have been obtained in an audit or a review of the historical financial statements; if not, the practitioner should design and perform procedures to obtain it. These procedures may include inquiry of client management and review of another practitioner's working papers, particularly those dealing with financial reporting practices.

Presentation of Pro Forma Financial Information

The SSAE on pro forma information requires that

- The pro forma financial information be appropriately distinguished from the historical financial information. (The column of pro forma amounts in the financial statements is usually labeled ''pro forma.'')

- The transaction or event reflected in the pro forma financial information be described, along with the source of the historical financial information on which it is based.
- The significant assumptions used in developing the pro forma adjustments, together with any significant uncertainties about those assumptions, be disclosed.
- The pro forma financial information include statements to the effect that it should be read in conjunction with the related historical financial information and that it is not necessarily indicative of the results that would have been attained had the transaction or event actually taken place earlier. (Article 11 of Regulation S-X provides further guidance with respect to the presentation of pro forma financial information in SEC filings.)

Reporting

As in other attest engagements, two levels of assurance may be provided on pro forma information—positive assurance based on an examination or negative assurance based on a review. As noted earlier, examination procedures generally encompass a combination of inspection, confirmation, and observation, and review procedures generally include inquiry and analytical procedures.

The objective of examination procedures applied to pro forma financial information is to limit attestation risk to an appropriately low level to allow the practitioner to provide positive assurance about whether

- Management's assumptions provide a reasonable basis for presenting the significant effects directly attributable to the underlying transaction or event.
- The related pro forma adjustments give appropriate effect to those assumptions.
- The pro forma column reflects the proper application of the adjustments to the historical financial statements.

In a review, the procedures should be sufficient to limit attestation risk to a moderate level, so that the practitioner can provide negative assurance with respect to the three items stated above.

Ordinarily, assurance that the pro forma adjustments "give appropriate effect" to management's assumptions means that the adjustments have been prepared in conformity with generally accepted accounting principles relevant to the proposed transaction or event. If applicable, that would include the consistent application of GAAP in both the historical financial statements and the pro forma adjustments.

The practitioner's report should be dated as of the completion of the appropriate procedures. The report may be combined with the report on the historical financial information or may be separate. If the reports are combined and the date of completion of the procedures on the pro forma financial information is after the date of completion of the field work on the historical financial information, the combined report should be dual dated. (See Chapter 21 for an explanation of dual dating.)

Examination Report. The following example of a standard report on an examination of pro forma financial information is based on the SSAE (AT Section 300.16):

> We have examined the pro forma adjustments reflecting the transaction [or event] described in Note 1 and the application of those adjustments to the historical amounts in the accompanying pro forma condensed balance sheet of X Company as of December 31, 19X1, and the pro forma condensed statement of income for the year then ended. The historical condensed financial statements are derived from the historical financial statements of X Company, which were audited by us, and of Y Company, which were audited by other accountants, appearing elsewhere herein [or incorporated by reference]. Such pro forma adjustments are based upon management's assumptions described in Note 2. Our examination was made in accordance with standards established by the American Institute of Certified Public Accountants and, accordingly, included such procedures as we considered necessary in the circumstances.
>
> The objective of this pro forma financial information is to show what the significant effects on the historical financial information might have been had the transaction [or event] occurred at an earlier date. However, the pro forma condensed financial statements are not necessarily indicative of the results of operations or related effects on financial position that would have been attained had the above-mentioned transaction [or event] actually occurred earlier.
>
> [*Additional paragraph(s) may be added to emphasize certain matters relating to the attest engagement.*]
>
> In our opinion, management's assumptions provide a reasonable basis for presenting the significant effects directly attributable to the above-mentioned transaction [or event] described in Note 1, the related pro forma adjustments give appropriate effect to those assumptions, and the pro forma column reflects the proper application of those adjustments to the historical financial statement amounts in the pro forma condensed balance sheet as of December 31, 19X1, and the pro forma condensed statement of income for the year then ended.

Like an audit report on historical financial statements, an examination report on pro forma financial information may be modified to describe circumstances, such as scope limitations, uncertainties, or reservations about the propriety of the assumptions. Examples of such reports are included in the SSAE.

Review Report. As discussed earlier, a practitioner's review report on pro forma financial information expresses negative assurance with respect to the assumptions underlying the proposed transaction or event and how it might have affected the historical data. Following is the standard report on a review of pro forma financial information:

> We have reviewed the pro forma adjustments reflecting the transaction [or event] described in Note 1 and the application of those adjustments to the

historical amounts in the accompanying pro forma condensed balance sheet of X Company as of March 31, 19X2, and the pro forma condensed statement of income for the three months then ended. These historical condensed financial statements are derived from the historical unaudited financial statements of X Company, which were reviewed by us, and of Y Company, which were reviewed by other accountants, appearing elsewhere herein [or incorporated by reference]. Such pro forma adjustments are based upon management's assumptions described in Note 2. Our review was conducted in accordance with standards established by the American Institute of Certified Public Accountants.

A review is substantially less in scope than an examination, the objective of which is the expression of an opinion on management's assumptions, the pro forma adjustments and the application of those adjustments to historical financial information. Accordingly, we do not express such an opinion.

[*Same paragraph as second paragraph of examination report.*]

[*Additional paragraph(s) may be added to emphasize certain matters relating to the attest engagement.*]

Based on our review, nothing came to our attention that caused us to believe that management's assumptions do not provide a reasonable basis for presenting the significant effects directly attributable to the above-mentioned transaction [or event] described in Note 1, that the related pro forma adjustments do not give appropriate effect to those assumptions, or that the pro forma column does not reflect the proper application of those adjustments to the historical financial statement amounts in the pro forma condensed balance sheet as of March 31, 19X2, and the pro forma condensed statement of income for the three months then ended.

PROSPECTIVE FINANCIAL INFORMATION

The usefulness of prospective financial information has become widely recognized, and such information is in demand by the financial community, including investors and potential investors. Prospective financial information is presently used in a wide variety of situations, ranging from public offerings of bonds or other securities and arrangements for bank or similar financing, to internal microcomputer "spreadsheet" software programs designed to facilitate the preparation of various financial analyses, including short-range plans (budgets), long-range plans, cash flow studies, capital improvement decisions, and other plans.

Prospective financial information is any financial information about the future. The information may be presented as complete prospective financial statements or limited to one or more elements, items, or accounts. To qualify as *prospective financial statements*, the presentation must meet specific criteria (discussed later). Other, more limited presentations of prospective financial information are referred to as *partial presentations*. The two types of prospective financial information are discussed separately in this chapter.

Although in many instances it is easy to determine what does not fall under the definition of prospective financial information, in others an answer may not be readily apparent. Carried to an extreme, almost any financial presentation could arguably be deemed to be prospective financial information, since many amounts contained in historical financial statements are calculated in light of future expectations.

For practical purposes, presentations that contain dollar amounts based on assumptions of future events in each of a number of future years generally fall under the definition of prospective financial information. On the other hand, financial information based on historical values, such as annual depreciation expense or scheduled principal payments of debt, would not be considered prospective financial information. Also, information based on assumptions of future events that is used only in determining current values typically would not be considered prospective financial information. Thus, future cash streams that are projected to future periods and then discounted to their present values would not usually be considered prospective financial information, nor would actuarial calculations of current pension obligations.

The growing interest in prospective financial information created a need for guidance on its preparation and presentation, along with guidance for practitioners associated with the information. In response, the AICPA developed the following materials to organize and refine what had been a patchwork of standards for prospective financial information:

- AICPA Statement on Standards for Accountants' Services on Prospective Financial Information, *Financial Forecasts and Projections* (AT Section 200). This statement, which carries authority equal to that of a Statement on Auditing Standards, applies when a practitioner reports on or submits to the client or others prospective financial information that he or she assisted in assembling and reasonably expects to be used by a third party. The statement specifies the procedures to perform and the reports to issue and sets forth "minimum presentation guidelines" for prospective financial statements.

- AICPA *Guide for Prospective Financial Statements*, which is a companion document to the statement. It includes all the standards set forth in the statement and provides guidance for preparers of prospective financial statements and additional guidance for engagements covered by the statement, as well as for other prospective financial information engagements.

- AICPA Statement of Position (SOP), *Questions Concerning Accountants' Services on Prospective Financial Statements*. The SOP was developed to clarify and expand on certain reporting and procedural guidance in the guide.

Prospective Financial Statements

Prospective financial statements are either financial forecasts or financial projections that present financial position, results of operations, and cash flows, and include summaries of significant assumptions and accounting policies.

Financial forecasts are prospective financial statements that present, to the best of the responsible party's (generally, management's[1]) knowledge and

[1]See the discussion later of "Responsibility for Prospective Financial Statements."

belief, an entity's expected financial position, results of operations, and cash flows. A financial forecast is based on management's assumptions reflecting *conditions it expects to exist* and the *course of action it expects to take*. A financial forecast may be expressed in specific monetary amounts as a single-point estimate of forecasted results or as a range. In the latter instance, management selects key assumptions to form a range within which it reasonably expects the item or items subject to the assumptions to fall. For example, forecasted financial statements that present expected results for a proposed apartment complex may contain a range showing the sensitivity of the forecast to variations in occupancy rates. The range must not be selected in a biased or misleading manner, for example, a range in which one end is significantly less expected than the other.

Financial projections are prospective financial statements that present, to the best of management's knowledge and belief, given one or more *hypothetical assumptions*, an entity's expected financial position, results of operations, and cash flows. A financial projection is sometimes prepared to present one or more hypothetical courses of action for evaluation, as in response to a question such as, "What would happen if . . . ?" A financial projection is based on management's assumptions reflecting conditions it expects would exist and the course of action it expects would be taken, given one or more hypothetical assumptions. For instance, a financial projection of a company's operations and cash flows may be based on assumptions about the construction of an additional plant facility. A projection, like a forecast, may be expressed as a range.

Commonly presented prospective financial statements include

- Forecasts in feasibility studies and preliminary feasibility studies. These studies may cover hospitals, sports complexes, homes for the elderly, real estate ventures, and so on. Generally, they involve various types of capital expenditures.
- Forecasts or projections relating to new or expanded projects or operations or existing operations of an entity over specified future periods. The prospective financial statements may be, for example, forecasts of target companies the client is considering acquiring, forecasts of the client company for purposes of conducting discussions with lenders, forecasts prepared on behalf of creditors (for example, in troubled financial situations, such as bankruptcies), or forecasts for the client company in contemplation of a refinancing or eliminating a line of business.
- Forecasts filed in connection with applications for government assistance grants.
- Rate studies for municipalities and public utilities, reported in financial statement format.
- Forecasts, including the actuarial components thereof, of insurance companies. Such forecasts may be filed, for example, with insurance commissions of states in which an insurance company wishes to be licensed to do business.

- Forecasts or projections of future results of a syndicated tax-oriented investment. Syndicated projects may involve real estate, oil and gas, alternative fuel programs, research and development programs, farming transactions, and equipment leases.
- Forecasts prepared in connection with a revenue bond issue.

A practitioner may be engaged to prepare a financial analysis of a potential project. Such an engagement includes obtaining the information, making appropriate assumptions, and assembling the presentation. For example, management may wish to analyze prospective data before making a decision, but may lack the expertise to formulate appropriate assumptions and assemble the data. Such an analysis is not, and should not be characterized as, a forecast or a projection and would not be appropriate for general use, because management does not take responsibility for the assumptions and presentation. The requirements of AT Section 200 and the related guide do not apply to a practitioner preparing a financial analysis.

Presentations of prospective financial statements may take the form of complete financial statements (the details of which may be summarized) or may be more limited, as long as they include, at a minimum, all of the following items that are applicable[2]:

a. Sales or gross revenues.
b. Gross profit or cost of sales.
c. Unusual or infrequently occurring items.
d. Provision for income taxes.
e. Discontinued operations or extraordinary items.
f. Income from continuing operations.
g. Net income.
h. Primary and fully diluted earnings per share.
i. Significant changes in financial position.[3]
j. A description of what management intends the prospective financial statements to present, a statement that the assumptions are based on information about circumstances and conditions existing at the time the prospective information was prepared, and a caveat that the prospective results may not be achieved.
k. Summary of significant assumptions.
l. Summary of significant accounting policies.

Items a through i represent the minimum items that constitute prospective financial statements. A presentation that omits one or more of these applicable

[2]An applicable item is one that would be presented for historical financial statements. For example, earnings per share would not be an applicable item for a nonpublic entity, since earnings per share are not required to be presented in historical financial statements of such entities.

[3]When the prospective financial statements take the form of basic financial statements, this requirement is met by presenting a statement of cash flows and related disclosures in accordance with SFAS No. 95, *Statement of Cash Flows* (Accounting Standards Section C25).

items would be considered a partial presentation, unless the omitted item was derivable from the information presented. Partial presentations, which are ordinarily not appropriate for general use, are discussed later in the chapter. Items j through l should accompany all prospective financial statement presentations. A presentation that omits one of the latter items would not be a partial presentation but a deficient presentation, because of the lack of required disclosures.

Prospective financial statements usually should be prepared on a basis consistent with the accounting principles expected to be used in the historical financial statements covering the prospective period. Sometimes, however, the special purpose of the presentation requires that it be prepared based on a comprehensive basis of accounting other than GAAP. In that event, the use of a different basis of accounting should be disclosed.

Uses of Prospective Financial Statements

Prospective financial statements may be for either general use or limited use. *General use* refers to use of the statements by persons with whom management is not negotiating directly, for example, in an offering statement of an entity's debt or equity interests. Because recipients of prospective financial statements distributed for general use are unable to communicate directly with management, the most useful presentation for them is one that portrays, to the best of management's knowledge and belief, the expected results. Thus, only a financial forecast is appropriate for general use.

Limited use of prospective financial statements refers to use of the statements by management alone or by management and third parties with whom it is negotiating directly. Examples include use in negotiations for a bank loan, submission to a regulatory agency, and use solely within the entity. Third-party recipients of prospective financial statements intended for limited use can ask questions of and negotiate terms directly with management. Any type of prospective financial statements that would be useful in the circumstances would normally be appropriate for limited use. Thus, the presentation may be either a financial forecast or a financial projection.

Responsibility for Prospective Financial Statements

Prospective financial statements, including the underlying assumptions, are the responsibility of the responsible party, usually the client's management. In certain circumstances, this may be a party outside the entity being reported on (for example, a party considering acquiring the entity).

The party responsible for the prospective financial statements cannot guarantee the achievement of the financial results set forth in them, because achievability depends on many factors that are outside its control. However, that party may influence the operations of an entity through planning, organizing, controlling, and directing its activities, and therefore is in a position to develop reasonable or appropriate assumptions.

At times the party responsible for the prospective financial statements may wish to enlist the assistance of outside parties in preparing the statements. For example, a practitioner may provide this assistance by helping the party identify key factors, develop assumptions, gather information, or assemble the statements. Such activities ordinarily would not affect the practitioner's independence in examining the prospective financial statements.[4] Regardless of the extent of the accountant's participation, however, he or she is not responsible for the assumptions. The practitioner may assist in the formulation of assumptions, but management or another party is responsible for evaluating the assumptions, making key decisions, and adopting and presenting the assumptions as its own.

Services on Prospective Financial Statements for Third-Party Use

There are three services practitioners may apply to prospective financial statements for use by third parties—compilation, examination, and application of agreed-upon procedures. The practitioner is required to perform one of the three services whenever a third party, including specified users (see below), might reasonably be expected to use prospective financial statements that the practitioner assisted in assembling. (The AICPA statement does not permit practitioners to review prospective financial statements.)

Examinations of and application of agreed-upon procedures to prospective financial statements correspond to those services for attest engagements generally. Compilations of prospective financial statements are not attest engagements, because they do not result in the expression of a conclusion on the reliability of the assertions contained in the financial statements. Compilations are covered by the statement and guide, however, because they are valuable professional services involving a practitioner's expertise as an accountant, though not as an attestor.

Compilation.   A compilation of a financial forecast or projection involves

- Assembling the prospective data, to the extent necessary, based on the responsible party's assumptions.
- Obtaining satisfaction that the underlying assumptions are not obviously inappropriate.
- Reading the prospective data and considering whether it appears to be presented in conformity with AICPA presentation guidelines.

Assembling data refers to the manual or computer processing of mathematical or other clerical functions related to the presentation of the prospective financial statements. For instance, working with the client, discussing assumptions and other relevant data, and participating in writing up the prospective

---

[4]The SEC staff has expressed concern about a practitioner's independence regarding prospective financial statements or historical financial statements covering the forecast period when a practitioner has assisted in preparing the prospective financial statements. Accordingly, the practitioner should consider the issue of independence if he or she is requested to assist in preparing prospective financial statements for an SEC registrant or for an entity that may become an SEC registrant during the forecast period.

financial statements ordinarily would meet the definition of assembling data. On the other hand, merely reproducing and collating such statements or allowing the responsible party to use the practitioner's computer processing hardware or software generally would not represent assembling data.

As discussed earlier, in a compilation, the practitioner does not provide assurance on the prospective data or the underlying assumptions. Consequently, the practitioner's procedures are limited, consisting principally of obtaining background knowledge of the industry and the entity, making inquiries, reading the data, and confirming with the responsible party the latter's responsibility for the assumptions. The AICPA guide specifies the procedures the practitioner should apply in performing a compilation of a financial forecast or projection.

Examination. An examination of a financial forecast or projection is the highest level of service offered by a practitioner with regard to prospective financial statements. An examination involves evaluating the

- Preparation of the forecast or projection.
- Support underlying the assumptions.
- Presentation for conformity with AICPA presentation guidelines.

In examining a projection, the practitioner need not obtain support for the hypothetical assumptions, but should consider whether they are consistent with the purpose of the presentation.

The practitioner's objective in examining a forecast or projection is to limit attestation risk to an appropriately low level. Thus, he or she should select from among all available procedures to assess inherent and control risk and to restrict detection risk.

Applying Agreed-Upon Procedures. When a practitioner applies agreed-upon procedures to a financial forecast or projection, specified users of the forecast or projection participate in establishing the nature and scope of the engagement and take responsibility for the adequacy of the procedures to be performed. Generally, those procedures may be as limited or extensive as the specified users desire, as long as the users take responsibility for the adequacy of the procedures. Mere reading of the prospective financial statements, however, is not in itself a sufficient procedure. Consistent with other attest engagements involving the application of agreed-upon procedures, distribution of the practitioner's report when agreed-upon procedures are applied to a financial forecast or projection is restricted to the specified users. The report enumerates the procedures performed and states the practitioner's findings; it may not express any form of negative assurance on the financial statements taken as a whole.

Reporting on Prospective Financial Statements for Third-Party Use

The statement and guide set forth reporting standards for compilations, examinations, and engagements to apply agreed-upon procedures.

Standard Compilation Report.   A practitioner's standard report on a compilation of a forecast that does not contain a range follows:

> We have compiled the accompanying forecasted balance sheet, statements of income, retained earnings, and cash flows of XYZ Company as of December 31, 19XX, and for the year then ending, in accordance with standards established by the American Institute of Certified Public Accountants.
>
> A compilation is limited to presenting in the form of a forecast information that is the representation of management and does not include evaluation of the support for the assumptions underlying the forecast. We have not examined the forecast and, accordingly, do not express an opinion or any other form of assurance on the accompanying statements or assumptions. Furthermore, there will usually be differences between the forecasted and actual results, because events and circumstances frequently do not occur as expected, and those differences may be material. We have no responsibility to update this report for events and circumstances occurring after the date of this report.

For a projection, the practitioner's report would include a separate paragraph describing the limitations on the usefulness of the presentation.

A practitioner may compile prospective financial statements for an entity with respect to which he or she is not independent. In such circumstances the practitioner may issue the standard compilation report, but should specifically disclose the lack of independence; however, the reason for the lack of independence should not be described.

Modifications to Standard Compilation Report.   In some circumstances a practitioner may wish to expand the report to emphasize a matter regarding the prospective financial statements. Such information may be presented in a separate paragraph of the report. For instance, an emphasis-of-a-matter paragraph may be used to bring to the reader's attention conditions that could significantly affect the prospective results, such as the impact the repeal of a current regulation would have on the company's sales. In emphasizing such a matter, however, the practitioner should ensure that he or she does not appear to be expressing assurance or expanding the degree of responsibility being taken with respect to the information. For example, the practitioner should not include statements in a compilation report about the mathematical accuracy of the statements or their conformity with presentation guidelines.

An entity may request a practitioner to compile prospective financial statements that contain presentation deficiencies or omit disclosures other than those relating to significant assumptions. The practitioner may compile such prospective financial statements provided the deficiency or omission is clearly indicated in the report and is not, to his or her knowledge, undertaken with the intention of misleading those who might reasonably be expected to use such statements.

Standard Examination Report.   Following is the practitioner's standard report on an examination of a forecast that does not contain a range:

> We have examined the accompanying forecasted balance sheet, statements of income, retained earnings, and cash flows of XYZ Company as of December 31,

19XX, and for the year then ending. Our examination was made in accordance with standards for an examination of a forecast established by the American Institute of Certified Public Accountants and, accordingly, included such procedures as we considered necessary to evaluate both the assumptions used by management and the preparation and presentation of the forecast.

In our opinion, the accompanying forecast is presented in conformity with guidelines for presentation of a forecast established by the American Institute of Certified Public Accountants, and the underlying assumptions provide a reasonable basis for management's forecast. However, there will usually be differences between the forecasted and actual results, because events and circumstances frequently do not occur as expected, and those differences may be material. We have no responsibility to update this report for events and circumstances occurring after the date of this report.

When a practitioner examines a projection, the opinion regarding the assumptions should be predicated on the hypothetical assumptions; that is, the practitioner should express an opinion on whether the assumptions provide a reasonable basis for the projection given the hypothetical assumptions. Also, the report should include a separate paragraph that describes the limitations on the usefulness of the presentation. An example of an opinion paragraph that meets this requirement follows:

In our opinion, the accompanying projection is presented in conformity with guidelines for presentation of a projection established by the American Institute of Certified Public Accountants, and the underlying assumptions provide a reasonable basis for management's projection assuming the granting of the requested loan for the purpose of expanding XYZ Company's plant as described in the summary of significant assumptions. However, even if the loan is granted and the plant is expanded, there will usually be differences between the projected and actual results, because events and circumstances frequently do not occur as expected, and those differences may be material. We have no responsibility to update this report for events and circumstances occurring after the date of this report.

Modifications to Standard Examination Report. The following circumstances require the practitioner to modify the report:

- If the prospective financial statements depart from AICPA presentation guidelines, the practitioner should issue a qualified or an adverse opinion. However, if the departure is the failure to disclose assumptions that appear to be significant, the practitioner should issue an adverse opinion.
- If the practitioner believes that one or more significant assumptions do not provide a reasonable basis for the forecast, or a reasonable basis for the projection given the hypothetical assumptions, he or she should issue an adverse opinion.
- If the examination is affected by conditions that preclude application of one or more procedures considered necessary in the circumstances, the practitioner should disclaim an opinion and describe the scope limitation in the report.

When there is a scope limitation and the practitioner also believes there are material departures from the presentation guidelines, those departures should be described in the report.

The circumstances described below, although not necessarily resulting in modifications to the practitioner's report, would result in the following types of explanatory language in the standard examination report.

Emphasis of a Matter.   As discussed earlier, in some circumstances the practitioner may wish to emphasize a matter regarding the prospective financial statements, but nevertheless intends to issue an unqualified opinion. The practitioner may present other information and comments, such as explanatory comments, in a separate paragraph of the report.

Evaluation Based in Part on Report of Another Practitioner.   More than one practitioner may be involved in the examination, and the principal practitioner may decide to refer to the report of another practitioner as a basis, in part, for his or her own opinion. In that event, the principal practitioner should disclose that fact in stating the scope of the examination and should refer to the report of the other practitioner in expressing the opinion. Such a reference indicates the division of responsibility for the performance of the examination.

Comparative Historical Financial Information.   Prospective financial statements may be included in a document that also contains historical financial statements and a practitioner's report thereon. The historical financial statements that appear in the document may also be summarized and presented with the prospective financial statements for comparative purposes. In such situations, the practitioner's report on the prospective financial statements would include a reference to the historical financial statements and the report on them.

Reporting When the Examination Is Part of a Larger Engagement.   When the practitioner's examination of prospective financial statements is part of a larger engagement, for example, a financial feasibility study or business acquisition study, it is appropriate to expand the report on the examination of the prospective financial statements to describe the entire engagement.

Prospective Financial Statements for Internal Use Only and Partial Presentations

The AICPA has issued a proposed SOP, *Guidance on the Accountant's Services and Reports on Prospective Financial Statements for Internal Use Only and Partial Presentations of Prospective Financial Information.* The document, when issued in final form, will replace guidance included in the AICPA guide. An overview of the proposed SOP follows.

Internal Use Only.   In many circumstances, a practitioner may be engaged to provide services on prospective financial statements that are restricted to internal use only. Examples are giving advice and assistance to a client on the tax consequences of future actions or on deciding whether to buy or lease an asset. The practitioner may perform compilation, examination, or agreed-upon procedures services in accordance with AICPA standards for prospective financial statements for third-party use, as described earlier. Alternatively, the practitioner may perform other services or procedures, such as merely assembling the statements, tailored to the particular engagement circumstances.

In obtaining satisfaction that the prospective financial statements will be restricted to internal use, the practitioner may rely on either the written or oral representation of the responsible party, unless information comes to the practitioner's attention that contradicts the responsible party's representation.

The proposed SOP does not require the practitioner to report on services performed on prospective financial statements for internal use only. For example, a practitioner may submit computer-generated prospective financial statements without reporting on them, provided the statements are restricted to internal use only. When prospective financial statements intended for internal use only are accompanied by a practitioner's written communication (for example, a transmittal letter), however, the communication should state that the prospective results may not be achieved and that the statements are for internal use only.

Partial Presentations.   A partial presentation is a presentation of prospective financial information that excludes one or more of the items required to be included in prospective financial statements, as described earlier in this chapter. A partial presentation may include either forecasted or projected information and may be either extracted from a presentation of prospective financial statements or prepared specifically as a partial presentation. The following are examples of partial presentations:

- Sales forecasts.
- Presentations of forecasted or projected capital expenditure programs.
- Projections of financing needs.
- Other presentations of specified elements, accounts, or items of prospective financial statements (for example, projected production costs) that might be part of the development of a full presentation of prospective financial statements.
- Forecasts that present operating income, but not net income.
- Projections of taxable income or forecasted tax returns that do not show significant changes in financial position.
- Items that provide enough information to be translated into elements, accounts, or items of a financial forecast or projection. Examples include a forecast of sales units and unit selling prices, and a forecast of occupancy percentage, number of rooms, and average rates. In contrast, a forecast presenting unit selling prices alone would not be considered a partial presentation.

Partial presentations may be appropriate in many "limited use" situations. For example, in analyzing whether to lease or buy a piece of equipment, or in evaluating the income tax implications of a given election, it may be necessary only to assess the impact on one aspect of financial results rather than on the financial statements taken as a whole. Partial presentations are not ordinarily appropriate for general use.

A practitioner who is engaged to issue or does issue a written communication expressing a conclusion about the reliability of a written partial presentation that is the responsibility of another party should examine or apply agreed-upon procedures to the partial presentation. A practitioner may also compile a partial presentation.

The proposed SOP provides guidance for preparing partial presentations, discusses each of the practitioner's services, and includes illustrative reports.

25

Compliance Auditing

Laws and governmental regulations play an integral part in an entity's operations, and failure to comply with them may affect its financial statements. Management is responsible for ensuring that the entity complies with applicable laws and regulations. To meet that responsibility, management identifies those laws and regulations and establishes internal control structure policies and procedures designed to provide reasonable assurance of compliance. The auditor's responsibility for testing and reporting on compliance with laws and governmental regulations varies according to the type of entity being audited and the terms of the engagement.

During the mid-1980s, reports of illegal activities caused concern in Congress and among the public and raised questions about auditors' responsibility for detecting and reporting violations of laws and governmental regulations— referred to as illegal acts. In response, the Auditing Standards Board issued two new Statements on Auditing Standards (SASs): No. 53, *The Auditor's Responsibility to Detect and Report Errors and Irregularities* (AU Section 316), and No. 54, *Illegal Acts by Clients* (AU Section 317). Together they define the auditor's responsibilities in this area under generally accepted auditing standards (GAAS).

Those responsibilities, including those related to illegal acts, apply to *all* audits performed under GAAS. A governmental entity, not-for-profit organization, or business enterprise may engage an auditor, however, to audit its financial statements in accordance with government auditing standards issued by the Comptroller General of the United States or, if it received federal financial assistance, in accordance with the federal Single Audit Act of 1984. In performing an audit in accordance with those requirements, the auditor assumes responsibilities beyond those encompassed by GAAS. To fully understand how the consideration of illegal acts affects the scope of such audits, the auditor must be familiar with the requirements of government auditing standards and the Single Audit Act of 1984 as well as GAAS. This chapter discusses each of these sources of audit guidance regarding an entity's compliance with laws and regulations.

GENERALLY ACCEPTED AUDITING STANDARDS

The auditor's responsibilities with respect to illegal acts under GAAS are to design the audit to provide reasonable assurance of detecting illegal acts that could have a *direct and material* effect on financial statement amounts, and to make the audit committee aware of any illegal acts that come to the auditor's attention. Those responsibilities are described in Chapter 4. If the auditor concludes that noncompliance with laws and regulations could have a direct and material effect on the financial statements, he or she must design the audit to obtain reasonable assurance that noncompliance will be detected: He or she should assess the control structure as it applies to compliance with laws and regulations and, if necessary, based on that assessment, design substantive tests of compliance. SAS Nos. 53 and 54 do not require the auditor to issue a report on the client's compliance with laws and regulations.

SAS No. 54 states that an audit conducted in accordance with GAAS does not ordinarily include auditing procedures specifically designed to detect illegal acts that might have only an *indirect* effect on financial statements. Those kinds of illegal acts (which SAS No. 54 refers to simply as "illegal acts") may come to the auditor's attention, however, through procedures performed to support the audit opinion, for example, reading minutes and inquiring of management and legal counsel concerning litigation, claims, and assessments. In addition, the auditor may inquire of management about compliance with laws and regulations, its policies for preventing illegal acts, and whether it issues directives and obtains periodic representations from management concerning compliance with laws and regulations. Any of these or other procedures may point to the possibility of an illegal act. SAS No. 54 provides additional guidance with respect to detecting and reporting illegal acts generally, and is discussed in Chapter 4.

SPECIAL CONSIDERATIONS IN PLANNING A GOVERNMENTAL AUDIT

In auditing a governmental entity, compliance with laws and regulations is particularly important, because governmental organizations are usually subject to more specific rules and regulations than other business entities. The audit risk of failing to detect instances of noncompliance is correspondingly greater. Since many of those rules and regulations may have a *direct and material* effect on the determination of financial statement amounts, the auditor should take them into consideration when designing procedures to reduce overall audit risk—the risk that the financial statements are materially misstated—to the appropriately low level required by professional standards.

To determine an appropriate audit testing plan, the auditor considers preliminary judgments about materiality in addition to the assessment of inherent and control risk. In a governmental audit, the auditor needs to consider materiality not only in relation to the individual fund balances, but also in relation to federal financial assistance programs. Failure to consider this in the planning stages may cause a duplication of efforts later in the audit. The auditor's understanding of a governmental entity client should include consideration of the possible financial statement effects of laws and regulations that auditors generally recognize as having a direct and material effect on the financial statements of governmental entities. The auditor should also assess whether management has identified those laws and regulations. Procedures for accomplishing this consist of considering knowledge obtained in prior-year audits; inquiry of management, legal counsel, appropriate oversight organizations, and program administrators; obtaining written representations from management; reading relevant agreements; reviewing minutes of meetings of relevant legislative bodies; and reviewing other relevant information. Furthermore, two statements should be added to the management representation letter required by SAS No. 19.

- A statement that management acknowledges its responsibility for the entity's compliance with applicable laws and regulations.
- A statement that management has identified and disclosed all laws and regulations having a direct and material effect on the determination of financial statement amounts.

SAS No. 53 (AU Section 316.09) states that "in developing an audit plan, the auditor should consider factors influencing audit risk that relate to several or all account balances and obtain an understanding of the internal control structure." SAS No. 55, *Consideration of the Internal Control Structure in a Financial Statement Audit* (AU Section 319), requires the auditor to obtain an understanding of the internal control structure sufficient to plan the audit and to assess control risk for the assertions embodied in the financial statements. This includes knowledge of internal control structure policies and procedures the entity has placed in operation to ensure compliance with laws and regulations that have a direct and material effect on the determination of financial statement amounts. In auditing a governmental entity, the auditor also needs to determine whether the requirements of the Single Audit Act, discussed later, apply.

In assessing control risk with respect to compliance, the auditor should consider policies and procedures in all three elements of the internal control structure: the control environment, the accounting system, and control procedures. Control environment factors that are particularly relevant to the auditor's assessment of control risk relating to compliance with laws and regulations are

- Management's awareness or lack of awareness of relevant laws and regulations.
- Policies regarding matters such as acceptable operating practices and codes of conduct.
- Assignment of responsibility and delegation of authority over matters such as organizational goals and objectives, operating functions, and compliance with regulatory requirements.

The auditor's activities in obtaining an understanding of the internal control structure and assessing risk are similar to those in audits of nongovernmental entities, explained in detail in Chapter 8.

As discussed later in this chapter, government auditing standards require that "a test should be made of compliance with applicable laws and regulations." In planning and conducting the necessary tests of compliance, the auditor should

- Determine which laws and regulations could, if not complied with, have a direct and material effect on the financial statements.
- Assess, for each significant law or regulation, the risk that material noncompliance could occur. This includes assessing the internal control

structure policies and procedures the entity has placed in operation to ensure compliance with laws and regulations.

- Based on that assessment, design procedures to test compliance with laws and regulations to provide reasonable assurance that intentional or unintentional instances of noncompliance that could have a material effect on the financial statements have not occurred.

In developing the audit testing plan for a governmental entity, the auditor should consider all the applicable performance and reporting requirements in combination, to design the most efficient plan. There are three sources— GAAS, government auditing standards, and the Single Audit Act—each with different requirements, that the auditor needs to be aware of when considering a governmental entity's compliance with laws and regulations. Because the provisions of these three sources overlap, the Auditing Standards Board issued SAS No. 63, *Compliance Auditing Applicable to Governmental Entities and Other Recipients of Governmental Financial Assistance*, which provides guidance for applying SAS Nos. 53 and 54, government auditing standards, and the Single Audit Act, as they apply to compliance with laws and regulations. The remainder of this chapter outlines the provisions of government auditing standards and the Single Audit Act of 1984.

GOVERNMENT AUDITING STANDARDS

In 1988, the U.S. General Accounting Office (GAO) issued a revised edition of *Government Auditing Standards—Standards for Audit of Governmental Organizations, Programs, Activities, and Functions* (often referred to as the "Yellow Book"). The Yellow Book prescribes generally accepted governmental auditing standards (GAGAS), which are applicable for audits of state and local governmental units; not-for-profit organizations, like universities and hospitals, that receive government aid or grants; and mortgage companies subject to the provisions of Housing and Urban Development audit guides. Certain laws, like the Single Audit Act, and regulations, like Office of Management and Budget (OMB) Circulars, also require public accountants to follow the standards in the Yellow Book for financial audits. The standards do not apply to providers of goods and services to the government unless specifically required by the supply contract between the parties.

The Yellow Book contains standards for two types of governmental audits, financial and performance. This chapter discusses only financial audits, since they are the type an independent auditor is more likely to perform. Generally accepted governmental auditing standards incorporate GAAS, including SAS Nos. 52 through 61, and include some additional standards. Like GAAS, GAGAS are divided into three categories: general, field work, and reporting standards. Following is a summary of the additional standards an auditor must adhere to when performing an audit in accordance with GAGAS.

General Standards

The GAGAS general standards cover four areas: qualifications (i.e., adequate professional proficiency), independence, due professional care, and quality control. The qualifications standard imposes certain education and training requirements, beyond those required by GAAS, which must be met by January 1, 1991, and on a continuing basis thereafter. Specifically, the standard requires at least 80 hours of continuing education and training every 2 years for all members of the engagement team. For members of the engagement team responsible for directing the field work and reporting on the audit, at least 24 of the 80 hours must be directly related to the governmental environment and governmental auditing.

The independence standard is similar to that prescribed by GAAS for an audit of financial statements. The standard regarding due professional care is worded the same in both GAAS and GAGAS. However, the Yellow Book (p. 3-13) contains the following statement:

> In government audits the materiality level and/or threshold of acceptable risk may be lower than in similar-type audits in the private sector because of the public accountability of the entity, the various legal and regulatory requirements, and the visibility and sensitivity of government programs, activities, and functions.

The GAGAS quality control standard calls for the auditor's participation in an external quality control review program, which goes beyond what is required by GAAS. Auditors can meet this requirement by participating in an external quality control review program, like those conducted through or by the AICPA, National State Auditors Association, Intergovernmental Audit Forums, GAO, or the Institute of Internal Auditors.

Field Work Standards

Additional field work standards under GAGAS deal with audit planning and evidence. For example, there is a documentation requirement that the audit program be cross-referenced to the working papers. While some auditors may do this on all engagements, it is not a part of GAAS. The Yellow Book also includes a standard explicitly requiring tests of compliance with applicable laws and regulations; that is, laws and regulations that could have a direct and material effect on the financial statements. This standard does not extend the auditor's responsibility beyond SAS Nos. 53 and 54; however, entities subject to the provisions of the Yellow Book are likely to be subject to extensive laws and regulations.

Reporting Standards

Additional reporting standards under GAGAS are designed to satisfy the unique needs of governmental financial audits. The standards include the following:

- The auditor's report should state that the audit was conducted in accordance with GAGAS as well as GAAS.

- The auditor should issue a report on the entity's compliance with laws and regulations that could, if not complied with, have a direct and material effect on the financial statements. This report should include all material instances of noncompliance.

- The auditor should issue a report on his or her understanding of the entity's internal control structure and the assessment of control risk made as part of a financial audit.

The additional reporting requirements for audits conducted under the Yellow Book are discussed below.

Standard Report on Compliance with Laws and Regulations.   The key features of the standard report on compliance with laws and regulations are the statements of both positive and negative assurance. The auditor expresses positive assurance on items tested for compliance and negative assurance on items not tested. The Yellow Book (pp. 5-2–5-3) states

> Positive assurance consists of a statement by the auditors that the tested items were in compliance with applicable laws and regulations. Negative assurance is a statement that nothing came to the auditors' attention as a result of specified procedures that caused them to believe the untested items were not in compliance with applicable laws and regulations.

An example (contained in SAS No. 63, para. 22) of an auditor's report on compliance with laws and regulations that disclosed no material instances of noncompliance follows[1]:

> We have audited the financial statements of [*name of entity*] as of and for the year ended June 30, 19X1, and have issued our report thereon dated August 15, 19X1.

> We conducted our audit in accordance with generally accepted auditing standards and *Government Auditing Standards*, issued by the Comptroller General of the United States. Those standards require that we plan and perform the audit to obtain reasonable assurance about whether the financial statements are free of material misstatement.

> Compliance with laws, regulations, contracts, and grants applicable to [*name of entity*] is the responsibility of [*name of entity*]'s management. As part of obtaining reasonable assurance about whether the financial statements are free of material misstatement, we performed tests of [*name of entity*]'s compliance with certain

---

[1]SAS No. 58 (AU Section 508.08) specifies that a title that includes the word "independent" is one of the basic elements of the standard audit report. The illustrative standard reports in AU Section 508 use the title "Independent Auditor's Report." This and subsequent illustrative audit reports present only the body of the report and omit the title, as well as the date of the report and signature of the auditor's firm.

provisions of laws, regulations, contracts, and grants. However, our objective was not to provide an opinion on overall compliance with such provisions.

The results of our tests indicate that, with respect to the items tested, [*name of entity*] complied, in all material respects, with the provisions referred to in the preceding paragraph. With respect to items not tested, nothing came to our attention that caused us to believe that [*name of entity*] had not complied, in all material respects, with those provisions.

This report is intended for the information of the audit committee, management, and [*specify legislative or regulatory body*]. This restriction is not intended to limit the distribution of this report, which is a matter of public record.

Compliance Tests Not Performed.   Based on the assessment of control risk or an assessment that the transactions and balances directly affected by laws and regulations are not material to the financial statements taken as a whole, the auditor may decide not to perform any tests of compliance with laws or regulations. In this instance, the report should be modified to contain a statement that the auditor did not test for compliance with laws and regulations. The auditor should not include a statement of positive assurance; however, his or her assessment of risk and materiality in conducting the audit of the financial statements provides a basis for expressing negative assurance.

Reporting Noncompliance.   The glossary to the Yellow Book defines noncompliance with laws and regulations as

A failure to follow requirements, or a violation of prohibitions, contained in statutes, regulations, contracts, grants, and binding policies and procedures governing entity conduct. (p. G-8)

When an auditor's procedures disclose a material instance of noncompliance, the auditor must evaluate its potential effects and should either qualify the statements of positive and negative assurance in the report on compliance or consider issuing an adverse opinion. The standard report should also be modified to include

- The definition of material instances of noncompliance.
- An identification of material instances of noncompliance.
- A statement that noncompliance noted was considered in forming an opinion on whether the entity's financial statements are presented fairly, in all material respects, in conformity with generally accepted accounting principles.

The auditor is responsible for reporting material instances of noncompliance even if the resulting misstatements have been corrected in the financial statements. In that instance, the auditor may wish to include in the report a statement that the misstatements resulting from the instances of noncompliance have been corrected for purposes of financial statement presentation. The auditor is not required to disclose in the report instances of noncompliance that are not considered material. The auditor should, however, report them to the entity in a separate communication, preferably in writing. This separate communication, or management letter, should be referred to in the report on compliance.

Reporting on the Internal Control Structure.   As discussed in Chapter 8, SAS No. 60, *Communication of Internal Control Structure Related Matters Noted in an Audit* (AU Section 325), requires the auditor to communicate, either orally or in writing, reportable conditions noted during an audit. Reportable conditions are defined as

> Matters coming to the auditor's attention that, in his judgment, should be communicated to the audit committee because they represent significant deficiencies in the design or operation of the internal control structure, which could adversely affect the organization's ability to record, process, summarize, and report financial data consistent with the assertions of management in the financial statements.

In addition to the requirements of SAS No. 60, government auditing standards require a *written* report on the internal control structure in *all* audits. They also require the auditor's report to identify and disclose material weaknesses in the internal control structure. Finally, GAGAS require the auditor to communicate in writing the following matters, which are not covered by SAS No. 60:

- Identification of the elements of the internal control structure.
- Description of the scope of the auditor's work relating to the control structure and control risk assessment.
- Description of deficiencies in the control structure not considered by the auditor to be significant enough to be reportable conditions. This description may be communicated separately, as discussed below.

A report on the internal control structure in which the auditor has noted reportable conditions should include the following major items:

- A statement that, as a part of the audit of the financial statements, the auditor considered the entity's internal control structure for purposes of expressing an opinion on the financial statements and not to provide assurance on the internal control structure.
- A listing of the categories into which the significant internal control structure policies and procedures have been classified. The classification may be by cycle (e.g., revenue), financial statement caption (such as accounts receivable), or accounting application (e.g., billings).
- A statement that the auditor obtained an understanding of the design of the control structure policies and procedures and determined whether they had been placed in operation; and a statement that the auditor

assessed control risk. To comply with SAS No. 60, the report should also define reportable conditions, describe the reportable conditions noted, define material weaknesses, and state whether the auditor believes any of the reportable conditions noted are material weaknesses.

Following is a report (taken from SAS No. 63, para. 38) on the internal control structure, noting reportable conditions:

We have audited the financial statements of [*name of entity*] as of and for the year ended June 30, 19X1, and have issued our report thereon dated August 15, 19X1.

We conducted our audit in accordance with generally accepted auditing standards and *Government Auditing Standards*, issued by the Comptroller General of the United States. Those standards require that we plan and perform the audit to obtain reasonable assurance about whether the financial statements are free of material misstatement.

In planning and performing our audit of the financial statements of [*name of entity*] for the year ended June 30, 19X1, we considered its internal control structure in order to determine our auditing procedures for the purpose of expressing our opinion on the financial statements and not to provide assurance on the internal control structure.

The management of [*name of entity*] is responsible for establishing and maintaining an internal control structure. In fulfilling this responsibility, estimates and judgments by management are required to assess the expected benefits and related costs of internal control structure policies and procedures. The objectives of an internal control structure are to provide management with reasonable, but not absolute, assurance that assets are safeguarded against loss from unauthorized use or disposition, and that transactions are executed in accordance with management's authorization and recorded properly to permit the preparation of financial statements in accordance with generally accepted accounting principles. Because of inherent limitations in any internal control structure, errors or irregularities may nevertheless occur and not be detected. Also, projection of any evaluation of the structure to future periods is subject to the risk that procedures may become inadequate because of changes in conditions or that the effectiveness of the design and operation of policies and procedures may deteriorate.

For the purpose of this report, we have classified the significant internal control structure policies and procedures in the following categories [*identify internal control structure categories*].

For all of the internal control structure categories listed above, we obtained an understanding of the design of relevant policies and procedures and whether they have been placed in operation, and we assessed control risk.

We noted certain matters involving the internal control structure and its operation that we consider to be reportable conditions under standards established by the American Institute of Certified Public Accountants. Reportable conditions involve matters coming to our attention relating to significant deficiencies in the design or operation of the internal control structure that, in our judgment, could adversely affect the entity's ability to record, process, summarize, and report financial data consistent with the assertions of management in the financial statements.

[*Include paragraphs to describe the reportable conditions noted.*]

A material weakness is a reportable condition in which the design or operation of the specific internal control structure elements does not reduce to a relatively low level the risk that errors or irregularities in amounts that would be material in relation to the financial statements being audited may occur and not be detected within a timely period by employees in the normal course of performing their assigned functions.

Our consideration of the internal control structure would not necessarily disclose all matters in the internal control structure that might be reportable conditions and, accordingly, would not necessarily disclose all reportable conditions that are also considered to be material weaknesses as defined above. However, we believe none of the reportable conditions described above is a material weakness.

This report is intended for the information of the audit committee, management, and [*specify legislative or regulatory body*]. This restriction is not intended to limit the distribution of this report, which is a matter of public record.

Often an audit will reveal deficiencies in the internal control structure that the auditor believes are not significant enough to be reportable conditions as defined by SAS No. 60. As noted earlier, these conditions are not required to be included in the report on the internal control structure, but should be separately communicated to the entity, preferably in writing. When the auditor communicates these conditions in a separate management letter, the report on internal control structure should be modified to include the following statement:

We also noted other matters involving the internal control structure and its operation that we have reported to the management of [*name of entity*] in a separate communication dated [*date of letter*].

SAS No. 60 (AU Section 325.17) specifically prohibits the auditor from issuing a written report representing that no reportable conditions were noted during an audit. Therefore, if no reportable conditions were noted, the paragraphs of the report on the internal control structure illustrated earlier that describe reportable conditions and material weaknesses would be replaced by the following paragraph (SAS No. 63, para. 39):

Our consideration of the internal control structure would not necessarily disclose all matters in the internal control structure that might be material weaknesses under standards established by the American Institute of Certified Public Accountants. A material weakness is a condition in which the design or operation of one or more of the specific internal control structure elements does not reduce to a relatively low level the risk that errors or irregularities in amounts that would be material in relation to the financial statements being audited may occur and not be detected within a timely period by employees in the normal course of performing their assigned functions. We noted no matters involving the internal control structure and its operation that we consider to be material weaknesses as defined above.

No mention is made of reportable conditions. The report refers only to the fact that no matters involving the internal control structure and its operation were noted that the auditor considered to be material weaknesses. This language both satisfies GAGAS and is permissible under SAS No. 60.

SINGLE AUDIT ACT

Background

Before the enactment of the Single Audit Act of 1984 (the Act), a federal agency that issued a grant to a state or local government had the authority to establish its own audit guidelines. There was no oversight body or any other means of controlling the scope or number of audits required for a particular agency or other entity receiving federal financial assistance. Often the federal assistance came from several different federal agencies. As a result, the same internal control procedures and transactions often were tested more than once, frequently by different independent auditors, and sometimes even simultaneously. These duplicative audits caused organizational inefficiencies and led to increased audit costs.

The Single Audit Act created a single, coordinated audit (often called a "single audit," "organization-wide audit," or "entity-wide audit") of all federal financial assistance provided to a recipient agency during a fiscal year. The Act emphasizes audits of those federal financial assistance programs that the federal government has defined as major, as discussed later. The objectives of the Act are to

- Promote the efficient and effective use of audit resources.
- Improve state and local governments' financial management of federal financial assistance programs through more effective auditing.
- Establish uniform requirements for audits of federal financial assistance provided to state and local governments.
- Ensure that federal departments and agencies, to the greatest extent practicable, are audited in accordance with the requirements of the Single Audit Act.

The Office of Management and Budget is responsible for setting policies regarding the frequency and scope of audits required for federal agencies to meet government auditing standards. In 1985 the OMB issued Circular A-128, "Audits of State and Local Governments," to facilitate the implementation of the Single Audit Act. Together, Circular A-128 and the Act require (1) an audit of the entity's general-purpose or basic financial statements, (2) the performance of additional audit tests for compliance with applicable laws and regulations related to grants received, and (3) tests of control structure policies and procedures designed to ensure compliance with laws and regulations of applicable federal financial assistance programs. In addition, Circular A-128 prescribes the responsibilities for monitoring those requirements.

In 1976, the OMB issued Circular A-110, which set forth audit requirements for institutions of higher education, hospitals, and other nonprofit organizations receiving federal grants. However, the audit requirements were not clear and were often misunderstood. At the time of this writing, the OMB has proposed Circular A-133, "Audits of Higher Education and Other Non-profit Agencies," which, when issued, would extend to colleges and universities and nonprofit agencies receiving federal financial assistance, requirements similar to those contained in Circular A-128. Hospitals, other than those associated with a university, are specifically excluded from Circular A-133.

Applicability of the Single Audit Act

The requirements of the Act apply to each state and local government that receives a total amount of federal financial assistance of $100,000 or more in a fiscal year. A government that receives $25,000 or more, but less than $100,000 in any fiscal year, may elect to implement the Single Audit Act requirements in lieu of the separate financial and compliance audit requirements of the various applicable federal financial assistance programs. Governments receiving less than $25,000 in any fiscal year are exempt from the requirements of the Act, as well as all other federal audit requirements.

Certain not-for-profit organizations that are primary recipients of assistance from federal agencies may be required by a state or local government to be audited in accordance with the Act. These single audits are performed by state or local governmental auditors or public accountants who meet the Yellow Book's independence and qualification standards.

Auditing Compliance with Specific Requirements of Major Federal Financial Assistance Programs

Under the Single Audit Act, the auditor must report on whether the entity has complied with laws and regulations that have a material effect on each *major* federal financial assistance program. The Act defines a major federal financial assistance program based on the total expenditures of federal financial assistance during a program year. These major programs are listed in the *Catalog of Federal Domestic Assistance*; examples include the National School Lunch program and Headstart programs.

Management is responsible for identifying those federal financial assistance programs from which it receives funding. OMB Circular A-128 states

> In order to determine which major programs are to be tested for compliance, state and local governments shall identify in their accounts all federal funds

received and expended and the programs under which they were received. This shall include funds received directly from federal agencies and through other state and local governments.

On a single audit, it is the auditor's responsibility to test for compliance with the specific requirements of every applicable major federal financial assistance program. This is in addition to the GAGAS requirement to design tests to assess the risk that noncompliance with laws and regulations could have a direct and material effect on the financial statements. The Single Audit Act requirement is much more stringent; thus, after testing compliance with the requirements of the Single Audit Act, the auditor may often consider that no further testing of compliance with laws and regulations is necessary to fulfill the GAGAS requirement.

The single audit must include the selection and testing of a representative number of charges from each major federal financial assistance program identified. The extent and selection of items to be tested depends on the auditor's professional judgment. For *all* major programs, Circular A-128 requires the auditor to specifically consider

- *Types of Services Allowed*—Is the entity using financial assistance to purchase goods and services allowed by the program?
- *Eligibility*—Were the recipients of the goods and services eligible to receive them?
- *Matching Requirement*—Did the entity contribute the necessary amount from its own resources toward projects paid for with financial assistance?
- *Reporting*—Did the entity file all the reports required by the federal financial assistance program?
- *Special Tests and Provisions*—Are there other federal provisions with which noncompliance could materially affect the federal financial assistance programs?

The details of these items vary with each federal financial assistance program. To help the auditor determine which federal compliance requirements should be tested, the OMB publishes the *Compliance Supplement for Single Audits of State and Local Governments* (the *Compliance Supplement*), which specifies program compliance requirements and suggests auditing procedures for the larger federal financial assistance programs. The *Compliance Supplement* also includes references to the *Code of Federal Regulations* and other applicable statutes. The auditor should consult this supplement when considering the nature, timing, and extent of procedures to perform as a basis for expressing an opinion on compliance.

In addition to the specific requirements that recipient agencies must comply with and that the auditor must test, Circulars A-128 and the proposed A-133 require that independent auditors determine whether

- Financial reports and claims for advances and reimbursements contain information that is supported by the books and records used to prepare the basic financial statements.

- Amounts claimed or used for matching were determined in accordance with the particular grant requirements.

The Circulars require that the auditor's report on compliance (illustrated later in this chapter) specifically address the above requirements. In determining whether these requirements have been met, the auditor should consider the following, as appropriate, when testing charges to federal financial assistance programs:

- Are the charges necessary and reasonable for the proper administration of the program?
- Do the charges conform to any limitations or exclusions in the federal assistance agreement?
- Were the charges given consistent accounting treatment and applied uniformly to both federally assisted and other activities of the recipient?
- Were the charges net of applicable credits?
- Were only costs applicable to federal financial assistance programs charged to those programs?
- Were the charges properly recorded (that is, correct purpose, amount, date) and supported by source documentation?
- Were the charges approved in advance, if required?
- Were the charges incurred in accordance with competitive purchasing procedures, if required by the particular financial assistance program?
- Were the charges allocated equitably to the activities that benefited, including nonfederal activities?

Materiality Under the Single Audit Act

The concept of materiality for financial statements covered by the Act differs somewhat from that prescribed by GAAS. Under the Act, materiality is considered in relation to each major federal financial assistance program. Also, a material amount pertaining to one major program may not be considered material to another major program of a different size or nature.

Risk Assessment Under the Single Audit Act

Risk assessment in an audit performed under GAGAS is identical to that under GAAS. Under the Single Audit Act, however, the auditor has responsibilities over and above those of GAAS and GAGAS, namely, testing and reporting on the entity's compliance with the specific requirements of a particular program and the general requirements (discussed later) that apply to all programs. Thus, in assessing risk in a compliance audit of a major federal program, the auditor must also consider the risk that he or she may fail to appropriately modify his or her opinion on compliance with such a program. This risk has three aspects.

- Inherent risk—the risk that material noncompliance with requirements applicable to a major federal financial assistance program could occur assuming there were no related control structure policies or procedures.
- Control risk—the risk that material noncompliance that could occur in a major federal financial assistance program will not be prevented or detected on a timely basis by the entity's internal control structure policies and procedures.
- Detection risk—the risk that the auditor's procedures will lead him or her to conclude that noncompliance that could be material to a major federal financial assistance program does not exist when in fact such noncompliance does exist.

The following paragraphs summarize the requirements of the Single Audit Act that pertain to each of the risk components, and explain how the requirements, taken together, provide a basis for the auditor's report on compliance.

Inherent Risk. The auditor's assessment of inherent risk conditions is pervasive to the entire entity. In other words, the inherent risk conditions that exist would most likely affect both the entity's ability to record financial transactions and its compliance with laws and regulations. Therefore, a separate assessment for financial and compliance purposes may be unnecessary.

Control Risk. Under the Single Audit Act the auditor is required to determine and report whether the government has internal control structure policies and procedures to provide reasonable assurance that it is managing federal financial assistance programs in compliance with applicable laws and regulations. Circular A-128 elaborates on the auditor's responsibility, as follows:

> The auditor must make a study and evaluation of internal control systems used in administering federal financial assistance programs. The study and evaluation must be made whether or not the auditor intends to place reliance on such systems. As part of this review the auditor shall:
>
> (1) Test whether these internal control systems are functioning in accordance with prescribed procedures.
>
> (2) Examine the recipient's system for monitoring subrecipients and obtaining and acting on subrecipient audit reports.

The auditor should obtain a sufficient understanding of each of the three elements of the entity's internal control structure relating to federal financial assistance programs to plan the audit of the entity's compliance with the specific requirements of those programs. Control structure policies and procedures relating to those programs may be separate from policies and procedures applied to other transactions the entity enters into. For example, the policies and procedures in place to ensure eligibility might be totally separate from those relating to the processing of financial transactions. The auditor's understanding should include knowledge about relevant control environment factors and the design of policies, procedures, and records used in administering federal financial assistance programs and whether they have been placed in operation. The understanding should include knowledge about the design and extent of the supervisory control procedures in place to ensure that laws and regulations are being complied with. This understanding may be documented separately from the auditor's understanding of the overall control environment, the accounting system used to process financial transactions, and related control procedures.

The total amount of major federal financial assistance program expenditures may be less than 50 percent of the recipient organization's total federal financial assistance expenditures. In such circumstances, the auditor should extend the understanding to include the largest nonmajor programs so that at least 50 percent of federal financial assistance program expenditures are documented.

The auditor's understanding should be sufficient to enable him or her to

- Identify the types of potential material noncompliance.
- Consider matters that affect the risk of material noncompliance.
- Design effective tests of the entity's compliance with applicable requirements of major federal financial assistance programs.

Once the auditor has obtained the understanding of control structure policies and procedures relating to compliance, he or she should perform tests of controls, or consider tests of controls performed concurrently with obtaining the understanding, to determine whether the design and operation of relevant policies and procedures are effective for preventing or detecting material noncompliance. This assessment of control risk helps the auditor evaluate the risk that material noncompliance exists in a major federal financial assistance program.

Detection Risk. OMB Circular A-128 requires that in an audit including major federal financial programs, a representative number of charges from each major program be selected for testing. The objective of these tests of compliance with requirements is to restrict detection risk. Just as in a financial statement audit, in a single audit the auditor determines how much substantive testing is necessary to reduce detection risk to an appropriately low level on the basis of the risk assessment activities. As the assessed level of control risk decreases, the acceptable level of detection risk increases.

General Requirements Applicable to Federal Financial Assistance Programs

The OMB *Compliance Supplement* identifies six general requirements that are applicable to all or most federal financial assistance programs. These requirements involve significant national policy, and failure to comply could have a material effect (though not necessarily a *direct* effect) on an organization's financial statements. The *Compliance Supplement* requires, as part of all audits of state and local governments that receive federal financial assistance, that compliance with applicable general requirements be tested, if failure to comply could materially affect the entity's financial statements. Therefore, where applicable, the auditor is required to perform tests that address compliance with these requirements.

- *Political Activity* (Hatch Act and Intergovernmental Personnel Act of 1970, as amended)—Federal funds cannot be used for political activity of any kind.
- *Construction Contracts* (Davis–Bacon Act)—Laborers and mechanics employed by contractors of federally funded projects must be paid wages not less than those established by the Secretary of Labor as the prevailing local wage rate.
- *Civil Rights*—No person shall be excluded from participation in, or be subjected to discrimination in connection with, a federally funded program because of race, color, national origin, sex, or physical impairment.
- *Cash Management*—Cash should be withdrawn only in amounts necessary to meet immediate needs or cover program disbursements.
- *Relocation Assistance and Real Property Acquisition*—Federally funded programs involving the acquisition of property must provide certain services for the households and businesses they displace.
- *Federal Financial Reports*—Specified financial reports must be periodically submitted.

The *Compliance Supplement* does not include two additional general requirements, which should also be tested for compliance.

- *Indirect Costs*—A portion of operating costs may be charged to federal programs as indirect costs. To be eligible for reimbursement under those programs, indirect costs must be allocated in conformity with an indirect cost allocation plan prepared in accordance with OMB Circular A-87 or other similar directives.
- *Drug-Free Workplace Act of 1988*—Regulations requiring grant recipients to certify that they have a drug-free workplace were issued by 35 federal agencies. The regulations apply to grants approved or awarded on or after March 18, 1989, and require that grantees
  - •• Publish a statement notifying employees that the illegal manufacturing, distribution, dispensation, possession, or use of a controlled substance is prohibited in the workplace.
  - •• Implement a drug-free awareness program to provide information on the availability of drug counseling and rehabilitation.
  - •• Notify the granting agency within ten days after receiving notice of an employee's conviction under any criminal anti-drug statute and impose a sanction on any employee convicted of such a crime.

These general requirements are expected to be included in the next revision of the *Compliance Supplement*.

Nonmajor Programs

The discussion of the Single Audit Act thus far has related to those programs defined as major federal financial assistance programs. Many state and local governments, however, receive some or all of their federal financial assistance from programs that do not meet the federal definition of major programs. These programs are referred to as nonmajor programs. The procedures required to be performed on nonmajor programs are substantially more limited in scope than those for major programs. As part of the audit of the financial statements or of considering the internal control structure, the auditor may have selected for testing some transactions from nonmajor programs; if so, he or she should test those transactions for compliance with the applicable requirements. The auditor is not required to address compliance with the general requirements or the specific requirements of other transactions from the nonmajor program.

SAS No. 63 cites, in paragraph 86, an example of the extent of testing necessary for a nonmajor program.

> If in the audit of the general-purpose or basic financial statements an auditor examined a payroll transaction that was charged to a nonmajor program, the auditor should determine that the position could reasonably be charged to that program and that the individual's salary was correctly charged to that program.

Reporting Under the Single Audit Act

The reporting requirements of the Single Audit Act are more extensive than those under GAAS and GAGAS. In addition to the report required by GAAS on the financial statements and the reports required by GAGAS on the internal control structure and on compliance with laws and regulations, the auditor performing a single audit must issue reports on

- Compliance with specific requirements applicable to major federal financial assistance programs.
- Compliance with the general requirements applicable to those programs.
- Compliance with requirements applicable to nonmajor federal financial assistance programs.
- The supplementary schedule of federal financial assistance (discussed later).
- The internal control structure, based on the assessment made as a part of the audit of the general-purpose or basic financial statements and the additional tests relating to systems used in administering federal financial assistance programs.

Reporting on Compliance with Specific Requirements of Major Federal Financial Assistance Programs. The auditor is required to report on the governmental entity's compliance with the specific requirements applicable to major federal financial assistance programs. As illustrated in the report that follows (SAS No. 63, para. 74), an unqualified report expresses positive assurance on such compliance.

> We have audited the City of _____'s compliance with the requirements governing types of services allowed or unallowed; eligibility; matching, level of effort, or earmarking; reporting; [*describe any special tests and provisions*]; claims for advances and reimbursements; and amounts claimed or used for matching that are applicable to each of its major federal financial assistance programs, which are identified in the accompanying schedule of federal financial assistance, for the year ended June 30, 19X1. The management of the City of _____ is responsible for the City's compliance with those requirements. Our responsibility is to express an opinion on compliance with those requirements based on our audit.
>
> We conducted our audit in accordance with generally accepted auditing standards, *Government Auditing Standards*, issued by the Comptroller General of the United States, and OMB Circular A-128, "Audits of State and Local Governments." Those standards and OMB Circular A-128 require that we plan and perform the audit to obtain reasonable assurance about whether material noncompliance with the requirements referred to above occurred. An audit includes examining, on a test basis, evidence about the City's compliance with those requirements. We believe that our audit provides a reasonable basis for our opinion.
>
> The results of our audit procedures disclosed immaterial instances of noncompliance with the requirements referred to above, which are described in the accompanying schedule of findings and questioned costs. We considered these instances of noncompliance in forming our opinion on compliance, which is expressed in the following paragraph.
>
> In our opinion, the City of _____ complied, in all material respects, with the requirements governing types of services allowed or unallowed; eligibility; matching, level of effort, or earmarking; reporting; [*describe any special tests and provisions*]; claims for advances and reimbursements; and amounts claimed or used for matching that are applicable to each of its major federal financial assistance programs for the year ended June 30, 19X1.

Scope Limitations.   Any restrictions on the scope of the audit, that is, on the auditor's ability to perform all the procedures considered necessary in the circumstances, may require the auditor to qualify the opinion or disclaim an opinion. This decision depends on the auditor's judgment about the nature and magnitude of the potential effects of the scope limitation and their significance to each applicable major federal financial assistance program. Paragraph 76 of SAS No. 63 illustrates the appropriate wording when a qualification or disclaimer of opinion is necessary.

Material Noncompliance.   The auditor is also precluded from issuing an unqualified opinion on compliance when the auditing procedures performed reveal instances of noncompliance that the auditor believes could have a material effect on a program. In these circumstances, the auditor must use his or her professional judgment to determine if a qualified or an adverse opinion is required. Report language for both a qualified and an adverse opinion is illustrated in SAS No. 63, paragraphs 78–79.

Regardless of the auditor's opinion on compliance, Circular A-128 requires him or her to report *any* instance of noncompliance found and any resulting questioned costs. The Single Audit Act does not require the auditor to report likely questioned costs; that is, the auditor does not project known questioned costs to the population to arrive at likely questioned costs. The auditor reports only those questioned costs that are known to have been incurred.

Reporting on Compliance with the General Requirements of Major Federal Financial Assistance Programs.   As previously noted, the auditor is required to test compliance with the applicable general requirements. The auditor's report on compliance with the general requirements contains a disclaimer of opinion on compliance with the general requirements. It does, however, express positive assurance that the results of procedures performed on the items tested disclosed no material instances of noncompliance, if that is the case, and negative assurance with respect to items not tested. In addition, the report states that the auditor's procedures were limited to the applicable procedures described in the *Compliance Supplement*, or describes alternative procedures.

Reporting on Compliance with Nonmajor Programs.   The auditor's report on compliance with requirements applicable to nonmajor federal financial assistance programs contains a disclaimer of opinion on compliance with nonmajor programs and statements of both positive and negative assurance similar to those in a report on the general requirements, discussed above.

Reporting on Internal Control Structure Policies and Procedures Used in Administering Federal Financial Assistance Programs.   The Single Audit Act requires the auditor to issue a report on the internal control structure policies and procedures used in administering federal financial assistance programs. SAS No. 63 does not contain an example of such a report. Following is an illustrative report that meets the requirements of the Act:

> We have audited the financial statements of [*name of entity*] as of and for the year ended June 30, 19X1, and have issued our report thereon dated August 15, 19X1.
>
> We conducted our audit in accordance with generally accepted auditing standards, *Government Auditing Standards*, issued by the Comptroller General of the United States, and OMB Circular A-128, ''Audits of State and Local Governments.'' Those standards and OMB Circular A-128 require that we plan and perform the audit to obtain reasonable assurance about whether the financial statements are free of material misstatement.
>
> In planning and performing our audit of the financial statements of [*name of entity*] and of its compliance with laws and regulations governing federal financial assistance programs for the year ended June 30, 19X1, we considered its internal control structure, including applicable control procedures used in administering

federal financial assistance programs. Our consideration of the internal control structure was undertaken to provide a basis for determining the auditing procedures to perform for the purpose of expressing our opinions on the financial statements and on the organization's compliance with laws and regulations governing federal financial assistance programs.

The management of [*name of entity*] is responsible for establishing and maintaining the internal control structure used in administering federal financial assistance programs. In fulfilling this responsibility, estimates and judgments by management are required to assess the expected benefits and related costs of internal control structure policies and procedures. The objectives of the internal control structure used in administering federal financial assistance programs are to provide management with reasonable, but not absolute, assurance that resource use is consistent with laws, regulations, and policies; resources are safeguarded against waste, loss, and misuse; and reliable data is obtained, maintained, and fairly disclosed in reports. Because of inherent limitations in any internal control structure, errors or irregularities may nevertheless occur and not be detected. Also, projection of any assessment of the structure to future periods is subject to the risk that procedures may become inadequate because of changes in conditions or that the effectiveness of the design and operation of policies and procedures may deteriorate.

For purposes of this report, we have classified the significant internal control structure policies and procedures used in administering federal financial assistance programs in the following categories [*Identify categories*]:

For all of the control categories listed above, our consideration of the internal control structure consisted of obtaining an understanding of the design of relevant policies and procedures used in administering major federal financial assistance programs, determining that they had been placed in operation, performing test of controls, and assessing control risk.

With respect to the internal control structure policies and procedures used solely in administering the nonmajor federal financial assistance programs of [*name of entity*], our consideration of relevant policies and procedures was limited to obtaining an understanding of their design, and for those nonmajor programs selected for testing, determining that the relevant policies and procedures had been placed in operation.

Based on our consideration of the policies and procedures as described in the two immediately preceding paragraphs, we noted certain matters involving the internal control structure used in administering federal financial assistance programs and its operation that we consider to be reportable conditions under standards established by the American Institute of Certified Public Accountants. Reportable conditions involve matters coming to our attention relating to significant deficiencies in the design or operation of the internal control structure used in administering federal financial assistance programs that, in our judgment, could adversely affect the organization's ability to record, process, summarize, and report financial data consistent with the assertions of management.

[*Include paragraphs to describe the reportable conditions noted.*]

A material weakness is a reportable condition in which the design or operation of one or more of the internal control structure elements does not reduce to a relatively low level the risk that errors or irregularities in amounts that would be material in relation to the financial statements being audited may occur and not be detected within a timely period by employees in the normal course of performing their assigned functions.

Our consideration of the internal control structure used in administering federal financial assistance programs would not necessarily disclose all matters in the internal control structure that might be reportable conditions and, accordingly, would not necessarily disclose all reportable conditions that are also considered to be material weaknesses as defined above. However, we believe none of the reportable conditions described above is a material weakness.

We also noted other matters involving the internal control structure used in administering federal financial assistance programs and its operation that we have reported to the management of [*name of entity*] in a separate communication dated August 15, 19XX.

This report is intended for the information of the audit committee, management, and others within the organization and [*specify regulatory agency or other third party*]. This restriction is not intended to limit the distribution of this report, which is a matter of public record.

Report on Supplementary Schedule of Federal Financial Assistance.   OMB Circular A-128 requires an auditor's report on the schedule of federal financial assistance program expenditures. This schedule must show the total expenditures for each federal financial assistance program as identified in the *Catalog of Federal Domestic Assistance*. The schedule of federal financial assistance is a type of additional information in an auditor-submitted document, as discussed in Chapter 23. The auditor's report on the schedule falls under the reporting guidelines of SAS No. 29, *Reporting on Information Accompanying the Basic Financial Statements in Auditor-Submitted Documents* (AU Section 551), and might read as follows:

We have audited the general-purpose financial statements of the City of _____ for the year ended June 30, 19XX, and have issued our report thereon dated September 8, 19XX. These general-purpose financial statements are the responsibility of the City's management. Our responsibility is to express an opinion on these general-purpose financial statements based on our audit.

We conducted our audit in accordance with generally accepted auditing standards and *Government Auditing Standards*, issued by the Comptroller General of the United States. Those standards require that we plan and perform the audit to obtain reasonable assurance about whether the general-purpose financial statements are free of material misstatements. An audit includes examining, on a test basis, evidence supporting the amounts and disclosures in the general-purpose financial statements. An audit also includes assessing the accounting principles used and significant estimates made by management, as well as evaluating the overall financial statement presentation. We believe that our audit provides a reasonable basis for our opinion.

Our audit was made for the purpose of forming an opinion on the general-purpose financial statements of the City of _____ taken as a whole. The accompanying schedule of federal financial assistance is presented for purposes of additional analysis and is not a required part of the general-purpose financial statements. The information in that schedule has been subjected to the auditing procedures applied in the audit of the general-purpose financial statements and, in our opinion, is fairly presented in all material respects in relation to the general-purpose financial statements taken as a whole.

PART 5

Auditing Specialized Industries

Introduction to Part 5

The discussions of auditing concepts, principles, and procedures in Parts 1 through 4 of this book are presented principally within the framework of enterprises engaged in manufacturing, selling, and service activities. In contrast, the chapters in Part 5 deal with auditing a number of specific industries. While every industry has at least some characteristics that set it apart from other industries, those characteristics do not necessarily require unique audit strategies or procedures. In some industries, however, the risks, accounting principles, control structure, transactions, and accounts are sufficiently different to require specialized knowledge on the part of an auditor. Fifteen such industries are covered in the chapters in Part 5.

The following chapters present detailed descriptions, as appropriate, of the business, economic, and regulatory environment and activities of organizations in the industry, the risks they typically face, unique accounting principles that have implications for auditing, typical transactions and key control structure policies and procedures that are unique to the industry, and suggested auditing procedures. The relative emphasis given to each of those topics and the organization of the chapters vary by industry and were dictated by the nature of the industry and the environment in which it operates. The intent is to describe only the characteristics and auditing considerations that are unique to each industry. Accordingly, when reading any of the chapters in Part 5, the reader should also review the discussion of auditing standards and procedures in the first 25 chapters of the book; material from those chapters that is applicable to audits of specialized industries is generally not repeated in Part 5.

26

Auditing Banks

OVERVIEW OF THE INDUSTRY

Banks are primarily in the business of money brokerage. By accepting deposits and extending credit, banks act as conduits between those with funds to invest and borrowers. Bank loans and investment securities, which are essentially another form of loan, are earning assets, and the interest income they generate is the principal source of revenue for the banking industry.

Several different types of institutions within the banking industry perform financial intermediary and service functions. Some of the typical activities of those institutions are listed below.

Type of Institution	*Typical Activities*
Commercial banks	Accept deposits, make loans, facilitate payments and collections, invest in securities, perform trust services, and provide financial services, such as discount brokerage and advisory services.
Thrift institutions (savings and loan associations, savings banks, and credit unions)	Accept deposits, make mortgage and consumer loans, invest in securities, and provide other financial services.
Trust companies	Manage funds and other assets, the beneficial interest in which remains with the owner and not the bank.

While the differences among the activities of financial institutions were at one time fairly well pronounced, legislation and aggressive business development in recent years have blurred the traditional distinctions. As a result, the differences between banking institutions and others in the financial services industry, such as insurance companies and securities brokerage firms, are disappearing rapidly. For practical purposes, this chapter focuses on commercial banks.

A bank may accept deposits in the form of demand deposits, which bear no or low interest, and time deposits, which ordinarily bear a market rate of interest. Time deposits consist of savings accounts, certificates of deposit, individual retirement accounts, negotiable orders of withdrawal (NOW) accounts, club accounts, and commercial and public fund time deposits. Bank earnings are generated principally by making loans to businesses and individuals and investing in U.S. government and municipal securities. Many banks also act in a fiduciary capacity by providing trust, investment management, and safekeeping services. In addition to charging fees for account services, other income-producing activities include providing credit cards, safe deposit boxes, cashier checks, money orders, foreign currency exchange, travelers' checks, and savings bonds.

Commercial banks in the United States are either federal or state chartered. Federal-chartered banks must include "national" or "N.A." (national association) in their name, are supervised by the Office of the Comptroller of the

Currency, and are required to be members of the Federal Reserve System (FRS) and to have their deposits insured by the Federal Deposit Insurance Corporation (FDIC). State-chartered banks are supervised by the banking authorities of the chartering state, are required to obtain FDIC insurance coverage, and may elect to join the FRS. Commercial banks may be organized as unit banks, branch banks, or bank holding companies, depending on the laws of the state in which they operate. They may also engage in foreign operations using a foreign department, foreign offshore branches, an Edge Act Corporation, or a foreign subsidiary or affiliate.

A bank may hold assets that have been entrusted to it and for which it acts as agent or fiduciary for the customer. While the bank may have physical possession of the assets, they are not carried on its general ledger. Nonbank assets may include a variety of items, such as marketable securities, real property, and personal assets. In many banks, the value of nonbank assets often approximates or exceeds the total assets shown in the bank's financial statements.

BANK REGULATION AND ACCOUNTING PRINCIPLES

Bank regulation is based on the philosophy that it is essential to the national interest that the banking system be sound, so as to merit complete and continued public confidence. As a result, banks are subject to strict governmental regulation and supervision. There are four primary bank regulators, each with distinct but sometimes overlapping jurisdiction.

- *The Office of the Comptroller of the Currency (OCC)*. The Comptroller of the Currency is the appointed official in the U.S. Treasury Department responsible for the chartering and supervision of national banks.
- *The Federal Reserve Board (FRB)*. The Federal Reserve System is the centralized banking system of the United States. It is guided by the Federal Reserve Board, which includes among its functions the examination and supervision of member banks.
- *The Federal Deposit Insurance Corporation*. The Federal Deposit Insurance Corporation examines state banks that are not members of the Federal Reserve System. Sometimes these examinations are conducted simultaneously with those of state banking departments.
- *State Banking Authorities*. State banking authorities are responsible for and examine state banks that they have chartered. If a state bank is a member of the Federal Reserve System, the examination is sometimes a joint state and federal examination. If a state bank is not a member of the Federal Reserve System, the examination may be a joint state and FDIC examination.

The Securities and Exchange Commission (SEC) exerts significant influence over the financial reporting practices of publicly held bank holding companies. Historically, the SEC has deferred to the bank regulators on matters of disclosure by banks. Securities issued or guaranteed by a bank (as contrasted with a bank holding company) have been exempt from the registration provisions of the Securities Act of 1933 since its adoption. In addition, few publicly held banks have been subject to the usual registration and reporting provisions of the Securities Exchange Act of 1934 because they are subject to other regulatory agencies. Generally, the bank regulators must conform their regulations with those of the SEC, and thus there is a relatively high degree of consistency in reporting. Bank holding companies, however, do not come under the narrow exemption from the securities laws that was granted to banks. The SEC reviews registration statements filed by bank holding companies that offer securities pursuant to the 1933 Act and administers the registration, reporting, and insider trading provisions of the 1934 Act for bank holding companies with 500 or more shareholders and over $1 million in assets.

All of the authorities mentioned, except the SEC, are required to examine the banks under their regulation. There are significant differences between the scope of their examinations and the scope of an independent audit. The reports of those examiners are reviewed with the bank's board of directors. Independent auditors should request to attend those meetings and, at a minimum, obtain and review the reports, since the findings represent an important additional source of information for use in planning and performing a bank audit.

Banks are required by the various regulatory authorities to maintain certain standards of capital adequacy. Items included in capital for purposes of generally accepted accounting principles (GAAP) and for regulatory purposes differ. The two regulatory calculations of capital are primary capital and secondary capital. Primary capital generally consists of equity under GAAP plus the bank's reserve for loan losses; secondary capital generally includes primary capital plus certain liabilities that are convertible into equity or have equity characteristics, as specified by banking regulatory authorities.

The form and content of bank and bank holding company financial statements are based on GAAP, which, in turn, is influenced by the reporting requirements of the various applicable regulatory authorities and the SEC. Thus, the auditor of a bank should be familiar with, as appropriate, the rules and regulations of the Comptroller of the Currency (for national banks) and of the FDIC (for state banks that are not members of the Federal Reserve System), the regulations of the Board of Governors of the FRS (for state member banks), and the instructions to the annual report forms of the Board of Governors of the FRS applicable to bank holding companies. In addition, the regulations of the appropriate state banking authorities and of SEC Regulation S-X (particularly Article 9) and Guide 3 should be consulted.

RISK ASSESSMENT AND AUDIT STRATEGY

Engagement Planning

Several characteristics of the operations and business of banks are unique to the industry and require the auditor's consideration in assessing risks, determining the audit strategy, and performing auditing procedures. Some of the more important characteristics are

- A bank's assets are highly negotiable and liquid. Thus, they are subject to greater risk of loss than are the assets of other businesses.
- Banks are subject to substantial regulatory reporting requirements that sometimes go beyond GAAP. Information needed to satisfy these reporting requirements must be anticipated in planning the audit.
- Banks frequently have complex internal control structures that provide substantial independent review of transactions.
- Banking is one of the more technologically advanced industries, and traditional "manual" audit techniques may be ineffective or inefficient. Determining the need for and coordinating the work of different specialists who may be involved in the audit may be a complicated task.

The AICPA industry audit guide, *Audits of Banks*, issued in 1983, provides guidance on specialized accounting principles and reporting practices for the banking industry and on auditing procedures applicable to banks. At the time of this writing, the AICPA is in the process of issuing an updated industry accounting and audit guide on savings and loan institutions.

Risk Factors

Banks are exposed to a variety of inherent risks that are unique to the industry. With respect to lending activities, banks face three major types of inherent risk: credit risk, interest rate risk, and liquidity risk.

Credit Risk.　Extending credit is inherently a risky activity; that is, the bank assumes the risk that the borrower may not repay the loan. The decision to grant a loan is based on the credit information available at the time the loan is made. As economic and other factors change, however, the borrower's ability to repay the loan may also change. In addition, changes in the fair market value of assets and changes in the creditor's financial status represent risks in nonrecourse and recourse lending.

A principal risk factor for certain banks is excessive concentration of loans by type of entity (e.g., subsidiaries of controlled groups), industry (such as automotive, oil and gas, or real estate), or geographical area. Geographical factors relate to distinctions between areas of the United States (e.g., the Sun Belt versus the Northeast) and, for banks that transact business internationally, between domestic and foreign operations, including those in lesser-developed countries where currency restrictions often apply. There is also political risk in foreign operations, namely, the possibility that a change in government might result in nationalization of the banks and businesses in that country. The auditor should evaluate the collectibility of all loans, with particular attention to the relative amounts of recourse and nonrecourse loans.

Another credit risk faced by banks relates to "due from" accounts, which are amounts due from other banks for check clearing. These assets are similar to loans; however, they are included with cash on the balance sheet. The risk concerns the financial viability of the other banks. The auditor should apply the same procedures to these accounts to evaluate their collectibility as are applied to the bank's loan portfolio.

Interest Rate Risk.   Interest rate risk relates to the sensitivity of earnings to changes in interest rates. Banks assume interest rate risk as a basic function of accepting deposits and making loans, and derive income for undertaking this risk. Steps taken to neutralize interest rate exposure normally serve to minimize earnings potential.

Market interest rate fluctuations may affect management's intent and ability to hold securities and loans until maturity and may expose a bank to the risk of reduced net interest margin. Since banks must make investments and loans for extended periods, an inability to match these rate-sensitive assets with similarly rate-sensitive liabilities funding the assets can cause the net interest margin to diminish or disappear entirely.

Liquidity Risk.   Liquidity risk refers to banks' need to have funds available at all times to repay fully all maturing liabilities on a timely basis. Banks and bank holding companies act as financial intermediaries to assume liquidity risk by borrowing for shorter periods than those for which they lend.

Because of the substantial volume of transactions and daily settlement requirements, all bank transactions must be processed on the day they are received. Banks have suspense accounts that relate to processed transactions that cannot be identified; debits in those accounts that cannot be identified may be properly chargeable to expense, while unidentified credits often are in fact liabilities. The risk related to these accounts is that all items will not clear, resulting in an unbalanced position. Accordingly, the auditor should analyze suspense accounts on a regular basis to ensure that they clear on a timely basis. The net amounts in the suspense accounts are usually immaterial, but the auditor should analyze individual amounts in determining which debits and credits are related.

Other Risks.   Banks face additional inherent risk from investment activity. Banks may deal in futures and options in an effort to improve their net interest margin. This can involve risks, however, because bank management predicts changes in interest rates to compensate for a mismatched portfolio. Inherent risk also results from repurchase agreements, reverse repurchase agreements, and various trading strategies involving securities and loans. The auditor should ascertain whether those types of transactions are hedges or speculations and whether it is necessary to recognize the related risk currently by marking the accounts to market.

Regional and money center banks that are involved in foreign operations are also exposed to the risks of currency fluctuations. The auditor should evaluate the matching of dates of buy and sell positions on an individual-contract basis.

In addition, banks are exposed to both internal and external risks relating to deposits. Internal risks include manipulation of dormant accounts, unauthorized overdrafts, fraudulent debits, and withholding and lapping of deposits. Overdrafts are a form of extending credit; therefore, the auditor should review the bank's overdraft list for the adequacy of the reserve for overdrafts. Externally imposed risks include forgeries, new-account frauds, the inability to collect checks deposited by customers, and inadvertently permitting customers to draw on funds that are the result of kiting. In computerized systems, a lack of general control procedures magnifies such risks, since there may be unauthorized changes to bank records, programmed procedures, and reports.

Banks may be exposed to risks from commitments and loss contingencies relating to loans and securities transactions. For example, a bank may have an unrecorded commitment to purchase securities at a fixed price that is unfavorable or to continue to provide financing to an enterprise that is no longer considered a satisfactory risk. In those and similar circumstances, if the commitment is binding, the bank should provide for the related losses before additional credit is granted. The auditor will need to ensure that the bank has complied with the requirements of Statement of Financial Accounting Standards (SFAS) No. 5 in accruing or disclosing loss contingencies.

Banks sometimes transfer securities from their investment portfolios to their trading accounts. Because these two categories of securities are treated differently under GAAP, there is a risk that a loss resulting from a decline in market value of a trading account security may not be recognized on a timely basis for financial statement purposes. The auditor should plan to test transfers between accounts and determine management's intent with regard to securities transactions to ensure proper classification.

An auditor of a multi-affiliate holding company who is reporting separately on one affiliate should be aware of the risk that losses from related party transactions between affiliates could be deferred improperly or disguised. For example, one entity could sell a loan to another entity at more than fair market value to avoid loss recognition by the selling bank. The auditor should simultaneously examine all entities in the group that are under common control and should be alert for related party transactions.

Planning Considerations

Unlike most other businesses, banks traditionally close their books daily and release their earnings results soon after year-end. Therefore, it is often important that the audit be completed quickly. Providing the necessary data on a timely basis requires extensive planning and coordination, which can be accomplished by establishing timetables that indicate when various phases of the year-end closing are to be completed. Sometimes a detailed checklist organized by department or activity is used as the control mechanism for the year-end audit. Such checklists identify the data that the auditor requires, the client personnel responsible for preparing or providing it, when it is to be available, and the audit personnel responsible for that phase of the audit. The dates requested are based on the client's clearance schedule and the related estimated audit time. These schedules must be monitored closely to identify problem areas on a timely basis and to ensure that all deadlines are met.

The audit program for a bank often provides for substantive procedures to be performed throughout the year, with an update at year-end. When this is done, the auditor should ensure that the professional standards on early substantive testing are met, as described in Chapter 9. This "continuous audit" approach has several benefits, including

- Identification and resolution of issues prior to year-end.
- The opportunity to broaden audit personnel's understanding of the industry because one person may become involved in several areas of the bank.
- Less disrupting of the bank's operations because the work of the external auditor can be coordinated with that of the internal audit department.
- The ability to perform a substantial amount of audit work before year-end and to be prepared to release earnings results promptly.

Another significant factor in determining the audit strategy in the banking industry is the efficiency of testing control structure policies and procedures and thus reducing to a significant extent the amount of substantive testing. Because of the complex control structures generally found in banks, tests of controls are often performed. The control structure is frequently characterized by a high level of automation and electronically initiated transactions. Assessing the control structure in computerized systems is discussed in detail in Chapters 8 and 11.

The existence of an internal audit function is probably more prevalent in banking than in most other industries. If an internal audit function is objective, competent, and well supervised, the external auditor's procedures often include assessment of the internal audit function for purposes of using the work of the internal auditors. Determining the way in which and the extent to which the internal audit function is to be utilized is part of developing the audit strategy. The internal auditors should participate in that process to ensure that everyone involved has a clear understanding of the work to be performed and its timing. Chapter 6 discusses the auditor's responsibilities when the work of internal auditors is used.

In addition, banks often have a separate credit review function that reviews loan quality and documentation. The auditor should ascertain to whom the credit review department reports and its annual scope. If the credit review function is independent of the chief lending officers and other loan department personnel, the auditor may be able to use the work performed by the credit reviewers, in much the same way as the work of the internal audit department is used.

Analytical Procedures

Banks generate considerable analytical information for regulators and others that may be useful to the auditor in the planning stage. The auditor should become familiar with the types of analytical information contained in management's monthly financial reports to the board of directors. Banks often capture historical data throughout the year so that they can prepare a statement of condition on the basis of average daily balances. Such statements are issued as supplementary information to the year-end balance sheet. Wherever possible, the auditor should use average daily figures to develop ratios that may be useful for performing analytical procedures. In addition, there are commercial services that provide specific data that is useful in comparing an entity's operations with those of its local and national peer groups within the industry. Figure 26.1 presents some significant ratios used in the banking industry.

Interest Rate Sensitivity, Liquidity Management, and Capital Adequacy

Banks, in common with other financial institutions, are actively involved on a daily basis in various unrelated transactions affecting their asset and liability portfolios. Because of variations in both amounts and timing, these transactions cannot be matched perfectly in terms of interest sensitivities and maturities. Thus, the bank is left with an imbalance in its asset and liability positions that makes it sensitive to changes in interest rates.

Figure 26.1   Selected Ratios Used in the Banking Industry

Ratio	*Significance*
Securities divided by total assets	Indication of earning asset mix
Securities by type divided by total securities	Measure of investment portfolio mix
Net loans divided by total assets	Indication of earning asset mix
Net loans divided by total deposits	Indication of funding sources for loan base
Loans by type divided by total loans	Measure of loan portfolio mix and indication of lending strategy and risk
Loan delinquencies divided by respective type of loan outstanding	Measure of past-due loan risk
Loan loss valuation reserve divided by total loans net of unearned discount	Measure of loan portfolio risk coverage
Loan loss recoveries divided by previous year's charge-offs	Measure of charge-off policy and recovery experience
Nonperforming loans to total loans Reduction in interest income on nonperforming loans, net of tax effect, to net income	Measure of impact of nonperforming loans on net income
Investment income divided by average total securities	Measure of investment portfolio yield
Loan income divided by average net loans	Measure of loan portfolio yield
Total interest paid divided by average total deposits	Measure of cost of funds
Net income divided by average total assets	Measure of return on assets
Net income divided by average capital	Measure of return on equity
Primary capital to assets	Measure of capital adequacy

Figure 26.2   Illustrative Interest Rate Sensitivities

(In millions)	1 month or less	3 months or less	6 months or less	1 year or less
Assets	$1,000	$1,400	$1,600	$1,700
Liabilities	1,300	1,600	2,200	2,400
Gap	($ 300)	($ 200)	($ 600)	($ 700)

Management attempts to control the spread, or gap, between asset and liability positions of different maturities in order to reduce interest rate risks to acceptable levels. The net interest rate sensitivity gap illustrated in Figure 26.2 indicates that, because of the projected imbalance, an increase in interest rates in the next six months could result in substantially higher interest costs and a decrease in net interest income.

A concept closely related to interest rate sensitivity is liquidity management. Liquidity describes a bank's ability to meet financial obligations that arise during the normal course of business and is measured based on loan maturity. Figure 26.2 also indicates the bank's liquidity at each interval. If all liabilities due in one month or less were not refinanced, the bank would have to liquidate longer-term assets to cover the amount by which those liabilities exceeded assets convertible into cash in the same period.

In addition, as mentioned earlier, banks must maintain certain levels of capital as specified by regulatory authorities. The auditor should focus on the minimum acceptable regulatory ratio of capital to risk-based assets and should ensure that those capital requirements are being met. From a regulatory standpoint, a bank's capital position could affect its ability to enter into mergers and acquisitions, since acquisitions can result in a dilution of capital.

Materiality

Assessing materiality in the banking industry has several unique aspects. Because banks are so highly leveraged, balance sheet components are usually too large to be used as a practicable measure of materiality. Two income statement line items, net interest income and net income, and the accounts included in the capital adequacy computations are focal points in assessing materiality. The illustrative financial statements of a bank contained in the AICPA bank audit guide and the federal bank regulatory authorities' capital adequacy requirements indicate the accounts that are included in those items.

TYPICAL TRANSACTIONS, CONTROL STRUCTURE POLICIES AND PROCEDURES, AND AUDIT TESTS

Operations

Deposits.   One of the primary objectives of a bank is to obtain deposits, which it in turn lends to customers and invests in other earning assets. The deposit function, while not in itself revenue producing except for fees for various services, is important since it provides the funds for producing revenue through the lending and investment cycles.

Generally, demand deposit operations are computerized, and tellers handle a large variety of micro-encoded (MICR) documents. Daily transactions involving demand deposits, savings deposits and withdrawals, installment loan payments, mortgage loan payments, teller cash tickets, and official checks, as well as departmental debits and credits, flow together from the tellers in individual branches into a central proof department.

Savings department operations parallel those of demand deposits; they include procedures for opening accounts and posting deposit and withdrawal transactions. Savings operations comprise interest computations, payments, and maintaining records for certificate-type time accounts.

For both types of deposit transactions, the teller is responsible for verifying the account number and name, the account balance, and the validity of the customer's signature on the transaction ticket. Many computerized systems allow the teller to make immediate inquiry of a customer's account and recent activity. That capability facilitates the determination of the validity of customer transactions.

Auditing procedures in the area of deposits are not significantly different from procedures performed on comparable transactions and accounts in other industries. Because of the automated nature of bank accounting systems, most tests of deposit operations are directed toward control procedures related to the completeness and accuracy of data input and updated to master files. Control procedures related to authorization, other than teller verification, generally operate on an after-the-fact basis, with the bank relying on third parties to corroborate that transactions in deposit accounts are authorized. The authorization control procedures that are tested typically are those relating to changes to master files, such as interest rates paid, service charge levels, and new types of accounts. In addition, specific emphasis should be placed on dormant-account activity.

The principal substantive test of deposit balances is direct confirmation with customers. Confirmation procedures usually are coordinated with the internal audit department. In addition, accrued interest should be tested. This may be done through a bulk proof test of accrued interest and general ledger account analysis, including tracing entries to source journals and reviewing unusual transactions.

Substantive tests should include review and tests of client reconciliations of detail ledgers to general ledger balances; review of the handling of significant holdover items to be presented on the next day, overdrafts, rejects, and returned items; confirmation of significant "due to" (interbank clearing) accounts; and tests of period-end interest accruals.

Electronic Funds Transfer Systems. An electronic funds transfer system (EFTS) is a computer-based network designed to transfer funds through an electronic medium, thus eliminating paper-based transactions. EFTS was developed primarily in an effort to reduce check processing costs in view of the increased volume of transactions. The most commonly used adaptations of

EFTS are direct deposit systems, automated clearinghouse systems, and auto-mated teller machines.

A direct deposit system involves the direct deposit of payments into the recipient's account without the use of a check. The process begins when the recipient submits a standing authorization form to the paying organization. Subsequently, when a payment is due, the payer submits to its bank a magnetic tape containing transaction information, and the tape is processed through the bank's system. Transactions to be credited to an account at the payer's bank are extracted and held in a temporary file until the transaction date. Other transactions are captured on a master tape, which is sent to an automated clearinghouse (ACH), where the items are transmitted to the appropriate financial institution to be cleared.

A direct deposit system may also include preauthorized payment. In a preauthorized payment system, recurring payments are made directly by the payer's bank to the recipient's bank without the payer writing a check. The process begins when the payer provides the recipient with written authoriza-tion to debit an account at a particular bank. When a payment is due, the recipient produces a form containing the payer's account number and amount, and the recipient deposits these check facsimiles in the bank, which then processes the check facsimiles through the proof department and credits the recipient's account.

An automated clearinghouse is a centralized computer that receives, sends, and controls specific EFT messages between member banks and other ACHs. In a non-ACH system, a large part of the transfer of funds is also done electronically, but only after the checks or other paper documents have been micro-encoded, sorted, and read to a computer file. In an ACH system, the check is eliminated, and the payment is cleared through the ACH automat-ically. Inputs to and outputs from the ACH are in electronic form.

Automated teller machines (ATMs) are remote banking terminals that allow customers to make deposits, withdrawals, or transfers between accounts and to inquire as to current balances. A plastic card with a magnetic stripe on the back and a personal identification number (PIN) are required to activate the machine. Most ATMs process transactions in an on-line mode. Additionally, certain decision logic is programmed into the ATMs that enables them to process off-line.

Control procedures in an EFTS consist of system software, such as that related to access, asset protection, and documentation, in addition to the control procedures that would be performed in a teller-based operation. As suggested earlier, those computer control procedures are frequently tested by the auditor.

Loans

The organization of the lending function depends on the size of the bank and the complexity of its lending activities. A separate department usually handles each of the numerous types of loans.

Types of Loans.   Loans are categorized by type of borrower, purpose, matur-ity, and risk. Categorization is necessary for accounting control, reporting to various supervisory authorities, and management information. Generally, loans are categorized as commercial, real estate, or consumer.

Commercial financing includes

- Demand loans, which have no fixed maturity and are payable on demand. Interest, earned daily, is billed to the borrower periodically, usually monthly. These are the most liquid loans in a bank's portfolio.
- Time loans, which are usually made for a 30- to 120-day period. Interest may be payable at maturity, billed monthly, or discounted from the proceeds of the loan.
- Term loans, which are obligations with maturities from one to ten years. These loans provide intermediate or long-term financing.
- Factoring, which occurs when a lender purchases accounts receivable at a discount. The bank may purchase the receivables without recourse to the borrower.
- Assigned accounts receivable financing, which is the pledging of accounts receivable to the bank as collateral for a loan. The bank usually lends from 60 to 90 percent of the face amount of the receivables, depending on their quality.
- Lease financing, in which personal property is purchased by the bank and leased to a customer on a net-lease, full-payout basis.

Real estate financing includes

- Residential mortgage loans, which consist of conventional, Federal Housing Administration insured, and Veterans Administration partially guaranteed loans. These loans are secured by mortgage liens on real property.
- Commercial and construction mortgage loans, which generally carry terms of one to three years, are secured by liens on real property, and are used to finance real estate development projects such as the construction of single-family dwellings, apartments, industrial complexes, commercial buildings, and land development.

Consumer financing includes

- Installment loans, which are frequently discounted and generally made to customers to finance the purchase of consumer goods and services.
- Credit card loans, which are utilized to consolidate a consumer's charge purchases from participating merchants into a single revolving charge account.
- Cash advance loans, which are lines of credit established by consumers and are drawn on by writing a special check or by drawing a check on a checking account in excess of the funds on deposit.

Loan Policy and Enforcement. In formulating policy, decisions must be made as to what percentage of deposits and capital should be invested in loans, what types of loans should be made, and the probable character, likely diversification, and anticipated volume of commercial and consumer loans. Limits for each line of business should be established. Directors and management must decide whether the bank will grant formal lines of credit and must determine the requirements for annual or seasonal liquidations of debt, interest rates, and compensating balance requirements. The loan policy should prevent an overinvestment in loans and should result in an acceptable ratio of loans to deposits. If this ratio becomes too high, regulatory authorities may require an increase in the bank's capital. Once the loan policy has been formulated, it must be enforced. The effect on bank operations should be reviewed periodically, and the policy should be updated when necessary.

Generally, loans are approved by the board of directors or its designated committee. Large loans are approved directly by a formal resolution in the minutes of the board or committee. Many banks have a committee that reviews all loans over a stipulated amount on a frequent basis. In banks that do not have a separate credit review function, the internal audit department usually reviews loan documentation and quality. The auditor normally performs tests of controls in the area of credit granting, loan approval, and documentation; typically those tests consist of reviewing the minutes of the loan committee (to ensure that approvals are appropriately documented) and examining credit files for compliance with bank policy.

Income Recognition.   Interest and fees charged by a commercial bank on its loan portfolios are generally its principal source of income. The major types of fees and costs are shown below. SFAS No. 91 (Accounting Standards Section L20) requires that *nonrefundable* fees and costs be deferred as an adjustment of loan yield using the interest method. As indicated below, most such fees and certain direct origination costs (or initial direct costs of leases) must be deferred and amortized over the life of the loan (or lease) as a yield adjustment.

Description	*Required Accounting*
Loan origination fees	Deferred as an adjustment of loan yield, generally using the interest method.
Commitment fees	Deferred as an adjustment of loan yield, generally using the interest method for commitments that are integral to the lending process; recognized during the commitment period for commitments that are considered a separate service.
Syndication fees	Cash basis unless a portion of the loan is retained by the manager and the yield is lower than other participants' yield.
Origination costs (internal and external)	Deferred as an adjustment of loan yield, generally using the interest method.

Other fees for services should be taken into income when the service has been performed. Such fees may include debt placement fees that are similar to underwriting fees of investment bankers and are not adjustments to interest rates.

The audit objectives for the various service fees charged by banks relate to the timing and amount of revenue recognition. Generally, the auditor performs tests directed at the proper recording of amortization.

Loan Reviews. The impact of loan collectibility on a bank's financial position has compelled banks to use an ongoing form of credit evaluation. Many banks have a loan evaluation function that reports directly to, or indirectly through, the internal audit function, which in turn reports to the examining/audit committee of the board. In addition, bank regulators, as part of their examination procedures, designate individual loans as either classified or nonclassified; classified loans, which warrant monitoring and a specific allowance, are further labeled as either loss, doubtful, substandard, or special mention.

Evaluating loans and determining the adequacy of the allowance for loan losses is a complex process. It requires the ability to evaluate relative risk in the lending area based on types and volumes of lending activity. The auditor who reviews loans must be aware of the internal system for grading loan quality, including the procedures used to identify and monitor past-due and nonperforming loans, and quantifying potential losses. Nonperforming loans, also referred to as nonaccrual loans, are loans on which interest payments are delinquent or collection of the principal has become doubtful and on which the bank has as a result ceased to accrue interest income. Federal supervisory agencies and the SEC have established regulatory reporting guidelines for nonaccrual loans. The bank's policies for classifying loans as nonaccrual and for charging loans off, either partially or in full, are critical considerations in the auditor's loan review. In addition, the auditor should be familiar with the regulator's classification of loans as included in its report on the bank (discussed earlier).

The existence of internal loan review and the structure, size, and complexity of the bank should be considered in determining the extent of the auditor's loan review. The ultimate quality of the loan review depends on the exercise of business judgment.

Some of the more significant factors affecting the evaluation of individual loans and the overall loan portfolio are

Types and volumes of lending activity.

Dynamic nature of lending markets.

Management's lending policies.

Competence of lending officers.

Control procedures for monitoring the loan portfolio and reporting on its status.

Internal loan review function.

Industry and portfolio concentrations.

Past collection records.

Policy on nonaccrual of interest.

Policy on charging off loans.

Policy on providing for loan losses.

Loan collectibility often depends on the worth of the collateral, particularly when loans are in default. Consequently, the auditor should review the value of collateral on a liquidation basis rather than on a going concern basis. Not all secured loans are completely collateralized. Also, although collateral is pledged, its value may not be sufficient to cover the entire loan principal. The loan portion not secured is the same as an unsecured loan and is subject to the same collection risks. Therefore, loan grading is usually subjected to tests of controls directed at completeness and accuracy, and the adequacy of the current-year provision as well as the allowance for loan losses should be substantively tested through individual loan review and overall portfolio analysis.

Investments

Normally, the funds management department of a bank is governed by a funds management committee or an assets and liabilities management committee. The committee usually consists of senior executive officers such as the president, executive vice president(s), and heads of related departments, for example, loans, investments, and deposits. Their responsibility is to plan and periodically evaluate the funds allocation strategy and the specific portfolio decisions on loans, deposits, and other sources of funds. Traditionally, banks have not been allowed to invest in equity securities; investment has been limited to debt instruments.

Control Objectives and Auditing Procedures. The following major control objectives should be considered in assessing the control structure relative to investment and trading account securities:

- Purchases and sales of securities should be initiated only on the basis of appropriate authorization to ensure compliance with corporate policies and with legal, regulatory, and liquidity requirements.
- All authorized security transactions should be recorded accurately and on a timely basis.
- Adequate asset protection procedures should be maintained for securities located in the bank and in the possession of correspondents or other independent custodians.
- All income earned on investment and trading account securities should be recorded accurately and collected on a timely basis.

Auditing procedures for investment and trading account securities include both tests of controls and substantive tests; they do not differ significantly from the procedures applied to investments of entities in other industries, as described in Chapter 17. Banks also engage in selling (buying) securities under agreements to repurchase (resell) them. Known as repurchase agreements and reverse repurchase agreements, respectively, these instruments and related audit tests are discussed in Chapter 39.

Investment Account Securities.   Investment securities generally represent a very significant asset and source of income for banks. The primary goals of the investment department are to maximize its contribution to the bank's overall profitability while maintaining liquidity and stability. Investment strategies should complement other facets of the overall operating strategy.

To meet both liquidity and income objectives, the investment portfolio should be managed so that maturity schedules are balanced. To do this, management must anticipate deposit trends and the credit needs of loan customers, without exposing the bank to significant security losses in times of rising interest rates. Orderly spacing of investment maturities permits re-employment of proceeds at more favorable yields in times of rising interest rates. Although the credit risks inherent in the investment portfolio may be minimal, because of the general character of commercial bank investments, the exposure to market declines resulting from market yield fluctuations is always present.

Normally, securities are purchased at a premium or discount. Amortization of premiums and accretion of discounts should be accounted for using the interest method, which results in a constant rate of return based on the adjusted book value of the security.

When securities are held to maturity, the accretion of discounts and amortization of premiums eliminate the recognition of gains or losses for financial reporting purposes. Commercial banks, however, often are affected by fluctuating loan and deposit levels that necessitate selling investment securities for liquidity purposes before their maturities, with possible gains or losses.

Trading Account Securities.   Banks frequently purchase and hold debt securities for resale; in engaging in this activity, banks essentially are acting as dealers in securities. The trading account should include all securities purchased solely for resale. Unlike investment securities, which have a relatively long holding period, trading account securities are intended to be held for sale at a profit. Management should document its intention at the date of acquisition.

When acting as a dealer, a bank may, either alone or in concert with other commercial banks in a syndicate, purchase an issue of municipal general obligation securities directly from the municipality at an agreed-on price arrived at through competitive bidding. The bank then sells the municipal securities to institutional investors or on the open market. The markup in price is compensation for distributing the securities and assuming the risk of a change in market value during distribution.

As mentioned earlier, trading account securities are accounted for differently from investment securities because they are held for resale and are not intended to be held until maturity. According to the audit guide, trading account securities should be carried at current market value, with increases or decreases in unrealized gains or losses included in the income statement. The banking regulators generally permit the use of the cost, market, or lower-of-cost-or-market method of accounting for trading account securities; however, use of the cost method is discouraged.

Fiduciary and Other Activities

The primary concern in the audit of nonbank assets is the bank's contingent liability from not properly fulfilling its responsibilities as fiduciary or agent. The auditor should review a bank's various trust agreements and determine that the bank is in compliance with them. Consideration should be given to physically counting assets held in trust or testing the internal audit department's counts to obtain satisfaction about their safeguarding. Testing in this area usually comprises a combination of tests of controls and substantive tests, with significant emphasis on testing the bank's reconciliations.

The auditor should also determine the extent to which a bank has engaged in other off-balance-sheet activities that create commitments or contingencies, including innovative transactions involving securities and loans (e.g., transfers with recourse or put options), that could affect the financial statements, including disclosures in the notes. Inquiries of management relating to such activities should be formalized in the representation letter normally obtained at year-end. The auditor should also review the bank's documentation to determine whether particular transactions are sales or financing arrangements.

27

Auditing Colleges, Universities, and Independent Schools

OVERVIEW OF THE INDUSTRY

The business operations of a college or similar institution, and hence its accounting practices, differ from those of a commercial organization in three significant respects. First, such institutions generally do not have owners. This should not affect the audit because the responsibility to report to the trustees, creditors, and other providers of resources does not differ significantly from the auditor's responsibility to the shareholders of a corporation. Second, a college's resources are not completely fungible; some expenditures are subject to donors' restrictions or the designation of the trustees. The auditor should recognize these restrictions and test expenditures for compliance with them. These restrictions may not be significantly different from those placed on a commercial enterprise through its budgetary process; the restrictions that differ most significantly are those that separate expendable operating resources from capital (principal) funds such as endowments, which may not be spent. The third and most obvious difference between educational institutions and commercial enterprises is that the receipts of the former include contributions, entitlement grants, and appropriations.

Nonprofit educational institutions differ from commercial enterprises in other ways as well.

- Service, not profits, is the objective of educational institutions. Nonprofit organizations do not spend to produce revenues; instead, they spend to accomplish their mission. As a result, a primary objective of financial reporting is accounting for resources received and used rather than determining net income.
- In some ways, nonprofit organizations are more stringently regulated and controlled than are profit-oriented enterprises. Nonprofit operations may be affected by legal and contractual requirements in the form of federal and state statutes, grant stipulations, judicial decrees, charters, bylaws, trust agreements, or contracts with grantors.
- Once student enrollment is set for a school term, financial results for that period are relatively predictable. For this reason, most colleges and universities put a great deal of effort into establishing enrollment goals and budgeting. The budgets are then monitored closely, and normally they are extremely accurate.
- Under Internal Revenue Code Section 501, a variety of nonprofit organizations, including educational institutions, may gain tax-exempt status; however, they may become subject to an income tax on income from a business enterprise not related to their exempt purpose.

ACCOUNTING PRINCIPLES

The differences listed above do not suggest basic changes in the procedures to be applied in auditing educational institutions; they do, however, require refinements in the accounting principles used by such institutions. Accounting principles for American colleges and universities have evolved over many years, beginning with *Standard Forms for Financial Reports of Colleges, Universities, and Technical Schools*, published in 1910 by the Carnegie Foundation, and *College and University Finance*, by Trevor Arnett of the University of Chicago, published in 1922. Current accounting principles for colleges and universities are codified in the AICPA's audit guide, *Audits of Colleges and Universities* (issued in 1973 and revised in 1975 to include Statement of Position 74-8, *Financial Accounting and Reporting by Colleges and Universities*); those for independent schools, in the AICPA's 1981 audit and accounting guide, *Audits of Certain Non-Profit Organizations*. Basically, those principles call for educational and other nonprofit institutions to maintain their accounts in a series of self-balancing individual funds.

Fund Accounting

Often the resources received by an educational institution are restricted by the contributor and may be used only for specific purposes and activities. For example, a college may receive a gift that can be used only for scholarships or a grant from a governmental agency that is limited to specific research. In accepting those restricted resources a nonprofit organization also assumes the accompanying custodial obligations. The organization has the fiduciary duty to ensure that such resources are used in accordance with the contributor's stipulations and often is required to report on compliance with those stipulations. Fund accounting is employed to monitor restricted or earmarked resources and to ensure and demonstrate the institution's compliance with legal and administrative requirements.

Statement of Financial Accounting Concepts (SFAC) No. 6 does not use the term "fund" or "fund balance"; rather, it uses the term "net assets." The distinction between these terms is that "fund" refers to a common *group* of assets and liabilities (e.g., the plant fund), and "fund balance" refers to the assets minus the liabilities in that fund. "Net assets"—which is the equivalent of equity in a commercial enterprise—represents the difference between each *class* of the entity's assets and liabilities. There are three classes of net assets: permanently restricted, temporarily restricted, and unrestricted. Although financial statement reporting may be based on these classes, colleges and universities often maintain their records by fund group. For this reason, the accounting principles set forth in this chapter are described in terms of fund accounting.

As used in nonprofit accounting, a fund is an accounting entity with a self-balancing set of accounts for recording assets, liabilities, the fund balance, and changes in the fund balance. Separate accounts are maintained for each fund to ensure that the limitations and restrictions on the use of resources are observed. While the fund concept involves separate accounting records, it does not necessarily entail physical segregation of resources. Fund accounting is basically a mechanism to assist in exercising control over the purpose of particular resources and amounts of those resources available for use. For reporting purposes, funds that have similar characteristics or common purposes may be combined into fund groups.

The major fund groups for colleges and universities and their presentation in financial statements are described as follows:

- *Current Funds*—Operating funds, consisting of unrestricted and restricted funds available for current operations. Unrestricted current funds are subject only to budgetary limitations; restricted current funds are subject to limitations imposed by the donors. The balance sheet of the current funds includes the usual asset and liability accounts such as cash, short-term investments, accounts receivable, inventories, prepaid expenses, accounts payable, accrued liabilities, deferred revenues, and restricted and unrestricted fund balances.

- *Loan Funds*—Resources that may be lent to students, faculty, and staff. The fund balance sheet consists of cash, temporary investments, notes receivable (less an allowance for uncollectible loans), and fund balances.

- *Endowment and Similar Funds*—Funds invested for the purpose of producing income, which may be either spent currently or added to principal. These funds may consist of "true" endowment funds in which the principal must remain intact in perpetuity and is nonexpendable. Endowment funds also include "term" endowments, which are set aside for a specified time, and funds designated to "function as endowment" by the board of trustees, usually termed "quasi-endowment funds" and sometimes referred to as "funds functioning as an endowment," which are established from current or other funds. Board-designated funds may be transferred back to their original current or other fund at the board's discretion.

- *Annuity and Life Income Funds*—Funds acquired by an institution subject to annuity contracts, living trust agreements, or gifts and bequests that reserve life income to one or more beneficiaries.

- *Plant Funds*—Funds intended for the construction, acquisition, and renovation of existing physical properties used for institutional purposes; funds already expended for plant properties; funds set aside for the renewal and replacement of plant properties; and funds accumulated for the retirement of indebtedness on plant properties. This fund group includes all debt incurred for physical facilities.

- *Agency Funds*—Funds over which an institution has custodial control for a third party. For example, a student organization may ask the college to maintain its cash account and bill membership fees. The college collects and distributes monies as directed by the student organization.

Financial Statements

Following the applicable AICPA audit guides, educational institutions normally prepare three basic financial statements: a balance sheet, a statement of changes in fund balances, and a statement of current funds revenues, expenditures, and other changes.[1]

The balance sheet is divided into self-balancing fund groups, such as current funds, loan funds, endowment funds, and plant funds, according to their major

---

[1]The FASB discussion draft on financial statement display would require a cash flows statement and a statement of changes in net assets in addition to a balance sheet.

purpose. Current unrestricted and restricted funds may be segregated on the balance sheet, or they may be combined, with the fund balances identified separately.

The statement of changes in fund balances is presented by fund group, using the same groups as on the balance sheet. The statement reports the following information:

- Revenues and other additions to fund groups:
  - Operating income—current unrestricted fund.
  - Gifts and grants—all funds.
  - Investment income—all funds.
  - Expended for plant facilities—plant fund.
- Expenditures and other deductions from fund groups:
  - Operating expenditures—current fund.
  - Plant facilities expenditures—plant fund.
  - Retirement of indebtedness—plant fund.
  - Disposal of plant assets—plant fund.
  - Annuity and life income payments to beneficiaries—annuity and life income fund.
- Other changes:
  - Addition to plant facilities—plant fund via current fund.
  - Deduction for retirements of plant facilities—plant fund.
  - Mandatory transfers among funds.
  - Nonmandatory transfers among funds.
- Net increase (decrease) in fund balance for the year.
- Fund balance at the beginning of the year.
- Fund balance at the end of the year.

The statement of current funds revenues, expenditures, and other changes shows the financial activities of unrestricted and restricted funds related to the current reporting period; it does not purport to present the results of operations or net income or loss for the period. The net increases or decreases reported on this statement should be the same as the amounts reported as net changes in unrestricted and restricted current funds in the statement of changes in fund balances. The statement of current funds revenues, expenditures, and other changes includes the following, either on the face of the statement or in the notes to the financial statements:

- Revenues:
  - Unrestricted—same as revenues in statement of changes in fund balances.
  - Restricted—recognized only to the extent of restricted expenditures.
- Expenditures and mandatory transfers:
  - Detailed by nature of expenditures (such as instruction or research).

•• Unrestricted—same total as operating expenditures and mandatory transfers in statement of changes in fund balances.

•• Restricted—same total as operating expenditures in statement of changes in fund balances.

This statement reconciles to the statement of changes in fund balances if the "excess of transfers to revenues over restricted receipts" (decrease in fund balance) or "excess of restricted receipts over transfers to revenues" (increase in fund balance) is included in this statement.

The AICPA audit guide includes recommendations for financial statement presentation and illustrative auditor's reports.

RISK ASSESSMENT AND AUDIT STRATEGY

An auditor assigned to a college or university engagement for the first time may find that its operations are decentralized and greatly varied, that management relies on a great many disparate accounting and information systems, and that the financial statements are complex. Because financial position and changes in fund balances are reported for each fund, there are often more accounts to examine for a college or university engagement than for an industrial engagement.

For certain accounts, such as payroll, the auditor may find it most efficient to perform tests of controls of the institution's control structure policies and procedures in order to be able to assess control risk as low and thus to significantly restrict substantive tests. For other accounts, such as major gifts, the most efficient strategy may be to employ primarily substantive tests. The audit strategy should be reconsidered annually, because sources of revenue and types of expenditures may change dramatically as an institution adapts its operations to the marketplace.

Some variations exist between the authoritative pronouncements for colleges and those for independent schools, particularly in the treatment of pledges, depreciation, and restricted funds. At the time of this writing, some of these areas are in the process of change; the auditor should consult the latest pronouncements of the Financial Accounting Standards Board, Governmental Accounting Standards Board, and AICPA. None of those differences, however, is likely to affect the basic audit concerns described in this chapter. Generally, the auditor's focus shifts with the size and complexity, rather than the type, of organization under audit. Hence, the audit of a large university is likely to resemble the audit of a large museum or foundation (or of any large, decentralized corporation) more closely than the audit of a small college, and the audits of a small independent school and a charitable or social organization are likely to be similar.

While universities' costs have been rising, their traditional sources of revenue have been adversely affected. The college-age population began to decline in the 1970s. State and municipal governments have fewer resources available to support their educational systems. The federal government has cut back on research, training, and financial aid programs that in the past had provided support to education. Finally, various changes in the Internal Revenue Code and regulations have affected colleges, universities, and independent schools. Some changes, such as those that limit the benefits to certain donors from supporting educational and other philanthropic organizations, have adversely affected gift revenues. (In reducing individuals' tax rates, the tax code has raised the effective cost of giving to colleges and universities.) Other changes, particularly those brought on by the Tax Reform Act of 1986, have made fringe benefits more expensive. Finally, more detailed compliance regulations for the IRS information return (Form 990) have increased the paperwork burden at such institutions.

Colleges, universities, and independent schools have responded to these financial pressures in various ways, including cutting costs, retrenchment, seeking to attract new students, developing new sources of revenue, more aggressive investment strategies, interfund borrowings, and external debt. Each of these responses increases the risk—both inherent and control risks— that must be recognized by independent, internal, and government auditors practicing in the education industry. Figure 27.1 summarizes many of those risks.

Figure 27.1   Risks in an Educational Environment

Financial Pressure	*University Responses*	*Potential Risks*
Inflation	Cutting costs	Reduced control structure policies and procedures because of cutbacks in administrative staff
		Incentives to postpone accounting recognition of liabilities
		Unauthorized appropriation of university assets by underpaid employees
		Use of restricted funds for expenses outside donor's original intent
	Retrenchment	Potential difficult judgments in the accounting treatment of excess facilities
Adverse demographics	Expanding continuing education programs	Increased contracts with and receivables from corporations and other sponsoring third parties instead of income from students, who pay in advance

(Continued)

Figure 27.1   Continued

Financial Pressure	University Responses	Potential Risks
		Inadequate control procedures for billings to and collections from part-time students
	Aggressive marketing strategies	Doubtful collectibility of receivables and student loans
Federal budget deficits	Increased scrutiny by IRS	Additional compliance requirements of federal government for student financial assistance programs
Reduced sources of funds	Aggressive investment strategies	Valuation of real estate, venture capital, and other investments for which market values may not be readily determinable
		Need to determine physical existence of borrowed or loaned securities by confirmation or observation
		Accounting for complex transactions such as income from options and mortgages with equity participation
	Creation of unrelated affiliates and other new revenue sources	Increased risk from operations outside management's traditional understanding and control
		Increased receivables from and contracts with nonstudents
		Valuation of investments in new business ventures
		Nonobservance of restrictions imposed by sponsors on use of funds, particularly compliance with federal regulations for research administration
		Valuation of funds advanced under deferred giving programs

Figure 27.1 *Continued*

Financial Pressure	*University Responses*	*Potential Risks*
		Appraisal of value of gifts in kind
		Exposure to taxation of unrelated income
	Interfund borrowings	Borrowing from restricted funds, possibly against donor's intent
		Possible use of inappropriate interest rate for interfund loans
		Possible nonpayment of interfund loans
		Inappropriate or illegal expenditures of endowment principal
	External debt	Possible noncompliance with covenants
		Responsibility to report to holders of publicly held debt
		Need to capitalize interest
Need to modernize facilities	Capital expenditures	Expenditures on new space while deferring maintenance on old space
		Assumption of role of general contractor without requisite expertise

Materiality poses a unique problem in auditing not-for-profit organizations. SAS No. 47 (AU Section 312) requires the auditor to consider materiality for planning purposes in terms of the smallest aggregate level of misstatements that could be considered material to any one of the financial statements. Since even the largest institutions adopt a balanced budget, their operating margin is likely to be quite small. Hence, it may not be meaningful to emphasize net results of financial activities at colleges and universities in making materiality judgments. Instead, many auditors consider materiality in terms of each of the various fund groups, total expendable resources or capital funds, or other measures, such as the annual change in endowment value. Obviously, such judgments must be made on a case-by-case basis. Expenditures that do not conform to fund restrictions expose the institution to legal penalties; they should be disclosed to management and considered for adjustment, no matter how small.

AUDITING THE REVENUE CYCLE

Classes of transactions in the revenue cycle that are unique and significant to colleges and universities include

- Tuition and other service fees (such as application fees, laboratory fees, museum admissions, and patient-care fees at affiliated hospitals), some of which may be similar to revenue transactions of commercial organizations.
- Financial aid programs (which have extensive compliance requirements).
- Gifts (which are classified depending on donor restrictions).
- Investments (which involve proper income allocation).
- Grants (which have extensive compliance requirements).
- The operation of hospitals or clinical practices (by larger universities), which may require both management and the auditor to consider operating factors and standards outside the traditional educational realm.

Tuition and Other Service Fees

Applications for admission are first solicited and received from prospective students. Once students are admitted, their names and other data are entered on a master file from which billings are generated at the start of each school term. Normally, students must pay tuition and related fees in order to register. Accordingly, it would be unusual for a significant number of student accounts to be outstanding at the end of the fiscal year. Balances may exist with outside scholarship providers or other third parties, however, and the auditor should review them for collectibility. Accounts received from third parties for their employees' attendance in continuing education programs may merit special attention. In addition, it is becoming increasingly common for students to pay a deposit in one fiscal year that is applied to tuition in the following period; the auditor should ascertain that tuition revenue is recognized in the proper period.

Tuition and other student revenues are usually a sensitive audit area because of the large transaction volume and the resulting need for effective control structure policies and procedures. These policies and procedures should address the control objectives of completeness, accuracy, and authorization. Specifically, policies and procedures should ensure that all students enrolled are billed, that tuition billings to individual students are appropriate, that financial aid was authorized, and that appropriate fees for room, board, and other services were billed and allocated to the proper accounts. In addition, policies and procedures should be in place to ensure that cash receipts, scholarships, loans, and other credits are applied to the correct accounts and that all transactions are reflected accurately on individual students' records. Also, there should be follow-up procedures to collect outstanding balances.

In examining student revenues, the auditor may find the following analytical procedures effective:

- Comparing students who received grade reports with those who paid bills.
- Comparing students registered at standard tuition rates with total tuition revenue.
- Comparing revenue recognized with budgets.
- Testing tuition rates by comparing student status at the time of application (in-state, out-of-state, full-time, part-time, and so on) with amounts charged.

Continuing education revenues may not lend themselves to such analytical procedures.

The automation of most student revenue systems suggests that general (i.e., computer) control procedures, especially those relating to maintenance of master files, may be of particular importance. Also, the auditor must be alert to the assignment of tuition, particularly for summer programs, to the proper fiscal year. Finally, in considering tuition revenues at a public institution, the auditor must recognize the distinction between funds received from day and other degree students (which may be subject to the appropriation process) and those received for nondegree, adult education courses (which often are not).

Student Loans and Financial Aid

Loans may be made from both governmental and institutional loan funds. After loan funds have been applied for and received by the institution, loans are granted to individual qualifying students. (For certain programs, a "needs analysis" must be performed on an individual-student basis to match the student's resources with aid that may be available from governmental programs.) The loan recipient executes a note, and a loan receivable is created; after the recipient's graduation, collection procedures are put into effect for outstanding principal and interest balances. Annual reporting by the institution to the federal government on loan activity involving federal programs is required, and periodic independent audits of those programs are required to address compliance as well as the financial administration of the program.

Major audit concerns include policies and procedures for establishing loan collectibility allowances and maintaining accurate loan records. Many institutions follow governmental reporting practices and record loan interest on a cash basis. A major audit planning procedure involves coordinating tests of student loan accounts with government financial aid audits performed by internal auditors, the institution's independent auditor, or other auditors to ensure that work is not duplicated. (See the discussion of this topic later in the chapter under "Audits of State and Federal Programs at Colleges and Universities.")

Gifts and Other Contributions

Colleges, universities, and independent schools have developed sophisticated means of soliciting support from individuals, foundations, corporations, and other sources. Most systems provide for recording pledges, summarizing fund-raising performance, and comparing performance with campaign goals. The sophistication of those systems may highlight the need for the auditor to understand the solicitation process and its results; the auditor's objective, however, remains the same—determining that contributions are completely and accurately recorded and that management has a means of recognizing any restrictions placed by donors on the use of contributions.

College financial management often includes separate systems for alumni giving and other development activities. Comparing alumni giving records with the college's accounting records may provide evidence that all gifts have been recorded. The auditor may compare amounts recorded for the current year with those contributed in the past or may review the terms of pledges to see that stipulations in the gifts have been recorded properly. Trustees often acknowledge receipt of major contributions; the auditor should review minutes of their meetings for mention of specific gifts. A review of selected correspondence files may provide the auditor with information about the process by which support is solicited and used. Finally, the auditor should consider the use of correspondence, pledge cards, acknowledgments, and other documentation to obtain satisfaction that donor restrictions have been properly recognized and classified. Certain universities have a policy of rejecting gifts that carry onerous restrictions, such as institutional matching or support of particular political views. The auditor's review of correspondence files may reveal whether all organizational units within the institution are following such policies.

Gift accounting by educational institutions has certain features of which the auditor should be aware.

- *Pledges* may be recorded as receivables at their estimated value, but most colleges and universities choose the alternative available to them of disclosing the amount in a note to the financial statements. Accounting principles for independent schools require that pledges be recorded as assets; the auditor should be particularly attentive to their collectibility.
- *Deferred giving programs* generate life income and annuity funds that are available to colleges and universities only at the time specified in individual agreements. In addition, such receipts often are subject to a university's commitment to pay stipulated amounts (annuity funds) or a certain percentage return (life income funds) periodically to the donor or other designated individual. Sometimes gifts may be restricted to certain securities as well. The auditor must ascertain that the institution has distinguished properly between such gifts and other funds for which principal or income may be available for immediate use. The auditor should also refer to life expectancy and interest tables to determine a school's potential liability for annuity payments in excess of earnings. The auditor should note gifts held in trust outside the university; such funds are not recorded as assets, but income derived from them should be disclosed in a note to the financial statements.
- *Gifts in kind* are recorded at market value or at a nominal amount if a value cannot be readily obtained.

At the time of this writing, the FASB is considering a project on accounting for "nonreciprocal transfers," such as gifts and contributions. A distinction is made between nonreciprocal transfers (gifts that are truly nonreciprocal and add to an institution's net assets) and contractual obligations, which should be recorded in the same way as a liability and perhaps be considered unrestricted. The FASB project also covers pledges. The preliminary discussions suggest that unconditional pledges (i.e., those whose use is not conditioned on certain events but that may be restricted when used) would be recognized immediately. Conditional pledges would not be recognized until the condition is satisfied. Contributed goods, including collections of art and artifacts, would be recorded at fair value and recognized in financial statements at the time of their donation. (The FASB has also discussed retroactive capitalization of such collections.) Contributed services, on the other hand, would not generally be valued and recognized unless they created an asset.

Investments and Investment Income

Investments, which often constitute the largest component of the balance sheet of a college or an independent school, may be valued for financial reporting purposes at either cost or market. For institutions following the "total return" concept, which emphasizes total investment return (both yield and gains and losses), market value is more appropriate. Statement of Financial Accounting Standards (SFAS) No. 12 (Accounting Standards Section I89) and other pronouncements that specify valuation at the lower of cost or market do not apply, but the auditor of an institution that values investments at cost should evaluate recorded investment values in situations in which a diminution that is other than temporary has occurred. Auditing procedures for investments include periodic determination of their physical existence and tests of market value. In testing investment income, the auditor should use procedures appropriate for investment companies, including tests of unit-value calculations for pooled investments and of the distribution of income from pooled investments to individual funds. Restricted securities and funds limited to a particular type of investment should not enter into a general investment pool.

Investment returns of certain educational institutions may exceed budgeted "spending rates," with the excess being added to "income stabilization reserves." Additions to such reserves should be considered revenue of the period, along with other investment income, rather than as transfers to the respective reserves. On the other hand, if an institution spends a portion of gains from quasi- or true endowment funds, that portion should be considered a transfer between funds rather than revenue. If such gains are appropriated from endowment and other funds under the "total return" concept, the auditor should compare market values for each such fund with the original value of the gift to ensure that the gains are available for use.

Educational institutions may hedge their fixed-income portfolios with financial futures or options and may seek to increase investment income through securities lending, repurchase agreements, and options trading. The auditor should review the relevant control structure policies and procedures to ascertain that the school maintains a traceable record of the physical existence of the related securities, and should determine that such transactions are properly collateralized, that the net proceeds from the transactions are recognized as capital or income transactions in the appropriate period, and that the arrangements (if material) are disclosed. Realized and unrealized capital gains or losses, and profits or losses on options trading, are considered increases or decreases in the principal of endowment and other funds rather than investment income.

Grants and Contracts

Many university activities, such as research and training, are conducted with the direct support of external sponsors. Revenues associated with direct costs of federally sponsored projects are recognized when the related expenses are incurred, but often reimbursement for indirect costs and employee benefits is recorded at predetermined rates that are later adjusted to reflect actual expenditures. The difference between actual and estimated overhead costs usually is not recognized as revenue in the year in which the costs are incurred; instead, it is reflected as an adjustment in the college's overhead rate in the future. The restrictions frequently placed on expenditures by grant and contract sponsors may require special audit attention.

Specific audit objectives in this area include ascertaining that

- Payroll charges, materials, and other direct costs are accurately summarized and distributed to individual contracts, and overhead is applied at current rates and on an appropriate basis.
- Research revenues are recorded completely and accurately, sponsors are billed on a timely basis, and adequate follow-up procedures exist for outstanding receivables.
- All cash receipts are accurately recorded, and advance payments or letter-of-credit advances are applied to the proper accounts.
- Budgets are recorded accurately and procedures to monitor cost overruns are functioning.

If such activity is significant, the auditor should examine grants and contracts to ascertain that contract charges, including indirect cost allowances, are recorded in accordance with contract provisions.

Federal grants and contracts impose particular administrative burdens on recipient schools. The auditor should review reports of government auditors and correspondence with sponsors to determine whether a contingent liability for disallowed costs should be recorded or disclosed in accordance with SFAS No. 5 (Accounting Standards Section C59).

AUDITING THE BUYING CYCLE

The buying cycle of a college or school does not differ materially from that of a commercial enterprise. Both types of organizations employ separate capital and operating budgets, both face certain restrictions on the use of funds by operating divisions, and payrolls and other expenses of both are subject to various levels of management approval. (The buying cycle for commercial enterprises is discussed in Chapter 13.) Accounting for college buildings and equipment has some special characteristics, however, such as fund restrictions, that the auditor should be aware of.

Capital Assets

The cost of college buildings and equipment is considered a capital outlay or expenditure of the fund that supports the purchase. Such acquisitions are also recorded in the plant fund as assets. Potential audit concerns in the area of capital assets are as follows:

- Particularly at decentralized schools, there may be a question as to whether all capital assets have been recorded.
- The distinction between expense and capital items may not be applied consistently.
- The acquisition of assets through external borrowing may subject the institution to restrictions on the use of related revenues and to other debt covenants.
- Deferred maintenance may present a serious financial risk that may not be reflected in the financial statements.

Over the past decade, many colleges have incurred external or internal debt to finance plant acquisitions or renovations. Internal borrowing from endowment or current funds is particularly common. Some accountants believe that it is preferable for such internal (that is, interfund) borrowings to bear interest to reimburse the lending funds. The auditor must determine the likelihood of repayment of interfund borrowings; if repayment is not likely, they should be treated as permanent transfers. The auditor should review provisions of long-term external borrowing agreements to observe that all debt covenants have been met. The nature and extent of pledged assets and revenues should be disclosed in the financial statements. The auditor should also determine that SFAS No. 62, *Capitalization of Interest Cost in Situations Involving Certain Tax-Exempt Borrowings and Certain Gifts and Grants* (Accounting Standards Section I67), has been properly applied. That statement calls for the capitalization of interest during construction on fixed assets purchased with external debt, except that capitalized amounts are recorded net of income earned on unexpended construction funds financed with tax-exempt borrowings that are externally restricted to finance specified assets or to service the related debt.

SFAS No. 93, *Recognition of Depreciation by Not-for-Profit Organizations* (Accounting Standards Section D40), as amended by SFAS No. 99, requires all not-for-profit organizations to recognize depreciation on long-lived tangible assets, such as buildings, equipment, and, with some exceptions, their collections of art, library books, historical treasures, and so forth. This requirement, which became effective for fiscal years beginning January 1, 1990, is likely to have several implications for colleges, universities, and independent schools.

1. Their financial statements will be more comparable with those of commercial enterprises, but net assets will decrease significantly, particularly with the required retroactive application of the SFAS in the first year.
2. Attention will be focused on funding capital renewal.
3. Fixed asset, space management, and budget systems may require upgrading.
4. Cost allocation and recovery procedures can be expected to improve.
5. There will be a new emphasis on assets not previously capitalized, including art collections, library books, and historical treasures.
6. Record-keeping demands may increase administrative cost.

Expenditures of Restricted Funds

Colleges and universities do not record revenues of restricted funds until the funds are expended; thus, restricted revenues equal expenditures on the statement of current funds revenues, expenditures, and other changes. Occasionally, the distinction between restricted and unrestricted expenditures is not clear. For example, donors often contribute funds for purposes such as "faculty enrichment" or "library purchases," which may be substituted for unrestricted funds and vice versa in certain circumstances. In other cases, such as government contracts, the restrictions are much more binding. The auditor may consider it appropriate to examine some expenditures charged to restricted funds to ensure that restrictions have been met.

EDP AUDITING IN THE UNIVERSITY ENVIRONMENT

College and university EDP operations usually combine two completely different computerized systems. What is generally referred to as "administrative computing" is the counterpart of financial data processing operations in most other businesses. Administrative computing involves payroll, general ledger, and other accounting processing functions, as well as admissions and other university functions. The other aspect of university EDP operations often is referred to as "academic computing." This is the component of university computer use involved in instruction and research. The auditor should, as one of the first steps in planning the audit of a university, determine how the two components interface.

It is not uncommon for data processing or computer science students to be employed as computer operators for the administrative system. While this is not necessarily an audit risk, there must be adequate separation of duties and supervision. In considering student accounts receivable, for example, the auditor should determine whether student operators have access to information that could be considered sensitive.

Another aspect of the university EDP environment that demands special attention is the proliferation of both personal and institutional microcomputers. "Hacking" has become a national pastime and, with some universities now requiring students to own a personal computer, use of micros has become a key area of audit concern; the auditor should be alert to the need for general control procedures to prevent or detect unauthorized access to computer files.

AUDITS OF STATE AND FEDERAL PROGRAMS AT COLLEGES AND UNIVERSITIES

During the 1960s and 1970s, individual federal agencies such as the National Institutes of Health, the National Science Foundation, the Defense Department, and, most significant, the Office (later Department) of Education became the largest "donors" to many educational institutions. Consistent with the practices of universities' original donors in the early 1900s, these agencies commissioned audits of each of their own separate grants at each grantee institution. The growth of those grants soon outstripped the resources provided by the granting agencies to perform individual project or program audits at colleges and universities. In 1979, the U.S. General Accounting Office (GAO) reported that federal audit coverage of colleges and universities was spotty at best. Office of Management and Budget (OMB) Circular A-110 took effect at that time for most educational institutions. That pronouncement requires educational institutions to engage their independent or internal auditors to study and evaluate their financial management systems relating to federal projects and to determine that their transactions comply with federal regulations—in effect to perform an audit, similar to a single audit (as discussed in Chapter 40), in which the university, rather than the individual funds, is considered the entity subject to audit. Today, independent auditors of educational institutions that receive federal funds are likely to be asked to add federally related procedures to the financial statement audit. (At the time of this writing, the OMB has proposed Circular A-133, which, when issued, would supersede Circular A-110. Circular A-133 would clarify the audit requirements for educational institutions as well as other nonprofit organizations.)

The objective of those procedures is not to provide a basis for forming an opinion on the school's financial statements or federal programs. Rather, the auditor's objective is to determine whether

- The institution has implemented and utilized appropriate financial and administrative systems and procedures to discharge management responsibilities effectively and to protect the federal interest.
- The institution is in compliance with the uniform federal administrative requirements of Circular A-110.
- Financial reports submitted to federal agencies contain reliable financial data.

In meeting that objective, the auditor determines that costs incurred under federal contracts

- Are necessary and reasonable.
- Conform with any limitation or exclusion in the award.

- Are accounted for consistently and uniformly with other institutional activities.
- Are net of "applicable credits."
- Are approved in advance if required.
- Are incurred in accordance with competitive procurement procedures.
- Absorb indirect costs at the proper rate.

Financial, internal control, and compliance reports should be issued in accordance with government regulations (as specified in the GAO's *Standards for Audit of Governmental Organizations, Programs, Activities, and Functions*, commonly called the "Yellow Book").

28

Auditing Construction Companies

OVERVIEW OF THE INDUSTRY

The U.S. government, in its Standard Industrial Classification Code, divides the construction industry into three main categories.

- *Building construction*—Single-family dwellings, apartment houses, some industrial plants, hospitals, office buildings, warehouses, and similar structures.
- *Nonbuilding construction*
  - •• Heavy construction—Dams, large bridges, tunnels, refineries, and electric power plants.
  - •• Highway and street construction.
- *Specialty trade construction*—Plumbing, heating and air conditioning, painting, electrical work, masonry, carpentry, and so on.

Within those classifications, the form of business varies widely, from large-scale international corporations to various forms of joint ventures and small, family-operated businesses. Many contractors engage in more than one type of construction activity. The discussion in this chapter also applies to performance under construction contracts with the U.S. government.

The construction industry is very sensitive to changes in economic conditions. During recessionary periods, construction budgets are generally the first to be cut back as a company's resources are redirected to current operations. During those times, construction companies are more likely to accept less-profitable, riskier contracts as a means of utilizing overhead and retaining experienced personnel. The impact of an economic downturn, however, is not immediately reflected in a construction company's financial statements. Instead, the effect is postponed because contracts in process and extending over a period of years are normally completed, providing revenues for the near future. New construction, however, is likely to be canceled.

Government regulations and policies have a significant effect on the operations, although not on the financial reporting requirements, of construction companies. The industry is required to comply with local building codes and zoning ordinances and with regulations of several federal regulatory agencies, such as the Occupational Safety and Health Administration, the Equal Employment Opportunity Commission, and the Environmental Protection Agency. Constant changes in government regulations are the reason for contractors' common practice of disclaiming responsibility, in contracts, for obtaining all government approvals, licenses, and permits required for a construction project. This responsibility must be borne by the owner.

ACCOUNTING FOR CONSTRUCTION CONTRACTS

Accounting principles for the construction industry are prescribed mainly in Accounting Research Bulletin (ARB) No. 45, *Long-Term Construction-Type Contracts* (Accounting Standards Section Co4); the AICPA audit and accounting guide, *Construction Contractors*; the AICPA industry audit guide, *Audits of Government Contractors*; and Statement of Position 81-1, *Accounting for Performance of Construction-Type and Certain Production-Type Contracts* (SOP 81-1). The FASB, in Statement of Financial Accounting Standards (SFAS) No. 56, paragraph 8 (Accounting Standards Section A06.112), has indicated that the specialized accounting principles in SOP 81-1 and the construction contractors guide have been designated as preferable for purposes of justifying a change in accounting principle for long-term construction-type contracts.

The primary focus for recognizing revenues, accumulating costs, and measuring income by companies in the construction industry is the profit center, which is usually the individual contract. SOP 81-1 provides criteria to be used in determining the appropriate profit center, a process that sometimes is quite complex. In certain circumstances, if the criteria in SOP 81-1 are met, a group of contracts (known as combining) or a phase or segment of a single contract (known as segmenting) may be used as a profit center. The profit center can have a significant impact on the amount of profit and loss recorded in a period (discussed later). For the purposes of this chapter, the profit center will be a single contract.

There are two generally accepted methods of accounting for contract performance: the percentage-of-completion method and the completed-contract method. (The units-of-delivery method is a modification of the percentage-of-completion method.) Guidance for determining which method to use is contained in SOP 81-1 and is discussed in this section.

Percentage-of-Completion Method

Under this method, revenue and income are recognized based on the actual performance under a contract for a given period. When the criteria for using it (discussed later) are present, recognizing revenue under the percentage-of-completion method is preferable because it better reflects the economic results of contract performance. It also better relates revenues to period costs and provides more useful information about the volume of a contractor's economic activity.

A key aspect of the percentage-of-completion method is determining how to measure progress toward completion. A number of methods are used to measure the extent of completion on a contract. Generally, they can be grouped into input measures (based on efforts devoted to a contract, like costs or hours of labor), and output measures (based on results achieved, like contract milestones or units produced). One commonly used input measure is referred to as the cost-to-cost method and is described in Chapter 12. The measure or measures adopted should be applied consistently to contracts with similar characteristics.

Completed-Contract Method

Under the completed-contract method, revenues and costs are recognized when the contract is substantially completed. Practice varies with respect to determining when substantial completion has occurred. As a general rule, substantial completion is reached when the contractor's remaining costs and potential risks are insignificant. Factors to be considered in determining if substantial completion has been achieved may include departure from the construction site, acceptance by the owner, and compliance with performance specifications. The specific criteria adopted should be used consistently for contracts with similar characteristics.

Choosing the Preferable Alternative

The two methods of accounting for contract performance are not acceptable alternatives in the same circumstances. SOP 81-1 recommends using the percentage-of-completion method when

- Reasonably dependable estimates can be made of the extent of progress toward completion and the amount of total contract revenues and costs;
- There is a clear specification in the contract of the enforceable rights regarding goods and services to be provided, the price or its method of determination, and the method and terms of settlement; and
- There is the expectation that both parties can fulfill their contractual obligations.

The completed-contract method is recommended only if

- Financial position and results of operations under this method would not vary materially from those resulting from the use of the percentage-of-completion method (e.g., if the entity has primarily short-term contracts); or
- The percentage-of-completion method is inappropriate because "inherent hazards" beyond management's control make estimates of contract revenues and costs doubtful or other criteria for using the percentage-of-completion method are not met.

The SOP indicates that "inherent hazards" do not relate to doubtful estimates resulting from inadequate estimating procedures. Instead, those hazards relate to external factors or contract conditions that raise questions about contract estimates and about the ability of the contractor or owner to perform the contractual obligations. While inadequate estimating procedures may influence an entity's ability to prepare reasonably dependable estimates, the presumption is that contractors have the ability to make estimates that are sufficiently dependable to justify using the percentage-of-completion method of accounting. Persuasive evidence to the contrary is necessary to overcome that presumption.

Provision for Anticipated Losses

Under either method of accounting, if at any time the estimated total cost exceeds the total contract price, indicating a loss on the contract, the entire loss ordinarily should be recognized. There are, however, some rare exceptions to this principle, such as in loss-type contracts that are, in substance, research and development arrangements. For example, a government contract may be entered into with the intent of developing a prototype whose cost is to be shared by the contractor. If the prototype is successful, profitable contracts are expected to follow. The costs are appropriately treated as research and development costs, and thus should be expensed as incurred but should not be anticipated. In addition, SOP 81-1 provides criteria for combining related contracts with different profit margins in determining the need for a provision for losses. Provisions for losses should be shown separately as a liability or as a deduction from any related accumulated costs.

Capitalization of Interest Cost

Paragraph 9 of SFAS No. 34 (Accounting Standards Section I67.105a–b) requires capitalization of interest on assets that an enterprise constructs for its own use and assets intended for lease or sale that are constructed as "discrete projects." In the contractor's accounting, an asset being constructed under a long-term contract qualifies as a discrete project, even though title to all materials and improvements acquired or constructed by the contractor generally rests with the owner. Thus, it is not appropriate to offset advance payments on one contract against costs of another or to apply the aggregate advance payments against the total accumulated costs on the balance sheet to determine the amount of interest to be capitalized. Instead, the determination should be made on an individual-contract basis.

Although SFAS No. 34 is applicable to construction contractors, capitalization of interest cost may not have a material effect on the financial statements because of the financing arrangements typical in the construction industry. Generally, a construction contractor's financing requirements are for working capital purposes, and working capital loans are usually tied to individual contract requirements and made for a short period (e.g., 30 to 60 days). In addition, the contractor often arranges for advance payments or for payments to vendors to be made only on receipt of billings from the owner, resulting in a small net asset balance. Consequently, capitalization of interest cost may not be material.

The effects of not capitalizing interest are even less likely to be material when the percentage-of-completion method of accounting is followed. Under that method, income is recognized currently and thus may offset, in whole or in part, the effect of expensing interest currently. The effects are more likely to be material under the completed-contract method, since accumulated costs are carried in the balance sheet and income is not recognized until the project is completed. In determining whether capitalization of interest will have a material effect on the financial statements under the completed-contract method, the auditor should also consider the pattern of contract completion, since the effect on income is less likely to be material if the contractor completes a number of contracts annually.

Deferred Income Taxes

The Tax Reform Act of 1986 significantly narrowed the differences in accounting for construction contracts for income tax purposes and financial accounting and reporting purposes. However, to the extent there are differences, they would be timing differences under APB Opinion No. 11, *Accounting for Income Taxes*, or temporary differences under SFAS No. 96, *Accounting for Income Taxes*, and the deferred tax consequences of such differences must be appropriately accounted for.

As explained in Chapter 19, SFAS No. 96, as amended by SFAS No. 100, was to be effective for years beginning after December 15, 1989. In December 1989 the FASB voted to defer the effective date of SFAS No. 96 to fiscal years beginning after December 15, 1991. Because of the uncertainty of further possible amendments to SFAS No. 96, this chapter does not include a detailed discussion of accounting principles related to income taxes.

Financial Statement Presentation

Construction contractors use either a classified or an unclassified balance sheet. The AICPA construction contractors audit and accounting guide states that classified balance sheets are preferable for enterprises with operating cycles of one year or less and that unclassified balance sheets are preferable if the operating cycle exceeds one year. The guide presents guidelines both for statement presentation in accordance with those preferences and for appropriate disclosures. Most contractors present classified balance sheets, and it is common for such contractors to consider the assets and liabilities arising from long-term contract activities as current, even though the operating cycle of such contracts may extend over several years.

CONSTRUCTION CONTRACTS, INTERNAL CONTROL STRUCTURE POLICIES AND PROCEDURES, AND TESTS OF CONTROLS

The significant cycles in a construction firm usually include contract revenues, job costs (and related cycles), and contract evaluation and control, including estimating and bidding.

Types of Construction Contracts

The contract is the key document in construction companies. It is usually extensive and contains all the technical, legal, and financial details associated with a project. As presented in the AICPA audit and accounting guide, there are four basic types of contracts.

- *A fixed-price (lump-sum) contract* provides for a single price for the total amount of work to be performed on a project.

- *A unit-price contract* provides that a contractor will perform a specific project at a fixed price per unit of output.
- *A cost-plus contract* (referred to in the guide as a "cost-type" contract) provides for reimbursement of allowable or otherwise defined costs incurred, plus a fee for the contractor's services. Usually, the contract requires only that the contractor's best efforts be used to accomplish the scope of the work. Cost-plus contracts occur in a variety of forms; often they contain terms specifying reimbursable costs, overhead recovery percentages, and fees. Fees may be fixed or based on a percentage of reimbursable costs.
- *A time-and-materials contract* is similar to a cost-plus contract and generally provides for payments to the contractor on the basis of direct labor hours at fixed hourly rates (the rates cover the cost of indirect labor and indirect expenses, and profit) and cost of materials or other specified costs.

The guide notes that "all types of contracts may be modified by target penalties and incentives relating to factors such as completion dates, plant capacity on completion of the project, and underruns and overruns of estimated costs." This is true even for guaranteed maximum price and target estimate contracts. Under cost-type contracts with the federal government, statutory limitations have been imposed on fees negotiated at the outset of the contract. In addition, the federal government has significant contractual rights not generally found in contracts between commercial enterprises. Among them is the right to renegotiate the aggregate annual profits earned from contracts with specified federal departments and agencies.

Many factors influence the type of contract that is negotiated. Risk is the primary consideration addressed in negotiating a contract; other factors that influence the terms of the contract are the nature of the project, construction techniques to be used, industry practice, method of financing, pricing practice, and billing terms.

In conjunction with assessing the type of contract to negotiate, the construction company must estimate the cost of the project. The entire strategy for performing the contract must be considered in estimating the contract, including, but not limited to, availability of materials, labor, and equipment; weather; financing and subcontracting; competition; and provisions for profit and risk. Cost estimates should be prepared in detail; all costs for which the contractor has responsibility or risk should be included. The preparation of the estimate should be systematized, with detailed written systems and procedures and requirements for review and approval by responsible officials. The more disciplines involved (e.g., engineers, architects, attorneys, insurance and tax experts, and procurement specialists), the more likely that all items will be evaluated properly.

The Revenue Cycle

The auditor should be concerned with the amount and timing of revenue based on accurate and timely job forecasts. The method of revenue recognition should conform to GAAP and be consistent with prior years.

To meet those key control objectives in the revenue cycle, construction companies generally establish control structure policies and procedures for the following activities:

- Documenting total estimated contract revenues.
- Issuing, approving, and recording change orders, claims, and back charges.
- Identifying jobs in loss positions.
- Recognizing changes in contract terms and the impact of penalty provisions.
- Segregating reimbursable and nonrecoverable costs, especially on cost-plus and time-and-materials contracts.
- Computing and reviewing forecasts used in estimating extent of completion and costs to complete.
- Preparing and approving billings based on job forecasts.
- Recording job revenues and billings properly and on a timely basis.

If the auditor determines that evidence of the effectiveness of those policies and procedures is likely to be available and efficient to obtain, he or she will generally plan to perform tests of controls as a basis for reducing substantive tests. As described in Chapter 8, the tests of controls consist of inquiry, observation, examination of evidence, and, if appropriate, reperformance of the client's policies and procedures.

Job-Cost and Related Cycles

Job or contract costs are an accumulation of purchases, internal cost allocations for equipment and overhead, payroll costs, and possibly material costs assigned from inventory. Some auditors treat these different costs as different transaction classes in the job-cost cycle. The most common transaction classes are

- Vendor purchases and payments.
- Subcontractor payments.
- Payroll.
- Internal allocation of equipment costs.
- Indirect cost allocations.

Generally, the different types of costs are accumulated from various journals into what is commonly referred to as the job-cost report. Total costs in the job-cost report at any time reconcile to the general ledger; the job-cost report is also equal to the aggregate of costs incurred for each separate contract. Within the contract the costs are further subdivided by the type of work performed and the project phase. For example, the job-cost report on a building contract might show total job costs of $250,000, part of which would be recorded under the description "concrete work on the foundation." By segregating those costs, contractors can determine if they are over or under budget on a particular segment of a contract, and this helps in preparing accurate job forecasts.

Another reason for segregating job costs is that some may be recoverable under a contract. Certain costs may be for additional work performed at the owner's request or may result from specification alterations and may serve as a basis for a claim or change order. In such cases, the auditor is concerned with proper accounting for the related revenues, including the timing of their recognition.

Internal Control Structure Policies and Procedures

Policies and procedures are necessary to ensure that all job costs incurred are recognized in the proper period. The contractor is concerned with achieving a proper cutoff at each job site, even though the accounting is done by the home office. Procedures are also needed to ensure that subsidiary cost records agree with the control accounts.

Key control procedures for vendor purchases and subcontracting costs include

- Authorization of vendor purchases, supported by purchase orders. (Bids are generally obtained for major purchases.)
- Approval of vendor invoices by job site personnel to ensure that goods or services have been received; comparing invoices with quantities received and purchase order prices.
- Coding of invoices by personnel familiar with the job. (Many companies indicate job-cost codes on the purchase order to avoid miscoding.) Recoverable and nonrecoverable costs are usually assigned different account codes in the job-cost report.
- Comparing subcontractor invoices with the subcontract for terms, retentions, prices, and related data. Aggressive subcontractors may attempt to overbill or "front end load" their billings. Accordingly, job site personnel review and approve the percentage of completion stated on subcontractor invoices, so that payment is made only for work performed.
- Requiring subcontractors to submit performance bonds. Lien waivers are normally obtained from subcontractors on final payment.
- Recording anticipated costs of materials used based on reasonable estimates if vendor invoices have not been received at the end of an accounting period; review of the accrual by supervisory personnel. (Purchases of materials at the end of an accounting period that have not been used are considered inventory.)
- Approval of back charges, claims, and extras before recording and payment.

Control procedures related to other parts of the job-cost cycle include

- Proper accumulation and recording of payroll costs in the correct cost codes in the job-cost report.

- Maintaining records of equipment on the job. Charges to the job are generally made monthly based on those records and the contractor's rates for company-owned equipment.
- Periodic reviews of equipment rental rates to ensure that they reflect actual equipment costs. On cost-plus contracts, the rates are based on contract specifications.
- Recording materials taken from inventory (such as gravel used by a paving contractor) based on inventory cost records.
- Proper calculation of overhead cost allocations, based on rates that are periodically updated and approved.

Tests of Controls

Job-cost cycle control procedures are often tested as a basis for restricting substantive tests. This strategy allows the auditor to perform a significant amount of the work at an interim date and determine early in the audit whether the job-cost report can be used for testing job forecasts, whether cutoff problems exist that may require extensive payables searches or other substantive procedures, and whether detailed records are being properly posted and agreed to the general ledger. The objectives of tests of controls in the job-cost cycle do not differ from those in the buying cycles of manufacturing enterprises.

Contract Evaluation and Control, and Costs to Complete

Contractors constantly monitor projects in process to ascertain the percentage of completion for billing and revenue recognition purposes and determine whether the projects are over or under budget. Cost overruns might indicate significant problems requiring immediate resolution to avoid losses, large cash outlays, and potential litigation. Constant monitoring also allows the client to evaluate its staff and obtain data that may be useful in future bidding, estimating, and project control.

Estimating and Bidding.   The beginning stage of every contract is the estimating process and submitting a bid based on project specifications from the owner. A lack of control structure policies and procedures relating to these activities can result in unprofitable contracts or inaccurate estimates of percentage of completion, leading to possible misstatements of the financial statements.

The contractor's procedures usually include recalculating the clerical accuracy of estimates and reviewing bids to determine that they cover all contract specifications. Bids are broken down by contract area (e.g., concrete work, plumbing, and electrical) to permit later budget analysis, project administration, and documentation of claims.

Bids obtained from vendors or subcontractors are generally documented. Requiring performance bonds on subcontractors ensures performance of the subcontracts. Unit costs used in bidding are obtained from recent job-cost records or current price quotations. Bids are approved by a responsible official before they are submitted, especially on low-margin jobs and jobs where profit margins are expected to change. Finally, the contractor evaluates successful as well as unsuccessful bids to determine whether they were reasonable and competitive.

In assessing the aforementioned control procedures, the auditor should consider testing the documentation of project bids, the comparison of bids with actual results on completed jobs (to provide an indication of the contractor's estimating results and profit margins), and the bid review and approval process.

Job Forecasts.   Control procedures generally exist to ensure that forecasts are reasonable, timely, and based on an acceptable and consistent method, such as cost to cost, efforts expended, or units of work performed. In larger companies, a separate forecasting department may evaluate projects, either at the job site or in the home office. In smaller companies, the field project manager or even the company president or owner may do the forecasting.

In reviewing contracts, management evaluates each phase or major component of the project. Costs incurred to date are compared with budgeted amounts for each contract phase, and the job forecast is updated based on variances. The following are common control procedures for forecasting the progress on a job:

- Reviewing records of open purchase orders and commitments (to ensure that all remaining major costs are considered).
- Comparing actual costs with the final budget that was prepared from the bid.
- Examining correspondence from the field staff and the owner. Field staff should submit progress reports to the forecasting department periodically if the two departments are separate.
- Reviewing changes in contract terms, prices, claims, and penalties.
- Approving forecasts by responsible officials.
- Updating forecasts on a timely basis.
- Reviewing forecasts to determine that they are based on actual costs incurred or efforts expended to date.
- Reviewing comparisons of costs to date with budgeted amounts and noting whether variances are explained and properly reflected in the forecasts.
- Reviewing the reporting of quantities of physical work performed to ensure that actual unit costs incurred are accurate and that forecasted unit costs for remaining work are appropriate.

Other Control Structure Policies and Procedures

In addition to the previously mentioned cycles, the contractor's control structure should include policies and procedures relating to major equipment items, claims, change orders, accounting for joint ventures, and job site accounting. With the exception of job site accounting, the auditor seldom performs tests of controls in those areas; instead, substantive procedures are usually performed.

Job Site Accounting. The contractor's control structure may be centralized in the home office or decentralized and located at the various job sites. If the contractor uses job site accounting, the auditor must be concerned with and assess the policies and procedures that relate to significant account balances. If the control structure for the previously mentioned cycles is located at the job site, the auditor should assess it as if each job site were a separate company or division. As discussed later, only policies and procedures relating to transactions that could have a material impact on the financial statements would be considered for testing.

Often the job site staff may be small and temporary, and segregation of duties, especially over cash, may be lacking. As a result, management may consider using internal auditors to review job site accounting records. It is a good practice to periodically have internal auditors or home office personnel distribute payroll checks. An official who does not control and reconcile the cash accounts is usually designated to approve purchases and disbursements, based on proper documentation.

Cash receipts from contract billings are directed either to the home office or into a job site account maintained at a zero balance. Lockboxes or automatic transfer accounts may be utilized for that account. This method of cash management allows the company optimum utilization of its cash while reducing the opportunities for job site personnel to manipulate liquid assets.

Job Site Visits. Job site visits are not required in all circumstances, but they can be helpful to the auditor in obtaining an understanding of a contractor's operations. In addition, such visits can provide invaluable first-hand information about the physical status of projects and operational problems. Job site visits are required when the auditor intends to assess control risk at the site as low or when the related accounts cannot be substantiated by other procedures.

While the level of accounting functions (and related control procedures) varies depending on the size of the project, one objective of a site visit, regardless of the size of the project, is obtaining information and supporting documentation to evaluate the reasonableness of the progress of the project to date. The auditor may perform such procedures as

- Identifying uninstalled materials that should be excluded when measuring progress toward completion, and noting the physical security over such materials.
- Discussing with the contractor's personnel who are familiar with the contract, the status of labor hours incurred to date and estimates to complete, including evaluating those estimates by observing the physical progress of the project. If the project is complex, such evaluations may be beyond the auditor's capabilities, and he or she should consider engaging the services of a specialist.

- Observing contractor-owned or rented equipment.
- Discussing with the contractor's personnel who are familiar with the project, other information required to evaluate the project's status or that may affect the estimated total gross margin (such as problems encountered or operational inefficiencies).

RISK ASSESSMENT AND AUDIT STRATEGY

In auditing commercial enterprises, the auditor usually emphasizes procedures directed at the reasonableness of the opening and closing balance sheets. While procedures are also performed directly on income statement accounts, usually such procedures are limited. In the audit of a contractor's financial statements, however, the auditor's primary concern is ascertaining the reasonableness of the estimated total gross margin of each contract and the recognition and measurement of gross margin for the period. High inherent risk is often associated with the management judgments underlying estimates that affect not only the amount and timing of revenue and expense, but also the resultant balances in the various asset and liability accounts. In auditing the financial statements, the auditor must keep in mind how construction accounting affects key relationships between accounts. For example, depending on the accounting method used, the measurement of progress toward completion can affect the determination of revenues, cost of revenues, accounts receivable, unbilled receivables, retentions receivable, and inventory.

Another difference between the audit of a typical commercial enterprise and that of a construction contractor is the nature of the evidential matter. In the audit of a commercial enterprise, evidential matter obtained to support management's assertions in the financial statement is typically factual. For example, revenues may be supported by shipping documents like bills of lading; cost of sales may be supported by suppliers' invoices. Such evidential matter requires limited evaluation on the part of the auditor.

In the audit of a construction contractor, the forms of evidential matter that support financial statement assertions are more varied and usually require greater judgment on the part of the auditor. For example, to audit earned revenues and the cost of such revenues, the auditor must review the estimates of progress toward completion and estimated gross profit, both of which require judgments to determine that income recognized during the period under audit has been calculated properly based on total projected gross profit for the contract at completion and on the work performed to date. Furthermore, judgment is required to evaluate whether the method utilized to measure progress produces reliable and meaningful measurements of the work performed to date.

If a project is evaluated at year-end and an incorrect percentage of completion is determined, it can have a significant impact on revenue recognized in the financial statements for both the current and subsequent years. In addition, contracts with potential losses and cash flow or other problems may not be identified. Therefore, project evaluation and control is a significant risk area for the auditor.

The auditor should consider such additional risk factors as the reasonableness of projected completion dates and related risks of incurring penalties for liquidated damages or overruns in projected job overhead costs. The auditor should also consider the status of relations with the owner and the potential for disputes over whether unanticipated work performed should be considered as an unpriced change order or a claim.

One of the most common errors of auditor judgment is spending numerous hours testing job costs to date and then accepting blindly (or with little scrutiny) the percentage of completion (based on estimated costs to complete) used by the client in recognizing revenue. From an audit risk standpoint, procedures to gain assurance about percentage of completion can be as important as job-cost testing.

In developing the audit strategy, the auditor may determine that evidence of the effectiveness of control procedures that affect significant account balances is available and that it would be efficient to obtain it. The auditor should consider testing those control procedures if doing so would be more efficient than performing substantive procedures. For example, it may be more efficient to test control procedures for accumulating job costs to date than to perform substantive tests by examining numerous invoices and payrolls. On the other hand, the revenue cycle usually lends itself to substantive procedures because contract prices, billings, current and retention receivables, and special terms can easily be confirmed.

In smaller companies where there are few open contracts at year-end, the auditor may find it efficient to substantiate job forecasts. If there are numerous large contracts open, the auditor may choose to test control structure policies and procedures in the forecasting cycle to determine if the forecasts are reliable for determining the percentage of completion at year-end and the possibility of loss contracts. If the auditor's tests indicate that the contractor's control procedures for project forecasting are adequate and result in accurate forecasts, it should be possible to limit substantive testing, perhaps to comparing the percentage of completion (and related estimate of cost to complete) used in revenue forecasts with the most recently approved forecast.

Certain construction projects are so large that many of the control structure policies and procedures are located at the job site rather than the contractor's headquarters as described earlier. In those cases, job site visits may be a necessary element of the planning process, and many key auditing procedures may have to be performed at the site. On medium-sized projects, only certain aspects of the control structure may be located at the job site. Transactions such as direct labor and miscellaneous disbursements may be processed at the construction site, while material purchases may originate from the contractor's headquarters. Small projects may have few or no control functions performed at the construction site. Control functions typically performed at the job site include preparing and approving time sheets; payment is subsequently made at the contractor's headquarters.

In determining which job sites to visit and when, the auditor should consider the usual risk and materiality factors. Job site visits should be planned well in advance. The auditor should arrange for the appropriate contractor personnel to be present and should ensure that any necessary accounting or other information (if not available at the job site) is gathered and brought to the site. Similarly, since the site may be a great distance from the contractor's headquarters, the auditor should ensure, before leaving the site, that all procedures have been performed and the required documentation has been gathered.

SUBSTANTIVE TESTS OF BALANCES

The amount and timing of income to be recognized on contracts depend primarily on the methods and bases used to account for the contracts. Thus, to form an opinion on the reasonableness of the amount and timing of income to be recognized, the auditor must first evaluate the method of accounting for each contract, using the previously discussed criteria for the percentage-of-completion and completed-contract methods, and determine whether it is appropriate.

Next, the auditor considers the revenues and costs associated with each contract. Based on information about total contract revenues and costs, the auditor must evaluate management's determination of the amount of income to be recognized (for contracts accounted for under the percentage-of-completion method) or the amount of loss to be recognized (for both completed-contract and percentage-of-completion methods). As discussed earlier, the critical factor in that determination is what method was used to measure the level of contract completion.

To evaluate the method used to determine the level of completion, the auditor should consider obtaining and reviewing documentation of estimates of contract revenues and costs, and the extent of progress toward completion for a sample of contracts, and consulting, if necessary, with construction managers and production personnel and with engineers, architects, and other specialists. An excellent audit tool for reviewing and evaluating contract revenues and costs is a summary of contract data, as presented in Figures 28.1 and 28.2 (reproduced from pages 92 and 93 of the construction contractors audit and accounting guide). This summary provides an overview of the status of the contracts, permits the auditor to analyze the relationship between costs and revenue by individual contract, and highlights areas where adjustments may be required. Figure 28.3 summarizes many of the substantive tests appropriate for evaluating the timing and amount of income recognized during the period and for substantiating the related balance sheet accounts.

Contract Revenue

Estimating contract revenue can be a complex process. Although the estimate is based largely on the terms of the contract, numerous factors subject to a variety of uncertainties must be considered throughout the life of a contract. The estimates are made for the purpose of recognizing revenue in the appropriate period under the percentage-of-completion method of accounting, and to determine whether a loss has been incurred under both the completed-contract and percentage-of-completion methods.

Figure 28.1 XYZ Company, Inc.
Fixed-Price Contracts in Process
Summary of Original and Revised Contract Estimates
as of Balance Sheet Date

Contract Identification	Original Contract Price	Original Estimate of Contract Costs	Original Estimate of Gross Profit		Net Changes in Contract Price	Revised Contract Price	Revised Estimate of Contract Costs			Revised Estimate of Gross Profit		% of Completion Measured by
			Amount	%			Costs to Date	Estimated Costs to Complete	Revised Total Costs	Amount	%	
	(1)	(2)	(2)	(2)	(3)		(4)	(5)				(6)
A	$100,000	$ 55,000	$45,000	45%	-0-	$100,000	$ 42,000	$ 18,000	$ 60,000	$ 40,000	40%	Cost to cost
B	130,000	110,000	20,000	15.4%	20,000	150,000	80,000	40,000	120,000	30,000	20%	Cu. yds. completed
C	175,000	125,000	50,000	28.6%	25,000	200,000	125,000	75,000	200,000	-0-	—	Labor hours
D	250,000	200,000	50,000	20%	150,000	400,000	270,000	330,000	600,000	(200,000)	—	Cost to cost

(1) Per original contract.
(2) Per original bid.
(3) Supported by change orders and/or claims meeting accounting criteria for inclusion.

(4) Per audit of contract costs.
(5) Per audit of estimated costs to complete.
(6) Reviewed for appropriateness and consistency.

Source: Reproduced from AICPA audit and accounting guide, *Construction Contractors*, p. 92.

Figure 28.2 XYZ Company, Inc.
Fixed-Price Contracts in Process
Analysis of Contract Status
as of Balance Sheet Date

	Per Contractor's Books and Records						Auditor's Adjustments				Adjusted Gross Profit					
					Gross Profit to Date			Revised		Provision for Projected Loss		To Date		Prior Periods		Current Period	
Contract Identification	Contract Billings to Date	Costs Incurred to Date	% Completed	Revenue Earned to Date	Amount	%	Revised % Completed	Earned Revenue to Date	Revenue Adjustments	Adjustments	Amount	%	Amount	%	Amount	%
	(1)	(2)	(3)	(4)			(5)	(6)	(7)	(7)	(8)	(8)	(9)	(9)	(8)	(8)
A	$ 80,000	$ 42,000	70%	$ 80,000	$38,000	47.5%	70%	$ 70,000	($10,000)(A)		$ 28,000	40%	$20,250	45%	$ 7,750	31%
B	82,500	80,000	65%	97,500	17,500	17.9%	67%	100,500	3,000 (B)		20,500	20%	8,500	18.9%	12,000	21.6%
C	150,000	125,000	55%	110,000	(15,000)	—	62.5%	125,000	15,000 (C)		-0-	—	28,600	28.6%	(28,600)	—
D	300,000	270,000	45%	300,000	30,000	10%	45%	180,000	(120,000)(A)	110,000(D)	(200,000)	—	—	—	(200,000)	—

(1) Per audit of contract billings.
(2) Per audit of contract costs.
(3) Management's estimate of completion.
(4) Per contract revenue accounts on books.
(5) Per auditor—based on review and analysis of costs, billings, management's estimate of completion, job-site visits, etc.
(6) Result of applying revised percentage of completion to revised contract price.
(7) Adjustments to be reviewed with and accepted by management.
(8) Should be compared with prior periods and with similar contracts.
(9) Per audit of prior periods.

(A) Adjustment necessary to reduce recorded earned revenue and recognize excess billings.

(B) Adjustment necessary to increase recorded earned revenue and recognize unbilled revenue.

(C) Adjustment necessary to increase recorded earned revenue and reduce recorded excess billings in order to reflect projected "break-even" on contract. Remaining revenue ($75,000) now equals estimated costs to complete.

(D) Adjustment necessary to provide for balance of the total projected loss on contract. Remaining revenue ($220,000) now equals estimated costs to complete ($330,000) less provision for projected loss ($110,000).

Source: Reproduced from AICPA audit and accounting guide, Construction Contractors, p. 93.

Figure 28.3 Contract Revenue Cycle

Audit Objectives	Earned Revenue	Accounts Receivable	Unbilled Revenues (costs in excess of billings)	Advance Billings (billings in excess of costs)	Substantive Procedures
Accuracy of contract value, including all change orders.	X				1. Confirm original contract price and subsequent change orders directly with the owner. Examine signed original contract and subsequent change orders.
Accuracy of measured progress toward completion, including reasonableness of method used.	X				2. Review and test client's procedures, including estimates and calculations. See "Contract Costs" later in this chapter.
Accuracy of calculation of owner billings, including consistency with provisions of the contract.		X	X	X	3. Agree cumulative amounts billed plus unbilled revenues (or less advance billings) at the balance sheet date to earned revenues recorded through the balance sheet date. Confirm amounts billed with the owner. Alternative procedures—review amounts billable by referring to contract terms and recalculating; examine subsequent cash receipts.

(Continued)

Figure 28.3 Continued

Audit Objectives	Earned Revenue	Accounts Receivable	Unbilled Revenues (costs in excess of billings)	Advance Billings (billings in excess of costs)	Substantive Procedures
Accuracy and completeness of cash receipts.		X			4. Confirm payments made with the owner. Alternative procedure—examine subsequent cash receipts.
Collectibility of amounts reflected as outstanding.		X	X		5. Review owner's financial statements to ascertain owner's financial condition and ability to pay total contract price yet to be billed, as well as unpaid billings, and availability of financial resources obtained through a third party. Review third party's financial statements and related arrangements entered into with owner. Review owner's past payment performance. Examine subsequent cash receipts. Review bonding arrangements and lien rights.

The principal factors the auditor considers in reviewing the contractor's estimate of total contract revenue are original contract price, change orders, claims, contract options, and additions. Those factors, together with related substantive procedures, are discussed in this section.

Original Contract Price.   The original contract price is the total amount expected to be realized from the contract. This amount may be fixed or variable, depending on the type of contract. Fixed-price and unit-price contracts usually contain a stated contract price for a defined amount of work; however, they may also have provisions for adjustments to the stated price. Typical adjustments are escalation clauses (changes based on prescribed economic indices); bonus or penalty adjustments associated with target cost, completion dates, or performance levels; and price redetermination based on periodic or retroactive assessments of target cost or performance levels.

The auditor should obtain a summary of the key contract provisions affecting revenues, along with management's current assessment of the amounts associated with price adjustments. The original stated contract price can be substantiated by comparing the data with the signed contract or by direct confirmation with the owner; escalation price adjustments can be recalculated using formulas set forth in the contract or can be confirmed directly with the owner. Evaluating the likelihood of price redetermination and bonus or penalty adjustments requires a careful review of the contract and the contractor's past and projected performance, and may also entail consultation with engineers, architects, or other specialists to evaluate the probability of future outcomes.

Cost-plus contracts occur in a variety of forms. Generally, the contract includes provisions for reimbursement of defined costs (often a maximum amount of reimbursable costs is set forth in the contract), overhead recovery percentages, and payment of a fee (which may be fixed or a percentage of defined reimbursable costs). Bonus or penalty provisions similar to those in fixed-price contracts may also be included. If a cost-plus contract involves management services only, and all costs are fully reimbursable (i.e., there is no risk to the contractor), only the fee should be included in determining revenue. If, however, the contractor is responsible for purchasing and managing materials and hiring workers and subcontractors (i.e., costs on which the fee is based or for which the contractor is at risk, even though they are reimbursable), these costs are properly included in determining revenue. The auditor should determine that disallowed or disallowable costs have been charged off.

As with fixed-price contracts, the auditor should obtain a summary of key contract data affecting revenues (e.g., reimbursable costs, percentages of cost recovery, and the fee) and corroborate that information by referring to signed contracts or by confirming with the owner. Audit emphasis for cost-plus contracts is on accumulating contract costs that serve as the basis for calculating the fee and overhead recovery amounts. The auditor should ensure that the contractor adequately distinguishes reimbursable costs associated with the contract (i.e., costs that give rise to contract revenues) from costs that are not reimbursable. If the contract includes bonus or penalty provisions, auditing procedures similar to those described for fixed-price contracts should also be performed.

Time-and-materials contracts have characteristics of both fixed-price and cost-plus contracts. Accordingly, the auditor should consider the various auditing procedures described in the preceding paragraphs, depending on the particular contracts involved.

Change Orders.   Change orders modify the original provisions of a contract and may or may not affect the original contract price; they may be initiated by the owner or the contractor. The accounting for change orders depends on the underlying circumstances, so each change order must be analyzed individually. The auditor should determine whether the contractor has an adequate control structure to ensure that all change orders have been identified. Often the work to be performed under a change order is defined, but the adjustment to the contract price is not specified. Under the percentage-of-completion method, if there is evidence that the additional costs will be recovered, total contract revenues and costs may be adjusted accordingly; alternatively, the related costs may be deferred (i.e., excluded from income determination) until the amount is known. Anticipated revenues in excess of costs related to unpriced change orders should not be recognized, however, until realization is assured beyond a reasonable doubt. If change orders have not been processed, have not been approved for scope and price, or are in dispute, the accounting described below for claims is appropriate.

Auditing procedures for change orders that have been approved by the owner and are not in dispute are no different from those for contract revenues and costs incurred to date. If the change orders have not been approved or are in dispute, the auditor should evaluate the existence and collectibility of the related additional revenues and the propriety of the underlying accumulated costs. The auditor may be able to confirm the amounts of unapproved change orders with owners. If not, the auditor should review and discuss the contract terms with the contractor's legal counsel and knowledgeable contractor personnel. It may be appropriate to obtain written representations from the contractor's legal counsel regarding contract disputes. Testing the underlying accumulated costs generally involves examining supporting documents, seeking evidence of owner authorization for incurring those costs (if appropriate), and evaluating whether the costs relate to work within or outside the scope of the contract.

Claims.   Contractors often seek to recover amounts over the agreed-on contract price for unanticipated costs caused by others, such as errors in construction drawings or design, owner-caused delays, or disputed or unresolved change orders. These claims may take the form of legally filed documents or negotiations in process which, if allowed, would result in increased revenues. Such anticipated revenues should be reflected in total contract revenues only if it is probable that the claims will be upheld and the amount can be reasonably estimated, and only to the extent that they do not exceed related costs incurred. SOP 81-1 specifies the conditions that will satisfy those requirements. The auditing procedures for claims are similar to those for change orders.

Contract Renegotiation and Termination. The federal government retains the right to terminate contracts at its convenience or alter their scope significantly. Federal regulations govern the termination or material modification of government contracts so as to protect contractors that do business with the government.

Revenue recognition on terminated contracts can be complex. If the government and the contractor agree on the settlement payments, revenue recognition follows the normal method. If, on the other hand, litigation appears likely, revenue recognition should follow the guidelines established for claims. Additional guidance on accounting for renegotiated and terminated government contracts is provided in Chapter 11B of ARB No. 43 and in the industry audit guide, *Audits of Government Contractors*.

Contract Options. Some contracts may include options that, if exercised by the owner, effectively increase the scope of work and total contract revenue. Generally, if the change in scope and price is predetermined in the contract, the accounting for contract options should be the same as that for change orders; that is, the options become part of the profit center containing the related contract. The options should be considered a separate profit center (i.e., segmented) if the scope of work is significantly different from that specified in the original contract, or if the scope is similar but the revenue and cost relationships differ significantly or the price was negotiated without regard to the original contract. The auditor should evaluate the appropriateness of the decision to combine or segment, by considering the circumstances in light of the criteria for combining and segmenting presented in SOP 81-1. The auditing procedures for contract options are similar to those for change orders.

Additions. Contract additions are agreements that increase the scope of work beyond that in the original contract. The criteria described in the preceding paragraph should determine whether additions are segmented from the original contract or combined with it. The auditing procedures for additions are similar to those for change orders.

Contract Costs

Contract costs consist of two elements, costs incurred to date and estimated costs to complete. Costs incurred to date are based on the actual costs incurred in conjunction with a contract and are relatively easy to substantiate. Estimated costs to complete are more difficult to substantiate, since they require projecting future costs related to a contract.

Costs Incurred to Date. Accumulating costs incurred to date is essentially no different from accumulating inventory costs, and related auditing procedures are basically the same as those used in connection with inventories of commercial and industrial companies. Generally, the elements of contract costs are governed by the authoritative pronouncements applicable to inventories. Costs not clearly related, either directly or indirectly, to a contract should be excluded from contract costs and reflected as costs of the period they relate to.

The following general principles apply to accounting for contract costs, as prescribed by SOP 81-1:

• All direct costs, like material, labor, and subcontracting costs, should be included in contract costs.

• Indirect costs allocable to contracts include the costs of indirect labor, contract supervision, tools and equipment, supplies, quality control and inspection, insurance, repairs and maintenance, depreciation, and amortization. For government contractors, other types of costs that are allowable or allocable under pertinent government contract regulations may be allocated to contracts as indirect costs if otherwise allowable under GAAP. Methods of allocating indirect costs should be systematic and rational. Appropriate bases for allocating costs include direct labor hours and direct labor cost. The method used should be tailored to the particular circumstances of a contract.

• General and administrative costs ordinarily should be charged to expense as incurred, but may be accounted for as contract costs under the completed-contract method of accounting or, in some circumstances, as indirect contract costs by government contractors.

• Generally, selling costs should be excluded from contract costs and charged to expense. Precontract costs (including estimating and bidding costs) that are incurred for a specific anticipated contract and that will result in no future benefits unless the contract is obtained should not be included in contract costs before receipt of the contract. Such costs may otherwise be deferred only if they can be directly associated with a specific anticipated contract and if their recoverability from that contract is probable; they should be included in contract costs on receipt of the anticipated contract. Costs related to anticipated contracts that were charged to expense as incurred, because their recovery was not considered probable, however, should not be reinstated by a credit to income on the subsequent receipt of the contract.

• Interest costs capitalizable according to the criteria discussed earlier in this chapter should be included in contract costs.

The auditor should ascertain that all proper costs to date have been recorded. Usually the cutoff for costs is tested in the search for unrecorded liabilities. Inquiry of knowledgeable contractor personnel and review of job-cost reports and contract files may indicate unusual costs that should be recorded. Overhead costs that are allocated to contracts in accordance with GAAP should be reviewed for proper and consistent allocation methods.

Costs or units to date reported in the job-cost report are often audited through tests of controls, as noted earlier. If the costs are substantiated, the auditor should review and test vendor and subcontractor invoices for proper coding to the correct job and job category and should note that the costs are properly allocable to the job.

Labor costs (or hours) should be tested to ascertain that the costs are coded properly to the job and reflect all labor-related costs. Payroll audit tests should be performed to test the propriety of the costs, and equipment charges should be tested for reasonableness and consistency. Equipment rental rates may be compared with actual company cost or "blue book" rates. Invoices should be examined to determine that costs assigned from inventory are based on actual costs and that overhead allocations are consistent, reasonable, and computed accurately (subject to contract limitations, if appropriate).

The auditor should consider comparing material, labor, and overhead costs incurred to date and estimates to complete the contract with costs on similar contracts completed during the year, reviewing estimates and procedures from the prior year, and inquiring about and observing the client's procedures. (It may be possible to test key control procedures applied to the estimating process.)

The auditor may review individual annual employee earnings records for reasonableness and recalculate the allocation of labor to individual contracts based on some common element (e.g., materials or contract price). The reported allocation should be compared with actual labor reported, and significant discrepancies should be investigated. Labor costs allocated to individual contracts should be reconciled to total payroll costs.

On cost-plus contracts, the auditor should determine that recoverable and nonrecoverable costs are segregated in the accounting records and that the records are adequate to withstand the scrutiny of owners' auditors, if required. The review of contract revenues should satisfy the auditor that nonrecoverable costs are not being billed. Year-end billings and job-cost reports should be examined to ensure that all recoverable costs have been billed on a timely basis and that the related revenues have been recognized. On cost-plus contracts with a guaranteed maximum price or fee ceiling, an analysis should be made of the costs and fees recognized to date. The analysis should consider the stage of completion of the project and the remaining costs and fees to be earned.

Estimated Costs to Complete.   Periodically, the costs to complete a contract must be reestimated. Since revenue is fixed (unless contract provisions permit specified changes), a change in estimated costs requires recognizing a change in the ratio of revenue to cost for accounting purposes. Since costs commonly change, regular, conscientiously prepared estimates are essential. Preparing estimates of costs to complete is one of management's most difficult tasks, and evaluating them is correspondingly difficult for an auditor. An auditor who understands the contractor's operations and business conditions will be better able to understand the estimate of costs to complete. If the estimates are prepared diligently and responsibly and if communication between auditor and contractor is open and candid, an auditor can obtain reasonable assurance that the estimates are attainable. Guidance on auditing accounting estimates is contained in SAS No. 57 and Chapter 9 of this book.

Most contractors prepare estimates of costs to complete in a systematized manner, with detailed written policies and procedures, including review and approval by responsible officials. The estimates generally include detailed analyses of original bills of material, with items still to be obtained included at current prices, unless purchase commitments at specified prices exist. Initial estimates of various kinds of labor are analyzed in detail and compared with experience to date. Judgment is needed in extrapolating current experience into the future, particularly with respect to labor rates, fringe benefits, and overhead costs. The smaller and more specific the items extrapolated, the smaller the risk of error. The more often a contract is examined and judgments are made, the more reliable the estimates are likely to be.

In evaluating the estimate of costs to complete, the auditor should

- Review the contractor's procedures for preparing the estimates.
- Test the compilation of the estimates by reviewing the underlying data, such as manning tables, labor and overhead rate schedules, bills of material, and schedules of material received and still to be received (open purchase orders).
- Perform analytical procedures, like comparing the details of the estimate of costs to complete with the details of the original cost estimate supporting the contract bid, or comparing evidence of physical completion (e.g., number of units completed) with the percentage of completion indicated by cost estimates.
- Consult with the engineering and production supervisors who make the critical judgments entering into the estimates in order to understand the reasons for their judgments and the degree of confidence with which they are made, and to determine that the estimating process adequately recognizes anticipated changes in future costs resulting from collective bargaining agreements, known price changes, estimated inflation rates, and other similar events and circumstances.
- Assess management's ability, based on past experience, to estimate with reasonable accuracy the eventual outcome of contracts in progress.
- Be alert for long-lasting jobs likely to have cost overruns, and ensure that the implications of delays have been considered in estimating costs to complete.
- Be alert for the inclusion of reserves in estimated costs to complete and ascertain that the contractor's method of determining and including those reserves is consistently applied and is in conformity with the requirements of SFAS No. 5 for the accrual of loss contingencies.

However well organized or carefully performed and documented estimates of costs to complete are, they can never be more than estimates. Errors in judgment are inevitable, but can be minimized if the estimates are made according to a well-established, well-controlled routine. When estimates are revised, the related effect on contract costs should be recorded in the period in which the facts underlying the revision became known. If a revision is the result of a mechanical or factual error in a previous estimate, however, it should be accounted for as a prior-period adjustment pursuant to APB Opinion No. 20, *Accounting Changes.*

Contract Losses

Auditing procedures should be designed to ensure that potential contract losses are identified and properly accounted for; losses that meet the criteria for accrual under SFAS No. 5 should be recognized in the financial statements in the proper period and other loss contingencies should be disclosed properly.

Procedures the auditor may use in reviewing contract loss reserves include considering the nature of the contract and the historical results of similar contracts. The auditor should review job correspondence files, including correspondence with the owner; the reasonableness of the specific contract estimate; the aging of accounts receivable, including long-outstanding retentions (see below); and accounts receivable billings and collections in relation to total contract revenue. Certain comparisons may also be helpful in assessing the existence and amount of estimated or contingent losses, like comparing total budgeted costs with final costs incurred on similar jobs in the past, revised with original budgets, other contract factors with corresponding budgeted items (e.g., labor hours and material used), total costs incurred with budgeted amounts, and the client's bid with bids of competitors, if available. The auditor should be alert for overlooked change orders and claims that may ameliorate losses. The auditor should also consider the client's control procedures applied to the estimating process.

Contract Billings

The amount of revenue recognized on a contract does not always coincide with the amount billed to the owner, especially for contracts accounted for on the completed-contract basis. Often billings (amount and timing) are prescribed as part of the terms of the contract. When billings to owners are more or less than the amount of revenue recognized, the following situations result:

- *Unbilled Receivables*. Revenue has been recognized but cannot be billed because of the terms of the contract. Such amounts are recorded in the balance sheet as accounts receivable.
- *Billings in Excess of Revenue*. Owners are billed in accordance with the terms of the contract, and the excess of billings over revenue is recorded as a liability. (Progress payments may be received, as stipulated in the contract, without regard to stage of completion.)

Auditing procedures in connection with receivables generally are the same as those performed on audits of commercial and industrial companies, except that certain alternative procedures must be applied to unbilled receivables. The auditor should evaluate billing data based on accumulated cost information and the terms of the contract, ascertain that the unbilled amounts were subsequently billed, and assess the ultimate collectibility of the receivables.

A portion of amounts billed over the duration of a contract will not be paid until the contract has been completed to the owner's satisfaction. These amounts are referred to as retentions. While auditing procedures for retentions are basically the same as for accounts receivable, the auditor must be especially concerned with evaluating the collectibility of these amounts, since payment may not be due for several years and is subject to owner claims for rework or other costs.

Contract Liabilities

Contract liabilities result from purchases of materials, work performed by subcontractors, equipment rentals, accruals of payroll and related fringe benefit costs, penalty accruals, and accrued losses on contracts. The auditor must be satisfied that all liabilities have been recorded and properly classified and disclosed. Amounts due subcontractors are sometimes confirmed because subcontractor invoices may be received late and because the confirmation procedure provides evidence that supports the amounts and terms of retentions payable and may identify claims and disputes with subcontractors. If subcontractors' payables are not confirmed, the auditor should consider the need to reconcile payable balances to subcontractors' statements. In addition, the auditor should consider confirming the terms of long-term purchase commitments.

The auditor should ask the contractor about existing claims or disputes against the company that have not been recorded. Old outstanding payables may also indicate contract problems, such as inadequacies in the work performed or penalties. The auditor should determine the need to accrue costs on the related claims in accordance with SFAS No. 5.

Sometimes, contractors do not use the cost-to-cost method to compute the percentage of completion. When other methods are used, the costs expensed to date in the financial statements represent the estimated final costs multiplied by the percentage of completion. The difference between the actual costs incurred and the costs expensed is recorded as a liability for costs to be incurred (or a deferred asset account).

29

Auditing Emerging Businesses

A 1980 report by the White House Commission on Small Business[1] recognized the need to encourage individual enterprise, independent business, and innovation. Since the report was issued, significant legislation benefiting smaller business has been enacted, such as the Regulatory Flexibility Act, the Small Business Innovation Development Act, the Small Business Development Center Improvement Act, and the Tax Reform Act of 1986 (primarily in the potential tax benefits available under Subchapter S election). Several studies have indicated that small businesses generate the majority of new jobs in the private sector while also promoting innovative investment in research and development. Venture capital groups, major banks, and other financial institutions have identified this sector of the economy as a primary target in their strategies for growth. New business magazines have grown rapidly by aiming their content at the needs of entrepreneurs. In many respects, we are in an entrepreneurial era.

The need for standard-setting organizations to respond to the concerns of smaller businesses has also been recognized. Concluding that auditing standards were not adequately considering variations in the size of companies, the Cohen Commission and the Oliphant Committee recommended that additional guidance be established on the nature and extent of auditing procedures for small enterprises.[2] The American Institute of Certified Public Accountants responded to the recommendations by issuing a 1985 auditing procedure study, *Audits of Small Businesses*, as well as by acknowledging the effect on small businesses of several of the ''expectation gap'' auditing standards issued in 1988.

In addition, the Financial Accounting Standards Board (FASB) sponsored research to learn whether the financial statements of private and smaller public companies met the needs of users of such information. The studies concluded that user needs did not significantly vary with the size of the entity.[3] Some accountants have suggested, however, having less stringent disclosure requirements for smaller or privately held entities. The FASB's effort to mitigate the disclosure pressures on small businesses is evident in Statement of Financial Accounting Standards No. 87, *Employers' Accounting for Pensions*, which delayed the effective date of implementation for nonpublic enterprises for two years.

CHARACTERISTICS OF EMERGING BUSINESSES

Emerging and smaller businesses have unique characteristics that affect how the auditor develops the audit strategy, assesses risks, and performs substantive procedures. Those characteristics include

[1]White House Commission on Small Business, *America's Small Business Economy* (Washington, DC: U.S. Government Printing Office, April 1980).

[2]Commission on Auditors' Responsibilities, *Report, Conclusions, and Recommendations* (New York: 1978); and *Report of the Special Committee of the AICPA to Study the Structure of the Auditing Standards Executive Committee* (New York: AICPA, 1978).

[3]Financial Accounting Standards Board, *Financial Reporting by Privately Owned Companies— Summary of Responses to FASB Invitation to Comment* (Special Report) (Stamford, CT: FASB, 1983); and A. R. Abdel-khalik, *Financial Reporting by Private Companies—Analysis and Diagnosis* (Research Report) (Stamford, CT: FASB, 1983).

Entrepreneurial management. Emerging entities reflect the drive, determination, and motivation of their entrepreneurial founder or chief executive. Business and organizational objectives are usually congruent with the personal objectives of the entrepreneur.

Owner-manager involvement. The vast majority of emerging and smaller businesses are closely held. Typically, the shareholder-owner(s) and family members also fill key managerial posts. In addition, an owner-manager usually has the authority to override prescribed procedures.

Limited financial expertise. Many owner-managers are manufacturing, research, marketing, or sales oriented, but are not fully conversant with financial, accounting, and administrative issues.

Limited middle management expertise. Professional managers to serve in key technical and middle management positions are often not recruited until later in a company's life cycle, if at all. Thus, the objective analytical tools a professional manager would demand are not present in many emerging and smaller entities.

Limited policy-making group. The group above management, such as a board of directors, typically consists of individuals whose names were used merely to obtain a corporate charter, rather than an effective policy-making group.

Lack of supervision and segregation of duties. With limited resources and thin middle management, separation of duties and supervision are often lacking. Their absence may be compensated for, in part, by the watchful concern and involvement of the owner-manager.

Informal accounting system. The limited resources of emerging businesses often lead to their having informal accounting systems with inadequate control procedures.

High leverage and undercapitalization. The entrepreneur usually relies on banks, commercial finance companies, and vendors for financing. The owner's personal resources available for investment in the company, particularly in the early stages, frequently are limited. Therefore, emerging businesses are often undercapitalized and highly leveraged.

Related party transactions. Business transactions between the owner-manager and the company, or with entities under common ownership or owned by close relatives, are customary in entrepreneurial situations. Often these are motivated by income tax or estate tax considerations.

AUDIT STRATEGIES FOR EMERGING BUSINESSES

An audit strategy should always be designed to achieve maximum efficiency and timeliness without sacrificing audit effectiveness. Efficiency and timeliness are particularly important in auditing an emerging business because

- Generally the company's accounting staff is limited, and an audit necessarily disrupts operations.
- Credit grantors often require financial statements within specified periods.

- The cost of professional services is an important concern.
- The owner-manager often makes certain operating decisions based on the audited financial statements.

To design an effective and efficient audit strategy and provide the services the owner-manager expects, the auditor must be knowledgeable about the operation of the business, including the products or services the company sells, how it manufactures or obtains its products, the market it serves, its competitive position, and the way it markets its products or services. The auditor must also understand the control structure, which consists of the control environment (particularly management's objectives, plans, operating style, and philosophy), the accounting system, and control procedures. Finally, the auditor must assess the risks associated with the company's operations and control structure. Chapter 8 discusses the various means of obtaining insight into a company's business and its control structure.

Risk Assessment

The following factors are relevant to the auditor's consideration of inherent risk in the emerging business environment:

- Owner-managed companies often depend on outside financing, and credit grantors typically impose financial requirements, such as maintaining a minimum equity, working capital, or current ratio.
- Continued or increased financing by credit grantors may be dependent on the company's financial position and current operating results.
- Banks, vendors, customers, and investors may rely more heavily on the annual auditor's report as a basis for credit decisions.
- The management of an emerging business enterprise may adopt accounting practices based solely or primarily on their income tax effects.
- The business may be dependent on one or a few products that, in a rapidly changing technological environment, may suddenly become obsolete, or on a key supplier or one key customer.
- As noted earlier, family-owned businesses may engage in related party transactions like leasing arrangements, loans, and sales to or purchases from affiliated persons or companies.

The auditor should consider a range of matters affecting the industry the company operates in, the company's present and planned operations, and its financial condition. For example, the auditor should inquire about possible adverse trends in the industry and should compare the company's operating results with the industry average. Many operational characteristics are indicative of the various types of risks faced by an enterprise, like the possibility of technological changes making the company's products obsolete, its dependence on only a few suppliers or customers, substantial dependence on the success of a particular project, unusual transactions with related parties, a significant decline in sales or gross margins, or a recent easing of credit policies. The

auditor should also consider whether the company's income or financial flexibility has deteriorated compared with prior years, whether it has exhausted its
lines of credit with banks, and whether it plans to use the financial statements
for an equity or debt offering to restructure its present capital or debt ratios.

The risk of errors or irregularities occurring in the financial statements of
emerging businesses is usually concentrated in the accounting system for
revenues and receivables, or inventory, depending on the nature of the business. The major risk for smaller service companies tends to be in the area of
revenues and receivables, especially if the company recognizes service revenue
in stages, such as on a proportional performance basis or, if appropriate, on a
straight-line time basis. A major audit concern is that revenue recognized
reflects work actually performed. Other principal concerns for service companies are billed and unbilled receivables, and the allowance for uncollectible
accounts, since those accounts are likely to be subject to owner-manager
control. The auditor should be particularly alert to ascertaining that a proper
revenue cutoff was achieved and that the allowance for uncollectible accounts
appears adequate, since there may be limited past experience to go by. For
smaller manufacturing or distribution companies, inventories are the high-risk
area because owner-managers often may try to minimize income taxes by
understating ending inventories and gross margins. The auditor's attention
should be directed particularly to determining that proper receiving and
shipping cutoffs were achieved, along with the other usual auditing procedures
for inventories (described in Chapter 14).

In assessing control risk in an emerging business, the auditor should be
aware of the frequent lack of segregation of duties in accounting functions.
This results from limited staff, easy accessibility to financial records and assets
by clerical and administrative personnel, and informal and undocumented
authorization and supervisory procedures. The involvement of the owner-
manager can compensate for a lack of formal control procedures, provided the
level of involvement is ongoing. The owner-manager, however, typically has
the authority to override the few control procedures that may exist in an
emerging business. For example, accounting personnel could be instructed to
back-date sales invoices to enhance or smooth revenues for a particular period,
to make unauthorized shipments to customers, or to hold out credit memos.
The auditor's assessment of all these risks should influence the audit strategy.

Selecting the Audit Strategy

The auditor's procedures in obtaining and evaluating audit evidence are the
same for an emerging business as for any other business enterprise. They
consist of tests of controls, substantive tests of details, and analytical procedures, and are explained in detail and illustrated in the chapters in Part 3 of
this book on auditing transactions and account balances. Materiality considerations, which enter into the choice of an audit strategy as well, are also the
same for an emerging business as for an established one.

Because owner-manager businesses typically have small accounting staffs,
low transaction volume, and limited segregation of duties and supervision, the
most efficient strategy is usually one that emphasizes substantive tests of year-

end account balances. Nonetheless, on each engagement the auditor must assess control risk. Based on this assessment, the auditor determines whether, and to what extent, performing tests of controls may be efficient. Also, different strategies may be used for different accounts on an engagement.

Auditing Research Monograph No. 5, *Audit Problems Encountered in Small Business Engagements*, indicated that many auditors of smaller businesses "at least occasionally accept management's representations as audit evidence when completeness of recorded transactions cannot otherwise be substantiated."[4] This suggests that a practice problem may exist that auditors of emerging businesses should be aware of; it also points to the need for auditors to devise an audit strategy to meet the completeness objective, even when faced with deficiencies in control procedures directed at completeness.

Chapter 7 indicates some of the effects of inadequate completeness control procedures on the conduct of an audit. If those control procedures are not effective, substantive testing may have to be changed or increased. Evidence concerning completeness often can be obtained through analytical procedures, substantive tests of details of related populations, and other substantive tests that are available but are not ordinarily performed. An example of a substantive test of a related population would be testing cash disbursements in the subsequent period to search for liabilities that were unrecorded at the balance sheet date. Confirming accounts payable, including those with known vendors with zero balances, for the same purpose, is an example of a substantive test that is not ordinarily performed, except in extremely poor control structures. Particularly in the emerging business environment, the auditor may have to be skillful in designing substantive tests to achieve the completeness objective; in most instances, some evidence will probably have to be sought from tests of controls, particularly of the control environment and relevant control procedures. If sufficient competent evidence cannot be obtained, a scope limitation may result, and the auditor should consider the effect on the audit opinion.

RELATED SERVICES

Owner-managers of emerging businesses generally require audited financial statements when

- Significant ownership interests are held by parties other than the owner-manager.
- The owner-manager needs greater assurance about the functioning of the control structure, especially the protection of assets.
- Operations are decentralized, so that the owner-manager must rely on a reporting system to control the business.
- Relatively large amounts of debt are owed to trade creditors, banks, or other financial institutions.

[4]D. D. Raiborn, *Audit Problems Encountered in Small Business Engagements*, Auditing Research Monograph No. 5 (New York: AICPA, 1982), p. 74.

- Plans exist to raise relatively large sums of money in the near future.
- Plans exist to go public or sell the business in the near future.
- Audited financial statements are required under joint venture or third-party contracts (such as royalty agreements, franchise agreements, field warehouse agreements, and bonding requirements).

If an audit is not required, an accountant may nonetheless be associated with the financial statements on two other levels of service—reviews and compilations. As discussed in Chapter 23, the AICPA in 1978 began issuing Statements on Standards for Accounting and Review Services (SSARSs), which established standards for such services.

Review Service

Although a review is less extensive than an audit, review procedures provide a basis for expressing limited assurance that the accountant did not become aware of any material changes that should be made to the financial statements. Essentially, a review is designed to enable an accountant, without applying comprehensive auditing procedures, to assess management's representations and to consider whether the financial statements appear to be in conformity with generally accepted accounting principles. To perform a review, the accountant must be familiar with the company's business and the accounting practices of its industry. Based on this knowledge, the accountant inquires about the company's accounting practices and procedures, financial statements, and other matters, and performs analytical procedures, all as outlined in SSARS No. 1 (AR Section 100), to identify unusual items or trends.

A review service may be appropriate for an emerging business if

Owners are active in managing the company and are knowledgeable about operations, personnel, and finances.

Little need exists for nonmanagement shareholders to have the higher level of assurance provided by an audit.

Creditors have a long-standing personal relationship with management, and there is relatively little debt outstanding.

No plans exist to go public, sell the business, or raise sums of money.

Debt is backed by collateral or personal guarantees.

Compilation Service

The scope of a compilation does not give the accountant a basis to express any assurance, since neither auditing nor review procedures are performed. Instead, relying on familiarity with industry accounting practices and with the company's business, the accountant helps prepare financial statements using data provided by the company. This allows the accountant the opportunity to consider whether the financial statements are appropriate in form and are free from obvious material misstatements; however, the accountant does not probe beneath the surface unless it is apparent that the data provided is incomplete or in error. The accountant's report that accompanies compiled financial statements indicates that a compilation service was performed, but, because neither an audit nor a review was performed, it expresses no assurance.

Companies find a compilation service useful mainly for internal needs or as a by-product of other services, like preparing income tax returns. It may also be appropriate when management engages the accountant to prepare monthly financial statements.

The Independent Accountant as Business Advisor

To a great extent, the entrepreneur perceives the independent accountant not only as an auditor but also as an advisor to management. When serving the entrepreneur, the accountant is often called on to provide advice on such diverse topics as buying or leasing plant or equipment; achieving the maximum coverage, at the least cost, from employee benefit programs; implementing tax deferral and tax savings programs; attracting and retaining key management personnel; obtaining financing; and expanding or contracting product lines.[5] Advising management in these areas also requires that the accountant thoroughly understand the business.

An accountant who understands how the emerging business fits into the overall economy can apply technical accounting and financial skills to enhance the entity's growth or profitability. By making an effort to discuss, challenge, and help shape the entrepreneur's business objectives and personal financial goals, the independent accountant will earn the owner-manager's confidence and respect necessary to fulfill the important role of business advisor. Once confidence and mutual respect develop between an independent accountant and an owner-manager client, the accountant can find opportunities to provide many services that are important to the survival and growth of an emerging or smaller business. Some typical services provided to such clients include

- Corporate, personal, and estate tax planning to take advantage of opportunities in the tax law and minimize the cash flow drain from income and other taxes.
- Helping to prepare income and other tax returns to comply with federal, state, and local laws or regulations.
- Advising on cash management techniques.
- Helping the owner-manager determine the financial effects of contemplated business decisions or transactions and analyzing their impact on the strategic position of the business.
- Compiling and evaluating budgets or forecasts and applying an independent, professional objectivity, as well as knowledge of the company, to help ensure that goals are achievable and plans practicable.

[5]Many of the factors discussed in this chapter that should be considered by the entrepreneur of an emerging business in developing plans and strategies are further elaborated on in *The Coopers & Lybrand Guide to Growing Your Business* by Seymour Jones, M. Bruce Cohen, and Victor V. Coppola (New York: John Wiley & Sons, 1988).

- Determining sources of financing needed to meet growth objectives and identifying key issues and provisions of financial agreements to anticipate their future impact on business activities.
- Developing, implementing, and evaluating reporting, operating, and cost control systems to ensure that management information systems grow with the business.
- Assessing control procedures, particularly in newly established computer installations, to ensure that assets are protected and transactions are authorized and executed in accordance with the owner-manager's intentions.
- Advising on the installation, modification, and upgrading of executive compensation and employee benefit plans to attract, motivate, and retain key employees.
- Evaluating financial, tax, and other consequences of potential mergers and acquisitions, including, where appropriate, the strategic positioning of the company to maximize its value on sale or liquidation.

Because of the limited accounting expertise of many small businesses, the independent accountant typically provides bookkeeping and accounting services in addition to advising on such diverse areas as financial and tax planning. Certain requirements under Interpretation 101-3 (ET Section 101.05) of the Rules of the AICPA Code of Professional Conduct (see Chapter 3) apply when an independent accountant performs manual or automated bookkeeping services. Those requirements are intended to avoid the appearance that the accountant is an employee and therefore lacks independence in the eyes of a reasonable observer.

THE MICROCOMPUTER AND EMERGING BUSINESSES

The reduced cost and increased capabilities of microcomputers and the availability of high-quality application software packages have created a revolution in information processing and management for all segments of the economy, particularly for smaller and emerging businesses. Virtually every smaller company that has not already done so should seriously consider using a computer to maintain its accounting records and other management information.

For many smaller entities, the need to develop specialized custom software is rapidly disappearing. High-quality generalized software is available for such applications as general ledger, financial reporting, budgeting and forecasting, accounts receivable, inventory, and asset management. Word processing, job scheduling, and most planning procedures can be performed easily by non-technical personnel utilizing relatively inexpensive microcomputer software.

The accountant should be prepared to assist the emerging business in identifying microcomputer hardware and software that are most appropriate for the business and in implementing their use. In addition, the auditor is qualified to assess control procedures and advise management of deficiencies.

Equally important is the use of microcomputers as a service tool for the auditor. For example, information from prior reviews or audits, including ratio and other analytical information, can be maintained in a data base, and standard working papers can be prepared, stored, and updated throughout the year. In addition, the computer can be used to prepare a trial balance and related account details. The auditor can enter appropriate adjustments, corrections, and reclassifications directly into the computer to produce an adjusted trial balance. The computer can also be used to prepare financial statements, ratio and trend analyses, and other comparisons.

Graphics, like bar or pie charts, portraying important ratios or other pertinent relationships can be produced by computer. These visual displays often enhance users' understanding of the financial statements. The data base can sometimes be used in preparing the company's federal and state income tax returns, and the same data may also serve as the basis for updating three- to five-year financial forecasts. Finally, analytical programs may be used to help the auditor and owner-manager compare current-year or forecast data with expected results, past history, and regional or national industry averages.

The microcomputer has had an especially significant impact on the information systems of emerging and smaller businesses and on how auditors serve these clients. Communications software can even link client and auditor systems. The use of the microcomputer as a service tool will expand further as more auditors gain experience with it. The successful auditor of the future will be creative in utilizing existing and developing computer technology to enhance efficiency and cost effectiveness and add value to both audits and the special services discussed earlier. The auditor's use of the computer is the subject of Chapter 11.

30

Auditing Health Care Institutions

OVERVIEW OF THE INDUSTRY

Health care is one of the fastest-growing industries in the United States. The system of health care delivery organizations is extensive, encompassing the following segments:

- Hospitals.
- Nursing homes.
- Health maintenance organizations and other providers of prepaid care.
- Continuing care retirement communities.
- Home health agencies.
- Medical group practices.
- Clinics.
- Other ambulatory care organizations.

Health Care Services

The different segments of the health care delivery system provide various combinations of services. The specific combination offered depends on a variety of factors that prevail in a location, including state and local licensing laws, reimbursement structures, availability of medical personnel and facilities, and the demographic details (such as age and industrial distribution) of the potential patient population. The unique aspect of the health care industry from an audit perspective is the health care delivery system—the revenue cycle. The other cycles are essentially similar to those in manufacturing or selling enterprises and thus are not emphasized in this chapter.

Services are generally described by a six-level classification. Those levels indicate, but do not strictly define, the type of organization, the level of medical treatment involved, or the severity of or prognosis for the medical situation. The levels are

Preventive—Health education and prevention programs provided by business and other organizations, such as schools and family planning clinics.

Primary—Early detection and routine treatment of health problems, such as often are provided by physicians' offices, industrial and school health units, and hospital outpatient and emergency departments.

Secondary—Acute-care services, typically provided by medical personnel, through hospitals, using elaborate diagnostic and treatment procedures.

Tertiary—Highly technical services, such as for psychiatric and chronic diseases, provided through specialty facilities and teaching hospitals.

Restorative—Rehabilitative and follow-up care, typically provided by home health agencies, nursing homes, and halfway houses.

Continuing—Long-term, chronic care, typically provided by continuing care retirement communities (CCRCs), geriatric day care centers, and nursing homes.

The types of providers of those services have increased in recent years. In addition to hospitals, there are ambulatory surgery centers, freestanding specialty clinics, a predominance of physician group practices, hospices, day care centers for the elderly, specialized home health agencies, rehabilitative care centers, nursing homes, CCRCs, and health maintenance organizations (HMOs), among others.

The growing economic magnitude of the health care system has led to increased regulatory activities focusing on health care. This increase in regulation interacts with a growing demand for more health care and for increasingly technical and complex methods of providing it. The largest and most evident regulatory activity involves reimbursement by federal and state governments; this is covered later in this chapter under ''Third-Party Reimbursement or Payment.'' Other regulatory activities are concerned in varying degrees with the availability and quality of health care. There are continued initiatives by federal and state governments to link such regulations to reimbursement in order to enforce compliance.

The presence of multiple regulatory systems influences the demand for and the nature of professional accounting services required by health care institutions. Those systems often emphasize reporting requirements, and health care institutions tend to view compliance reporting as a major use of accounting data. Auditing services in particular are affected because the regulatory agencies rely heavily on the attest activities of the health care institution's independent accountants.

Often, four or more parties may be involved in arranging health care services, including

- The patient.
- The physician.
- A health care entity that provides institutional or other services (hospital, nursing home, ambulatory surgical center, etc.).
- A third-party payor (Medicare, Medicaid, Blue Cross, commercial insurance company, HMO, etc.).

Self-pay and charity patients, who do not have access to third-party coverage for their health care service needs, also utilize such services.

The Hospital Segment

Hospitals continue to be the largest segment of the health care industry measured by both dollars of revenue and the variety of professional services delivered. Accordingly, the emphasis in this chapter is on auditing hospitals, although many of the principles and practices discussed are also applicable to other types of health care providers.

There are approximately 6500 hospitals in the United States; the number fluctuates as facilities are opened, closed, and merged—changes that occur in response to population shifts and economic and regulatory pressures. Patient care is the essential function of a hospital. Other vital roles include medical education and research. Many larger general hospitals have become total community health centers, providing a wide range of outpatient services in addition to traditional inpatient care. One characteristic of the growth of the health center concept has been the emergence of such diverse related organizations as real estate holding companies and medical management companies. These organizations are a response to changes in the reimbursement, regulatory, tax, and financial environment facing hospital management. Such nontraditional organizational structures and patterns of activity are needed to provide adequate financial resources to support the delivery of health care by hospitals. Some observers see these changes as leading to major multihospital systems, so that in the future a few major health entities may control the majority of the hospital beds in the country.

Hospitals may be classified by type of ownership and mode of operation, as follows:

- *Government*—Hospitals operated by governmental agencies and providing specialized services to specific groups and their dependents, such as the military, veterans, government employees, the indigent, and the mentally ill.
- *Investor-owned (proprietary)*—Hospitals owned by individual proprietors or groups of proprietors or by the public through stock ownership. The objective of such hospitals is to operate for profit.
- *Voluntary nonprofit*—Hospitals operated under the sponsorship of a community, religious denomination, or other nonprofit entity. This is the largest category (in numbers of hospitals), comprising two major types, teaching hospitals and community hospitals.

     Teaching hospitals—Generally university-related hospitals (government or private), their health care service activities combine education, research, and a broad range of sophisticated patient services. Large community hospitals affiliated with medical schools and offering intern and resident programs are also considered teaching hospitals.

     Community hospitals—Hospitals that traditionally are established to serve a specific area, such as a city, town, or county, and usually offer more limited services than teaching hospitals.

Hospitals may also be categorized by the type of care provided, as short-term (acute), general, long-term general, psychiatric, and other special care. The mode of a hospital's operation and the type of care occur in various combinations, such as government psychiatric or short-term pediatric.

Third-Party Reimbursement or Payment

A major difference between health care entities and commercial enterprises is that the recipient of health care services—the patient—in most cases does not pay directly for the services. Instead, payment is made by some other organization. The payment is often referred to as ''reimbursement,'' and the other organization is referred to as a ''third party.'' Typically, a hospital's most significant patient revenue sources are its reimbursement contracts with third parties. The third party may be Medicare, Medicaid, some other governmental agency, Blue Cross, an HMO, another provider of prepaid care (known as a Preferred Provider Organization, or PPO), or a commercial insurance company. In each case, there is an identifiable group of patients whose health care services are paid for, in whole or in part, by the third party. The amount of the reimbursement, as well as the eligible class of patients and other administrative matters, is covered by regulations (for governmental third parties) or contracts (for Blue Cross plans, HMOs, PPOs, etc.).

The major third parties, in dollar volume, are the governmental agencies. Of these, the federal government is the largest. Federal involvement became a major element of reimbursement beginning with the enactment of the Social Security Act of 1965, which created the Medicare and Medicaid programs to reimburse health care institutions, such as hospitals, nursing homes, and home health agencies, for their costs of providing services to the elderly and the indigent. Medicaid is a state-administered third-party reimbursement program designed to underwrite hospital costs of the medically indigent and those eligible for certain types of public welfare. Medicare is a third-party reimbursement program administered by the Health Care Financing Administration of the U.S. Department of Health and Human Services. Medicare underwrites the medical costs of persons 65 and over and some qualified persons under 65. ''Part A'' covers hospital services and ''Part B'' covers physicians' services.

State governments have long been involved in reimbursement for health care services, and their involvement has increased through participation in the Medicaid program. The continued growth of third-party expenditures for reimbursement has fostered a number of state-based cost control programs. Of increasing importance are a wide variety of controls at the state level, usually referred to by terms such as ''state rate control.'' The federal government has been quite active in encouraging or supporting such programs.

The impact of governmental and commercial third parties on hospitals focuses on when the reimbursement or payment is determined and its basis. Third-party reimbursement or payment systems are either retrospective or prospective. Retrospective refers to systems that determine the amount to be paid after the services have been performed. In prospective payment systems, the amount is determined before the services have been performed. Reimbursements or payments are usually based on a fixed amount per case, sometimes coupled with a payment for certain of the hospital's costs of services performed for eligible patients or a percentage of the amounts charged by the hospital for such services. The relevant regulations or contracts contain specific provisions designed to ensure that only certain fixed payments, costs, or charges enter into the determination of the reimbursement or payment. There are also provisions to ensure that reimbursement or payment is made only for services to eligible patients. Third-party payors can be expected to continue to refine their approach as the volume of payments increases. The difference between the hospital's established rates for services rendered and the amounts received or receivable from third-party payors is known as a contractual allowance or adjustment and is usually shown as a deduction from gross patient revenues on the statement of revenues and expenses or is otherwise disclosed.

Prior to 1983, Medicare payments to hospitals were generally based on defined allowable costs. In 1983, the federal government adopted the Prospective Payment System (PPS), which is based on a predetermined and generally fixed payment rate for each Medicare inpatient discharge. The rate of payment depends on a medical classification system, called Diagnostic Related Groups (DRGs), which takes into account patient diagnostic, clinical, and other medical factors. Under this system, discharge diagnoses are classified into major diagnostic categories, which are then subdivided into specific types of health problems. Incorporated into the system is the concept of relative value, which provides hospitals with higher payments for care associated with more difficult diagnoses, for example, heart attacks, than for simpler diagnoses, such as pneumonia.

Hospitals seeking payment under Medicare's PPS are subject to utilization and quality reviews conducted by Peer Review Organizations (PROs). The PRO determines whether hospital services paid by Medicare are reasonable, necessary, and performed in the most economical settings consistent with quality care. The PRO also validates DRG assignments and reviews length of stay and services received by inpatients as well as outliers (patients with an unusually long stay compared with the DRG average length of stay, or patients who have incurred extremely costly treatments relative to other patients in their DRG class). The PRO also determines whether physician attestation statements are signed and on file for purposes of the Medicare Anti-Fraud and Abuse Legislation. If the PRO deems the DRG to be improper or judges the admission to be unnecessary, it will change or deny payment for services rendered.

Certain allowable costs incurred by hospitals subject to PPS continue to be reimbursed by Medicare on the reasonable-cost basis, subject to certain limitations. Such allowable costs include capital costs (depreciation, interest on debt incurred for capital additions or renovations, operating leases, rents, and other capital-related costs), costs of medical education programs (intern, resident, and nursing school programs), and certain outpatient services. Some hospital inpatient units, such as psychiatric and rehabilitation, are also specifically excluded from the PPS program. However, the reimbursement for such units by Medicare continues, but is limited to target rates of allowable cost increases as provided under the Tax Equity and Fiscal Responsibility Act (TEFRA) of 1981.

Medicare reimbursement for nursing homes and home health agencies is based on allowable costs incurred, subject to certain limitations. Medicare payments for covered physicians' services are determined on the basis of the lowest of "customary charges," "prevailing charges," or "actual physician charges." Customary and prevailing charge limits are established on a periodic basis by the Medicare program. States use various methods to pay health care providers for covered services under their Medicaid programs. All state programs must be approved by the federal government.

Medicare, Medicaid, and certain state Blue Cross programs require filing of a year-end cost report in order to settle on an annual basis with hospitals, nursing homes, and home health agencies for services provided to beneficiaries of these programs. Even hospitals included in the PPS system must use cost reporting principles and cost report forms to determine reimbursement for services not covered by predetermined and fixed payment rates.

Some states have received waivers from the federal government and are permitted to determine payment rates for Medicare patients in accordance with a statewide rate-setting method different from the method developed by the Medicare program. In return, the Medicare program typically requires that total Medicare expenditures not exceed prescribed limits. If those limits are exceeded, the excess may be refundable to the federal government, depending on the conditions of the waiver. This payment would come from the hospitals. Accordingly, hospitals operating in a waiver state may have to consider Statement of Financial Accounting Standards (SFAS) No. 5 with respect to loss contingencies if payments are anticipated.

Sources of Long-Term Financing

A major source of not-for-profit hospital financing has been tax-exempt debt. This has resulted from the increase in construction costs and the decline in traditional sources of hospital capital, such as philanthropy. Approximately three-fourths of all not-for-profit hospital debt issued since the late 1970s has been tax-exempt bonds, generally revenue bonds. In many jurisdictions, not-for-profit hospitals may not directly issue such bonds, but legislation usually permits revenue bonds to be issued through financing authorities, which then make the proceeds available for use by the hospitals. The involvement of the financing authorities often gives rise to complex accounting issues.

The Term "Not for Profit"

Terms such as "not for profit" and "nonprofit" are commonly used to refer to voluntary hospitals—those that are not privately owned or operated by a governmental agency. This usage has served as partial support for those who argue that voluntary hospitals should not make a profit, that is, have net income. The merits of such arguments are not addressed in this book. An auditor of a hospital client, however, should be aware of the exempt organization provisions of the federal income tax laws and regulations, which grant exemption to specified organizations that meet a variety of tests. One of those tests, the not-for-profit test, requires that the hospital not be organized for purposes of providing net income for investor-owners. From the standpoint of financial management, however, an organization's revenues must exceed its expenses in an inflationary economy, or continued operations will in effect liquidate the organization unless it has sources of financing other than operations.

ACCOUNTING PRACTICES

Fund Accounting

Many governmental and nonprofit health care providers are subject to terms and conditions on how funds from donations, grants, and tax support may be used. Such entities have historically utilized fund accounting for record-keeping and financial reporting purposes. Under fund accounting, restricted funds are accounted for and reported on separately from funds that are available for general purposes. Fund accounting, however, is not required for health care entities' general-purpose financial statements.

Revenue from Health Care Services

Usually, the majority of a health care entity's revenue is received from third-party payors. Such third-party payors, however, typically do not pay for services based on the entity's established rates for the services. As previously noted, the difference between the established charges and the payment rates is referred to as a "contractual adjustment."

Gross patient service revenue and accounts receivable from patients are normally recorded on the accrual basis utilizing the health care entity's established rates. Income statement provisions and related allowances for contractual adjustments, charity care, and uncollectible accounts are also recorded on an accrual basis in the period in which the related services are provided. These provisions are deducted from gross patient service revenue to determine net patient service revenue. Provisions for charity care and uncollectible accounts are recorded at the health care entity's established rates. Because of the inability of most entities to differentiate between bad debts and other types of allowances, the Accounting Standards Executive Committee (AcSEC) concluded in 1989 that bad debt expense of health care entities, unlike commercial enterprises, should be presented as a deduction from gross patient service revenue instead of as operating expenses. Some health care entities, however, continue to report bad debt expense as part of operating expenses.

Third-Party Payor Considerations

As previously noted, Medicare, Medicaid, some Blue Cross plans, and certain other third-party payors retrospectively determine final amounts due to or due from health care entities for services provided for their beneficiaries. Many such third-party payors pay periodic interim amounts based on estimates until this final retrospective determination can be made. The third parties audit the cost reports, often resulting in cost disallowances and subsequent appeals, which may take many years to resolve. Final settlements may, and often do, have a significant impact on a health care entity's results of operations. Therefore, a reasonable estimate of the final settlement amount should be made in the period in which related services are provided. Auditing such estimates requires an understanding of the financial aspects of each significant third-party payment program. The auditor often needs to use the work of experts.

Pledges Receivable

Pledges of contributions, less an allowance for estimated uncollectibles, should be recorded in the financial statements. The amount of the allowance generally is not disclosed because of concern that it may adversely affect the ultimate collection of pledges. Unrestricted pledges are recorded as nonoperating revenue in the period in which they are made unless they apply to a future period; in that instance, they are recorded as deferred revenue. Restricted pledges should be reported in the appropriate restricted funds.

Capitalization of Interest

Statement of Financial Accounting Standards (SFAS) No. 62, *Capitalization of Interest Cost in Situations Involving Certain Tax-Exempt Borrowings and Certain Gifts and Grants* (Accounting Standards Section I67), amends certain provisions of SFAS No. 34, *Capitalization of Interest Cost.* Under SFAS No. 62, interest earned is required to be offset against interest costs when qualifying assets are acquired with the proceeds of tax-exempt borrowings that are externally restricted to either finance the acquisition of specified qualifying assets or service the related debt. The amount to be capitalized is the interest cost of the borrowing, less interest earned on investments acquired with the proceeds of the borrowing from the date of the borrowing until the assets are ready for use. SFAS No. 62 also excludes assets acquired with restricted gifts and grants from the interest capitalization requirement. The exclusion applies to the extent that such gifts and grants are restricted to acquisition of particular assets and to the extent that funds are available from the gifts and grants.

Accounting for Contracts with Hospital-Based Physicians

Hospitals may have a number of different arrangements with physicians for services performed in the hospital. The nature of the arrangement governs the reporting of related revenues and expenses. In general, when an employee or contractual relationship exists between the hospital and physician covering normal hospital ancillary services (e.g., radiology, pathology, cardiology, and emergency room), a charge is made by the hospital for the service, and the hospital records the revenue. If a physician's services are billed separately under the physician's name and collections are turned over to the physician, either gross or net of an administrative fee, neither the billings nor the payments to the physician should be recorded in the hospital's accounts. Under these arrangements, the hospital is merely performing an administrative service for the physician.

University-affiliated hospitals may have arrangements under which salaried staff physicians are permitted to treat private patients and retain a portion of the related billings. Such arrangements usually result from teaching or research physicians' need for continued clinical experience. Commonly, employment contracts provide that any excess billings are to be placed in a restricted fund and used for purposes to be jointly agreed on by the hospital and the physician. In such instances, the revenues should be excluded from the statement of operations and reflected as an increase in the restricted fund.

Deferred Third-Party Reimbursement and Payment

Certain reimbursable costs under retrospective third-party reimbursement contracts differ from the amounts recorded for financial accounting purposes. Some of those differences are timing (temporary) differences and should be treated similar to book/tax timing differences. Some health care organizations have established deferred reimbursement charges and credits based on the estimated reimbursement effect of existing timing differences. Examples of retrospective reimbursement timing differences include depreciation, interest during construction, and losses on advance refunding of debt. Under the Medicare PPS, deferred reimbursement charges and credits should be recorded only for timing differences related to amounts that are reimbursed based on cost, such as capital-related items.

Authoritative Guidance

The hospital industry follows the principles and concepts recommended by the AICPA *Hospital Audit Guide*, issued in 1972, and subsequent amendments, which have been issued as Statements of Position. At the time of this writing, a revision and update of the audit guide to make it applicable to all health care entities is close to being finalized. The *Chart of Accounts for Hospitals*, a publication of the American Hospital Association, is helpful in understanding the terminology and accounting followed by hospitals.

The Statements of Financial Accounting Concepts issued by the FASB have identified different sets of financial reporting objectives for business enterprises and for nonprofit[1] organizations. The major distinguishing characteristics of nonprofit organizations are noncommercial revenue sources, lack of a profit motive, and absence of defined ownership interests. The FASB stated that nongovernment, nonprofit hospitals whose operating needs are financed largely through revenues from the sale of goods and services and whose capital needs are financed largely through the proceeds of debt issues should follow the authoritative accounting standards applicable to business enterprises.

---

[1]Statement of Financial Accounting Concepts (SFAC) No. 4, *Objectives of Financial Reporting by Nonbusiness Organizations*, uses the term ''nonbusiness'' to describe what in this book is called a ''nonprofit'' organization.

The following AICPA Statements of Position (SOPs) apply to health care entities:

- SOP 78-1, *Accounting by Hospitals for Certain Marketable Equity Securities.*
- SOP 78-7, *Financial Accounting and Reporting by Hospitals Operated by a Governmental Unit.*
- SOP 81-2, *Reporting Practices Concerning Hospital-Related Organizations.*
- SOP 85-1, *Financial Reporting by Not-for-Profit Health Care Entities for Tax-Exempt Debt and Certain Funds Whose Use Is Limited.*
- SOP 87-1, *Accounting for Asserted and Unasserted Medical Malpractice Claims with Health Care Providers and Related Issues.*

Investments in Marketable Equity Securities (SOP 78-1). SOP 78-1 specifies the accounting for and reporting of investments in marketable equity securities by not-for-profit hospitals. The provisions of the SOP are the same as those of SFAS No. 12, which originally did not apply to not-for-profit organizations.

Financial Accounting and Reporting by Hospitals Operated by a Governmental Unit (SOP 78-7). This SOP provides that hospitals operated by a governmental unit should follow the requirements of the *Hospital Audit Guide*, which in effect recommends the use of enterprise fund accounting.

Reporting Practices Concerning Hospital-Related Organizations (SOP 81-2). This SOP clarifies accounting and reporting by hospital-related organizations such as auxiliaries and foundations. Accounting Research Bulletin (ARB) No. 51, *Consolidated Financial Statements*, provides guidance on whether the financial statements of such organizations should be consolidated or combined. For purposes of applying SOP 81-2, a separate organization is considered to be related to a hospital if the hospital controls the organization and one of the following three conditions exists:

- The organization has solicited funds in the hospital's name and those funds are intended for the hospital.
- The hospital has transferred resources to the organization and they are held in the hospital's name.
- The hospital has assigned certain hospital functions to the organization.

The hospital's financial statements should disclose summarized information concerning the related organization if the financial statements have not been consolidated or combined in accordance with ARB No. 51. Financial reporting for hospitals is discussed later in the chapter.

Financial Reporting by Not-for-Profit Health Care Entities for Tax-Exempt Debt and Certain Funds Whose Use Is Limited (SOP 85-1). As noted earlier, many hospitals have issued debt to raise capital. A significant amount of this debt is tax exempt. Indenture agreements often specify that the hospital must set aside funds with a trustee for the protection of bondholders and to service the debt. In addition, third-party reimbursement contracts frequently require that organizations fund depreciation (i.e., segregate liquid assets in a separate account) in order to be reimbursed for the expense.

SOP 85-1 sets forth the following major recommendations:

- Tax-exempt debt obligations of health care entities should be recorded as a liability of the general funds.
- Restricted funds should include only assets restricted by a donor or grantor. Accordingly, trustee-held bond funds and funded depreciation should be reported as assets in the general funds.
- Interest income on *borrowed funds* held by a trustee should be reported in the operating section of the statement of revenues and expenses. Investment income related to funded depreciation and other *nonborrowed funds* should be reported in the nonoperating section.

Medical Malpractice Claims (SOP 87-1). The cost of malpractice claims can be significant to health care entities, many of which are uninsured or self-insured for these claims. SOP 87-1 provides specific guidance for applying SFAS No. 5 and covers the following topics: the ultimate cost of malpractice claims, estimating the amount of the loss, reported and unreported incidents, disclosure issues, discounting, claims-made policies, retrospectively rated premiums, captive insurance companies, and trust funds. Many of these topics are discussed in Chapter 16.

Continuing Care Retirement Communities

Also referred to as residential care facilities, continuing care retirement communities (CCRCs) provide the elderly a broad spectrum of services in a controlled environment, including residential facilities, meals, recreational activities, and nursing home care. The array of CCRC financial arrangements has resulted in a diversity of accounting practices. This led to the issuance in 1989 of an exposure draft of a proposed SOP on accounting and reporting by continuing care retirement communities. The proposed SOP addresses transactions related to fees, future obligations, and acquisitions of continuing care contracts. It addresses accounting in five areas.

- Refundable fees.
- Fees repayable to residents from reoccupancy proceeds.
- Nonrefundable fees.
- Obligation to provide future services and use of facilities.
- Initial direct cost of acquiring continuing care contracts.

A summary of the issues and proposed conclusions follows.

Issues	*Conclusions*
Refundable fees	• Report as a liability. • Reclassify to deferred revenue when refund obligation is eliminated.
Fees repayable to residents from reoccupancy proceeds	• Record as deferred revenue. • Amortize over life of facility.
Nonrefundable fees	• Record as deferred revenue. • Amortize on straight-line basis over the individual resident's life expectancy.
Obligation to provide future services and use of facilities	• Accrue liability based on current residents, using net present value. • Reflect reductions only to extent of previous accruals.
Indirect cost of acquiring contracts	• Capitalize only direct cost of acquiring contracts. • Amortize on a straight-line basis over the average life of residents.

Financial Statement Presentation

Health care entities present classified balance sheets. As noted earlier, the financial statements of most not-for-profit health care entities historically have been segregated into general funds and restricted funds. Interest has been growing in single-fund (aggregated) reporting, under which separate funds would be eliminated and financial statements presented for the entity as a whole. This approach is consistent with guidance set forth in SFAC No. 6, *Elements of Financial Statements*.

For entities that follow fund accounting, the statement of changes in fund balances is a basic hospital financial statement. Its format may be "standard," which permits easy comparison with the prior year, or "columnar," which facilitates an understanding of the interfund relationships of certain transactions.

One acceptable format for a hospital's statement of revenues and expenses includes the following major categories:

- Patient service revenue, which is stated at gross (customary) charges before deducting contractual or other allowances and may be classified as to source (inpatient or outpatient, daily hospital service or ancillary) or shown in total.
- Deductions from revenues, including reductions in gross patient service revenue for free care, courtesy allowances, bad debts, and third-party contractual adjustments. (Some providers do not show gross patient

service revenues and deductions on their statement of revenues and expenses but rather start the statement with net patient service revenues.)

- Other operating revenue from nonpatient-care services to patients and from sales to people other than patients and other activities, such as cafeteria operations, sales of supplies, sales of scrap, and parking lot revenue.

- Total operating revenue, which consists of patient service revenue, net of deductions, plus other operating revenue. Total operating revenue shows the amount the hospital generates through services that is available to cover expenses.

- Operating expenses, which may be reported by major functional classification (e.g., nursing, administration) or by natural classification (e.g., salaries, supplies). Certain expenses, such as rent expense, depreciation, and interest, must be reported separately on the statement of revenues and expenses or in the notes to the financial statements. Expenses incurred in fund-raising activities should be disclosed separately in the financial statements.

- Nonoperating revenues are not directly related to patient care or sales of related goods and services. Nonoperating revenues are reported after net income or loss from hospital operations. This presentation segregates the results of recurring hospital operations from nonoperating income, much of which is of a nonrecurring nature. Significant categories of nonoperating revenues include unrestricted contributions and investment income. Other, less-significant categories, such as income from rental properties, are generally reported net of related expenses.

An alternative to the above grouping of revenues, which is appropriate for all health care entities, breaks down revenue as follows:

1. Revenue from providing health care services to patients or residents.
2. Revenue from agreeing to provide or arrange for such services.
3. Other revenue.

Under this approach, revenue from providing health care services to patients or residents is typically shown net of deductions. Revenue from agreeing to provide or arrange for health care services under prepaid arrangements with HMOs and PPOs is labeled "premiums earned." For revenue from other sources, revenue resulting from activities that are major and central to ongoing operations ("operating") is distinguished from revenue resulting from peripheral or incidental activities ("nonoperating"). Thus, similar revenue could be classified differently by different health care entities, depending on how such revenue was generated.

Cash Flow Reporting.   Not-for-profit entities were excluded from the requirements of SFAS No. 95, *Statement of Cash Flows* (Accounting Standards Section C25), because at the time of its issuance the AICPA was conducting a research project on not-for-profit financial statement display issues. However, many health care entities follow SFAS No. 95, and the AICPA has since recommended to the FASB that the provisions of SFAS No. 95 be applied to all health care entities, not only those operating on a for-profit basis.

RISK ASSESSMENT AND AUDIT STRATEGY

Inherent Risk

Health care entities operate in a competitive, rapidly changing industry, which is characterized by the following inherent risk conditions:

- Governmental budgetary constraints, which affect a health care entity's Medicare and Medicaid revenues, as well as reduced payments from all third-party payors.
- Stiff competition for physicians and patients, particularly in metropolitan areas where there are numerous health care entities with overlapping and/or common service areas.
- Increased salaries of nurses and other health care professionals.
- Reduced cash flow, which could affect the ability to meet debt service payments and debt covenants.
- Declining HMO payments to hospitals.
- Increased board pressure on management to improve financial condition and operating results.
- Shortages of skilled personnel, particularly nurses and technicians.
- Limited availability and high cost of adequate insurance coverage, particularly medical malpractice coverage.

Inherent risk considerations in the health care industry revolve largely around the third-party reimbursement structure. A key concern is billing procedures, which are complicated by the very significant involvement of third parties, few of which pay the hospital's gross charges. The auditor should be particularly concerned about the accuracy of cost reports and allocations and of the statistics on which they are based. For prospective payment systems, the greatest risk is the denial of reimbursement by a third party because of unnecessary utilization of services, referred to as "utilization denial." The auditor should consider whether the hospital has adequate utilization review procedures to monitor denials. Since testing medical records to determine the medical necessity of services performed is beyond the technical expertise of auditors, past history of denials may provide guidance in determining the extent of risk in this area.

Audit Strategy

In developing an audit strategy for a hospital engagement, the auditor must have a thorough understanding of the hospital's patient mix, which is influenced by the geographical location of the hospital, the range of services it provides, and state regulations. In particular, the audit strategy will vary depending on whether services are rendered on a charge-paying or cost-reimbursement basis. If most of the hospital's services will be paid on a cost-reimbursement basis, the propriety of costs incurred is a primary audit concern. The accuracy of expense classifications and of statistics used to allocate indirect costs to service departments is also significant. In addition, the accuracy of departmental revenue classification is important in the cost apportionment process. If payment is made either directly by the patient or by third parties based on actual charges billed, auditing statistical data and departmental cost classification is deemphasized since that data does not affect revenue. In prospective payment systems like the Medicare DRG system, the auditor must be concerned with the procedures used to abstract patients' medical records and to assign each case to the proper DRG, since that assignment determines the revenue to be received.

Control structure policies and procedures in the patient revenue cycle are often effective, and the auditor may, depending on efficiency considerations, plan to perform tests of controls in this area. In an effort to control costs and comply with various regulatory requirements, hospitals often have sophisticated expense budgeting systems. Budgetary reviews and analyses of expenses reflected in the monthly financial statements are often performed by hospital management; such procedures help ensure that underlying expense data has been processed correctly. In addition, management reviews of the third-party reimbursement structure and of cost reports are often performed.

In situations where the entity has a sizable accounting staff, a sufficient volume of transactions, and a well-controlled EDP department, the auditor may determine that it would be efficient to perform tests of controls as a basis for reducing substantive tests. On the other hand, tests of controls may not be efficient for hospitals that typically have small accounting staffs and a general absence of segregation of duties and supervision.

Deadlines for filing third-party cost reports may make performance of substantive procedures before year-end particularly appropriate and efficient for accounts receivable, the allowance for uncollectible accounts, and fixed assets. See the discussion in Chapter 9 on timing of substantive tests.

In planning a hospital audit, it is important to have an understanding of the hospital's current financial position and financial trends. Analyzing financial ratios may lead to a fuller understanding of the hospital's operations and problems than could be obtained from reviewing raw data. For example, the knowledge that a hospital has 75 days of its revenue tied up in uncollected accounts receivable may be more meaningful and cause a different level of concern than the knowledge that the accounts receivable balance is $4 million.

It is also helpful to compare the hospital's operations and financial position with those of other institutions. A variance from industry averages could point to problems. In making comparisons with industry data, the auditor must ensure that the sources and compilation of data are consistent and relevant; for example, industry statistics used should be for hospitals of similar size (measured by number of beds) and geographical location. Industry statistics are published quarterly in *Healthcare Financial Management* or annually in the Healthcare Financial Management Association's *Financial Analysis Service*. Information may also be compiled on a statewide basis by regulatory bodies, nonprofit agencies, or financial information services.

Materiality

Materiality guidelines for hospital audits should be based on the specific circumstances of each hospital. For not-for-profit hospitals, the excess of revenues over expenses may be less important as a basis for materiality judgments, because nonprofit hospitals often have access to alternative capital sources (e.g., contributions and grants) and do not provide a return to investors. Parameters frequently used by the auditor in evaluating materiality in hospital financial statements include current ratios, debt–equity ratios, and debt coverage ratios; restricted or unrestricted fund balances; and specific line items.

Single Audit Act and Related Audit Considerations

Health care entities that receive financial assistance from a governmental agency may be required to have their financial statements audited in accordance with the provisions of the Single Audit Act of 1984 and OMB Circular A-128, "Audits of State and Local Governments," or A-110, "Uniform Requirements for Grants to Universities, Hospitals, and Other Non-Profit Organizations." Financial assistance may take the form of grants, contracts, loans, loan guarantees, property, cooperative agreements, subsidies, and insurance or direct appropriation. SAS No. 63, *Compliance Auditing Applicable to Governmental Entities and Other Recipients of Governmental Financial Assistance*, provides guidance for audits of certain entities that receive governmental financial assistance and explains the relationship between those requirements and the requirements of the *Government Auditing Standards*, issued by the U.S. General Accounting Office. Additional guidance on audits in accordance with the Single Audit Act of 1984 is provided in the AICPA audit and accounting guide, *Audits of State and Local Governmental Units*. All of the above-mentioned sources are discussed in Chapter 25 of this book.

TYPICAL TRANSACTIONS, CONTROL STRUCTURE POLICIES AND PROCEDURES, AND AUDIT TESTS

Patient Revenue Cycle

The major source of revenues in a hospital is services provided to patients. Revenue is recorded, at the hospital's established rates, on the accrual basis at the time services are performed. Patient service revenues are recorded separately by source (such as laboratory revenue) and by patient type (such as inpatient or outpatient). Additionally, the source of payment for each patient is essential information that should be captured by the accounting system. Hospitals generally bill inpatients after completion of a patient's stay in the hospital.

The actual amount received by the hospital may vary depending on contractual arrangements between the hospital and the patient or a third-party payor. Contracts with third-party payors may or may not provide for reimbursement that coincides with a hospital's standard uniform rate structure. Instead, amounts due may be based on the hospital's costs, volume, intensity of service, and so forth. The various third-party payors utilize different payment mechanisms. Some arrangements with third parties provide hospitals with interim cash flow until final reimbursement can be calculated. Services rendered to private-paying patients are billed at the established rates except that courtesy allowances may be granted to doctors, employees, or members of religious orders, and charity allowances may be granted as determined by patient needs and hospital policy.

To understand the hospital's patient revenue cycle, the auditor should become familiar with the various functions and departments that may serve patients and should also understand how those functions and departments relate to accounting for patient revenue. Auditing a hospital's patient revenue cycle is discussed in the context of the following typical functions and departments involved in serving patients.

Admitting Function.   A patient is admitted to the hospital either in an emergency situation or based on a licensed physician's recommendation. The first step in the admitting function is acquiring credit and insurance information about the patient. The auditor should review the procedures for gathering and recording this information to gain an understanding of the patient classification system. Accurate patient classification is essential for determining the accuracy of patient accounts receivable. Frequently a patient's classification is redetermined after the patient has been admitted; the hospital should have control procedures to ensure that classification changes are monitored.

The next step in the admitting function is initiating accounting documents. The primary document that begins the revenue accounting cycle is generally the admissions form. The auditor needs evidence of the completeness and accuracy of admissions forms; this is generally obtained by comparing them with other records produced by the accounting system.

Finally, the admitting function is responsible for the location, by bed, of all patients in the hospital. The rate charged is based on the patient's location, which encompasses both accommodations and intensity of care. For example, the rate for a private room is higher than that for a semiprivate room, and intensive care is more costly than routine care. The auditor is concerned about the accuracy of revenue based on patient location; relevant audit evidence can be obtained by comparing daily census reports with patients' accounting records.

Daily Hospital Service Charges.   Daily hospital charges for room, board, and general nursing care provided to patients are recorded as revenue on a per diem basis. Daily hospital service departments typically include routine or general care, intensive care, coronary care, and nursery. Routine care is further categorized by room accommodations, such as private or semiprivate. Since most third-party contracts reimburse hospitals for daily hospital services based on patient-day statistics, the auditor should test those statistics for completeness and accuracy. If the hospital has effective control procedures for accumulating the statistics, the auditor may test those procedures; alternatively, the auditor may perform substantive tests of the statistics.

Ancillary Service Charges.   Diagnostic or therapeutic services other than room, board, and general nursing care are referred to as ancillary services and include use of operating rooms, recovery rooms, anesthesiology, and nuclear medicine facilities. Unlike daily hospital service charges, ancillary charges are generated for each instance of service provided instead of on a per diem basis. Testing the distribution of ancillary revenues to the appropriate departments is an important auditing procedure, since many third-party payors reimburse hospitals for ancillary services based on the relationship of the ancillary department revenues applicable to third-party payors to total ancillary department revenues applied to the ancillary department's reimbursable operating costs.

Outpatient Service Charges.   Outpatient services may include emergency room treatment; laboratory, radiology, or other testing procedures; or clinic services. Other terms for some of these admissions are short stay and same-day surgery.

Outpatient records may be processed by the admitting function from the emergency room, clinic, or other location in the hospital; the procedures are similar to those for inpatients. An assigned admission number generally identifies the patient as an outpatient or inpatient. Ancillary services are provided to outpatients on the same charge basis as is used for inpatients. Outpatient service charges are recorded separately because different third-party reimbursement arrangements may apply to inpatients and outpatients. Since the two revenue sources are similar, it is appropriate for the auditor to test only those procedures unique to the outpatient revenue cycle in connection with the testing of inpatient revenues.

A patient may be admitted for outpatient services but may remain in the hospital as an inpatient. In those instances, the revenue generated from the outpatient services is reclassified as inpatient revenue.

Discharge and Billing Functions.   Notification that a patient is leaving the hospital results in discontinuance of the daily hospital service charge. During the patient's stay, routine and ancillary charges are recorded in the individual's subsidiary ledger account as part of "in-house accounts receivable." After discharge, this account is transferred to the "suspense" file, sometimes referred to as a "discharged but not billed" file. The patient's account remains there for several days to ensure that all charges for services are recorded properly in the account.

After the suspense period, billings are prepared for all hospital services, and the account is transferred to the "billed" accounts receivable file. In many instances, the hospital calculates and records the third-party contractual allowance at this time. Credit and collection procedures are then applied to the billed accounts receivable. To aid in these efforts and to provide a basis for assessing the allowance for uncollectible accounts, the billed accounts receivable file is classified by payor category (e.g., Medicare, Blue Cross, or private-paying), since collection procedures differ by payor. Additionally, aging analyses by payor classification are needed to evaluate the probability of collection for each category.

Substantive Tests of Accounts Receivable.   Hospital receivables have several characteristics not normally found in receivables of commercial organizations. First, full-rate charges to patients for services received may be settled for an amount less than the full rate because of contractual arrangements with third-party payors or courtesy, charity, or other policy discounts. Since revenue is initially recorded at the hospital's standard gross charges, patient accounts must be adjusted to their net realizable value through a contractual allowance. Typically, inpatient accounts are adjusted at the billing date, although some hospitals may adjust at time of discharge or remittance. Outpatient accounts are typically adjusted on remittance. The difference between the gross charges and the amount of interim reimbursement from the third party is the contractual allowance. The hospital may also maintain a separate cost report settlement account to establish estimates of the difference between the interim reimbursement and final cost settlement.

Payment may be made by a single third-party payor or a combination of payors (e.g., commercial insurance, Medicare, Medicaid, workers' compensation, and the patient). Since a patient may have more than one insurer, it is possible for duplicate payments to be made on the patient's account. This results in credit balances in accounts receivable, which are characteristic of hospitals with aggressive billing procedures. The auditor should review the components of these credit balances and, if they are significant, consider reclassifying them. Since the hospital must refund duplicate payments, the auditor should determine that refund checks are for authorized credit balances and that they are payable to the proper payee.

In most hospitals, accounts receivable are classified according to the patient's billing status, generally using the following categories:

- Inpatient
  - Admitted but not discharged (commonly referred to as "in-house patients").
  - Discharged but not billed (accounts awaiting final or "late" charges, or unbilled as a result of a backlog in billing procedures—which might indicate a control structure deficiency).
  - Discharged and billed.
- Outpatient
  - Unbilled.
  - Billed.

These categories of inpatients and outpatients may be expanded further to indicate private-paying status or third-party responsibility for payment.

The accuracy and existence of accounts receivable are tested predominantly by reviewing subsequent cash receipts. The completeness and accuracy of admitted-but-not-discharged patient receivables can be tested by comparing accounts with the daily census report. Confirming balances with patients may be difficult, and the auditor should consider confirming other items, such as number of days spent in the hospital, types of insurance coverage, or, at least, the policy number and insurance company. This information confirms that the patient was in the hospital.

Third-Party Payors

Almost every hospital receives reimbursement under some type of third-party arrangement. Although programs vary from state to state and plan to plan, almost all third-party programs require an annual report to determine the final settlement for the accounting period. The final settlement, less amounts paid by the program during the period, is the settlement due to or from the third-party program. This annual third-party report is referred to as the statement of reimbursable cost, or the cost report. The auditor's review of the cost report for completeness and accuracy is an important procedure in determining that the settlement is proper and that it has been appropriately reflected in the financial statements. The balance sheet and income statement accounts usually affected by this report include third-party settlements receivable or payable, contractual allowances, and the reserve for contractual allowances.

The auditor should determine the mix of third-party payors and should consider the control procedures for billing in each classification. Audit tests tailored to the specific situation should be performed to substantiate the contractual allowances for each third-party payor. In addition, the auditor should ascertain that appropriate allowances have been deducted from patient accounts receivable for third-party payments that will be less than the full charge reflected in accounts receivable. Patient accounts billed to third parties may be disallowed in whole or in part and rebilled to patients. Accordingly, the auditor should evaluate the hospital's past experience with receivables disallowed by third parties to determine that probable losses have been adequately provided for. If significant amounts of patient accounts receivable are in cost-reimbursement payor classifications, the auditor should consider whether substantive tests of receivables would be the most efficient way of obtaining evidence of the realizable value of accounts receivable at year-end. The auditor should be alert to delays in these settlements and should take them into consideration in making his or her evaluation.

Although the Medicare DRG system does not use cost reporting for rate determination purposes, cost reports are still necessary to determine the reimbursement for pass-through costs (i.e., costs excluded from the DRG rates), outpatient services, and excluded units. It is necessary for the auditor to test the hospital's summarization of capital costs to determine the amounts due from Medicare for such costs.

Medicare requires hospitals to report annual statistical and financial data concerning costs incurred. The data required for the Medicare cost report is as follows:

- Expenses by cost center as recorded in the hospital's general ledger, which are then adjusted and reclassified to exclude nonallowable costs (the A Schedules).
- Overhead costs of nonrevenue-producing departments, allocated to revenue-producing departments (the B Schedules).
- The full cost of each revenue-producing department, apportioned between the relevant payor and all other payors based on utilization of days or charges for that department (the C Schedules).
- A summary and comparison of Medicare costs with interim payments received or receivable by the hospital.

As a result of the timing of the year-end cost report filing and of audits by Medicare, one or more prior-year cost reports may be unsettled at any point in time.

As noted earlier, various third-party reimbursements are determined using numerous statistics, including patient-days. Substantive tests of statistics typically include reviews of the method of their accumulation, adequacy of supporting documentation, adherence to prescribed regulations, comparability with prior years, and reasonableness.

Hospitals generally maintain logs of billings to and remittances from third-party payors, with details of patient-days, departmental revenues, coinsurance, deductibles, and other data. The auditor should test the accuracy of the logs because the final settlement will be based on information contained in them. Normally patient data recorded in the logs is tested by comparison with remittance advices and billing forms.

Computer software packages are useful in assisting the auditor in this area. The client may use software packages to prepare the cost report, or the auditor may use them to test the client's cost report. A software package would also be useful in comparing the current-year cost report with the prior-year report for the same provider and identifying items with significant changes.

Nonpatient Revenues

Revenues from sources other than patient charges consist of interest on invested funds, unrestricted gifts and grants, transfers from restricted funds, and expenditures of restricted fund assets for the benefit of unrestricted (general) funds. Auditing procedures for material nonpatient revenues should include, but not be limited to

- Confirming investment activity with banks or an external trustee.
- Reviewing data and documents underlying gifts, grants, and bequests, such as board minutes, correspondence, and acknowledgment receipts.

- Reviewing research or grant documentation.
- Confirming pledges and evaluating their collectibility.

Buying Cycle

Payroll.   Hospital employees may be classified as professional and nonprofessional. Examples of professional staff are registered nurses and licensed vocational nurses. Nonprofessional employees include orderlies, housekeeping and maintenance personnel, kitchen staff, and administrative personnel. Control over both professional and nonprofessional time is critical since salaries constitute a significant portion of hospital costs.

Generally, the same payroll auditing procedures used in other organizations of comparable size also apply to hospitals. Testing of total payroll costs should cover classification of costs by department, which is important for purposes of reimbursement and also for cost reporting. Misclassification of a reimbursable cost to a nonreimbursable cost center could result in failure to receive reimbursement for that cost. The auditor typically reviews the appropriateness of the account distribution and traces amounts to the payroll register or distribution summaries. Those registers or summaries are tested for mathematical accuracy and then agreed to the appropriate general ledger accounts.

Other Expenses.   Hospital expenses are typically classified by departmental function (such as nursing services and laboratory services). Proper classification of costs by department is important for financial statement purposes as well as cost reporting and reimbursement. The auditor should test the propriety of the general ledger account distribution by reference to purchasing documentation.

Inventories

While supplies and drugs are significant expenses to hospitals, usually inventory amounts for supplies and drugs are insignificant to the balance sheet. Therefore, substantive procedures for inventory, for both income statement and balance sheet accounts, are often limited to fluctuation analysis, such as gross profit analysis, and inquiry.

If the auditor determines that it is necessary to observe the inventory-taking, the procedures are generally no different from those followed for a commercial company. The auditor should make adequate arrangements prior to the date of the inventory to facilitate an accurate count. It is necessary to ensure that all inventory is counted; this may take careful planning because items usually are not tagged and supplies may be located in several different areas of the hospital.

Pharmacy inventories are often taken by an independent service, which issues a report on the results of the physical count. The auditor generally reviews the qualifications of the independent service team, discusses procedures utilized with the team leader, and makes independent test counts, as necessary.

Fixed Assets

Auditing procedures for a hospital's property, plant, and equipment are typically the same as those of a commercial enterprise and are discussed in Chapter 18. Some hospital departments own and use expensive, highly specialized equipment, such as nuclear magnetic resonance devices. Department heads should, of course, be closely involved in capital budgeting and purchasing decisions, but that involvement should not extend to overriding control procedures that have been instituted for purchases generally.

Tests of Restricted Funds

For entities that use fund accounting, the audit of restricted funds should include reviews of

- The instruments applicable to the assets, to ensure compliance with their restricted purpose.
- Transfers to unrestricted (general) funds, to ensure that expenditures were made for their intended purpose.
- Investment activity, including independent confirmation of investments held by trustees, to ensure the segregation of funds.
- Solicitation and collection procedures, to ensure adequate control over cash receipts.

Analytical Procedures

Because of the numerous statistics maintained by hospitals for measuring patient care activities (patient-days, laboratory tests, pharmacy requisitions, X-ray tests, etc.) and because hospitals usually record revenues and expenses on a departmental basis, analytical procedures are easy to construct for testing revenues and expenses. For example, routine service revenues can be tested by use of patient-day statistics and applicable room rates. Departmental expenses usually relate to departmental revenue. Gross margins on pharmacy and supply items are fairly constant, because consistent markup percentages are normally used.

Malpractice Insurance

Increased patient volume, more-complex treatment methods, and a consumer-oriented legal climate have combined to increase malpractice cases against hospitals. As insurance costs continue to rise, many hospitals have changed their insurance practices and are seeking other ways of covering and limiting their exposure to litigation. Insurance coverages vary from complete self-insurance to insurance with large deductibles. Insurance coverage may be on a claims-made basis or on an occurrence basis. Insurance premiums may be retrospectively rated. Entities may establish trust funds to cover a portion of their self-insurance program or may place their insurance coverage with a captive insurance company. Each of these variations in insurance coverage requires a different accounting treatment and is explained in SOP 87-1. As a basis for designing substantive tests and ensuring compliance with SOP 87-1, the auditor needs to understand the entity's insurance program and its procedures for identifying and accruing losses.

For hospitals with a self-insurance or modified self-insurance program, the auditor should perform detailed reviews of "incident" reports. ("Incident" for this purpose is defined as "an event that could expose the hospital to liability.") The hospital should have established procedures for reporting incidents; those procedures may include preparing a narrative report of all incidents, interviewing hospital staff, obtaining evaluations of independent insurance adjusters, and, if appropriate, referring to legal counsel.

The auditor should review case-by-case reports of the status and estimates of potential liability for asserted and unasserted claims and obtain and review the opinions of independent consultants. In addition, the auditor should inquire into the hospital's reporting and investigation procedures for identifying and estimating potential liability. Confirmation requests should be sent to the hospital's incident investigator and the insurance adjusters and investigators as well as to its attorneys. Such incidents should also be covered in management's representation letter.

31

Auditing High Technology Companies

OVERVIEW OF HIGH TECHNOLOGY COMPANIES

One of the fastest growing segments of American industry today is high technology, commonly defined to include computers and related equipment and software, electronics and components (including semiconductors), computer-assisted design/manufacturing/engineering/software engineering (CAD/CAM/CAE/CASE), telecommunications, instrumentation, robotics, biotechnology, medical technology, and other applied sciences. The high technology industry deals essentially with scientific theories and applications and reflects the use of technology to create products and applications that in many instances are entirely new and significantly enhance productivity. Those new products and applications are characterized by

- Continuing dependence on investments in research and development (R&D) to either develop new products or maintain market advantages.
- Short product life cycles. Getting the right product to market faster requires both controlling the R&D effort and an effective marketing organization to track customer needs.
- High gross margins. The pricing structure is not based on manufacturing costs. The expense of developing products and maintaining them in the field can outweigh the cost of production.
- Decreasing percentage of direct labor costs. Controlling material and overhead, including indirect labor, costs is key, as is having the proper cost accounting systems to identify cost drivers for corrective actions and product profitability for business decisions.
- High product servicing costs and an increasing proportion of revenues derived from service. The unique nature of the products as well as customer performance requirements create ongoing servicing needs with commensurate costs.
- Early entry into global markets. The product uniqueness, worldwide applicability, and need to preempt competitor actions create immediate opportunities for marketing abroad.

High technology companies often are characterized by rapid growth. Accordingly, auditors should focus on the risks that result from a growth environment. Management can reduce those risks to some degree by consulting the auditor before making major decisions, particularly with respect to installing or modifying accounting and other information systems and determining accounting policies. Auditors should look to the experiences of larger companies during their formative years for indications of the kinds of problems and issues likely to confront smaller, emerging high technology companies. (Also see Chapter 29.)

With the exception of computer software and service companies and R&D–oriented entities, high technology companies have many of the characteristics of manufacturing enterprises, and accordingly many of the audit issues discussed in Part 3 of this book apply to them. This chapter highlights the unique aspects of the high technology environment, including software and research companies, and the auditing implications of that environment.

RISK ASSESSMENT AND RELATED AUDIT CONSIDERATIONS

As noted in Chapter 6, the risk that misstatements will occur and remain undetected by the client has two elements—control risk and inherent risk. The preceding paragraphs suggest that for many high technology clients, control risk may be relatively high. Managers of such companies often are entrepreneurial and not averse to accepting risk. Accordingly, in some instances, the accounting system and related control procedures may receive less attention than the R&D and sales functions.

The speed of technological change in the industry tends to increase inherent risk; for example, rapid obsolescence is not uncommon.

Generally, high technology companies continue to receive much of their financing from venture capitalists, who expect both the security of a preferred position and the potential rewards of equity financing. To attract venture capital, companies must be prepared to negotiate such features in their financing arrangements as instruments that are convertible into stock, provisions for additional payments based on earnings performance, preferred stockholder rights, antidilution provisions, and involvement in the company's board of directors. In addition, a high technology company's initial financing is usually from private sources, so the auditor is one of few people outside the company to review the related documentation. Therefore, auditors should review the provisions of financing agreements carefully and understand them thoroughly.

Inherent risk may be high for two other, related reasons: the unique uncertainties associated with many of the transactions typically entered into by high technology companies and the difficult accounting issues created by both those uncertainties and the varied forms of those transactions, particularly when compared with transactions of established manufacturing enterprises. This chapter discusses those uncertainties and accounting issues and suggests how auditors can respond to them to reduce audit detection risk.

Revenue Recognition

High technology products are innovative, and frequently customers' sophistication and expectations about them are uneven. Moreover, product performance is often unproven, the installation process is lengthy and often subject to customer approval, or there is a prolonged period when customers may be entitled for various reasons to cancel a sales agreement and return the product. For all those reasons, inherent risk associated with revenues and receivables is likely to exist. Decisions about the appropriate time of revenue recognition may be particularly sensitive, necessitating careful evaluation by the auditor.

If the level of uncertainty surrounding customer acceptance of a product, product performance, collectibility of receivables, and the amount of returns or warranty claims is low or predictable, revenue is often recognized on shipment, since in those instances the earning process is substantially complete at that time. If, on the other hand, product performance and evaluation are uncertain, customer acceptance (i.e., the time at which the product can no longer be returned) is the preferred point of revenue recognition. Using customer acceptance as the basis for revenue recognition, however, makes it difficult for many companies to predict revenue, since recognition then depends on customers' actions as well as on the completion of the earning process as customarily understood. Whatever point is selected for revenue recognition, the auditor should understand thoroughly the contractual relationships that have been entered into, monitor the entity's experience with the transactions, be sensitive to fluctuations in receivables, monitor fluctuations in warranty expense, and watch for unusual levels of credits and returns. In situations where those procedures do not provide the auditor with sufficient evidence as to customer acceptance, he or she should consider using the positive method of confirming receivables. Statement of Financial Accounting Standards (SFAS) No. 48, *Revenue Recognition When Right of Return Exists* (Accounting Standards Section R75), as well as Chapter 12 of this book should be consulted. Revenue recognition issues for software sales are discussed later in this chapter.

The untried and often experimental nature of many high technology products has also led to innovative selling arrangements, which further complicate revenue recognition. Those arrangements include products held by customers on a trial basis, products shipped on consignment, contingent sales, and rentals with purchase options. In evaluating the accounting for all these types of transactions, the auditor should review contract documentation, focusing on identifying nonstandard clauses that alter the economic substance of otherwise standard transactions and on the substance of the transactions, which may differ from their form.

As part of understanding the revenue cycle, the auditor should be aware of the unique channels of distribution that often exist with customers of high technology companies. For example, many high technology companies deal with original equipment manufacturers (OEMs) or value-added resellers (VARs), which use hardware purchased from the high technology company in conjunction with other hardware and/or OEM-provided computer or proprietary software and resell the combined products to end users. Unique sales arrangements are often negotiated with these resellers, involving such terms as volume discounts, rebate arrangements, rights of return, and pay-on-reorder arrangements. The auditor should understand those provisions and evaluate the related accounting judgments. Also, in auditing OEM and value-added reseller receivables, the auditor should be aware that these companies may be undercapitalized and susceptible to severe cyclical swings, either of which might affect rates of equipment returns or the allowance for uncollectible accounts.

Lower-priced hardware is frequently sold through distributors, again often involving unique sales arrangements. In addition to volume discounts or rebates similar to those in OEM sales, distributors of products may be protected against price declines by manufacturer guarantees to match the lowest price available (price protection). Manufacturers also generally allow returns, to protect distributors against inventory imbalances (stock rotation). Initial sales of products to distributors are often significant; however, the auditor should be aware that in some circumstances reorders may be a better indication of user demand than shipments, since initial orders may be subject to higher levels of returns if user demand does not materialize.

Transferring product rights by licensing or royalty agreements is common among high technology companies. Sometimes it is difficult to ensure that all products or processes involving licensing or royalty payments have been identified and properly controlled. Thus it is important for the auditor to understand the products and related services being sold.

The uncertainties associated with revenue recognition have implications for accounts receivable. The collectibility of receivables is affected by customer perception of product performance and by support and maintenance expectations. The auditor should evaluate problems identified for their potential applicability to all similar receivables.

Field-Service Operations

Many high technology manufacturers have field-service operations that support the installed equipment base. Revenues from field-service operations may be based on contracts or individual service calls, depending on the underlying service or maintenance agreement with the customer. The auditor should be alert to service and maintenance costs that should not be billed to customers because they were covered by warranty agreements.

Field-service operations tend to be geographically dispersed and characterized by a large volume of low-dollar-value transactions. The geographical dispersion often requires large amounts of test equipment and parts inventories at many locations. Accordingly, controlling those operations requires effective procedures and management systems, which may not be fully developed. Internal audit participation in this area is often critical to facilitate adequate audit coverage.

Field-service inventory valuation practices vary. Because it is necessary to support the product base for its entire life cycle, valuation methods differ. Many companies carry field-service inventories as they would any other type of inventory, that is, at historical cost with provisions for obsolescence and inventory shrinkage. Other companies value field-service inventories as if they were depreciable assets. The auditor must evaluate these methods to ensure that asset valuation and cost allocation are appropriate.

Components are frequently removed from customer equipment and returned to inventory to be refurbished. The carrying value of returns should be assessed by identifying the cost to refurbish the components; they should be recorded at the lesser of replacement cost less cost to refurbish, or net realizable value. Other inventory valuation problems include identifying historical costs for parts manufactured in previous years but still in inventory, and physically counting small inventory quantities in many locations.

Another significant auditing problem in field-service operations involves consigned inventory. The auditor should be alert to documentation, control structure policies and procedures, valuation, and balance sheet classification relating to consigned inventories.

Frequently, warranty expense is incurred through field-service operations; costs generally represent installation expenses (which for field-service operations are not differentiated from maintenance expenses) and expenses for service and maintenance during the warranty period. The warranty liability should be accrued on the basis of expected warranty expenses.

Computer Software Sales

Many high technology companies sell software, generally by means of a license for its use in perpetuity or for a fixed term. The revenue process may vary substantially because software may be standard or customized, or may necessitate significant installation support. In addition, customer acceptance may be uncertain, and the selling agreement may provide for extended payment terms, trial periods, or liberal termination features.

The principal events in the software earning process include signing a licensing agreement, delivering and installing the product, and the customer's acceptance of the product. Shipment may or may not be significant to the earning process. For example, when a vendor licenses off-the-shelf deliverable software to an end user and has no other obligations, and collectibility is reasonably assured, revenue should be recognized at shipment. When the vendor has other obligations that are not separable from the software license and are to be performed after delivery, not all revenue should be recognized on delivery. If obligations include significant vendor performance in addition to delivery of a license to a software product, contract accounting is appropriate.

Because of all the uncertainties described above, the auditor should ensure that revenue recognition occurs only after the right to use has been granted, the customer has accepted the software and incurred an obligation to pay, and the seller's performance is substantially complete. In 1987, the AICPA Accounting Standards Executive Committee forwarded an issues paper to the Financial Accounting Standards Board (FASB) setting forth alternative views on revenue recognition for software sales in different circumstances. The FASB discussed the issues paper in 1988 and encouraged the AICPA to issue it in the form of a Statement of Position (SOP). At the time of this writing, the AICPA is preparing a draft SOP that is expected to incorporate most of the views expressed in the issues paper.

Postdelivery customer support services may be priced separately or included in the software product price. Service revenues should be separately identified and recognized ratably in relation to the performance of services under the contract. Similarly, revenues from maintenance contracts that provide for updating or otherwise enhancing software should be recognized over the term of the contract. Recognition of postdelivery customer support services was also included in the AICPA issues paper mentioned above.

SFAS No. 86, *Accounting for the Costs of Computer Software to Be Sold, Leased, or Otherwise Marketed* (Accounting Standards Section Co2), outlines accounting for the costs of internally developed and purchased software. The costs of R&D–

related activities, which must be expensed in the period incurred, are differentiated from the costs of production activities, which are capitalized. The difference between these two activities is based on the concept of "technological feasibility." To qualify for capitalization, costs must meet the specified requirements for technological feasibility. Software rights purchased or leased for use in the manufacture of products for resale must also meet the requirements for technological feasibility to be capitalized.

The auditor must make a judgment regarding technological feasibility; to do this, he or she reviews the product plan and software development methodologies. The auditor must ensure that software is not carried in excess of net realizable value, and that revenue forecasts, on which amortization expense is based, are reasonably constructed, adequately documented, and realistic in view of the company's established channels of distribution and financial resources.

Bioscience and Technology

Bioscience and technology involve applying biological science and engineering in a variety of industries, including pharmaceuticals, health care, and agriculture. Bioscience and technology companies have the same attributes as other high technology companies, but are particularly characterized by operating losses and the intensity of the R&D effort. They often have corporate sponsorship and partnership arrangements, which typically give larger companies the right to manufacture and sell products in exchange for R&D funding and royalty payments.

Bioscience and technology revenues are derived from contractual development arrangements, royalty agreements, or product sales. Appropriate revenue recognition depends on the company's state of development. Therefore, the auditor needs to understand the details of research and production contracts, assess the achievement of project milestones, and understand related product licensing and royalty arrangements. Revenue recognition methods should be reevaluated as the company moves out of the prototype and initial production phases into commercial production.

Classification of costs is another important accounting and tax issue for bioscience and technology companies. Substantial judgment is required to determine the appropriate accounting for patent costs, purchased and sponsored R&D, licensed technology, and organizational expenses. This is discussed later in the chapter.

Foreign Operations

High technology companies typically enter foreign markets early in their development. Because of the opportunities presented by large foreign markets, many high technology companies consider various aspects of globalization, including what countries to penetrate, market entry strategies, distribution channels, and form of investment (e.g., direct or joint venture). Often, sales begin with direct exports and then occur through a local distributor, with field-service technicians added to support the installed base. Eventually, a separate sales office and a branch or subsidiary may be established. Companies may also choose to manufacture or to conduct R&D activities offshore.

Foreign operations create many statutory reporting, legal, and tax compliance issues that both the client and the auditor need to recognize. Additionally, expenses of operating abroad may be higher than comparable domestic costs, particularly because of additional duty, freight, insurance, and administrative costs. The auditor should be aware that the costs of duty requirements are often significant and subject to review and audit by customs authorities on a retroactive basis.

Foreign markets also create foreign currency translation and transaction problems arising from translation of asset and liability positions and revenue and expense transactions in currencies other than the U.S. dollar. The response to foreign currency exposure by high technology companies is determined to some degree by their relative size: Smaller, newer entrants into foreign markets often quote prices in U.S. dollars, while larger, more sophisticated companies frequently manage their net exposure for individual currencies and sometimes hedge those exposures. The appropriate accounting for exposures and related hedges is set forth in SFAS No. 52 (Accounting Standards Section F60).

Product Inventory Valuation

Obsolescence of inventory components used in manufacturing and servicing high technology products is often a significant valuation issue. High technology products are susceptible to frequent engineering change orders to upgrade performance, life cycles are short, and competitive products sometimes have superior price and performance characteristics. Additionally, in an effort to market new products quickly, companies may not conduct appropriate market research on products. To assess obsolescence of parts inventory, companies generally analyze the demand for it by extending the product's sales backlog and/or forecast by each component in the product's bill of materials, and compare this estimated usage of the components plus expected usage in servicing the product with the number of components on hand. The auditor needs to assess the reasonableness of the sales forecast and to ensure that the bill of materials is current and accurate. Industry association information, as well as data obtained from high technology market research firms, is often helpful in assessing sales forecasts.

Direct Materials Valuation

Because the costs of raw materials in high technology products often decrease over time, generally that component of inventory is valued on the average cost or FIFO basis; the use of LIFO valuation is less common than in many other industries. Many high technology companies are assemblers of components and are therefore material-intensive; vertical integration tends to be fairly limited. Accordingly, audit tests should focus on procedures for acquiring materials, accounting for purchase price variances, the existence of and appropriate accounting for purchase commitments, and the proper treatment of volume discount arrangements with vendors. See the discussions of auditing the buying and production cycles in Chapters 13 and 14 for further details.

Overhead Accounting

Rapid growth and a short product life cycle create significant expenditures for new plant and new products. Start-up costs associated with new plants and products generally should be expensed and not capitalized as part of inventory. Consistent measurement of these costs is difficult. In periods of fluctuating growth rates, excess capacity should be assessed and the related costs excluded from inventory. These assessments are also difficult, but they are necessary to ensure that inventory does not include costs that have no earning potential.

Because direct labor is a decreasing percentage of total costs in high technology products, allocating overhead to production based on direct labor may not be the most appropriate method to match overhead costs to specific products. The auditor must determine the reasonableness of overhead allocations based on the products' cost structures in order to assess the reasonableness of the carrying costs.

Certain products (e.g., semiconductors) are manufactured by methods for which a process cost accounting system is appropriate. In those instances, the auditor must ensure that valuation procedures for work-in-process inventories appropriately account for lost or spoiled units. Similarly, the auditor should ensure that the "yield" assumptions underlying the standard costs established for completed products are realistic and supported by actual experience. Essentially, this involves assessing whether the average number of usable products completed absorbs the total cost associated with the number of products started at each stage of the manufacturing process.

Research and Development Costs

One of the investment community's key performance measures of high technology companies is the level of expenditure for research and development, including that funded by others. SFAS No. 2 (Accounting Standards Section R50) provides guidance on accounting for R&D costs. The 1986 Tax Reform Act, while reducing the rate from 25 percent to 20 percent, maintained tax credits for qualified R&D spending. The auditor should be aware of the detailed guidelines on what activities qualify for tax credits and should ascertain that expenditures are appropriately classified for both accounting and tax purposes.

Another tax issue is the limitations on deductions of R&D and software development costs by a personal holding company. Such a company is defined as one where five or fewer of its shareholders own 50 percent or more of its stock, and over 60 percent of its gross income (sales) is from passive sources. Since in certain circumstances income from selling licenses for software use is considered passive income for tax purposes, many of these expenses would not be currently deductible.

Research and development may be funded by a variety of legal arrangements that are often influenced by federal and state income tax and securities regulations. Those arrangements include debt and equity interests and contracts to provide services. The auditor should consider the nature of the obligation incurred. SFAS No. 68, *Research and Development Arrangements* (Accounting Standards Section R55), specifies how an enterprise should account for its obligation under an arrangement for the funding by others of its R&D activities. The enterprise should determine whether its obligation extends beyond performing research and development; to the extent that the enterprise is obligated to repay the other parties, it should record a liability and recognize R&D expenses when the costs are incurred.

High technology companies often purchase technology through either acquisition of a company, direct purchase of a license, or other arrangements. Purchased R&D should be expensed immediately; existing products may be capitalized and amortized over their estimated useful life; the purchase of an ongoing business gives rise to goodwill, to be amortized over an appropriate period. The auditor needs to ensure that the classifications, as well as amortization periods, are appropriate.

Intercompany Transactions and Taxes

Tax issues for high technology companies generally relate to foreign manufacturing, sales, service operations, and R&D activities. In the past, American companies operating abroad avoided much of the U.S. tax burden on foreign earnings by claiming credits for foreign taxes paid. The 1986 Tax Reform Act decreased the U.S. tax rate and added major administrative burdens to the use of foreign tax credits. As a result, accounting and record-keeping requirements affecting foreign subsidiaries have increased significantly.

Intercompany prices may be structured to reduce foreign taxes on business income in high-tax nations. Companies can accomplish this by carefully analyzing their transfer pricing alternatives, management fees, interest, and royalties. The auditor should ascertain that all intercompany profits have been eliminated from inventory for financial reporting purposes. The auditor should also be alert to intercompany profits in self-constructed assets. Consolidating entries for eliminating intercompany profits should be made net of tax effects.

While in the past, technology was often licensed to related foreign entities at an arm's-length price set at the time of agreement, the 1986 Tax Reform Act imposed a "superroyalty" provision. Now, U.S. companies may be required to periodically revise their licensing agreements or intercompany pricing policies with foreign affiliates to reflect current returns from the technology abroad; foreign tax liabilities, however, may not be correspondingly decreased. The auditor should be aware of such periodic revisions to the tax code.

Because of numerous complex foreign tax issues, considerable judgment is needed to apply relevant regulations. The auditor and a tax specialist should work closely together in evaluating the tax provision.

32

Auditing Insurance Companies

OVERVIEW OF THE INDUSTRY

The primary purpose of insurance is to spread risks among people or entities exposed to similar risks. When an insurance policy is issued, the insured makes a payment in advance of the possible occurrence of an insured event, such as death (life insurance) or financial catastrophe (property and liability insurance). The insurance company generally does not know if a claim will result, when it will occur, or how much will be paid under the policy. The fundamental difference between the insurance industry and other industries is that insurance companies accumulate cash first and pay claims costs in the future. In other industries, generally costs are incurred first and cash is received later, after a company's products have been sold or services performed.

The insurance industry has changed substantially over the years. For life insurance companies, the profitability of new products has been challenged by competition and interest rates. In addition, the AIDS epidemic is affecting the marketing, underwriting, and pricing strategies of companies selling life and accident/health insurance.

Property and liability (also known as property and casualty) companies are also facing challenging profitability issues. Claims costs have risen because of legislated benefits. Claims for asbestos and other environmental pollution have increased significantly because of various rulings and legal decisions that established coverage and lengthened the coverage period. There is an increase in the number of troubled companies with which reinsurance has been placed, causing a potential overstatement of reinsurance receivables and recoverables.

These are only a few of the key industry conditions the auditor must understand in order to assess risks and design auditing procedures.

Structure of the Industry

There are three main types of insurance companies: life, property and liability, and title insurance companies. Companies are further divided into direct or primary writers and reinsurers. Life insurance companies provide financial assistance at the time of death and also during a person's lifetime in the form of annuity, endowment, and accident and health insurance policies. Premiums are often level, even though the policy benefits and services provided by the insurance company (insurance protection, sales effort, premium collection costs, and claims) are not expected to occur evenly over the contract period.

Property and liability insurance companies provide protection against damage to or loss of property caused by various perils, like fire and theft, or legal liability resulting from injuries to other people or damage to their property. Property and liability insurance companies also issue accident and health insurance contracts. Premiums received on property and liability contracts are intended to cover expected claims costs resulting from insured events that occur during a fixed period of short duration. Life insurance companies and property and liability companies are quite similar in their major operations, underwriting procedures, claims processing, and investment activities.

Title insurance companies issue title insurance contracts that indemnify real estate owners, buyers, and mortgage lenders against loss or damage arising from defects in, liens on, or challenges to their title to real estate. Title insurance contracts usually cover an extended period, such as the period of ownership.

Most insurance companies are organized as either stock or mutual companies. A stock company is owned by stockholders and earns income for their benefit by performing services for its policyholders. A mutual company is owned by the policyholders and operates for their benefit; most policies issued are participating policies, under which profits are distributed to the policyholders as policy dividends. Stock companies may also issue participating policies, which entitle policyholders to share in the company's earnings through dividend distributions. Other types of organizations are reciprocal exchanges, which consist of a group of ''subscribers'' that exchange insurance contracts through an attorney-in-fact, and fraternal benefit societies, which are similar to mutual insurance companies and provide life or health insurance to their members.

Insurance companies in the United States are licensed as either life or general insurance companies (property/liability and title companies). Usually companies that do business in both markets are holding companies with separate life and property/liability subsidiaries, or companies licensed in one field with a subsidiary that is licensed in the other.

Reinsurance

Reinsurance is a means by which the original or primary insurer, also known as the ceding company or the reinsured, transfers all or a portion of its risk under an insurance policy or a group of policies to another insurance company, known as the assuming company or the reinsurer. The assuming company may in turn transfer all or part of the risk to one or more other companies. The policyholder continues to hold the original insurance policy and usually does not know that the policy has been reinsured. Company policy regarding reinsurance is based on the desire to limit losses, stabilize underwriting results, and protect surplus. Property and liability companies also use reinsurance to avoid concentration in a single geographical area and thus reduce the possibility of a large number of claims resulting from one event. In transferring all or part of a risk, an insurance company still maintains its liability to the insured. Thus, to the extent that an assuming company might be unable to meet its obligations, a contingent liability exists on the part of the ceding company. The AICPA has issued Statements of Position on auditing life and property and liability reinsurance, which outline the steps that should be followed in auditing reinsurance activities.

Regulatory Environment

Insurance company operations are significantly affected by state regulatory requirements; consequently, auditors must know the specific state statutes applicable to their clients. (Except for SEC jurisdiction over public companies, there is no federal insurance regulatory organization.) Statutes in all states provide for a state insurance department to supervise insurance companies and enforce compliance with the law. In addition, the National Association of Insurance Commissioners (NAIC) has been formed in an attempt to establish uniform rules and regulations. This association has no legal status, and any rules it adopts must be passed as law in the individual states before they become binding.

While the statutes vary by state, their main objective is the development and enforcement of measures designed to promote solvency, appropriate premium rates, fair dealing with policyholders, and uniform financial reporting. In the majority of states, insurance companies cannot be organized or sell policies without insurance department authorization. Each state has its own statutory requirements for minimum capitalization, solvency margins, and dividend restrictions. Those requirements may also vary depending on the type of company (life or property and liability, stock company or mutual company) and the type of business conducted (marine or casualty, life or accident and health insurance).

Investment restrictions also vary from state to state. Regulations specify how funds are to be invested and valued. Values for stocks and bonds are published by the NAIC each January in a manual entitled *Valuations of Securities.*

To promote uniform financial reporting, the statutes provide for annual (and, in some states, quarterly) statements in prescribed form to be filed with the insurance departments, and for insurance companies to be examined by the insurance departments at stated intervals. The annual statement (generally referred to as the "convention blank") includes a balance sheet, summary of operations, surplus statement, statement of cash flows, many supporting exhibits and schedules, and supplemental questionnaires and reports; the data in those statements is extracted from the company's accounting and statistical records. It is essential for auditors to have a working knowledge of the statutory annual statement, since it is usually convenient to use its various schedules and exhibits as a basis for substantive tests of details and analytical procedures.

In addition to the statutory requirements, authoritative accounting principles for the insurance industry have been issued by the Financial Accounting Standards Board in SFAS No. 60, *Accounting and Reporting by Insurance Enterprises* (Accounting Standards Section In6), No. 61, *Accounting for Title Plant* (Accounting Standards Section Ti7), and No. 97, *Accounting and Reporting by Insurance Enterprises for Certain Long-Duration Contracts and for Realized Gains and Losses from the Sale of Investments* (Accounting Standards Section In6). The AICPA insurance industry audit guides, *Audits of Stock Life Insurance Companies* and *Audits of Fire and Casualty Insurance Companies*, contain specialized accounting principles and practices. In addition, Statements of Position on *Accounting for Property and Liability Insurance Companies, Accounting for Investments of Stock Life Insurance Companies,* and *Accounting for Title Insurance Companies* and industry-specific issues papers contain useful background information. The form and content of financial statements of insurance companies subject to SEC regulation are governed by Article 7 of Regulation S-X.

STATUTORY- AND GAAP-BASIS ACCOUNTING PRACTICES

Statutory financial accounting is required by the state insurance departments and prescribed by the NAIC. One of the main purposes of statutory-basis financial statements is to provide information about the solvency of an insurance company and its ability to pay all ultimate claims of policyholders. Assets that cannot be used to pay policy claims (like furniture and fixtures, automobiles, prepaid expenses, and agents' balances receivable over 90 days) are irrelevant to that purpose; therefore, they are deducted directly from surplus (i.e., they are "nonadmitted" assets).

Statutory accounting starts with "ledger assets," which are account balances arising from cash and premium transactions. The ledger assets are adjusted for accruals and reserves (including unearned premiums and claims or benefit reserves), which are referred to as nonledger assets and liabilities since they are not under general ledger control. These nonledger accounts are controlled by a separate accounting system and are posted to the trial balance for financial reporting purposes. Nonadmitted assets are then deducted to arrive at net admitted assets on a statutory basis. Conservative assumptions generally dominate statutory accounting principles.

The purpose of GAAP-basis financial statements for insurance companies, on the other hand, is the same as for any other type of company. Thus it differs from the purpose of statutory accounting. GAAP-basis financial statements include assets that are not admitted for statutory accounting purposes, and they are based on more realistic assumptions regarding accounting estimates. This section of the chapter describes the major accounts that are unique to insurance companies and the differences between statutory- and GAAP-basis accounting.

Premium Revenue

Premiums are consideration received from an insured in exchange for the insurance company's contractual obligation to assume risk, and are an insurance company's principal source of income. Premiums are considered to be of short or long duration, depending on the terms of the insurance contract. SFAS No. 60 (Accounting Standards Section In6.107) defines these terms as follows:

> *Short-Duration Contract.* The contract provides insurance protection for a fixed period of short duration and enables the insurer to cancel the contract or to adjust the provisions of the contract at the end of any contract period, such as adjusting the amount of premiums charged or coverage provided.

> *Long-Duration Contract.* The contract generally is not subject to unilateral changes in its provisions, such as a noncancelable or guaranteed renewable contract, and requires the performance of various functions and services (including insurance protection) for an extended period.

As stated in Section In6.108, examples of short-duration contracts include most property and liability insurance contracts and certain term life insurance contracts, like credit life insurance. Examples of long-duration contracts are whole-life contracts, guaranteed renewable term life contracts, endowment contracts, annuity contracts, universal life type contracts, and title insurance contracts.

Premiums from short-duration contracts should be recognized as revenue over the period of the contract in proportion to the amount of insurance protection provided. Premiums from long-duration contracts should be recognized as revenue when they are due, unless the product has been classified as an investment contract, limited-payment contract, or universal life contract as defined in Statement of Financial Accounting Standards (SFAS) No. 97, which sets forth the accounting treatment for products meeting that definition. Investment contracts that do not contain significant mortality or morbidity risk are no longer accounted for as insurance contracts but as interest-bearing financial instruments. Gross premiums in excess of net premiums on limited-payment contracts must be deferred and recognized over the benefit period. SFAS No. 97 requires use of the retrospective deposit method for universal life type products. Under the retrospective deposit method, premiums are no longer reported as income. Instead, premiums are credited to policyholder accounts, which are charged periodically for mortality and administrative and other expenses.

Unearned Premiums

Unearned premiums represent deferred income from policies written. Normally, unearned premiums are computed from a file of policies currently in effect, known as a premium in force file, based on either a monthly or daily proration. A monthly proration assumes that all policies with an effective date in a certain month are written evenly throughout the month. When the daily pro rata method is used, the unearned premium is calculated by multiplying premiums in force by the unexpired number of days divided by the total number of days for which the policy is effective. Unearned premiums are calculated for both statutory and GAAP accounting purposes. The calculation applies mainly to property and liability insurance companies, although group accident and health policies issued by life insurance companies also typically have unearned premiums.

Policy Acquisition Costs

Policy acquisition costs on new and renewal contracts (e.g., commissions, premium taxes, underwriting and issue expenses, and inspection reports) are charged to operations as incurred for statutory reporting. For products accounted for under SFAS No. 60, the entire premium is not earned when the policy acquisition costs are expended. Therefore, acquisition expenses that vary with and are related mainly to the production of new business should be deferred and amortized over the period of premium revenue recognition for GAAP reporting purposes. For universal life type products, deferred policy acquisition costs should be amortized at a constant rate based on the present value of the estimated gross profit for GAAP reporting purposes.

Valuation of Investments

For statutory accounting, investments are carried at values specified by the NAIC. Generally, common stocks are carried at market value, preferred stocks at cost for life insurance companies and at market for property and liability companies, and bonds at amortized cost. For GAAP purposes, common stocks and nonredeemable preferred stocks should be carried at market; bonds and preferred stocks that must be redeemed by the issuer or are redeemable at the option of the investor should be carried at amortized cost if the company has both the ability and the intent to hold the securities until maturity. Investments in policy loans and mortgage loans are reported at the outstanding principal balance, and investments in real estate are stated at cost less accumulated depreciation. If a decline in the value of an investment carried at cost or amortized cost is considered to be other than temporary, the investment should be reduced to its net realizable value.

Nonadmitted Assets

For statutory purposes, nonadmitted assets include all assets that are not permitted to be reported as admitted assets in the annual statement and are charged directly to surplus. Nonadmitted assets, including receivables outstanding for more than 90 days, are restored to the balance sheet for GAAP purposes. The auditor should review these receivables for collectibility and evaluate the need for an allowance for uncollectible accounts.

Realized and Unrealized Investment Gains and Losses

Realized gains or losses are recognized in determining net income for GAAP reporting and for statutory reporting by property and liability companies. Realized gains and losses are reported in the income statement as a component of other income on a pretax basis. Life insurance companies record realized gains or losses directly in surplus for statutory purposes. Unrealized gains and losses are credited or charged directly to stockholders' equity in all instances. Effectively, the difference between the current valuation of investments on hand at the balance sheet date and cost resides in stockholders' equity.

Mandatory Securities Valuation Reserve

The mandatory securities valuation reserve (MSVR) for life insurance companies is computed according to a formula prescribed by the NAIC to provide for possible losses on investments. The MSVR is not a valuation reserve but an appropriation of surplus; therefore, it is restored to stockholders' equity in GAAP financial statements. Such a reserve is not required in the statutory statements of property and liability companies.

Investments in Subsidiaries

Investments in subsidiaries may not be consolidated under statutory reporting requirements but must be accounted for, as prescribed by the NAIC, using methods similar to those for investments in common or preferred stocks. Generally, the carrying value of common stock of subsidiaries is established by the company based on the book value or equity of the subsidiary at the balance sheet date. GAAP financial statements should follow the requirements of SFAS No. 94 regarding the inclusion of insurance subsidiaries for consolidation purposes.

Income Taxes

The Tax Reform Act of 1984 established a single-base tax structure for life insurance companies. This structure embodies the tax rules applicable to corporations in general while retaining provisions that reflect the unique nature of the life insurance industry and its products. The Tax Reform Act of 1986 (TRA 86) had a significant impact on property/casualty companies. TRA 86 reduced the deduction for unearned premiums from 100 percent to 80 percent and also requires property/casualty insurers to discount loss reserves and loss adjustment expenses.

For statutory reporting purposes, insurance companies do not provide for deferred income taxes. Under GAAP, companies must record deferred income taxes for specified differences between GAAP income and taxable income.

Policy Reserve (Future Policy Benefits) Valuation

Policy reserves represent the future guaranteed benefits of life policies payable under the contract provisions of the policies. Policy reserves are actuarially computed to show the present value of future benefits reduced by the present value of future net premiums. Policy reserves are the largest liability on a life insurance company's balance sheet.

Statutory reserves for life insurance companies are calculated assuming conservative estimates for interest earned on premium revenue that is collected and invested and for mortality (probability of death or proportion of persons expected to die at particular ages per thousand persons). Published actuarial tables, sometimes modified to reflect a company's experience, are used by life insurance companies; approval of a state insurance department is required. Morbidity tables that indicate the probability of incidence, by age, of becoming mentally or physically diseased or of becoming physically impaired are used for accident and health insurance. No assumption for withdrawals in the form of lapsed (or, for cash value life insurance policies, surrendered) policies is made in statutory reserve calculations, since statutory reserves are usually expected to equal or exceed cash surrender values.

Statutory reserves are subject to limitations and methods prescribed or permitted by regulatory authorities that are at variance with GAAP. Under GAAP, the interest assumption should reflect the current investment return, the mortality or morbidity assumptions should reflect recent experience, and a withdrawal assumption should be included. Those assumptions should also include a provision for adverse deviation in light of the long-term nature of life insurance and the inherent inability to predict the future with certainty. GAAP require that the original assumptions continue to be used (i.e., to be "locked in") as long as reserves are sufficient to provide for future benefits and expenses. If a deficiency occurs, the assumptions are revised for loss recognition purposes, as discussed later. Revised assumptions may be applied to new issues as necessary.

Loss or Claim Reserves

Determining whether loss or claim reserves are adequate is by far the most difficult aspect of auditing a property and liability insurance company. In many instances, the auditor needs actuarial assistance to determine the adequacy of the reserves. Some accounting firms employ actuarial consultants and have also developed software packages to calculate the reserve amounts under various methods. Auditing liability claim reserves is particularly difficult, because of the long period that elapses before claims are finally settled. Under both statutory and GAAP accounting practices, losses are recognized when incurred. Estimated liabilities are established for losses that have been reported, and additional estimates are made for losses that have been incurred but have not yet been reported (IBNR). SFAS No. 60 (Accounting Standards Section In6) neither prohibits nor mandates discounting of estimated liabilities. At the time of this writing, the FASB is in the early stages of a project on the issue of discounting in general.

In establishing the estimated IBNR liability, a company accumulates its past reported losses by line of business and attempts to project the ultimate cost of settling all losses for a given year. In addition to past experience, a company must also consider other factors, like changes in inflation rates, reinsurance programs, and lines or volume of business written, so as to best estimate its IBNR reserve.

Statutory and GAAP accounting methods also provide that costs associated with settling losses (loss adjustment expenses) should be accrued in the period when the related losses were incurred. These costs include amounts paid for outside services like claims adjusters and attorneys, and direct and indirect internal costs associated with claims settling. Under GAAP, estimates of recoveries on unsettled claims for salvage and subrogation should be deducted from the liability for unpaid claims, although this treatment is not permitted under statutory accounting practices. Salvage is an amount received by the insurance company from the sale of property on which a total loss has been paid to the insured. Subrogation is the statutory or legal right of the insurance company to recover amounts from a third party that is wholly or partially responsible for a loss the insurance company paid.

Earned But Unbilled Premiums

Some property and liability companies write a significant volume of business, such as workers' compensation, for which the initial payment is in the form of a deposit premium. After part or all of the policy period has passed, the insured's reported payroll is audited and a billing made to adjust the premium. When a company writes this type of business, the amount of additional premium receivable at the financial statement date should be estimated and recorded. Statutory accounting for earned but unbilled premiums varies by state.

RISK ASSESSMENT AND AUDIT STRATEGY

To formulate the audit strategy for an insurance company, the auditor must understand the environment in which the company operates, including the products it offers and how long it has been involved in specific product lines. In addition, the auditor should be aware of the regulatory constraints of the individual states where the company does business.

If a company has handled certain product lines for a considerable time, it usually has effective control structure policies and procedures the auditor can test. Tests of controls are often efficient because of the massive amounts of data typically processed by insurance companies. In addition, in many companies management reviews profit and loss analyses by line of business or product as a basis for reacting to decreases in premium revenue or increases in claims or benefits, which may call for changing product pricing, underwriting standards, or reinsurance. If such reviews are made, the auditor may consider it efficient to test them.

Specifically, the auditor should understand the company's statutory minimum surplus requirements, which depend on the types of business written and the state of domicile. In addition to periodic audits by the states, the company's operating results are scrutinized through a series of Insurance Regulatory Information System Tests (known as Early Warning Tests) prescribed by the regulatory authorities. These tests consist of a series of separate analytical financial ratios and relationships for both life and property and liability companies and are designed to measure normal levels of financial stability. To the extent that the results of a number of the tests do not fall within acceptable parameters, closer scrutiny or more frequent audits may be considered necessary. This information generally is not made public.

In developing the overall audit strategy, the auditor should fully utilize the statutory information the insurance company generates to comply with state regulations. Information like annual statements, Early Warning Test results, and state examination reports are invaluable tools for assessing a company's financial position and operating results. In addition, many insurance companies have sophisticated management decision-making systems for assessing profitability and monitoring progress in meeting budgets and business plans. The auditor should obtain an understanding of management's objectives and methods of controlling the business as a basis for assessing the inherent and control risks associated with the company and its products.

One of the most significant assets of an insurance company is its portfolio of bonds. As indicated previously, bonds are reflected in the financial statements at amortized cost. If interest rates are high, there is a risk that the market value of the bonds may be significantly lower than their amortized cost. Accordingly, the auditor should assess the company's ability and intent to hold the bonds to maturity; the possibility of adjusting the carrying value of the bonds to market may have to be considered. If a company is faced with the prospect of a negative cash flow, this may affect its ability to hold the bonds to maturity.

Most companies rely rather heavily on reinsurance. Accordingly, the ceding company must assess and monitor the financial stability of its reinsurers. To the extent that procedures for accomplishing this are not in place, the auditor should consider the possibility of contingent liabilities from reinsurer failures.

Assessing the adequacy of loss reserves is critical for an auditor of a property and liability company. A company establishes its loss reserves based on reported claim data and historical information plus considerations such as changes in its underwriting philosophy and mix of business, reductions or increases in retention for its own account (use of reinsurers), unusually large or nonrecurring losses, and dramatic increases in either inflation rates or current awards by juries or judges in liability cases. It is important for the auditor to assess the company's experience in these areas in light of the planned audit strategy.

The competitive environment in both the industry and the financial services sector in general has a significant impact on both life and property and liability companies. For instance, during the late 1970s and early 1980s, high interest rates generated a need for new interest-sensitive products. Those products led to policies like universal life and single-premium deferred annuities, which enable the policyholder to reap the benefits of higher interest rates and, in the case of universal life policies, still retain an element of life insurance coverage.

These products, which did not exist until the late 1970s, now have a dominant position in the industry. Obviously, the auditor is faced with new issues in evaluating the impact of these products and the company's use of appropriate reserving procedures.

TYPICAL TRANSACTIONS AND CONTROL STRUCTURE POLICIES AND PROCEDURES

The flow of operations of a typical insurance company is as follows:

1. The company determines the appropriate premium, bills the insured, and collects the premium.
2. Some of the premium is used to pay immediate expenses, like commissions and operating costs.
3. Most of the premium is invested to pay claims in the future.
4. Investment income and proceeds from sales of investments are used to pay claims as incurred.
5. Profits, if any, are returned in part to the stockholders or policyholders as dividends.

Those operations may be viewed as falling into three major transaction cycles.

- The premium cycle.
- The claim/benefit cycle.
- The investment cycle.

The investment cycle includes buying and selling investments and receiving investment income. Auditing an insurance company's investment cycle is the same as auditing other businesses that maintain investment portfolios (see Chapter 17) or investment companies (see Chapter 33); thus it is not described in this chapter. The other two cycles, which are unique to the insurance industry, are discussed below.

The Premium Cycle

The premium cycle includes all phases of premium recognition, from application to expiration of the policy. They can be divided into four functions.

Policy writing.
Policy underwriting.
Recording premiums.
Collecting premiums.

The accounts related to the premium cycle are premium income, reinsurance ceded, commission expense, premiums receivable, premiums payable, future policy benefits (policy reserves), and unearned premiums.

Policy Writing.   The policy-writing function consists of writing and issuing insurance policies. A policy is a contract between the insurer and the insured and contains all the terms and conditions agreed to. In a life insurance company, policies generally are prepared at the home office; a number is assigned to each policy. The initial premium is usually paid when the policy is delivered, although many companies encourage payment with the application. Close control must be kept over policies delivered but not paid for. As soon as a policy is issued, an in-force file is created; this is probably the most important file used by a life insurance company. It is a perpetual inventory of all policies issued and in force at a given time and is the source for preparing or calculating premium billings, commission payments, premium taxes, policyholder dividends, and the actuarial reserve liability. Once a policy has been issued, all information on the application, including age, sex, premium, and limits of coverage, is entered on this file. The policy is the source document for the master file.

In a property and liability insurance company, policy writing may be done by agents, at a branch, or at the home office. It may be completed before or after risk underwriting, depending on who writes the policy. If an agent writes a policy, the home or branch office underwrites the policy after it has been written, based on a copy or abstract of the policy called a "daily." An agent is a person who has a relationship with a particular insurance company and has the authority to bind the company on the coverage for the insured. In contrast, a broker has a relationship with various insurers and does not have the authority to bind a company but can only submit an application for coverage. If the branch or home office writes a policy, the company underwrites from the application sent by a salesperson.

The major control objective in the policy-writing function is the prompt, complete, and accurate reporting of all policy-writing transactions to the company or home office. This objective is achieved mainly by controlling blank policies issued to agents or employees, policies issued to agents and insureds after they have been written and recorded, and dailies processed at the home office. If based on the understanding of the control structure the auditor expects to be able to assess control risk as low, the audit strategy generally is to perform tests of controls relating to the policy-writing function.

Policy Underwriting.   Underwriting is the assumption of risk for designated loss or damage in exchange for a premium. It includes evaluating the acceptability of the risk, assessing the company's capacity to assume the entire risk (i.e., considering whether reinsurance is required), and determining the premium if the risk is accepted. In a life insurance company, applications require information about age, sex, occupation, health history, and any additional facts that might affect insurability. The information on the application, the medical and inspection report, and the company's own guidelines are used to rate the applicant as a standard, substandard, or uninsurable risk. Applicants subject to a higher than normal mortality are substandard risks. Some companies refuse to insure substandard risks, and others insure them at higher than normal rates. The premium charged is based on the insured's age and risk group and is determined by the underwriter, using company premium rate books. Normally the quality of the underwriting is not apparent until a substantial period of time has passed. The company's reinsurance limits must also be considered in underwriting policies. Policies to be reinsured because they are in excess of company retention limits or are substandard risks must be coded when they are issued and reported to the reinsurance department for processing.

In a property and liability insurance company, evaluating the acceptability of risks involves reviewing the exposure and potential loss, which is based on information on the dailies and endorsements (amendments or changes to existing policies). Both individual company policies and state laws often specify procedures for investigating risks; for example, information about applicants for automobile insurance may be requested from the State Department of Motor Vehicles.

Premiums on policies written by the company are determined and premiums on policies written by agents are reviewed by referring to bureau or company rate manuals or applying underwriting expertise. For policies written by agents, cursory reviews are made in the field office and the dailies are recorded. Although the coverage can be canceled by the company after the underwriting has been completed, it is customary to record the policy before acceptance; if the policy is subsequently rejected, it is canceled and the records are adjusted.

In policy underwriting, the major control objective is the prompt, accurate, and complete recording of all risks that have been accepted in accordance with the company's predetermined standards and the documenting of all policy underwriting transactions. In obtaining an understanding of the control structure policies and procedures applied to policy underwriting, the auditor should consider whether premium, commission, and reinsurance rates coded on dailies or underwriting worksheets are proper. Often the auditor examines policies to determine whether the risks accepted are within the company's established retention limits, reinsurance has been considered, and there is evidence of review by a supervisor in the underwriting department. The auditor should also determine whether the findings are consistent with the assumptions that will be used in auditing loss reserves. Past loss trends may not be a valid basis for predicting future losses, if underwriting standards are changed, the control structure is ineffective, definitions of risk categories are revised, or reinsurance limits are changed.

Recording Premiums.   When a premium is received by a life insurance company, usually the amount is credited to either premium income, a policyholder account, or premium suspense. Premium suspense is a liability account used to record amounts that are intended as premiums but cannot be credited to income until a particular event occurs, like approval and issuance of the policy or allocation of amounts received to appropriate premium income or policyholder accounts.

When statutory-basis financial statements are prepared, uncollected premiums (premiums currently due but unpaid as of the statement date) and deferred premiums (premiums applicable to the current policy year but not yet due) must be calculated. Depending on the size and sophistication of the company, the calculation may be computerized or performed manually. The gross amount of uncollected and deferred premiums adjusts premium income from the cash to the accrual basis for the statutory summary of operations.

In property and liability companies, premium recording includes coding and processing transactions (dailies and endorsements) to produce the premiums written account, and maintaining statistical data to produce the premium in force and premium earned accounts. Dailies and endorsements may be coded at the time the policy is underwritten or later.

Premiums written are premiums billed less premiums returned for endorsement or cancellation. If there are endorsements, the premiums written account includes a pro rata portion of the related original premium. The original premium amount is the premium for the full term of a policy for the current coverage at the latest premium rate shown in the policy or the endorsement.

The major control objective of the policy-recording function is maintaining accurate records of the policies in force. That objective calls for control procedures to ensure the completeness and accuracy of input and updating of the in-force records. Entries to the policy master file are made mainly from the premium cycle, although in a life insurance company entries are also made from the claim cycle. The auditor should assess control procedures applied to all entries with financial significance.

The auditor often agrees the information contained in the policy, such as policy number, name and address of policyholder, issue date and term of policy, plan code, mode of payment, face amount of insurance, and premium, to the in-force listing. In addition, the auditor usually considers tests of the company's control procedures designed to ensure that all risks are recorded (i.e., batch controls and numerical sequencing of policies and applications).

Collecting Premiums. The premium-collecting function includes billing, receiving cash, applying receipts to agents' balances, and paying commissions. In a life insurance company, generally insureds are billed directly, and they pay the company directly. An unpaid premium file is kept by either policy number or insured's name, rather than by agent, and commissions are paid directly to agents. Premiums may be paid monthly, quarterly, semiannually, or annually depending on the policyholder's preference or the company's marketing strategy.

In a property and liability insurance company, three basic methods are used for billing premiums.

- The company bills the agents, who, in turn, bill the insureds. The monthly statements to the agents usually include policy number, name of insured, effective date of policy, gross premium, commission rate, and amount of commission. The agents transmit the premiums, after deducting their commissions, to the company as they are collected.

- The unpaid premium file is kept by the agents, who bill the insureds, collect the premiums, and transmit the payments to the company after deducting their commissions. Agents transmit a monthly statement listing all transactions for which premiums are due. In general, these transactions have already been recorded by the company from dailies previously received or issued.

- Insureds are billed directly by the company and pay the company directly. The company then pays commissions to the agents, usually on a periodic basis.

The major control objectives of premium billing and collecting are to calculate receivables, commissions, and related accounts accurately; to determine that billing file data agrees with the in-force file data; to bill promptly; to investigate and resolve differences between company records and agents' records; and to control cash receipts.

Usually tests of controls are performed on the premium billing and collection system, although substantive tests like confirmation of receivables and review of subsequent cash receipts from agents and insureds normally are also performed. In addition, the auditor will often review specific transactions selected from throughout the period and test the summarization and recording procedures, including recalculation of commissions to agents and brokers. Tests of controls relating to cash receipts and to the accuracy and authorization of cash disbursements, premium revenue, and commission general ledger entries arising from the premium cycle are no different than for any other type of business.

The Claim Cycle—Benefit Payments

The claim cycle encompasses disbursing benefits and recording paid and unpaid claims, and includes the following functions:

- Notification of loss.
- Verifying the loss.

- Evaluating the loss.
- Settling and recording the loss.

To match premium revenue with the related claim expense, the insurance company's liability should be recorded when a loss is incurred. Because an insurance company cannot always determine the exact amount of claims incurred, the liability often must be estimated. The claim cycle is concerned with reported claims and their settlement, and the accumulation of statistical data to facilitate estimating and evaluating liabilities at year-end. The financial statement accounts affected by the claim cycle are claims expense and reinsurance recoveries, future policy benefits, provision for outstanding claims, and reinsurance balances.

Notification of Loss.   Although loss reporting is not controlled directly by the insurance company, knowledge of its characteristics is necessary to enable the company to carry out other claim functions. A loss (or claim) report by a claimant is the company's first notification of a loss occurrence. The claimant may be the policyholder, a beneficiary named in a life insurance policy, or a third party entitled to benefits under the terms of the policy. A claimant contacts either the insurance company directly or the insured's agent or broker. This results in a written notice of loss, which becomes the original documentation of the claim.

The primary control objective relating to notification of losses is the prompt, accurate, and complete recording of all claims, since those records are the basis for determining the company's liability. The objective may be achieved by promptly creating a loss file and assigning a claim number to each claim reported, matching incoming correspondence with the claim, and following up on claims that have been open for a long time. Control over claim numbers is important to ensure that the company is aware of all reported claims and can identify them as either open or closed.

Audit tests include determining whether there are abnormal delays between reporting dates and dates claims are filed and abstracts prepared, and between dates claim notices are received at branches and dates they are received at the home office; testing the numerical sequence of claim numbers; examining documentation of the matching of claim notices to related dailies, policies, or applications; determining that loss abstracts have been authorized; and determining that all documents are included in the claim file.

Verifying the Loss.   The insurance company verifies a claim by obtaining evidence that a loss occurred and that it was covered under the terms of the policy, and determining that the policy was properly in force.

Death claims are generally easy to verify, because the occurrence of the loss is definite. The company investigates whether the policy is in force and obtains proof of death, such as a physician's statement (death certificate), and any other evidence considered necessary to substantiate that the claim is valid and the loss was within the terms of the policy. The validity of a property or liability claim is determined by comparing the loss report with the record of insurance coverage in force. After the insurance coverage has been verified, an adjuster is assigned to investigate the loss and determine that it actually occurred and is valid.

The basic objective of verifying the claim is to ensure that only valid claims are included in the company's claim liability. Although the specific tests vary from company to company, they usually include examining documentation of verification that the policy was in force, of the existence of reinsurance, and of verification of the claim.

Evaluating the Loss. The insurance company's liability under the terms of the policy may be clearly stated in the policy or may require an estimate based on the judgment of someone familiar with the details of the particular claim. Any amounts that may be recoverable from a reinsurance company are calculated, and the reinsurer is notified of the pending loss. Often the liability for a life insurance claim is clearly stated under the terms of the policy and, therefore, can be established easily. The occurrence and extent of property losses are not difficult to evaluate either, and usually the estimate of the company's liability is easily determinable also.

The adjuster estimates the amount or cost of the loss and the approximate amount of any potential salvage or subrogation, both of which reduce the loss paid by an insurance company. Also, the existence of any deductible under the terms of the policy should be noted in the loss file. Both the ultimate cost of the loss and expenses to be incurred in settling it are estimated. These expenses are called loss adjustment expenses and may include payments for the services of the claims adjuster, legal expenses, and other costs.

For certain liability losses, estimates of the ultimate cost of the loss to the company are highly subjective. Not only is there often a long reporting and settlement lag, but the extent of the loss may be difficult to determine and there may be the possibility of unknown injuries.

The major control objectives are prompt establishment of reasonable initial claim reserves in accordance with company policy, and prompt adjustment of reserves for changes in circumstances or knowledge of new facts. Tests of controls may include determining whether the company's policy for evaluating losses is documented, adjusters are adequately supervised to ensure that losses are estimated in accordance with company policy, there are procedures to ensure that incoming correspondence is matched promptly with the appropriate claim documents and that reserves are revised accordingly, and open claim files are periodically reviewed.

Settling and Recording the Loss. Losses incurred include paid and unpaid (outstanding loss reserve) portions, both of which are recorded. Details on losses incurred are maintained on a gross basis, before reinsurance, with reinsurance records maintained separately. Financial statements show losses on a net basis.

A claim may be settled by payment or by the decision not to pay. Once the claim has been settled, the loss file is reviewed to ensure that

- The final payment or other settlement resulted in removal of any remaining amount from the outstanding loss reserve account.

- A release has been obtained from the claimant that the claim was settled satisfactorily.
- Reinsurers have been notified of their liability, and the receivable has been recorded properly.
- The policy is canceled if risks covered no longer exist.
- Statistical data has been updated properly.
- The loss file has been marked "closed" or "paid."

In liability insurance, many factors, including the incidence of litigation, the likelihood of a court settlement, the judgment of the court, the effects of inflation, and state laws (especially in workers' compensation cases) affect costs. Familiarity with the delay characteristics of loss types is important, because knowing what factors influence the final settlement of losses is necessary to evaluate the loss reserves required. After a final payment has been made, the policy generally stays in force. It should be annotated regarding the loss for future underwriting considerations.

The major control objectives are similar to those in any payment cycle, including prompt payment of valid claims, proper authorization for disbursements, and accurate recording of payments. These can be achieved by establishing procedures for approving disbursements, following up long-outstanding claims, and recording disbursements.

Audit tests in this cycle often include testing the approval of documents before processing; tests of the completeness and accuracy of recording payments; tests of postings to ledger and nonledger accounts; tests of salvage and subrogation recoveries; and comparison and reconciliation of accounting data with statistical data.

SUBSTANTIVE TESTS OF SELECTED ACCOUNTS

This section describes accounts that are unique to the insurance industry and the procedures used in auditing them. Guidelines for auditing life and property and liability insurance companies are contained in the AICPA industry audit guides, *Audits of Stock Life Insurance Companies* and *Audits of Fire and Casualty Insurance Companies*.

Policy Reserves

The actuarial reserve liability of a life insurance company is computed based on the record of policies in force. This record is similar to a perpetual inventory. Moreover, the auditing procedures are the same as for the inventory of a commercial entity: reviewing appropriate sections or parts of policies, testing the application of the appropriate actuarial factors, and recalculating the extensions. Auditing the statutory actuarial liabilities of a life insurance company requires the ability to recognize the appropriate tables and rates used in connection with the various groupings of the units in the inventory. Therefore, the auditor should consider having a life insurance actuary assist in recalculating the reserves.

As indicated earlier, the auditor ordinarily tests the company's control procedures to ensure the completeness and accuracy of updating the master file, or inventory of policies on file. In addition, the auditor performs substantive tests of the master file similar to those used in auditing any inventory. Those tests include recalculating extensions of reserve factors and comparing selected policies with the inventory listing. The auditor generally traces reserve factors used in the computation to the appropriate factor tables and compares the number of policies and face value of insurance with the exhibit of life insurance included in the statutory annual statement and with the policy master file. Some auditors have developed customized audit software to test policy reserves of life insurance companies for both statutory and GAAP purposes.

As already noted, the main difference in auditing policy reserves calculated in conformity with GAAP compared with statutory reserves relates to determining the reasonableness of the assumptions and the propriety of the actuarial factors used. If a complete inventory of policies in force is used in the GAAP reserve computation, the tests directed at completeness and accuracy are the same as those performed in auditing the statutory reserves. Often, however, companies use a model of their policy inventory to determine the GAAP reserves; in that event, the auditor should be satisfied that the model is appropriate.

In using models, the derivative reserve factors for key plans are extended to other plans that can properly be placed in the same category. An appropriate model would include those plans, age groupings, and durations required to make the model sensitive to material changes in the plan and age distribution. At a minimum, the auditor should be satisfied that the model effectively reproduces the statutory results for insurance in force, premiums, expenses, and reserves. In most cases, the auditor considers it necessary to test the model under varying conditions to determine whether it is properly responsive. This testing is often done using audit software.

For many plans, the factors for statutory reserves are published. A company calculating GAAP reserves, however, should develop its own factors based on assumptions that are reasonably conservative and include a provision for the risk of adverse deviation. The auditor must be satisfied as to the following:

- The reasonableness and appropriateness of the basic assumptions (interest, mortality, expenses, and withdrawals) underlying the calculations of the reserve factors, including the reasonableness of the provision for the risk of adverse deviation.
- The appropriateness of the actuarial formulas.
- The accuracy of the factors resulting from applying formulas to the assumptions.

Reported Losses

The auditor should obtain listings of losses reported but unpaid and reinsurance recoverable thereon at the statement date, including estimates of unpaid loss adjustment expenses calculated on an individual-case basis. The auditor should test them for arithmetical accuracy and trace the totals to the financial statements. Claims processing should be reviewed to ensure that it is consistent with prior years and that year-end cutoff dates are appropriate.

If loss estimates are based on average costs, the auditor should review the methods used in determining them, including the logic applied, trends over a period of years, and whether the volume is sufficient to produce credible results. The auditor should also consider how reinsurance recoverables are treated in calculating average costs, particularly if there is a substantial amount of reinsurance as well as salvage and subrogation.

As part of tests performed in the claim cycle, the auditor should review the company's loss experience statistics for a number of years. Normally, a long development period is needed to determine with reasonable accuracy the actual settlement costs of liability claims. The difficulty of accurately estimating the costs of settling outstanding claims is further complicated by inflation and the current litigious environment.

Unreported Losses

The reserve for losses incurred but not yet reported provides for claims occurring before year-end but reported to the insurer in later periods. This requires estimating the number of such claims and the corresponding dollar amount required for final settlement. The methods used in these estimates are numerous and varied, as previously discussed, but generally they are based on past experience and should in all cases reflect the application of sound judgment.

Since IBNR claim reserves are based on estimates, the auditor needs to understand the company's estimating approach. Prior-year results in estimating IBNR reserves are a valuable guide to the effectiveness of the approach used. This type of comparison is usually made by means of a ''runoff'' that lists all payments on claims that were incurred but not reported as of the previous year-end. The total of this runoff and any remaining liability is compared with the IBNR reserve established at that time. In analyzing loss reserves, management must use judgment about past experience and trends. The auditor must be able to evaluate the methods used by the company's management, including whether they are consistent between years.

It is also important to consider whether statistics can be used in making a projection. In particular, adjustments to industry statistics may be necessary to take into account

- Changes in the mix of business written and related loss data in the current year.
- Reserving policy—A change in claims department personnel or a decision by management to change its reserving or claim settling policy may cause an increase in the average loss reserve per case.
- Catastrophes like earthquakes or hurricanes.
- Inflation—Reserves should take into account increases in the expected costs of loss settlements caused by inflation.

- Reinsurance—The presence or absence of reinsurance coverage or a change in the level or type of reinsurance could have a significant effect on loss statistics.

The auditor should use all available statistical data in determining the reasonableness of the loss reserves. Regardless of the methods used by the company, the auditor should be satisfied that the information used for the loss reserve analysis agrees with actual experience and that the methods are reliable and valid. The auditor should review and test the data used in developing the percentages and ratios entering into the IBNR computation. Basically, the same methods and auditing procedures used in evaluating loss reserves are used in auditing loss adjustment expenses.

Deferred Acquisition Costs

A life insurance company normally develops cost studies that segregate acquisition costs from costs attributable to maintaining policies. These cost studies also isolate development and other similar expenses so that it can be determined whether any of those costs should be deferred. Deferring development or similar expenses requires judgment on the part of both management and the auditor; they should give overriding consideration to future benefit, consistency, amortization period, and probability of recovery. If cost studies are not available, it is necessary to estimate acquisition costs, based on information used in determining the premiums to be charged. The audit of cost studies should be the same as for any other cost system.

Under GAAP, a premium deficiency must be recognized when it is probable and quantifiable. Thus, all or part of the unamortized balance of deferred acquisition costs of a life insurance company may have to be written off if the future revenue stream that the costs are to be amortized against becomes impaired. Through a procedure known as loss recognition or recoverability test, impairments in the revenue stream are identified by comparing actual with expected interest rates, mortality experience, and policy continuations as well as by reviewing the effects of rising expenses and general economic conditions. After future premiums have provided for all policy benefits and expenses, the remaining margins must be sufficient to amortize the deferred costs. Since GAAP do not allow losses on unprofitable business to be deferred, the present value of these losses should be written off in the year when the loss becomes evident. If the premium deficiency exceeds the deferred acquisition costs to be written off, a liability should be established for the excess amount.

Generally, acquisition costs to be deferred for property and liability insurance companies are determined by calculating ratios of acquisition costs to written premiums and applying those ratios to unearned premiums. Testing such ratios is relatively simple; however, the auditor must carefully evaluate whether the costs included in the calculations are proper and ascertain that the expenses vary with and are related to the production of new business. In addition, the auditor should review the business groupings used by the company to determine whether the basis for deferral is reasonable and consistent, and whether deferring acquisition costs to future periods is justified in the light of prevailing operating conditions.

When premiums are established for a property and liability company, it is expected they will be sufficient to pay losses and expenses, including amortization of deferred acquisition expenses, and to provide a margin of profit over the contract period. There are circumstances, however, in which the premium is not sufficient to cover anticipated losses, loss expenses, deferred acquisition costs, and other costs subsequent to acquisition. Any such premium deficiencies should be determined by reasonable groupings of the business, consistent with the company's operations. If it is expected that losses and loss adjustment expenses, maintenance expenses, and unamortized deferred acquisition expenses will exceed the related unearned premiums, the expected premium deficiency should be provided for by writing off any unamortized deferred acquisition costs. If the premium deficiency is greater than the unamortized deferred acquisition costs, a liability should be established for the excess deficiency.

Use of Audit Software

Computerization of accounting and other systems in the insurance industry is extensive. The auditor often finds it efficient to test general control procedures to obtain evidence of their effectiveness, as discussed in Chapter 11. Also, there are usually numerous opportunities for using various software packages of the types described in Chapter 11. Customized software developed for use in auditing life insurance companies was noted earlier. Similar software has been developed for several applications in property and liability companies. Among its uses are testing unearned premium calculations, the completeness of the data in a company's in-force file, and the accumulation of data necessary for testing loss reserves.

33

Auditing Investment Companies

OVERVIEW OF THE INDUSTRY

An investment company serves as a vehicle for investors with similar investment objectives to benefit from professional investment management and diversification of investments without incurring the substantial costs that would be associated with smaller portfolio positions. The business of an investment company consists of selling its capital shares to the public; investing the proceeds, principally in securities, in a manner that seeks to achieve its established investment objectives; and distributing to its shareholders the net income from, and net gains realized on sales of, its investments.

The management investment company is the most dominant of several types of investment companies. The shares issued by a management investment company do not represent either obligations to pay a stated amount or individual interests in securities. (Those types of investments, such as variable annuities, collective trust funds, unit investment partnerships, and offshore funds, are offered by other categories of investment companies.) Within the management investment company classification, the two main types are open-end (i.e., mutual) funds and closed-end funds. The discussion in this chapter is presented principally in terms of mutual funds, which predominate in the industry. Investors in mutual funds invest and disinvest directly with the fund on a continuous basis. Closed-end funds do not redeem capital shares on a continuous basis; instead, investors disinvest by selling capital shares to others, as with securities in general.[1] Investment companies operate in an environment that is highly regulated by the Securities and Exchange Commission (SEC), extremely competitive, and subject to specialized tax treatment.

In the early 1980s, the investment company industry emerged from a principally equity-oriented environment to one dominated by mutual funds investing in debt and money market instruments. Since that time, mutual fund products have continued to develop in response to customer demand and the availability of innovative investment vehicles, such as international/global funds, junk bond funds, sector funds, tax-exempt funds, multiple portfolio series funds, and mortgage-backed security funds. New investment strategies utilizing options, futures, and forward contracts have been used to enhance yields and to hedge investment risk. In addition, closed-end funds with a variety of objectives, including foreign and domestic equity growth as well as fixed-income bond portfolios, have found increased favor with the investing public.

The conduit, or "pass-through," concept underlies the operations of the entire industry. By complying with specific SEC regulations and certain sections of the Internal Revenue Code (described later), a management investment company can distribute as dividends to its shareholders, net investment income earned and capital gains realized, with no federal income taxes being assessed against the fund; the shareholder pays the appropriate tax and thus double taxation is avoided. Net investment income on a GAAP basis comprises income from dividends and interest on an investment company's investments, plus all other income except realized and unrealized gains or losses from

---

[1]Except for this aspect, closed-end funds are very similar to mutual funds, and auditors of closed-end funds should consider the relevant sections of this chapter.

security transactions, minus operating expenses other than federal and state income taxes on realized gains from security transactions. In addition, the eligibility of dividends for certain favorable federal income tax considerations can be retained by the fund and passed through to its shareholders. Failure of a fund to comply with SEC and Internal Revenue Service (IRS) regulations could subject it to the tax rules applicable to ordinary corporations.

The auditor should be aware of a number of specific tax and regulatory constraints on mutual funds. First, to qualify as a regulated investment company (RIC), discussed later, for tax purposes, an investment company must

- Meet several diversification-of-assets tests on a quarterly basis. These tests are particularly important for start-up funds, because certain requirements *must be met* at the end of the first quarter of a fund's initial year.
- Derive less than 30 percent of its gross income from gains (disregarding losses) on the sale or disposition of securities held for less than three months.[2]
- Derive at least 90 percent of its "gross income" from dividends, interest, and gains from the sale or other disposition of securities, foreign currencies, or other qualifying income, including, but not limited to, gains from options, futures contracts, or forward contracts.
- Distribute to shareholders at least 90 percent of the fund's "net investment company taxable income."

While this is not a requirement to maintain RIC status, recent tax legislation requires a mutual fund to distribute to its shareholders by December 31 at least 98 percent of its capital gains income (for the 12-month period ended October 31) and 97 percent of its ordinary income (for the 12-month period ended December 31), or pay a nondeductible 4 percent federal excise tax on the undistributed amount.

Second, to qualify for exemption from taxes on net investment income and capital gains realized, an investment company must distribute 100 percent of such income annually to its shareholders. Other tax matters that must be considered include the following:

- For federal income tax purposes, net short-term capital gains are considered ordinary income to the extent they exceed net long-term capital losses.
- Certain corporate actions, such as a return of capital, affect capital gain or loss determination.
- A fund may elect not to distribute long-term capital gains, but may retain them and record and pay a federal income tax liability thereon.
- Capital gains need not be distributed if the fund has an equal or greater amount of capital loss carryovers available. Funds may carry capital losses forward for eight years.

---

[2]Securities held for less than three months are called short-three securities, a category that applies only to investment companies that function under the conduit concept.

- The SEC usually permits only two distributions of long-term capital gains in a tax year.

In addition to Subchapter M of the Internal Revenue Code, as amended (Sections 851–855 and 4982), the auditor of a mutual fund should be familiar with the following federal regulations, which address all aspects of fund operations, including the contents of a fund prospectus, investment portfolio diversification, record keeping, advertising, and related party transactions, as well as financial statement reporting and disclosures:

- The Investment Company Act of 1940, as amended (the 1940 Act).
- The Investment Advisors Act of 1940, as amended (the Advisors Act).
- The Securities Act of 1933 (the 1933 Act).
- Article 6 of Regulation S-X.
- The AICPA industry audit and accounting guide, *Audits of Investment Companies*, 3rd ed. (1987).

The auditor should also understand the differences among the following designations relating to mutual funds, some of which have been formulated by the regulatory and taxing authorities:

Regulated Investment Company—An investment company that qualifies for special tax treatment provided by Subchapter M of the Internal Revenue Code by meeting the requirements of Subchapter M and following the conduit concept of passing its income to its shareholders.

Registered Investment Company—An investment company that has filed a registration statement with the SEC in accordance with the requirements of the 1940 Act, which statement has been declared effective by the SEC.

Diversified Investment Company—A management investment company having at least 75 percent of its total assets in cash and cash items (including receivables), government securities, securities of other investment companies, and other securities, with no more than 5 percent of its total assets in any one issuer, and not holding more than 10 percent of the voting securities of any one issuer (Section 5 of the 1940 Act).

Load Fund—An open-end investment company that adds a sales charge (of up to 8½ percent) to the net asset value in computing the offering price to provide for underwriters' and dealers' commissions.

No-Load Fund—A mutual fund selling its shares to the public at net asset value without a sales charge.

12b-1 Plan Fund—A load or no-load mutual fund that covers certain expenses of promoting the sale of fund shares through payments by the fund to an advisor or a service organization under a Rule 12b-1 plan approved and adopted by the fund's directors and shareholders. 12b-1 plan funds may include a contingent deferred sales load, which is imposed under certain conditions when the shareholder redeems shares.

Series Fund—A mutual fund offering several distinct portfolios from which a purchaser can choose. The assets of each series are segregated from the assets of the other series in the fund. While each portfolio of a series is considered a separate corporation (trust) for tax purposes, all portfolios of a series are considered as one registrant with the SEC. This treatment leads to many efficiencies, particularly in the registration process.

The maintenance and reliability of accounting records and the issuance of financial reports are the responsibility of a mutual fund's officers and trustees. The accounting and administrative functions are either performed by fund employees ("internalized" funds) or provided by other organizations, usually under contract (managed funds). Typical organizations that provide services to funds are

- *Investment Advisor (Manager)*. A manager generally provides investment advice, research services, and certain administrative services under a contract that provides for an annual fee, which is usually based on a specified percentage of average net assets (although some agreements provide for a fee based on gross investment income as well as average net assets). The contract must be approved by a majority of the trustees who are disinterested persons, as defined by the SEC, and by a majority of the fund's shareholders.

- *Distributor*. A distributor, often referred to as the principal underwriter, acts as an agent or a principal and sells the fund's shares at net asset value with or without sales charge (load), either as a wholesaler through an independent dealer or as a retailer through its own sales network. Some funds adopt distribution plans under Rule 12b-1 that use fund assets to pay for distribution expenses. One of the requirements of that rule is that the disinterested trustees must approve the plan each year.

- *Transfer Agent*. A transfer agent issues, transfers, redeems, and accounts for the fund's capital shares under an agreement with the fund. In addition, the transfer agent usually processes the distribution of dividends and realized gains on securities, including any reinvestment of dividends by shareholders. The transfer agent function may be performed by a bank or a private company or by a related party, such as the investment advisor, distributor, or other affiliated company.

- *Custodian*. Custody of a fund's cash and portfolio securities usually is entrusted to a bank that has prescribed minimum aggregate capital, surplus, and undivided profits, and that is responsible for the receipt, delivery, safekeeping, and often the evaluation of the securities. An investment company using a bank as custodian may allow the bank to deposit qualifying securities in a central securities depository, that is, The Depositor Trust Company (DTC). Most U.S. traded securities are held by this depository on behalf of the securities industry. With respect to global or international funds, the custodian typically has a subcustodian network that holds foreign securities and receives cash dividends, interest income, and other distributions such as stock splits or dividends. The subcustodian must comply with Rule 17f-5 of the 1940 Act.

Clearing organizations use "book entry" methods to record transfers of securities, thus obviating the need for physical movements of the securities. Custodians may also use the Federal Reserve or treasury book entry system as a depository for U.S. government and agency securities. Rule 17f-4 of the 1940 Act contains special rules applying to the use of book entry systems.

ACCOUNTING PRINCIPLES

Under the 1940 Act, mutual funds are required to maintain certain accounting records, including

Transaction journals that contain the details of investment and related cash activity.

Securities ledger(s), which contain a detailed listing of securities held by the fund.

An order book, showing the details of orders for each purchase or sale of portfolio items.

A fund's assets and liabilities typically are valued daily at current fair value. The valuation of securities according to the fund's policies, as described in its prospectus, often constitutes one of the custodian's most significant responsibilities, since the net asset value per share of the fund's outstanding capital stock is required to be released each business day 75 minutes after the close of the New York Stock Exchange. Valuation sources include prices reported by national stock exchanges, over-the-counter markets, brokers, specialized pricing services, and foreign exchanges; trustees' valuations; and other specialized methods.[3] The net asset value per share is computed by dividing the value of all the assets of the fund, less liabilities, by the number of shares outstanding at the end of the day.

Restricted securities, which cannot be offered for public sale without first being registered under the 1933 Act, are generally valued in good faith by the board of trustees. The objective is to state the securities at the amount the owner could reasonably expect to receive for them in a current sale. A pricing agent usually furnishes prices daily for tax-exempt funds based on information about market transactions and quotations from recognized municipal securities dealers.

Money market funds usually seek to maintain a constant net asset value per share of $1. To accomplish this, many money market funds value their portfolio securities on the basis of amortized cost. Other money market funds use the penny-rounding method (rounding the net asset value per share to the nearest cent based on a share value of $1). Both of those methods are allowed by Rule 2a-7 of the 1940 Act.

Income equalization is a practice unique to the investment company industry; it applies to funds that do not pay dividends daily. Income equalization is

---

[3]A matrix is one type of specialized pricing method used by funds. Matrix pricing is an EDP technique for valuing securities based on an aggregate of a variety of factors and without exclusive reliance on quoted market prices.

used to prevent a dilution (caused by the continuous sales and redemptions of capital shares) of the continuing shareholders' per-share equity in undistributed net investment income. The method involves applying a portion of the proceeds from sales and the costs of repurchases of capital shares to undistributed net investment income (which excludes all capital gains and losses); the portion is equivalent to the amount, on a per-share basis, of distributable net investment income on the date of the related transaction. Income equalization is based on the concept that the net asset value of each share sold or repurchased is composed of both undistributed net investment income and capital components.

Reporting requirements for mutual funds include

- Annual audited financial statements to shareholders.
- Semiannual and annual reports to the SEC on Form N-SAR. The annual report must include a letter to the SEC from the auditor on the adequacy of the fund's internal control structure as of the year-end.
- Semiannual financial statements to shareholders (not required to be audited).
- Post-effective amendments to registration statements on Form N-1A, Parts A, B, and C (annual updating of selling prospectus).
- Federal Tax Form 1120 RIC, if operating in a corporate or Massachusetts or Maryland business trust form.
- Federal Form 8613 (Excise Tax), if a distributable amount exists.
- Federal Form 1099 DIV to shareholders.

The form and content of financial statements for SEC purposes are governed by Article 6 of Regulation S-X and by the AICPA audit and accounting guide for investment companies. The requirements of Article 6 are generally more comprehensive than those of the guide, and encompass the following financial statements:

- Statement of assets and liabilities.
- Statement of operations.
- Statement of changes in net assets for the past two reporting periods.[4]
- Investment portfolio.

In addition, while not considered a basic financial statement, supplementary per-share information for the past ten years is required to be presented.

RISK ASSESSMENT AND AUDIT STRATEGY

The two main areas of audit concern in a mutual fund relate to portfolio accounting (accounting for investments purchased and sold, investment valua-

---

[4]In certain circumstances (see SFAS Nos. 95 and 102), a statement of cash flows is required and replaces the statement of changes in net assets.

tion, income received, and other corporate actions) and share transfer accounting (accounting for ownership, sales, redemptions, and payment of dividends, including dividend reinvestment). In determining the audit strategy for a mutual fund, the auditor may be confronted with one of several different processing environments, ranging from a comprehensive in-house system to one principally provided by third-party organizations. As described earlier, third-party organizations under contract to funds usually provide services involving bookkeeping, custody of cash and investments, maintenance of shareholder accounts, and pricing of certain portfolio investments. In most instances, the accounting system is computerized, particularly with respect to shareholder records. Many auditors believe the latter function is the most critical, since the number of capital shares is not constant, as in an industrial corporation or closed-end fund, but contracts or expands daily. This "breathing capital structure" increases inherent risk associated with capital accounts beyond that typically found in other corporations.

In determining the audit approach, the auditor must obtain an understanding of the fund's control structure and assess control risk as a basis for determining the substantive tests to be performed. If a fund has an in-house system that encompasses the record keeping for the fund's transactions and the maintenance of shareholder accounts, the auditor generally has ready access to the system and can, with minimal difficulty, carry out the procedures necessary to assess its effectiveness.

For accounting and control procedures provided by service organizations, the auditor should consider performing certain additional procedures. Specifically, since a custodian usually maintains the records for a mutual fund, most of the audit work is performed at the custodian's location. The audit strategy for a mutual fund generally calls for obtaining an understanding of and assessing procedures performed by the custodian, because they are usually effective and subject to periodic review by the fund's management and board of trustees. As mentioned earlier, most custodians of mutual fund investments maintain customers' U.S. traded securities on deposit with the DTC and not in their own vaults. Of particular importance to the auditor are the custodian's procedures for performing periodic reconciliations of its records of the fund's securities with those of the DTC. The auditor should review the reconciliations and assess their effectiveness, including how frequently they are performed.

To assess control risk as low in a third-party environment, the auditor either arranges to perform certain tests of controls, including those of general control procedures, or relies on a third-party assessment made and reported on by other independent auditors. In this connection, the auditor should apply the procedures specified by SAS No. 44, *Special-Purpose Reports on Internal Accounting Control at Service Organizations* (AU Section 324). (See also the discussions in Chapters 6 and 23.)

CONTROL STRUCTURE POLICIES AND PROCEDURES, AND TESTS OF CONTROLS

Control procedures established by investment companies or provided for them by custodians generally include the following:

- Procedures for the receipt and delivery of securities as authorized by responsible officials and for recording cash paid and received.
- Appropriate valuation of the portfolio of investments and proper recording of cost for financial reporting and tax purposes.
- Safeguarding securities.
- Procedures to ensure compliance with restrictions on the company's investment objectives and policies (as stated in its prospectus).
- Procedures to ensure the custody, pricing, and timely notification of corporate actions with respect to foreign securities.

The auditor's tests of controls, if called for by the audit strategy, will generally focus on obtaining evidence of the effectiveness of those control procedures. If a pricing agent is relied on for quotations used in valuing investments, the auditor should also consider periodically visiting the pricing service's facilities to review the procedures used in obtaining daily quotations.

Investment companies have large volumes of cash receipts and cash disbursements, many of which are handled by wire. Control structure policies and procedures are needed to ensure that such transactions are accompanied by sufficient information to allow amounts to be recorded in the proper customer's account. Because of the volume of these transactions, reconciliations are performed frequently, sometimes even daily. The auditor should review the reconciliations, including procedures for investigating and resolving differences. In general, policies and procedures applied to investment accounts, income from investments, accruals, and expenses are similar to those found in commercial and manufacturing enterprises.

Control procedures relating to shareholder accounting, including those of the fund's transfer agent, should also be reviewed and, if called for by the audit strategy, tested. Since a fund's capital changes daily, specialized procedures are frequently found in this area. At a minimum, the auditor should gain an understanding of procedures for processing

- Sales of fund shares and related collections.
- Repurchases and related payments.
- Payments of dividends in cash and additional shares.
- Inactive or dormant accounts.
- Cancellations of sales and repurchases.
- Wire orders in federal funds.
- Check writing and telephone redemptions.
- Electronic funds transfers.
- Pending or incomplete transactions (such as unidentified wire orders and incomplete purchase applications).
- Sales or redemptions for which processing is delayed beyond the normal trade date ("as of" trades).
- Incoming mail (i.e., ensuring that it is properly time–date stamped).
- Shareholder correspondence.

Under Rule 17A(d)-13 of the 1940 Act, certain registered transfer agents are required to obtain a report by an independent accountant on their internal control structure policies and procedures. A third-party auditor's report may be issued by the transfer agent's own independent auditor or by an auditor engaged specifically to issue such report. The fund's auditor should obtain this report and consider both discussing it with the third-party auditor to determine the nature and scope of work performed in connection with issuing the report, and reviewing the relevant working papers. If the report and work of the third-party auditor are deemed acceptable and there is other evidence that the transfer agent had an effective control structure in place from the "report date" to the "audit date," a separate review of the transfer agent's control procedures by the fund's auditor will be unnecessary.

SUBSTANTIVE TESTS

Substantive tests for a mutual fund generally can be grouped into four major financial statement areas: investments, income, expenses, and shareholders' equity. Because of specialized industry practices and regulatory requirements, many of the procedures are unique to mutual funds. The following discussion is limited to these industry practices and related auditing procedures.

Investments

Investments represent the most significant asset in a mutual fund's statement of assets and liabilities. The auditor's concerns about investments are related to custody, unsettled trades, valuation, proper recording of financial reporting and tax cost, and adherence to the fund's investment restrictions. Tests of the accuracy of the fund's records are the same as for other industries and thus are not discussed here.

In connection with the audit of investments, the auditor should confirm with the custodian all portfolio positions held at the audit date and all open (unsettled) investment transactions. With the exception of certain situations described under Rule 17f-2, it is generally not necessary for the auditor to count securities held by the custodian unless the client requests it. All unsettled investment transactions should be confirmed with the appropriate brokers. SEC rules mandate the sending of a second confirmation request if there is no response to the initial request after a reasonable time. Alternative auditing procedures usually are employed to substantiate unconfirmed open transactions at the audit date. The confirmation procedures followed are detailed in the scope paragraph of the auditor's report. (See Figure 33.1.)

Financial Reporting Release No. 404.03 requires that values assigned to all investments be substantiated by the auditor. Auditors use several different means of obtaining prices to substantiate the values assigned to investments by a custodian, depending on the type of fund under consideration. Some auditors have developed computer software packages that compare market prices obtained from an independent source with the security prices used by the fund. These packages also permit the auditor to recalculate the client's extensions and footings. Other auditors purchase and use commercially available software packages designed to accomplish the same objectives. In all instances, the auditor should use a different source from the one that provided quotes to the fund.

For domestic publicly traded common and preferred stocks and corporate bonds, daily quotes from national stock exchanges are available to the auditor from several published sources. The auditor must determine whether the client used closing exchange prices or composite exchange prices (which are more widely published). Daily quotes from international exchanges, which usually close earlier in the day than do the U.S. exchanges, generally are provided to the custodian by a broker or pricing agent for foreign common and preferred stocks and corporate bonds. The auditor should consider obtaining quotes from independent sources by using correspondent firms or foreign offices of the auditing firm, which should provide the quotes from local published or electronic financial sources. If the fund uses a computerized pricing service, the auditor should become familiar with the information provided by the service.

For thinly traded securities, it may be necessary for the auditor to obtain quotes from brokers that deal specifically in certain equity securities. For corporate bonds without quotes, generally the auditor should obtain quotes from several brokers in order to evaluate the reasonableness of the quotes used by the fund or should compare recent trade prices with broker-provided quotes.

The auditor should review the reasonableness of the procedures followed to identify and value restricted securities. Disclosure of restricted securities must be made in the financial statements, together with certain other information required under amendments to Article 6 of Regulation S-X.

The auditor can substantiate prices for tax-exempt funds, which are usually furnished by a pricing agent, by obtaining quotations from market makers and comparing them with the furnished prices, comparing selected proceeds from sales during the period with the value used on the day preceding the sale, or obtaining a portfolio valuation from a second pricing service.

As discussed earlier, many money market funds value their securities at amortized cost, either based on exemptive orders granted by the SEC or as allowed by Rule 2a-7. If a fund follows an exemptive order, the auditor should review a copy of the order and ascertain that the fund has procedures in place for monitoring adherence to the conditions enumerated in the order. If a fund adopts Rule 2a-7, the auditor should review that rule and ascertain that the fund has procedures in place for ensuring that the conditions in the rule will be met. Among those conditions are that investments are to be limited to short-term, high-quality debt instruments, and a requirement that the trustees determine that using either the amortized cost method or the penny-rounding pricing method (described earlier) is in the best interests of the fund and its shareholders, and ensure that a stable price per share is maintained.

Both exemptive orders permitting use of amortized cost valuation and Rule 2a-7 require a fund to price its portfolio periodically, using available market quotations, to determine if the net asset value deviates from $1 per share. The auditor should review those pricings and determine whether, during the period under audit, a deviation occurred and, if so, what corrective action was taken by the trustees. The auditor should also obtain market quotations (usually given in yields) directly from a major market maker at the audit date to determine whether there was a deviation in price from $1 a share. (The fund should be requested to price its portfolio at market at the audit date.)

In addition to SEC and IRS restrictions on a fund's investments, which deal principally with diversification and classification, there are generally restrictions in the fund's prospectus relating to the quality of investments, geographic dispersion, type of security, and so on. The auditor should review the fund's portfolio for compliance with all of those restrictions.

Further, because of significant and extensive changes to the tax law, incorporated in the Tax Reform Act of 1986 and subsequent amendments, as well as the need to apply existing tax rules regarding trading in options, futures, and forward contracts within the already complex investment company environment, the auditor must be constantly aware of tax compliance.

Investment Income and Realized Gains

Because of the conduit concept underlying mutual funds, recording and classification of investment income and realized gains from sales of investments are of paramount importance to the auditor. Investment income usually is composed of dividends and interest earned. The auditor should determine that all income earned during the period has been recorded for financial reporting purposes. New investment vehicles, such as convertible securities, "deep discount" bonds, "payment-in-kind" bonds, and "securitized" or "collateralized" obligations, must be carefully reviewed to ensure proper accounting and recording of income. With respect to dividends, the auditor usually substantiates domestic dividends and other corporate actions (such as stock splits and issuance of stock rights) by referring to published sources. Software packages are available that allow the auditor to compare the client's tape with a tape from an independent source. (The same software packages can also be used to compare the pricing tapes mentioned earlier.) Pricing services exist for foreign securities; however, the auditor may wish to make arrangements, usually with correspondents, to identify corporate actions such as cash dividends, stock dividends or splits, and stock rights. The auditor should also review the federal taxability of such corporate actions, as well as the related foreign currency gains and losses, to assist fund management in determining investment company taxable income available for distribution.

Mutual funds are required by the IRS to accrete original-issue discount on all securities by use of the yield method and to amortize bond premium on tax-exempt bonds using the straight-line method. Funds have the option of amortizing premium on other bonds and may use either the yield method or the straight-line method. The auditor usually recalculates such computations or tests the formulas used.

In auditing investment sales and the related realized gains and losses, the auditor should test the classification of capital gains and losses (as short term or long term) for tax purposes. Of particular concern is the determination of financial reporting and tax cost. Many mutual funds still use specific identification for both purposes; some funds use the average method for financial reporting purposes only. The use of specific identification permits a fund to choose the particular lot of shares to be sold and thereby accomplish specified performance objectives (or manage the utilization of capital loss carryforwards).

The test of the classification of gains and losses should include a review for wash sales. A wash sale occurs when securities are sold (or otherwise disposed of) and, within a period beginning 30 days prior to the sale date and ending 30 days after that date (a 61-day period), the investment company has acquired (or has contracts to acquire) substantially identical securities. A loss sustained on such a sale (or other disposition) is not allowed by the IRS. Instead, for tax purposes the amount of loss is added to the basis of the "substantially identical" security. Determining the extent to which wash sales have occurred is necessary to enable a fund to properly distribute its investment company taxable income and long-term capital gains and to maintain its RIC status.

Accruals and Expenses

The auditor should determine that expenses assumed by the investment company are in accordance with the provisions of the investment advisory contract, prospectus, or other related agreements. Usually the auditor recalculates the management fee, which is the largest expense incurred by an investment company. Other expenses, such as printing, distribution ("12b-1 fees"), transfer agent and custodial fees, and professional fees, should be reviewed for authorization by a fund officer and should be traced to invoices and agreements. State income and franchise taxes should be recalculated. The auditor ordinarily analyzes changes in significant expense categories between the current and prior periods.

For a fund that declares dividends daily (as money market funds usually do), the auditor should ascertain that management reviews expense accruals periodically and allocates expenses ratably over the year. For funds that do not declare dividends daily, the SEC has informally taken the position that expenses need not be accrued daily if the cumulative accrual, when netted, would not be material.

The securities laws of the states ("Blue Sky" laws) in which an investment company's securities are sold generally limit certain investment company expenses. A more restrictive limitation may be provided for in the investment advisory contract or cited in the prospectus. In addition, during the start-up period of a new fund, the investment advisor may voluntarily limit the expenses of the fund by agreeing to reimburse the fund for certain expenses in excess of a specified percentage of the average value of the fund's net assets during the year. Such reimbursable amounts should be reviewed and recalculated by the auditor, because they may not qualify for the 90 percent income test (discussed earlier). The auditor must be aware of their potential impact on the fund's Subchapter M tax compliance.

Capital Accounts

Auditing capital or shareholders' accounts does not require any unusual considerations other than reviewing and testing the internal control structure of the transfer agent, as previously discussed, and testing the computations of the net asset value per share used in the daily purchase and sale transactions of a fund's shares.

To determine whether the fund followed the procedures specified in Rule 2a-4 of the 1940 Act in calculating the current net asset value of its outstanding shares for purposes of distributing and redeeming such shares, the auditor should select a number of days and review the fund's net asset value computations as shown on the price make-up sheets. The review should include

- Comparing quantities and description of portfolio securities owned with data in the investment ledger.
- Tracing quoted market prices to independent sources.
- Testing the clerical accuracy of market value extensions and footings.
- Reconciling amounts for other assets and liabilities to the general ledger accounts.
- Reviewing the reasonableness of income and expense accruals.
- Reconciling the number of the fund's shares outstanding to the general ledger accounts.
- Recalculating the net asset value per share by dividing total assets minus liabilities by the number of shares outstanding.

If the fund follows the practice of income equalization (described earlier), the auditor should test the breakdown between the income and capital components of the net asset value of shares for several days during the period under audit; often nonstatistical sampling is involved in this procedure.

Supplementary Information and Investment Portfolio

There are two unique aspects of reporting on the financial statements of an investment company. The first involves the table required by Regulation S-X showing a fund's per-share data for the past ten years. This information is covered by the auditor's opinion. The other unique reporting feature for funds is that every security position in the fund's portfolio is shown in the financial statements and is covered by the auditor's report, including number of shares held, face amount, description, fair value, category (industry or similar grouping), and type of security. Figure 33.1 shows the standard auditor's report for an investment company.[5]

---

[5]As indicated earlier, Regulation S-X requires supplementary information for ten years. As illustrated in Figure 33.1, GAAP requires this information for five years. As a practical matter, most investment companies present this information for ten years.

The report in Figure 33.1 is for a fund. The same report, with appropriate wording changes, would be used for a series of funds.

Figure 33.1   Auditor's Standard Report

<u>Independent Auditor's Report</u>

We have audited the accompanying statement of assets and liabilities of XYZ Investment Company, including the schedule of portfolio investments, as of December 31, 19XX, and the related statement of operations for the year then ended, the statement of changes in net assets for each of the two years in the period then ended, and the selected per-share data and ratios for each of the five years in the period then ended. These financial statements and per-share data and ratios are the responsibility of the Company's management. Our responsibility is to express an opinion on these financial statements and per-share data and ratios based on our audits.

We conducted our audits in accordance with generally accepted auditing standards. Those standards require that we plan and perform the audit to obtain reasonable assurance about whether the financial statements and per-share data and ratios are free of material misstatement. An audit includes examining, on a test basis, evidence supporting the amounts and disclosures in the financial statements. Our procedures included confirmation of securities owned as of December 31, 19XX, by correspondence with the custodian and brokers, and other auditing procedures. An audit also includes assessing the accounting principles used and significant estimates made by management, as well as evaluating the overall financial statement presentation. We believe that our audits provide a reasonable basis for our opinion.

In our opinion, the financial statements and selected per-share data and ratios referred to above present fairly, in all material respects, the financial position of XYZ Investment Company as of December 31, 19XX, the results of its operations for the year then ended, the changes in its net assets for each of the two years in the period then ended, and the selected per-share data and ratios for each of the five years in the period then ended, in conformity with generally accepted accounting principles.

[*Signature*]

[*Date*]

34

Auditing Mining Companies

OVERVIEW OF THE INDUSTRY

The principal difference between hard-rock mining companies and companies involved in oil and gas producing activities, discussed in Chapter 35, relates to the nature, timing, and extent of expenditures incurred for exploration, development, production, and processing of minerals.

Generally in the mining industry, a period of as long as several years elapses between the time exploration costs are incurred to discover a commercially viable body of ore and the expenditure of development costs, which are usually substantial, to complete the project. Therefore, the economic benefits derived from a project are long term in nature and subject to the uncertainties inherent in the passage of time. In contrast, the costs related to exploring for deposits of oil and gas are expended over a relatively short time.

The mining industry is highly capital intensive. Substantial investments in property, plant, and equipment are required; usually they represent more than 50 percent of a mining company's total assets. The significant capital investments of mining companies and the related risks inherent in any long-term major project may affect the recoverability of capitalized costs. The auditor must be cognizant of these factors, among others, and must assess the risk that costs will not be recovered.

The operational stages in mining companies vary somewhat depending on the type of mineral, because of differences in geological, chemical, and economic factors. The basic operations common to mining companies are exploration, development, mining, milling, beneficiation and agglomeration, smelting, and refining.

Exploration is the search for natural accumulations of minerals with economic value. Exploration for minerals is a specialized activity involving the use of complex geophysical and geochemical equipment and procedures. There is an element of financial risk in every decision to pursue exploration, and explorers generally seek to minimize the costs and increase the probability of success. As a result, before any field work begins, extensive studies are made concerning which types of minerals are to be sought and where they are most likely to occur. Market studies and forecasts, studies of geological maps and reports, and logistical evaluations are performed to provide information for use in determining the economic feasibility of a potential project.

Exploration can be divided into two phases, prospecting and geophysical analysis. Prospecting is the search for geological information over a broad area. It embraces such activities as geological mapping, analysis of rock types and structures, searches for direct manifestations of mineralization, taking samples of minerals found, and aeromagnetic surveys. Geophysical analysis is conducted in specific areas of interest localized during the prospecting phase. Rock and soil samples are examined, and the earth's crust is monitored directly for magnetic, gravitational, sonic, radioactive, and electrical data. Based on the analysis, targets for trenching, test pits, and exploratory drilling are identified. Drilling is particularly useful in evaluating the shape and character of a deposit. Analysis of samples is necessary to determine the grade of the deposit.

Once the grade and quantity of the deposit have been determined, a decision must be made regarding the technical feasibility and commercial viability of developing the deposit for mining activity. The value of a mineral deposit is determined by the intrinsic value of the minerals present and by the nature and location of their occurrence. In addition to the grade and quantity of the ore, such factors as the physical accessibility of the deposit, the estimated costs of production, and the value of joint products and by-products are key elements in the decision to develop a deposit for commercial exploitation.

The *development* stage of production involves planning and preparing for commercial operation. Development of surface mines is relatively straightforward. For open-pit mines, which are surface mines, the principal procedure is to remove sufficient overburden to expose the ore. For strip mines, an initial cut is made to expose the mineral to be mined. For underground mines, data resulting from exploratory drilling is evaluated as a basis for planning the shafts and tunnels that will provide access to the mineral deposit. Substantial capital investment in mineral rights, machinery and equipment, and related facilities generally is required in the development stage.

The goal at the *mining* stage of production is to break up the rock and ore to the extent necessary for loading and removal to the processing location. A variety of mining techniques exist to accomplish this. The drilling and blasting technique is utilized frequently; an alternative is the continuous mining method, in which a boring or tearing machine is mounted on a forward crawler to break the material away from the rock face.

After removal from the mine site, the ore is ready for *milling*. The first phase of the milling stage involves crushing and grinding the chunks of ore to reduce them to particle size. This is performed in several steps; water is generally used in the grinding process, and the end product of this phase is a slurry, or combination of finely ground ore and water.

The second milling procedure is concentration, which involves the separation of the mineral constituents from the rock. This is usually done using separation techniques such as flotation, and leaching and precipitation. Flotation is a process in which heavy metallic substances are made to cling to the bubbles of an oily froth and rise to the surface, from which they can easily be skimmed off. This process is used primarily for concentrations of ores that contain compounds of sulfur. Since most of the metal production in the United States comes from sulfide ores, flotation is the most commonly used concentration process in this country. Flotation is used not only to separate the desired mineral from the waste rock, but also to separate different minerals from each other. Leaching and precipitation are particularly important for concentrating oxide ores. Leaching is a process of extracting the metallic compound from the ore by selectively dissolving it in a suitable solvent, such as water, sulfuric acid, or hydrochloric acid. The metal is then removed from the solution using chemical or electrochemical precipitation techniques. In recent years, heap leaching, another method for recovery of various minerals, primarily gold and silver, from low-grade ore deposits, has become a significant factor in gold production. Even though the recovery of the minerals in heap leach operations is often much lower than in other processes, heap leaching is nevertheless a cost-effective process.

Beneficiation and agglomeration relate to ferrous (iron) mining. Beneficiation is the dressing or processing of ore for the purpose of regulating the size of the desired product, removing unwanted constituents, and improving the quality, purity, or assay grade of the ore. Beneficiation techniques include crushing, screening, and washing, and also involve the use of gravity, magnetic, and flotation methods. Small particles of iron ore generally are subjected to an additional process called agglomeration. Agglomeration is a process in which the beneficiated particles are fused together into larger bits or pellets that are easier to handle.

Smelting is the process of separating the metal from impurities with which it may be chemically bound or physically mixed too closely to be removed by concentration. Most smelting is accomplished through fusion, which is the liquefaction of a metal under heat. In some cases, chemical processes are used instead of, or in combination with, heating techniques. Since metals occur in a variety of combinations with other elements, the smelting technique utilized depends on the characteristics of the concentrate. The principal phases of the smelting process include roasting, "true" smelting, and converting. Roasting is a heating process used primarily for sulfide ores as a means of driving out the sulfur. "True" smelting is the process of separating the metal from its chemical bonds by melting. Converting entails blowing oxygen-enriched air through molten metal, causing oxidation and removal of sulfur and other impurities from the metal.

Refining is the last step in isolating the metal. The primary methods utilized are fire refining and electrolytic refining. Fire refining is similar to smelting. The metal is kept in a molten state and treated with pine logs, hydrocarbon gas, or other substances to enable impurities to be removed. Fire refining generally does not allow the recovery of by-products. Electrolytic refining uses an electrical current to separate metals from a solution in such a way that by-products can be recovered. In electrolytic refining of copper, plates of impure copper (anodes) are suspended between thin plates of pure copper (cathodes), and both are then submerged in a solution of copper sulfate and sulfuric acid. When an electrical current is passed through the solution, pure copper from the anodes is deposited on the cathodes. Gold and silver are important by-products of the electrolytic refining of copper.

ACCOUNTING FOR EXPLORATION AND DEVELOPMENT COSTS

Accounting and reporting issues in the mining industry are discussed in AICPA Accounting Research Study No. 11, *Financial Reporting in the Extractive Industries* (1969). In 1976, the Financial Accounting Standards Board (FASB) issued a discussion memorandum, *Financial Accounting and Reporting in the Extractive Industries*, which analyzed issues relevant to the extractive industries. Neither of these attempts, however, culminated in the issuance of an authoritative pronouncement for mining companies. At present, therefore, the accounting practices prevalent among mining companies are the principal source of generally accepted accounting practices for the industry.

Exploration and development costs are major expenditures of mining companies, and auditors of such companies should have an understanding of the activities involved in those processes and the related accounting principles.

The characterization of expenditures as either exploration, development, or production usually determines whether they are capitalized or expensed. For accounting purposes, it is useful to identify five basic phases of exploration and development: prospecting, property acquisition, geophysical analysis, development before production, and development during production.

Exploration Costs

Prospecting usually begins with obtaining (or preparing) and studying topographical and geological maps. Prospecting costs, which are generally expensed as incurred, include options to lease or buy property; rights of access to lands for geophysical work; and salaries, equipment, and supplies for scouts, geologists, and geophysical crews.

Property acquisition includes both the purchase of property and the purchase or lease of mineral rights. Costs incurred to purchase property are capitalized; costs attributable to the purchase or lease of mineral rights are expensed as incurred until a commercial body of ore is identified, or they are deferred until it is determined whether a project is commercially feasible. Acquisition costs may include lease bonus and lease extension costs, lease brokers' commissions, abstract and recording fees, filing and patent fees and other legal expenses, and costs of land and lease departments.

Geophysical analysis is performed to discover specific deposits of minerals. The related costs (commonly referred to as exploration costs) are accounted for in a number of different ways. Most companies expense all those costs as incurred; others capitalize them until such time as the existence or absence of an economically recoverable mineral reserve is established. If no reserve is established, the costs are written off. Some companies capitalize previously expensed costs at the time a project is considered to be commercially feasible, while others capitalize only costs incurred in the later development stage of a project and do not capitalize previously expensed exploration costs. A "full cost" concept (discussed at length in Chapter 35) has not gained general acceptance in the mining industry.

Development Costs

A body of ore reaches the development stage when the decision has been made to develop it for mining. Development costs include expenditures associated with drilling, removing overburden (waste rock), sinking shafts, driving tunnels, building roads and dikes, purchasing primary cleaning or processing equipment and equipment used in developing the mine, and constructing supporting facilities to house and care for the work force. In many respects, the expenditures in the development stage are similar to those incurred during exploration. As a result, it is sometimes difficult to distinguish the point at which exploration ends and development begins. For example, the sinking of shafts and driving of tunnels may begin in the exploration stage and continue into the development stage. In most instances, the transition from the exploration to the development stage is the same for both accounting and tax purposes.

Generally, all costs incurred during the development stage before production starts are capitalized; usually they are reduced by the proceeds from the sale of any production during the development period. Development ore (ore extracted in the process of gaining access to the body of ore) is normally incidental to the development process.

Development also takes place during the production stage. The accounting treatment of development costs incurred during the ongoing operation of a mine depends on the nature and purpose of the expenditures. Costs associated with expansion of capacity are generally capitalized; costs incurred to maintain production are normally included in production costs in the period in which they are incurred. In certain instances, the benefits of development activity will be realized in future periods, such as when the "block caving" and open-pit mining methods are used. In the block caving method, entire sections of a body of ore are intentionally collapsed to permit the mass removal of minerals; extraction may take place two to three years after access to the ore is gained and the block prepared. In an open-pit mine, there is typically an expected ratio of overburden to mineral-bearing ore over the life of the mine. The cost of stripping the overburden to gain access to the ore is expensed in those periods in which the actual ratio of overburden to ore approximates the expected ratio. In certain instances, however, extensive stripping is performed to remove the overburden in advance of the period in which the ore will be extracted. When the benefits of either development activity are to be realized in a future accounting period, the costs associated with the development activity should be deferred and amortized during the period in which the ore is extracted or the product produced.

Determining the Start of the Production Phase

Determining when the production phase begins is important for accounting purposes because, in general, at that time development costs are no longer capitalized and revenue from the sale of ore is included in sales revenue rather than as a reduction of capitalized development costs. The point at which production is considered to begin is sometimes stipulated in loan agreements and may initiate debt payments. Determining the commencement of production is also significant for federal income tax purposes. The point at which a mine is considered to begin production is generally the same for both accounting and tax purposes.

Statement of Financial Accounting Standards (SFAS) No. 7, *Accounting and Reporting by Development Stage Enterprises* (Accounting Standards Section De4), states that "an enterprise shall be considered to be in the development stage if it is devoting substantially all of its efforts to establishing a new business" and "the planned principal operations have not commenced" or they "have commenced, but there has been no significant revenue therefrom." Although SFAS No. 7 specifically excludes mining companies from its application, the definition of a development stage enterprise is helpful in defining the point at which a mine is considered to be in the production phase.

Mining companies usually follow one of three assumptions as to when the production phase begins.

1. When the value of the ore extracted is greater than the cost of extraction and milling.
2. When both the mine and the mill produce on a regularly scheduled basis at the planned activity levels.
3. When ore is extracted on a regular basis without regard to the milling capability.

When the mine begins production, the capitalized property acquisition, exploration, and development costs are recognized as costs of production through their amortization, generally on the unit-of-production method, over the expected productive life of the mine.

It is generally preferable to expense as incurred start-up costs of mill facilities, smelters, and refineries. Start-up costs are defined as costs incurred after operations have begun but before the facilities have reached anticipated productive capacity and an economically viable level of commercial production.

RISK ASSESSMENT AND AUDIT STRATEGY

Among the risk factors inherent in the mining industry are the very long time it generally takes to bring a mine from the exploration and development stages to the commercially viable production stage, the capital intensity of the industry, the significant use of riskier forms of capital—debt financing and joint ventures—to finance new projects, and financial pressures on the industry from various sources. From an audit standpoint, those risk factors may have an effect on the recoverability of capitalized costs carried on the balance sheet at large dollar amounts.

Auditing mining companies requires the auditor to evaluate many types of management judgments for which it is usually extremely difficult to obtain "hard" data. For example, for purposes of both auditing cost accumulations and their allocation to current production and assessing the recoverability of highly material capitalized costs through production and sales, the auditor must evaluate (1) the reasonableness of management judgments about proved and probable mineral reserves, (2) the metal content of those reserves, (3) estimated future production costs, (4) the lives of mining properties and equipment with economic lives and values that are determined largely by future metal prices, and (5) the precise dates when a mine passes from the exploration stage to the development stage and then to the production stage. These management judgments have a pervasive effect on the financial statements of mining companies. For example, as discussed later, the estimate of mineral reserves affects balances in the property, plant, and equipment accounts as well as the product inventory and cost of sales accounts.

Another area in which the auditor must evaluate management judgments in the absence of relatively reliable audit evidence involves a decision by management to shut down operations. Volatile metal prices may make active operations uneconomical from time to time, and, as a result, mining companies will shut down operations, either temporarily or permanently. A significant concern of the auditor when operations are temporarily shut down is the carrying value of the related assets. If a long-term diminution in the value of the assets has occurred, a write-down of the carrying value to net realizable value should be recorded. This decision is extremely judgmental and depends on projections of whether viable mining operations can ever be resumed. Those projections are based on significant assumptions as to prices, production quantities, and costs; because most minerals are worldwide commodities, the projections must take into account global supply and demand factors. The auditor can corroborate management's assumptions as to prices by using independent price projections; assumptions relating to production quantities can be evaluated by comparing historical metal recoveries with projections and overall mine capacity; and cost assumptions can be evaluated based on historical and projected inflation rates and cost increases. A temporary shutdown of a mining company's facility may raise questions as to whether the company can continue as a going concern, and it may be necessary for the auditor to include an explanatory paragraph in the audit report, particularly if the facility represents a major part of the company's assets.

Valuation of product inventory is also affected by worldwide imbalances between supply and demand for certain metals. Companies sometimes produce larger quantities of a metal than can be absorbed by the market. In that situation, management may have to write the inventory down to its net realizable value; determining that value, however, may be difficult if there is no established market or only a thin market for the particular metal. The auditor must evaluate management's judgments about the value of its inventory. Furthermore, the valuation of the company's property, plant, and equipment accounts may be affected if imbalances persist for a long time.

In planning the audit of a mining company, occasionally the auditor may decide to use the services of surveyors, engineers, geologists, or other specialists that are independent of the client. The auditor should also be aware, in the planning stage, of the unusual problems often associated with physical counts of mineral products and metals, particularly considerations relating to the form or shape in which the inventory is stored and to determining the metal content of minerals in the various stages of production. Other planning considerations that are unique to the mining industry include the need to evaluate certain computations made for income tax purposes on the basis of individual mining properties, as discussed below.

The audit strategy for mature mining companies generally calls for tests of controls and early substantive testing. Established mining companies usually have an effective control structure for all transaction cycles, including production, and the auditor typically is able to obtain the evidence necessary to assess control risk as low. Control procedures to safeguard inventories of precious metals, while typically very effective, are particularly important to the auditor's assessment of control risk. For some accounts, the only substantive tests performed may be analytical procedures.

The production cycle is particularly significant in the mining industry; each year management attempts to determine, based on market and other factors, its year-end inventory position. The auditor's testing plan for the production cycle may depend largely on the inventory level expected at year-end and the company's method of costing inventory. If a company uses the LIFO method and an inventory buildup is not expected, the auditor is not likely to encounter inventory costing problems. On the other hand, if a company uses another costing method or if an inventory buildup is expected, as may happen during an economic downturn, the risk of misstatement in costing out the inventory will likely increase and the auditor may plan to perform detailed substantive tests of inventory balances.

Management of new mining companies, often called "venture mining companies," is generally not as control conscious as management of mature companies. For venture mining companies, the auditor usually performs detailed substantive tests of account balances, with emphasis on capitalized costs, which typically represent a large proportion of a venture company's assets.

Audit strategy decisions are further affected by the degree of vertical integration of an enterprise's operations. Companies that are not vertically integrated generally sell to only a few large customers; consequently, receivables can be substantively tested efficiently. In general, the greater the degree of vertical integration, the more likely the auditor is to plan to perform tests of controls, because of the larger number of individual transactions and customers.

In addition to the inherent and control risks found in all types of entities, as described in Chapter 6, there are some unique risks in the mining industry. These risks relate to a company's compliance with governmental and other requirements concerning toxic waste, reclamation, and a wide range of other environmental matters such as land destruction and air and water pollution. Mining companies are also subject to regulations concerning occupational hazards to the health of their employees and public health considerations. The auditor should evaluate a mining company's potential legal exposure arising from failure to meet those requirements, compliance with required disclosures, and the impact of any noncompliance on the audit opinion. Typically, these matters are addressed in letters from the client's attorneys.

While the usual materiality considerations apply to the mining industry, the auditor should note that the property, plant, and equipment accounts are likely to be relatively more significant than they are in many commercial and industrial enterprises because of the capital intensity of the industry. As explained later in this chapter, the auditor is also likely to find large materials and supplies inventories. Both of those areas may require audit attention beyond what is usual in other enterprises.

TYPICAL TRANSACTIONS, CONTROL STRUCTURE POLICIES AND PROCEDURES, AND AUDIT TESTS

The Revenue Cycle

Depending on the degree of vertical integration, mining companies may derive revenue from sales of minerals in the form of ore, concentrate, or finished metal; tolling; royalties; or mineral property conveyances. A company may also have gains and losses from commodity futures transactions.

Sales of Minerals. Generally, minerals are not sold in the raw-ore stage because of the insignificant quantity of minerals relative to the total volume of waste rock. (There are, however, some exceptions, such as iron ore and coal.) The ore is usually milled at or near the mine site to produce a concentrate containing a significantly higher percentage of mineral content. For example, the metal content of copper concentrate typically is 25 to 30 percent, as opposed to between one-half and 1 percent for the raw ore. The concentrate is frequently sold to other processors; occasionally, mining companies exchange concentrate to reduce transportation costs. After the refining process, metallic minerals may be sold as finished metals, either in the form of products for remelting by final users (e.g., pig iron or cathode copper) or as finished products (e.g., copper rod or aluminum foil).

Sales of raw ore and concentrate entail determining metal content based initially on estimated weights, moisture content, and ore grade. Those estimates are subsequently revised, based on the actual metal content recovered from the raw ore or concentrate, if settlement is based on actual recoveries. Estimates generally are made by both the seller and the buyer; the difference is usually split, but sometimes an ''umpire'' is required to determine the metal content sold.

Sales prices are often based on the market price on a commodity exchange such as the COMEX (New York Commodity Exchange) or LME (London Metal Exchange) at the time of delivery. Sometimes a time other than delivery is used to set the price; for example, the average of daily COMEX prices for the two-week period subsequent to delivery of the minerals could be used. In those circumstances, it might be necessary to record revenue based on an estimate of the total sales value of the shipment at the point of sale and adjust the amount when the sales price has been determined.

If the planned audit strategy calls for tests of controls in a mining company's revenue cycle, the tests are similar for the most part to those performed in other industries. As noted earlier, some companies may sell to a small number of large customers; in that event, accounts receivable are easily tested using only substantive tests. Collectibility of receivables is usually not a major problem for mining companies.

Tolling. Companies with smelters and refineries may also realize revenue from tolling, which is the processing of metal-bearing materials of other mining companies for a fee. The fee is based on numerous factors, including the weight and metal content of the materials processed. Normally, the processed minerals are returned to the original producer for subsequent sale. To supplement the recovery of fixed costs, companies with smelters and refineries frequently enter into tolling agreements when they have excess capacity.

Royalties. For a variety of reasons, companies may not wish to mine certain properties that they own. Mineral royalty agreements may be entered into that provide for royalties based on a percentage of the total value of the mineral or of gross revenue, to be paid when the minerals extracted from the property are sold.

Mineral Property Conveyances. A mining company may also enter into arrangements, often as a means of obtaining financing, to convey a portion of its mineral reserves to others. In addition to the more usual forms of conveyances (joint ventures—both incorporated and unincorporated—outright sales, and partnerships), these conveyances take the form of, for example, sales of minerals-in-place (i.e., in the ground), sales of fractional interests in undeveloped mining properties, conveyances with the right of return after a specified period (which are usually termed sales, but are accounted for as leases), bullion loans (loans that will be repaid from the proceeds of sales of gold), and any number of other possible combinations. The auditor should analyze such transactions carefully to determine their economic substance for purposes of evaluating the revenue recognition principles applied by the company.

Recognizing Revenues. Generally, revenue should be recognized only when all of the following conditions have been met:

- The product has been shipped and is no longer under physical control of the seller (or title to the product has already passed to the buyer).
- The quantity and quality of the product can be determined with reasonable accuracy.
- The selling price can be determined with reasonable accuracy.

Mining companies often encounter problems with the last two conditions because final quantities and prices may not be established at the time of delivery. Provisional invoices commonly are recorded using estimated quantities and prices that are adjusted when details of the deliveries are finalized. The auditor can ascertain that estimated quantities and prices are reasonable by comparing final invoices with the provisional invoices, paying particular attention to the trend of revisions.

Commodity Futures Transactions. Mining companies usually have significant inventories of commodities that are traded in worldwide markets, and frequently enter into long-term forward sales contracts specifying sales prices based on market prices at time of delivery. To protect themselves from the risk of loss that could result from price declines, mining companies often "hedge" against price changes by entering into futures contracts. Companies sell contracts when they expect selling prices to decline or are satisfied with the current price and want to "lock in" the profit (or loss) on the sale of their inventory. To establish a hedge when it has or expects to have a commodity (e.g., copper) in inventory, a company sells a contract that commits it to deliver that commodity in the future at a fixed price. The company usually closes out the futures position before the delivery date by buying the contract back at the current market price.

As an example of a hedging transaction, assume the following facts:

- A mining company enters into a forward sales contract on March 14 to deliver 20,000 pounds of copper on June 3 of the same year at the COMEX spot market price per pound at that time.
- The company's cost to produce is 69 cents a pound, which is not expected to change.
- On March 14, the COMEX copper price for June delivery is 75 cents a pound.
- On June 3, when delivery on the sales contract is due, the COMEX price for June delivery is 65 cents a pound.

If the company wants to "lock in" its profit of 6 cents per pound (the 75-cent price on March 14 for June delivery minus the 69-cent production cost), it will hedge the sale. To do so, on March 14, the company enters into a June futures contract on the COMEX to sell 20,000 pounds of copper at 75 cents a pound. In June, the company will offset its position by buying a futures contract for 20,000 pounds on the COMEX at 65 cents a pound. In so doing, the company will realize a profit of 10 cents a pound on closing out the futures contract and a loss of 4 cents a pound (the 69-cent production cost less the 65-cent selling price) on the sales contract. By hedging the sales commitment, the company has locked in the profit of 6 cents a pound that was determinable on March 14, regardless of whether the price of copper for June delivery rises or falls between March 14 and June 3.

The accounting for commodity futures contracts depends on whether the contract qualifies as a hedge under Statement of Financial Accounting Standards No. 80, *Accounting for Futures Contracts* (Accounting Standards Section F80).

To ensure that transactions are accounted for appropriately, the auditor must understand the mining company's trading philosophy and control structure relating to futures trading. Control structure policies and procedures include overall authorization, often by the board of directors, of the maximum hedged and risk positions, periodic reconciliations of positions, and confirmation of open positions. The auditor should understand, and in some situations may test, the company's control procedures for authorizing, processing, and recording trades and should obtain satisfaction that the inventory of open positions is adequately maintained. Accounting Research Bulletin No. 43, Chapter 4, requires the company to consider whether a write-down of inventory to lower of cost or market is necessary, regardless of whether it has entered into hedging transactions.

The Expenditure Cycle

The audit strategy for the expenditure cycle often calls for tests of controls as a basis for significantly restricting substantive tests. Tests of controls are usually performed for payroll accounts in the mining industry and are often performed for purchases of materials and supplies, especially if the auditor expects inventory levels to be material at year-end. If purchase costs are expected to flow through to cost of sales by year-end, the auditor may perform a combination of analytical procedures of cost of sales and detailed substantive tests of the related quantities instead of performing tests of controls in the production cycle.

Exploration and Development Costs.   Exploration and development activities and accounting for costs associated with them were discussed earlier. This section of the chapter covers control structure policies and procedures and both tests of controls and substantive tests for exploration and development activities.

The auditor should determine whether the mining company has policies and procedures relating to acquiring exploration rights and maintaining proper title or mining rights to properties being explored. The auditor should review the company's procedures for accumulating and allocating exploration expenditures to various properties, to determine that costs related to properties that have not demonstrated economically recoverable ore have not been capitalized or inappropriately allocated to other properties.

Additional auditing procedures may include reviewing management, engineering, and geological reports to establish that properties identified as successful are in fact successful. The auditor might want to discuss the company's accounting policy with its engineering and geological experts to make them aware of the policy and its ramifications. This may be helpful in determining whether the company's accounting personnel receive the expert information necessary to implement the policy. As with any accounting policy, the auditor should determine whether the policy is applied consistently from period to period.

The auditor should understand the company's control procedures for accumulating and allocating development costs. Since the generally accepted practice is to capitalize all development costs related to a mining property, it is important for the auditor to examine evidence corroborating the characterization of expenditures as development expenditures. Because similar expenditures may be classified as either exploration or development, the company should have procedures in place to ensure proper classification. For example, drilling costs usually must be apportioned among exploration, development, and production activities; this may be accomplished on the basis of feet drilled or hours of drill use. The auditor should review the bases of allocation and determine that they are appropriate.

The auditor should review the mine plan detailing the projected costs and revenues of a project to evaluate management's judgment about its economic viability. This plan should have been developed by the company's engineering and geological staff and should reflect the input of industry experts and economists regarding the economic viability of the project. Discussions should be held with senior management about its intention to continue to expend amounts for the project and ultimately to begin production. Significant projects should be subject to the board of directors' approval; the auditor should review the approval and should also evaluate the company's ability to obtain necessary financing for the project. Although these procedures are initially performed when a company begins capitalizing costs, annual updates are usually necessary to evaluate their carrying value.

The auditor must be aware of important decisions that affect accounting policies at the time a new mine makes the transition from the development stage to the production stage. Among them are the accounting treatment of ore processed during the development stage (development ore) and costs incurred to bring mill facilities, smelters, and refineries to commercial levels of production (start-up costs). The proceeds from sale of development ore sold before completion of the development stage normally are credited against capitalized development expenditures. The auditor should review the company's procedures for identifying such proceeds to ensure that they are recorded properly. If the company's policy is to inventory development ore and record sales proceeds as sales, the auditor should review the company's procedures for identifying, controlling, and taking inventory of development ore quantities and related costs. Companies often capitalize costs incurred in excess of normal costs as development costs; in that event, the auditor should review the basis for determining normal costs to ensure that both production costs and development costs are stated properly.

Inventory. A mining company's inventory generally has two major components—metals and minerals, and materials and supplies that are used in mining operations.

Metals and Minerals. Metal and mineral inventories usually comprise broken ore; crushed ore; concentrate; materials in process at concentrators, smelters, and refineries; metal; and joint and by-products. The usual practice of mining companies is not to recognize metal inventories for financial reporting purposes before the concentrate stage, that is, until the majority of the nonmineralized material has been removed from the ore. Thus, ore is not included in inventory until it has been processed through the concentrator and is ready for delivery to the smelter. This practice evolved because the amounts of broken ore before the concentrating process ordinarily are relatively small, and consequently the cost of that ore and of concentrate in process generally is not significant. Furthermore, the amount of broken ore and concentrate in process is relatively constant at the end of each month, and the concentrating process is quite rapid—usually a matter of hours.

Determining inventory quantities during the production process is often difficult. Broken ore, crushed ore, concentrate, and materials in process may be stored in various ways or enclosed in vessels or pipes. The auditor should consider the dimensions of piles or containers, density of the material, moisture content, and assay factors, and should ensure that measurement methods are applied consistently from period to period. The auditor should also review the various engineering formulas used, to determine that they are reasonable and comparable between periods. If production inventories are taken by surveying techniques, such as piles of concentrate, the auditor should observe the surveying as it occurs. In some circumstances, the auditor may want to discuss the surveying techniques with the client or to consider using the services of an independent surveyor. Quantities of production inventories on hand in enclosed vessels, pipes, or tanks should be compared with capacity factors of the various containers. Density, moisture, and assay factors should be examined for reasonableness and comparability between periods. The auditor may collect samples and have them tested for the various factors by an independent laboratory; in most circumstances, however, the client's laboratories may be used provided the source of the samples is not identified.

Examining the metallurgical balances reconciliation, which is prepared periodically by the company's technical staff, is a useful auditing procedure. That reconciliation may be performed for both ore and concentrate quantities; it reconciles opening amounts on hand to ending balances by accounting for additions and reductions during the period.

Processed metal is generally easier to measure than broken ore and concentrate because it is substantially uniform in purity and is cast into specific shapes and forms. The auditor should observe the counting or weighing of amounts on hand and also may want to obtain independent assays. In addition, the auditor should determine that the company has adequate procedures to ensure that scales are calibrated periodically, since it is seldom practicable for the auditor to test the accuracy of the scales independently.

With few exceptions, mining companies carry metal inventory at the lower of cost—determined on a LIFO, FIFO, or average basis—or market. Occasionally, mining companies value inventories of precious metals in finished and salable form at net realizable value, which approximates market but exceeds cost. Although this policy is acceptable, it is rarely applied, and then only if there is an assured market at quoted prices.

Product costs for mining companies usually reflect all normal and necessary expenditures associated with cost centers such as mines, concentrators, smelters, and refineries. Inventory costs comprise not only direct costs of production, but also an allocation of overhead, including mine and other plant administrative expenses. Depreciation, depletion, and amortization of capitalized exploration, acquisition, and development costs also should be included in inventory.

When production inventories are in the form of ore or concentrate, a primary audit concern with respect to valuation is determining the metal content of such inventories. The company normally has procedures in place to monitor the percentage recovery, assay, and moisture content factors used. The auditor should be satisfied that those factors are reasonable and consistent with current expectations of the client and independent assayers. Actual settlement assays agreed to by the seller and buyer during the year may provide evidence that current estimates are either reasonable or unreasonable. In the latter instance, the auditor may consider it appropriate to seek independent corroborative evidence.

If a company engages in tolling (described earlier), it may have significant production inventories on hand that belong to other mining companies. Usually it is not possible to physically segregate inventories owned by others from similar inventories owned by the company. Memorandum records of tolling inventories should be maintained and reconciled periodically to physical counts. The auditor should review the reconciliations and ascertain that differences have been resolved satisfactorily.

Materials and Supplies. Materials and supplies usually constitute a substantial portion of the inventory of most mining companies, sometimes exceeding the value of metal inventories. This is because a lack of supplies or spare parts could cause the curtailment of operations. In addition to normal operating supplies, materials and supplies inventories often include such items as fuel and spare parts for trucks, locomotives, and other machinery. Occasionally, because of the significance of the cost of certain spare parts and the need to have them on hand to ensure the uninterrupted operation of production equipment, mining companies capitalize spare parts and treat them as equipment (accounting for them as "emergency spare parts" or "insurance spares") rather than inventory. These emergency spare parts are depreciated over the same period as the equipment with which they are associated. Most mining companies use perpetual inventory systems to account for materials and supplies because of their high unit value.

The auditor should understand the company's procedures for ordering, purchasing, issuing, and counting materials and supplies inventories. Because of the value of these parts, mining companies commonly have comprehensive cycle count procedures, the results of which are summarized and reported to upper-level operating management for scrutiny and review. The auditor should observe the cycle count procedures, perform test counts, and ascertain that book-physical differences are resolved and unusual trends and variations are adequately explained.

Materials and supplies inventories normally are valued at cost minus a reserve for surplus items and obsolescence. The auditor should understand the company's procedures for identifying surplus and obsolete items, parts for equipment that is no longer in use, and damaged or deteriorated items, and should obtain satisfaction that those procedures are functioning properly.

Property, Plant, and Equipment.   Because mining companies are capital intensive, the auditor should be particularly concerned with the control structure policies and procedures for authorizing and recording capital expenditures. Auditing procedures in this area do not differ from those used in other industries; however, the importance of the control structure may be greater because of the volume and high dollar value of transactions.

When operations are temporarily shut down, the related facilities usually are placed in a "standby mode" that provides for care and maintenance so that the assets will be retained in a reasonable condition that will facilitate resumption of operations. Care and maintenance costs are usually recorded as expenses in the period in which they are incurred. Examples of typical care and maintenance costs are security, preventive and protective maintenance, and depreciation. On occasion, it may be desirable to accrue the total anticipated costs at the beginning of the care and maintenance period, provided that both the time period and amount of costs involved can be reasonably estimated.

Expenses.   Three expense accounts—depreciation, depletion and amortization, and royalties—are discussed in the following paragraphs because they ordinarily are significant to companies that engage in mining operations.

Depreciation.   The principal difference between computing depreciation in the mining industry and in other industries is that useful lives of assets that are not readily movable from a mine site must not exceed the estimated life of the mine, which in turn is based on the remaining economically recoverable ore reserves. In some instances, this may require depreciating certain mining equipment over a period that is shorter than its physical life.

Depreciation charges are significant because of the highly capital-intensive nature of the industry. Moreover, those charges are affected by numerous factors, such as the physical environment, revisions of recoverable ore estimates, environmental regulations, and improved technology. Thus, the auditor must critically review the depreciation rates used for the various categories of fixed assets. The point at which depreciation begins is also of concern to the auditor; the appropriateness of dates selected should be evaluated. In many instances, depreciation charges on similar equipment with different intended uses may begin at different times. For example, depreciation of equipment used for exploration purposes may begin when it is purchased and use has begun, while depreciation of milling equipment may not begin until a certain level of commercial production has been attained.

Depletion and Amortization. Depletion of property acquisition, exploration, and development costs related to a body of ore is calculated in a manner similar to the unit-of-production method of depreciation. The cost of the body of ore is divided by the estimated quantity of ore reserves or units of metal or mineral to arrive at a depletion charge per unit. The unit charge is multiplied by the number of units extracted to arrive at the depletion charge for the period. This computation requires a current estimate of economically recoverable mineral reserves at the end of the period; the auditor must be satisfied with this estimate.

It is often appropriate for different depletion calculations to be made for different types of capitalized exploration and development expenditures. The auditor should evaluate the categories utilized and determine their appropriateness. For instance, one factor to be considered is whether capitalized costs relate to gaining access to the total economically recoverable ore reserves of the mine or only to specific portions.

Usually, estimated quantities of economically recoverable mineral reserves are the basis for computing depletion and amortization under the unit-of-production method. Therefore, the auditor should be satisfied that the ore reserve information is computed properly, which requires that the ore reserve unit and ore reserve base be determined. The choice of the reserve unit is not a problem if there is only one product; if, however, as in many extractive operations, several products are recovered, a decision must be made whether to measure production on the basis of the major product or on the basis of an aggregation of all products. Generally, the reserve base is the company's total proved and probable ore reserve quantities; it is determined by specialists, such as geologists or mining engineers. Proved and probable reserves typically are used as the reserve base because of the degree of uncertainty surrounding estimates of possible reserves. The imprecise nature of reserve estimates makes it inevitable that the reserve base will be revised over time as additional data becomes available. Changes in the reserve base should be treated as changes in accounting estimates in accordance with APB Opinion No. 20, *Accounting Changes* (Accounting Standards Section A06), and accounted for prospectively.

Under generally accepted auditing standards, the auditor may use the work of specialists in examining matters that are potentially material to the financial statements and that require special knowledge in areas other than accounting and auditing. Reviewing ore reserve data for purposes of calculating depreciation and depletion is a primary example of a circumstance in which the auditor may use estimates of ore reserve quantities provided by experts, such as geologists or mining engineers. Statement on Auditing Standards (SAS) No. 11, *Using the Work of a Specialist* (AU Section 336), and Chapter 6 of this book discuss the auditor's responsibilities and required procedures when using the work of a specialist.

Royalties.   Because royalties commonly are a significant expense to a mining company, the auditor should substantiate periodic payments by reference to underlying royalty agreements and should agree quantities and values to recorded amounts. The auditor should also ensure that royalty costs based on production are included in production costs for purposes of valuing the inventory.

Liabilities.   Mining companies usually are subject to various types of mineral taxes that must be accrued, including ad valorem, severance, and gross proceeds taxes. In addition, as a result of environmental considerations, mining companies may incur significant costs for restoration, reclamation, and rehabilitation of mining facilities after the mining process has been completed. Those costs should be accrued during the revenue-producing period.

The auditor should review the accruals for restoration and reclamation and ensure that estimated costs are reasonable and consistent with current expectations. Reading lease agreements and discussions with lawyers concerning environmental requirements, discussed earlier, may disclose the need for additional accruals.

Income Taxes

The most significant differences between financial reporting and income tax treatment for mining companies are mine development and exploration expenditures, impairment reserves, and percentage depletion.

For financial reporting purposes, mine development and exploration expenditures are generally capitalized and amortized over the life of the ore deposit; for tax purposes, they are currently deductible.[1] Additions to impairment reserves are expensed currently for accounting purposes, but do not generate a tax deduction until the underlying property is abandoned, sold, or exchanged.

Percentage depletion is a statutory allowance designed to encourage mining and is, therefore, computed without regard to the cost or adjusted basis of the property. The excess of tax percentage depletion over the cost depletion expensed in the financial statements is usually the principal difference between financial and tax reporting for many mining companies. While an in-depth

---

[1]A corporate taxpayer is presently allowed only 70 percent of development and exploration expenditures as a current deduction. The remainder is amortized over 60 months.

analysis of percentage depletion is beyond the scope of this book, there are certain concerns of which the auditor should be aware.

The deduction for tax depletion is a percentage of the gross income from a mining property limited to 50 percent of the taxable income from the property. Because this computation is made for each mining property, the determination of revenues and costs for individual properties is significant to a mining company. The auditor should understand the company's procedures for accumulating the amounts necessary to compute percentage depletion. In particular, the auditor should understand the method of determining taxable income for each property and gross income from mining.

Areas of particular concern in determining taxable income from a property include the appropriate allocation of indirect costs, such as selling expenses, general and administrative overhead, state and local taxes, and interest costs if a borrowing is directly related to a specific property. In addition, the auditor should ensure that the computation is in accordance with current tax regulations; the assistance of a qualified tax specialist should be sought when necessary. These procedures should provide reasonable assurance that tax liabilities in excess of amounts accrued will not be assessed by the taxing authorities as a result of their review of percentage depletion deductions.

The determination of gross income from mining is based on the value of the mineral at the cutoff point (i.e., before application of nonmining processes). To the extent that minerals are sold to independent third parties at the cutoff point, the sales price generally determines gross income from mining. For an integrated mining company, gross income is generally determined under the proportionate profits method (which attributes an equal amount of profit to each dollar of mining and nonmining cost incurred), unless the company can establish the existence of a representative field or market price for an ore or mineral of similar kind and grade. The auditor should ensure that direct mining and nonmining costs are properly identified and that indirect costs (i.e., costs not directly identifiable with a particular mining or nonmining process) are reasonably apportioned.

Corporations are subject to an Alternative Minimum Tax (AMT), which is applicable if it exceeds the regular tax liability. While an in-depth analysis is beyond the scope of this book, certain general concepts of the AMT are outlined here. The AMT taxes a much broader income base than the regular tax, although at a lower rate. To compute AMT liability, the corporation's regular taxable income is recomputed to reflect certain adjustments and preferences. The resulting amount, referred to as Alternative Minimum Taxable Income (AMTI), is multiplied by the corporate AMT rate to arrive at a tentative minimum tax (TMT). The TMT is compared with the regular tax liability, and the greater of the two amounts must be paid.

The major impact of the AMT on mining companies lies in the rule that a deduction for percentage depletion that, combined with prior-year depletion deductions, is in excess of a mineral property's basis is generally not allowable for AMT purposes. In addition, exploration and development expenditures are generally amortized over ten years for AMT purposes. Consequently, many mining companies may find themselves subject to the AMT.

A credit for minimum tax paid (minimum tax credit, or MTC) is allowed to offset regular tax liability in future years. However, the MTC may not reduce the regular tax below the tentative minimum tax for the taxable year in which the credit is utilized. To the extent that a taxpayer is subject to the AMT because of "exclusion" items as defined in the tax code (for example, the percentage depletion preference), however, the MTC will be reduced or even eliminated. An extremely important issue for the mining industry relates to the interplay of percentage depletion and net operating loss carryforwards in calculating the MTC. The auditor should consult appropriate tax personnel with respect to this issue.

As explained in Chapter 19, SFAS No. 96, *Accounting for Income Taxes*, as amended by SFAS No. 100, was to become effective for fiscal years beginning after December 15, 1989. In December 1989, the FASB voted to defer the effective date of SFAS No. 96 to fiscal years beginning after December 15, 1991. Because of the uncertainty of further possible amendments to SFAS No. 96, this chapter does not include a detailed discussion of accounting principles related to income taxes.

Supplementary Financial Statement Information—Ore Reserves

SFAS No. 89, *Financial Reporting and Changing Prices* (Accounting Standards Section C28), eliminated the requirement that certain publicly traded companies meeting specified size criteria must disclose the effects of changing prices and supplemental disclosures of ore reserves. However, Item 102 of Securities and Exchange Commission Regulation S-K requires that publicly traded mining companies present information related to production, reserves, locations, developments, and the nature of the registrant's interest in properties.

35

Auditing Oil and Gas Producing Activities

Statement of Financial Accounting Standards (SFAS) No. 19, *Financial Accounting and Reporting by Oil and Gas Producing Companies* (Accounting Standards Section Oi5.101), defines oil and gas producing activities as those that "involve the acquisition of mineral interests in properties, exploration (including prospecting), development, and production of crude oil, including condensate and natural gas liquids, and natural gas." This chapter covers those activities; it does not address the refining, marketing, and distribution of petroleum products.

OVERVIEW OF OIL AND GAS PRODUCING ACTIVITIES

The oil and gas industry is extremely complex, primarily because of (1) the risks involved in the exploration and production process, including low exploration success rates, volatility of prices, and fluctuations in supply and demand for oil and natural gas, and (2) the variety of business strategies used to raise capital and share risks. The auditor's understanding of these areas is critical to the application of appropriate auditing procedures. In addition, the auditor should be generally familiar with the operating characteristics of companies involved in oil and gas producing activities. The AICPA *Guide for Audits of Entities with Oil and Gas Producing Activities* contains guidance for this industry.

Oil and Gas Producing Operations

Oil and gas producing activities begin with the search for prospects—parcels of acreage that management thinks may contain formations of oil or gas that will be economically viable to produce. For the most likely prospects, the enterprise may contract with a geological and geophysical (G&G) company to conduct various tests to assess the types of subsurface formations and their depths. Based on the G&G studies, the enterprise evaluates the various prospects, rejecting some and accepting others as suitable for acquisition of lease rights. (Prospecting may be done before or after obtaining lease rights.)

Specialists called landmen may be used to obtain lease rights. A landman is in effect a lease broker who searches titles and negotiates with property owners. Although the landman may be part of the company's staff, oil and gas companies often acquire lease rights to properties through independent landmen. Consideration for leasing the mineral rights usually includes a bonus (an immediate cash payment to the lessor) and a royalty interest retained by the lessor (a specified percentage of subsequent production minus applicable taxes).

Once the leases have been obtained and the rights and obligations of all parties determined, exploratory drilling begins. Because drilling costs run to hundreds of thousands or millions of dollars, many companies reduce their capital commitment and related risks by seeking others to participate in joint venture arrangements. Participants in a joint venture are called joint interest owners; one owner, usually the enterprise that obtained the leases, acts as operator. The operator manages the venture and reports to the other, nonoperator participants. The operator initially pays the drilling costs and then bills those costs to the nonoperators.

The operator acquires the necessary supplies and subcontracts with a drilling company for drilling the well. The drilling time may be a few days, several months, or even up to a year or longer depending on many factors, particularly well depth and location. When the hole reaches the desired depth, various instruments are lowered to "log the well" to detect the presence of oil or gas. The joint interest owners evaluate the drilling and logging results to determine whether sufficient oil or gas can be extracted to justify the cost of completing the well. If the evaluation is negative, the well is plugged and abandoned as a dry hole. If the evaluation indicates the presence of sufficient quantities of crude oil or natural gas (hydrocarbons), the well is completed and equipment is installed to extract and separate the hydrocarbons from the water coming from the underground reservoir. Completion costs may exceed the initial drilling costs.

To transport the oil or gas from the well, a trunk line may be built to the nearest major pipeline; for crude oil, the alternative exists of storing the oil in tanks as it is produced and removing it later by truck to a crude oil pipeline or refinery.

Gas may be first sent to a natural gas processing plant for removing "natural gas liquids" (NGLs), such as propane and butane, for sale. Removing the NGLs converts the "wet" gas to "dry" gas for sale. Often, the gas is first sold to gas pipeline companies, which sell to local distribution companies (LDCs). The LDCs, in turn, sell to "end-users" such as homeowners and industrial users of natural gas. Since the mid-1980s, more and more natural gas producers have been selling directly to LDCs or industrial users, and paying the intermediate pipelines to transport the gas.

Before production begins (sometimes even before the well is drilled), oil and gas purchasers are selected and sales contracts are negotiated. Crude oil is typically sold in the United States on a spot basis at "posted prices" shown on the purchaser's "posted price bulletin" in effect at the time of sale. The bulletin may show price adjustments for the location and quality of the oil production. Sales terms for natural gas vary greatly. Natural gas may be sold on a spot basis at a negotiated price for the coming month's production. Some gas is sold under long-term contracts covering 10 or 20 years or more. Some gas is sold at substantially less, some at substantially more, than spot market prices because of federal government price regulations or pursuant to long-term contracts.

The oil or gas purchaser issues a division order, which is signed by the seller(s), acknowledging who is to receive what share of the sales proceeds. Many oil division orders specify that the purchaser will send separate checks to each owner of an economic interest in the production. Many gas division orders specify that the purchaser is to send one check to the well operator. The operator must then distribute the appropriate amounts to the other joint interest owners and the lessor(s). Ownership is discussed in more detail later in this chapter.

Various factors determine the economic success or failure of oil and gas exploration activities. Those factors include many uncertainties, some of which are discussed below, that set the oil and gas industry apart from other capital-intensive industries.

- *Anticipated Success of Drilling.* According to figures compiled by the American Petroleum Institute and the American Association of Petroleum Geologists, only 15 to 20 percent of exploratory wells have traditionally been successful, while the success rate for development wells (wells in areas known to contain oil or gas) approximates 80 percent. In addition to the risks associated with finding commercial quantities of oil and gas, exploration activities are affected by drilling risks such as stuck drill pipes, blowouts, and improper completions.

- *Taxation.* A substantial portion of the revenues from the sale of crude oil and natural gas goes directly or indirectly to the federal and state governments in the form of severance taxes, ad valorem taxes, and income taxes. After the various taxes, royalties to the landowner, and production costs have been deducted, the producer's income from the sale of crude oil and natural gas may be only a small percentage of gross revenues.

- *Product Price and Marketability.* U.S. producers typically do not encounter problems selling the oil they produce. Although the price received is not controlled by the U.S. government, it is dependent, in part, on prices set by the Organization of Petroleum Exporting Countries (OPEC). The OPEC countries control a very high percentage of the free world's oil reserves, thus giving them significant influence over the price of oil. Conservation and increased exploration for oil reserves outside of the OPEC countries in the late 1970s and early 1980s caused OPEC's market share of world oil sales to drop significantly from 1973 to 1986. With the new reserves in the North Sea, Mexico, and the North Slope displacing OPEC sales, the OPEC countries were forced to curtail production in order to support the price of oil on the world market.

  Marketability of natural gas varies significantly in different areas of the United States. Producers of natural gas are dependent on the needs of the local pipeline company that purchases and transports it. Typically, pipeline companies curtail or completely stop purchasing natural gas from some wells during periods of excess supply. The U.S. government no longer regulates the price of most natural gas. Since natural gas is not as easily stored as oil and transportation methods are also more limited, the price may also vary significantly depending on the time of year. For example, the demand for natural gas is usually much stronger during winter, and prices may increase during this period. Natural gas prices are controlled to some extent by oil prices because a large proportion of users can alternate between oil and gas, depending on prices.

- *Timing of Production.* How quickly oil and gas are produced directly affects the payback period of an investment and its financial success or failure. The timing of production varies with the geological characteristics of the reservoir and the marketability of the product being produced. Reservoirs may contain the same gross producible reserves, yet the timing of production causes significant differences in the present value of the future revenue stream.

- *Acreage and Drilling Costs*. The availability of quality exploration acreage and drilling personnel and supplies has increased, while the related costs have dropped significantly since the boom period of the late 1970s and early 1980s.

Raising Capital and Sharing Risks

In light of the high risks and significant capital requirements involved in exploring for oil and gas, funds are raised and risks are shared by a wide variety of techniques, some of which are motivated by the availability of varying tax benefits to investors.

Many mature companies use the cash flow from existing oil and gas production to finance additional drilling activities. Banks also represent a traditional source of capital; however, banks typically lend no more than 50 percent of the estimated value of proved developed oil and gas properties. Sales of bonds or stock are also used to finance drilling activities. Consistent with other industries, the availability of such debt or equity funds varies significantly depending on the perceptions of the investment community.

Two other traditional methods of raising drilling capital and sharing risks have been used by oil and gas companies. An oil and gas company owning valuable mineral rights can often attract other exploration companies, individuals, or partnerships to participate in a joint venture. The joint venture participants pay all or a major portion of the drilling costs in return for a lesser portion of the operating income from the well. Companies may also sponsor drilling funds structured as limited or general partnerships in which individual investors participate in the drilling activity by funding substantial portions of the drilling costs. Changes in the tax laws disallowing offsetting of ''passive'' losses generated by limited partnerships against ''active'' income, accompanied by volatility of oil prices, have reduced the popularity of limited partnerships.

During periods when traditional financing sources are not available, the industry has developed more innovative methods of raising capital, including

- *Completion Funds*. A completion fund is a limited partnership similar to a drilling fund, except that the money raised is invested in completion activities and production equipment after a well has been initially evaluated as being capable of producing sufficient reserves to justify the completion costs.
- *Production Purchase Funds*. Also known as income funds, these limited partnerships invest in producing wells, using either leveraged or non-leveraged acquisitions. The primary risks to the investor are that future prices may be less than anticipated when the property was purchased or that reserve quantities may decline as a result of changes in estimates.
- *Mezzanine Financing*. Through pooled funds raised primarily from institutional sources, funds are loaned to operators for completion expenses, development drilling, and acreage acquisition (activities typically not funded by banks). The loans, which are collateralized by interests in the financed properties, are typically made at interest rates somewhat below

market. The lower interest rate is compensated for by an equity interest in the properties, and accordingly the mezzanine financier may have a higher overall return, commensurate with the increased risk, than a bank would earn.

• *Oil Field-Services Joint Ventures.* An operator holding relatively low-risk developmental drilling prospects may enter into a joint venture with a drilling contractor or other oil field-services vendors. The vendors provide services in exchange for an interest in the properties being developed and receive a return from future production from the wells drilled, with or without recourse to the operator.

• *Exchange Offers.* Also known as roll-ups, these transactions involve one entity's issuance of common stock, partnership units, or debt in exchange for several entities' limited partner interests, working interests, or other direct or indirect interests in oil and gas production. Through an exchange offer, numerous investors with small interests in existing production may more efficiently reinvest cash flow in new exploration and development ventures. The Securities and Exchange Commission (SEC) has prescribed rules for accounting for these transactions in Staff Accounting Bulletin (SAB) No. 47. The surviving entity may be a master limited partnership (MLP) for which the limited partner interests may be freely traded.

These financing methods are important to the auditor's understanding of an oil and gas client's business. They are typically accompanied by complex agreements, sharing ratios that change during the life of the project, and tax treatment that may differ from accounting treatment, all of which must be considered in assessing inherent risk.

During much of the 1980s the industry underwent a period of capital starvation, falling oil and gas prices, and significant loss of technical personnel. The late 1980s saw greater volatility of oil prices and seasonality of gas prices. Accordingly, the availability of new capital has been and will continue to be limited.

Oil and Gas Ownership Interests

An oil or gas company typically acquires ownership of a prospect by obtaining a lease from the mineral owners. The lease is for a specified term (for example, three years) and usually includes a provision perpetuating the lease as long as oil or gas is commercially produced.

Ownership is transferred to joint venture participants by means of an assignment. The lessee creates an "assignment of oil and gas lease," specifying the location of the lease, the lessor, that the assignment is subject to the royalty interest reserved by the lessor (and any prior assignments), and the amount of ownership interest assigned to the joint venture participant.

Leases and assignments are legal documents and are generally placed on record with the appropriate governmental agency (for example, the Registry of Deeds in the county where the property is located). Before drilling begins, an attorney is engaged to perform a title search. If a well is successful, the attorney issues a division order title opinion to the oil and gas purchaser, naming the owners of the oil and gas interests and the amount of the interest. Based on this, the purchaser prepares division order instruments and forwards them to the appropriate oil and gas owner for signature. The purchaser distributes monthly revenue to the owners based on the percentages in the division order. Often, the attorney's division order title opinion shows two interest percentages—the net revenue interest and the working interest—for each owner. The purchaser distributes revenue based on the net revenue interest, and the operator prepares monthly billings for operating cost based on the working interest.

A net revenue interest entitles the owner to a share in the revenues generated by an oil or gas well; a working interest obligates the owner to pay a portion of the cost associated with drilling and operating a well. For example, if an oil company (the operator) leases mineral rights, granting a one-eighth royalty, and then obtains a joint venture participant who agrees to participate equally in drilling an exploratory well, the following situation exists:

	Net Revenue Interest	Working Interest
Lessor (royalty interest)	12.50%	0 %
Lessees:		
Operator	43.75	50.00
Joint venture participant	43.75	50.00
Total	100.00%	100.00%

If the well costs $1 million to drill and complete and generates $100,000 of revenue during the first month of operation, the joint venture participants each would be entitled to $43,750 of revenue (a 43.75 percent net revenue interest) and would be obligated to pay $500,000 in drilling and completion costs (a 50 percent working interest). The lessor's royalty interest would be $12,500.

In practice there may be several joint venture participants (working interest owners), as well as overriding royalty interest owners. An overriding royalty interest is similar to the lessor's royalty in that it entitles the owner to a percentage of revenues without obligation to pay the costs of drilling, completing, and operating the well. Overriding royalty interests are created for geologists who generate the prospect, for independent landmen as compensation for obtaining the lease from the owner, as part of "farmout" agreements (discussed later in this chapter), or for a variety of other reasons.

ACCOUNTING PRINCIPLES

Successful Efforts and Full Cost Accounting

The following pronouncements set forth generally accepted accounting principles unique to oil and gas producing activities:

- SFAS No. 19, which describes a "successful efforts" method of accounting.
- SFAS No. 25, which recognizes that other methods may be appropriate.
- SEC Regulation S-X, Article 4, Section 10 (also referred to as S-X Rule 4-10), which prescribes two acceptable methods for public entities—either the successful efforts method described in SFAS No. 19 or a "full cost" method, as described in S-X Rule 4-10.
- SFAS No. 69, which requires supplementary disclosures of oil and gas producing activities.

Additional guidance and interpretations are found in FASB Interpretations, SEC Staff Accounting Bulletins, surveys of industry accounting practices, and petroleum accounting journals.

The primary differences between the successful efforts and full cost methods center around costs to be capitalized and those to be expensed. In essence, as the name implies, under the successful efforts method, only those costs that lead to the successful discovery of reserves are capitalized, while the costs of unsuccessful exploratory activities are charged directly to expense. Under the full cost method, all exploration efforts are treated as capital costs under the theory that the reserves found are the result of all costs incurred. Both methods are widely used; however, larger companies tend to follow the successful efforts method.

The following examples of accounting policy footnotes briefly describe each of the two methods prescribed in S-X Rule 4-10:

Oil and Gas Properties—Full Cost Method

The Company follows the full cost method of accounting for oil and gas producing activities whereby all costs, by country, of acquiring, exploring for, and developing oil and gas reserves are capitalized and charged against earnings, as set out below. Capitalized costs include lease acquisition costs, geological and geophysical costs, lease rentals and related charges applicable to nonproducing properties, costs of drilling both productive and nonproductive wells, and overhead charges applicable to acquisition, exploration, and drilling activity.

Such costs are not capitalized in an amount that exceeds the sum of (a) the present value of future net revenues from proved reserves, computed using current prices and costs and a 10 percent annual discount factor, plus (b) the lower of cost or estimated fair value of unproved properties, plus (c) the cost of properties not being amortized, less (d) the income tax effects related to differences between the book and tax bases of the properties involved. All costs capitalized are amortized using the unit-of-production method based on estimated quantities of total proved reserves. [Amortization may also be computed using units of revenue produced. Also, as discussed later in this chapter, certain capitalized costs may initially be excluded from the amortization computation.]

Sales of oil and gas reserves in place and abandonments of properties are accounted for as a reduction of capitalized costs, with no gain or loss recognized, unless the reduction would significantly alter the relationship between capitalized costs and proved oil and gas reserves.

Oil and Gas Properties—Successful Efforts Method

The Company follows the successful efforts method of accounting for oil and gas producing activities. Under this method, exploration costs, including geological and geophysical costs, delay rentals on undeveloped leases, and exploratory dry hole costs are charged to expense as incurred. Drilling and development costs are capitalized on wells in progress, successful wells, and development dry holes. Lease acquisition costs are capitalized as incurred and are charged to expense when a property is abandoned or its value is substantially impaired, based on a property-by-property evaluation. [Impairment of lease acquisition costs may also be recognized on a group or aggregate basis.]

Capitalized acquisition costs are depleted on the unit-of-production method based on estimated quantities of total proved reserves. Capitalized drilling and development costs are depleted on the unit-of-production method based on estimated quantities of proved developed reserves.

Gains and losses from sales of proved properties are included in the results of operations. Proceeds from sales of unproved properties in which the company retains an economic interest generally are credited against property costs. No gain is recognized until all property costs have been fully recovered and the Company has no substantial commitment for future performance.

SFAS No. 25, issued in 1979, allowed private companies to use other generally accepted methods of accounting for oil and gas producing activities. At that time, many private companies had been using variations of the successful efforts and full cost methods prescribed in S-X Rule 4-10. Some private companies and limited partnerships prepare financial statements on an income tax basis.

Below is an example of an accounting policy footnote for tax-basis financial statements.

Oil and Gas Properties—Income Tax Method

The accounting records of the Company are maintained and the accompanying financial statements have been prepared in accordance with accounting practices permitted for federal income tax purposes. This method of accounting differs from generally accepted accounting principles primarily in the following ways: (a) revenue and expenses are recognized when the related cash is received or disbursed; (b) receivables and payables, other than those arising from cash transactions, are not recognized in the financial statements; (c) all exploration and development costs (including intangible drilling costs and delay rentals), except leasehold and equipment costs on producing properties and certain geological and geophysical costs, are expensed as incurred; (d) depletion of producing leasehold costs is calculated in accordance with the provisions of the Internal Revenue Code; (e) depreciation of lease and well equipment is computed using accelerated methods; and (f) leasehold costs are expensed when they become deductible for income tax purposes.

Obviously, the method of accounting for oil and gas producing activities does not increase or decrease the chances for success or failure in exploring for oil and gas, nor does it alter the real return on investment. Nevertheless, it can significantly affect the perception of creditors, investors, and others who use historical cost financial statements in evaluating the potential success or failure of a company. From the auditor's perspective, the accounting method followed affects the procedures performed in auditing the oil and gas properties. Accordingly, the auditor should tailor auditing procedures in this area not only to the company, but also to the method of accounting.

Accounting for Joint Operations

Accounting systems for oil and gas producing activities are generally the same as for most other activities. There are significant differences in the data gathering and reporting requirements, however, depending on whether the entity is an operator or a joint venture participant (nonoperator). The two major systems unique to oil and gas producing activities are the joint interest billing system and the revenue distribution system. The operator's joint interest billing system must properly calculate and record the operator's net cost as well as the costs to be billed to the nonoperators. Likewise, the revenue distribution system should properly allocate cash receipts among venture participants; this entails first recording the amounts payable to the participants and later making the appropriate payments.

As discussed previously, joint interest operations evolved because of the need to share the financial burden and risks of oil and gas producing activities. Joint operations typically take the form of a simple joint venture evidenced by a formal agreement, generally referred to as an operating agreement. The operating agreement defines the geographical area involved, designates which party will act as operator of the venture, defines how revenue and expenses will be divided, and sets forth the rights and responsibilities of all parties to the agreement. The agreement also establishes how the operator is to bill the nonoperators for joint venture expenditures and provides nonoperators with the right to conduct "joint interest audits" of the operator's accounting records for the joint venture.

Accounting for joint operations is basically the same as accounting for operations when a property is completely owned by one party, except that in joint operations, revenues and expenses are divided among all of the joint venture partners. The following section discusses accounting for joint operations, first from the operator's standpoint and then from the nonoperators' perspective.

Operator Accounting.   The operator typically records revenues and expenses for a well on a 100 percent or "gross" basis and then allocates the revenues and expenses to the nonoperators based on ownership percentages maintained in the division order and joint interest master files. The usual approach is to first record the full invoice or remittance advice amount and then use a contra or clearing account to set up the amounts due from or to the nonoperators. Recording transactions by means of contra accounts facilitates generating information used by management in reviewing operations on a gross basis.

Before drilling and completing a well, the operator prepares an authorization for expenditure (AFE) itemizing the estimated costs to drill and complete the well. While AFEs are normally required by the operating agreement, they are so useful as a capital budgeting tool that they are routinely used for all major expenditures by oil and gas companies, even if no joint venture exists. In addition to AFEs, the operator's field supervisor or engineer at the well site prepares a daily drilling report, which is an abbreviated report of the current status and the drilling or completion activity of the past 24 hours. That report may be compared with a drilling report prepared by the drilling company (also called a ''tour'' report). Some daily drilling reports indicate estimated cumulative costs incurred to date.

For shallow wells that are quickly and easily drilled, the AFE subsidiary ledger, combined with the daily drilling report, may provide the basis for the operator's estimate of costs incurred but not invoiced. For other wells, however, the engineering department prepares an estimate of cumulative costs incurred through year-end as a basis for recording the accrual and, if material, of commitments for future expenditures. Since an oil and gas company's accruable liabilities are primarily costs related to wells in progress, the engineering estimates may in some instances replace the auditor's usual tests for unrecorded liabilities in this area.

The operator normally furnishes the nonoperators with a monthly summary billing that shows the amount owed the operator on a property-by-property basis. The summary billing is accompanied by a separate joint operating statement for each property. The joint operating statement contains a description of each expenditure and shows the total expenditures for the property. The statement also shows the allocation of expenditures among the joint interest participants. The operator does not always furnish copies of third-party invoices supporting items appearing on the joint interest billing, but the third-party invoices can be examined and copied during the nonoperators' audit of the joint account. The operator may also furnish the nonoperators a production report.

Nonoperator Accounting.   From the nonoperators' standpoint, the accounting for joint operations is basically the same as that followed by the operator. It is not unusual for a company to act as an operator on some properties and a nonoperator on others. To be able to make comparisons and evaluations that include both types of properties, nonoperators should also record items on a gross basis. A nonoperator should develop a control procedure for a timely review of the joint operating statement to determine whether the operator is complying with the joint operating agreement, is billing the nonoperator only authorized charges at the appropriate percentages, and is distributing the appropriate share of revenues.

Other Accounting Procedures.   The operating agreement may permit the operator to charge the joint venture a monthly fixed fee to cover its internal costs incurred in operating the joint venture. Alternatively, the agreement may provide for reimbursement of the operator's actual costs.

The parties in a joint operation may agree either to share costs in a proportion that is different from that used for sharing revenues or to change the sharing percentages after a specific event takes place. Typically, that event is "payout," the point at which certain venturers have recovered their initial investment. All parties involved in joint operations encounter payout situations at some time. Control procedures must be designed to monitor payout status to ensure that all parties are satisfied that items have been properly allocated in accordance with the joint operating agreement.

Gas Accounting Issues

Gas Imbalances.   Generally, any of the working interest owners of a gas well may take their share of production in kind. Owners may disagree about when and to whom gas is to be sold. If one or more owners cannot, or will not, sell their shares of current production, the remaining owners can sell the entire production as if it were their own and keep the revenues. In such cases all owners have an understanding that a "gas imbalance" has been created that should be reversed in the future.

By prior agreement, the owners that did not sell (i.e., the under-produced owners) are allowed to take and sell in the future an additional quantity of gas in excess of their proportionate share to eliminate the imbalance. However, the gas imbalance may grow substantially over several months or even years to the point where full reversal through disproportionate gas sales may not be possible. The agreement may provide for cash settlement, typically for imbalances remaining when gas production ceases.

The operator generally issues a monthly gas balance statement apprising each working interest owner of the difference between the cumulative gas sold and credited to the owner and its economic share, or true ownership, of gas produced for sale. The auditor may utilize these operator statements (perhaps in combination with confirmations or other procedures) to substantiate the quantities of gas reflected in the client's recorded imbalance.

A 1985 study by the Revenue Committee of the Council of Petroleum Accounting Societies (COPAS Study) found that gas producing companies used the entitlements method, the sales method, or combinations thereof to account for gas imbalances. These methods are described below. The COPAS study also found that some companies adopted the entitlements method for significant imbalances, but used the simpler sales method for insignificant imbalances.

Under the entitlements method, each working interest owner recognizes gas revenues based on its proportionate share of gas production owned, not on revenues received. Over-takes are recorded as liabilities or deferred revenues, depending on the anticipated method of settlement. Under-takes are recorded as receivables. Collectibility of the receivables is dependent on the terms for settlement of imbalances, the plans for settlement, and the adequacy of underlying reserves.

As discussed in the COPAS Study's report, the liability or receivable is generally classified as current, and the carrying value of the imbalance may be based on historical cost, current market price, or other recognized accounting method. The auditor must evaluate the method used for reasonableness and consistency.

Under the sales method, each working interest owner recognizes gas revenues based on actual sales. This continues as long as the owner has not over-produced its reserves (i.e., has not sold more than its share of ultimate expected gross production). Once an owner over-produces, a liability—not revenue—is recognized. The under-produced owner may recognize revenue and a receivable, recorded in the same way as under the entitlements method and subject to the collectibility considerations mentioned earlier.

Adjustments to production expenses—depreciation, depletion, and amortization (DD&A)—and underlying reserves may be necessary to reasonably match expenses with revenues under the sales method. Such adjustments would generally not be necessary under the entitlements method.

Take-or-Pay Gas Contracts. During the late 1970s and early 1980s, many contracts for selling natural gas required the purchaser to take a minimum quantity each year or pay the producer as if the gas were taken. The purchaser could "recover" such payments by taking (without payment) gas in a future year in excess of that year's minimum quantity.

However, when regional gas producibility exceeded demand and gas prices fell, the take-or-pay commitments were not always honored by gas purchasers. They claimed legal principles relating to "*force majeur*" conditions and the impossibility of performance. Some gas purchasers made cash payments or similar settlements to producers for relief from take-or-pay obligations.

General industry practice is for gas producers not to accrue a receivable for minimum quantities not taken. When payment is received for gas not taken and the gas purchaser has the right to recover the payment through future takes, normal accounting for producers is to record the payment as a deferred credit. Revenue is recognized at the time of later recovery or when recovery is no longer possible. A similar approach may be appropriate in accounting for take-or-pay settlements.

RISK ASSESSMENT AND AUDIT STRATEGY

Inherent Risk

OPEC politics, the extent of volatility in crude oil prices, the demand for natural gas, the level of interest rates, changes in the U.S. tax law, and changes in capital and credit market perceptions significantly affect industry economics and behavior. In addition, changing prices and demand affect the value of oil and gas reserves used as collateral for bank loans. As a result, companies may find it impossible to service their bank debt, pay trade accounts, and meet drilling commitments. In recent years, significant numbers of financially troubled oil and gas companies have sought relief from their problems through bankruptcy protection, debt restructuring and debt service deferral, property sales, mergers, settlement of trade debt with stock or leasehold interests, and reducing overhead costs through salary cuts and personnel layoffs.

The auditor should consider those factors in assessing inherent risk. Specifically, the following internal and external factors should be considered in assessing inherent risk, both overall and at the account balance level:

- *Liquidity and Financial Resources.* The auditor should consider the availability of adequate cash flow from internal and external sources, the impact on cash flow of revised timing and pricing of oil and gas production, the ability to meet fixed commitments and debt service requirements, and the implications of evidence that may bring into question the entity's continued existence as a going concern.

- *Asset Realization.* The auditor should address the collectibility of joint interest receivables, the possible impairment of undeveloped properties resulting from declining leasehold values and the entity's inability to carry and develop properties, the potential impairment of producing properties as a result of the reduced value of the related reserves, and whether lease and well equipment inventory should be written down because of excess supply.

- *Product Marketability.* Production of gas wells may be suspended because of excess supply or uncertainty about gas pricing and regulation. The auditor should ensure that nonproducing gas wells have been identified and should become aware of significant gas contract provisions (e.g., take-or-pay arrangements for producers and "market-out" clauses for purchasers)[1] and consider their potential impact on the financial statements.

- *Joint Interest Operations.* Joint ownership increases the likelihood of exposure to financially distressed operators. The auditor of a nonoperator may need to be concerned about the extent and findings of joint interest audits, the adequacy of the operator's internal control structure, any conflicts of interest or related party transactions involving the operator, and the operator's ability to meet its financial and operating commitments. The auditor may also consider whether the operator is using funds and properties in accordance with agreements and whether the nonoperator has legal and unencumbered ownership of properties and production revenues.

- *Reliability of Reserve Estimates.* The reliability of reserve estimates depends primarily on the use of reputable and qualified petroleum engineers, and the availability, nature, completeness, and accuracy of the data needed to develop the reserve estimates. The reliability of reserve estimates has a direct impact on the calculation of DD&A and on ceiling and impairment tests (which are described later in this chapter and relate to the realization of the carrying values of assets).

- *Debt Compliance.* Complying with debt covenants may be difficult for oil and gas companies in a depressed economic environment. Technical defaults require written waivers and close review by the auditor.

---

[1]Market-out clauses allow a party (usually the buyer) to adjust the price or terminate the contract when the existing contract price is inconsistent with the market. Typically, the seller may either accept the new price offered or terminate the contract. The seller may be allowed to take the matter to arbitration or to demonstrate that another buyer will pay a higher price.

- *Variety and Complexity of Agreements.* The extensive use of innovative financing methods involving complex sharing and commitment terms that require accounting recognition or disclosure is common in the industry. Complying with the specific terms of partnership, joint venture, and operating agreements may be difficult. Contract terms otherwise regarded as inconsequential (e.g., dissolution, buyouts, and additional financing commitments) take on increased importance to both the company and its auditor in an economic downturn.

- *Adequate Insurance Coverage.* Both operators and nonoperators usually maintain adequate insurance coverage for the high cost of personal injury and property damage from well blowouts; however, industry practice typically is not to insure for the loss of a well or the cost of capping the well in the event of a blowout.

- *Complex Income Tax Considerations.* The oil and gas industry is subject to very complex taxation, and as a result income tax accruals of oil and gas companies are unusually complicated. Virtually every oil and gas company is faced with a variety of transactions that either must or may be treated differently for tax purposes than for financial reporting purposes. The Tax Reform Act of 1986 provides additional complexities in dealing with issues such as the alternative minimum tax. It is necessary to maintain several sets of records to meet the IRS and financial reporting requirements resulting from complex income tax regulations. Tax considerations affect the economics of many transactions in the industry to such an extent that they may become a determining factor in investment decisions. The auditor must have an adequate understanding of the principal income tax considerations affecting oil and gas companies.

- *Related Party Transactions.* Related party transactions are often extensive; they may result in possible conflicts of interest among investors, operators, and general partners.

Control Risk

There are several unique aspects of control risk in oil and gas companies. Smaller oil and gas companies ordinarily do not have adequate segregation of duties, although senior management's knowledge of the industry and the company's operations may compensate, in part, for that lack. Many companies, especially nonoperators, do not compare actual costs incurred with amounts projected on AFEs as a means of monitoring drilling activities on a timely basis. Many companies also do not have sophisticated accounting systems capable of tracking the detailed revenue and expense information that must be maintained at the well level to comply with federal income tax regulations and provide management with the information necessary to compute DD&A and identify uneconomic wells. Independent reserve determinations and reserve "audit" reports typically contain the caveat that the independent engineer has accepted key data from the client at face value. In addition, because accounting personnel do not participate in the search for oil and gas, they may not be adequately informed on a timely basis about new contracts, abandonment of properties, or other important transactions.

Audit Strategy

There are certain industry-related factors that the auditor should consider in determining the audit testing plan for an entity with significant oil and gas producing activities. The type of operations (e.g., whether the entity is an operator or a nonoperator, whether it manages limited partnerships, and whether it owns a small percentage of many properties or a larger percentage of a few properties) also influences audit strategy decisions—that is, whether it is likely to be efficient to perform tests of controls in order to significantly restrict substantive tests. In addition, the audit strategy will be affected by the company's accounting method. In full cost accounting, there is a possibility of error in measuring depletion and in overall valuation relating to the ceiling test. Successful efforts companies have a large number of cost centers, requiring accurate records and depletion calculations.

The auditor of both a company that acts as general partner and the limited partnerships it manages often finds it efficient to perform tests of controls relating to joint interest billings and revenue. In a typical general partner/limited partnership situation, virtually all transactions affecting the partnership flow through the general partner's accounting system. Only isolated revenue and expenses flow directly to the limited partnerships.

As suggested earlier, in difficult economic times, oil and gas companies typically experience serious cash flow problems. This may result in their extending payment terms on accounts payable and attempting to negotiate forms of payment other than cash. In certain circumstances, vendors that provided services or materials in connection with oil and gas operations may demand payment from the nonoperators in an oil and gas property, even though the nonoperators already advanced funds to the operator to satisfy their proportionate share of the billing. In addition, owners of nonoperating working interests and royalty interests may experience difficulty in collecting oil and gas revenues from the operator. In those situations, the auditor should consider inherent risk and materiality associated with nonoperated properties. In certain instances, the auditor of a nonoperator might consider visiting the operator of the properties to evaluate the operator's financial stability, ensure that monies advanced to the operator have been used for payment of costs related to the properties, ascertain that the operator is releasing revenue checks on time, determine that delay rentals are being paid properly, and assess any possible contingencies resulting from serious financial difficulties on the part of the operator.

The volume of transactions and complex allocations of costs and revenues associated with joint operations have prompted the industry to develop computerized systems not only to handle joint interest billings and revenue distribution, but also to maintain lease records and property files. Computer software has been developed for both larger mainframes and microcomputers. With the development of this software, especially for microcomputers, comes increased risk of manipulation or unauthorized use of computerized data files. The auditor must gain an understanding of how the various software programs process data and what control procedures have been implemented to prevent such manipulation or unauthorized use.

Some auditing firms have developed sophisticated software programs to assist in audit testing. The programs range from complex programs tailored to individual accounting systems to microcomputer spreadsheet programs that assist in analytical procedures and certain detailed computations (e.g., amortization and impairment calculations). These packages can enhance significantly the efficiency of audits of companies with oil and gas producing activities.

Developing the audit strategy also entails an assessment of the audit team's professional capabilities. In recognition of the unique problems and complexities of accounting for oil and gas exploration and production, the overall audit strategy may call for the presence of audit staff with special training or the use of industry specialists. Some accounting firms provide employees with training courses that address oil and gas operations, accounting, taxation, and auditing. In addition, capabilities are enhanced if the firm has access to a specialist, such as a petroleum reservoir engineer, who can perform selected procedures in the area of oil and gas reserves. Current auditing standards, however, do not specifically require the auditor to use such a specialist.

SUBSTANTIVE TESTS: AUDIT OBJECTIVES AND PROCEDURES

The following discussion addresses the principal audit areas unique to oil and gas producing activities. The audit objectives and procedures are not intended to be all-inclusive, nor are all of the procedures likely to be applicable to any one audit. The auditing procedures used on an engagement should be tailored to the specific accounting method followed and the company's internal control structure.

Joint Interest Billings Receivable

As noted previously, oil and gas operators frequently have difficulty in collecting joint interest billings when there is a slowdown in the industry and nonoperators experience liquidity problems. In evaluating the collectibility of receivables, the operator often estimates the future net revenues that it can withhold from properties operated on behalf of nonpaying parties. An auditor confronted with that situation should obtain evidence from the operator that a valid claim exists against future revenues. If the operator projects recovery of amounts over a period of more than one year, classification between current and long-term assets must be considered.

When it becomes apparent that delinquent accounts are uncollectible, operators often contemplate charging them to the cost of oil and gas properties rather than to the allowance for uncollectible accounts or current-period expense, as appropriate. Receivables that have been determined to be uncollectible should be charged to the allowance account or to current-period operations as bad debt expense, unless the operator has obtained or will obtain an assignment of the nonpaying party's interest in the properties. At a minimum, the portion of those uncollectible receivables realizable from future production may be capitalized as a cost of oil and gas properties. These capitalized costs would then be subject to the operator's normal accounting policy for the disposition of capitalized oil and gas property costs.

Audit objectives and related auditing procedures for joint interest receivables can be summarized as follows:

Audit Objective	*Typical Auditing Procedures*
Joint interest receivables included in the balance sheet represent amounts owed to the company for authorized charges incurred on behalf of other participants in joint operations.	Examine third-party charges billed to others to determine that they have been charged to the proper well and are classified appropriately as to type of cost.
	Consider confirming significant receivables.
	Test ownership percentage used in billing by examining operating agreements, lease assignments, AFEs, title opinions, and division orders.
Joint interest receivables include all amounts due to the company relating to joint operations.	Obtain a list of all properties for which the company acts as operator. Determine that the company has recorded all costs incurred related to its operated properties, including amounts to be billed to others and its own pro rata share.
Joint interest receivable listings are accurately compiled and the totals are properly included in the financial statements.	Test the clerical accuracy of joint interest receivable listings.
Joint interest receivables are collectible and reduced to estimated realizable value when appropriate.	Review joint interest receivables for potential uncollectible accounts. Procedures should include testing of the aging of amounts due, review of subsequent receipts, discussions with client personnel, and examination of assignments and reserve reports for receivables that are collateralized by the participant's interest in a well.
	Discuss potential for significant problems relating to joint interest owners who have elected ''nonconsent'' status, that is, have elected not to participate in certain activities.

Audit Objective	*Typical Auditing Procedures*
Joint interest receivables are classified properly in the balance sheet (current versus long-term) and the appropriate disclosures of amounts due from related parties have been made.	Review reserve reports to determine timing of receipt if collection is dependent on future revenues from production. Review disclosure of categories of joint interest receivables.

Oil and Gas Property Costs

The audit aspects of oil and gas property costs vary according to the method of accounting, although some are common to both methods.

Full Cost Method.   Under the full cost method of accounting for oil and gas producing activities, the major audit issues relate to determining an appropriate realizable value or "ceiling" for capitalized oil and gas property costs, which costs are capitalizable, and the method of amortization that should be used. S-X Rule 4-10 prescribes how a public company should make those determinations. At the time of this writing, the SEC is considering proposed changes to the S-X Rule 4-10 computation of the ceiling.

Under the full cost method of accounting, capitalized costs should not exceed the realizable value of the related properties. Typically, the most critical aspect of auditing a full cost company is determining that the full cost ceiling test has been applied properly. For many companies, the greatest risk that the financial statements will be materially misstated arises from misapplication of that test.

In computing the ceiling limitation, one unique aspect that must be addressed is the related income taxes. SAB No. 47, Topic 12, Item D-1, specifies how income taxes are to be treated in computing the ceiling limitation and illustrates a computation of the ceiling test.

If net capitalized costs in the full cost pool exceed the ceiling, a write-down may be avoided if consideration of subsequent events, such as price increases or additional reserves on properties owned at year-end becoming proved, eliminates the excess. Such subsequent events must occur before the audit report date and must relate to properties owned at year-end. The avoidance of a write-down must be adequately disclosed, but the subsequent events should not be considered in the disclosures required by SFAS No. 69 of the client's proved reserves and future net revenues. SAB No. 47, Topic 12, Item D-3b, contains further details.

S-X Rule 4-10 states that a company following the full cost method should capitalize all costs directly related to acquisition, exploration, and development activities. This would appear to include at least a portion of a company's labor and overhead costs if its personnel participate in any of those activities.

This area is very subjective, however, and the portion of labor and overhead costs capitalized varies significantly from company to company. Whatever practice is adopted, it must be reasonable and applied consistently from year to year; there should also be audit evidence available to support management's assertions about the level of labor and overhead capitalized.

For full cost accounting, Financial Reporting Release (FRR) No. 14 provides for two alternative methods of determining the treatment of costs of investments in unproved properties and major development projects: immediate inclusion of all costs incurred, or temporary exclusion of all acquisition and exploration costs that relate directly to unevaluated properties. Examples of costs that relate directly to unevaluated properties include leasehold acquisition costs, delay rentals, geological and geophysical costs, exploratory drilling, and capitalized interest. The cost of drilling an exploratory dry hole (i.e., a well not finding proved reserves) should be included in the amortization base upon determination that the well is dry.

Excluded costs must be reassessed for impairment at least annually, and preferably quarterly, either individually for each significant property (if the cost relating to a property exceeds 10 percent of the net full cost pool) or in the aggregate for insignificant properties using the successful efforts approach, as discussed in Rule 4-10(c)(1) (i.e., by including the excluded property costs in the amortization base ratably on the basis of such factors as the primary lease terms of the properties, the average holding period, and the relative proportion of properties on which proved reserves have been found previously). The concept of impairment of unproved properties is addressed in greater detail later in this chapter.

S-X Rule 4-10 provides for two alternative methods of computing the amortization rate.

- Equivalent physical units of production based on relative energy content, with gas converted to oil or vice versa, usually at a rate of 6000 cubic feet (6 mcf) of gas to 1 barrel of oil.
- Units of revenue, based on current gross revenues in relation to future gross revenues based on current prices, except as contractually stipulated.

Differences in the two methods may result from a disparity between the approximate 6:1 gas to oil ratio of physical units and the relative sales values of the gas and oil, typically caused by a gas contract price that is far above or below the current economic value of the equivalent Btu content of the gas. SAB No. 85 expresses the SEC staff's belief that the revenue method may be more appropriate than the units-of-production method when oil and gas sales prices are disproportionate to the relative energy content.

Successful Efforts Method.   S-X Rule 4-10 requires the costs of dry exploratory wells to be charged to expense, while the costs of dry development wells are capitalized. Therefore, it is important that wells be classified properly. Rule 4-10 defines a development well as "a well drilled within the proved area of an oil or gas reservoir to the depth of a stratigraphic horizon known to be productive.'' An exploratory well is ''a well drilled to find and produce oil or gas in an unproved area, to find a new reservoir in a field previously found to be productive of oil or gas in another reservoir, or to extend a known reservoir.'' Generally, an exploratory well is any well other than a development well, a service well, or a stratigraphic test well.

Those definitions do not always coincide with definitions commonly used in the industry (e.g., the industry definition of a development well may be more liberal than the SEC definition). This results in two auditing problems. First, certain exploratory dry holes may be improperly classified as development wells, a situation that occurs primarily with stepout or delineation wells drilled at the edges of a producing reservoir. Second, there may be inconsistencies between the SFAS No. 69 disclosures and the drilling statistics found in Item 2 of Form 10-K (which is usually prepared by nonaccounting personnel). The auditor should examine the data (such as maps and reserve reports) supporting the classification of significant wells and discuss the classifications with appropriate company personnel. A company that reports a large number of unsuccessful development wells may not be classifying wells correctly, since development wells are generally successful.

The auditor should consider reviewing the status of wells, particularly gas wells, in which production has been suspended. The criteria under which management continues to capitalize the costs of exploratory wells whose outcome is uncertain should be determined. S-X Rule 4-10 identifies the criteria that must be met for continued capitalization of those costs. The auditor should review budgets, AFEs, and other documentation supporting management's firm commitments and plans to further develop areas in which exploratory wells are located as well as the company's ability to make appropriate future expenditures.

FASB Interpretation No. 36, *Accounting for Exploratory Wells in Progress at the End of a Period* (Accounting Standards Section Oi5), requires that if an exploratory well is in progress at year-end and is determined to be a dry hole in the following year, but before the financial statements are issued, the accumulated costs at year-end should be charged as a loss in the year in which they were incurred, while the costs incurred in the subsequent year should be charged to expense in the subsequent year. If the amount to be expensed in the subsequent year is deemed material, the auditor should consider whether disclosure as a subsequent event is appropriate.

In assessing impairment of unproved properties on an individual property basis under S-X Rule 4-10, the auditor should consider the nature of a company's activities. For example, if a company sells undeveloped leases (either to other oil and gas companies or to partnerships), impairment should be evaluated based on expected selling prices for the acreage rather than on drilling plans. The key audit issue is identifying management's intent with regard to each property and relating that intent, and the enterprise's ability to achieve it, to the impairment recognized. The auditor should be aware that most companies do not formally segregate on their books the undeveloped properties into two categories (i.e., to be sold as an undeveloped lease or to be drilled); instead, the segregation occurs quarterly and at year-end when the company assesses impairment. The auditor should seek evidence from exploration personnel who are involved with the properties on a daily basis.

Assessing impairment of proved properties under the successful efforts method is not as rigidly defined as impairment under the full cost method. Assessment on a property-by-property basis or on a field-by-field basis is common in the industry. Computations using either discounted or undiscounted future net revenues are acceptable in practice. At the time of this writing, neither the FASB nor the SEC has released definitive guidelines for assessing impairment under the successful efforts method.

Capitalization of Interest.   There are several issues involved in applying SFAS No. 34, *Capitalization of Interest Cost* (Accounting Standards Section I67), to successful efforts companies and to full cost companies that exclude unevaluated property costs from amortization. Undeveloped leases qualify for interest capitalization as long as exploration activities necessary to prepare the lease for its intended use are in progress. Qualifying activities include predrilling administrative and technical work, title opinion curative work, and obtaining drilling permits from regulatory agencies. For an unproved property covering a large number of acres, the auditor should review the circumstances and activity carefully to determine whether the work being done on a portion of the acreage allows interest capitalization on the entire block. If drilling activities are continuous, drilling costs qualify for interest capitalization until the property is capable of producing and delivering oil or gas.

Two related problems exist with regard to the capitalization period. The first concerns the temporary suspension of activities. If substantially all activities related to acquisition of an asset are suspended, interest capitalization should cease until they are resumed. For example, if a company determines that an exploration project is too expensive or risky to pursue without joint venture partners and suspends activities until joint venture partners are located, interest capitalization should cease. When activities resume, the project again qualifies for interest capitalization.

The second problem relates to the cessation of capitalization on completion of activities. Generally, when a well is completed, interest capitalization is suspended unless external factors (e.g., the failure of the pipeline company to complete construction) prevent the well from producing. If significant costs are required to hook up a well, capitalization should recommence when those activities begin and should cease again when the hookup is completed. Interest capitalization may cease sooner under the full cost method as a result of unevaluated properties' being transferred into the amortization base on determining that proved reserves exist, even if production has not yet commenced.

Workover Costs.   Operations to restore or increase production from an already producing well are referred to as a ''workover.'' The accounting for workover costs depends on whether the project is designed to increase the quantity of proved reserves assigned to the property. If it is, the workover costs should be treated as part of the capitalized costs of oil and gas properties. If, on the other hand, the workover project is designed to restore or maintain production or enhance the rate of production without significantly increasing proved reserves, the workover costs should be treated as lease operating expenses. Completion costs incurred within a geological formation to which proved developed nonproducing reserves have been assigned previously are considered to be development costs, not workover costs.

Audit Objectives and Related Auditing Procedures.   Audit objectives and related auditing procedures for costs of oil and gas properties can be summarized as follows:

Audit Objective	*Typical Auditing Procedures*
Oil and gas properties included in the balance sheet physically exist and the company has legal title or similar rights of ownership to the properties.	Examine drilling reports, AFEs, operating agreements, mineral leases, and assignments. Compare listing of producing wells with revenue records. Determine that delay rentals have been paid or that leases are currently under production.
Oil and gas properties recorded include all mineral interests owned by the company.	Reconcile data maintained by the land department (for undeveloped leases), exploration department (for wells in progress), and production department (for producing wells) to the general ledger and properties listed in the joint interest billing and division of interest master files. Perform a reasonableness test of the relationship of costs incurred as recorded in the general ledger to documentation about net wells and net acreage maintained outside the accounting department. Compare listing of well activity with AFE log.
Oil and gas property listings are accurately compiled and the totals are properly included in the financial statements.	Test the clerical accuracy of oil and gas property listings.
Oil and gas properties are properly stated at the lower of (1) cost less accumulated DD&A or (2) unimpaired value.	Examine canceled checks for lease bonus payments, and supporting documents for other direct acquisition costs. Determine that well costs incurred in the current year are supportable, recorded at the company's proper ownership percentage, and properly classified as to cost type. Determine well status (i.e., exploratory versus development). Ascertain that internal costs capitalized are supportable and in

Audit Objective	*Typical Auditing Procedures*
	compliance with the method of accounting followed.
	Determine that interest cost capitalized during the current year relates to qualifying property on which qualifying activity has occurred.
	Review the client's DD&A computations for accuracy, use of appropriate data, and conformity with GAAP and S-X Rule 4-10.
	For full cost companies, review the client's ceiling test and analysis of unamortized property impairment for accuracy, use of appropriate data, and conformity with GAAP and S-X Rule 4-10.
Sold, abandoned, or transferred properties have been properly identified and accounted for.	For successful efforts companies, determine whether proved and unproved property costs have been impaired.
	Examine supporting documentation (e.g., cash receipts, farmout agreement, or lease assignment) and determine that the disposition is properly recorded. Recalculate the gain or loss, if applicable. Compare wells listed as assets with revenue records.
Wells in progress at year-end are reflected appropriately in the financial statements.	Review results of drilling up to the issuance of the financial statements. Determine that all costs incurred through year-end have been properly accrued.
Oil and gas properties are properly classified in the balance sheet and appropriate disclosures have been made.	Review drafts of financial statements, possibly with the aid of a specialized disclosure checklist or other practice aid.

Oil and Gas Revenues and Related Expenses

Except for sophisticated computerized revenue systems (which record revenue on the true accrual basis using monthly production data), usually revenues are accounted for initially on the cash basis; the remittance advice prepared by the purchaser is used as the source document. The cash basis is often used by smaller, less sophisticated companies and companies that do not operate properties, because they either do not receive monthly production data from the field or lack the capability to compute accurately from internal data the production and revenues by well.

Use of the cash basis requires a company, for purposes of accrual basis reporting, to accrue unpaid production at least quarterly and at year-end. The accrual is composed of two parts, amounts related to the typical one- to two-month lag in collections for mature wells and amounts held in suspense because of title problems on new wells. The auditor must focus on the amount accrued, the proper inclusion of all operated and nonoperated properties, the use of appropriate production data and sales prices, and the proper accrual of related taxes and operating expenses.

Generally in the continental United States, oil remaining in storage tanks at period-end (i.e., inventory) is not specifically accounted for. Accrued revenue typically is based on either production data (which includes amounts in storage) or cash remittances (which exclude amounts in storage). The method followed should be applied consistently.

Audit objectives and related procedures for testing oil and gas revenues can be summarized as follows:

Audit Objective	*Typical Auditing Procedures*
Recorded oil and gas revenues represent the company's proper ownership share of actual quantities produced and sold. Recorded oil and gas revenues do not include amounts owned by others.	For selected wells or individual amounts recorded, agree recorded revenue and quantities sold to supporting remittance advices. Compare recorded production with production reports. Agree ownership percentages to signed division orders.
All oil and gas produced and sold during the year is reflected in the accounting records.	In conjunction with the review of the client's year-end revenue accrual, determine that the appropriate number of months' revenue has been recorded for all significant wells. Compare amounts recorded with remittance advices or production reports.
	Compare recorded revenue with amounts projected in the company's reserve report and with prior-year production. Investigate accounting for imbalances.
	Analyze monthly production revenue by well and investigate unusual fluctuations.
Oil and gas revenues are recorded at the proper price.	Compare unit sales prices by well with sales contracts or posted prices.
	Compare average unit prices by well or lease with prior-year prices. Investigate significant unusual fluctuations.

Lease and Well Equipment Inventory

Declines in drilling activity are often accompanied by higher levels of inventory of tubular goods and wellhead equipment than are needed for planned drilling activities. It has become standard industry practice to classify tubular goods and wellhead equipment as inventory in the current assets section of a company's balance sheet. This inventory actually has two components. One is the portion of inventory to be "sold" to joint interest partners at the time the goods are used in drilling activity. The accounting procedures called for in standard operating agreements allow new material to be transferred to the joint account at the manufacturer's prevailing base price. This component of inventory should be carried at the lower of cost or the amount that will be recovered from the joint interest partners. If the company has more than a one-year supply of inventory to be sold to joint venture partners, classification of the excess portion as a noncurrent asset should be considered. (Such classification does not mitigate the necessity to consider impairment.) The other component of this inventory is the portion that will be transferred to the company's own oil and gas property accounts as it is used in drilling.

If the company has more inventory on hand than can reasonably be used in its operations and consequently intends to sell the excess at current market prices, impairment should be considered. This may be done by comparing the carrying amount with market prices and, if appropriate, charging the excess to current-period earnings. In determining the amount of the impairment, it is acceptable to apply the lower of cost or market test to either individual items or the entire inventory in the aggregate. The auditor should also consider observing the inventory, paying particular attention to the condition of the lease and well equipment. It is not adequate to rely entirely on confirmation from independent trucking yards where the lease and well equipment is stored. (Trucking yards are similar to independent warehouses, discussed in SAS No. 43 [AU Section 901.26–.27] and in Chapter 14 of this book.)

Mineral Conveyances

Mineral interests in oil and gas properties are conveyed to others for a variety of reasons, including to spread risks, obtain financing, improve operating efficiency, and achieve tax benefits. A transaction may involve the transfer of all or part of the rights and responsibilities of operating a property (an operating or working interest); the transferor may or may not retain an interest in the oil and gas produced. Sometimes an interest in a property entitles the owner to a share of revenues from the property but does not obligate the owner to pay the costs of operating the property (a nonoperating interest such as a royalty, overriding royalty, or net profits interest). A transaction may, on the other hand, involve transferring a nonoperating interest to another party and retaining the operating interest or transferring part of an operating interest and retaining the remaining part. One example of a mineral conveyance is a farmout arrangement, in which the farmor (or holder of the lease right) allows another entity (as farmee) to earn a working interest in the lease in exchange for paying all costs of drilling and completing a well. Usually the farmor retains a small overriding royalty that is convertible to a stated working interest at payout.

S-X Rule 4-10 contains detailed guidance on how the various types of mineral conveyances should be accounted for under the successful efforts method of accounting. FRR No. 17 amended the SEC full cost rules to generally prohibit income recognition in connection with sales or other conveyances of oil and gas properties. It also clarified the circumstances in which income may be recognized for management fees and compensation relating to contract services.

In measuring the relationship between costs and proved reserves for the purposes of income recognition under FRR No. 17, the auditor should consider the effect of the sale or transfer on the future amortization rate.

Typically, the auditor should examine individual mineral conveyances in detail to discern the true economic substance of the transaction. In auditing mineral conveyances, the auditor should remember that under the successful efforts method, while income recognition is possible when an economic interest is retained, it is not appropriate if the original cost has not been fully recovered. Under the full cost method, as mentioned earlier, income recognition has been virtually eliminated by FRR No. 17. Accordingly, the auditor should review carefully any income recognized from mineral conveyances. Special attention should be paid to situations in which income is recognized by sponsors of limited partnerships.

Supplementary Financial Disclosures

SFAS No. 69 details supplementary disclosure requirements for the oil and gas industry, most of which are required only by public companies. Both public and nonpublic companies, however, must provide a description of the accounting method followed and the manner of disposing of capitalized costs. Audited financial statements filed with the SEC must include supplementary disclosures, which fall into three categories.

- Historical cost data relating to acquisition, exploration, development, and production activity.
- Proved reserve quantities.
- Standardized measure of discounted future net cash flows relating to proved oil and gas reserve quantities (also known as SMOG [standardized measure of oil and gas]).

The supplementary disclosures are required of companies with significant oil and gas producing activities; significant is defined as ten percent or more of revenue, operating results, or identifiable assets. SFAS No. 69 specifies that the disclosures are to be provided as supplemental data; thus they need not be audited, but must be labeled clearly as unaudited.

Because of the reliance placed on the supplementary reserve information by financial statement users and because certain audited information (i.e., amortization and impairment information) is derived directly from the reserve data, the auditor should have a basic understanding of how reserve data is developed and of the inherent risks associated with it. Proved oil and gas reserves are the estimated quantities of crude oil, natural gas, and natural gas liquids that have been demonstrated with reasonable certainty, based on geological and engineering data, to be recoverable in future years from known reservoirs under existing economic and operating conditions (i.e., using prices and costs in effect on the date of the estimate). Proved reserves are inherently imprecise because of the uncertainties and limitations of the data available.

Most large companies and many medium-sized companies have qualified engineers on their staffs to prepare oil and gas reserve studies. Many companies use independent engineering consultants to determine, review, or audit reserve estimates. Usually, reserve studies are reviewed and updated at least annually to take into account new discoveries and adjustments of previous estimates.

Auditors of oil and gas companies generally use the reserve studies prepared by petroleum engineers. Because of the expertise required to estimate reserve quantities, however, the auditor typically does not have the necessary qualifications to fully evaluate an engineer's estimate. Therefore, as required by SAS No. 11, *Using the Work of a Specialist* (AU Section 336), discussed in Chapter 6, and a related auditing interpretation (AU Section 9336.03), the auditor ordinarily should be satisfied as to the reputation and independence of outside engineers or the qualifications and experience of in-house engineers who estimate the reserve quantities, should obtain an understanding of the engineer's methods and assumptions used in preparing the reserve estimates, should appropriately test the accounting data provided to the engineer, and should consider whether the engineer's report supports the related information in the financial statements.

Appropriate testing of the accounting data varies with the circumstances of the engagement. It may include (1) performing analytical procedures on summarized reserve information, (2) comparing reserve information with the current year's actual production and operating costs, and (3) testing the accuracy and completeness of selected properties' historical production, ownership interests, payout determinations, year-end prices, and cost rates.

In addition, if the SFAS No. 69 supplementary reserve information accompanies audited financial statements, AU Section 558, *Required Supplementary Information*, discussed in Chapter 22, and interpretations thereof (AU Section 9558) require that the auditor

- Inquire about management's understanding of the specific requirements for disclosure of supplementary oil and gas reserve information.
- Inquire about the qualifications of the person who estimated the reserve quantity information.
- Compare recent production with reserve estimates for significant properties and inquire about disproportionate ratios.
- Compare reserve quantity information with information used for the amortization computation and inquire about differences.
- Inquire about the methods used to calculate the SMOG disclosures.

- Inquire about whether the methods and bases for estimating reserve information are documented and whether the information is current.

If the auditor believes that the information is not presented within the applicable guidelines, AU Section 558 requires additional inquiries. Because of the nature of estimates of oil and gas reserve information, however, the auditor may not be able to evaluate the responses to additional inquiries; this limitation must be reported in accordance with professional standards.

Statement of Cash Flows

SFAS No. 95, *Cash Flows Statement*, requires inclusion of a statement of cash flows in financial statements. This pronouncement has had a significant impact on the oil and gas industry, with perhaps the most difficult aspect being proper classification between operating, investing, and financing activities. For example, exploration costs appear to be investing activities; however, successful efforts companies have to add back the activities that have been expensed (such as dry hole cost) to net income in order to derive cash flow from operating activities. The purchase of equipment inventory appears to be both an operating activity (to the extent the inventory will be sold to third parties) and an investing activity (to the extent inventory will be transferred to oil and gas properties upon completion of wells).

Another issue is presentation of changes in joint interest billings receivable or payable. For nonoperators, presentation as an operating activity appears appropriate; however, for operators, classification as a financing or investing activity may be more appropriate under the assumption that the transaction spreads risk or that the operator is either loaning funds to or borrowing funds from nonoperators. The difficulty in gathering information to comply with SFAS No. 95 often makes application costly for oil and gas companies.

Income Tax Accounting

As explained in Chapter 19, SFAS No. 96, *Accounting for Income Taxes*, was to become effective for fiscal years beginning after December 15, 1989. In December 1989, the Financial Accounting Standards Board voted to defer the effective date of SFAS No. 96 to fiscal years beginning after December 15, 1991. Because of the uncertainty of further possible amendments to SFAS No. 96, this chapter does not include a detailed discussion of accounting principles related to income taxes.

36

Auditing Pension Plans

Pension plans operate by investing contributions of sponsors and employees in income-producing assets, the income from which is intended to be used to pay benefits to retirees or their beneficiaries in the future. In recent years, pension plans have taken on increased importance and have also become more complex as a result of changes in tax and other legislation, concern over the costs involved, and heightened awareness of the significance of such plans on the part of participants.

Employer contributions to pension plans usually are based either on actuarial calculations (in the case of defined benefit plans) or on amounts or rates stipulated under the terms of the plan (in the case of defined contribution plans). A defined benefit plan is one in which benefits are determined in advance by a fixed formula that is usually related to the employee's compensation, years of service, or both. Actuarial calculations are used to establish the amount of contributions required to meet those benefits. In a defined contribution plan, the employer is generally required to contribute a fixed or determinable amount to the individual account of each participant. The plan must provide for the allocation of plan earnings and losses, and, in some plans, forfeitures, to participants' accounts. Benefits are based solely on the accumulated contributions and income thereon. Pension plans may be single employer plans (i.e., sponsored by one company) or multiemployer plans, which are sponsored by several companies under, for example, a collective bargaining agreement. Some plans are contributory; that is, the participants bear part of the cost.

A plan is established and maintained pursuant to a plan instrument that specifies the plan's provisions. Plan records, including accounting records, may be maintained at several locations, such as the offices of trustees, insurance companies, actuaries, plan administrators, and plan sponsors.

BACKGROUND OF PENSION PLAN ACCOUNTING AND AUDITING

Prior to 1975, relatively little attention was given to preparing financial statements for pension plans, and those statements were rarely examined by independent auditors. Passage by Congress of the Employee Retirement Income Security Act of 1974 (ERISA) created a new era in pension plan accounting, financial reporting, and audits; it also significantly expanded government's involvement in the design, operations, and reporting of pension plans. ERISA requires plans to file an annual report with government agencies, including, among other things, financial statements and certain supplemental schedules. In addition, depending on the number of plan participants, an audit of the statements and schedules may be required to be performed by an independent auditor.

The absence, at the time ERISA was enacted, of authoritative accounting pronouncements addressing pension plan accounting and financial reporting requirements, coupled with auditors' limited experience with pension plans and the minimal guidance initially provided by ERISA, created serious problems for auditors. The Department of Labor (DOL) has since issued regulations providing guidance on accounting and reporting matters, prescribing minimum disclosures, and reducing the confusion regarding audits of plans.

After much work, debate, and several exposure drafts, the Financial Accounting Standards Board (FASB) issued, in 1980, Statement of Financial Accounting Standards (SFAS) No. 35, *Accounting and Reporting by Defined Benefit Pension Plans* (Accounting Standards Section Pe5). This statement is the authoritative pronouncement on accounting principles and financial reporting standards for defined benefit plans; it reduced the options previously available to such plans. SFAS No. 35 also applies to plans not covered by ERISA. Although it is limited to defined benefit plans, it also provides useful guidance with respect to accounting and financial reporting by defined contribution plans.

Through its Employee Benefit Plans and ERISA Special Committee, the AICPA developed an audit guide entitled *Audits of Employee Benefit Plans*, which was issued in 1983. This guide, although not exhaustive, was the first pronouncement to thoroughly discuss audits of both defined benefit and defined contribution pension plans as well as health and welfare plans.

This chapter covers accounting principles and financial reporting for pension plans and presents auditing standards and procedures specifically applicable to pension plans.[1] The auditor of a pension plan should be familiar with the provisions of SFAS No. 35, the AICPA audit guide, and the government regulations, as well as the instructions to the ERISA reporting forms. Where the plan's auditor is also the auditor of the sponsoring company, many of the auditing procedures discussed in this chapter will be performed as part of the audit of the company's statements; those procedures need not be repeated in auditing the pension plan. Auditing employers' accounting for pensions is discussed in Chapter 16.

FINANCIAL STATEMENTS AND ACCOUNTING METHODS

In SFAS No. 35, the FASB concluded that the primary objective of a defined benefit pension plan's financial statements is to provide financial information that is useful in assessing the plan's present and future ability to pay benefits when they come due. This objective recognizes that plan financial statements should address the needs of plan participants, because pension plans exist primarily for their benefit. Those needs entail principally assessing the performance of plan administrators and other fiduciaries in managing plan assets. Accordingly, the FASB concluded that the pension plan rather than the fund holding the assets is the reporting entity.

To accomplish that objective, a pension plan's annual financial statements should include

- A statement of net assets available for benefits as of the end of the plan year.

[1]For a more in-depth study of pension plans, see Richard M. Steinberg and Harold Dankner, *Pensions: A Financial Reporting and Compliance Guide*, 3rd ed. (New York: John Wiley & Sons, 1987).

- A statement of changes in net assets available for benefits in the plan year.
- Information regarding the actuarial present value of accumulated plan benefits as of either the beginning or end of the plan year.
- Information regarding the effects, if significant, of certain factors on the change in the actuarial present value of accumulated plan benefits.

The statement of net assets available for benefits should be presented in enough detail to allow users to identify which of the plan's resources are available for benefits. Generally, all assets (except contracts with insurance companies) are presented at fair value. Similarly, the statement of changes in net assets available for benefits should contain sufficient detail to enable significant changes in net assets during the year to be identified. Paragraph 15 of SFAS No. 35 specifies the minimum disclosure requirements for information regarding changes in net assets available for benefits.

Accumulated plan benefits of participants are required to be shown at the present value of the future benefit payments attributable under the plan's provisions to employees' service rendered to the date of the actuarial valuation (discussed further in the section, ''Actuarial Benefit Information''). Disclosure of the actuarial present value of accumulated plan benefits (which can be made in the financial statements or accompanying notes) should be segmented into at least the following categories:

- Vested benefits of participants currently receiving payments.
- Other vested benefits.
- Nonvested benefits.

Present employees' accumulated contributions as of the benefit valuation date (including interest, if any) must also be disclosed.

The actuarial benefit calculations as of the end of the most recent plan year may not be completed at the time the financial statements are prepared; accordingly, the actuarial present value of accumulated plan benefits is often presented as of the beginning of the year. In these circumstances, a statement of net assets available for benefits as of the beginning of the year, a statement of changes in net assets available for benefits for the preceding plan year, and information regarding changes in the actuarial present value of accumulated plan benefits must also be presented. This additional information is necessary to satisfy the basic objective of a plan's financial statements.

Information regarding the effects of certain factors on the change in the actuarial present value of accumulated plan benefits may be presented either in the notes or in financial statement format. Effects of plan amendments, changes in the nature of a plan (e.g., a merger with another plan), and changes in actuarial assumptions, if significant, are required to be disclosed; significant effects of other factors may also be identified. If a statement format is used and only the required information is disclosed, an additional ''other'' category will be needed to balance the statement. If a note format is used, the actuarial present value of accumulated plan benefits as of the preceding benefit information date should also be disclosed. Illustrative financial statements and note disclosures for a defined benefit pension plan are set forth as an appendix to SFAS No. 35. Similar disclosures for a defined contribution pension plan are contained in the AICPA audit guide.

Some pension plans have traditionally maintained their books and records on a cash or modified cash basis, which omits significant assets and liabilities. SFAS No. 35 requires the use of the accrual method for financial reporting purposes; this conforms to ERISA reporting requirements, although the DOL permits financial statements in the annual report to be prepared on a basis of accounting other than GAAP if the differences are described in a note. SFAS No. 35 also requires that changes in accounting principles made to conform to its provisions be accounted for by retroactively restating prior-period financial statements. Accordingly, a change from the cash to the accrual method or a change in the method of investment valuation from cost to fair value should be accounted for retroactively.

AUDITING PLAN ASSETS, LIABILITIES, REVENUES, AND EXPENSES

The audit strategy for a pension plan varies depending on the nature and operation of the plan. In planning the audit, the auditor should obtain sufficient information to identify significant aspects of the engagement and to assess inherent and control risks. The auditor's understanding of the control structure may need to include accounting and control procedures that are maintained by others. The audit guide provides guidance in this area as well as a discussion of the use of third-party audit reports on internal control. (See also SAS No. 44, *Special-Purpose Reports on Internal Accounting Control at Service Organizations* [AU Section 324], and Chapters 6 and 23 of this book.) In addition, the auditor may need to examine evidence that is not part of the plan's records (e.g., employer payroll records and actuarial reports). In single employer plans, this ordinarily presents no problem, since the employer is usually also the plan administrator.

Contributions

Accounting Principles.   Revenue reported in the plan's financial statements should include all contributions (by both the employer and employees) applicable to the year under audit. All amounts due to the plan as of the plan year-end are shown as contributions receivable, and include those pursuant to formal commitments as well as to legal or contractual requirements. Normally, employer contributions under defined benefit plans subject to ERISA should comply with the minimum funding standards established by ERISA. An allowance should be provided for estimated uncollectible amounts, if appropriate.

Control Structure Policies and Procedures.   A single employer plan should have control procedures to determine that contributions meet the authorized or required amounts and are appropriately recorded on a timely basis. Control procedures include ensuring that the records contain documentation (formal commitments, plan instruments, and an actuary's report) supporting the basis of contributions reported as revenue or receivables of the plan. Employer payroll records should be compared with employee contributions as reported by the plan or reflected on trustee statements.

Employer contributions to a multiemployer plan are made on a self-assessed basis and represent the majority of the plan receipts. Contributions generally are determined by the number of hours or days worked or gross earnings of the participant at a standard contribution rate and are reported on standard preprinted forms. The plan should have a procedure for establishing initial accountability over the reporting forms immediately on receipt (e.g., by document number or dollar or other control total). The forms should be controlled throughout processing, from the time of receipt of contributions to final posting to the participant's eligibility records and employer's contribution records.

The plan control procedures should be adequate to allow missing or delinquent employer reports and contributions and employer overpayments or underpayments to be identified for follow-up. Procedures may include audits of the employer's records on a systematic or exception basis, periodic requests that participants report any discrepancies in hours worked or contributions reported on their behalf by the employer, or a reconciliation of employee status reports furnished by a union to employer contribution reports.

Generally, contributions are mailed directly to a bank for credit to the plan's account or are received at the plan's office; in the latter event, prenumbered receipt forms should be used. The numerical sequence of the forms should be reviewed and subsequent deposit of the cash in the bank should be ascertained. Contributions received should be deposited intact on a timely basis and should not be used for payment of plan expenses.

A cumulative record of the employers' contributions should be maintained because the plan is required to report annually on contributions made by employers. The total contributions should be reconciled periodically to participants' records and the cash receipts records.

Audit Objectives and Procedures. The audit objectives for revenue and contributions receivable include determining whether amounts received during the year and due at year-end have been authorized and are accurate and complete, and whether an appropriate allowance for uncollectible receivables has been established. In auditing contributions, consideration must be given to evidence of employers' formal commitments as well as legal or contractual requirements. Specific auditing procedures relating to contributions receivable depend on whether the plan is a single employer or multiemployer plan. Auditing procedures for both types of plans include obtaining explanations for significant fluctuations in contributions for the year.

Suggested auditing procedures for single employer plans are shown in Figure 36.1. In most cases, audit efficiency is enhanced if the auditing procedures for contributions are coordinated and performed simultaneously with procedures applicable to employer records, referred to in the audit guide as participants' data and discussed later in this chapter under "Actuarial Benefit Information." The audit objectives applicable to participants' data (which

Figure 36.1   Suggested Auditing Procedures for Contributions Received and Receivable in Financial Statements of Single Employer Pension Plans

---

Contribution Records

Trace contributions recorded in the plan's general ledger to the cash receipts records and to deposits shown by bank statements or trustee reports.

Review amounts received subsequent to the statement date for consistency with reported contributions receivable.

Review adequacy of the allowance for uncollectible amounts.

Confirm contributions recorded as received and receivable by direct correspondence with the employer or by comparison with employer records.

For contributory plans, confirm employee contributions directly with participants on a test basis, as appropriate.

Employer Records

Reconcile total gross earnings shown by employees' earnings records to total wages shown by the general ledger and payroll tax reports.

Compare payroll data (e.g., salary, hours worked, hiring date, sex, birth date) for a selected group of employees with the employees' earnings records, time records, and personnel files.

Compare payroll data with participants' data furnished to the actuary.

Ascertain the completeness and accuracy of the basic data (see discussion under "Actuarial Benefit Information") used by the actuary (e.g., work force size, hours worked, and sex of employees), including tracing key data from the actuary's report (if shown therein) or confirming such data with the actuary. Normally, these procedures are performed on individual data as well as summary totals. If contributions are not based on actuarial determinations, as in most defined contribution plans, test the data (e.g., hours worked and covered compensation) used in calculating contributions.

Determine whether contributions received and accrued comply with the applicable provisions of the plan instrument and, where applicable, with the collective bargaining agreement.

Actuary's Report

For defined benefit plans, review the actuary's report for consistency with reported contributions for the year.

If the work of an actuary is used, follow the guidance in Statement on Auditing Standards (SAS) No. 11, *Using the Work of a Specialist*, as discussed later in this chapter.

Conformity with GAAP and ERISA

Review the criteria used by the plan in accruing employer contributions, to determine whether the criteria have been applied consistently and contribution amounts comply with generally accepted accounting principles (GAAP) and the provisions of ERISA.

---

includes demographic, payroll, and benefit data) entail determining whether covered employees are properly included in the employee eligibility records or contribution reports and whether accurate data for eligible employees has been provided to the plan and, if applicable, the actuary. Accordingly, procedures to achieve these objectives are also suggested in Figure 36.1.

Auditing contributions to multiemployer plans is more complex than for single employer plans; thus the auditor may need to apply additional procedures to obtain the required assurance about reported contributions. The auditor should determine whether the plan maintains adequate records of the contributions of the various employers and of the cumulative benefit credits of the individual plan participants.

Often this involves performing tests of the plan's control procedures relating to employers' contribution reports (which usually accompany periodic payments under the terms of the plan) for the purpose of reviewing the total hours worked and dollars earned (or other basis used for determining contributions) and allocating benefit credits to individual plan participants. The auditor should inquire about the methods used by the plan administrator to compensate for missing or incomplete participants' data.

Specific auditing procedures might include those shown in Figure 36.2. The auditor of a multiemployer plan should be aware of any risks arising from economic difficulties experienced by participating companies, since they could affect the collectibility of contributions receivable.

Figure 36.2 Suggested Auditing Procedures for Contributions Received and Receivable in Financial Statements of Multiemployer Pension Plans

---

Contribution Records

Reconcile total cash receipts as shown by the cash receipts records for a selected period to (1) total amount credited to the general ledger contribution accounts, (2) total amount posted to employers' contribution records, and (3) deposits shown by the bank statements or trustee reports.

If employer contributions are deposited in a central bank account, test amounts transferred to other bank accounts.

Compare selected individual employer contribution payments as shown by the cash receipts records with (1) amount shown on the employers' contribution reports and (2) amount posted to the individual employer contribution record, and trace selected postings from the employers' contribution records to the cash receipts records and the employer's contribution report.

Test the arithmetical accuracy of a selected number of contribution reports and ascertain whether the correct contribution rate was used.

Review employers' contribution reports to test the accuracy of the postings to participants' records, and trace entries on the participants' records to the contribution reports on a test basis. For defined contribution plans, determine that the contribution allocation to individual accounts conforms with the plan instrument.

Reconcile total participants' credits posted to the records for a selected period to the total credits shown by employers' contribution reports.

Determine the reasonableness of contributions receivable at the statement date by comparison with collections received subsequent to the statement date; also, review the related employers' contribution reports to ascertain that the receipts apply to the year under audit. If the plan's records are held open after the year-end, ascertain that amounts received in the next year that pertain to the year under audit have been recorded properly as accounts receivable.

Continued

Figure 36.2   *Continued*

Ascertain, by tests considered appropriate in the circumstances, the nature and amount of any delinquent or unreported contributions.

Review the adequacy of the allowance for uncollectible amounts.

Confirm contributions recorded as received during the period under audit on a test basis, by direct correspondence with selected employers.

Employer Records

Perform the auditing procedures under "Employer Records" in Figure 36.1 for selected employers.

Compare employers' contribution data for a selected number of participants with data shown on the employees' earnings records, and trace selected employees' earnings records to employers' contribution reports to ascertain that they have been properly included in or excluded from the reports.

Actuary's Report

For defined benefit plans, review the actuary's report for consistency with the amount of contributions.

If the work of an actuary is used, follow the guidance in SAS No. 11, *Using the Work of a Specialist* (discussed later in this chapter).

Conformity with GAAP and ERISA

Review the criteria used in accruing employer contributions to determine whether the criteria have been applied consistently and contribution amounts comply with GAAP. For defined benefit plans (other than certain insured plans), money-purchase plans, and target benefit plans, determine that the contributions required to be made are in accordance with the provisions of ERISA.

Employer Records.   For all plans, examining employer records is necessary to enable the auditor to gain assurance about contributions reported. For a defined contribution plan, employer records are the source of hours worked, pay rates, or other data on which contributions are based. Similarly, employer records are the source of pertinent data used by the actuary in determining contribution amounts for a defined benefit plan. For both types of plans, the auditor needs assurance that the information used in the determination of contributions is complete and accurate.

In some circumstances, the auditor may be unable to examine employer records; in that event, he or she should attempt to perform appropriate alternative auditing procedures to obtain satisfaction that the information on which contributions and other actuarially determined amounts are based is reasonable. For a single employer plan, the auditor should attempt to obtain a report from the employer's auditor stating that the appropriate auditing procedures have been performed.

The auditor of a multiemployer plan may likewise attempt to obtain reports from the auditors of selected employers, stating that appropriate auditing procedures have been performed. Alternatively, if the plan or related union maintains a complete record of participants, the auditor may deem it appropriate to correspond directly with participants. Such correspondence, which should request the participant's confirmation of employer, hours, pay rates, and so on, may be administered by the auditor, or by the plan or union under the auditor's control. Other alternative procedures might be appropriate in particular circumstances.

In addition to reviewing reports obtained from other auditors, the plan auditor should obtain satisfaction as to the independence and professional reputation of the other auditors and perform other procedures considered appropriate in the circumstances, as described in AU Section 543.04.

Investments

Accounting Principles. All plan investments (which represent a plan's largest asset), including equity and debt securities, real estate, and bank common or commingled trust funds, but not contracts with insurance companies (discussed later), should be stated at fair value as of the date of the financial statements. The fair value of an investment is the amount a pension plan could reasonably expect to receive for it in a sale between a willing buyer and a willing seller. The relative difficulty of determining fair value depends on the nature of the investments held. For securities traded in an active market, published market quotations should be used as the basis for the determination; the closing price on the financial statement date is usually the fair value. If a plan's investments include restricted securities, which cannot be offered to the public without first being registered, the board of trustees or the administrative committee must consider the effect of the restriction on determining fair value. Fair value should be adjusted to reflect brokerage commissions and other selling expenses if these are significant.

Various special procedures may be required to determine fair value of other investments without readily determinable values such as securities of closely held corporations or real estate. If there is no active market for an investment but there is such a market for similar investments, selling prices in that market may be helpful in estimating fair value. If a market price is not available, expected cash flows discounted at an appropriate interest rate may aid in estimating fair value. The use of independent experts qualified to estimate fair value may be necessary for certain investments.

Purchases and sales of securities should be reflected on a trade-date basis. Thus, if a plan's accounts are maintained on a settlement-date basis, they should be adjusted to a trade-date basis to reflect year-end transactions, unless the effect of the adjustment would not be material to the financial statements taken as a whole. Similarly, dividend income should be recorded on the ex-dividend date, rather than on the record or payment date. Income from other investments, such as interest and rent, should be recorded as earned, and appropriate accruals should be made.

Footnote disclosures for investments of pension plans are set forth in SFAS No. 35 and include, among other items, identification of individual investments that represent 5 percent or more of the net assets available for benefits.

Control Structure Policies and Procedures.   Policies and procedures for plan investments depend largely on the form of trustee arrangement and the physical location of the plan's records and investments. Such policies and procedures should ensure that investment transactions are recorded at appropriate amounts and on a timely basis. That is usually accomplished by maintaining detailed subsidiary records that are reconciled regularly to the plan's general ledger. If securities are held by trustees who issue periodic reports to the plan but retain the documentation of transactions, the plan should either have procedures to ensure the accuracy of such reports or maintain its own transaction records.

To ensure that investment income and expense are recorded at appropriate amounts, the plan should have procedures for reviewing commissions and fees for reasonableness and for comparing interest and dividend income with reliable reference sources. Investments carried at fair value should be compared with quotation sources and appraisal reports. Valuation methods, including good-faith estimates, should be documented in plan committee minutes.

The plan's investment policy and criteria and the responsibility for custody of its securities should be established and authorized by the board of trustees. The trustees should abide by any restrictions that may be imposed by the trust agreement or by government regulations.

If the plan administrator is directly responsible for investment decisions, significant transactions should be approved by the board of trustees or an appropriate committee. If investment decisions are made by a custodian who also acts as trustee, the plan's agreement with the custodian-trustee should be approved by such board or committee. The board or committee should also monitor investment performance.

Investments held by the plan should be adequately protected from loss and misappropriation by physical and other control procedures and should be counted or confirmed periodically.

Audit Objectives and Procedures.   Although the audit objectives and procedures parallel those used by other entities whose principal assets are investments, various adaptations are necessary because of the nature of pension plan operations and the requirements of ERISA. Further, the audit of investments is significantly influenced by the nature of trustee arrangements, as discussed under "Custodial Relationships."

The audit objectives for investment transactions include determining that all investments are recorded and exist, are owned by the plan, and are free of liens or pledges; that all investment transactions (including income thereon) are recorded; and that the investments are properly valued in conformity with GAAP. (Auditing investments is covered in Chapter 17.)

The audit strategy for investments (i.e., determining whether it is efficient for the auditor to perform tests of controls) depends to a large degree on the volume and portfolio mix of a plan's investment transactions and the plan's control structure. Procedures that may be performed include

Determining that investment transactions were properly authorized by tracing transactions to minutes of meetings indicating approval.

Examining brokers' advices, cash records, and other supporting documentation for the historical cost or selling price, quantity, identification, and acquisition and disposal dates of investments.

Comparing recorded prices of purchases and sales with published market price ranges on the trade dates.

Recomputing realized gains and losses.

The auditor should perform analytical procedures to determine the overall reasonableness of investment income, considering the composition of the plan's investment portfolio and changes therein during the year. Such procedures include comparing current income with the corresponding period of the prior year, referring to industry indices for investment companies or mutual funds with similar portfolios, and reading and analyzing reports prepared for the plan's investment committee that compare actual returns with expected returns. In addition, the auditor should observe the trend of investment values in relation to the portfolio mix; an investigation of fluctuations may uncover errors or other events that may require recognition in the plan's financial statements.

The auditor can substantiate the existence of securities either by inspecting and counting them or by obtaining a confirmation from the custodian. To be able to rely on a confirmation, the auditor must be satisfied with the custodian's legal responsibility for assets held in trust, reputation, and financial resources. (See "Custodial Relationships" for further discussion.) The auditor should inspect deeds, title policies, insurance contracts, and leases covering real property. Loan and mortgage instruments should also be examined, and the balances and terms should be confirmed, with appropriate consideration of collectibility.

The auditor should substantiate the fair value of investments and test the computation of the net change in fair value. Determining fair value of publicly traded securities presents no difficulty. The fair value of investments for which market quotations cannot be readily obtained should be determined by the plan's administrative committee for single employer plans or its board of trustees for multiemployer plans. The auditor is not an appraiser and is not expected to substitute his or her judgment for that of management; the auditor should only ascertain whether the procedures followed by management were adequate and the results obtained appear to be reasonable. The auditor is justified in expecting that the plan's administrative committee or board of trustees will have documented its judgment of fair value and that the documentation will be made available for the auditor's evaluation.

The auditor should review and test the various reports, analyses, computations, appraisals, and other sources used in determining fair value as of the statement date. Written representations from appropriate specialists may be used in considering the reasonableness of values reported by the plan. When using a specialist, the auditor should apply the procedures contained in SAS No. 11 (AU Section 336).

The auditor should determine whether the plan's investments violate any restrictions or limitations imposed by the plan instrument or policy on types of investments. (In addition, the auditor should inquire whether the plan's investments violate the provisions of ERISA.) If approval of investment transactions by the board of trustees or administrative committee is required, the auditor should examine evidence of such approval and should also review transactions for evidence of liens, pledges, or other security interest in investments. The auditor should test interest and dividend income received and receivable by computation, reference to appropriate published sources, or review of cash receipts and related documentation. Such procedures should include tests for unrecorded amounts.

Detailed procedures and illustrative audit programs for investments of pension plans are presented in Chapter 8 of the AICPA audit guide.

Custodial Relationships

As noted previously, many pension plans use some form of trust arrangement for investments. The plan's auditor must be aware of such arrangements and consider their impact on the audit.

Trust Arrangements.   Trust arrangements are either directed or discretionary. In a directed trust, the trustee acts as custodian of the plan's investments and is responsible for collecting the investment income; the plan directs the trustee as to investment transactions and usually maintains the investment records, together with the supporting documentation. Accordingly, the auditor may perform the normal auditing procedures, as discussed earlier, with respect to investments.

In a discretionary trust, the trustee has discretionary authority over investment decisions and generally exercises control over the investments. The trustee usually issues periodic reports to the plan, but retains the documentation supporting transactions. Although the plan may have control procedures to ensure the accuracy of such reports and may maintain its own records of transactions, the lack of supporting documentation, such as brokers' advices, normally requires the auditor to alter the normal procedures.

Many auditors believe that in auditing discretionary trusts, it is acceptable to obtain a report (often referred to as a ''single-auditor'' report) from the independent auditor of the bank's trust department stating that the auditor has performed a review of pertinent control structure policies and procedures of the trust department. Ordinarily, the plan auditor does not review the trust department auditor's working papers, but obtains satisfaction as to the independence and professional reputation of the trust department auditor. The single-auditor report allows the plan auditor to use the trust department's report of plan transactions and is acceptable under the audit guide.

Some auditors believe, however, that a report on the control structure does not provide the plan auditor with sufficient assurance of the adequacy of the trust department's periodic reports of plan transactions. They maintain that reports of the trust department's independent auditor should state that substantive tests, including examination of brokers' advices, were performed with respect to plan transactions. If they are unable to obtain such a report, those plan auditors would examine pertinent records at the bank. These additional procedures normally are not considered necessary by the audit guide if a single-auditor report is available.

If a single-auditor report cannot be obtained, the audit guide specifies that the plan auditor, in order to express an unqualified opinion on the plan's financial statements, would need to visit the bank to assess the relevant policies and procedures of the bank's trust department. Since it is normally not practicable for the plan auditor to do that, however, the guide indicates that if the plan auditor is unable to obtain a single-auditor report on the trust department's control structure, a scope limitation ordinarily results.

Common or Commingled Trust Funds. Bank common or commingled trust funds and insurance company pooled separate accounts contain assets of two or more plans that are pooled for investment purposes. In a common or commingled fund, a pension plan acquires units of the fund, generally referred to as units of participation. Pooled separate accounts are similar to common and commingled funds, and a plan's share of pooled separate accounts is also determined on a participation-unit basis. Periodically (e.g., each month or quarter), the unit value is determined based on the fair values of the underlying assets. The amount of a plan's equity in a common or commingled fund or pooled separate account is determined by multiplying the unit value by the number of units held. Assets invested in a common or commingled fund are held in trust for the plan, while assets invested in a pooled separate account are the property of the insurance company, and the plan has specified rights thereto.

The accounting and financial reporting for plan investments in common or commingled funds and pooled accounts are not addressed in SFAS No. 35, but DOL reporting and disclosure regulations prescribe the accounting for these funds for plans subject to ERISA. Some auditors believe that investments in common and commingled funds and pooled separate accounts should be reported as a separate line item in the statement of net assets available for benefits and that the change in value should be similarly reported in the statement of changes in net assets available for benefits. The plan's financial statements should not otherwise report the proportionate share of the underlying investments and transactions of these funds and accounts. This method of accounting and reporting is consistent with DOL regulations.

If a plan holds investments in common or commingled funds, the auditor should normally apply the following procedures:

- Physically examine or confirm with the trustee the number of units of participation in the fund held by the plan.
- Examine supporting documents for selected plan transactions in units of participation.
- Review the financial statements of the common or commingled fund and relate the per-unit information reported therein to amounts reported by the plan, including fair value, purchase and redemption values, and income amounts; if the fund's financial statements have been audited by an independent auditor, the plan auditor should obtain a copy of the fund auditor's report. The plan auditor should be satisfied as to the independence and professional reputation of the fund auditor, in accordance with AU Section 543.04. If the financial statements of the common or com-

mingled fund have not been audited by an independent auditor, the plan auditor should obtain a copy of a single-auditor report, if available, relating to the common or commingled fund's activities and control structure, or should apply appropriate auditing procedures at the bank, including assessing control risk relating to the income amounts and unit values of the common or commingled fund. (If the plan auditor is unable to apply these procedures, a scope limitation will result.)

Auditing procedures for insurance company pooled separate accounts are described later in this chapter.

Master Trusts.   Master trusts hold assets only of plans maintained by a single employer or members of a controlled group of companies. Each plan with assets in a master trust has an undivided interest in the assets of the trust, and ownership is represented by a proportionate dollar interest or units of participation.

As with common and commingled funds, the accounting and reporting for master trusts are not addressed in SFAS No. 35. Current DOL regulations require each plan participating in a master trust to report pursuant to ERISA, using the single-line presentation. Previous regulations had required a plan to report its allocable share of the individual assets in and activities of a master trust. Some auditors believe that one-line presentation is preferable, although either presentation has been and may continue to be acceptable for financial reporting. DOL regulations require a master trust to file more detailed financial information with governmental agencies.

The ERISA reporting requirements for master trusts do not affect the need to apply auditing procedures to the trust's financial records. Because of the significance of the master trust to the plan's financial statements, sufficient procedures, normally those already set forth for investments, should be applied to the financial records of the master trust to enable the auditor to form an opinion on the plan's financial statements. The auditor is not required, however, to issue an opinion on the financial statements of the master trust.

If the same auditor audits more than one individual plan with assets in a master trust, normally it is more efficient to first apply auditing procedures to the master trust and then determine how ownership is attributed to the individual plans. The auditor should review the trust agreement to obtain satisfaction that the accounting for the individual plan interests is consistent with the allocation method set forth in the agreement. If the accounting is not specified in the agreement, the auditor should determine that all administrators of the plans participating in the master trust agree with the method of allocation.

Contracts with Insurance Companies

Pension plans may invest some or all of their assets with insurance companies under several types of arrangements. The funds invested may be held in separate accounts by the insurance company or commingled with the insurance company's general assets (often referred to as general accounts). Separate accounts generally pool the funds of several plans (pooled separate accounts), although they may be established separately for one plan (individual separate accounts).

Accounting Principles.   Insurance contracts should be recognized and measured for financial statement purposes in the same manner as called for under ERISA. The recognition of insurance contracts under ERISA depends on their classification. Generally, the various types of insurance contracts can be classified according to whether the payment to the insurance company is currently allocated to purchase immediate or deferred annuity contracts (allocated contracts) for individual participants or is accumulated in an unallocated fund (unallocated contracts) that is used to meet benefit payments directly when they come due or to purchase annuities for individual participants on retirement (or earlier termination of service if the participant's benefits are partially or fully vested).

Under an allocated contract, plan benefits are fully guaranteed on payment of the premiums to the insurance company. Examples of allocated contracts include individual life insurance or annuity contracts, group permanent insurance contracts, and deferred group annuity contracts. Under unallocated contracts, plan benefits are guaranteed only to the extent that funds are available. Deposit administration (DA) group annuity contracts and immediate participation guarantee (IPG) contracts are examples of unallocated contracts. Under ERISA, unallocated insurance contracts should be recognized in the plan's financial statements, and allocated contracts should be excluded because the insurance company has assumed responsibility for the plan benefits.

ERISA requires investments in separate accounts to be carried at fair value, but permits other insurance contracts to be valued at either fair value or amounts determined by the insurance company in accordance with the terms of the contract (referred to as "contract value"). Contract value is almost invariably used in plan reporting of other contracts, since normally insurance companies do not report fair value to the plan. Stating insurance contracts at contract value, however, is inconsistent with the required accounting for all other plan investments at fair value. The FASB, in its consideration of this inconsistency, indicated in SFAS No. 35 that a fair-value approach for insurance contracts would necessitate additional calculations that might be extremely complex. Accordingly, the FASB concluded that such contracts should be presented in the same manner as that used when they are included in filings with governmental agencies pursuant to ERISA, along with appropriate disclosures.

Control Structure Policies and Procedures.   The control objectives—authorization, approval, and protection from loss—and the policies and procedures applicable to insurance contracts are similar to those for investments in general. These should include procedures to ensure that premiums and interest are recorded appropriately on a timely basis. This can be accomplished by comparing premium statements with contracts, recalculating interest, and reviewing current participant listings.

Audit Objectives and Procedures. The audit objectives applicable to plan assets held by an insurance company are establishing the physical existence of the assets represented by the contract, substantiating their reported value in conformity with GAAP, and determining compliance with the terms of the contract.

As with investments in securities, the auditor should perform analytical procedures to determine the reasonableness of income recorded by the plan on insurance contracts, including comparisons with industry indices or other publicly available insurance return information. Since not all assets represented by insurance contracts are included in a plan's financial statements, the auditor should review all insurance contracts to determine whether they should be reported as assets in plan financial statements. The auditor should correspond directly with the insurance company to confirm information such as that summarized in Figure 36.3. Additional procedures depend on the type of contracts, as discussed in the following sections.

Separate Accounts. An individual separate account is operated similar to a bank discretionary trust fund. Sometimes such accounts are audited by independent auditors, in which event the plan auditor may review the other auditor's report. Otherwise, the auditing procedures are similar to those for discretionary trust funds (discussed earlier in the chapter). They include obtaining a copy of a single-auditor report relating to the insurance company's separate-account control structure or applying appropriate auditing procedures at the insurance company.

Pooled separate accounts are similar to bank commingled funds, and the additional auditing procedures are similar to those discussed under ''Common or Commingled Trust Funds.'' They include auditing the balance of and transactions in the plan's units of participation in the pooled account and

---

Figure 36.3   Suggested Information to Be Confirmed with Insurance Companies Holding Pension Plan Assets

> The contract value of funds in a general account or the fair value of funds in a separate account at the plan's year-end and the basis for determining such values.
>
> Contributions (premium payments) made during the year, including the dates received by the insurance company.
>
> Interest and dividends, changes therein, and whether such amounts have been earned or credited during the year on an estimated or actual basis.
>
> Refunds and credits paid or payable by the insurance company during the year because of termination of plan members.
>
> Dividend or rate credit given by the insurance company.
>
> Annuities purchased and/or benefits paid or payable during the year from unallocated insurance contracts.
>
> Asset management fees, commissions, sales fees, premium taxes, and other expenses (sometimes collectively referred to as ''retention'') charged or chargeable by the insurance company during the year.
>
> Amounts of transfers among various funds and accounts.
>
> Special conditions applicable on termination of a contract.

obtaining the report of an independent auditor on the financial statements of the pooled separate account, obtaining a copy of a single-auditor report relating to the separate-account control structure, or applying appropriate auditing procedures at the insurance company.

Deposit Administration Group Annuity and Immediate Participation Guarantee Contracts. Contributions under DA or IPG contracts are deposited with the insurance company and credited to an unallocated account. When an employee retires, the amount required to purchase an annuity to provide for the retiree's pension is charged to the account. Under one form of IPG contract, pension payments are made directly from the account. DA contracts provide interest on the account at a guaranteed rate, and dividends or rate credits (generally net of contract expenses) are determined solely at the discretion of the insurance company. IPG contracts provide interest based on the insurance company's actual investment income, so there is an "immediate participation" in the insurance company's investment performance. Expenses under an IPG contract are charged directly to the account.

The following auditing procedures, in addition to those previously set forth for contracts with insurance companies in general, should be considered if plan assets are invested pursuant to a DA or an IPG contract:

- For DA contracts, evaluate the reasonableness of the interest credited to the contract in relation to the guaranteed rate stipulated in the contract.

- For IPG contracts, consider the plan administrator's conclusion regarding the reasonableness of the investment income credited to the contract. Reference should be made to insurance yield data furnished to the plan by the insurance company. Generally, this evaluation is sufficient to satisfy the auditor as to the aggregate investment yield. If, however, the amount credited does not appear to be reasonable, the auditor should apply additional procedures, such as asking the insurance company about its compliance with the method of computing investment yield under the terms of the contract. If the auditor is still not satisfied with the reasonableness of the investment return credited to the plan, consideration should be given to requesting the plan administrator to contact the insurance company to arrange for its independent auditor to perform agreed-on procedures and issue a report. Those procedures would be applied to the insurer's determination of investment return in accordance with the terms of the contract.

- If benefits are paid directly from the fund, determine that benefit payments were made to eligible beneficiaries and in the correct amounts. The auditor should consider applying the procedures for auditing benefit payments set forth in Figure 36.4. If annuities are purchased for employees on retirement or earlier separation, determine that the purchases were made based on rates stipulated in the contract and on benefit levels set forth in the plan document.

- Determine whether expenses charged to the fund are in accordance with the insurance contract or are otherwise authorized by the plan.

Figure 36.4   Illustrative Procedures for Auditing Benefit Payments

Review, on a test basis, the approved applications for benefits and ascertain that the current benefit amounts have been properly approved.

Review, on a test basis, employees' eligibility for the payment of benefits and evaluate the plan's procedures for monitoring continuation of benefits.

Recalculate, on a test basis, the benefit payments and ascertain whether an independent individual has reviewed the calculation.

Compare data (including endorsements) on paid benefit checks with payment records and ascertain that long-outstanding checks are investigated.

On a test basis, examine canceled checks for, or confirm by direct correspondence with selected participants or beneficiaries, benefits recorded as paid during the period under audit. Compare signatures with those on applications for benefits or with other appropriate plan documents.

Ascertain that payments made to participants or beneficiaries over an unusually long number of years are still appropriate.

For defined contribution plans, trace the amount paid to the individual participants' account records.

Other Assets

Generally, other assets are limited to pension plan assets used in operations (e.g., building, equipment, and furniture and fixtures), which should be presented at cost less accumulated depreciation. This conflicts with DOL regulations concerning ERISA annual reports prepared under "the alternative method" of compliance,[2] since the regulations do not distinguish between operating and other assets, and require assets to be stated at current value. Practice in ERISA filings under the alternative method, however, has been to state operating assets at cost less accumulated depreciation. The control structure and audit objectives and procedures for such assets are similar to those for other entities.

Liabilities

Generally, the principal liabilities of a pension plan are accrued expenses (discussed under "Administrative Expenses") and amounts owed for securities purchased (see the section, "Investments").

Benefit Payments

Benefit payments to retired or other eligible participants, including expenditures to purchase allocated insurance contracts, represent the largest item of operating expenses of a pension plan.

[2]Annual reports may be prepared in accordance with ERISA or under an "alternative method" prescribed by the DOL. The alternative method is by far the more frequently used of the two.

Control Structure Policies and Procedures. The plan's policies and procedures should ensure that benefit payments are recorded on a timely basis and that they are determined and authorized in accordance with the plan document. Procedures should include use of signed applications for the commencement of benefit payments; applications should be controlled and carefully processed. An individual not involved in the original processing procedures should review applicants' eligibility and ascertain that retirement benefits have been determined in conformity with payroll and personnel records and with the plan documents or insurance company records. The board of trustees (for a multiemployer plan) or administrative committee or its designee (for a single employer plan) should approve all applications for benefits. Control totals of monthly pension benefits should be maintained.

Control procedures should be established to ensure that individuals receiving benefits are eligible for the continuation of such benefits. Procedures might include periodic comparisons, by an individual not involved in processing benefit applications, of endorsements on paid checks with signatures in personnel records or on benefit applications; sending greeting cards to pensioners, returnable to the plan in the event of nondelivery; reviewing obituary notices; and visiting pensioners.

Audit Objectives and Procedures. The audit objectives applicable to benefit payments include determining that recipients are eligible beneficiaries, that payments were made in correct amounts pursuant to plan provisions, and that people no longer eligible for benefit payments are removed from the benefit records. Auditing procedures, including both tests of controls and substantive tests, that may be performed to achieve these audit objectives are set forth in Figure 36.4. Often, tests of controls are performed in auditing benefit payments. For more detailed information about those tests, see the audit guide.

The auditor should also compare benefit payments made by the plan in the current period with those made in the prior period and obtain explanations for significant fluctuations that may have an impact on other audit areas.

Administrative Expenses

Accounting Principles. Plan administrative expenses should be recorded in the financial statements in conformity with GAAP. Commonly, in many single employer plans, the employer bears all administrative expenses of the plan; this fact should be disclosed.

Control Structure Policies and Procedures. Control structure policies and procedures for administrative expenses should ensure that such expenses are recorded at appropriate amounts on a timely basis, are authorized by a responsible official or board, and are supported by documentation. Procedures to ensure that unauthorized or duplicate payments are detected on a timely basis are also necessary.

In multiempíoyer plans, although the trustees are responsible for approving all administrative expenses, responsibility for approving routine expenses is usually delegated to the administrator or other employees of the plan. Because of their fiduciary responsibility, the trustees should make certain that control procedures for administrative expenses are adequate. The board of trustees generally retains the authority to approve expenditures over a stated amount. Contract or professional administrators are paid according to various criteria (e.g., the number of participants covered by the plan or the number of employers' reports processed). Therefore, it is important that the plan's records provide the information necessary to determine the reasonableness of such payments.

Audit Objectives and Procedures. The audit objectives for administrative expenses include determining whether the expenses are in accordance with agreements, properly approved, properly classified, and recorded in appropriate amounts. In accordance with these objectives, the auditor reviews the terms of the plan agreement and minutes of the meetings of the board of trustees or administrative committee to determine whether administrative expenses were properly authorized. The auditor also analyzes the account and examines contracts, agreements, invoices, and other supporting documentation. If the plan uses a contract administrator, the propriety and reasonableness of the payments should be evaluated by testing the basis of the contract payment.

If one office functions as a service organization for several plans, the auditor should review the organization's allocation of administrative expenses not directly associated with a specific plan to ascertain that the allocation is based on an equitable method. The auditor should also determine that the method selected was approved by the board of trustees.

AUDITING ACTUARIAL BENEFIT INFORMATION AND OTHER FINANCIAL STATEMENT DISCLOSURES

Actuarial Benefit Information

Background and Requirements. SFAS No. 35 requires defined benefit pension plans to report specified actuarial benefit information in accordance with the objective of plan financial statements. The benefit information to be presented is the actuarial present value of accumulated plan benefits. Accumulated plan benefits are future benefit payments that are attributable, under the plan's provisions, to participants' service rendered prior to the benefit information date. Accumulated plan benefits comprise benefits expected to be paid to retired or terminated employees or their beneficiaries, beneficiaries of deceased employees, and present employees or their beneficiaries. They include nonvested benefits as well as vested benefits.

Accumulated plan benefits should be reported only to the extent that related assets are included in the financial statements. Thus, for plans in which benefits are fully guaranteed by an insurance company and the related assets are not reflected in the financial statements, the actuarial present value of accumulated plan benefits should exclude fully insured benefits.

Plan administrators of defined benefit plans use the services of actuaries in determining benefit information. The assumptions to be included by an actuary in the accumulated benefit calculations are prescribed by SFAS No. 35, which sets forth specific guidelines for determining accumulated plan benefits. The actuarial present value of accumulated plan benefits is determined by applying actuarial assumptions to the accumulated plan benefit amounts. The actuarial assumptions are used to adjust those amounts to reflect the time value of money (discounts for interest) and the probability of payment (decrements such as mortality, disability, withdrawal, and early retirement) between the benefit information date and the expected date of payment. The actuarial assumptions should be based on an ongoing plan and should reflect the best estimate of the plan's future experience with regard to those assumptions.

The benefits should be discounted at assumed rates of return that reflect the rates expected during the periods for which payment of benefits has been deferred. Those assumed rates should be consistent with the returns realistically achievable on the types of assets held by the plan, the plan's investment policy, and the rates of inflation assumed in estimating automatic cost-of-living adjustments. Expected rates on existing assets and those available in the marketplace, expected rates from the reinvestment of actual returns from those investments, and rates on investments expected to be held in the future all enter into the determination of the assumed rates. Thus, accumulated plan benefits generally are not discounted solely at rates of return on existing investments. To the extent that assumed rates of return are based on values of existing plan assets, however, the values used should be the same as those presented in the plan's financial statements. The rates of return may be adjusted to account for administrative expenses of the plan.

In lieu of the assumed rate of return, SFAS No. 35 allows plans to use assumptions inherent in the estimated cost, at the benefit information date, of obtaining a contract with an insurance company to provide participants with accumulated plan benefits, whether or not that is the intent. Thus, the settlement rate concept set forth in SFAS No. 87, *Employers' Accounting for Pensions* (i.e., use of a rate that reflects the amounts at which the pension benefits could be effectively settled), is an acceptable alternative under SFAS No. 35. Since the use of a settlement rate by the plan would eliminate the need for different valuations by the employer and the plan, use of a settlement rate by plans is likely to become more common.

Financial statement disclosures should include a description of the methods and significant assumptions (e.g., assumed rates of return) used to calculate the actuarial present value of accumulated plan benefits. If administrative expenses expected to be paid by the plan are reflected by adjusting the assumed rates of return, that should be disclosed. Changes in the methods or assumptions should also be disclosed.

Financial statements of defined contribution plans normally present only the net assets currently available for plan benefits, since benefits to be paid are not determinable until payment. Such plans may disclose the vested portion of benefits credited to participants' accounts, which does not require actuarial calculations.

Audit Objectives and Procedures. Auditing actuarial benefit information requires testing certain participants' data in addition to performing procedures relating to the use of the work of an actuary. The participants' data to be tested in a pension plan audit varies with the factors on which contributions and benefits are based. Such data is identified in the plan document and may include demographic or census data, payroll or salary data, and benefit data. Generally, as discussed earlier, it is more efficient to perform this testing in conjunction with the testing of plan contributions. In addition, since benefit payments are ultimately based on the participants' data, the results of the testing discussed under "Benefit Payments" should be considered in auditing actuarial benefit information.

The principal audit objective for actuarially determined information is to obtain satisfaction as to the reasonableness of the information to be disclosed in the plan's financial statements. Many of the auditing procedures (described below) relating to use of the actuary's report are performed in auditing the pension cost reported on the employer's financial statements; if so, they need not be repeated at the plan level.

In determining the reasonableness of the actuarial information prepared by the actuary, the auditor needs to obtain and review sufficient competent evidential matter. Normally this is accomplished by reviewing the actuary's report. Guidance on using the work of a specialist is provided by SAS No. 11 (AU Section 336), which requires auditors to satisfy themselves as to the professional qualifications and reputation of the actuary. Usually this can be done by determining that the actuary is a member of a recognized professional actuarial society (e.g., a Fellow of the Society of Actuaries or a member of the American Academy of Actuaries). Alternatively, the auditor might consider whether the actuary is an "enrolled actuary" under ERISA or might obtain competent professional advice on the actuary's qualifications from another actuary who is known by the auditor to be qualified.

The auditor may need to consult with the actuary when report items require clarification or explanation. Such consultation may be substantially reduced by ascertaining in advance that the actuary's report will contain all the information required by the auditor. Also, if the auditor becomes aware of changes in conditions that might affect the actuary's determinations, it would be appropriate, after discussing the matter with the client, for the auditor to advise the actuary. Other auditing procedures with respect to using the work of an actuary are outlined in SAS No. 11.

Procedures that the auditor may find useful in implementing the requirements of SAS No. 11 are set forth in Figure 36.5. In following those procedures, the auditor should not expect to rely on an actuary's conclusion as to the conformity of actuarially computed amounts with GAAP. Such a conclusion requires a knowledge of accounting principles, including the concept of materiality. Conversely, the auditor should refrain from making actuarial judgments.

SAS No. 11 indicates that the understanding among auditor, client, and actuary regarding the actuary's representations as to any relationship with the

Figure 36.5   Suggested Auditing Procedures for Actuarially Determined Information

---

Determine whether the actuary is familiar with the current terms of the pension plan and has properly recognized them in the calculations. This may be accomplished by reviewing the actuary's report or, with the client's consent, contacting the actuary directly.

Determine the professional reputation and qualifications of the actuary.

Determine whether the actuary is unrelated to the client.

Review and test the employee data given to the actuary on which the actuarial calculations are based. Procedures outlined in Figure 36.1 under "Employer Records" should be used as a guide.

Determine whether the actuarial methods used by the actuary to determine pension costs and accumulated plan benefits are appropriate and whether the same methods were used in the prior period.

Determine that each significant actuarial assumption used to determine the actuarial present value of accumulated plan benefits reflects the best estimate of the plan's future experience solely with respect to that individual assumption.

Ascertain that the value of pension fund assets used in actuarial calculations to determine pension costs is not unreasonable.

Determine whether the effect of any changes in actuarial methods and assumptions has been disclosed.

Determine whether the actuarially determined information contained in the plan financial statements agrees with the actuary's report.

Review the period from the date of the actuarial valuation to the fiscal year-end (and through the subsequent events period, to the extent known) to see whether any significant events (e.g., plant closings, changes in plan, and changes in market value of securities) have occurred that would materially affect amounts reflected or disclosed in the financial statements. If such events have occurred, consult with the actuary and obtain an estimate of the dollar effect of such amounts.

---

client should preferably be documented. Some auditors believe that the actuary should be requested to set forth in writing the circumstances of any relationship with the client. The auditor may also wish to ask the actuary to send him or her a copy of the actuary's report as well as to confirm certain other information not contained in the actuary's report. An illustrative letter requesting this information (and also requesting information as to any relationship with the client) is presented in the AICPA audit guide.

The audit objectives applicable to defined contribution plans require the auditor to determine that net assets have been allocated to individual participant accounts in accordance with the plan document and that participant accounts agree in the aggregate with total net assets. These objectives are accomplished by performing auditing procedures such as

- Reviewing the plan documents to understand the basis of allocation.
- Testing the allocation of investment income, company contributions, appreciation (depreciation), and other items to the accounts.
- Testing individual employee contributions to the respective account for contributory plans.

- Determining that the sum of the individual accounts agrees with the total net assets.
- Confirming information with participants as appropriate.

Other Financial Statement Disclosures

Requirements.   SFAS No. 35 requires the following disclosures in the plan's financial statements, in addition to the disclosures already described:

- Brief general description of the plan agreement, including vesting and benefit provisions.
- Description of significant plan amendments adopted during the year ending on the latest benefit information date; if amendments were adopted between the latest benefit information date and the date of the financial statements, disclosure should be made that the actuarial present value of accumulated plan benefits does not reflect those amendments.
- Brief description of the priority of participants' claims to the assets of the plan on plan termination and, for plans subject to ERISA, benefits guaranteed by the Pension Benefit Guaranty Corporation (PBGC), including a discussion of the application of the PBGC guarantee to any recent plan amendments.
- Funding policy and any changes in such policy. If a plan is contributory, the method of determining participants' contributions should be disclosed. Noncash contributions, if any, by the employer should be described. Plans subject to ERISA should disclose whether the minimum funding requirements of ERISA have been met. If a minimum funding waiver has been granted by the IRS or if a request for a waiver is pending, that should be disclosed.
- The federal income tax status of the plan if a favorable letter of determination has not been obtained or maintained.
- Plan administrative expenses. If significant plan administrative costs are absorbed by the employer, that fact should be disclosed.
- Significant transactions in which the plan is involved jointly with the plan sponsor, the employer company, or employee organizations.
- Unusual or infrequent events or transactions occurring after the latest benefit information date but before issuance of the financial statements that might significantly affect the usefulness of the financial statements in assessing the plan's present and future ability to pay benefits; for example, a plan amendment adopted after the latest benefit information date that significantly increased future benefits attributable to participants' services rendered before that date. If they are reasonably determinable, the effects of such events or transactions should be disclosed; if such effects are not quantified, an explanation of why they are not reasonably determinable should be provided.

Notes to plan financial statements prepared pursuant to ERISA reporting and disclosure requirements include some of the disclosures required by SFAS

No. 35 as well as additional disclosures. Disclosures required by ERISA but not specifically by SFAS No. 35 are

Description of material lease commitments and other commitments and contingent liabilities.

Description of any agreements and transactions with persons known to be parties of interest.

Information concerning whether a tax ruling or determination letter has been obtained. (SFAS No. 35 requires disclosure of the federal income tax status of the plan only when a favorable letter of determination has not been obtained or maintained.)

Any other information required for a fair presentation.

Compliance with ERISA calls for a description of any variances between GAAP and the principles followed in the financial statements, and an explanation of any differences between the financial statements and amounts reported on Form 5500.

The disclosure requirements described for financial statements prepared pursuant to ERISA reporting and disclosure requirements apply to both defined contribution and defined benefit pension plans. Disclosures prescribed by SFAS No. 35 relating to the actuarial present value of accumulated plan benefits, minimum funding requirements, and PBGC plan termination provisions, however, do not apply to defined contribution plans.

Auditing Procedures.   The following is a summary, and is not all-inclusive, of the auditing procedures applicable to other financial statement disclosures for pension plans. Several of these procedures may be performed in conjunction with the audit of the sponsoring company; if so, they should not be repeated at the plan level.

Read and abstract key portions (employee coverage or eligibility, vesting, benefit determination, priority of claims, and so on) of the plan document, noting changes or amendments in the plan. This should be performed annually in conjunction with the actuary's report, which normally summarizes changes in the plan.

Read the minutes of meetings of the board of trustees or administrative committee for amendments adopted, funding policy changes, or other matters affecting the plan.

Request an analysis (generally in the actuary's report) of the plan's compliance with minimum funding requirements.

Examine the tax determination letter and inquire about changes therein.

Inquire about the existence of (a) significant plan transactions with the employer, (b) parties-in-interest transactions, and (c) material lease or other commitments.

OTHER AUDIT CONSIDERATIONS

Subsequent Events

In common with audits of other entities, the auditor of a pension plan should consider events subsequent to the date of the financial statements through the date of the auditor's report, to determine whether adjustment of or disclosure in the financial statements is required. Subsequent events are discussed in general in Chapter 21. Auditing procedures might include, but are not necessarily limited to, those shown in Figure 36.6, which is based on the AICPA audit guide. Since investments normally represent the major part of a pension plan's assets, the auditor should be alert for material changes in the market value of securities subsequent to the statement date, particularly if the opinion is dated near the end of the filing period permitted by ERISA. If the auditor becomes aware of any such material changes, consideration should be given to whether there is adequate disclosure in the financial statements. (AU Sections 560.05 and 560.07 contain further guidance.)

Audit Requirements Relating to ERISA

Certain requirements of ERISA result in the modification of auditing procedures or the performance of additional procedures. Those features fall into three principal categories: plan compliance with ERISA, transactions prohibited by ERISA, and reporting and disclosure requirements of ERISA.

Plan Compliance with ERISA.   The auditor should consider whether the terms of the plan relating to participation, vesting, joint and survivorship coverage, and certain other provisions comply with pertinent ERISA requirements. Normally, the auditor can use one of two approaches in this connection.

Figure 36.6   Suggested Auditing Procedures in the Subsequent Period

> Review minutes of board of trustees' or administrative committee meetings held through the completion of field work.
> If available, obtain interim financial statements of the plan for a period subsequent to the audit date, compare with the financial statements being audited, and investigate unusual fluctuations.
> Inquire of and discuss with the plan administrator:
>
> > Abnormal disposal or purchase of investments since year-end.
> > Amendments to plan and trust instruments and to insurance contracts.
> > Unusual terminations of participants, such as terminations arising from sale of a division or layoffs.
> > Changes in commitments or contingent liabilities of the plan.
>
> If there is a significant period of time between the date of the response of the plan's legal counsel and the date of completion of field work, obtain supplemental legal representations.

If it can be determined that the plan is a qualified plan under the provisions of the Internal Revenue Code, the auditor may conclude that the plan complies with the provisions of ERISA. Ordinarily, the auditor may gain reasonable assurance that a plan is qualified under the code by examining a tax qualification letter, if such a letter has been issued by the IRS covering the current plan provisions. Alternatively, the auditor can obtain satisfaction that the plan's provisions comply with ERISA by obtaining a letter from the client's legal counsel stating that the plan's provisions comply with either ERISA or the code.

The above procedures for determining plan compliance with ERISA would be appropriate for the first year in which a plan has been amended or for new pension plans. In recent years, the plan qualification provisions of the code have been subject to frequent change, and corresponding changes have been made to ERISA. Accordingly, plans have been required to be amended to conform to these changes, and qualification letters are usually obtained regarding the plan amendments. In theory, if there are no plan amendments thereafter, little or no additional work related to plan compliance would be needed in subsequent years. In practice, however, a tax qualification letter or other evidence of plan compliance tends to carry less weight with the passage of time, since the IRS is concerned not only with the plan provisions themselves, but also with the manner in which the plan operates in accordance with those provisions. Therefore, in subsequent years, the auditor should be alert to changes in the manner in which plan provisions are applied.

If the auditor of the plan also audits the financial statements of the employer, this work may be done in connection with the audit of the employer and need not be duplicated. If the plan's auditor does not audit the employer, a report may be obtained from the employer's independent auditor that indicates the procedures followed and the audit findings with respect to plan compliance with ERISA. Such a report may be used as evidence only if the plan's auditor is satisfied as to the independence and professional reputation of the employer's auditor and performs procedures considered appropriate, as described in AU Section 543.04. (See "Using the Work of Other Auditors" in Chapter 6.)

Transactions Prohibited by ERISA. Transactions prohibited by ERISA could give rise to significant receivables because a plan fiduciary is liable for losses to the plan resulting from a breach of fiduciary duties and for restoring to the plan profits made by the fiduciary through the use of the plan's assets. Accordingly, the auditor should apply procedures to ascertain whether there has been a breach of fiduciary duties or prohibited transactions have occurred and, if so, whether a receivable or other disclosure should be reflected in the financial statements. Procedures for accomplishing this include

Inquiring whether any activities or transactions that might be prohibited have occurred.

Obtaining from the plan administrator a list of all parties in interest (to use as a reference point during the audit), reviewing the administrator's procedures for identifying parties in interest, and examining related documentation to determine whether the list appears to be complete.

Ascertaining whether any prohibited transactions have been disclosed as a result of past IRS or other governmental examinations.

Because the auditor should, as a result of the ordinary audit work, be familiar with significant transactions that might be prohibited, few, if any, additional procedures should be necessary in most instances.

Reporting and Disclosure Requirements of ERISA. As part of the audit, the auditor will usually consider whether the financial statements and supplemental schedules have been prepared in conformity with ERISA and the related DOL reporting and disclosure regulations. The auditor need not be unduly concerned, however, about whether the other reporting and disclosure requirements of ERISA have been complied with, because penalties imposed for noncompliance are not likely to have an impact on the plan. Nonetheless, the auditor should be alert to instances of noncompliance with respect to such items so as to be in a position to advise the client of the need to consider corrective action.

Supplemental Schedules. The normal auditing procedures should be sufficient to permit the auditor to report on most of the information included in the supplemental schedules. The auditor may perform some additional procedures, however, with respect to certain schedules, such as the schedule of 5 percent reportable transactions.

Prohibited transactions should be reported on a schedule of parties-in-interest transactions. That schedule need not include any transactions exempted from the prohibited transaction rules, but the notes to the financial statements should include a description of all agreements and transactions with parties in interest. SAS No. 45 (AU Section 334) and SFAS No. 57 (Accounting Standards Section R36) offer useful guidance in this regard; however, the ERISA definition of parties in interest is somewhat broader than the definition of related parties.

Other Considerations

Bonding. The auditor should determine whether the plan maintains at least the required minimum amount of fidelity insurance in accordance with provisions of ERISA.

Transaction Approval. The auditor should be acquainted with the collective bargaining agreement, declaration of trust, insurance contract, and other plan documents and should be alert for any transactions that require the approval of the board of trustees (for a multiemployer plan) or administrative committee (for a single employer plan).

Potential Plan Termination. When reading minutes of meetings of the board of trustees and administrative committee and performing other auditing procedures, the auditor should be alert for any evidence of a potential pension plan termination. In addition, the auditor may wish to inquire of the employer's management as to the possibility of a plan termination. If a plan termination is more than a remote possibility, the auditor should ensure that the situation is appropriately reflected or disclosed in the financial statements.

Letter of Representation and Legal Counsel Letters. Immediately before completing the field work, it is desirable for the auditor to obtain a letter of representation from management, worded to fit the individual circumstances of the engagement. In addition to representations obtained in accordance with SAS No. 19 and discussed in Chapter 21, the letter should normally include representations related to compliance with ERISA, any potential plan termination, changes in plan provisions, parties-in-interest transactions, value of investments (including those stated at fair value as determined by the board of trustees or administrative committee), and other pertinent matters. The representation letter should be signed by officials of the plan, generally the plan administrator and the individual equivalent to the chief financial officer. If the sponsoring employer is the plan administrator, one or more company officials responsible for administration of and accounting for the plan should sign the letter. In addition, the auditor should obtain a letter from the plan's legal counsel concerning litigation, claims, and assessments, in accordance with SAS No. 12 (AU Section 337). (See the discussion of "Lawyers' Letters" in Chapter 21.)

AUDIT REPORTS

An auditor's report on pension plan financial statements is included for most pension plans as part of the annual report required to be filed under ERISA. This section of the chapter discusses and illustrates standard reports and commonly encountered departures from standard reports. These reports are consistent with the guidance provided in AICPA Statement of Position (SOP) 88-2, *Illustrative Auditor's Reports on Financial Statements of Employee Benefit Plans Comporting With Statement on Auditing Standards No. 58, "Reports on Audited Financial Statements."* Reference to the SOP should be made for additional examples.

Standard Report

If the auditor has audited a pension plan's financial statements in accordance with GAAS and concludes that they have been prepared in conformity with GAAP, an unqualified report is appropriate. An illustrative standard auditor's report covering defined benefit pension plan financial statements prepared in accordance with SFAS No. 35 is shown in Figure 36.7. In the illustration, it is assumed that the required information regarding the actuarial present value of accumulated plan benefits and the changes therein is presented in separate financial statements. Figure 36.7 assumes that the actuarial benefit information is presented as of the end of the plan year.

Figure 36.7   Illustrative Unqualified Auditor's Report on a Defined Benefit Plan

---

Independent Auditor's Report

We have audited the accompanying statements of net assets available for benefits and of accumulated plan benefits of XYZ Pension Plan as of December 31, 19X2, and the related statements of changes in net assets available for benefits and of changes in accumulated plan benefits for the year then ended. These financial statements are the responsibility of the Plan's management. Our responsibility is to express an opinion on these financial statements based on our audit.

We conducted our audit in accordance with generally accepted auditing standards. Those standards require that we plan and perform the audit to obtain reasonable assurance about whether the financial statements are free of material misstatement. An audit includes examining, on a test basis, evidence supporting the amounts and disclosures in the financial statements. An audit also includes assessing the accounting principles used and significant estimates made by management, as well as evaluating the overall financial statement presentation. We believe that our audit provides a reasonable basis for our opinion.

In our opinion, the financial statements referred to above present fairly, in all material respects, the financial status of the Plan as of December 31, 19X2, and the changes in its financial status for the year then ended in conformity with generally accepted accounting principles.

[*Signature*]

[*Date*]

Under GAAP, if information regarding the actuarial present value of accumulated plan benefits is presented as of the beginning rather than the end of the year, prior-year statements of net assets available for benefits and of changes in net assets available for benefits are required. Further, under the alternative method of complying with ERISA's reporting and disclosure requirements, plans must present comparative statements of assets and liabilities. In that event, the auditor's report in Figure 36.7 would be modified.

Reporting on Supplemental Schedules Required by ERISA.   Annual reports filed pursuant to ERISA are required to contain certain supplemental schedules that must be covered by the auditor's report. SAS No. 29, *Reporting on Information Accompanying the Basic Financial Statements in Auditor-Submitted Documents* (AU Section 551), provides reporting guidelines when the auditor submits to a client or others a document that contains information in addition to the basic financial statements.

Reference to Confirmation of Investments.   Investments held as of the plan year-end may be confirmed with the custodian rather than inspected and counted. If the securities are confirmed, some auditors refer to this fact in the scope paragraph of the report. For example, language such as the following might be added to the scope paragraph: "Investments owned at December 31, 19X2 were confirmed to us by the custodian." While this practice has been considered acceptable, the audit guide does not address the issue and such wording is not included in the illustrative auditor's report in Figure 36.7.

Departures from the Standard Report

Limited Scope Audit Pursuant to DOL Regulations.   In practice, many plan administrators limit the scope of the audit to exclude financial information

Figure 36.8   Illustrative Auditor's Report—Audit Scope Restricted by Plan Administrator Regarding Information Certified by Bank or Insurance Carrier

---

Independent Auditor's Report

We were engaged to audit the financial statements and schedules of XYZ Pension Plan as of December 31, 19X1 and for the year then ended, as listed in the accompanying index. These financial statements and schedules are the responsibility of the Plan's management.

As permitted by Section 2520.103-8 of the Department of Labor's Rules and Regulations for Reporting and Disclosure under the Employee Retirement Income Security Act of 1974, the plan administrator instructed us not to perform, and we did not perform, any auditing procedures with respect to the information summarized in Note X, which was certified by ABC Bank, the trustee of the Plan, except for comparing the information with the related information included in the 19X1 financial statements and supplemental schedules. We have been informed by the plan administrator that the trustee holds the Plan's investment assets and executes investment transactions. The plan administrator has obtained a certification from the trustee as of and for the year ended December 31, 19X1 that the information provided to the plan administrator by the trustee is complete and accurate.

Because of the significance of the information that we did not audit, we are unable to, and do not, express an opinion on the accompanying financial statements and schedules taken as a whole. The form and content of the information included in the financial statements and schedules, other than that derived from the information certified by the trustee, have been audited by us in accordance with generally accepted auditing standards and, in our opinion, are presented in compliance with the Department of Labor's Rules and Regulations for Reporting and Disclosure under the Employee Retirement Income Security Act of 1974.

[*Signature*]

[*Date*]

---

prepared by a bank, a similar institution, or an insurance carrier. This is permitted under DOL reporting and disclosure regulations if the institution is regulated and supervised and is subject to periodic examination by a state or federal agency and if the information is certified as complete and accurate by the institution.

If the scope of the audit has been restricted in this way, the plan auditor should compare information covered by the certification of the institution with related information in the financial statements and supplemental schedules and determine that it is presented in compliance with DOL regulations. Also, if the certified data is based on information supplied by the plan administrator, the auditor should be satisfied that amounts reported by the institution as received from or disbursed at the discretion of the plan administrator are determined in accordance with the terms of the plan. The auditor's report in Figure 36.8 assumes that the plan administrator has restricted the audit scope with respect to financial information prepared and certified to by a bank, a similar institution, or an insurance company.

Scope Limitation Relating to Employer Records.   SAS No. 58, paragraphs 40–42 (AU Sections 508.40–.42), provides guidance when the auditor is unable to examine employer records or to perform appropriate alternative auditing procedures, as discussed earlier in the chapter.

Investment Valuation.   Most pension plans state investments other than insurance contracts at fair value, as required by SFAS No. 35 for defined benefit plans and DOL reporting and disclosure regulations governing the alternative method of compliance. If marketable securities are carried at cost and market value is substantially lower than cost, the auditor should be guided by the AICPA auditing interpretation entitled "Evidential Matter for the Carrying Amount of Marketable Securities" (AU Section 9332.01).

37

Auditing Public Utilities

OVERVIEW OF THE INDUSTRY

Electric, gas, and local telephone utilities are granted monopoly status within their designated service areas because those services are considered essential to the public welfare and an exclusive franchise is needed to avoid duplication of the substantial and costly facilities required. With this monopoly status has come governmental regulation of the rates charged for the services.

Public utilities are capital-intensive businesses. It is not unusual for an electric utility to spend several billion dollars constructing a large generating station. The investment by electric and gas utilities in plant facilities necessary to transmit and distribute their services is equally significant, and telephone utilities' costs of providing service are also substantial. As a result of these capital requirements, the plant account is the most significant asset of a utility and usually approximates the long-term debt and equity capital on the balance sheet.

Public utilities may be either investor owned or publicly owned (by either governmental agencies or customers). The majority of utilities offering electric, gas, or telephone services are owned by stockholders. In certain areas, the federal, state, or local government provides utility services. Cooperative systems usually serve rural areas and are owned by the customers of the services.

Operating Characteristics

Electric Utilities.   Electricity is produced at large generating plants. Typically, except for hydroelectric plants, a heat source such as coal, oil, gas, or nuclear fuel is needed to produce electric power. The power is delivered in bulk throughout the utility's service area by its transmission system. Power is made available to individual customers via the utility's distribution plant.

Electric power cannot be stored; it must be produced as it is needed.[1] This places unusual capital requirements on the utility, which must have sufficient generating capacity to meet peak load requirements that might exist only for short periods during a day or during certain times of the year. In addition, an electric utility must have sufficient excess or reserve capacity so that it can operate even if one or more of its largest generating units are unavailable. Utilities can reduce the need to build reserve plant capacity, however, by joining power pools, integrating their systems with those of neighboring utilities, and contracting with other utilities, independent power producers, and cogenerators to purchase their excess capacity.

Cogenerators are often major commercial or industrial customers who install generating facilities for their own use. These facilities generate electricity and a by-product, such as steam, which are used by the cogenerator in its operations or production. Current federal regulations provide an incentive to commercial and industrial customers to build their own generating facilities, since any excess electricity generated must be purchased by the local utility at the utility's avoided cost. Avoided cost is determined differently in each juris-

---

[1] Recent developments in superconductivity may change the way energy is stored and transported in the future.

diction, but the goal is to determine the cost the utility would have incurred to generate the electricity.

Although cogeneration provides an alternative to a utility's investment in costly generating facilities, it poses certain risks to the utility, which is frequently obligated to provide replacement energy in the event of an outage at the cogeneration facility. Since the cogeneration facility is not operated by the utility, the maintenance program may not be under the utility's control and may not be adequate. In addition to the additional risks for the utility in managing its capacity, it loses the customer sales for which it has already constructed facilities.

Gas Utilities.   While electric utilities are beginning to separate production from transmission and distribution of electricity, these functions traditionally have been performed by separate companies in the gas industry. The extraction of natural gas from the ground is a nonregulated operation. Regulated gas pipelines purchase gas from the wellhead, transport it, and sell it to distributors at wholesale prices. Regulated gas distribution companies sell and deliver the gas to ultimate consumers at retail. Recent rule making by the Federal Energy Regulatory Commission (FERC) is changing the structure of the natural gas industry. The goal is to allow "open access transportation," enabling end users to purchase gas on the spot market directly from producers. As a result, the role of the pipeline companies will expand from wholesale supplier to transporter or "common carrier."

Another distinction between electric and gas utilities is that gas can be stored pending customers' use; therefore, gas utilities do not require significant reserve plant capacity. However, gas distributors are more susceptible to changes in competitive fuel prices. Many large gas customers have dual fuel capabilities that enable them to burn either oil or gas in the same boiler with minimal conversion time or cost. These customers are very sensitive to differences between the prices of gas and oil. Gas companies have responded by obtaining approved rates (tariffs) that allow their price to change with the price of oil. This can move a significant portion of the gas utility's business into the nonregulated arena, complicating the application of Statement of Financial Accounting Standards (SFAS) No. 71. (The criteria for applying SFAS No. 71 are described later in this chapter.)

Telephone Utilities.   Telephone service is provided by a sophisticated network of wiring, cables, and switching equipment. Telephone utilities transmit both local and long distance calls by routing them through central offices that house the switching equipment used for transmission. For local calls, this is a relatively simple procedure; however, for long distance calls, it can result in an indirect routing process depending on the available capacity of switching equipment. As with electric utilities, this places a significant capital requirement on telephone utilities to maintain transmission equipment that will provide the capacity to meet peak requirements.

The divestiture of the Bell Operating Companies by American Telephone and Telegraph Company (AT&T) in 1983 began a new era in telecommunications. The divestiture created seven regional holding companies, which own the local telephone companies that provide local exchange services to most areas of the United States. AT&T and other interexchange carriers continue to provide long distance service. At the time of the divestiture, a system of local access and transport areas (LATAs) was implemented, with many states divided into multiple LATAs. Under this system, revenues from intra-LATA calls generally belong to the local telephone company, and revenues from inter-LATA calls, to the interexchange carrier. The local telephone company, however, charges the interexchange carrier an access fee to hook the carrier's long distance network into the local network.

The Economic Environment

Electric and Gas Utilities. Beginning in the 1970s, the gas and electric utility industry, which before then was considered to be financially sound, was dealt a series of economic blows. Environmental regulations began to increase construction time and costs significantly. Energy conservation began to take effect following the OPEC oil embargo in 1973–74, and construction projects were delayed or even canceled. Public utility securities, once considered a secure income investment, became less attractive to investors as inflation devalued dividend income. Earnings coverage of fixed charges declined toward (or even below) the minimum required under existing indentures before new debt securities could be issued. The dependence of many utilities on the capital markets became more and more costly as stocks sold below book value and bonds sold at record interest rates. The nuclear accident at Three Mile Island in 1979 dealt another significant blow to the electric utility industry.

The 1980s brought a focus on deregulation and on the prudence of management's decisions and actions. Regulators began to scrutinize the construction costs of recently completed generating facilities, particularly nuclear power plants, disallowing excess or imprudent costs. With the rising concern over excess capacity, the scrutiny extended to the appropriateness of management's initial decision to build new facilities. Significant increases in both costs and federal regulation, combined with growing consumer concern over nuclear power, caused many utilities to abandon the construction of nuclear power plants. Recently completed facilities could not meet the new federal licensing standards, creating serious financial difficulties for the utilities. Public Service of New Hampshire declared bankruptcy after its Seabrook Nuclear Power Station did not receive an operating license. Long Island Lighting Company fell victim to the same change in regulation during the construction of its Shoreham Nuclear Power Station, which it was forced to close. At the same time, analysts in the mergers and acquisitions arena began to view public utilities with completed construction programs as possible targets for hostile takeovers.

Telephone Utilities. In contrast to electric and gas utilities, telephone utilities generally have not suffered from burdensome environmental regulations or increased construction costs, and until the late 1970s the local telephone utilities were considered financially sound. Since then, however, the advent of competition, the rapid introduction of advanced technology into the telecommunications industry and the consequent shortening of what had been abnormally long depreciation lives, and the divestiture of the local operating companies by AT&T have caused increases in both local telephone rates and the business risks faced by telephone utilities. The telephone industry now faces such issues as competition, recovery of asset costs, bypass technology, and deregulation. As local phone rates continue to rise, regulators are looking for innovative means of cost containment. Also, many telephone companies are in favor of deregulation as a means to meet increasing competition. Although these issues are not expected to significantly affect telephone utilities in the near future, the long-term structure of the industry is likely to change.

THE REGULATORY ENVIRONMENT

The rate-making process determines the selling price of services provided by a utility; it specifies the overall level of revenues, the types and amounts of rates that may be charged, and the various classes of users to which the different rates apply. Rate making also influences the application of accounting principles by a public utility, because the regulatory body often prescribes accounting methods for utilities under its jurisdiction, which may or may not conform with generally accepted accounting principles (GAAP) appropriate for non-regulated businesses.

The Rate-Making Process

The rates that a public utility charges its customers are a matter of administrative law; its revenues are predetermined and subject to the scrutiny of interested parties and the approval of regulatory bodies. The public utility proposes rates, designed to cover its costs and provide a return on its investment, to the federal or state regulatory commission having jurisdiction. The regulatory authority then reviews the rate proposal and allows interested parties such as consumer groups or major industrial customers to respond to, and often challenge, the proposal. After the commission has considered the arguments of the utility and interested parties, it determines the amount of revenue the utility should be permitted to receive (usually less than the utility's original proposal) and approves the corresponding tariffs to be charged to various classes of customers. The rates of publicly owned power agencies usually are set by their own governing boards, as empowered by statute or contract.

The Rate-Making Formula

Determining the amount of revenue a utility should be allowed to earn (the revenue requirement) can be summarized in the following equations:

$$\text{revenue requirement} = \text{cost of service}$$

$$\text{cost of service} = \text{operating expenses} + \text{return}$$

$$\text{return} = \text{rate base} \times \text{rate of return}$$

Cost of Service.   Cost of service is the amount that will permit the utility to meet all expenses properly chargeable to current utility operations and incurred to provide utility services, plus provide a return on amounts invested in assets necessary to provide such services. Operating expenses include salaries, materials, fuel costs, supplies, miscellaneous expenses, taxes, and depreciation of plant.

Developing the operating expenses component of cost of service begins with the utility's historical accounting records of operating costs incurred, recorded in accordance with the uniform system of accounts prescribed by the regulator. The utility selects a test period to be used in the rate application. Ideally, the test period selected should be as close as possible to the period for which the rates to be fixed will be operational; in most instances, the test period will not coincide with the utility's fiscal year. Normally, test-period costs are adjusted for anticipated or known changes in expenses during or after the test period. For example, annualized union wage increases during the test period and any contracted future cost increases would be taken into account in determining cost of service. In some jurisdictions, utilities have been allowed to use a projected future test period. In these instances, the utility applies for rates to go into effect at a future date and projects the cost of service at the effective date.

If a utility develops a cost of service study that is reasonable in relation to costs incurred (or to be incurred) and is able to justify those costs, and if the regulatory commission agrees that the costs are reasonable, the utility should receive adequate revenues to operate successfully. That means that if the utility is operated efficiently, it should provide adequate service and be able to attract additional capital as needed. Unexpected changes in cost or sales volume, however, may preclude the utility from achieving the results anticipated in the rate application.

The terms ''above the line'' and ''below the line'' are commonly used in rate making. The ''line'' is net operating income (i.e., operating revenues net of operating expenses, including income taxes). Costs above the line are operating expenses that are part of the cost of service and are reflected in the revenue requirement. Other revenues and expenses, referred to as nonrate items (e.g., rental income from nonutility property), do not constitute operating income or expense and therefore are not part of the cost of service; they are shown below the line as other income or expenses and are borne, in effect, by the common shareholders.

Return.   Return is the amount that should induce investors to invest in, or retain their investments in, a public utility. The first step in calculating the amount of a utility's return is determining the utility's rate base.

Rate Base.   The rate base represents a utility's total investment in facilities used to provide service, generally measured at its original cost. This is the base to which rate of return is applied to arrive at the level of operating earnings (i.e., return) at which the utility should be able to operate successfully. The principal components of rate base are as follows:

- *Plant-in-Service.* Plant-in-service includes the cost of facilities used and useful in providing service to the public, net of accumulated depreciation. (The inclusion of depreciation in cost of service provides a recovery of the investment; hence accumulated depreciation is deducted from the rate base.)
- *Construction-Work-in-Progress (CWIP).* Although it appears that the "used and useful" principle would automatically eliminate CWIP from inclusion in the rate base since CWIP will not be used or useful until some time in the future, some commissions include all or part of CWIP in the rate base. In some cases, CWIP is included to allow a utility that has significant construction projects to remain financially viable. This is a sensitive issue since the inclusion of CWIP in the rate base requires current customers to pay for a plant that generally is considered to benefit future customers.

In many jurisdictions, CWIP is excluded from the rate base. From the utility's viewpoint, however, the investment in CWIP is no different from any other investment and therefore merits a return. This is recognized, in those jurisdictions in which CWIP is excluded from the rate base, by capitalizing, as a cost of construction, an estimated return commonly referred to as an allowance for funds used during construction (AFDC). The effect of recording an AFDC is to recognize that the utility has sacrificed the alternative use of the funds invested in CWIP and that the return on amounts invested in construction represents part of the cost of completed construction. While the utility industry tends to view the AFDC from a return perspective, capitalizing the carrying costs of construction projects is a generally accepted accounting principle. Accounting for the AFDC is explained later in this chapter. Telephone utilities follow similar practices but refer to the capitalized return as "interest charged construction."

- *Deferred Income Taxes.* Since a utility recovers the full provision for income taxes from its customers as an operating expense, net deferred tax credits generally are deducted from the rate base. This is done to recognize that the positive cash flow resulting from deferred taxes provides the utility with cost-free capital that is supplied by the ratepayers. Not deducting deferred income tax credits would have the effect of providing the utility's investors with a return on a portion of the rate base for which they did not provide the capital. Utilities that have adopted SFAS No. 96, *Accounting for Income Taxes*, are required to record deferred tax liabilities and assets that previously were not recorded because of the interplay of rate regulation and SFAS No. 71 (discussed later). The utilities and their regulators have to identify the additional deferred taxes that were not provided by ratepayers, so that the amounts are not applied to reduce the rate base. As explained in Chapter 19, in December 1989, the Financial Accounting Standards Board (FASB) voted to defer the effective date of SFAS No. 96 to fiscal years beginning after December 15, 1991; however, some utilities have elected early implementation of the standard.
- *Working Capital.* Regulators recognize that a utility cannot operate without continuously available funds and therefore permit an allowance for working

capital to be included in the rate base. This allowance may represent a specified number of days of a utility's cash requirement; however, regulators may require utilities to submit a study to justify the amount of working capital claimed.

The rate base, as determined through the rate-making process, is the total value on which the utility is permitted to earn a return.

Rate of Return. The authorized rate of return is the return expressed as a percentage of the utility's rate base, and it is based on the utility's cost of capital.[2] The authorized rate of return is not a guarantee of a certain level of earnings and is rarely attained because of delays in the rate-making process (regulatory lag) and revenues and expenses that vary from expected levels (attrition). A utility's actual (realized) rate of return is the amount it earns expressed as a percentage of the rate base after deducting operating expenses, including depreciation and taxes. In the landmark case *Bluefield Water Works and Improvement Company* v. *Public Service Commission of West Virginia*,[3] the U.S. Supreme Court discussed rate of return as follows:

> A public utility is entitled to such rates as will permit it to earn a return on the value of the property which it employs for the convenience of the public equal to that generally being made at the same time and in the same general part of the country on investments in other business undertakings which are attended by corresponding risks and uncertainty; but it has no constitutional right to profits such as are realized or anticipated in highly profitable enterprises or speculative ventures. The return should be reasonably sufficient to assure confidence in the financial soundness of the utility and should be adequate, under efficient and economical management, to maintain and support its credit and enable it to raise the money necessary for the proper discharge of its public duties.

In determining the authorized rate of return, an appropriate cost for each of the utility's various sources of capital—long-term debt, preferred stock, and common equity, including retained earnings—is identified. For long-term debt and preferred stock, the coupon interest rate, appropriately adjusted for premiums or discounts, or dividend rate is the cost of capital. Determining an appropriate cost of capital for common equity (including retained earnings) is usually more subjective.[4] The overall cost of capital is the weighted average return on all sources of capital. In the telephone industry, other types of rate regulation are being considered, including price caps (allowing the telephone company to earn whatever it can using a maximum price set by the regulator), sharing of cost savings, and deregulation of certain services and products.

---

[2]Cost of capital is calculated as a weighted average of the cost of the various components of the utility's capital structure—its debt, preferred stock, and common shareholders' equity. Most corporate and managerial finance textbooks discuss at considerable length the concept of the cost of capital, how to calculate it, and the factors that affect it.

[3]262 U.S. 679, 692 (1923).

[4]Determining an appropriate rate (or rates) of return on common equity is discussed in most finance textbooks.

ACCOUNTING PRINCIPLES FOR RATE-REGULATED ENTERPRISES

The principal authoritative sources of accounting principles for public utilities include

- SFAS No. 71, *Accounting for the Effects of Certain Types of Regulation* (Accounting Standards Section Re6).
- SFAS No. 90, *Accounting for Abandonments and Disallowances of Plant Costs* (Accounting Standards Section Re6).
- SFAS No. 92, *Accounting for Phase-in Plans* (Accounting Standards Section Re6).
- SFAS No. 101, *Regulated Enterprises—Accounting for the Discontinuation of Application of FASB Statement No. 71* (Accounting Standards Section Re6).
- FASB Technical Bulletin No. 87-2, *Computation of a Loss on an Abandonment* (Accounting Standards Section Re6).
- Prescribed systems of accounts issued by FERC for electric and gas utilities, the Federal Communications Commission (FCC) for telephone utilities, and state regulatory commissions.

These statements incorporate the economic effects of the rate-making process that are not considered in other authoritative pronouncements.

The Interrelationship of Rate Making and Accounting

As part of the rate-making process, rate orders (from FERC, FCC, or state commissions) often require rate-regulated enterprises to observe accounting practices that would be at variance with GAAP for a nonregulated entity. An example is the accounting for research and development costs; while GAAP require their immediate recognition as a period expense, public utility commissions often require a utility to defer research and development costs and amortize them over the future periods in which compensating revenues will be provided through the rate-making process.

The FASB recognizes the economic effect of regulation on public utilities. SFAS No. 71 requires companies to capitalize costs if regulation ensures that incurred costs will be recovered in the future through the rate-making process. For example, a commission may permit excessive repair costs incurred in one fiscal period to be recovered in a future period through increased customer rates. For accounting purposes, the excessive repair costs should be deferred until the increased rates are effective and should be amortized as the revenues are collected. Similarly, if current rates are provided for costs that are expected to be incurred in the future, such as the costs of potential storm damage repairs, SFAS No. 71 requires companies to recognize those current additional receipts as liabilities. SFAS No. 71 applies to regulated operations of an enterprise that meet all of the following criteria:

- The enterprise's rates for regulated services or products are established by an independent third-party regulator or by its own governing board.

- The regulated rates are designed to recover the specific enterprise's costs of providing the regulated service or products.
- It is reasonable to assume that the rates described above can be charged to and collected from customers, in view of the demand for the regulated service or product and the level of competition.

In December 1988, the FASB issued SFAS No. 101, *Regulated Enterprises— Accounting for the Discontinuation of Application of FASB Statement No. 71* (Accounting Standards Section Re6). SFAS No. 101 specifies that an enterprise that ceases to meet the criteria for application of SFAS No. 71 should report that event in its general-purpose financial statements by eliminating from its statement of financial position the effects of any actions of regulators that had been recognized as assets and liabilities pursuant to SFAS No. 71. However, the carrying amounts of plant, equipment, and inventory measured and reported pursuant to SFAS No. 71 should not be adjusted unless those assets are impaired; in that event, their carrying amounts should be reduced to reflect the impairment. The net effect of the adjustments should be included in income of the period of the change and classified as an extraordinary item.

The Board has provided guidance for the application of SFAS No. 71 to specific situations. In addition, SFAS No. 71 has been amended for three types of events that have become more frequent in the electric utility industry— abandonments of plants, disallowances of costs of recently completed plants, and rate phase-in plans for recently completed plants. This section discusses these items and certain elements of financial statements that are accounted for differently for rate-regulated enterprises than for other entities.

Abandoned Plant Losses and Disallowances

Rate-regulated enterprises, particularly electric utilities, sometimes terminate the construction of a plant because of economic or other considerations. In similar circumstances, a nonregulated enterprise would be required to immediately write off its investment in the plant. A rate-regulated enterprise may be able to recover the cost of the abandoned plant from its customers and therefore may not be required to write off its investment. The utility should write off the investment, however, when it becomes probable that the cost of the abandoned plant will not be recovered from customers. FASB Interpretation No. 14, *Reasonable Estimation of the Amount of a Loss* (Accounting Standards Section C59), provides guidance on estimating the amount of a loss.

Generally, when it becomes probable that a utility will abandon an operating asset or an asset under construction, SFAS No. 90 requires the cost of the asset to be removed from CWIP or plant-in-service. Estimated termination charges are added to the recorded costs. The enterprise must determine the likely recovery of the total costs to be provided from future rates, as permitted by its rate regulator. Only the amounts probable of recovery may be deferred; the remainder is recognized as a loss.

If the regulator permits the utility to recover the costs of an abandoned plant over a period of time, the utility must consider whether it will be allowed to earn a return on the investment. The concept of return is described earlier in this chapter. If it is likely that recovery of cost plus a full return will be granted, SFAS No. 90 requires that the costs be reported as a separate new asset and amortized in the same manner as used for rate-making purposes.

Often the regulating body does not allow the utility to earn a return on its investment in abandoned plant. If no return or a partial return is allowed, only the present value of the future revenues expected to be provided is reported as a separate new asset. Any excess of the total cost of the abandonment over the present value of the estimated future revenues is recorded as a loss. Disallowances of a portion of the costs of new facilities follow the same accounting.

Because of regulatory lag, these accounting decisions are generally made before the final rate order is issued. During that time, the investment in abandoned plant (deferred debit) represents a loss contingency. After a final rate order is issued, any adjustments to the calculations described above must be recorded. FASB Technical Bulletin No. 87-2 provides examples of the calculations and implementation guidance.

Phase-in Plans

The construction costs of electric utility plants have escalated over the past decade, and consequently the completion of a new facility and its addition to the rate base can result in a significant increase in rates. To avoid placing a financial strain on individual ratepayers, ''phase-in plans'' were developed to moderate the initial rate increase. The objective of such plans is to increase rates gradually by deferring some of the rate increase to future years and providing the utility with a return on investment in deferred amounts. SFAS No. 92 allowed costs deferred under a phase-in plan to be capitalized as deferred charges provided that substantial physical construction had been performed on the plant prior to January 1, 1988. In addition, the costs must be deferred pursuant to a formal plan that specifies the timing of recovery (not to exceed ten years) and limits the scheduled annual increases in rates each year in order to prohibit a back-end loading of the recovery. Costs deferred for plants on which substantial construction had not been completed prior to January 1, 1988, are not allowed to be capitalized for financial reporting purposes.

Allowance for Funds Used During Construction

As described earlier, in those jurisdictions in which CWIP is excluded from the rate base, rate-regulated enterprises capitalize a return on their investment in CWIP. That return takes into account the cost of different funding sources. Unlike nonregulated enterprises, utilities are permitted by SFAS No. 71 to recognize an equity return (and thereby recognize current-period income) on CWIP. The FASB considers this practice to be acceptable because the cumulative AFDC, including the equity return recognized while the plant is under construction, later becomes part of the cost of the plant for rate-making purposes. When construction is completed and the asset is placed in service, the total cost of the asset, including the AFDC, is recognized in the rate base on which the utility is permitted to earn a current return. As a result, the utility recovers the total cost of the plant, including the AFDC, through depreciation charges that are part of the cost of service to be recovered from customers over the estimated life of the plant. SFAS No. 90 added a restriction that AFDC may be capitalized only if its subsequent inclusion in allowable costs for rate-making purposes is probable, and further limited capitalization to AFDC recorded during construction or as part of a qualifying phase-in plan.

The AFDC return is normally divided into two components. For electric and gas utilities, each of these is reported separately on the income statement. They are the interest component, or the allowance for borrowed funds, and the equity component, or the allowance for other funds. Telephone utilities, which do not separate the AFDC into components, commonly refer to the AFDC as "interest charged construction."

Some rate regulators have recognized the significant financing burdens faced by a utility in financing its CWIP by permitting the utility to collect a current cash return on some of its CWIP. In this way, a utility earns a current cash return to compensate for the carrying cost (borrowings and equity capital) of financing CWIP. If a utility is allowed to earn a current return on a portion of its CWIP, then it is not permitted to recognize any AFDC on that portion of CWIP. From the utility's perspective, it is preferable to earn a current cash return on CWIP; the resulting cash flow can be used to pay the carrying charges on CWIP, thereby lessening the overall financing requirements. In general, utilities that are permitted to earn a current return on CWIP are considered to have a better quality of earnings than those that do not earn a current cash return. In some cases, state and federal regulators have elected differing treatments.

Revenue Subject to Refund

Sometimes regulated enterprises are granted temporary rate increases by a regulatory authority subject to the condition that all or a portion of the additional revenues may be refundable to customers. If the rates finally authorized are lower than the temporary rates, usually the utility is required to refund the excess revenues. The provisions of SFAS No. 5, *Accounting for Contingencies*, determine whether a provision for estimated refunds should be accrued for this loss contingency. Generally, a utility records a liability to refund revenues previously collected from customers when it is probable that a refund will be due and the amount of the refund is reasonably determinable. In practice, these conditions often are met only when the regulator issues an order for a refund; however, in some circumstances, the conditions of SFAS No. 5 may be met before a formal rate order is issued. SFAS No. 71 does not permit any refunds to be recognized as prior-period adjustments; instead, refunds must be recognized in the accounting period in which the requirements of SFAS No. 5 are met. The utility is required to disclose the effect of the refund on net income of the current year and to indicate the years in which the refunded revenue was recognized.

Unbilled Revenues

Utilities normally bill their customers on a cycle basis during each month, which allows the utilities to spread the workload of meter reading (for electric and gas utilities), billing, and collection more evenly. At a given time, therefore, a portion of the service utilized by customers is unbilled. If a utility's sales volume and rate per unit of sales do not fluctuate significantly from year to year, the impact of unbilled revenues on annual income is immaterial. The frequency of rate increases and changes in sales volume, however, can affect a utility's operating results, and as a result many public utilities accrue unbilled revenues based on estimated unbilled usage at the end of a period. Other utilities determine their revenues for rate-making purposes on a meters-read or bills-rendered basis and therefore do not accrue unbilled revenues. This practice is acceptable provided that it is consistent with the utility's rate making. Telephone utilities typically accrue unbilled revenues based on prorated basic service charges plus actual unbilled calls and other charges. The Tax Reform Act of 1986 required utilities to report unbilled revenue as taxable income.

Deferred Energy Costs

Since the mid-1960s, many electric and gas utilities have had energy adjustment clauses in their rate structures as a means of automatically passing through to their customers energy costs (fuel expense for internally generated power, purchased gas costs, and the energy component of the cost of purchased power) above or below the approved base cost per unit as identified in the tariff. An energy adjustment clause enables a utility to recover cost increases sooner and provides greater assurance that actual costs of energy will be recovered from customers. If regulatory approval were required for each rate change, the delays resulting from the administrative proceedings would adversely affect the utility's earnings. Even with energy adjustment clauses, a lag usually exists between the time energy costs are incurred and when they are billed to customers.

The energy cost increases experienced as a result of the OPEC oil embargo in 1973-74 gave rise to the practice of deferring unbilled energy costs until related revenues were collected in subsequent periods. As customers are billed, the related deferred energy costs are written off. If actual costs are less than provided for in the base rates, the difference is recognized as a deferred credit and refunded to customers. Energy adjustment clauses vary substantially among regulatory jurisdictions, and the auditor should become familiar with the operation of the energy clause of the individual utility and ascertain that it is being applied properly.

Leases

SFAS No. 71 requires rate-regulated enterprises to report capital leases, as defined in SFAS No. 13, as capital leases in their financial statements. In many cases, those leases are treated as operating leases for rate determination purposes. Therefore, it is necessary for utilities to adjust the aggregate income statement charges resulting from capital lease accounting to reflect the accounting that would have resulted from operating lease treatment.

Generally, this requires that the excess of the expense under capital lease treatment over the expense under operating lease treatment be deferred in the early years of a lease. The deferred charge is reduced and eventually eliminated in the later years of the lease, when the operating lease method results in higher expenses than does the capital lease method. This accounting results in aggregate income statement charges being recognized in an amount approximately equal to the revenues provided to cover the rate-making determination of allowable expenses on an operating-lease basis. Aside from this deferred charge, capital leases are presented on the balance sheet as required by SFAS No. 13.

Deferrals of Gains and Losses

Nonregulated companies are required to record a gain or loss on reacquisition of debt under APB Opinion No. 26, as amended by SFAS No. 4. The difference between the reacquisition price and net carrying amount of the extinguished debt is classified as an extraordinary item. Rate regulators, however, generally require that utilities amortize these gains and losses over the remaining life of the issue unless the commission with the primary rate jurisdiction specifically allows an alternative treatment. If, by rate order, future revenues are to be adjusted to compensate for the gain or loss on early extinguishment of debt, SFAS No. 71 requires that the utility capitalize the gain or loss and amortize it over the period during which it will be allowed for rate-making purposes. Amounts amortized would not be classified as extraordinary items. If the gain or loss is not deferred and amortized, it should be recognized currently as an extraordinary item.

Rate regulators often permit utility companies to defer and amortize certain unusual costs over a specified period. The accounting treatment must conform with the company's rate-making procedures. Examples of such unusual costs are storm damage, abandonments of construction programs, and development of electronic data processing systems.

Income Taxes

In the past, the recognition of income tax expense under GAAP was generally consistent with rate-making policies. SFAS No. 96, whose effective date is fiscal years beginning after December 15, 1991, as noted earlier, will remove many of the exceptions previously permitted rate-regulated enterprises. Thus, while the distinctions in financial reporting of income taxes between regulated and nonregulated entities are narrowing, the gap between financial reporting and rate making may expand. It is essential for the auditor to thoroughly understand the rate regulator's policies and practices with respect to recognizing deferred income taxes.

Historically, most public utilities used the flow-through method of accounting for certain timing (temporary) differences. Under this method, income tax expense is recognized on the basis of taxes paid or payable. A small number of differences were accorded deferred tax treatment (commonly called normalization, from a regulatory standpoint), primarily because of IRS regulations. Normalization generally results in higher operating expenses for utilities and, therefore, higher revenue requirements. SFAS No. 71 allowed flow-through accounting to be used for financial reporting if certain criteria were met.

Utilities that have adopted SFAS No. 96 have to change the way deferred taxes are calculated and have to use the liability method to record deferred taxes on temporary differences, whether they are normalized or flowed through for regulatory purposes. In addition, the definition of temporary differences encompasses the equity component of AFDC, which utilities historically recorded on a net-of-tax basis.

Many regulators may continue to require flow-through accounting for income taxes for rate-making purposes. If flow-through accounting is prescribed by the regulator and deferred taxes not currently provided under that method meet the recovery criteria set forth in SFAS No. 71, the differences between the flow-through method and the liability method would be recorded as regulatory assets or liabilities on the balance sheet. In determining the amount of deferred taxes to be established, SFAS No. 96 focuses on the probable future revenue to be recovered through rates. SFAS No. 96 recognizes that the future revenues will include recovery of the tax expense generated on the revenues as well as the deferred tax liability. The tax-on-tax item is recorded as a regulatory asset on the balance sheet, with the offset to the deferred tax liability.

Excess deferred taxes created by a reduction in the enacted tax rate are removed from the deferred income tax liability; however, these changes are not generally recognized in the income statement. The average rate assumption method provision contained in the 1986 Tax Reform Act prohibits excess deferred taxes related to "protected" depreciation differences from being used to reduce customer rates more rapidly than over the life of the asset giving rise to the difference. In addition, the utility is likely to be held accountable for other deferred taxes collected from customers. Consequently, the excess deferred taxes generally become liabilities to customers.

An increase in the enacted tax rate would probably not result in an immediate provision for income taxes. An increase in the deferred tax liabilities would cause a need for higher rates in the future in order to satisfy the liability. If it is probable that the regulator would grant such higher rates, the charge resulting from the increase in deferred tax liabilities would be carried as a regulatory asset in the utility's balance sheet.

Financial Statement Presentation

The format of the financial statements of a public utility is often different from that of other enterprises. The financial statements reflect the capital-intensive nature of the utility's operations and are presented from the rate regulator's viewpoint. The primary sources and the primary uses of capital are presented first on the balance sheet; thus utility plant is the first asset classification and capitalization is the first grouping shown in the liabilities and equity section. Many utilities traditionally group long-term debt, except for the current portion, with preferred stock and common equity as total capitalization.

The focal point of the income statement is operating income. In theory, operating income is the return on the investment or rate base. Revenue and expense items that do not relate to utility operations are reported below the line, or after operating income. Income taxes are considered operating expenses and are reported above the line. Interest and the related AFDC are presented below the line.

RISK ASSESSMENT AND AUDIT STRATEGY

Inherent Risk

In formulating the audit strategy for a rate-regulated enterprise, the auditor should consider inherent risk, especially risk factors relating to the regulatory structure of the industry. The recovery of regulatory assets, such as deferred energy costs, abandoned plant assets, and phase-in assets, depends on the rate-making process. The auditor should assess the risk that those costs will not be recovered and should determine that they have been accounted for properly. The disposition of revenue subject to refund also depends on the rate-making process. The auditor should evaluate the adequacy of the reserve pending resolution of a rate case.

The construction of new generating facilities is an increasing risk in the current regulatory environment, where prudence reviews result in disallowances and phase-in plans result in deferred costs. The alternative to construction also has risks. Cogeneration and contracts to purchase power eliminate the utility's control without a corresponding decrease in responsibility to provide service. In addition, cogeneration and other factors can result in over- or undercapacity.

As local telephone rates continue to increase, regulators are reviewing rates of return and cost allocations between inter- and intrastate operations. New FCC and state regulatory commission rules continue to be promulgated on cost allocations between regulated and unregulated operations. Improper allocating of these costs can lead to improper collection of revenues.

Competition is becoming a significant factor in the gas and electric industry. Electric utilities compete with neighboring utilities as well as cogenerators. Gas utilities compete with alternative fuel sources, because many large commercial and industrial gas customers have the ability to switch from gas to fuel oil and do so when the price of fuel oil drops below the price of gas. The evolution of open access transportation poses risks for all companies in the natural gas industry. Telephone utilities face increasing competition stemming from the inter-LATA market and bypass of local facilities. Competition will continue to grow as the industry faces the opportunities of deregulation.

The economic environment is also changing. During the 1980s, a major investor-owned utility declared bankruptcy. At the same time, public utility companies past the construction stage were identified as potential hostile takeover candidates.

Control Risk

Utilities are under constant scrutiny by regulators, which contributes to the development of an effective control environment. Both management and regulators require extensive, accurate, and timely financial and operating information for use in the rate-making process, in accessing the capital markets, and in complying with SEC reporting requirements.

Typically, accounting information is generated by large, highly automated, and complex systems. Much of the accounting data is system derived. For example, in the telephone industry, customer calls are recorded via magnetic tape. The information on the magnetic tape is rated, billed, and controlled by the system. Electric and gas utilities follow a similar process, using magnetic tapes in industrial meters and using electronic meter-reading devices that enable company personnel to input usage directly on a tape that can be read by the system. Other amounts are also calculated by the system, such as deferred energy costs and nuclear fuel amortization. Given the amount of information that is derived from the accounting system, utilities generally have effective systems that incorporate many control procedures. The control structure is strengthened by the general characteristic of utilities to employ a sufficient number of operating and accounting personnel to afford adequate segregation of duties.

For all of those reasons, it is generally efficient to perform tests of controls in the audit of a rate-regulated enterprise. This strategy is generally used to accomplish audit objectives for accounts that are part of the revenue and buying cycles. The control objectives in these cycles that are specific to utility companies are highlighted below.

TYPICAL TRANSACTIONS, CONTROL STRUCTURE POLICIES AND PROCEDURES, AND TESTS OF CONTROLS

The Revenue Cycle

In common with other service businesses, a public utility's revenue cycle is concerned with processing transactions that generate service revenues. The related accounts that are unique to or particularly significant in the utility industry are unbilled revenues, customer deposits, and deferred energy costs.

Tests of controls are usually directed at policies and procedures intended to ensure that

All service installations are authorized.

All meter or telephone installations or terminations are recorded at the time of installation or discontinuance.

Billing records are set up on a timely basis for all completed service and meter installations.

All usage is measured by meter or other means and recorded on a regular and timely basis.

All usage is billed.

Bills are accurately calculated using the rates approved by the applicable regulatory commission for the particular customer class.

Customer deposits are safeguarded and recorded.

Cash receipts are safeguarded and recorded in the proper accounts.

Write-offs of customer accounts receivable are authorized and recorded.

The tests of controls would include an appropriate combination of inquiring about the client's control procedures, observing that they have been placed in operation, examining evidence that they are designed and operating effectively, and in some instances reperforming control procedures.

The Buying Cycle

The buying cycle encompasses several classes of transactions that may differ from those found in other commercial enterprises.

- Purchases or construction of utility plant.
- Fuel purchases.
- Purchases or sales of power.
- Incurring and accounting for costs through a work-order system.

Purchases or Construction of Utility Plant. Accounting for transactions related to additions to and sales of utility plant differs from the accounting for similar transactions in nonregulated entities because of several specialized industry practices (described earlier) involving a utility's plant accounts. Tests of controls are ordinarily directed to policies and procedures to ensure that

Additions to and disposals of property, plant, and equipment (including CWIP) are authorized.

AFDC is calculated in accordance with defined policies and at rates approved by the regulators.

Overhead items are accumulated and distributed accurately in accordance with accounting policies governing the capitalization of overhead.

Completed construction is transferred to plant-in-service on a timely basis so that depreciation accruals start and AFDC accruals cease at the appropriate time.

Depreciation rates and policies conform to those prescribed by regulatory authorities.

The cost and accumulated depreciation of property, plant, and equipment are accurately recorded.

Plant retirements are reported on a timely basis, and the original cost of retired property (together with the costs of removal less salvage value) is eliminated appropriately against accumulated depreciation.

Idle or abandoned assets are excluded from plant-in-service, as applicable.

Fuel Purchases. Coal, oil, and gas are commonly referred to as fossil fuels; consumption of these fuels is one of the principal operating costs of an electric utility. The cost of purchased gas is similarly significant for a gas distribution utility. In addition, the use of deferred energy accounting, described earlier, may result in significant deferred energy costs. Accounting for the purchase and consumption of fossil fuel and purchased gas must be controlled effectively; the procedures are similar to those for purchasing and using inventories in general.

If a utility owns a nuclear generating station, the auditor should assess the control procedures for purchases of nuclear fuel and the amortization of its cost and other related expenditures (e.g., spent fuel storage and reprocessing costs). The amortization is calculated by a unit-of-production method based on the estimated total usable heat content of the nuclear fuel and the heat content expended in a given period. As mentioned earlier, the amortization amount may be generated by the accounting system. Because of the lead time involved in procuring and processing nuclear fuel, industry practice is to capitalize an AFDC on nuclear fuel while it is being processed from uranium ore to fabricated fuel assemblies available for service. Control procedures for buying, storing, using, and disposing of nuclear fuel are similar to those for plant assets generally.

Purchases or Sales of Power.   Electric utilities frequently buy and sell temporarily surplus energy or plant capacity. Most electric utilities enter into these agreements through interchanges (i.e., arrangements with neighboring utilities to exchange power to promote overall efficiency and reliability) that operate independently of the utilities and coordinate the production of electric power of member companies to achieve maximum economy. Gas utilities occasionally enter into contractual agreements with neighboring utilities for the purchase or sale of surplus gas. Normally, both purchase and sale transactions with interchanges are subject to similar procedures.

The auditor's tests of controls generally focus on policies and procedures to ensure that

Contracts are authorized.

The quantities of power or gas purchased or interchanged are monitored and measured.

All purchase and sale transactions are recorded accurately.

Required disclosures of long-term purchase commitments have been made.

Incurring and Accounting for Costs Through a Work-Order System.   The work-order system, sometimes referred to in the telephone industry as a clearing account system, is an integral part of the accounting system of most public utilities. In a work-order system, costs of all types enter the system, are summarized, and are allocated to general ledger accounts according to a predetermined arrangement. The arrangement may be based on a study of the activities of a particular group of employees to determine which functional activities of the utility are benefited, or it may be the result of a management decision made at the time a special project is authorized. The allocations determine whether various charges are classified as capital items or expense items. The work-order system is of particular concern to the auditor since a substantial amount of costs flow through it before ultimately being charged to a general ledger account. In some companies, all labor costs are initially charged to a work order (departmental work order) and subsequently allocated to the appropriate general ledger (capital or expense) accounts. Many of the costs that enter the work-order system originate in other subsystems or feeder systems, such as materials and supplies, payroll, and miscellaneous purchase transactions.

Tests of controls over the work-order system are usually directed at policies and procedures to ensure that

Work orders are initiated on the basis of proper authorization.

All charges to work orders are reviewed for accuracy and approval.

Adequate records are maintained of all work-order charges.

The allocation of departmental work-order costs to the general ledger accounts is reasonable and has been documented appropriately.

As noted in discussing the revenue cycle, the tests of controls would involve inquiry, observation, examination of evidence, and, if appropriate, reperformance.

SUBSTANTIVE TESTS

Certain areas can be audited more effectively by means of substantive testing. A number of those areas do not have any unique features that differentiate them from comparable accounts of entities in other industries. Thus, accounts receivable other than from customers of the utility's services; prepaid insurance, taxes, and interest; accounts payable and accrued liabilities; long-term debt; and the capital stock accounts are tested in the same way as in other industries and are not discussed here. Other accounts, however, are unique to utilities, and the substantive procedures typically performed on them are described in this section.

Allowance for Funds Used During Construction

Because of the capital-intensive nature of rate-regulated utilities, the AFDC is an important audit area. The auditor should understand how CWIP is treated for rate-making purposes. If the accrual of an AFDC is appropriate based on the rate making, the auditor should ascertain that the AFDC rate has been computed in a manner consistent with the rate regulator's prescribed method. Further, the auditor should determine that the AFDC accrual has been applied only to appropriate CWIP and that it has been calculated properly.

Regulatory Assets

Regulatory assets are capitalized costs incurred by the utility that are probable of future recovery as a result of rate actions of a regulator. Such costs would be recorded as expenses by nonregulated enterprises. Regulatory assets typically include such items as deferred energy costs, losses on reacquired debt, deferred operating and maintenance costs under a phase-in plan, and abandoned utility plant.

Because regulatory assets are recorded only to the extent that it is probable that future revenues will be provided to recover them, the auditor must have a thorough understanding of the regulatory environment. If the regulator has already acted on the recoverability of the deferred cost, the auditor should review the rate order to ascertain that the asset exists. If the regulator has not yet acted on recovery of the deferred cost, significant judgment must be exercised to conclude that it is probable of recovery and therefore an asset. Although probable does not mean that recovery is certain, it implies a very high expectation that the regulator will grant future recovery. In evaluating management's assertions concerning the probability of future recovery in the absence of regulatory action, the auditor should consider the past experience of the utility in the regulatory jurisdiction, the experience of other utilities in the regulatory jurisdiction, the views of the utility's rate counsel, and other relevant evidence.

Unbilled Revenues

If the auditor has performed tests of controls in the revenue cycle and has been able to assess control risk as low, substantive tests may be limited to a review of the reasonableness of the estimates used in the accrual and analytical procedures applied to the unbilled revenues. Analytical procedures may consist of comparing the unbilled revenues with the prior year and with billed services, taking into account changes in customer usage and rates.

Deferred Energy Costs

Deferred energy costs are calculated monthly, based on data generated from both the revenue and buying cycles. In addition to assessing their recoverability (discussed earlier), the auditor should test the client's procedures for making the calculation or review the calculation itself.

Nuclear Fuel

Since nuclear fuel purchases are made somewhat infrequently, it may be more efficient to substantiate the nuclear fuel account balance and related amortization than to test control procedures.

Analytical Procedures

The analytical procedures most useful to an auditor of a public utility involve comparing financial information with information for prior years and considering relationships among current-year accounts. Examples of analytical procedures in an electric and gas utility audit are

> Comparing base revenue per kilowatt-hour by class of customer with the prior-year amounts and considering the reasonableness of any changes against rate orders.

Comparing monthly sales volumes with corresponding months of prior years and reviewing any changes in light of changes in rates, temperature, and similar factors.

Relating energy adjustment clause revenues to energy costs in the current period.

Comparing fuel expense per kilowatt-hour by type of generation with prior-year amounts. The percentage change may be related, for example, to the percentage change in oil cost per barrel. Changes in the mix of fuel use and in the cost of purchased energy may be reviewed for reasonableness. The total sources of energy (internal generation plus purchases) may be compared with uses of energy (sales, internal use, and losses).

Relating AFDC as a percentage of the average CWIP balance to the rates used by the company to accrue the AFDC for the year.

In a telephone utility audit, analytical procedures such as the following may be performed:

Comparing access charges with the related minutes of use.

Comparing revenues with the number of messages.

Comparing local service revenues with the number of access lines.

Relating depreciation expense as a percentage of plant to authorized rates.

Comparing maintenance expense with total telephone plant or with number of access lines.

38

Auditing Real Estate Companies

OVERVIEW OF THE INDUSTRY

The boundaries of the real estate industry are difficult to define because many entities that engage in real estate transactions also derive substantial revenues from other sources. For the purposes of this chapter, a real estate company is one that derives its principal revenues from activities involving the control, ownership, or sale of land and buildings. This definition encompasses companies that engage in

Owning undeveloped land for wholesale or retail sale.

Land development.

Improving and selling real property as a primary product (e.g., a home builder).

Acquiring and improving property to be held as an investment for the production of current income and for future appreciation.

Many companies are involved in more than one of those activities and, in addition, derive revenues from a variety of ancillary services associated with real estate, such as financing, property management, insurance, subcontracting, and brokerage. In addition, a number of other types of businesses, such as brokerage, leasing, management, and financing, are closely associated with real estate ownership and operations.

Organizational Forms

Companies in the real estate industry are organized under various legal forms, including sole proprietorships, general partnerships, limited partnerships, corporations, joint ventures, and trusts. The form of organization is governed largely by the objectives of the business. For example, a contractor or builder normally selects the corporate form of organization to obtain the benefits of limited liability because of the business risks associated with this type of operation. Owners of an individual project may organize as a limited partnership to obtain the benefits of both limited liability for the passive investors and the pass-through of tax losses that may be deductible in certain situations.

Real estate is particularly sensitive to changes in economic conditions, and real estate companies usually avoid assembling large central staffs and making heavy capital investments, so that overhead can be reduced to a minimum during difficult economic times.

Limited Partnerships

The limited partnership form of organization is especially well suited to real estate ventures. It has many of the favorable tax attributes of a general partnership, but provides limited liability for the limited partners. These limited partners are generally responsible only for the capital that they have committed to the partnership, although in some instances they may be required to return cash previously withdrawn from the partnership. The limited partnership form enables the general partners, who are usually developers or investors, to obtain equity from outside sources for real estate projects and may permit limited partners to sell their interests (e.g., the trading units in a master limited partnership), thus providing the limited partners with liquidity.

In the past, investors in a limited partnership would receive a share of the partnership losses, which they would use to offset taxable income from other sources. Income from the sale of real estate would have resulted in a capital gain, which received preferential tax treatment. Under the Tax Reform Act of 1986 (TRA 86), losses from an investment in a limited partnership are classified as passive losses that can only offset other passive income and may subject the investor to the alternative minimum tax. TRA 86 also eliminated the preferential tax treatment of capital gains.

Partnership Agreements

The partnership agreement is a significant document that states the scope of activities in which the partnership may operate, sets forth the term of existence on the partnership and defines the conditions under which the partnership may be terminated or dissolved before the stated termination date, and details the rights and obligations of the respective partners. The agreement affects not only the accounting for the partnership, but also the profit recognized by the developer/general partner. The following provisions of a typical partnership agreement are of particular interest to the auditor:

- *Capital Contributions and Borrowings.* The agreement sets forth the total amount of the partner's investment and the payment schedule on which capital contributions are to be made. The amount and timing of contributions materially affect both the investor's return on the investment and the cost of the project. Normally, an investor is required to sign a promissory note for the capital contributions that are payable after the date of admission. Terms of default and remedies for the general partners are defined, and normally the use of all capital contributions is specified in the partnership agreement. Most agreements also grant the partnership the right to borrow moneys from other sources and establish certain requirements for and limitations on such borrowings.
- *Capital Accounts, Profits and Losses, Cash Flow, and Distributions.* The agreement states the accounting method (cash or accrual) and the fiscal year of the partnership (which is normally a calendar year). Cash flow and profits and losses are normally defined, and the method of allocation among partners is stated. In addition, the allocation of gain or loss and of the proceeds on a sale of the project and the distribution of proceeds from a refinancing are specified.
- *Rights and Obligations of Partners.* The agreement defines the rights and liabilities of the limited partners. Limited partners usually have the right to call meetings, vote for amendments to the limited partnership agreement, and vote for removal or substitution of the general partners; participation in management by the limited partners is prohibited. The agreement also sets

forth the general partners' responsibilities for managing the partnership. These generally include the right to execute the mortgage note, construction contract, management agreement, and other documents required in connection with the construction and operation of the project, and the power to appoint the managing general partner. The agreement generally specifies whether an audit or review of financial statements will be provided within a specified time frame. The most relevant provisions from the auditor's viewpoint relate to the general partners' right to pay or receive specified fees as compensation for organizing and developing the partnership and for managing the construction phase of the project. Also significant are the general partners' obligations to initiate and support rental operations. Usually the general partners and managing general partner do not receive any compensation for managing the affairs of the partnership in their capacity as general partners. They may, however, receive fees through related parties, such as management fees to affiliated management companies, for providing services other than those that are part of their role as general partners.

The specific terms of partnership agreements vary widely. The auditor should be familiar with the partnership agreement so as to determine whether the accounting principles applied by the partnership are in conformity with the agreement, and whether the general and limited partners have complied with the restrictive provisions of the agreement. The terms of the partnership agreement can significantly affect the amount and timing of the profit a developer/general partner may recognize on a transaction with the partnership.

Real Estate Investment Trusts

Real Estate Investment Trusts (REITs) allow investors to purchase units in a REIT at a stated price per unit. The units may be listed on an exchange and actively traded, thus providing investors a means of liquidity. An investor generally receives a payout each year, since the REIT rule requires that 95 percent of earnings be distributed. Income from a REIT is considered portfolio income and thus cannot be used to offset passive losses.

The Regulatory Framework

Real estate transactions have become increasingly subject to regulations. An auditor must be knowledgeable about those regulations and ensure that they are properly considered in planning the audit and for purposes of financial statement disclosures. Statement of Financial Accounting Standards (SFAS) No. 5, *Accounting for Contingencies* (Accounting Standards Section C59), provides guidance for determining whether accrual or disclosure is required with respect to pending or threatened litigation and possible assessments for noncompliance with federal, state, and local regulations. (Accounting for contingencies is discussed in Chapter 21.)

Investments in real estate, generally in the form of an interest in a real estate limited partnership, may be subject to the same Securities and Exchange

Commission registration and reporting requirements as are other investments. A seller of a public or private investment should prepare a complete disclosure document (prospectus or offering memorandum) to ensure against future claims by buyers that disclosures were inadequate or misleading. If such disclosures are not presented, the auditor must be alert to possible claims by buyers for recision of a transaction and refund of the purchase price.

The Department of Housing and Urban Development (HUD), through the Federal Housing Administration (FHA), regulates the development and operation of all projects for which it insures the mortgages or provides rent subsidies. In addition, most agreements and documents governing the development, construction, and financing of such projects are required to be approved by HUD and, in most instances, must be filed on specified forms. State housing agencies impose similar restrictions and requirements.

The Interstate Land Sales Full Disclosure Act requires developers to make full disclosure in connection with the sale or lease of certain undeveloped subdivided land. The Act makes it unlawful for a developer to sell or lease, by use of the mail or any other means of interstate commerce, any land offered as part of a common promotional plan unless the land is registered with the Office of Interstate Land Sales Registration (OILSR); a printed property report must be furnished to prospective purchasers or lessees. Similarly, the Federal Trade Commission has authority to act on unfair or deceptive trade practices with respect to real estate sales, particularly as related to marketing and selling activities of real estate companies.

Regulation Z of the Consumer Credit Protection Act (the truth-in-lending law) has a significant effect on real estate financing transactions, since many real estate purchases are made on credit. Regulation Z outlines requirements for both creditors and borrowers for the full disclosure of credit costs and is applicable to all real estate transactions, regardless of amount, in which individual borrowers are involved in nonbusiness transactions.

ACCOUNTING PRINCIPLES

Equity Investments

Joint ventures are common in the real estate industry; they may be incorporated or operated as general or limited partnerships. Most joint ventures are for single projects and are of limited life. With the exception of a few partnership accounting issues, there are no accounting practices that are unique to joint ventures, and the only codified generally accepted accounting principles (GAAP) covering accounting by joint ventures are in two nonauthoritative sources—a 1979 AICPA issues paper and Statement of Position (SOP) 78-9, *Accounting for Investments in Real Estate Ventures*.

Accounting for an investment in a real estate venture is governed by APB Opinion No. 18, *The Equity Method of Accounting for Investments in Common Stock* (Accounting Standards Section I82), SOP 78-9, SFAS No. 94, *Consolidation of All Majority-Owned Subsidiaries* (Accounting Standards Section C51), and SEC Regulation S-X. At the time of this writing, the FASB is studying the requirements for and application of consolidation and equity accounting. SFAS No. 94 requires consolidation of all majority-owned subsidiaries unless control is temporary or does not rest with the majority owner. Determining an investor's ability to exert control over an investment in a joint venture organized as a partnership is sometimes difficult. A partnership that is controlled by an investor, that is, one in which the investor has a majority voting interest, should be considered a subsidiary of the investor for reporting purposes; thus, it should be consolidated and intercompany profits and losses not yet realized in transactions with third parties should be eliminated. Since partnerships do not have voting stock, the condition that usually indicates control is ownership of a majority (over 50 percent) of the interest in profits and losses. Control may also exist with a lesser percentage of ownership, as specified by terms included in contracts, leases, partnership agreements, or court decrees that give the investor a majority voting interest. Alternatively, if major decisions—such as the right to replace general partners, approve the sale or refinancing of the principal assets, or approve the acquisition of principal assets—require approval by the limited partners, ownership of a majority of the interest in profits and losses may not in itself constitute control. A noncontrolling investor in a general partnership generally should account for the investment by the equity method, although SOP 78-9 notes that there are circumstances in which the cost method may be appropriate.

· Real property owned by undivided interests (e.g., as tenants in common) is subject to joint control if decisions concerning financing, development, sale, or operation require the approval of two or more of the owners. Most real estate ventures in the form of undivided interests are subject to some level of joint control, and they should be presented in the same manner as investments in noncontrolled partnerships. Occasionally, in a joint venture in which the participants have undivided interests, approval of two or more of the owners is not required for major decisions, each investor is entitled only to its pro rata share of income and expenses, and the investors are severally liable only for the indebtedness each incurs in connection with its interest in the property. In those circumstances, the investment may be presented by recording each investor's pro rata share of assets, liabilities, revenues, and expenses of the venture.

In practice, pro rata consolidation is also used other than in the limited circumstances described above. Under SOP 78-9, an entity is not required to change from pro rata consolidation if it followed that practice prior to the issuance of the SOP.

Investors may contribute, in exchange for an ownership interest in an entity, real estate that has a fair value in excess of its book value. SOP 78-9 indicates that generally an investor should not recognize any profit on the contribution and that the investor and investee should record the transaction at the historical cost of the real estate. If one investor contributes real estate and another investor contributes cash in proportion to their respective ownership interests, however, certain of those transactions may in essence be sales. The SEC has expressed (in Staff Accounting Bulletin No. 48) the position that transfers by promoters and shareholders of nonmonetary assets to a company in exchange for its stock usually should be recorded at the transferor's historical cost basis.

Venture agreements may designate different percentage allocations among the investors for profits and losses, cash distributions from operations, and distributions of cash proceeds from liquidation. To ascertain the economic substance of the investor's share of the venture net income or loss, such agreements should be analyzed to determine how an increase or a decrease in net assets of the venture will affect cash payments to the investor over the life of the venture and on its liquidation. Specified profit and loss allocation ratios alone should not be used to determine an investor's equity in venture earnings if the allocation of cash distributions and liquidating distributions is determined on a different basis. Often the investor's equity is determined by assuming the liquidation of all assets and liabilities at their book values and the distribution of the proceeds to the venture participants; the change in each participant's equity position during the year should equal its share of venture profit or loss on a GAAP basis.

Real Estate Properties and Deferred Costs

A variety of costs are incurred in the acquisition, development, leasing, sale, or operation of a real estate development project. SFAS No. 67, *Accounting for Costs and Initial Rental Operations of Real Estate Projects* (Accounting Standards Section Re2), provides guidance on when costs should be capitalized, deferred, or expensed.

Property taxes and insurance costs incurred on real estate projects should be capitalized only during the period in which activities necessary to get the property ready for its intended use are in progress. Such costs incurred after the property is substantially complete and held available for occupancy should be charged to expense as incurred. Paragraph 22 of SFAS No. 67 states that "a real estate project shall be considered substantially completed and held available for occupancy upon completion of tenant improvements by the developer, but not later than one year from cessation of major construction activity."

SFAS No. 34 (Accounting Standards Section I67) generally requires capitalization of interest during construction and development. Assets qualifying for interest capitalization include real estate developments intended for sale or lease that are constructed as discrete projects. Land that is not undergoing activities necessary to prepare it for its intended use does not qualify for capitalization. When development activities are undertaken, however, expenditures to acquire land qualify for interest capitalization while the development activities are in process. If the resulting asset is a structure, the interest capitalized on land expenditures becomes part of the cost of the structure; if the resulting asset is developed land, the capitalized interest is part of the cost of the land. SFAS No. 34 provides guidance on determining the appropriate amount of interest to be capitalized. (See also the discussion in Chapter 28.)

After a determination is made to capitalize a cost, it is allocated to the specific parcels or components of a project that are benefited. Guidance for situations where specific identification is not practicable is provided by SFAS No. 67.

Incremental revenue from incidental operations in excess of related incremental costs should be accounted for as a reduction of capitalized project costs.

Incremental costs in excess of incremental revenue should be charged to expense as incurred, because the incidental operations did not reduce the costs of developing the property for its intended use.

Estimates and cost allocations should be reviewed at the end of each financial reporting period until a project is substantially completed and available for sale. Costs should be revised and reallocated as necessary on the basis of current estimates. Revisions of estimates and cost allocations on projects for which sales revenue has not been recognized are not accounting changes as defined by APB Opinion No. 20, *Accounting Changes* (Accounting Standards Section A06), and their effects should therefore be accounted for as additional capitalized costs.

Real estate held for investment should be carried at cost, unless a decline in value is other than temporary. Real estate held for sale, including repossessed real estate obtained through foreclosures, should be carried at the lower of cost or estimated net realizable value. Estimated net realizable value is the estimated selling price of the property in the open market, allowing a reasonable period of time to find a purchaser, reduced by (a) estimated costs to complete or improve such property to the condition contemplated in determining the estimated selling price, (b) estimated direct selling expenses, and (c) estimated direct costs to hold the property to the point of sale. Since real estate held for sale is, in effect, inventory, a recovery of value after such property has been written down should not be recognized. Costs to complete or improve and direct holding costs should be capitalized when incurred, as long as the carrying amount does not exceed estimated net realizable value. Direct holding costs include property taxes, management fees, insurance, maintenance, security, and other operating costs.

Capitalized costs of abandoned real estate should be written off as current expenses or, if appropriate, should be charged to allowances established for that purpose. They should not be allocated to other components of a project or to other projects. Donations of land to municipalities or other governmental agencies for uses that will benefit the project are not abandonments. The costs of the donated land should be allocated as a common cost of the project.

Changes in the use of real estate may arise after significant development and construction costs have been incurred. In such circumstances, paragraphs 15 and 16 of SFAS No. 67 note that development and construction costs incurred before the change should be written off, except as follows:

- If the change is made pursuant to a formal plan for a project that is expected to produce a higher economic yield, the write-off may be limited to the amount by which the capitalized costs incurred and to be incurred exceed the estimated value of the revised project at the date of substantial physical completion.

- In the absence of a formal plan for a project that is expected to produce a higher economic yield, the write-off may be limited to the amount by which total capitalized costs exceed the estimated net realizable value of the property, determined on the assumption that it will be sold in its present state.

Leasing, Sale, and Operational Period

In addition to capitalized costs, project owners generally incur certain other preoccupancy costs not specifically identifiable with construction activity but necessary to make a project operational or to stimulate sales or rentals. Depending on the type of business in which a real estate company is engaged, such deferrable costs might include financing, tenant leasing, and selling costs. In general, such costs may be deferred and amortized in future periods if they are associated with future revenues and if their recovery is reasonably assured.

Financing or loan costs include loan fees, finders' fees, legal fees, commissions, document printing costs, and other costs and expenses directly related to financing. The accounting for financing costs applicable to construction loans is the same as that for construction period interest. Costs applicable to permanent financing should be classified as deferred financing costs and amortized over the terms of the related mortgages, preferably using the interest method.

SFAS No. 67 recommends criteria for deferring and expensing selling costs. Costs incurred to sell real estate projects (project costs) should be classified with and accounted for in the same manner as construction costs if both of the following tests are met:

- The costs are reasonably expected to be recovered from sales of the project or from incidental operations.
- The costs are incurred for tangible assets that are used directly throughout the selling period to aid in the sale of the project or for services that have been performed to obtain regulatory approval for sales.

Examples of selling costs that ordinarily meet these criteria are expenditures for model units and related furnishings, sales facilities, legal and other fees incurred to obtain regulatory approval for sales, and semipermanent signs.

Other costs incurred to sell real estate projects should be classified and accounted for as prepaid expenses if they do not meet the criteria for project costs and they are incurred prior to receipt or use of the related goods or services and are expected to benefit future periods. Expenditures for future advertising, brochures, and similar selling tools, and draws against future commissions are examples of selling costs that ordinarily meet those criteria. Certain prepaid expenses (e.g., sales commissions under the installment method) can be identified with specific future revenue and therefore should be charged to operations in the period in which the related sales revenue is recognized. Costs that do not meet the criteria for capitalization or deferral should be expensed as incurred.

SFAS No. 13, paragraph 19 (Accounting Standards Section L10.115), governs accounting by lessors for "initial direct costs" of operating leases. Initial direct costs, as defined in SFAS No. 13 and further expanded on in SFAS No. 17 (Accounting Standards Section L10), are to be deferred and allocated over the lease term in proportion to the recognition of rental income. Examples of initial direct costs given in SFAS No. 17 are commissions, legal fees, costs of credit investigations, costs of preparing and processing documents for executed leases, and certain compensation. Examples of other costs that might meet the criteria for initial direct costs are expenditures incurred for tenants' improvements or alterations necessary to obtain a lease and other monetary concessions made that may be directly associated with acquiring a tenant. Costs related to unsuccessful leasing activities should be expensed as incurred. SFAS No. 67 allows the deferral of certain leasing costs, such as model units and their furnishings, that are related to and recoverable from future rental operations. Such costs should be amortized over the lease term if they can be identified with a specific lease; otherwise, they should be amortized over the expected period of benefit.

Profit Recognition on Sales of Real Estate

Accounting principles for recognizing real estate sales and profits are found in SFAS No. 66, *Accounting for Sales of Real Estate* (Accounting Standards Section Re1). It emphasizes that, after determining the economic substance of a transaction, the matters with the greatest impact on the timing of profit recognition are

1. The extent of the buyer's investment in the property acquired and the certainty of collection of the seller's receivables.
2. The continuing involvement of the seller with the property sold.

SFAS No. 66 prescribes that revenue and profit be recognized at the time real estate is sold, provided that the amount of the revenue is measurable (which is a collectibility issue) and the earning process is complete or virtually complete (i.e., the seller has no obligations to perform activities subsequent to the sale in order to earn the revenue). In addition, the statement specifies that the economic substance, as opposed to the legal form, of the transaction determines the timing, amount, and designation of revenue. Because many real estate transactions are designed to maximize income tax benefits, and in some instances profits, the economic substance of a real estate transaction may differ in many aspects from its legal form.

Real estate sales differ from revenue transactions in many other industries in that consideration for a significant portion of the sales value is often a long-term, nonrecourse note receivable that is usually collateralized only by the property sold. Since the uncertainty about the collectibility of a receivable arising from the sale of real estate is usually greater than in other business transactions, SFAS No. 66 requires that, for profit to be recognized on the accrual basis, both a buyer's initial investment and subsequent payments on the note receivable must be adequate to demonstrate a commitment to pay for the property. If a buyer's initial down payment or continuing payments do not meet the requirements of accrual-basis profit recognition, the deposit, installment, reduced-profit, or cost recovery method should be used. Those methods are discussed in SFAS No. 66.

The requirements in SFAS No. 66 relating to the down payment and continuing investment are designed to satisfy the revenue measurement criterion for the recognition of revenue and profit. The second set of requirements relates to the criterion that the earning process be complete or virtually complete. After the date of sale, the seller may be obligated to arrange financing, develop or construct facilities on the property sold, manage the property, guarantee a return on investment, or provide leasing or other forms of support in operating the property. In general, SFAS No. 66 requires that an evaluation of the effect of the seller's continued involvement be made. In some instances, such involvement may have little effect on the amount or timing of profit recognition; in other instances, recognition of all or part of the profit from the sale should be deferred until the seller's performance of required continuing obligations. A sales agreement or contract should not be recorded as an accrual-basis sale if the seller's continued involvement results in the retention of the same kinds of risks as the retention of ownership would entail. For example, if a seller is obligated to operate the property subsequent to its sale and may suffer operating losses, a sale has not occurred. If the amount of the seller's loss resulting from continued involvement is limited by the terms of the sales agreement or by business considerations, profit recognized at the time of sale must be reduced by the maximum amount of exposure to loss. Profit may be recognized when realized if the agreement allows the seller to participate solely in future profit from the operation or resale of property with no risk of loss. SFAS No. 98, *Accounting for Leases* (Accounting Standards Section L10), however, provides that a sale-leaseback transaction that includes any continuing involvement other than a normal leaseback during which the seller-lessee intends to actively use the property should be accounted for by the deposit method or as a financing.

If, under the terms of a real estate sales agreement, the seller is required to obtain or provide permanent financing on the property for the buyer, no sale should be recognized until such financing has been obtained. A sales agreement may require the seller to provide management or other services relating to the property after the sale, without compensation or with compensation in an amount less than prevailing rates. In these circumstances, the seller's profit on the sale should be reduced by the anticipated costs to be incurred for those services and by a reasonable profit, which will be brought back into income as the services are performed.

Agreements for the sale of undeveloped or partially developed land often include a requirement that the seller develop the property, provide off-site improvements, or construct facilities on the land. The accounting for the seller's performance of development and construction should be the same as the accounting for long-term construction contracts, namely, the percentage-of-completion basis should be used, unless the seller cannot reasonably estimate total cost and profit. In that case, the completed-contract method would be used. The same rate of profit should be used on the recognition of the land sale and the development and construction activity.

Profit may also be recognized by real estate lessors if a lease transaction meets the criteria in SFAS No. 13 for classification as a sales-type lease and the criteria in SFAS No. 66 and SFAS No. 98 for full and immediate profit recognition. Since a lease usually involves no down payment and SFAS No. 66 requires a minimum down payment, that requirement effectively prohibits sales-type leases of real estate.

Extinguishment of Debt

SFAS No. 76, *Extinguishment of Debt* (Accounting Standards Section D14), describes the circumstances in which a company should consider its debt to be extinguished for financial reporting purposes; in describing these circumstances, the statement provides specific criteria that must be met for debt to be considered extinguished. In addition, the statement clarifies that a gain or loss should be recognized immediately when debt is considered to be extinguished.

Repayment is the most common circumstance for extinguishment of debt and includes a company's reacquisition of its debt in the open market, regardless of whether the securities are canceled or held as treasury bonds. All repayments of debt are considered extinguishments if the company is relieved of its obligations with respect to the debt.

The accounting rules for extinguishing debt by third-party assumption are particularly important to companies that sell real estate. SFAS No. 76 specifically provides that when a nonrecourse mortgage is assumed by a third party in conjunction with the sale of property, the legal release criterion has been met and the seller may consider the mortgage to be extinguished. In the event of a sale of property subject to a recourse mortgage, the transaction must be evaluated to determine whether the seller has been legally released from the primary repayment obligation. If the legal release criterion has not been met, the financial statements of the seller should continue to reflect the mortgage payable, and a "receivable" from the purchaser should be recorded for the mortgage payments to be made by the purchaser.

Operating Rental Revenues

Most reporting on operating rental properties is directed to individual projects. Although this accounting is not required, rental income should preferably be shown on a gross basis, with a deduction for vacancies to arrive at net rental income. Presenting only the net amount reduces the usefulness of the information to management, investors, and lenders. Nonoperating and service income, such as payments for services, interest income, and assessments, are classified separately. Lease terms vary depending on the type of properties being leased and special terms that are agreed on in lease negotiations. Common types of charges to tenants include base rental income, percentage rents, expense rebillings, and common area charges.

Base rental income is the basic rental charge stated in a lease and is applicable to all types of property. Sometimes it is adjusted for prior-year increases in the consumer price index. A question frequently arises regarding the accounting for rent concessions given to a new tenant at the inception of a lease. Payment of a tenant's prior lease or lease cancellation charges should be deferred and amortized on a straight-line basis over the initial term of the new lease. Generally lease income should be recognized on a straight-line basis unless there is an economic justification for using some other method. Accordingly, if the tenant is not required to pay rent during the initial months of a lease, it is appropriate to allocate the aggregate rental revenue related to the initial noncancelable lease term over that entire term.

Percentage rents are found principally in retail leases and call for additional amounts based on the lessee's sales activity. Because sales normally increase over time, the lessor is partially protected from the effects of inflation over the life of the lease. Leases usually contain definitions of the terms used (e.g., gross receipts) and state how the percentage rent is to be calculated. Terms can vary widely from lease to lease, and the auditor must understand the specific lease terms. Determining the accrual for percentage rents at the end of an accounting period can be difficult because tenants normally are not up-to-date in reporting their gross receipts and because sales reporting periods may be different from financial reporting periods. Therefore, a method of estimating the gross receipts expected by tenants for the period is needed. If the property has been in operation for a few years, historical data may be available to form a basis for an estimate. If not, it may be necessary to contact tenants for an estimate or to use industry data.

Rebilling increases in expenses to tenants is common in most types of commercial properties. Some examples of expenses rebilled to tenants are real estate taxes, utility costs, and maintenance expenses. The types of expenses that may be rebilled are specified in the lease. Generally, the amount is based on a comparison of current expenses with base-year amounts, that is, amounts incurred during the first year of the lease. Terms vary from lease to lease, based on the date the lease was negotiated and the negotiating ability of the parties involved. Rebilled expenses should preferably be reflected in the income statement as revenue rather than netted against the related expense, since the lessor is responsible for their incurrence and that presentation is likely to be more informative.

Determining revenue from rebilled expenses can be complex if one or more of the following situations exists:

- There are several leases that began at different dates and have different base years.
- Lease terms specify that only increases over a certain amount are to be rebilled after the base year.
- Different factors are used to determine each type of rebilled expense.
- Leases provide different bases for allocating costs, such as gross area, net rentable area, and gross occupied area.
- Base-year or current-year expenses are required to reflect pro forma amounts at some different (generally higher) level of occupancy.

Common area charges are made for common areas in shopping centers and, in some cases, in low-rise, multiple-use office buildings. Some examples of common areas are indoor and outdoor malls, parking areas, and lobbies. Normally, charges for areas used in common by tenants are based on an agreed-on amount per square foot as stated in the lease or on actual costs incurred. In some cases, percentage rents paid by a tenant may be reduced by the common area charges. Sometimes tenants agree to maintain the common areas adjacent to their space instead of paying these charges; many ''anchor'' tenants (tenants that rent a significant area, e.g., a major department store in a shopping mall) select this method.

RISK ASSESSMENT AND AUDIT STRATEGY

The audit strategy for a real estate company depends largely on the volume of its transactions and its internal control structure. If, for example, a company is involved in the development and sale of only one or a few projects during the period under audit, it would probably be more efficient to emphasize substantive testing, even if the control structure appears to be effective. Particularly for smaller companies, which generally have a limited number of transactions during a year, it is usually more efficient to perform substantive tests of transactions and account balances. Furthermore, many real estate companies are closely held by entrepreneurial builders who do not place a great deal of emphasis on control procedures. For such companies, a substantive testing approach may be the only feasible strategy.

Other real estate companies, particularly those that are large and publicly held, have adequate control structures and transaction volumes to warrant an audit strategy based on the performance of tests of controls to reduce the assessed level of control risk to low. For example, tests of controls would be appropriate for a multilocation home builder that sells hundreds of units a year and has an effective control structure. The auditor should also consider the composition of the various account balances. If an account balance comprises a large number of items with relatively low individual values, such as a large number of houses produced by a builder, testing controls is generally more efficient because of the impracticability of substantiating a large dollar amount of the total. The procedures for the closing and legal recording of a sale of a residence are standardized within a state, as are the documents that the auditor would examine. In addition, applying the principles in SFAS No. 66 to the sale of residences is seldom complicated unless exceptionally small down payments are received. Even in that instance, it would seem inefficient to substantiate a multitude of individual sales transactions; instead, tests of controls coupled with year-end cutoff procedures would be more practical.

Historically, HUD, through the FHA, has been closely associated with real estate projects through its mortgage insurance and rent subsidies programs. State governments, through housing finance agencies, have been increasing their involvement in the housing industry, primarily as lenders but in some instances as developers or insurers. The activities of HUD, however, are limited to insuring mortgages on residential real estate and in some cases rent subsidies. It neither plans nor builds housing and it does not loan funds directly to mortgagors. The mortgagor, general contractor, and subcontractor all agree to abide by the rules and regulations prescribed by HUD. HUD Handbook 4470.2, *Cost Certification Guide for Mortgagors and Contractors of HUD-Insured Multifamily Projects* (August 1978), and Handbook IG 4200.1A, *Audit Guide for Auditing Development Cost of HUD-Insured Multifamily Projects for Use by Independent Public Accountants* (March 1978), are the two primary sources for cost certification rules. Auditors are often requested to provide a special report to satisfy the requirements of HUD or the state. The specific reporting rules are complex and are found in the applicable federal or state publications. The auditor should be familiar with those rules and reports and should take them into consideration in planning the engagement.

SUBSTANTIVE TESTS

The transaction cycles and typical control structure policies and procedures of real estate companies do not differ significantly from those in commercial and industrial companies, described in Chapters 12, 13, and 14, and accordingly are not discussed further here. If the auditor plans to test control procedures, the tests of controls suggested in those chapters should be performed. The remainder of this chapter discusses substantive tests that are of particular importance in auditing real estate companies.

Developer's Receivables

Individual accounts and notes receivable of a developer may be material to the enterprise, and their collectibility may depend on the economic conditions of a myriad of entities or their limited partners. Collectibility may be further complicated by the developer's role as general partner of the debtor entity. Accordingly, for material receivables, the auditor should review the financial position of the debtor entity in evaluating the collectibility of amounts due from general and limited partners. If the receivables are without recourse, the auditor should evaluate the realizable value of the underlying collateral property or its ability to generate sufficient cash to realize the receivable.

The auditor must also address related party transactions and the required disclosures. Reviewing the sales contracts, partnership agreements, offering documents, and construction and management operating contracts assists the auditor in determining if the financial statement disclosures comply with SFAS No. 57, *Related Party Disclosures* (Accounting Standards Section R36), as discussed in Chapter 6. The auditor should be particularly sensitive to transactions between the enterprise and related parties and should ensure that such transactions are not prohibited by contracts or agreements.

Property Acquisition and Development Costs

The following audit objectives are of particular significance in auditing capitalized acquisition and development costs:

- Determine whether the client's cost capitalization and allocation policies and procedures conform with GAAP and are appropriate in the circumstances.
- Determine whether costs are charged to cost of sales on a systematic, rational, and timely basis.
- Ascertain that projects to which costs have been charged physically exist.
- Obtain satisfaction about the recoverability of capitalized costs.

In testing acquisition and development costs, the auditor must examine documentation that is appropriate to each particular type of cost. Figure 38.1 suggests the appropriate documents for the major types of capitalized costs.

As noted earlier in this chapter, real estate held for sale should be reported at the lower of cost or estimated net realizable value. The concept of estimated net realizable value presumes the existence of a willing seller and a willing buyer, but economic conditions may create situations in which no willing buyers exist other than at distress prices. If the auditor is satisfied that the client's valuation method, not based on distress prices, is nevertheless reasonable and that the client intends and has the financial strength to hold the property for a reasonable period of time, and if the auditor's knowledge and inquiries lead to the conclusion that the lack of buyers appears to be a temporary condition, the auditor may accept that valuation. Determining what constitutes a reasonable period of time requires the use of judgment, considering all the circumstances, for example, whether the property is currently ready for sale or whether the owner intends and is able to complete and sell the property. The estimated selling price should contemplate a sale in the reasonably near future, which may exceed one year but should not be an indefinite period. If the period exceeds two years, the auditor should consider this fact in deciding whether to modify the opinion because of uncertainties as to realizability of the carrying value.

The auditor may find it necessary to request the client to have an appraiser value a property or to review another appraiser's work. Appraisers are specialists, as defined in SAS No. 11, *Using the Work of a Specialist* (AU Section 336). The auditor should follow the guidance in that statement in determining whether to request an appraisal, in considering the client's selection of an appraiser, in using the appraiser's findings, and in evaluating the work. Reliance may be placed more heavily on an appraiser who is not related to the client. If the appraisal is made by client personnel, the auditor should consider carefully the qualifications of the individuals making the valuation judgments and their objectivity. If the auditor concludes that independent appraisals are required for specific problem properties, the client should be asked to engage outside appraisers. The auditor should review the appraisal report to determine that the computations affecting the estimates of value are arithmetically correct and that the assumptions appear reasonable and do not conflict with known facts. The AICPA audit and accounting guide, *Guide for Use of Real Estate Appraisal Information*, presents concepts and considerations regarding valuation and appraisal data. The auditor should refer to the guide when appraisal information is to be used on an engagement.

In determining net realizable value, the auditor should consider

- Current status or nature and condition of the property.
- Current and future intended uses of the property, as related to the general economic conditions and population growth in the area.
- Special qualifications in an appraisal that do not agree with existing conditions (e.g., repairs that are assumed to have been made, a five-year holding period to find a willing buyer, new landscaping, and so on).
- Overall suitability of the property for its current or intended use.

Figure 38.1   Evidential Matter for Real Estate Acquisition and Development Costs

Type of Cost	Documents to Be Examined (If Applicable)	Information Derived
Vacant land	Deed	Ownership
	Purchase contract	Price
	Title policy	Restrictions
	Mortgage	Financing terms
Developed property	Deed	Ownership
	Purchase contract	Price
	Title policy	Restrictions
	Mortgage	Financing terms
	Closing statement	Prorations of costs
	Security agreement	Security interest
	Insurance policies	Coverage and value
	Certificates of occupancy	Legal occupancy
Land improvements	Contracts	Price, performance
	Subcontracts	Price, performance
	Vendor invoices	Costs billed to date
	Insurance policies	Coverage and value
Structures and equipment	Construction loan	Construction financing
	Construction contract	Price, performance
	Subcontracts	Price, performance
	Vendor invoices	Costs billed to date
	Permanent loan (mortgage)	Financing terms
	Insurance policies	Coverage and value
Indirect project costs	Vendor invoices	Costs billed to date
	Company-prepared analyses indicating cost allocations	Reasonableness of cost allocations
Property taxes and insurance costs	Vendor invoices	Costs billed to date
	Real estate bills	Applicable amount and period
Legal fees, recording fees, survey fees, appraisal fees, and similar charges associated with real estate properties	Vendor invoices and billings	Costs associated with acquisition of properties

- Various restrictions, including zoning.
- Comparable prices of other properties in the area.
- Holding costs, including taxes, assessments, prior liens, and security services.

Real Estate Sales

Except for retail lot sales, sales transactions usually occur infrequently and involve large sums of money. Sales of land, apartment complexes, shopping centers, office buildings, and other large projects are often complex transactions, which usually require an audit approach that emphasizes substantive testing. The objective of the audit of sales transactions is to determine that the proper amount of revenue has been recognized in the appropriate period and that the proper charge to cost of sales has been made, all in accordance with the authoritative accounting pronouncements discussed earlier in this chapter. Emphasis should be placed on the method of revenue recognition, the adequacy of the down payment and continuing payments on any notes received, and the nature of any continuing responsibilities of the seller. The economic substance of a real estate sale often varies from its legal form, and close attention must be paid to the sales agreements and related documents, including, but not limited to, agreements of sale, notes receivable, escrow instructions, management agreements, lease agreements, partnership agreements, and construction contracts. All of those documents could contain provisions affecting the timing and amount of revenue recognition in sales transactions. The auditor must also be aware of the possibility of related party transactions and should apply the procedures necessary to identify related parties, as discussed in Chapter 6.

If revenue from sales of real estate has been recognized using the installment method, the enterprise should have control procedures in place to ensure that the appropriate amount of deferred (unrealized) profit is recognized as earned in the proper period. Either through testing those procedures or through substantive tests, the auditor should obtain evidence that the amount of revenue recognized in the current period from current- and prior-period sales is appropriate.

Operating Rental Revenues

Following is an efficient approach to testing base rentals:

- Obtain a rent roll for one month during the year.
- Examine selected leases to ascertain the correctness of the rental income.
- Annualize the rental income of the month tested and compare the result with the amount recorded in the general ledger.
- Investigate significant variations between recorded revenues and the computed amounts and obtain documentation to support reasons for the differences.

That approach may be applied to all types of rental operations; however, if the number of tenants is large, such as in apartment buildings, and the desired audit coverage cannot be achieved without examining a significant number of leases, additional or alternative procedures may be needed. Possible procedures include

- Testing rental revenues according to type of unit (appropriate for properties that have standard rents) by
  - • Determining total possible rental revenues to be collected, using full occupancy at current rents.

- •• Deducting amounts for vacancies, based on vacancy rates shown in rent rolls.
- •• Obtaining documentation to support the reasons for significant variations between recorded revenues and the computed amount.
- • Testing rental revenues by
  - •• Tracing rents received to cash records.
  - •• Tracing cash receipts records to bank statements and the general ledger.
- • Confirming lease terms (should be performed in conjunction with auditing rents receivable and security deposits).
- • Obtaining the rent rolls and examining apartments indicated as vacant to ascertain that they are in fact vacant.

The following procedures may be used in auditing percentage rents:

- • Obtain an analysis, by tenant, detailing the activity in percentage rentals and showing accruals at the beginning of the period, collections, income for the period, and accruals at the end of the period.
- • Select several tenants for detailed testing of percentage rentals by
  - •• Examining sales reports in support of receipts for the period.
  - •• Testing the accuracy of percentage rental computations.
  - •• Tracing percentage rental rates and minimum rents to leases on file.
  - •• Reviewing tenants' sales reports and obtaining explanations for significant fluctuations between months or periods.
- • Review the reasonableness of the estimate of year-end sales and test the computation of rents accrued; compare estimates with prior-period amounts.
- • Review procedures and results of percentage rent audits performed by client personnel.
- • Examine subsequent receipts of sales reports and percentage rents.

Income from rebilled expenses is often an increasing part of total property income; therefore, it should receive appropriate audit attention. As with percentage rents, determining the accrual for rebilled expenses as of the close of a period is complex because lease periods may be different from reporting periods. Therefore, amounts to be rebilled may be determined on the basis of estimated expenses. One possibility is to use budgeted expenses as a basis for rebilling, if they are determined to be reasonable.

Procedures to consider in auditing rebilled expenses are as follows:

- • Obtain an analysis of rebilled expenses showing beginning accruals, receipts, rebillings for the current year, and ending accruals.
- • Select several tenants for testing by
  - •• Examining leases to ascertain which expenses are to be rebilled, the base year, and the base amount that should be used in the current-year computation.

- •• Testing the client's computation to see if it is in accordance with lease provisions.
- Recalculate and review the reasonableness of client estimates used to determine rebillable amounts.
- If the client bills on an interim basis, determine whether accrued income is recorded properly at year-end.
- Review past-due amounts to determine whether any disputes exist between the client and the tenant. Consider whether adjustments of the accruals are necessary.

In most cases, income from common area charges is not significant in relation to total property income and no special auditing procedures are performed. If considered significant, these accounts may be tested in connection with tests of lease rental income. If common area charges are based on actual expenses incurred, audit tests are similar to those performed in connection with expense billings.

Depreciation Expense

Depreciation is a substantial noncash expense for real estate companies that lease property. Depreciation on a project begins when the property or a phase is substantially complete and available for occupancy (as defined in SFAS No. 67). Documents such as the certificate of occupancy and contractor invoices can assist the auditor in determining when it is appropriate to begin recording depreciation. In reviewing the reasonableness of the calculations, the auditor can compare useful lives with tax guidelines, real estate literature, or engineering studies. The auditor should also review the depreciation methods used for consistency.

39

Auditing Securities and Commodities Broker-Dealers

THE CHANGING ENVIRONMENT

Factors ranging from changing investor demands to shifting global economic conditions shape the environment in which securities and commodities broker-dealers operate. Several significant changes have occurred within the industry over the past decade in response to the fiercely competitive environment. Considerable consolidation occurred in the late 1970s and early 1980s among broker-dealers. In addition, several large organizations that were not previously part of the industry have made substantial investments or acquired firms in the industry. More recently, increased numbers of foreign companies, most notably Japanese firms, have made significant investments in U.S. broker-dealers, while U.S. broker-dealers continued to expand in international markets.

At first, the consolidation and influx of capital prompted diversification of firms providing financial services. Several firms that previously offered specialized services in only limited areas added new, diverse product lines and became "financial supermarkets," offering products or services in a broad range of investment areas such as commodities, government securities, asset-backed securities, limited partnerships in real estate, venture capital and oil and gas investments, annuities, mutual funds, program or portfolio trading, home equity loans and brokering, real estate, and insurance. As the rapid expansion of firms continued—in addition to the development of innovative products—broker-dealers have become involved in more capital-intensive activities such as underwriting, providing bridge loan financing for acquisitions and leveraged buyouts, and taking large equity positions in deals as a merchant bank. To be competitive, firms' needs for capital grew, and many firms met those needs by issuing more subordinated debt, forming alliances with business partners, and selling their shares to the public.

In the mid- to late 1980s, a number of factors surfaced that have caused a reassessment of the trend toward diversification by broker-dealers. These factors include the effects on the industry of the unfavorable publicity resulting from insider trading scandals and other alleged securities law violations, the October 1987 market crash, and the development of internal frictions among departments of firms as profits from one area were seen as being used to offset losses in other areas. As a result, by the end of the decade, the environment had stabilized in terms of the growth in size and type of services being offered by broker-dealers. "Boutique" firms formed by individuals formerly associated with full-service broker-dealers began offering specialized services, including merger and acquisition consulting, merchant banking, asset management, and specialized securities trading. At the same time, large, full-service firms were divesting themselves of certain product lines in an effort to refocus their resources and capital.

The changing environment was accompanied by unprecedented growth and volatility of the financial markets. The Dow Jones Industrial Average went from 875 in 1972 to a high of 2,722 in August 1987, with daily average volume on the New York Stock Exchange (NYSE) increasing from 22 million shares in 1972 to over 600 million shares traded during the market crash of October 19, 1987. NYSE volume during the week preceding and including that crash exceeded the volume for the entire year 1968. Within the following two years, most world stock markets met and exceeded the high of 1987, although at substantially reduced volume levels. Many people attribute the record highs to the merger and acquisition boom in 1988 and 1989.

Change has also been prevalent in the commodities industry in terms of volume and types of contracts. Major factors underlying this change can be traced to the Commodity Futures Trading Commission Act of 1974, which expanded the definition of commodities and began to regulate certain previously unregulated commodities; the establishment of limited partnership commodity funds, which allowed smaller investors to participate through a ''pooling'' of resources with similar investors; and the use of financial futures and options to hedge price-level risks. The number of futures contracts traded annually has grown from 18 million in 1972 to 112 million in 1982 to 246 million in 1988. The leading contract types traded have also changed significantly. In 1972, the ten leading contract types traded were physical commodity futures; in 1988, six of the ten (including the top two) were financial futures. The industry has been able to accommodate this range in business primarily because of advances in computer technology and other technological innovations such as centralized clearance and certificate depository facilities.

The securities and commodities industry is currently characterized by a proliferation of new financial products and services; the entry of new enterprises and investors into the industry, some of which are not familiar with the environment; innovative and complex trading and other business strategies involving foreign currency, arbitrage, options, futures, global trading, and other complicated financing arrangements; and sophisticated computerized systems for processing and controlling transactions. All these developments have had dramatic effects on the risks associated with doing business in the securities and commodities industry. In the 1960s and through most of the 1970s, most firms in the industry were subject to risks related primarily to the amount of paperwork entailed in processing transactions and to business risks related to swings in the economy, that is, fluctuations in the value of securities and commodities investments and in levels of trading volume on which their commission revenue was based. In the current environment, there are increased risks related primarily to the complexity of trading strategies and the proliferation of highly leveraged investment vehicles, as well as a heightening of the traditional credit, liquidity, and operational risks. For example, both the pace of change in the industry and the increased volatility of the marketplace (coupled with new means of financing, such as interest rate swaps) have increased business risk for many firms. Auditors of broker-dealers must understand the new products and services being offered, the underlying trading and financing strategies, the means of executing and processing the transactions, and the risks associated with all of those factors.

To further complicate matters, the industry operates in a global marketplace where 24-hour trading is quickly becoming a reality. Many countries are reducing the regulatory and legal barriers in their financial markets, and more firms are actively pursuing business operations in these countries. These developments heighten the risks assumed by a firm in this industry. For example, control procedures to monitor and assess market and credit risk must now extend to global operations.

To leverage from a strong capital base, enhance investment banking relationships, and maximize profits, firms have become involved in merchant banking transactions. In a typical merchant banking transaction, a firm will not only perform the usual investment banking functions (such as structuring a transaction, providing bridge loan financing, and issuing high-yield or "junk" bonds to finance a leveraged buyout), but it may also purchase an equity stake in the company being purchased. For the auditor, such equity positions usually raise questions as to the proper valuation of the company and the associated profit recognition on the investment banking fees earned by the firm.

Indictments and allegations of securities law violations involving insider trading, accommodation/accumulation transactions (i.e., "parking") and practices that favor the firm or its employees instead of customers (i.e., "front running") have created a growing concern among management, auditors, and lawyers alike over corporate responsibility and supervision of employees with regard to compliance with securities regulations. This concern has resulted in increased internal audits and compliance reviews and the refinement or development and enforcement of firms' codes of ethics and conflict of interest policies.

As a result of the October 1987 market crash, intense focus has been placed on securities regulations and the effectiveness of the current regulatory system. This scrutiny has come from the public as well as the federal government and has taken the form of various studies on the regulatory environment before, during, and after the crash, with particular emphasis on protection of investors. While the exact causes of the crash will be debated for years to come, the studies have revealed some pertinent findings and have led to the imposition of "circuit breakers" (that is, temporary halts in trading to control a significant surge of volatility within the market). While the present regulations, for the most part, are believed to be effective, there is ongoing debate as to whether one overall regulator is needed to oversee, among others, the NYSE, Commodity Futures Trading Commission (CFTC), and National Association of Securities Dealers (NASD).

The ramifications of the October 1987 market crash are evident. Retrenchment and strategic refocus of Wall Street firms, and cost-containment measures, have become leading topics of conversation in board rooms. Regulators have heightened their focus on the overall effectiveness of the regulatory system and their "policing" function. The federal government has expressed its concern over the protection of the investing public, especially small investors. Finally, broker-dealers have had reinforced the need for adequate internal control structures and effective management reporting systems.

The regulatory environment in which broker-dealers operate is also constantly changing. Regulatory standards have been revised to monitor and control the activities of securities and commodities firms more effectively. As a result of the paperwork and financial crises experienced by many firms in the late 1960s, which reduced investor confidence to levels matched only by those experienced after the stock market crash of 1929, Congress created the Securities Investor Protection Corporation (SIPC) to insure customers' funds and securities held by securities firms up to a specified amount. The Securities and Exchange Commission (SEC) then established additional rules to improve the protection of investors' property, particularly Rule 15c3-3 under the Securities Exchange Act of 1934. That rule, commonly referred to as the "customer protection rule," prescribed standards for the protection of customers' property. Similar rules have been developed by the CFTC for firms engaged in commodities brokerage. Further, in response to the collapse of a few government securities dealers, Congress passed the Government Securities Act of 1986, which regulates a previously unregulated area of the financial markets. All of these regulations are discussed in more detail later in this chapter.

The various regulatory bodies are engaged in an ongoing effort to promulgate new regulations required because of new products and increasingly complex trading strategies. This process is likely to continue as long as traders devise new strategies and transactions, and product developers offer new investment vehicles to an increasingly sophisticated investing public. As a result of this rapidly changing environment, the AICPA has revised its audit guide, *Audits of Brokers and Dealers in Securities*, and at the time of this writing is finalizing a commodities industry audit guide entitled *Audits of Future Commission Merchants and Commodity Pools*.

THE REGULATORY FRAMEWORK FOR SECURITIES BROKER-DEALERS

The October 1987 market crash gave support to the basic effectiveness of the capital requirements and various other regulations designed to protect customers and preserve the liquidity of the markets. The regulatory system caused firms to assess their capital adequacy; in a few instances, firms either were able to obtain additional capital or had to reduce or close down their business. During this period of extreme market volatility, the regulatory environment governing the buying and selling of securities also performed, for the most part, as intended. Since 1987, however, the regulators have been performing their policing function with more vigor, and various additional regulatory solutions are being explored to more effectively address the interrelationship of the stock, futures, and options markets.

Also, in response to the advent of a worldwide financial marketplace, many countries, most notably Japan, the United Kingdom, and members of the European Community, are adjusting their regulatory environment to permit entry by foreign broker-dealers. This requires auditors to review management's procedures for ensuring compliance with complex regulatory structures around the world. In addition, the SEC, in conjunction with self-regulatory organizations, is promulgating new rules for the regulatory treatment of foreign transactions and the interaction of foreign broker-dealers with U.S. customers.

Finally, as a consequence of the securities law violations noted earlier, the role of a firm's compliance department has become increasingly important.

Most firms' compliance departments are responsible for developing and monitoring policies and procedures to prevent or detect violations of various securities regulations and laws. The auditor should consider the adequacy of the firm's compliance function in assessing its control environment.

Net Capital (Rule 15c3-1)

SEC Rule 15c3-1 under the 1934 Act prescribes net capital requirements for broker-dealers.[1] It was amended in 1975 to establish a uniform and comprehensive net capital standard for the industry—a standard that was adopted by all the national securities exchanges.[2] Previously, many firms, in addition to complying with the SEC's net capital rule, were required to be in compliance with separate net capital rules of the various national securities and commodities exchanges of which they were members.

As defined, net capital comprises the net worth of a firm plus certain subordinated liabilities, less deductions for (a) assets that are essentially not readily convertible into cash, (b) percentages (''haircuts''[3]) of the various components of a firm's trading and investment accounts, and (c) percentages or market-value amounts of certain other open or unsettled securities and commodities transactions with customers and other broker-dealers.

The required level of capital may be computed under one of two methods. Under the first method, broker-dealers must maintain a maximum specified ratio of aggregate indebtedness, as defined, to net capital, as defined. Aggregate indebtedness generally comprises all liabilities pertaining to a firm's customer business. Under this method, the broker-dealer must maintain a minimum dollar amount of net capital. If the ratio of aggregate indebtedness to net capital exceeds 10 to 1, a firm may no longer expand its business; if the ratio exceeds 12 to 1, a firm is required to contract its business; and if the ratio exceeds 15 to 1, the firm must discontinue operations.

The alternative method of computation, which is presently used by most firms, is designed to measure a firm's net capital in relation to balances owed to the broker-dealer relating to its business with customers.[4] If a broker-dealer utilizes this alternative method of computing required net capital, the haircut percentages applied to the securities positions and other operationally oriented

---

[1]The provisions of the rule require broker-dealers to be in compliance with the capital requirements at all times. Although the rule does not require daily computations of net capital, broker-dealers are obligated to maintain adequate bookkeeping records to ensure compliance on a daily basis.

[2]The amendment adopting the uniform net capital rule also required the registration, for the first time, of broker-dealers engaged exclusively in the sale of municipal securities. This led to the creation of the Municipal Securities Rulemaking Board (MSRB), which, together with the SEC, oversees such broker-dealers.

[3]Haircuts are a means of recognizing the market risk associated with securities that are either owned or have been sold short by a broker-dealer. Haircuts are based on the marketability and volatility of the individual investments and are higher for positions that are more volatile and less marketable.

[4]A broker-dealer that has elected to compute net capital requirements pursuant to the alternative method must request permission from the SEC to change from it.

deductions made in arriving at net capital are substantially reduced. Under the alternative net capital rule, a broker-dealer must maintain a minimum dollar amount of net capital and cease to expand its business if net capital falls below 5 percent of aggregate debits (i.e., debit balances associated with customer transactions) included in its reserve formula computation (required pursuant to Rule 15c3-3, discussed next) as of the same date. The firm must contract its business if net capital falls below 4 percent of aggregate debits; the firm must cease operations if net capital falls below 2 percent of aggregate debits. At the time of this writing, the SEC is considering revisions to the net capital rule that would raise the minimum capital requirement under the first method and equalize the haircut percentages applied to securities positions.

Reserve Formula and Possession or Control of Customer Securities (Rule 15c3-3)

The problems encountered in the early 1970s in connection with the first liquidations of broker-dealers under the Securities Investor Protection Act and the desire for more timely clearing of transactions between securities firms led to the need to design additional financial responsibility regulations to ensure the protection of customers' assets held by securities firms. SEC Rule 15c3-3 was adopted to ensure the protection of customers' assets held by securities firms. It requires the following:

- *Weekly Computation of Reserve Formula.* Securities firms must perform weekly calculations, known as the computation of the reserve requirement pursuant to Rule 15c3-3, that account for all debit and credit cash balances attributable to customers, as defined. All customers' cash balances are considered to be fungible, and the total debit balances are subtracted from the total credit balances attributable to customers. If the result of this computation is a net credit balance, the firm must deposit that amount of cash or cash equivalents in a "special reserve bank account" for the exclusive benefit of customers. If the result of the formula is a net debit balance, no deposit is required. In determining the amounts to be included in the formula, a firm may use either specific identification of customer versus firm transactions or any other rational and systematic method of allocation.
- *Possession or Control Requirement.* Securities firms must maintain a system for identifying all customer securities that are fully paid for or are held as excess collateral in connection with margin transactions. Further, firms must develop systems for issuing instructions to segregate these securities and promptly "reduce them" to the firm's possession or control, as defined.

The rule specifies various time periods, considering the business environment, in which securities firms must take the prescribed actions. For example, customers' fully paid or excess margin securities may be reported in "fail to receive"[5] for 30 days or less; however, older fails may be required to be

---

[5]This and other terms used are discussed later in this chapter under "The Trading Cycle."

"bought-in" by the broker-dealer to protect customers. On the other hand, customers' fully paid or excess margin securities are not permitted to be "located in," for example, bank loans; if this occurs, the broker-dealer must immediately reduce such securities to possession or control. Firms that neither clear transactions for customers nor carry customer accounts, of course, are exempted from these requirements.

Financial Reporting and Annual Audit Requirements (Rule 17a-5)

Through the mid-1970s, most securities and commodities firms were burdened by myriad financial and operating reports required by various self-regulatory authorities, many of which were duplicative and costly to prepare. In addition, periodic audit examinations had to be performed on a surprise basis using prescribed auditing procedures. To reduce the reporting burden, the SEC adopted, effective January 1, 1976, a streamlined uniform regulatory report to be filed periodically by all broker-dealers. Known as the Financial and Operational Combined Uniform Single Report (FOCUS Report), it is also required by the NYSE, NASD, and other self-regulatory organizations. Periodic regulatory reporting for securities broker-dealers, as well as annual auditing requirements, are stipulated by SEC Rule 17a-5.

Regulatory Reporting.   Every broker-dealer registered under Section 15 of the Securities Exchange Act of 1934 must periodically file the FOCUS Report with the SEC on Form X17A-5 or, if certain conditions exist, with a designated self-regulatory organization (i.e., either a national securities exchange or a registered national securities association) that transmits the information to the SEC. Part I of the FOCUS Report is filed monthly (either 10 business days or, for NYSE firms, 17 business days after month-end) by broker-dealers that carry customer accounts or clear transactions for customers. Part I is a one-page summary of 26 key indicators designed to highlight the broker-dealer's financial and operating condition.

All broker-dealers must file either Part II or Part IIA of the FOCUS Report at the end of each calendar quarter. Part II is a comprehensive set of financial statements, comprising a statement of financial condition, statements of income and of changes in subordinated liabilities and stockholders' equity or partners' or sole proprietor's capital, and supplementary schedules, including reserve formula (Rule 15c3-3) and net capital (Rule 15c3-1) computations, and possession or control (Rule 15c3-3) information. Part II is intended to be generally consistent with similar financial statements prepared in conformity with generally accepted accounting principles (GAAP). Part IIA is an abbreviated version of Part II and is used by broker-dealers that do not carry customer accounts or clear transactions for customers, or that are registered solely to sell shares of investment companies and do not clear transactions entered into on their own behalf.

Audited Financial Statements.   Every broker-dealer registered under Section 15 of the Securities Exchange Act of 1934 must file, pursuant to paragraph (d) of Rule 17a-5, audited financial statements (either calendar- or fiscal-year) within 60 days following year-end. The broker-dealer may adopt a fiscal year-end for purposes of this rule that differs from its fiscal year-end for tax or other financial reporting purposes; however, once a year-end has been established, it cannot be changed without SEC approval.

In adopting the FOCUS Report, the SEC amended Rule 17a-5 to eliminate previously prescribed auditing procedures. It replaced those procedures with language that permits independent auditors to exercise professional judgment in establishing the nature, extent, and timing of auditing procedures to be applied. Pursuant to Rule 17a-5 (paragraph [g]),

> The scope of the audit and review of the accounting system, the internal control and procedures for safeguarding securities shall be sufficient to provide reasonable assurance that any material inadequacies existing at the date of the examination . . . would be disclosed. Additionally, as specific objectives, the audit shall include reviews of the practices and procedures followed by the client:
>
> (i) in making the periodic computations of aggregate indebtedness and net capital under Rule 17a-3(a)(11) and the reserve required by Rule 15c3-3(e);
>
> (ii) in making the quarterly securities examinations, counts, verifications and comparisons and the recordation of differences required by Rule 17a-13;
>
> (iii) in complying with the requirement for prompt payment for securities of Section 4(c) of Regulation T of the Board of Governors of the Federal Reserve System; and
>
> (iv) in obtaining and maintaining physical possession or control of all fully paid and excess margin securities of customers as required by Rule 15c3-3.

In conjunction with an audit performed in accordance with the requirements specified by Rule 17a-5, the independent accountant must comment on any material inadequacies existing at the date of the audit in the accounting system, the internal accounting control procedures, the procedures for safeguarding securities, and the practices and procedures reviewed as specified in items (i)–(iv) above. The term "material inadequacy" is defined in the rule as

> Any condition which has contributed substantially to or, if appropriate corrective action is not taken, could reasonably be expected to (i) inhibit a broker or dealer from promptly completing securities transactions or promptly discharging his responsibilities to customers, other broker-dealers or creditors; (ii) result in material financial loss; (iii) result in material misstatements of the broker-dealer's financial statements; or (iv) result in violations of the Commission's record-keeping or financial responsibility rules to an extent that could reasonably be expected to result in the conditions described in parts (i), (ii), or (iii) of this subparagraph.[6]

[6]The portion of Release No. 34-11935 in which the amendments to Rule 17a-5 are summarized, under the caption "Accountants' Reports," includes language to the effect that determining a material inadequacy generally requires (1) completion of auditing procedures in the particular area, (2) appropriate review at the decision-making level by both management and the independent accountant, and (3) possible consultation with counsel. Consequently, there could be a reasonable period of time between the date a potential condition considered to be a material inadequacy is first identified and the date such determination is finally made.

If the audit did not disclose any material inadequacies, the independent accountant's report should so state. Comments on material inadequacies must be submitted with the broker-dealer's audited financial statements and must, if applicable, indicate corrective action taken or proposed by the broker-dealer.

In addition, paragraph (h)(2) of Rule 17a-5 provides that, if at any time during the course of the audit or related interim work, the independent accountant determines that a material inadequacy exists, it should be brought to the attention of the chief financial officer of the broker-dealer. That officer must then notify the SEC and the designated examining authority by telegram within 24 hours, as set forth in Rule 17a-11; a copy of the telegraphic notice must be furnished to the independent accountant. If the accountant fails to receive that notice from the broker-dealer within the 24-hour period or disagrees with the statements contained in the notice, the accountant must report the material inadequacy to the SEC and the designated examining authority within 24 hours, as set forth in Rule 17a-11.

The annual audit report is required to include the following financial statements and supplementary schedules, all of which must be prepared in conformity with GAAP:

- Statement of financial condition.
- Statement of income (loss).
- Statement of cash flows.
- Statement of changes in stockholders' equity, partners' capital, or sole proprietor's capital.
- Statement of changes in liabilities subordinated to the claims of general creditors.
- Supplementary schedules
    - •• Computation of net capital under SEC Rule 15c3-1.
    - •• Computation of reserve requirements under SEC Rule 15c3-3.
    - •• Information relating to possession or control requirements under SEC Rule 15c3-3.
    - •• A reconciliation of the computation of net capital pursuant to Rule 15c3-1 and the computation of the cash reserve requirement under Rule 15c3-3 to the corresponding computations included in the unaudited FOCUS Report as of the same date, if these computations differ materially. If no material differences exist, a statement to that effect is required.[7]

Annual audited financial statements are treated by the SEC as public documents. To achieve some degree of confidentiality, however, a firm may

[7]The statement should be included on the schedules computing the reserve requirement under Rule 15c3-3 and net capital under Rule 15c3-1, and should be worded as follows: "There were no differences between this computation of net capital (or, if applicable, reserve required pursuant to Rule 15c3-3) and the corresponding computation prepared by (name of broker-dealer) and included in its unaudited Part II (IIA) FOCUS Report filing as of the same date, which differences are considered to be material."

file two sets of financial statements. The set that is to be treated as a public document is required to contain the broker-dealer's statement of financial condition, the related notes, and the auditor's report thereon and the auditor's report on material inadequacies. The second, complete set of financial statements and supporting schedules, and the auditor's report thereon, should be marked "Confidential."

Rule 17a-5 also prescribes requirements for obtaining filing extensions as well as for written notification to the SEC of the appointment and termination of auditors. In addition to providing audited financial statements to regulatory organizations, SEC Rule 17a-5 requires that broker-dealers, within specified time frames, furnish their customers with semiannual statements of financial condition, one of which must be audited, together with appropriate footnotes.

The Government Securities Act of 1986

In response to some highly publicized failures of government securities dealers, Congress passed the Government Securities Act of 1986 (GSA). The purpose of the GSA was primarily to establish capital adequacy, record-keeping, and financial disclosure guidelines for government securities dealers, who, before enactment of the GSA, were largely unregulated. The capital requirements of the GSA essentially track relevant regulations already applicable to securities firms, most notably Rule 15c3-1, with certain variations to enable the regulators to better monitor the risks that are more common to government securities dealers. The most significant variation relates to the required haircut calculations for a government securities dealer's inventory. In recognition of the unique characteristics of government securities, haircuts have been designed to measure market risk and credit risk as well as the broker-dealer's liquidity.

The GSA is administered by the U.S. Treasury Department and monitored by the SEC. A government securities dealer who is required to adhere to the GSA is subject to annual audits of its financial statements and must make quarterly unaudited filings with the regulators. If a government securities dealer is subject to other regulations as a securities broker-dealer (e.g., Rules 15c3-1 and 17a-5), because of the similarities of the rules the dealer is exempted from the requirements of the GSA.

Other Rules and Regulations

Auditors should be familiar with other SEC rules under the 1934 Act pertaining to broker-dealers, particularly Rules 8c-1 and 15c2-1, 17a-3, 17a-4, 17a-11, and 17a-13. Rules 8c-1 and 15c2-1 deal with fraudulent practices and hypothecation of customers' securities; Rule 17a-3, with records required to be maintained; Rule 17a-4, with record retention; Rule 17a-11, with notification concerning violations of SEC rules; and Rule 17a-13, with quarterly security counts, verifications, and comparisons. Auditors should also be aware of the pertinent regulations of the Board of Governors of the Federal Reserve System—Regulation T, which governs the amount of credit that broker-dealers may extend to customers; Regulation U, concerning the amount of credit that banks may grant to customers for the purpose of buying securities on margin; and Regulation X, which specifies conditions borrowers must meet when obtaining credit for the purpose of purchasing or carrying securities. The regulations of the CFTC and the rules and regulations of the pertinent national stock exchanges or NASD are also relevant to audits of broker-dealers. During the audit, the auditor should review the report on the most recent examination by the broker-dealer's "designated self-regulatory examining authority" as part of the process of evaluating the firm's compliance with regulatory requirements.

THE REGULATORY FRAMEWORK FOR COMMODITIES BROKER-DEALERS

As a result of increased investor activity in commodity futures transactions, the CFTC was established by Congress in 1974, as part of the amendment of the Commodity Exchange Act (CEA), to regulate transactions involving contracts of sale of commodities for future delivery traded on domestic commodity exchanges. In addition, the amendment expanded the definition of commodities beyond farm products to include "all other goods and articles . . . and all services, rights and interests in which contracts for future delivery are presently or in the future dealt in." Thus, regulated commodities include diverse items ranging from sugar, corn, pork bellies, and metals, to interest rate futures, stock index futures, treasury bonds, and foreign currencies. In 1988, CFTC regulations were promulgated to protect U.S. customers in transactions on foreign futures exchanges.

Since its inception, the CFTC has enacted rules governing trading in commodity futures and the financial soundness of firms that conduct business in commodity futures, and standards to ensure the protection of customers' funds relating to transactions in commodity futures. The SEC and CFTC are making a concerted effort to coordinate their financial responsibility and reporting rules to eliminate duplicative reporting practices.

As the principal regulator of the commodities industry, the CFTC has exclusive jurisdiction over contract markets (commodity exchanges), floor brokers, clearing organizations, trading advisors, commodity pool operators, and futures commission merchants (FCMs) and their agents. CFTC regulations that directly affect audits of financial statements of FCMs concern minimum capital requirements, segregation and protection of customers' funds, and financial reporting requirements.

Minimum capital requirements are set forth in CFTC Regulation 1.17, which calls for FCMs to maintain specific amounts of adjusted net capital based on a dollar amount or percentage of an FCM's segregated funds required under Section 4d of the CEA and CFTC Regulation 1.20. FCMs that are also securities broker-dealers meet this requirement by complying with SEC Rule 15c3-1, covering net capital (discussed previously). Although the net capital requirements of the SEC and CFTC are similar, auditors should be aware of the unique characteristics of the two rules.

Regulations for protection of customers' funds are enumerated in Section 4d of the CEA and CFTC Regulations 1.20 and 30.7, which require FCMs to segregate and separately account for customers' funds in domestic and foreign markets. In addition, CFTC Regulations 1.21 to 1.30 set forth regulations for the use, investment, records, and deposit parameters of customers' funds held by FCMs. As part of the audit, the auditor is required to review an FCM's practices and procedures for daily computation of the domestic and foreign segregation requirements and funds on deposit.[8]

In addition to filing financial reports with the CFTC on registration, each FCM is required by CFTC Regulation 1.10 to file quarterly and annual financial reports. This rule specifies the format (Form 1-FR) and the filing dates of such reports and allows FCMs who are also registered securities broker-dealers to satisfy this requirement by filing a copy of their FOCUS Report with the CFTC in lieu of Form 1-FR. Similar to the SEC requirements for securities broker-dealers, CFTC Regulation 1.16 requires auditors to examine and report on the annual financial statements; to review and report on an FCM's accounting systems, internal control procedures, and procedures for safeguarding customer and firm assets; and to report material inadequacies.

Auditing procedures applicable to FCMs do not differ substantially from those relating to securities broker-dealers. The auditor should review an FCM's procedures for complying with CFTC segregation and net capital requirements and should review the calculation of such requirements as of the date of the financial statements to ascertain that sufficient funds are segregated appropriately and minimum net capital requirements are met. In this connection, the auditor should obtain a copy of the Commodity Exchange Act and the CFTC regulations to gain an understanding of areas unique to the commodities industry.

TYPICAL TRANSACTIONS, CONTROL STRUCTURE POLICIES AND PROCEDURES, AND TESTS OF CONTROLS

Generally accepted auditing standards require auditors to obtain an understanding of the internal control structures of securities and commodities broker-dealers and to assess control risk. As noted previously, SEC and CFTC rules impose responsibilities for reporting on material inadequacies in internal control. As part of assessing control risk, the auditor may perform tests of controls within a firm's major transaction cycles. Although the specific transaction cycles for which this strategy is used depend on the complexity of a particular broker-dealer's operations and the diversity of its product lines, three cycles are significant to most firms in the industry: the trading cycle, the financing cycle, and the underwriting cycle.

---

[8]Like the SEC, the CFTC imposes specific record-keeping and record retention regulations for reporting FCMs. Auditors should be familiar with CFTC Regulations 1.31 to 1.39, which discuss these requirements.

The Trading Cycle

The trading cycle is concerned with the processing of transactions that generate commissions or trading revenues of a firm. This cycle may relate to transactions in corporate securities, commercial paper, options, commodity futures, or government issues.

As a general rule, firms enter into transactions either on their own behalf or on behalf of customers. When a firm acts on its own behalf, it acts as principal in purchasing or selling for its own account. Generally, the purpose of such activities is to hold securities for subsequent resale or to sell securities short to take advantage of anticipated market declines. Most firms also engage in trading strategies involving arbitrage of securities (described later) and hedging by means of options or futures transactions. These transactions, which have gained widespread acceptance within the financial community, are complex. To understand them, the auditor must understand the economic considerations underlying each type of transaction, the pertinent regulatory considerations, and the associated elements of business risk (both market risk and credit risk). The auditor's ability to understand and evaluate business risk is critical, particularly in light of the many new, innovative, and complex financial instruments continually being introduced to the marketplace. Without fully understanding the economics of these instruments, an auditor may not be able to properly evaluate the various risks and potential contingencies associated with their use.

Usually the revenues or losses generated through a firm's executing transactions on its own behalf are classified as trading income or loss. Alternatively, when a firm executes transactions on behalf of a customer, it acts in an agency capacity. Commissions charged customers constitute the revenues earned through this activity.

The trading cycle encompasses control structure policies and procedures for the processing of transactions from the inception of orders to their final disposition in the general ledger. The processing of trades is essentially the same for corporate securities, listed options, government securities, and commodity futures; however, each type of transaction has certain unique aspects. These unique aspects generally relate to the time required for a transaction to settle (corporate securities transactions generally settle in five business days, while commercial paper, listed options, government securities, and commodity futures transactions generally settle in one day), the mode of clearance (broker to broker or through the facilities of a clearing organization), or the terminology used. Nevertheless, the control structure and audit objectives for the different types of transactions are essentially the same.

Standard industry practice is to record securities transactions on a settlement-date basis. This practice is not in conformity with GAAP, which requires the recording of securities transactions on a trade-date basis. At a minimum, this practice must be disclosed in the notes to the financial statements. In addition, the auditor should measure the impact of this practice on the financial statements being audited to determine whether an adjustment to the financial statements is required to reflect trade-date accounting.

To demonstrate the flow of a transaction in this cycle, an equity securities transaction is illustrated. If the trading transaction is entered into on behalf of the firm, the trading decision is made in the firm's trading department (in larger firms, typically under the direction of the head trader); if the transaction is on behalf of a customer, the order is transmitted by the customer to a registered representative or salesperson. Buy or sell orders are then submitted by the firm to the floor of an exchange for execution. (For securities not listed on an exchange, the transaction is executed directly with a firm that makes a market in the particular security being traded.) Once the order has been executed, a confirmation is sent back to the trading firm, which then processes the order through its internal processing system, ordinarily using in-house or service organization computer facilities.

Between the time a transaction is executed and the time it settles (generally five business days for corporate securities transactions in the United States), the firm performs several comparisons with information generated by the clearing facilities of the exchanges or other brokers, to ensure the correctness of the executed trades. During this time, the firm also submits trade confirmations to customers or, for transactions executed on its own behalf, to firm traders to ensure agreement with their records.

Comparisons and confirmations are important control procedures that the auditor may test to obtain evidence of their effectiveness in meeting control objectives relating to completeness, accuracy, and authorization of securities and commodities transactions. For example, a control structure deficiency might be identified by evidence of an unusually large number of unresolved differences relating to clearinghouse comparisons or of significant differences related to confirmations with other broker-dealers. Most securities and commodities transactions entered into by broker-dealers are with third parties, usually settle in a short time, and are confirmed by third parties on a regular basis. Accordingly, the existence of aged transactions could be an indication of ineffective control procedures.

On the settlement date, the firm records the transaction in its general ledger. The detailed customer and firm inventory records are updated as part of this process, and the stock record is also updated to reflect the transaction. A stock record is a detailed listing, by security position, of all securities attributable to customers, other brokers, and the firm. One side of the stock record indicates the ownership of the security (e.g., customer, firm, or failed to deliver to another broker-dealer), and the other side shows its location (e.g., vault, at the transfer agent, or failed to receive from another broker-dealer). The ownership side of the stock record is commonly referred to as the "longs" and the locating side as the "shorts." For each security issue, the record must be in balance (i.e., the longs must equal the shorts).

As part of the settlement process, the firm must maintain records of amounts payable and receivable from the clearing organizations and other brokers as well as of the related securities to be received or delivered. These balances, commonly referred to as "fails," are an integral part of the securities business. A fail occurs when securities are not received or delivered on the settlement date, and a firm has an open position with another firm or with a clearing organization. When a firm fails to receive securities, its general ledger shows a payable for the contract value of the securities, and the stock record shows a short position for the number of shares not received. Conversely, when a firm fails to deliver, it has a debit balance in its general ledger for the amount receivable from the sale of the securities; the stock record shows a long position on behalf of the firm to which the securities are deliverable.

In addition to applying control procedures to these positions to ensure that amounts receivable and payable are complete and accurate and that pertinent regulatory requirements are being met, many firms have instituted sophisticated procedures for these positions as part of the cash management system. In all businesses, attention must be given to the collection of outstanding receivables as a means of providing operating funds. In the securities industry, the focus is on obtaining securities that a firm is failing to receive so that they may in turn be delivered, thereby freeing cash to be used in operating the business.

In commodity futures trading, the equivalent of the security ledger is commonly referred to as the point balance. Detailed ledgers, including money balances, are maintained for each customer's domestic and foreign transactions, and firm transactions, with the net offsetting balance representing the position with the commodity clearing organization. Commodity futures clearing organizations settle the unrealized gains or losses on a position daily with the broker-dealer. The daily payment is reconciled through the point balance, and the unrealized gain or loss is included in a customer's account balance in the general ledger.

The auditor often performs tests of controls in the trading cycle to obtain evidence that

- Orders are executed and processed based on proper authorizations.
- Executed orders are recorded and summarized completely and accurately.
- Transactions are compared with information received from clearing organizations and other broker-dealers, and discrepancies are identified and resolved.
- All transactions are accurately recorded in the general ledger, stock record (point balance), and detailed firm, customer, and fail accounts.
- Securities are received and delivered appropriately, and related receipt and payment of cash are recorded completely and accurately.
- Securities in-house and at depositories are under proper control.
- Extending credit to customers is within prescribed guidelines, and open balances are collected.
- Regulatory requirements with respect to extending credit, executing transactions, and monitoring open positions are complied with.

The Financing Cycle

All transactions entered into by a securities firm require financing of some kind. The financing may be provided by several sources.

In common with all other profit-oriented businesses, securities firms require permanent financing. For corporations, permanent financing is generally provided through the sale of common and preferred stock; for partnerships or sole proprietorships, it is provided through contributions to capital. Permanent financing may also be provided through subordinated lending agreements under which funds or securities are provided to a firm for its use in financing operations. Subordinated lending arrangements are evidenced by formal agreements and are entered into for defined periods of time. The claims of these lenders, in the event of liquidation of a broker-dealer, are subordinated to the claims of the firm's customers and general creditors. Subordinated loans, which must be approved in writing by the designated examining authority (a national stock exchange or NASD) to be acceptable to the SEC, may be treated as capital for computing net capital pursuant to SEC Rule 15c3-1. Since permanent financing is obtained at regular, planned intervals and is not used to fund day-to-day operations, these financing activities are audited as part of capital.

Financing also occurs in the normal course of business in the securities industry. For example, fails to receive may be considered as a means of financing fails to deliver. In addition, certain trading strategies on the part of firms and their customers that generate short positions may be considered as financing certain customer and firm long positions. Financing through fail transactions is audited as part of the trading cycle. Trading strategies are considered in auditing the inventory accounts.

Three major sources of financing in the securities industry, all of which are ordinarily part of a firm's daily operations, are bank loans, stock lending, and repurchase agreements. Historically, bank loans have been the primary source of financing in the securities and commodities industry. Loans normally are obtained on a short-term basis to meet day-to-day operating needs and may be collateralized by securities or commodities. The market value of such collateral is governed by Regulation U of the Federal Reserve Bank. Pursuant to this regulation, firms are required to maintain prescribed ratios of collateral to loan balances based on whether the loan is on behalf of the firm or on behalf of its customers. This collateral must also be accounted for separately by loan type and may not be commingled. Since firms are required, pursuant to SEC Rule 15c3-3, to maintain possession or control of customers' fully paid or excess margin securities, only marginable securities in customers' margin accounts may be used to collateralize bank loans obtained on behalf of customers. The rate of interest charged for bank loans is generally the broker call loan rate, which approximates the prime lending rate.

Traditionally, securities lending has been used by broker-dealers to meet delivery commitments that could not be met otherwise because of a firm's failing to receive securities from other brokers or clearing organizations. In today's environment, securities lending activity has greatly increased to satisfy settlement demands imposed by regulations and to support trading techniques and has become an important business activity of many broker-dealers. In a stock-lending transaction, there is a simultaneous exchange of a specific security for cash value. (Letters of credit may be used in lieu of cash.) The lending broker rebates to the borrowing broker a certain percentage, usually ranging up to 80 percent of the broker call loan rate, of the interest earned on the cash collateral received. The rebate rate is negotiated on an individual-transaction basis. For example, a lender earns interest by lending available firm and client securities and using the cash collateral received to decrease broker call loans or invest in money market instruments. The borrower also earns interest on the cash collateral until the securities are returned. This method has gained wide acceptance in the securities industry as a less expensive means of financing a firm's operations.

As part of daily procedures, firms commonly mark their stock-lending and borrowing transactions to market, a process whereby contract value is compared with current market value, and collateral is then either increased or decreased to maintain the agreed-on relationship between the value of the securities and cash collateral.

Because of the prevalence of stock-lending transactions in the securities industry, many firms act as intermediaries by locating dealers willing to lend securities to other dealers. The income that such firms earn on these transactions is the difference between what they pay (rebate) to the borrowers of securities and what they charge (rebate) the providers.

Generally, government securities dealers act as market makers in government securities and other money market instruments. Since those dealers maintain inventories for the firm accounts to be subsequently sold to customers, they usually hold positions that they either cannot immediately dispose of or have purchased for purposes of speculation. These positions generally require some form of outside financing, because they may equal many times a firm's permanent financing. A firm may pledge these securities to obtain bank financing; the interest rate charged for bank loans is the government-dealer loan interest rate. Recently, firms that deal extensively in these types of securities have resorted to a less expensive means of financing their inventory by entering into repurchase agreements (commonly referred to as "repos") with investors.[9]

In a repurchase agreement, a dealer sells to an investor who has funds to invest overnight, a specified amount of securities in exchange for cash, which is deposited in the dealer's bank account. Concurrently, the dealer agrees to repurchase the securities from the investor at a specified date at a slightly higher price, the difference in prices representing the interest to be earned by the overnight investor. Securities that are sold pursuant to a repurchase agreement are treated as financing transactions and not as sales of trading or investment positions. Since the interest rate is lower than the government-dealer loan interest rate, this is a relatively less expensive means of financing dealers' inventories.

Although repurchase agreements can be entered into on an overnight basis, they may be negotiated on a fixed-maturity basis or for a term agreed on by the buyer and seller. The advantages of repos have been described as follows:

> From the point of view of investors, overnight loans in the [repo] market offer several attractive features. First, by rolling overnight [repos], investors can keep surplus funds invested without losing liquidity or incurring a price risk. Second,

---

[9]For a more complete analysis of repo transactions, see "Report of the Special Task Force on Audits of Repurchase Securities Transactions" issued in June 1985 by the AICPA.

because [repo] transactions are secured by top-quality paper, investors expose themselves to little or no credit risk.

On term, as opposed to overnight [repo] transactions, investors still have the advantage of their loans being secured, but they do lose some liquidity. To compensate for that, the rate on [a repo] transaction is generally higher the longer the term for which funds are lent.[10]

In light of several failures of firms that engaged in significant repurchase transactions, the auditor should be mindful that those transactions are not, in fact, risk-free (as suggested by the quote) and should encourage the client to address credit risk appropriately.

As in security-lending transactions, many firms act as intermediaries by investing in reverse repurchase transactions. (In these transactions, a firm purchases a security under an agreement to resell it—the reverse repurchase— at a specific price on a specified date and finances those positions by entering into repurchase agreements.) These transactions are called ''matched re-purchase transactions''; firms entering into them earn income in the amount of the difference between the interest charged on the repurchase agreement and the interest earned on the reverse repurchase agreement. For financial statement reporting purposes, matched repurchase transactions should be recorded on the statement of financial condition as both assets and liabilities. A firm engaging in repurchase transactions should mark the securities under-lying the transactions to market on a daily basis, which would indicate the need for additional collateral in the event of significant market fluctuations.

The auditor should note the terms of repurchase agreements vis-à-vis the terms of reverse repurchase agreements or inventory positions. To the extent that repurchase agreements expire before the maturities of the inventory positions or reverse repurchase agreements, the firm may be required to refinance those positions. Depending on prevailing interest rates, financing may be at higher rates than the related investments and could result in a loss to the firm.

The auditor often performs tests of controls in the financing cycle to obtain evidence that

- Management determines the firm's financing needs and monitors its financing activities.
- Appropriate stock-lending and repurchase agreements are obtained for each customer with whom the firm conducts such business.
- Collateral balances are maintained in accordance with good business practices and in conformity with the appropriate regulatory require-ments.
- The amount of loans and the value of collateral pledged are authorized and are recorded completely and accurately.
- Interest paid and collected is completely and accurately recorded.

[10]Marcia Stigum, *The Money Market*, rev. ed. (Homewood, IL: Dow Jones–Irwin, 1983), p. 41.

- Open stock-lending and repurchase transactions are marked to market and additional collateral is obtained, as appropriate.
- Credit checks and continued credit surveillance are performed.
- The collectibility of stock-lending receivables is evaluated.
- Financial statement disclosures are appropriate.

The Underwriting Cycle

Many firms offer investment banking or underwriting services to assist corporations and state and local governments in raising funds, primarily through the private or public sale of securities. If a broker-dealer engages in substantial underwriting activity, the auditor may identify underwriting as a separate cycle.

Generally, securities offered to the public must be registered with the SEC pursuant to the Securities Act of 1933. Securities offered pursuant to a private placement are exempt from SEC registration, although they may be required (as may publicly offered corporate securities) to be registered with the states in which they are offered. In a private placement, the securities are offered to a limited number of investors and generally are restricted as to resale. Ordinarily, private placements are less costly and burdensome than public offerings, primarily because SEC registration is not required. Bonds offered to the public by state and local governments, commonly referred to as "municipal underwritings," are also exempt from SEC registration, although the MSRB, as well as the SEC, closely supervises firms conducting business in these securities.

Firms may underwrite securities on either a "firm-commitment" or a "best-efforts" basis. If securities are underwritten on a firm-commitment basis, the underwriter agrees to purchase the security issue from the issuer at a specified price; the firm then sells the securities to the public at a higher price. When an underwriting is undertaken on a best-efforts basis, the underwriter agrees to sell as much of the security issue as possible. Investment bankers generally prefer the best-efforts basis for securities of emerging companies that do not have proven performance records. Most private placements are underwritten on a best-efforts basis.

Ordinarily, underwritings are costly to complete and require a capital commitment on the part of the underwriting firm, which may be required to purchase unsold securities and to take haircuts pursuant to Rule 15c3-1 on these securities as well as on underwriting commitments and "when-issued" transactions (described below). Also, in computing regulatory net capital, the underwriting firm is required to deduct from capital certain good-faith deposits and receivables attributable to underwritings. As a result, firms that engage in this activity usually form underwriting syndicates to sell the securities. An underwriting syndicate normally comprises one or two firms that act as manager and a number of other firms that participate in underwriting the securities. Underwriting syndicates are formed on an individual-offering basis. Typically in large firms, a high-level commitment committee comprising senior management determines whether to participate in an offering.

Before the securities are sold to the public, a due diligence meeting is held between the issuer of the securities and the broker-dealers that intend to manage and participate in the underwriting. At this meeting, financial and other information that relates to the company and the securities to be issued is reviewed. Such information will be included in the registration statement. Another purpose of this meeting is to reach a preliminary understanding concerning the general terms of the formal underwriting agreement between the issuer and the underwriters.

Shortly after this meeting, an underwriting agreement is executed between the issuer and the manager of the underwriting syndicate. The agreement specifies the terms of the transaction, including the underwriting spread, which is the difference between the price at which the securities are to be sold and the proceeds to be received by the issuer. (Before the formal agreement, which is usually effective on the date the registration statement is completed, the manager and the issuer operate pursuant to a letter of intent.) The manager, in turn, executes agreements with the underwriting participants for their respective portions of the underwriting commitment.

At the manager's discretion, a selling group of firms that generally are not members of the underwriting syndicate may be formed to supplement the sales effort. The underwriting manager has authority to allocate shares to be sold by the members of the selling group. Normally, there are no formal written agreements between the manager and the selling group, which functions as agent for the underwriters. The underwriting syndicate is responsible for selling any unsold shares allocated to the selling group.

The manager has the authority to retain a portion of the securities, usually for sale to large institutions such as banks and insurance companies. It is more efficient for the manager to handle sales of this nature directly; in addition, it eliminates the inconvenience of institutional purchasers having to purchase several smaller blocks from various members of the underwriting syndicate. These transactions are termed "group sales" and constitute what is commonly referred to as the "pot."[11]

The newly issued securities may begin trading in the open market in a stock exchange or in the over-the-counter market in what is commonly referred to as the aftermarket. Practical problems may occur for the underwriting syndicate if the securities trade in the aftermarket at a price below that at which they are being sold by the underwriters. In that event, the underwriting agreement may require the manager to stabilize the price by entering a bid for the securities at a price at or close to the offering price. This practice is permissible under the Securities Exchange Act of 1934, but it must be carried out within strict guidelines. Any securities purchased by the underwriter in this fashion are taken into inventory to be sold at a future date.

On the other hand, if the securities sell in the open market at a price above the offering price, investor demand for the offering may be so great that the underwriters may oversell the position by committing to sell to customers

---

[11]The manager usually receives a selling concession fee for securities sold in this fashion, and the remaining underwriting income minus appropriate expenses is distributed to the members of the underwriting syndicate.

more shares than are being offered, that is, by assuming a short position for the excess. If all the customers honored their commitments, the manager of the underwriting would have to purchase shares on the open market to meet the syndicate's commitments; the resulting gain or loss (usually there is a loss) would be allocated to those members of the syndicate that had oversold positions.

In addition to performing the preceding tasks, broker-dealers that function as manager in an underwriting maintain the books and records for the underwriting and account for sold and unsold securities positions for the entire underwriting. They also maintain detailed income and expense accounts so that the profit or loss on the underwriting can be distributed to the participants on termination of the underwriting syndicate. All participants also maintain records to the extent of their involvement in the underwriting.

For services performed in connection with the underwriting, the manager receives a management fee, which is deducted from the underwriting spread. Members of the selling group also receive a fee for their services, called the selling concession, which is a percentage of the underwriting spread. The selling concession is also deducted from the underwriting spread. The remaining portion of the underwriting spread minus related expenses is allocated to the other members of the underwriting syndicate based on their respective participations.

Rule 415 under the Securities Act of 1933 allows corporate issuers of securities to register in advance with the SEC debt or equity securities that are expected to be offered for sale within a two-year period, commonly referred to as a "shelf registration." This rule provides issuers of securities with increased flexibility and enables them to achieve cost savings by reducing the effort associated with completing separate registrations for each issue of securities offered within a two-year period. Issuers that decide to take advantage of Rule 415 must, of course, update the financial information in the registration document by filing the appropriate amendments.

Transactions in securities that have not been issued because the underwriting has not been completed are considered to be "when-issued" transactions. When-issued transactions are contracts to purchase or sell securities when, and if, they are issued. These transactions are not recorded in a firm's asset and liability accounts, but are accounted for separately in subsidiary records and in the detailed customer accounts.

The auditor often performs tests of controls in the underwriting cycle to obtain evidence that

- Commitments for the underwriting of corporate or municipal securities are appropriately authorized in advance and are documented by formal agreements.
- Provisions for losses arising from unfulfilled commitments are recorded and are approved by management.
- Open contractual commitments and when-issued transactions are completely and accurately recorded in general ledger and detailed customer accounts.

- Transactions relating to a syndicate are authorized and are completely and accurately recorded in the detailed accounts of that syndicate.
- The firm clearly distinguishes between positions undertaken on its own behalf and on behalf of customers.
- Gains and losses relating to underwritings are completely and accurately recorded.
- Income from underwriting transactions is recognized appropriately.
- Aged receivables are monitored.
- Financial statement disclosures are appropriate.
- For firms that manage underwritings, procedures are in effect for stabilizing the market for securities underwritten and for accounting for oversold positions.
- Appropriate due diligence meetings are held before registrations become effective, the appropriate parties (participating underwriters, counsel, independent auditors, and officers of the issuer) are invited to attend, and appropriate procedures are followed at the meetings.

RISK ASSESSMENT AND AUDIT STRATEGY

Determining the audit strategy requires a thorough assessment of the inherent and control risks specific to the firm. Partially as a result of high capital leverage, some of those risks are unusually high for securities and commodities broker-dealers. The degree of risk associated with a particular firm depends on a number of factors, including

- The "tone" set by top management (e.g., management's risk philosophy, focus on control procedures, exercise of oversight and supervision, and emphasis placed on profitability).
- The types of financial instruments the firm trades.
- The effectiveness of the control structure and internal reports to alert management to adverse situations that may expose the firm to losses.
- The internal audit function.

In assessing the impact of the above factors, the auditor must exercise particular judgment concerning policies and procedures designed to ensure the completeness, accuracy, and authorization of transactions. Judgment also plays an important role in assessing revenue and expense cutoffs, valuations of the firm's investments, and financial statement disclosures.

In planning an audit of a broker-dealer, the auditor should also assess the impact of the regulatory environment, with particular emphasis on changes that have occurred, and the expectations of the client, its customers, and regulators. In reaching conclusions about audit scope, the auditor should consider, among other factors, inherent risk, the effectiveness of the broker-dealer's internal control structure, materiality, and the possible need to synchronize the timing of certain auditing procedures (described later).

Of particular importance for an auditor in the securities and commodities industry are the presence of "cumulative" control procedures and third-party confirmation. Cumulative control procedures will not detect a misstatement until a report is generated as a result of some specific action, such as a periodic bank, depository, or clearinghouse reconciliation. (Such reconciliations are an integral element of the settlement process.)

Third-party confirmations are important procedures at broker-dealers. Various regulations require confirmations to be sent to the counterparty on most transactions, such as purchases and sales, and repo and reverse repo transactions. In addition, third parties confirm, directly or indirectly, certain other transactions, such as through daily settlement and position sheets received from depositories, physical receipts and deliveries of securities, and the mailing of customer statements. These confirmations are in addition to those required by Rule 17a-13, previously discussed. Given the level of transactions subject to third-party scrutiny, an auditor may obtain assurance by reviewing confirmation procedures.

The regulatory environment has a major impact on audit strategy decisions because of the requirements that a broker-dealer's independent auditor report on the adequacy of the firm's internal control structure and on its compliance with specific rules dealing with financial responsibility and record keeping. Accordingly, usually some tests of controls are performed even if the auditor would not otherwise elect to do so; however, the extent of tests of controls considered necessary for regulatory reporting purposes varies widely in practice. In addition, the volatility and risk factors in the industry, and the level of activity of some accounts affect the auditor's decision about performing interim substantive tests, such as confirming various balances. On the other hand, because most assets and liabilities are presented at market value, the auditor typically is not concerned about cost and its realization. Moreover, assets generally are not classified as current or noncurrent on the statement of financial condition, so the auditor does not have to be concerned about the distinction between those categories. Such a distinction has little meaning for broker-dealers, since, theoretically, all assets except furniture and fixtures and certain other miscellaneous assets are readily convertible into cash.

Rule 17a-5 paragraph (h)(1) requires auditors to be "mindful" of the need to consider synchronizing the application of certain auditing procedures and performing tests in certain areas simultaneously. Accordingly, although auditors can exercise their professional judgment in making these strategy decisions, they may be expected to justify a choice not to synchronize certain substantive tests (such as confirming customer transactions and open or unsettled transactions with other broker-dealers and transfer agents and substantiating stock record positions by counting securities or through other appropriate means).

Recognizing the operating risks they face, many broker-dealers have established risk analysis departments and devised specialized computerized "exposure reports," which may be prepared daily, to highlight for senior management certain areas of exposure. In addition, many firms set "trading limits" for each individual responsible for trading securities or commodities for a firm's own account. Exposure reports typically identify exposure in repo and reverse repo agreements and stock loan/borrow transactions, trading limit violations, and aged suspense and receivable accounts. Furthermore, many firms have sophisticated credit functions and internal audit procedures to address risk analysis. The auditor should consider the effect of those control procedures on the audit strategy by ascertaining the completeness and accuracy of the exposure reports, the thoroughness of management's review of them, and management's responsiveness to adverse exposures reflected by the reports and to recommendations for improvements noted in internal audit reports.

In assessing risk, the auditor should be mindful of the environment in which a broker-dealer operates. That environment usually involves

Volatile securities markets, which, combined with global trading, increase the intra-day risk a broker-dealer is exposed to.

Use of highly sophisticated computers that often allow on-line access by registered representatives, firm traders, and key accounting personnel.

Daily, weekly, and monthly comparisons of the firm's records with those of clearing organizations and other firms.

Journal entries that record not only dollar amounts but also the corresponding movements and values of the underlying commodities or securities positions.

Regulatory pronouncements that govern virtually every aspect of the business, along with periodic examinations by self-regulatory authorities.

A number of transactions typically entered into by firms in the securities and commodities industry have certain inherent risks associated with them that are unique to the industry. A pervasive risk inherent in the securities trading area is the possibility that no liquid market exists for the securities held by a firm. There should be procedures in place to monitor the profitability of securities in the firm's inventory account, especially securities with a limited market. Another risk, from both a business and a regulatory viewpoint, is undue concentration in securities of a single issuer. Concentration situations should be reported to management on a timely basis. The reports typically identify all securities of a single issuer and its affiliates held by a broker-dealer, including equities, bonds, options, and repurchase agreements.

As discussed earlier, one of the major sources of financing in the securities industry is bank loans. In addition to the risks faced by all businesses concerning collateralized bank loans, broker-dealers are subject to a unique risk resulting from regulations governing collateral. Rule 15c3-3 prohibits broker-dealers from utilizing customers' fully paid or excess margin securities as collateral for customers' bank loans. In addition, under Regulation U, the required ratios of the value of collateral to the amount of loans differ between loans for purposes of financing customer-related activity and loans on behalf of the firm. Thus firms must maintain separate records for customer and firm loans and related collateral.

Securities lending has become a principal financing source for brokerage firms. The inherent risks associated with securities lending are

Potential failure by one party to return securities or collateral called by the other party, resulting in the need to buy or sell the securities at a possible loss.

Possible nonpayment of interest rebates.

Possible unauthorized payments between employees of borrowing and lending firms, and abuse of expense accounts such as for unauthorized entertainment, which is sometimes a factor in this activity.

The inherent risks associated with repo transactions (discussed earlier) are essentially the same as those in stock-lending transactions and relate to the creditworthiness of firms or other parties with which an entity does business. Because repo transactions are intended to be fully collateralized, they were not included in Rule 15c3-3 dealing with protection of customers' securities. There is, however, risk involved in these transactions, and new regulations have been issued governing them. Among other things, these rules require broker-dealers to obtain repo agreements specifying the contract terms, to maintain certain records, and to confirm repos with the counterparty to the transactions. The auditor should be alert to the procedures for complying with those rules and for evaluating the credit risks assumed by the business.

Another type of transaction securities firms may engage in is risk arbitrage, in which a firm invests in securities that are generally involved in mergers or tender offers. In a merger situation, the risk, or exposure, to the firm relates to the possibility that the proposed merger may be unsuccessful. Such aborted mergers often result in a loss to the firm. In a tender offer, one company makes an offer for a specific number of shares of another company, reserving the option to accept all stock tendered over the minimum as well as a lesser number of shares. In this type of transaction, the price offered usually is substantially higher than the current market price of the securities. The risk, or exposure, to the firm relates to the possibility that the shares may not be accepted.

The inherent risks unique to underwriting securities include the possibility that underwriters may be required to purchase unsold securities positions offered pursuant to a firm-commitment underwriting. This would result in the need to finance those securities, assume the market risk of ownership, and take haircuts pursuant to Rule 15c3-1. Lawsuits may also be initiated by the purchasers of the securities under Section 11 of the Securities Act of 1933, under which all persons (including underwriters) connected with a registration statement have responsibility for material misstatements contained therein. In addition, customers who have committed to purchase securities being underwritten may refuse to honor the transactions, resulting in the underwriter's having to purchase the securities.

SUBSTANTIVE TESTS OF BALANCES

Based on the assessment of inherent and control risk, the auditor plans the nature, timing, and extent of substantive procedures. The discussion in this section is limited to accounts unique to the securities and commodities industry.

Special Reserve Bank Account

The auditor should confirm the existence of the special reserve bank account, which is required to be maintained in an amount equivalent to the net credit balance, pursuant to the Rule 15c3-3 computation, attributable to a firm's customers. Similarly, CFTC Regulations 1.20 and 30.7 require segregation of commodity futures or commodity option customer funds. Such funds may be deposited in a bank account (or with a clearing organization or another FCM). The auditor should determine that the special account is subject to a written agreement that, in the event of liquidation, the balance is to be used solely to satisfy customers' claims.

Deposits with Clearing Organizations

Clearing organizations function as adjuncts to securities exchanges to facilitate the settlement of transactions; their growth has enhanced the ability of broker-dealers to process increasing numbers of transactions. Examples of clearing organizations are the National Securities Clearing Corporation, which clears transactions executed on the New York and American stock exchanges; the Stock Clearing Corporation of Philadelphia, which serves as an adjunct to the Philadelphia Stock Exchange; and the Options Clearing Corporation, which clears all listed options transactions.

Clearing organizations net individual transactions in the same security to arrive at one position for each security to be delivered or received between a clearing organization and a firm, and one net monetary balance to be received or paid. Money is received or paid daily, and the monetary balance in each firm's account typically equals the contract value, which approximates the market value, of all its open positions. These receivables from and payables to clearing organizations are typically reconciled daily. The reconciliations are key control procedures and thus are usually tested by the auditor to obtain evidence that they are operating effectively throughout the year and that any unreconciled items are appropriately disposed of at year-end.

Deposits with clearing organizations are receivables for advances made to secure open positions at the clearing organizations. Deposits may be made in cash or securities. (The types of securities suitable for this purpose are defined by each clearing organization and generally comprise U.S. Treasury bills.) The auditor usually confirms deposits with clearing organizations as to type and amount. If securities are on deposit, their market values should be substantiated by reference to independent pricing sources.

Deposits with the clearing organizations of regulated futures exchanges differ from those with securities exchanges. Futures transactions represent legally binding contracts between a firm or its customers (as either buyer or seller) and a futures exchange clearing organization. Such contracts obligate the trading parties to buy or sell a standardized quantity of a commodity at a specific future date and price. Since the clearing organization guarantees performance on the contract, it requires a margin deposit. Margin rates vary based on the specific commodity traded. On the date the transaction is entered into, the clearing organization requires an initial margin deposit, and the contract is marked to market daily, with any difference resulting in a variation margin payable or receivable. All margin amounts are determined at the close of the applicable exchange's business day and are settled on the following day.

Deposits made with clearing organizations of regulated futures exchanges may consist of cash, certain obligations of the U.S. government, or letters of credit, as determined by the various exchanges. These deposits are segregated between customers' and firm deposits and are accounted for separately. Auditing procedures should include tests of the separate identification of customers' and firm margin amounts.

Receivables from Broker-Dealers

Receivable balances consist of open trades with other firms, including receivables attributable to fails to deliver, floor brokerage fees receivable, and receivables from clearing organizations. Fails to deliver result from sales of securities (either as principal or as agent on behalf of customers) to another broker-dealer in which the selling broker-dealer cannot deliver the securities to the buying broker-dealer by the settlement date. These transactions appear as long positions on the stock record and as receivables in the general ledger stated at the contract amount.

Auditing procedures for fail-to-deliver balances should include confirmation with the other parties to the transactions. Additionally, the auditor should review the aging of these balances and the relationships of monetary balances to market values of securities. This review should be directed toward determining a firm's compliance with regulatory requirements for the delivery of these items, as well as toward identifying potential collectibility problems. The auditor may wish to review the subsequent collection of these balances.

Transactions for exchange-listed securities are executed on the floors of the various exchanges by floor brokers. As a general rule, firms are entitled to floor brokerage representation by virtue of their ownership of stock exchange seats. Some firms execute transactions as floor brokers for other firms that either do not have floor brokerage facilities or have difficulty executing trades during peak-volume periods. Firms performing this service charge a floor brokerage fee for each transaction executed.

Normally, the auditor confirms floor brokerage fee balances with the firms from which they are receivable. In addition, the auditor should review the aging of the receivables and, in certain circumstances, examine subsequent collections.

FCMs deal directly with the clearing organizations of futures exchanges when buying or selling regulated commodities. When dealing in nonregulated commodities, such as forward contracts, FCMs deal directly with other counterparties. A forward contract is a transaction that will settle on a specified later date and at a specific price; however, unlike futures contracts, for which quantity and delivery date are fixed by a futures exchange, the quantity and delivery date of forward contracts are negotiated by the contracting parties. In addition, forward contracts, unlike futures contracts, do not usually require margin payments, nor are they guaranteed by a clearing organization; therefore, settlement of these transactions depends on the creditworthiness of the counterparties. FCMs measure gain or loss on these transactions daily by comparing the current day's value of the forward contract with the amount specified in the contract. If the current day's value is different from the contract value, the difference is generally recorded as an unrealized gain or loss, and as a receivable or payable, as appropriate.

Receivables from or payables to FCMs associated with forward contracts, as well as the existence and terms of the forward contracts, may be confirmed with the counterparties. Since confirming these transactions can sometimes be difficult, the auditor should consider procedures such as reviewing settlement of open forward contracts subsequent to year-end. In addition, the auditor should test the FCM's methodology for the daily valuation of forward contracts, which could involve complex calculations and the exercise of judgment. Furthermore, the auditor should understand the client's procedure for assessing the financial viability of the counterparty to determine whether collectibility appears to be a concern.

Receivables from clearing organizations represent the net amount by which securities that a firm fails to deliver exceed its fail-to-receive positions. These balances should be confirmed with the clearing organizations.

Deposits for Securities Borrowed

Deposits for securities borrowed represent amounts paid by a firm to lending brokers for securities that the firm has borrowed; the deposits are collateralized by the borrowed securities. Generally, the market value of the borrowed securities approximates the cash given to the lending brokers. The securities borrowed should be marked to market daily on an individual-security basis. If the value of the borrowed securities declines, the firm should request additional securities as collateral. If the value of the securities increases, the firm may be required by the lender to increase the cash deposit to equal the agreed-on relationship of cash to the value of securities.

The auditor should normally substantiate these deposits and the related collateral by direct confirmation with the lending firms. Furthermore, the auditor should review the relationships of monetary balances to the values of securities to determine whether any material discrepancies exist. The auditor should also determine that the appropriate capital charge is taken in accordance with Rules 15c3-1 and 15c3-3.

Receivables from Customers

Receivables from customers comprise debit balances in customers' accounts, which the AICPA broker-dealer audit guide defines as including "all accounts resulting from normal securities and commodities transactions other than with other broker-dealers or with persons whose securities or funds either are part of the net capital of the broker-dealer or are subordinated to claims of general creditors." Receivables from customers may include receivables from a firm's employees but may not include balances owed by partners, officers, directors, stockholders, or certain other "noncustomers" as defined by the regulators.

Customers' debit balances arise from the purchase of securities, either in a cash account or on margin, for which the firm has not been fully paid. These receivables are collateralized by the customers' securities held by the firm, which may be used by the firm to obtain financing. In purchases of commodities, customers' debit balances arise when an initial or variation margin deposit is due. These receivables are usually satisfied within one or two business days. Generally, the margin requirements of an FCM are in excess of the requirements of the applicable exchange. The use of the FCMs' margin requirements, and daily variation margin calls, allows FCMs to reduce their risk with respect to commodity customers' debit balances. The auditor should confirm customers' account balances and securities and commodities positions. Consideration should also be given to confirming accounts closed during the year and accounts with zero balances.

The relationships between debit balances and the value of securities in each account should be reviewed. (For example, based on regulations in effect at the time of this writing, the value of securities in margin accounts should approximate a minimum of 140 percent of the related debit balances, and normally there should not be any significant unsecured debits or short securities positions, or accounts that are not fully secured.) Based on this review, the auditor should assess the reasonableness of the firm's allowance for uncollectible accounts and ascertain the impact of any doubtful accounts on the capital computation under SEC Rule 15c3-1 and on the reserve computation pursuant to SEC Rule 15c3-3. The auditor should evaluate the firm's procedures to ensure the adequacy of margin in customers' accounts and the issuance of calls for additional margin and should review the firm's procedures for compliance with Regulation T of the Board of Governors of the Federal Reserve System. Computerized audit techniques may facilitate these reviews.

Securities Purchased Under Agreements to Resell

Securities purchased under agreements to resell (reverse repo agreements) represent receivables for funds that have been loaned by the firm and generally are collateralized by government securities or by various forms of commercial paper. The auditor should confirm these balances, the terms of the agreements, and the related collateral (including its location). In addition, the relationships between the receivables and the underlying collateral should be reviewed to assess collectibility of the receivables and determine the capital charges required.

In examining these balances, the auditor should be cognizant of the credit risks associated with the related transactions and should determine that the broker-dealer is diligent in obtaining the necessary collateral. In addition, for reverse repo agreements that are matched with repo agreements, the auditor should ascertain whether any exposure exists with respect to repo agreements that expire before the maturities of the related reverse repo agreements, in which case the auditor should also determine the broker-dealer's ability to refinance these positions.

Firm Inventory Accounts

Firm inventory accounts include securities that are owned by the firm; they are classified as either trading or investment accounts. Trading accounts contain securities purchased for resale to customers or other brokers and are a firm's stock-in-trade. Investment securities are intended to be held for longer periods than are securities in trading accounts and are purchased with the expectation of capital gain.[12]

For financial statement purposes, firm inventory accounts should be classified into marketable securities and securities that are not readily marketable. Securities in firm inventory accounts are valued at current market value for financial statement purposes. Unrealized appreciation and depreciation in values are included in determining net income; as a result, deferred taxes should be computed if appropriate. The auditor should reconcile the securities in the firm investment accounts to the stock record. In addition, the market values of the securities should be substantiated by reference to financial journals or other independent sources. On larger engagements, ordinarily this is performed using computer software programs that compare price tapes obtained from independent sources with those used by the client. The capital charges (haircuts) taken for securities positions in firm inventory pursuant to the requirements of SEC Rule 15c3-1 should also be reviewed.

Market values may not be available for all securities positions. For example, market quotations for some bonds issued by municipalities are not readily available. For those bonds, values are determined by management, based on various factors such as the rating of the bond, its coupon rate, the prime lending rate, unique redemption provisions of the bond, and its maturity date. In addition, firms may hold other securities for which there are no quoted market prices. These may include securities purchased in a merchant banking transaction that cannot be sold or offered because of a restriction or that are pending registration pursuant to the Securities Act of 1933. In these instances, management of the broker-dealer should value the securities based on the earnings records of the companies in conjunction with other factors, such as book values, yields, and current market conditions.

In evaluating the market value assigned a security, the auditor should consider the liquidity of the security. For example, the market value of a thinly traded or restricted security may not necessarily be its closing price on an exchange. The auditor should review the information considered by management and ascertain that the procedures followed are reasonable in the circumstances. Although the auditor may determine that the underlying documentation supports the fair-value estimates, he or she may conclude that because the range of possible values is significant, the opinion should be modified. The modification would relate to an adjustment that might have been required if a ready market value existed. If the auditor is unable to obtain reasonable assurance as to the market values of securities, the opinion on the financial statements may have to be appropriately qualified.

Firm inventory trading accounts also include spot commodities, that is, physical commodity, futures, and forward contracts, and options owned by the

---

[12]The distinction between trading account securities and investment account securities that is made for accounting purposes is not necessarily the same as that made for tax purposes. Reference should be made to the appropriate tax regulations for the tax aspects of that distinction.

firm. Commodities, like securities, are valued at current market value for financial statement purposes. While the auditor, by reference to financial journals, can substantiate market values for spot commodities and futures contracts that are traded on exchanges, market values of forward contracts and options (and nonregulated spot commodities and futures contracts) are determined by FCMs using often-complex calculations. Such calculations, which will involve a certain degree of subjectivity, consider factors such as current interest rates, period of time until settlement, volatility, transportation costs with respect to commodities purchased in foreign markets, and closing time of foreign markets. The FCM attempts to determine what the commodity would be worth in the normal course of business at the FCM's location. The auditor should review the FCM's assumptions and substantiate the calculation, or use a recognized pricing model to review the FCM's calculation. The capital charges for commodities are described in CFTC Regulation 1.17(c)(5)(ii).

Memberships in Exchanges

Exchange memberships are either owned by the broker-dealer or contributed to the firm under a subordinated lending agreement. The carrying value of exchange memberships for financial statement purposes is cost. Generally, a valuation reserve is not established unless a reduction in market value is considered to be other than temporary.

The ownership of exchange memberships and their current market values (usually the last price of a membership sold) may be confirmed directly with the exchanges. The AICPA broker-dealer audit guide states that the propriety of considering exchange memberships as assets of the broker-dealer should be evaluated by reference to partnership agreements or other documents.

Bank Loans

Bank loans are obtained by securities firms as a means of financing customer and firm positions. Loan balances, as well as the related collateral, should be confirmed with banks. If formal lending arrangements exist, such as those made for compensating balances and commitment fees, the auditor should confirm those arrangements. In addition, the collateral (customer or firm securities) should be reviewed to determine the firm's compliance with SEC Rule 15c3-3 and Regulation U of the Board of Governors of the Federal Reserve System.

Payables to Broker-Dealers and Clearing Organizations

Items in this category include payables arising from fails to receive and net payables to clearing organizations. A fail to receive results from a purchase of securities (either as principal or as agent on behalf of customers) from another broker-dealer in which the securities are not received from the selling broker-dealer by the settlement date. A firm has exposure with respect to a fail to receive if the market value of the securities increases and the delivering broker-dealer does not deliver them. At this point, a firm may have to purchase the securities in the marketplace, and a loss will be recognized in the amount of the appreciation on the securities.

These balances should be confirmed with the other broker-dealers. The auditor should also review the aging of the fails to receive and the relationship of market value of the securities to the monetary balance contract value of each fail.

For FCMs, payables to broker-dealers relate primarily to a mark to market on forward contracts. The auditor should be aware that this amount represents the FCM's market risk with respect to the forward contracts based on the current value of the commodity versus the forward contract prices. The auditor should confirm the existence and terms of the forward contracts with the counterparty, and review the calculation of the mark to market on the contracts and the creditworthiness of the counterparty.

Payables to clearing organizations represent net amounts due for securities that a firm fails to receive in excess of its fail-to-deliver positions. Payables to clearing organizations for commodities represent the amount due for the day's change in margin requirements resulting from a mark-to-market loss on the underlying futures contract. These balances are confirmed with the clearing organizations. Additionally, if appropriate, the auditor should review the aging of the individual positions and the relationship of market value of the securities to the monetary balance or contract value of each fail.

Securities Sold Under Agreements to Repurchase

The auditor should confirm balances related to financing transactions involving repo agreements as well as the terms of the agreements and the related collateral and should focus on the relationship of the payables to the collateral received by the firm. The auditor should also determine that there are adequate procedures for ensuring that appropriate collateral is obtained for these positions.

Payables to Customers

Payables to customers comprise credit balances in securities customers' accounts that are owed in connection with sales of securities, or open trade equity and securities or other collateral on deposit for commodities customers' accounts. These balances are audited as part of the customer account confirmation process.

Securities Sold But Not Yet Purchased

These generally consist of securities that a firm sold but did not have in its inventory, securities sold that are "covered" by call options, and securities that are arbitraged against proprietary long positions.

A firm sells securities short to take advantage of anticipated market declines; eventually it must purchase these securities. If their value increases, the firm incurs a loss equal to the difference between the amount paid for the securities and the amount previously received on sale. In auditing short securities positions, common audit tests would be testing the market value of the security and agreeing the position to the stock record.

Hedging short securities positions with call options is a trading strategy utilized by many firms. In its most basic form, it is used by a firm in an attempt to protect itself from price increases by fixing the price at which it will be able to buy the securities through exercise of the call options. In reviewing these positions, the auditor should ascertain the exercise price of the option relative to the market value of the short securities. In addition, the auditor should determine that the options have not expired. In recent years, many complex trading strategies involving options have gained wide acceptance. In applying auditing procedures in this area, the auditor should obtain an understanding of the transactions, evaluate the risk to the firm, and determine that the firm has given appropriate recognition to regulatory considerations, especially the charges that enter into the computation of net capital under SEC Rule 15c3-1.

Arbitrage Transactions

Securities firms may engage in riskless arbitrage and risk arbitrage transactions. In riskless arbitrage transactions, the investor purchases and sells similar securities in a like market. Convertible and when-issued securities are the principal trading instruments in this form of transaction. In risk arbitrage transactions (described earlier), the firm invests in securities that are generally the subject of mergers or tender offers. The auditor should understand the nature and purpose of arbitrage transactions entered into by the client. In addition, the auditor should determine that the appropriate haircut is taken pursuant to Rule 15c3-1.

Commodities firms can also engage in a type of arbitrage transaction. In such commodity transactions, the FCM or customer purchases one commodity contract and concurrently sells another contract for the same commodity. These types of transactions have increased through global trading of commodities as traders seek price variations in the same commodity on a global basis. For example, an FCM can purchase a forward contract for gold in London and sell a gold futures contract for a like amount on the Commodity Exchange in New York.

Subordinated Liabilities

Subordinated liabilities are borrowings, pursuant to formal lending agreements, that are subordinated to the claims of general creditors. Typically, a subordinated lender provides cash in return for the firm's formal agreement to pay a stipulated interest rate. A subordinated agreement could also take the form of a secured demand note, under which the lender provides the firm with securities or other collateral that may be used by the firm to borrow funds to finance operations. In a secured demand note transaction, the firm records a receivable for the amount of the subordinated loan, which should be less than the value of the securities that serve as collateral. The auditor must ascertain whether subordination agreements have been approved by the appropriate regulatory bodies, whether the balances of the liabilities are stated fairly, and whether the value of the related collateral is accurately computed. This may be confirmed directly. The AICPA broker-dealer audit guide states that the auditor should confirm as well the expiration dates of the agreements, the extent of the amount subordinated, any limit as to that amount, and the exact nature of the liability to the subordinating party.

For financial statement purposes, subordinated debt may be included with capital as long as the total amount is appropriately captioned total subordinated liabilities and stockholders' equity or partners' or sole proprietor's capital, as appropriate.

Securities Positions

The auditor should review the stock record to determine that all positions, both long and short, are audited appropriately. For example, the auditor should determine that securities related to fails to receive or fails to deliver are confirmed in connection with the fail confirmations, that securities at clearing organizations and depositories are confirmed, that securities positions attributable to customers are confirmed in connection with the audit of customers' accounts, and that securities held in the firm's custody are counted. In addition, the auditor should review the mathematical accuracy of the stock record and ensure that any out-of-balance conditions are appropriately resolved.

Pursuant to Rule 17a-5, the auditor should determine that the firm has complied with all other provisions of SEC Rule 17a-13. Specifically, on a quarterly basis, the firm is required to count or confirm all securities positions in its possession or control. These are generally considered to be securities in the broker-dealer's vault, securities at custodians or depositories, fails to deliver, stock loans, and securities in transfer. Accordingly, it is customary to count securities in the physical possession of the broker-dealer or observe and test the count performed by the broker-dealer's personnel. In the latter instance, the auditor should ensure that the broker-dealer's procedures result in a complete and accurate count. In addition, the auditor should perform some independent test counts.

The auditor should ensure that all securities are counted, including those for which the broker-dealer exercises custodial and fiduciary responsibility. In that regard, customers may leave their fully paid securities with the broker-dealer to be held on their behalf. Those securities may be in the names of the individual customers or in the broker-dealer's "street name" (i.e., the name of a nominee of a broker-dealer). Typically, securities registered in customers' names would be located in areas of the broker-dealer's stock record identified as "safekeeping." Customers' fully paid securities registered in the street name would typically be at a depository and would be identified in the stock record in a location designated as "free." Such designation indicates that the securities have not been pledged as collateral for a bank loan.

The auditor should evaluate the procedures for recording and summarizing count differences and determine that those differences are appropriately resolved. The auditor should also determine the cause and disposition of unresolved differences and their impact on the financial statements and other regulatory reports.

SEC Rule 17a-13 requires that broker-dealers perform quarterly securities counts or employ cycle count procedures that result in every security position being counted at least once every quarter. This rule also requires that the employees who perform the counts not have other responsibilities involving the physical handling of securities.

For purposes of determining the adequacy of the control structure pursuant to the requirements of Rule 17a-5, the auditor should review and observe count and confirmation procedures of the broker-dealer to ascertain that they have been performed in accordance with Rule 17a-13 and that differences have been appropriately recorded and resolved. The observation of the broker-dealer's count can be made either at interim or at year-end, depending on the auditor's assessment of control risk. Also, as part of auditing the securities positions, the auditor should determine the nature and value of securities held by transfer agents, securities in transit, and securities held at branch offices. Appropriate tests should be performed based on the materiality of those securities in relation to the financial statements of the firm and on the control structure policies and procedures applied to them.

FCMs maintain a physical commodity inventory similar to a stock record. Generally, physical commodities are represented by warehouse receipts, which are negotiable instruments. These warehouse receipts, which may be held in an FCM's vault or by a custodian, are numbered and state the commodity type and quantity. The inventory record should include this information from each warehouse receipt and indicate the location of the warehouse receipt and ownership (firm or customer) of the physical commodity. In testing the accuracy of the inventory record, the auditor should examine the warehouse receipts in the FCM's possession and confirm those held by custodians.

In addition to a physical commodity inventory, FCMs prepare a "point balance," which is a listing by commodity type of all open futures contracts. This report shows the contract price, the current market value, and the gain or loss caused by the difference. This difference should be the balance of the amounts due from, or to, the respective futures exchange clearing organization. While the CFTC requires this report monthly, most FCMs prepare it daily to facilitate their reconciliations with clearing organizations.

Omnibus Accounts

Broker-dealers may perform clearing functions for other firms, such as processing trade information, comparing executed transactions with records of other broker-dealers and clearing organizations, and accounting for open positions with other broker-dealers and clearing organizations. The net effect of all transactions with clearing organizations and other broker-dealers is contained in an "omnibus account" of the introducing broker-dealer. If the clearing organization clears transactions on behalf of the introducing firm on a "fully disclosed basis," the introducing broker-dealer's customers' accounts are recorded by the clearing firm. The clearing firm treats those accounts as if they were its own accounts and is responsible for ensuring that they are collateralized and maintained in compliance with the appropriate regulatory requirements.

In auditing an introducing broker-dealer, the auditor should confirm balances in the omnibus account and should review the clearing agreement and evaluate the firm's procedures for ascertaining the clearing firm's compliance with the clearing agreement (e.g., the procedures for substantiating clearing fees). In addition, the auditor should assess, by reference to the clearing agreement, any risks or exposure assumed by the introducing broker-dealer with respect to executed transactions or open positions maintained by the clearing firm on the introducing broker-dealer's behalf.

In auditing a clearing firm, the auditor should confirm the balance in the omnibus account and assess the firm's procedures for ensuring compliance with the clearing agreement. The open positions with other broker-dealers, clearing organizations, and customers' accounts should be substantiated in connection with the previously described auditing procedures applicable to those accounts.

Suspense and Error Accounts

The auditor should determine the composition of securities and cash balances in suspense accounts. Generally, suspense items are attributable to transactions that cannot be readily identified as to the appropriate customer, broker-dealer, or firm account. Thus they are "suspensed" until the necessary research is performed to determine their disposition. As a rule, balances should remain in suspense accounts for only a short time.

In reviewing suspense balances, the auditor should determine their appropriate resolution and their impact on the financial statements and on other auditing procedures. For example, balances in suspense accounts that are resolved against customers' accounts may, if material, cause the auditor to amend the confirmations sent to customers. The auditor should also review the broker-dealer's procedures for the timely resolution of suspense balances and determine their impact on SEC Rule 15c3-1 and Rule 15c3-3 computations.

Error accounts contain cash or securities balances, as well as profit and loss amounts, that are attributable to errors on the part of a broker-dealer, usually in processing orders on behalf of the firm or its customers. For example, if as the result of an incorrectly prepared order ticket, 100 shares of ABC Company are purchased on behalf of a customer instead of 100 shares of XYZ Company, the ABC shares would be placed into an error account until they are sold. Any profit or loss realized on the subsequent sale, as well as any profit or loss incurred in connection with the purchase of the XYZ shares, would also be placed into the appropriate "error" profit and loss account. (In many firms, securities positions attributable to errors are recorded in the proprietary trading accounts and the profit or loss resulting from the liquidation of those positions is included as trading profit or loss.)

The auditor should ascertain the extent of control procedures for error accounts as a basis for determining the nature, timing, and extent of auditing procedures. The auditor should also determine that management performs sufficient review and follow-up procedures to ensure that appropriate corrective action is taken on a timely basis.

Dividends Receivable or Payable

Cash or stock dividends receivable should be reviewed as to completeness and as to age and collectibility. The auditor should review the broker-dealer's procedures for recording dividends payable. Based on this review, the materiality of the individual balances, and the assessment of control risk, the auditor may decide to test the accuracy of recording these balances.

Many firms record dividends receivable and payable on the payable date rather than on the record date. The auditor should review the amount of dividends receivable and payable attributable to record dates and payable dates that straddle the balance sheet date to ascertain the materiality of those amounts and should consider their impact on the financial statements. The auditor should also review procedures for recording unclaimed dividends to ascertain the broker-dealer's compliance with the pertinent state escheat laws.

Supplementary Information Under Rule 17a-5

The auditor should perform auditing procedures with respect to the computation of net capital under SEC Rule 15c3-1, the computation of reserve requirements pursuant to Rule 15c3-3, and the information relating to possession or control requirements under Rule 15c3-3, all prepared as of the date of the financial statements. Those procedures may include reperforming the calculations, reasonableness tests, and analytical procedures directed at significant items in the determination of the various computations. The nature, timing, and extent of those auditing procedures should be based largely on the auditor's assessment of control risk. Furthermore, in applying auditing procedures to these schedules, the auditor should consider that such information is not a basic part of the financial statements prepared in conformity with GAAP, but is supplementary information required by Rule 17a-5, and that the schedules must be considered in relation to the basic financial statements taken as a whole.

Underwriting Agreements

The auditor should review underwriting agreements to ascertain the terms and amounts of open contractual commitments and should confirm them with the issuers of the securities. In measuring the amounts of those commitments, the auditor should determine the underwriter's liability for unsold positions. That liability may be either divided—meaning that each participant in the underwriting syndicate is responsible for purchasing a specified maximum number of shares of stock or principal amount of bonds—or undivided—in which case each participant is liable for a designated percentage of unsold securities. The auditor should also confirm when-issued transactions with the customers that committed to purchase those securities. If the amounts are material, the broker-dealer should consider the need to disclose those transactions in a note to the financial statements. The auditor may also review the subsequent settlement of those transactions.

With respect to private-placement transactions, the auditor should review with management the agreements between the broker-dealer and the companies issuing the securities to ascertain whether the broker-dealer has any obligations that require disclosure in the financial statements.

Generally, good-faith deposits are required in connection with the purchase of new issues of securities. When a firm acts on behalf of a syndicate, each member's share of the good-faith deposit is given to the manager. As part of the audit of the managing underwriter, the good-faith deposit may be confirmed with the issuer, and the liability for participants' deposits may be confirmed with the participants. In auditing a participant, the auditor may confirm the good-faith deposit with the managing underwriter. The auditor should review the aging of good-faith deposits to ascertain that the appropriate capital deductions have been taken pursuant to Rule 15c3-1.

There is customarily a lag between the time an underwriting is completed and the time all expenses are accounted for and the profit or loss allocable to the participants is distributed. In an attempt to expedite this settlement process, Rule 15c3-1 imposes capital charges for receivables relating to underwritings. In applying substantive procedures to those balances, the auditor should focus particularly on any unusually old balances. In auditing the accounts of the managing underwriter, the auditor should consider the adequacy of procedures for recording revenues and expenses pertaining to these items, including necessary accruals. In an audit of a participant in an underwriting, the auditor should review agings of receivables and, as appropriate, examine subsequent collections. Also, the auditor should review the receivable balances in light of Rule 15c3-1 to ascertain that the appropriate capital deductions have been taken.

To obtain additional assurance as to the completeness and accuracy of the client's records of underwriting commitments, the auditor may review for a selected period the "tombstone" advertisements that appear in newspapers and financial journals announcing the offering of securities. The auditor's purpose in this review is to determine that the broker-dealer has recorded the commitments pertaining to the offerings in which its name appears as manager or participant. Tombstone advertisements, however, are not necessarily published for each underwriting.

As part of the evaluation of litigation, the auditor should ascertain the existence of any lawsuits or pending claims resulting from underwriting activities and determine their impact on the financial statements. Specifically, the auditor should determine whether the participants in an underwriting syndicate are jointly or severally liable for legal claims arising in connection with the underwriting. If the participants are severally liable, each participant is liable only to the extent that claims relate to its portion of the securities underwritten. If the participants are jointly liable, each participant is responsible for all claims to the extent that they are not satisfied by the other participants of the syndicate.

In addition to their underwriting activities, many firms provide corporate finance services in which they advise businesses in connection with mergers and acquisitions and with corporate reorganizations, assist in tender offers for securities, and provide various types of investment advisory services. The auditor should review the receivables resulting from fees attributable to those activities and apply appropriate substantive procedures, such as confirming the balances or examining underlying agreements, letters of arrangement, and so forth; reviewing the aging and subsequent collection of the balances; and ascertaining that income as well as any related expenses are recorded in the proper accounting period.

Effects of EDP on the Audit

During the early to mid-1980s, two major developments influenced the role of EDP in the audit of securities and commodities broker-dealers. Many financial services firms began undertaking major software development projects. These efforts were precipitated by the realization on the part of many securities and commodities firms that their EDP operations had become outdated and were only marginally capable of handling current and anticipated increases in transaction volumes, new types of financial instruments, and the acquisition of other firms. The new, state-of-the-art systems are designed to respond to those needs and are easier to maintain and enhance.

The other major development was a renewed awareness of the importance of exercising control over EDP operations. In determining the audit testing plan and performing auditing procedures, the auditor should take maximum advantage of the client's control structure policies and procedures. An effective control structure, including user control procedures, can enable the auditor to reduce substantive tests considerably. That strategy depends to a large extent on the adequacy of general control procedures, that is, procedures that are applied within a firm's data center. (See the discussion of general control procedures in Chapter 11.)

The use of sophisticated audit software designed to assist in performing audit tests has expanded greatly. Auditing firms have developed programs for confirming customers' accounts and balances held by other broker-dealers, preparing account listings, testing compliance with regulations (e.g., requirements for margining of customers' accounts), testing market valuations used by firms, and performing allocations pursuant to Rule 15c3-1. Properly utilized, these software packages can contribute significantly to audit efficiency.

40

Auditing State and Local Governmental Entities

OVERVIEW OF THE STATE AND LOCAL GOVERNMENTAL ENVIRONMENT

State and local governmental accounting and auditing are in a period of significant change. A new accounting standard-setting body, swiftly changing governmental accounting principles, and new federally mandated auditing requirements and standards testify to the extensiveness and rapidity of that change. Increasing numbers of governmental units are preparing financial statements in conformity with generally accepted accounting principles (GAAP) and having them audited in accordance with generally accepted auditing standards (GAAS). The expanding use of financing vehicles by port, housing, development, and transportation authorities and similar entities has also broadened the field of governmental accounting and auditing. Increasing attention has been focused on the appropriate spending of federal funds and on the auditor's role in preventing the misappropriation of taxpayers' dollars. Because of this, standards covering financial reporting, disclosure, and testing have become more uniform throughout the industry.

Users of governmental financial statements are different from and represent a more diverse range of interests than users of a business entity's financial statements. In addition to investors, labor organizations, oversight agencies, policy makers, and operating management—all of which have counterparts in the commercial environment—governmental entities also provide information to senior levels of government (for such purposes as grant compliance or data analysis) and, most important, their constituencies, which are most directly affected by decisions about obtaining and using resources. The needs of this wide variety of users differ. Holders of bonds are interested in fiscal performance and soundness of financial condition. Resource providers, whether taxpayers, other governmental entities, or legislatures, wish to ensure that the governmental unit is expending those resources efficiently and in the manner prescribed by law. The objectives of bondholders and constituents may conflict; for example, a large fund balance is desirable to bondholders but not to constituents. Management of a governmental entity must strike a balance between the objectives of the two groups.

A characteristic of the governmental environment of particular significance to the auditor is the greatly increased number of regulations that govern expenditures at all levels. Probably the most pervasive regulations are those embodied in a governmental entity's budgetary system; budgets that set revenue and expenditure levels have a greater effect on the operations of governments than budgets do in most other organizations. In addition, a network of regulations is embodied in laws that must be complied with by department, program, or grant administrators at a particular level of government or at lower levels. Thus, a department cannot overspend its budget, and its expenditures must meet the requirements of contracts, awards, laws, and regulations that govern the allowability of costs charged to specific contracts or programs.

Auditing guidelines and regulations established by federal, state, and local governments do not supersede generally accepted auditing standards, but may prescribe additional requirements with which the auditor should comply.

Generally accepted governmental auditing standards (GAGAS) for federally assisted programs are set forth in *Standards for Audit of Governmental Organizations, Programs, Activities, and Functions*, popularly referred to as the "Yellow Book," first published by the U.S. General Accounting Office (GAO) in 1972 and most recently revised in 1988. The AICPA has provided guidance to the auditor in its 1986 audit guide, *Audits of State and Local Governmental Units* (ASLGU), as amended by Statement of Position 89-6, which presents examples of auditors' reports. In addition, when auditing a state or local governmental unit that receives federal financial assistance, the auditor must comply with the requirements of the Single Audit Act of 1984 (the Act) as described in Circular A-128, "Audits of State and Local Governments," issued by the U.S. Office of Management and Budget (OMB). In 1989, the AICPA issued Statement on Auditing Standards (SAS) No. 63, *Compliance Auditing Applicable to Governmental Entities and Other Recipients of Governmental Financial Assistance*, which explains the relationship among generally accepted auditing standards (GAAS), the Yellow Book, and the Act. Compliance auditing is the topic of Chapter 25 of this book.

GOVERNMENTAL ACCOUNTING AND REPORTING PRINCIPLES

Governmental accounting principles and reporting practices are unique in several respects and reflect the fundamental differences between commercial enterprises and governmental units.

Fund Accounting

The most notable distinction between governmental and commercial accounting is the concept of fund accounting and the presentation of financial statements by fund types. In the governmental environment, the entity being audited is not viewed as an integrated accounting unit; instead, each of the individual fund types encompassed by the entity is considered and shown (although not necessarily reported on) separately. Transactions involving more than one fund should be recorded using interfund receivable and payable accounts. Fund accounting is used by governments as a means of controlling and accounting for various types of restricted resources and related expenditures.

The three broad types of funds typically found in governmental accounting systems are governmental, in which the primary concern is accounting for service delivery and demonstrating compliance with resource restrictions; proprietary, in which the concern is cost recovery (through user charges or fees) or cost determination for specific activities; and fiduciary, which account for assets held by a government as trustee or agent. These types of funds have been further subdivided and defined by the Governmental Accounting Standards Board (GASB).

Governmental Funds. Governmental funds and their purposes are as follows:

General Fund—Accounts for all financial resources except those required to be accounted for in another fund.

Special Revenue Funds—Account for the proceeds of specific revenue sources (other than special assessments, expendable trusts, or major capital projects) that are legally restricted to expenditures for specified purposes.

Capital Project Funds—Account for financial resources to be used for the acquisition or construction of major capital facilities (other than those financed by proprietary funds and fiduciary funds).

Debt Service Funds—Account for the accumulation of resources for and payment of general long-term debt principal and interest.

Proprietary Funds. The two kinds of proprietary funds are

Enterprise Funds—Account for operations that are financed and managed in a manner similar to private business enterprises. The governing body may have decided that the costs (including depreciation) of providing goods or services to the general public on a continuing basis should be financed or recovered primarily through user charges, or that periodic determination of revenues earned, expenses incurred, and net income is appropriate for capital maintenance, public policy, management information, accountability, or other purposes.

Internal Service Funds—Account for financing of goods or services provided by one department or agency to other departments or agencies of a governmental unit or to other governmental units on a cost-reimbursement basis.

Fiduciary Funds. Also called trust and agency funds, fiduciary funds account for assets held by a governmental unit in a trustee capacity or as agent for individuals, private organizations, other governmental units, or other funds. Fiduciary funds include expendable trust funds, nonexpendable trust funds, pension trust funds, and agency funds.

Account Groups. In addition to the three fund types, there are two account groups that are used to establish accountability over fixed assets and long-term obligations. The general fixed assets account group reflects a governmental unit's fixed assets, except those used in enterprise or internal service fund activities and therefore recorded in those proprietary funds. Historically, governments have not recorded "infrastructure" assets such as streets, sidewalks, bridges, and storm drains on the theory that they were immovable and not subject to theft. There is a growing trend, however, to record these items both for better accountability and for more accurate service cost information. Similarly, depreciation on these assets normally is not recorded, but increasing concern over the deterioration of the nation's infrastructure has prompted renewed interest in doing so. Such records would be helpful, for example, in ensuring accountability and in developing indirect cost systems. A government's policy for recording fixed assets and related accounts should be disclosed.

Originally the general long-term debt account group was established to account for all governmental debt not carried as a liability of another fund. Its use has expanded to include other noncurrent liabilities, such as lease commitments, claims and judgments, and compensated absences.

Modified Accrual Basis Accounting

Another distinguishing characteristic of governmental accounting is the use of a modified accrual basis of accounting for reporting purposes. For governmental funds and expendable trust funds, the accrual basis of accounting is modified to focus on a measurement of financial flows, that is, to show the increase or decrease in net current financial resources. Revenues and other financial resources (such as bond proceeds) are recognized in the accounting period in which they become available and measurable. Expenditures are recognized on the accrual basis, except for

- Unmatured principal and interest on general long-term debt.
- Inventory, which is usually recorded as an expenditure when purchased.
- Prepaid items, such as insurance, which are usually recorded as an expenditure when paid.
- Capital outlay items, which are expenditures of the acquiring fund.

In August 1989, the GASB issued a revised exposure draft entitled *Measurement Focus and Basis of Accounting—Governmental Fund Operating Statements*, which proposes the use of the full accrual basis for all financial resources (current and noncurrent). If adopted, it will radically change many of the revenue and expenditure concepts described later in the chapter. Under present plans, it is expected to become effective in 1993, or thereafter, in conjunction with future GASB statements on pensions, capital reporting, financial reporting, risk financing, and compensated absences. The statement on financial reporting (not yet drafted) may radically change the balance sheet.

Encumbrances

Encumbrances are another unique aspect of governmental accounting. The GASB defines encumbrances as "commitments related to unperformed (executory) contracts for goods or services." Encumbrances should be recorded in governmental funds for which an annual budget has been adopted; their purpose is to aid in budgetary control and accountability, and they are also useful for cash planning. Encumbrances outstanding at year-end are neither expenditures nor liabilities. In some governmental units, budget appropriations lapse at year-end, while in other units they are carried forward. If appropriations are carried forward, outstanding encumbrances should be recorded by reserving part of the fund balance as a reserve for encumbrances. If appropriations lapse but the governmental unit intends to honor the commitments, outstanding encumbrances should be disclosed either by a reservation of the fund balance or in a note to the financial statements. The unit's policy as to appropriations and encumbrances should be disclosed in the accounting policy footnote.

Standard Setting for Governmental Accounting

In 1984 the GASB was established under the auspices of the Financial Accounting Foundation for the purpose of establishing accounting principles for state and local governmental units. Prior to that time the National Council on Governmental Accounting (NCGA) performed that function. One of the GASB's first actions was to address the then-current status of governmental accounting principles and to adopt certain of the NCGA statements and interpretations as part of generally accepted accounting principles for governmental entities. Those statements and interpretations as well as all GASB statements, interpretations, and technical bulletins are included in the GASB's 1987 *Codification of Governmental Accounting and Financial Reporting Standards*. The AICPA has designated the GASB as the body to establish financial accounting principles for state and local governmental entities under Rules 202 and 203 of the AICPA Code of Professional Conduct. Since its formation, the GASB has issued one concepts statement and ten accounting standards.

In the agreement that established the GASB, a hierarchy of generally accepted accounting principles applicable to state and local governments was specified in which GASB pronouncements take precedence over Financial Accounting Standards Board (FASB) pronouncements. The agreement also provided that, if the GASB had not issued a pronouncement on a particular matter, governmental entities were to be guided by FASB pronouncements. In 1989, this agreement was changed, placing FASB pronouncements issued since the formation of the GASB at a lower level; effectively, such FASB pronouncements do not need to be followed.

Financial Reporting

NCGA Statement No. 1 specifies that for fair presentation of financial position and results of operations in conformity with GAAP, a governmental unit should prepare and issue general-purpose financial statements (GPFS), consisting of

- Combined balance sheet—all fund types and account groups.
- Combined statement of revenues, expenditures, and changes in fund balances—all governmental fund types and expendable trust funds.
- Combined statement of revenues, expenditures, and changes in fund balances—budget and actual—general and special revenue fund types (and similar governmental funds for which annual budgets have been legally adopted).
- Combined statement of revenues, expenses, and changes in retained earnings/fund balances—all proprietary fund types and similar trust funds.
- Combined statement of changes in financial position—all proprietary fund types and similar trust funds.

The GASB also recommends that a governmental unit issue a comprehensive annual financial report (CAFR) containing an introductory section, a financial section, and a statistical section. The introductory section contains financial highlights and organizational information. The financial section consists of the financial statements listed above plus combining statements by fund type, individual fund and account group statements, detailed budgetary data, and schedules. The statistical section may indicate compliance with legal or contractual provisions, present historical trend data, or simply report in greater detail information presented elsewhere in the CAFR. The auditor should ensure that any financial data in the introductory and statistical sections is consistent with that in the financial section.

The auditor should be aware that defining the entity to be included in the GPFS and CAFR is not always straightforward. NCGA Statement No. 3, *Defining the Governmental Reporting Entity*, states that in identifying other agencies (such as housing authorities, utility systems, or school boards) that should be included as part of the governmental entity, the primary criterion is "the exercise of oversight responsibility over such agencies by the governmental unit's elected officials." That criterion causes the reporting entity to be defined broadly and results in the inclusion in the reporting entity's financial statements of governmental units that may be audited by auditors other than that of the reporting entity. This could result in financial statements in which all or the majority of the components of a fund type are not audited by the auditor who is expected to issue the opinion. The ASLGU provides guidance in this situation. At the time of this writing, the GASB has issued an exposure draft of a statement on the reporting entity, which is intended to clarify the determination of entities to be included and the manner of inclusion.

TRANSACTION CYCLES

Many governmental units use the cash basis of accounting throughout the year, with budgetary controls for expenditures, and adjust their accounting to the modified accrual basis at year-end for financial statement presentation purposes. By contrast, most commercial enterprises use the full accrual basis of accounting, which provides a degree of control over both revenues and expenditures by permitting analysis of interim financial statements as well as the timely comparison of control accounts with their supporting detail. Because of these differences in bookkeeping methods, the auditor of a governmental entity often devotes more attention to the flow of transactions than to the resulting balance sheet accounts. He or she must therefore have a thorough understanding of the transaction cycles and of the laws and regulations that govern the entity's transactions.

The Budget Cycle

A government's budget is a financial plan that contains the legal authority to spend money and incur liabilities. The budgetary process and the role that budgets play in governments differ from comparable considerations in business enterprises. Because a government's budget has the force of law once it has been adopted, it has great significance to both the governmental unit and the auditor. NCGA Statement No. 1 specifies that annual budgets should be adopted by every governmental unit (whether or not required by law or regulation), budgetary control should be provided through the accounting system, and budgetary comparisons should be included in the appropriate financial statements.

The annual budget should be established in accordance with applicable legal requirements, which might require, for example, holding public budget hearings, publishing the proposed or final budget, and approval of the budget by a higher level of government or the citizenry. The budget must conform to any applicable revenue and expenditure limitation laws or regulations; supplemental appropriations and budgetary transfers must also be in accordance with governmental regulations and limitations.

The adopted budget and subsequent supplemental appropriations should be recorded in the accounting system as a means of controlling expenditures and permitting management to monitor compliance with the budget on an ongoing basis. Budgetary control procedures frequently provide for a review of the remaining appropriation before final approval is given for an expenditure. Encumbrance accounting, described earlier, also enhances budgetary control by reducing the remaining appropriation when purchase orders are issued.

Because the budget cycle is central to the operations of a governmental unit, the auditor usually places particular emphasis on the cycle when assessing control risk. That is, the auditor will seek evidence that the control structure, as it affects the budget cycle, has been properly designed and placed in operation, and is operating effectively.

The Revenue Cycle

Governmental revenues can be classified conveniently into seven types.

- Assessed taxes.
- Self-assessed taxes.
- Intergovernmental revenue.
- Revenue received for governmental services.
- Licenses, fees, permits, and fines.
- Investment revenue.
- Contributions and donations.

Those aspects of each type of revenue that are unique to governments are discussed in this section. Control procedures for cash receipts are similar to those in commercial and industrial enterprises.

Assessed Taxes. The primary sources of revenue in this category are property and special assessment taxes, which are levied according to the various state and local tax regulations. Many municipalities assess, levy, and collect their own property taxes. Sometimes, the assessing, billing, and collecting are performed by one governmental entity for a group of entities. In such cases, a portion of the funds is retained by the collecting entity and the remaining amounts are recorded as "additions to agency funds" for future distribution to the other governmental entities. The auditor should have a clear under-standing of the control procedures for the tax assessing and collection process as well as procedures for appealing and changing valuations.

Self-Assessed Taxes.   Revenue in this category is based on taxpayer assess-ments; the accurate determination and reporting of amounts due are the responsibility of individual taxpayers. Examples of self-assessed taxes are income, sales, excise, utility, and personal property taxes. As with assessed taxes, sometimes one governmental entity collects self-assessed taxes for a group of entities. The recording of taxes collected by this process is the same as for assessed taxes. Income taxes may present an audit problem because the source documents—the tax forms—may be covered by a confidentiality law that prevents the auditor from obtaining and testing them. In that event, the auditor may have to use the work of the governmental entity's internal audi-tors, which may involve testing their work or even designing specific pro-cedures for them to follow. For other self-assessed taxes, such as sales taxes, the auditor should consider the existence of a master file of taxpayers and the government's procedures applied to the file, including examinations.

Intergovernmental Revenue.   Intergovernmental revenue received by state and local governments can take one of three forms.

- Entitlements and shared revenue, which are based on a legally established or predetermined amount.
- Collections, which result from collections made by another governmental entity.
- Expenditure reimbursement type grants, which are received as partial or full reimbursement of expenditures that meet certain preestablished cri-teria.

The auditor has two concerns about intergovernmental revenue. The first is that the normal completeness and accuracy control procedures have been properly designed and placed in operation. Second, the auditor needs to deter-mine that the governmental unit is in compliance with the terms of the law or regulation establishing the revenue. As discussed under "Contingent Lia-bilities from Grant Noncompliance," noncompliance with a law or regulation may cause accounts to be uncollectible, or require repayments.

Other Governmental Revenues.   Transactions involving revenues from serv-ices; licenses, fees, permits, and fines; investment revenue; and contributions and donations are generally recorded on the cash basis. Control objectives for such transactions relate principally to completeness of input.

The Buying Cycle

The buying cycle consists of two distinct parts (goods and services, and payroll). The auditor's primary concern for both is that transactions are properly authorized. In a governmental unit, the objective of proper authorization of expenditures has implications beyond those in other enterprises. Proper authorization implies that the expenditure is part of a legally adopted budget, that the persons contracting for the goods or services and approving their payment are properly authorized to do so, that the goods or services have been received, and that all laws and regulations affecting the expenditure (e.g., a requirement to obtain competitive bids) have been complied with.

In obtaining an understanding of the control structure and assessing control risk for the buying cycle, the auditor needs to be aware that some important control procedures may not be applied as part of financial transaction processing. For example, payment made to or on behalf of an individual under a government grant may require the individual to meet certain requirements in order to be eligible to receive the payment. The determination of eligibility, which is an important part of the authorization and payment process, is often accomplished separate from the routine processing of the payment.

A significant and unique control procedure in government payroll systems is known as "position control." Governments budget specific numbers of people in prescribed employment categories or positions at specified salary levels. For example, a department may be assigned one manager, two assistant managers, and four clerks. A position master file, similar to the employee master file, is created and maintained, based on the budget. In obtaining an understanding of the control structure and assessing control risk, the auditor should consider procedures established to ensure that changes made to these files are properly authorized. The auditor generally performs tests to determine that the position master file and the employee master file match, that salaries conform with the budget, and that the positions and salaries are authorized by the budget.

Government payroll systems are often structured so that employees, once they are included in the employee master file, continue to receive paychecks unless some positive action is taken to remove them from that file. That is, the payroll system typically is not based on time reporting by employees. As a result, there is the possibility of phantom employees. In assessing control risk, the auditor should consider whether procedures exist to ensure that only employees who are properly includable on the payroll are paid and that they are paid in accordance with required attendance. Other auditing procedures for payroll expenditures are discussed in Chapter 13.

Payroll costs (and related overhead charges) may be chargeable to grants and thus reimbursable. Control procedures often are established to ensure that work was actually performed on grants, and that payroll costs are appropriately classified and allocated to those grants. Under the "single audit" approach, discussed in the following section, compliance with the terms of some grants is tested as part of the requirements of OMB Circular A-128. In addition, the auditor may wish to test whether payroll rates related to federal

grants comply with the applicable local ordinances. The union scale requirements of the Davis–Bacon Act are also important for entities or projects with
federal grants.

RISK ASSESSMENT AND AUDIT STRATEGY

This section discusses factors that affect the audit strategy in a governmental
environment.

Types of Governmental Audits

Both the auditor and the governmental unit should understand the type and
scope of the audit to be performed. The Yellow Book describes two types of
governmental audits, as follows:

Financial Audits

Financial audits include financial statement and financial related audits.
a. Financial statement audits determine (1) whether the financial statements of
    an audited entity present fairly the financial position, results of operations,
    and cash flows or changes in financial position in accordance with generally
    accepted accounting principles, and (2) whether the entity has complied with
    laws and regulations for those transactions and events that may have a
    material effect on the financial statements.
b. Financial related audits include determining (1) whether financial reports
    and related items, such as elements, accounts, or funds are fairly presented,
    (2) whether financial information is presented in accordance with established
    or stated criteria, and (3) whether the entity has adhered to specific financial
    compliance requirements. (pp. 2-1–2-2)

Performance Audits

Performance audits include economy and efficiency and program audits.
a. Economy and efficiency audits include determining (1) whether the entity is
    acquiring, protecting, and using its resources (such as personnel, property,
    and space) economically and efficiently, (2) the causes of inefficiencies or
    uneconomical practices, and (3) whether the entity has complied with laws
    and regulations concerning matters of economy and efficiency.
b. Program audits include determining (1) the extent to which the desired results
    or benefits established by the legislature or other authorizing body are being
    achieved, (2) the effectiveness of organizations, programs, activities, or func-
    tions, and (3) whether the entity has complied with laws and regulations
    applicable to the program. (p. 2-3)

Performance audits traditionally have been performed by federal or state
government auditors. If during the course of a financial audit, however, an
independent auditor identifies an opportunity for improved economy or efficiency, the recommendation should be communicated to management.

Single Audit Considerations

The auditor is frequently engaged to perform an audit of a governmental unit in accordance with OMB Circular A-128 and the Single Audit Act. This requires that the auditor perform procedures beyond those required by GAAS and GAGAS, in terms of both the nature and the extent of the procedures. The requirements of the Act are covered in Chapter 25. For audit efficiency, the auditor should consider the requirements of Circular A-128 and the Act when planning the engagement. For instance, federal regulations specify criteria for selecting grant costs to be tested in a single audit. The Act also specifies that the auditor obtain an understanding of the internal control procedures used in administering federal financial assistance. Early identification of the requirements of the Act can prevent unnecessary duplication of efforts.

Risk and Materiality Considerations

The auditor should be sensitive to certain elements of inherent and control risk that are unique to formulating a strategy for a governmental audit. For example, the absence of a unified, consistent level of overall financial management in many governmental units suggests that the strength of management and the performance of specific departments or programs may vary widely.

The auditor should also be sensitive to the materiality implications of autonomous, decentralized, individual entities and programs. A single department, program, or grant that is discovered not to be in compliance with laws, regulations, or contract terms may generate publicity and attendant effects far out of proportion to the normal materiality considerations in a commercial or industrial environment. In this regard, the Yellow Book states, ''In government audits the materiality level and/or threshold of acceptable risk may be lower than in similar-type audits in the private sector because of the public accountability of the entity, the various legal and regulatory requirements, and the visibility and sensitivity of government programs, activities, and functions.'' Therefore, in developing the audit testing plan, the auditor should consider external pressures exerted by the political process and the nature of the client's constituency. Much can be learned about the expectations of those constituencies by reading newspapers and minutes of council and legislative proceedings, hearings, and investigations.

The auditor should consider the level of financial statements on which his or her opinion is to be expressed. If the auditor has been engaged to express an opinion on the combined, or general-purpose, financial statements (GPFS), materiality should be determined separately for each fund type and account group. In this case, the fund type and account group columns are considered to be elements of the GPFS. In circumstances where the auditor has been engaged to express an opinion on the individual fund statements, materiality should be established at that level. In addition, there are no working capital or income measurements in governmental accounting, so the auditor must look to other measures of materiality, such as total assets, liabilities, fund balances, revenues, and expenditures.

Overall Audit Strategy and Planning Considerations

As mentioned earlier, governmental accounting uses the modified accrual basis, which focuses on the measurement of financial flows as opposed to profit or loss. As a result, the balance sheet often does not include productive assets, such as inventory and fixed assets, that enter into the determination of income. In addition, receivables on the balance sheet usually are not derived from the revenue cycle, but are recorded as assets independently of a cycle. For these reasons, it is often more efficient to test the flow of transactions and the resulting operating accounts separately from the balance sheet accounts. For example, based on the assessment of inherent risk and the understanding of the control structure, the auditor may decide to perform tests of controls directed at the authorization and accuracy of input of transactions and at the file control objective for the buying cycle. If those tests support a low assessment of control risk, the auditor might restrict substantive testing of the operating accounts affected by the buying cycle to analytical procedures, but might perform detailed substantive tests to satisfy the audit objectives for accounts payable.

Computer software can be used to enhance the efficiency of governmental audits. For example, governmental entities frequently combine the cash balances of their agencies in order to be able to invest in assets with higher yields than would otherwise be available or to facilitate the treasury function in other ways. Software can be used to test both the distribution of interest to the various agencies and the accuracy of the equity positions of the individual agencies in the pooled cash fund. Similarly, software may be used to test assessed tax rolls, including calculation of the tax on individual properties and its distribution to the appropriate governmental agencies or units.

Client Representation Letter

In addition to the items applicable to audits of business enterprises generally, a governmental client representation letter should cover several areas that are specific to governmental units and activities, namely, the inclusion of all component units, the proper classification of fund types and account groups, and compliance with budgets, laws, and regulations and with grant requirements. Changes in government administrations may cause difficulty in obtaining representations from former officials, and their replacements may not be willing or able to provide representations about periods and events that occurred before they took office. This could lead to a scope limitation that would require a qualified opinion.

SUBSTANTIVE TESTS

This section discusses those aspects of substantive tests that are unique to audits of governmental units and activities. Most audit objectives and procedures to meet them are, of course, similar to those for business enterprises and are not discussed here.

Balance Sheet Accounts

Receivables from Taxes. As noted earlier, revenue presently is recognized under the modified accrual basis of accounting when it becomes measurable and available. (This may change in 1993 or thereafter.) The concept of measurable and available has not been quantified for all sources of revenue. NCGA Interpretation No. 3, however, specifies that property taxes that are due as of the balance sheet date and are expected to be collected within 60 days of year-end should be recognized as revenues; other taxes that have been assessed are reported as deferred revenues. The auditor often tests the accuracy and collectibility of tax receivables by examining cash receipts after year-end; material receivables resulting from collections by other governmental units can be confirmed. Total property tax revenues can be reconciled to the value of assessed property.

Due to and Due from Other Funds, and Other Interfund Accounts. Most interfund account balances are liquidated before year-end; those that are not should be examined to support their treatment as loans rather than as equity contributions. A typical auditing procedure is to reconcile all funds to each other (total due to's should equal total due from's) and to determine that there is a reasonable purpose for the interfund balance (i.e., that it was created by a normal operating interfund activity). The auditor should also determine that the receivable balances can be considered current available resources in the governmental funds. Amounts that are currently available should be accounted for as reserves.

Restricted Assets. Revenue bond indentures frequently require that a specified amount of cash be restricted for debt service or system rehabilitation. Such restricted assets should equal the sum of payables from restricted assets and the equity reserved for the restricted purpose. The auditor should determine that the amount of the restriction has been determined properly in accordance with the regulating instrument.

General Fixed Assets Account Group. The general fixed assets account group is used to provide accountability for capital assets, even though their cost is charged to expenditures when incurred. This practice was not always followed in the past, with the result that records of cost may not be currently available. When the governmental unit establishes fixed asset values, the auditor should determine that the procedures for estimating cost are reasonable and consistent. The same is true for assets donated to governmental activities.

Liabilities. Governmental accounting systems sometimes do not distinguish between actual liabilities in the form of accounts payable and encumbrances. There is no need to make that distinction for budgetary reporting purposes since both are deductions from budgeted appropriations. The distinction is necessary for reporting under GAAP, however, because expenditures and encumbrances are reported differently, and the auditor should ensure that it is made. The auditor should also perform tests to determine whether the reserve for encumbrances is supported by authorized commitments.

Judgments payable, litigation claims, and unfunded pensions and other employee-related accruals should be evaluated to determine that they will be payable from expendable available financial resources. If so, they should be treated as liabilities of the appropriate governmental fund; if not, they are presently treated as liabilities in the general long-term debt account group.

Fund Equity.   Changes in aggregate fund balances should normally result only from differences between revenues and other financing sources and expenditures and other financing uses on the operating statement, residual equity transfers as defined in NCGA Statement No. 1, and prior-period adjustments (Statement of Financial Accounting Standards No. 16, *Prior Period Adjustments* [Accounting Standards Section A35]). It is not uncommon, however, for governmental entities to record operating items directly in equity accounts. Accordingly, the auditor should review activity in all fund equity accounts to ensure that all charges and credits that should go through the operating statement have in fact done so.

Reserves are established to identify the existence of assets that are not available to be spent currently or assets that have claims against them that are not liabilities at the date of the balance sheet, such as encumbrances. Designations of fund balances are the result of voluntary management decisions to earmark resources for specific future uses. Designated fund balances should be supported by specific plans approved by senior management and, if appropriate, a legislative body.

Contingent Liabilities from Grant Noncompliance.   As noted earlier, grants frequently specify conditions with which the recipient must comply. Although some of those conditions are nonfinancial, such as those that relate to environmental and employment practices, others are of a financial nature, for example, those that specify costs properly chargeable to a grant. If costs are disallowed or a grant is rescinded by the granting agency, a contingent liability could result.

Conceptually, there can be no quantitative materiality guidelines for evaluating the extent of a contingent liability that could result from a grant violation. In many cases, an entire grant could legally or contractually be canceled as a result of a minor violation. As a practical matter, however, the act of noncompliance generally has to be very serious to cause the recipient to lose grant funds that are material in relation to the financial statements. That presumption may be tested by reviewing historical records of the grantor's acceptance of performance under similar grants and the effects of disallowed costs.

Comparisons of Budget and Actual and Other Operating Statements

As noted earlier, a combined statement of revenues, expenditures, and changes in fund balances—budget and actual is required by NCGA Statement No. 1 for general and special revenue fund types and similar governmental funds for which annual budgets have been legally adopted. The auditor's responsibility for and approach to that statement are the same as for the other financial statements. In addition to the auditing procedures appropriate under GAAS and GAGAS, usually the auditor is subject to a regulatory requirement to test the governmental unit's compliance with statutory and other regulations by comparing budgeted with actual expenditures at the level of detail at which the budget is legally controlled. Actual expenditures reported on this and the other operating statements should be subjected to analytical procedures—budget to actual and current year to prior years—and explanations for variances sought.

The budget versus actual comparison should be made using the basis of accounting used to develop the budget. If the budget has been prepared on the modified accrual basis, it may contain GAAP exceptions. Sometimes budgets may be prepared on the cash basis or may include encumbrances. The basis used to prepare the budget should be disclosed and differences between it and GAAP should be reconciled on the face of the statement or in the notes. The auditor may wish to test the current-period encumbrances and the control procedures for reappropriating these amounts, if applicable to the particular governmental unit. As discussed earlier, encumbrances are a means of measuring total commitments made against a particular budgetary amount. If (as is most often the case) the governmental entity intends to honor these commitments, and if the budget does not include encumbrances because it is prepared on the cash basis, encumbrances will be a reconciling item between the GAAP- and budget-basis reports. The auditor may wish to expand the normal cutoff procedures to include encumbrances.

Index

Pages in **boldface** refer to the page on which the term is defined or to a block of pages that includes the definition of the term.

About the Editor

The editor of the sixth edition of *The American Tradition in Literature* is George Perkins, Professor of English at Eastern Michigan University. He received his Ph.D. from Cornell University and has taught at Washington University, Baldwin-Wallace College, Fairleigh Dickinson University, and the University of Edinburgh. In 1981 he was a Fellow at the Institute for Advanced Studies in the Humanities at the University of Edinburgh. Author of essays on American and English literature and folklore, Professor Perkins is General Editor of *The Journal of Narrative Technique.* His books include *The Theory of the American Novel, Realistic American Short Fiction, American Poetic Theory,* and (with Northrop Frye and Sheridan Baker) *The Practical Imagination* and *The Harper Handbook to Literature.*